A HISTORY OF THE CROWN JEWELS OF EUROPE

Lord Twining

LONDON

B. T. BATSFORD LTD

First published, 1960

© Lord Twining, 1960

MADE AND PRINTED IN GREAT BRITAIN BY
WILLIAM CLOWES AND SONS, LIMITED, LONDON AND BECCLES
FOR THE PUBLISHERS B. T. BATSFORD LTD
4 FITZHARDINGE STREET, PORTMAN SQUARE, LONDON, W.1

A HISTORY OF THE
CROWN JEWELS
OF EUROPE

PREFACE

It was nearly thirty years ago that the idea of producing such a work as this was first conceived. The original plan was for the book to be in two parts. The first part was to be a series of studies tracing the origin, the development of, and the meaning attributed to each of the royal ornaments, with additional chapters on Orders of Chivalry, precious materials and symbolism. The second part was to take the form of a *catalogue raisonné* with a historical background, dealing chapter by chapter with each of the various Christian kingdoms of Europe. It soon became clear that the information required to undertake Part II had to be available before any attempt could be made to write Part I. It also became apparent that Part II would be a large book in itself. It was therefore decided that Part II should be published first under the title *A History of the Crown Jewels of Europe*, and that Part I should be published subsequently under a different title.

The present volume is intended to provide accurate information of an encyclopaedic nature about crown jewels and regalia in Christian Europe. The subject covers a vast canvas over a period of seventeen centuries. It has necessitated the study of a mass of literature of varying quality in nearly a score of languages, besides visiting most countries in Europe. Although this has led to the collection of a great mass of material, it cannot be said to be complete. Those readers who are sufficiently interested to wish to pursue further studies will find in the bibliographies and footnotes a reasonably wide selection of sources to consult.

In my task I have received assistance and advice from a very large number of people and it would be difficult to compile a full list. First I must express my humble appreciation for the gracious permission given by Her Majesty Queen Elizabeth II to publish information about the English Crown Jewels not included among the regalia and for some of these items to be photographed for the first time. H.R.H. Prince Ernest August, Duke of Brunswick, has also been gracious enough to give assistance and advice about the Hanoverian regalia.

The following is a list, by no means complete, of those who have rendered me assistance and which I acknowledge with gratitude:

Austria: Dr Otto Demus, Dr Hermann Fillitz; *Bavaria:* Dr Hans Thoma; *Bohemia:* Dr Josef Cibulka; *Bulgaria:* Professor D. P. Dimitrof of the National Archeological Museum, Sofia; *Denmark:* the late Dr Andarap, Dr G. Boesen, the Inspector of Rosenborg Castle, Dr Rasmussen, Dr Olaf Olsen of the National Museum, Copenhagen; *England:* The Lord Chamberlain, Major-General H. D. W. Sitwell, Keeper of the Jewel House, Sir Owen Morshead, G.C.M.G., late Librarian at Windsor Castle, Mr M. R. Holmes, London Museum, Mr C. C. Oman, Department of Metals, Victoria and Albert Museum, Mr R. H. Dolly, Department of Coins and Medals, British Museum,

Mr Mackworth Young, Librarian at Windsor Castle, Mr A. C. Mann, Crown Jeweller; *France :* M. Pierre Verlet of the Louvre; *Germany :* The British Consul General, Munich; *Hanover :* Mr G. M. Willis; *Holy See :* The Rev. Father J. J. Keane of the Society of the White Fathers; *Hungary :* Dr Alexander Mihalik, the Director of the Hungarian National Museum; *Italy :* Mr G. E. Stockley, British Consul General, Naples, Mr E. Bateman, M.B.E., British Consul, Turin; *Norway :* The President of the Crown Regalia Commission, Mr K. R. Kjeldesperg, British Vice-Consul, Trondheim; *Poland :* Dr Adam Bochnak of Wawel, Cracow; *Portugal :* Dr João R. S. Couto, the Director of the National Museum of Antique Art (Lisbon), the late José Rosas, Jnr; *Prussia :* the Director of the former Hohenzollern Museum, Schloss Monbijou, Berlin; *Russia :* The Director of the Kremlin Museum; *Saxony :* M. Seyderich, Director of the State Art Museum, Dresden; *Sweden :* The late Baron Caederström, the late Dr T. Lenk and Dr B. Hullner, Director of the Royal Armoury, Stockholm, Dr Lars O. Lagerqvist of the National Historical Museum, Stockholm.

In addition I have received considerable assistance from H.M. Ambassadors in Vienna, Oslo, Lisbon and Moscow, and from the British Council representatives in Vienna, Stuttgart, Cologne and Paris. Miss E. S. DuBuisson has rendered me indefatigably the greatest assistance from the book's inception, in translations, research, typing and proof-reading. Colonel R. A. Hay has been most helpful in checking translations and proof-reading, and I have to acknowledge the assistance of various other translators. For several years Miss Marjorie Sharp, now Mrs Kenyon, undertook the formidable task of typing the first drafts, which work was completed by Mrs Sussex. I owe a debt of gratitude to my son, the Hon. J. P. Twining, who has been largely responsible for the important chapter on Spain. Finally I must express my most grateful thanks and appreciation to Miss Thelma Nye of B. T. Batsford Limited who has been responsible for the editing and much of the technical side of the production of this book and who has shown great patience and intelligence in this work.

London, 1960   **TWINING**

CONTENTS

CONTENTS

LIST OF ILLUSTRATIONS

XV

WURTEMBERG

YUGOSLAVIA

ACKNOWLEDGMENT

The author and publishers wish to acknowledge the following for the use of photographic material:
His Grace the Duke of Abercorn for Plate 214, c; the Administrator, the Minster, Aix-la-Chapelle for Plates 106, a, b, c, d and 107, a; Alinari for Plates 116, c, 126, a, c, 129, a, 210, d; Ampliaciones y Reproducciones Mas for Plates 208, a, b, 209, b, c, 210, a, b, c, 211, b, c, 212, a; the Director, Austrian National Library, Vienna for Plate 205, c, d; Antikvarisk-Topografiska Arkivet, Stockholm for Plates 222, a, b, c, d, 223, a, c, d, e, 224, a, d, 225, a, b, c, d, 228, b; Archives Photographique d'Art et Histoire, Paris for Plate 84, a; Asscher's Diamond Works for Plate 71, a, c, d; the Administrator, Barcelona Cathedral for Plate 210, a; the Director, Bavarian National Museum for Plates 18, d, 29, a, b, 97, a, 109, d; the Director, Bavarian State Library for Plate 96, c; His Grace the Duke of Bedford for Plate 49, a; the Director, Bibliothèque Nationale for Plate 78, a; the City Librarian, Birmingham Public Libraries for Plates 58, a, 60, b; the Trustees of the British Museum for Plates 41, b, 44, 45, a, b, c, 56, b, c, d, 57, c, 68, a, 113, a, b, 125, c, 209, c; the Director, Cambridge University Library for Plate 46, a; the Administrator, Catania Cathedral for Plate 128, d; His Grace the Archbishop of Canterbury and the Library Trustees, Lambeth Palace for Plate 46, d; Messrs Christie for Plates 26, a, b, c, 173, b; the Director, Cluny Museum, Paris for Plate 207, a; the Administrator, the Treasury, Cologne Cathedral for Plate 99, b; the Director, the Courtauld Institute of Art for Plate 49, b; the Administrator, the Treasury, Cracow Cathedral for Plates 136, a, b, c, d, 140, a; Crown Copyright used with the permission of the Controller of H.M. Stationery Office, Plates 58, b, 65, b, 67, b, c, d, e; Crown Copyright reserved to Her Majesty The Queen by permission of the Lord Chamberlain, Plates 50, b, 51, b, c, 55, b, c, 56, a, 58, b, 59, 60, a, b, 61, a, b, 62, a, b, 63, b, c, 64, a, b, c, 65, a, b, 66, a, b, c, d, 67, a, 69, c, 70, a, b, 71, b, 72, a, b, 73, a, b, 74, a, b, c, d, 75, a, b, c, 76, 77, a, b, 205, a, b, 212, c; Crown Copyright by permission of the Ministry of Works, Plate 206, a; Crown Copyright by permission of the Director and Secretary of the Victoria and Albert Museum, Plate 121, b; the Director, Czartoryski Museum, Cracow for Plate 137, a, d; De danske Kongers Kronologiske Samling for Plates 40, a, 41, a, c, e, g, 42, b; through the courtesy of Dr Otto Demus, President Bundes-denkmalamtes for Plate 14, a, b, c; Deutsche Fotothek, Dresden for Plate 141, a, b, c, d; the Director, Dijon Museum for Plate 78, d; the Director, Diocesan Museum, Vienna for Plate 1, a; The Dropmore Press Limited for Plate 63, e, f; the Administrator, the Minster, Essen for Plate 97, d; the Marquis of Exeter for Plate 49, b; Ernesto Farina, Monza for Plates 125, b, 126, b; G. Félici for Plate 116, a, b; the Director, Danish National Museum, Fredericksborg for Plate 40, b, c; Plate 110, a, b, c, d by gracious permission of H.R.H. Ernst August; Ernst Matthaus Fürbock for Plate 2, a, b, c, d; Gabinetto Photografico Nationale for Plate 129, d; the Director, Hamburg City Library for Plate 39, a, b, c, d; the Director, German National Museum, Nuremberg for Plate 5, c; Giraudon for Plates 78, a, c; 88, b, 89, e, 96, a; the Administrator, Granada Cathedral for Plate 211, b, c, d; the Director, Herzog Anton Ulrich Museum, Brunswick for Plate 99, c; the Administrator, the Treasury, Hildesheim Cathedral for Plate 107, b; the Director, Historical Museum, Basle for Plate 6, b, d, 48, a, b, c, d; the Director, Historical Museum, Dresden for Plates 141, a, b, c, d, 197, a, b, c, d, 198, a, b, c, 200, a, b, c, d, 202, d, e, f, 203, a, b, c, d, e, f, 204, a, b, c, d, e, f; the Director, Historical Museum, Stockholm for Plate 228, a, b, c, d; the Director, former Hohenzollern Museum for Plates 153 to 164; the Director, Hungarian National Museum for Plates 121, a, 122, a, b, c, 123, a, b, c, d, e, f; the Directors, The Illustrated London News for Plate 165, a, b, c; Ingeborg Limmer, Bamberg for Plate 16, c; the Director, Johanneum, Graz for Plate 2, c, d; the Administrator, Klosterneuburg Abbey for Plate 1, b, d; the Director, Kremlin Museum for Plates 166, a, b, c, d, 167, a, b, c, 168, a, b, c, d, e, f, 169, a, b, c, 170, a, b; the Director, Kunsthistorisches Museum, Vienna for Plates 4, a, 5, a, b, 10, a, b, c, 11, c, 13, c, e, f, g, h, 100, a, 101, 102, a, b, 104, a, b, c, 105, b, c, 107, a, 127, c; Landesbildstelle, Salzburg for Plate 3, a, c, d; K. Livrustkammaren, Stockholm for Plates 215, b, 216, e,

ACKNOWLEDGMENT

217, c, 219, a, b, c, 221, a, b, d, e, f, 224, b, 227, b; the Director, London Museum for Plates 54, c, 57, a, b, c, 58, c, 60, d; the Director, The Louvre for Plates 78, b, 83, a, 84, a, 86, a, b, c, d, 87, c, 89, b, c, d, 96, a; Bildarchiv Foto Marburg for Plates 97, d, 106, a, c, d, 117, 118, a, b, 119, b, c; the Administrator, Mariastein Church for Plate 3, b; Plate 96, b, by courtesy of the Metropolitan Museum of Art, New York; the Ministry of Foreign Affairs for Plates 52 and 53; the Administrator, the Treasury, Monza Cathedral for Plates 125, b, 126, a, c, d; the Administrator, the Treasury, Namur Cathedral for Plate 30, b; the Director, National Museum, Copenhagen for Plates 37, a, b, c, 38, a, b, c; the Director, National Museum, Florence for Plates 125, a, 210, d; the Director, National Museum, San Martino, Naples for Plates 130, a, b, c, 213, a; the Director, National Museum, Sofia for Plate 36, a, b, c; the Director, National Museum of Antique Art, Lisbon for Plate 143, a, b; the Director, National Museum of Antiquities, Edinburgh for Plate 206, b, c; the Director, National Museum, Stockholm and the Administrator, Upsala Cathedral for Plates 218, b, 221, a, b, c, d, 222, a, b, c, d, 223, a, b, c, d, e, 224, a, b, c, d, 225, c, d, e, f, 226, a, b, 227, c; the Trustees, National Portrait Gallery for Plates 50, a, 69, a; the Administrator, Nonnberg Abbey for Plate 3, a, c, d; the Director, Neues Museum, Wiesbaden for Plates 155, a, b, c, d, 156, b, c; Nordisk Pressefoto, Copenhagen for Plate 40, c, d; the Director, Nymphenburg Castle for Plate 19, a, b; Oesterreichische Lichtbildstelle for Plates 4, b, 6, c; the Administrator, Papal Treasury, the Vatican for Plates 114, a, b, c, d, 115, a, b, c, d; Messrs Frank Partridge for Plate 211, a; the Director, The Pierpont Morgan Library, New York for Plate 47, a; the Administrator, Plock Cathedral for Plate 137, b, d; Public Record Office for Plate 69, b; Bruno Reiffenstein for Plate 1, b; the Director, Residenz Treasury, Munich for Plates 15, a, b, c, 16, a, c, 17, a, b, 18, a, b, c, 19, c, 20, a, b, c, d, e, 21, a, b, c, d, 22, a, b, c, d, 23, a, b, c, 24, a, b, 25, a, b, c, 27, a, b, 28, a, b, 29, c, d, 96, d, 100, b, c, d, e; M. José Rosas for Plates 144 to 152; the Inspector, Rosenborg Castle for Plates 40, a, d, 41, a, c, d, e, f, g, 42, a, b, c, d, e, 43, a, b, c, d; Routledge and Kegan Paul Ltd for Plate 63, a; the Director, Royal Armoury, Madrid for Plate 207, b; the Director, Royal Armoury, Stockholm for Plates 214, a, b, c, 215, a, b, 216, a, b, c, d, e, 217, a, b, c, d, 218, a, c, d, e, 219, a, b, c, d, e, 220, a, b, c, d, 227, b; the Director, Royal Museum of Art and History, Brussels for Plate 30, a; the Administrator, St Eusebius Cathedral, Vercelli for Plate 97, b; the Administrator, the Treasury, St Vitus's Cathedral for Plates 31, a, b, 32, a, b, 34, a, 35, a; the Director, Santiago University Library for Plate 208, a; the Director, former Schloss Museum, Berlin for Plate 108, a; Anton Schroll and Co. for Plates 7, 8, a, b, 12, a, 13, a, 105, a; the Director, Silesian Museum, Wroclaw for Plate 123, d; Messrs Sotheby and Co. for Plate 68, b; Captain Edward G. Spencer-Churchill for Plate 51, b; the Administrator, the Treasury, Speyer Cathedral for Plates 46, b, 98, a, b, c, d, e, f, g; the Administrator, Split Cathedral for Plate 230, b; the Director, State Armoury, Stockholm for Plates 215, a, b, c, 216, a, b, c, d, e, 217, a, b, c, d, e, 218, a, b, c, d, 219, a, b, c, d, e, 220, a, b, c, d; the Administrator, Strengnäs Cathedral for Plate 226, a, b, c, d; Studio Nobile for Plate 85, c, d; the Administrator, Toledo Cathedral for Plate 208, c; the Treasury, Vienna for Plates 1, c, 4, a, 5, a, b, 6, a, b, 9, a, b, c, 10, a, b, c, 11, a, 12, a, b, c, 13, a, b, c, d, e, f, g, h; Vatican Photographic Archives for Plates 111, a, c, 112, a, b, c, 113, c, d; the Administrator, Vesterås Cathedral for Plate 227, a; O. Vœring for Plate 134, a, b, c; the Director and Secretary of the Victoria and Albert Museum for Plate 68, a; the Keeper of the Wallace Collection for Plate 71, b; the Keeper, the Royal Castle, Wawel for Plate 140, b, c; the Dean and Chapter of Westminster Abbey for Plates 46, c, 47, b, c, d; Kunstverlag Wolfram for Plates 1, d, 4, b, 6, c, 9, c, 11, a, b, 12, a, b, 102, a, b, 127, a, 104, a, c; the Director, Wurtemberg Landesmuseum, Stuttgart for Plate 229, a, b, c, d; Zaiks (Kolowca Stanislaw) Cracow for Plates 136, a, 138, a, b, 139, a, b, c, d, e, 140, a, b, c, d; Stencuv Graficky Zavod, Prague for Plates 32, a, b, 33, a, b, c, 34, a, b, 35, b, 120, c. Acknowledgment is also made to Macmillan and Co. Limited for permission to use the quotation on page 168 from Sir John Wheeler-Bennett's *King George VI: His Life and Reign*.

As the photographs have been collected from various sources over the course of thirty years it has been difficult to keep a complete list of their origin. The author therefore wishes to express his thanks to any persons who have supplied photographs and whose names do not appear in this list.

INTRODUCTION

Any person reading the title of this book may reasonably ask 'What is a crown jewel?'. It will therefore be as well to try to provide an answer to this question, though the subject is too complex to allow of a precise definition.

In the early days of monarchy in Europe it became customary for the kings to assemble the tangible wealth of the nation in their royal treasuries. Here were kept not only the coin and bullion but also other valuables including part of the national archives, the royal insignia, gold and silver plate and jewelled ornaments. The plate and jewellery were used in normal times to provide a suitable magnificence for the royal state, though in times of need they could be turned into money.

In the early period the national insignia were not necessarily intrinsically valuable, but were given a certain importance for sentimental and national reasons. When the anointing and coronation of kings were first introduced little thought was given to the need for a permanent set of coronation ornaments, but as nationhood was firmly established the power of the Church became a potent factor in relation to the State. Gradually the right of the Primate to crown the king was accepted and, to make doubly sure that no candidate could be crowned without the approval of the Church, claims were established for ecclesiastical authorities to have the custody of the royal ornaments. Thus in France the Royal Abbey of St Denis became the repository of the regalia at an early date, while in England the abbot and monks of Westminster claimed that they possessed the crown and other relics of St Edward which were to be used at the coronations of English kings. At Monza too the clergy were at pains to assert that they were the guardians of the Lombard Crown and they may even have fabricated a crown to strengthen their claim. In Bohemia in the XIII century the coronation regalia were entrusted to the authorities of the Cathedral of St Vitus at Prague, and there are other similar examples. In some countries, however, the regalia were kept in the royal treasury, and in Germany in particular the possession of the Imperial Treasure was an important factor in enhancing the prospects of a candidate for election as German King. It thus became almost a general practice for a special set of regalia to be used for the coronation, and these ornaments were accorded a national status.

This fact made it impossible, or at least difficult, for the regalia to be used on other occasions and a second set of royal ornaments was necessary. These insignia were usually kept in the royal treasury, and as their use was governed by formal restrictions it was found convenient for kings also to possess personal crowns. This was more than ever necessary when a tradition became established that the national regalia should not be taken out of the kingdom. In England we find that John had a different set of ornaments for his use in France, and Henry III had a crown and sceptre made in 1229 when he visited Brittany. One of the charges preferred against Richard II was that he had taken the regalia out of the kingdom. In 1911 when King George V went to India for his coronation Durbar a special crown had to be made for the occasion as it was found that it would be unlawful for the English regalia to be taken out of the country. Again in 1940 when King Haakon and his Government left Norway in the face of the German invasion, the state treasure of gold coin and bullion was taken out of the country, but the national regalia were left behind.

Generally speaking, the coronation ornaments, the state regalia and the personal crowns were all regarded as crown jewels. As recently as 1939 King George VI directed that the personal crown, which Queen Victoria had had made at her own expense because she found the regulations for the removal of the State Crown irksome, should be placed with the regalia in the Tower of London and regarded as a crown jewel.

The variety of occasions on which kings wore their crowns also demanded different sorts of crowns as, for example, when a king wore armour he wore a crown on his helmet so that all could see his rank, and this necessitated a special crown for the purpose. Another factor was the change in fashions to which kings were as susceptible as anyone else and often preferred to use the products of contemporary art rather than appear with an old-fashioned crown and other royal ornaments.

Apart from the ornaments which were attributes of royalty, the royal treasuries contained a miscellaneous collection of jewellery for the use of the king, his consort and his family. The status of these objects is sometimes difficult to determine. They were frequently taken into use, were altered and the stones reset, while at times some items were lost or given away as presents. No very careful record of their whereabouts seems to have been kept, although they were from time to time enumerated in lists and inventories; but generally speaking they were regarded as coming within the general term crown jewels.

Francis I of France was the first king to conceive the idea of forming a collection of splendid jewels which were to be the inalienable property of the crown for use, in perpetuity, by the future kings and queens of France. Despite the protection of formal legal documents this arrangement ran into difficulties, as the pieces were frequently changed and the jewels reset while additional stones from the royal caskets were inserted. Moreover royal mistresses were allowed their use and were often reluctant to return them when they fell into disfavour. Nevertheless in France the idea of a state collection of personal jewellery persisted down to the fall of the Second Empire in 1871. In England James I endeavoured to form a like royal treasure of inalienable personal jewellery, but this arrangement broke down in the next reign when Charles I had to sell all the jewels he could lay his hands on to pay for the Civil War. Subsequently, certain pieces of jewellery were made over to the Crown even as recently as the reign of George V. Similar arrangements were made in other countries, Prussia and Sweden for instance, while in Denmark Queen Sophie Magdalena bequeathed some fine jewellery for the use of future queens of Denmark. Elsewhere conditions varied. In some countries the reigning dynasty was so closely associated with the state that crown jewels and family jewels were indistinguishable. This was particularly the case in Austria and to some extent also applied to Bavaria and Russia. In other countries the sovereigns were careful to maintain their collections of jewels as personal property, especially when the position of the monarchy was by no means secure. An example to be noted is the case of Queen Isabel II of Spain, who in 1878, some years after her abdication, sold some of her jewels. There was considerable discussion in the Cortes as to whether or not they were crown jewels but the Queen was able to establish that they were her personal property. In a period when so many monarchies have fallen the question as to what are crown jewels is obviously a delicate matter and for the purpose of this book a broad interpretation of the term has been followed regarding collections of jewels which are or have been in royal treasuries. With a few exceptions jewellery which is the personal property of royal families has been excluded.

There are vast royal collections of jewelled ecclesiastical ornaments, *objets d'art* and plate which could strictly speaking be included in the term 'crown jewels', but it has not been found possible to enumerate these with the exception of a few pieces of particular interest. But there is a third category which can be said to belong to our subject and included in this are burial and funeral crowns, nuptial crowns, votive crowns, crowns made to contain relics and crowns on reliquary busts.

Many royal tombs have been opened, particularly in Bohemia, England, France, Germany, Hungary, Italy, Poland and Sweden and in some cases it has been found that kings and queens were buried with crowns on their heads and with other royal ornaments at their side. This practice seems to have been followed from about the x to the xvi centuries, but with few exceptions these ornaments were specially made of gilded metal adorned with semi-precious or imitation stones. When the practice of burying regalia with kings was given up it became usual in some countries for funeral regalia to be placed on the royal coffins and there are a few examples, in Sweden for instance, of a special funeral crown being kept among the regalia.

In Hanover, Prussia and Russia we find crowns which were kept for use at royal weddings. There are a number of votive crowns still extant, which were the gifts of kings or queens, to be hung before an altar. In some cases these may have been crowns which had been worn but others were specially made for the purpose. It is interesting to record that when some of the votive crowns found at Guarrazar were acquired by the Cluny Museum in Paris, the Spanish Government tried to establish a claim to them on the grounds that they were crowns which had been worn and were therefore crown jewels and should be returned to Spain. During the period of the cult of relics it became the practice for royal personages to present crowns to churches as receptacles for thorns from the Crown of Thorns and other holy relics. Some examples of these survive, such as the crowns in the Treasuries of the Cathedrals of Amiens and Namur and the so-called Crown of St Louis in the Louvre. Finally there is a considerable group of crowns made for reliquary busts. Some, such as the Crown of St Wenceslas at Prague and perhaps the crown on the bust of Charlemagne at Aix-la-Chapelle, were used for the coronations of kings. Others were royal gifts for reliquary busts of either kings or saints. There are also many, particularly on statues of the Virgin, which were gifts of private persons. The criterion for their inclusion in this book is whether or not they have a royal association.

Despite the most careful precautions which have been taken to safeguard the regalia and crown jewels, often with the protection of the most solemn legal forms, these objects were frequently vulnerable. The coronation regalia, especially if regarded as relics, were less susceptible to danger than were the secular ornaments, for special steps to safeguard them were usually taken in times of foreign invasion or civil war, while there are but few instances of their being pledged. But it was not so with the secular regalia and crown jewels. There are innumerable instances of state and personal crowns being pawned or broken up and sold to provide funds for the national cause, while personal jewellery was disposed of for the same purpose, though such treasures rarely fetched the price that had been put upon them. The pages of this book give countless instances of the important part that this wealth played in the destiny of nations. Even the Papacy was not immune. In 1456 Pope Calixtus III disposed of all his treasure to equip a fleet against the Turks and in 1797, by the Treaty of Tolentino, Pope Pius VI had to sell the gold and jewelled ornaments in all the treasuries under his control in Italy in order to meet the indemnity demanded by Napoleon. But the greatest losses were those resulting from pillage. When Constantinople was sacked by the Crusaders the priceless treasures which had been accumulated in the greatest centre of civilisation were looted and destroyed in sheer barbarism. The historian of the fourth Crusade wrote: 'Since the creation of the world such a vast quantity of booty had never been taken from one city.' The sack of Rome in 1527 was another notable occasion which saw the loot of great treasure. There are other examples such as the pillage of the Treasury of St Denis during the Wars of Religion in the XVII century. In England in 1642 the Puritanical Government of the Commonwealth ordered the complete destruction of the Ancient Regalia, an act of vandalism which can only be equalled by the systematic dispersal of the relics of the French monarchy at the time of the Revolution.

We must now consider the main sources of information which are available for the study of this subject. They may be divided into three main groups: actual ornaments; literary sources and pictorial representations. The number of actual royal ornaments that has survived is surprisingly large and this book deals with some 200 crowns, besides many hundreds of other ornaments and pieces of jewellery still extant. But it is necessary to appraise these with caution as sources of historical information, for there are but few which have not been repaired, refreshed, restored or have been subjected to such major alterations as to make them very different objects from the originals. Most of these objects have been studied by art historians whose conflicting views and prejudices in favour of particular *ateliers*, nations or religions make most interesting, if confused reading which often makes it difficult to come to a final judgment.

Literary sources are abundant but owing to the tendency for one writer to per-petuate the errors of another, it is most necessary to undertake as much original research as possible and to cross check information. The literature on the subject may be con-veniently divided into various categories. First there are the early chroniclers or historians who, when writing about contemporary events which they had witnessed themselves or heard from first-hand witnesses, are reasonably reliable. When they wrote about bygone days they were dependent on legends and traditional stories which they were often inclined to embellish. Many were skilful propagandists who shamelessly perverted the truth to satisfy the needs of the religious or political protagonists who employed them or whom they supported. During the present century much work has been done in the reassessment of history not only in an objective manner but supported by the easier access to archives. Some surprising new facts have come to light causing fresh appraisals to be made.

Encyclopaedias are useful sources of information, though there are but few which are absolutely reliable. Ancient works, such as that of Isidore of Seville, provide much that is of value but some modern encyclopaedias are spoiled by a national bias.

State archives contain a great deal of information, but their very size makes general research difficult, costly and often unrewarding. In some countries the most important documents have been collected together by subjects and edited. In others, Spain for example, the available material is immense, but a great deal more work requires to be done on it. In most countries there are gaps owing to the ravages of war, civil disturbances, earthquakes and fire, to say nothing of such acts of vandalism as occurred in England in the XIX century when tons of most valuable documents were sold as waste paper.

Modern research has shown that a number of important documents are forgeries, the most notable perhaps being the Donation of Constantine, but the number includes Papal Bulls and other documents to support the claims of Westminster and St Denis to be the repositories of the regalia, and the Austrian *Privilegium Maius*. It must be stated, however, that these documents were usually based on traditional beliefs and frequently their purpose was merely to give a formal stamp of authority to an existing position. The consciences of the monkish writers were perhaps salved because of this. The importance of these documents is that at the time at which they were produced they were usually accepted as genuine and therefore served their purpose to give confirmation to a popular belief.

Lists of royal ornaments first make their appearance in about the XII century. In the XIII century we begin to find inventories, which became more informative with the passage of time. They were frequently made on a change of custodian and in many cases they were compiled by monks. It seems to have been a leisurely occupation and some of those of the XV and XVI centuries run into many pages, enumerating each precious stone. But here again caution is necessary, as if more than one person was employed on making an inventory the same standards may not be found on each page. Moreover in one case, at least, that of the 1634 inventory of the Treasury of St Denis, items are included which were not in the Treasury at the time. In modern times when royal treasuries have been open to the public there has been a tendency for inventories to be replaced by catalogues which are not so informative. The ideal inventory is that made for Duke Albert V of Bavaria in the mid-XVI century. He employed an artist, Hans Mielich, to represent on the page opposite the description an exact drawing of each item. Today with the high quality of photographic technique it should be possible for each item listed to be supported by a photograph. Unfortunately although there are massive photographic archives they are usually kept separate from the written records.

Another important written source is in the coronation *ordines*. Of these there are a great many. Some give us no more information than the general lines on which the coronation ceremony should be conducted. Others are more precise. But they are valuable in the way in which they record the development of the coronation rite, the introduction of the royal ornaments and in the prayers, the meanings which the ecclesiastical authorities liked to attribute to them. Since the XVI century these have been supplemented by official accounts of individual coronations, which describe the ceremonies in great detail and are usually authoritative, though occasionally there are lapses in exactitude. An example of this is in the sumptuous account of the coronation of George IV by Nayler, which includes a picture of St Edward's Crown being carried by Lord Anglesey, although St Edward's Crown was not present at the ceremony and Lord Anglesey had lost both his legs at the Battle of Waterloo six years previously.[1]

In the XIX century magnificent works on regalia were commissioned by the Emperors of Austria and Russia which, despite the need for revision in the light of modern research, still stand as monumental records of great worth.

During the present century there has been a spate of works on regalia. Well-known scholars have covered much of Europe, though they have usually confined themselves to a selected period or a particular country. P. E. Schramm and his associates in *Herrschaftszeichen und Staatssymbolik* have dealt very fully with the development and use of regalia in most European countries down to the end of the mediaeval period. Schramm has also made notable contributions on Germany while his works on European coronations are quite outstanding and make him the leading expert on the subject. Alföldi and Deér have supplemented Schramm's work with equally valuable studies. In Austria Weixlgärtner, Schlosser and Fillitz; in Bavaria Thoma; in Bohemia Cibulka; in Denmark Liisberg and Boesen; in England Sitwell and Holmes; in France Verlet; in Hungary Bárány-Oberschall and Kelleher; in Sweden Caederström and Thordeman, to quote but a few, have written with authority on the subject.

In this book it has not been possible to give a full bibliography, as it would be too large and in any case the list would include books of varying quality. But a select bibliography is given at the end of most chapters which is supplemented by numerous references as to where information may be found on particular points and by a short general bibliography.

When we turn to pictorial sources the most continuous evidence is provided by numismatics. Valuable though the information to be gained from coins, seals and medals undoubtedly can be, some caution is needed. In early times kings borrowed from classical representations of Roman Emperors and they liked to be depicted enthroned in majesty, bearing the imperial emblems used in Rome or Byzantium. Gradually as the royal ornaments came into accepted use in Western Kingdoms, the kings were depicted with those which they used themselves. Coins and seals were frequently made in foreign mints and forms used in the country of manufacture would be copied in preference to native practice. Moreover, for practical reasons, a die used for making seals or coins was sometimes employed in more than one reign, despite the fact that there might have

---

[1] Another most valuable source of information is the accounts kept by royal treasuries and jewellers' bills.

been changes in the regalia meanwhile. Nevertheless much valuable data can be found by intelligent study of this type of material.

There is still a rich field of illuminated MSS., miniatures and other early drawings. These are worth close study, with the same reservations as have been made in regard to other sources and due allowance given for the fanciful notions of the artists. Neither must we overlook the marks and signs, which are little roughly drawn pictures including crowns and sceptres, which were sometimes made on royal documents in England. Some of these are reproduced in Palgrave's *Ancient Kalenders of the Treasury*. These, while of course not showing great detail, probably give a clear contemporary representation of the royal ornaments they purport to depict.

From the xv century onwards we have an increasing number of royal portraits, some of which give careful, even exact, representations of the royal ornaments. In the xviii century they are not always so reliable, as the painters of state portraits often kept sets of dummy ornaments in their studios.

Monumental effigies are another source of pictorial representation. Sometimes we may take the royal ornaments depicted as very closely resembling the actual regalia, although usually there was considerable scope for artistic licence. But they do show the type of royal ornament in use at the time. In many cases, however, their value has been reduced by restoration.

Yet another source is tapestry and needlework. Occasionally some evidence can be obtained from these works of art and in some cases—for example the Bayeux Tapestry and those in the National Museum at Copenhagen depicting the Danish kings—show with a good degree of accuracy the ornaments in contemporary use.

These then are some of the sources available, and all with the exercise of careful cross checking give us a reasonably clear idea of many royal ornaments which have been used down the ages.

A word must be said about the illustrations in this work. They have been selected and produced for the purpose of illustrating the text and not as an attempt to provide technical evidence. Many of the objects illustrated have been specially photographed for this book and some have not been published before.

Some photographs have been included which are not perhaps up to modern standards. These, such as the jewellery formerly among the Austrian and French royal treasures, are reproduced because of their special interest.

It has not been possible in this volume to include a co-ordinated study of the development of the use of royal ornaments in Western Europe. But it may be useful here, even at the risk of over-simplification, to outline some of the salient points connected with the introduction of various types of royal crowns. It is a complex story going back to Old Testament, Eastern and Teutonic sources influenced by the usages developed by the Emperors both in Rome and Byzantium.

The pre-Christian Roman Emperors adopted the laurel wreath as a formal head-dress. Several Emperors aspired to wearing the diadem, but this was only possible, at least in public, when the idea of monarchy had become firmly established. Aurelian was probably the first Emperor to introduce the diadem, which had for long been the royal head-dress of Persian kings. It was a piece of broad ribbon tied at the back of the head and adorned with two strings of pearls between which was set a row of precious stones. The diadem was worn by all the later Roman Emperors. Under Constantine the Great, the first Christian Emperor, a change was made by the introduction of the *stephanos*, a stiff golden circlet over which the diadem was worn. Constantine also introduced the practice of the Imperial State helmet being worn not only by the Emperor as war lord but also by the military chiefs and the Imperial Bodyguard. The helmet had taken the form of a rigid metal circlet with one or two arches passing over the head for protection from sword blows. The intervening space was filled in by leather, light metal plates or a textile material. It became customary for the Imperial helmets to be gilded and for the circlet and arches to be ornamented. In the case of the Emperor, his rank was denoted by the diadem being worn round the circlet.

In the VI century a change took place and the name *stemma* first appears in official documents to signify the Imperial Crown. A striking difference between the *stephanos* and *stemma* was the development of the pendants, richly decorated with pearls and gems, which hung over the ears, and were known as *cataseistae*. It was the exclusive right of the Emperor to wear the *cataseistae*, and they thus formed an essential part of the *stemma*. It retained the feature of the original diadem of a double row of pearls with precious stones set between, the most notable, either round or square, set in the centre. A trefoil which some writers have taken for a cross, was placed on top of the circlet in front.

In the IX century under the Macedonian Dynasty the *stemma* was closed with two cross-bands or arches. Reiske, in his *Commentaries*, describes the type in use in the X and XI centuries as: '. . . the *stemma* was a head covering, originating from the helmet, with gold hoops, of which one circled the head horizontally and two semi-circular ones which intersected each other; a cross was generally placed on top, the rest of it was made of rich fabric, embroidered with gems and pearls.'

With the introduction of the *stemma* the *stephanos* was no longer worn by the Emperors, but it became the insignia of the Caesars, who wore it without a cross, of the Sebastocrator, of the children of the Emperor, and of the nobles of the highest rank. It was also given by the Emperor to foreign princes.

At the end of the XI century the Comnenus Dynasty introduced a new type of crown called the *kamelaukion*. It had a textile cap covering the head with two cross-pieces of gold which later on became a complete hemisphere. Anna Comnena described the crown of her father, the Emperor Alexius Comnenus, thus: '. . . the Imperial diadem circles the head like a perfect hemisphere, adorned on all sides with pearls and gems, partly inlaid, partly pendant. From both sides strings of pearls and gems hang touching the face. This is a special accessory to the Imperial State adornment. On the *stephanoi* of the Sebastocrators and the Caesars there are but few pearls and gems without a hemispherical shape.'

The *kamelaukion* was in fact a type of crown developed from the head covering called *camelaucum* first mentioned at a very early date and which was adopted by the Greek and Syrian Popes in the late VII and early VIII century. It was referred to in the *Vita* of Pope Constantine (*obiit* 715) and may be regarded as the head-dress of the Pope of Rome which developed into the Papal Tiara. The *kamelaukion* continued in use as the Imperial Crown until the end of the Byzantine Empire.

The West was not slow to imitate Imperial practice, and rulers liked to be depicted on their coins and seals wearing the laurel wreath and other Imperial insignia. After the anointing of Pepin in 751, the crown placed on the head of the anointed king became to be regarded as a special royal emblem. The word *corona* was used metaphorically to refer to the sovereign status of a ruler and was frequently described by the term *regnum*.

The lily which had been introduced by Constantine the Great as an Imperial and Royal badge was also borrowed by the West and can be seen on the crown on the small statue of an Emperor, formerly at Metz and now in the Louvre; and also on the crown on the head of the Emperor in a miniature in the Book of the Gospels of Charles the Bald. It was soon borrowed by other western kingdoms. In England the lily crown replaced the Teutonic golden helmet at the coronation of Edgar in 973, though the crown was certainly known there earlier.

In the IX century the arched crown first appeared in the West—whether borrowed from the Byzantine Emperors or developed directly from the Teutonic helmet is not certain. Lothair I and Charles the Bald are both depicted with arched crowns, and there is a drawing by Pieresc in the Bibliothèque Nationale of King Boso of Burgundy (*obiit* 887) wearing an arched crown. In England it was introduced by Edward the Confessor towards the end of his reign. The arches seem to have been regarded as an Imperial emblem, but Otto I introduced the single arch on the Imperial Crown probably to enable the mitre, taken from Old Testament usage, to be worn. Thereafter, the single arch became a feature of the German Imperial Crown and of the later personal mitre-crowns used by the Emperors, but the open circlet with or without the lily ornament continued to be worn.

The helmet crown had been introduced in the XI century for the purpose of distinguishing the king's rank when in armour, and the first evidence appears in the reign of Henry I in England. This practice necessitated the use of a large open crown which could be conveniently worn on top of the helmet. In France the open lily crown was distinctly developed. After the Battle of Bouvines in 1214 the prestige of the French Monarchy led to the widespread adoption of great lily crowns.

In the Middle Ages it was customary not only for kings to have several crowns but also different types of crowns, and Conrad III, perhaps to distinguish his Imperial rank from that of lesser sovereigns, adopted a crown with two intersecting arches sloping upwards surmounted by the orb and cross. This was copied by Henry V in England, probably in 1416, and was adopted in Portugal in 1481, in Scotland in 1488, in France c. 1497, in Spain in 1554, in Sweden in 1561, in Poland in 1597 and in Denmark in 1624.

Although the cross had been worn on the Imperial Crown by Byzantine Emperors, possibly from the IV century, it was not introduced in the West until much later. This may have been because the cross-bands forming the arches were regarded as forming the sign of the cross on the head of the Lord's anointed. It first occurs in the German Imperial Crown which did not have the double arch; when it is not quite certain but not later than the time of Conrad II and possibly as early as Otto I. In England a single cross first appears when Mathilda brought the crown of her husband, the Emperor Henry V, to this country and it continued to be used in this form. It was not until the reign of

Henry VI that the four crosses alternating with fleurs-de-lis became a feature of the English crown, and this was probably due to the necessity to distinguish between the king's dual position as King of England and King of France.

In the Middle Ages the spirit of nationalism led to the coronation crowns being given the name of a sainted king or national hero. Thus we find St Edward's Crown in England, the Crown of Charlemagne in France, and the crowns of St Wenceslas in Bohemia, St Sylvester in the Holy See, St Stephen in Hungary, St Olaf in Norway, Constantine Monomachus in Russia and the Crown of Boleslas Chrobry in Poland.

In modern times it has been generally accepted, at least heraldically, that the upward sloping arches are an Imperial emblem and arches which are flat or depressed at the centre denote royal rank. This may date from the marriage of Queen Mary of England to Philip of Spain, when the crowns of England and Spain were displayed armorially. For the Crown of England, the Crown of St Edward, which was a closed *stemma* was taken as the model, and this with its flat or slightly depressed arches became the proto-type. Modern crowns with their rigid circlets bordered with pearls and with precious stones set between, having a stone of special merit set in the centre, and with arches surmounted with the orb and cross, continue traditions originating in the Byzantine *stemma* and the Teutonic helmet with features added to emphasise some historical event.

Some remarks must be made about precious stones, though it is intended to deal more fully with the subject in a subsequent volume. Fashions in precious stones have undergone great changes. This is partly due to the mystical properties and ideas that were attributed to precious stones in the Middle Ages, to the availability and rarity of particular sorts of precious stones and to the introduction of new methods of cutting stones which added to their appearance, brilliance and lustre.

In early times red stones were particularly prized and were given a place of special prominence in crowns and other ornaments. Oriental rubies of large size have always been rare and are but poorly represented in European royal treasuries. Their place was taken by balas rubies which are a kind of spinel and which were in fairly good supply including some of notable size. Garnets too, which were mined in Europe, were also favoured. Diamonds began to take their place as stones of exceptional merit in the XIV century, although they did not enjoy the highest esteem until the art of cutting was introduced into Europe. The modern method of cutting diamonds by the use of diamond powder was probably introduced by Louis de Berquem in 1476 when the wearing of diamond ornaments by women was already an established fashion. But there is evidence of the existence of polishers in Nuremberg as early as 1373. The rose cut was introduced in 1520 and as it avoided a waste of material it soon became popular. In the middle of the XVII century the brilliant cut was introduced, it is said by Cardinal Mazarin. The diamond then became the pre-eminent stone quite eclipsing coloured stones, and not only were many stones which had been cut in older forms recut, often at a great sacrifice in weight, but ornaments began to appear with brilliants as the sole stone used to adorn them and they have held that position ever since.

Emeralds, sapphires and pearls were also highly prized and there are many notable examples of them among crown jewels. Some stones, such as amethysts, which were at one time popular and of high value, went out of fashion when the supply became so great that they fetched but a fraction of their former price and the increased availability of good quality sapphires, emeralds and other coloured stones brought them into eclipse.

In the Middle Ages the weight of precious stones was but rarely stated. This was perhaps because of the varying standards of weight in use in different countries. At one time the carat had ten different values in Europe and three in the Orient. The name carat seems to have had different origins. Some suppose it is the weight of the seed of an African leguminous tree *Erythrini Abyssinia*, the native name of which was *kuara* and the weight of which was constant. Others claim that it is the *rati*, an Indian unit which was the weight of the scarlet and black bean-like seed of the plant *Abrus precatorius*. But the weight of this was not constant and a carat varied in different places and at different times from 1.86 to 2.25 grains troy. In 1876 a proposal was made that the carat should be universally standardised at 205.00 milligrams. The weight was eventually fixed in 1878 at 200.00 milligrams. It is not surprising that confusion arose and that large stones are often picturesquely described as being the size of a pigeon's egg or a bantam's egg or if the stone was very large of a hen's egg or even as large as a man's fist. Another difficulty in determining the weight of stones is that they were not always weighed before being set and as a result many subsequent recorded weights are often only jewellers' estimates.

While I have been at pains to include in this book all crowns and other regalia in the principal Christian kingdoms of Europe, there may be some which have been omitted for one reason or another. For instance, in the Bargello in Florence there is a crown with crosses, probably of German origin, and in the German National Museum at Nuremberg there is a crown with fleurs-de-lis, probably from Norway, but there is no certainty that these had any royal associations. A crown of the sovereign Grand Prior of Malta is still preserved in the Palazzo di Malta but this does not belong to any country included in this book. In the British Museum there is an engraving of the ancient crown of Candia or Crete, once in the Treasury of St Mark's, Venice. In the Treasury of St Maurice, Valais, Switzerland, there is a bust of St Candide wearing an arched crown. Undoubtedly there are others, including some in private ownership. I learned the other day of a lady who collected crowns as a hobby but I have been unable to ascertain whether her collection contains any of royal origin. During my researches I have on several occasions found royal ornaments put away and forgotten, which has given me a lumber-room complex. It seems more than likely that there are a number of crowns and other insignia lying mouldering in attics or in the vaults of banks, some of which from time to time will surely be rediscovered and brought to light. It is not impossible too that new finds will be made of treasures, including crowns, that have been buried and that more royal tombs will be opened to reveal their contents.

Apart from European regalia there are several crowns still extant which have been used by Christian sovereigns in countries situated in other continents. Those which are still in use today include the crown, sceptre and orb of the Emperor of Ethiopia which are kept at Addis Ababa, and the two crowns of the Queen of Tonga. The Kabaka of Buganda who was crowned according to a Christian coronation rite has a crown which is a circlet set with precious stones, inside of which is a richly embroidered tall, cylindrical hat like a fez. Others which are now but museum pieces include crowns and other regalia of the Emperors of Brazil in the museum of Petropolis near Rio de Janeiro, the crown of the Emperor Maximilian in the National Museum in Mexico City, two crowns of the Hova queens of Madagascar in the former Royal Palace at Tananarive, the crown of the Emperor Faustin Soubouque in Port au Prince, Haiti, and the regalia of the kings of Hawaii in the Museum in Honolulu. In the Ryks Museum in Amsterdam there is a royal crown of gilded base metal which was captured from a British ship by the Dutch. It was a present from King James II to the King of Guinea. There are a number of such crowns in the possession of African chiefs in West Africa and there is also a fragment of a crown, a present from an English king to an American Indian king, in the Massachusetts Museum.

London, 1960   TWINING

CHAPTER ONE

AUSTRIA

The rulers of Austria who first styled themselves dukes, then archdukes and from 1804 to 1918 emperors, owed their position to their hereditary possession of the land. Because of this there was no coronation ceremony in Austria, but on the accession of each ruler there was a ceremony of investiture at which he ratified the old privileges and freedoms and received the Homage. The fact that many of them became Emperors of the Holy Roman Empire and Kings of Bohemia and Hungary did not affect their relationship to Austria.

The heart of the state was the Mark, which lay along the south bank of the Danube and was originally formed about A.D. 800 as a defence for the Frankish kingdom against the Slavs. Otto the Great established the little border state as a distinct entity and in 976 his successor appointed a prince of the House of Babenberg as ruler. Shortly afterwards it became known as Austria.[1] In 1156 the Emperor Frederick I raised Austria to the rank of duchy and conferred upon it exceptional privileges. In order to ensure that the duchy would remain in the same dynasty, even though there might be a failure of male issue, the investiture was bestowed not only upon the Duke but also upon his wife. The Duke was assigned a rank next after the Prince Electors. The successive dukes of the Babenberg dynasty acted as almost independent rulers. They made treaties with neighbouring kings and arranged marriages with many of the great families of Europe. The Emperor only interfered in order to settle boundary disputes. The family became extinct with Duke Frederick II, who was killed in battle against the Hungarians in 1246.

The Emperor Frederick II then claimed as vacant fiefs of the Empire the Duchy of Austria and also that of Styria, which the Babenbergs had acquired and entrusted their rule to Duke Otto of Bavaria. The Pope, however, bestowed the duchies upon Hermann, Margrave of Baden, who had married the niece of the last of the Babenbergs. Although invested by the German king, Otto was unable to establish his authority. On the death of Hermann in 1251 the Estates of Austria met and chose Ottakar, son of Wenceslas I of Bohemia, as their Duke in order to end the prevailing unrest.

The origin of the Austrian ducal insignia is uncertain. We know, however, that in 1228 the Emperor Frederick II, by a patent, granted to Duke Leopold and the other three dukes of the Empire the right to use the *piletus ducalis circumdatus ferto pinnito*.

In 1273 Rudolph of Hapsburg, the Landgrave of Alsace, who had been elected German king, defeated and killed Ottakar, who had by that time become King of

---

[1] Austria in German is *Oesterreich*, meaning 'East Realm'. The name first occurs in a charter of 996 in the phrase *in regione vulgari nomine Ostarrichi*.

Bohemia. Rudolph invested his sons Albert and Rudolph with the duchies of Austria and Styria. This marked the beginning of the Hapsburg domination of Austria. Rudolph's successors continued to rule as Dukes of Austria, and in the XIV century Duke Rudolph IV (1358–65) unsuccessfully solicited from his father-in-law, the Emperor Charles IV, the higher title of Archduke. Despite this failure he sought to combine all the privileges previously bestowed, and in a document known as the *privilegium maius*, which today is considered to be a forgery, it was ordained that the Dukes of Austria should wear a prince's mantle and a crown surmounted by gables over the ducal hat. Representations of this ornament are depicted in a portrait of Rudolph IV (*Plate 1, a*) in the Diocesan Museum in Vienna and also in portraits of his successor. This form of ducal hat combines two symbolic elements, the hat which was the emblem of the ducal title and the single arch and cross borrowed from the Imperial Crown, which symbolised royal power and thus marked the special position of Austria.

In 1437 Duke Albert was elected Emperor. At that time the principle of primogeniture was not practised in the House of Hapsburg and the duchies were ruled by two or sometimes three members of the family. Albert's successor, Frederick III, who was crowned as Emperor at Rome in 1453, ratified the claims made by Rudolph IV and raised Austria to the status of an archduchy bestowing upon the ruling Duke the title of King which, however, does not appear to have been used. There were indeed important reasons why the title should not be handed down to Frederick's successors as sovereigns of Austria. Frederick himself was already a king and wished to establish the dignity of Austria as being equal to other kingdoms in Central Europe, but its use might have led to the introduction of the elective principle for the rulers of Austria, whereas the hereditary principle was considered to be essential as the power sprang from the ownership of land.

Although Austria had become an archduchy, the Hapsburgs were not yet in undisputed possession, and, in fact, in 1487 the Hungarians, having defeated the Austrians, became for a time possessed of Austria, Styria and Carinthia. The Emperor Maximilian I (1493–1519) recovered the archduchy and re-established the House of Hapsburg as rulers. He reorganised the lands over which his descendants were destined to rule and established his authority. At that time the archduchy comprised the land above and below the River Enns which later became known as Upper and Lower Austria. Maximilian was succeeded by his son Charles of Spain, who was known as the Emperor Charles V from 1519 to 1556. Charles, in order to save himself from the direct responsibility of the Hapsburg domains, resigned these lands and titles to his brother, Ferdinand I, who was elected Emperor on Charles's abdication in 1558, and who in turn was succeeded by his son Maximilian II in 1564. On Maximilian's death in 1576 his son Rudolph II was elected Emperor. Towards the close of his reign Rudolph was afflicted by a mental disease, and this and his childless marriage led to his deposition by his brother Matthias, who had new problems important to the future position of Austria to face. The Turkish menace and the spread of Protestantism made it desirable that Austria should be assured of unity under a Roman Catholic dynasty, but the succession was a matter of considerable complication. To ensure a closer connection between the Roman Catholic Church and the ruling dynasty of Austria, the Archduke

b   *Austrian archducal hat, 1616.*
Abbey of Klosterneuburg (p. 3)

a   *Portrait of Duke Rudolph IV (1358–65) wearing*
Austrian archducal hat. Diocesan Museum, Vienna
(p. 2)

c   *Painting of archducal hat of Joseph II, 1764.*
Treasury, Vienna (p. 4)

d   *Crown on reliquary of St Leopold, 1616.*
Abbey of Klosterneuburg (p. 3)

a   *Styrian ducal hat on tomb of Duke Ernest the Iron (obiit 1424). Monastery at Rein (p. 4)*

b   *Portrait of the Emperor Frederick III, c. 1460, wearing Styrian ducal hat. Monastery at Vorau (p. 4)*

c   *Sceptre and sword of the Styrian Land Marshal, XVII Century. Johanneum, Graz (p. 4)*

d   *Styrian ducal hat, XV Century. Johanneum, Graz (p. 4)*

Maximilian III, associating its trusteeship with his forebear, St Leopold, had a new archducal hat made and solemnly handed it over to the Monastery of Klosterneuburg.[1] This Hat was made by a goldsmith of Prague and took a form different from that of its predecessors, being closed with two arches and surmounted by an orb and cross. The document by which the Monastery of Klosterneuburg was entrusted with the safekeeping of the archducal hat stated that it was given 'in love of the Roman Catholic Church and in memory of St Leopold, the founder of his House as Margrave of Austria'. The 15th November 1616—the Feast of St Leopold—was chosen for the ceremony of handing over the archducal hat, and at the same time the reliquary of the saint adorned with a rich crown was presented to the monastery. At the ceremony the eternal punishment of God was invoked upon those who took the hat away, although to the Archduke was reserved the right to remove it for the ceremony of investiture, provided that it was returned within thirty days. It was on several occasions removed from the monastery for greater safety and in 1645 was taken to Seckau for four years to prevent it from falling into the hands of the Swedes. In 1683 it was removed, during the Turkish invasion, to the Abbey of St Nikola near Passau. In 1718 it was taken to the Treasury, Vienna, and in 1791, when danger from the French was feared, it was removed to Pressburg. In 1791 it went to Prague, in 1800 to Hungary and in 1813 it again went to the Vienna Treasury. This archducal hat was used at the investiture of Archduke Ferdinand II in 1620 and subsequently at all such ceremonies down to that of the last reigning archduke, Ferdinand the Good, at Vienna in 1835 and in the Tyrol in 1838.

The Austrian Archducal Hat (*Plate 1, b*) made in 1616 is still kept in the Treasury of the Monastery of Klosterneuburg. The hat itself is of a stiff red material. Fastened with silk to the hat are eight plates in the form of isosceles triangles. The four triangles at the front, back and sides are surmounted by single pear-shaped pearls and from behind these spring the arches. The other four triangles are surmounted by round pearls. All the plates are of gold richly decorated. The point of each plate is emphasised by a lozenge-shaped diamond, in the centre of each plate is a large stone in a circular setting, in the axial plates are balas-rubies and in the others emeralds. They are surrounded by collets of small table-cut stones from which extend elaborate designs in red, blue and green enamel embodying other precious stones. The edges of the plates are picked out in spots of white enamel inside which is a border with a design in enamel. The arches are flat and decorated both on the top surface and on their sides with a design carried out in pearls, table-cut precious stones and enamel. At the point of juncture of the arches rises an orb formed of a round sapphire set *à jour* in a ring, on the summit of which rests a small cross. The hat is lined with ermine which is turned up outside and eight semi-circular tufts rise between the plates. The present ermine lining is believed to be a recent addition. Formerly there was probably one of smaller dimensions which did not hide the plates. Expert opinion considers that this ornament was made by the same craftsmen who made the Austrian imperial sceptre and orb, the workmanship and style being very similar.

The crown on the reliquary of St Leopold (*Plate 1, d*) in the Monastery of Klosterneuburg is very different from that on the archducal hat. It is very much more ornate and resembles more a royal crown. The arches are composed of ropes of seed pearls and surmounted by an orb and cross.

1 For these circumstances and the subsequent description of the Archducal Hat and the Crown of St Leopold, see W. Pauker and E. Kris: 'Österreichs Erzherzogenhut im Stift Klosterneuburg' published in the *Jahrbuch der Kunsthistorischen Sammlungen in Wien*, N.F., Bd III, 1933.

In 1764 Joseph II was crowned Emperor at Frankfurt during the lifetime of his parents, and it was considered appropriate that he should wear the archducal hat for his state entry into the city. As the ceremony was not an archducal investiture the clergy at the Monastery of Klosterneuburg asserted that the archducal hat in their possession could not be made available as it 'was not conformable with the privileges granted by the Holy Roman Emperors and Kings to the Most Serene Ducal House of Austria'. It was, therefore, necessary for a new hat to be made for the occasion. This followed more or less the earlier model, having twelve gables and a single arch. A contemporary painting of this ornament (*Plate 1, c*) is still preserved in the Vienna Treasury, and the frame deprived of its jewels is kept in the storeroom of the Treasury.

Besides the archducal hat the insignia used at the ceremonies of investiture consisted of the sword and two banners for Upper and Lower Austria respectively, and since the time of Matthias a sceptre and orb. In Styria, too, a ducal hat was introduced. It is first represented on the tomb of Duke Ernest the Iron (*obiit* 1424) (*Plate 2, a*) at the Monastery of Rein, and can also be seen in a portrait of the Emperor Frederick III dating from about 1460 which is now in the Monastery of Vorau (*Plate 2, b*). This ducal hat was removed to Vienna in the time of Maria Theresa, but there were requests from Styria for its return to Graz, where it had formerly been kept. In 1766 before its return it was restored and the pearls were added and a new cap provided. Today it is preserved in the Johanneum at Graz (*Plate 2, d*). It is of silver gilt and consists of ten gables each topped by a drop-shaped pearl. It is closed by a single arch surmounted by a cross. Also preserved in the Johanneum at Graz are a sceptre and a sword (*Plate 2, c*) which were used as emblems of authority by the Land Marshal.

In Carinthia there was a ceremony of investiture and a ducal hat, but these are no longer preserved. In the Tyrol there were no separate insignia and the only ceremony of investiture was that held in 1838 when the Austrian archducal insignia were used. However, a ducal hat and a sceptre (*Plate 3, b*) are preserved in the Treasury of the church at Mariastein in the Tyrol. The hat is of gilded copper and consists of ten gables closed with two arches and surmounted by an orb and cross. Semi-precious and imitation stones are used in its decoration. Inside is a cap turned up with ermine. Both ornaments belong to the first half of the XVI century but their origin is uncertain. They have sometimes been called the Hat and Sceptre of the Emperor Matthias, and one theory is that they were that Emperor's insignia as Duke of Bavaria and were given by him to the church at Mariastein. In 1613, whilst on a visit to Innsbruck, the Archduke Maximilian III sent for them but appears to have considered them as unsuitable for use.

There is in Austria another group of crowns which are not well known and although perhaps they do not properly belong to our subject they are worthy of a brief mention. At Salzburg is situated the ancient Abbey of Nonnberg, the foundation of which is, by tradition, attributed to a Merovingian princess, about A.D. 600.[1] At one time the nuns were drawn from noble families and the abbess was of princely rank. Today in the Abbey there is still kept a crown (*Plate 3, a*) probably of French origin which is

---

[1] There may be similar crowns in other abbeys which were royal foundations. One such was in the Carolingian Convent of Frauenchiemsee until 1921 and was worn by the Abbess. It can still be seen in portraits preserved in the Convent.

considered to belong to the middle of the xv century. It was originally placed on the head of the reliquary bust of the founder of the Abbey—St Ermintrude—but was replaced by a baroque crown in 1712 when the earlier crown was placed round the saint's neck as a necklace. Today it is kept separately and is worn by the abbess in processions on great feast days. The crown is characteristic of a princess's crown of the period and consists of twelve silver gilt fleurs-de-lis decorated with precious stones and pearls and joined by hinges on the front of which are small plates bearing figures in enamel and surmounted by jewelled trefoil ornaments on pins. The baroque crown (*Plate 3, c*) is in the form of a royal crown closed with two arches and surmounted by a cross. It is richly decorated with pearls and a few precious stones, and on the front arch is a small plaque bearing an enamelled picture of the Virgin Mary with St Ermintrude. It was made either in 1654 or 1712 and replaced the original crown on the bust. This crown was in turn replaced on the head of the bust by a very elaborate crown which is said to date from 1753. The reliquary bust dates from 1316. The fourth crown (*Plate 3, d*) was found in the tomb of Abbess Anna von Weggarten (1435–39) when it was opened in 1629. It is a simple circlet but of interest because it is closed with two arches.

When Napoleon was proclaimed Emperor of the French on 14th May 1804 the great House of Hapsburg became in danger of being relegated to a position inferior to the Bonapartes, whom they regarded as upstarts, as it seemed probable that either the Holy Roman Empire would collapse or Napoleon would be elected Emperor in succession to Francis II. In order to forestall such an eventuality, and to preserve the position of his house, Francis II, on 11th August 1804, assumed the style of 'Francis I, Hereditary Emperor of Austria', while still keeping the title of Roman Emperor elect. In 1806 Austria, by the Treaty of Pressburg, lost Venice and the Tyrol, while the confederation of the Rhine broke the unity of Germany. On 6th August 1806 Francis formally resigned the imperial dignity in an instrument which announced that, finding it impossible in the altered state of things to fulfil the obligations imposed by the engagements taken at his election, he considers as dissolved the bonds which attached him to the Germanic body, releases from their allegiance the States of which it consisted and retires to the government of his hereditary dominion under the title of 'Emperor of Austria'.[1]

Francis II (Francis I, Emperor of Austria), having been crowned at Frankfurt in 1792, was not crowned again on the occasion of the change of his title and status. When the question of proclaiming the Austrian Empire was receiving consideration, Cobenzl addressed the Emperor on 5th November 1804 to the effect that 'the octagonal coronation crown' was the real Imperial Crown of the Holy Roman Empire and 'under these circumstances the House Crown could be used as the hereditary Imperial Crown, which makes it unnecessary to purchase a very costly crown for the new imperial honour, and Your Majesty, or Your Majesty's successors can be crowned with it'.[2]

The so-called 'House Crown' is a beautiful example of the Renaissance work of German goldsmiths. Since Sigismund had in 1424 removed the Imperial Regalia to

---

[1] The original document is quoted in full in Meyer's *Corpus Iuris Confoederationis Germanicae*, Vol. I, p. 70. [2] O. Kralik: *Die Oesterreichische Kaiserkrone*, 1917.

Nuremberg the German Imperial Crown was no longer available, except for very special occasions, and a personal crown for the Emperor was more than ever necessary. Frederick III (1440–93) had introduced a personal crown with the mitre in a permanent form and similar crowns were made for Maximilian I (1493–1519) and Charles V (1519–56), but these were sold in Madrid in 1561. Rudolph II had an exceptional opportunity of having a crown of outstanding artistic merit made. He was a notable patron of the arts and particularly fond of precious stones. He established an *atelier* in the Hradshin at Prague to which he attracted not only distinguished artists but engaged Milanese craftsmen—the *Miseroni*—who were experts in cutting precious stones. Moreover, at about that time the Tsar of Russia had made a rich present of gold to Rudolph. It has not been accurately determined who designed and made the crown, but it may have been the work of several craftsmen. At one time it was thought to have been the work of David Altenstetter of Augsburg, but more recent research[1] attributes it to a Dutch goldsmith, Jan Vermeyen, probably assisted by Jan Moors, and a noted jeweller Jost Gelwe (Gulwe). In the course of time this crown came to be known officially as the House Crown, the first documentary evidence being in the will of Ferdinand II. Rudolph's successor, Matthias, added a sceptre and orb to the House Regalia and these were made in the same workshop as the crown in Prague in 1615.

With the change of title of the Austrian archdukes in 1804 to that of Hereditary Emperor it was necessary for a new coat of arms to be adopted. From the XIV century onwards the emperors had used a mitre crown heraldically, although at times a formal royal crown was used; this was decorated with alternate scallops and pearls and was closed with arches surmounted by an orb and cross. On 11th August 1804 Francis II issued an ordinance defining the new arms which were to be surmounted by the Austrian Hereditary Imperial Crown. This was a formalised version of the Rudolph Crown with an orb and cross instead of the distinctive sapphire which surmounted the actual crown. The Emperor of Austria was also King of Bohemia, of Hungary and from 1815 to 1867 of Lombardo-Venetia. He was also titular King of Dalmatia and Grand Duke of Zara and Ragusa, and for these dominions heraldic crowns, somewhat more ornate than those in use in Western Europe, were used heraldically.

No occasion arose for Francis to use the regalia until the coronation of his son Ferdinand the Kind as King of Hungary at Pressburg in 1830. Four sketches for regalia and robes to be worn by the Emperor on this occasion were prepared by Philipp von Stubenrauch and are still preserved in the Vienna Treasury. The Matthias sceptre and orb and the sword which had been made in the XVII century to complete the set were naturally chosen as the Emperor's regalia. As there was no suitable mantle available, a new one was made. A portrait of Francis in full robes and regalia as Emperor of Austria was painted by Friedrich von Amerling (*Plate 4, a*), and this was the only time that the Rudolph Crown was worn as the Imperial Crown of Austria. A 'substitute' crown was made for Francis to wear at his son's coronation ceremony. Although it conformed with the general design of the Rudolph Crown, it was simpler and lighter. It was melted down in 1871.

[1] Arpad Weixlgärtner: *Die Weltliche Schatzkammer in Wien. Neue Funde und Forschungen*, I, II. *Jahrbuch der Kunsthistorischen Sammlungen in Wien*, N.F. Bd I (1926), Bd III (1928).

a   *Royal crown, XV Century.
Nonnberg Abbey* (p. 4)

b   *Ducal or archducal hat and sceptre, XVI Century.
Mariastein Church* (p. 4)

c (left)   *Baroque crown for reliquary bust of
St Ermintrude, 1712. Nonnberg Abbey* (p. 5)

d (right)   *Crown from tomb of Abbess Anna von Weggarten (obiit
1439). Nonnberg Abbey* (p. 5)

a *Portrait of the Emperor Francis I with regalia of Emperor of Austria by Friedrich von Amerling, 1830. Treasury, Vienna*
(p. 6)

b *Accession ceremony of the Emperor Francis Joseph, 1848* (p. 7)

On Francis's death in 1835 Ferdinand became Emperor of Austria, but there was no coronation. The Imperial Regalia were, however, displayed at the accession ceremony, as they were on similar occasions for Ferdinand's successors (*Plate 4, b*). In 1838 Ferdinand was crowned King of Lombardo-Venetia at Milan and a special set of regalia was made consisting of an outer frame of a crown to contain the Iron Crown of Lombardy, a sceptre, an orb, a mantle and a sword. The sceptre, orb and the frame of the crown were broken up in 1871–2. An aquatint by A. Weissenböck depicting Ferdinand wearing these insignia is still preserved in the Vienna Treasury, together with the sword and mantle. Ferdinand abdicated in 1848 and was succeeded by Francis Joseph, who died in 1916 when Charles I became Emperor, but was forced to abdicate at the end of the First World War in November 1918, and thus the long rule of the House of Hapsburg over Austria came to an end.

During the XVI century many of the treasures of the Hapsburgs were stored in a set of rooms in the north-east tower of the ancient palace in Vienna. It was not until 1890–1, following the opening of the Art Historical Museum, that the regalia, emblems, jewels and other objects of historical value were assembled in one collection and housed in a wing of the Hofburg, now known as the *Weltliche Schatzkammer* or Secular Treasury. Here was assembled the treasure of the House of Hapsburg. This included the Austrian archducal regalia, other than the 1616 Archducal Hat; the Imperial Austrian regalia; the regalia, coronation robes and relics of the Holy Roman Empire; heralds' tabards and staves and other ceremonial insignia; the insignia of various Orders of Chivalry; the treasure inherited from the Dukes of Burgundy, including the ornaments of the Golden Fleece; the Hapsburg family jewellery and heirlooms; relics of the Empress Marie Louise, the Duke of Reichstadt and the Emperor Maximilian of Mexico and other miscellaneous items including pictures, miniatures, tapestries, trinkets and the like. At one time or another the Crown of St Stephen of Hungary; the Crown of Bohemia; the Iron Crown of Lombardy and the Austrian and Styrian archducal hats were kept in the Treasury, but were returned to their own national repositories. During the Napoleonic Wars the treasure was moved when danger threatened Vienna. In 1805 it went to Offen; in 1809 to Temesvar; in 1813 it had been placed on board a ship on the Danube, but news came of the victory of the allies and it became unnecessary for it to be removed again.

On 1st November 1918 on his abdication the Emperor Charles ordered the jewels which were the private property of the imperial family to be removed and taken to his place of exile in Switzerland. Other objects were claimed by various countries after the First World War but only the coronation regalia used by Napoleon as King of Italy and a few objects associated with Hungary were given up. When Hitler occupied Austria in 1938 he fulfilled a promise he had given to the city of Nuremberg and sent the regalia and the relics of the Holy Roman Empire there. Consequently the Treasury which had first been opened to the public in 1827 was closed. During the Second World War the contents of the Treasury were evacuated to a place of safety. In 1946 the United States Occupation Authorities in Germany, into whose hands they had fallen, returned the regalia and relics of the Holy Roman Empire, and on 1st July 1954 the Treasury was opened once more to the public, and the collection, which had been enriched with important items which had previously been deposited in the Art Historical Museum, has since been exhibited in the old rooms but rearranged to greater advantage. There are some 190 items in all in the Treasury, but only those which belong to our subject can be described here.

The first group consists of ornaments belonging to the Insignia of the Archducal Hereditary Homage.

The sceptre and orb (*Plate 5, a*) are of simple Gothic design in silver gilt, and their origin is unknown. In the German National Museum at Nuremberg there is a portrait of Sigismund, who became King of Bohemia in 1419, bearing his personal regalia, including a sceptre and orb of very similar but not exact design (*Plate 5, c*). The picture was painted between 1510 and 1512, so that there is no proof that they had been the actual regalia used by Sigismund. It is thought by some that they were part of the personal regalia of George of Poděbrad and remained among the Bohemian regalia until the time of Matthias. In the Vienna Treasury there is a portrait of Matthias as King of Bohemia, of which country he became king in 1616, in which these ornaments can be recognised (*Plate 5, b*). From the time of Matthias they were used at the investitures of Austrian archdukes, and down to the last investiture in Austria in 1835 and in Tyrol in 1838 they were carried by high Court dignitaries at the ceremony.

The Sword of Investiture (*Plate 6, c*) dates from the last quarter of the xv century, and although there is no reliable information as to its use before the xix century, it may have been first used at the investiture of Archduke Maximilian V (the Emperor Maximilian I) in 1497. It was evidently the ceremonial sword of Maximilian and is the only object of his personal regalia which is still known to exist. The slender, delicately shaped handle consists of three distinct parts, of which the first is the octagonal pommel of browned iron with shields cut in relief and ornamented with damascened work. The shields terminate in an archducal coronet and a royal crown. Two pieces of open brass work are attached to the quillons and represent a royal crown with the Austrian arms, the royal eagle and another *M* all worked in arabesque. When the hilt is disjoined, the lobes of the quillons show the armourer's mark near the tang, *MAISTER M.S. VON H.* The blade bears three rows of deeply incised lozenges and is decorated along its whole length with designs cut in gold foil and soldered to the blued steel. The designs represent coats of arms, inscriptions and foliage. The sword was restored in 1871.

The Hereditary Banner of Upper and Lower Austria has the shape of a cavalry guidon and is made of crimson silk damask terminating in two points and edged with a fringe of crimson and gold. A border of gold and silver runs along the edges. The centre shows on one side the embroidered arms of the Archduchy of Lower Austria (a white crossbar on a red field and five golden eagles on a blue field) and on the other the arms of Upper Austria. A smaller coat of arms, that of the Counts of Abensberg and Traun, hereditary bannerets, is inserted in the border. The fluted shaft, to which the Banner is fastened by golden nails, is painted red and decorated with gold and silver stripes. It has a clasp to which the shoulder-belt, also richly embroidered in silver and gold, is attached. The metal points of the shaft bear on one side the coat of arms of the Counts of Traun, and on the other side the intertwined initial letters of their name.

There is also a Hand of Justice which dates from the xvii century (*Plate 6, a*). It is of silver gilt and the upper extremity takes the form of an outstretched hand reminiscent of the Hand of Justice in the French regalia, but on a miniature scale. According to tradition it was the emblem of authority of the Governor of the Hapsburg

a   *Sceptre and orb in Austrian archducal insignia, XV Century. Treasury, Vienna* (p. 8)

b   *Portrait of Matthias as King of Bohemia by Hans von Aachen. Treasury, Vienna* (p. 8)

c   *Portrait of the Emperor Sigismund by Albrecht Dürer (1510–12). German National Museum, Nuremberg* (pp. 8 and 127)

a   *Hand of Justice used as emblem of authority of the Governor of Hapsburg's land in Alsace and Breisgau. XVII Century. Treasury, Vienna (p. 8)*

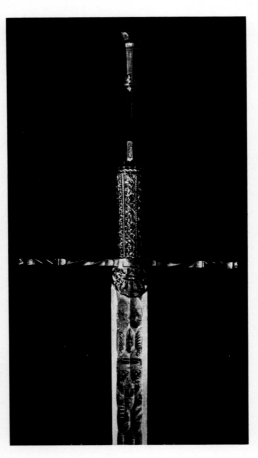

c   *Sword belonging to Austrian archducal insignia. XV Century. Treasury, Vienna (p. 8)*

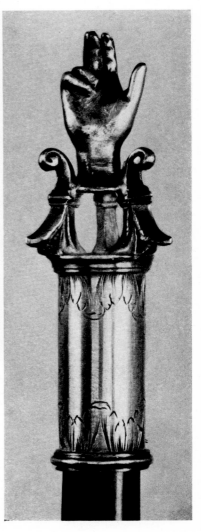

b   *Hand of Justice, XVII Century. Historical Museum, Basle (p. 9)*

d   *Hand of Justice, XVIII Century. Historical Museum, Basle (p. 9)*

b and d were probably used for similar purposes as a.

Austrian Imperial Crown, 1602, front view. Treasury, Vienna (p. 9)

a *Imperial Crown, right side* (p. 9)

b *Imperial Crown, left side* (p. 9)

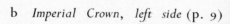

Lands in Alsace and the Breisgau. In the Historical Museum at Basle there are two such Hands of Justice dating from the XVII and XVIII centuries, which are thought to have been used for a similar purpose.

The other objects, such as staves of office and tabards, do not call for any special note. But there are some interesting and curious items such as the dog collar of green velvet and oak leaves in gold with mountings of silver which was worn by the leading hound of the Grand Master of the Hunt and the hawking pouch, hawks' hoods and decoy of green velvet embroidered with gold which were the attributes of the Chief Falconer.

The second group consists of the ornaments of the Austrian Imperial Regalia. The Imperial Crown of Austria in its present form is substantially as it was originally made in 1602 (*Plates 7* and *8*), though it has been subjected to a loss of jewels on various occasions. In 1764 pearls and precious stones were removed to adorn the archducal hat of Joseph II. In 1830 some stones were taken for the so-called substitute crown made for Ferdinand. Again in 1867 stones were removed for the brilliant crown of the Empress Elizabeth on the occasion of her coronation at Budapest. In 1871 the Keeper of the Treasury, Quirin von Leitner, ordered the jeweller Kochert to make good the losses.

The Imperial Crown has as its base a gold circlet bordered top and bottom with well-matched pearls, 91 on the upper rim and 81 on the lower. On the band table-cut diamonds are set alternately with beautifully enamelled daisy-shaped ornaments in the centre of each of which is set a large button-pearl. Including the stone in the front which is said to be a white sapphire, there are 8 large table-cut stones, each set in a square setting bordered by 15 smaller diamonds.

The circlet is surmounted by eight fleurs-de-lis, four large and four small. The frame of the design is of gold delicately enamelled with the outline thrown into relief by a graduation of pearls. The fleurs-de-lis in the front and back have in their centres great red stones which are uncut but polished and held in light settings *à jour*. Although it is claimed that they are rubies, this is unlikely and, indeed, their colour is not deep enough for spinels. It is more probable that they are garnets, rich deposits of which occur in Bohemia. Each is surrounded by 4-point or table-cut diamonds. The side fleurs-de-lis have had faceted spinels in their centre, each of which is surmounted by 4-point or table-cut diamonds. The fleur-de-lis in front is surmounted by a drop-shaped pearl. The fleur-de-lis at the back is also surmounted by a fine drop-shaped pearl but smaller than the one in front. The two fleurs-de-lis at the sides are surmounted by smaller drop pearls. The four smaller fleurs-de-lis are also outlined and surmounted by pearls. In the centre, from a base of 3 stones, rises a graduated row of 7 rubies.

The frame of the mitre-shaped cap is in two parts, each part consisting of two triangular gold plates, joined on the inner edge by a broad band on which there is rich enamelling in varied design of birds, butterflies and flowers. The centre edges of these bands are edged with a row of spendidly matched pearls. The gold plates themselves show in exquisite workmanship four scenes in bas-relief. On the first Rudolph II is depicted as a conqueror, armed, bareheaded, holding the sceptre in his right hand and with five *Victoriae* of which one with wings holds a laurel wreath above his head. Turkish trophies lie at his feet. The second shows Rudolph II, in armour, wearing the archducal hat and bearing the sceptre in his right hand, passing in procession with halberdiers in the background. This is thought to represent the coronation procession at Prague. The third plate depicts Rudolph II on horseback on a hillock, brandishing a sword. He is dressed in armour and wears an open royal crown. This scene resembles the traditional part of the Hungarian coronation ceremony when the newly-crowned king mounts his charger, rides on to a mound composed of soil from each of the Hungarian counties, and, brandishing his sword, swears to defend the boundaries of the kingdom. It, therefore, probably depicts the coronation at Pressburg. The fourth plate shows the imperial coronation at Frankfurt. A mitred bishop places the Imperial Crown on the head of the Emperor, while six men wearing electoral hats stand nearby.

Connecting the front of the crown with the back, and thus dividing the two sides of the mitre-shaped cap, is a hoop or arch of gold, embellished with diamonds and pearls and finished with delicate white and blue enamel work. The crown is surmounted by a small cross of gold with a diamond set in the centre. From the upper part of the cross branch two golden arms which hold in place a large sapphire uncut but polished. Inside the arch is the inscription:

RVD (OLPHVS) ROM (ANORUM) IMP (ERATOR) HVNG
(ARIAE) ET BOH (EMIAE) REX CONSTVXIT MDCII.

On the gold circlet the upper row of pearls, according to Kunz,[1] totals 960 gr and the lower 840. Between these pearls are others of 440 gr, while the large drop pearls weigh 2,052 gr. The largest pearl is drop shaped and had belonged to Rudolph II. It weighs 104 gr. This may be the pear-shaped pearl which, according to Gomara,[2] was secured in 1515 from the Indians at Terarequi in the Gulf of Panama and came into the possession of Charles V. In 1610 Shah Abbas sent an emissary to Prague with many valuable gifts for the Emperor. Among these were 'three oriental pearls exceeding big'. These may be among the pear-shaped pearls in the crown. The original cost of the crown was 700,000 talers, which in those days was an enormous sum. There is a leather case with gold pressing for the crown which was made in the early part of the XVI century.

The Imperial Sceptre (*Plate 9, a*) was made in 1615 by Andreas Osenbruck who, from 1613 to 1617, was Court Goldsmith to the Emperor Matthias, the successor of Rudolph II. On the handle and concealed by a capsule is another capsule bearing on the outside the monogram of the Emperor Matthias and the year of his election—1612—while inside is engraved the signature *ANDREAS OSENBRUCK fecitt anno 1.6.1.5*. The staff of the sceptre is of ivory, but the handle at the bottom shows an abundance of delicately executed enamel work of a different design from that of the crown and orb. The top of the ivory rod is surmounted by an elaborate gold and enamel bulb which shows similar work to that of the band of the orb. The edgings of pearls, both on the handle and the upper part, are similar to those on the crown and orb, as are the settings of the diamonds and rubies. The sceptre is topped by a large uncut but polished sapphire, smaller than the one in the crown and of lighter colour. Kunz states that the pearls in the sceptre weigh 300 gr.

The Imperial Orb (*Plate 9, b*) is ornamented very similarly to the crown and sceptre. The globe is of pure gold and is surrounded in the middle by a broad band, richly decorated with enamel and from top to bottom by a narrower band also decorated with enamel. The broad band carries a row of pearls on its upper and lower edges, 50 in the former and 48 in the latter. On the front and back and at the two sides of this band are 4 single table-cut diamonds, each in a square setting edged with 16 smaller diamonds. Between all the diamonds is rich enamel work, in the middle of which are two daisy ornaments of similar design to those on the crown. The daisy ornaments have a large pearl set in the centre of each. The narrow band is decorated with multi-coloured enamels of birds, butterflies and flowers, of similar designs to those on the crown. The bottom of the globe is flat. At the sides, above and below the broad band, are isolated enamel decorations, two on each side. On the top of the globe is a richly decorated pedestal on which

---

[1] G. F. Kunz: *The Book of the Pearl*. It is not known where Kunz obtained this information, as there is no record in the inventories of the weight of the pearls. It may be a jeweller's estimate.

[2] Francisco Lopez Gomara : *Historia General de les Indias*.

rests a cross, having the side and top extremities in the shape of stunted fleurs-de-lis. Each of these fleurs-de-lis has, in the centre, a large table-cut diamond surrounded by 3 small diamonds. In the centre of the cross there is a similar table-cut diamond surrounded by 4 small diamonds and by 4 large table-cut rubies. On the enamelled pedestal are 4 small diamonds. At the junction of the horizontal and perpendicular pieces of the cross 4 pear-shaped pearls protrude, while the two side fleurs-de-lis are pointed with pearls. Surmounting the cross in a gold clasp is a beautiful uncut sapphire which, unfortunately, has been pierced by a gold rod that secures it to the clasp.

There is some doubt as to whether the orb is of the same workmanship as the crown, but it is generally thought that both the orb and the sceptre were made for the coronation of the Emperor Matthias by the same craftsman. Kunz states that the pearls in the orb weigh 1,615 gr.

A noteworthy feature common to these imperial ornaments and to the archducal hat is that each is surmounted by a large uncut but polished sapphire. In the Middle Ages special qualities and powers were attributed to precious stones. Such superstitions were given a new lease of life in Rudolph II's Court. The Emperor's physician, Anselmas de Boodt, in his *Gemmarum et lapidium historia*, has described in detail the miraculous properties of sapphires. He claims that they possessed the power to alleviate the heat of fevers, to heal wounds, to preserve the wearer from the temptations of Venus and to make his heart strong. It is not unnatural, therefore, that the great sapphire should be given so conspicuous a place in the crown, and even if the superstitions lost some of their hold in the following reign, the similarity in the general ornamentation of the other three pieces of regalia demanded from the aesthetic point of view that each should also be adorned with a notable sapphire.

The weapon designated the Austrian Imperial Sword (*Plate 9, c*) does not belong to the other ornaments in the set. It is mentioned in the Inventory of the Treasury taken in 1750, but from 1826 to 1870 it was in the Court Hunting and Harness Room and only became an ornament of the regalia in 1871. It was made in the first quarter of the XVII century but the maker's name is not known. The grip, the pommel, the cross bar and the handguard are of iron inlaid with beaten gold and ornamented with deeply set rubies and pearls and devices in enamel. The blade is flat, ribbed and ornamented with deeply set pearls and rubies, devices in enamel and with a delicate pattern of beaten gold. The designs bear no resemblance to those used on the other ornaments of the regalia. The scabbard is covered with crimson velvet, the mouth and chape being ornamented in the same style as the hilt.

When Francis attended the coronation of Ferdinand in 1830 no suitable mantle was available for him to wear with the full regalia of the Emperor of Austria. A painter named Philipp von Stubenrauch was commissioned to produce four designs, and the water-colour sketches of these are preserved in the Treasury. The mantle made from the design chosen is of cherry red velvet embroidered in gold with the imperial double-headed eagle with the escutcheon. The original ermine collar was destroyed in 1874 but was replaced in 1955. On all other great occasions including the accession ceremony of Francis Joseph in 1848 the robes and insignia of the Sovereign of the Order of the Golden Fleece were worn.[1]

With the demise of the Holy Roman Empire in 1806 the venerable regalia, relics and coronation robes of the former emperors became relegated to the position of

[1] Among the treasures of the Order of the Golden Fleece are a beautiful cross and the chain or potence (*Plate 12, a*).

museum pieces. The important role which they played in German history makes it more appropriate to describe them in Chapter Nine which deals with Germany.

When in 1471 Charles the Bold, the last of the Dukes of Burgundy of the House of Valois, died without a male heir, his rich treasure was inherited by the House of Hapsburg through the marriage of his daughter, Mary, to Maximilian I. The Court of the Dukes of Burgundy during the xv century was the richest and most luxurious in Europe.[1] The objects from this inheritance still preserved in the Vienna Treasury are:

The Burgundian Court Goblet, a superb specimen of workmanship of the second half of the xv century. It is 46 cm in height, of rock crystal in a setting of gold, decorated with enamel, pearls, diamonds and rubies. It was the property of Duke Philip the Good.

The Unicorn Sword (*Plate 10, a*), which has a hilt and scabbard of narwahl horn, a material which was highly prized in the Middle Ages and was identified with the unicorn. Both sides of the pommel are decorated with small oval plaques in enamel, representing respectively the Crucifixion and the Virgin. The sword is mentioned in an inventory of Charles the Bold, Duke of Burgundy, who was killed at Nancy in 1477. Maximilian I, to meet the heavy cost of his election as Emperor, had to pawn it in 1486, and it did not return to the Hapsburg Treasury until in 1630 one of the descendants of the nobleman to whom it had been pawned presented it to the Emperor Ferdinand II at the Diet of Ratisbon.[2]

A ring of gold (*Plate 10, b*) set with diamonds in the form of the letter *M* which in reverse forms the letters C.H.I., which is an abbreviation for the names of Jesus. According to tradition it was the engagement ring of Mary of Burgundy. It dates from the second half of the xv century.

A brooch (*Plate 10, c*) which is perhaps the finest example of xv-century brooches extant. The setting is a delicate wreath of gold and supports the traditional design of a pair of lovers. Their faces and hands are enamelled white; the man's hair is partly of gold wire and their dresses of pale cold blue enamel. The ground is filled with minute flowers and foliage in high relief. Between the lovers' heads is a triangular diamond and beneath it a *cabochon* ruby. On either side are large single pearls with 3 more at the base.[3]

A dish of oriental agate 29 in. in diameter and made from the biggest piece of agate known. According to tradition it was brought to Europe by the Crusaders as booty after the fall of Constantinople. It is probably of Oriental origin and workmanship and it dates from the second quarter of the IV century. According to legend it was associated with the Holy Grail, probably because in the XVII and XVIII centuries it was thought that an inscription which had been erased had included the name of Christ.

Among the miscellaneous objects in the Treasury are two important items of regalia. The first is a crown known as the Crown of Stephen Bocksay, Prince of Transylvania, who received it, together with a banner and sceptre and a sword, from the Sultan Achmed I by the hand of his Grand Vizier, who sent it to the Prince, who

---

[1] H. Clifford-Smith: *Jewellery*, London. Several inventories of the ducal jewels have been preserved—for those of Philip the Hardy (1392–1404) see B. J. H. Prost: *Inventaires Mobiliers et Extraits des Comptes des Ducs de Bourgogne*, 2 Vols. 1902–14. For those of Philip the Good (1396–1467) and Charles the Bold (1433–77) see A. de Laborde: *Les Ducs de Bourgogne*, Part 2, Vol. II, 1849.

[2] There is another piece of narwahl horn in the Treasury 94 in. long and 2·2 in. wide at the base. It was given to Ferdinand I by the Polish King Sigismund II in 1540. The staff of the sceptre of the Austrian Imperial Regalia may also be made of narwahl horn and not true ivory.

[3] Joan Evans: *The History of Jewellery 1100–1870*, London 1951.

was his vassal and the leader of an insurrection against Rudolph II. The crown which alone survives was brought to Vienna in 1610.

The crown takes the form of a Byzantine *Kamelaukion*, being spherical in shape and completely closed on the top. It is divided into eight fields of meridional stripes. The whole frame is made of silver plates ornamented with pearls, precious stones and niello. The leaves of the lower part of the circlet contrast with the background of alternate light green and rose-coloured silk. On the front is a small cross which was added by Stephen Bocksay (*Plate 11, c*). There is a case for the crown made of wood and covered with Persian silk brocade which shows a woman reading in a garden with a youth offering her a vessel of wine. The book which the woman holds is signed with the word *GHYIAS* in whose workshop the silk brocade was designed and made. Ghyias worked at the Court of the Shah Abbas the Great towards the end of the XVI century.

The second item of regalia is the Hungarian Sabre of Maria Theresa (*Plate 11, b*). It was originally made for Charles VI as King of Hungary in 1712, but it was worn by Maria Theresa at her coronation on 28th June 1741, and at the Pressburg Diet. It is from its association with these ceremonies that it takes its present nomenclature. The hilt and scabbard are of gold engraved with arabesques and richly set with diamonds and flat stones. The blade bears an Arabic inscription.

Other items which are of sufficient interest to deserve mention are the Golden Rose bearing the mark *GIUS. SPAGNA ROMA* which was consecrated and presented by Pope Pius VII to the Empress Caroline Augusta in 1810. The Prussian field-marshal's baton, presented by the Emperor William II to Francis Joseph, is adorned with Prussian eagles and crowns in silver, diamonds, rubies and enamel on a ground of blue velvet. Among the relics of the Empress Marie Louise and the Duke of Reichstadt are the cradle of Napoleon's son, presented by the city of Paris on 11th March 1811 to Napoleon and Marie Louise on the occasion of the birth of the son who took the title King of Rome and later Duke of Reichstadt. Another present made on the same occasion, this time by the city of Milan, is a basin and tripod of coloured bronze and silver gilt, being a copy of an antique model in the museum at Naples. Marie Louise's jewel casket is richly decorated with ornaments in stamped and chased silver plate, originally gilt, and was made by Biennais. There are two egg-cups, one of which had belonged to Louis XVI and one to Napoleon, and also a tumbler of Napoleon's, and another memento is a golden ring with a silhouette of Queen Marie Antoinette surrounded by pearls.

There are also certain ornaments which belonged to the Emperor Maximilian of Mexico, the brother of the Emperor Francis Joseph. These include his Imperial Mantle—erroneously called the Coronation Mantle, there being no coronation in Mexico. It is made of sapphire-blue satin with a collar of the Mexican Order of the Eagle embroidered in gold on the bottom, the eagle holding the serpent in its claws. There are the collars of the Order of the Eagle and of the Mexican Order of Guadelupe; a golden ring set with an emerald; three sceptres, two of which are also receptacles, for documents. The Imperial Crown of Maximilian is in the National Museum in Mexico City.

When on 1st November 1918 Count Berchthold, the High Chamberlain of the Imperial Court, was ordered by the Emperor Charles to remove the personal jewels from the Treasury he took only those objects which were regarded as the personal property of the imperial family. As a result there are but few pieces of personal jewellery in the Treasury today and they are of little interest. There are, however, some notable semi-precious stones. The first of these is a splendid hyacinth of 416 carats known as *La Bella* (*Plate 13, a*), bought by the Emperor Leopold I from the Hungarian family of Humanay in 1687. This is set in an enamelled double-headed gold eagle and forms the breast. Another stone is an opal which is said to be the largest example known. It is pear-shaped and mounted on three clasps and weighs 17 oz. In spite of its weight and size, which is that of a man's fist, it has been worn as a pendant. It is known as the 'Hungarian Opal' (*Plate 13, b*) and came from the opal mines at Cernowitz in Hungary which have been worked since 1400. In the middle of the last century it is said that an offer of £50,000 was refused for this stone.

Another stone is a very large pear-shaped amethyst in a mount (*Plate 13, d*), shaped like a gold crown set with emeralds. This was a present made by King Charles of Spain to the Emperor Leopold I. There are also 2 large topazes set in gold and one set with 2 pearls, a milk opal and an aquamarine (*Plate 13, c, e, f, g and h*) which was acquired in about 1600 and weighs 492 carats.

The personal jewellery that was removed included the following items:

Eight Golden Fleeces:

A *Toison d'or* set with 7 large brilliant solitaires of a total weight of over 89 carats, two are yellow diamonds.

A *Toison d'or* with 3 brilliants in the centre and the lamb in brilliants.

The 'Little' brilliant *Toison d'or*, the lamb being made of gold. This was so called in the reign of the Emperor Ferdinand III, and the decoration was placed in the cradle of newly born archdukes.

A *Toison d'or* with 3 large yellow sapphires (erroneously described as oriental topazes) set with brilliants. This decoration was, until 1765, in the private collection of the Emperor Francis I.

A *Toison d'or* with 2 large chrysolites.

A *Toison d'or* with 3 large garnets. It was transferred from the private collection of the Emperor Francis I on 4th December 1765.

A small brilliant *Toison d'or* with the lamb in gold.

A *Toison d'or* with 150 solitaire brilliants of the finest water and in the middle a rose-coloured brilliant of $26\frac{1}{8}$ carats.

The diamond crown which was originally made for the Empress Maria Anna was re-set for the coronation of the Empress Elizabeth as Queen of Hungary in 1867 (*Plate 11, a*). It was also used by the Empress Zita at her coronation at Budapest in 1916. The circlet was bordered with pearls and set with a profusion of diamonds. It was surmounted by eight fleurs-de-lis set with large diamonds, each with a pear-shaped pearl on top. The two arches were richly decorated with diamonds and where they intersect were slightly depressed and surmounted by a fine diamond and pearl cross. Inside is a cap of purple velvet. The finest brilliants, distinguished by their size and purity, were used. They were of the old Dutch cut and were taken from among the jewels which had belonged to the Empress Maria Theresa.

The Chaton suite, which consisted of 95 brilliants with gold links on two strings and 700 brilliants on fourteen strings and six *breloques*, each with a brilliant drop in a setting of small brilliants. These stones came from the insignia of the great military Maria Theresa Orders which belonged to the Emperor Francis and were set with 920 brilliants. By an order of the Emperor Joseph II, dated 4th January 1783, these insignia were broken up. The brilliants were removed, restrung and in this condition were stored in the Treasury for the Emperor to use in any way he wished.

The suite of pearls which consisted of a string of 114 large pearls and, as a clasp, the so-called

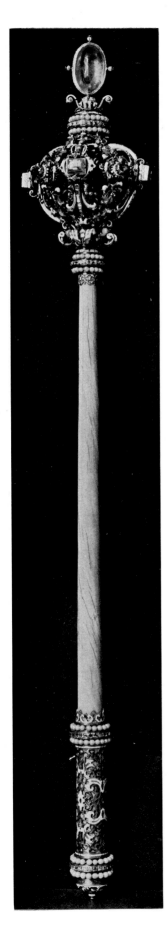

a (left) *Imperial Sceptre, 1615.*
Treasury, Vienna (p. 10)

b (right) *Imperial Orb, 1615.*
Treasury, Vienna (p. 10)

c (below) *Hilt of Imperial Sword.*
XVII Century. Treasury, Vienna
(p. 11)

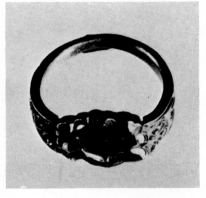

b (i) and (ii)   *Gold ring set with diamonds in the form of an M. Said to be the engagement ring of Mary of Burgundy. Second half of XV Century. Treasury, Vienna (p. 12)*

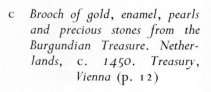

a   *The Unicorn Sword from the Burgundian Treasure. Treasury, Vienna (p. 12)*

c   *Brooch of gold, enamel, pearls and precious stones from the Burgundian Treasure. Netherlands, c. 1450. Treasury, Vienna (p. 12)*

a   *Diamond crown originally made for the Empress Maria Anna and subsequently worn by the Empresses Elizabeth and Zita. Formerly in the Treasury, Vienna.* (p. 14)

b (below, left)   *The Hungarian sabre, 1712. Treasury, Vienna* (p. 13)

c (below, right)   *Crown of Stephen Bocksay, XVII century. Treasury, Vienna* (p. 13)

a (left)   *Cross and chain, or potence,*
of the Order of the Golden Fleece (p. 11)

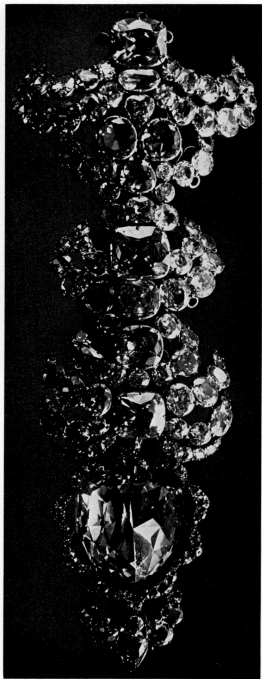

b (right)   *The Florentine diamond*
set in a hat ornament. Formerly in
the Treasury, Vienna (p. 16)

a (left) *'La Bella'
hyacinth of* 416
carats (p. 14)

b (right) *The
Hungarian Opal*
(p. 14)

c *Large topaz set as a brooch with gold and
enamel. XVI Century* (p. 14)

d *Large pear-shaped
Amethyst* (p. 14)

e *Topaz with pearls in gold setting.
XVII Century* (p. 14)

f *Oriental aquamarine of* 492 *carats in a gold
setting,* c. 1600 (p. 14)

h *Large topaz in gold setting.
XVII Century* (p. 14)

g (left) *Milk white opal in gold
setting,* c. 1600 (p. 14)

All these are in the Treasury, Vienna

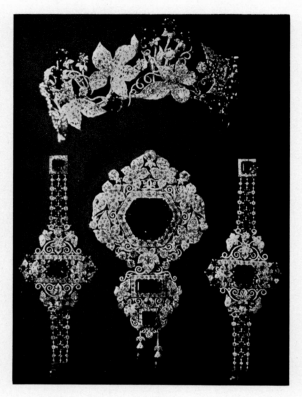

a   *Diadem, corsage and bracelets of emerald suite* (p. 15)

b   *Collar and brooches of emerald suite* (p. 15)

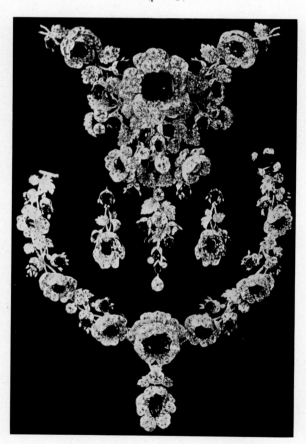

c   *Collar and breast ornament and ear-rings of ruby suite* (p. 15)

d   *Girdle of ruby suite* (p. 15)

These ornaments were formerly in the Treasury, Vienna

'Baden Solitaire' of 30 carats; a necklace and three rows of pearls, 121 in all, with a larger some-what flatter solitaire brilliant of $14\frac{1}{22}$ carats as a clasp[1]; two bracelets set with 240 medium-sized pearls with two brilliant clasps; a *sévigné* with brilliants weighing 49 carats and 6 pearls of 75 carats. This pearl set was formed out of the pearls given up on 14th October 1765 by the Empress Maria Theresa from the family jewels and out of the Tuscan pearls given up to the Treasury on 24th January 1792 by order of the Emperor Leopold II. The history of the 'Baden Solitaire' has not been recorded.

The emerald suite, known as the Maria Theresa Emeralds, which consisted of a diadem, a corsage, a necklace, two bracelets (*Plate 14, a* and *b*), two slides and a watch with chatelaine. The principal stones were taken from a very large corsage which had belonged to Maria Theresa and was afterwards worn by the Empress Marie Louise, wife of Leopold I. In 1800 the corsage was divided into eleven pieces and replaced in the Treasury. In 1810 the pieces were assembled into a suite consisting of a tiara, necklace and corsage. The present setting dates from later, probably the years 1877 and 1886. The watch had also belonged to the Empress Maria Theresa. The irregular oval case consists of a single piece of emerald. The chatelaine for the watch is set with brilliants and emeralds and was made in 1879.

The suite of rubies which was a complete parure consisting of a tiara, a girdle (*Plate 14, c* and *d*), a necklace and a pair of earrings, a corsage and a watch. The main components came from the Treasury of the Queen Marie Antoinette and were brought into safety during the French Revolu-tion. They were bought by the Emperor Francis II from Princess Maria Theresa, daughter of the unfortunate French queen, on the occasion of her marriage to the Duke of Angoulême, and added on 26th October 1801 to the other private jewellery of the Imperial House in the Treasury. The last resetting of the ruby suite took place in 1854 on the occasion of the marriage of the Emperor Francis Joseph to the Empress Elizabeth.

The diamond tiara which had the Frankfurt Solitaire as the centre piece. It was a brilliant cut diamond of the finest water weighing $44\frac{5}{8}$ carats. This stone was bought by the Emperor Francis I together with a ring in 1764 at Frankfurt-on-Main with 28,000 *louis d'or* and originally mounted in a hat buckle. After the death of the Emperor, the Empress Maria Theresa had the whole of her late consort's private jewellery, including the Frankfurt Solitaire, given over to the Treasury for safe custody in 1765.

The so-called rose necklace which consisted of fourteen rose-shaped ornaments set with brilliants. In each, one large stone was set among a number of smaller ones and there were eleven pendants set with large and splendid solitaire brilliants. With the necklace there were a pair of ear-rings with two large brilliant drops. The greater part of the brilliants used for this ornament came from the so-called 'Esclavage' which the Empress Maria Theresa received as a wedding present from her mother-in-law, the Duchess Elizabeth Caroline of Lorraine. The Duchess Elizabeth had similarly received this magnificent ornament from her mother-in-law, the widowed Queen of Poland, Eleanor, sister of the Emperor Leopold I, and afterwards consort of Duke Charles V of Lorraine. This necklace and a pair of ear-rings were placed in the Treasury for safe custody by the Empress Maria Theresa on 14th October 1765. The order relating to the ear-rings had the following note added to it by the Empress in her own hand: 'Therefore it is also the intention of Her Majesty the Empress that these ear-rings should be retained and regarded for all time as a family souvenir.'

An aigrette in the Hungarian national colours, set with emeralds, brilliants and rubies. It was

---

1 According to Kunz: 'The weight of the pearls in the first necklace was 3,400 gr, 3 of the pearls weighed 92 and 100 gr each. The weight of the second necklace was 3,780 gr. The pearls in the two bracelets weigh 2,800 gr.'

placed in the Treasury for custody in 1766 as 'belonging to the hood of the Order of St Stephen'.

A set of buttons of gold and enamel, each with five table-cut precious stones let in. These date from the time of the Emperor Rudolph II.

A breast ornament in the Hungarian national colours set with brilliants, emeralds and rubies. It was set with stones taken from the jewel casket of the imperial private treasure in 1867 for the Emperor Francis Joseph.

A small *sévigné* of brilliants with 1 rose-drop brilliant. The stones came from the family treasure of the Empress Maria Theresa.

A set of brilliants, in the centre of which is a large yellow sapphire which was worn by the Empress Maria Theresa on the ribbon of her muff during ceremonial sleigh drives.

A hat buckle with 3 yellow sapphires set round with brilliants. This ornament came from the Florentine treasure, and the Emperor Francis I wore it at his coronation as a clasp on his mantle. Later he occasionally wore it in his hat.

A ring with a small white diamond which was worn by the Emperor Francis I.

A ring with a diamond of yellowish colour.

An ornament of the Order of the Star and Cross for the use of the Patroness of the Order.

A set of brilliants with the Star and Cross Order reset in 1854 from broken objects of the imperial private treasure.

A corsage of brilliants with 380 brilliants weighing $266\frac{31}{32}$ carats.

A pair of bracelets of brilliants with 494 brilliants and two connecting pieces weighing $330\frac{1}{4}$ carats.

A set of emeralds, rubies and brilliants with the Cross of the Royal Hungarian Order of St Stephen also set with emeralds, rubies and brilliants. This ornament was worn by the Empress Maria Theresa as Grand Master of that Order on ceremonial occasions.

A pearl necklace of 86 pearls set in two rows with a clasp of brilliants with three rosettes of brilliants connected by a double row of *chatons*.[1] This ornament was an heirloom of the Empress Caroline Augusta.

An aigrette for a kalpak with semi-precious stones and diamonds of old-fashioned cut.

A brilliant pin with a triangular solitaire and two pendant brilliant drops. The pin was reset from broken ornaments of the imperial private treasure in 1854. The triangular solitaire diamond before that formed the centre piece of a Golden Fleece belonging to the Emperor Francis I and was placed in the Treasury for safe keeping on 22nd January 1766.

A necklace of 30 grey pearls with a centre piece in brilliants.[2]

The 'Florentine' Diamond.

The 'Star of Este'.

The most important stone among the Hapsburg jewels was the Florentine Diamond (*Plate 12, b*). It is yellow-tinted and weighs $133\frac{1}{3}$ Viennese carats (approximately $139\frac{1}{2}$ French carats) and may still be regarded as one of the great diamonds of the world. The official description in the catalogue of the objects contained in the Treasury of the Imperial and Royal Houses of Austria in 1880 reads:

The 'Florentine', also called the 'Great Florentine' Diamond, at present forming part of a hat buckle, is known as one of the largest diamonds in the world. It weighs $133\frac{1}{2}$ carats, but it is of rather a yellow colour. The stone is cut in nine surfaces covered with facets forming a star

1 According to Kunz: 'The weight of the pearls was 2,600 gr.'
2 According to Kunz: 'The total weight of the pearls was 1,040 gr, the largest being 48 gr.'

with nine rays. This jewel was once the property of Charles the Bold, Duke of Burgundy, who, according to the custom of the day, carried all his valuables into the battlefield, first to have them always in sight, and, secondly, on account of the mysterious power then attributed to precious stones. Charles lost this stone in the Battle of Morat on 22nd June 1476. Tradition relates that it was picked up by a peasant who took it for a piece of glass and sold it for a florin. The new owner Bartholomew May, a citizen of Berne, sold it to the Genoese, who sold it in turn to Ludovico Moro Sforza. By the intercession of the Fuggers it came into the Medici Treasury in Florence. When Francis Stephen of Lorraine exchanged this duchy for the Grand Duchy of Tuscany, he became owner of the Florentine Diamond. Through this Prince, who later became the consort of the Empress Maria Theresa, this diamond came into the private treasury of the Imperial House at Vienna. At the coronation of Francis Stephen as Emperor of Germany at Frankfurt-on-Main on 4th October 1745 the Florentine Diamond adorned the crown of the House of Austria.

Streeter[1] disagrees with much of this story and reconstructs the history on the following lines:

Charles the Bold, according to Robert de Berquem, handed over in 1476 three diamonds to his great uncle L. de Berquem, the inventor of the art of diamond cutting. These he cut, one triangular, which Charles gave to Louis XI; one thin, which he gave to Pope Sixtus IV; and one thick, which he had set in a ring. The diamond in the ring could not have been as large as the Florentine, and in any case, according to De Comines, Charles lost all his large jewels, including his great diamond which was one of the largest in Christendom, not at Nancy in 1477 but at Granson in 1476. According to one story a Swiss soldier, finding it together with a valuable pearl in a box, mistook it for a piece of glass, threw it aside, but on second thoughts he picked it up from under the wagon where it had fallen. He then sold it for a florin to a priest at Montigny who in his turn disposed of it for three florins to the Bernese authorities. At that time there was residing at Berne a wealthy merchant named Bartholomew May who had many relations, both of a commercial and private character, with Italy. Having purchased the gem for 5,000 florins and a present for the Mayor, William von Diessland, through whose mediation the sale had been effected, May sold it for a small profit to a Genoese dealer. The Milanese regent, Ludovico Moro Sforza, bought it for some 10,000 florins, and when the treasures of Milan were distributed Pope Julius II purchased it for 20,000 ducats.

But according to J. J. Fugger we learn that the diamond was bought from the Bernese Government not by Bartholomew May but by his own great uncle Jacob Fugger, head of the great Augsburg family of that name, together with the Cap of Maintenance and other jewels belonging to the Duke of Burgundy, all for 40,000 florins. In a document illustrated by himself and published by Lambecius in the *Bibliotheca Caeserea*, Fugger gives an account of these jewels. His description of Charles the Bold's large diamond does not correspond with any of the large diamonds existing today and least of all the Florentine. He describes it as a pyramid $\frac{5}{8}$ in. square at the base with the apex cut into a four-rayed star, coinciding with the middle of each face of the pyramid. It was the central piece of a beautiful pendant of diamonds, rubies and pearls and remained for some years in the Fugger family, who sold it to Henry VIII of England in 1547 shortly

1 E. W. Streeter: *The Great Diamonds of the World.*

17

before his death. It continued to form part of the English crown jewels until the reign of Queen Mary, who presented it to her husband, Philip II of Spain, in 1554. Thus, after a period of seventy-six years, the stone returned to the descendant of the original owner, Charles the Bold of Burgundy. This stone could not have been the Florentine and, in fact, there is no evidence to show that the Florentine was ever in the possession of Charles the Bold.

We find the Florentine, however, in the possession of the Grand Duke of Tuscany in the middle of the XVII century when the Duke on more than one occasion showed it to Tavernier. It was the largest diamond in Europe at the time, but owing to its citron or yellow colour it did not command the same esteem as it would have done had it been pure white. The diamond is cut on all sides in facets which suggests that it was cut by Indian lapidaries. It is likely that the stone came to Italy direct from the East. The Florentine passed into the possession of the Austrian branch of the Hapsburgs when Maria Theresa married Francis, Grand Duke of Tuscany. Some writers have confused the Florentine with the Sancy and others have called it the Maximilian. When Fugger broke up Charles the Bold's Cap of Maintenance, Maximilian II purchased one of the stones described as a good-sized diamond, but it had no connection with the Florentine. Francis I is said to have worn the Florentine in his House Crown at his coronation in 1745, but subsequently it was set in a hat ornament surrounded by other diamonds.

Another large diamond was the 'Star of Este', which only came into possession of the Hapsburg family at a comparatively recent date. The Este family was one of the oldest of the former ruling houses of Italy. The male line became extinct in 1803, but the only daughter of the last scion had married the Archduke Ferdinand, third son of the Emperor Francis I. In 1875 this branch of the Hapsburg family died out and the title and possessions passed on to the Archduke Ferdinand, who was murdered at Sarajevo, and thus they were inherited by his heir, who became the Emperor Charles. The stone was a comparatively small one weighing $25\frac{1}{2}$ carats, but was noted for its perfection of form and quality.

It is believed that all these jewels, with the single exception of the Florentine Diamond, have been disposed of. I have it on the authority of Baron Mirbach, a member of the household of the Archduke Otto, that the emeralds of Maria Theresa and the 'Star of Este' had to be sold to provide for the needs of the exiled imperial family and that the Baden Solitaire and the Rosencollier were stolen by an unworthy trustee, and it is doubtful whether they will reappear as their form has probably been changed.

According to one author[1] the Hapsburg pearls were sold to furnish the funds to purchase the aeroplane in which the Emperor Charles attempted to regain his throne.

[1] Mary Abbott: *Jewels of Romance and Renown*, London 1933.

BIBLIOGRAPHY

BOCK, DR FRANZ — *Die Kleinodien des Heiligen Römischen Reiches Deutscher Nation*, Leipzig 1864.

CHYTIL, DR K. — *Korona Rudolf II*, 1921. With additional footnotes, 1928 and 1929 (in Czech with French summary).

DREXLER, K. — *Das Stift Klosterneuburg*, Vienna 1894.

FILLITZ, HERMANN — *Katalog der Weltlichen und der Geistlichen Schatzkammer*, Vienna 1954.
Catalogue of the Crown Jewels, Vienna 1956.
Article in the Year Book of the Art Historical Collections, Vol. LII, Vienna 1956.

KLAPSIA, H. — *Goldschmiedearbeiten in dem Chorherrnstift Klosterneuburg bei Wien*, 1897.

KRALIK, O. — *Die Oesterreichische Kaiserkrone*, Innsbruck 1917.

MAYER, MATH — *Mariastein in Unter-Intal, Selbstverlag des Verfassers in Going, Post Ellmau Tyrol*, Teil II, 1933. *Geschichte der Kirche, Wallfahrt und Siedlung*.

PAUKER, W. AND KRIS, E. — 'Oesterreichs Erzherzogenhut im Stift Klosterneuburg' in the *Jahrbuch der Kunsthistorischen Sammlungen in Wien*, N.F., Bd VIII, 1933.

SCHLOSSER, JULIUS VON — *Die Schatzkammer des Allerhöchsten Kaiserhauses in Wien*.

SIEGENFELD, A. R. VON — *Das Landeswappen der Steiermark*, Graz 1900.

TITZE, H. — 'Die Denkmale des Stiftes Nonnberg in Salzburg' *in der Oesterreichen Kunst Photographie*, Bd VII, Vienna 1911.

TURBA, G. — 'Die Kaiserliche Hauskrone', in *Historisches Jahrbuch 46*, pp. 72–80.

WEIXLGÄRTNER, ARPAD — *Die Weltliche Schatzkammer in Wien. Neue Funde und Forschungen*, I, II. *Jahrbuch der Kunsthistorischen Sammlungen in Wien*, N. F., Bd I (1926); Bd III (1928); Bd LII (1956).
Guide to the Weltliche Schatzkammer, 1933.

Führer durch die Schatzkammer des Allerhöchsten Kaiserhaus, Vienna 1898.

Guide to the Vienna Schatzkammer, 1900.

DUKES

BABENBERG DYNASTY

1156 Henry II
1177 Leopold V
1194 Frederick I the Catholic
1198 Leopold VI the Glorious
1230 Frederick II the Warlike
1281 Ottakar of Bohemia

HAPSBURG DYNASTY

1276　Rudolph I. German King from 1273
1282　Albert I. German King from 1298. With his brother Rudolph II
1308　Frederick I and Leopold I (and occasionally two younger brothers)
1326　Frederick I alone. German King from 1314
1330　Albert II and his brother Otto
1339　Albert II alone
1358　Rudolph IV, sometimes called the Founder
1365　Albert III
1395　Albert IV
1404　Albert V. German King (as Albert II) from 1438. Also King of Hungary and Bohemia
1439　Ladislas Posthumous. Also King of Hungary and Bohemia
1439　Frederick V, Regent. German King from 1440. Emperor (as Frederick III) from 1452

ARCHDUKES OF AUSTRIA

1453　Frederick V (see above) and Albert VI
1463　Frederick V alone
1493　Maximilian I. German King from 1485. Emperor Elect from 1508
1519　Charles. Elected German King 1519. Emperor 1530 (as Charles V)
1556　Ferdinand I. German King from 1531. Emperor from 1558. Also King of Bohemia and Hungary
1564　Maximilian II. German King from 1562. Emperor from 1569. Also King of Bohemia and Hungary
1576　Rudolph V. German King from 1575. Emperor from 1576. Also (as Rudolph II) King of Bohemia and Hungary
1612　Matthias. German King and Emperor from 1612. Also King of Bohemia and Hungary
1619　Ferdinand II. German King and Emperor from 1619. Also King of Bohemia and Hungary
1637　Frederick III. German King 1636. Emperor 1637. Also King of Bohemia and Hungary
1656　Leopold I. German King and Emperor from 1658. Also King of Bohemia and Hungary
1705　Joseph I. German King 1690. Emperor 1705. Also King of Bohemia and Hungary
1711　Charles. German King and Emperor (as Charles VI) from 1711. Also King of Bohemia and Hungary
1740　Maria Theresa. Also Queen of Bohemia and Hungary. Her husband German King and Emperor (as Francis I) from 1745
1780　Joseph II. German King and Emperor from 1765. Also King of Bohemia and Hungary

1790   Leopold II. German King and Emperor from 1790

1792   Francis II. The last German King and Emperor from 1792–1806. Also King of Bohemia and Hungary

EMPERORS OF AUSTRIA

1804   Francis I (formerly Francis II)

1835   Ferdinand I

1848   Francis Joseph I

1916   Charles I. Abdicated 1918

N.B. This list includes those who were the lawful rulers of Austria. The position is complicated by the fact that the Hapsburgs associated the several members of the family at one time with the government of their dominions. Moreover as German Kings and Emperors and as Kings of Bohemia and Hungary they were frequently absent from their Austrian lands and appointed sons, brothers or nephews as Governors, who took the title of Archduke in Austria, Duke in Styria and Carinthia, and Count in Tyrol. These are not included in the above list but some are mentioned in the text. Another cause of confusion is that some Archdukes of Austria were elected German King during the lifetime of their father and their German coronations sometimes took place before their accession as Archdukes of Austria. As a result they could be known by two numbers, e.g. the Emperor Rudolph II was the Archduke Rudolph V.

CHAPTER TWO

BAVARIA

The ancient and important House of Wittelsbach has played a leading part in the history of Europe. First as dukes, then as electors and finally as kings, it was for over seven centuries associated with the governance of Bavaria. Three members of the family were elected to the imperial throne, two became Kings of Bohemia and another King of Greece; others again were Margraves of Brandenburg from 1323–73 and Kings of Sweden from 1654–1718, while their marriages to other royal houses, particularly the Hapsburgs and the Stuarts, further increased their prestige, influence and wealth. It is not surprising then that the Wittelsbach Treasury should rank amongst the foremost of such collections in Europe. Today the catalogue of the Treasury contains no less than 975 items which represent the changing fortunes of the family over a long period.

From an early date the Wittelsbach family had been of importance in Germany and especially in Bavaria. In 907 Luitpold, cousin and general of the Carolingian Emperor Arnulf, was Margrave of the Eastern March and Duke of Bavaria, which latter title was retained until the year 938. In the XI century the head of the family took the title of Count of Scheyern, the ruined castle of that name being situated near Pfaffenhofen in Upper Bavaria, and here the family remained until 1112, when they moved to Kelheim. Later, Otto V, Count of Scheyern, moved the family residence to Wittelsbach and transferred that name to himself and his family. At about this time Otto had been recognised as Count Palatine of Bavaria. In 1180 his son, Otto VI, having rendered valuable assistance to the Emperor Frederick I, was invested at Altenburg with the Dukedom of Bavaria. In 1208 Otto V's great nephew Louis, who had succeeded to the titles and lands, destroyed the ancestral castle at Wittelsbach, the site of which is to this day marked by a church and an obelisk, and in 1255 the lands were divided between the two sons of Duke Otto the Illustrious. The elder, Louis II, received the Palatine of the Rhine and Upper Bavaria and the younger, Henry I, was given Lower Bavaria.

In 1314 the younger son of Louis was elected to the imperial throne as Louis IV, or Louis the Bavarian, and occupied it until his death in 1347. There had been other partitions of the family lands in the Palatinate, and from 1329 to 1356 the electoral vote had been exercised alternately by the two sons of the Emperor Louis IV. In 1353, however, the younger, Rupert, became the sole ruler, and in 1356, in exchange for some land in Upper Bavaria, was given the electoral dignity of Count Palatine of the Rhine by the Emperor Charles IV. In 1390 the Palatine of the Rhine passed to Rupert's nephew, whose son became German king in the year 1400. The electoral vote of the Palatine was confirmed by the Golden Bull, in spite of the opposition of the Duke of Bavaria, who claimed either this vote or, alternatively, that given to the King of

Bohemia. To have given two votes to one family would have placed it in a dangerously strong position and the Bavarian claim was refused. In the Golden Bull the vote was given to a definite territory which was declared indivisible and its descent was ordered to be by primogeniture instead of by partition. The Counts Palatine also became Arch-Stewards of the Empire with the right to carry the orb at imperial coronations and to use it as their emblem.

In 1402 the Elector Louis III married Princess Blanche, daughter of Henry IV of England, and the crown that she brought with her is still preserved in the Treasury.

The Protestant Frederick V, the ill-starred 'Winter King', who was crowned King of Bohemia on 4th November 1619 at Prague, was decisively defeated in the following year and the senior branch suffered eclipse. Frederick had married Elizabeth, daughter of James I of England whose Wittelsbach descendants are considered by some to be the pretenders to the Stuart inheritance and thus to the throne of Great Britain. Frederick's son regained the Palatinate at the Peace of Westphalia in 1608, but not the electoral vote, as this had been transferred to the Duke of Bavaria in 1523. An eighth electorate was then created for the Counts Palatine of the Rhine, together with a new imperial office of Treasurer. The Wittelsbachs thus obtained a second electoral vote and consequently greatly increased their power as a family.

On 19th March 1565 Duke Albert V and his consort the Princess Maria Anna of Hapsburg decided to form a collection of the treasures of their House. The document ordering the foundation of this collection still exists. It lays down that after their death the treasure was to be preserved, if possible, in perpetuity for their princely house and was to remain in Munich. Seventeen objects were specified as inalienable, to which ten others were shortly added. Among them were contemporary objects made in Munich to the Duke's orders and others purchased by his agents in Italy. Seven remain: a ceremonial chain by Hans Mielich, a gold and enamel cup set with gems, three gold pendants, a silver-gilt casket and the Albertine coffer by Fontana. Additions were made to the collection by the first elector, Maximilian I (1597–1651), including two more gold cups by Hans Mielich and some rock crystal and semi-precious stones very finely cut in Milan. He also founded the *Reiche Kapelle*, a private oratory in which was assembled a store of church works of art which was later added to the treasure in the Residenz. In the XVIII century the Elector Albert, later the Emperor Charles VII, added greatly to the collection. When the Bavarian dynasty died out and the Wittelsbachs succeeded, further large additions were made to the treasure, mainly from Heidelberg, Düsseldorf and Mannheim. In the XIX century the secularisation of the Bavarian monasteries and cathedral foundations added many late Carolingian and Ottonian donations.

In 1742 the Palatine branch of the family became extinct and the Sulzbach branch became the senior. The year 1742 also saw the election to the imperial throne, in opposition to the husband of Maria Theresa, of Charles Albert, the Elector of Bavaria, who was crowned at Frankfurt as the Emperor Charles VII. The reign of Charles VII, however, only lasted for two years during which time he was rather a pathetic figure. At the very time that he was being crowned, his hereditary dominions in Bavaria were being overrun by Austrian troops. He described himself as being 'attacked by stone

a *Crown of the Empress Kunigunde c. 1010. Residenz Treasury, Munich (p. 26)*

b *XIV-Century lily crown Residenz Treasury, Munich (p. 26)*

c *The Kunigunde and lily crowns joined together. Residenz Treasury, Munich (p. 26)*

a   *Crown of the Emperor Henry II (St Henry), XIII–XIV Century. Residenz Treasury, Munich* (p. 27)

c   *Imperial burial crown attributed to St Henry, XIV–XV Century. Cathedral Treasury, Bamberg* (p. 28)

b (left)   *Crown of Princess Blanche, XIV Century. Residenz Treasury, Munich* (p. 27)

a   *Ceremonial chain of gold, con-
    sisting of sixteen links of enamel-
    led scroll work, c. 1560.
    Residenz Treasury, Munich
    (p. 29)*

b   *Statue of St George in Renais-
    sance armour on a richly capari-
    soned horse 1590. Residenz
    Treasury, Munich (p. 29)*

a (above, left) *The Franconian sword, XV Century, c. 1460–65. Residenz Treasury, Munich* (p. 29)

b (above, right) *Sword of Duke Christopher, XV Century, c. 1480. Residenz Treasury, Munich* (p. 29)

c (left) *The Palatine sword, XVI Century. Residenz Treasury, Munich* (p. 30)

d (right) *Ceremonial sword of Duke Maximilian I, XVI Century. Bavarian National Museum, Munich* (p. 30)

a (above, left)   *Portrait of the Emperor Charles Albert with coronation regalia by G. Desmarées 1742. Nymphenburg Castle, Munich* (p. 32)

b (above, right)   *Portrait of the Empress Maria Amelia by G. Desmarées. Nymphenburg Castle, Munich* (p. 32)

c   *So-called 'Bohemian orb'. Residenz Treasury, Munich* (p. 31)

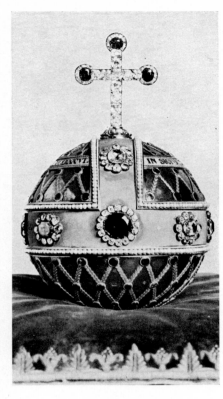

a   *Royal crown, 1806* (p. 32)

b   *Royal orb, 1806* (p. 33)

c   *Royal
sceptre, 1806*
(p. 33)

d   *Royal state
sword, 1806*
(p. 33)

e   *Queen's crown, 1806 and 1867* (p. 32)

These items are all in the Residenz Treasury, Munich

a   *Cross of the Order of St George set with rubies and diamonds, 1729. Residenz Treasury, Munich (p. 33)*

b   *Cross of the Order of St George set with rubies and brilliants, 1760. Residenz Treasury, Munich (p. 34)*

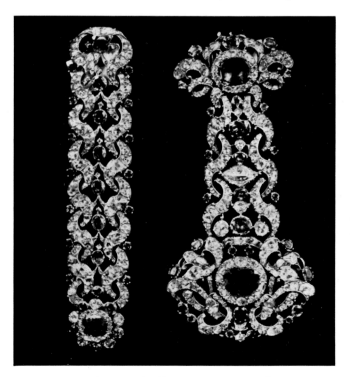

c   (i) *Loop of silver, brilliants and rubies of the Order of St George, 1760;* (ii) *Hat ornament of silver, brilliants and rubies of the Order of St George, 1760. Residenz Treasury, Munich (p. 34)*

d   *Star of the Order of St George with brilliants and rubies, 1760. Residenz Treasury, Munich (p. 34)*

a   *Cross of the Order of St George with emeralds, brilliants and rubies, 1830. Residenz Treasury, Munich (p. 34)*

b   *Star of the Order of St George with emeralds, brilliants and rubies, 1830. Residenz Treasury, Munich (p. 34)*

c   *Cross of the Order of St George with rubies, brilliants, emeralds and peridot, 1874. Residenz Treasury, Munich (p. 34)*

d   *Cross of the Order of St George of silver, rubies and brilliants, 1905. Residenz Treasury, Munich (p. 34)*

a   *Gold collar of the Order of St Hubert, 1708. Residenz Treasury, Munich (p. 35)*

b (left)   *Cross and star of gold and silver set with emeralds and brilliants of the Order of St Hubert, 1708. Residenz Treasury, Munich (p. 35)*

c   *Star of the Order of St Hubert of silver-gilt set with brilliants, 1708. Residenz Treasury, Munich* (p. 35)

a (left)   *Order of the Golden Fleece
with brilliants, 1763. Residenz
Treasury, Munich* (p. 35)

b (right)   *Order of the Golden Fleece with brilliants,
1763. Residenz Treasury, Munich* (p. 35)

and gout, ill, without money or land and in distress comparable to the sorrows of Job'. In 1777 the Bavarian branch of the Wittelsbachs likewise became extinct and the succession passed to the Elector Palatine, Charles Theodore.

In 1799 the Zweibrücken branch of the family succeeded to the titles and lands, and in 1803, as a result of Napoleon's policy of suppressing the ecclesiastical states, Bavaria gave up the outlying provinces of the Rhine and received in exchange the bishoprics of Würzburg, Bamberg, Augsburg, Freisingen, part of that of Passau, and seventeen cities and villages and twelve abbeys, this adjustment of territory forming a compact unit. In that year the objects of temporal authority were brought into the Munich Treasury. In the three successive years there were further adjustments and finally in 1806 Bavaria was advanced to the rank of Kingdom and the Elector took the title of King Maximilian I.

King Maximilian I wished to introduce a coronation ceremony, but as a Concordat with the Holy See had not been signed it was found to be impossible. Nevertheless a set of royal ornaments was made as the State regalia of the kingdom. The ceremony performed at the succession of each new king was one of swearing the oath to the constitution in the throne-room of the royal palace at Munich before the ministers and other persons of distinction and at this ceremony the regalia were displayed near the king. Of the six Bavarian kings the second, Louis I, abdicated for political reasons; the fourth, Louis II, abdicated owing to a serious mental disease; the fifth, who became afflicted with a mental disease similar to that of his brother and predecessor, never actually reigned; and the sixth king, Louis III, was forced to abdicate at the end of the First World War. Otto, the brother of the third king, was elected to the throne of Greece in 1833, but was deposed in 1863.

Formerly the crown jewels had been kept in the *Schatzkammer* or Treasury of the Residenz at Munich but during the Second World War the Treasury was closed and the contents taken to a place of safety. In 1945 the Residenz at Munich was seriously damaged by aerial bombardment, and it was not until 1958, when a part of the palace had been restored, that a new Treasury became available for the magnificent collection to be exhibited again to the public. The treasure is arranged in ten rooms and the greatest care has been taken to display it effectively; the result has been an out-standing success. Although many ornaments formerly in the Treasury have been removed, others have now been included which makes it one of the richest collections of its kind still in existence. Not only has it great historical interest, but it gives some idea of what the royal treasuries of England and France and the other great kingdoms of Western Europe—the contents of which we only know from inventories—must have been like. There are cups, beakers and other vessels, ecclesiastical ornaments and relics, trinkets and curiosities in the rarest and most precious materials, and in many cases with high artistic merit. Among the precious materials used are: gold and silver; enamel; diamonds; pearls; precious stones; many kinds of semi-precious stones; rock crystal; rose quartz; agate; onyx; sardonyx; chalcedony; jasper; heliotrope; serpentine; nephrite; lapis lazuli; cornelian; prase; coral; ruby-glass; amber; mother-of-pearl; mussel shell; nautilus shell; ivory and rhinoceros horn. It would be impossible to deal with every item and many are beyond the scope of this work. Our attention, must, therefore, be confined to such items as can be included in the term 'regalia' or 'crown jewels'.

The first room contains works of the Middle Ages, some of which are not only rich and rare works of art but of great antiquity. Among them are four crowns. There were in the Bamberg Cathedral Treasury two crowns bearing the name of St Kunigunde which were transferred to the Munich Treasury in 1803. These two crowns can be joined together to make one, although in origin they are separated by several centuries. St Kunigunde was the wife of the Emperor Henry II, known as Henry the Saint, who was Duke of Bavaria in 985. He married Kunigunde, daughter of Siegfried, Count of Luxemburg, in 1001, and in 1002 he was elected and crowned as German king. Both he and his wife were renowned for their devotion to the Church and they were both canonised. According to a XII-century tradition they took vows of chastity.

The first crown (10)[1] dates from about the year 1010, and at any rate not later than 1025, in which year the Empress gave it to the Cloister of Kaufungen. Kunigunde was first crowned at Paderborn in 1002, so this could not have been the crown used on that occasion, and we have no evidence as to whether it was that used at her imperial coronation at Rome in 1014. It is considered that it may have been made at Metz, of the See of which her brother Theoderich (*obiit* 1044) was bishop.

The gold circlet (*Plate 15, a*) consists of five oblong rectangular shields, all riveted to the foundation of thin gold plate. These little shields are attractively decorated with squares and round designs, picked out by strong filigree borders. The points of these round quadrangles are set off by a small pearl in a gold setting, while their centres are in most cases filled with large sapphires. Little stones in plain settings—recognisable as rubies, sapphires and amethysts—surround the four sides of the variously rounded quadrangles. The rest of the surface is covered with gold filigree decorations, like those on the bindings of the Gospels of Henry II in the Town Library at Bamberg, the Minster Treasury at Aix and in the Comelian Collection in the State Library at Munich, which are characteristic of the XI century. The filigree work serves as settings for the precious and semi-precious stones which, besides those already mentioned, include topazes, chrysolites, molten glass and pearls. The five plates are joined together with hinges.

The second crown (15) is of much later date and is considered to be of the mid-XIV century, about the reign of the Emperor Louis of Bavaria.

This crown (*Plate 15, b*) is of similar width to the first crown and was joined to it (*Plate 15, c*) when, on Church festivities, it was placed upon the skull of the Empress, who was the patron saint of the town and bishopric of Bamberg. It consists of eleven silver gilt pieces joined by hinges, each piece being surmounted by a fleur-de-lis as a *pinna*. The eleven hinges are fixed by as many gold pins, each of which was formerly surmounted with a light sapphire with a pearl on top, but only 6 of these remain. The surfaces of the eleven plates and also the lily-shaped *pinnae*, are all decorated with little inset rubies, which in groups of 3 surround a central large gem. The eleven divisions are nailed into a gilded copper rim. The front fleur-de-lis is considerably larger than the others and is surmounted by a cross, the centre of which is set with a sapphire of fine water. To the four sides of the sapphire are attached 3 rubies in a trefoil design in a plain gold setting which form the arms of the cross. On the back is placed a small gold cruciform receptacle with a lid decorated with a chased crucifix, which was intended to serve as a reliquary, possibly to contain

[1] Numbers in brackets without a letter prefix refer to the 1955 Catalogue.

a piece of the Crown of Thorns. Below the main crown is a narrow circlet of two gold wires on which a decoration of 3 pearls alternates with carved vine leaves.

It was not until Henry and Kunigunde had been canonised that special interest was centred in these crowns. After 1380 a bust was fashioned of the head of the Empress, on which a crown was placed. This was dedicated by an unknown duchess. The crowns were cleaned in 1653 and repaired in 1706 as they were badly damaged. In the inventory of 1793 they appear for the first time described as 'The Imperial Crowns of St Kunigunde'.

A third crown (15) from Bamberg Cathedral Treasury is described in the catalogue as the so-called 'St Henry's Crown'.

The crown (*Plate 16, a*) is of silver gilt and Gothic in shape and decoration and was said to have adorned the head of a bust of the saint in Bamberg Cathedral. It consists of six plates, each of which carries a large fleur-de-lis above the base. The fronts of the plates are adorned with oak leaves which are raised up on the flat under-surface. Between the foliage pattern stand up large precious stones in claw settings arranged in such a way that on the circlet the centre stone on the base of each plate has two smaller stones on each side. Each fleur-de-lis is decorated in the same manner with four precious stones which, with the one in the centre of the base, form a cross. The hinge pins are surmounted by little knobs covered with the chased foliage work. From behind this foliage work rise cast figures of angels which fill the spaces between the fleurs-de-lis. The central stones in the front and the back of the crown are cameos, the one in front a sardonyx, bearing the head of Minerva and dating from the late Roman Empire, while the one at the back is of XVI-century origin. On the inside of the crown there are slots on the front and back plates for fixing the imperial arch and cross, and there is a spare slot provided on the plate to the left of the one at the back so that the crown could be made smaller by the removal of one plate and yet bear the arch and cross. The slot on the back plate is damaged. This feature suggests that the crown was not made for a reliquary bust but made in an adjustable form so that it could be worn. It is considered to belong to the late XIII or early XIV century. Undoubtedly changes have been made in the decoration of the crown as is exemplified by the addition of the XVI-century cameo. Muratori considered that the angels were added when the crown was redecorated in the XIV century.[1]

The fourth crown (16) (*Plate 16, b*) came from the Palatine Treasury in 1872. It is a beautiful crown that was brought from England in 1402 by Princess Blanche, the daughter of Henry IV of England, who in that year married the Elector Louis III of the Palatinate. It is considered that the crown may be of either French or English origin, but no attempt has been made to assign definitely whence it came or what craftsmen made it. The catalogue states that in 1399 it was already referred to in England as 'old jewellery'. Possibly this reference alludes to the description of this crown which is contained in an indenture of 1399 testifying 'the delivery made out of the King's Chamber, of jewels in gold and silver plate, etc., heretofore belonging to Edward III, Richard II, Queen Anne the Duchess of York, the Duke of Gloucester, and Sir John Golafre'. Item 175 reads as follows:

Item I. *corone de XI. ovages garnis de XI. Saphirs XXXIII baleys t cxxxii. ples xxxiii. dyamantz dont viii. contrefaitz. Itm. vi. florons chescun de un baleys v. saphirs chescun de ix ples dont defaut en tout vii. ples. Itm. vi meiners florons chescuns d'un saphir iiii. petitz baleys i. emeraude dont defaut un esmeraud t. ii petitz ples en chescun pois.*[2]

1 This crown is further discussed in Chapter Nine—Germany, p. 310.
2 Sir Francis Palgrave: *Antient Kalendars and Inventories of the Treasury*, Vol III.

This description fits exactly this crown, except that it mentions eleven *ovages* whereas there are now twelve. The crown can be altered in size by the removal of one or more plates, so a reduction in size would account for there being one *ovage* less. It is described in the catalogues of the Treasury as the so-called 'Bohemian Crown'. This designation is derived from a tradition that the crown fell into the hands of Duke Maximilian I of Bavaria who was commanding the Imperial Army which defeated Frederick, the so-called 'Winter King', at the Battle of the White Mountain. This story is today discredited in the absence of evidence to support it and because it is not mentioned in the inventory of the Treasury of the Elector of Bavaria until 1764. The possibility of Elizabeth, the wife of the 'Winter King', having taken this crown with her to Prague, cannot be lightly dismissed. It is possible, too, that this crown originally belonged to Anne of Bohemia, daughter of Charles IV and consort of Richard II of England.[1]

There were formerly in the Bamberg Cathedral Treasury two women's crowns which disappeared in the XIII century but of which we have engravings.[2] Deér[3] considers them to have been of Sicilian workmanship, probably brought to Germany by Henry VI with the treasure of the Norman kings, which were taken to Trifels. He suggests that they were presented to Bamberg by Philip of Swabia and his wife on the occasion of their coronation in 1199 or on the transfer of the remains of St Kunigunde in 1201.

There is still preserved in the Cathedral Treasury at Bamberg an imperial crown which was probably made for a reliquary of Henry II and repaired in 1653 (*Plate 16, c*). In 1793 it is mentioned as a crown with which Kunigunde was buried, and later it was claimed as having been found in Henry II's grave, but neither of these suppositions are possible.

> It consists of a brass circlet covered with white silk and gold braid with jewels set in embroidery of acorns and flowers. On the top is a wreath of lilies, wound at the back with white silk and the front edge is decorated with brass spirals, pearls and jet. This is the work of the XIV or XV century and later, probably in the XVI century, four arches were added, made of brass with green silk wound around them.

The second room of the Treasury contains objects of the late Gothic and early Renaissance period and the third room is devoted to two superb ornaments. The first

[1] The author's attention has been drawn to an opinion expressed by Schramm in *Herrschaftszeichen und Staatssymbolik*, Vol. III, p. 993 footnote 3. He states: 'There is no basis for Thoma's theory . . . that the crown goes back "at least" to Richard II, perhaps even to Edward III. We shall see that the shape itself excludes this possibility.' It is possible that Schramm had not seen the extract quoted above from an inventory, which refers to a crown of the reign of Richard II which is clearly of the same shape and the description almost exactly fits the Crown of Princess Blanche. Moreover in a document of the eighteenth year of Richard II's reign, which refers to Queen Anne of Bohemia, who had died the previous year, there is the following mark which shows that crowns of this type were used in England then and which may well be a rude drawing of the crown in question. Richard II is depicted wearing a crown of this type in a miniature of Henry of Monmouth being knighted. British Museum MS. Harl. 1319.

[2] Johann Peter von Ludewig: *Scriptores rerum episcopatus Bambergensis*, Bamberg 1718.

[3] Josef Deér: *Der Kaiserornat Friedrichs II.*

is a magnificent ceremonial chain (55) of German workmanship, probably made in 1560 for Albert V from a design of Hans Mielich, the drawing of which is in the Bavarian National Museum. The disposition of 1565 calls the style of the setting 'Spanish work' and states that 3 large fine drop pearls were used to decorate an emerald pendant. In 1730 they were replaced by another ornament of gold and enamel, which was made in 1600, but more recently that too was removed and remains in the Treasury as a separate item. On the institution of the Order of St George in 1729 by the Elector Charles Albert this chain was used at the festivities of the Order.

The chain (*Plate 17, a*) is of gold and consists of sixteen links of enamelled scroll work. In each link is set a precious stone or pearl; in the side links there are 4 emeralds and 3 spinels set alternately with 8 large half-pearls. The central link is especially richly decorated with griffin and lion heads; the remaining simpler links repeat two different styles of ornamentation—one style for the pearls and the other for the gems. To the central link is attached a pendant consisting of a big hexagonal emerald in a similar claw setting to that of the gems in the chain. The total length is 111 cm. Clifford-Smith[1] writes: 'the size and quality of the stones and the great beauty of the enamelled setting render it without doubt the finest article of its kind in existence'.

The second ornament (56) is a magnificent piece with St George in Renaissance armour on a richly caparisoned horse (*Plate 17, b*). The horse's body is carved out of chalcedony and the rest of the group is of gold richly enamelled and decorated with table stones, rubies and emeralds. The front of the pedestal is decorated with a shield bearing the Bavarian arms, decorated with sapphires and enamel, the Electoral Hat and the chain of the Golden Fleece held by two lions and an inscription. The whole pedestal is richly decorated with gold, enamel and precious stones. This ornament was made in 1590 for William V and was kept in the goldsmith's cabinet of the dukes.

The fourth room contains ornaments of ecclesiastical art. The fifth room contains regalia and insignia of Orders of Chivalry with some personal jewellery, almost every item of which must attract our attention.

The Franconian Sword (210) was made for the Prince Bishop Johann III von Grumbach (1455–66), and on his tomb in Würzburg Cathedral the effigy of the Bishop is shown wearing it as an emblem of his temporal power in the Duchy of the Franks, which power had been exercised by the Würzburg bishops since the time of Bishop Gottfried II of Hohenlohe.

The sword (*Plate 18, a*) was made in Würzburg and is 130 cm in length. The hilt is of silver covered with violet velvet and studded with silver gilt nails hammered into a pattern of three broad rows of flowers. The pommel is formed of a big octagonal jasper. On the guard on both sides are the intermingled arms of the Duchy of the Franks, the Bishopric of Würzburg and the Barony of Grumbach, in silver gilt and niello borne by two embossed savages. The guard ends are in the form of dogs' heads. The scabbard is of silver gilt of five pieces joined by hinges; three pieces are decorated with chased Gothic tendril work, while the remaining two are covered with purple velvet with silver gilt studs. The tip of the scabbard is formed by a fantastic animal's head.

The Sword of Duke Christopher of Bavaria (1449–93) (211), who died at Rhodes and was buried there, is of Rhenish origin and appears to have been made at Strassburg, about the middle of the xv century (*Plate 18, b*).

1 H. Clifford-Smith: *Jewellery*, London 1908.

Its total length is 130 cm. The hilt and scabbard are of silver. On the hilt are four male and four female figures in niches, of which each two pairs are alike. The corners of the niches are set with rubies; on the quadrangular twisted pommel the Bavarian arms are twice engraved, the lion gilded and the incised places filled with lacquer; at the junction of blade and hilt there are on both sides two coats of arms—those of Bavaria and the Order of St John—in similar styles. The guard is covered with chased silver foliage and tendril work. The scabbard is composed of four parts joined by hinges and, like the guard, is covered with chased and embossed leaf work, consisting of a repeated design of two bunches of grapes and two vine leaves, soldered on to a smooth ground; between the leaf tendrils are set an ape or a bird. The tip is formed by the head of a monster. On the narrow flat blade the mark x is cut and filled in with gold. The Cross of St John on the sword is the same as that which is to be found on contemporary medals of the Order of St John, with whose knights Duke Christopher fought against the Turks at Rhodes. This sword was apparently brought to Munich from Rhodes with the other possessions of the Duke. The earliest mention of it is in a travel book of 1664, when it was apparently in the *Kammergalerie*. The rubies were added at a later date—in the XVII or XVIII century. It was for a time in the keeping of the Knights of the Order of St George and was transferred from their keeping to the Treasury in 1907.

The Palatine Sword (212) (*Plate 18, c*) was made in 1653 for the Palatine Elector Charles Louis (1632–80) by Abraham Drentwett, an Augsburg craftsman, who achieved renown in 1649 and died in Augsburg in 1666.

Its length is 119 cm. The scabbard and hilt are of silver gilt. The hilt takes the form of a lion rampant, of which the body displays the sinews. In the front paws he holds an enamelled shield with the Bavarian Palatine arms, the Electoral Hat and the orb, surmounted by the inscription *Honi soit qui mal y pense*, and above the coat of arms *G.L.P.C.Ao.1653 Juny*. In the hind paws are two shields with the orb. The guard, on which the lion's hind paws rest, is of *Knorpelwerk*[1] which on both sides merges into the lion's body. It bears on one side the Palatine, and on the other the Bavarian arms. The scabbard has chased ornaments with *Knorpelwerk*, on either side of which are three enamelled shields, a golden lion on a black field (Palatinate), blue lozenges (Bavaria) and a red regalia shield with the orb. On the blade there is engraved the inscription *JESVS NAZARENVS RNVX PESALVAMES/SANCTA MARIA ADIVNYX PESALVAM* and *JESVS NAZARENVS REX IVEORVN YX/SANCTA MARIA ADIVNYX PESALVAM*. The date, 1483, is on both sides. There is also the Hall and Master's mark. The blade is really XIV century and apparently the inscription was engraved by an illiterate, as that would explain the mistake in the text, for the date should read 1384. This sword is mentioned in the inventory of the inheritance of the Elector Charles Louis and it was transferred from the Palatine Treasury in 1803.

There are in the Bavarian National Museum at Munich three swords which belonged to Duke Maximilian I. The first is a ceremonial sword (*Plate 18, d*), the second a knight's sword, and the third the personal sword of the Duke.

The origin and purpose of the so-called 'Bohemian Orb' (216) is not quite certain. It is probably of Augsburg workmanship of the early XVII century and may have been made for the Elector Palatine Frederick V (1610–32). Possibly it was made as the symbol of the Office of the Imperial Arch-Steward who possessed the privilege of carrying the Imperial Orb at the coronation of the Emperor, a dignity which was lost by the Palatinate in 1632. In the Mannheim inventory of 1738, however, it is described

[1] This is a characteristic decoration of the late XVI century and early XVII century.

as the 'Bohemian Orb'.[1] When the consort of Frederick V was crowned as Queen of Bohemia at Prague in 1619, she, like the king, received an orb at the ceremony. As there was only one orb available among the Bohemia regalia it is possible that this Bavarian one, being at hand, was used for the Queen and thus came to be known as the 'Bohemian Orb' (*Plate 19, c*).

It is of gold and is 20 cm in height and 11 cm in breadth. There are four vertical and one horizontal bands, the same number as in the Imperial Orb, but whereas in the Imperial Orb the vertical bands encircle the globe, in this orb they rise from the horizontal band. The bands are set with rubies, emeralds, sapphires, amethysts and table-cut diamonds, forty-four stones in all, the bands themselves being decorated with a simple scroll work. Above rises a cross, similarly decorated, seventeen stones being used. In 1806 5 sapphires were removed to be used in the decoration of the new Bavarian Royal Orb.

The imperial regalia of Charles VII consist of two imperial crowns, a sceptre and an orb, which were made for his coronation at Frankfurt in 1742. He was the son of Maximilian II and had succeeded as Charles Albert, Duke of Bavaria, in 1725 and, on the death of the Emperor Charles VI in 1740, he renewed the claims of the Dukes of Bavaria to the Imperial Throne and the Hapsburg inheritance. As the claim was strenuously opposed by Francis, the husband of Maria Theresa, it was not until 1742 that he was elected Emperor with the designation of Charles VII, although in the previous year he had been recognised and crowned at Prague as King of Bohemia. As the Imperial Regalia were not available, he had a substitute set of ornaments made. Only seventeen days elapsed between his election and his coronation at Frankfurt, which would hardly have been time enough for their manufacture. It has been established that for his Bohemian coronation on 19th December 1741 he brought to Prague a crown from Munich as the Bohemian regalia were not available. It may, therefore, be presumed that he had anticipated his needs and had ordered these insignia in good time—at least by the autumn of 1741. It may be said with certainty that the two crowns were made by Nicholas Nell, a master of Frankfurt (*obiit* 1751), and by Jacob Philip Drentwett, master in Augsburg (*obiit* 1754). The names of the makers of the sceptre and orb are unknown, but the sceptre is considered to be of Augsburg workmanship.

The Emperor's crown (217) was intended to conform in general appearance to the Imperial German Crown now in Vienna. Instead of eight plates as in the original, this crown is composed of seven of which two are engraved with representations of the Apostles Peter and Paul and the remainder with scroll work ornamentation. From behind the central plate in front there rises a cross with straight arms from the back of which springs a single arch. The crown is of silver gilt and was originally set with precious stones and pearls and provided with a cap of red velvet. It is 26 cm high and 8 cm wide and has the maker's name engraved on it.

The second crown for the Empress (218) is somewhat similar in shape and design being also of silver gilt and formed of seven plates of crosses and a single arch. Two of the plates bear embossed figures of St Peter and St Paul and the other five *rocaille* ornamentation. It was originally set with precious stones and gems. It is 26 cm in height and 20 cm in breadth. The 1937 catalogue states

---

[1] Its traditional association with Bohemia was the same as that of the so-called 'Bohemian Crown'.

that it resembles a funeral crown in the Treasury of St Vitus's at Prague, but this is misleading as the latter is in quite a different style, though having the main features of an imperial crown.

The sceptre (219) of silver gilt was intended to resemble the Imperial Sceptre. It is a round rod with four leaves at the top. Originally there were small ornaments at the top to represent an orb.

The Imperial Orb (220) is of silver gilt originally set with precious stones. From the top rises a cross, the ends of which are set with pearls.

Portraits of Charles VII and his consort Maria Amelia wearing these crowns and the Emperor bearing the sceptre and orb are at Nymphenburg Castle near Munich (*Plate 19, a* and *b*).

The precious stones and pearls were removed from the ornaments in the time of Maximilian III Joseph and were employed in the decoration of the insignia of the Orders of Chivalry and other jewellery.

When Bavaria was raised to the status of a kingdom in 1806, a set of royal ornaments consisting of a king's crown, a queen's crown, a sceptre, an orb and a sword were made in Paris by Martier Guillaume Biennais in the so-called Empire style. The king's crown, the sceptre and the orb bear the maker's mark—*I.B.L.*—in a lozenge. The sword bears the maker's name of M. G. Biennais. The queen's crown was probably made by the same firm, but was altered in 1867 by the Court jeweller in Munich, Gottfried Merk, by the order of King Louis II. On the inside is engraved 'G. Merk K.'. The old pattern of the crown can be seen in the portrait of Queen Theresa, the wife of Louis I, by J. Stieler, which is in the Neue Pinakotek in Munich.

The King's Crown (223) (*Plate 20, a*) is of gold and takes the formalised shape of a modern royal crown, being closed with four arches, depressed at the centre. They are, in fact, only half-arches, and if so described are eight in number, for where they meet at the centre they form an ogee and the ends curve backwards and downwards, held in position by an octangular gold collar. They are so arranged that there is no arch in the centre of the circlet. The circlet of undecorated gold is set with eight coloured stones within circles of diamonds and alternating with these are 8 large diamonds with sixteen coloured stones set singly between them. The upper and lower rims of the circlet are bordered with strings of well-matched pearls. Resting on the circlet and running right round the crown is an elaborate design of scroll work in which a row of 32 large diamonds amidst a number of smaller ones effectively stand out. Each arch springs from behind a strawberry leaf in the centre of which is set a large coloured stone in a circle of diamonds. The arches are decorated with palm sprays chased in gold and each bears five large coloured stones in a circle of diamonds. The orb surmounting the crown is formed of open filigree work. In front is a large piece of blue molten glass which can be replaced by the Blue Brilliant when required. The equator and meridional bands of the orb are decorated with coloured stones set in circles of small diamonds, while the whole is covered with a net pattern picked out with diamonds. From the orb rises a simple cross set with 7 brilliants. The coloured stones in the crown are rubies and emeralds, while the diamonds are all brilliant cut. The stones were taken from various other ornaments including two Imperial Crowns of Charles VII.

The Queen's Crown (224) (*Plate 20, e*) is a small crown of four ascending arches, which meet at the centre and form an ogee and are held together by a jewelled collar. The circlet is bordered by two rows of small pearls and is decorated with large brilliants, each bordered by two smaller ones and set alternately with coloured stones in circles of brilliants. Resting on the upper rim is a scroll-work decoration containing in all 32 large brilliants. On this rest eight strawberry leaves;

in the centre of each there is a large pearl and the veins of the leaves are picked out by rows of smaller pearls with brilliants set between. Behind these rise the arches in the form of an ogee, each of which has a row of brilliants on either side. The orb is richly set with brilliants. Between each arch is a large pear-shaped pearl.

The Bavarian Orb (225) (*Plate 20, b*) is made of gold and is set with brilliants, emeralds, sapphires and rubies. It is elaborately decorated in an unusual manner; the whole globe is covered with gold network in the form of a double band of laurel leaves and at the junction of each band there is a set of small coloured stone in a round gold setting. The broad equator and single meridional bands are embroidered with small pearls set in a groove. On the equator are set four coloured stones within circles of brilliants, set alternately with brilliants within circles of brilliants. Similarly on each side of the meridional band is a large diamond in a circle of brilliants. The spacing of these stones leaves a somewhat severe expanse of gold, which nevertheless is very effective. Level with the large diamond on the meridional band there runs round the globe a small gold collar bearing the following inscription embossed in gold: *IN SIGNUM, CONCORDIAE PATRIS AC PATRIAE, ANNO DOM. MDCCCVI*. In all, the orb is 20 cm high and 13 cm broad. From the top there rises a graceful cross resting on a golden pedestal. The limbs of the cross are decorated entirely with diamonds, except at the circular ends, in which are set sapphires in collars of diamonds.

The Bavarian Sceptre (226) (*Plate 20, c*) is a gold rod and has a similar origin to the Royal Crown and Orb. In all, it is 89 cm in length. Apart from a plain polished gold handle at the lower end, the whole is richly embellished with cast foliage work with rosettes, the dividing points being set with brilliants, emeralds, sapphires and pearls. The top is surmounted by a small royal crown, decorated with small precious stones. Around the central part is a scroll which bears the inscription: *CUI NON CIVIUM SERVITUS TRADITA, SED TUTELA*. The sceptre bears both the maker's and inspector's marks. It is indeed a very handsome ornament which, though not embellished with the profusion of precious stones to be found on some of the more magnificent sceptres in Europe, has a most striking appearance. It first came into the Treasury with the Crown and Orb in 1807.

The State Sword (227) (*Plate 20, d*) is 96 cm in length and is made of gold decorated with chased ornamentation; the hilt and guard are set with brilliants, sapphires and rubies and with a large emerald. The scabbard is of gold with similar ornamentation, the foundation being covered with red velvet. On the blade, in gold capitals, is the inscription: *NEC TEMERA, NEC TIMIDE*, together with the Bavarian coat of arms and the lion. There are also the maker's and inspector's marks. The belt is of reddish velvet, embroidered with gold and Medusa heads. The clasps bear the maker's mark of M. G. Biennais.

In 1729 the Elector Charles Albert instituted the Order of St George. This Order had originally been founded in the XII century as a crusading order and had been revived by the Emperor Maximilian I in 1492. The Elector Charles Theodore confirmed the order in 1798, since when there have been certain changes in its constitution.

The Insignia of the Order in the Treasury are:

A cross (240), a star (241) and a hat agraffe (242) made for the Elector Charles Albert in 1729 by a Munich jeweller. They are of silver gilt set with rubies, brilliants and molten glass. In the middle of the cross is St George in gold, with the letters *I.V.P.F.*[1] similarly decorated (*Plate 21, a*). This was known as the Red Suite.

---

1 *Justis ut palma florebit.*

A cross (244), a star (245) and a hat agraffe (246) decorated with large emeralds, rubies and brilliants, made for the Elector Maximilian III Joseph (1745–77) and known as the Green Suite.

A cross (248) (*Plate 21, b*), a star (249) (*Plate 21, d*) and a hat ornament (250) of brilliants, rubies and glass paste set in silver, made in 1760 for the Elector Maximilian III Joseph.

A hat ornament (251) (*Plate 21, c*) and a loop of silver (252) (*Plate 21, c*) set with rubies and brilliants made for the Elector Maximilian III Joseph in 1760.

A fragment of the gold collar (253) of the Order of St George which was first mentioned in the inventory of 1774.

A cross (254) (*Plate 22, a*), a star (255) (*Plate 22, b*) and a hat agraffe (256) and an epaulette (257) in silver set with emeralds, rubies, brilliants and glass paste, set in silver, made in 1830 for King Louis I.

A cross (258) and star (259) in silver with rubies, brilliants and glass paste made in 1830.

A star (260) made in 1869 by Gottfried Merk, of silver set with rubies, brilliants and blue glass paste.

A sword (261) of the Order of St George made in 1870 by Johann Stroblberger of silver, with the grip in mother-of-pearl.

A cross (262) (*Plate 22, c*), a hat agraffe (263) and an epaulette (264) of gold set with rubies, brilliants, emeralds and peridot made in 1874 by A. Hausinger.

A cross (265) and star (266) made in 1902 by Gottfried Merk, of silver set with rubies, brilliants and glass paste.

A cross (267) (*Plate 22, d*) and a star (268) made in 1905 by Gottfried Merk, of silver set with rubies, brilliants and glass paste.

The Order of St Hubert was founded in 1444 by Gerhard V, Count of Ravensberg and Duke of Jülich and Berg in Upper Bavaria. It is one of the oldest and most distinguished Orders in Europe. The Order was founded to commemorate the defeat at Ravensberg of Egmont, Duke of Geldern, in the time of St Hubert. After the death of Adolphus, Duke of Jülich, in 1437, whose lands Gerhard V inherited, Egmont was dissatisfied with his inheritance and tried to enforce his claims by arms, but was severely defeated. To reward and encourage his knights, Gerhard instituted the Order in honour of the Trinity and under the protection of St Hubert. At first the Order was called 'The Order of the Horn' because each knight wore a gold chain composed of hunting horns. The seat of the Order was originally at the collegiate church of St Christine Nydecken, but in 1569 it was removed to Jülich. On the extinction of the House of Jülich in 1609 there was disagreement over the succession, and because of this and the Thirty Years War the Order fell into abeyance. In 1708 it was revived by the Elector Palatine, John William, and took its final form in 1808 under the first King of Bavaria.

The staff and shield of the Order is made of green lacquered wood covered with silver gilt on which red lions are painted. On top is an enamelled shield on both sides of which are the Arms of Bavaria, the Palatinate, Jülich, Berg, Cleves and Geldern in coloured enamel. There is also a representation of the Imperial Orb in blue enamel surrounded by the chain of the Order. Above the shield is a figure of St Hubert kneeling before a stag also in enamel and the device of the Order: *IN TRAV VAST.*[1] Round the shield are embossed coats of arms and three trophies in silver gilt and above the Elector's Hat in silver gilt set with pearls. Below hang two enamel crosses of St Hubert.

[1] 'Steadfast in truth.'

The foot of the shaft is sheathed with iron and has two silver gilt rings. The staff dates from the beginning of the XVIII century and is either Augsburg or Heidelberg work.

The items of Insignia of the Order now in the Munich Treasury are:

Two gold collars (270, 271) of the Order (*Plate 23, a*) made probably in Mannheim or Heidelberg in 1708.

A cross (272) and star (273) of gold set with brilliants and rose diamonds which were probably made in Heidelberg in 1708.

A cross (274) and a star (275) (*Plate 23, b*) of gold and silver set with emeralds, and brilliants, probably made at Mannheim about 1708.

A star (280) of the Order of gold set with brilliants and rose diamonds made by Gottfried Merk in Munich in 1880.

A star (*Plate 23, c*) of this set is of silver gilt set with brilliants with a similar inscription on a red shield.

The insignia were probably made by a German goldsmith on the occasion of the revival of the Order in 1708.

In the 1879 catalogue[1] other insignia of the Order are listed. They include:

A cross and star (C.64 and 65) with rubies and brilliants made for the Elector Maximilian III Joseph in 1792 by the jeweller Caspar Mayr of Munich.

Three sets (K.26, F.52 and 53 and M.43 and 44) which are described as being of gold and enamel, and another three sets (C.103 and 104, D.57 and 58, E.45 and 46), which are not described.

There are seven Orders of the Golden Fleece and two additional collars dating from the XVIII century:

The first (281) belonged to Philip V of Spain, who gave it in 1742 to Maximilian III Joseph, who later became Elector on the occasion of the imperial coronation in Frankfurt. It consists of a collar with clasp and a 'Spanish *Toison*' set with 176 brilliants. It is probably of Spanish workmanship.

A Golden Fleece (288) (*Plate 24, a*) with a yellow brilliant set in the body was made for the Elector Maximilian III Joseph in 1763 by a Munich jeweller, old stones in the Treasury being used.

A collar (282) and Golden Fleece which are probably of Munich workmanship and date from the middle of the XVIII century. They are decorated with 6 large and 129 small diamonds, the larger ones being triangular in shape.

A collar (286) and Golden Fleece of XVIII-century German workmanship set with rubies and brilliants with a large oriental garnet of 134 carats in the centre.

A collar (287) and Golden Fleece in which the Blue Brilliant is set.

A collar (285) and Golden Fleece of silver gilt, probably made in Munich in 1750, set with 68 brilliants and 2 large sapphires.

A collar (289) (*Plate 24, b*) and Golden Fleece made by Johann Staff, Court Jeweller in Munich to Maximilian III Joseph in 1763. They are decorated with white and yellow brilliants which were taken from the stock of loose stones in the Treasury and valued at 320,000 florins.

A collar (283) with a small Golden Fleece made for Elector Maximilian III Joseph in Munich in 1750 decorated with 37 brilliants and 6 rubies. The largest ruby weighs seven carats.

Another collar (284) dating from about the same time is set with brilliants.

---

[1] The numbers in brackets prefixed by a capital letter refer to the enumeration in the 1879 catalogue.

The former richness of the Wittelsbach cabinet of jewellery can best be appreciated by reference to the 1879 catalogue of the Wittelsbach Treasury. Apart from the ornaments that have already been described only a few pieces of importance are included today. Some pieces have been appropriated for the private use of members of the royal family and some were sold in 1931 at Christie's in London. The outstanding stone in the Wittelsbach Treasury is the 'Blue Brilliant', sometimes called the *Hausdiamant* (287) or the 'Wittelsbach Blue'. This blue brilliant was brought into the Wittelsbach family as part of the bridal treasury when Princess Maria Amelia of Austria, the daughter of the Emperor Joseph I, married the Elector Charles Albert of Bavaria, who afterwards became the Emperor Charles VII. The Empress wore it as a breast ornament. She died in 1756 and in 1761 this stone, with her other ornaments, came into the Wittelsbach Treasury at Munich. In the inventory of this Treasury of 1722 it was valued at 240,000 florins. The Elector was very fond of wearing this insignia but later, when Bavaria was raised to a Kingdom, the stone was placed in the front of the orb surmounting the royal crown when the crown was used. At other times its place was taken in the crown by a piece of blue molten glass.

> The stone is a magnificent blue diamond (*Plate 25, a*) weighing 35·32 carats and has a slightly oval shape with a fine blue tint. It is set in a circle of brilliants, with a border of larger brilliants in a floral design. Suspended from this is a loop or bow of brilliants with horizontal rays radiating from a large, oblong, brilliant-cut diamond of pinkish tint in the centre. Altogether 700 brilliants are used in the setting. From the bow hangs the Golden Fleece.

It was first set in its present form by order of Maximilian III Joseph in 1761. In December 1931 this ornament, but without the Golden Fleece, was offered for sale by auction at Messrs Christie's in London, but the highest bid—£5,072 10s.—not reaching the reserve price, it was withdrawn from the sale. The other stones in this ornament were taken from a hat ornament and from a pair of shirt buttons. Although this stone cannot compare in size or beauty with the famous Tavernier or Hope Blue diamonds, it is a stone of great rarity and distinction. Its earlier origin remains obscure. It is not known how it came into the Austrian ownership.

The second jewel of importance in the Wittelsbach Treasury is a black and white pearl known as the 'Pearl of the Palatinate' (870) and also called the 'Eye of the Palatinate' (*Plate 25, c*). It first appears in the Düsseldorf inventory of 1711 where it is described as decorating the cover of a box. It was known to have been in the possession of the Elector John William (1690–1716) and possibly it was bought by the Elector himself through the jeweller Jan Walrawn, who was much thought of by the Düsseldorf Court. It was brought from the Palatine Treasury in 1782.

> The pearl is drop-shaped and weighs not quite 12 carats. It is set in a diamond ornament, the pedestal of which is in the form of garlands, on which rest three interwoven snakes, their heads making a cup-like setting for the pearl. The pearl itself is an abnormality, its rounded top being quite black but with good lustre. Black pearls are not uncommon.

The Treasury was formerly particularly rich in pearls and in the 1879 catalogue the following important ornaments were included:

A necklace (B.19) of five rows of oriental pearls of a total weight of 1,601 carats.

A collar (B.20) of 96 round pearls.

A collar (B.21) of 90 pearls.

A necklace (B.22) of 66 large round pearls, the total weight of which are $334\frac{11}{16}$ carats.

A necklace (B.23) of 29 large pearls weighing $154\frac{11}{16}$ carats.

A necklace (B.24) of 232 pearls.

A group of 22 large pearls (B.25).

A necklace (B.26) of 184 pearls.

A monogram M.I. (Maximilian Joseph) (B.49), set with 97 oriental pearls weighing 627 carats and 31 Bavarian pearls of 296 carats.

A pair of bracelets (B.97) composed of 220 oriental pearls with two gold slides set with 4 brilliants made for the Empress Josephe Maria Antonia about 1729 who was the daughter of Charles VII Albert and consort of the Emperor Joseph II.

Five strings of well-matched oriental pearls (C.68, C.69, C.70, C.71, C.72) totalling 2,092 carats.

A monogram L.T. (B.111) set with 21 fresh-water pearls.

Three single pearls (C.38, C.40 and C.42), two of which were round and weighed $28\frac{9}{16}$ carats and $9\frac{11}{16}$ carats respectively and 1 pear-shaped of $22\frac{5}{16}$ carats.

The only ornament now in the Treasury entirely composed of pearls is a necklace of 90 Bavarian pearls (297) which was brought into the Treasury in 1917. The first Bavarian pearls were produced in the xv century, and the pearl-fishing industry reached its fullest development between 1814 and 1857, during which period 158,880 pearls were won. There is also a breast ornament of silver set with diamonds and pearls (Plate 25, b)

Since 1918 the so-called pearl diadem (230) which belonged to King Otto of Greece and was worn by his consort has been kept in the Treasury (Plate 28, a). It consists of a row of well-matched round pearls on which stands an elaborately ornamented frame of brilliants bearing 16 large pear-shaped pendant pearls with 16 large pear-shaped pearls set in an upright position.

According to the 1879 catalogue the Treasury was also very rich in diamonds. Apart from the Blue Brilliant already described there were a number of notable diamond ornaments and other stones of a large size. At a sale of Christie's in London in 1931 three diamond ornaments were sold and these were described in the catalogue as:

An important brilliant pendant (Plate 26, b), composed of three large stones, the centre one of circular shape and the other two of drop shape, the upper and centre stones connected by brilliant scroll work of smaller stones; the setting being of silver gilt, the back of one drop-shaped stone being enamelled blue and green. According to an inventory of 1774, of the jewels of Maximilian III Joseph, the pendant was mounted in its present form by the Munich jeweller, C. Rieländer, and sold for £4,000.

An important brilliant tiara (Plate 26, a), designed as a collet band of 49 graduated brilliants surmounted by a broad trellis band, within the sections of which are suspended 36 briolettes of varying sizes. The trellis band is surmounted by floral sprays with an expanded rose in the centre with a large single stone and a drop brilliant above forming a rosebud. This tiara was originally mounted by the Parisian jeweller, Borgeois, in 1817, and reset in 1832, on the instructions of King Louis I by the Munich jeweller, Kaspar Rieländer, and sold for £7,000.

A fine oblong cinnamon-yellow brilliant, weighing 30·25 carats, set in a gold ring and sold for £1,300.

Other important diamond ornaments in the 1879 catalogue include:

A solitaire (B.39) of reddish tint weighing $29\frac{1}{4}$ carats.

A solitaire brilliant (B.48) of greenish-yellow tint set in a ring *à jour* weighing $29\frac{1}{4}$ carats.

A hat pin (C.6) of brilliants set with a great brilliant clasp of $26\frac{5}{16}$ carats.

A collar of white brilliants (B.3) set *à jour* in gold with a slide set with a long round-cut brilliant, the three large stones in the middle set between smaller brilliants. In all there were 30 brilliants of the first water. This collar was made by the Court Jeweller, Rieländer, in 1827.

A *sévigné* (B.7) of brilliants with a large brilliant of 11 carats in the centre made for King Louis I by Rieländer in 1828.

A group of 6 large flat rose-cut diamonds (B.41) of beautiful quality in a silver setting, the largest stone weighing $18\frac{1}{4}$ carats, and the smallest 12 carats.

A breast ornament (B.99) of brilliants and pearls set with 1,116 rose diamonds, 35 drop pearls and 3 half-pearls.

A pair of ear-rings (B.6) each with a yellow rose-cut diamond set with 12 smaller white rose-cut diamonds, the total weight of the stones being 15 carats.

A pair of ear-rings (B.9) of brilliants, the largest of about 8 carats and 8 pear-shaped brilliant pendeloques. These were part of a set which included the diamond tiara sold at Christie's.

A pair of ear-rings (B.16) of pearls and brilliants each in the form of a pearl with a circlet of brilliants with 3 pendant pear-shaped pearls made by Rieländer in 1825. This item is still in the Treasury.

A pair of ear-rings (B.102) set with rose-diamonds.

A hair ornament (B.50) with a large yellow brilliant of $12\frac{7}{16}$ carats set in gold.

A hair ornament with a three-cornered brilliant of $11\frac{1}{2}$ carats ánd a small round brilliant.

A hat agraffe (C.6) of white brilliants of a gross weight of 30 carats, a large brilliant weighing $26\frac{5}{16}$ carats set in the middle; made by Rieländer in 1822.

A hat agraffe (C.7) of rose and brilliant diamonds made by the Court Jeweller Johann Staff in Munich in 1765.

A hat ornament with a solitaire (C.8) of 9 carats set with 455 brilliants in silver gilt.

A brilliant (B.61) in the form of a pear-shaped pendoleque.

Twenty-one coat and seventeen vest buttons (B.18) of rose-cut diamonds. The stones were bought by Elector Maximilian II Emmanuel in Amsterdam and were fashioned by orders of Maximilian III Joseph in 1768 and made into buttons by Rieländer.

Two pairs of buckles (C.60) with 88 large and 44 brilliants in silver setting.

A sword hilt (C.27) set with 789 brilliants made for Elector Maximilian III Joseph.

The Treasury contained what must have been one of the most remarkable collections of emeralds. The following were included in the 1879 catalogue:

A hat ornament (B.32) with a beautiful emerald and brilliants.

A large emerald (B.34) of 70 carats in a silver gilt setting.

An emerald (B.35) of 52 carats in a silver gilt setting.

A great six-sided emerald (B.38) of $27\frac{13}{16}$ carats.

An uncut emerald (B.51) of 120 carats. In 1565 it was set in a gold and enamel goblet.

An emerald (B.52) of 80 carats.

Eighteen single emeralds (B.57), the largest of which weighed 24 carats. One was set with brilliants.

A sword hilt (C.62) of gold set with 548 brilliants and 322 emeralds which belonged to Elector Maximilian III Joseph.

a   *Order of the Golden Fleece with the Wittelsbach Blue Diamond, 1761. Residenz Treasury, Munich* (pp. 35 and 36)

b (above, right)   *Breast ornament of silver set with diamonds and pearls. Residenz Treasury, Munich* (p. 37)

c (right)   *The Pearl of the Palatinate. The pearl itself is an abnormality, its rounded top being quite black. It is set in a diamond ornament. Residenz Treasury, Munich (p. 36)*

a   *Brilliant tiara. Sold at Christie's 1931* (p. 37)

b (left)   *Brilliant pendant. Sold at Christie's 1931* (p. 37)

c (right)   *Large emeralds. Sold at Christie's 1931* (p. 39)

In 1931 nine emeralds from the Treasury were sold at Christie's (*Plate 26, c*):

A magnificent oblong emerald weighing 53·75 carats, and sold for £5,600.
A magnificent square emerald weighing 39·75 carats and sold for £2,000.
Another weighing 42·25 carats and sold for £1,450.
Another weighing 38·31 carats and sold for £1,450.
Another weighing 28·16 carats and sold for £1,580.
A magnificent large square emerald weighing 61·35 carats and sold for £750.
A magnificent large emerald of hexagonal shape weighing 98·98 carats and sold for £3,100.
An emerald of similar shape weighing 28·69 carats and sold for £2,750.
A large *cabouchon* emerald drop weighing 85·45 carats with a gold setting in the centre, the base
   enamelled, and sold for £573 10s.

Even allowing for the difference between the old German weight and standard weights these stones are difficult to identify among those in the 1879 catalogue.

Rubies and sapphires are not so well represented in the collection but there is a suite of balas rubies which is still preserved in the Wittelsbach Treasury. This was made by the order of Louis I for his wife Theresa in 1830 by the Munich jeweller, Kaspar Rieländer. The stones were already in the Wittelsbach Treasury and a number were taken from the so-called ruby collection of the Elector Maximilian III Joseph. The suite consists of:

A cockade (235) of favour (*Plate 27, b*) 14 cm in length consisting of 3 big and several small rubies
   set in silver gilt and numerous brilliants set in silver.
A collar (234) (*Plate 27, b*) 50 cm in length consisting of nine links each containing 1 big balas-ruby.
   Each link is joined to the next by brilliants. The rubies are set in gold and the brilliants in silver.
   The largest ruby weighs 22 carats.
A diadem (233) (*Plate 27, a*) 13 cm in height and 19 cm in diameter of tendril work composed of
   142 brilliants set in silver gilt with 140 rubies set in gold. The largest ruby weighs $36\frac{15}{16}$ carats.
A pair (236) of ear-rings each with 3 rubies above which is an oval leaf of 5 large and many small
   brilliants. The settings are of silver gilt and the length is 10 cm.
A pair of bracelets (238–9) (*Plate 28, b*) of brilliant tendril work inset with rubies, in the centre of
   which is a large single stone.
In all there are 72 rubies and 40 brilliants, the total weight of the stones being $76\frac{7}{32}$ carats.

Another ruby ornament is a hat agraffe made in Munich in 1875 by Gottfried Merk for King Louis II which consists of a lily in brilliants with a large drop ruby.

Apart from the Golden Fleece set with sapphires already described, the only notable sapphire ornament which still is preserved in the Treasury is a hat ornament consisting of brilliants set in the shape of a rose with 4 big sapphires and 1 large brilliant at the centre in a silver gilt setting. Engraved at the back 'G. Merk 1874'. This ornament was made for Louis II by the Court Jeweller Merk. Louis wore it daily in his hat.

The other five rooms contain numerous ornaments and plate made with rare materials, but with few exceptions they do not belong to our subject; attention can be drawn to a few objects of particular interest:

The first is a figure of St George of gold and studded with brilliants. St George is on horseback, piercing the dragon with his lance. The figure rests on a three-cornered pedestal of heliotrope adorned with carved and enamelled ornamentation. The figure of St George belonged to the insignia of the Order of the Garter given to Frederick, Count Palatine and King of Bohemia, on the occasion of his wedding. The original design was made by Holbein in 1547 for Henry VIII. This jewellery is first mentioned in the description of the Munich mansion of Marchese Pallavicini. It first appears with the mount in the Munich inventory of 1680. The Garter of the same set of insignia was picked up on the battlefield of the White Mountain when Frederick was defeated in 1620 and handed over to Duke Maximilian of Bavaria.

From a number of pendants the following are deserving of mention:

A pendant in gold and enamel bearing a chased bust of Cleopatra with the asp in her bosom. The face and hands are of cut hyacinth and she holds a green enamel viper twisted round her arm against her bosom. Her head is adorned with a six-pointed diamond diadem. The dress is of blue enamel. The figure is surrounded by enamel ornamentation and the whole set with emeralds, rubies and table diamonds. It is of German workmanship of the middle XVI century but the stone cuttings were probably of Italian work of that time. The pendant was once the chief ornament of a large necklace.

A gold pendant (*Plate 29, d*) with serrated enamel scroll work with branches of fruit between. Two big stones are set in the scroll work above which is a quadrangular aquamarine supported by two angels in enamel, one holding a cornucopia and the other a palm. Below is a rectangular red stone. The back is decorated with enamel scroll work. It is of German workmanship (c. 1560), perhaps from a design by Hans Mielich. The aquamarine was inset in 1730. Originally the place of the aquamarine had been taken by a large table-cut stone.

A gold pendant (590) (*Plate 29, c*) or corsage ornament in the shape of a lion rampant in brown enamel set with a table-cut stone, rubies and pearls. The lion holds in its four paws an open circlet of emeralds which originally held a big emerald or a medallion and wears a crown decorated with rubies and pearls. Three pearls hang from it. It has a chain composed of seven links, each containing a table-cut diamond in a box setting. It is of German workmanship of the mid-XVI century and came from the Palatine Treasury in 1794. In the Mannheim inventory of 1738 it is described as 'The Bohemian Order'; in that of 1783 as 'The Bohemian Crowned Lion'.

A pendant of rock crystal pear-shaped in an enamel and gold cast setting of scroll work and fruits with a recumbent *Putto* on either side. There are 4 table diamonds in the setting. It is of German workmanship of mid-XVI century, probably identical with No. 11 of Albert V's disposition of 1565 when the rock crystal replaces a big deep-coloured ruby.

A gold and enamel pendant in the shape of a little bear overlaid with amber and sitting on a monkey at the foot of which are two little dogs, the whole set with rubies, table diamonds and pearls. The pendant hangs from three chains. It is of German workmanship of mid-XVI century; a legacy from the Electoral Prince Joseph, son of the Elector Maximilian Emmanuel to whom it was given by the wife of Archduke Maximilian Philip *née* Princess de la Tour d'Auvergne.

A gold and enamel pendant in the shape of an elephant with a serpent twined round its foot. Over its body is a cloth, having on one side a big baroque pearl surmounted by four rosettes and on the other the Bavarian arms in enamel. On its back is a little quadrangular pedestal in front of which is a spinel ruby and at the back an enamelled peacock. On the pedestal sits a lion and in front of it the mahout is sitting, both in gold enamel. It is of German workmanship (c. 1560).

a   *Diadem of ruby suite, 1830. Residenz Treasury, Munich* (p. 39)

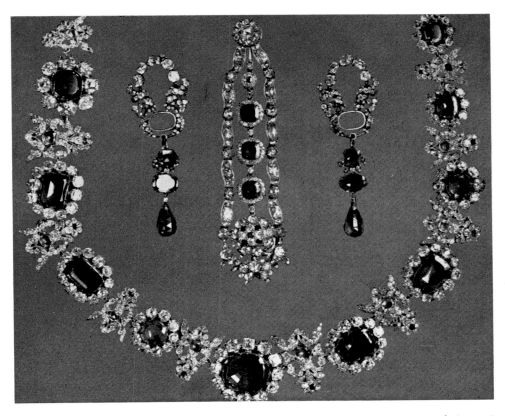

b   *Collar, cockade and pair of ear-rings of ruby suite. Residenz Treasury, Munich* (p. 39)

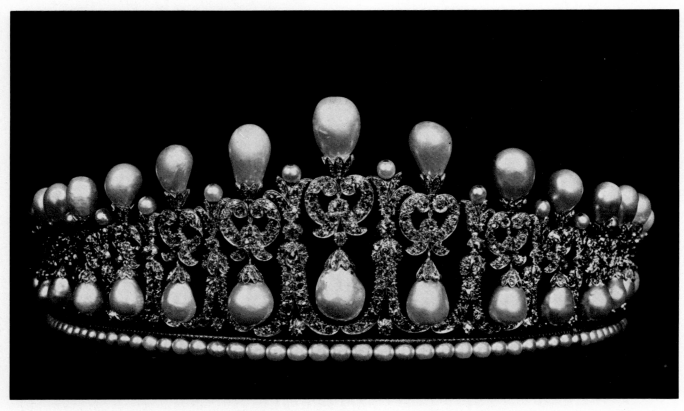

a   *Pearl diadem. Residenz Treasury, Munich* (p. 37)

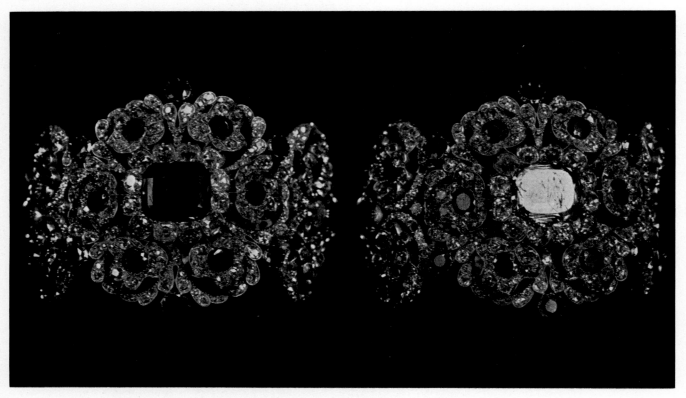

b   *Pair of bracelets of ruby suite, 1830. Residenz Treasury, Munich* (p. 39)

A pearl was set in place of a table diamond in 1730. It can be seen being worn by the Duchess Anna in a miniature illustration of 1559 by Hans Mielich.

A pendant in the form of a little round glass box in a gold and enamel setting. Inside is an antique warrior in cast gold and enamel in a chariot, drawn by two galloping red-enamelled horses all set with rubies, diamonds, pearls and emeralds. From the back hangs a gold and enamel parrot with a big baroque pearl on its breast and 5 emeralds and 3 rubies on its back. It is of German work, probably late XVI century; formerly a little cross of rubies hung from the box. The parrot was probably added in the XVII century.

A pendant of pierced gold and enamel scroll work on which the name of Jesus and *I.H.S.* stands in Gothic script in table stones of an old-fashioned cut in gold setting, surrounded by similarly set stones. It is of Italian workmanship of the mid-XVI century. The pendant is mentioned in Albert IV's will as a gift from the Duke of Mantua with whose family there was close relationship. An inventory of 1572 states that Duke William V wore it round his neck every day.

A pendant of gold filigree work, in the centre an octagonal agate on which is a picture of St Anthony and the Holy Child in beaten gold. It is Italian work of the XVI century and came from the Palatine Treasury.

A pendant in the form of a trophy of arms of silver gilded in places. Below the weapons sit two Turks in chains, painted in cold enamel. The whole is richly set with brilliants, rubies, emeralds and 2 big pearls. The back of the trophy is very realistically painted in cold enamel to represent a runner with a battering ram. Each of the 2 big pearls weigh 60 carats. It is of German workmanship, possibly Augsburg, of the second half of the XVII century and it came from the Palatine Treasury.

Another ornament is a hat brooch in the form of a trophy in gold and enamel. In the centre is a breast plate in velvet enamel and above a helmet in blue enamel. Behind are arms, a banner and a shield arranged in the shape of a trophy. At the upper edge a plume of feathers in which is a big table diamond, above which is an 18-carat table diamond. Above these is a plume made up of 4 big and 2 small drop pearls, between which are table diamonds of various sizes from which spring the feathers set with small stones. 245 table diamonds are introduced into the ornament. Enamelled on the back in the court colours is a lozenge-shaped flag with the Bavarian arms and Ducal Hat, surmounted with the inscription: *Dominus Virtutem Nobiscum MDC III*. It is described in Maximilian I's will as third in order in the Treasury. It is of German, probably Augsburg, workmanship of 1603 by the Augsburg goldsmith Georg Peyerle. According to the accounts of the Court Treasury in 1610, the goldsmith received 1,300 florins for his work.

Among the semi-precious stones is a drinking vessel in the shape of a shell made from a single piece of amethyst and in the 1879 inventory a large and small aquamarine (R.12).

Duke Albert V employed as Court painter Hans Mielich (1516–73). On the Duke's orders he prepared an inventory which was illustrated with exact copies in miniature of the Duke's jewels and those of his wife Anne of Austria. These drawings are now in the Royal Library at Munich and in the Bavarian National Museum (*Plate 29, a* and *b*).

41

BIBLIOGRAPHY

BASSERMANN-JORDAN, E. AND SCHMID, W. *Der Bamberger Domschatz*, Munich 1914.

BOCK, DR FRANZ *Die Kleinodien des Heiligen Römischen Reiches Deutscher Nation*, Leipzig 1864.

DEÉR, JOSEF *Der Kaiserornat Friedrichs II.*

HAEBERLEIN, FRITZ *Schatzkammer der Residenz München*, 1937.

PALGRAVE, SIR FRANCIS *Antient Kalendars and Inventories of the Treasury of H.M. Exchequer*, 1836.

SCHAUSS, DR EMIL VON *Historischer und Beschreibender Katalog der Königlich Bayerischen Schatzkammer zu München*, 1897.

SCHRAMM, P. E. *Herrschaftszeichen und Staatssymbolik.*

STERN, DR HEINRICH *Führer durch die Schatzkammer der Münchner Residenz*, 1931.

THOMA, DR HANS *Schatzkammer der Residenz München, Katalog 1958.*

THOMA, DR HANS AND HEGE, WALTER *Kronen und Kleinodien. Deutscher Kunstverlag, 1955.*

DUKES

1070	Guelph I	1294	Rudolph I and Louis, later Emperor Louis IV
1101	Guelph II		
1120	Henry IX, the Black	1347	Stephen II and Albert I
1126	Henry X, the Proud	1375	Stephen III, Frederick and John II
1138	Leopold IV, Margrave of Austria	1397	Ernest and William III
1142	Henry II of Austria	1438	Albert III, the Pious
1156	Henry the Lion	1460	John IV and Sigismund
1180	Otto, Count of Wittelsbach	1465	Albert IV, the Wise
1183	Louis I	1508	William IV
1231	Otto II, the Illustrious	1550	Albert V
1255	Louis II, the Severe	1579	William V

ELECTORS

1596	Maximilian I, the Great	1745	Maximilian III Joseph. End of the younger line of Wittelsbach
1651	Ferdinand		
1679	Maximilian II Emmanuel	1778	Charles Theodore, Elector Palatine of the Rhine
1726	Charles Albert, Emperor		
		1799	Maximilian IV Joseph

KINGS

1806	Maximilian I	1886	Otto I
1825	Louis I. Abdicated		Luitpold as Regent
1848	Maximilian II		Louis as Regent
1864	Louis II	1913	Louis III. Abdicated 1918

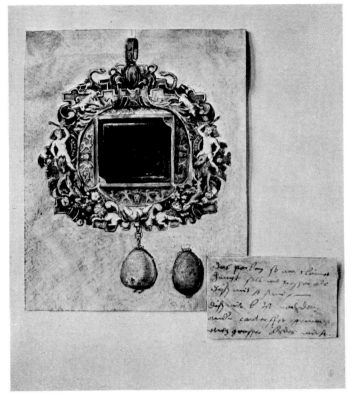

a (left)   *Hat ornament with ostrich plumes by Hans Mielich from Inventory of Duke Albert V. Bavarian National Museum, Munich (p. 41)*

b (above right)   *Large ruby in an enamel setting with pearl pendant by Hans Mielich from Inventory of Duke Albert V. Bavarian National Museum, Munich (p. 41)*

c (left)   *Pendant for ceremonial chain possibly from a design of Hans Mielich in the form of a Bohemian Lion, 1570–80. Residenz Treasury, Munich (p. 40)*

d (right) *Pendant for ceremonial chain from a design of Hans Mielich, 1560. Residenz Treasury, Munich (p. 40)*

a   *XIII or XIV-Century crown. Royal Museum of Art and History, Brussels* (p. 44)

b   *Reliquary crown, XIII Century. Treasury of Namur Cathedral* (p. 44)

CHAPTER THREE

BELGIUM

The Kingdom of Belgium was established as a liberal constitutional monarchy in 1831. In 1813, on the restoration of the Orange dynasty in Holland, Belgium had been annexed and William, the Prince of Orange, had been proclaimed Sovereign Prince of the United Netherlands. In 1815 he assumed the title of King of the Netherlands and made a state entry into Brussels where he underwent a ceremony which is sometimes erroneously referred to as a coronation. In 1830 a revolution broke out and a provisional government was set up which proclaimed Belgium's independence, and two months later Belgium was acknowledged as an independent state by the Powers. In 1831 the Duke of Nemours was elected King, but his father, the French King Louis Philippe, refused his consent. On 12th July, Prince Leopold of Saxe-Coburg accepted the throne of Belgium and on 19th July made his state entry into Brussels. The procedure on this occasion has been followed at the accession of each successive sovereign and has become the traditional and established ceremony in place of a coronation. The king rides into the city on horseback by a circuitous route, showing himself to his people. In 1951, however, King Baudouin varied the first day's procedure by driving to and from the Parliament House in a carriage procession instead of riding on horseback. On arrival at the Parliament House, the king enters the Chamber of Deputies where the senators, the deputies and the representatives of foreign powers are assembled. Standing before the throne, which bears the words: *L'union fait la force* and with arm outstretched, he declares in French and in Flemish: 'I swear to observe the constitution and the laws of the Belgian people and to preserve the independence of the nation and the integrity of its territory.' Then, seated on the throne, he reads his speech from the throne. The king then proceeds, on horseback, to the Royal Palace. On the following day he drives in state to the cathedral where a solemn *Te Deum* is sung.

Although a set of regalia was used by William in 1815 as King of the United Netherlands, he took this with him to Holland when he abdicated the Belgian throne in 1830. Today there are no regalia in Belgium. This is probably because the short time available between the acceptance of the throne by Leopold I and his state entry into his capital did not permit a set to be made. As there was no coronation ceremony it was, no doubt, considered unnecessary to go to the expense of having a set of regalia made, and this would have been in keeping with the liberal ideas of the times.

According to Jones in his *Crowns and Coronations*, a crown was made for the queen in the latter part of the XIX century by the Court jeweller. It is described as a very elaborate work of art, composed of 40 pearls, 20 pear-shaped and of enormous size; 40 large brilliants and nearly 5,000 small ones; the whole being set in gold and wrought in open work. It was said to resemble a coronal of flame, simple in form but of great elegance. Its weight was less than half a pound. Enquiries have failed to elicit any information except that there are no crown jewels in Belgium, all the jewellery worn by the Queen being the private property of the royal family, and it is therefore possible that the crown referred to does still exist among the royal jewels. In the accounts of the funeral of Queen Astrid it was stated that a crown rested on the coffin.

Streeter[1] describes a diamond of 50 carats called *La Reine des Belges* which was given to Queen Marie by her mother, the Archduchess, wife of the Archduke Joseph, Palatine of Hungary.

For heraldic purposes the Kingdom of Belgium has adopted a formal royal crown with four arches, a long sceptre surmounted by the Belgian lion and a hand of justice.

In the Royal Museum of Art and History in Brussels there is a crown which has been variously ascribed to the XI, XIII and XIV centuries (*Plate 30, a*). Its origin is unknown, but it was acquired from a private collection in the XIX century.

The circlet is a narrow band formed of ten straight pieces of silver gilt, with a corded edge. From behind the plates rise fleurs-de-lis, originally ten in number, but only six remain intact. The crown is decorated with precious stones, but some of the settings are empty. Some of the settings take the form of rosettes while others have an oak leaf design.

The crown was probably found in a grave but may have been worn, as it conforms generally with the circlets worn by royal ladies characteristic of the XIII century.

In the Treasury of the cathedral at Namur is a rich golden crown in the form of a circlet made of eight flat gold plates joined together with hinges and pins, each of which is surmounted by a pearl (*Plate 30, b*). From the centre of each plate rises a fleur-de-lis. Those at the front and back carry a receptacle in each of which is preserved a thorn from the Crown of Thorns. The whole crown is richly decorated with pearls, precious stones and filigree work. There is a beautifully chased leather box for the crown. Bock[2] expressed the opinion that this crown was a gift to the cathedral by Philip the Good in the early part of the XV century, but later investigation has shown that it was made specifically for the purpose of containing the two holy relics and was given by the Eastern Emperor Baldwin I in 1204 to his brother Philip the Noble, Count of Namur. There is in the British Museum a fragment of a crown which was purchased through art dealers half a century ago. It bears a close relationship to the Namur crown.

In the Gallerie d'Apollon in the Louvre there is a crown which was given by St Louis to the Monastery of the Dominicans at Liège.[3] It is described in the chapter on France.

---

[1] E. W. Streeter: *The Great Diamonds of the World.*
[2] Dr Franz Bock: *Die Kleinodien des Heiligen Römischen Reiches Deutscher Nation* (Leipzig 1864).
[3] Jules Helbig: *Relics and Reliquaries given by St Louis, King of France, to the Monastery of the Dominicans of Liège* in *Mémoires* published by the Royal Academy of Belgium, Vol. XLIV, 1882, p. 16.

BIBLIOGRAPHY

BOCK, DR FRANZ	*Die Kleinodien des Heiligen Römischen Reiches Deutscher Nation*, Leipzig 1864.
BORCHGRAVE D'ALTANA, COMTE JOS. DE	*Description sommaire des collections des Musées royaux d'art et d'histoire*, Brussels.
BORCHGRAVE, D'ALTANA, COMTE JOS. DE AND CRICK-KUNTZIGER, M.	*Musées Royaux d'Art et d'Histoire Descriptive Sommaire des Collections. Tome 2, Section des Industries de l'Art*, Brussels 1936.
COURTOY, F. AND SCHMITZ, J.	*Memorial de l'Exposition, 1930 à Namur.*
JONES, W.	*Crowns and Coronations*, London 1898.
MELY, M. F. DE	'Les reliques de Constantinople au XIII Siècle' in *Revue de l'Art Chrétien*, 1902.
	'Les Reliques de Constantinople' in *Revue de l'Art Chrétien*, 4th Series, 1899–1900.
STREETER, E. W.	*The Great Diamonds of the World*, London 1882.

KINGS OF THE BELGIANS

1831	Leopold I
1865	Leopold II
1909	Albert
1934	Leopold III
1951	Baudouin

CHAPTER FOUR

BOHEMIA

Although the Czechs appear to have become masters of Bohemia in the v century, it is not until the introduction of Christianity that the history of the country emerges from obscurity. Christianity was first introduced by the Germans, but owing to an innate distrust of them, little progress was made until the conversion of the Bohemian Prince Bořivoj (c. 837). The early Christian rulers of Bohemia supported the new religion with energy and forged links with Bavaria and the Saxon dynasty. In 921 the Duchess Ludmilla was murdered for her Christian beliefs, and in 935 Wenceslas, surnamed The Holy, one of the most famous rulers of Bohemia, was slain by his brother Boleslav. Both Ludmilla and Wenceslas were subsequently canonised by the Church of Rome. To this day Wenceslas is revered as the national saint and his name is particularly associated with the Bohemian regalia (*Plate 31, a*). Under Boleslav, who succeeded Wenceslas, and his son Boleslav II, the Bohemian rulers gained control of Moravia and a large part of Silesia and a part of Poland. The State was even sometimes referred to as the Bohemian Empire, though in reality it was only a principality. The foreign possessions were soon lost to Boleslav the Great, King of Poland, and the Přemyslide dynasty was replaced by Boleslav the Great's brother Vladivoj who secured German aid and not only agreed to pay the Germans tribute, as had been done by several previous Bohemian rulers, but became a vassal of the German Emperor and accepted the German title of Duke.

On Vladivoj's death the Přemyslide dynasty was restored in the person of Břetislav (1037–55), who, in order to secure more stable conditions, persuaded the nobles to consent to the oldest member of the House of Přemyslide's succeeding when the throne became vacant. During this reign German suzerainty was finally established. Břetislav was succeeded by his eldest son Spitihněv.

Bohemia was anxious at that time for its status to be raised to a higher rank than that of Poland and senior to that of Hungary whose ruler in the year 1000 had been made king by agreement between the Emperor and the Pope. At the same time the Papacy wished to gain a greater influence in Eastern Europe. In 1059 Duke Spitihněv received from Pope Nicholas permission to wear the mitre, which privilege was granted as a special favour, not in the ordinary way bestowed upon laymen. In return Spitihněv agreed to pay 100 lb of silver a year as census or Peter's Pence, which, however, did not carry with it any recognition of feudal dependence. When Vratislav succeeded his brother, Spitihněv, he too had a similar right conferred upon him in 1072 by Pope Alexander II, and in a letter which Pope Gregory VII sent to the Duke on 22nd September 1074 not only is the annual payment of 100 lb of silver a year referred to, but mention is made of a gift of silver equivalent to the Duke's bodily weight. These payments, however, lapsed. Schramm[1] draws attention to a painting dating from the second half of the XI century, apparently of Bohemian origin, depicting Christ placing a tiara-shaped hood with three circlets and surmounted by a cross on the head of Duke St Wenceslas. He suggests that this may represent the actual mitre bestowed upon the Bohemian dukes. At the Battle of Flarcheim in 1080, when Duke Vratislav was the ally of the Emperor Henry IV he captured the royal lance of Rudolph the anti-king, which had a relic in the blade. Henry gave Vratislav permission to have this carried in front of him in ceremonial processions in Bohemia, on the great feast days of the Church, when the Duke wore his regalia. This gave the Duke a special prestige in relation to the Hungarian king, who already had a royal lance.

In the great struggle between Henry IV and the Papacy over the question of investitures, Vratislav assisted the Emperor, who, as a reward, conferred upon him personally, but not on his successors, the title of King. The Emperor on his return from Italy in 1086 came to Bohemia in person, and at a gathering at Mohuc he handed Vratislav a royal crown. On 15th June 1086 Vratislav and his consort Svatara, clad in royal robes, were crowned in St Vitus's Cathedral at Prague. Egilbert, Archbishop of Treves,[2] conducted the service, but the crown was placed on the King's head by the Bishop of Prague.

Bohemia at this period had obligations towards the Empire, but had no part in its government. This was rectified to some extent when the German King, Conrad III, conferred on the Bohemian Prince Sobeslav (1125–40) the title of Hereditary Cup Bearer of the Empire, thus granting a certain influence on the election of the emperors. The relations between Bohemia and the Empire were still further strengthened when in 1156 the Emperor Frederick I Barbarossa ceded Upper Lusatia to the ruling Bohemian Prince Vladislav II and conferred upon him the personal title of King in return for his taking part in Frederick's Italian campaigns.[3] The Emperor himself on 11th January 1158 placed a royal crown on the King's head at Zezno before the Diet, the legislative body of the State of Bohemia. The new king took the title of Vladislav I.

It was intended that this title should henceforth be hereditary, but owing to the struggles between the Přemyslide princes which followed the abdication of Vladislav in 1173, the title again fell into abeyance. In consequence of the constant internal struggles, the German influence grew stronger. In 1197 Přemysl Ottakar became undisputed ruler of Bohemia and he was crowned King at Mainz at the same time as Philip received the German crown on 15th August 1198, but we have no details of the ceremony. In 1212 Ottakar's royal title was confirmed by a Bull of the Emperor Frederick II, and thereafter it became hereditary, the Emperor retaining the investiture of the kingdom, but recognising the right of election. In order to ensure the proper

[1] P. E. Schramm: *Herrschaftszeichen und Staatssymbolik*, Vol. 3, 1955.

[2] The Archbishop of Treves was one of the three Rhenish prelates who enjoyed pre-eminence and played an important part in the election of the German kings and at their coronations at Aix.

[3] He supplied 300 knights for the Emperor *Romzug* who distinguished themselves. See C. W. Prévite-Orton: *The Shorter Cambridge Mediaeval History*.

succession Ottakar had his son, Wenceslas I, crowned with his wife Kunhuty during his own lifetime on 6th February 1228.

Wenceslas I introduced a ceremony of crown wearing. In 1249, on the day of the Assumption of the Holy Virgin, the Bishops of Prague and Olonunetz placed a crown on his head and invested him in the royal robes. The sceptre and orb were placed in the King's hands, and thus attired he took part in the solemn Mass in St Francis's Church. This ceremony was continued by several of Wenceslas's successors.

Wenceslas I reigned from 1230 until 1253 and was succeeded by his son, Přemysl Ottakar II, who was crowned in Prague on 25th December 1261 with his wife Kunhuty. Přemysl Ottakar II was one of the greatest of the Bohemian kings and considerably extended the boundaries of the kingdom.

In 1273 on the death of Richard of Cornwall, Rudolph of Hapsburg was elected German king. Ottakar himself had been suggested as a candidate for election, but he first of all declined, one of his reasons being that his Slav origin would not be acceptable to the Germans, but when his declared enemy had been chosen, he attempted to obtain the German crown with the aid of the Pope.[1] On Ottakar II's death in 1283 his son Wenceslas II succeeded, but as he was only a boy of seven years of age a guardian was appointed, and he was not crowned until 2nd June 1297. He had already married Guta, daughter of Rudolph of Hapsburg, and their coronation was solemnised with great splendour. The King was anointed and crowned by Gerhard, Archbishop of Mohuc, and he also received the sceptre. The insignia and robes are said to have been most sumptuous. The crown was valued at 2,000 *hryvnas*. The sword and shield which were carried in front of the King were estimated to have cost 3,000 *hryvnas*. The shield bore the lion of Bohemia, which was made of pearls with 4 large rubies set in the claws. The coronation robes were richly embroidered with golden leaves, each adorned with five precious stones. The belt and hat were also of great value. The day after the coronation the King attended the foundation ceremony of the Zbraslavsky Monastery, and after Mass he put on his crown and with his sceptre in his hand conferred knighthood on various persons.

In 1300 Wenceslas, at the request of the Polish nobles, became King of Poland and in the following year, on the extinction of the old royal family of Hungary, there was a movement in that country to elect him as king, an offer he declined although agreeing to his son Wenceslas, then aged twelve, being so elected. On Sunday 26th April 1303 Wenceslas married his second wife Elizabeth, called Reitshka, a Polish princess. The ceremony took place in St Vitus's Cathedral and Reitshka was crowned Queen of both Bohemia and Poland.

In 1305 Wenceslas II died and was buried in the Zbraslavsky Monastery. It is recorded that the body was adorned with the insignia of royalty—a crown on his head and a sceptre and orb in his hands, the ornaments being made of silver gilt.

His son Wenceslas III, who was already King of Hungary, was only aged sixteen at his succession. Within a year he was assassinated. He was not crowned as King of Bohemia, but his father on his death-bed had insisted that his son swore an oath upon the head of St Wenceslas and the sacred relics.

1 Count Franz von Lützow: *Bohemia, an Historical Sketch.*

With the death of Wenceslas III in 1306 the male line of the Přemyslide dynasty came to an end. There only remained in the royal family the widows of Wenceslas II and Wenceslas III and the four daughters of Wenceslas II. The eldest daughter married Henry, Duke of Carinthia, which made him the popular choice for the throne, but the German King Albert declared Bohemia a vacant fief of the Empire and nominated his eldest son Rudolph his candidate as king, and he was duly elected by the nobles, who also agreed to his brothers being in the line of succession if Rudolph should die childless. In order to appease the national feelings and to give some token of continuity of the native dynasty, a marriage was arranged between Rudolph and Elizabeth, the widow of Wenceslas II, but Rudolph died in the first year of his reign and before he had been crowned. He was, however, buried with royal insignia, and when his grave was opened in 1870 a crown, sceptre and orb were found in his tomb and these are still preserved in the Treasury of the Cathedral of St Vitus at Prague (*Plate 34, a*).

The crown was originally an octagon composed of eight plates riveted together, four sur-mounted by crosses and four by fleurs-de-lis. One lily is now missing. The plates were adorned with a pattern of incised branches. The crown is closed with two arches and at the point of inter-section is an exquisite little medallion in the form of a quatrefoil bearing a relief of the Annunciation of the Virgin Mary. The sceptre, which is also silver gilt, is a six-sided hollow rod, the lower handle being missing. At the top is an ornament of six leaves alternately pointing upwards and downwards. On top is a small globe. The orb is of silver and is a flattened spheroid, the halves of which are joined together by a number of tabs. On top is a plain cross.[1]

Within one year the nobles of Bohemia were twice faced with the problem of choosing a new king. One party supported the hereditary rights of the House of Hapsburg, others supported the candidature of Henry of Carinthia, who, after a stormy meeting of the Diet, was elected and accompanied by his wife entered Prague amidst popular acclamation. But civil war broke out, and as Henry's incapacity became apparent, all parties agreed to the need to choose another as king and in 1310 elected John, Count of Luxemburg, the only son of the new German King Henry who became the Emperor Henry VII. John was married to Elizabeth, the second daughter of Wenceslas II and took possession of Bohemia without any substantial resistance. He and his consort were crowned in St Vitus's Cathedral on 7th February 1311 with a great dis-play of splendour. The regalia were carried by dignitaries of the kingdom in accordance with established custom and the younger members of the nobility, who before the ceremony had been knighted, held the crown over the head of the Queen at Mass. The ceremony was performed by the Archbishop of Mohuc, Peter of Aspelt, an adherent of the Hapsburg family. After the coronation a banquet was held at the Monastery of St James in the old city of Prague, and there were tournaments and money was distri-buted to the people. On 18th April 1337 John's second wife Beatrix of Bourbon was crowned Queen of the Kingdom of Bohemia in St Vitus's Cathedral. The time was one when a financial depression was being experienced and the ceremony was carried out in a very modest way. King John was present, but neither wore his royal robes nor

[1] See Dr K. Chytil, Dr A. Podlaha, Dr K. Vrba: *Korunovachi Klenoty Kralovstvi Ceskeho*, Prague 1912, and Dr A. Podlaha: *Illustrierter Katalog des Prager Domshatzes*, Prague 1930.

the kingly regalia. It has been suggested[1] that this was because the King in his financial difficulties had been compelled to sell or pawn his crown jewels. It is, however, expressly stated by one writer[2] that Queen Beatrix was crowned with the *corona regni Bohemiae*. After the ceremony the coronation banquet was held at the Monastery of St James.

Although John has come down in history as a paragon of chivalry[3] and has become famous because of his heroic death at Crécy when he was suffering from complete blindness, he was not popular in Bohemia which he rarely visited. Bohemian historians assert that he only visited his kingdom when he wished to extract money from the people. He was particularly fond of France with whose Royal House he had close family connections. He sent his second son Wenceslas, when aged seventeen, to the French Court to be educated and at his confirmation the young prince was given the name of Charles after the French King Charles IV. In 1346 on the death of his father at Crécy, Charles, who had also fought on the battlefield, became King of Bohemia, having been declared heir to the throne with the consent of the nobles in 1341.

Charles possessed a very different outlook and qualities from his father. He had for a period during his father's lifetime been given full power as regent to govern Bohemia and Moravia during which time he restored order, re-established the country's financial position and made peaceful arrangements with Hungary and Poland. He became very popular with his future subjects, and more important still, he acquired a great and lasting affection for Bohemia. He had been elected German King on 12th July 1346 when his father was still alive. As such he held a meeting of the Estates of Bohemia at which he confirmed all the privileges previously conferred on the kingdom, some of which had been in abeyance. The monarchy was made hereditary according to the rule of primogeniture, but in the event of the royal family having no heir, the rights of the Estates to choose their king was made sure. Charles did many things to improve the social and political position of Bohemia, including the founding of the University and the establishment of a High Court of Law at Prague, and he fostered the use of the Bohemian language which especially endeared him to the people. Whether with justification or not, Bohemian historians claimed that the German princes had never allowed Bohemia its true place in Europe. Charles as Emperor as well as King of Bohemia rectified this. Perhaps the most important thing which he did to achieve this was to make Prague his principal city not only of the Court but from which he ruled the Empire.

When he was Margrave of Moravia and Regent of Bohemia in his father's lifetime, Charles had given thought to bringing the arrangements for the coronation of the kings of Bohemia more into line with those in the great kingdoms in Western Europe. He raised the Bishopric of Prague to the status of an Archbishopric and obtained a Bull from Pope Clement VI at Avignon, dated 5th April 1344, which granted the Archbishop of Prague the right of crowning the kings of Bohemia, a right which had previously belonged to the Archbishop of Mohuc. He himself confirmed the Archbishop's right

[1] Palacky and Tomek: *History of Prague*, I, 545.
[2] *Zbraslav Chronicle*, Fontes IV, 335.
[3] Edward III called him *Corona Militiae*.

in 1347 when he was making preparations for his own coronation. In 1346, or possibly a little earlier, a crown was made which, according to a Bull of Pope Clement VI issued in April 1346,[1] was to adorn the skull of St Wenceslas and to be used for the purpose of the coronation of the Kingdom of Bohemia and other royal functions. The reign of Charles was in fact a turning point in the history of the Bohemian coronation service and regalia, and it is convenient to take stock of the information that is available regarding the royal ornaments which had been in previous use. We know that the regalia which the kings up to this time had received at their coronations were the crown, the sceptre and the orb. In addition the sword was carried before the king and also used for giving the accolade. The shield which was also carried before the king did not count as a royal ornament. The queen received the crown and sceptre. The royal emblems had been borne on coins since the XI century, but these do not provide trustworthy evidence of what the actual ornaments looked like, although they may be taken to approximate with the general design of the regalia in use. Thus the crown on a coin of Wenceslas II is decorated with lilies which strongly suggests that that form of crown was in use at that time. The burial ornaments of Rudolph may provide us with better evidence, but it must be remembered that Rudolph only reigned for a short time and that his Court may have been influenced by German custom. It is unlikely, however, that the lilies and crosses or the arches would have been used on Rudolph's burial crown unless they were already accepted as being the customary emblems for a king of Bohemia.[2]

Charles laid down a new ceremonial to be followed at the coronation of the kings and queens of Bohemia which shows a strong French influence. The king proceeds from the Castle of Prague to St Vitus's Cathedral and is anointed and vested with alb, dalmatic, shoes, gloves and the royal mantle and receives the bracelets, sword, ring, sceptre, orb and crown. The queen[3] is led bare-footed to the altar, she is anointed and receives a sceptre, ring and crown. It was laid down that the 'noble Abbess of the Convent of St George should be present' at the crowning of the queen. This foundation was specially associated with the martyred saint, Duchess Ludmilla, whose relics were kept there.

In considering the reasons for Charles ordering a bust of St Wenceslas and a crown to adorn it, it must be remembered that the King had been brought up at the French court at a time when the cult of Charlemagne was very strong there. When he became King of the Romans he showed his devotion to Charlemagne in various ways. According to some authorities it was he who had the golden bust made to contain the great Emperor's skull and ordered an imperial crown to be placed on the head of the bust. Even if he was not responsible for the making of the bust, he would have been familiar

---

[1] See *Archives of the Metropolitan*, Chapter VIII (7), published in *Monumenta Vaticana*, No. 650.

[2] Cibulka: *Korunovačni Klenoty* in *Umění*, Prague 1930, asserts that formerly all the royal ornaments had been the personal property of the kings and that there was no special coronation crown. Certainly the kings were likely to have had their own personal regalia, but the reference to the *corona regni Bohemiae* in the *Zbraslav Chronicle* strongly suggests that one crown was kept specially for coronations.

[3] It was laid down that she should be crowned on the same day as the king, but later it became the custom for the queen's coronation to be performed on the following day, or even a few days later.

with it and this no doubt determined him to do something similar for the Bohemian national saint. Thus he ordered to be made a golden bust of St Wenceslas to contain the saint's skull and to adorn the head he also ordered, according to the Bull of Pope Clement VI, 'some sufficiently precious royal diadem out of reverence and devotion to St Wenceslas'. Further, he placed in the crown a relic of the Crown of Thorns which gave it a very special status. Charles laid down that the crown was to be kept on the saint's head in the place where he was buried and was only to be removed for the coronation of a new king or such other solemnities as would require the wearing of the royal crown. The crown had to be returned on the same day as it had been used and it was made clear that it was only loaned (*concedatur*) to the king who had to pay the church 200 *hryvnas* each time it was used. Thus as the Crown of St Wenceslas it became the national coronation crown of the kings of Bohemia.

The oldest inventory of the regalia is that of 1354 and there were four more taken during Charles's reign in 1355, 1365, 1368 and 1374. The first one includes the crown from the bust of St Wenceslas; *vasculum christallinum pro repositione crismatis sive olei sacri pro unccione regum Böemiae et reservari mandavit*; an orb and sceptre of silver gilt; a golden ring with a balas; and the crown of Queen Anna of gold and precious stones which adorned the tomb of St Wenceslas. We have no information as to whether the sceptre, orb, ring and ampulla were provided by Charles or were part of the older coronation ornaments. In the other four inventories the crown is described in more detail and from that of 1355 onwards it is stated that the crown contained a mitre, probably that which the Pope had placed on Charles's head at the imperial coronation in Rome that year. There is no mention of the ampulla or of the crown of Queen Anna. In all the inventories the globe is described as being of gold and the sceptre of silver gilt.

Charles and his first consort Blanche were crowned on 2nd September 1347, the ceremony being conducted by Arnost of Pardubice, Archbishop of Prague. Charles's latter wives, Anna, daughter of Rudolph II, Count Palatine of the Rhine, Anna of Chweidniz and Elizabeth of Pomerania were all crowned with great splendour, while on 15th June 1363 his son Wenceslas was crowned at the age of two, and in 1370 the boy's youthful wife Joanna of Bavaria was also crowned.[1]

In the year 1348 Charles had begun to build a large fortified castle in a very strong position on the summit of a steep rock to the west and not far from Prague. He named the castle Karlstein and intended it as a stronghold for the royal family in time of danger, as a repository for the crown jewels and for the safe-keeping of the archives. In 1350, after his coronation at Aix-la-Chapelle, he sent the imperial regalia to Prague where it was received with great state and after being kept in the capital for a time, it was taken to

---

[1] Charles seems to have broken all records in his attendance of coronations. He himself was first crowned King of the Romans at Bonn on 26th September 1346; again as King of the Romans at Aix-la-Chapelle on 25th July 1349; as Charles I, King of Bohemia, on 2nd September 1347; as King of Italy on 6th January 1355; as the Emperor Charles IV on 6th June 1355 and as King of Burgundy on 4th June 1365. He was also present at the coronations of his second, third and fourth wives as Queens of Bohemia, of his son Wenceslas as King of Bohemia in 1363 and as King of the Romans at Aix-la-Chapelle on 6th July 1376 and of his daughter-in-law as Queen of Bohemia in 1370.

Karlstein, but removed to be publicly displayed in Prague once a year. When the Bohemian regalia were first taken to Karlstein is not certain, the first reliable mention being in 1420 in the reign of Sigismund.

There were two other events in Charles's reign which call for mention. The first was the famous Golden Bull which he issued in 1356 in his capacity as Emperor to regulate the election of the German kings. From the point of view of Bohemia it was important because it formally confirmed all the privileges previously granted to the kingdom; it firmly established the position of the King of Bohemia as the senior elector and in its last clause it specifically laid down that the sons of the lay electors were to be taught the Bohemian language on reaching the age of seven. The second was that Charles championed the reform of the Church which led to a temporary estrangement with the Holy See and was the beginning of the movement that was to have a profound effect far beyond the boundaries of Bohemia. At Charles's funeral on 11th December 1378 the regalia were carried in procession and the Emperor lay in his coffin clad in purple, a crown on his head, an orb, sceptre and sword beside him. These must have been special ornaments made to be buried with him and may have been copies of the imperial regalia rather than the royal ornaments of Bohemia. On his coffin were placed the imperial banner and shield with the imperial eagle.

Charles was succeeded by Wenceslas IV, whose second wife Sophia of Bavaria was crowned at Prague on 15th March 1400. Another inventory had been taken in 1387 in which it is stated that the crown had to a great extent been remade[1] and is described in yet greater detail than before. The orb, sceptre and the ring are described as before. Wenceslas had a troublous reign. At first he was in continual conflict with the nobles who actually twice imprisoned their sovereign. He neglected his duties as German king and on 21st August 1400 the four Rhenish electors deposed him. In Bohemia the demand for Church reform continued and the great schism in the Church of Rome alienated the Bohemian people who, with the support of Queen Sophia, espoused the cause of Huss, her confessor, who demanded definite and far-reaching reforms. When Huss was burnt at the stake as a heretic, civil war broke out in Bohemia which the vacillating king was powerless to control. This led to the Hussite Wars which involved Bohemia in a long period of confusion and bloodshed. In 1410 three of the electors chose as German King Sigismund, who had become King of Hungary by his marriage to Queen Mary in 1387, and who was the younger step-brother of Wenceslas. He was crowned at Aix-la-Chapelle in 1414, but the imperial insignia were still at Karlstein and Wenceslas, despite repeated demands, refused to give them up. In 1411 Wenceslas and Sigismund were reconciled and Sigismund promised to arrange for his brother to be crowned Emperor at Rome and for him to retain the imperial regalia and relics as long as he lived. Wenceslas did not go to Rome, however, and in 1416 Sigismund again expressly acknowledged that his brother should during his lifetime be styled King of the Romans and that he would not claim the relics and regalia of the Holy Roman Empire. On the death of Wenceslas in 1419 Sigismund became King of Bohemia. On 30th June 1420 with a large army he occupied the castle of Prague and gained possession of Karlstein. On 20th July he was crowned King of Bohemia in St

[1] *Multum reformata de novo.*

a   *The Bohemian Regalia. St Vitus's Cathedral, Prague* (pp. 47 and 68)

b   *Crown of St Wenceslas, front view. St Vitus's Cathedral, Prague*
(pp. 53 and 64)

a   *Crown of St Wenceslas, back view* (p. 53)

b   *Crown of St Wenceslas, view from above*
(pp. 53, 64 and 136)

Vitus's Cathedral with the national regalia which had been brought from Karlstein. They were returned there on 30th July and the list of the royal ornaments at Karlstein included the sword and sheath of St Wenceslas and a sceptre and orb, but not the crown. The coronation was held under rather special circumstances and was not attended by representatives from all over the kingdom. Shortly after the coronation Karlstein was in danger, so Sigismund had the imperial and Bohemian regalia and some documents relating to privileges secretly removed, first to Blindenburg Castle near Ofen (Buda) and later to Ofen itself. On 22nd March 1424 he had the imperial regalia removed to Nuremberg for perpetual safe-keeping. On 7th June 1421 the Diet of the Bohemian Estates accused Sigismund of having removed the Bohemian crown and the imperial regalia and relics and gave this as one of the reasons for deposing him. In 1435 the Diet requested Sigismund, who in 1433 had been crowned Emperor at Rome, to return all that he had taken away as a prerequisite to any agreement which the Diet might come to with him.

After further negotiations Sigismund pledged himself to return the documents relating to privileges and he issued a decree confirming all the ancient rights of Bohemia. It was agreed that he could return as king if he delivered up the crown and the documents. Sigismund's chancellor, Kaspar Slik, was sent with a suite to Vienna and Pressburg and brought the documents to Iklava (Iglau) on 10th August. On 13th August the 'crown of gold adorned with precious stones' was examined and at a ceremony of splendour Sigismund was received as king and thanked for safeguarding the crown and regalia. Master Menhart of Khradetz, as Supreme Burgrave, then took the regalia to Karlstein in his custody. With Sigismund's death in 1437 the House of Luxemburg became extinct. Sigismund had designated his son-in-law Albert as his successor and he was crowned as King of Bohemia on 29th June 1438 at Prague according to the established procedure, although some new details of ceremonial were introduced. His reign was, however, short as he died in 1439. His unexpected death without an heir was further complicated by the fact that it was known that his wife, Queen Elizabeth, was shortly to give birth to a child. On 22nd February 1440 Queen Elizabeth gave birth to a son who was given the name of Ladislas Posthumous and became the rightful heir to the kingdom. But there were divided factions and a state of anarchy. So disturbed was the condition of the country that in 1448 Master Menhart of Khradetz secretly removed the national regalia to his castle at Velhartice, where, after his death, they were in the custody of his son Oldrich until 1450 when they were returned to Karlstein. In 1453 they were handed over by Oldrich to George of Poděbrad, who was administering the kingdom for the coronation of Ladislas on 20th August of that year. The following November they were returned to Karlstein by George of Poděbrad. Ladislas died on 23rd November 1457 when only seventeen years of age. There being no heir, the Emperor Frederick III, head of the House of Hapsburg, claimed the throne, but after some difficulties the Estates, exercising their privilege, unanimously elected George of Poděbrad as King. Thus a native of Bohemia for the last time ascended the throne. George of Poděbrad was crowned in St Vitus's Cathedral on 17th April 1458 and on the following day his wife Joanna of the family of Rotzmital was crowned. The crown and other royal ornaments had been brought from Karlstein for these ceremonies and were subsequently returned by the Burgrave, King George's son. On the death of George of Poděbrad in 1471, Ladislas Jagiellon of Poland was elected king and was crowned at Prague on 22nd August of that year. During his reign steps were taken to frame regulations for the better safe custody of the regalia. Two burgraves were appointed, one from the nobility and one from the thanedom, to take charge of the castle and its contents and to keep records of all the objects kept there. Detailed rules were drawn up, including the special oaths which had to be taken by the burgraves. These were published in 1500.

The regalia and the documents relating to the privileges were kept in the Chapel of the Holy Cross which was situated in the big tower. The chapel was divided into two parts by an iron grille. The crown regalia and some reliquaries were kept in the innermost part in a trellised quadrangular niche painted blue on the inside with white glass. The chapel could only be opened when the regalia were required, or the records needed to be consulted. The Diet appointed two special commissaries on each occasion to unseal the door of the chapel and to seal it up again. The keys were kept in the chancery of the Castle of Prague. In 1546 the castle suffered from a great fire and the keys melted. Subsequently when the Chapel of the Holy Cross was to be inspected, the authorities had to take with them a sworn locksmith and mason in order to obtain entry.

Ladislas Jagiellon died in 1516 and was succeeded by his son Louis who had been crowned King of Bohemia on 11th March 1509 at the age of four. In 1522 on the occasion of the coronation of his wife Maria of Hapsburg, he had to renew the royal oath on the Crown of St Wenceslas in the saint's chapel before the ceremony, the regalia having been brought from Karlstein for the occasion. On this occasion and at the subsequent coronation, that of Ferdinand I, there was a disagreement between the great officers of State as to which of the royal ornaments were to be carried in the procession. The matter on this occasion was settled by the arrangement that the King should wear his crown and carry the sceptre and orb. Like his father, Louis spent most of his time in Hungary to the detriment of Bohemia, and in 1526 when leading his army of 25,000 against the Turkish host of 300,000, he perished on the battlefields of Mohacs. The Archduke Ferdinand of Austria now claimed the Bohemian throne because he was married to Anna, the daughter of King Ladislas Jagiellon. He was elected King by the Diet, thus beginning a permanent line of Hapsburg sovereigns. The new king was crowned on 24th February 1527 and on the following day his consort Anna was crowned. In order to assure the hereditary succession, Ferdinand caused his son Maximilian to be crowned King of Bohemia on 20th September 1562. Ferdinand, who had been crowned Emperor in 1556, attended the ceremony wearing his Imperial Robes and with the Imperial Crown on his head. Maximilian's wife Maria was crowned Queen on the following day.

In 1547 when Prague was in open resistance to Ferdinand, it was rumoured that the regalia had been moved from Karlstein which was, however, untrue. There were occasions when royal visitors wished to view the regalia. One such occurred in April 1555 when Ferdinand's son, the Archduke Ferdinand, was in Prague and again in 1556 when the Archdukes Ferdinand and Charles wished to see the crown and regalia and the relics. On each occasion the special permission of the Diet had to be obtained. Ferdinand died in 1565 and the crown, the sceptre, the orb and the sword were carried in the funeral procession from the castle to the Church of St Stephen and on the journey to Prague.

In 1575 the Diet recognised Maximilian's eldest son Rudolph as his successor and agreed to his coronation. This took place on 21st September 1576, the regalia being brought from Karlstein in a particularly solemn manner two days before the ceremony and deposited in the Chapel of St Wenceslas. In 1576 Maximilian died at Rezno. His body was brought to St James's Church in Prague and an old Bohemian manuscript in the University of Prague, which was almost certainly written by a Florentine called Marcus Bydozorinus, who died in 1612, gives a detailed description of the ceremony of which he was an eye-witness. The superscription of the manuscript is *Rudolphus rex Bohemiae XXI*. Its text in translation runs as follows:

In 1577 the corpse of the Emperor Maximilian was borne in state from its former place of burial in the cloister of St James in the old town and was interred with ceremony in the Church of St Vitus on the altar of Prague near his father Ferdinand I. The banners of the kingdoms and lands and the funeral hearse were followed by numerous singers and His Majesty's Chaplains; after them in long ranks came the Priors, Canons and Abbots; then the Bishops before whom were carried the holy vessels and the Crozier shining with gold, silver and pearls. First came those most worth seeing in which were the costly and most important regalia of the Hungarian, Bohemian and Roman Kingdoms. In front rode Jaroslav Smiřický von Smiřec who carried the sword in a beautiful and costly scabbard; close to him came Michael Spanesky von Lisovo, the highest *landschriber*, with the golden sceptre. By his side was Burian Trčký, Vice Chamberlain, and Johann Wchynský von Wchnic, Burgrave of Karlstein. In the third row followed Adam of Schwamberg, High Sheriff, who carried the golden orb with the cross. On his right rode Wratislav von Pernstein, High Chancellor, and on the left Johann von Waldstein, Judge of the High Court. Now came Wilhelm Ursinus von Rosenberg, Head Burgrave of Prague, who bore the beautiful pure golden crown richly decorated with costly pearls and precious stones of the glorious kingdom of Bohemia. In 1347 Blanche, the wife of Charles IV, had caused this crown to be made at great cost [*sic*].

In the same order the Hungarian nobles bore the regalia of their kingdom, the sword, sceptre and orb and the Holy Crown which they affirmed was sent down from heaven in 1022 at the entreaties and prayers of their King, St Stephen.

Then came others of His Majesty's especial insignia: namely the insignia of the Golden Fleece on a cushion; the helmet overlaid with gold which had over it a golden crown; and lastly the Emperor's personal vestments. At the end the Princes of the Empire stepping one behind the other bearing the sword, the sceptre and the orb and likewise the crown shining with gold and pearls and extraordinarily richly decorated. Then came the heralds of the Holy Empire and at last the corpse borne by twenty-four Lords of different countries. Behind the bier walked the Emperor Rudolph in mourning apparel, his face covered with a black veil.

(Here follow the names of the high personalities who attended the funeral procession)

Besides these rode one on horse-back who was commanded by the Magistrates to throw the magnificent medals struck in commemoration of the funeral among the people assembled before the *Rathaus* of the old town; and when the others saw this they pressed so closely round him and threw themselves upon the medals in such a way that they were jammed together and some were thrown down and suffocated; whereupon there arose great alarm and outcry so that the soldiers standing round mingled with the crowd. Then the Lords who were already in the alley before the

Rathaus and the Prelates, Abbots and Bishops were overtaken by a great terror for they feared treason and they must have remembered that which they had heard shortly before (namely that the Jesuits had brought and collected many weapons), fearing a repetition of St Bartholomew's Eve. Then fled everyone who might. Some hid themselves in the houses, others in the cellars, some fell head-over-heels.

Thus one of the Abbots broke his crozier in his haste. Others lost the rings from their fingers, others several of the ornaments, whereby they received no little damage.

By this means the Bohemian sceptre and orb were damaged.

When the Emperor heard the uproar he took the black cloth from his head and commanded that there should be peace. Order was restored immediately and the funeral procession reached the Church of St Vitus without further hindrance.

Bock[1] has taken this as evidence that the damage done to the sceptre and orb necessitated new ones being made, but the official report to the Diet says nothing about any damage to any of the royal ornaments. It relates that:

the Supreme Burgrave Wilhelm von Rosenberg covered the crown he was carrying with his cloak. The Supreme Lay Magistrate Michael Spanesky Lisovo who was carrying the golden sceptre was said to have made his escape and only when order was restored did he come back to the procession carrying the sceptre of the Bohemian Royalty under his cloak.

In both reports the sceptre is described as gold, although that in the inventories was always referred to as silver gilt. But the new description may not have been accurate. Rudolph was a great collector and showed a keen interest in the regalia. In June 1598 the Diet sent a commission to Karlstein, led by Peter Vok of Rosenberg and Christopher of Lobkowitz, to make an inventory of the treasure kept in the castle. The Archbishop Zbynck Berka of Dube with the clergy and the two burgraves of Karlstein were present. The regalia and relics were placed upon the altar and some of the rare objects, including the so-called Horns of Roland,[2] were entrusted to the Chancellor who took them to show Rudolph. They were returned and Rudolph sent some artists to the castle to make drawings of the regalia. On 13th June the crown was replaced in its box and we learn it was put into an iron chest which also contained the sceptre, the orb and the bases of two golden crosses. For coronations the regalia were conveyed to Prague in this chest and the ornaments were taken out and placed upon the altar in St Wenceslas's Chapel with the sword of the saint. The Karlstein burgraves and vassals, together with some other noblemen and knights, kept guard throughout the night. After the coronation the regalia were taken back to the altar and kept under guard until returned to Karlstein. In 1611, during a period of danger when the Archduke Leopold invaded Bohemia and threatened Prague, the Diet ordered the regalia to be removed to St Vitus's Cathedral, where they were placed in St Wenceslas's Chapel under the guard of 300 musketeers. It is generally accepted that the present sceptre and orb were made on Rudolph's directions either at the end of the XVI century or in the first years of the XVII century. The times were propitious because Rudolph had set up an *atelier* to which he had invited German and Dutch artists and Italian craftsmen and here was made the Hapsburg House Crown, now in Vienna. The Bohemian sceptre and orb

[1] Dr Franz Bock: *Die Kleinodien des Heiligen Römischen Reiches Deutscher Nation* 1864.
[2] Now in the Treasury of the Cathedral of St Vitus.

were probably made in the same *atelier*. Some Bohemian writers have expressed surprise as to whether Rudolph could have obtained the money required for such costly ornaments, but Rudolph had at about that time received a rich present of gold from the Russian Government which no doubt was used among other things for this purpose.

In 1611, after the invasion of the Archduke Leopold, the Estates forced Rudolph to abdicate. He had for some time been in failing health, being struck with a mental disease. In 1612 he died and his brother Matthias, King of Hungary, became King of Bohemia and was crowned at Prague on 21st May 1611. Matthias was childless, as were his two brothers, and the question of succession was deliberated in the Diet on 5th June 1617. The next heir in the Hapsburg family was Archduke Ferdinand of Styria, but owing to some dissension he was not elected, though was recognised as king and with but little delay was crowned with great solemnity on 19th June of the same year. Ferdinand II was a fanatical adherent of the Roman Catholic Church and had cruelly persecuted the Protestants in Styria. On Matthias's death in March 1618 the Bohemian Estates formally deposed Ferdinand II and elected Frederick, Elector Palatine, as King. Accompanied by his wife Elizabeth, daughter of James I of England, he was crowned at St Vitus on 4th November 1619 and his consort on 7th November. Both sovereigns were Protestants and the traditional forms were adapted to the circumstances, while Dicastus, the Administrator of the Protestant Consistory, officiated at both ceremonies. It is possible that in the procession from the castle to the church the Queen wore a crown which is now in the Wittelsbach Treasury and is known as the so-called Bohemian Crown. This may originally have belonged to Queen Anne of Bohemia, the wife of Richard II of England, and had been given by Henry IV to his daughter Blanche who married Louis III, the Elector Palatine. In the description of the ceremony it is stated that contrary to former practice the Queen received an orb at the ceremony. No doubt those who organised the coronation looked to other countries where a Protestant rite had been introduced and found that in Sweden the queen was invested with an orb. In the Wittelsbach Treasury at Munich there is an orb which in the 1738 inventory of the Treasury of Mannheim was described as the 'Bohemian Orb' (*Plate 33, a* and *b*). It was so designated because it was thought that, together with the so-called Bohemian Crown also in the Munich Treasury, it fell into the hands of Duke Maximilian of Bavaria after the Battle of the White Mountain, but some doubt is today cast on the reliability of this story.

The Sword of St Wenceslas, which had always been kept in the Treasury of St Vitus, was handed over on demand to the civil authorities after Matthias's death. This was done under certain conditions on 15th October 1619 and it was used at Frederick's coronation. The crown and regalia were also moved from Karlstein and placed in the Chancery of the castle at Prague. Frederick's reign was very short and in 1620 an Imperial Army invaded Bohemia and defeated the Bohemian forces at the Battle of *Bila Hora*, or the White Mountain. Frederick immediately left his kingdom.

Ferdinand II had always maintained his rights in Bohemia on the grounds of the election and coronation in the lifetime of his father and he now resumed the government of the kingdom and published a decree suppressing the ancient free constitution of

Bohemia and proclaimed the Bohemian crown to be hereditary in the House of Hapsburg. After the Battle of the White Mountain the Commander of the Imperial Army, Maximilian Duke of Bavaria, ordered the regalia to be moved to St Vitus and deposited in St Wenceslas's Chapel. The Thirty Years War made Karlstein no longer a safe place for the regalia and it was never returned there. In 1625 the office of the Burgraves of Karlstein was abolished by Ferdinand II's order and was never subsequently restored.

On 21st November 1627 Eleanora of Mantua was crowned in Prague in the presence of her husband, Ferdinand II, and four days later her son Ferdinand III was crowned King of Bohemia. That the Hapsburgs continued to attach importance to the Bohemian coronation is demonstrated by the fact that Ferdinand IV who, however, pre-deceased his father Ferdinand III, was crowned at St Vitus's in August 1646 and the third wife of Ferdinand III, Eleanora, also of the House of Mantua, was crowned Queen of Bohemia on 11th September 1656 while Leopold I, son of Ferdinand III by his first wife, was crowned King of Bohemia on 14th September 1656. At the coronation of Ferdinand II and Ferdinand IV the sovereigns appeared attired in the imperial vestments and bearing the regalia of the Holy Roman Empire, while at all these ceremonies the sovereigns about to be crowned put on the Bohemian royal vestments in St Wenceslas's Chapel. At the coronations of the two queens the regalia of the Holy Roman Empire was borne in the procession.

No coronation was solemnised for another sixty-seven years as Joseph I was not crowned at Prague. His brother and successor Charles VI was crowned on 5th September 1723 and his wife Elizabeth Christina of Brunswick-Lüneburg three days later. On Charles's death, Charles Albert of Bavaria was crowned in St Vitus's Cathedral on 19th December 1741. At that time the Bohemian regalia had been taken to Vienna and therefore were not available, and as Charles Albert's title to the Empire was in dispute, the Imperial Regalia were also not at his disposal. He was crowned with a crown which had been brought by him from Munich. For his coronation at Frankfurt in the following year he had a special set of regalia made, and these ornaments—two crowns, a sceptre and an orb—are still preserved, deprived of their stones, in the Munich Treasury. These may have been ready in time for the coronation at Prague.

At Vienna the Bohemia regalia were deposited in the Imperial Secular Treasury and placed in the cabinet in which the Hapsburg House Crown was kept. When required for a coronation the ornaments were taken to Prague and kept in the Royal Apartments of the castle, except for the actual coronation ceremony for which they were taken to St Wenceslas's Chapel. Care was apparently taken on these occasions to check that the regalia were intact, for it is related in the official description of the coronation of Ferdinand IV in 1646 that the King repaired to the Chancery, where he handed over the crown to the Supreme Burgrave, the orb to the Supreme Judge and the sceptre to the Supreme Chancellor. Having disrobed, he proceeded to the House of the Diet and from there accompanied by the Emperor to the Royal Apartments in the castle. The royal ornaments were carefully inspected for recognition and confirmation. In the reigns of Joseph I and Charles VI there was a movement to get the regalia returned to Prague. The subject was discussed in the committee which dealt with the constitution in 1708 and 1709 and also from time to time between 1710 and 1723. The committee reported that the great officers of state had been given an assurance that the Sovereign and succeeding kings would assume an obligation not to remove from Prague without good reason the regalia, the state papers and the crown archives. It seems, however, that they must have been removed after Charles VI's coronation in 1723 as they were not available for that of Charles Albert in 1741.

When Maria Theresa was crowned some changes were made in the coronation ceremony, as it was the first time that a queen regnant had been crowned. She had already been crowned as Queen of Hungary, but her husband had not yet been crowned Emperor. The regalia and vestments were taken from the Queen's apartments in the castle to St Wenceslas's Chapel on the day of the coronation. In the procession from the castle to the church the Sword of St Wenceslas in its scabbard with an unsheathed sword beside it were borne before the Queen. The regalia were carried by the great officers of state according to custom which had been established in the XVI and XVII centuries. The cap was carried separately to the crown. In front of the regalia were borne the banners, two loaves of bread, one gilded and the other of silver plate and two chalices, one containing red and the other white wine. On arrival at the church the Queen went to the Chapel of St Wenceslas and put on the royal mantle and in the procession before the actual coronation she wore the Hapsburg House Crown. After the ceremony the regalia were returned to Vienna, where they were locked away out of view and not until 14th April 1782 by a decree of the Emperor Joseph II were they again exhibited in a cabinet of the Treasure Chamber so that they might be seen by visitors. It is curious that the Bohemian regalia were not included in the Inventory of the Treasury made in 1750.

Maria Theresa's son, Joseph II, had become Emperor in 1765 and in 1780 succeeded to the Kingdoms of Hungary and Bohemia. He has been described as an enlightened despot, but he showed no respect for the historical traditions of either kingdom and even planned to turn the great castle of Prague into military barracks. He refused to be crowned King of Bohemia. His brother Leopold II, who succeeded to the throne in 1790, endeavoured to conciliate the national feeling. The question of the return of the regalia was revived and a Bohemian delegation went to Vienna to make such a request in March 1790. Leopold agreed and on 26th August of that year he issued a decree ordering their return and another one on 8th November announcing his decision to be crowned at Prague. The whole matter was discussed in the Diet in 1790 and a committee recommended that the regalia should be kept in the ancient sacristy adjoining St Wenceslas's Chapel. On 17th July 1790 the Diet debated the ceremonial which should be used for bringing back the crown and for its subsequent safe-keeping. The Diet appointed a delegation of four representatives, each with two deputies representing the clergy, the nobility, the knighthood and the burgraves and Lord Mayor of the old city of Prague, but war appeared imminent and the delegation's departure was delayed, word being sent to the Emperor of the decisions which had been made. When the arrangements for the coronation were ready, the delegation set off. The whole ceremonial of the coronation, including the oath of fidelity and the oath of homage, were discussed by the Diet and a request was made that Queen Maria Louisa should also be crowned. Leopold in a decree of 25th April 1791 gave his approval to the details of the ceremony. The document contained regulations for the route to the place of coronation, the rights to be observed, the preparations that were to be made in the city and enumerated the regalia and other insignia that were available and indicated what had to be obtained. In general the previous coronations of 1723 and 1741 were taken as models.

The delegation arrived at Vienna on 22nd July 1791 and was joined by other delegations from Moravia and Silesia. Leopold having heard the requests made by the Diet ordered the regalia to be delivered to the delegation by the Lord Chamberlain on 4th August. The following day a procession of carriages carrying the regalia, accompanied by the delegates and representatives of Bohemia, Moravia and Silesia and an escort of cavalry, set out from Prague via Znoiem, Jihlava, Caslavsko and the Castle of Koledei, arriving at Prague on 9th August. The regalia were taken to the castle in solemn procession and deposited in the Chapel of St Wenceslas. Leopold appointed two guardians of the regalia and the Archbishop, the Supreme Burgrave, the Dean of the Chapter, the President of the Courts of Justice (or his deputy), the Councillor of the Courts of Appeal, a knight and the Lord Mayor of Prague were given the right of custody of the keys of the place where the regalia were to be kept. This was the former sacristy, which had been strengthened with iron and secured by solid locks, in which was placed a special chest which had been constructed by the Royal Upholsterer, Sorbee, and an architect from Archet.

Leopold II was crowned on 6th September 1791 and his consort six days later. Leopold died early in the following year and his son Francis I was crowned on 9th August 1792 and his wife, Maria Theresa, two days later. On the death of Francis I in 1835, his successor Ferdinand V the Kind was crowned at St Vitus on 7th September 1836 and his consort Maria five days later. On this occasion the Emperor wore the Austrian Imperial Mantle in the procession to the church. This is still preserved in the Vienna Treasury. This was the last Bohemian coronation.

In 1866 when there was threat of war with Prussia the Governor of Bohemia came to an agreement with the *Zemsky Vybor*, or Provincial Board, and in a decree dated 11th April of that year it was laid down that the coronation insignia were to be taken to Vienna temporarily and kept in the Emperor's Treasury. In August 1867 they were returned to Prague where they were solemnly received with great ceremony. They were placed in the same room adjoining St Wenceslas's Chapel in which they had formerly been kept, the security of which had been improved. A new iron door to St Wenceslas's Chapel was secured with seven locks and the chest in which the regalia were kept had seven identical locks. The keys were entrusted to the Archbishop of Prague; the Governor of the Kingdom of Bohemia; the representatives of the Provincial Board; the Dean and Chapter of Prague and the Lord Mayor of the City of Prague. While the improvements to the room were being undertaken, the regalia were temporarily deposited in the National Archives in the castle. When they were taken to their proper repository the room became known as the Crown Vault, and there they have remained ever since. On 28th September 1929 on the occasion of the millenary of St Wenceslas's death[1] the Treasury was opened and the regalia displayed on a

---

[1] Count Franz von Lützow: Op. cit. gives the date of St Wenceslas's death as 935.

cushion which was made in 1868. Although no opportunities were given for expert examination of the crown and other ornaments, they were all photographed.

The oldest coronation ornament which still survives is the Sword of St Wenceslas with which the Kings of Bohemia were girt at their coronations. The sword was also used to give the accolade to newly created knights on the occasion of coronations. There is no definite evidence as to the origin of the sword, but from its shape, workmanship and decoration it is considered to date from the x century. In the inventories of 1354 it is described as:

Item: A sword with scabbard of gold, gems and pearls made for St Wenceslas.

In 1387 the inventory is given as:

Item: The sword of St Wenceslas with scabbard of which the lower part is broken, ornamented with gems and pearls.

This mention of the broken scabbard probably explains why the present scabbard, obviously of much later date than the sword itself, should have been substituted for the earlier richly decorated one. There is no documentary proof of this, but it is probable that at some time during the succeeding century the scabbard sustained further damage and that at some time towards the end of the Middle Ages the present scabbard was made. That this scabbard dates from the first half of the xv century is evident both from the characteristic embossing of the diagonal bands, which encircle it, and to which the fastening rings are attached, and by the trefoil decoration along both borders. This trefoil or foliage ornament is to be found frequently on many ecclesiastical and secular objects of the late Gothic period.

That the sword itself is obviously much older than the scabbard is evidenced by the guard and pommel. The blade is very similar to those of the Sword of St Maurice and the Imperial Ceremonial Sword now in Vienna, while the simplicity of the guard agrees with the plain design of the Helmet of St Wenceslas. It is cruciform in shape, like so many x- and xi-century swords. The crystal pommel is also typical of that period, the use of rock crystal for decorative purposes being very common during the late Roman period of art. It is quite probable, therefore, that this sword did actually belong to St Wenceslas; at any rate it dates from the x or early xi century. The material covering the grip from guard to pommel is, however, obviously of later date.

The sword and scabbard are still preserved in the Ecclesiastical Treasury of St Vitus (*Plate 33, c*) where there is another ancient sword which by tradition is that of St Stephen of Hungary.

There are also in the Treasury the helmet and coat of mail of St Wenceslas which have been included in the inventories since the xiv century and although they do not belong to the regalia, they are deserving of some mention because of their great age and because of the veneration in which they have been held by the people of Bohemia as relics of their patron saint.

The helmet is, like all mediaeval helmets, beaten out of one piece of metal. It is basin-shaped with a border running from back to front and has no visor. The border, and also a nose piece, are fixed to the helmet with nails and are decorated with damascened work in silver. The border does not run right round the helmet, but leaves a gap of about 2 in. at the back. The pattern of the silver damascening somewhat resembles the lettering of initials of late Carolingian manuscripts. Here and there the silver plate shows traces of having been repaired by the welding on of small pieces of iron plate. These repairs were probably done soon after the helmet was made; they are common in damascened work of the period, the repeated application of heat necessary in order to weld the plate to the foundation metal causing the former to become perforated. The nose piece is ornamented with a curious distorted representation of a human figure which appears to be intended for the crucified Christ. The outstretched arms, the hands and the torso and loincloth are easily recognisable, but the place of the head is taken by a somewhat formless decoration. The figure is composed of the iron foundation work of the helmet raised up to the level of the covering silver plate. This decoration makes it possible that the helmet may be of earlier date than Wenceslas and may have belonged to his father, Borivoj I, who was baptised by St Methodius. In his time it may have been inexpedient, for fear of antagonising his heathen subjects, for the ruler to wear openly any sign of Christianity. It is more probable, however, that the helmet was made for Wenceslas himself. As it is doubtful whether at that date the Bohemians had sufficient skill in ironwork, it seems probable that it was acquired from some tribe or nation which had attained proficiency in the art of weapon-making. We know from an old biography that Wenceslas attached great importance to the provision of fitting arms for the equipment of his fighting men. From the marked resemblance of this helmet to early English specimens, both in shape and decoration, it is possible that it is of Anglo-Saxon workmanship.

The coat of mail is also attributed to St Wenceslas. This piece of armour is of chain mail, of a high technical finish. Both in shape and workmanship it resembles those closely fitting coats of mail worn at that time. Some of the links are made of gold; their edges can be clearly seen. It is doubtful whether this coat of mail, judging from its shape and craftsmanship, can be considered as earlier than the XII century.

The lance which Duke Vratislav captured from Rudolph, anti-King, in 1080, fell into disuse when Vratislav received the title of King in 1085–6. In the XII century Duke Sobeslav caused his chaplain to fetch the flag of St Adalbert, Bishop of Prague, which was hidden in a wall of the church, and in 1126, at the Battle of Kalm, it was affixed to a lance and used as a field ensign. In the XII century a flag of St Wenceslas is mentioned but neither lance nor flag seem to have been regarded as of much significance. In the inventory of Prague Cathedral, 1354–5, there is mentioned the *vagina aureae b. Wenczlai* and there was also mentioned the *crux parria aureae quae fuit supi vagina lancae*. There are still preserved in the Ecclesiastical Treasury of the Cathedral of St Vitus two lances, one of which, according to the catalogue, contains a *clavus domini* and the other is the top of an iron lance from the Middle Ages, which are possibly the two lances referred to above.

The Crown of St Wenceslas of Bohemia (*Plates 31 and 32*) is one of the finest examples of the great mediaeval lily crowns that has survived. It consists of four golden plates each taking the form of a fleur-de-lis, two intersecting arches which are surmounted by a cross in which is a thorn from the Crown of Thorns, and inside are two caps. Although we know from coins and from the burial crown of Rudolph of Hapsburg that earlier Bohemian crowns were decorated with fleurs-de-lis, there cannot be much doubt but that the inspiration for this crown came from France. Charles IV had been brought up at the French Court at a time when the cult of Charlemagne was very strong and when much importance was attached to relics and treasures associated with the past. In the Treasury of the Abbey of St Denis there were a number of crowns including the three great French crowns—the so-called Crown of Charlemagne used as the French

Coronation Crown; the Crown of St Louis and the *Sainte Couronne*. All these crowns were composed of four great fleurs-de-lis and the *Sainte Couronne* was closed with two intersecting arches and in the crown as a relic was a thorn from the Crown of Thorns.[1] The Crown of St Wenceslas has, therefore, features in common with the *Sainte Couronne* which can hardly have been accidental.[2]

The circlet of the crown is composed of four separate parts, each of double plates of gold, the bases of which are hinged together with pins and form a circlet. From the middle of each plate rises a large and striking fleur-de-lis. There has been some confusion as to which part was the front of the crown and which the back. The old inventories designate the lily with 4 large rubies and whose base has a large sapphire in the centre with a ruby on either side as the front or first part. If this is the front part, the one at the back has 5 rubies on the lily, while on the base is a sapphire larger than the one on the first part with 5 rubies set in either side to form a cross. In either case the centre stone of the base and the stones on the lilies are so set as to form a cross. Besides the 1387 inventory, several writers, including Hajek, Bock-Pollach, the Rzehalo Lithograph and Legis-Glueckseliga all placed the first part as belonging to the front of the crown. Dr Bock,[3] however, considers the back part should be in the front, pointing out that the three crosses formed by the precious stones are the symbol of a Christian monarch. It is difficult, however, to conclude that the crown was wrongly described in the early inventory and as the first part contains the most valuable stones, it must be regarded as the front of the crown.

The two side portions each have 8 precious stones. The left one has a large ruby with a sapphire on either side on the base and 5 sapphires set in the form of a cross on the fleur-de-lis. The right one has a large balas ruby in the centre with a large sapphire on either side in the base, while in the fleur-de-lis the centre stone is a large sapphire with 3 sapphires and a lynx sapphire set around. Each of the four lilies are topped by a fine pearl. The stones are set in heavy gold funnels and are held in position by claws. Each of the two pins that lock the hinges has a ruby set on top.

The arches are, in fact, double gold plates linked by clasps. The lower ones are affixed to the back of the lilies and are unadorned with precious stones. On top of these are narrow gold strips which are shorter and which are richly decorated with rubies, emeralds, pearls, but no sapphires. These upper strips which form the arches are evidently of different origin to the rest of the crown and the settings of the stones are quite different in character. Instead of protruding gold funnels they are set in gold frames with a beaded edge. Dr Cibulka[4] has suggested that the jewelled parts of the arches are formed from parts of a queen's crown and he considers that they may possibly have come from the crown of Queen Anna which, according to the 1354 inventory, was on the tomb of St Wenceslas, but it is not mentioned in subsequent inventories. Unfortunately the descriptions of the crown in the inventories of 1354, 1355, 1365, 1368 and 1374 are not detailed enough to tell us more than that there were jewelled intersecting bands over the cap on top of which rested the cross. These descriptions suggest that they may have been jewelled strips not unlike those on the crown found in the tomb of the Empress Constance at Palermo, or the stones may have been set on what are now the lower strips. If the former theory is correct, they

---

[1] The first two crowns are depicted somewhat summarily perhaps in the plates of Félibien's *Histoire de Saint Denys*. The *Sainte Couronne* is depicted on the head of Charles Martel in a picture, by an unknown artist, known as The Mass of St Giles.

[2] Dr Josef Cibulka, in a article in *Umění*, Vol. III, Prague 1930, rejects the suggestion that the crown was inspired from the style of the French crown but he seems to have overlooked the three Court lily crowns at St Denis.

[3] Op. cit.   [4] Op. cit.

would hardly have formed a firm enough base for the cross and this may provide the reason why some reconstruction of the crown became necessary between 1374 and 1387 as is mentioned in the 1387 inventory. Another point is that subsequent to the coronation of Charles IV and his consort Anna, the Queens of Bohemia were crowned with St Wenceslas's Crown and not with a special crown of their own. This was probably one of the reasons for it to become the custom for the queens to be crowned on a different day to their husbands, as it would have been inconvenient to use the St Wenceslas Crown twice at one ceremony. It would, therefore, have been especially fitting for the Crown of St Wenceslas to contain an element of the crown of the consort of Charles IV thus combining a king's and a queen's crown. Apart from the change in the arches the other alterations which were made between 1374 and 1387 included the removal of a string of 60 large pearls which adorned the circumference of the lower edge of the circlet, the holes by which the string was affixed are clearly visible in photographs of the crown. The emeralds which, according to earlier inventories, had decorated the four fleurs-de-lis were also removed.

The golden Latin cross which surmounts the crown has a sapphire on top and a ruby at the end of each arm. In the middle is a small sapphire framed in the form of a cross and set *à jour*. On one side is a carved relief of the Crucifixion and on the other side half figures of the Virgin Mary and St John. In the golden cross is a receptacle in which a relic of the Crown of Thorns is inserted, though not visible and on the surface of the arms of the cross is an inscription in Gothic letters which reads: *+HIC+EST+SPINIA—DE CORONA—DOMINI*. The origin of the relic is not known, but Charles IV was a great collector of relics and may have acquired it during his stay at the French Court. It is known that St Louis, who acquired the Crown of Thorns, detached a few single thorns which he gave to members of his family. The cross has become slightly bent and the screw and nut which affixes it to the arches have become loose; this has led to the cross swivelling round which has added to the confusion as to which part of the crown is the front and which is the back. It may be mentioned that looking down on the crown from above the arches also form a cross which probably had the symbolic meaning of the sign of the cross placed over the head of the Lord's anointed.

It is at first somewhat puzzling to find two caps in the crown. One is hemispherical in shape, stiff and attached to the circlet. The outside is of red damask woven with gold with a leaf pattern. This cap dates from the XVIII century. Bock[1] considered that the old cap, or *pileus*, was made of a heavy unpatterned red velvet which effectively gave the gold of the crown a more striking appearance. The other cap, *Haueblein*, was carried in the coronation procession on a silver gilt tray by the Lord Chamberlain who placed it on the King's head just before the Archbishop crowned the King. In the early inventories the cap was specifically called a 'mitre'. Before the time of Charles IV the emperors who received the mitre at their coronation were not usually depicted wearing it, but at Karlstein there are several pictorial representations of Charles IV wearing the mitre inside his crown with the horns to the front and back of his head and not over the ears, which was the manner in which it was finally incorporated into the Imperial Crown. It is possible, therefore, that he had an imperial mitre incorporated into the Bohemian Crown, but it is more probable that he had it placed there because two Dukes of Bohemia had had the mitre bestowed upon them by the Pope as a personal mark of favour. This special distinction could easily have become a tradition of the type which had a special appeal to Charles and the nationalistic-minded Bohemians. Certainly as an ordinary *pileus* or crown cap it would not have been borne in the coronation procession as a separate ornament or ceremoniously placed on the King's head.

Although Dr Franz Bock, Bock-Pollach and Count Luzansky were given an opportunity of inspecting the crown before its transfer to Vienna in 1866 it has never been scientifically

[1] Op. cit.

examined. Dr Vrba, the Court Chancellor, had intended to examine the stones mineralogically when the crown was inspected on 10th August 1911, but only sufficient time was available for the taking of photographs and to examine the stones through lenses.

The gold of the crown has never been properly assayed, the most accurate examination placing its quality at 21 carats. There is some doubt about its weight. Dr Bock estimated it at 4 lb 13¾ loths, but it is believed that the cap had been removed. The true weight with the two caps is believed to be 2,499 gr.

In the 1387 inventory the crown had 92 stones and 20 pearls. Later accounts gave numbers varying from 91 to 96 stones, but the number of pearls has remained the same at 20. The present number is 91 stones and 20 pearls. The stones may be divided according to their colour—46 are of various shades of red and have been usually called rubies, although some are undoubtedly spinels or balas rubies. There are 20 blue stones of a more or less deep colour. The largest is in the middle of the front part of the circlet. Most of them appear to be genuine sapphires, but 4 have been described as lynx or lux sapphires.[1] The green stones are all emeralds and number 25 all of which are set in the arches. All but two of the stones are rough uncut and polished. The two show traces of cutting which was possibly done in the Orient. Legis-Glueckseliga in 1836 estimated the weights of some of the stones. The large sapphire in the front he estimated at 70 carats; that in the centre of the right fleur-de-lis at 60 carats; in the centre of the front fleur-de-lis the red stone was estimated at 80 carats and the largest in the right plate at 50 carats. The pearls are of good quality and despite their great age are well preserved.

The crown is in much the same state as it was in 1387. There are a few traces of repair. At the coronation of George of Poděbrad one stone fell out, which was considered to be a bad omen. In the XVI and XVII centuries some of the stones were changed.

There is a leather case for the crown which was made in 1347, the year of the coronation of Charles IV. On the outside it is ornamented with engravings partly coloured with the colour faded in places. The pattern consists of twigs and leaves, the leaves being green on a dark background and the twigs being red. Between the leaves are shields bearing the arms of Arnost of Pardubice, Archbishop of Prague. On the other side is a shield bearing the arms of the Archbishopric of Prague. On the lid there are also shields, one bearing a black eagle on a yellow field with wings outspread and another the white Bohemian Lion.

The descriptions of the sceptre and orb in the earlier inventories are very meagre. In that of 1354 the entry is:

Item: *POMUM REGALE ET SCEPTRUM ARGENTEUM DEAURATUM*

and in that of 1387:

Item: *POMUM AUREUM CUM CRUCE ET SCEPTRUM ARGENTEUM DEAURATUM.*

Apart from the fact that between 1354 and 1355 the orb became described as being of gold instead of silver gilt, the only information we can gain is negative to the effect that they must have been simple ornaments unadorned with precious stones. In the Vienna Treasury there is still preserved a Gothic sceptre and orb attributed to the Kingdom of Bohemia. Some authorities consider they may have been the private ornaments of George of Poděbrad, but in the German National Museum at Nuremberg there is a portrait of the Emperor Sigismund by Dürer with a sceptre and orb distinctly like those in the Vienna Treasury, although differing a little in detail. It is true that the

---

1 Lynx or lux sapphires is the name usually applied to cordierite which is also known as iolite or dichroite, see G. F. Herbert Smith: *Gem Stones*.

portrait was painted about a century after Sigismund's death, but the Emperor is known to have had his private regalia and they may have been kept at Nuremberg and have been available for Dürer to sketch between 1510 and 1512. In the Vienna Treasury there is also a portrait of the Emperor Matthias, as King of Bohemia, by Hans von Aachen and the sceptre and orb he bears can be recognised as these ornaments. They were subsequently used at investitures of the Archdukes of Austria. Whether the existing Bohemian sceptre and orb were made for Rudolph II because the original ornaments in the Bohemian regalia were damaged at Maximilian's funeral, is at least questionable. It is more likely that the art-loving Rudolph considered the simple Bohemian ornaments to be unworthy and with the means at his disposal he ordered new and more elaborate ornaments to be made.

The Bohemian sceptre (*31, a*) is a masterpiece of the early Renaissance and it is from the best period of the school of Benvenuto Cellini. The name of the maker is, however, unknown and no mark giving any clue to this has been discovered.

The sceptre is 67 cm in length and is divided into five parts. In spite of great variety of ornamentation, each section of the sceptre harmonises in such a way as to give a splendid effect. The lower end is composed of seven simple, embossed rays, the lowest of which is surrounded by a finely chiselled laurel wreath. The second ray has a gilded foundation on which are set 23 well-marked pearls of the first water. On this ray rises a golden cylinder, which forms the grip or handle. On the smooth golden surface is inset an elaborate design of vine leaves and tendrils of very delicately detailed translucent enamel. The tendrils are dark green, or blackish, transparent enamel; green and blue ornaments are set among the leaves. Above this cylinder is a *pomellum*, the widest part of which is decorated with a band of 24 pearls. Above this rises a second cylinder with beautifully chased ornamentation of natural foliage work. The middle of this cylinder is wider than the rest and is adorned with roses, smelted on, the leaves of which are covered with red and white enamel on a transparent background. This cylinder terminates in a polished gold *pomellum* which serves as a socket for the next section of the sceptre. This next cylinder is also adorned with finely chased foliage, which is of the acanthus leaf type. The next two divisions narrow towards the top and are also decorated with delicately chased foliage ornaments. They are divided by a narrow band, set between two rings with a surface of white enamel, on which are set little flower ornaments of engraved gold. At the top of the shaft is a *pomellum* with a wreath of carved leaves set with 10 big pearls from which rises the unusual head-piece of the centre. This elaborate ornament consists of four S-shaped decorations with an acanthus leaf design among which are set precious stones and pearls like fruit.

The sceptre weighs 1,013 gr and the purity of the gold is 15 carats. It is richly set with pearls, there being 25 in the lower circle and 24 in the middle circle and 10 in the upper circle, while 4 more are set in the ornament at the top which also contains 4 rubies and 4 sapphires. Surmounting the sceptre is a very fine ruby which Legis-Glueckseliga estimated at 25 carats and Dr Franz Bock at 23 to 24 carats. If it is indeed a true oriental ruby, it is a very unusual stone. Most of the so-called rubies mentioned in the inventories of Royal Treasuries are really balas rubies. Large oriental rubies are very rare and those over 10 carats are more valuable than any other precious stone of the same size. This stone has scarcely been cut, is oblong in shape and its smooth surface is polished. Bock[1] suggests that it probably belonged to an old sceptre of Charles IV and was inherited by Rudolph, but this is doubtful as both the imperial and Bohemian sceptres at that time were severely simple and unadorned with precious stones.

[1] Op. cit.

a   *Bohemian orb, front view* (p. 59)   b   *Bohemian orb, back view* (p. 59)

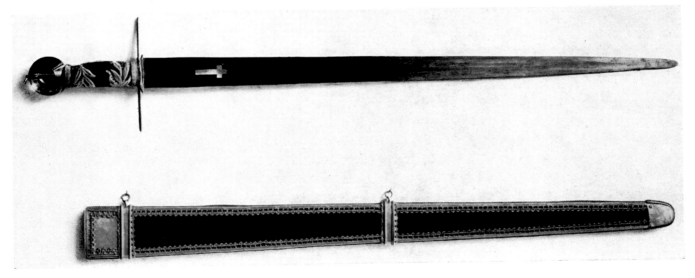

c   *Sword and scabbard of St Wenceslas. Treasury, St Vitus's Cathedral* (p. 63)

a   *The burial regalia of Rudolph of Hapsburg, 1306. Treasury, St Vitus's Cathedral*

b   *Funeral regalia, XVII Century. Treasury, St Vitus's Cathedral* (p. 73)

The orb (*33 a*, and *b*), like the sceptre, is a masterpiece of goldsmiths' art of the Renaissance period, the two parts of the globe itself and the surmounting cross are combined into one artistic whole.

It is 9·8 cm in height and the width with the band is 12·2 cm and without the band 10 cm. In addition the height of the cross and the base on top of the globe is 12·2 cm and the width of the arms is 7 cm. It is of gold, the purity of which has been assayed at 18 carats. The weight of the whole ornament is 780 g. In order to lessen the weight, the globe has been hollowed out in the centre and filled either with some resinous substance or with light wood. A broad horizontal band divides the globes into two halves. The borders of this band are embossed and the space between it is studded at regular intervals with eight precious stones, 4 rubies and 4 sapphires set in gold. Between these stones are set trefoil ornaments containing 3 pearls. Each trefoil has as its centre a rose engraved in gold and covered in enamel. From these spread three vine tendrils also in enamel. Scenes from the Old Testament are skilfully carved in high relief worked with stamp and chisel on both halves of the globe.

There is disagreement between Dr Franz Bock and Dr Chytil about the description of these scenes. Bock describes the lower half as representing the story of the creation and says that the first group shows God the Father leaning from the clouds, his robe held by an attendant angel giving his commands to Adam and Eve. According to him the second group shows the Creator summoning the animals together and delivering them over to the first man that he might name them and that they might serve him. He describes the last group as showing the Fall; Adam and Eve with the crowned serpent nearby stand before the Creator to be told the consequence of their sin.

Chytil, on the other hand, asserts that the three scenes are taken from the Book of Genesis relating the history of Adam and Eve as the parents of the human race. He says the first scene shows the Lord and Adam, the Lord with a beard and long hair, his right hand raised, walks from the left side towards the right. He is clad in a large draped mantle with a train carried by a little winged angel. In front of the Lord, Adam is depicted on his knees, his hands folded. Between the two figures to the right of the Lord, the sun displays its rays and clouds extend in the background to the left towards the Lord. Underneath, beside the angel's wing, is the setting crescent moon. On the right of the group is a bush and above this the bare boughs of the trees. He describes the second scene as the Lord leading Adam into paradise and bestowing on him power over all creation. The Lord is in a flowing garment with a cloak buckle on his breast. By his right hand he leads the naked Adam and waves with his left hand. On the left of Adam, between the trees, are deer, a fox and a bird flying in the air. On the right of the Lord is a tree with boughs; beside it a horse and other creatures. He describes the third scene as the Lord forbidding Adam and Eve to eat from the forbidden tree. Beside the Tree of Knowledge—as indication of the fall of the first people—the serpent is as if withdrawing. The serpent has a human face with a coronet. To the right are Adam and Eve on whom the Lord imposes the ban by a sign. The Lord is clad in a long loose garment. Between this group and this scene are bushy trees.

Bock's version of the upper half is that it depicts the scenes from the life of David. First we see David vanquishing Goliath. The giant lies on the ground and David is about to strike off his head. In the background are the rejoicing Israelites and the fleeing hosts of Philistines. Next comes the Prophet Samuel anointing David as king and finally Samuel and Jesse offering sacrifices in the presence of Saul. Chytil's version does not disagree with this to any important extent.

Above these scenes on the upper half of the globe runs a narrow band on which is inscribed in dark blue enamel in Latin capitals: *DOMINE IN VIRTUTE TUA LAETABITUR REX ET SUPER SALUTARE TUUM EXSULT[ABIT]*. From this springs the pedestal on which the cross stands, at the base of which are six small sphinxes. These sphinxes crouch on a base of acanthus leaves and give the appearance of supporting the pedestal of the cross. This arrangement has a symbolic meaning and represents the triumph of the faith of the Cross over the defeated pagan gods and beliefs.

The orb is surmounted by a cross as a sign of holiness and a symbol of the power and might which should guide the newly crowned king. It also served to remind him that all dominion comes from above and that he ruled his people as ambassador of Christ the Crucified. Beautiful though the whole orb is, the artist has excelled himself both in the design and the technical execution of the cross. It measures $8\frac{3}{4}$ in. in height and glows with pearls and precious stones in a setting of chiselled gold and enamel work. It is set with rubies and sapphires, cut in six facets and of oblong shape. In the centre is a ruby of the purest water; 4 sapphires surround this, while at the foot of the cross is another ruby. The upper and lateral beams of the cross are surmounted by spiral ornaments, covered in places with many coloured enamels; at the end of each of these ornaments stands a pearl. From the angles of the arms of the cross spring four foliage ornaments, each with a pierced pearl at the end. The back of the cross is similarly decorated, except that at the back of the central ruby is fixed a small gold plate with the following inscription in black enamel: *Deus celum regnat et reges terre.* The design of this orb and cross is remarkable for its beauty and unity of conception and for the relation of its component parts of each other. The proportions are the same as those of the German orb.

According to Bock both from the design and from the technical skill of the execution, it is certain that this orb was the work either of an artist trained in the Italian school of Benvenuto Cellini or of a member of the celebrated Guild of Augsburg and Nuremberg Goldsmiths. The carving of the figures in the groups is very similar to that of the medallions of the time of Rudolph II which bear the monogram *A.A.*, so that it is possible that they were executed by the master hand of Rudolph's famous Italian maker of medals, Antonio Abbondio. It cannot be stated with certainty that the settings of the precious stones and the enamel work are by the same hand as the reliefs, but it appears quite possible.

It has already been mentioned that in the inventory of 1354 one item is described as: *vasculum christallinum pro repositione crismatis sive olei sacri pro unccione regum Böemiae et reginarum quem idem rex pro coronacionibus ipsorum dedit et reservari mandavit.* In the 1387 inventory the English translation of the description is a crystal vase in a manner of a pyx in which is carried the oil for anointing the king. It seems evident that the ornament was provided by Charles IV as part of the coronation apparatus mentioned in the 1354 Inventory. After his coronation it appears to have been placed in the Ecclesiastical Treasury of St Vitus's Cathedral. It was usual in other kingdoms for the ampullae required for the anointing to come from the church treasury and not to be included among the regalia.[1] There are still in the Treasury of St Vitus's Cathedral two ampullae, one of which is in a silver gilt setting and is considered to belong to the middle of the XIV century. Bock considered that this was the one provided by Charles IV, and, although there is no evidence, it probably is so. The other one is of later date, probably in the early part of the XV century.

A ring was included in the regalia in the 1354 inventory and described as: *anulus aureus cum lapide; qui palaas discitur, per dictum regem donata et pro coronacione regum*

---

[1] In France and England there were special ampullae for traditional reasons and ampullae are found in the regalia of the three Scandinavian kingdoms after the Reformation.

Böemiae successorum suorum ad usum per ipsum deputata. In the 1387 inventory it still appears and is described as: *anulus aureus cum palasio de intersigniis regalibus . . .*, but in the course of time it became the practice for no special ring to be used and the ring set with the balas ruby disappears. In the XVI and XVII centuries the descriptions of coronations merely mention the investiture with the golden ring. At the coronation of Charles VI a valuable diamond ring was used, and for the coronation of Maria Theresa a valuable ring was brought from the Royal Treasury.

Besides the regalia several of the coronation vestments have been preserved. At the time of Charles IV these consisted of the dalmatic, mantle, alb, girdle and sandals. Charles IV's dalmatic is described in Smilo's inventory of 1387 as being of red velvet interwoven with gold threads. It was decorated to match the chasuble with beautifully woven designs on which were embroidered in pearls little oak leaves with acorns of silver gilt plate. There were also apparently made of the same material and of the same pattern, a beautiful cape especially described as that which the emperor wore at Bohemian coronations and a subtile, or sub-deacon's vestment. The inventory goes on to state that shortly after the death of Charles and evidently just prior to 1387, the subtile was cut up and various ecclesiastical vestments were made from the foundation material. It appears from the end of the statement in the inventory that the dalmatic was also cut up and that the pearls were taken out and given to the archbishop to be used for other purposes.

Another document, the *Pergament Codex* in Aix-la-Chapelle archives, describes in full detail the coronation of Maximilian II as King of Bohemia at Prague in 1562 and gives a description of the coronation robes. It states that the King was arrayed by the High Chamberlain and wore white breeches, doublet and half-boots.

Over this came a long coat of crimson satin and then a cloak of white linen, like a priest's. He was girt with a crimson silk cord over an alb of cloth of silver, after which the maniple and stole of crimson velvet set with many beautiful pearls and precious stones were put on, and lastly a rich mantle of cloth of gold, decorated with countless very large pearls and precious stones of incomparable value.

According to Bock the robes kept in the St Vitus's Treasury are of the same period as the orb and sceptre.[1]

The mantle consists of stiff cloth of gold, the warp of gold thread and the woof of red silk. The effect of this weaving is to give the cloth a red-gold sheen, which looks light or dark according as the light falls on it. It is patterned at regular intervals with a design in red silk, the shape and style of which show the cloth to be of Genoese or Milanese weaving of the last half of the XVI century. It is interesting to note the difference in shape and cut from that of earlier mantles. Instead of being of circular shape, like an ecclesiastical *pluvial* or *cappa*, it resembles a court dress, with flowing folds and a long train. It is lined with plain red *gros de Naples*, and the collar, front, and part of the train are trimmed with ermine. This valuable fur was taken off the mantle after each coronation and given to a furrier for safe-keeping. The stole and bands are of the same material as the mantle; the ends of the stole are trimmed with gold fringe.

At the earlier Bohemian coronations a *tunica talaris* of red satin with simple gold embroideries was also worn; it reached to the feet and served to replace the former alb or tunicle.

When towards the middle of the last century it became necessary, during the course of restorations, to open the tomb of Charles IV, it was found that the body was

1 Chytil, op. cit., considers the mantle to be of a later date than that assigned by Bock.

arrayed in silk and satin garments, which may very probably have formed his state apparel during his lifetime and, as such, merit notice here.

The upper garment was of a rich and costly velvet material. The foundation is of stiff satin of a dark yellow colour on which was a raised foliage design in pile velvet of a brownish colour. This design consists in the repetition at regular intervals of a little curving branch, with a leaf attached and having at the top a cluster of fruit woven in gold thread. The texture of the material, the design and the woven gold threads show that the stuff actually does date back to the time of Charles IV and that the corpse has not been re-clothed at a later period. Although the weave and pattern does not reach that technical and artistic excellence which the silk industry had attained by the end of the XIV century, it is an advance on anything known in Bohemia at that time and is very probably the work of the oriental silk weavers established by the Emperor Charles at Laurenzberge near Prague, in order to introduce the valuable and lucrative silk industry to the people of his beloved city of Prague.

The stole is of the same material as the mantle. Schramm[1] says:

As the English Coronation Order of the XIV century was used to enrich the Bohemian one, it is no surprise to find the temporal stole also in Bohemia from that century onwards. It is, therefore, included among the Bohemian crown insignia together with a purple mantle and a girdle.

There is, however, good reason to believe that the stole did not come into use in Bohemian coronations before the coronation of Ferdinand I in 1527 and more probably not until that of Maximilian in 1562 and that its source was German and not English. There is no mention of the stole in the XIV century, but in the XVI century it became the practice of those of the kings of Bohemia who were also emperors to walk in the procession from the castle to the church attired in their imperial robes and insignia and they changed into the Bohemian royal garments in St Wenceslas's Chapel. They would, therefore, have been wearing the Imperial Stole, and it would have been natural for them to include it in the Bohemian coronation vestments.

In the Treasury of St Vitus there are two relics of the Duchess Saint Ludmilla which deserve notice. She was the wife of Borivoj and they were the first rulers of Bohemia to be received into the Christian Church. She was martyred in 921 and was subsequently canonised. A reliquary bust of the martyred Duchess made of silver gilt is kept in the Treasury. According to the catalogue it dates from the second half of the XIV century and was formerly in the Convent of St George. On the head is what is described as a princess's crown (*Plate 35, a*) dating from the XVII century. It is closed with two arches and the whole is richly decorated with pearls. It bears a resemblance to the crown on the bust of St Leopold at Klosterneuburg which was made in Prague in 1616. Both the bust of St Ludmilla and the crown are deserving of closer study. It seems likely that Charles IV would have wished to perpetuate in some permanent form the memory of Bohemia's earliest martyr in the same way that he had given a bust of St Wenceslas to the Cathedral of St Vitus. The abbess of the Convent of St George had a privileged position at the coronation of Bohemian queens (*Plate 35, b*) and there is reason to believe that the bust was taken to St Vitus's Cathedral for these occasions. There is also in the Treasury an arm reliquary of the saint which dates from the XV century.

[1] Op. cit.

There is also in the Treasury of St Vitus's Cathedral a set of imperial insignia—a crown, sceptre and orb (*Plate 34, b*)—which in the inventory are described as facsimiles. They are all gilded copper and date from the early part of the XVII century and were used to place on the catafalque of members of the imperial family. They do not call for any special comment.

On 13th November 1937 a crown and eight ear-rings were discovered during the dredging of the Danube at Budejovice (Budweis); the circlet is a silver band in which there are holes at the back to join it together. On the lower edge are thirty-four holes to suspend pendants, of which nineteen are still preserved. The surface of the circlet is stamped with figures in two rows—some of these repeat the same design of a ruler enthroned but the details are indistinct. The crown is of inferior work and a primitive copy in Western style of a Byzantine woman's crown. It is probably of the XII century and Vladimir Denkstein, who wrote a paper on the crown, considers it possible that it was intended as a present.

BIBLIOGRAPHY

BOCK, DR FRANZ — *Die Kleinodien des Heiligen Römischen Reiches Deutschen Nation*, Leipzig 1864.
'Die Kroninsignien Böhmens' in *Mitteilungen der K.K. Central Commission zur Erforschung und Erhaltung der Baudenkmale*, Vol. II, Vienna 1857.

CHYTIL, DR K., PODLAHA, DR A. AND VRBA, DR K. — *Korunovačni Klenoty Království Ceského*, Prague 1912.

CIBULKA, DR JOSEF — *Český Řád Korunovační A Jeho Pŭrod*, Prague 1934.
Korunovační Klenoty in *Umění*, Vol. III, Prague 1930.

LEHNER, F. J. — *Ceska Skola Malinska*, XI Vetzu, Prague 1902.

LÜTZOW, COUNT FRANZ VON — *Bohemia, an Historical Sketch*, London 1896.

PAVEL, JAKUB — 'České Korunovační Klenoty' in *Zprávy Pamatkore Pece*, 6–8–XV–1955.

PODLAHA, DR ANTON — *Illustrierter Katalogdes Prager Domschatzes*, Prague 1930.

PREVITE-ORTON, C. W. — *The Shorter Cambridge Mediaeval History*.

SCHRAMM, P. E. — *Herrschaftszeichen und Staatssymbolik*, Stuttgart 1956.

TANNER, E. — *Hrad královsky a Hradčany, Ottovy Ceiky III*, 1885.

Actus Coronationis serenissima Frederici, Com: Pal: Rheni et Dom. Elisabethae in Regem et Reginam Bohemiae (Prague 1619).

KINGS AND CORONATIONS

1086 Vratislav granted title of King and given golden crown by the Emperor Henry IV. Crowned in Prague with his consort, Svatara

1125 Sobeslav

1158 Vratislav or Vladislas II has title of King conferred upon himself and his successors by the Emperor Frederick Barbarossa. Crowned in 1158

1198 Přemysl Ottakar. Title of King conferred upon Bohemian sovereigns at all times by the Emperor Philip. Crowned as King of Bohemia at Mainz in 1198 at the same time as Philip received the German crown

1203 Crowned a second time at Merseburg when the Emperor Otto and the Pope confirmed his hereditary title of King and guaranteed all the privileges obtained from the German monarchs

1228 Wenceslas I. Crowned on 6th February with his consort, Kunhuty, in the lifetime of his father

1253 Přemysl Ottakar II. Crowned at Prague with his wife, Kunhuty, 25th December 1261

1283 Wenceslas II. Crowned King of Bohemia 1297, King of Hungary 1283 and King of Poland 1300. Second wife, Elizabeth, crowned 26th April 1303

1305 Wenceslas III, not crowned

1306 Rudolph I, not crowned

1307 Henry of Carinthia, not crowned

1311 John. Crowned with his consort, Elizabeth, at Prague 7th February 1311. Second wife, Beatrix, crowned at Prague 18th April 1337

1346 Charles I (IVth as Emperor). Crowned with wife at Prague 2nd September 1347. His second, third and fourth wives were also crowned

1363 Wenceslas IV. Crowned at age of two at Prague, in father's lifetime, 15th June 1363. First wife, Johanna of Bavaria, crowned in 1370, his second, Sophie of Bavaria, crowned in 1400

1419 Sigismund. Crowned at Prague 20th July 1420

1438 Albert of Hapsburg. Crowned at Prague 19th June 1438

1453 Ladislas Posthumous. Crowned at Prague 28th October 1453

1458 George of Poděbrad. Crowned at Prague 17th April 1458. His wife, Joanna, crowned the following day

1469 Matthias Corvinus proclaimed King at Olmutz, 3rd May 1469, but was not crowned

1471 Ladislas II. Crowned at Prague 22nd August 1471

1509 Louis I. Crowned at Prague at age of four, 11th May 1509. His consort, Marie, crowned at Prague 9th June 1522

1526 Ferdinand I. Crowned at Prague 25th February. His consort, Maria Anna, crowned on the following day

1565 Maximilian. Crowned at Prague in father's lifetime on 20th September 1562. His consort, Marie, crowned on the following day

1575 Rudolph II. Crowned at Prague 21st September 1575

1611   Matthias. Crowned at Prague 21st May 1611. His consort, Anna, crowned 10th January 1616

1619   Frederick of the Palatinate. Crowned at Prague 4th November 1619. His consort, Elizabeth, crowned at Prague 7th November 1619

1617   Ferdinand II. Crowned 17th June 1617. His consort, Eleanora of Mantua, crowned at Prague 21st November 1627

1637   Ferdinand III. Crowned at Prague 25th November 1637 in father's lifetime. His third wife, Eleanora, crowned 11th September 1656

1646   Ferdinand IV. Crowned at Prague August 1646 in father's lifetime, whom he predeceased

1658   Leopold I. Crowned at Prague 14th September 1656 in father's lifetime

1705   Joseph I, not crowned

1723   Charles II (VIth as Emperor). Crowned at Prague 5th September 1723. His consort, Elizabeth Christina, crowned 8th September 1723

1741   Charles III (VIIth as Emperor). Crowned 19th December 1741

1743   Maria Theresa. Crowned at Prague 12th April 1743. Her husband, Francis, refused to be crowned

1780   Joseph II, not crowned

1791   Leopold II. Crowned at Prague 6th September 1791. His consort, Marie Louise, crowned 12th September 1791

1792   Francis I. Crowned at Prague 9th August 1792. His consort, Maria Theresa, crowned two days later

1836   Ferdinand V. Crowned at Prague 7th September 1836. His consort, Maria Anna Caroline, crowned at Prague 12th September 1836

1848   Francis Joseph refused to be crowned

a *Crown from reliquary bust of St Ludmilla. XVII Century. Treasury, St Vitus's Cathedral* (p. 72)

b *Coronation of Maria Anna, 1836. The Abbess of the Convent of St George, wearing the crown from the reliquary bust of St Ludmilla, assists in the act of coronation* (p. 72)

a (above, left) *Mural painting in the Church of Boyana, near Sofia, of Constantine Asen (1257–77) and his wife Irene* (p. 78)

b (above, right) *Miniature from a Book of the Gospels of Tsar Ivan Alexander (1331–71) with his family. National Archeological Museum, Sofia* (p. 78)

c *Miniature of Ivan Alexander from the* Chronicle of Manasses. *National Archeological Museum, Sofia* (p. 78)

CHAPTER FIVE

BULGARIA

Of the first Bulgarian Empire we have knowledge only from external sources. In 864 the ruler, Boris, was converted to Christianity and was baptised by the two monks, Saints Cyril and Methodius, who subsequently were regarded as the patron saints of the kingdom. Under his younger son, Symeon (893–927), who assumed the title of Tsar or Basileus of the Bulgars and Romans, the nation achieved a rank among the civilised powers of the earth.[1] But in 970 disaster overtook the Tsar Boris II, who was defeated by the Russian prince, Svatoslav. Svatoslav in his turn was defeated by the Byzantine Emperor, John Tzimisces. We have a description of the triumphal return of the Emperor into Constantinople, bringing with him the captive Bulgarian Tsar Boris. Runciman quotes from Leo Diaconus and from Cedrenus[2]:

> A long splendid procession wound from the Golden Gate down the Triumphal Way to St Sofia. After rows of warriors and captives, there came a golden chariot in which was borne the most precious of all the spoils, the Icon of the Virgin of Bulgaria. When this icon came we do not know, but the Emperor revered it exceedingly and draped it in the Imperial Mantle of the Tsars. Behind it rode the Emperor John on his white horse and after him, on foot, there came the Tsar of the Bulgarians. At the Cathedral John laid the Icon and the Crown Jewels of Bulgaria on the altar of God's Wisdom: the crown itself was a thing of marvellous richness and beauty. The court then moved to the Palace and there, before all the dignitaries of the Empire, Boris of Bulgaria abdicated his throne.

Although under his son Samuel the empire revived, in 1018 the ruling dynasty became extinct and with it the first Bulgarian Empire disappeared.

In 1186 Ivan Asen, who claimed descent from the old Shishmanovitch Dynasty, assumed the title of Tsar of the Bulgars and Greeks. He made Trnovo his capital and there, having acknowledged the spiritual supremacy of the Pope, he received from the hands of the Papal Legate the gift of a royal crown. Under Asen's younger brother, Kalojan, and Asen II the power of the Bulgarian Empire greatly increased. Asen II formed an anti-Latin alliance of Orthodox Leaders and established an Orthodox Patriarchate in Trnovo, thus severing the connection between Bulgaria and the Papacy. This Second Bulgarian Empire lasted until 1330 when, following their defeat by the Serbians under Stephen Urosh III at the Battle of Velbuzhd, the Bulgars became subject to Serbia and formed part of the short-lived Empire of Stephen Dushan until 1335 when they came under the domination of the Turks. The Bulgarian Empire finally disintegrated in 1393.

1 Edward Gibbon: *Decline and Fall of the Roman Empire.*
2 Steven Runciman: *A History of the First Bulgarian Empire.*

The only knowledge we have of the regalia of the Second Bulgarian Empire is from mosaics and frescoes depicting the Tsars. One of these shows Asen I (1186–95) wearing a heavy crown with jewelled arches, and bearing in one hand a cross and in the other a sceptre. The King is wearing a close-fitting under-robe over which is a lorium and a royal mantle lined with ermine. A mural painting in the Church of Boyana shows the Tsar Constantine Asen (1257–77) and his consort Irene in coronation robes. There are also two miniatures of Tsar Ivan Alexander (1331–71) one of which, from a Book of the Gospels, depicts the Tsar with his family; the other is from the *Chronicle of Manasses*. These contemporary pictures show that the Bulgarian rulers followed very closely the practice of the Byzantine Court. The Tsar in each is depicted wearing a camelaucium and bearing the labarum. He wears a tunic or sakhas and the Loros, a broad, jewelled and embroidered scarf, the end of which was carried over the left arm. The Empress wears a crown of the shape described as *modiolus*, which was wider at the top than at the base and was decorated with rays. She also bears a sceptre.

In 1908 the ruling Prince, Ferdinand, publicly proclaimed Bulgaria an independent kingdom. This ceremony took place at the church of the Forty Martyrs at Trnovo, the ancient capital, but there was no ceremony of coronation. In 1918 King Ferdinand abdicated and was succeeded by his son, Boris, whose title was King, or Tsar, of the Bulgars. King Boris continued to rule until his death in 1943: his son, Simeon, then became King and reigned until 1946 when the monarchy was abolished, neither King Boris nor King Simeon having been crowned.

No regalia were made for the modern kingdom but the Tsar was sometimes depicted wearing the robes and bearing the regalia of a Byzantine emperor. A heraldic crown in the Byzantine style was adopted. Photographs of Queen Eleonore, the consort of King Ferdinand, show her wearing a royal crown of Byzantine design.

BIBLIOGRAPHY

FILONE, B.   *L'ancien Art Bulgaire.*
GIBBON, EDWARD   *Decline and Fall of the Roman Empire.*
OSTROGORSKY, G.   *History of the Byzantine State*, translated by Joan Hussey, Oxford 1956.
RUNCIMAN, STEVEN   *A History of the First Bulgarian Empire*, 1930.

RULERS OF BULGARIA

FIRST BULGARIAN EMPIRE

852   Boris I Michael
889   Vladimir
893   Symeon
927   Peter
969   Boris II

BULGARIA

MACEDONIAN EMPIRE

976 Samuel
1014 Gabriel Radomir
1015 John Vladislav

SECOND BULGARIAN EMPIRE

1187 Asen I
1196 Peter
1197 Kalojan
1207 Boril
1218 Ivan II Asen
1241 Koloman
1246 Michael Asen
1257 Constantine Asen
1278 Ivaljo
1279 Ivan III Asen
1280 George I Terter
1292 Smiletz

INTERREGNUM

1300 Caka
1300 Theodore Svetoslav
1322 George II Terter
1323 Michael Sisman
1330 Ivan Stephen
1331 Ivan Alexander
1371 Ivan Sisman
(1365–96 in Vidin, Ivan Stracimir)

SOVEREIGN PRINCES

1879 Alexander of Battenberg. Abdicated 1886
1887 Ferdinand of Saxe-Coburg-Gotha

KINGDOM PROCLAIMED

1908 Ferdinand. Abdicated 1918
1918 Boris
1943 Simeon II. Abdicated 1946

CHAPTER SIX

DENMARK

There were originally three kingdoms in Denmark. The ancient legends all relate that in primitive times the chosen leader was made king and was elevated on a shield or mounted on a stone so that he might be seen by the assembled people. He was consecrated to the protection and happiness of his subjects by an inviolable oath on the sacred ring and according to the *Havamal* this 'Ring Oath' was taken even by Odin.[1] It is also recorded that at the meeting of the courts of justice the leader wore the bracelet on his arm. At a later time it became the custom to choose as successor the nearest male relative of the deceased king or at any rate a member of the royal family. In each of the three kingdoms there was a place of election and elevation; one near Lunden in Scania; one at Leyra in Zealand and the third near Viborg in Jutland.

Before the introduction of coronation into Denmark two or possibly three Danish kings had been crowned as Kings of England. In 1017 Canute the Great was elected as King of all England and was anointed and crowned by the Archbishop of Canterbury in London. He was succeeded by his son, Harold, who was elected at the Witena-gemot at Oxford, where he also received a crown. It appears, however, that Elnoth, the Archbishop, withheld his benediction and, placing the regal insignia upon the altar, refused formally to deliver them, contending that they belonged with better right to the sons of the late King Ethelred. Canute II, or Hardicanute, succeeded to the throne in 1039 but there is no record of the place or manner of his coronation.

In 1027 Canute the Great journeyed to Rome with Rudolph III, King of Burgundy, and attended the imperial coronation of Conrad II. As King of England Canute was in a position of special honour and was not obliged to render service to the Emperor. In fact, he made an agreement of alliance with Conrad and arranged a marriage between their children. As King of Denmark his position would not have been so sure for early in the Carolingian period Denmark had established contact with the neighbouring German kingdom and in 826 the Emperor Louis the Debonair received the homage of the Danish King Harold on the occasion of his baptism at Mainz. In the confusion that followed the fall of the Carolingian dynasty, the Kingdom of Denmark recovered its independence, only to lose it again as a result of the victories of Otto the Great over King Harold Blue Tooth during whose reign the conversion of Denmark to Christianity really took place (A.D. 960). There followed a period in Danish history which was chaotic and the process of incorporating Denmark finally into Christendom was slow. But King Canute IV, who was murdered in 1086, was made a saint and the kingdom

---

[1] The ring was *Baugr* which means a bracelet. This ornament was specially revered in Scandinavia.

could, therefore, claim to be honoured by a holy king before England or Germany. The German hold over the kingdom had not been of long duration and the boundary receded to the River Eider, on whose banks might be seen the inscription *Eidora Romani terminus Imperii*[1]; the Danes, however, found it expedient to be tolerably submissive to the German emperors until the death of the Emperor Frederick II, in 1250, and on several occasions the kings did homage. King Canute Lavard had become in Mecklenburg the vassal of the German King Lothair II, and when the Danish king was murdered by his cousin Magnus, Lothair attacked Denmark in 1131. On the Danes agreeing to pay tribute and to furnish hostages, peace was re-established. But in 1134, by which time Lothair had been crowned Emperor, a new cause for quarrel arose. Magnus, fearing that the Emperor might support the murdered Canute's brother went to Halberstadt where Lothair was holding a court and took his kingdom in fee with him. Lothair placed a crown on Magnus's head and on Whit Sunday, when the Emperor went to church in full regalia, Magnus rendered service as a token of vassalage by carrying the sword before him. When Magnus died he was succeeded by his rival, Eric, the brother of Canute Lavard, who took no steps to renew the feudal relationship with the Emperor. But in 1152, when King Peter named Svend ascended the throne and was faced with a rival claimant to the throne, the German King Frederick I Barbarossa took the Danish king's side. In return King Svend had to submit to feudal dependency, and in 1152, shortly after Frederick's imperial coronation, he attended the Diet of Merseburg where the Emperor placed a crown on his head and enfeoffed him with the sword of his rival. Svend did homage and rendered service by carrying the sword before the Emperor. In 1157 Svend was killed and was succeeded by Valdemar I, another son of the murdered Canute Lavard, who rendered homage to the Emperor. This was the last occasion as his son Canute VI, who succeeded to the throne in 1182, refused to do so.

The reign of Valdemar I marks the turning point in Danish history. In 1170, in order to secure succession he had his son Canute VI crowned as King,[2] and with this act of coronation the principle of primogeniture was recognised. No doubt he was actuated by the fact that coronation had been introduced into Norway in 1164 and that Denmark could not be inferior in this respect, especially as they possessed a sainted king in Canute Lavard, who was Valdemar's father. This ceremony, which included the anointing, took place on the canonisation of Canute Lavard and the Church, undoubtedly, was strongly in favour of the rite's being performed. Apart from this action, the first reference to the coronation of a Danish king is that of Valdemar II, who was crowned in 1202.[3] There is no evidence of the actual details of these ceremonies, but it is probable that the *Ordo Romanus* was followed in the main, though there may have been one or two national peculiarities. The crown and sceptre were foreign to Denmark and the other northern kingdoms as emblems of kingship. The crown was in common use as a mere ornament worn by men and women of noble birth on solemn festive occasions. That worn by women usually took the form of a wreath and was called

[1] Lord Bryce: *The Holy Roman Empire.*

[2] *Danmarks Riges Historie*, Vol. I, pp. 579–670, Copenhagen 1897–1905. See also Saxo: *Gesta Danorem*, Books 10–16, Strassburg 1886.

[3] *Tractatus Varii*, etc., *apud Elzev*, 1629, p. 86.

a *Tirstrup Crucifix, XII Century.*
National Museum, Copenhagen (p. 83)

b *Aaby Crucifix.*
National Museum, Copenhagen (p. 83)

c *Crowned figures of Christ the King and the Blessed Virgin Mary on Liisberg altar frontal.*
National Museum, Copenhagen (p. 83)

a   *Tapestry depicting King Christian III with regalia. National Museum, Copenhagen (p. 86)*

b   *Tapestry depicting King Frederick II with regalia. National Museum, Copenhagen (p. 86)*

c   *Tapestry depicting King Christian II with his crown upside down on the ground and the sceptre broken in his hand to symbolise his dethronement. National Museum, Copenhagen (p. 87)*

'Head-Gold' and even to this day there is observed the custom of the use of bridal crowns at weddings. Formerly, the bracelet had been the symbol of leadership and while the Church would not give recognition to an ornament which was so closely linked with paganism, doubtless it was felt that there was some relationship between the bracelet and the open circlet of gold placed upon the king's head. Perhaps it was in order to command respect for the crown as a royal emblem that the Church introduced the practice of placing crowns, corresponding closely with the kings' crowns, on the head of Christ on crucifixes.[1] Several of these are preserved in the National Museum at Copenhagen, characteristic examples being that from Tirstrup in Jutland (*Plate 37, a*), which dates from the middle of the XII century and has four crosses alternating with four fleurs-de-lis and one from Aaby (*Plate 37, b*). But it was some time before the crown was given precedence among the royal ornaments because in the north the sword was the symbol of law and of power and of justice and in Denmark, as in Sweden, the sword[2] took first place, not only by being carried immediately after the king in the coronation procession but by being the first ornament of the regalia to be presented to him. The king, sword in hand, proceeded to the chancel and made a valiant thrust in the direction of the four quarters of the globe in order to show that thus would he protect the people and the true religion from all enemies.[3]

On the death of Valdemar III in 1375 his daughter Margaret, who had married Haakon VI, King of Norway, became Regent. Her son Olaf was elected King of Denmark but died while still a youth and Margaret became Regent of Norway and Denmark. In 1388 she was elected 'Sovereign Lady and Ruler of Sweden'. She proclaimed her cousin the infant Eric of Pomerania, who was King of Norway, to be King of the three Kingdoms of Denmark, Norway and Sweden, and he was crowned at Kalmar in 1397. He was deposed in 1439 in favour of Christopher of Bavaria who was crowned King of Denmark in that year; and subsequently King of Norway and also King of Sweden at Upsala in 1441. On the death of Christopher in 1488 a distant cousin, Count Christian of Oldenburg, was elected King. The union of the kingdoms was never very strong or popular in Sweden and was finally broken up in 1523. The union of the Kingdoms of Norway and Denmark continued until 1814 when it was formally dissolved. The Danish kings were crowned in the other two kingdoms up to the early part of the XVI century; Christian I at Upsala in 1457, Christian II at Oslo in 1514, and John II at Stockholm in 1520.

The earliest account we have of a post-Reformation coronation is that of Frederick II in 1559.[4] Unfortunately the description is written in verse by the Poet Laureate,

[1] Crowned figures of Christ the King and the Blessed Virgin Mary were probably for the same purpose. There is a very fine example on the altar frontal from Liisberg in the National Museum, Copenhagen (*Plate 37, c*).

[2] H. C. Bering Liisberg: *The Danish State Regalia and Crown Jewels at Rosenborg.*

[3] The brandishing of the sword appears in the Roman imperial rite from the XII century onwards. It does not appear in the Roman rite for the coronation of a king until the XVI century. There is little actual evidence as to whether the part played by the sword, as described above, was a feature of the Danish coronation prior to the Reformation, but probably it was.

[4] From the occasion of the crowning of Christian IV down to the last coronation in 1840 the ceremony took place in the Chapel of the Royal Castle at Fredericksborg.

Hieronymus Hosius,[1] and no forms are given which make it difficult to make comparisons with other rites.

The King went to the church, which had been decorated with red hangings for the occasion, in procession, accompanied by the nobles carrying the regalia and proceeded to his throne set up before the altar, upon which the regalia were deposited. When he had finished his private devotions, the officiating minister delivered an admonition to him and then the *Veni Creator* was sung. After the hymn, the King and the nobles standing before the minister, who remained seated, the Lord Chancellor presented the King as lawful heir to the throne and demanded that he be crowned, and the minister replied that in response to the demand he would proceed with the coronation. He then addressed another admonition to the King on the subject of his kingly duties and the King took the oath, in which he swore to preserve the peace of the Church, to defend the realm, and to maintain justice. Another anthem praying for the prosperity of the King was now sung, after which the minister anointed Frederick between the shoulders and on both wrists, using a form which expressed the significance of the unction. After the anointing and during the singing of the *Te Deum*, the King was arrayed in his regal vestments. The minister delivered the sword, with an admonitory form containing something of the ideas of the old form of the Church, and girded it on the King. He then addressed the people, warning them of their sovereign's power and authority to punish, and the King drew the sword and brandished it towards the four corners of the compass. There followed the crowning, the minister and as many of the nobles as conveniently might setting the crown on the King's head together, after which the minister delivered the sceptre into the King's right hand, charging him to rule well, and the orb and the cross into his left, addressing him at length upon the meaning of the ornament. The singing was now resumed and the King delivered the regalia to the nobles appointed, and returned to his throne. Homage was then done and the King, according to custom, created eight knights.

Although we do not possess the forms, there is much in the order that is obviously based on the Roman rite. The presentation of the king by the Chancellor has taken the place of the presentation by the bishops; the king is anointed as in the Roman rite; the brandishing of the sword, while of native origin, is also in the Roman rite; and there is no ring. No mention is made of the Holy Communion, nor is there any reference to the queen.

The subsequent history of the Danish coronation ceremony is somewhat obscure. Two influences—political and religious—made necessary a number of alterations and omissions. The most important of such changes came about as a result of the substitution of absolutism for an elective and limited monarchy, during the reign of Frederick III. The first step was the establishment of the monarchy on a hereditary basis, and it resulted from the failure of Charles X of Sweden in his second war against Denmark, which did not succeed owing to the heroic defence of Copenhagen, under the leadership of Frederick III. The Danish aristocracy, by their cowardice, incapacity, egotism and treachery during the national crisis, had forfeited the respect of every other section of the community and the people of Copenhagen, conscious of having saved the country, took the lead in the affairs of state. The courage and resource displayed by Frederick III during the time of national danger had won him an extraordinary popularity, and in

---

[1] 'Regis Friderici Coronatio descripta carmine ab Hieronymo Hosio', in *Schiardius Redivivus sive Rerum Germanarum scriptores varii*, T. III, pp. 65 ff.

October 1660 the leading citizens of Copenhagen declared the monarchy to be hereditary in Frederick III and his posterity. Finally, in January of the following year, an act entitled *Instrument, or Pragmatic Sanction*, declared that all the prerogatives of majesty and all regalia as an absolute lord, had been made over to the King. The future constitution of *Lex Regia Perpetua* was set out in the *Kongelov*, or 'King's Law', a document of remarkable literary excellence. The supreme spiritual authority was claimed, and it expressly stated that it was not becoming for anyone to crown him because the moment the king ascended the throne the crown and sceptre belonged to him by right. The person of the king thus became, in the eyes of the ultra-royalists, not merely autocratic but sacrosanct.

The new position was made quite clear on the accession of Frederick's successor, Christian V, who was anointed on 7th June 1671. The ceremony was no longer a coronation for the King went into the church already crowned. But the service symbolised the submission of the new autocrat to the Almighty, and the officiating Bishop of Zealand delivered an oration in which he declared that the King was God's immediate creation and His vice-regent on earth, and that it was the bounden duty of all good subjects to serve and honour the Celestial Majesty as represented by the terrestrial majesty of the King. This ceremony continued to be performed until 1840, and we have a description of it on the accession of Christian VIII in that year.[1]

The King and Queen came to the church in separate processions. Three bishops met the King at the entrance to the church and conducted him to his throne, during the singing of the Introit, and then met the Queen's procession and conducted her to her throne. The Introit over, the Bishop of Sjaelland delivered a first address, after which the Bishop of Olgaard read a lesson, which was expounded by the Bishop of Sjaelland. A copy of the Statutes, together with the anointing vessel, were then deposited on the altar and the Bishop of Sjaelland delivered a further address with special reference to the Constitution. The three bishops then knelt before the altar, the Bishop of Sjaelland beginning the Lord's Prayer. The King in the meanwhile laid aside his royal ornaments, the crown, the sceptre and the orb with which he had entered the church, in preparation for the anointing. First was sung in Latin *Veni Sancte Spiritus*, and *Emitte Spiritum Sanctum Domine*, with the response *Et renovabis faciem terrae*, etc., followed by the collect of Pentecost, *Deus qui corda fidelium*. A hymn followed during which the Bishop of Sjaelland went to the altar, opened the vessel containing the oil and consecrated it with a secret prayer. The King, who had resumed his ornaments during the singing and prayers, being now summoned by the Bishop to be anointed, went to the altar with his crown on his head, his sceptre in his right hand and the orb in his left. There he again laid aside the regalia together with his right-hand glove, while the Lord Chamberlain unfastened the clothing covering his breast. Then as the King knelt before the altar, the Bishop, dipping the tips of two fingers in the oil, anointed him in the form of a cross on forehead, breast and right wrist, using a suitable form. The ornaments being resumed, General Superintendent Callisen read Psalm xxi, 2–8, and the Bishop delivered another discourse, after which a hymn was sung. The Queen was now summoned and anointed on forehead and breast, with a suitable form, and after a further hymn a last discourse was delivered by the Bishop and the Hymn of Praise was sung. The King once more laying aside the regalia, the Bishop intoned *The Lord Be With You*, with the response *And With Thy Spirit*,

1 A. Seidelin: *Allernaadigst approberet Ceremoniel ved Deres Majestaeter Kong Christian den Ottendes og Dronning Caroline Amalias Forestaaende*, Copenhagen 1840.

and sang the special collect and then gave the Blessing. After a final hymn, the King resumed his ornaments and the Royal procession left the church.

This ceremony cannot be considered as a coronation as the King came to the church already wearing the crown which he had placed on his own head and bearing the sceptre and orb which were not delivered to him by the clergy. It was rather a ceremony of anointing and was favoured by the Lutheran Church in order to meet a peculiar political situation and to retain some power for the Church, although unction was foreign to Protestant ideas.

The new constitution of 1848 limited the power of the monarchy and the logical sequence was that the ceremony should be dropped as meaningless for the hereditary nature of the monarchy still meant that the regalia and all that it symbolised passed by inheritance to the new king, while the need for expressing the Divine Right of the kingship no longer existed. Thus Christian VIII's successor, Frederick VII, on his accession, was merely proclaimed and this custom has been subsequently followed.[1]

While the monarchy was elective it was customary for the kings to provide their own crowns and other royal ornaments and to pay for them from their private exchequer. Usually when a king died his regalia were buried with him, or were broken up and the material used for a new set of ornaments. When Christian IV ascended the throne there were two crowns in the Royal Treasury in the Castle of Copenhagen which had belonged to his two predecessors, Christian III and Frederick II, but these were melted down in 1628 during the wars and the consequent financial difficulties which the kingdom was experiencing.

The only evidence available as to the nature of the early regalia is from coins and seals, sepulchral effigies of the tombs of kings in Roskilde Cathedral and the important set of tapestries of which seven are now in Kronborg Castle and eight in the National Museum at Copenhagen. The coins and seals do not tell us much as the designs of the royal ornaments are formalised. Nor can we be sure of the accuracy of those represented on the funeral monuments at Roskilde. The crown of Margaret, for instance, was renewed about the year 1600. The tapestries are, however, deserving of close study. They were ordered by Frederick II and were manufactured in Copenhagen between 1581 and 1585 by Van Mandern and other Flemish weavers from the designs of the Flemish painter Hans Kniper. They represent 111 Danish kings up to Frederick II himself and his son Christian IV. The designs of the royal ornaments depicted must have been fanciful, except perhaps in the case of the life-sized tapestries of Christian III (*Plate 38, a*) and Frederick II (*Plate 38, b*). The crowns of these two kings were still preserved in the Royal Treasury at the time when Hans Kniper made the designs. Since great attention was paid to depicting even the smallest detail, it is reasonable to suppose that the artist was given an opportunity to make accurate sketches of them. Each crown is depicted as an open circlet with eight leaf-like gables set with pearls and precious stones. Both kings also carry a sceptre and orb and are girded with a state sword. Of

---

[1] Frederick VII was the last of the Oldenburg line and the crown passed to Prince Christian, youngest son of Duke William of Schleswig-Holstein-Sonderburg-Glücksburg, the husband of Louise of Hesse, the niece of King Christian VIII. This family produced an Empress of Russia, a Queen of England, and two new dynasties—those of Norway and Greece.

a, b, c and d *Designs of crown for King Christian IV by Corvinianus Sauer. Hamburg State Library* (pp. 87–88)

a *Crown of King Christian IV, 1594. Designed by Corvinianus Sauer. Rosenborg (pp. 87 and 88)*

b *Detail from portrait of King Frederick III by Abraham Wuchters, c. 1660, showing arches added to the crown. Museum of National History, Fredericksborg (p. 89)*

d *Miniature of King Frederick III showing arches added to the crown. Rosenborg (p. 89)*

c (left) *Portrait of King Christian IV by Peter Isaacsz, c. 1612, showing arches added to crown. Museum of National History, Fredericksborg (p. 89)*

the other kings it is interesting to note that Eric of Pomerania, who was deposed, is depicted with the crown lying on top of the sceptre at his feet, while in the case of Christian II (*Plate 38, c*), who was also dethroned, the sceptre in his hand is broken in two and his crown is on the ground upside down.

The State Sword of Christian III (*Plate 41, d*) was made in Copenhagen in 1551. The King had ascended the throne in 1533 at the time of the Reformation and accepted Lutheranism in 1536.

> It is the oldest ornament in the regalia. The hilt and sheath are made of silver gilt with an elaborate chased pattern of flowers, tendrils, framework and fantastic figures of men and animals set with table diamonds characteristic of the early Renaissance. The work was done by Johann Siebe of Flanders, a skilful jeweller employed by the King and who also made clocks, watches and compasses.

The oldest crown in the regalia is a beautiful open crown made for the coronation of Christian IV (*Plate 40, a*). It was designed by Corvinianus Sauer, a noted travelling artist, who had been born at Augsburg and had learned his trade in France and in Venice. He was employed by Dirik Fÿring, a master goldsmith from North Germany, who had come to Odense before 1581 and had made ornaments in precious metals for Frederick III and his Queen and for Duke Christian, the heir designate to the throne. Christian had ascended the throne in 1588 at the age of eleven and in 1594 preparations were set in hand for his coronation to be performed in the following year, and Dirik Fÿring was commissioned to make the crown. Corvinianus Sauer has left a number of drawings of ornaments which he designed for the Danish Court and these were incorporated in a book of designs by Jacob Mores[1] which was preserved in Copenhagen until 1788 when it was taken to Hamburg where it is still in the city library.

According to Bering Liisberg[2] the King took a keen personal interest in the designs for his crown (*Plate 39, a, b, c, and d*). The first two designs, which carried a single arch and mitre similar to the Imperial Crown, were quite foreign to the established shape of Danish crowns. It has been suggested that this was taken from the Imperial Crown of Rudolph II, but this was not made until some years later (1602). The Emperors Frederick III, Charles V and Maximilian II all had personal imperial crowns with single arches and mitres inside and these would have been known to jewellers at the time. In the first design Sauer evidently had in mind that Christian was King not only of Denmark but also of Norway, as it not only took the form of an imperial crown, but carried the royal crown on top. The second design showed three crowns, two of which were closed with arches while the lowest of the three was shaped as an imperial crown with a mitre. It is thought that this may have been intended to represent the King's claim to the kingdom of Sweden as well as to the throne of Denmark and Norway. But there had already been trouble with Sweden owing to the fact that Denmark had refused to remove the three Swedish crowns from the Danish coat of arms after the dissolution of the Union in 1523. If there had, indeed, been any intention of adopting such a symbol, the Government might have found it necessary to exercise a veto on the design.

1 R. Stettiner in 'Das Kleinodienbuch des Jakob Mores' *der Hamburgischen Stadtbibliotek.*
2 H. C. Bering Liisberg: *Christian den Fjerde og Güldsmedene.*

Sauer's next three designs followed the general pattern of open crowns previously in use in Denmark, but they were discarded, perhaps because the King considered them to be too heavy. The final design, which was much lighter, was accepted.

The crown (*Plate 40, a*) is built up according to traditional form as a broad open circlet, with a series of Gothic gables and points on the upper edge which in the two older crowns had assumed the shape of the antique palmette. Though in its architecture the crown is thus mainly Gothic, yet in its decoration of luxurious tendrils, flowers and volutes, ornamented throughout in beautiful enamel, with genii and symbolic figures, also in enamel, and with an abundance of sparkling diamonds and softly luminous pearls, it bears the stamp of the Italian Renaissance.[1]

The foundation of the crown is the head-band itself, which is made of a thin plate of gold 6·5 cm in height, hammered out and slightly convex. From it springs the gables, six of which are large and six somewhat smaller with a triangular diamond in a setting ornamented with volutes and a large pear-shaped pearl with a smaller one above. The six larger gables are made up of a foliage and a tendril pattern, with a star of diamonds in the centre, winged genii on either side, and a large pear-shaped pearl on top. The six largest gables are formed in the same way, but with a symbolic figure in the centre under a canopy of diamonds and with a large pear-shaped pearl having a diamond at each point. Of the symbolic figures, two represent the pelican feeding its young with its own life-blood, a symbol of self-sacrifice; two represent maternal love, a woman with a child at her breast; and the remaining two are Justice, a female figure with a sword and scales, and Strength, a man riding a lion and carrying two columns. Below each of the largest gables the circlet itself is ornamented with two winged genii in enamel, carrying between them a large table-cut diamond with a large pearl above and below. Beneath each of the lesser gables there is a smaller stone, with pearls but without the genii, and between these, below each of the smallest points, there is a star of diamonds, all these ornaments being set in a thin band of light filigree work of gold, fastened above and below to the frame by a round bar of cast gold set with diamonds, flowers and geometrical figures of bright clear colours in enamel work. In all 54 pearls and 294 diamonds are used in the decoration of the crown. The inside also calls for attention, first for the way in which the ornaments are affixed, and secondly for its decoration. Owing to the profuseness of the rich enamel work it was not possible to solder the ornaments to the golden frame and they are affixed by screws and bolts. Unlike so many crowns, the inside of this one is also beautifully decorated, the pattern being followed at the back as well as the front, but without the use of diamonds. In the centre of each of the leaf ornaments there is a coat of arms in enamel.

This crown is particularly interesting, not only as a very fine specimen of the contemporary goldsmith's art, but as a notable example, of which so few still exist, of open royal crowns. There is a picturesque description of the first occasion on which it was used, on the King's State entry into Copenhagen after his coronation at Fredericksborg:

Never since has Copenhagen seen anything to compare with the sight of the young King riding across the 'High-bridge' towards the ancient and picturesque castle of Copenhagen on a brilliant summer day, ships gay with flags on either hand. Prominent on his horse in a Spanish dress of red and cloth-of-gold, he wore this marvel of gold, jewels and pearls upon his head. In his right hand he carried the sceptre and at his side the great Sword of State. The orb was not carried by the King himself, but borne in front of him by Sten Brahe.

[1] Bering Liisberg: *The Danish State Regalia*, op. cit.

There are several indications that at one time arches were added to the crown. In a portrait of Christian IV by Peter Isaacsz (*Plate 40, c*), a Dutch artist who painted in Copenhagen between 1607 and 1625, which is now in the Castle of Fredericksborg, the King is depicted wearing the crown with two intersecting arches. A crown of similar arches is also shown on the effigies of Frederick III, on medals dated 1624 in the National Museum at Copenhagen, and at Fredericksborg, and also in two portraits of Frederick III (*Plate 40, b*) at Fredericksborg and a miniature at Rosenborg (*Plate 40, d*). A crown with two upward sloping arches began to be used heraldically in Denmark from 1620 and the artists may have copied this, although this feature detracted from the artistic merit of the crown. On the other hand there are holes for screws for holding slots for the arches, which can be seen on the crown so that it is possible that actual arches were added on occasions. Denmark probably adopted the arched crown in imitation of Sweden where it had been introduced in 1561.

Later in the reign, however, Christian's disastrous participation in the Thirty Years War in 1625, and his costly war with Sweden a decade later, forced him to dispose of his crown, with many other articles from his Treasury. No doubt the old King felt deeply humiliated when, in order to 'save his honourable name', as he himself puts it, he had to pawn the crown with which he had been crowned in his youth. Fortunately the crown was not broken up and when Frederick III succeeded him it was redeemed and was restored for his coronation in 1648. Although not to be used again after that reign, it has been preserved, and although some of the points are bent and there are traces of damage caused through the ages, it still retains a brilliant position among the other Danish royal ornaments at Rosenborg Castle.

Christian IV had a sword made for bestowing the accolade and it is known as the Sword of Investiture. The sword is of standard type; the hilt and cross-bar having been decorated by Corvinianus Sauer, while the blade bears the name of the maker, D. E. Tomas De Aila. In 1660 at a revolutionary assembly in Copenhagen the power of the nobles was abolished and the monarchy was declared to be absolute and hereditary. Frederick III considered that this new state of affairs should be emphasised by a great outward show of splendour, and despite the impoverished state of the kingdom he decided to have made a new and permanent regalia for the hereditary kings. The King had no doubt foreseen that with the changed conditions there would be no coronation of future kings as there was no person but the king himself 'sufficient and capable of placing the crown on the king's head' as he took possession of it by inheritance and that, therefore, the old regalia were no longer appropriate.

In 1665 the jeweller Paul Kurz was commanded to make a new crown (*Plate 41, a*), and another jeweller Paul Prieur was given the order to make a new sceptre. The King also ordered an orb and a sword. Fearing the Queen Dowager might make this an occasion for plotting against him and placing her son, Prince George, on the throne, the work had to be carried out secretly and the ornaments were placed in one of the vaults of the Castle under the King's own chamber. Only the King's confidential secretary, Peder Schamacher, was in the secret, and he was entrusted with the key of the vault, and he alone knew the King's wishes as to what was to be done with the new regalia after the King's death.

The crown consists of a circlet of gold bordered by two narrow bands and is decorated with a formal raised design picked out with small diamonds, larger stones being used to emphasise the pattern of the scroll-work. In front and at the back are set large sapphires. That in front weighs 84 carats and that behind 144 carats, both being table-cut. On the centre part of the sides of the circlet are set a spinel of 107 carats and a garnet of 90 carats. On the circlet rise eight curved leaves or palmettes, a form of decoration which is to be found on earlier Danish crowns. Each of these has a large stone set in the centre, that in front being engraved with the monogram of Christian V on its under-side, while the veins of the leaves are picked out in small diamonds. From behind these ornaments spring the arches, four in number and depressed at the centre. Each is decorated with a row of small diamonds and at the point of intersection of the arches rests an orb and cross. The orb is enamelled blue and the equator and meridional bands are set with diamonds, while a floriated diamond cross rises from it. Inside is a cap of crimson velvet. There is an engraving of this crown made in 1729, now in the British Museum (*Plate 41, b*).

The crown is usually described as 'The Crown of the Absolute Monarch,' but this is but a museum description and it is, in fact, the Crown of Denmark and as such is used heraldically and on the rare occasions when a crown is needed—in modern times only at the lying-in-state of the king.

There does not seem to have been any crown or coronet provided for the Crown Prince, but such a crown is depicted painted on a panel at Rosenborg dating from about 1694–9. This was probably intended only for heraldic use. The crown corresponds in general with the king's crown with a sapphire in front. A design for a prince's crown (*Plate 41, f*) is similar but a large drop pearl takes the place of the orb and cross surmounting the crown.

According to Bering Liisberg[1] there is a romantic history attached to the sapphire set in the front of the circlet, although some authorities regard the story as fanciful. This stone is known as the 'Blue Mountain' because it is said to give the effect of a luminous blue mountain. While its exact origin is unknown, Liisberg considers that there is a probability of its being identical with the stone which was given to Christian I by the Duke of Milan in 1474. The gift was made while the King was on a pilgrimage to Rome and consisted of a necklet containing a rare and costly sapphire. A century later this stone is said to have been in the vaults of the Castle of Gottorp, as the joint property of the King of Denmark and the Duke of Holstein. Each prince possessed a different key to the vaults, so that they could be opened only when both agreed to do so. In 1597 the Duke presented Christian IV with his share of the jewel, and in the same year the King sent a trustworthy man to Gottorp with his key, asking the Duke to go with the man to remove the jewel. It appears that the necklet was duly brought to the King, but at the time necklets with large stones were no longer fashionable in high circles and the sapphire was certainly too huge to be placed in a piece of jewellery among any of the delicate ornaments which Christian prized so much, some of which have fortunately been preserved. It is possible, therefore, that the King let the jewel remain in his Treasury until the wedding of his son in 1634, for it may be that this was the stone, 'a beautiful sapphire estimated at 80,000 dalers', which came to adorn the forehead of the bridegroom's horse, just as

[1] Bering Liisberg: *The Danish State Regalia.*

another beautiful stone, which will be described later, was said to have been carried as a fly-piece on the horse's harness. The assumption is that when, after 1660, Frederick III wanted to have everything in readiness for the ceremony of the anointing of his successor, who would be the first king to be invested with the attributes appropriate to the new regime, he was glad, in view of the emptiness of his Treasury, to have this magnificent stone to set in the new crown.

The Siberian Amethyst (*Plate 42, a*) is a large stone which has been coupled by Bering Liisberg with the 'Blue Mountain' in the story given above, according to which it was used as a fly-piece on the harness of the horse that bore the son of Christian IV at his wedding in 1634. Some doubts have been cast on this story, but it is at any rate certain that Christian V ordered the jewel to be placed in a central position as a pendant from the canopy of his throne. There it has appeared at each successive coronation ceremony, and on other occasions when the throne has been used. The stone is of unusual size, and is held in a setting of gold which carries a wreath of palms with the royal monogram in the centre. It is octagonal in shape, and on the upper side is an attachment with a golden ring from which it can be suspended. The lower end is terminated by a gold filigree ornament. It must be remembered that at that time amethysts were very highly prized, being valued even with diamonds. Since then their value has declined considerably, and today neither the size nor the quality of this stone would be considered to be of outstanding note. In colour it is somewhat pale, and during the course of time its surface has suffered from scratches. Its weight is recorded as 1,305 carats. Even if its past glory has declined in the light of modern discovery, it is of interest to show the prestige that amethysts at one time enjoyed.

From an artistic point of view the royal sceptre (*Plate 41, c*) is the best piece among the regalia of the hereditary monarchy. It was made by the skilful jeweller of Frederick III, Paul Prieur, and its chief glory lies in the beautiful enamel work which is the principal feature of decoration.

> The rod is slender and elegant, being divided in the middle by a round ornament decorated with enamel and diamonds. At the base is an elaborately decorated handle, formed by two inverted golden flowers with a boss at the lowest extremity and a tapering design above, both richly encrusted with diamonds, the design at the top carrying a circle of pearls. The head of the sceptre is formed of a beautiful bluish-white lily on which rests a royal crown surmounted by an orb and cross, all of which are encrusted with diamonds.

The queens of Denmark were not invested with the sceptre, but one queen, Elizabeth, wife of Christian II, carries a sceptre on her monumental effigy. This can be explained by the fact that the Queen died in Brussels and that the effigy was designed by an artist at the Court of the Emperor Charles V who was unfamiliar with Danish customs. Margaret is also depicted sometimes with a sceptre.

The orb (*Plate 41, g*) was made at the same time as the crown and sceptre and is a golden globe with an equator and two lateral bands crossing over the top, outlined in diamonds. A simple diamond cross rises from the summit. The orb was introduced into the regalia by the Oldenburg dynasty and Christian I is the first king to be depicted carrying an orb.

The Danish regalia and crown jewels are displayed in the king's chamber in Rosenborg Castle at Copenhagen.[1] The Castle was built by Christian IV between 1613 and 1617. Early in the XIX century the State art collection was broken up and some of its valuables relating to the Royal House were removed to Rosenborg and combined with the collection of royal souvenirs already preserved there. This collection was gradually arranged and enlarged and Frederick VII in 1859 gave permission for the castle to become a museum in which were gathered portraits, miniatures, curios, objects of precious metals and stones and furniture from other castles and collections. These have been arranged into a chronological collection of the Danish kings which is the only royal collection of its kind in Europe. It is open to the public.

Frederick III decided that a new sword must be provided to replace the huge State Sword of Christian III. It is called the Coronation or Gala Sword (*Plate 41, e*), the latter description being more appropriate.

> The hilt, whose guard is formed of mussel shells, is set with diamonds, rose-cut stones and brilliants having now superseded the table-cut stones of an earlier date. The scabbard is covered with red velvet on which the arms of the component parts of the kingdom form a descending row. These coats of arms are in enamel with a small crown of brilliants over each. This sword ranks fourth amongst the ornaments of the regalia and was only used at the ceremony of the anointing of the king.

After the monarchy had become absolute and hereditary in 1660 and the coronation ceremony had become one of anointing, it was necessary to provide an ampulla for the oil as the Lutheran Church did not possess such vessels.

> The anointing vessel (*Plate 42, c*) takes the form of a beautiful little gold box, cylindrical in shape and decorated with a pattern of flowers delicately ornamented in enamel. To set off this pattern a number of small square-shaped diamonds have been set at convenient distances in symmetry. The top of the box takes the form of a hinged lid. In shape it takes the biblical form of a vial, instead of that of a horn as is found in Sweden. The enamel work shows that it was made probably by the artist who made the sceptre, Paul Prieur.

At the time of the making of the regalia, Frederick also ordered the keeper of the cabinet of curiosities, Bendix Grodtschilling (1662–5) to have a royal throne made from the tusks of the narwahl, in the style characteristic of the High Seat of a Scandinavian chief. This distinctive throne is remarkable for the material from which it is made, and is in this respect unique. The somewhat flamboyant metal decorations were in keeping with the tastes of the time and it is a notable object, even though in modern times it may not be regarded as being particularly artistic. It was from the centre of the canopy in front that the Siberian Amethyst hung. This throne is still used on occasions of state. At the same time as he ordered the throne, Frederick also commanded Ferdinand Küblich to make three colossal silver lions which were to be placed before the throne that they might 'show their fiery spirit and yet tremble before the throne', and thus give a striking illustration of the power and might of the hereditary and absolute monarch of Denmark. These celebrated lions are beautifully chased in

[1] Until a few years ago they were displayed on a pyramid, which has been replaced by a four-sided pedestal on which they are shown to better effect.

silver. It has been suggested by some authorities that this custom was borrowed from the Spanish Court, but there the lions were only two and they stood on either side of the throne. There can be little doubt that the idea originated from the description of the throne of Solomon.[1] The splendid effect of these lions can be seen in the picture of the coronation of Frederick IV. They are still used to this day at solemn ceremonies, at the Opening of Parliament and at royal funerals.

Preserved among the regalia is the beautiful coronation cup, a huge flagon or cup of welcome on a stem with a cover shaped like a flattened globe. It was made at The Hague in 1663 by H. C. Brechtel and shows the various animals which are included in the Danish Arms. The decoration of the cover consists of a circle of swans supporting on their backs a diminutive crown and sceptre. It recalls more than anything else an illustration of one of the tales of Hans Andersen. This vessel was used only at coronation banquets as the drinking cup of the king.

The queens of Denmark were crowned up to the last coronation in 1649. Thereafter they wore a crown at the anointing ceremony at which they received the unction. A crown was probably made for Queen Charlotte Amalie, consort of Christian V for her anointing in 1671, and this may have been used by Queen Louise at her anointing in 1699. A portrait of Queen Louise at Rosenborg shows the crown lying on a table near the Queen, who has her hand on it (Plate 42, e). The rims of the circlet are bordered with pearls and set with a number of large diamonds. This no doubt was the crown with which the King crowned Queen Anna Sophie Reventlow one Sunday morning shortly after the death of Queen Louise. The frame of the crown, deprived of its jewels, was preserved until the end of the XVIII century and is mentioned in the inventory of 1784.

Frederick IV's successor, Christian VI, was married to Sophie Magdalena, Princess of Brandenburg-Bayreuth. For her anointing in 1731 she had a new crown made because she could not entertain the idea of wearing a crown that had been profaned by being worn by Anna Sophie Reventlow, who was of noble but not of royal descent.[2] For the same reason she discarded the throne which had been made for the queens of Denmark, and despite its incongruous appearance when placed beside the narwahl throne of the King, she used one which had been in her audience chamber when Crown Princess and which she had decorated with silver and various emblems. The new crown was made by Fabricius and became the permanent crown of the queens.

The crown (Plate 42, b) is delicate and graceful in shape. The circlet is bordered by stones, the Queen's monogram being engraved on a diamond in the front. From the circlet rise eight leaves which, while taking the shape of the strawberry leaf that by this time had been adopted as the formal ornamentation of royal crowns in Europe, were modified to appear not unlike the ornamentation on the King's crown. The centre and the veins of these leaves are picked out with diamonds and from behind them spring the four depressed arches, bordered by small stones with a row of larger ones running down the centre. At the juncture of the arches is placed the orb, enamelled a

---

[1] 1 Kings x,19–20. 'The throne had six steps . . . and two lions stood beside the stays. And twelve lions stood there on the one side and on the other upon the six steps.'

[2] Bering Liisberg: The Danish State Regalia.

pale blue, with the usual bands and a simple cross set with small diamonds. Inside the crown is a cap of crimson velvet.[1]

Displayed among the regalia is a fourth sword which was made as the wedding sword of Frederick VII.

The Order of the Elephant which, because of its exclusiveness, takes its place in the first rank of European Orders of Chivalry, is said to have been founded by Christian I. A still earlier derivation has been assigned to it, but its real origin is surrounded by obscurity. It is also not known why the elephant was chosen as the emblem of the Order, although it is generally thought that it symbolises Danish connections with the Orient. As at present constituted it dates from 1693, and as it was not in being at the time of the coronation of Christian V, the insignia did not form part of the original regalia but was added later. Membership of the Order is limited to reigning sovereigns and their sons and to thirty knights who must be of the Protestant faith.

The insignia of the Order consist of a chain or collar and star, the chain being composed of twenty-two small elephants of massive gold, facing each other in pairs. Each elephant has a blue housing and tower on its back with a cloth on which is inscribed 'D' for Dacia, and a negro in enamel rides on the animal's neck. The elephants alternate with small crenellated castles to which they are joined by chains. From the chain, or collar, a larger gold and enamelled elephant is suspended.

The eight-pointed star is of silver with a purple medallion bearing a cross surrounded by a laurel wreath. The ribbon of the Order is light watered blue and the motto is: *Magnanime Pretium.*

Displayed on the pyramid (*Plate 43, a*) with the regalia are the Star of the Order in brilliants, worn with the coronation dress; a large star in pearls made in the time of Christian V for the coronation robe; a star of the Order with pearls and diamonds for the dress of the Order, and the chain of the Order, the large elephant suspended from which is set with diamonds.

The oldest specimen of the Order of the Elephant at Rosenborg was made for Frederick II and bears the King's portrait and monogram. Another early example was made by Corvinianus Sauer in 1617 and is combined with the Order of the Mailed Arm (founded by Christian IV in 1616) with a picture of the King. There is also preserved the insignia of the Order of the Elephant set with diamonds, rubies and sapphires and bearing the monogram of Frederick V. Another set of insignia bears the monogram of Christian VI. A small Order of the Elephant with the tower made into a whistle was used by Christian V when hunting.

The Order of Dannebrog, according to Danish tradition, is of miraculous origin, having been founded by Valdemar II in 1219 as a memorial of a victory over the Estonians, which was won by the appearance in the sky of a red banner bearing a white cross. Historically, however, the Order dates from its formal foundation in 1671 by

[1] Dr G. Boesen has published in a paper entitled *Fabritius—Arbejder i Rosenborgsamlingen* some details of the jeweller's account for making the crown. The total cost was 2,102 Rigsdaler. One brilliant cost 360 RD, twelve medium-sized stones 45 RD, 906 small diamonds and sixty-four loths of gold 576 RD.

Christian V, on the occasion of the birth of his son Frederick. The Statutes were published in 1693. The Order was originally restricted to fifty knights, and was granted as a family decoration. In 1808 Frederick VI reconstituted it as an Order of Merit, further alterations being made in 1811 and 1864. It now consists of three classes.

The insignia of the Grand Cross are a chain and star. The chain consists of cyphers *W* and *C V*, the initials of Valdemar and Christian V, alternating with small crosses of Dannebrog all connected by small chains. The star is even-pointed and of silver, bearing a large Danish cross in white enamel with red and gold borders, with the letter *W* in the centre and the inscription *Gud Og Kongen* (for God and King) on the four arms. The ribbon is white with a red edging.

Since the coronation of Frederick IV the insignia of the two Orders have been worn as part of the coronation dress and the Sovereign's Star of the Order of Dannebrog set with diamonds and the chain of the Order are displayed on the pyramid with the regalia.

The Danish Ensign is also named the Dannebrog, and has the same legendary origin as the Order. It is swallow-tailed and the white cross is not tapered out into a point but ends squarely, the inner edges of the red tails leading off from the upper and lower edges of the bar. This is one of the oldest national flags in continuous use.

The coronation robes consisted of a heavily embroidered tunic and breeches; silk stockings with gold clocks; shoes of white satin and a royal mantle of purple velvet lined and trimmed with ermine and embroidered with a profusion of royal crowns. The coronation costume and mantle of Christian V are still preserved at Rosenborg. Useful evidence as to the coronation costume and the anointing ceremony can be obtained from the following pictures at Rosenborg:

The anointing of Christian V in the Chapel of the Castle of Fredericksborg, 1671. Preliminary grisaille work for an engraving, probably by Peder Andersen.

The anointing of Frederick IV in the Chapel of the Castle of Fredericksborg 1700. Water-colour by Bendix Grodtschilling III 1706.

Frederick IV in coronation costume, attributed to B. le Coffre.

Christian VI in royal robes signed by Jens Juel 1771.

Frederick VI in coronation robes, sketched by Vilh Bendz 1830.

The coronation procession of Charles VIII across the court-yard of Fredericksborg Castle, 28th June 1840, painted by I. V. Gertner.

The anointing of Christian VIII in the Chapel of Fredericksborg Castle, painted by I. V. Gertner.

A drawing of the anointing of Queen Caroline Amalie by I. V. Gertner.

A sketch of the anointing of Christian VIII, by Major S. P. L. Schack, and a drawing by I. V. Gertner.

The baptismal vessels (*Plate 43, b*) which are displayed on the pyramid consist of a gold dish and ewer and a pair of candlesticks, but they bear no religious symbolism and Liisberg in his description says: 'Everything breathes pure heathenism.' They are believed to date from the baptism of Frederick IV and to have been procured at the same time as the silver baptismal font which is in the Knights' Hall at Rosenborg. On the bottom of the font, which is of Hamburg work, possibly by Carsten Mundt, is a relief representing the Baptism of Christ. The vessels have been used for all the baptisms of royal princes and princesses since 1671.

There are also preserved among the regalia at Rosenborg Castle those crown jewels which are at the disposal of the reigning queen. The majority have come down either from Queen Sophie Magdalena or from Princess Charlotte Amalie, the daughter of Frederick IV. As regards jewels of an earlier date, the will of Queen Sophie Magdalena mentions only the necklet of large round Scottish pearls. In her will she directed that 'all jewels particularly mentioned in my will are to go to my son, Frederick V, and must always remain in the royal house', so that her daughter should be unable to claim any of them.

In course of time most of the ornaments have been altered and the stones have been reset in accordance with the various changes of fashion. The following is a list of the ornaments comprising this collection (*Plate 43, c*):

A spray of white and yellow brilliants (*Plate 42, d*).
A necklet of brilliants with seven drop stones and a pair of brilliant ear-rings[1] (*Plate 42, f*).
A coronet of emeralds with brilliants, and a brooch, necklet and ear-rings to match.
Two bracelets with pearl and ruby clasps.
A necklet of Scottish pearls.
Two rows of rose diamonds and a corsage.
A breast ornament of brilliants and rubies with pendant pearls.
A brooch and a crescent-shaped aigrette in brilliants.
A brooch to match the Scottish pearls.
Fourteen sprays of rose diamonds for the hair.
A pearl necklet.
A string of pearls with tassels.
A pair of pendeloque ear-rings.[2]

The Scottish pearls are very large, but of bad shape and poor lustre. There are, however, three very fine and large drop-shaped pearls. As we have seen, the necklet of Scottish pearls is the only item older than Queen Sophie Magdalena's bequest, and it is possible to recognise only the necklet of brilliants with seven drop stones and the fourteen sprays of rose diamonds for the hair as the jewels of that Queen. Some of the others doubtless have been reset to include her stones, while the remainder are those bequeathed by Princess Charlotte Amalie in 1775.

There are in the collection at Rosenborg many items which give evidence of the close association between the Danish and English Courts. Among these is a jewelled casket of chased gilded silver ornamented with about 2,000 small diamonds. This was a present from Anne who became Queen of England, to Queen Sophie Amalie, the mother of her husband, Prince George. In 1794 when there was a fire at Christianborg, the casket was stolen, but the thief was caught.

The most important items of English origin are various insignia of the Order of the Garter. The oldest is the insignia with the collar given by Queen Elizabeth to Frederick II. The Garter insignia which was given to Christian IV is ornamented with pearls. Christian V was given the Garter in 1662 when, as Crown Prince, he was on a visit to England, and the Star and Garter of his insignia are set with diamonds.

---

[1] The largest pendeloque weighs 23 carats and the largest round stone 20 carats. The large stones in the ear-rings weigh 14 carats each.   [2] The pendeloques weigh 14 and $12\frac{1}{2}$ carats.

a *King's crown, 1665. Rosenborg* (p. 89)

b *Engraving of the royal crown of Denmark, 1729. British Museum* (p. 90)

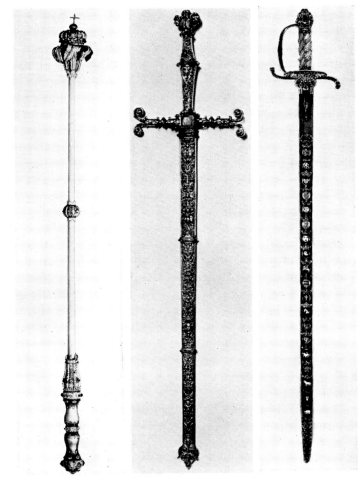

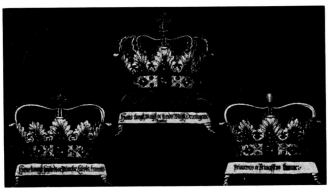

f *Panel depicting designs for the crowns of the Crown Prince and royal princes, 1694–9. Rosenborg* (p. 90)

c *Royal sceptre, 1665* (p. 91)

d *State sword of King Christian III, 1551* (p. 87) *Rosenborg*

e *Coronation sword, 1671* (p. 92)

g *Royal orb. Rosenborg* (p. 91)

a (above, left) *Siberian amethyst of 1,305 carats. Rosenborg* (p. 91)

b (above, right) *Queen's crown. Rosenborg* (p. 93)

c (left) *Box for anointing oil. XVII-Century. Rosenborg* (p. 92)

d (right) *A spray of white and yellow brilliants among the Queen's state jewellery. Rosenborg* (p. 96)

e *Portrait of Queen Louise with her crown. XVII–XVIII Century. Rosenborg* (p. 93)

f *A necklace of brilliants and a pair of brilliant ear-rings among the Queen's state jewellery. Rosenborg* (p. 96)

BIBLIOGRAPHY

BERING LIISBERG, H. C.   *The Danish State Regalia and Crown Jewels at Rosenborg.*
Christian den Fjende og Güldsmedene, Copenhagen 1929.

BOESEN, DR G.   *Fabritius—Arbejder i Rosenborgsamlingen.*

JORGENSEN, A. D.   'De danske Regalier', in *Tidskraft fur Kunstindustrie*, 1892.

MACKEPRANG, M. AND   *Kronborgtapeterne*, Copenhagen 1950.
CHRISTENSEN, S. F.

NØRLUND, P.   *Gyldne Altre*, Copenhagen 1926.

SEIDELIN, A.   *Allernaadigst approberet Ceremoniel ved Deres Majestaeter Kong Christian den Ottendes og Dronning Caroline Amalias Forestaaende höie Kronigst- og-Salvings-Act paa Frederiksborg Slot, etc.,* Copenhagen 1840.

STETTINER, R.   *Das Kleinodienbuch des Jakob Mores* in *Hamburgischen Stadtbibliotek.*

Catalogue of the Chronological Collections of Danish Kings in Rosenborg Castle. Official Guide to the Museum of National History at Fredericksborg Castle.

KINGS

941   Harold Blue Tooth. Baptised 960
991   Sweyn I. Forked-beard
1014   Canute II the Great. Also King of England and Norway
1035   Canute III. Also King of England
1042   Magnus the Good, King of Norway
1047   Sweyn II
1076   Harold the Simple
1080   Canute IV
1086   Olaf IV, the Hungry
1095   Eric I, the Good
1105   Nicholas I
1135   Eric II
1137   Eric III, the Lamb
1147   Sweyn III
      Canute V
1157   Valdemar the Great
1182   Canute VI. Crowned 1170 at age of seven years as father's co-Regent
1202   Valdemar II, the Victorious. Crowned 1201
1241   Eric IV
1250   Abel
1252   Christopher I
1259   Eric V
1286   Eric VI
1320   Christopher II

1340 Valdemar III

1375–1376 Interregnum

1376 Olaf V

1387 Margaret. Queen of Sweden, Norway and Denmark

1397 Margaret and Eric VII. Eric crowned King of the three Kingdoms at Kalmar, 17th June 1397

1412 Eric VII

1439 Christopher III, King of Sweden, Norway and Denmark. Crowned at Copenhagen 1442

1448 Christian I. King of Sweden, Norway and Denmark. Crowned at Copenhagen 25th October 1449

1481 John. Crowned in Denmark 1483

1513 Christian II. King of Denmark and Norway. Crowned 4th November 1520

1523 Frederick I. Crowned at Copenhagen 7th August 1524

1533 Christian III

1559 Frederick II. Crowned at Copenhagen 1559

1588 Christian IV. Crowned at Copenhagen 1596

1648 Frederick III. Crowned at Copenhagen 1649

1670 Christian V. Crowned at Fredericksborg 7th June 1671

1699 Frederick IV. Crowned at Fredericksborg 1699

1730 Christian VI. Crowned with Queen Sophie Magdalena at Fredericksborg 1731

1746 Frederick V. Crowned at Fredericksborg 1747

1766 Christian VII. Crowned with Queen Caroline Mathilda at Fredericksborg 1767

1808 Frederick VI. Crowned at Fredericksborg 1809

Loss of Norway 1814

1839 Christian VIII. Crowned with Queen Caroline Amalie 28th June 1840 at Fredericksborg

1848 Frederick VII. Coronation abandoned

1863 Christian IX

1906 Frederick VIII

1912 Christian X

1947 Frederick IX

a (extreme left) *Pyramid displaying regalia and the insignia of the Danish Orders. Rosenborg* (p. 94)

b (left) *Pyramid displaying regalia and gold plate* (p. 95)

c (right) *Pyramid displaying regalia and the queen's state jewellery* (p. 96)

d (extreme right) *Pyramid displaying regalia*

Coins depicting the development of the English crown

1	2		3	4
		5		
6	7		8	9
		10		
	11		12	
14	13			15
16	17		18	

1 AR penny of Athelstan, c. 930; 2 AR penny of Edgar, c. 970 (both 1 and 2 show Kings wearing an open crown with points and cataseistae); 3 AR penny of Canute, c. 1017–23 (shows King wearing a lily crown); 4 AR penny of Canute, c. 1023–9; 5 AR penny of Edward the Confessor, c. 1053–6 (both 4 and 5 show Kings wearing the Galea or helmet); 6 AR penny of Edward the Confessor, c. 1059–62; 7 AR penny of Edward the Confessor, autumn 1065?; 8 AR penny of Edward the Confessor, summer 1065? (6, 7 and 8 show the Confessor first with a lily crown and then wearing a closed crown); 9 AR penny of Harold II, 1066; 10 AR penny of William the Conqueror, c. 1066–8; 11 AR penny of William the Conqueror, c. 1068–71; 12 AR penny of William the Conqueror, c. 1071–4 (9, 10, 11 and 12 show the Kings wearing closed crowns); 13 AR penny of Henry II, c. 1180–9 (shows the introduction of the cross in front of the crown in the reign of Henry II); 14 AR groat of Edward I, 1279–80 (shows the great lily crown of Edward I which continued to be the style for a time); 15 AV guiennois of Edward III, 1360 (Anglo-Gallic series, shows the helmet crown of Edward III); 16 AR groat of Henry VII, c. 1490; 17 AR testoon of Henry VII, c. 1504–9 (shows the arched crown at the time of Henry VII); 18 AR groat of Mary, 1553–4 (shows the Queen wearing a crown with flatter arches). British Museum (pp. 102 and 105)

CHAPTER SEVEN

ENGLAND

The English coronation ceremony and regalia, despite the break caused by the Commonwealth in 1649, has a longer and more continuous history than that of any other country in Europe. Today, apart from the Papacy, it is only in England that the coronation service survives and, therefore, only the kings and queens of England are entitled to wear the royal crown. In his important book *The History of the English Coronation Ceremony*, Professor Schramm,[1] has traced the development of the coronation of the Anglo-Saxon kings. He dismisses the possibility of Celtic influence and writes:

> the factors that determined the consecration of an Anglo-Saxon king were Teutonic custom, Christianity and the idea of a kingship prevalent under the Carolingian and Saxon emperors.

He draws attention to certain outside influences including the Anglo-Saxon mission to Germany in the VIII century, the correspondence between Boniface and Alcuin and the latter's visit to the Court of Charlemagne, which must have made him acquainted with the introduction of the anointing in the Frankish monarchy in 751, and of the fact that Charles's sons were anointed by the Pope in 781. The Anglo-Saxon kings were related to several of the royal houses of Europe which provided a link between the English and Continental Courts.

But there were two other important factors which influenced the development of the coronation ceremony in England and of the style and use of royal ornaments, at any rate up to the time of the Tudors. The first was the strong desire to make it clear to people at home and abroad alike that the King of England was in no way inferior to the Emperor or to the King of France, or to any other sovereign. We will come across various examples of this influence as the story is unfolded. The second factor was a dynastic one. Whenever there was a change of dynasty the first king of the new line seemed anxious to associate himself with what had gone before in order to emphasise continuity and to strengthen his claims to the throne which were not always very sure. At the same time something new was introduced which was characteristic of the new order and gave it a dynastic mark.

BEFORE THE CONQUEST

Little is known about the regalia or the rites of the installation of the pagan kings. Some 'diadems' and crowns have been found in what are believed to be rural Roman-British shrines and have been described as priests' regalia. In March 1956 three sheet-bronze diadems were ploughed up on a site which has yielded Roman material of the

1 P. E. Schramm: *The History of the English Coronation Ceremony*, Clarendon Press, Oxford 1937.

II and IV centuries A.D. Early in 1957 two more diadems and a crown (*Plate 45, a* and *b*) were found on the same site, which is in the parish of Hockwold-cum-Wilton on the southern boundary of Norfolk. These ornaments have been acquired by the British Museum and the official description is:

> Each diadem has an adjustable head-band and a high front ornamented with applied silver plaques. Each plaque bears one or two types of *repoussé* design, either a very barbarous version of the classical vase and two birds motive, or a crudely rendered male human figure holding a crook-like object and a sphere. Such diadems are extremely rare, only one other similar find from Cavenham in Suffolk being known from Britain.

The crown is more elaborate than the diadem and consists of a head-band from which rise four strips meeting on the top of the head. At the apex is a spike or knob and at each junction of the vertical strips of the head-band is a medallion bearing a mask. The only other object of this nature and period that has been discovered was a similar crown from Leckhampton, Gloucester, which has now been lost.

Another find of recent years was the royal burial ship at Sutton Hoo in Suffolk. Among the objects which had been buried were some which are considered to be emblems of sovereignty. One is a stone like a whetstone which has tapering ends terminating in a lobed knob originally painted red and encased in a bronze framework. A human mask is cut on each of the four stone faces on either side. It is considered by some to be a sort of sceptre or staff. The other object is an iron standard over 6 ft high, surmounted by a bronze standard with spreading antlers and so fashioned on its lower end that it could be stood upright on the ground.

Although the Anglo-Saxon monarchies were hereditary, primogeniture was not practised and it was not even necessary for one of the king's sons to succeed to the throne. Nevertheless, the ancestry of the Anglo-Saxon dynasties was invariably traced back to the gods, usually to Woden. Later it was claimed that this ancestry could be traced back to Noah or even to Adam.

The first Christian consecration of an Anglo-Saxon king which is recorded is that of Ecgferth whose father, Offa, had obtained effective authority over a large part of what was to become the Kingdom of England. In 787 Offa displayed his power at a synod held at a place called Celchyth where, with the approval of the Pope, he recognised the Episcopacy. He took advantage of the occasion to assure the succession by having his son, Ecgferth, consecrated as his colleague, and the prince subsequently signed charters as *Rex Merciorum*. On this and other similar occasions the ceremony is described with the phrase 'to cyninge gehalgod'. *Gehalgian* is the word which was normally used in Anglo-Saxon texts for the consecration of bishops and churches, and its use in connection with the ceremonies of installing kings indicates that the Church had already gained a powerful influence.[1] It may be presumed that the principal part of the ceremony was the anointing. The next such ceremony recorded is that of Eardd-wulf, who was consecrated and enthroned as King of Northumbria at York on 26th May 796. The Northumbrian annals also relate that Coenwulf received the diadem of the Kingdom of Mercia in the same year—*diadema regni Merciorum suscepit*. In 802 Egbert,

[1] P. H. Blair: *Anglo-Saxon England.*

on his succession to the Kingdom of Wessex, placed the diadem of the whole kingdom upon his head—*diadema totius regni capiti imposuit*.[1] It is worth noting that Egbert had hastened home from the Court of Charlemagne where he had been for thirteen years in exile and had served as one of Charlemagne's captains. He would, therefore, have been aware of the German customs in these matters.

In 853 Egbert's son and successor, Ethelwulf, sent his youngest son Alfred, then five years old, to Rome. The *Anglo-Saxon Chronicle* relates that Alfred was consecrated by Pope Leo IV and later writers mention that the prince brought back to England the regalia which had been bestowed upon him on this occasion. It came to be accepted that he had been anointed and crowned by the Pope. Actually, Alfred was not heir to the throne at that time and a fragment of a letter from Pope Leo to Ethelwulf makes it clear that the Pope confirmed the prince and invested him with the insignia of a Roman consul. Nevertheless, the idea persisted that Alfred brought back a crown from Rome and that this had been preserved and used as the coronation crown of England. Robert of Gloucester (*c.* 1270) is the first to draw attention to what may have been a general belief at that time. He writes, referring to Alfred's visit to Rome: 'The pope Leo him blessed when he thither came and the king's crown of this land, that in this land yet is.' There is no mention of King Alfred's crown either in any coronation *ordo* or account of a coronation. In the xvii century the coronation crown was sometimes described as King Alfred's, but this was probably owing to the Reformation and the consequent wish to break away from the reliquary association of St Edward's Crown.

On his death, Ethelwulf's three elder sons reigned in quick succession, but there is no record of any ceremonies connected with their accession. In 886 Alfred was chosen king and was crowned at Winchester in 891. He was succeeded by his son, Edward the Elder, who, according to some writers, was crowned in 901 at Kingston-on-Thames and according to others at London.

The first coronation of a queen took place in 856 when Ethelwulf married Judith, daughter of Charles the Bald. After the marriage rite had been completed by the handing over of a ring, the Princess was anointed and crowned. His successor, Athelstan, is the first king we can say with certainty was crowned at Kingston-on-Thames, where the coronation stone is still preserved. This was in 924. He was succeeded by his two brothers, Edmund and Edred, who were crowned at Kingston in 940 and 946. Edwy, the eldest son of Edmund, was crowned in 955, but it is not recorded where. His brother, Edgar, although succeeding in 959, was not crowned until 973. One explanation for the delay is that in 973 Edgar reached the age of thirty years, the minimum canonical age for ordination to the priesthood.[2] Edgar had recalled St Dunstan from exile which had been spent in a monastery at Ghent. While the King supported the Archbishop in his zeal for introducing reforms into the Church, he received in return the backing of the Church in strengthening his position, especially against the magnates who were antagonistic to the King and Church alike. One of the reforms which Dunstan introduced was a Sacramentary which had been compiled from continental usage and

1 Symeon of Durham: *Historia Regum.*
2 Blair: op. cit.

which contained a coronation *ordo*.[1] Hitherto there had been no such form of ceremony. The Dunstan *ordo* was in two recensions. The first of these kept the old elements of anointing and enthronement, while the second introduced crowning in the form of a Teutonic golden helmet to be placed on the king's head by the clergy. It also added the investiture with the short sceptre and long rod. These two recensions were compiled between 960 and 973, but when a decision was taken for Edgar to be crowned in 973, the Egbert recension was revised and amplified. The revision drew freely from the Bible and from continental practice and the compilers had before them not only the *ordines* used by the West Franks and the Germans, but Hincmar's *ordo* for the coronation of Charles the Bald as King of Lotharingia in 869. The result was a coronation *ordo* introduced into England which was superior to any used on the Continent. The helmet was replaced by a crown, and the ring and sword were added to the short sceptre and the long rod. Provision was also made for the anointing and coronation of the queen in which the West Frankish practice was closely followed. Both king and Church gained by this *ordo*, the king because of the increased solemnity and dignity with which the former secular parts of the ceremony, such as the investiture with the insignia and the enthronement were now conducted by the clergy, and the Church because of the special right given to the clergy in the ceremony of the installation of a new king. It is to be noted in the description that Edgar came to the church wearing his crown, though it was taken off and placed on his head again by the Archbishop after the anointing. This emphasises the change from the old to the new practice.

We must now see what evidence there is regarding the use of crowns. The first portrait of an Anglo-Saxon king on a coin was in respect of a king of Mercia in the VII century, and it was almost slavishly copied from the common coin of Constantine the Great.[2] The kings continued to be depicted on their coins in the Constantinian tradition and this included the diadem worn by the Eastern emperors. The first king to be depicted wearing a crown instead of a diadem was Athelstan, and it occurs thereafter from time to time on occasional coins of other kings, though the diadem is usually depicted (*Plate 44*). But did the Anglo-Saxon kings actually possess diadems or crowns? We find use of expressions such as *cynehelm* or king's helmet which is referred to in place of a crown in the earliest coronation *ordines* and which it is generally accepted was used in place of a crown. We also come across words such as *couldon-bag* or circlet of fame, or *coven-beag*, circlet of the Elected One.

In 926 Athelstan received an embassy from Hugh the Great, father of Hugh Capet, who sought the hand of the King's fourth sister. The embassy brought rich presents, including:

> a diadem precious from its quantity of gold, but more so for its jewels, the splendour of which threw the sparkles of light so strongly on to the beholders that the more steadfastly any person endeavoured to gaze so much the more he was dazzled and compelled to avert his eyes.[3]

[1] P. E. Schramm: *The History of the English Coronation Ceremony*.

[2] R. H. Dolley: *Explanatory Note on the Coins, Medals, Dies and Seals*, in the catalogue of an Exhibition of Royal Portraits in the Royal Academy 1953.

[3] *William of Malmsbury's Chronicle*, which says that the crown was given to the Monastery of Malmsbury.

We also learn from Dunstan's biographer that the young King Edwy, or Edwin, absented himself from the coronation feast and Dunstan with another priest was sent to fetch him. They found the royal crown, wrought with gold, silver and precious stones, lying neglected on the floor. It is from the coronation of Edgar that the continuous history of the English coronation begins when the crown replaced the helmet as the first of the royal ornaments. In contemporary MSS. at the British Museum[1] Edgar is depicted wearing a crown with three trefoils, an ornament which was to develop in a stylised form into the fleur-de-lis.[2]

Edgar's son, Edward the Martyr, was crowned at Kingston in 975, and after his murder his brother Ethelred the Unready was crowned in 979 and his son, Edmond Ironside, in 1016. We may take it that the Dunstan *ordo* was used on these occasions.

The sceptre, which was first introduced to the coronation ceremony for Edgar, appears as an innovation on the coins of Ethelred the Unready in the year 1000. When Canute conquered England he had struck in every mint coins depicting himself wearing the English lily crown, though on later coins he returned to the diadem and added the sceptre.[3] Although there is no evidence of a sceptre being introduced among the coronation ornaments, the long sceptre and rod had been used as a secular emblem of sovereignty from an earlier date. Mention has already been made of the object found at Sutton Hoo, which is regarded as a sceptre. We have, too, an ornament known as the Alfred Jewel which is in the Ashmolean Museum, Oxford, and which Schramm[4] considers is the head of a sceptre which belonged to Alfred the Great. There is not much evidence of other royal ornaments of this period. Malmsbury mentioned that the sword with which Athelstan cut the rock at Dunbar was deposited in the Treasury. In those days there was very little real antiquarian interest but relics were assiduously collected and in this case, the story having been connected with a miracle, the sword was no doubt kept because it associated chivalry with real life. Malmsbury also gives a description of the gifts in addition to the diadem already mentioned which the embassy of Hugh the Great brought to Athelstan. These included:

the sword of Constantine the Great on which the name of its original possessor was read in golden letters; on the pommel, upon thick plates of gold might be seen fixed an iron spike, one of the four which the Jewish faction prepared for the Crucifixion of Our Lord: the spear of Charles the Great, which whenever that invincible Emperor hurled in his expeditions against the Saracens, he always came off conqueror; it was reported to be the same, which, driven into the side of Our Saviour by the hand of the centurion, opened, by the precious wound, the joys of paradise to wretched mortals; the banner of the most blessed martyr Maurice, chief of the Theban legion; with which

[1] *Cotton MSS. Vespasianus A.VIII: Claudius B.IV* and *Tiberius A.III* and *C.VI.* The first of these (*Plate 45*, c) depicts the Charter of the foundation of New Minster Abbey, Winchester, by King Edgar in A.D. 996 written in book form in gold miniature, on a purple ground, representing the King, between the Virgin and St Peter, offering the Charter to the Saviour.

[2] The trefoil emblem which became formalised into the fleur-de-lis was adopted by Constantine the Great as an imperial and royal badge. It continued in use and was borrowed by the West, where it began to be used to decorate the circlets of crowns a few years before Edgar's coronation. Thereafter English royal crowns have always borne the fleur-de-lis although at first in a primitive form.

[3] R. H. Dolley: op. cit.

[4] P. E. Schramm: *Herrschaftszeichen und Staatssymbolik*, Vol. I, p. 320.

the same king, in the Spanish war, used to break through the battalions of the enemy however fierce and wedged together, and put them to flight: . . . part of the holy and adorable cross enclosed in crystal; where the eye, piercing through the substance of the stone, might discern the colour and size of the wood; a small portion of the Crown of Thorns, enclosed in a similar manner, which, in derision of his government, the madness of the soldiers placed on Christ's sacred head.

William of Malmsbury was writing some time about 1125, but he states that he had taken the story from the writings of a poet of about the middle of the x century. That some such relics did exist is shown by the entries of two inventories of the Exeter monastery which had been reformed by Athelstan, who had made presents to it, including the Lance of Charlemagne. Down to the XIV century other historians referred to the Lance and to the Sword of Constantine, but they are only quoting William of Malmsbury and are at pains to emphasise that the King of England was in no way inferior to the Emperor who possessed the St Maurice Lance which contained a Nail of the Cross, or to the King of France whose coronation sword contained the tip of the Lance of Longinus which had pierced the side of Our Lord.

One of the puzzles of history is the extent of the influence of Byzantium in England. We have noted that the English coinage was copied from that of Constantine the Great, and that although the English crown came to be introduced on some coins, the diadem of the Eastern Empire persisted, in fact it continued to be used until the early part of the reign of Edward the Confessor. We have noted, too, the presence of a sword which was said to have belonged to Constantine and which contained a precious relic. From the time of Athelstan, the English kings used the Byzantine title *Basileus*, and some authorities have tried to explain this by suggesting direct administrative and political contact with Byzantium in the x century.[1] There were three possible routes through which Byzantine influences could come—direct contact by sea, through Italy or up the Danube. There is little evidence of such direct influence and it was more likely to have been indirect through the German Court, especially during the Ottonian period when the relationship between the two Courts was close and intimate.[2] The title *Basileus* was generally taken in England to be the equivalent of 'King', but there was a tendency for the kings to assume imperial pretensions. Drögereit[3] has shown that the seventeen charters of Athelstan, Edmund, Edwy and Edgar in which the terms *Imperator* or *Imperialis* appear are forgeries, or at least not above suspicion. Moreover, there is no trace of empire in the coinage, in the coronation ritual, in the *Anglo-Saxon Chronicle* or in the *Law Codes*. In fact, there is no positive contemporary evidence to support the use of the imperial titles by these Anglo-Saxon kings. The claims were put forward at a later date by chroniclers and others: and as one writer says: 'the constitutional significance of the imperial title within these islands did not exist'.[4] Nevertheless, we do later find the imperial title being used in a new coronation *ordo* compiled between 1066 and 1085. We find the expression *regale imperium*, while the sceptre is described

[1] R. S. Lopaz: 'Le Problème des Relations Anglo-Byzantines du 7ième au 10ième siècle', in *Byzantion 1948*.   [2] D. Talbot Rice: *The Byzantine Element in late Saxon Art*.
[3] Richard Drögereit: *Kaiseridee und Kaisertitel bei den Angelsachsen*, in *Zeitschrift der Savigny-Stiftung für Rechtsgeschichte*, 69. Germ. Abt., 1952.
[4] H. R. Loyn: *The Imperial Style of the Tenth Century Anglo-Saxon Kings in History*, N.S. Vol. XL, 1955.

as *Imperiale et Regale*. The Court poets in the Conqueror's reign emphasised that he is not just 'King' but 'King of other Kings'. Writers used the argument that the Anglo-Saxon kings ruled over the several kingdoms of England and after the Conquest the king ruled over Normandy as well as England, but one purpose at least which they had in mind was to establish the claim that the King of England was in no way inferior to the Emperor, or to the King of France. The seal of this claim was, perhaps, made when the *Laudes* was introduced into the coronation service by William the Conqueror which proclaimed the fact that there was now a third kingdom in the community of western states enjoying equal rights and status.[1] It might be thought that the Anglo-Saxons would have made capital out of the English connection with Constantine the Great. The first Christian emperor had been elected at York. We do find the legend of St Helena, his mother, very strong in England and it was claimed erroneously that she was a British princess and a coin was struck posthumously bearing her effigy, while many churches were dedicated to her.

Edward the Confessor, the son of Ethelred II, was taken to the Norman Court at Rouen by his parents in 1013 on the recognition of Sweyn as King of England. Here he remained until his recall in 1041 when he was recognised as the heir to the throne by Hardicanute who died in 1042. In 1043 Edward was crowned at Winchester and in 1045 he married Edith, daughter of Earl Godwin, father of the future Harold II and leader of the cause of national independence. Edward did not possess many kingly qualities and his upbringing at the Norman Court gave him a lasting affection for France which influenced his outlook, especially as he surrounded himself with French courtiers. This has been fully dealt with by Freeman.[2] But his piety and sanctity earned him the surname of 'Confessor' and this, together with the fact that he was the last king of Anglo-Saxon royal descent, made him a national figure.

The foundation of the great Abbey of St Peter at Westminster, which was consecrated in his absence as he lay dying, was an achievement which has linked his name especially with subsequent English history. The Abbey was not only destined to hold his shrine but to become the coronation church of the kings of England, the burial place of many, the national Pantheon and, for a time, the repository of the regalia. The coronation ornaments became especially associated with his name and many writers have sought to prove that the English coronation crown was the actual crown of the Confessor. It is, therefore, worth examining closely such evidence as exists regarding the royal ornaments which he used. The principal sources are his coinage, his seals and the Bayeux Tapestry.

On the first five types of coins, the King is depicted in the traditional style with a helmet and diadem (*Plate 44*). In 1057 a revolutionary change took place and he is depicted enthroned wearing the English lily crown, a long sceptre with a cross in his right hand and an orb with a cross in his left, held at a pronounced angle.[3]

---

[1] Schramm: *The History of the English Coronation Ceremony.*
[2] Dr E. A. Freeman: *The History of the Norman Conquest,* Vol. II.
[3] For this symbolism see Abbot Auber: *Histoire et Théorie de Symbolisme Religieux*, Paris 1884, and Sir Francis Oppenheimer: *Frankish Themes and Problems.* The slanting cross sometimes obtained an angle of eight degrees representing humility in that it is in imitation of Christ carrying the cross.

The first seal of the Confessor was in use from 1053 to 1065. It may have been made on the Continent and it bears some resemblance to that of Henry I of France. The King is enthroned wearing a crown with three trefoil points, in his right hand is a sceptre surmounted by a trefoil and in his left hand an orb. On the counter seal he has in his right hand a sceptre with a bird and in his left hand a sword. The two later seals of his reign are similar. The seal itself with the representation of the King Enthroned in Majesty and some of the royal ornaments with which he is depicted were innovations borrowed from the Continent. The sceptre with the bird appears for the first time and has remained one of the English royal ornaments down to the present day. The bird has been taken to be a dove and has been variously described as the special emblem chosen by the Confessor to represent either the Holy Ghost or the King's love of peace. If the representation of the seal is compared with those of the Emperors Conrad II (1034–9) and Henry IV (1056–1108)[1] it can be seen that there is a striking similarity which suggests that it was adapted from the Franconian or Salic emperors who had introduced the bird on their sceptres as their emblem. It is probable that in Germany the bird was a phoenix adopted from Roman imperial practice. Since we have no record of an actual orb until very much later, it seems probable that the kings were content to use it iconographically, when depicted Enthroned in Majesty.[2]

On the eighth type of coinage introduced by Edward, the King is depicted wearing an arched crown. Arched crowns had been introduced into the west by the Carolingians, whether as being derived from the helmet crown or from the Byzantine *stemma*[3] it is difficult to say. Those who support the view that Byzantine influence in such matters was very strong, especially in the Ottonian period, will claim that the Confessor's crown was a Byzantine arched *stemma* with a rigid circlet upon which rested ornaments represented by points and closed with two arches. From the sides hang the *pendiliae* or *cataseistae* which in Byzantium were reserved for the Emperor alone.

The other source of knowledge about the Confessor's regalia is the Bayeux Tapestry which dates from about 1077. Here King Edward is first depicted wearing the English open lily crown, but more massive than had previously been depicted. The King also holds a sceptre with a lily at the top. In the second representation the King

---

An example can be seen on an early Christian sarcophagus in the Church of St Francisco (formerly St Pietro Maggiori) at Ravenna; on the crosses surmounting the orbs on the Great Seals of Henry I, Stephen and Henry II; in a XIV-century drawing on parchment formerly in Bamberg Cathedral and now in the library of the Castle of Pommersfelden. The same symbolism is found in certain early churches in England and France which have the chancel askew.

[1] The Confessor's half-sister, Gunhild, married the Emperor Henry III and relations between the Courts were very intimate. The Emperor sent an embassy to attend the Confessor's coronation.

[2] This is usually claimed to be the first representation of the use of an orb in England, but Taylor in his *Glory of Regality* quotes Strutt as stating: '. . . in the first plate of 'The Royal and Ecclesiastical Antiquities' which represents King Edgar between two saints adoring Christ, one of the saints bears his sceptre and the other the globe with the cross on top; this delineation was made in the year 996.' P. E. Schramm, in his *Sphaira, Globus, Reichsapfel*, suggests that the Confessor copied the use of the orb from Canute who had borrowed it from his kinsman, the Emperor Conrad II. There is insufficient evidence to establish this definitely.

[3] The *stemma* also owed its origin to the helmet.

wears a very similar crown, but in place of the short sceptre carries a staff. The question of whether a crown of the Confessor became the coronation crown of England will be discussed later (see page 112).

We know little about Harold's coronation except that it was held on the same day as the funeral of the Confessor. It is not certain whether it was held in St Paul's Cathedral or Westminster Abbey. But in view of the shortage of time, the distance of St Paul's and the sanctity with which the newly consecrated Abbey must have been regarded, Westminster would seem to be the most probable venue. On the Bayeux Tapestry Harold is depicted Enthroned in Majesty with the English lily crown on his head, the sceptre in the right hand and the orb in the left. On his right side a noble carries the Sword of State. From this we need not assume that an actual orb existed for there is no evidence to support this.

But a new feature in the sceptre is that it carries foliations, the meaning of which has not been explained. It seems that there are three possibilities. In Germany the Emperor Henry II is shown with a lance bearing fruit which symbolises the Tree of Life[1] but there is no special reason why Harold should have adopted this, and in any case it is not fruit that is depicted on his sceptre. The second possibility is that it was taken from the Biblical reference to Aaron's Rod.[2] In 1427 when Henry VI was King we find reference to an ornament in the Treasury designated Aaron's Rod and this probably refers to an old foliated sceptre, the original symbolism of which had been forgotten. The third possibility is that it symbolises Edward the Confessor's death-bed vision of the Allegory of the Green Tree. According to his biographer, the dying King had a trance in which two monks he had known in his youth came to him. Having foretold the sorrows of England, Edward asked: 'What shall be the time or the way in which we may look to these threatenings to come to an end?' 'In that day,' they answered, 'when a green tree shall be cut away from the midst of its trunk, when it shall be carried away to the space of three furlongs from its root, when without the help of man it shall join itself of its trunk, and shall again put forth leaves and bear fruit in season. Then shall be the time when the woes of England shall come to an end.' Although Archbishop Stigand thought it was the babbling of an old man worn out by sickness, various meanings were put upon the dying King's words. The most authentic interpretation was that the tree, removed from the root for the space of three furlongs, means the crown transferred to usurpers during the reigns of Harold and the two Williams. The tree returns to root when Henry I marries Matilda, daughter of Margaret; it bears leaves at the births of her children, but on the death of the son William Athling, it dies. At the births of the Empress Matilda and of her son Henry II it brings forth new leaves.

It may be asked how such a meaning could have been shown on the Bayeux Tapestry. In the first year of the Conqueror's reign various interpretations were put to the allegory and, in fact, there appears on one of his coins a sceptre with two leaves. It is noteworthy that it disappears until the time of the young Henry, son of Henry II, on whose seal there is a long floriated staff, which feature appears again on the seals of Richard I to Henry III and disappears until the Rod of Aaron is found in the reign of Henry VI.

1 Revelation xxii,2.   2 Numbers xvii.

After the defeat and death of Harold at the Battle of Hastings on 14th October 1066 William occupied London and was crowned in Westminster Abbey on Christmas Day. Perhaps because he attached great importance to coronation and because he feared that the English regalia would not fall into his hands, he brought with him his own royal ornaments which he had had specially made. We have a description of the crown from Bishop Wido (Guy) of Amiens[1] which reads as follows:

> In quas promeritam disponit ferre coronam
>> Et ducis abjecto nomine rex fieri.
> Auro vel gemmis jubet ut sibi nobile stemma
>> Illud quo deceat fiat ab artifice.
> Misit Arabs aurum, gemmas a flumine Nilus,
>> Graecia prudentem dirigit arte fabrum,
> Qui Salomoniacum, vix deterior Salomone,
>> Mirificum fecit et diadema decens.
> Principio frontis medium carbunculus ornat;
>> Posthinc jacinctus lucifer insequitur;
> Et tunc aurifico resplendet in orbe topazon;
>> Saphirus quartum ditat honore gradum;
> Sardonicus quintus regales obsidet aures,
>> Cui calcedonius ordine sextus adit;
> Septimus est jaspis, procul a quo pellitur hostis;
>> Sardius octavus ignivomus rutilat;
> Figitur in nona cella lux chrysolithana;
>> Tuque, berylle, locum clarificas decimum;
> Undecimum viridis numerum smaragdus adimplet;
>> Huic quoque chrysoprasus fert duodenus opem;
> Verticis in summo stat margarita suprema,
>> Quae sibi subposito luce replet lapides;
> In cujus dextra laevaquae parte locata
>> Est amethisti lux, cui color est geminus.
> Æthereus veluti propulsis nubibus axis
>> Insitus ignitis syderibus rutilat,
> Aurea lucifluis distincta corona lapillis
>> Undique sic renitet lumine clarifico.
> Sceptrum cum virga componit post diadema,
>> Commoda quae pariter significant patriae;
> Nam sceptro tumidae regni moderantur habenae,
>> Dispersos virga colligit ac revocat.
> Tempore disposito quo rex sacrandus habetur,
>> Terrae magnates et populosa manus.

Insufficient attention has been paid to this by writers on the English regalia. There are several things to be learnt from it. First, the crown is described as a *stemma* and has an arch, or arches, thus William's crown is equal in status to that of the Emperor. Moreover, it was made by a Greek jeweller. But more important perhaps is the special

[1] 'De Bello Hastingense Carmen', in *Mon: Hist: Britannica*, ed. H. Petrie, London 1848.

significance in the choice of precious and semi-precious stones which are meticulously listed. The use of these particular stones, twelve in number, is based on allegorical meanings and was evidently borrowed from the imperial crown,[1] now in Vienna, which is now considered to have been made for the Emperor Otto I.[2] The allegorical meaning of this figure twelve and of the stones themselves were taken from the Bible and refer to the jewels on the breast-plate of the High Priest[3] and the figurative foundation stones of the Heavenly City.[4] The use of such stones in the English coronation crown has been passed down almost accidentally, it would seem, to the present day and more will be said about them later.[5] Bishop Wido further relates that besides the crown, William also brought a sceptre and a verge to England.

On his first seals the Conqueror is shown wearing the English lily crown with three points and he holds a sword erect in his right hand and in his left an orb and cross *pattée fitchée*. In 1068 William's Consort, Matilda, came to England and on 11th May was anointed and crowned at Winchester.

THE NORMANS

The Norman kings made a practice of wearing their crowns on solemn occasions and William made it a rule that there should be three crown wearings a year—on Christmas Day at Gloucester; on Easter Day at Winchester, and on Whitsunday at Westminster. On each of these occasions the Witenagemot, or State Assembly, met and the King attended and had the crown placed on his head by the Archbishop or a prelate appointed by him. In 1070 at the Easter feast at Winchester this office was performed by the Papal Legate, which was taken to be a sort of confirmation by the Pope of the King's consecration.

According to William of Malmsbury, the Confessor wore his crown on Easter Day 1065 and again on Christmas Day of that year. This custom was in use in Germany and France and may have been introduced to England at the end of the Confessor's reign but it was William who made it a hard and fast rule which was copied on the Continent. This rule lasted until the reign of Edward I, although in Stephen's reign the civil war led to a break in practice. Henry II wore his crown in 1157 and 1158 and his Consort, Queen Eleanor of Aquitaine, although not crowned in England, wore her crown on the same occasions. This would have been considered lawful as she had already been crowned in 1137 at Bordeaux as Queen Consort of Louis VII of France. It was at the crown wearing of 1158 which took place at Worcester that Henry II took off his crown and placed it on the altar and said he would not wear it again. This

1 H. Deckerhauf: 'Herrschaftszeichen und Staatssymbolik', Vol. I, Chap. 25 in *Schriften der Monumenta Germaniae Historica*, 13/1.

2 Otto I, 936–73, whose first wife was Edgitha, daughter of Edward the Elder and sister of Athelstan.

3 Exodus xxviii,17–20. See also the covering of the King of Tyre, though only nine stones are mentioned in Ezekiel xxviii,13, but twelve are given in the Septuagint.

4 Revelation xxi,19,20.

5 See p. 137 referring to Sir J. Fernes's *Glory of Generosity* 1556, and p. 167 to the present arrangement of stones in St Edward's Crown.

has been ascribed by the chroniclers as an example of the King's humility, but as this was not a quality he possessed, later historians have looked for other reasons. Spending a great deal of time in his overseas possessions, it was impossible for him to continue regular crown-wearings, and he was no doubt aware that in France, too, they were falling into disuse. The custom was finally dropped by Edward I, who had an aversion to wearing his crown in public. Nevertheless, the practice of the sovereign wearing the crown when meeting Parliament has survived until the present day.

William the Conqueror died at Rouen on 9th September 1087 and was buried at Caen, where his son, William Rufus, raised a very rich shrine to receive the coffin. This tomb was destroyed by the Huguenots in 1562 and the Conqueror's remains were scattered and lost with the exception of a single thigh bone which was placed in the restored tomb in 1642. There is no evidence that the King was buried with any regalia or ornaments. The dying King sent his son, William Rufus, to England where he was accepted as King and crowned at Westminster by the Primate Lanfranc on 26th September 1087. William used his father's seal until about 1096 when a matrix was executed for him. He wears the English lily crown, but with five points surmounted by trefoils and with the *cataseistae*. In his right hand is held a sword erect and in his left an orb *pattée pommettée*. On his coins Rufus wore the arched *stemma* of William the Conqueror. On William's death on 2nd August 1100 he was succeeded by his brother Henry I. His succession was popular as he had assimilated English ways and outlook. He was elected at Winchester but hurried to London and was crowned at Westminster two days later on 5th August. He greatly strengthened his position in the eyes of his subjects by his almost inspired marriages with Edith, the daughter of King Malcolm III of Scotland, and Margaret, the sister of Edgar Athling. The Queen was crowned by Archbishop Anselm, who had been absent when Henry succeeded to the throne, and to please the Normans she changed her name to Matilda. Henry had several seals. In his first he is shown with the same regalia as William II. We learn that the *cataseistae* were put to practical use as straps fastened under the chin to keep the crown firmly on the head. Gervase of Canterbury relates a remarkable anecdote of Archbishop Ralf, successor of Anselm, snatching the crown from the King's head, because he had disregarded the Archbishop's right to place the crown on his head, and breaking the *ansula* or clasp. Another version states that when requested by the Archbishop to remove his crown, the King undid the knot under his chin, saying it did not sway on his head. This incident occurred at Windsor on the occasion of the King's second marriage. It had been the custom in England for the cheek-piece of the helmet to be tied under the chin in this way. Apparently the proper significance of the *cataseistae* was not understood.

In the second seal the King carries in his left hand an orb with a small cross surmounted by a bird, a feature which is repeated in the subsequent reign. The only similar representation is on the cover of the Book of Gospels of the Ratisbon School now in Cracow which shows the Emperor Henry IV between his sons, Henry V and Conrad, all of whom carry in their right hand an orb surmounted by a bird. Although the bird was the emblem of the Salic emperors, it is difficult to say whether this use of it was borrowed by the English king from the German court, or vice versa: the latter

a (above, left) *Diadem found at Hockwold - cum - Wilton. British Museum* (p. 100)

b (above, right) *Crown found at Hockwold - cum - Wilton. British Museum* (p. 100)

c *Miniature of King Edgar in the* New Minster Charter. *British Museum* (p. 103)

a   *Scene depicting the coronation of Harold from a XII-Century MS.*
Cambridge University (p. 112)

b (right)   *Gravestone of the Emperor Henry V. The crown in both of these*
illustrations is possibly intended to represent the imperial crown of the Emperor
Henry V brought to England by his widow, Matilda. The crown has a cross
inset above the brow. Historical Museum, Speyer (p. 112)

c   *Henry V enthroned. The work dates from the*
reign of Henry VI and is the earliest representation
of the arched imperial state crown introduced by
Henry V. Westminster Abbey (p. 127)

d   *Edward IV, his consort, Elizabeth Woodville, and*
the future Edward V receiving a book from Caxton,
taken from the MS. Dictes and Sayings of Philosophers. *Lambeth Palace Library. The King and*
Queen wear arched crowns and the King carries
an orb (pp. 129 and 131)

seems to be more probable if the dating of the work as belonging to the reign of Henry V is correct as that Emperor did not ascend the throne until 1106, whereas Henry's first seal dates from 1100. On another seal Henry is depicted wearing a helmet encircled with a crown. On the coins of the later part of the reign there is a change in the crown, and the King is depicted wearing a large crown, with fleurs-de-lis, closed with arches. This is repeated on the first coins of the reign of Stephen.

Henry died on 1st December 1135 and was buried at Reading. After his son was drowned in the disaster of the *White Ship* there was no direct heir to the throne. Although the claim of Matilda, the widow of the Emperor Henry V and the King's daughter, was recognised by some, Henry I's nephew, Stephen, was chosen King and was crowned at Westminster on 22nd December 1135. Matilda had come to England during Henry I's reign, bringing with her two crowns which had belonged to her husband the Emperor which she lent to her father. She married as her second husband Geoffrey Plantagenet, Count of Anjou, and she returned to England on 30th September 1139. In 1141 she was received at Winchester by her supporters and a religious service was held, but she was neither anointed nor crowned. There followed a period of unrest and civil war which lasted almost until Stephen died on 25th October 1154. During this time Stephen's crown fell into the hands of Matilda at Winchester. Stephen had two seals and the regalia shown is similar to that on the later seals of Henry I, but on his coins the crown is the arched lily crown used by Henry I, though later the arches disappeared. Which crown could this be? It was not the Conqueror's *stemma*. It could possibly have been the old English lily crown with arches added, but this is hardly likely. The imperial crown brought to England by Matilda did not have arches but had a new feature, a cross which was fixed prominently over the brow and this is not depicted on the coins. It seems possible that it may have been the second and smaller crown brought over by Matilda which, if it did not have arches, could have had them added.

THE PLANTAGENETS

On the death of Stephen on 25th October 1154 the Norman dynasty came to an end and Henry II, son of the Empress Matilda and Geoffrey, Count of Anjou, ascended the throne as the first king of the Plantagenet dynasty and was crowned on 20th December, at Westminster.

On the death of the Emperor Henry V, the Empress Matilda had handed over the imperial regalia to the Archbishop of Cologne, but she kept those ornaments which she considered to be her husband's own property. These included two, or possibly three crowns: a relic of the Apostle St James and some imperial vestments which she deposited at the Abbey of Bec Helouin near Rouen.[1] Two crowns and the relic, however, were brought to England and the latter was given to the Abbey of Reading. According to Deér,[2] and as has been mentioned, Matilda lent the crowns to her father, Henry I. There was another crown which was possibly that described by Abbot Suger of St Denis which decorated a vessel *cum quibusdam floribus coronae imperatricis*.

---

[1] Etienne of Rouen: *Draco Normanicus.*   [2] Josef Deér: *Der Kaiserornat Frederichs II.*

The first crown is described in the inventory as:

> the largest crown massive with gold and precious stones with which King Henry, son of the Empress, appeared after he had been crowned. It is of such weight that it is supported on both sides on two silver rods whenever the Emperor or King is crowned with it. When it is replaced in the Treasury the whole crown is divided into segments. When, however, it is joined together on the wearer's forehead there is a very large and valuable stone with a cross of solid gold mounted above it.

There are certain special features in this crown which were new to England. It was very massive and heavy, necessitating it being supported when worn either by two noblemen or by two rods. It could be taken to pieces, and there were seven pieces in the shape of lilies and a cross which was set above the brow below which was a great stone considered worthy of special mention. It does not seem to have had an arch, although at that time crowns were sometimes provided with slots into which arches could be fitted and there is no mention of *cataseistae*.

This crown was used by Henry II at his coronation on 19th December 1154 and became for a time the dynastic crown of the Plantagenets. We have no reliable picture of the crown. It is depicted summarily on the coins of Henry II where it can be recognised by its cross. It is, however, worth drawing attention to two different crowns which have a common feature and may purport to depict this crown. The first is on a stone dug up at Speyer and now in the Historical Museum there (*Plate 46, b*). Schramm[1] has suggested that the relief on the stone might represent Henry V or Frederick I, although in a later work he ascribes it to Frederick I. The Emperor is shown wearing a crown which consists of a rigid circlet set with large jewels with a cross placed, possibly inset, immediately above the brow. The second is a XIII-century picture of the 'Coronation of Harold' (*Plate 46, a*).[2] Although the picture is somewhat fanciful, there is on the middle of the front ornament of the crown a cross which has the same distinctive shape as that on the Speyer crown. The King is holding on to the crown with both hands. This might be a reference to the legend that Harold had crowned himself, or perhaps he was merely adjusting the crown on his head after he had been crowned. A third possibility, however, can be advanced that the crown was so heavy that he was holding it up from his head. There are several references in contemporary writers of the necessity of supporting this heavy crown. In one of the *Cotton MSS.* in the British Museum it is mentioned that one of the duties of the Earl Marshal of England was to support the crown and the MS. says: 'When the crown is put on the head the Earl should put his hand on the flower in front to hold up the crown because he is Marshal in peace and war.'

Roger de Hovenden, in his account of the coronation of Richard I, mentions that the coronation crown was so heavy that it was supported over the King's head by two earls. Because of its weight, before leaving the church, the King changed it for a lighter one, a custom which has been followed ever since. The second crown, which Matilda brought to England, may have been the lighter crown to be exchanged for the heavy one after the crowning, or after the central part of a crown-wearing ceremony was over.

[1] P. E. Schramm: *Die Deutschen Kaiser und Könige in Bildern, 751–1152.*

[2] Cambridge University Library MS. Ee III 59 entitled *La Estoire de Saint Aedward le Roi Translatie du Latin.*

a   *Apotheosis of St Edmund from a MS. probably dating from the XIII Century. Formerly in the Holford Collection, now the property of the Pierpont Morgan Library, New York, U.S.A.* (p. 136)

b   *Effigy of Henry III (obiit 1272) on his tomb in Westminster Abbey. It is the work of William Torel, goldsmith of London, in the year 1291–2. The King is wearing an open lily crown* (pp. 116 and 350)

c   *Coronation of Henry V from his Chantry Chapel in Westminster Abbey. The King is wearing a low crown with arches and alternating crosses and fleurs-de-lis. Although it is meant to represent St Edward's Crown the latter form of ornamentation was not used on English crowns until the reign of Henry VI from which this work dates* (p. 136)

d   *Contemporary portrait of Richard II. Westminster Abbey* (p. 123)

Drawings of pieces of jewellery lost at the Battle of Granson by Charles the Bold, Duke of Burgundy, in 1476
now in the Historical Museum, Basle

a   *The Order of the Garter given to Charles the Bold by Edward IV on the occasion of the marriage of his sister*
Margaret of York, 1475 (p. 128)

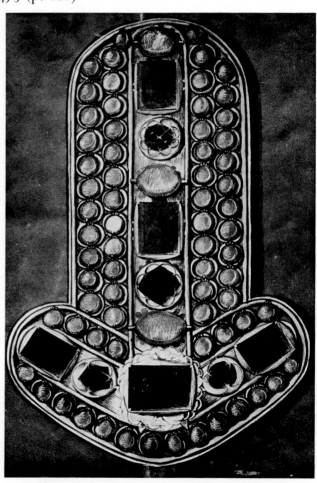

b   (above) '*The Three*
Brethren', *subsequently*
purchased by Henry VIII
(p. 146)

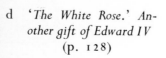

d   '*The White Rose.*' *An-*
other gift of Edward IV
(p. 128)

c   '*The Feather*'. *Probably also a gift of Edward IV*
(p. 128)

When Henry II's eldest son died, he secured the succession of his next son, the young Henry, by making him co-Regent and by having him anointed and crowned in 1170. The young Henry died, however, in 1183, and was buried in his coronation robes. In 1185 Pope Urban III sent a legate to Henry II with a golden crown decorated with peacock's feathers with which to crown John, the King's youngest son, as King of Ireland, but nothing came of this and the crown is not heard of again.

Henry II died on 6th July 1189 and was succeeded by his son Richard I, Cœur de Lion, who was crowned on 3rd September of that year. Cœur de Lion was the least English of the Kings of England and spent less than a year of his reign in England. Henry's death occurred at Chinon and Matthew Paris describes that:

> he was carried to burial with his face uncovered, clothed in royal apparel, wearing a golden crown on his head and gloves in his hands: foot-gear woven with gold and spurs on his feet: a great ring on his finger and in his hand the sceptre and girded with a sword, and in this array he was buried.

We have a full account of the coronation of Richard I by Roger de Hovenden, though there are several others. The regalia and royal vestments were carried on a board. The King was vested with the tunic and the dalmatic and after the sword and spurs had been delivered he put on the mantle. He was then crowned and the sceptre and rod were placed in his hands. Afterwards the King put on a light crown for the banquet. There is mention, too, of a *pilleus regius* being carried in front of Richard. Richard was married in Cyprus to Berengaria of Navarre on 12th May 1191.

Richard Cœur de Lion was taken prisoner by the Emperor, and he was compelled not only to pay an enormous ransom but to become a vassal of the Emperor. Perhaps this was the principal reason why he underwent a second coronation at Winchester in 1194. The crown was actually placed on his head in the King's Chamber, where he also received the sceptre. The King then went into church in procession. In July 1195 the Emperor Henry VI vested Richard with the Burgundian Kingdom of Arles and sent him a very valuable golden crown as a sign of their mutual friendship. There is no record of Richard ever having used it. Richard died on 6th April 1199, and was buried at Fontevraud. The *Annals of Winchester* relate that Richard was buried in the crown he had worn for the Winchester ceremony of 1194 but that probably means that it was placed on the King's head for the lying-in-state and that a less valuable burial crown was substituted.

He was succeeded by his brother John, who was crowned on 22nd May 1199. He was crowned a second time on the occasion of his marriage in 1200 and a third time in 1201. John had already been installed as Duke of Normandy at Rouen on 25th April 1199. At this ceremony he was girt with the sword of the duchy and a circlet adorned with rosettes was placed on his head.

We now begin to find matters relating to the regalia being documented. In the fifth year of his reign, the King by Letters Patent dated 11th October 1203 acknowledges to have received at Caen from John, Bishop of Norwich, *Regalia nostra. scilicet. magnam coronam nostram. gladium deauratum. tunicam. pallium. dalmaticam. baudrieam. sandalia. cirotecas. frettas et calcaria.*

In December of the same year John left France and took his regalia with him. In 1204 on 18th December a receipt was issued from Reading for robes and regalia. These included a gold crown made at London; the mantle of red samite bordered with sapphires, cameos and pearls with a brooch stone sewn on in front; a dalmatic of the same stuff bordered with orfreys; a tunic of white diaper; a silken cloth, four-square for the King's seat; sandals and buskins of the same red samite; bands of orfrey work; a belt of the same samite studded with cameos and other precious stones; white gloves jewelled with a sapphire and an amethyst, and the sword which was made for the King's coronation with a scabbard of orfrey work.[1] Three years later another receipt for the regalia is entered in patent roll dated 9th December 1207 at Clarendon. The mantle, which now appears under its future name *Pallium regale*, was of purple with a gold clasp and brooch, and the tunic and sandals were of the same colour. The dalmatic was of a deeper hue, black purple. The belt is described as of leather work with stones and the buskins were of the same stuff. The gloves were only mentioned by name and the silk cloth borne over the King at his coronation is included instead of the cloth for his seat. Two swords are specified—one called Tristram's; the other belonging to the regalia, and besides the crown the King received his great sceptre, the golden rod with the dove and the golden spurs. It will be seen that the items described in these two lists are different and it is reasonable to suppose that the list of 1207 contained the coronation ornaments only used on special occasions, while the 1204 list refers to ornaments of state or personal ornaments worn on lesser occasions, or for use abroad.

John gave a golden crown to the Foundation that he had established at Beaulieu, where it was said to have been made into a shrine or casket. Another of John's crowns was found to be in the Treasury of Adam de Stratton. Either of these could have been the 'London' crown, but there is insufficient evidence to tell. It is improbable that King John lost any of his royal ornaments in the disaster of The Wash. It was his baggage train that was lost, and it is unlikely that the regalia would have travelled in the baggage train. Moreover, there is evidence of the survival of all the important ornaments.

John died on 19th October 1216. His tomb at Worcester was opened in July 1797 and it was found that instead of a crown on his head he was wearing a monk's cowl which was said to be a passport through the regions of purgatory. A sword was found which had been in his left hand. He was succeeded by his son Henry III, who was crowned at Gloucester on 28th October 1216 when a boy of nine, the French being in possession of London and Westminster. At Gloucester the proper regalia not being available, he was crowned with a simple gold circlet which romantic writers have suggested was his mother's bracelet. But the tradition that the Kings of England must be crowned at Westminster was already so strong that Henry was again crowned in the Abbey on Whitsunday, 16th June 1220. There is an inventory which gives a full list of the regalia and robes required for the ceremony which is quoted:

These are the regalia which Eustace de Faucenberg, Treasurer and Chamberlain, received from

---

[1] The full text in Latin is given in W. H. St John Hope's article on the 'King's Coronation Ornaments' in the *Ancestor*, Vol. I.

the Bishop of Winchester at Westminster on the Thursday next after the Feast of St Dunstan. A golden crown entirely adorned with diverse stones; golden spurs; a rod of silver gilt; a golden sceptre; a tunic and dalmatic of red samite with a jewel and precious stones in the orfray; a girdle with golden fittings and precious stones; a pall of red samite with precious stones; a golden ring with a ruby; two golden brooches for the pall and dalmatic, in the one of which is a sapphire and in the other a pearl; one pair of new sandals and stockings of red samite with an orfray; two orfrays with gold fringe to embroider the King's sandals; a pair of old stockings of red samite with orfrays; and a pair of old stockings embroidered with gold which belonged to King John: a tunic of white diaper with a dalmatic of red samite; an old pall of red samite; three swords which were at Corfe Castle covered with leather; two swords covered with red samite embroidered with orfrays; two pairs of gloves.

On the occasion of Henry's wedding with Eleanor of Provence in 1236, the King wore his crown and was arrayed in the royal robes. The sceptre and the rod and the three swords were borne before him. The account of this coronation makes the first mention of the sword called 'Curtana' which Matthew Paris describes as the Sword of St Edward. On this occasion various claims were put forward for rendering services which was probably the origin of the Court of Claims. We know something of the personal jewellery of the Queen.[1] She possessed nine chaplets at the time of her marriage and purchased eleven more.

We know of several other crowns of Henry III. In 1229 the King went on an expedition to Brittany, and for this he had a new set of regalia made consisting of a crown, a sceptre and staff of silver gilt with sandals and gloves and a suit of white cloth of silk.[2] We have already noted that it was apparent that John had a special set of regalia with him in Normandy and not the coronation regalia. It seems that Henry III also found it necessary to pursue this custom. In 1235 his sister, Isabella, married the Emperor Frederick II as his third wife, and she took with her a crown bearing the representation of the four Holy Kings whom the English claimed, which Schramm suggests meant that Henry III was placing his sister under their protection. Henry III had accepted Pope Innocent IV's offer to make his second son, Edmund Crouchback, King of Sicily. In 1255 a crown which had belonged to the Emperors Frederick II and Conrad IV was pledged from the Imperial Treasury to the merchants of Siena. Pope Alexander IV, who had succeeded to the Papacy, persuaded Henry to buy the crown for 10,000 oz of gold. Owing to the opposition of the baronage, Edmund did not achieve the Sicilian throne.

Matthew Paris relates that when in 1247 Henry knighted his half-brother William of Valence, Earl of Pembroke, the King was seated on his throne in a splendid robe, having a circlet of gold upon his head commonly called a 'garland'. In an inventory of the jewels belonging to Henry III made in 1272, a large and valuable crown is recorded, followed by three crowns of gold enriched with precious stones, valued at £336 13s. 4d. There was also an imperial cap, or hat, embellished with jewels and five garlands of gold of Paris's work valued at £27 13s. 9d. An interesting record is of a payment from the

---

1 Mme A. de Barrera: *Gems and Jewels 1860*.
2 Close Rolls 1227–1272. Public Record Office 232.

Treasury on 24th April 1242, of 45 pence for 4½ dwt of pure gold to repair the sceptre of the Blessed Edward.[1] Henry III died at Westminster on 16th November 1272 and was buried in the Abbey. His effigy on his tomb shows him wearing an open crown ornamented with lilies and formerly adorned with imitation precious stones (*Plate 47, b*). The original two sceptres which he held have disappeared. The effigy was made by William Torel in 1291–2.

Henry III was succeeded by his eldest son who had been christened Edward in honour of the Confessor, and thus restoring an Anglo-Saxon name to the Kings of England. Edward I and Queen Eleanor of Castile were crowned at Westminster on 19th August 1274. Not many details are known of the ceremony but there is one important one which tells us that the Great Crown was relegated to the position of a State crown. A wardrobe account of 1299–1300[2] describes it as 'a great crown of gold with square balays, emeralds, sapphires, oriental rubies and oriental pearls . . . which is appointed to be carried over the heads of the Kings of England when they leave the church on the way to the banquet on the day of the coronation'. The fact that it was 'carried over the heads of the Kings of England' suggests that it was the German, i.e. the Plantagenet crown. In the same account three other crowns are mentioned belonging to the Lady Blanche of Spain—one with rubies, emeralds and great pearls valued at £600; another *super perlis indies* worth £310; a third of one piece with rubies and emeralds worth £320. Besides these crowns the Queen possessed three big brooches set with gems; two square brooches; one with a large balas and the other with a large sapphire in the centre, each surmounted by pearls and other stones; a pair of brooches linked by a chain for fastening a mantle; two larger brooches, one shaped as an eagle set with rubies and emeralds, and the other with figures of a king and queen wearing mantles of fleurs-de-lis. The King also had two large brooches set with gems; a ring brooch with a ruby and small garnets which he usually wore, and another set with rubies and emeralds as a present from the Queen. Besides some silk belts ornamented with gold he had a gilded pendant set with a large sapphire to be worn next to his skin so that its properties might be effective.[3]

According to Rymer's *Foedera*, the crown or coronet of Llewellyn ap-Griffiths, Prince of Wales, became the property of Edward I in 1283 when his brother, David ap-Griffiths, was captured. We also learn that Alphonso X, King of Castile (1252–85), offered a crown and other jewels to the shrine of St Edward.

In the past the regalia had been kept at various places, but Henry III appointed a Keeper of Jewels and established a Treasury for the safe-keeping of the King's valuables at the Tower of London. The relics of St Edward and other treasures were nevertheless kept at Westminster. When the Abbey Treasury was robbed with the apparent connivance of some of the monks, it does not appear that any of the ornaments in the regalia were lost. The coronation ring of Henry III and the Privy Seal of the King were found scattered on the floor. The King ordered the regalia to be moved to the Tower

[1] Frederick Devon: *Issues of the Exchequer.*
[2] Society of Antiquaries, London, MS. 119, f. 285, quoted by W. H. St John Hope.
[3] Joan Evans: *The History of Jewellery, 1000–1870.*

of London, but that part of the coronation ornaments which were regarded as relics of St Edward remained at Westminster.

Edward I died on 7th July 1307 and was buried in Westminster Abbey. His tomb was opened on 2nd May 1774.[1] On his head was an open crown, or fillet, of gilded tin on which rested trefoils. In his right hand was a copper gilt sceptre with a cross 2 ft 6 in. long, and in his left hand a rod surmounted by a bird, 5 ft ½ in. in length.[2]

Edward II and his Queen Isabella were crowned on 25th February 1308. The issues of the Exchequer[3] record that the sceptre was repaired for the coronation. There is also an entry on 26th November 1317 indicating a payment of '20 marks to Roger Frowyk, goldsmith of London, by his own hands, in advance of making a crown of gold for the Lord King'. There follows a note 'there is yet coming to the same Roger for making the same Crown £23 6s. 8d.'

There is a very full list of jewels and plate contained in an indenture of articles delivered to the Treasurer and Chamberlain of the Exchequer which Thomas Ousefleet, the King's clerk, made in 1324. It contained, apart from a large number of pieces of gold and silver, gilt and silver plate, ten crowns which are described in some detail:

(1) A crown of gold with ten *fleurons*, the principal stones being emeralds and balays and with 80 pearls. Valued at £66 13s. 4d.

(2) A crown of gold with fourteen *fleurons*, the principal stones being rubies and emeralds with 56 pearls. Valued at £60.

(3) A crown of gold with ten *fleurons*, the principal stones being rubies, emeralds and balays. Valued at 200 marks.

(4) A crown of gold with eight *fleurons*, the principal stones being beautiful emeralds and balays and with 4 great oriental pearls, besides sapphires. Valued at £200.

(5) A crown of gold with ten *fleurons*, the principal stones being rubies and emeralds with smaller rubies, emeralds and pearls. Valued at £60.

(6) A gold crown of eleven *fleurons*, the principal stones being sapphires, garnets and pearls. Valued at 100 shillings.

(7) A crown of ten *fleurons*, with rubies, emeralds and Scottish pearls. Valued at £53 6s. 8d.

(8) A crown of gold with ten *fleurons* with large Scottish pearls and some round sapphires. Valued at £50.

(9) A small crown of gold with twenty-two *fleurons*, garnished with small rubies and emeralds. Valued at 100 shillings.

(10) A crown of silver of Paris work of nine *fleurons*. Valued at 100 shillings.

1 *Archaeologia*, III, 376–413.

2 In the church of Leybourne in Kent there are two iron crowns and on the wall beneath them is the inscription: 'these crowns are believed to be venerable gifts to Leybourne Church by Edward I and his Queen on the occasion of their royal visit paid to the son of King Edward's old friend and comrade in arms at Leybourne Castle on 25th October 1286.' The old friend was Sir William de Leybourne, the first Englishman to be given the title of admiral. Although Edward's visit can be confirmed there is no record of any reliquary gifts. The crowns are, in any case, of much later date and it is possible that they were made in connection with the celebrations for the restoration of the monarchy in 1661 when there was great rejoicing in Kent, or in connection with the arrival of William and Mary.

3 Devon: op. cit.

In addition there were two golden circlets and nine golden chaplets.[1] Other items of jewellery included two ring brooches; one brooch of gold; two fleurs-de-lis and two pontifical rings.

Edward II was dethroned on 20th January 1327 and murdered at Berkeley Castle on 21st September 1328. His body was buried at Gloucester.

We must now consider certain significant developments in the regalia during the reigns of the first six Plantagenets. It is quite clear that step by step the monks of Westminster turned their claim of being the possessors of the relics of St Edward into the actual use of them as part of the coronation regalia (see p. 132). In the XI century the king's own sword was carried close at hand in case of danger, but this led to rival claims and several swords came to be used. At the coronation of the young Henry, son of Henry II, in 1170, more than one sword was used, and perhaps this custom may have been started as early as the coronation of Stephen. At the coronation of Richard I three swords were used, and the number was later increased to four. In the case of Henry III it may have been five, as, in addition to two ceremonial swords, three others covered with leather were brought from Corfe. John had two swords, one of which was made for his coronation and the other called the Sword of Tristram which, according to Palgrave,[2] had been presented, or more probably restored, by the King's nephew, the Emperor Otto IV. He suggests that this sword may be identical with *Curtana*. He mentions, however, that in the Treasury there was a companion weapon known as the Sword of Smith Welland which was brought forth for the knighting of Geoffrey Plantagenet and had been in the Treasury among the regalia for a long time. The sword called *Curtein* first appears at the coronation of Eleanor of Provence in 1236. The name *Curtein* was that given to the sword of Ogier the Dane, one of Charlemagne's twelve peers whose fame was spread abroad in the Romances of Charlemagne.[3] It is related that whilst assaying his sword on the *perron* or steel block, before Charlemagne's palace at Aix-la-Chapelle, Ogier broke half a foot off his blade, leaving a blunt end for which reason it was called *Curtein*. According to the story, Ogier married a daughter of Edgar, King of England. This traditional link with the English royal family probably accounts for attaching the name *Curtein*, later changed to *Curtana*, to one of the swords in the English regalia. Since its origin must come from the Romances of Charlemagne, it would have been more likely to have been attached to the sword of Smith Welland rather than to that named after Tristram. At this period it was customary to give romantic names to the swords of heroes and great captains. England led the way in respect of the coronation sword, as the French coronation sword was not named *Joyeuse* until 1275.

We first hear of spurs as royal ornaments at the burial of Henry II, and they first appear at the coronation of Richard I. A pair of golden spurs are included in the lists of regalia in John's reign. A special pair was made for Henry III's coronation and the King subsequently gave them for the new Lady Chapel at Westminster, the foundation stone of which was laid on the Vigil of Pentecost, the day before the coronation.

[1] 'Chaplets' in the inventories seem unquestionably to refer to garlands or a form of head-dress and not to rosaries which were also sometimes called 'chaplets'.

[2] Sir Francis Palgrave: *The Antient Kalendars and Inventories of the Treasury of H.M. Exchequer.*

[3] Raynbert de Paris: *Ogier the Dane.*

With regard to the sceptre and the rod, a good deal of confusion has arisen. It is frequently asserted that the sceptre with the cross is the orb in another form. This is strictly speaking not so as both ornaments had their own symbolism. Until 1191 neither on the Continent nor in England had the orb been regarded as a coronation ornament. It was a secular ornament symbolising the sovereignty of the world under the cross of Christianity and was originally filled with dust to remind the sovereign of human corruptibility. It was shown iconographically when the king was Enthroned in Majesty and may have actually been held, but not delivered by the clergy, in the left hand at the enthronement at the end of the coronation service. At the coronation of the Emperor Henry VI in Rome in 1191, it was delivered by the Pope, and in 1198 it formally became a coronation ornament in the *ordo* of the coronation of Otto IV as King of the Romans. Before that, however, there was an actual orb among the imperial regalia and at coronation ceremonies this was placed on the altar with all the other imperial regalia and relics, several of which were not presented.[1] It was hardly likely that the King of England would not also wish to use an orb, but the difficulty was that he had only two hands in which to receive three ornaments. At the coronations at Aix-la-Chapelle and Rome at this time the sovereign received only one sceptre, so that the difficulty of having a free hand to receive the orb did not arise. This difficulty in England was overcome by adding a large sceptre-like stem to a globe and this form of hybrid royal ornament continued for some time. Whether an actual ornament combining the two was made before Richard II is open to doubt, although literary evidence of such an actual ornament existing appears in the directions to a royal funeral, probably that of Edward III in 1377. In any case it was not correct, and ultimately the error was put right and the two ornaments given their proper status. Richard's sceptre-cum-orb was floriated. This symbolism of the Confessor's allegory of the Green Tree had not been used after Harold until the young King Henry (1170–82), who on his seal held a long floriated rod.

Although a bird had been borrowed from the Salic emperors to surmount the rod this had not been used by the first two Norman kings, but having been used by Henry I and Stephen, Henry II continued the practice. It is not, however, until the reign of John that the bird is described as a dove. The bird borrowed from the Salic emperors was probably originally a phoenix which had been used by some Roman emperors to surmount their orbs, and was changed by the German emperors into an eagle. The dove, with its association with the Holy Ghost, would have been considered as a much more appropriate emblem of St Edward than a phoenix or an eagle.[2] Down to Henry III the king was always shown on the Great Seal enthroned and holding a sword in his right hand. In 1259, by the Treaty of Abbeville, Henry III renounced all claims to the Duchy of Normandy and the Provinces of Anjou, Touraine, Maine and Poitou and undertook to do homage for Guienne, Limousin and Quercy. In a new seal in that year it was noticed with shame that the King had changed the sword for a sceptre. There is a monkish verse quoted by Sandford[3]:

1 H. Fillitz: *Die Insignien und Kleinodien des Heiligen Römischen Reiches*, Vienna 1954.
2 The Five Martlets on the Confessor's Coat of Arms date from the reign of Richard II.
3 *Genealogical History*, Book II, Chap. 4, p. 91. See also *Liber de Antiquis Legibus*.

To France range you.
New seals are made.
Old seals forsaken.
Down laid the blade.
Sceptres up taken.[1]

Edward III was crowned on 25th January 1327 and his Queen was crowned on the first Sunday in Lent of the same year. There are several detailed accounts available of Edward III's plate, jewels and regalia. The first is dated 1339 and lists the jewels found in the Treasury when R. de Wodehouse entered upon the office of Treasurer. Apart from plate, of which there was a considerable quantity, we find one crown of gold 'of the old fashion' with twelve *fleurons* adorned with sapphires. A second crown of gold with ten *fleurons* with rubies, emeralds, and Scottish pearls. A third crown of gold with ten *fleurons* with rubies, emeralds and pearls. These were personal crowns. There is also a golden circlet with fleurs-de-lis and in addition twenty-four chaplets are listed. There was also a small crown of gold of twenty-two *fleurons* decorated with small emeralds and rubies. The list enumerates a large number of jewels, including rings and brooches, many of which can be identified as having been in the 1324 indenture.

From 1346 there is a list of relics and other articles of value delivered to William de Edyndon, Treasurer, and to the Chamberlain by William de Cusaunec. There are three items which call for notice. A rod called the Rod of Moses and two ampullae, one of crystal containing the oil of St Nicholas, and the other of glass containing the oil of the 'Blessed Virgin de Sardeneye'. In Constantinople the Eastern emperors possessed an ornament known as the Verge or the Rod of Moses which was a relic said to have been brought there by Constantine the Great. It was carried in processions with the cross of Constantine. It was kept in the oratory of St Theodore among the objects of ceremony used by the Emperor. The Verge of Moses was not a symbol of authority like other rods and sceptres and it is not recorded how it came into Constantine's possession.[2] It is possible that the Verge or Rod of Moses of Edward III was in some way connected with that at Constantinople. It may have been sold by the Emperor at the time he sold the Crown of Thorns and other relics to St Louis. It could have been a present from St Louis, or the idea may have been brought back to England by the Crusaders. It was a wooden rod covered with gilt and its possible connection with the ornament afterwards called 'St Edward's Staff' will be discussed later.

The place of the ampullae is difficult to determine. It was usual, when there was no special ampulla available, as in France, for the ordinary ecclesiastical vessels from the Church Treasury to be used at coronations. The King of England was still only anointed with *oleum sanctificatum* and not with the chrism which the Kings of France alone among Christian kings received. Wickham Legg[3] gives the text of a letter from Pope John XXII to Edward II about the oil of coronation, relating how when Thomas à Becket was in

---

[1] Since the sword had indicated the position of the King as Duke of Normandy, the change, in fact, was correct.

[2] A. Vogt: *Constantin VII Porphyrogenéte. Le Livre des Cérémonies. Commentaire.*

[3] L. G. Wickham Legg: *English Coronation Records.*

exile in France the Blessed Virgin Mary appeared telling him that the fifth King of England from the one then reigning would be a good man and a champion of the Church: 'wherefore for him and his successors she gave the said Saint a phial with most Holy Oil'. The letter goes on to recount how the Blessed Virgin Mary gave the oil to a monk named Nicholas to hide secretly. It is significant that the two ampullae that turned up in the next reign should be recorded as relics and named after the Blessed Virgin Mary and St Nicholas.

From 1356 there is an inventory of jewels from several treasuries which were delivered to John, Bishop of Rochester, on his appointment as Treasurer by William, Bishop of Winchester, the late Treasurer. Among the objects in the Treasury of the Cloister of Westminster Abbey were four crowns: the Great Crown of the King recently pledged in Flanders; another crown with four *manicles* of gold garnished; the third crown and the fourth crown.

They are all described as *nient preice*, which is usually translated as to mean 'worth nothing'. This is hardly likely to be the case as the crowns were obviously very valuable and, in fact, one had been pledged for a very large sum of money. The phrase could mean 'priceless', but it is more likely to mean without value in the sense that they had not been valued.

In the Treasury of the High Tower of London there were, apart from some royal robes, two pairs of spurs for the coronation of the king; two sceptres, gilt, with doves on top, two short sceptres with gold with crosses on top. The sword called *Curtana* and two other swords, a scabbard for one of which was enamelled in silver while the other had a scabbard of red samite bordered with gold. There was also the Golden Rose given to Edward I by the Pope. There are further inventories dated 1361 and 1367. In the latter the Great Crown is still described as recently pledged in Flanders.

In 1272 Henry III had deposited a large part of his treasure in Paris with his sister as a security. The list includes many rings; sixty-nine belts adorned with gold or jewels and forty-five brooches, besides plate, but none of the ornaments of the regalia were included. Edward III was the first king to pledge a crown, though it later became customary. In 1334, to defray the expense of the French wars, a crown—no doubt the Great Crown—was pledged in Flanders to Tidman de Lymberg, a great loan contractor. In 1335 the King issued a mandate to Paul de Monte Florum to return the gold crowns that had been pledged for 8,000 marks which had been repaid. In 1340 the King pledged his crown to the Bishop of Treves for 25,000 florins, another crown for 5,500 florins and a certain small crown for 4,256 florins. In 1343 Philip de Weston and Hugh de Ulseby were appointed to redeem the Great Crown and other jewels pledged in foreign parts. In 1344 the King ordered Thomas and William de Melchebourn to deliver the Great Crown to the Treasurer and Chamberlain and issued a warrant to the latter to receive it.[1]

Edward III had at least two new crowns made for his use. On 6th May in the thirty-seventh year of his reign Beatrix, widow of Thomas de Berewose, was paid 200 marks which the King had commanded to be paid in discharge of a debt of £133 6s. 8d. for a

---

[1] Thomas Rymer: *Foedera*.

certain crown purchased for the King's use.[1] Again, in the forty-first year of his reign, Edward III commanded the payment to Simon Roger of the sum of 1,100 marks for a certain crown purchased for the King's use.

Edward, Prince of Wales, the eldest son of Edward III, later known as the Black Prince, was very fond of jewels and there are records of many purchases made by him.[2] Among purchases in 1352 were 2 rubies bought for £30 8s. 10d., pearls for £8 2s. 0d., and sixty-six sets of buttons for £38 6s. 8d. In 1353 the Prince bought 4 rubies for £5 6s. 8d., a single ruby for £18, 779 pearls at 2d. each plus 5s. 2d., 20,000 seed pearls for £80, twenty-four round buttons of silver gilt and enamel for £41 and one button set with pearls and stones for £5. In 1355 his purchases included an oriental ruby for £10, twenty-seven rings, some set with rubies, some with diamonds and some with pearls, ten gold brooches set with stones and pearls and a helmet set with many great pearls and a leopard's crest. In 1358 the Prince bought a small ruby ring and two diamond rings while in 1361 the purchases included 8,559 pearls for £115 16s. 8d., 480 pearls for 1,005 marks, a ruby for 100 marks, and a fine ruby bought from John de la Mare at Kenyngton for £1,883 6s. 8d. This last stone must have been of exceptional size. In 1352 the Prince had bought for his own use a circlet costing £40, and in 1356 a crown belonging to King John II of France fell into his hands when the King was taken prisoner at Poitiers. It was described as of gold, diamonds, sapphires, rubies and other great pearls. It was pawned on 24th July 1359 to Sir Richard, Earl of Arundel, together with a gold star set with rubies, diamonds and sapphires and great pearls for £2,000. Both these ornaments were redeemed on 22nd October 1359.

Edward III died on 21st June 1377 and was succeeded by the son of Edward the Black Prince who was crowned as Richard II at Westminster on 16th July 1377. This is the earliest occasion of which we have a record of the Court of Claims and probably at which the *Liber Regalis* was used. This is the fourth recension of the English coronation *ordo* incorporating the various changes and additions that had been made. The regalia are not yet officially given the name of St Edward, though the stone chalice of the Confessor is mentioned. The royal ornaments included the sleeveless tunic, shaped like a dalmatic which later came to be called the *colobium sindonis*; a long tunic reaching to the ankles, woven with great golden images; the buskins, sandals and spurs; the sword and its girdle; the armils; the royal mantle, four square, and woven throughout with the golden eagles; the crown; the ring; the gloves; the golden sceptre with the cross and the golden sceptre with the dove.

The bracelets, or armils, had been included in the Anselm *ordo* about 1100 and used thereafter. The meaning which came to be given to them was that they were 'a sign of honesty, wisdom and enclosure by God'. Confusion arose between the bracelets and the stole which had been introduced by Edward I, who borrowed it from the practice in Germany, Sicily and Aragon. At the coronation of Edward II, the instruction said: 'the armillae are to hang from the neck and from both sides of the shoulders down to the elbows like a stole. They should be tied to the elbows by silken cords to emphasise

1 Frederick Devon: *Issues of the Exchequer.*
2 Register of Edward the Black Prince, 1351–65. Public Record Office 1933.

the meaning.' There were, therefore, two ornaments called 'armillae'. At the coronation of Richard II the King first received the stole and then the bracelets.[1]

We have a full description by Walsingham, a monk of St Albans,[2] of Richard II's coronation, and he makes an interesting reference to the orb: *consurexit de rotundo globo auerum, quem tenebat, in manu chirothecato, et habebit in summitate signum crucis.*

In one version of the *Liber Regalis*[3] the orb is mentioned in connection with the sceptre with the cross: *Et in dextra manu sua ponetur pila rotunda deaurata in qua virga deaurata erit fixa a manu ipsius usque ad pectus protensa in cuius virgae summitate erit signum Dominicae crucis quod super pectus eiusdem principis honeste debet collocari.*

We have already noted the probable explanation of these two ornaments despite their different origin and symbolism. We may take it that from this time there was in the regalia an ornament which was an orb surmounted by a rod with a cross on the top similar to that depicted in the contemporary portrait of Richard II in Westminster Abbey. Richard II adopted a new style of crown which consisted of five tall *fleurons* with small ones in between. This is shown in his portrait in Westminster Abbey (*Plate 47, d*), and the so-called Bohemian Crown, now in the Munich Treasury,[4] is of a similar style and may have been the crown of Richard II's consort, Anne of Bohemia, who was crowned on 22nd January 1382.

There is little evidence about the jewels of Anne of Bohemia but an *Issue of the Exchequer of 6 Ric. II* of 4th August refers to 100 marks paid to John Palying of London, goldsmith, for a worked fillet, the decoration of which included a large ruby and 2 sapphires and also for three rings each with 1 great diamond placed in the middle, for the use of Queen Anne costing £66 13s. 4d.[5]

Palgrave[6] publishes a document giving a schedule or inventory of regalia and jewels consisting of: a crown of gold of Spain; a pallet of Spain; a sword of Spain; and a saddle of Spain.

All these are minutely described. The description of the crown is as follows:

A Schedule or Inventory of Regalia and Jewels

(L: 3; 21; 13) 1. Une *Corone* d or d *Espaign* pois vi.mᵃrz v unc rebatuz pʳ croye t perrie ii mᵃrz preis } xlii li

Un gross baleys round pois ciiiiˣˣi qarr chescun qarr a v mᵃrz q amont } DCiiiˡⁱvⁱˢ viiiᵈ

vi gross baleys en la Gᵃnde *Corone* en la sercle preisez a   DC. li.

vii gross baleys en les gᵃntz florons en mesm la corone preisez a } iiiiˣˣxiiiˡⁱ vⁱˢviiiᵈ

vii baleys en les petitz florons preisez a   xxxv li

[1] P. E. Schramm: op. cit.
[2] Thomas Walsingham: *Historica Anglicana.*
[3] *Missale Westmonastriense*, fase II, col. 734.
[4] See Chapter Two—Bavaria, pp. 27–8.
[5] A document dated 9 Ric. II, 28 August, quoted by Palgrave, Vol. II, p. 51, which refers to Queen Anne, bears a sign of the distinctive shape of the Crown now in the Munich Treasury.
[6] Sir Francis Palgrave: op. cit.

vii rubies en les gᵃntz florons preisez a	xxi li.
vii saphirs en la sercle preisez a	lvi li.
xxi saphirs en vii gᵃnts florons preisez a	cv. li.
vii saphirs en les petitz florons preisez a	xiiii li.
lxx gross ples en les gᵃntz florons preisez a	cv. li.
iiiiˣˣiiii meyndres ples en les gross florons preisez a	xxx li.
xl petitz ples en les petitz florons en mesm la *Corone* preisez a	xv li.

M¹DCC xix li xiii s iiii d

The list is undated and there is no seal, but the handwriting is of the reign of Richard II. There are two other references to the Spanish Crown in the reign of Richard II. The first is an entry in the *Issues of the Exchequer* dated 23rd September of the fourth year of the reign recording £1,719 13s. 4d. paid on the delivery of the crown which is the exact amount of the valuation in the inventory. The second is in the twentieth year of the reign (1397–8), which records that the crown of the King of Spain was delivered by the Treasurer and Chamberlain to Guy More, Keeper of the Privy Seal, at the Feast of Pentecost.[1] A detached *fleuron* corresponding to the description of the *fleurons* of this crown appears as item 35 of an inventory of regalia and jewels of Henry VI in Edward IV's reign,[2] the implication being that the crown had been broken up some time previously. It is likely that the crown was the state crown of Peter of Castile.

The sword of Spain and the *pallet d'or* also make frequent appearances in the inventories up to the end of Henry VI's reign.

In 1396 Richard married as his second wife Isabella of France, a girl of seven years old. Despite her youth, rich presents were showered upon her. Richard gave her a circlet with large baleys, sapphires and pearls. From the Duke of Gloucester she received a crown of eight *fleurons* and a jewelled eagle. Her father gave her a very rich fleur-de-lis ornament set with jewels and pearls. The Duke of Aumale gave a circlet of stones set as *fleurons*. At Dover and Canterbury the citizens gave her other crowns and the city of London a jewelled circlet. At Eltham Richard gave her other presents, including a collar of diamonds, rubies and large pearls; a belt of golden feathers and a circlet and a chaplet formed of clusters of large pearls set as roses and sewn on red velvet.

During this reign we find several instances of crowns being pawned. On 6th September of the third year of the reign, the King pledged to certain citizens in London jewels including a great crown which is minutely described.[2] At Easter in the eighth year of the reign the crowns of Edward III and Queen Philippa were pledged to one Anthony Bache in France to pay for the King's troops in France. In the tenth year of the reign the royal crown was pledged to the Mayor and commonality of London for £4,000. In Rymer's *Foedera* other transactions are recorded. In 1378 there was an acquittance for three crowns and other jewels delivered in the Exchequer by William Bishop of London, and Richard, Earl of Arundel, who held them as pledges for £10,000, lent to the King by John Philpot and other merchants. In 1382 there was a receipt for

1 Sir Francis Palgrave: op. cit. Vol. II, p. 53.　　　　2 Devon: op. cit.

the King's crown and other jewels from the Corporation of London, to whom they had been pledged, and in 1391 a licence was given to Bartholomew Lumbard and Louis Daport of Lucca to bring to England for sale two crowns and other jewels.

When Richard was deposed in 1399, the Plantagenet dynasty came to an end. Froissart in his account of the ceremony at the Tower of London states that the King took off his crown and handed it to Henry of Lancaster saying: 'Harry, fair cousin and Duke of Lancaster, I present and give to you this crown with which I was crowned King of England and all the rights dependent on it.' He adds that the crown and sceptre were subsequently packed up and taken to the Treasury at Westminster Abbey. One of the charges levelled against Richard was that he had taken the regalia to Ireland. Though there does not seem to have been any hard and fast rule, it does seem to have been understood that the heirlooms of the Crown should not leave the shores of Britain, although this does not appear to have applied to personal regalia.

THE HOUSE OF LANCASTER

Henry IV, the first king of the House of Lancaster, was crowned on 13th October 1399, sixteen days after the dethronement ceremony of Richard II. Although he had been elected by a convention of Estates, his claim to the throne was not very firm, especially as there was the reproach that he had deposed an anointed king. As already related there had been a legend at least since the reign of Edward II of miraculous oil brought to Becket by the Blessed Virgin Mary. This obviously was intended to satisfy the claim of the English monarch that he was in no way inferior to the French who had the sacred oil sent from heaven in the *Sainte Ampoule*. It was later said to be in a glass phial contained in a golden eagle which had been hidden at Poitiers where it had been discovered by Edward the Black Prince. It was found again by Richard II in the Tower, but his demand to be anointed with the sacred oil was refused by the Primate on the grounds that Richard had already been anointed. Henry IV, in order to strengthen his questionable claims to the throne, was anointed with it. No special mention of it was made in the coronation *ordo* and it does not seem to have created the profound effect intended. For the first time meanings were attached to the sword. One was called 'The Sword of Justice' and the other 'The Sword of the Church'. The King's second wife, Joan of Navarre, was crowned on 2nd March 1403.

A few weeks after the coronation, the jewels and gold and silver plate formerly belonging to Edward III, Richard II, Queen Anne the Duchess of York, the Duke of Gloucester and Sir John Golafre were delivered into the King's Chamber and a detailed list has been preserved and is published by Palgrave.[1] There are no less than 338 items, including a number of royal ornaments among them:

The Sword of Spain.
A pair of gold bracelets decorated with 14 emeralds, 12 garnets and 56 small pearls.
A silver gilt sceptre surmounted by a crucifix.
A silver gilt sceptre surmounted by a cross.
A silver gilt sceptre surmounted by a dove.

1 Sir Francis Palgrave: op cit., Vol. III, p. 313.

Two long, iron sceptres with silver gilt blades surmounted by doves.

A small gilt crown and six *fleurons* decorated with emeralds, garnets and counterfeit stones.

A beautiful crown which corresponds to that described as the so-called Bohemian Crown in the Bavarian Royal Treasury at Munich.[1]

An old crown of gold of seven large and six small *fleurons* set with 14 large and 28 small balas rubies and 14 emeralds.

A large crown of silver gilt decorated with counterfeit stones.

A number of plates of *fleurons* which had probably come from older crowns which had been broken up.

Moses Yard, a long rod of silver gilt.

Henry IV died on 20th March 1413 and was succeeded by his son, Henry V, who was crowned on 9th April of that year. His consort, Catherine of France, was crowned on 24th February 1420. Henry V had a crown which became famous because of the incidents which are said to have occurred to it at the Battle of Agincourt on 25th October 1415. Several writers refer to the crown worn by Henry at the battle. It is said that after Mass on the morning of the battle, a very handsome bascinet, upon which was a very rich crown, was brought to the King. During the battle it was struck twice and injured by blows. The Duke of Alençon broke off a part with his battle axe, and two *fleurons* were cut off by a French Esquire who, with seventeen others, had sworn to perform such a feat or perish. This crown is usually identified as the one described[2] as 'The Golden Crown for the Bascinet', garnished with rubies, sapphires and pearls valued at £679 5s. 0d. There was another crown of state among the King's baggage which was taken by the French, together with the seals and a state sword when the royal camp was looted. The Sieur de Gaucourt instituted proceedings for the recovery of the crown and jewels. The crown seems to have been returned but the sword fell into the hands of the future Duke of Burgundy, Philip the Good, and some of the jewels were never recovered. Another crown was known as 'The Harry Crown' and had a fleur-de-lis in front decorated with a great balas ruby, 1 other balas, 1 ruby, 3 great sapphires and 2 great pearls. Each angle of the crown had 2 great sapphires, 1 balas and 6 pearls. The great balas is thought by some to be the stone known later as the Black Prince's Ruby. The 'Harry Crown' is also regarded by some writers as the same as 'The Golden Crown for the Bascinet'. It was pledged to Thomas Duke, a goldsmith, in 1415, for the payment of wages. A crown, the description of which suggests it was the Plantagenet crown, was pawned by Henry V to the Mayor of Norwich for £800 and was redeemed by Henry VI. Another described as the crown of King Richard was also pawned and not redeemed until 1429.

We hear of yet another crown which was in the possession of Richard, Earl of Cambridge, a near relation of Henry V, who had married Anne Mortimer, a sister of the Earl of March. There was a plot in July 1415 whereby the King was to be assassinated and the Earl of March was to be proclaimed King at the Welsh border and crowned with a Spanish crown in the Earl's possession. It was to be carried in the van of the army and passed for the Crown of England. The plot failed because of March's refusal to participate, and the Earl of Cambridge was executed. The Spanish Crown referred to was

---

1 See Chapter Two—Bavaria, pp. 27–8.   2 Rolls of Parliament, Vol. IV, p. 251.

probably that inherited by the Earl of Cambridge from his father, Edmund of Langley whose second wife was Isabel, the younger surviving daughter of Peter I of Castile.

On the chantry of Henry V at Westminster Abbey the King is twice depicted, once wearing the coronation crown which is arched (*Plate 47, c*), and in the other wearing an arched state crown (*Plate 46, c*). Henry V introduced the state crown with arches and it continued to be used thereafter. The occasion for this innovation was probably the visit of the Emperor Sigismund to England in 1416 to seek Henry's support for securing the abdication of the three rival popes. Hitherto in the Empire the English had been considered to form part of the German 'nation' and had only been formally recognised as a separate nation for the first time at the Council of Constance. Of course, in England no such tutelage was accepted, but the feeling of the time is illustrated by the story that relates that when the Emperor Sigismund visited Henry V at London, he was met by the Duke of Gloucester, who, riding into the water to the ship where the Emperor sat, required him at the sword's point to declare that he had not come purposing to infringe on the King's authority in the realm of England. Sigismund answered: *Nihil se contra superioritatem Regis praetexere.* It is obvious that it would have been regarded as important that the crown of the King of England should appear to all to be of equal status to that of the Emperor. At the time Sigismund was not in possession of the imperial regalia and had his own personal crowns which he elected to wear on solemn occasions. On his seals and other contemporary portraiture Sigismund is shown wearing a crown with two high intersecting arches.

Henry V died on 31st August 1422 and was succeeded by his son, Henry VI, who was eight months old on his succession. In 1429, though still a child, he was crowned at Westminster on 6th November. The young King was carried to the Abbey by Lord Warwick and a special crown was made for him, the large one, which would have been unsuitable, being still unredeemed in pawn. In the procession the prelates each carried a relic: the prior a rod, *Virga Regia*, and the abbot the King's sceptre. On this occasion special meanings were given to the swords. *Curtana* became 'The Sword of Mercy'. One of the others became 'The Sword of Justice to the Spirituality', and the third 'The Sword of Justice to the Temporality'. These names are still used today. At the Court of Claims of Edward VII in 1902 a claim was put in for the right to carry the orb which it was asserted had been carried by the claimant's ancestors at the coronation of Henry VI.

As a result of the wars of the previous reign, Henry VI also became King of France and on 7th December 1431 was crowned at Notre-Dame in Paris by the Cardinal Archbishop of Paris. He left the church with one crown on his head and another carried before him. His Queen, Margaret of Anjou, was crowned at Westminster on 30th May 1445. On his earliest seal we find, for the first time, the crown with three crosses *pattées* with pearl points in between. This was, no doubt, to differentiate between the English and French crowns, the latter having only fleurs-de-lis. On his seal for French affairs he has a sceptre with a Hand of Justice. There are two records, dated February of the fifth year of the reign, of an ampulla containing oil, a pair of bracelets and a verge called 'The Rod of Aaron', being taken out of their case by the Duke of Bedford and locked in a chest in the Great Treasury of Westminster. This is the only time we come across a sceptre so designated. Its name suggests that it must have been foliated. It may thus have been one that had fallen into disuse. In a list of armour, standards, etc., in the Tower of London[1] is an item 'Breast with box for Eagle'. Is it possible that this was used to carry the ampulla in the coronation procession of 1429? In 1450 an inventory of the regalia kept at Westminster Abbey was made by a monk named Sporley, a translation of the text of which is:

> Relics of Holy Confessors. St Edward, King and Confessor, for the memory of posterity and for the dignity of the royal coronation caused to be preserved in this church all the royal ornaments with which he was crowned namely his tunicle, supertunica, armilla, girdle and embroidered pall, a pair of buskins, a pair of gloves, a golden sceptre, one wooden rod, gilt, another of iron.
> Also an excellent golden crown, a golden comb and a spoon.
> Also for the coronation of the Queen a crown and two rods.
> Also for the communion of the Lord King on the day of his coronation one chalice of onyx stone with foot rivets and a paten of the best gold, all of which are to be considered precious relics.

Henry VI was deposed on 4th March 1461 and is said to have been murdered in the Tower on 20th June 1471 and with him the House of Lancaster came to an end.

THE HOUSE OF YORK

Edward IV, son of Richard, Duke of York, was acclaimed King and assumed the royal title in March 1461. He was crowned at Westminster on 29th June 1461. His Consort, Lady Elizabeth Woodville, was crowned on 26th May 1465.

There is an inventory of the regalia and jewels of Henry VI dated 13th March of the second year of Edward IV's reign. At the head of the list is:

> the Kynges grete crowne of gold which is closed within a little coffin of leather and bound with iron and locked with divers locks and keys and is also sealed without with divers lords seals which is in the King's Great Treasury at Westminster.

The only other item of regalia mentioned is the Sword of Spain which had probably come into the Treasury as part payment for troops employed in the Black Prince's Castilian campaign of 1367, and which from time to time was placed in pawn. There are mentioned, however, several fleurs-de-lis or pinnacles from crowns which had been broken up.

When Charles the Bold, Duke of Burgundy, married Margaret of York (1475), the sister of Edward IV, she took with her some rich and valuable presents from her brother. These included a beautiful nuptial crown now in the Treasury of the Minster of Aix-la-Chapelle[2] and a jewel called 'The White Rose' (*Plate 48, d*) consisting of a large spinel and enamel work set in gold. Edward IV conferred the Order of the Garter upon Charles the Bold. This Garter was decorated with 9 rubies, 4 diamonds, pearls and had twenty letters in diamonds with enamel (*Plate 48, a*). Another item which was probably a present from Edward IV was a hat ornament known as 'The Feather' (*Plate 48, c*). It was decorated with 5 balas rubies, 4 diamonds and 75 pearls set in gold

---

[1] Enrolled Acts, 33 Henry VI (1455), in Public Records Office.
[2] It was restored in the XIX century.

and one of the ornaments is in the form of a white rose. After the Swiss had routed Charles's army at the Battle of Granson, they captured the Burgundian camp with all its treasures. Soon after the battle the Burgundian treasure was offered for public sale, with the exception of these four precious jewels, which were sold with great secrecy by the authorities to Fugger of Augsburg in 1504 for 40,000 Rhenish florins. Three water-colour paintings on vellum were made of these jewels at about that time, or possibly a little earlier. These paintings are now in the Historical Museum at Basle.

Edward IV died on 9th April 1483 and was succeeded by his son Edward V, who had reigned for only two months and thirteen days when he was deposed and is said to have been murdered in the Tower. Preparations were made for the coronation but it did not take place. Richard III, brother of Edward IV, was then proclaimed King and was crowned on 6th July 1483. We have detailed descriptions of the ceremony. These coronations followed more or less the procedure laid down, but we find an arched crown is definitely established. The names attached to the sceptres underwent some changes. At the coronation of Elizabeth Woodville one was called St Edward's or the Spiritual Sceptre, and was carried by a bishop and the other, the Sceptre of the Realm or the Sceptre of England, which is described as a temporal sceptre was borne by an earl. At the coronation of Henry VI St Edward's sceptre was delivered and Richard III received it when he paid a formal visit to the Abbey before his coronation. This change may have been introduced because the actual orb, without a sceptre surmounting it, was introduced into the regalia. It is depicted in a contemporary MS. of Edward IV and his Queen, Elizabeth Woodville (*Plate 46, d*),[1] both of whom too are wearing arched crowns. It is an orb with a cross on a short stem and is quite separate from the King's sceptre. In the coronation *ordo* of Richard III there is mention of a sceptre in the King's left hand and the 'ball with the cross signifying monarchy' in his right. St Edward's Staff appears in this designation for the first time. It may have been one of the relics carried by a Prelate at the coronation of Henry VI in 1429. At the coronation of Richard III it is stated to have been carried as a relic. The only relic we find in the form of a staff is 'The Rod of Moses', and it seems likely that this became St Edward's Staff. Meanings were given to some of the ornaments, the gilt spurs signifying knighthood; the sceptre with the dove, peace, and the ball with the cross, monarchy.

Richard's reign did not last long for on 22nd August 1485 the King was beaten by his rival, Henry Tudor, and slain at Bosworth Field. The battered crown from Richard's helmet was placed on Henry's head by Lord Stanley and he was acclaimed King by the army. It was probably this crown which Henry VII bequeathed to Westminster Abbey, according to the following passage in his will:

> Also we will let our executor cause to be made an image of a king, representing our own person, the same to be of timber carved and wrought with plate of fine gold in the manner of an armed man and upon the same armour a coat of our arms of England and France enamelled with a sword and spurs accordingly; and the said image to kneel upon a table of silver and gilt and holding betwixt its hands the crown which pleases God to give us with the victory of our enemy at our first field and which image and crown we bequeath to Almighty God, our Blessed Lady Saint Mary and Saint Edward the Confessor.

1 From MS. of *Dictes and Sayings of the Philosophers*, Lambeth Palace Library.

During the reigns of six kings of the House of Lancaster and York a number of changes were made in the royal ornaments. The idea that the relics of St Edward were preserved and included his crown, which had become the Coronation Crown, had been confirmed in the coronation *ordo* and in an inventory of the Treasury, at Westminster Abbey. The arches had been added to the state crown of Henry V to emphasise the status of the King of England, and although at first they were only occasionally used, they appear on the seals from the time of Henry VI. Crosses, too, had been added to alternate with the fleurs-de-lis of the crown to distinguish between the English and the French crowns. The orb which had mistakenly been combined with the sceptre with the cross became a separate ornament. The swords had been given a meaning and the coronation services had been consolidated.

THE HOUSE OF TUDOR

With the accession of the Tudor dynasty, these changes were still further developed and consolidated into a pattern which, despite the destruction of the regalia in 1649, has lasted more or less intact down to the present day. We have more information about the crown jewels from fuller and more frequent inventories than had been available in the past and from the accounts of the destruction of the regalia by order of the Commonwealth Parliament in 1649.[1] It will be convenient to deal with the period of the Tudor dynasty and the reigns of the first two Stuart kings together and this brings us down to the destruction of the regalia in 1649.

There were nine coronations between 1485 and 1649:

> Henry VII: 30th October 1485
> Henry VII's consort, Elizabeth, daughter of Edward IV: 25th November 1487
> Henry VIII and Catherine of Aragon: 24th June 1509
> Anne Boleyn: 1st June 1533
> Edward VI: 20th February 1547
> Mary I: 1st October 1553
> Elizabeth I: 13th January 1559
> James I: 25th July 1603
> Charles I: 2nd February 1626

It is clear from the inventories made in the reign of Henry VIII that most of the older royal ornaments were no longer kept at the Tower, but were kept at Westminster with the relics of St Edward and the other coronation regalia. At the Reformation the Abbot of Westminster was replaced by a dean who became responsible for the contents of the Treasury, and, of course, the relics were no longer regarded as such. In the Secular Treasury at the Tower of London we find the state regalia consisting of the Imperial Crown, one sceptre and an orb together with the queen's regalia and a few other ornaments, besides the extremely valuable collection of plate. It is possible that

---

[1] Inventories of 1521 and 1532 in the reign of Henry VIII; of 1550 in the reign of Edward VI; of 1559 and 1597 in the reign of Elizabeth. In the reign of James I, one of the crown jewels and plate at the Tower of London, of 1604, and one of 1606 of the regalia in Westminster Abbey. Finally there are those taken in 1649 when Parliament ordered the destruction of the regalia.

the state regalia[1] originated in the reign of Henry VII or even earlier, but it seems to be more likely that they owed their origin to the imperial pretensions of Henry VIII. Henry was a candidate for the imperial throne in 1516, and we find several indications of the importance attached to the equality of status of the King of England with the Emperor. Acts of Parliament contained certain references to the Imperial Crown of England.[2] There is also an illuminating remark as to the reason for the English crown being 'closed' given in a letter from Dr Cuthbert Tunstall (later Bishop of Durham) addressed to Henry VIII. He wrote:

> one of the chief points in the election of the Emperor is that the candidate must come from Germany and be subject to the Empire; whereas Your Grace is not, nor ever since the Christian faith were the Kings of England subject to the Empire, but the Crown of England is an Empire of itself much better than the Empire of Rome for which cause your brow weareth a closed crown.

But the most significant thing, perhaps, is that the state regalia were based on those of the Empire. The arched imperial crown bore a new feature in the form of figures of Christ, the Virgin Mary and St George on the fleurs-de-lis, reminiscent of the plates bearing Old Testament kings and prophets on the German imperial crown, now in Vienna. The single sceptre and orb among the state regalia also conformed with the imperial regalia.

The emperors[3] had placed a miniature orb and cross at the point of intersection of the arches on the summit of their personal crowns and this was adopted in England. It is uncertain whether this was done in the reign of Henry V, but it can be seen on a crown worn by Henry VI in a miniature on the Charter to King's College, Cambridge, in 1446. It can be seen, too, on the crown on the head of Edward IV in his portrait in MS. at the Lambeth Palace Library already referred to. It is also visible on the coins of Henry VII. This feature has continued to the present time and has been followed almost universally in Europe, with the notable exception of the crowns of the Bourbon Kings of France, although it can be seen on one of the great crowns of France on the King's head in the picture of the Mass of St Giles painted in the late XV or early XVI century. The orb is thus elevated beyond doubt to its proper symbolism of sovereignty of the world under the Cross of Christianity. It also came to be placed on top of the sceptre, but when or where this was first done is uncertain, although probably in England, at the time of the Tudors. A state sceptre of Henry VIII continued in use down to the reign of Charles I and it is depicted in Daniel Mytens' portrait of that King (*Plate 51, b*). This reveals that a small orb was placed on top of the sceptre surmounted by a cross on which rested a dove. Thus the state sceptre of Charles I combined the symbolism of the orb, the sceptre with the cross and the rod with the dove. This allowed for a full-sized orb to be carried in the left hand, thus conforming with imperial practice.

1 The difference between the coronation regalia and the state regalia has not attracted the attention it deserves.

2 E.g. Act 24 Henry VIII, Cap. 12 (*Statute of Appeals*), is said to be designed 'to keep the imperial crown of this realm from the anoyaunce of the See of Rome as from the autoritie of other foreiyne potentates attempting the diminution and violation thereof'. Act 25 Henry VIII, Cap. 22, 'The Lawful Kings and Emperors of this Realm.

3 This was probably started by Conrad III.

Although the inventories are of great importance and are worthy of a close study, it would be tedious to include them here in the text. At the time of the destruction of the regalia in 1649 there were five crowns in all: two at Westminster and three at the Tower; eight sceptres or rods; one globe; one pair of bracelets; three swords; one pair of spurs; the ampulla; a spoon and a comb; the chalice and paten and the coronation robes.

St Edward's Crown

The first crown at Westminster was described as King Alfred's Crown of gold wire work set with slight stones and two little bells weighing $79\frac{1}{2}$ oz valued at £3 per oz, the total value was £248 10s. od. This was the coronation crown which was referred to in the rubrics as the Crown of St Edward. The only other reference to its being called King Alfred's Crown is in Sir John Spelmann's *Life of King Alfred*, written in the first half of the XVII century. He records that on the box in which it was kept was an inscription: *haec est principatior corona cum qua coronabantur Reges Alfredus, Edwardus et ceteri*. Since there was no mention of King Alfred in Sporley's inventory (*c.* 1450), nor in that of 1606, this was a later invention and the most likely explanation is that with the Reformation everything was done to remove the taint of the coronation crown being a relic, and so it was given an additional historical origin, although the description still suggests that it was the crown that had been used as St Edward's.[1] Although the description is short and somewhat vague, we may assume the crown was arched as at the time the inventory was taken it was usual for open crowns to be described as circlets. The little bells are somewhat puzzling. *Tintinnabulae* were used on some imperial and royal robes and bracelets. The only extant crown with *tintinnabulae* is that on the reliquary of St Oswald, King of Northumbria, in the Hildesheim Cathedral Treasury, but this was because some plates from a bracelet were used in its restoration. It is more likely that the 'little bells' were the *pendulae* or *cataseistae*, the nature and meaning of which had never been properly understood in England, but which would have been a feature of a *stemma* dating from the time of Edward the Confessor and the Norman kings and which, no doubt, would have tinkled. But the most significant thing of all is the description of the stones as 'slight'. It might be thought that with the jealousy with which they regarded their status, the Kings of England would have adorned their coronation crown with rich and magnificent precious stones. For them to have tolerated 'slight stones' must have been due to some special reason. The fact that the crown was regarded as a relic is hardly a good enough reason for it was customary to 'improve' relics by the addition of great and valuable precious stones. The answer seems to lie in the allegorical meaning attached to precious stones in the Middle Ages and especially to their biblical association, which will be dealt with later.

This is a suitable place to discuss the vexed question as to whether the English Coronation Crown, which was given the appellation 'St Edward's Crown', could have

[1] S. M. Leake, Garter, expressed the opinion in *Notes and Queries*, First Series, xl, p. 422, that the pre-Commonwealth Crown of St Edward 'could not by the fashion of it be older than Edward IV'. He was obviously thinking in terms that the arched crown had been introduced in England by Henry V and had overlooked the fact that the Normans had used the closed *stemma*.

been an actual crown of the Confessor. Much has been written on this subject, various theories have been advanced, but not all the evidence seems to have been clearly examined and the question remains open.

It has been established that Edgar introduced the lily crown, which was an open circlet, surmounted by four trefoil ornaments which developed into fleurs-de-lis. It was used by Edgar's successors, including Edward the Confessor, and by Harold and is depicted on the Bayeux Tapestry.

Towards the end of his reign Edward the Confessor introduced the arched crown or closed *stemma* which is depicted on his eighth type of coinage. We have some information which may refer to the manufacture of this crown. In the *Chronicle of the Benedictine Abbey of Abingdon*[1] it is related that Spearhavoc, Bishop of London and previously Abbot of Abingdon, who was known to be a skilful workman, was employed to make an imperial crown in 1052. In fact he misappropriated part of the gold and jewels supplied for this purpose, and with the money from the episcopal treasury, left the country and was not seen again.

A crown of St Edward could have been preserved in two ways—it could have been buried with the King and removed on one of the occasions when the tomb was opened; or it could have been placed with other relics in the Abbey at Westminster which the King had founded.

We have little positive information to show whether the Confessor was buried with regalia. The 'Biographer' of Edward is silent on the matter. Dr Freeman states that the body was buried in royal robes with a crown on his head but this is probably fanciful and not taken from any authentic writer. Osbert de Clare, a sub-prior of Westminster and author of *A Life of Edward*, does not mention in his description of the burial that the King was buried in royal vestments and regalia. In Chapter XXX of his work, however, in which he describes the opening of the grave in 1102, he writes: 'The sceptre by his side and the crown on his head and all the royal adornments that are in the grave of a famous man, none of them appear to be wasted with old age.' But, as we shall see, Osbert de Clare was trying to gain for Westminster Abbey the status of the repository of the national regalia and therefore this statement is suspect. Maskell, quoting one writer[2] who describes the first translation of the body, says it was wrapped in costly linen and the best shrouds, but makes no mention of the regalia. In the Bayeux Tapestry the dying King Edward is shown wearing a lily crown. In the scene of his body being prepared for burial the crown has been removed and there is a blue cap on the King's head, while in the scene of the funeral no royal ornaments are shown.

The cult of the Confessor had gained strength in the reign of Henry I. Rumours quickly spread that King Edward worked miracles in his lifetime, that these were still wrought at his shrine daily and that his body was not corrupted. In 1102 the grave was opened and the body found in perfect condition. Bishop Gundulf, who tried to pull a hair of the beard as a souvenir, was unable to do so. As a result of this a movement was started to obtain canonisation for the Confessor. Osbert de Clare was sent to Rome in 1139 to seek the authority of Pope Innocent III for the canonisation of King Edward.

---

1 *Chronicon Monasterii de Abingdon*, edited by the Rev. Edward Stevenson, Rolls Series 1858.
2 W. Maskell: *Monumenta Ritualia Ecclesiae Anglicanae*, Vol. II, p. 78, quotes *Aelred Abbas Script.*

He failed in his mission but is said to have brought back a letter giving authority for the Confessor's regalia, which Osbert claimed the Abbey possessed, to remain at Westminster. The document reads:

> We notice also that the regalia of the illustrious King Edward, which you keep, and his insignia are so preserved in the same monastery unharmed and unspoiled that no one of whatever rank or reputation has the right to alienate them, either by sale or by transferring them to other use outside that holy place without unanimous consent of the brethren.[1]

Some twenty years later Osbert de Clare was again sent to Rome to make a new application for the canonisation of King Edward and on this occasion the King had given his support. Pope Alexander III this time acceded to the request and England had a sainted king from 1161.[2] On 13th October 1163 the body of St Edward was translated to a new shrine in the presence of Henry II. On this occasion the ring from the Confessor's finger, about which there had been so many legends, was removed and the royal robes were taken to be used as vestments on special occasions.[3]

Henry III showed great devotion to the memory of St Edward and rebuilt Westminster Abbey, where he erected a splendid new shrine to contain the body of the saint, to which it was translated on 13th October 1269 in the presence of the King, his son (the future Edward I) and many of the great men of the kingdom.[4] Holmes has suggested that Henry III, whose devotion to St Edward was notorious, could have removed the crown and preserved it as a relic.

The last time that the Confessor's tomb was opened was at the time when it was plundered in the XVII century. A pamphlet published in 1660 describes how the tomb was broken and the head of the corpse was found to be surrounded by a band or diadem of gold about an inch wide, and under the shoulder blades was found a crucifix of pure gold which 'Chas Taylour, Gent:' later gave to James II. The plunderer was the author of the pamphlet and the genuineness of his story is generally held as suspect.

We have already noted that the evidence that the Confessor was buried in his tomb with the regalia is slight and contradictory. We must examine the practice elsewhere in Europe. It has been recorded earlier in this chapter that Edward borrowed certain features of his regalia from the usage of the Franconian emperors, one of whom, Henry III, was his half-brother-in-law. The tombs at Speyer of several emperors of this dynasty have been opened and it was found that they were buried with crowns on their heads and with other royal ornaments. These were not crowns used during the lifetime of

---

[1] Holtzmann: *Papsturkunden in England*, I, 2 (Abhandl: der Gesellsch: der Wiss: zu Göttingen, Phil: Hist: KL N.F. 25), 1931. The Latin text reads: *Regalia quoque gloriosi regis Edwardi, quae apud vos habentur, insignia ita in eodem monasterio intacta et integra decernimus observari, ut nulli fas sit cuiuscumque ordinis aut dignitatis ea distrahere vel vendere aut extra eundem sacrum locum absque communi omnium fratrum assensu in aliquos usus prorogare.*

[2] The Emperor Henry II had been called 'The Saint' in 1156, but was not generally accepted as a saint by the Church. Louis IX of France was canonised at the end of the XIII century. England therefore was in a special position, with a sainted king.

[3] John Dart: *Westmonasterium.*

[4] M. R. Holmes: 'The Crowns of England', *Archaeologia*, Vol. LXXXVI, 1937, and 'New Light on St Edward's Crown', ibid., Vol. XCVII, 1959.

the emperors, but had been hurriedly made of copper or base metal specially for each burial. In France the practice was for the personal crowns of the king to be given to the Treasury of St Denis. In view of the Confessor's close relationship with the French Court, this custom would have been known at Westminster. Edward was buried the day after his death and there could hardly have been time to make even crude royal ornaments. The English lily crown was required for the coronation and, although the King may have had more than one crown, the only other we know of is the arched crown adopted on coins in the latter part of Edward's reign and probably made at Abingdon. The graves of many kings in different European countries have been opened and only in a few cases, and then for a special reason, was a real crown buried with its owner and these instances are of a much later date.

While the possibility that the Confessor was buried with his crown cannot be excluded it seems to be unlikely. If it was removed from his tomb it must have been before Osbert de Clare's visit to Rome in 1139, and thus the only occasion would have been the opening of the tomb in 1102.

Westminster Abbey had confirmed its right to be the place of coronation of English kings by the Papal Bulls of Nicholas I (1059–61) and Pascal II (1099–1118). These are today considered to be forgeries, carried out at Westminster about 1140. Another forged document of the XI century and ascribed to William the Conqueror states that Edward had given his crown and regalia to Westminster Abbey.[1] It is possible that the document brought back from Rome by Osbert de Clare in 1139–40 may also have been falsified. But these falsifications were usually based on some fact and were intended to give a formal seal of approval to what was already the practice. It seems of little account whether Osbert's document was false or true, because it was a credulous age and the claims of Westminster Abbey were widely believed and accepted. It is hardly likely that Osbert would have advanced this claim and brought back the document unless the Abbey had, in fact, some actual royal ornaments with which to substantiate the story. It would have been in accordance with contemporary practice for church vessels and other articles connected with King Edward to have been placed in the Treasury of the Abbey which he founded. We will presently show that the English coronation crown known as St Edward's was closed with arches, and the only arched crowns we know of in the XI century are the Abingdon crown and that brought to England by the Conqueror and described by Bishop Wido of Amiens.

Having established their claim to possess St Edward's Crown the monks of West-minster were no doubt anxious to use it as the coronation crown. The information we have, however, shows the association of the name of St Edward with the coronation regalia seems to have been of slow development. The first instance appears to have been at the coronation of Eleanor of Provence in 1236, when the Sword *Curtana* is called the Sword of St Edward. In 1242 there is a record of a sceptre being called the 'sceptre of the Blessed Edward'. The first mention of the Crown of St Edward is by Hemingburgh,

1 We have a possible example of a crown being forged in the case of Agilulf which was kept until 1797 at Monza. This may have been made by the monks in order to provide evidence to help them to establish their claim that Monza was the ancient place of Lombard coronations and the repository of the regalia. See Chapter Fourteen—Italy.

who states that when discussing the question of homage done by the Kings of Scotland to the English Crown, Edward I declared that he would have the due right of the kingdom 'and of the Crown of St Edward of which he was the guardian'.[1]

In the next reign we learn that the crown was used at the coronation of Edward II because great offence was caused by the fact that St Edward's Crown, as it was called, was carried by the 'iniquitous hands' of Piers Gaveston, the King's favourite. In Thomas Walsingham's account of the same coronation the tunic and dalmatic are called those of St Edward. Froissart's description of the coronation of Henry IV also speaks of St Edward's Crown. But it was not until the beginning of the xv century that the crown is officially referred to as St Edward's in the coronation *ordo* known as *forma et modus*.

Apart from the description of St Edward's Crown in the 1649 inventory in the time of the Commonwealth we have several pieces of evidence to show that it was closed with arches. Perhaps the earliest representation, which seems to have escaped notice, is a sign on a document of the fifteenth year of the reign of Richard II (1392). This shows a rough drawing of a crown with fleurs-de-lis, closed with two arches, with no ornamentation such as a cross on the top. We know of no other arched crown in England at this time and it is therefore probably intended to represent St Edward's Crown. The apotheosis of St Edmund in the xiii-century MS., *Miracula sancti Eadmundi* (*Plate 47, a*) from the Holford Collection depicts an arched crown with an orb and cross at the summit. Although the crown depicted is meant to be St Edward's the cross must be a fanciful addition.[2] Holmes[3] draws attention to a passage in the *Vita Sancti Edwardi* in which Earl Godwin, on his return from banishment, exhorts the King in the name of Christ 'the sign of whose holy kingdom thou wearest upon thy crown'. This probably refers to the sign of the cross formed by the two flat arches. There are several examples of crowns on the continent of Europe in which the flat arches, when viewed from above, unmistakably form the sign of the cross,[4] and which are otherwise unadorned with crosses, and it would have been in accordance with mediaeval ideas for the king to wear the sign of the cross on top of his anointed head. We have, too, Froissart's account of Henry IV's coronation in which he describes the crown as *Laquelle couronne estoit archée en croi*.

Henry V is depicted on his chantry in Westminster Abbey as being crowned with St Edward's Crown, which is arched without any surmounting cross and the crown in the portrait of Henry VI in *Holinshed's Chronicle* (1577 edition) conforms to this type.

To recapitulate, we can note that Edward the Confessor adopted an arched crown, which was probably made at Abingdon and that William the Conqueror brought to England a crown of similar form. One of these two crowns survived, either by being placed in the Treasury of the Abbey of Westminster or by being removed from the

[1] M. R. Holmes: op. cit.

[2] The MS. is at earliest xiv century and subsequent to the introduction of the cross as an emblem on English Crowns by the Plantagenets.

[3] M. R. Holmes: 'New Light on St Edward's Crown'.

[4] The Holy Crown of Hungary; the Crown of St Wenceslas (*Plate 32, b*) and the Reliquary Crown in the National Museum, Stockholm; and the crown on the statue of St Foy at Conques.

Confessor's tomb in 1102. In 1139 Osbert de Clare established the claim that St Edward's Crown was in the possession of the monks of Westminster, who were made its perpetual custodians. It then came to be used as the English coronation crown not later than the coronation of Edward II. When the state regalia were removed from the Abbey, the Crown of St Edward, as a relic, remained there. At the time of the Reformation, when relics were out of fashion, the ancient crown was given the name of King Alfred's Crown and continued to be used at coronations until it was broken up at the time of the Commonwealth. The manufacture of a new St Edward's Crown and the possibility of the survival of the frame, or at least of the gold of which it was made, will be discussed later.

It has clearly been shown that the German imperial crown, now in Vienna, was constructed on lines in which allegory, particularly on biblical themes, was all important. The description of William the Conqueror's crown by Guy of Amiens has already been quoted and it contains the same ideas. It might be thought that this meaning would have been lost in the course of time, but it is noteworthy that Sir John Fernes in his *Glory of Generosity* describes the crown with which Queen Elizabeth was crowned in 1559 and gives allegorical meanings to the twelve kinds of precious stones in the crown. Sitwell[1] has paraphrased the passage to which reference should be made. In the XVI century the idea that stones possessed special properties and powers was still widely held. The emphasis was, perhaps, more on worldly qualities than on biblical associations and the allegorical meaning had been given a more practical conception, but it is worth comparing the description of the stones used to decorate the following ornaments:

(a) The breast-plate of the High Priest. Exodus viii,17–20.
(b) The covering of the King of Tyre, from the Septuagint.
(c) The Foundation of Heavenly Jerusalem. Revelation xxi,19–20.
(d) Guy of Amiens's description of William the Conqueror's crown.
(e) Sir John Fernes's description of Queen Elizabeth's crown.

	1	2	3
(a)	Sardius	Topaz	Emerald
(b)	Sardius	Topaz	Emerald
(c)	Chalcedony	Sapphire	Jasper
(d)	Carbuncle	Jacinth	Topaz
(e)	Sardius	Topaz	Emerald

	4	5	6
(a)	Carbuncle	Sapphire	Sardonyx
(b)	Carbuncle	Sapphire	Jasper
(c)	Sardius	Sardonyx	Emerald
(d)	Sapphire	Sardonyx	Chalcedony
(e)	Chrysolith	Sardonyx	Sardius

1 Major-General H. D. W. Sitwell: *Crown Jewels and other Regalia in the Tower of London*, 1953.

	7	8	9
(a)	Jacinth	Agate	Amethyst
(b)	Jacinth	Agate	Amethyst
(c)	Topaz	Beryl	Chrysolite
(d)	Jasper	Sardius	Chrysolite
(e)	Jasper	Chrysoprase	Beryl

	10	11	12
(a)	Chalcedony	Beryl	Jasper
(b)	Chrysolite	Beryl	Sardonyx
(c)	Amethyst	Jacinth	Chrysoprase
(d)	Beryl	Emerald	Chrysoprase
(e)	Sapphire	Amethyst	Sardonyx

Considering the length of time, measured in centuries, between the biblical descriptions and that of the Crown used at the coronation of Queen Elizabeth, there is a remarkable similarity, and since modern mineralogy has a different classification for some of the stones bearing these names, it is not surprising that they do not absolutely agree. Ten of the stones are the same in each of the five descriptions, the others can be adjusted by colour. It will be noted that Sir John Fernes's arrangement of the three most important stones is the same as that of the two ornaments from the Old Testament.

This crown was used at the coronations of the sovereigns regnant down to that of Charles I, and also for the coronation of Anne Boleyn. The crown was totally broken up and defaced and the gold was to be sent to the mint for coinage. There is a story that the inventory of the regalia in the Treasury of Westminster Abbey was entrusted to a notorious republican named Henry Marten. When the iron chest was opened and the royal ornaments revealed, George Wither, the poet, who was present, was dressed up with them. Anthony Wood[1] describes the scene as follows:

> the crown, orb, sword and sceptre belonging antiently to King Edward the Confessor and used by all our kings at their inaugurations, and with the scorn greater than his lusts and the rest of his vices he openly declared that there should be no further use for these toyes and trifles. Wither, being crowned and royally arrayed, had first marched about the room with a stately garb and afterwards with a thousand apish and ridiculous actions exposed these sacred ornaments to contempt and laughter.

When Henry V had introduced the arched crown, the arches rose very steeply into what became known as the imperial shape. Later, although this feature was still retained, there was a tendency for them to be made flatter and the globe and cross is sometimes represented as fitting into a depression at the intersection of the arches. This, however, was probably due to artistic licence and not to any symbolic change. At the time of the Tudors the depression becomes more pronounced until two quite different types of crowns were evolved, one with upward sloping arches which was recognised throughout Europe as being the 'Imperial' shape, and the other with the arches definitely depressed at the centre which was adopted as the 'Royal' shape. It is

[1] Anthony Wood: *Athenae Oxonienses.*

difficult to say when this first occurred, but it is possible that it was formally adopted after the marriage of Mary I to Philip of Spain. Mary and her husband are often depicted with their royal ornaments shown heraldically, Mary sometimes having the Crown of England and Philip the Crown of Spain. We know that the Spanish crown was closed with arches at this time and the royal, not the imperial, shape was adopted. It seems likely that St Edward's, as the coronation crown, was taken as the model of the Royal Crown of England. A feature of the arched *stemma* in the XI and XII century, as depicted on the coins of the Norman kings, was that the arches were depressed at the centre. It may be, therefore, that St Edward's Crown became the prototype of the formalised 'Royal' crowns subsequently used in almost all the kingdoms of Europe.

The Queen's Crown

The second crown in the Treasury at Westminster Abbey was described in the 1649 inventory as 'Queen Edith's crown, formerly thought to be of massy gold but upon trial found to be of silver gilt enriched with garnets, foule pearls, sapphires and some odd stones. Weight 50½ oz valued at £16.' This is the first mention of Queen Edith's crown and it was probably invented to emphasise the historical rather than the reliquary origin of the coronation ornaments. This crown was no doubt that described as *corona prima reginarum Angaliae* in the 1606 inventory and as the Crown for the coronation of the Queen in Sporley's inventory. But it is not possible to determine its origin or when it was used. Its fate was the same as that of St Edward's Crown.

The Crown of State

We first find a description of the Tudor State Crown in the oldest preserved inventory of the period which was made in 1520–1. It had five crosses and five fleurs-de-lis and carried two arches which are described as the diadem. It is not necessary here to give a full description of the crown, as it is described in detail at various stages of its existence and several descriptions taken from the inventories have been published.[1]

The crown had a circlet garnished with 8 balas rubies, 8 sapphires and 5 pointed diamonds, 20 rubies and 19 pearls. From the circle rose the five crosses and five fleurs-de-lis all decorated with precious stones. The fleurs-de-lis had a feature new to English crowns for on each was a figure. On the first a representation of Christ, on the second of St George, on the third Our Lady with her Child and on the fourth and fifth further representations of Christ. Holmes[2] has pointed out that in order to overcome the religious susceptibilities following the Reformation the three figures of Christ were later described as the figures of kings, and the crown was depicted with the back view showing in the portrait of Charles I by Daniel Mytens. Moreover, the crown had been altered so as not to give the figure of the Virgin a prominent position. Collins has discussed the question as to when this crown was worn other than at the coronation. He suggests that because stones were frequently removed from the crown it was doubtful whether Henry VIII assumed it more than once in a quarter of a century. It is clear, however,

---

1 For the 1520 and 1521 inventory see *Associated Architectural Society's Reports & Papers 1883*, XVII, pp. 158–9. For the 1531 inventory see Palgrave, op. cit., Vol. II. For the 1574 inventory see *Jewels & Plate of Queen Elizabeth I* by A. J. Collins.   2 Holmes: op. cit.

from a detailed study of the 1521 and 1532 inventories that besides stones being removed there were some additions and alterations, and these would hardly have been made had the crown not been used. The practice of removing stones from the state crown when it was not in use continued until the reign of Queen Victoria. The crown would certainly have been worn at the coronation of Anne Boleyn in 1533 and when the King attended Parliament in person. The crown can also be recognised in numerous portraits of the King.[1]

Edward VI was crowned with three crowns. First with St Edward's Crown, secondly with the King's imperial crown and thirdly with a personal crown. Mary, too, was crowned with St Edward's Crown 'the Imperiall Crowne of this realme of Englonde' and thirdly with a very rich crown which had been purposely made for her. Queen Elizabeth was probably crowned with three crowns, though there is no record of a crown being especially made for her. No doubt she used her sister's personal crown. It is easy to explain that in each case the third crown was necessary because the imperial state crown was too heavy to be worn for any length of time by the boy king, Edward VI, or by the two queens regnant. But no satisfactory explanation has been given of the reasons for the imperial crown being imposed. It surely must be connected with the Tudor ideas of their imperial styles and title which we have seen had even been incorporated into Acts of Parliament. James I was also crowned with the imperial crown after he had received St Edward's. He may also have worn the personal crown of Edward VI at the end of the service.

The crown last appears in a detailed description in the 1649 inventory and it was recorded as being totally broken up and defaced. Sitwell,[2] quoting the Commonwealth inventory of the disposal of the Crown property of Charles I, states that the gold from the regalia went to the Mint for coining. The stones were sold, and an account of this is given in a record in the minute book, of the Society of Antiquaries dated 12th April 1748. This reproduces a list giving in detail the value of the stones in the regalia from the Tower of London which had been transcribed from the book of sales of the King's plate and jewels which was in the possession of Colonel John Dove.[3]

The Queen's Crown of State

According to the 1521 and 1532 inventories, the state crown of the Tudor queens was of gold with the border set with 6 sapphires, not all of which were fine; 2 lesser sapphires, 6 balas rubies 'not fine' and 4 small pearls 'not fine'. There were 6 fleurs-de-lis of gold, each set with a balas ruby, a sapphire and 5 small pearls, and it was closed with arches (the diadem) and a cross of gold. The 1649 inventory describes it as

the Queen's crown of massy gold, weighing 3 lb 10 oz enriched with 20 sapphires, 22 rubies balas and 8 pearls. The gold (5 oz being abated for the weight of the stones) was valued at £40 per lb, the sapphires at £120, rubies balas at £40 and the pearls at £41 10s. 0d., which in all amounted to £338 3s. 4d.

[1] Many have been reproduced by Erna Auerbach in her book *Tudor Artists*.   [2] Op. cit.
[3] The list is published in full in Sir John Hope: 'The King's Coronation Ornaments', *The Ancestor*, Vol. II; and Sitwell, op. cit.

This crown was probably used by the queen consorts after their coronation at Westminster Abbey. It was broken up and defaced in 1649, the gold was sent to the Mint and the stones were sold at £210, which was more than their valuation.[1]

Another crown which is sometimes taken to be Queen Edith's crown can be seen in some portraits of Elizabeth and in the portrait of Henrietta Maria by van Dyck. It has four very high arches set with large pearls, between which jewelled crosses were set. On top of the arches, a great irregular-shaped ruby was set *à jour*. This crown does not correspond with those described in any of the inventories, unless it is the coronet of gold under Item 5 of the inventory of James I, but that is more likely to have been one made for Anne of Denmark. It was more probably the personal crown made for Queen Mary.

It had for long been the custom of the queens to wear a regal circlet for the State Entry into London and in the procession to the Abbey, and this was removed for the anointing. We find descriptions of several of them. One was made for Catherine of Aragon and was of gold set with an emerald, 4 sapphires, 4 rose diamonds, 4 balas rubies and 14 pearls. In Sir A. Aucher's account of 1557 it is recorded as having been removed by the Protector Somerset (*obiit* 1552), and we hear no more of it. Others were made for Queen Mary's coronation,[2] and for Anne of Denmark. There is a warrant dated 16th June 1603 'for breaking up of certain jewels to make a circle for the Queen to be worn at her coronation'. Actually, although Anne had been crowned in Scotland in 1590, she was not crowned in England, but only watched the procession. In the 1604 inventory of James I, two circlets are recorded, one set with a great balas ruby, 8 table diamonds, 9 emeralds, 36 rock rubies and 56 round pearls. The other, described as newly made for the Queen, contained 8 fair diamonds of diverse fashions, 8 fair rubies, 8 emeralds and 8 sapphires garnished with 32 small rubies on the border, but they are recorded as being with the Queen.

The Crown of Edward VI

The third Tudor crown in the Treasury of the Tower of London in 1649 was described in the inventory as:

a small crown in an iron chest formerly under Lord Cottington's charge, enriched with diamonds, rubies, sapphires, emeralds, and pearls, the gold weighing 25 oz (whereof 3 oz being abated for the weight of the stones), valued at £3 6s. 8d. per oz, making a total of £73 16s. 8d. for the gold and £355 for the precious stones.

It is described in the 1604 inventory of James I, Item I as:

a Crown Imperial of gold set about the nether border with 9 great pointed diamonds and between every diamond a knot of pearls set with 5 pearls in a knot. In the upper border 8 rock rubies and

---

[1] The crown in the Armada portrait of Queen Elizabeth I does not in any way conform to the Crown of St Edward (*Plate 49, a*). It was probably a personal crown and may have been that made for the coronation of Mary and reconstructed for Elizabeth. It conforms to the general type of crown in use at the time of the Tudors and has certain features not introduced into English crowns before the xv century.

[2] Described in B.M. Add. 46348, p. 439.

20 round pearls. The four arches being set each of them with a table diamond, a table ruby, an emerald and upon two of the arches 18 pearls, and from the other two arches 17 pearls, and between every arch a great balas ruby set in a collet of gold and upon the top a very great balas ruby pierced.

This was the 'very Ryche' personal crown made for Edward VI by Everart Everdyes, the King's goldsmith and stone cutter. For the decoration of the crown, pearls were taken from collars and caps of Henry VIII. It will be noted from the description that contrary to the usual custom, the crown appears to have consisted of a circlet, arches and a cross on top without the alternating fleurs-de-lis and crosses on the circlet. It seems most unlikely, however, that such an omission should have been made and the explanation may be that the fleurs-de-lis and crosses formed part of the rigid circlet and were not separate detachable ornaments and that they were plain and unadorned with precious stones. This is borne out by what appears to be an accurate picture of a crown which cannot be identified as any other, on the Plea Roll (*Plate 69, b*) of the King's Bench of Michaelmas of 1553.[1]

The Sceptres

Although the Tudors had followed the imperial practice of having a single sceptre among their state regalia, it was as King of England that the sovereign was crowned, and thus it was with the ancient English ensigns of royalty with which he should be invested.

The coronation of Edward VI was the first to be held after the Reformation and a significant change is recorded. Although the crowns were imposed on the King's head by the Primate, who also delivered the ring and apparently St Edward's Staff, the other royal ornaments were delivered by noblemen, according to the Accounts of the Ceremony.[2] The sceptre was delivered by the Earl of Shrewsbury, the spurs by the Earl of Rutland and the ball of gold by the Duke of Suffolk. At the coronation of Mary the sceptre was delivered by the Earl of Arundel, St Edward's Staff by the Earl of Bute, the spurs by the Earl of Pembroke, and the ball of gold by the Marquess of Winchester. It will be seen that the sceptre, or rod with the dove, was delivered as before, but that the orb was also delivered and the sovereign, when enthroned in state to receive the homage, was invested in accordance with imperial practice with the crown, sceptre and orb. As the rod was delivered to Edward VI by the Primate, one is tempted to believe that it was one of the royal ornaments in the Treasury of Westminster Abbey, while those presented by noblemen were from the state regalia. Elizabeth, too, was invested with the orb which was described as the 'world'. For the coronation of Charles I the Church reasserted its rights, and in the Order drawn up for the ceremony the sceptre and the rod with the dove were delivered by the Primate. The orb was not delivered. St Edward's Staff, described as the Long Sceptre, was also carried in the procession. We find in Laud's footnotes and comments[3] a reference to St Edward's Staff or the Long Sceptre in which he remarks that it was not in the *Liber Regalis* but was

[1] P.R.O.K.B. 27/1168.

[2] Acts of the Privy Council of 13th February 1546–7 and two accounts of the ceremony in a manuscript volume belonging to the Society of Antiquaries, MS. CXXIII.

[3] *The Manner of the Coronation of Charles I of England at Westminster 2nd February 1626*, edited by Henry Bradshaw, Liturgical Text Society 1892.

said to have first been used at the coronation of James I when it was delivered to the Bishop of London, the King using the words: 'Doe you take this to hime, thears no other to carye it, for sure theare is no use for this.'[1] There is also to be found in the same document an account of the consecration and laying up in the Abbey of the three swords. This seems to be the only occasion on which the three swords were blessed.

In the 1649 inventory the royal ornaments in the Tower of London included two sceptres weighing 18 oz, valued at £60, and a long rod of silver gilt weighing 1 lb 5 oz, valued at £4 10s. 8d. In the Treasury of Westminster Abbey there were two sceptres: 'one set with pearls and stones, the upper end gold, the lower end silver, the gold weighing 25 oz and the lower end being horn and a little silver gilt. Another was of silver gilt with a dove, formerly thought to be gold, weighing 7¾ oz and the two were valued at £65 16s. 10½d. There was a staff of black and white ivory with a dove on top with binding and foot of gold, valued at £4 10s. and a large staff with a dove on top, formerly thought to be of gold, but upon trial found to be the lower part wood within and silver gilt without, weighing in all 27 oz, valued at £35.' It is possible to identify the sceptres in Westminster Abbey as those described as in the 1606 inventory. One of the two sceptres would have been the sceptre with the cross of gold and precious stones, and the other the long sceptre for the king with the dove on top, while the long rod of silver gilt was no doubt the long sceptre with the pike of steel which was St Edward's Staff. The other two were the queen's sceptres.

Of the two sceptres in the Tower of London, one was the state sceptre with the small globe on top surmounted by a cross on which rested the dove which was used by the sovereign when enthroned in majesty.[2] The queen's sceptre of gold with the dove would have been used on leaving the Abbey at the coronation. It would seem that it was also used at a masque attended by Anne of Denmark when it was damaged.[3] St Edward's Staff does not figure in the 1574 inventory, but was included in the Westminster Abbey inventory of 1606. It is not clear when it was taken to the Tower of London, possibly after Charles I's coronation in 1626.

In the 1574 inventory, Item 16 is a 'Yarde of Moyses garnished with gold and with the Arms of England and Castile'. It is not thought that this is the same as the previous ornament of that name, although the Arms might be those of Edward I and Eleanor of Castile, or of John of Gaunt who claimed to be King of Castile. It is more likely, however, that they were the Arms of Henry VIII and Catherine of Aragon whose shield was charged with Castile quartering Leon.

The Orb

The orb was described in the 1574 inventory as 'a round ball of gold with a cross on top'. In the 1649 inventory its weight is given as 1 lb 5¼ oz and it was valued at

---

[1] According to Sancroft's *Notes on the Coronation of Charles II*, St Edward's Staff was delivered to the King at the entrance to the church, and he walked with it in the procession.

[2] The title 'Majesty' was used only by the emperor until 1633 when the Imperial Chancery conceded it to the Kings of England and Sweden and in 1641 to the King of France. Zedler, *Universal Lexicon*, s.v. Majestät.

[3] A. J. Collins: op. cit.

£57 10s. We have seen that at least at three of the Tudor coronations it was delivered as one of the royal ornaments and it was carried at the coronation of Charles I. It was always depicted when the sovereign was shown Enthroned in State, or Majesty, and from the time of Charles I it was shown as one of the three royal ornaments in state portraits. It also features at the obsequies of the sovereign.

The Bracelets

In the 1574 inventory Item 6 is a pair of gold bracelets adorned with 6 balas rubies and some pearls. In the 1649 inventory their weight is given at 7 oz of which 1 oz was for the stones. The gold was valued at £20, the 3 balas rubies at £6, and the 12 pearls at £10. They were used at the last three Tudor coronations, but were omitted at the coronation of Charles I.

Other Ornaments

Among the other ornaments from Westminster Abbey in the 1649 inventory were a pair of silver gilt spurs with buckles set with twelve slight stones and crimson silk straps weighing 6¾ oz and valued at £1 13s. 4d. There were three swords with scabbards of cloth of gold valued at £3. According to the accounts of the purchase of necessaries for the coronation of Henry VII, the coronation swords seem to have been replaced with new ones, for we find an armourer named John Smythe provided a sword with a point for 8s., another with a point for 6s. 8d., and two pointless swords called *Curtana* for 16s. 8d. and 13s. 4d. respectively. There were also certain items for decorating the scabbard, including two pieces of purple lace which cost 8d., and the price of garnishing one sword was 12d. In the 1604 inventory of James I there is the great two-handed sword garnished with silver and gilt presented to Henry VIII by the Pope. The ampulla, previously called an eagle, is described in the 1649 inventory as a dove of gold set with stones and pearls weighing 8½ oz and valued with its box at £26. There was a silver spoon of 3 oz valued at 16s., and 'one old comb of horn worth nothing'.

Besides the regalia, the Tudors amassed numerous collections of plate and jewels. The first half of the xv century witnessed the English committed on the Continent in the Hundred Years War and the second half saw internal upheaval in England itself because of the Wars of the Roses. It is not surprising, therefore, that on his accession Henry VII found an empty Treasury, and the crown jewels and plate had been disposed of to pay for the wars. By careful administration he built up an exceptionally strong financial position and it is said that on his death there was £1,800,000 in the Treasury, an enormous sum for that time. He followed a policy by which very large sums were expended on plate and jewels which were put to good use, but at the same time furnished a valuable reserve on which to draw in time of trouble.

Henry VIII thus inherited a very rich treasure to which he added on a prodigious scale by purchase, by gifts, by legacies and by forfeitures.[1] He received a stupendous windfall by the confiscation of Church property at the Dissolution of the Monasteries.

[1] A. J. Collins: op. cit.

144

No less than 289,768⅞ oz of plate and jewels were surrendered, although only a relatively small quantity was retained in the Jewel House. Most of the metal was melted down for coining. Henry VIII loved jewellery and his example was followed throughout the country. There is no doubt that this was stimulated by foreign fashions, and the famous Field of the Cloth of Gold led to extraordinary rivalry in display between the English and French nobility. This state of affairs led to an influx of foreign jewellers and craftsmen. Clifford Smith[1] gives a list of the principal foreign jewellers patronised by the King. Outstanding among the designers was Holbein, who, however, was not a craftsman jeweller, and the actual work from his designs was undertaken by his friend, Hans of Antwerp. A collection of 179 designs, all apparently by Holbein, is now in the British Museum.[2] Among the most important jewelled ornaments worn by the King were the great collars. These were originally collars of livery and developed into the collars of the Orders of Knighthood and of Office.[3] The best known of these is the Collar of SS, the origin of which is obscure. It was used by John of Gaunt and through him it passed to his nephew, Richard II, and to his son Henry IV. Edward IV introduced a new collar of alternating suns and roses. Henry VII revived the Collar of SS but added the portcullis and Tudor Rose pendants and it became a badge of office in the King's Household.[4] Henry VIII ordered that the Collar of the Garter should be worn on state occasions. In the 1604 inventory of James I there are no less than fourteen collars including the two great collars of balas rubies of Henry VIII (*Plate 50, a*): the larger one had 13 great flat balas rubies, some square and some oval linked by ornaments of richly floriated gold on each of which was a large pearl; the smaller collar had 9 great balas rubies and collets of gold with ten knots, each containing 16 round pearls. There were too many jewels for us to notice here and we must confine ourselves to the most notable. The King continued to purchase jewels up to the time of his death, although not on the same lavish scale as in the early part of his reign. In 1546 Vaughan, his agent in Antwerp, wrote to Paget in London informing him of a splendid pendant formed of a large table diamond set in scrolls and masques upheld by a satyr and a nymph with a pendant pearl below, 'The time is unmeet', he wrote, 'to pester the King with jewels who already has more than most of the Princes of Christendom, and though I told him (John Carolo the owner of the jewel) that I would send the pattern to the King, I send it only to you.'[5]

One of the most celebrated pieces was a jewelled pendant known as 'The Three

[1] H. Clifford-Smith: *Jewellery*, London 1908.

[2] It is called *Holbein's London Sketch Book*.

[3] There are a number of references to the purchase of collars in Treasury records which are of interest. In *3 Henry IV* eight collars were purchased from Theodore, goldsmith, and sent to the King's sister, the Queen of Portugal, for his infant nephews. In *8 Henry IV* £385 6s. 8d. was paid for a collar of gold worked with the motto *sovreignez* and the letter *S*. In *98 Henry IV*, on 20th January, £550 was paid for a collar garnished with precious stones. In *6 Henry V* twenty-four collars of gold were purchased and sent to the King at Rouen. In *12 Henry VI*, six gold and twenty-four silver gilt, besides other collars of silver, were sent to the Emperor to be distributed to the knights and citizens of Basle, and there are further entries in the reigns of Edward IV and Richard III. For the Byzantine origin of the collar see pp. 376 and 526.

[4] Joan Evans: *The History of Jewellery, 1000–1870*.

[5] Joan Evans: op. cit.

Brethren (*Plate 48, b*). It had belonged to Charles the Bold, Duke of Burgundy, and on his defeat at the Battle of Granson in 1475 it was taken from his tent by a common soldier. It passed into the possession of the Magistrates of Berne who sold it to Jacob Fugger of the well-known merchant family of Augsburg. Just before his death, Henry VIII negotiated for its purchase. The transaction does not seem to have been completed until May 1551. Edward VI committed it to the custody of the Lord Treasurer on 7th June of that year, and on 31st October 1553 it was delivered to Queen Mary.[1] In the centre was a deep pyramid diamond $\frac{5}{8}$ in. square at the base, which was especially esteemed at the time as it was believed to have been the first to have been cut by Louis de Berquem, who had invented a new way of cutting diamonds. Set round it without foil were 3 very large balas rubies almost exactly equal in size and quality called 'The Three Brethren'. Between them were 4 very large pearls.

When Mary married Philip II of Spain, several notable jewels from the Spanish Treasury came into her possession. Among them a famous pearl known as *La Peregrina*.[2]

The collection of royal jewels was yet further enriched to an extraordinary extent in the reign of Elizabeth. She received many valuable presents especially each New Year's Day, as well as bequests, but she also acquired some important portions of the crown jewels of Scotland, Burgundy, Portugal and Navarre.

In 1567, the Earl of Murray, Regent of Scotland, found that Mary Queen of Scots had left a large collection of jewels, but an empty Treasury. He sold part of the jewels to furnish him with funds for his immediate necessities and Queen Elizabeth was a purchaser of some of these. Among the items she acquired was a case of pearls for which 12,000 crowns was paid. The history of these pearls will be related later. The diamonds of the House of Burgundy had been deposited in the Tower of London as security for a loan, and it was said they were worth three times the sum advanced. There is no record of their having been redeemed. According to Froude[3] Antonio de Castro, the natural son of the Infante Dom Louis of Portugal, had himself proclaimed King of Portugal on the death of the Cardinal King Henry. Philip II of Spain did not recognise his title and sent an army under the Duke of Alba which defeated Dom Antonio under the walls of Lisbon and annexed Portugal to Spain. Dom Antonio defeated, fugitive and dispossessed, escaped to London, taking with him the diamonds of the crown on which he hoped to raise funds to carry on the struggle against his rival. He endeavoured to interest Queen Elizabeth in his cause, who, in return for a promise of aid, took the Portuguese crown jewels, which included a large table-cut diamond of 30 carats known as 'The Mirror of Portugal' (*Plate 50, c*). When Dom Antonio was condemned to death *in absentia*, one of the charges was that he had taken the crown jewels from Portugal.[4]

The Crown Diamonds of Navarre were given to Queen Elizabeth as security for a loan to Henry, King of Navarre, who became Henry IV of France. Froude[3] states that there was disagreement between the Queen and the King of Navarre's emissary, Ségur, but as there is nothing to go on except Ségur's statement and the Queen's contradiction, it is difficult to decide the rights of the case. Ségur insisted that the Queen had lent

---

[1] B.M. Add. 46348, p. 439.   [2] See Chapter Twenty-five—Spain.
[3] J. A. Froude: *History of England*, Vol. II. [4] See Chapter Eighteen—Portugal.

a   *The Armada portrait of Elizabeth I showing one of the Tudor state crowns. Woburn Abbey* (p. 141)

b   *Portrait of Elizabeth I by M. Gheerardts. Burghley Collection. The great stone surmounting the headdress is possibly that described as 'a fair ruby great like a rocket ball'* (p. 181)

a   *Portrait of Henry VIII by Hans Holbein. The King is
wearing the great collar of balases. National Portrait
Gallery (p. 145)*

b   *Portrait of Elizabeth I by Isaac Oliver. The Queen is
wearing Mary Queen of Scots's pearls. Windsor Castle
(pp. 146 and 166)*

c   *The Mirror of Portugal from the portrait of Henrietta
Maria by Van Dyck. The Hermitage, Leningrad
(p. 146)*

his master 60,000 crowns, but Elizabeth said it was 300,000. Ségur demanded that either the jewels be given up to him or that they should be valued and that she should let his master have the surplus. Elizabeth contended that there was no surplus and that the diamonds were hers and she would keep them, which apparently she did.

THE HOUSE OF STUART

James I also added to the Treasury and his most notable purchase was the 'Sancy' diamond, which weighed 53 carats. This stone was among the French crown jewels and had been offered for sale all over Europe without success when suddenly at the end of March 1604 it was learnt that the French Ambassador in London, who was the brother of Nicholas de Sancy, had sold the great diamond to King James I for 60,000 écus, of which 20,000 was to be paid immediately, 20,000 on 10th September, and the rest of the money on 10th March of the following year. It features in the 1605 inventory of James I under an item which is described as 'a great and rich jewel of gold called "The Mirror of Great Britain" containing 1 very fair table diamond, 1 very fair table ruby, 2 other large diamonds cut lozenge-wise and one of them called the stone of the letter *H* of Scotland'. This was a diamond known as the 'Great Harry' from the Scottish crown jewels which James I (VI) brought to England with him and was garnished with small diamonds. Also 2 round pearls and 1 fair diamond cut in facets bought of Sancy.

The 1605 inventory of James I contains a number of jewels, some of which are worth noting but there are too many to quote in full.

Rings
Two gold rings, one set with a topaz and the other with a white sapphire.
A gold ring enamelled green and white with a fair rock ruby set with four claws.
A gold ring enamelled black, blue, white and green bearing a great rock ruby in four claws enamelled.

Buttons
Ten buttons set with 10 diamonds for the King's use.
Ten buttons of gold set with 10 table diamonds.
One button of gold set with a diamond and a great ragged pearl pendant.
Twenty buttons of gold, each set with 4 pearls and a true-love knot.
Twenty-four buttons of gold, each having a fair diamond of divers cuts.
Nineteen larger buttons, each having 1 diamond, some fairer than others.

Single Stones
A great blue sapphire unset.
A great amethyst set in gold.
A fair ruby balas without foil hanging in a case of gold enamel.
A fair great blue sapphire with foil and a long pearl pendant.

Pendants (called 'flowers' in the inventory)
A 'flower' of gold and rock ruby with a long pearl pendant.
A 'flower' with a very great table diamond set in gold called 'The Mirror'.[1]
A 'flower' of gold with a table diamond and a great pearl pendant.

1 This may have been 'The Mirror of Portugal' or another stone known as 'The Mirror of France'.

In addition there were five 'flowers' in the possession of the Queen.

In 1623, Charles I, as Prince of Wales, accompanied by Buckingham, went to Spain for the purpose of making an alliance which was to be sealed by his marriage to the Infanta—a journey which proved unprofitable. So as to make a good impression, James I arranged for a selection of the finest jewels in the Tower of London to be made by the jeweller Heriot. Besides 'The Three Brethren' those selected included a hat band adorned with 20 fair diamonds, and a diamond called 'The Mirror of France' described by James I as the 'Fellowe of the Portugall dymont' which Charles was told to wear in his hat like a black feather. 'The Mirror of Portugal' had the Cobham pearl as a pendant. There was a great Lorraine cross of diamonds, four other crosses and various other jewels.[1]

On 27th March 1605 King James I had promulgated an indenture in which he named the Imperial Crown of the realm and a number of royal and princely ornaments and jewels 'to be indivisible and inseparate for ever hereafter annexed to the kingdom of this realm'. As in France, an attempt was thus made to preserve the crown jewels for posterity, but it was a short-lived move, for in 1625 in the first year of his reign, Charles I found it necessary to dispose of a quantity of plate and jewels in the Netherlands, including 'The Mirror of Great Britain' and 'The Three Brethren' which had been specifically mentioned in the indenture.

By 1642 Charles was in desperate need of money and Henrietta Maria, on 23rd February of that year, sailed for the Netherlands with a quantity of plate and jewels which she endeavoured to sell. On 16th April she wrote to Charles that no loan was forthcoming on the rubies but she was going to pledge all her own precious stones. A month later she wrote:

> After much trouble we have found some money, but little as yet for the merchants are still somewhat afraid. Information had come from London that I had taken my gems surreptitiously and contrary to your wishes and that if money was loaned to me on them there would be no security for them . . . in the end they have had to be shown the authority signed by your hand.

The Queen pawned her own personal jewellery for wretchedly small sums but continued to have difficulty in disposing of the large pieces as there was no one who could afford to buy them. She was, for instance, unable to dispose of the ruby collar or the King's largest collar, although ultimately a merchant named William of Amsterdam advanced 140,000 guilders on the ruby collar and pendant pearls. In return for the money she sent the King powder, carbines and coin. It was not long before Parliament became acquainted with the facts and the legality of the King's action in sending the crown jewels out of the kingdom to be sold or pawned was questioned.[2] On 3rd March 1642 the King had left London for York and thus lost control of the Jewel House. Henrietta Maria returned to England but again left in 1644 for France whither she took all the jewels in the Royal Treasury, including some which were the property of the Crown. There is a document in the archives of the French Ministry of Foreign Affairs[3] which

[1] A complete list of the jewels removed from the Tower of London is given in *Archaeologia*, Vol. XXI, 1827, p. 148.

[2] The obscure legal position is discussed by A. J. Collins, op. cit., pp. 174-5, note 5.

[3] *Angleterre. Correspondence Politique*, Vol. 61, ff. 96-8, (*Plates 52* and *53*).

gives a list of jewels which she pledged through her agent, a Monsieur Cletstex of the Bank of Lombardy, Rotterdam. She received in all 1,006,275 livres and 11 sols of Dutch money. The Queen had to live in France in poverty and was forced to pawn her jewels one by one, both to support Charles I's partisans and to fulfil her own needs. She contracted loans with the Duke of Epernon to a total of 427,556 livres. As security the Queen gave the Duke's mandatory:

> a carcanet of massive gold covered with 60 round pearls of about 3 carats each intermixed 16 by 16 with rubies to the number of 10 of several shapes and sizes; a very large oriental ruby *en cabochon*; 4 balas rubies; two table cut; two *en cabochon*; 5 spinels also *en cabochon*.

It is possible to recognise this piece as the lesser of the ruby collars of Henry VIII. It was contained in a box of green velvet lined within with white satin and was valued at 130,000 livres. As the Duke was fearful that he would not be repaid the money, the Queen pledged the 'Sancy' diamond and 'The Mirror of Portugal', but later these were withdrawn from the Duke and sold to Cardinal Mazarin for 360,000 livres. In the list it is possible to recognise 'The Three Brethren', though it had been altered. It is described as having 1 pyramidal diamond; 3 balas rubies; 4 pearls with the addition of a table diamond of 30 carats and 2 pointed diamonds. It was sold through the Bank of Lombardy, Rotterdam, for 104,000 livres, but its subsequent fate is not known.

With the overthrow of the monarchy, the Commonwealth Parliament turned its attention to the disposal of the goods and personal estate of the late King, Queen and Prince. It was made clear later that this term included all plate and jewels[1] and Acts passed on 4th July 1649 authorised the retention of goods to the value of £10,000 for the use of the State. In September 1649 the Council of State was given powers to convert the metal into coin instead of selling it. This no doubt was due to the puritanical feelings of the Government of the Commonwealth who considered it immoral for the vanities of a goldsmith to be sold intact. Curiously enough it was their religious rather than their political feelings towards the monarchy that determined their course of action. Nevertheless, there were some things that could not be melted down and coined, such as the agate chalice of St Edward; the Queen's Ivory Rod and the coronation robes and vestments from the Treasury of Westminster Abbey. These were sold intact; the chalice for £110 15s., the black and white ivory staff with the dove on top for £5 and the robes for £5. Other personal ornaments and possessions, such as Charles I's coronation and Garter robes, his 'George' and some robes of Henry VIII and Anne of Denmark, and the Parliamentary robe of the Prince of Wales were sold without any fear that they might perpetuate the memory of the monarchy.

At first the Clerk of the Jewel House refused to give up the regalia and a number of orders were returned marked: 'Not obeyed', but in the autumn of 1649 the Trustees of Parliament broke into the Jewel House and took over the contents. The Dean of Westminster does not seem to have been any more obliging than the Clerk of the Jewel House, but finally all the regalia were removed and 'totallie broken and defaced'.

What is the chance of any of these items from those collections of ancient treasures having survived? Some of the personal ornaments have, we know, been preserved. Is

---

1 *Acts and Ord. of the Interregnum.* II, pp. 160–8.

it possible that the Queen's Ivory Rod is lying forgotten in some attic? Some jewels may have been returned by royalist supporters. Collins[1] quotes a passage from a letter dated 26th June 1660[2] which reports the Dutch Ambassador 'to be coming over with very rich presents . . . and all the jewels of the crown that were pawned there'. There is also a warrant dated 18th January 1661.

> Warrant to certain citizens of London who have discovered some of the King's plate, hangings, jewels, money, etc., of great value, lying concealed about Bishopsgate. The holders of them have removed from place to place, and declare they will burn them rather than the King shall have them.

But it seems unlikely that the Commonwealth Government would have kept such things as the frames of crowns or other royal ornaments. If they did keep any articles of precious metal, they would have been articles in everyday use. Oliver Cromwell was invested as Lord Protector in 1653. At the ceremony the Coronation Chair was brought over from Westminster Abbey, a sword of state was carried before him and a sceptre was presented to him by the Speaker. In 1656 there were suggestions of his being made King, and it is said a crown was made for him. At his funeral in 1658 he lay in effigy at Somerset House with an imperial crown of gold and jewels placed on a cushion on his chair of estate and with a sceptre and orb in his hand. As these ornaments do not appear in the list of funeral 'properties' it may be assumed that they already existed. The effigy remained in Westminster Abbey for some time, but in the reign of Charles II it was finally taken by a threatening mob to the Jewel Office in Whitehall, where, having first been stripped of its royal ornaments, it was hung out of a window with a rope round its neck. Holmes[3] suggests that the frame of that crown may have been used for the new St Edward's Crown made at the Restoration. Sitwell[4] has produced some new evidence in support of this theory and this will be discussed later. Cromwell's escutcheon and arms were surmounted by a royal crown with pronouncedly depressed arches and which was described as the Crown of England.[5]

The monarchy was restored on 29th May 1660, and Charles II was crowned on 23rd April 1661, there having been several delays and the postponement was probably due to the necessity of making new regalia.

Sir Edward Walker, Garter, in his account of the coronation, writes:

> because through the rapine of the late unhappy times all the royall ornaments and regalia heretofore preserved from age to age in the Treasury of the Church at Westminster, were taken away, sold and destroyed. The Committee met divers times, not only to direct the re-making of such royall ornaments and regalia but even to sette the form and fashion of each treasure; all of which doe now retayne the old names and fashion, although they have been newly made and prepared by orders given to Sir Gilbert Talbot, Master of the Jewel House.

---

[1] A. J. Collins: op. cit.
[2] *Report of the Royal Commission on Historical Manuscripts*, 5th Report, App. 154.
[3] Holmes: op. cit.
[4] Sitwell: op. cit.
[5] See p. 139.

He then goes on to give a list of the ornaments that were to be provided which were:

two imperial crowns set with precious stones, one to be called St Edward's Crown wherewith the King was to be crowned, and the other to be put on after his coronation before His Majesty's return to Westminster Hall.

Also an orb of gold with a cross set with precious stones.

A sceptre with a crown set with precious stones called 'St Edward's'.

A sceptre with a dove set with precious stones.

A long sceptre or staff of gold with a cross upon the top and a pike of steel at the foot called 'St Edward's Staff'.

A ring with a ruby.

A pair of gold spurs.

A chalice and plate of gold.

An ampulla for the oil and a spoon.

Two ingots of gold, one of a pound and the other of a mark for the King's two offerings.

All these were to be made by Sir Robert Vyner, the Court Goldsmith, who was in addition to supply:

a crown, mace, chain and badge for the Garter King of Arms; seventeen collars; seventeen Garters of the Order of St George; seventy-five badges of the Order of the Bath of Gold; divers parcels of gilt plate given to peers and others for new Orders, gifts and at christenings; eighteen large maces; divers other parcels of white and gilt plate.

It has frequently been taken that the phrase that the new ornaments were to retain the old names and fashions meant that they were to be replicas of the old regalia, but this, in fact, was not so. What the phrase means is that the same sort of ornaments were to be made anew so that the traditional regalia were used at the coronation. But this left a great deal of licence for the designers and craftsmen. Sitwell[1] has produced some new evidence from some interesting documents which had fallen into the hands of Robert Cole in 1830, when on the orders of Government many tons of Exchequer Records were mutilated and sold as waste paper. Cole acquired two tons of this paper which included an order for the Treasury dated 20th June 1662 to pay to Sir Robert Vyner, His Majesty's Goldsmith, the sum of £21,978 9s. 11d. in part payment of £31,978 9s. 11d., the total cost of the regalia and other articles made by him and provided for the coronation. Some writers have suggested that Charles II defaulted on the balance of £10,000, but Sitwell has pointed out that there is an entry in the Jewel House Letter Book that £10,000 had been paid in advance. Another of Cole's documents is a list showing the cost of regalia supplied to Charles II which is worth quoting. It was entitled: *A List of the Regalia Provided for His Late Majesty's Coronation, Charles II, and now in the Custody of Sir Gilbert Talbot, Master and Treasurer of His Majesty's Jewels and Plate.*

The document is dated 23rd April 1684, and seems to have been prepared in connection with the arrangements being made for the coronation of James II which took place in April 1685. The list contains the following information:

[1] Sitwell: op. cit.

	£	s.	d.
St Edward's Crown, 82 oz 5 dwt 16 gr.			
For the addition of gold and workmanship	350	0	0
For the loan of jewels returned	500	0	0
One Crown of State, 72 oz 1 dwt.			
For the gold, jewels and workmanship	7,870	0	0
One sceptre with a dove, 4 oz 3 dwt 20 gr.			
For the gold, jewels and workmanship	440	0	0
One sceptre with cross, 32 oz 11 dwt 10 gr.			
For the gold, jewels and workmanship	1,025	0	0
One St Edward's Staff, 45 oz 8 dwt 8 gr.			
For the gold and workmanship	225	6	2
One globe with a cross, 48 oz 7 dwt 12 gr.			
For gold, jewels and workmanship	1,150	0	0
One pair of spurs, 12 oz 18 dwt.			
For gold, jewels and workmanship	63	7	6
Two armillas, 6 oz 12 dwt 22 gr.			
For gold and workmanship	44	18	6
One ampulla or egret, 21 oz 8 dwt.			
For gold and workmanship	102	5	0
The Anointing Spoon, 3 oz 5 dwt.			
For silver and workmanship	2	0	0

Sitwell has drawn attention to the fact that the cost of St Edward's Crown, which contained 82 oz 5 dwt 16 gr of gold, was £350 plus £500 for the hire of jewels, and that although only minor alterations were made for James II's coronation, £305 16s. 5d. was charged plus £500 for the hire of jewels. He has suggested that since there was only a difference of £45 between the cost of providing the crown and the cost of refreshing it, the original must have been made from materials, perhaps even a frame, of an old crown which already existed in the Jewel House. If this is correct, it is reasonable to suppose that it was Cromwell's crown which, in turn, had been made of the materials from the Tudor Crown and which, indeed, had probably been made from the gold taken from older crowns. It is certainly an attractive hypothesis and the phrase used in the bill 'for the addition of gold' instead of 'for the gold', which is used for the other items, is surely sufficient to show that some material was available in the Jewel House and was used. Moreover there is no mention in the declared accounts of the Mint of an issue of coin being made from the metal of the original St Edward's Crown. It will be noticed that the new St Edward's Crown weighed less than 3 oz more than the original and that the document of 23rd April 1684 says that there was an addition of gold.[1]

On the question of whether there was a frame of an old crown which was brought into use, we can only speculate. From such records as exist we must accept that the

[1] If we calculate the cost of providing all the gold for the crown at the current price of £4 1s. per oz, the cost would have then been approximately £332. We get an idea of jewellers' charges in the bill for the regalia of the coronation of James II when Vyner was paid £45 for refreshing and setting precious stones in the crown. For designing and making a new crown the charge would, of course, have been very much higher. It will be seen, therefore, that the sum of £350 paid for St Edward's Crown in 1661 would have been quite inadequate.

a (above, left) *Portrait of Elizabeth of Bohemia by Daniel Mytens. The Queen is wearing the great ropes of pearls of Mary Queen of Scots, later known as the Hanoverian pearls. Royal Collection, St James's Palace* (p. 166)

b (above, right) *Portrait of Charles I by Daniel Mytens. The Tudor Imperial Crown of State and the state sceptre and orb can be seen in the picture. National Portrait Gallery* (p. 131)

c *Portrait of Charles II by Michael Wright. The King is wearing St Edward's Crown. Royal Collection, St James's Palace* (p. 153)

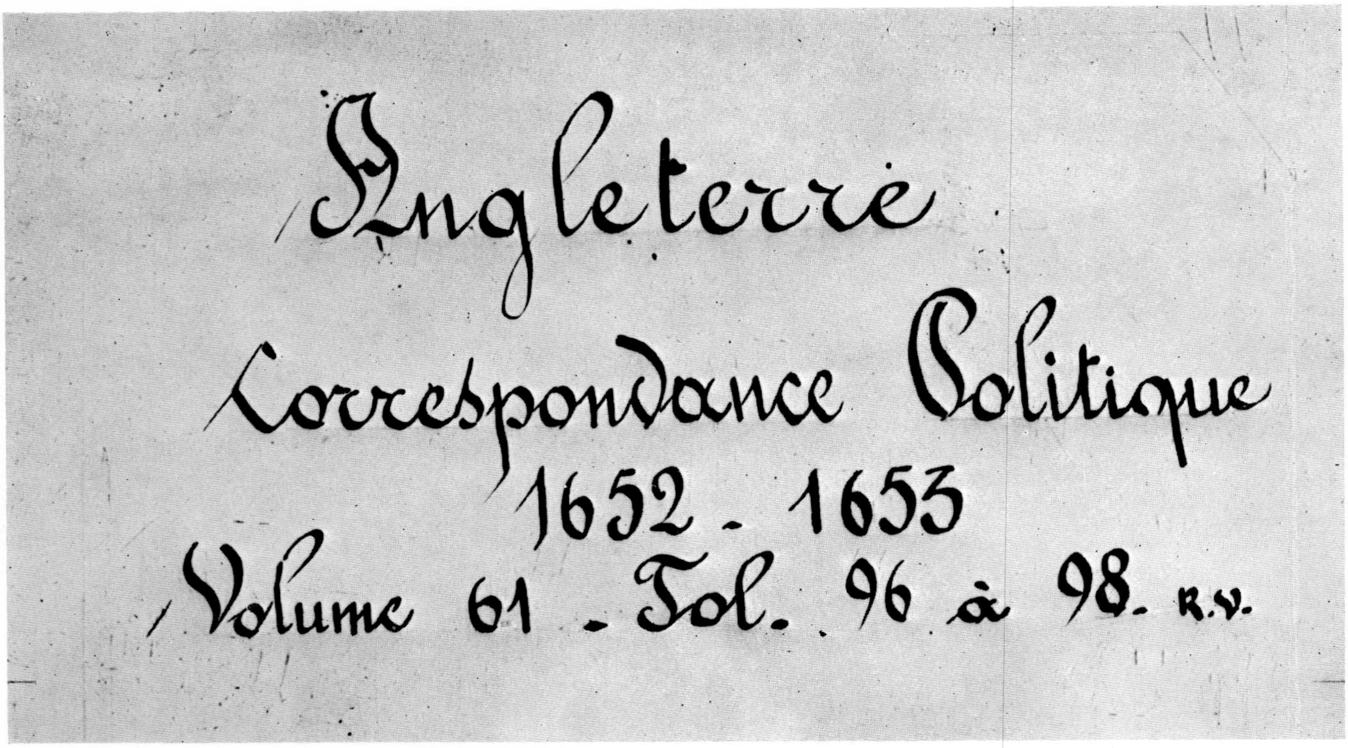

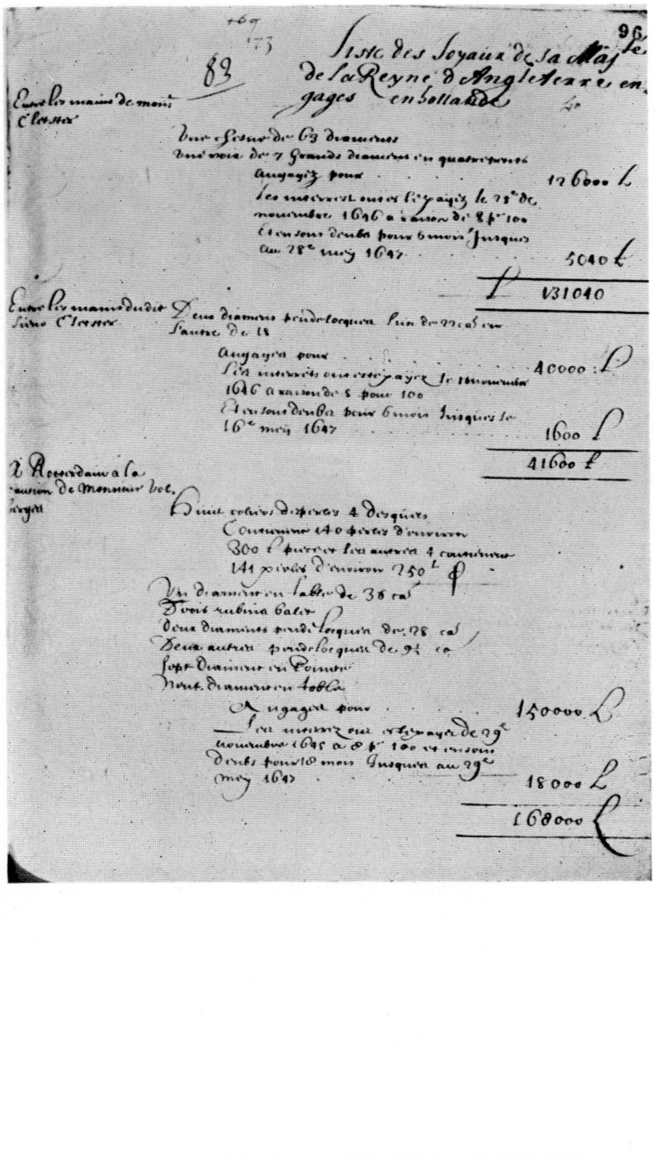

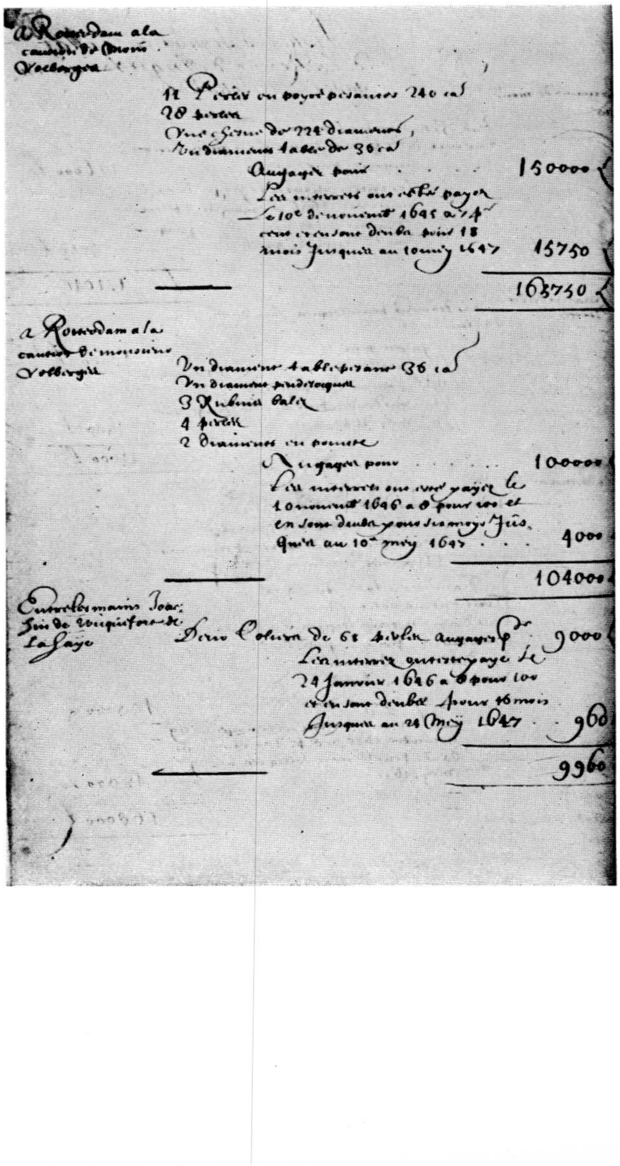

[Upper left — p. 84 / 97]

84   97

Un grand diamant table
Un autre grand diamant a casser
Ils avoient esté engagés pour
70000 ... a 8 pour cent mais
Il a esté payé 16000 La bon compte
au mois de Decembre 1645 en argent
de banque par monsieur y[...]
...   54000 L

Pour les interest Il faudra
Scavoir de Monsieur Avestu
quand ce aura esté payer Lequel
...   4320 L

     58320 L

3 Grands diamants en deux chastons
En chatton de 35 pierres
Engagés pour   20000 L
Les interest ont esté payer
Le 20 Janvier 1646 a 8 pour 100
et ensous deux pour 13 mois
Jusqu'au 20e may 1647   2133:6:8

     22133:6:8

No 1   34 Pierres
1 Grand diamant pendilocque
nommé La [...]
Engagé pour   20000 L
et interest ont esté payez le
5 auril 1646 a 8 pour 100 et en
sous deux pour 13 mois Jus.
Qu'il au 5 may 1647   1733:6:8

     21733:6:8

[Upper right]

No 2   1 Grand diamant nommé La [...]
Engagé pour   [...]
Les interest ont esté payé le
20 auril 1646 a 8 pour 100 et
ensous deux pour 13 mois
Jusqu'au 20 may 1647   [...]

     2445

No 3   35 pierres
1 Grand diamant
Engagé pour   1700
Les interest ont esté payé Le
20 auril 1646 a 8 pour 100 et
ensous deux pour 13 mois
Jusqu'au 20e may 1647   147[.]
     L   1047[.]

No 4   440 pierres
1 Diamant table qui manque
[...] Engagé pour   [...]
Les interest ont esté payer le
20 auril 1646 a 8 pour cent et en
sous deux pour 13 mois Jusqu'au 20
may 1647   21[.]

     271[.]

[Lower left — p. 85 / 98]

Plus au Lombard   85   98

No 5   1 Grand diamant pendilocque
1 Autre Grand diamant table
Engagés pour   35000 L
Les interest ont esté payer le
5 auril 1646 et en sous deux a
8 pour 100 pour 13 mois Jusqu'
au 5e may 1647   3033:6:8

     38033:6:8

No 6   1 Grand diamant table
1 autre grand diamant pendilocque
Engagés pour   35000 L
Les interest ont esté payer le
20 auril 1646 a 8 pour cent
et en sous deux pour 13 mois
Jusqu'au 20e may 1647   3033:6:8

     38033:6:8

Entre les mains du
St Jean Vestu
Une boiste d'argent fa[ite] des diamans
a la façon d'emire
Un richeur de 30 Emeraudes
Deux pendens des Emeraudes
Une Emeraude table
Une grande Emeraude blanc
[...] grande Emeraude Esposau
[...]
1336 pierres
160 pierres de 6 cas [...]
28 pierres
2 pierres en poyre de 52 cas
2 grandes pierres en poyre de 52 cas
Engagés pour   127391 L
Les interest ont esté payer le p[...]
de may 1646 a 8 pour cent et
sous deux pour 13 mois Jusque
au premier may 1647   10191 L

[Lower right]

Deposité entre les
mains de Monsieur
Avestu Engagemens

Un diamant table Longuene
en diamant pendilocque   pour [...]
deux chatons chasquine de 35 pierres   le Lombard
6 Rubits balests Retiré de Monsieur Avestu   Roterdam
par ordre du compte de

Abregé des Parties de sy
Contre

De Mr Cleene   131040
dud.   41600   / 17264[.]

Du Lombard de Roterdamme
dud.   168000
dud.   165700
dud.   104000   / 43770[.]

De Mons Wiquefort   9950
dud.   58320   / 6827[.]

De Charles Gerbier   / 2213[.]
Du Lombard de Amsterdam
ime   21733:6:8
dud.   21450
dud.   11473:6:8
dudit   27166:13:4
dud.   38033:6:8
Didit   38033:6:8   / 1678[.]

De Jean Vestu   / 13750
     / 10067[.]

Somme 1[...] 6275 L 11 S 8 d [...]

a *St Edward's Crown engraved by W. Sherwin, from* The History of the Coronation of the most excellent Monarch James II and his Royal Consort, Queen Mary, *by Francis Sandford, 1687 (p. 152–3)*

b *State crown as set for the coronation of James II engraved by W. Sherwin from Sandford (p. 154)*

c *Frame of state crown originally made for Charles II and last set for George IV. London Museum (p. 153 and 165)*

Tudor crowns were totally broken and defaced, and thus the only frame of a crown likely to have been available was that of Oliver Cromwell, the shape of which would have been taken from the Crown of England, depicted on his seal. This shape, with its depressed arches, which was probably copied from the original St Edward's Crown, would account for the very pronounced depression of the arches on the Crown of St Edward made in 1661. The additional gold would have been needed because the crown had to be made very large on account of the fact that the King, in accordance with the fashion of the day, wore a full-bottomed wig.

With the exception of the Imperial State Crown, the regalia made for Charles II are still in use today. All the ornaments, except St Edward's Staff, have, however, undergone changes and alterations.

In 1661 St Edward's Crown was set with precious stones, but the symbolism of the stones had been lost or forgotten. The State Crown differed considerably from the Tudor Crown. The circlet was bordered with pearls, between which were large stones alternating with jewelled rosettes. The five fleurs-de-lis and five crosses were reduced to four of each, and there were no figures on the fleurs-de-lis, which were set all over with diamonds and with four coloured stones. The crosses were also covered with diamonds with a large jewel set in the centre of each. It is generally assumed that the great irregular ruby was set in the cross *pattée* in the front of the crown for Charles II's coronation, but it is open to doubt whether it was in Charles II's crown at all during his reign. A document in Windsor Castle (No. 13015) describes George I's crown and states that the balas ruby was given to the crown by James II. It is not depicted in the portrait of Charles II by Eley or by Michael Wright. Sandford, in his account of the coronation of James II, is the first to mention it, saying the stone 'was esteemed worth £10,000'. The frame of Charles II's State Crown (*Plate 54, c*) now in the London Museum has a setting for the stone in the front cross *pattée*, and it is this that has led to confusion. The ruby was last set in the frame of this crown when it was altered for George IV. It is sometimes claimed that the Stuart sapphire was set in another cross, but this is uncertain. The arches rose in the imperial shape without any depression at the point of juncture. They were bordered with pearls, between which were set a row of coloured stones alternating with jewelled rosettes and surrounded with diamonds. The orb, or monde, on top was a large aquamarine.

The sceptre with the cross reverted to its old form without the dove, though the cross rested on an orb. The sceptre with the dove, however, retained the feature introduced into the Tudor state sceptre of the dove resting on the arms of the cross which surmounts the orb. The orb, or globe, followed the previous pattern but was heavier, weighing nearly $48\frac{1}{2}$ oz against 21 oz.

The armillae, or bracelets, were provided but not delivered at the coronation. The ampulla was fashioned in the traditional form of an eagle. The Master of the Great Wardrobe was ordered to provide the coronation vestments which were to be called St Edward's and the three swords, including *Curtana*, in addition to a sword of state. In another document[1] the Master of the Robes conceived it would be necessary to have another girdle and hangers with a sword for the King to put on after his coronation.

1 *Bodl. Ashm. MS.* 863, p. 344.

At the Restoration the new regalia, together with the royal plate, were placed in the Martin Tower at the Tower of London. No guards were provided, but an old man named Talbot Edwards, nearly eighty years of age, was made Assistant Keeper of the Jewel House and occupied the rooms in the upper storey of the Martin Tower. It was one of the perquisites of the Assistant Keeper to show the crown jewels to visitors for such fees as they agreed to pay. In 1671 there was the notorious attempt by Colonel Blood to steal the crown jewels. Blood was an Irishman who had risen to the rank of colonel in the Commonwealth Army. He was a man of great energy but a ruffian at heart. It appears that some weeks before the event Blood came to the Tower dressed as a parson and was accompanied by a woman who he passed off as his wife. Under the pretext of sudden indisposition on the part of the woman the unscrupulous pair traded on the sympathy of the old keeper, Edwards, and his wife, and rapidly fostered their friendship to the point of proposing a suitable marriage of the keeper's daughter with a so-called nephew of Blood's.

A day was arranged on which the intended bridegroom was to be introduced to the girl. The party arrived—Colonel Blood and three companions all secretly and heavily armed. Blood suggested that the old man should show them the crown whilst they waited for the girl to appear, so leaving one man on guard, they entered the Jewel House, where they immediately seized Edwards and bound him, threatening him with death if he made a noise. On his own evidence, Edwards did all he could to attract attention, whereupon he was knocked senseless, stabbed and left for dead. As the thieves were secreting the crown and orb, they were disturbed by the unexpected appearance of the keeper's son who immediately gave the alarm.

Leaving the remainder of the regalia the gang beat a hurried retreat. Overpowering the various guards, they rushed to St Catherine's Gate, where horses were awaiting them. However, after a tussle, Colonel Blood and one of his companions were caught, the others making good their escape. Several stones were lost from the crown in the struggle. As the jewels had been removed from St Edward's Crown, it must have been the State Crown that Blood attempted to steal.

The extraordinary sequel to this daring attempt was that instead of ordering his immediate execution, the King was so intrigued with the audacity and effrontery of the whole affair that the offenders were released and Blood himself was given a pension of £500 a year and a place with the King's Bodyguard.

For the coronation of James II in 1685 additional regalia had to be provided for his consort, Mary of Modena, who was also crowned. The accounts for the preparation of the regalia for this and subsequent coronations down to Queen Victoria have been published by E. A. Jones.[1] From these we learn that St Edward's Crown was reset with jewels hired for the occasion and provided with a new globe and cross. The State Crown was refreshed and repaired and several new stones were added. The sceptre was cleaned and some new gold added to the orb. For the Queen a coronet, or regal circlet, was provided to be worn up to the time of the anointing. It contained 16 oz 6 dwt, 18 gr of gold and was set with 172 diamonds, great and small, 1 ruby, 1 sapphire, 1 emerald and 78 large pearls, all of which were hired for the occasion. Vyner made the

[1] E. A. Jones: *The Old Royal Plate in the Tower of London.*

frame of the Queen's Coronation Crown and it weighed 21 oz 10 dwt, 12 gr. It was set with 419 diamonds great and small, 7 rubies, 7 sapphires, 2 emeralds and 46 very large pearls. All were hired at a cost of £530, though 1 pearl was lost. This crown had been lost sight of until recently, but early in 1956 a small crown was acquired by the Trustees of the London Museum, the frame of which has been identified as the Coronation Crown of Mary of Modena.[1] According to the official description of the coronation[2] an imperial crown of state was also provided and this is the one known as the Crown of Mary of Modena which is still kept in the Jewel House at the Tower of London. In the Jewel Book of the period, now in the Lord Chamberlain's Office, is a memorandum which related the receipt of Her Majesty's Crown of Estate, which weighed 17 oz 10 dwt and cost £70 17s. 6d. Although this is not included in the bills for the accounts for the coronation of James II quoted by Jones, it is referred to in the bills relating to the next coronation where we can recognise it by its weight and price, and it is further related that it was set with 38 very large diamonds, 523 great and small diamonds, 129 very large pearls and that these jewels were valued at £35,000, for which a charge of £1,000 was made and they were returned after the coronation.

There is no mention in the bills quoted by Jones of the Queen's rod with the dove, but in the Jewel Book of the period in the Lord Chamberlain's Office there is another memorandum which related the provision of 'one ivory rod curiously garnished with gold, enamelled, weighing 6 oz 14 dwt, 9 gr'. The gold cost £27 4s. and the ivory, the enamelling and the making cost £45.

To meet the religious feelings of James II, who was a Roman Catholic, Archbishop Sancroft was directed to revise the coronation ceremony. This he did somewhat drastically, which has been the cause of a good deal of criticism. One change on which the critics have been particularly severe is the delivery of the orb which they assert was another kind of sceptre and therefore two ornaments with the same symbolism are delivered, of which one, the orb, had to be handed back. We have already shown that the orb had quite a different origin to the sceptre and its own special symbolism. A difficulty had arisen in the XII century because of the natural desire of the English kings to adopt the orb already used on the Continent as an imperial symbol, and at the same time to retain the Anglo-Saxon sceptre and rod. The alternatives were for the orb to be delivered and handed back to free a hand for the rod, or to combine it with the sceptre. Richard II having chosen the latter method, this continued down to the middle of the XV century when the orb reverted to being a separate ornament in keeping with continental practice. Its actual use was obscure and uncertain, but it was considered an essential ornament for the sovereign to bear in the left hand when depicted seated Enthroned in Majesty. At the coronation of Charles II it had been carried in the procession along with the sceptre, but not delivered.

Sancroft no doubt would have looked to see what was the practice elsewhere. He would have found that at the imperial coronation and at other Roman Catholic royal coronations at which it was delivered, it was handed to the sovereign just after the sceptre without any special prayer. But when he turned his attention to the relatively

1 See *Illustrated London News*, 30th June 1956.
2 Francis Sandford: *The History of the Coronation of King James II*, London 1687.

new Protestant coronation rites, he would have found that a special form of prayer had been introduced in Denmark, Sweden and Bohemia. He also would have found that the *pallium* had a somewhat similar symbolism as it was cut foursquare, representing the four corners of the earth and he would therefore have thought it appropriate that the orb should be presented with the pallium with one prayer sufficing for both. He would, too, have been informed of the fact that the Church had persistently established the right to deliver the regalia to the sovereign, though on the occasion on which the orb may have been delivered in Tudor times it seems to have been handed over by a layman. Now the rights of the Church were established in respect of the orb too.

In the next reign owing to the joint sovereignty of William and Mary, which arose from the refusal of the King to act as Regent and the Queen to accept the crown without her husband as King, it was necessary for additional royal ornaments to be made so that the Queen could be crowned as Queen Regnant. The bills for the regalia for this coronation show that St Edward's Crown was lavishly decorated with 680 large diamonds, 14 large rubies, 8 sapphires, 12 emeralds, 492 large pearls valued at £20,000, for the hire of which a charge of £380 was made. The State Crown was partly reset and refreshed and a new cross was provided with 150 small diamonds at a cost of £200, but a deduction of £41 was made for the old diamonds and gold. The shape of the old state crown was changed from round to oval and the King, according to Evelyn,[1] wore it in Parliament six weeks before his coronation. One large ruby costing £60 was set in the King's sceptre which, together with the rod with the dove, were cleaned and refreshed. The jewels in the orb were reset and the enamel and gold were refreshed.

The Queen's Coronation Crown was that of Mary of Modena. It was set with jewels worth £15,000 which included 450 large diamonds, 7 large rubies, 7 sapphires, 9 emeralds, 123 pearls, 200 small pearls. £430 was charged for the setting and £600 for the hire of the jewels.

The circlet, now called the diadem, was also reset with 182 very large diamonds and other stones, and Queen Mary of Modena's Crown of State was refashioned. Gold to the weight of 2 oz 17 dwt and 12 gr was added and a new cross was made, and 'the King's great ruby' was set in the crown with a number of other stones. A new sceptre with a dove had to be made. It weighed 28 oz 12 dwt 7 gr and cost £165 18s. 6d. This and the Queen's sceptre with the cross were refurbished and adorned with precious stones at a cost of £380, but the most interesting item was the making of a second orb so that the Queen could receive the same symbol of sovereignty as the King, the orb only being delivered to a sovereign regnant. It was much smaller than the King's, weighing 21 oz 1 dwt and it cost £167 14s. In addition, there was a bill for £270 for adorning the orb with a large number of diamonds and precious stones.

In 1688 when James II attempted to flee the country, he was detained at Sheerness by some fishermen who searched him. Among the things which he took away was a diamond bodkin and the coronation ring which was said to have been the favourite ring of Mary Queen of Scots, who, at her death, sent it to James I through whom it came into the possession of Charles I, and on his execution was transmitted by Bishop Juxon to his son. It has also been said that James also took with him the aquamarine which

[1] John Evelyn: *Diaries*.

formed the monde of the crown. It was later found that the old aquamarine had been replaced by a piece of coloured glass which is still in the Tower of London.

For the coronation of Queen Anne on 23rd April 1702 a sum of £14,132 15s. was expended on the regalia. St Edward's Crown was set with hired jewels valued at £24,000, for which £960 was paid. As the King's crown was too heavy for the Queen, the State Crown of Mary of Modena was used[1] and was set with diamonds worth £79,500, the charge for the loan of which was £3,170.[2] The great ruby was set in the front cross of the crown where it had been when it was used by Queen Mary II. Mary of Modena's circlet, too, was set with diamonds worth £30,000. The two sceptres were reset with diamonds valued at £7,200. The orb, most probably that made for Mary II, was adorned with 1 very large sapphire, 1 very large and 220 large diamonds valued at £9,000. The jewels in St Edward's Crown were kept in the Lord Chamberlain's Office for a month after the coronation for the Queen to wear in Parliament, and £880 was charged for the extension of the loan.

In October 1702 the old State Crown was refurbished and reset with the old jewels. Three large diamonds for the fleur-de-lis and 78 small diamonds were added at a cost of £300 plus £350 for the workmanship. This was no doubt done so that it could be worn by the Queen at the Opening of Parliament.

At the Restoration the financial position did not permit of the same sort of accumulation of jewels as had taken place in the period of the Tudors and Stuarts though Charles II did bestow magnificent presents on his mistresses. Besides Vyner, Charles employed as Court Jeweller a celebrated French traveller and gem merchant, Sir John Chardin, who set up in London with a large collection of precious stones which he acquired in the East.

William III appointed as Court Jeweller Sir Francis Child in 1689 who supplied the King with many pieces of jewellery. Most of these pieces, however, were for presents to ambassadors, as it was fashionable at the time in the conduct of foreign affairs to exchange expensive presents. According to a document[3] Queen Mary on her death in 1694 owed a considerable sum to Mr Richard Beauvoir, a London jeweller, for diamond tags, buckles, sleeve clasps, loops, star and breast jewels. Queen Mary had inherited an historical jewel—a single pear-shaped pearl ear-ring which Charles I had frequently worn and which was said to have been rescued from the scaffold by a faithful follower who gave it to his daughter. Queen Mary gave it to the first Earl of Portland and it has descended to the present duke.[4]

James II was hardly in a position to emulate the extravagance of Louis XIV on the question of jewellery, but he did acquire some important pieces, and in 1702 he sold a diamond girdle and a buckle for £21,000 and a pair of diamond shoe-buckles for £3,000.[5] According to Horace Walpole[6] 'Queen Anne had but few jewels and those

---

1 See p. 155.
2 On this and other occasions it seems that 4% of the value of the jewels was the basis for the charge of the loan.
3 British Museum MS. Roy. 5751A f. 144.
4 Joan Evans: op. cit.
5 Joan Evans: *English Jewellery from the V century to A.D. 1800*, 1921.
6 Horace Walpole: *Reminiscences 1788*.

indifferent, except one pearl necklace given her by Prince George'. This necklace is still among the crown jewels.

THE HOUSE OF HANOVER

On the death of Queen Anne in August 1714 the direct line of the Stuart sovereigns came to an end, and by the Act of Settlement of 1701 the English throne passed to the Electress Sophia of Hanover, daughter of Elizabeth, Queen of Bohemia, who was the daughter of James I. The Electress Sophia died two months before Queen Anne. Her son, the Elector George, was then proclaimed King as George I. He was crowned at Westminster Abbey on 20th October 1714 and the regalia were again refreshed for the occasion. St Edward's Crown was but slightly adorned compared with previous occasions and only 120 large and small diamonds and 10 rubies and sapphires valued at £1,000 were used. In the procession to the Abbey the King wore a cap of estate of crimson velvet turned up with ermine, adorned with a circlet of gold enriched with diamonds. This was the circlet of Mary of Modena which was set with 20 large brilliants and roses, 120 larger brilliants and roses, and 360 smaller stones in addition to 120 diamonds round the rim. The total value of these stones was £32,000, and the usual 4% was charged for their hire. The King did not use the Crown of State of Charles II, but that which had been used by Anne,[1] probably because it was more convenient to wear with his full-bottomed wig. The diamonds with which it was set were valued at £116,700, for the hire of which the charge was £4,668. This Crown of State was set with a number of new stones on 12th March 1715 at the cost of £1,440. For the coronation the orb was set with 12 large diamonds, 30 rubies, sapphires and emeralds valued at £8,200, and the two sceptres with stones valued at £2,800.

There was no queen to be crowned but the Prince of Wales was present and he used the Coronation Crown of Mary of Modena, which was for the occasion set with stones worth £18,500. Charles II in 1660 had by warrant authorised a crown, or coronet, for the Prince of Wales which had a single arch, but from that time, until the reign of George I, there was no Prince of Wales. For the coronation one of the arches of the crown was removed.

In the British Museum is an ivory sceptre. It has the Royal Arms with motto surmounted by the royal crown and dated 1714. The case is stamped in gold with 'George I', a crown and '1714'. It is believed that this sceptre was made for use in Hanover because the English regalia were not allowed to leave the country.

[1] This crown is depicted in a lifesize and faithful water-colour drawing of the crown used at the coronation of George I, signed 'Joseph Grisoni, Delin: 1718', which is at Windsor Castle (*Plate 56, a*). Grisoni himself has written beneath it:

The Crown wherewith George King of Great Brittain was crowned; ye Cap is of crimson Velvet; ye Welt on wch. ye crown is fixed is of Ermin; ye circle & Barrs are beaten gold; ye ornaments are only silver & set with small diamonds; ye large Stones are Saphirs & Emerauds; & a few rubys very small; ye Balass in ye Cross in front was given to ye crown by King James II; ye ball on wh. ye Upper Cross is fixed is an Aque-marine, but ye lower part is gold enamelled green. Yis Cros is wore at ye Coronation and whenever ye King goes to ye Parliament: & is made new for every Coronation. It is kept in ye Tower of London. The number of the drawing is 13015.

a *Engraving of regal circlet of Mary of Modena by W. Sherwin. Sandford (p. 156)*

b (right) *Regal circlet of Mary of Modena as subsequently altered and reset. Last worn by Queen Adelaide. Tower of London (pp. 156–169)*

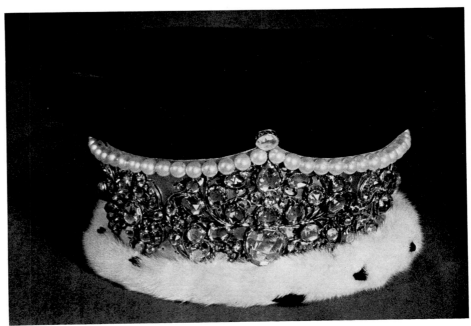

d *Engraving of State Crown of Mary of Modena by W. Sherwin. Sandford (p. 155)*

c (left) *State Crown of Mary of Modena altered and reset for Queen Anne. Tower of London (pp. 155 and 169)*

a   *Water-colour of the crown of George I by Joseph Grisoni.*
Royal Collection, Windsor Castle (p. 158)

b   *Engraving of the crown of George II by*
J. Sympson after J. Boeneke. British Museum
(p. 159)

c   *Engraving of the crown of George III by E. Rooker.*
British Museum (p. 159)

d   *Lithograph of crown of George IV by M. Gauie.*
British Museum (p. 160)

For the coronation of George II on 11th October 1727 St Edward's Crown was again but lightly set with stones. The King's circlet was richly adorned and the old State Crown was used with the addition of diamonds hired for the occasion valued at £109,200. Queen Caroline was crowned with Mary of Modena's Coronation Crown (*Plate 57, a*), the frame of which is now in the London Museum.[1] The Queen also wore the Queen's circlet in the procession to the Abbey and her Crown of State was that originally made for Mary of Modena. The three sceptres and the orb were also adorned with stones. The total value of the stones hired, excluding those in the King's State Crown, was £375,700. Opportunity was also taken to enamel the top of Mary of Modena's sceptre, to refresh St Edward's Staff and the bracelets and to fit the Sword of State and three other swords with new scabbards of cloth of gold.

We learn from Walpole[2] that Queen Caroline borrowed jewels to the value of £100,000 to adorn her petticoat, which was so immensely stiff and heavy that she could not kneel down and it was, therefore, fitted with pulleys to draw it up like a curtain. She wore the pearl necklace of Queen Anne and four other strings of pearls.

For the next coronation, that of George III and Queen Charlotte, on 22nd September 1761 the arrangements were very similar, and the value of the diamonds hired was £375,600, for which £15,024 was charged by the jewellers. The total bill came to £28,487 13s. 2d., with the following items:

			£
Fitting crown and provision of new cap	. . . . . .		9
Setting and adorning Crown of State	. . . . .		500
,,	,,	St Edward's Crown	180
,,	,,	the King's circlet	400
,,	,,	the Queen's Crown of State	400
,,	,,	the Queen's lesser crown	250
,,	,,	the Queen's circlet	300
,,	,,	the globe and three sceptres	550
,,	,,	three coronets and one circlet	600
Loan of diamonds @ 4%	. . . .		15,024
Making eight circlets	. . . .		95
Enamelling ivory sceptre, refreshing St Edward's Staff, enamelling and lining bracelets, repairing and refreshing eagle and spoon, spurs and Sword of State and three other swords	. . . .		68

The Queen's lesser crown was probably that which George III gave to Queen Charlotte on her arrival in England for the wedding. This later passed into the Hanoverian crown jewels and is still preserved.[3]

There is an item in the bill for gratuities amounting to £42 to the persons finding and bringing the jewels which broke and dropped from one of the sceptres at the coronation and other incidents. It was at this coronation that the Sword of State is said

[1] It has been discovered that the frame is not made entirely of gold and that those parts which were concealed by the velvet cap are made of brass plated with gold.
[2] Walpole: op. cit.
[3] See Chapter Eleven—Hanover.

to have been forgotten, making it necessary to borrow the ceremonial sword of the Lord Mayor. Answering the King's complaints, the Deputy Earl Marshal said: 'It is true, Sir, that there has been some neglect, but I have taken care that the next coronation shall be regulated in the exactest possible manner.' It is recorded, too, that when the King rose from the banquet the Sword of Justice was missing, as the person carrying it had slipped away to a brandy shop.[1]

In 1815 a woman forced her hands through the iron grille of the cage in which the regalia were kept in the Jewel House and wrenched the arches of the State Crown apart.

George III died in 1820 and was succeeded by his son George IV, who was crowned on 19th July 1821. There is some interesting information about the regalia, especially in connection with the coronation of George IV, in an unpublished account of the firm of Rundell, Bridge and Rundell, London jewellers, written between 1843, the year the firm was finally dissolved, and 1846, the year of the death of the compiler, George Fox.[2]

St Edward's Crown was set with crystals, coloured paste and imitation stones and apparently was not used. The King had had a very large and magnificent brilliant crown made which took the place of St Edward's Crown and the State Crown. It is true that the order of the procession mentions St Edward's Crown, but it is clear from Nayler's account that the King's new imperial crown was used throughout.[3] George Fox writes:

> The crown made for this occasion was really a magnificent one very many remarkable fine ornaments were introduced into it the principal one being a very fine round stone of the diameter of a shilling weighing –.[4] It was cut in the truest style and its proportions being mathematically correct. This stone was valued at the sum of £12,000 but on being sold in the year 1837, when many other large and fine diamonds belonging to Rundell and Bridges came to be auctioned by Messrs Sharp of Winchester Street at Willis Rooms, King Street, St James's, it was knocked down to Emmanuel Brothers for –.[4] These gentlemen bought it with other fine jewels at that sale for the Marquess of Westminster in whose possession the whole of the diamonds thus bought still remain.

The bill of the crown jewellers, Rundell and Bridge, was £735 for designing and making the crown and £6,525 for the hire of the brilliants. This charge was reckoned at 10% of the value of the stones against the usual 4%. The jewels were on loan from 1st April 1820 to 29th April 1823 and several subsequent charges were made for the extension of time. George IV wanted to adorn the crown with a design of roses, thistles and shamrocks instead of fleurs-de-lis, but the (Privy) Council was informed that the heralds held that this could not be done because the fleur-de-lis had been in use since before Edward the Confessor. The King, however, had his way by including these emblems in the regal circlet which he wore on his way to the coronation.[5]

[1] Walpole: op. cit.

[2] The original manuscript was presented to the Baker Library, Harvard University by Mrs Lyden Burgess Brownson, the great-granddaughter of the writer. A photostat copy is in the Victoria and Albert Museum.

[3] Sir George Nayler, Garter Principal King at Arms: *The Coronation of His Most Sacred Majesty King George IV*, (MDCCCXXIV).

[4] These figures are left blank in the original manuscript.

[5] For the subsequent history of which see p. 189.

a Coronation crown of Mary of Modena as reset for Queen
Caroline. London Museum (p. 159)

b Frame of crown of George IV.
London Museum (p. 160)

c Lithograph of crown of Queen Adelaide by Rundell Bridge
and Company. British Museum (pp. 161 and 163)

d Frame of crown of Queen Adelaide.
London Museum (p. 165)

a *Imperial State Crown of Queen Victoria.
Photograph by the late Sir Benjamin
Stone. Birmingham Reference Library*
(p. 163)

c *Frame of Imperial State Crown of Queen Victoria.
London Museum* (p. 167)

b (left) *Imperial State Crown of Queen Victoria as
reset for George V*

The old State Crown was also reset and a large sapphire furnished by the jewellers at the price of £700 was set in the diamond cross at the back. George Fox says:

> Two very badly shaped and worse coloured pearls were suspended from the cross. According to the Jewel Office these were deemed to be of enormous value and had been pawned to the Dutch Government for £50,000. For £5 Rundell and Bridge exchanged one for a better specimen and the originals were sold to a Jew dealer for £2.

George Fox also gives the value placed on some of the other ornaments, among which were St Edward's Crown, valued at £300, the Queen's crown, valued at £150, and the orb at £200.

The King's orb was provided with a new diamond, a coloured stone rosette, 402 new pearls and 1 large pearl on top of the cross, the cost being £149 15s. The King's gold sceptre was furnished with a new rose, thistle and shamrock on top and some new gold and stones added at a total cost of £127 10s. Some other minor repairs were made to the splendid new jewelled sword.

When William IV succeeded to the throne in 1831 he was very anxious to dispense with the coronation ceremony. When it was found that this could not be done, it was agreed to omit all but the ceremony in the Abbey and to conduct it on an economical basis. The total of Rundell and Bridge's bill for the preparation and cleaning of the regalia was only £1,349 11s. 8d., and this included the resetting of Queen Adelaide's crown. There was no charge for the hire of jewels and as the old Imperial State Crown of Charles II was the only one available set with jewels, it must have been that which was used. The King complained after the ceremony of the discomfort caused by the weight of the crown, which was aggravated by the fact that he was suffering from toothache. Greville[1] has left an interesting story about Queen Adelaide's crown. He related how on 8th August 1831 he rode to Windsor:

> to settle with the Queen what sort of crown she would have to be crowned in. I was ushered into the King's presence. . . . He sent for the Queen, who came with the Landgravine and one of the King's daughters . . . she looked at the drawings, meant apparently to be civil to me in her ungracious way and said she would have none of our crowns, that she did not like to wear a hired crown and asked me if I thought it was right that she should. I said, 'Madam, I can only say that the late King wore one at his coronation.' However, she said: 'I do not like it and I have got jewels enough so I will have one made up myself.' The King said to me: 'Very well, then, you will have to pay for the setting.' 'Oh no!' she said, 'I shall pay for it all myself.'

The Hanoverian kings accumulated a very large collection of personal jewellery. Queen Caroline had a fine pearl necklace of her own, one from Anspach, one from Zelland and another from elsewhere. After she had worn them at the coronation, the best pearls were taken from the four and made into one magnificent necklace. George II gave her many jewels and some very fine pearls, while the King's uncle, the Duke of York, sent her 6 pearls.[2] Queen Charlotte, too, received a large number of jewels. Her most splendid diamonds were given to her by the Nawab of Arcot. These consisted of 5 brilliants, the largest was 151 gr, oval in shape and was set in a necklace with the two smallest drop-shaped brilliants. The other two were set as ear-rings and weighed

---

[1] C. C. Greville: *Journal of the Reign of George IV and William IV*, Vol. II.

[2] Walpole: op. cit.

92 and $131\frac{1}{2}$ gr. In 1765 the Mogul Emperor, Shah Alam, transmitted through Lord Clive to George III a present of jewellery valued at several lakhs of rupees. These consisted of:

> an exceeding fine string of pearls with an awbray[1] studded with diamonds; a perfume box in the form of a casket on a tray, both objects being studded with diamonds; a dagger with a handle of jasper to fasten it to the girdle; a sword of gold mounted with diamonds, and with buckles of diamonds; a shield with four flowers of gold enamelled with a belt and buckles set with diamonds.

Apparently the acknowledgment of these gifts went astray, but in 1769 a letter was addressed to the Emperor from the King expressing regret that he had not received proper acknowledgment of 'the magnificent testimony of your friendship for us' and framed portraits of the King and Queen were sent with the letter.[2] Another gift to George III was a rose diamond of 63 gr given by the Grand Seigneur.[3] This is depicted in a drawing in the Victoria and Albert Museum, as also are the diamonds given to Queen Charlotte by the Nawab of Arcot and the brilliant of $125\frac{1}{2}$ gr worn in the crown of George IV.[4] The drawing describes them as a crown suite being in the possession of Rundell and Bridge. The Arcot diamonds were sold to Rundell and Bridge in accordance with Queen Charlotte's will, which included a clause about her 'personals' which read 'those of chief value being the jewels. First those the King bought for £50,000 and gave to me. Secondly those presented to me by the Nawab of Arcot . . . I give and bequeath the jewels received from the Nawab of Arcot to my four remaining daughters, or to the survivors or survivor in case they or any of them should die before me, and I direct that these jewels should be sold and that the produce . . . should be divided among them, my said remaining daughters or their survivors, share and share alike'.

Messrs Rundell, Bridge and Co. had been appointed jewellers and silversmiths to the Crown by George III and in 1834 on the death of John Bridge the firm was sold and his Executors ordered the sale of the diamonds. The sale took place on 20th July 1837 at Willis's Rooms and the two Arcot Diamonds, which were set as ear-rings and weighed 93 and $131\frac{1}{2}$ gr (57.30 carats) were bought for £11,000 by the Marquess of Westminster, who at the same time bought the large diamond of $125\frac{1}{2}$ gr which had been in George IV's crown for £3,500 as a birthday present for his wife.[5]

All these jewels came into the possession of George IV on the death of George III and we have an interesting comment on the matter by Greville.[6] George III had made a will in 1770 and in 1810 he had made another will, but for various reasons he always put off signing it. After his death, therefore, the only good will was the original one of 1770. This was produced and read, and the only legatee was the Duke of York.

---

[1] A breast ornament in the form of a cluster of jewels.

[2] For the correspondence see India Office Records. Home Misc., Vol. 134, p. 123.

[3] A title used by the Sultan of Turkey.

[4] See contemporary drawings in the Victoria and Albert Museum, Drawings, D.401–99.

[5] The Marquess also bought the Nassack diamond of 357 gr ($78\frac{5}{8}$ carats) for £7,200. It was sold by his successor nearly a century later. The two Arcot diamonds and the round brilliant were set in a tiara, which was sold at Sotheby's on 25th June 1959 for £105,000 to Mr Harry Winston of New York.

[6] Greville: op. cit.

Imperial State Crown of Queen Elizabeth II. Tower of London (pp. 167 and 168)

a   *Regal circlet in diamonds and pearls made for George IV* (pp. 160 and 189)

b   *Small diamond crown made for Queen Victoria. Tower of London* (pp. 166 and 170)

c   *Coronation crown made for Queen Alexandra. From the late Sir Benjamin Stone Collection. Birmingham Reference Library* (p. 166)

d   *Frame of regal circlet made for Queen Victoria to take the Koh-i-Nur. London Museum* (p. 189)

Now arose a difficulty whether the property of the late King demised to the King or to the Crown. The Chancellor said that the only person who had anything to say to the will was the Duke of York but the Duke and the King differed in regard to the right of inheritance and the Duke wishing to avoid any dispute or discussion on the subject begged to wash his hands of the whole matter. The King conceived that the whole of the late King's property devolved upon him personally and not upon the Crown and he consequently appropriated himself the whole of the money and jewels. The money did not amount to more than £120,000. So touchy is he about pecuniary matters that his Ministers have never dared to remonstrate with him, nor to tell him that he has no right so to act. The consequence is that he has spent the money and has taken to himself the jewels as his own private property. The Duke thinks that he has no right thus to appropriate their Father's property but that it belongs to the Crown. The King has acted in a like manner with regard to Queen Charlotte's jewels. She possessed a great quantity some of which had been given her by the late King on her marriage and the rest she had received in presents at different times. Those which the late King had given her she conceived to belong to the Crown and left them back to the present King. The rest she left to her daughters. The King has also appropriated the Queen's (Caroline's) jewels to himself and conceives that they are his undoubted private property. The Duke thinks that the Ministers ought to have taken the opportunity at the coronation when a new crown was to be provided to state to him the truth with regard to the jewels and to suggest that they should be converted to that purpose. This, however, they dared not do and so the matter remains.

It seems that the terms of Queen Charlotte's will respecting her jewels were not executed until after the coronation of William IV, although she had died in 1818. The Arcot diamonds and the circular diamond used in the crown of George IV can be seen in the lithograph of the crown of Queen Adelaide (*Plate 57, c*).

On the death of William IV, his niece Victoria ascended the throne and we enter a period which brings us down to the present day. The coronation took place in 1838, on 20th June. In accordance with the precedent of the coronation of William IV the ceremony was shorn of its procession and banquet. The bill of the Crown Jewellers, Rundell and Bridge, came to no more than £1,000 for 'resetting the whole of the diamonds and precious stones of the old crown into a new imperial crown with the addition of brilliants, pearls and a fine sapphire'. The other regalia were merely cleaned and repaired.

As at the two previous coronations, St Edward's Crown, no doubt because of its inconvenient size, shape and weight, was not used. It does not seem that it was present at the ceremony and the coronation service had degenerated to such an extent that St Edward's Crown was not even mentioned in the rubrics. Again, in the inventory taken in 1858 it is not described as St Edward's Crown but as 'the old Imperial Crown of gold set with imitation stones and imitation pearls with a red velvet cap', the gross troy weight being 82 oz 3 dwt.

For the first part of the ceremony the Queen wore a circlet made for George IV which was set with brilliants from the collection of state jewels. The new Imperial Crown is described as follows in the 1858 inventory:

The Imperial State Crown of her Majesty Queen Victoria was made by Messrs Rundell and Bridge in the year 1838 with jewels taken from old crowns and others furnished by command of Her Majesty.

It consists of diamonds, pearls, rubies, sapphires and emeralds, has a crimson velvet cap with ermine border and lined with white silk. Its gross troy weight 39 oz 5 dwt.

The lower part of the band and above the ermine border consists of a row of 129 pearls and the upper part of the band a row of 112 pearls, between which in front of the crown is a large, partly drilled sapphire purchased for the crown by His Majesty George IV.

At the back is a sapphire of smaller size and 6 other sapphires (3 on each side) between which are 8 emeralds. Above and below the 7 sapphires are 14 diamonds and around the 8 emeralds 128 diamonds.

Between the emeralds and sapphires are 16 trefoil ornaments containing 160 diamonds.

Above the band are 8 sapphires surmounted by 8 diamonds, between which are eight festoons containing 148 diamonds.

In the front of the crown and in the centre of a diamond Maltese cross is the famous ruby said to have been given to Edward, Prince of Wales, son of Edward III (called the Black Prince) by Don Pedro, King of Castile, after the Battle of Najera near Vittoria, A.D. 1367. This ruby was worn in the helm of Henry V at the Battle of Agincourt, A.D. 1415. It is pierced quite through after the Eastern custom, the upper part of the piercing being filled up by a small ruby. Round this ruby to form the cross are 75 brilliant diamonds.

Three other Maltese crosses form the two sides and back of the crown and have emerald centres and contain respectively 132, 124, and 130 brilliant diamonds.

Between the four Maltese crosses are four ornaments in the form of the French fleur-de-lis with 4 rubies in the centres and surrounded by rose diamonds containing respectively 85, 86 and 87 diamonds. From the Maltese crosses issue four imperial arches composed of oak leaves[1] and acorns, the leaves containing 728 rose, table and brilliant diamonds. 32 pearls form the acorns set in cups containing 54 rose diamonds and 1 table diamond.

The total of diamonds in arches and acorns is 108 brilliants, 116 table and 559 rose diamonds.

From the upper part of the arches are 4 large pendant pear-shaped pearls with rose diamond cups containing 12 rose diamonds and stems containing 24 very small rose diamonds.

Above the arch stands the mound containing in the lower hemisphere 304 brilliants and in the upper 244 brilliants. The zone and arc are composed of 33 rose diamonds.

The cross on the summit has a rose-cut sapphire in the centre surrounded by 4 large brilliants and 108 smaller brilliants.

The following is a copy of Rundell and Bridge's account at the period of their re-setting of the Imperial Crown:

Original Jewels

1 very large uncut ruby	170 carats
1 large full spread sapphire	104 $\frac{1}{8}$ carats
15 large sapphires	166 $\frac{1}{4}$ carats
11 emeralds	55 $\frac{1}{2}$ $\frac{1}{4}$ $\frac{1}{8}$ carats
4 rubies	6 $\frac{1}{4}$ carats
1,312 brilliants (various sizes)	265 $\frac{1}{2}$ $\frac{1}{8}$ $\frac{1}{16}$ carats
928 roses	256 $\frac{1}{4}$ carats
159 table diamonds	50 $\frac{1}{2}$ $\frac{1}{8}$ $\frac{1}{16}$ carats
3 drop-shaped pearls	71 $\frac{1}{2}$ carats

[1] The oak leaves and acorns are usually said to symbolise the incident of Charles II hiding in the oak tree at Boscobel. The oak leaves first appear in the engraving of the crown of George III (*Plate 56, c*) and the acorns in the crown of George IV (*Plate 57, b*).

Furnished by R. and B.

1	pearl drop	
32	pearls	373 carats
1	sapphire	$5 \frac{1}{8}$ carats
53	brilliants (table cut)	$23 \frac{1}{2} \frac{1}{4}$ carats
19	brilliants	$2 \frac{1}{8}$ carats
300	roses	$20 \frac{1}{2} \frac{1}{4}$ carats
13	roses	$\frac{1}{2} \frac{1}{8} \frac{1}{16}$ carats

There are two or three points to notice. This is the first official mention of the Black Prince's ruby, or that it was in the King's crown at the Battle of Agincourt. The fleurs-de-lis are attributed to the French form, although, as has been related in this chapter, it was adopted independently of French practice. The additional stones seem to have been furnished by the Crown Jewellers and not taken from a stock of state jewels as has sometimes been stated. The rest of the regalia were unchanged.

There are various stories about the coronation, which seems to have been carried out carelessly and with inadequate preparation and rehearsal. The critics of Archbishop Sancroft must have been pleased with the incident relating to the orb. The Queen had already said to Lord John Thynne, who officiated for the Dean of Westminster, 'Pray tell me what I am to do, for they do not know.' When the orb was put into her hand she said to him: 'What am I to do with it?' 'Your Majesty is to carry it, if you please, in your hand'. 'Am I?' she said. 'It is very heavy.' The ruby ring had been made for her little finger instead of the third on which the rubric prescribes that it should be put. When the Archbishop was to put it on she extended the former, but he said it must be on the latter. She said it was too small and she could not get it on. He said it was right to put it there and as he insisted she yielded, but had to take off her other rings and then this was forced on, but it hurt her very much and as soon as the ceremony was over she was obliged to bathe her finger in iced water to get it off. The noise and confusion was very great when the medals were thrown about by Lord Surrey, everybody scrambling in their might and main to get them and none more vigorously than the Maids of Honour. Lord Rolle, who was between eighty and ninety, fell down as as he was getting up the steps of the throne.[1]

About this time the frames of the old imperial state crowns of Charles II and the state crown of George IV and the crown used by Queen Adelaide became the property of Lord Amherst of Hackney. They are now on loan to the London Museum (*Plate 57, d*). That of Charles II is of silver, the other two are of gold.

Early in Queen Victoria's reign her uncle, Ernest Augustus, Duke of Cumberland, who had become King of Hanover, expected to receive that part of the jewellery left by William IV which could be regarded as Hanoverian property. A legal claim was made and despite the King pressing upon the Queen the necessity for bringing the dispute to a settlement, there were interminable delays and it was not until 1857 that the Commission which had been appointed made its award.[2] The jewels enumerated were handed over, but because of their pedigree, the celebrated so-called Hanoverian pearls

[1] Greville: *Journal of the Reign of Queen Victoria*, Vol. I.
[2] See Chapter Eleven—Hanover.

remained the property of the British royal family. They have a most interesting history. They had been given to Mary Queen of Scots by her husband the Dauphin and by his mother, Catherine de Medici, who had originally received them from her cousin's grandfather, Pope Clement VII, on the occasion of her marriage. After Mary's execution, they were sent to London for sale, and some information about these pearls is contained in a letter which De la Forest, the French Ambassador in London, addressed to Queen Catherine de Medici. He wrote from London on 8th May 1658:

> I enquired particularly as to the jewels of the Queen of Scotland which are here. I have found out that the large pearls for which Her Majesty once wrote to me are here, and as specified to me there are six strings on which they are strung like rosary beads and besides these there are 25 separate pearls even more beautiful and bigger than those which are strung, the greater part like nutmegs. They had not been three days before they were valued by divers merchants, the Queen (Elizabeth) wishing to take them for the sum at which they were valued. They were first shown to three or four goldsmiths and jewellers of this town who valued them at £3,000, i.e. 10,000 écus, offering to deliver them for that sum if desired. Several Italian merchants, too, saw them afterwards and priced them at 12,000 écus, which is about the price, according to what I was told, for which the Queen will take them. There is a Genoese who saw them after all the others who valued them at 16,000 écus, but I think that 12,000 will be the price.

These and her own pearls formed the nucleus of the great collection of pearls which have been passed down to the present day. They were inherited by James I, who gave them to his daughter Elizabeth, Queen of Bohemia, and were handed down by inheritance through the Electress Sophia to the Hanoverian Kings of England. In 1857 they were still recorded to be the finest pearls in Europe.[1]

Queen Victoria found the State Crown inconvenient not only because of its weight but because of the formalities needed for bringing it out of the Tower when required, and on 2nd March 1870 a new small imperial crown was made. This was placed in the Tower of London in May 1937 by the order of King George VI.

King Edward VII succeeded his mother in 1901, and the coronation which was to have been held in June 1902 had to be postponed until 9th August owing to his illness. It had originally been intended that St Edward's Crown should be used for the crowning and then replaced by the Imperial State Crown. To spare the King it was not used, in fact, but the official account of the ceremony written by H. Farnham Burke, Somerset Herald, makes it clear that St Edward's Crown was present throughout the ceremony.

A new crown was made for Queen Alexandra for the coronation. Although this retained the conventional shape of English crowns, there were new features, the frame being of platinum and not of gold. The arches, numbering four instead of two, are in the form of eight ogee-shaped half-arches. It was set entirely with brilliants with the Koh-i-Nur in the front cross *pattée*. The frame of this crown, set with paste, is now in the London Museum.

In 1907 the Cullinan Diamond was presented to King Edward VII by the Government of the Transvaal, and the King ordered the largest brilliant, a pear-shaped diamond

---

[1] The great ropes of pearls can be seen in the portrait of Queen Elizabeth I, by Isaac Oliver (*Plate 50, b*) and in the portrait of Elizabeth, Electress Palatine, Queen of Bohemia, by van Miereveldt, and of Queen Alexandra, by Sir Luke Fildes.

a   *St Edward's Crown, as set for King George V, 1911. Tower of London* (pp. 167 and 168)

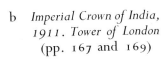

b   *Imperial Crown of India, 1911. Tower of London* (pp. 167 and 169)

a   *Queen Mary's crown 1911. Tower of London* (pp. 167 and 169)

b   *Crown of Queen Elizabeth, consort of King George VI. Tower of London* (pp. 167 and 169)

of $516\frac{1}{2}$ carats, to be added to the sceptre and known as the Star of Africa. The second Star of Africa, a brilliant of $309\frac{1}{3}$ carats, was placed in the brow of the State Crown, the Stuart sapphire being moved to the back.

THE HOUSE OF WINDSOR

For King George V's coronation on 22nd June 1911 St Edward's Crown was restored to its proper place and used for the act of crowning (*Plate 61, a*). It was entirely refurbished and the imitation stones were replaced by semi-precious stones. Although the original symbolic meanings do not seem to have been taken into account, this arrangement did in fact return to the traditional usage. It was worn, however, for only a few minutes and the Imperial State Crown was then substituted. A new crown was made for Queen Mary. It was in the traditional pattern with eight ogee-shaped half-arches. The Koh-i-Nur was set in the front cross *pattée*. The third stone from the Cullinan, known as the third Star of Africa, of 92 carats was set in the surmounting cross, and the fourth Star of Africa, a square-shaped diamond of 62 carats, was set in the circlet above the brow. Queen Mary presented this crown to her husband for the future use of queens consort of England. In 1911, when George V visited India to attend the Coronation Durbar at Delhi, it was found that it would be unconstitutional for the State Crown to leave England and a new crown, known as the Imperial Crown of India, was made for the occasion. It is now in the Tower of London. With the creation of the Dominions of India and Pakistan the Indian Empire was dissolved on 15th August 1947. An authoritative note on the future of the Imperial Crown of India is given by Sir John Wheeler-Bennett in his book *King George VI: His Life and Reign*. He writes:

> the question of the disposal of the Crown of India, specially fashioned for the Coronation Durbar at Delhi in 1911, also came up for discussion (in 1947). Whilst it had been purchased out of Indian revenues at the cost of £60,000 by the Secretary of State in Council on behalf of the Government of India and was vested in His Majesty, it was agreed between the King and the Prime Minister that as long as the two new Dominions remained in the Commonwealth it would seem proper that the Crown should be retained among the crown jewels but that if at a later date one or both of the Dominions of India and Pakistan were to secede it might be contended that in view of the fact that it had been purchased out of Indian funds the crown should be vested in some Indian authority.

King George VI was crowned with his consort on 12th May 1937. Queen Mary attended the coronation ceremony as Queen Mother and wore her crown without the arches, and it, therefore, was not available for Queen Elizabeth, for whom a new crown was made in which was set the Koh-i-Nur which now, by tradition, adorns the crowns of queens consort (*Plate 62, b*).

Queen Elizabeth II was crowned on 2nd June 1953. It was found that the frame of the old Imperial Crown was worn out and a new crown was made. The design was the same as that of Queen Victoria, except that the arches are flatter and give it a more pleasing appearance. The frame of Queen Victoria's crown is now in the London Museum (*Plate 58, c*). The only other change which took place in the regalia on this occasion was that a new pair of bracelets were made and presented to the Queen by the Governments of the Commonwealth and they were delivered to the Queen at the coronation.

Today there are kept in the Jewel House in the Wakefield Tower of the Tower of London:

> nine crowns;
> five sceptres;
> St Edward's Staff;
> two orbs;
> five swords;
> two pairs of bracelets;
> three coronation rings;
> one pair of spurs;
> the ampulla and spoon for the anointing;
> the old monde from George III's crown (*Plate 69, c*).

Besides these ornaments are the communion plate, the christening font and vessels, various items of plate, eight maces, fifteen silver trumpets, Maundy coins and the Insignia of the Orders of Chivalry.

St Edward's Crown (Plate 61, a)

The frame is of gold and probably unchanged since it was made by Vyner in 1661. It follows the conventional shape of a modern royal crown. The rigid gold circlet is bordered on its upper and lower edges with silver pearls. On the band are twelve precious or semi-precious stones in diamond clusters which were set in the crown on the occasion of the coronation of George V. The stones are sapphire, cape ruby, amethyst, tourmaline, white topaz, yellow topaz, spinel, peridot, carbuncle, garnet, jargoon and rose diamond.[1] On the circlet rests four crosses *pattée* and four fleurs-de-lis decorated with diamonds and precious stones. From behind the crosses spring the two arches which are depressed at the centre. They are bordered with silver pearls and the centre ornaments each consist of 5 diamonds alternating with semi-precious stones. At the junction of the arches rests a golden orb or monde with a jewelled girdle surmounted by a cross set with diamonds and precious stones from the arms of which hang 2 drop-shaped silver pearls. There are a total of about 440 stones, including sixteen large stones set in the circlet. Originally the crown was only set with precious stones on the occasions of coronations and it was used to crown Charles II, James II, William III, Anne, George I, George II, George III, George V, George VI and Elizabeth II. It was thus not used for four consecutive coronations and during that time it was set with paste and imitation pearls. It now is permanently set with diamonds precious and semi-precious stones. The circumference of the crown is 26 in., the height 12 in., and the weight 4 lb 15 oz.

The Imperial Crown of State made for Queen Elizabeth II in 1953 (Plate 59)

The crown follows the pattern of that made for Queen Victoria in 1838. The crown contains 3,250 diamonds and precious stones, including such historical stones as St Edward's sapphire, the Black Prince's ruby, Queen Elizabeth's ear-rings, the Stuart sapphire and the Second Star of Africa. A pearl from the River Conway was at one time placed in the State Crown but it is not known if it has survived or can be identified. The frame is of gold but the settings of the stones

[1] Some of the rose diamonds may be aquamarines.

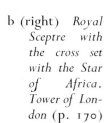

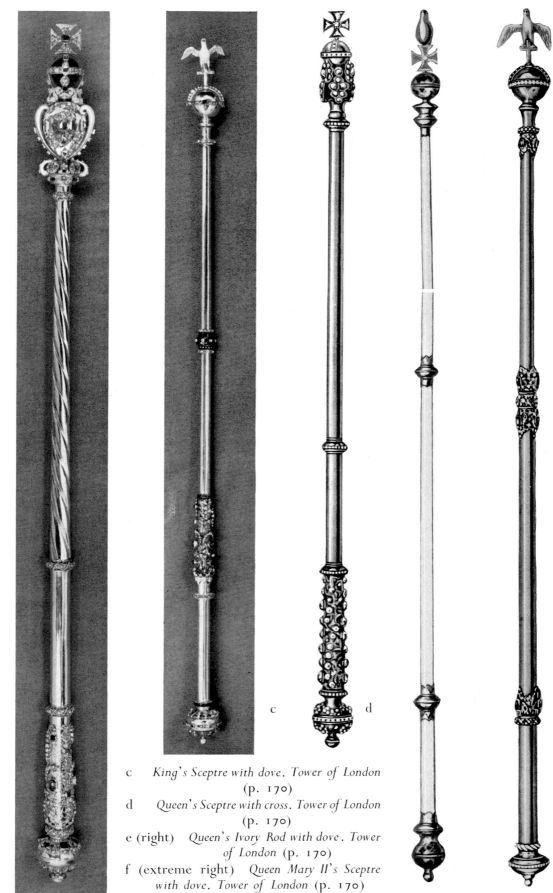

a   *Head of Royal Sceptre before introduction of the Star of Africa. From Cyril Davenport's* The English Regalia *(p. 170)*

b (right)   *Royal Sceptre with the cross set with the Star of Africa. Tower of London (p. 170)*

c   *King's Sceptre with dove. Tower of London (p. 170)*

d   *Queen's Sceptre with cross. Tower of London (p. 170)*

e (right)   *Queen's Ivory Rod with dove. Tower of London (p. 170)*

f (extreme right)   *Queen Mary II's Sceptre with dove. Tower of London (p. 170)*

a   *Royal orb. Tower of London*
    (pp. 153 and 171)

b   *Queen's orb. Tower of London*
    (pp. 156 and 171)

are silver. Inside is a Cap of Estate of purple velvet turned up with minever. This crown is used on state occasions such as the Opening of Parliament. The circumference is 23¾ in., height 12⅜ in. and weight 2 lb 13 oz.

The Imperial Crown of India (Plate 61, b)

This crown was made in 1911 at a cost of £60,000 and follows the general design of the Imperial State Crown except that there are eight ogee-shaped half-arches decorated with a pattern of lotus flowers. It is a beautiful and splendid crown decorated with 6,170 diamonds, 4 sapphires, 4 rubies and 9 emeralds of the first water. The emerald in the front is a stone of rare size and quality, weighing 36 carats. Another splendid emerald is set in the centre of the cross surmounting the monde. In the cross in front of the circle is a magnificent oriental ruby. Inside is a purple velvet cap of estate turned up with minever.

Queen Mary of Modena's Crown (Plate 55, c and d)

This was originally made as the Crown of State for Mary of Modena in 1685 but was remade for Queen Mary II and subsequently used by Queen Anne, George I and Queen Caroline. It is of gold set with rose-cut stones in silver and pearls with a red velvet cap. Gross weight 25 oz 15 dwt.

Queen Mary of Modena's Diadem (Plate 55, a and b)

This regal circlet was originally made in 1685, was reset for Queen Mary II and afterwards used by queens consort. It was also used by George I in the procession to his coronation. It was last used by Queen Adelaide in 1831 and has since been superseded by George IV's circlet. It is of gold set with rose-cut stones in silver and a row of pearls with a red velvet cap. Gross weight 14 oz 4 dwt.

Queen Mary's Crown (Plate 62, a)

This was made by Messrs Garrard & Company in 1911 and is a beautiful crown with the finest modern workmanship. Only diamonds are used in its decoration. The circlet is bordered by rows of small diamonds between which are set a number of diamond clusters with the Fourth Star of Africa of 61 carats in the front above the brow. The four crosses *pattées* and four fleurs-de-lis are set with diamonds and in the front cross the Koh-i-Nur of 106⅙ carats was originally set. From behind the crosses and fleurs-de-lis spring eight ogee-shaped half-arches which are detachable, as are the lesser Stars of Africa. These half-arches rise steeply and hold a diamond monde and cross in the centre of which is set the Third Star of Africa of 92 carats. Inside is a purple velvet cap turned up with minever. The circumference is 23⅝ in., height 11¼ in., weight 1 lb 9 oz.

Queen Elizabeth the Queen Mother's Crown (Plate 62, b)

This was made in 1937 by Messrs Garrard & Company. The crown follows the traditional pattern of a circlet with four crosses *pattées* and four fleurs-de-lis with four ogee-shaped half-arches. The diamonds for the circlet, including sixteen large stones, were taken from a circlet which had been made for Queen Victoria in 1858 and in which the Koh-i-Nur was mounted. The Koh-i-Nur is set in the front cross *pattée* and is detachable. The centre diamond on the band of the circlet was originally in a stomacher presented to Queen Victoria by the Sultan of Turkey. The diamonds in the arches, the monde and the surmounting cross *pattée* were supplied by Messrs Garrard & Co. The drop-shaped diamond in the surmounting cross was originally in a necklace from the Treasury of Lahore, presented to Queen Victoria in 1851 by the Honourable East India Company but was set in a diamond necklace. It weighed 22·60 carats which on trimming in 1937 was reduced to 22·48 carats. It is detachable for use on the necklace as before.

Queen Victoria's Small Diamond Imperial Crown (Plate 60, b)

This beautiful crown was made on 2nd March 1870. There are 1,162 brilliants and 138 rose diamonds weighing 132$\frac{17}{32}$ carats which were taken from a large fringe necklace.

The Prince of Wales' Crown (Plate 67, a)

This is of gold with a single arch and contains a red velvet cap. It weighs 29 oz 18 dwt. It was made for Frederick Louis, son of George II, on his creation as Prince of Wales and was carried before him when he was introduced into the House of Lords in 1783. It does not seem to have been used subsequently.

The King's Sceptre (Plate 63, b)

This is also used by queens regnant and is a gold rod 36$\frac{1}{4}$ in. long and weighs 2 lb 12 oz. It is ornamented with coloured enamel and set with precious stones in pommels. In all there are 272 diamonds, mostly rose or table cut, 25 rubies, 12 emeralds, and 1 sapphire. A fine round amethyst forms the monde. This has certainly been in the sceptre since the reign of James II[1] and possibly since 1661.

The First Star of Africa of 530 carats, the largest brilliant in the world, was added by Edward VII and makes it the most magnificent sceptre in Europe, a place previously held by the Russian Imperial Sceptre.

The King's Rod with the Dove (Plate 63, c)

This is 43$\frac{1}{2}$ in. long and is set with 199 rose and table-cut diamonds, 58 rubies, 10 emeralds and 4 sapphires. The sceptre is surmounted by an orb and cross, on the arms of which is a white enamelled dove with its wings displayed.

The Queen's Sceptre with the Cross (Plate 63, d)

This is 33$\frac{1}{2}$ in. long and was made for Mary of Modena. It is of gold set with crystals and weighs 23 oz 4 dwt.

The Queen's Ivory Rod (Plate 63, e)

This is 37$\frac{1}{2}$ in. long and was also made for Mary of Modena. It is an ivory rod mounted with gold and with two gold bands. At the bottom is a gold and enamelled knob and on the top is a gold and enamelled orb and cross on which sits a white enamelled dove with closed wings. The enamel on the knob and orb is of similar workmanship to that on the bracelets made in 1681. It weighs 11 oz 18 dwt.

The Queen's Sceptre with the Dove (Plate 63, f)

This was made for the coronation of Mary II as Queen Regnant. It is similar to the King's sceptre with the dove. It is 36 in. long and weighs 34 oz. It was only used on one occasion and was then lost sight of until 1814 when it was found behind the wainscoting of the old Jewel House.

St Edward's Staff

This is 56 in. long and is of gold, ornamented with acanthus and palm leaves and has a tapering steel point at the lower end with an orb and cross on the summit. The claim that it is to guide the footsteps of the king is a romantic idea based on the erroneous assumption that it is related to a bishop's crozier. It is not delivered to the sovereign nor is it carried by him, though it is borne by a nobleman at the coronation. The most likely explanation is that it is derived from the

---

[1] It can be seen in Kneller's portrait of that King.

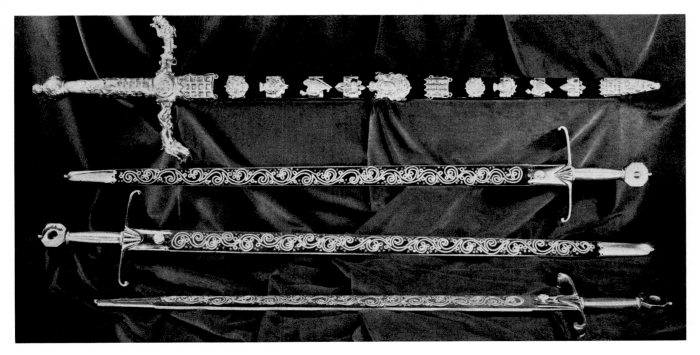

a   (i) *Sword of State*; (ii) *Sword of Justice to the Temporality*; (iii) *Sword of Justice to the Spirituality*; (iv) *Curtana or Sword of Mercy. Tower of London* (p. 172)

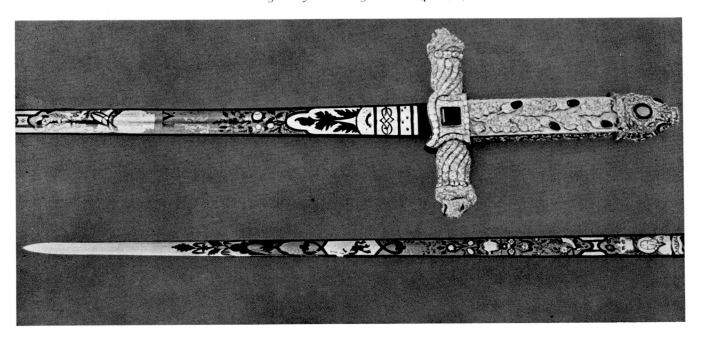

b   *Jewelled Sword of State. Tower of London* (p. 172)

c   *Jewelled Sword of State in scabbard* (p. 172)

a   *Ampulla and spoon. Tower of London*
(pp. 172 and 173)

b (i)   *Bracelets of Charles II.*
Tower of London
(p. 171)

b (ii)   *Coronation spurs.*
Tower of London
(p. 171)

c   *Coronation bracelets of Queen*
Elizabeth II. Tower of London
(p. 171)

old Anglo-Saxon verge or *baculus* which was a long staff that fell into disuse and was replaced by the shorter rod with the dove. At one time it contained a relic and it is possible that it was the same as the Verge of Moses. It weighs 56 oz 6 dwt.

The King's Orb (Plate 64, a)

This is of gold. The zone is composed of sixteen clusters containing 12 rubies, 6 emeralds, 6 sapphires and 128 rose-cut diamonds, bordered by two rows of 266 pearls. The arch is composed of six clusters containing 6 rubies, 2 emeralds, 2 sapphires and 48 rose-cut diamonds, bordered by two rows of 138 pearls, surmounted by an amethyst placed on a band of eight rows in which diamonds bearing a cross *pattée* composed of 1 emerald, 1 sapphire, 7 pearls and 182 rose-cut diamonds. It weighs 35 oz 11 dwt. The orb is probably in very much the same state as when it was originally made for Charles II in 1661. It was refreshed for James II. The stones were reset and some new gold added for William III. It does not seem to have been used at the next four coronations, but for George IV the old pearls were replaced by new ones and 1 new diamond and a coloured stone rosette were added. For Queen Victoria 6 small diamonds were added. It weighs 42 oz 7 dwt.

The Queen's Orb (Plate 64, b)

This was made for Queen Mary II. It is of gold and weighs 35 oz 11 dwt. From the Crown Jeweller's bills we learn that it was richly adorned with jewels hired for the occasion of the coronations of Anne and the first three Georges. Because of its smaller size and lesser weight it was no doubt found to be more convenient than the king's orb.

The Golden Spurs called St George's or the Knightly Spurs (Plate 66, b)

These were originally not part of the regalia but were part of the king's insignia as a knight. They are chased and furnished with buckles and velvet fittings which were altered for George IV. They weigh 10 oz 12 gr.

Bracelets (Plate 66, c)

Although the bracelets were not delivered to the sovereign at the time of the early Stuarts there was a pair among the regalia that were destroyed in 1649 which no doubt was the reason for a pair being included in the new regalia in 1661. Since the time of Charles II they have been carried at the coronation until that of Elizabeth II when a new pair was made with which the sovereign was invested. The pair made in 1661 are of gold enamelled with rose, thistle, fleurs-de-lis and harp, and lined with red velvet. They weigh 6 oz 4 dwt. The bracelets made for the coronation of Elizabeth II in 1953 were presented jointly by the Commonwealth Governments. They are of pure gold and quite plain, except for two narrow decorative bands of engraving and a single Tudor rose which serves as a clasp. They are lined with red velvet and the hallmark is a special coronation mark which includes an effigy of the Queen. They are 8¾ in. in circumference and 1½ in. in depth and the weight is 4 to 4½ oz troy.

The Ring

Usually a new ring was made for each sovereign for his coronation but it was kept afterwards as personal property. In the Tower of London there are, however, three coronation rings. The first is that made for William IV with a sapphire set with a cross of 5 rubies representing the Cross of St George upon a blue ground and the flag of St Andrew. Surrounding the sapphire are 14 brilliants. Other diamonds are set at the junction of the bezel of the ring. The ring was worn by Edward VII and George V. Queen Victoria's ring is copied on a small scale from the ring of William

IV. It is of gold set with a *cabochon* sapphire, just over $\frac{1}{2}$ in. at its greatest diameter. On the sapphire is a cross of 5 rubies enclosed in a framework of 24 small brilliants. The third ring is that which was made for Queen Adelaide and was subsequently worn by Queen Alexandra and Queen Mary. It is set with a ruby of $\frac{1}{2}$ in. surrounded by 14 brilliants and there are 13 small rubies set round the outside of the ring.

The Sword of State (Plate 65, a(i))

This is a two-handed sword. The length of the blade is 32 in. and the hilt of the sword is of gilt metal, the cross-piece representing a lion on the one hand and the unicorn on the other. The scabbard is covered with red velvet on which are gilt representations of the rose, thistle, harp, fleur-de-lis, and portcullis in silver gilt with the Arms of William and Mary in the centre.

The Sword of Justice to the Spirituality and the Sword of Justice to the Temporality (Plate 65, a(ii) and (iii))

These are straight, two-edged pointed swords with plain handles and guards. They have scabbards of crimson velvet ornamented with gold. The meaning of these two swords is derived from a passage from the Gospels.[1] In the second half of the XI century there arose the famous Contest of the Investitures between the Pope and the Emperor and the 'doctrine of the two swords' became prominent. In England, however, Henry I reached a compromise with the Pope and the two Swords of Justice to the Spirituality and Temporality are an assertion of the position of the king. They are purely temporal ornaments which are not consecrated. No prayers in relation to them are said at the coronation service, nor are they delivered but carried symbolically near the sovereign.

Curtana (Plate 65, a(iv))

The third sword is called *Curtana* because it has no point. We must look to the Romances of Charlemagne for the origin of its name. One of Charlemagne's twelve peers, Ogier the Dane, is reputed to have married a British princess. He struck the *perron* in front of the great Emperor's castle at Aix-la-Chapelle with his sword and the point broke and it was called 'Curtein'. Since the coronation of Henry VI it has also been called the Sword of Mercy.

The Jewelled Sword (Plate 65, b)

This was made for the coronation of George IV at the cost of £6,000. Its scabbard of dull gold is richly decorated with diamonds, rubies, emeralds in the designs of the Tudor rose, the thistle and the shamrock. At the bottom is a very fine turquoise set in diamonds and in the centre of the quillon is a very large and beautiful emerald, the value of which has been estimated at £2,500. The hilt and grip are thickly set with diamonds and some large coloured stones, while at the top is a large diamond. At coronations the peer who carries the Sword of State delivers it up to the Lord Chamberlain, who, in exchange, gives to him the Jewelled Sword which is then delivered to the Archbishop. The latter, after reciting a prayer, places it in the sovereign's right hand. The sovereign then stands and the Lord Chamberlain girds the sword about him. The sovereign then ungirds the sword and goes to the altar and places it there, still in its scabbard. The peer who has previously carried the sword then redeems it for 100s. At the coronations of William IV and Queen Victoria special swords were provided for the offerings.

The Ampulla (Plate 66, a)

This is a vessel of chased gold taking the form of a golden eagle with outstretched wings, standing on a pedestal. It is $9\frac{1}{2}$ in. high, 7 in. across the wings and $3\frac{1}{2}$ in. across the base. The head

[1] St Luke xxii,38.

screws off to allow it to be filled with oil, the capacity being 6 oz, and the beak has a hole in it to allow the oil to be poured out. The screw is of much earlier date than 1661, and the eagle probably dates from the end of the XIV century. It has never been definitely ascertained whether the present ampulla has any connection with that used before the Commonwealth.

The Spoon (Plate 66, a)

The spoon is of silver gilt and $7\frac{1}{2}$ in. long. Its origin is unknown. It is considered to date from the early part of the XIII century, or possibly from the later part of the XII century, but it is not the original coronation spoon.

The only occasions on which the full regalia are brought into use are at coronations, but the sovereign wears the Imperial Crown at the State Opening of Parliament on which occasion the Sword of State is carried before him and the Cap of Maintenance is also carried in the procession. If the sovereign opens Parliament before the coronation the crown is carried in the procession, but William III wore his crown on 22nd February 1689, a week after he had been proclaimed King, when he went to Parliament to pass the Act legalising his accession, as there was some doubt as to the validity of his acceding to the throne by a convention. On various other occasions of State, the Sword of State is borne before the sovereign, but it is not usual for the sovereign to wear the crown. There have been two special occasions at least when it has been suggested that the crown should be worn. The first was at Queen Victoria's Jubilee when the Queen said she would prefer to wear her bonnet. The second was for an elaborate service for the hallowing of the fighting men who would be engaged in the invasion of France in 1944, to be held at St Paul's on 12th May, the anniversary of King George VI's coronation and at which it was suggested the coronation regalia should be paraded. King George rejected this with distaste and with the comment that the coronation regalia was already consecrated to a unique purpose.[1] The crown, the sceptre and the orb are placed on the sovereign's coffin at the lying-in-state and at the funeral. At Queen Victoria's lying-in-state both orbs were placed on the coffin and no official reason was given at the time, but it has been conjectured subsequently that it was intended to symbolise her dual position as Queen of England and Empress of India.

For the investiture of Edward, Prince of Wales, at Carnarvon Castle in 1911, special insignia were designed by Sir Goscombe John, R.A. They were intended 'to combine the ancient tradition and symbolism while indicating the present day significance of the office which the heir to the throne now holds'. The whole of the gold used in the manufacture of the various pieces of the regalia was obtained from the vicinity of Carnarvon.[2] The official description given by the designer of the Prince of Wales' regalia was:

The chaplet (Plate 67, c) consists of a circlet of gold which is adorned with pearls and amethysts; fixed upon the circlet at intervals are four crosses pattées alternating with fleurs-de-lis of the orthodox pattern. The cross-pieces and the fleurs-de-lis are pierced and within the outlines of the former run sprays of the Rose of England and of the latter the Daffodil of Wales. The spaces between the cross pattée and the fleurs-de-lis are filled with rose-bud sprays. Some surprise may be felt at the use of the daffodil, but there is every authority to justify its use as a national emblem.

[1] J. W. Wheeler-Bennett: King George VI: His Life and Reign.
[2] The Story of Garrard's, 1721–1911.

The verge or rod (*Plate 67, b*)measures 2 ft 8 in. in length and is about ¾ in. in diameter at the foot, tapering gradually towards the head. In an ancient chronicle it is spoken of as a 'golden rod or verge betokeninge his goevernment'. It presents a much more aristocratic form than that carried by Prince Henry, son of James I, which was nothing so much like a billiard cue. The head of the verge is formed by three-winged *amorini*, supporting the Prince's coronet, the idea embodied being that of love supporting the crown. The cap of the coronet is formed of a large amethyst, that jewel being chosen for this and other portions of the regalia in accordance with the colour scheme of purple of the royal robes. Below the *amorini* is a design formed of the Prince's Badge of Feathers with the motto *Ich Dien* inscribed in bold letters underneath. Just where the hand will grasp the verge is a small amulet which forms a convenient place for holding. The tip of the verge is formed by the Dragon of Wales and below that the date MCMXI is given in Roman characters.

The ring (*Plate 67, d*) is of beautiful design in keeping with the description given, in an early record of the *Creation of the Prince of Wales*, of a 'ring of gold, to be put on the third finger of his left hand whereby he declareth his marriage with equity and justice. It is made of gold, the design being that of two Welsh dragons interlaced, their heads and claws forming the setting for a beautiful large amethyst'. It was from time immemorial customary for the Prince of Wales to be presented with 'a sword with the scabbard made of pure silk and gold' and the precedent was followed in 1911. As His Royal Highness was 'invested' and not 'girded' with the weapon it is worn 'bendwise' as the heralds say, or slung over the neck instead of being fastened round the waist. The hilt of the sword is 5 in. long and the blade 2 ft 7½ in. The great distinguishing feature of the pommel of the hilt is two Welsh dragons grasping or supporting the Prince's coronet, the design being symbolical of the dragons guarding the crown just as in the verge there is love supporting the coronet. On a collar just below the heads of the dragons the Prince's motto *Ich Dien* appears. The grip of the hilt is formed by the interlacing scaly bodies of these heraldic beasts and their curling tails make up the guard. The hilt is of silver gilt. One side of the blade of the sword—a beautiful specimen of polished steel—is adorned with the Prince's initial *E* surmounted by His Royal Highness's coronet, the motto *Ich Dien* and the date *MDCCCCXI*. On the other side of the blade appears the three feather-badge with an inscription in Welsh *Iorwerth Tywysog Cymru M.G.* which translated into English is 'Edward Prince of Wales Knight of the Garter'. The scabbard and belt are made of purple velvet corresponding with the colour of the robe, the former being wired in a reticulated pattern and the latter ornamented with characteristic scrolls of traditional design. The scabbard is tipped with gold and bears the motto *Ich Dien*. The clasp by which the Prince's purple velvet robe is fastened in front is composed of two brooches of Welsh gold of Celtic design which are connected by a loop and chain. Each brooch is 2 in. in diameter and circular in shape. Only metal—and no jewels whatever—has been employed in this part of the regalia.

These ornaments are now preserved in the National Museum of Wales at Cardiff.

The so-called Irish crown jewels, which gained notoriety because of their theft from Dublin Castle on 6th July 1907 while being the property of the Crown, were, in fact, the jewelled insignia of the Orders of St Patrick. They consist of a magnificent diamond and ruby star, a diamond brooch and five golden jewelled collars of the

a   Crown of the Prince of Wales. Tower of London (p. 170)

b   Head of the verge of the Prince of Wales. National Museum, Cardiff (p. 174)

c   Circlet of the Prince of Wales. National Museum, Cardiff (p. 173)

e   Regalia of the Prince of Wales. National Museum, Cardiff (p. 173)

d   Ring of the Prince of Wales. National Museum, Cardiff (p. 174)

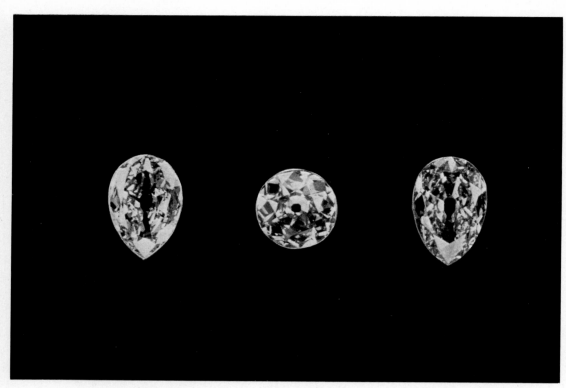

b *Two of the Arcot diamonds and circular diamond from the crown of George IV (pp. 160 and 162)*

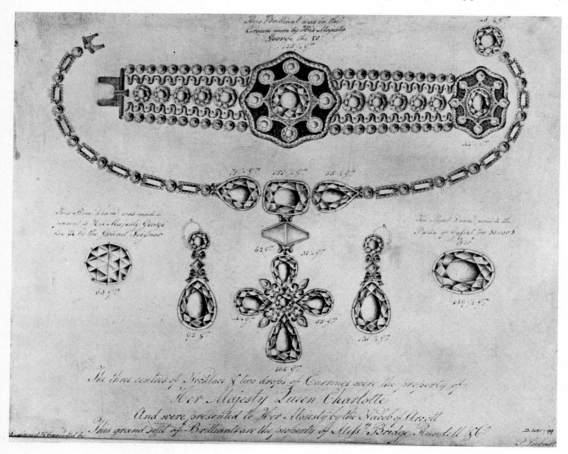

c *Brilliants of George IV from an engraving in the Victoria and Albert Museum (pp. 160 and 162)*

a (left) *Ivory sceptre of George I (p. 158)*

Knights Companion of St Patrick. They were stolen from the safe in the heavily guarded strong-room of Dublin Castle on the eve of a State Visit by King Edward VII and Queen Alexandra. The mystery of their disappearance has never been solved.

An outstanding feature of the English regalia is the number of stones of historical and traditional interest. There is no other collection in Europe which can compare with it in this respect. The following stones are deserving of special notice.

St Edward's Sapphire

In the cross surmounting the monde is a fine rose-cut stone.[1] At the second translation of the body of the Confessor in 1269, Laurence, Abbot of Westminster, removed the ring from St Edward's finger and no doubt preserved it in the Abbey as a relic. It had already been the subject of more than one legend and it was said to have the power of curing the cramp. At the coronation of Edward II a gold offering was made in the form of an image of the King offering the ring to the beggar of the legendary story.[2] How it survived the dissolution of the monasteries and the Civil War is not related, but the tradition is very strong that it is the sapphire from St Edward's ring and there is no reason to doubt it.

The Black Prince's Ruby

The first mention of this stone being associated with the Black Prince does not appear until the second half of the XVIII century. Horace Walpole, in his *Anecdotes of Painting* (1762–71), stated that Mr Speaker Onslow (*obiit* 1768) had a portrait of the Black Prince. It is an engraving by George Vertue (*Plate 69, a*) dated from 1732. Above the Prince's circlet there is a large ruby. This anecdote shows that there was a tradition associating the ruby with the Black Prince in the first half of the XVIII century. Previously the stone had been called 'The King's Great Ruby' at the coronation of William and Mary, and subsequently, in the Crown Jeweller's account for the coronation of George IV, it was called 'the large ruby'. By then, however, the traditional association with the Black Prince was strong. A member of the firm of Rundell, Bridge and Rundell, then the Crown Jewellers, in an unpublished account of the firm written between 1843 and 1846, wrote, in connection with the resetting of the Imperial State Crown at the time of the coronation of George IV:

> The principal jewel was a very large bad ruby balas said (on what authority we could never learn) to have belonged to Edward the Black Prince, who it was affirmed took it from the French king at the Battle of Crécy and afterwards wore as a jewel in his breastplate.[3]

The tradition became accepted officially when the 1858 inventory described the stone as:

> A ruby said to have been given to Edward, Prince of Wales, son of Edward III, called the Black Prince, by Don Pedro, King of Castile, after the Battle of Najera near Vittoria, A.D. 1367. The

1 A form of cutting introduced about 1520.
2 See Sitwell: op. cit.
3 See footnote 2, p. 160.

ruby was worn in the helmet of Henry V at the Battle of Agincourt, A.D. 1415. It is pierced through after the Eastern custom, the upper part of the piercing being filled by a small ruby.

This story has been retold and embellished by numerous writers, the usual version being that in about 1360 King Peter the Cruel of Castile treacherously murdered the King of Granada in order to gain possession of his jewels, among which was the great balas ruby, pierced in oriental style, which Peter subsequently gave to the Black Prince in gratitude for his victory at Najera in 1367 and which then passed into the English crown jewels. It is said to have been worn by Henry V at Agincourt and Richard III at Bosworth. It was then set in royal crowns under the late Tudors and early Stuarts, disappeared mysteriously under the Commonwealth and has been given a place of honour in the crown since the coronation of James II.

As this story is one of the most popular and frequently related about the English crown jewels it is worth examining in detail. The story of the King of Granada derives from the Chronicle of Lopez de Ayala,[1] a Castilian noble who, during the civil war between Peter and his natural half-brother, Henry of Trastamara, deserted his king and joined the usurper. According to Ayala in 1362 Bermejo, whose real name was Abu Said, having been defeated by Peter's army, went to Seville with a few followers and put himself at the mercy of the Castilian king. He had with him three balas rubies the size of pigeon's eggs and many other jewels. Peter coveted the jewels and so had the Moors seized while dining and put to death, Peter himself hurling the lance which killed Bermejo, while reminding him of occasions in the past when he had suffered from Bermejo's enmity. After the massacre many other jewels were found in the turban of a page.

Ayala's account should be taken with circumspection. When he wrote it he had attained high rank under the Trastamaran Dynasty and was at pains to explain away his inexcusable behaviour in breaking his oath to his sovereign by showing Peter as a tyrant whom no man of honour could serve. This fitted in with the Trastamaran policy of doing everything possible to blacken Peter's character both in Spain and abroad. So successful was this policy that Peter appears in the pages of history as an unspeakable monster who would stop at no crime. It was not until the xv century that he was seen in a better light, Isabel the Catholic refusing to allow him to be called 'The Cruel'. Modern historians have reassessed this period and see him as a tough, nationalistic king, unsympathetic to the romantically chivalrous knights from England and France, whose conduct was in fact little better than his own.[2] In particular Edward the Black Prince, held up to his contemporaries and to posterity as the model of chivalry, is revealed as a poor statesman and, on occasion, as vengeful as his contemporaries. In this particular story there seems no reason to doubt the facts as stated by Ayala, but the motive alleged by him seems inconsistent with these facts and with Peter's conduct on other occasions.

[1] Pero Lopez de Ayala: *Crónica del rey D. Pedro*, ed. E. Llaguno Y Amirola. *Crónicas de los reyes de Castilla*, Vol. I, Madrid 1779.
[2] The most important English reassessment is P. E. Russell: *The English Intervention in Spain and Portugal in the time of Edward III and Richard II*, Oxford 1955. For his assessment of the characters of Peter and Henry of Trastamara and of Ayala's reliability as a historian see pp. 16–23.

a (above, left) *Engraving of the Black Prince by George Vertue 1732, showing the ruby in his head-dress. National Portrait Gallery (p. 175)*

b (above, right) *Crown of Edward VI showing the Black Prince's ruby, from the Plea Roll of Michaelmas 1553. Public Records Office (p. 179)*

c *The Old Monde from the crown of George III originally thought to be an aquamarine but found to be glass. Tower of London (pp. 157 and 168)*

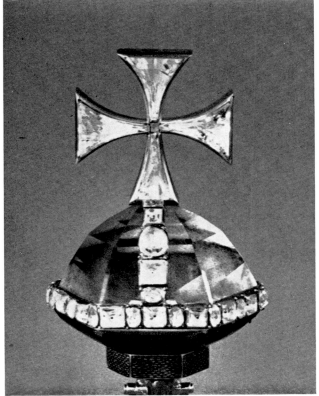

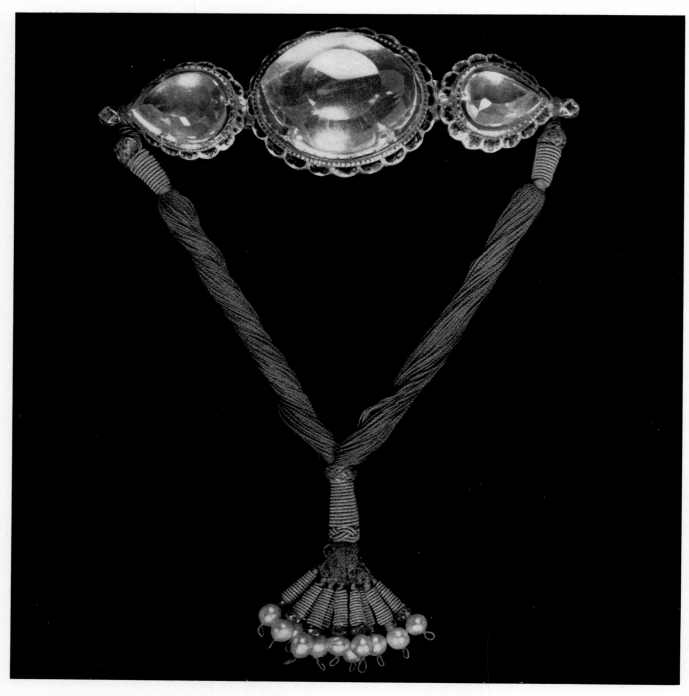

a *A model of the Koh-i-Nur in its original setting as an enamelled Indian bracelet* (p. 183)

b (left) *Detail of enamel work on back of the Koh-i-Nur*

It seems more likely that he killed Bermejo in revenge for past treacheries or reverses and took the jewels as a bonus.

One of the ways in which Henry of Trastamara endeavoured to impose his image of Peter as historical truth was by the systematic destruction of all the archives and state papers of Peter's reign. One important document which was saved and which was published by Ayala was Peter's unexecuted will dated 18th November 1362. This mentions two of Bermejo's great balas rubies among Peter's personal treasure. One was in a very large *alhayte* (a Moorish word meaning collar or breast ornament) which Peter had had made in Seville and which also contained two other large balases and two smaller ones, as well as numerous pearls and other stones: this was to be left to his second daughter Constance. He also intended to leave to Beatrice, his eldest daughter who was then betrothed to the heir to the Portuguese throne, a smaller *alhayte*, also made in Seville, in which there was another of Bermejo's balases. The third of Bermejo's three stones is not mentioned in the will and may well have been set in the Castilian state crown.[1]

In 1362 Peter had concluded a treaty of alliance with Edward III of England and in 1365, when Henry of Trastamara was about to invade Castile from Aragon, he invoked this alliance. The Black Prince, as the King's Lieutenant in Gascony, was responsible for relations with Spain, but he was too slow in his preparations for war to save Peter's throne. Peter, unable to meet Henry's mercenary companies in the field, fled from Seville in May 1366, taking with him on pack mules a great part of his personal fortune which was singularly rich in jewels. The implication of the *Dispensero Cronica* is that Bermejo's rubies were among these jewels. The Castilian state treasure, mainly bullion, was loaded on a galley which was treacherously seized and handed over to Henry.

Peter first fled to Portugal, but despite the betrothal of Beatrice to the heir to the throne he found no welcome there, so, breaking off the engagement, he then made his way to Bordeaux where the Black Prince was established. In order to ingratiate himself he gave to the Prince and his wife, Joan of Kent, many rich presents, among them a great gold retable, the 'golden Table' which figures in the chronicle of Bertrand du Guesclin[2] and which may be the *table d'Espaign* listed in several English inventories of the reigns of Richard II and Henry IV or, more likely, *notre grand table d'or et d'argent* which the Black Prince left in his will to the high altar of his foundation at Ashridge. Peter also gave the Prince an undertaking to pay the army which was being organised for the Castilian campaign. The cost was enormous, the subsidy which Edward III had given was soon exhausted and the Black Prince had to melt down his personal plate, while Peter had to dispose of all the treasure he had brought from Seville. The market became overloaded, prices slumped and the proceeds were disappointingly small. So hard pressed was Peter that he had to borrow 5,000 florins from the Black Prince to meet his personal needs. At length the expedition set off and on 3rd April 1367 the

---

1 See page 123 for the description of this crown and ruby in the English inventories, and page 595 for its identification with the state crown of Peter I and for a further consideration of the will.

2 C. Fernandez Duro: *La tabla de oro de Don Pedro de Castilla. Boletin de la Real Academia de la Historia,* tom, xv, p. 52. F. De Mely: *id tom,* xvi, p. 40.

Black Prince gained the overwhelming victory of Najera over the Trastamaran forces. There is no evidence whatsoever that Peter made any gifts to the Black Prince in gratitude for the victory. On the contrary they were on very bad terms, firstly about the disposal of prisoners and secondly over the financial settlement. Peter complained to Edward III through his ambassador that, as a result of the Black Prince's action, he had been forced to dispose of his jewels at unjustifiably low rates. Edward, in reply, instructed his son that the proper value of the jewels disposed of by Peter must be deducted from the funds claimed from him.[1]

The *Eulogium Historianum*, which is not renowned for its accurate placing of events, states that after Najera the Black Prince received £40,000 from Peter in gold and jewels 'among which he received a precious sword of Spain decorated with gold and precious stones'. If this is taken at face value it conflicts with surviving documentary evidence which shows that, although Peter tried to collect money to pay the debt and left his daughters in Bayonne as security, he never paid any of it. If, however, it is taken to refer to happenings before Najera, it fills a gap in the evidence and allows us to suppose that the sums Peter paid over for the maintenance of the army included pieces of jewellery, perhaps those which he could not dispose of for cash without difficulty. The sword may be identified both with that which Peter in his will intended to leave to his natural son, Juan, and with the *Espeie d'Espaign* of the English inventories. It is likely that the other Spanish items which appear in the same inventories came from the same source. Indeed the very form of the undated inventory, specifying the crown, *pallet d'or*, sword and saddle of Spain, with its detailed valuation of the pieces, is consistent with its being a list of regalia received in lieu of cash; there would be few other dealings with the regalia which would require such a detailed valuation to be made. The central stone of the crown was a great balas ruby weighing 181 carats and valued at £603 6s. 8d. It was most unusual in those days for the individual weight of any stone, however noteworthy, to be recorded, and the only occasion on which this would be done would be a financial transaction in order to ensure that its full value was obtained. In the inventory the ruby is described as 'round', which presumably means that it was *en cabochon* and not table cut.

The Black Prince was very fond of precious stones and the issues of the Treasury record numerous purchases, many of which were balas rubies, one of them costing £1,883 6s. 8d. This may have been the 'immense balas' later given by Edward IV to Charles the Bold, Duke of Burgundy, on the occasion of his marriage to Margaret of York, but it is difficult to conceive of it as being so immense that it was priced at over three times the value set on the stone in the Spanish crown, unless the latter was under-valued, as it may well have been if it had been received in Gascony at the time when the price of gems had been depressed by Peter's sales.

There is no evidence to support any of the other conceivable ways in which the Spanish crown and the other items could have come into the English Treasury. If the crown was a personal possession of the Black Prince, given or sold to him by Peter, or bought from one of the goldsmiths to whom Peter had sold it, there is nothing to show

---

[1] Public Record Office: Exchequer (Diplomatic Documents) No. 1553.

how it came into the Treasury; the Black Prince's will[1] contained no reference to any piece of regalia which might be identified with those in the undated inventory, while Joan of Kent died in 1385 and the crown at least was in the Treasury by 1382. Nor, if these items had been the personal possessions of Peter's two surviving daughters who in 1371 married the Black Prince's brothers, John of Gaunt and Edmund of Cambridge, is there any evidence to show how they passed into the Treasury, although we cannot entirely rule out that they might have been a contribution to the cost of the latter's expedition to Portugal in 1381–2. The circumstantial evidence supporting the theory that the crown in the undated inventory was handed over to the Black Prince as a part of the payment of the troops which were to regain Peter's throne is thus very strong. The balas in the crown is the only one of considerable size which features in the extant records and which has connections with both Spain and the Black Prince. It is possible that the latter acquired the other rubies of Bermejo if Peter had them with him, but again there is no positive evidence and no light is shed by the wills of the Black Prince and Joan of Kent. We are on less sure ground in identifying the ruby in the crown with one of those taken from Bermejo, but what evidence there is does tend to support the popular tradition.

Although there is no certain evidence to identify the great balas ruby in the Spanish crown with the Black Prince's ruby in the Imperial State Crown, a plausible case can be made out for it. In the Plea Roll of the King's Bench, of Michaelmas 1553, in the Public Record Office there is a reasonably accurate drawing of what must have been Edward VI's personal crown (*Plate 69, b*). Set on the top of it, held by a pin and having a cross fixed to its summit by another pin, is a stone which is unmistakably that now known as the Black Prince's ruby, although it is placed the other way up to its modern setting. In an inventory of 1550 Edward VI's crown is recorded as containing 'oon grete balas', clearly that on the top, weighing 1 oz 1 dwt, or about $157\frac{1}{2}$ carats. At first sight this seems to preclude identification with the balas in the Spanish crown, which was recorded as weighing 181 carats, but in the XIV century the weight in general use was equivalent to $\frac{14}{15}$ of troy weight, which was not officially introduced until 1526. We do not know for certain the weight of the carat in the time of Richard II, but if it bore the same relation to the earlier weight as did the later carat to the troy weight, the weight of the balas in the Spanish crown would be adjusted to approximately 168 carats.[2] The difference can be accounted for by the piercing of the stone.[3]

The piercing of this stone is an important point which needs further consideration, as it has always been attributed to 'Eastern custom'. Some writers suggest that it is only pierced at the top, whereas the 1858 inventory makes it clear that it is pierced right

[1] J. N.: *A Collection of all the Wills of the Kings and Queens of England, Princes and Princesses of Wales*, etc., London 1780.

[2] Moreover there are many balases mentioned in the various inventories and accounts of the XV and XVI centuries and although several of them were very large, there appears to have been no other stone in the 150–200-carat range.

[3] The whole question of mediaeval weights requires further research. For the introduction of troy weight, see J. A. Decouzdemanche: *Traité Pratique des Poids de Moyen Âge*, Paris 1915. The identification of the balas in the Spanish crown with the Black Prince's ruby has been considered by Collins (op. cit., p. 12 note) but he did not deal fully with the problem of the weights.

through: most have translated 'Eastern' as meaning 'Oriental', not appreciating that there is a difference, and giving the impression that the stone was pierced when the Black Prince acquired it. But 'Eastern' in terms of jewels can refer to the Eastern Empire and the Near East; 'Oriental' refers to India, Burma and the Far East. There can be no doubt that the Black Prince's ruby was 'Oriental' in origin because the only sources of supply were Burma and Siam. But in India and Burma it was not usually the custom at that time to pierce stones; in fact the lapidaries were at pains to avoid reducing the weight of the stone, for the qualities which counted were size, weight, shape and colour, but not brilliance. Only if there were a flaw in the stone or if the colour were poor would it be pierced. There is no mention of any stones in the Imperial Treasury of the Great Moguls or their predecessors being pierced until the XVII century when Tavernier in his *Mémoires* noted two large balas rubies as being pierced; in each case, however, there is a suggestion that the Moguls had acquired these particular stones from European travellers. On the other hand it was customary for Byzantine lapidaries to pierce stones, though usually small and medium-sized ones, and many were brought back by Crusaders from the Holy Land, Constantinople and Sicily. In fact some crowns still in existence, which were made in the ateliers under Byzantine influence, have pierced stones. The three great balas rubies given by St Louis to the Sainte Chapelle in Paris were undoubtedly brought back from the Crusades, as were probably the pierced balas rubies in the *Sainte Couronne* and two of the other great rubies in the French crown jewels, which were pierced, at least in the XVI century. In the Plea Roll representation the Black Prince's ruby is placed on end, with the cross set absolutely perpendicularly above it. This strongly suggests that the hole had been made for this particular purpose, and this is supported by the fact that there is no reference to this stone being pierced until an inventory taken in the reign of James I. By the middle of the XVI century Byzantine practices were becoming more widespread in Western Europe as a result of the fall of Constantinople, and there can be little doubt that the balas was pierced in England.

The evidence as to what happened to this stone in the 150 years which separate Richard II from Edward VI is slight. There is a very strong tradition that it was worn by Henry V at the Battle of Agincourt, and some writers have tried to connect this with the description of 'the golden crown for the Bascinet' which had four balases valued at £133 6s. 8d. As the current price of balas rubies was said to be £13 6s. 8d., the valuation suggests that one of the balases was of unusual size and worth some £87. Apart from the reluctance to weigh individual stones there was also a reluctance to give them separate values, and the fact that one of them seems to have had a separate value given it suggests that it was of particular importance; the vast discrepancy in the value from the stone in the Spanish crown could be explained by a great fall in the value of jewels. It would be unwise, however, to carry too far the argument about the reluctance to value separate stones. In France, for example, both among the crown jewels and in the regalia at St Denis, there were a number of large balas rubies with specific values. The evidence on which the Agincourt tradition can be supported is thus exceedingly slender and there is no evidence at all to substantiate the claim that the stone was worn by Richard III at the Battle of Bosworth.

It is possible that the great ruby was only placed in the crown on certain important occasions and thus would not feature in the inventories of crowns. In the time of the Tudors there was a number of large balas rubies in the State Crown of Henry VIII which were taken out of their settings for the King's use. An inventory of 1532 described one of these as 'A great Ballace broken'; in 1550 this had been replaced by 'A greate Ballace [w]hole'. Some writers have identified the former as the Black Prince's ruby, but a stone pierced for a particular manner of setting would hardly be described as 'broken'. 'A greate Ballace [w]hole' seems more likely to have been our stone. On the other hand, 'a fair ruby great like a rocket ball' which Elizabeth I showed the ambassador of Mary, Queen of Scots, is not likely to be this ruby; it might well have been the great ruby on the top of the headdress depicted in Gheerardts's portrait of Queen Elizabeth (*Plate 49, b*) in the Burghley Collection.

The next question is how the stone survived the depredations of the Commonwealth. Edward VI's personal crown contained several great balas rubies. Two of these were valued at £43 but there was another stone described as 'a pierced balas ruby wrapt in paper by itself'. It was valued at £4 and sold for £4 10s. Some writers have identified this as the Black Prince's ruby, while others have scorned the suggestion. For instance, in his paper on the crowns of England, Holmes says: 'His (Dove's) list incidentally kills the popular tradition that the Black Prince's ruby was sold for £4 as it shows that the price of rubies was from £3 to £6 (?) according to size.' Collins in his *Jewels and Plate of Queen Elizabeth I* says: 'To accept the identification is to impugn the integrity of the Commonwealth' and Sir Francis Sandford, writing forty years later, stated that the Great Ruby set in James II's crown was 'esteemed worth £10,000'. But the matter cannot be dismissed so easily. The pierced hole would undoubtedly have weakened the stone, which would have been removed from its setting when not in use to lessen the risk of its breaking. To find it as a separate stone wrapped in paper would therefore be quite natural. As to the price, balas rubies were no longer fashionable, nor were uncut stones, and an irregular pierced stone might have been difficult to dispose of except for cutting into smaller ones. The pierced stone would in any case severely restrict its use and would have much reduced its value. Moreover, as we have already noted, George Fox in his unpublished memoirs described it as a very large *bad* ruby balas. It must also be noted that there is no evidence of any other balas ruby being pierced or set among the regalia in such a way that piercing would be necessary. There seems to be every likelihood that this was in fact the stone now known as the Black Prince's ruby, though how it returned to the Treasury we cannot say.

An alternative possibility is that the stone, which was last depicted in Henrietta Maria's crown, was taken to Holland or to France by the Queen, but there is no record of it being disposed of and it is not mentioned in the list of jewels of Henrietta Maria in the French archives already cited. The only other possible explanation seems to be that it was sold and that the purchaser returned the stone after the Restoration. It is recorded that a great oriental ruby was bought for the coronation of Charles II from a jeweller, William Gomeldon. This ruby was not set in the crown of Charles II but was added to the State Crown of James II, when we find Sandford's exaggerated valuation of £10,000. But, if we look at the French crown jewels, we find three great balas rubies[1] valued at 60,000, 20,000 and 60,000 écus respectively. These valuations, once made, were never changed. The English Court in exile would have been familiar with French practice and the valuation of £10,000, while not representing the commercial worth, would have been in keeping with the manner in which the crown jewels were valued at the time.

In its new setting it was evidently necessary to strengthen the stone by the addition of gold foil at the back, which would not have been suitable for the setting of the stone *à jour* on the top of Edward VI's crown. The top hole was also hidden by an oriental ruby being set in it. In the 1858 inventory the weight of the stone is given as 170 carats, which was not an actual weighing but only a jeweller's estimate and includes the weight of the foil and the oriental ruby which would account for the discrepancy from the weight in the inventory of Edward VI.

There is one more point on which to comment and that is the tradition of giving the most prominent place in English crowns to a red stone.[2] We have already discussed the symbolic meanings of the stones of William the Conqueror's crown and in St Edward's crown at the time of Elizabeth I. In each case the place of honour was taken by a carbuncle. In modern times this means alamandine or the crimson garnet, but in earlier times it had the meaning of any deep rich red stone, including balas rubies.

Queen Elizabeth's Ear-rings

At the point of intersection of the arches of the Imperial Crown are 4 pear-shaped pendant pearls. When the crown was refurbished for George IV the jewellers found two very badly shaped and worse coloured pearls suspended from the cross. According to the Jewel Office they were declared to be of enormous value and had been pawned to the Dutch Government for £50,000. Rundell and Bridge exchanged one for a better specimen for £5. The original was sold to a Jew for £2.[3] When Queen Victoria's crown was made one was replaced by a new one. In recent years the story has become current that they were Queen Elizabeth's ear-rings. This seems to have first seen the light of day in an article on the crown jewels which appeared in *The Times* on 7th January 1911 just before the coronation of George V. It was said that after Queen Victoria's death, when a general check up was made of the huge quantity of goods accumulated in the royal palace during her reign, a paper packet was found which was marked 'Queen Elizabeth's ear-rings' and contained a pair of pendant pearl ear-rings. It was said that Edward VII ordered them to be placed in the crown. There appears to be no official record of this, but since there would be no cost for removing two pendant pearls and substituting two others, it would not appear in the accounts and there is certainly a possibility that the story is true. It is likely, however, that the Queen Elizabeth referred to would not be Queen Elizabeth I but Elizabeth, Queen of Bohemia, daughter of James I, whose pearls passed by inheritance to the Hanoverian kings and through them to Queen Victoria. The Stuarts seem to have had a particular liking for pear-shaped

---

[1] *The Côte de Bretagne* of 206 carats, The 'Roman A' of 121 carats and the *Œuf de Naples* of 241 carats.

[2] Also to be found in crowns in Austria, Bohemia, Denmark, France, Spain and Russia.

[3] George Fox: op. cit.

pendant pearl ear-rings.[1] Perhaps it was in memory of Charles I who was fond of wearing a single pearl and was even said to have worn one on the scaffold.

The Koh-i-Nur (Plate 70, a and b)

The Koh-i-Nur is one of the greatest historical stones in existence. There are legends which give it a vague history going back some 5,000 years, but there is nothing definite on record relating to the stone before the year 1112. Even so, the story about this stone must be taken with some reserve, but there is undoubtedly a great romance attached to it.

In 1526 the Sultan Baber wrote that, following a great battle in which the Rajah of Gwalior was defeated, his son was presented with a quantity of precious stones as a tribute. Among these was a great diamond which had been acquired by Sultan Ala-ed-din, who reigned from 1288–1321. Baber was presented with this stone by his son, and a judge of diamonds valued it as half the daily expense of the world. When it was originally found or how it came into the hands of Ala-ed-din is unknown, but from the time it came into the possession of Baber its history is well authenticated.

It remained in the hands of the Mogul emperors until the invasion of India by the Persians under Nadir Shah. The whole of the treasure of the Moguls fell into the conqueror's hands with the single exception of the famous Koh-i-Nur. All efforts to find its whereabouts were in vain, until a woman of the harem betrayed the secret that the vanquished Emperor kept it hidden in his turban.

Nadir was determined to secure the stone, and resorted to a clever trick. About to return to his own country, he held a great ceremony at which he reinstated the Emperor Mohammed. As a token of reconciliation and in order to cement the friendship they had sworn for each other, Nadir asked the Emperor to exchange turbans and immediately followed this by removing his own head-dress. With no time to remove the hidden stone and knowing that a refusal would mean death, the Emperor could do nothing but hand the conqueror his own simple turban and take in exchange the richly jewelled Persian head-dress. The Emperor so controlled his feelings and responded to the invitation with such apparent indifference that Nadir thought he had been misled. When the latter had an opportunity of withdrawing to his tent he greedily unfolded the turban and the long-coveted stone was revealed. 'Koh-i-Nur,' he exclaimed with rapture, and to this day this name, which means 'Mountain of Light', has been attached to the stone.

The stone was inherited by Nadir's feeble son who was put to the most fearful tortures and blinded by his enemies who coveted the stone. Nothing, however, could make him reveal where he kept it, and when at last Ahmed Shah, the founder of the Durani Afghan dynasty, came to his assistance, the dying owner of the Koh-i-Nur concluded an alliance with him and in exchange gave up the stone.

Timur, Ahmed's son, thus inherited the stone: then it was handed down to Timur's son, Zaman, who was deposed and blinded by his brother, Shuja. Zaman managed to

1 See portraits of Catherine of Braganza, by Jacob Huysmans and by Samuel Cooper; of Anne Hyde, wife of James II, by Sir Peter Eley; of Mary II, by William Wissing; of Sophia Dorothea, Electoral Princess of Hanover, by an unknown artist, and of Augusta, Princess of Wales, attributed to Allan Ramsay.

secrete the Koh-i-Nur in the mud walls of his prison, and it was a few years later, after some of the plaster had peeled off, before it was accidentally found.

Shuja in turn was dethroned and deprived of his sight, and was then sent into exile with his brother Zaman. He managed to retain possession of the great diamond and they were both well received by Ranjit Singh, the Lion of the Punjab, except that Ranjit extorted from them all their possessions including the Koh-i-Nur, for which, however, he paid. Ranjit Singh had it set in a bracelet which now, containing a model only of the original stone, is shown at the Tower of London.

The diamond remained in the Treasury at Lahore until 1849 when, following the mutiny of two Sikh regiments, the Honourable East India Company took possession of the Treasury and the stone was handed to Sir John Lawrence (later Lord Lawrence), who was to be responsible for its safe keeping. When the Board of the Company met a few weeks later to decide what should be done about the famous gem, one of the Board asked to see the stone and Lawrence, in some confusion, remembered that he had left it in his waistcoat pocket. In great haste he proceeded to his bungalow and found the stone still there. The Honourable East India Company decided to present it to Queen Victoria and in 1850 it arrived in England.

The gem had been cut in the way usually adopted by Indian lapidaries, which leaves the shape of the stone unaltered but covered with numerous facets. This shape, which exposed all the flaws in the stone, did not commend itself to the authorities in England whom the Prince Consort consulted. They advised that it should be cut as a brilliant, and it was so cut by the Crown Jewellers. While the jewellers did all that could be done to produce a fine brilliant from the stone, there has been much controversy as to the wisdom of the step. It has been argued that in its original state it was the historical Koh-i-Nur, and that now it had been reduced in size from 186 to 106 carats and that owing to the flaws it was necessary to make it a shallow brilliant of the finest water. Be that as it may, it is still a splendid stone and is unique from the historical point of view.

The Cullinan

Apart from the Koh-i-Nur the English crown jewels contain the two largest brilliants in the world and the story of these great stones is as follows.

On 26th January 1905 Captain M. F. Wells, whilst inspecting the Premier Mine, situated twenty miles north-west of Pretoria, saw a glistening spot in a rock, reflecting the manifold colours of a beautiful sunset. The glistening spot turned out to be an enormous diamond. The stone displayed three natural faces and one large cleavage face, as though it had been cut with a knife, thus indicating that it was only a portion of a larger stone. The stone was transparent, colourless and had only one small flaw near the surface. It weighed 3,025 carats which is about 1½ lb.

The stone was from the first called the 'Cullinan' after Sir T. M. Cullinan, Chairman of the Premier Diamond Company. The enormous size of the stone caused no little concern for it was unique in that it was more than twice the size of any stone yet discovered. Moreover, a stone weighing 1½ lb can scarcely be used as a piece of jewellery, and its value lay rather in the best way of cutting the largest number possible of brilliants from it.

a   The Cullinan Diamond in its natural shape. Messrs
Asscher, Amsterdam (p. 184)

b   The two lesser Stars of Africa
set as a brooch (p. 186)

d   Brilliants cut from the Cullinan Diamond (p. 186)

c (left)   The Cullinan Diamond after cleaving
(p. 185)

a   *Indian tiara in rubies and diamonds given to Queen Victoria in 1876 by Sir Jung Bahadoor. Originally set with opals*
(p. 190)

b   *Diamond fringe-pattern necklace mounted for wear as a tiara. Formerly the property of George III* (p. 191)

Fortunately, the discovery coincided with the healing of the wounds of the South African War and with two great leaders in power, Generals Botha and Smuts, who were at the time working incessantly to obtain the co-operation of all and to work with the British in building up the Union of South Africa. A resolution was moved in the Transvaal Legislative Assembly in August 1907 by General Botha, authorising his Government to acquire the diamond and present it to the King in token of the loyalty of the Transvaal people and in commemoration of the grant of responsible government. The resolution was carried by 42 to 19 votes, but the absence of unanimity and the feeling on the part of the British members that the offer came from the Dutch and not from themselves made the Home Government unenthusiastic about the King's acceptance of the jewel. When the question came before the Cabinet, Sir Henry Campbell-Bannerman, then Prime Minister, wrote to the King declaring that they 'did not really want to shirk the responsibility', but shirk it they did, the King being told that in matters of this sort his judgment was so good that the decision might safely be left in his hands. From his advisers he received conflicting opinions: Lord Esher, for example, definitely thought the gift should be refused. The King's own instincts were in favour of accepting, and in September, after the arrival of despatches from Lord Selborne, then High Commissioner of South Africa, advising that course he quickly made up his mind to take it as so on as the diamond was officially or formally offered by General Botha.[1] The formal offer was made by the Transvaal Government on 17th October, and the Cabinet having announced this on 5th November, the King wrote through the Secretary of State for the Colonies, Lord Elgin, on 7th November, accepting 'for myself and successors the valuable gift of the Cullinan diamond . . . as a token of the loyalty and attachment of the people of Transvaal, to his throne and person', and promising that he would cause 'this great and unique diamond to be kept and preserved among the historical jewels which form the heirlooms of the Crown'. The price paid for the stone by the Transvaal Government was £150,000.

The transport of such a valuable gem to England presented special difficulties. Detectives were sent to South Africa to guard the priceless stone. An insurance policy for a large sum was arranged but after due deliberation it was considered safest to despatch it by ordinary parcel post, while, as a blind, a dummy stone carefully sealed was placed in the captain's safe on the steamer and was assiduously guarded by detectives. The stone arrived safely in England and was duly presented to the King on his birthday. By the King's command the stone was placed beside the Imperial Crown and photographed.

The cutting of the stone was entrusted to the celebrated firm of Messrs I. J. Asscher of Amsterdam, and it was conveyed there under guard. A careful study of the stone showed that it had but one blemish—a black spot which necessitated the stone being cleaved. On 10th February 1908 this was successfully accomplished by Mr J. Asscher, and two pieces resulted, weighing 1,977½ carats and 1,040 carats. These were again cleaved into small pieces and two great brilliants weighing 516½ carats and 309¼ carats manufactured, besides a series of other stones. These two magnificent stones are the largest and the most valuable in the world and are of the purest water

---

1 The story is told by Sir Sidney Lee in his *Life of King Edward VII.*

and perfection. The largest, which is pear-shaped, was set in the royal sceptre and became known as the Star of Africa, while the second was set in the brow of the Imperial State Crown.

It had been arranged that Asschers should be allowed to keep the 'clippings' for their services and a small part was to go to Mr (later Sir) Arthur Levi and Mr Alexander Levi, who acted as expert supervisors of the operation. The 'clippings' meant the whole product except the two great stones. Of the remaining stones one, a marquise diamond of $11\frac{3}{4}$ carats, was acquired by King Edward, who gave it to Queen Alexandra as a present. The others, consisting of six large brilliants, ninety-six small brilliants and a quantity of unpolished fragments weighing 9 carats, were purchased by the Union Government in 1910, again at the instance of General Botha and on the suggestion of Messrs Levi, who feared that they would pass into private ownership. It was the intention that they should be presented to Queen Mary on the occasion of her proposed visit to South Africa with her husband, who was then Prince of Wales, for the purpose of opening the first Parliament in the Union. The visit had to be cancelled because of the death of King Edward and they were handed to Queen Mary at Marlborough House on 28th June 1910 by the High Commissioner of the Union of South Africa, the late Sir Richard Soloman, on behalf of the Government and the people of South Africa. The third stone, a pear-shaped diamond of 92 carats, and the fourth stone, a square-shaped diamond of 62 carats, became known as the Lesser Stars of Africa and were set in Queen Mary's crown, but in such a way that they can also be used as a brooch or pendant at will (*Plate 71, b*). The fifth stone was a heart-shaped diamond of $18\frac{3}{8}$ carats and was set in a brooch in similar heart-shaped form with other smaller diamonds. This brooch was worn by Queen Mary as the centre of the front cross *pattée* of the circlet of her crown at the coronation of George VI in 1938 in place of the Koh-i-Nur, which was mounted in the crown of Queen Elizabeth, consort of the King.

The marquise diamond given by Edward VII to Queen Alexandra is set as a drop pendant in a *cabochon* emerald and diamond necklace. The seventh stone, a marquise of $9\frac{3}{16}$ carats, and the eighth, a square-shaped diamond of $6\frac{5}{8}$ carats, are set in a brooch with other diamonds. The ninth stone, a pear-shaped diamond of $4\frac{9}{32}$ carats, is set in a ring.

The firm of Asschers received from King Edward, as a souvenir of the occasion, a silver cup which is still greatly prized by the firm. During the Second World War the factory was visited by Marshal Goering, who appeared acquainted with the story of the Cullinan Diamond and bluntly declared that he coveted the cup and would call for it the following morning, despite the protests of J. Asscher, Junior. After the Marshal had left, the cup was buried in a pile of rubble in the cellar, and the newspapers published a story that it had been stolen. It was found after the war and has resumed its honoured position in the Directors' Office.

The Stuart Sapphire

The Stuart Sapphire of 104 carats now set at the back of the State Crown is difficult to identify before the reign of Charles II. Large sapphires were not uncommon and were used to decorate ecclesiastical as well as royal ornaments. A large sapphire had been

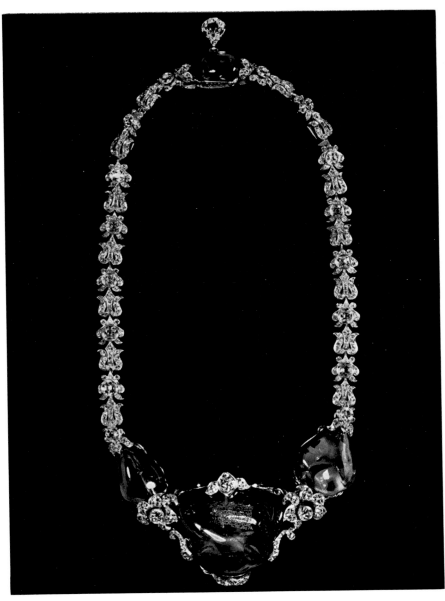

a The Timur Ruby. A necklace composed of 3 very large Indian cut rubies in the centre and one small one in the snap with a small drop diamond pendant. The chain portion is composed of clusters and trident-shaped links set with diamonds. Presented to Queen Victoria in 1851 by the Honourable East India Company from the Treasury of Lahore (pp. 187 and 191)

b (below) A girdle composed of 19 very large emeralds, 4 of which are carved enriched with lasque diamonds, pearls and small emeralds. From the trappings of a horse which formerly belonged to the Maharajah Ranjit Singh, mounted as a girdle for his successor, the Maharajah Shere Singh, and given to Queen Victoria by the Honourable East India Company in 1851 (p. 190)

a   *A cockade or cloak clasp in diamonds, formerly in five parts but altered to three parts by Queen Alexandra* (p. 190)

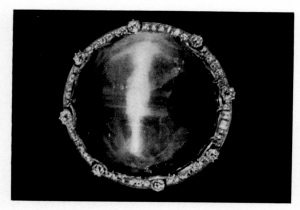

c   *The largest known catseye, $313\frac{1}{4}$ carats, on a diamond filet setting. Presented to Queen Victoria in 1886, formerly in the possession of the King of Kandy* (p. 193)

b   *Two diamond bows, made in 1859 by Garrards with diamonds supplied by Queen Victoria* (p. 193)

d   *A brooch with large sapphire and diamonds given to Queen Victoria by Prince Albert on their marriage* (p. 193)

set in the mitre of George Neville, Archbishop of York, and this was taken by Edward IV, who set it in his crown. It may have been this stone which was set in the front cross of the Imperial State Crown of Henry VIII. In the inventory taken in James I's reign in 1605 two large sapphires are recorded and there had been another in the crown of Edward VI. James II is believed to have taken the Stuart Sapphire to France with him when he fled the country and bequeathed it to his son, who passed it on to his grandson, Cardinal York, who wore it in his mitre. The Cardinal, shortly before his death, sold it to a Venetian merchant by the name of Arenberg. An Italian named Angiolo Benelli had been charged with the task of collecting the late Cardinal's papers and mementos.[1] Benelli bought the sapphire from Arenberg and then with some difficulty reached England in 1813 and gave the papers and other possessions of Cardinal York to George IV, who paid him £4,000. One item was the Stuart Sapphire, which was surrounded by 16 diamonds. The King gave it to Princess Charlotte, upon whose death it was returned as a crown jewel. Greville relates that in June 1821 the King dined at Devonshire House and Lady Conyngham wore the jewel in her head-dress. It was somehow retrieved from the Marchioness and later set in the State Crown of Queen Victoria.

The Timur Ruby (Plate 73, a)

Although not among the crown jewels in the Tower of London but forming part of a great necklace, an outstanding stone belonging to the British Crown is the Timur Ruby, or the Khiraj-i-alam, which means the 'Tribute to the World'. It is a spinel weighing 352½ carats and it has been claimed to be the largest ruby known. This, however, is not correct, for the spinel which surmounts the Imperial Russian Crown is recorded as weighing 414·30 carats (389 old carats). The term ruby is frequently applied to spinels as well as to the true or oriental ruby. The stone carries several inscriptions in the Persian language but in Arabic script.[2] The literal translation of the largest reads: 'This is the ruby among the twenty-five thousand jewels of the King of Kings, the Sultan Sahib Qiran, which in the year 1153 from the collection of jewels of Hindustan reached this place.' The date is that of the Hirja era and corresponds with A.D. 1740. The other inscriptions give the names and dates of the subsequent owners.

	Hirja	A.D.	
Akbar Shah . . .	1021	1612	Reigned 1556–1605
Jehangir Shah			1605–1627
Sahib Qiran Sani	1038	1628	1628–1658
Alamgir Shah	1070	1659	1658–1707
Badshah Ghazi Mahamad Farukh Siyar .	1125	1713	1713–1718
Ahmed Shah Duri-i-Duran . . .	1168	1754	1748–1772

The long inscription was cut by order of Nadir Shah and proves that it belonged to Amir Timur, the Tartar conqueror known in Europe as Tamerlane but known in Asia and the Moslem world as Shah Qiran, which means 'the Lord of the auspicious conjunction'.

1 Miss A. A. Taylor: *Stuart Papers at Windsor*.
2 For this and the subsequent history see a memorandum entitled *Engraved spinel rubies*, written by Sir J. R. Dunlop Smith, at the India Office, dated 21st March 1912.

This refers to the conjunction of Venus and Jupiter. Timur was born in A.D. 1336 and proclaimed himself ruler of Khorassan in 1370. After his conquest in Persia and Afghanistan he invaded India and took Delhi in 1398. He remained in India for a little over a year and returned to Samarkand in the spring of 1399. It is said that the ruby fell into the hands of Timur when he plundered Delhi. It is believed that it was in the possession of the fourth son of Timur—Mir Shah Rukh—who succeeded his father in 1408 and died in 1447 and was succeeded by his son Mirza Ulugh Beg, the famous astronomer, who reigned only two years when he was killed by his son Abdul Latif, who took the throne. It is believed that these three names were at one time inscribed on the stone but have been erased, possibly by Jehangir. The next we hear of the ruby is that it was presented to Shah Abbas I, the greatest of the Safavi Kings of Persia, whose dynasty was finally wiped out by Nadir Shah. Abbas reigned from 1587 to 1629 and it was he who, in conjunction with the British forces, took the island of Ormus from the Portuguese in 1622. He presented the ruby to the Emperor Jehangir, who at once had the names of himself and his father, the great Akbar, engraved upon it. When his favourite wife, Nur Juhan, remonstrated with him for spoiling the gem he said: 'This jewel will more certainly hand down my name to posterity than any written history. The House of Timur may fall but as long as there is a king this jewel will be his.' The jewel next passed to Shah Jahan, who had his name inscribed on it and set it in the Peacock Throne. On his deposition his son Aurangzeb gained possession of the ruby. The next two emperors' names were not engraved on the stone. When Nadir sacked Delhi in 1739 he took away most of the jewels set in the Peacock Throne. At this time the ruby was described as of 'upwards of three fingers in breadth and nearly two in length and was commonly called the Tribute of the World'. The words: 'this place' on the long inscription refer to Isfahan, where Nadir took it. In the confusion that followed the death of Nadir at Isfahan the ruby came into the possession of Ahmed Shah Durani in 1747. Taimur Shah, his son, succeeded to the gem on his father's death in 1772, and it eventually passed to Shah Shuja, his youngest son. During his detention in prison at Lahore he was forced to give up the ruby, along with the Koh-i-Nur, to Ranjit Singh. On the annexation of the Punjab in 1849 the Board of Administration took possession of all the state jewels. Some of the more valuable jewels found in the Toshakhana, including the Timur Ruby, were packed up in Lahore and sent via Karachi and Bombay to London. They were displayed at the Great Exhibition of 1851 and later presented by the Court of Directors of the East India Company, together with some pearls and an emerald girdle, to Queen Victoria. According to Herbert Smith,[1] another story is that Kirkin or Gurgin, King of Georgia, sent to Timur, through his envoys, 1,000 gold tankus struck in Timur's name, a thousand horses, fine stuffs and valuable articles including many vessels of gold, silver and crystal and a bright ruby of beautiful colour such as is rarely met with.[2] This stone approximates in weight to the largest ruby later found in the Mogul Treasury. It is narrated in the *Tuzuk* that the Prince Shah Jahan, after his victorious return from the Deccan, offered Jehangir the fine ruby which had been bought for the Prince's son at Goa for 200,000 rupees. It

[1] G. F. H. Smith: *Gem Stones*.
[2] Shafru'd Din: *Zafir Namur*. See also Doyle's *History of Timur Bec*.

seems hardly likely that there should be two rubies of such exceptional size and approximately of the same weight. It would, in any case, have made them two of the largest rubies known. It is likely that it had changed hands and found its way to Goa.[1]

In 1858 a new inventory was taken. It was headed 'Regalia in the Tower of London. Also Crown Jewels in the possession of H.M. Queen Victoria'. The necessity for this arose following the settlement of the dispute with the King of Hanover over the Hanoverian jewels, and some pieces had to be broken up in order to meet the claim. Opportunity was also taken to include in the inventory the interesting historical pieces which had been given to Queen Victoria in 1851 by the Honourable East India Company.

In 1901, in consequence of the death of Queen Victoria, an inventory of the crown jewels was again taken but this time those at the Tower of London were excluded. This inventory has been kept up-to-date and supplemented by six other lists:

1. Jewels left to the Crown by Her Majesty Queen Victoria.
2. Jewels left by Her Majesty the Late Queen Victoria, the property of His Majesty the King.[2]
3. Jewels the property of King George V.
4. Jewels left to 'His Majesty King Edward VII by Her Majesty Queen Victoria and hereafter considered as belonging to the Crown and to be worn by all future queens in right of it'.
5. Jewels given to the Crown by Her Majesty Queen Mary, 1912.
6. Jewels given to the Crown by His Majesty King George V, 1912.

These documents have never been published but with the permission of the Lord Chamberlain the author has been able to examine them. They contain a great deal of interesting information hitherto not available.

The first group of ornaments includes three regal circlets. The first is that made for George IV's coronation, for which the jewels were hired. The circlet has subsequently been reset with permanent jewels. In 1902 the band was remounted by order of Queen Alexandra and in 1937 a third row of cultured pearls was added. It became well known by being shown on the head of Queen Victoria on the stamps of her reign and in other portraits. It was subsequently worn by Queen Alexandra, Queen Mary, Queen Elizabeth and is worn by Queen Elizabeth II on her way to open Parliament. It is composed of four crosses *pattées* set with diamonds, in the centre of one of which is a straw-coloured diamond and four bouquets of rose, shamrock and thistle in diamonds. The band is of diamond scroll work and the original two rows of pearls consisted of 86 in the upper row and 94 in the lower which were changed to 81 and 88 respectively in 1902.

In 1858 a new regal circlet was ordered by Queen Victoria as a setting for the Koh-i-Nur. It was made by the Crown Jewellers and delivered in 1859. It consists of four fleurs-de-lis, four crosses *pattées* and sixteen quatrefoils each set with a large diamond. There were also four Greek honeysuckle ornaments of which one is designed to receive the Koh-i-Nur, set in a frame of small brilliants as a centre to the circlet. The centre diamond, a stone weighing $17\frac{1}{8}$ carats, was taken from the stomacher given to Queen Victoria by the Sultan of Turkey. The other diamonds were furnished by

1 Abdul Aziz: *The Imperial Treasury of the Indian Mughuls*.
2 These are not crown jewels although some items have subsequently been given to the Crown.

Queen Victoria, the large stones including 1 of 10 carats, 1 of $9\frac{7}{8}$ carats, 2 of 8 carats, 1 of $7\frac{6}{15}$ carats and 13 others from over 2 carats to under 5 carats each. In addition, 757 brilliants weighing $133\frac{31}{32}$ carats and 16 roses were employed in the circlet. In the fleurs-de-lis and cross *pattée*, 873 brilliants of $109\frac{15}{32}$ carats and 130 roses were used. The diamonds on the circlet were remounted by Messrs Garrard and Company for the crown of Queen Elizabeth in 1937. The frame of the old circlet is now in the London Museum (*Plate 60, d*). The Greek honeysuckle ornaments have been retained in their original form set with brilliants.

The third jewelled head-dress is a regal tiara of Indian design (*Plate 72, a*). It originally consisted of a leafage band surmounted by arches with leafage and opal centres and spires. There were 17 additional diamond collets set from the crown jewels in 1858 with the addition of 181 brilliants of $6\frac{13}{32}$ carats which could be used in lieu of spires. In June 1902 it was altered by order of Queen Alexandra, and it now consists of eleven principal pieces and eleven betweens on a band. The band has six centre pieces and five betweens which were remounted and 11 opals replaced by 11 rubies from the Indian necklace which was given to Queen Victoria by Sir Jung Bahadoor in 1876. The original 17 opals have been retained unset. In a memo of 1858 it states that there are 162 diamonds from part of the original tiara weighing $77\frac{5}{8}$ carats and 58 roses. In addition there were 899 brilliants of $139\frac{1}{8}$ carats and 30 roses from the general crown jewels, and 181 brilliants of $6\frac{11}{32}$ carats furnished by Messrs Garrards, a total of 1,242 brilliants of $173\frac{3}{32}$ carats and 84 roses. Part of the original tiara was broken up to satisfy the Hanoverian claims.

There are a number of jewelled Orders, those of the Garter including a very large brilliant Star and a Garter in the form of an armlet set with diamonds. There are nine Badges of the Order, one with the border, bar and loop set with large brilliants and the St George composed of diamonds, emeralds and rubies. Another large diamond, St George and the Dragon, is set with diamonds of various colours, and sapphires and rubies. In five others the St George is of carved onyx. There is also a brooch in the form of a bar for securing the riband on the shoulder. The Badge of the Order of the Thistle has a border of brilliants and a jewelled and enamelled St Andrew. The Badge of the Order of St Patrick is set with emeralds, rubies and diamonds and has a jewelled shamrock on a ruby cross.

At Windsor Castle are two swords (*Plate 77*), one a Court dress sword mounted in chased gold in the style of Louis XIV, the hilt and guard set with diamonds. The other a gold-mounted sword with a richly jewelled hilt and guard which follows the pattern of a sword worn by Napoleon. This sword belonged to Joseph Bonaparte.

A cockade (*Plate 74, a*), originally of five separate pieces set with brilliants, was altered for Queen Alexandra to a cloak clasp to consist of three pieces; the centre piece, set with a cluster of diamonds, and one side were kept in their original form and the other three pieces remounted as one to match the opposite side.

An important piece is a girdle (*Plate 73, b*) composed of 19 very large flat emeralds, 4 of which are carved, surmounted by 249 lasques,[1] 159 pearls and 56 emeralds.

---

[1] A lasque is a flat or oval-shaped stone.

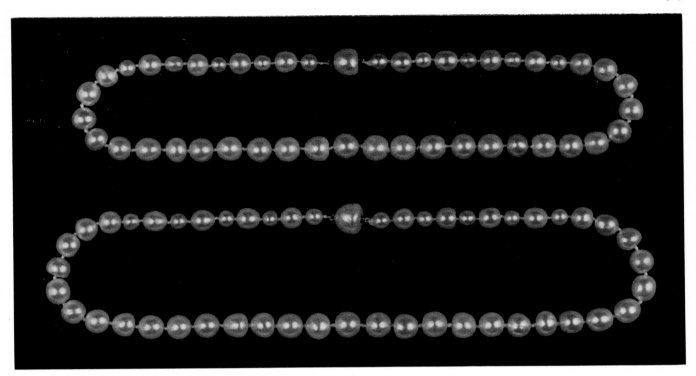

a   (i) Necklace of 46 pearls including the whole pearl snap which may have belonged to Queen Anne;   (ii) necklace of 50 pearls including the whole pearl snap which may have belonged to Queen Caroline, wife of George II (p. 191)

b   (i) Diamond necklace of 29 collets with a drop-shape diamond suspended from the centre collet; (ii) pair of large diamond collet top and drop-shape diamond ear-rings (p. 191)

c   Diamond collet necklace of 115 stones formed by a triple festoon in front and a single row at the back joined on either side with diamond triangular motifs (p. 192)

A necklace of trefoils, each with a pearl in the centre, graduated to a quatrefoil centre which is surmounted by a crown and has a large pearl pendant. This necklace was presented to Queen Victoria by The Daughters of the Empire on 24th June 1887 (p. 194)

The stones were originally set in the trappings of a horse belonging to the Maharajah Ranjit Singh and were remounted as a girdle by his successor, Maharajah Shere Singh. It was given to Queen Victoria by the Honourable East India Company in 1851 and is now in the Indian Room at Buckingham Palace.

Another ornament of great importance and interest is a necklace containing 3 very large uncut Indian rubies in the centre. A large diamond drop of 22·60 carats was originally set as a pendant from the centre ruby. It is now in the crown of Queen Elizabeth the Queen Mother but can be detached and used with the necklace. There are 2 other drop diamonds which were set on either side of the centre one, pendant from the diamond cluster between the rubies. These were taken from the original setting of the Koh-i-Nur but are now set as ear-rings. There is a small diamond pendant from the ruby snap, the chain is composed of clusters of trident-shaped links set with diamonds, two clusters of diamonds each between the 3 rubies. The rubies, which are spinels, weigh $352\frac{1}{2}$ carats, $94\frac{3}{16}$ carats and $72\frac{3}{16}$ carats. The first is one of the largest spinels known and is the famous stone called 'The Timur Ruby' or *Khiraj-i-alam*, which means 'Tribute of the World'.[1]

There are three fine diamond necklaces, the first (*Plate 75, b (i)*) was originally composed of 28 brilliant collets made with diamonds taken from the Garter Badge and a Sword. The largest stones are $11\frac{1}{2}$, $10\frac{1}{2}$, $9\frac{1}{2}$, $9\frac{1}{4}$, $8\frac{3}{4}$, $8\frac{9}{16}$, $8\frac{1}{2}$, $8\frac{3}{8}$ and $8\frac{1}{4}$ carats. The total weight of the brilliants is $161\frac{5}{16}$ carats. Two collets were removed in 1937 to make a pair of ear-rings (*Plate 75, b (ii)*) and were replaced by three from the other necklace to make up for length. The large brilliant from the crown of Queen Elizabeth the Queen Mother can be used as a pendant from the centre of the necklace.

The second necklace originally had 87 brilliant collets ranging from $\frac{3}{16}$ to $10\frac{1}{4}$ carats, but this had been reduced to 45 collets by removing 42. There is also a group of detached collets set with brilliants from which 1 was taken for the snap of the small necklace and 3 were used in the large necklace. There remain 154 collets.

There was formerly a necklace of a fringe pattern set in 1830 with brilliants which had been the property of George III. At one time they were mounted as a tiara (*Plate 72, b*) but have been remounted so that they can be used as a necklace.

A pearl necklace consisting of two rows of large pearls originally with 47 in each row but now consisting of 46, weighing 1,045 gr, in the upper row and 50 of 1,429·20 gr in the lower row (*Plate 75, a*). One row may have been a pearl necklace of Queen Anne's, to which reference has already been made, and the other belonged to Queen Caroline, wife of George II.

Other pearl necklaces are one of a single row of 81 pearls, one of one row of 116 pearls and one of four rows of pearls. The last was formerly the property of Ranjit Singh and was presented to Queen Victoria in 1851 by the Honourable East India Company. It consists of two rows of 55 pearls each, and two rows of 56 each with a square snap set with 2 large rubies and small diamonds and a red silk tassel pendant from it. This necklace has been restrung on several occasions, notably in 1910, 1937 and 1941 and each row has now a snap of 1 pearl enabling it to be worn as one long row.

Apart from diamonds and pearls made up as necklaces there were, in 1947, 239

[1] See p. 187.

diamond collets in a brown box not in use. In 1950 115 of these collets were formed into a three-row festoon necklace with a single row at the back and two triangular ornaments joining the front and the back (*Plate 75, c*).

An amethyst suite, which had belonged to the Duchess of Kent, mother of Queen Victoria, consists of a necklace, three brooches, a pair of ear-rings and a pair of side-combs. Amethysts were very popular in the late XVIII and early XIX centuries and were quite valuable. Queen Charlotte had an amethyst necklace worth £2,000, but today the stone is fairly common and owing to the change in fashion the necklace would now be valued at not more than £100.

There are twenty-one rings, all but four of which were sent to Windsor Castle on 24th November 1910 by the command of Queen Mary. They are:

A brilliant half-hoop with 5 brilliants in a carved gold shank.

A ruby half-hoop of 5 rubies in a plain gold shank.

A turquoise half-hoop with 5 turquoises in a forked gold shank.

A portrait ring.

A double diamond ring containing hair.

A ring with a long oblong head with diamond border; on it is engraved 'Charles Manners, Duke of Rutland, October 24, 1787'.

A ring with an oval head with hair in the centre and *Toujours chere* at the back.

A ring with a circular head with diamond border and cypher *J.P.* which denotes Rear-Admiral J. W. Pain, who died on 17th November 1803.

A ring with an oblong octagon head for hair with diamond border.

A ring with a portrait with diamond border and diamonds on shoulders engraved 'Queen Charlotte'.

An oval ring with birds in diamonds with *Toujours chere* in white enamelled scroll at the back.

An oval mourning ring with date 'October 20, 1784, Act 28' and the initials *M.L.* in diamonds.

A black enamelled ring with oblong diamond border engraved 'Edward, Lord Thurlow, ob. 12 September, 1806, Act. 76'.

A ring with a large oblong single stone diamond.

An old portrait ring with paste border.

A large oblong slide set with brilliants with a miniature engraved in sardonyx and also the word 'Dorset'.

A portrait ring engraved 'George II'.

A portrait ring engraved 'George III'.

A lasque ring set in plain gold.

An old oval diamond ring engraved 'Frederick, Duke of York'.

A large oval ring formerly with an opal with 6 brilliants on the shoulders. In 1936 the opal was removed and the ring reset with pink tourmaline which belonged to King Edward.

There are four bracelets; one is composed of five square foliage tablets set with brilliants; the second is of gold and blue enamel with oval head containing hair and cypher; engraved on the back is 'Hair of William Frederick, Duke of Gloucester, died 30 November 1834', bequeathed to the Duchess of Kent by the Duchess of Gloucester. Another bracelet is of 116 brilliants set in four rows. It was mounted in 1838. The fourth bracelet consists of four rows of 88 graduated pearls. This was also mounted in 1838.

A group of brooches includes one composed of diamonds and 8 pearls with 3 pendant pearls and three brooches, two large and one small, in the form of bows set with diamonds (*Plate 74, b*). These were mounted in May 1858 by Garrards and contain 497 pearls and 9 roses supplied by Queen Victoria. A brooch or snap in circular form set with 6 large brilliants and a cluster centre made in 1830 from the brilliant Badge of the Bath belonging to King George III. Six brooches or hairpins with a wheat-leaf design set with diamonds were made in 1830 from diamonds belonging to King George III; also an oval brooch with a diamond border; a pendant of circular form with a large ruby in the centre set around with small brilliants with a single diamond pendant and drop.

An interesting item is a Cat's Eye[1] mounted in gold and set with small rubies (*Plate 74, c*). It was taken from the King of Kandy when conquered and presented to Queen Victoria by Mr (later Sir) Edward Durney Lawrence. It is the largest Cat's Eye known and weighs $313\frac{1}{4}$ carats. It is now in a diamond setting. There are also a pair of brilliant ear-tops, which have large brilliant drops, taken from the ruby necklace and which were originally in the bracelet in which the Koh-i-Nur was set. Another pair of diamond top and drop ear-rings have emerald drops and swinging diamond fringes; a pair of single pearl ear-tops have two large drop-shaped pearls given by the Prince Consort in 1847, 2 collets from the necklaces were mounted as tops; a pair of large diamond solitaire ear-rings set with 2 brilliants taken from the large collet necklace; a large pair of ear-rings with rubies and diamond borders which was given by King George V to Queen Mary on 26th May 1926. Queen Mary added them to the ruby suite in the crown jewels in 1926.

The second list enumerates the jewels left to the Crown by Queen Victoria. The first item is an enamelled portrait of George IV set in diamonds with an oak wreath and acorns and a diamond crown at the top. This had been left to Queen Victoria by her aunt, the late Queen of Wurtemberg. Another bequest from this source in 1829 was a diamond whole hoop ring with the date '18 September, 1761', which had been Queen Charlotte's guard ring. These two ornaments are now at Windsor Castle. Another item is a small miniature of Queen Charlotte set in diamonds. There are also the Stars of the Orders of the Garter, the Bath, the Thistle and St Patrick.

A beautiful brooch with a very large sapphire set with 12 large diamonds was a present given to Queen Victoria by the Prince Consort on her marriage on 20th February 1840 (*Plate 74, d*). Another wedding present given to the Queen by her aunts, Princess Augusta, the Landgravine of Hesse Homberg, the Duchess of Gloucester and the Princess Sophia, was a large bracelet with 1 large emerald in the centre of it, set in diamonds. A suite designed by the Prince Consort consisted of a large oval brooch with a drop composed of opals with a diamond border. This was reconstructed in 1926 when the opals were replaced by rubies. A pair of ear-rings to match had been altered on 11th July 1902, when the opals were replaced by 3 rubies from the necklace given by Sir Jung Bahadoor, and 1 purchased by Queen Alexandra. A necklace originally of opals and brilliants consisted of 13 opal centres with borders of brilliants, but the opals were replaced on 27th April 1902 with rubies from Sir Jung Bahadoor's necklace. There is

---

[1] In the Inventory it is described as a 'Cakeye' which is obviously an error of transcription.

also an opal brilliant drop with a border of brilliants made into a brooch in which the opal has been replaced by a ruby. Another piece is a small oval brooch to match as a slide which was given to the Prince Consort by Queen Victoria in 1840. The original opal in the centre has been replaced by a ruby.

A present from the Empress of the French, given on 28th August 1855, was a flower holder of open gold work set with rubies, diamonds and pearls. In 1844 the Princess Sophia Mathilda of Gloucester bequeathed five rings which in 1910 were sent to Windsor by command of Queen Mary. They each contain small locks of hair of five of the young members of the royal family at the end of the XIX century.

Queen Victoria received a number of presents on the occasions of her Jubilee in 1887 and her Diamond Jubilee in 1897. These include a pendant composed of a gold repoussé, a George and the Dragon on a Garter, with a blue enamel background, the whole set in diamonds with 1 pearl drop. This was a present from the Household of the Prince and Princess of Wales in June 1887. From the Daughters of the Empire she received a necklace (*Plate 76*) composed of diamond trefoils graduated in size with 1 pearl in the centre of each, a large quatrefoil of diamonds with 1 large pearl in the centre and 1 pearl drop forming the centre of the necklace. It can be worn either as a brooch or a pendant. With it goes a pair of ear-rings to match, each composed of 1 pearl in a trefoil of diamonds. In 1897 the Queen's servants gave her a bracelet composed of diamonds, rubies and sapphires with a crown in the centre and '1837–1897' on the band. The Ladies and Gentlemen of Her Majesty's household on the occasion of the Diamond Jubilee in 1897 gave a pearl and diamond brooch with a pearl centre and a pearl drop pendant.

Another present was given to Queen Victoria by the Crown Prince and Princess of Prussia in 1862. It consists of an oxidised silver cross with 1 pearl in a crown of thorns in the centre containing a photograph of the Prince Consort and containing a lock of the Prince Consort's hair.

This list includes four other rings which do not require detailed descriptions.

The next list was of the jewels belonging to His Royal Highness the Prince Consort, and consisted of thirteen Badges and Stars of various Orders. There is a Garter composed of very fine diamonds which, together with the Star of the Garter, set with very fine diamonds and a cross of 5 rubies, was given to the Prince by Queen Victoria on 10th February 1840, together with a Badge of the Order composed of very fine diamonds with an onyx centre on a swivel with St George on one side and St Andrew on the other. There was another Badge of the Order also set with fine diamonds; a Badge of the Order of the Bath has four lions set in diamonds, the centre surrounded with small emeralds. Queen Victoria gave the Prince Consort on 26th August 1841 a fine Badge of the Golden Fleece set in diamonds with 3 fine opals in the centre, while the Prince of Wales gave his father a small Badge of the Golden Fleece set in diamonds with a sapphire centre. A Star and Badge of the Turkish Order Medjidi set with diamonds, a Star of India in gold with a diamond motto in blue enamel and a diamond star in the centre, a Badge of the Star of India, and a Badge of the Elephant Order of Denmark composed of enamel and diamonds are other items.

The next list were jewels left by Queen Victoria and the property of the King, and it is specifically stated that they were not Crown property. However, certain items were added to the India Collection in Buckingham Palace in January 1926. The most notable is a large Indian necklace consisting of 10 large square-shaped lasques, 4 small ones, 4 pearls, 3 emeralds, and 2 ruby solid drops in front with 6 *cabochon* rubies in the back connected by three rows of gold chain. This necklace was given to the Prince of Wales in India in 1876 by the Maharajah Scindia. It was reset in almost the original shape, with a few ornaments in red enamel and a snap with rubies added to it. The snap was made out of a large ring presented to the Queen with other jewellery by the Maharajah of Mysore in 1862. King George V gave it to the Indian collection.

A large ruby and diamond cluster necklace with a ruby clasp was given to the Prince of Wales in India in 1876 by Sir Jung Bahadoor. The rubies were taken out of this necklace in 1902 by order of Queen Alexandra and 11 were placed in the Indian tiara, 3 in a pair of top and drop ear-rings and 14 in a cluster necklace with drop.

A large sapphire ring with ruby cross with 5 diamonds encrusted surrounded by diamonds and diamond shoulders was given to Queen Victoria by the Duchess of Kent in 1838. It is engraved 'Queen Victoria's Coronation Ring, 1838'. Queen Alexandra gave it to Queen Mary in 1911, who, by the desire of King George V, sent it to the Tower of London in March 1919 to be added to the regalia.

The next section is a short list of items which were the property of King George V. There is then a list of items left by Queen Victoria to King Edward VII but to be considered as belonging to the Crown and to be worn by all future queens in right of it.

At the end of the first seven items there is a passage evidently taken from the Queen's Will which says: 'All these were given to me by my beloved husband.' The first item is a bracelet containing an enamel portrait of the Prince Consort, by Essex after Thornburns, in miniature, in armour set in a blue enamel garter with a bunch of five gold knots and four enamel York and Lancaster roses with a garter round each, the same as a collar of the Order. The Prince Consort gave this to the Queen at Christmas, 1844.

The next item is a bracelet with gold and blue enamel in six compartments and four pearls containing a portrait of the Queen's children given to the Queen on 24th May 1845. Another bracelet is similar to the above and contains mainly portraits of the Queen's younger sons. It dates from 26th August 1854.

A present given at Christmas 1849 was a shawl pin in silver and carbuncles, an exact model of an ancient Irish brooch at the Library of the Trinity College, Dublin. A present given on 21st November 1848 was a Cairn-Gorm picked up by the Prince Consort at Loch-na-Gar on 27th September 1848, and set as a Celtic brooch with alternate garnets set in blue enamel and flowers and small pearls, a ring pattern of blue and white enamel connecting the flowers and stones. It was worn on the shoulder by the Prince of Wales.

At Christmas 1858 the Queen received a brooch of English and French colours with the Turkish Crescent in diamonds, rubies and sapphires, bound by a Crimean ribbon. A present given to the Queen on 10th February 1842 was a brooch of Prince of Wales' feathers in white enamel with a coronet of gold and small enamel stones and pearls and a motto in a blue enamelled riband. Other items in this list were:

A bracelet portrait of the Princess Augusta by Sir William Ross set in gold with gold covering.

A bracelet of engraved gold containing a miniature of Princess Charlotte. The bracelet was designed by the Princess and given by the King of the Belgians on 24th May 1848.

A bracelet which had belonged to Princess Augusta of burnished gold containing a portrait of George III in the uniform of 'The Blues' with a cocked hat.

A bracelet containing the miniatures of the Queen of Portugal and King Ferdinand by Faja after Ross set in gold, rubies and diamonds, a small crown between the two miniatures, October 1853.

A bracelet left to the Queen by the Queen of the Belgians of gold and light blue enamel with 2 opals in the centre as shields, 1850.

A present from the Duchess of Kent on 21st November 1841 was a bracelet with a gold chain with dark blue enamel heart, Prince of Wales' feathers in gold containing the first hair of the Prince of Wales, also lockets with the hair of the other royal children.

Another bracelet of burnished gold in thirteen compartments contains the hair of George III and Queen Charlotte and of all their children.

A necklace of pearls from the Loch and River Tay consists of 61 pearls and a double pearl snap was given by Lord Breadalbane on 24th March 1849.

Four coloured photographs of the Prince of Wales, Prince Arthur, Prince Alfred and Prince Leopold could be worn at pleasure in a setting of diamonds and emeralds on black velvet bands.

The Queen received from her mother, the Duchess of Kent, a vinaigrette of light blue enamel with a gold-covered cup. A crochet of dark blue enamel and diamonds with watch seal and key was given by 'Madame Adelaide'. A ring of blue enamel found in an ancient Indian tomb was given to the Queen by the Princess Royal on 25th April 1857.

The next list contains two armlets given to the Crown by Queen Mary in 1912. They are now in the Indian collection at Buckingham Palace. The first was an armlet consisting of a long spinel ruby between 2 pearls strung on crimson silk. It was given to Queen Mary at Jeypore in December 1911 by the Maharajah of Jeypore, whose ancestor was Sahib-i-Koran Suliman, Emperor of Delhi 1038 H–A.D. 1620. The other is an armlet consisting of a long spinel ruby between 2 pearls strung on crimson silk. It was given to Queen Mary at Jeypore by the Maharajah whose ancestor received it from Shah Alam, Emperor of Delhi, 1111 H–A.D. 1692.

The final item is an armlet which was given to the Queen by His Majesty King George V in 1912 and is now in the Indian collection at Buckingham Palace. The armlet consists of a long pear-shaped spinel ruby engraved with the names of three of the Mogul emperors with seed pearl and silk ends, given to King Edward VII at his coronation by H.H. Rajah Sir Hira Singh of Nabha.

In addition to the crown jewels there are others which are family heirlooms and those which are the personal property of the sovereign, but these do not form part of our subject.

BIBLIOGRAPHY

AUERBACH, ERNA — *Tudor Artists*, London 1954.

AYLOFFE, J. — 'An account of the Body of King Edward the First in the year 1774', *Archaeologia*, Vol. III, 1775.

BLAIR, P. H. — *Anglo-Saxon England.*

CLIFFORD-SMITH, H. — *Jewellery*, 1908.

COLLINS, A. J. — *Jewels and Plate of Elizabeth I*, London 1955.

DART, J. — *Westmonsterium.*

DAVENPORT, CYRIL — *The English Regalia*, 1897.

DEVON, FREDERICK — *Issues of the Exchequer.*

DOLLEY, R. H. — 'Explanatory note on Coins, Medals, Dyes and Seals, in the Catalogue of an Exhibition of Royal Portraits in the Royal Academy of Arts', 1953.

ETIENNE OF ROUEN — *Draco Normannicus.*

EVANS, JOAN — *The History of Jewellery, 1000–1870*, London 1951. *English Jewellery from the V century to A.D. 1800*, London 1921

FOX, GEORGE — Unpublished Account of the Firm of Rundell, Bridge and Rundell, London Jewellers, 1843–6.

FREEMAN, DR E. A. — *The History of the Norman Conquest of England*, 1870.

FROUDE, J. A. — *History of England*, 1876.

GREVILLE, C. C. — *Journal of the Reigns of George IV and William IV*, Vol. II. *Journal of the Reign of Queen Victoria*, Vol. I.

HOLMES, M. R. — 'The Crowns of England', *Archaeologia*, Vol. LXXXVI, 1937. 'New Light on St Edward's Crown', *Archaeologia*, Vol. XCVII, 1959.

HOLTZMANN, W. — *Papsturkunden in England*, 1 and 2.

HOPE, W. H. ST JOHN — 'The King's Coronation Ornaments.' *The Ancestor*, Vols. I and II, 1902.

JONES, E. A. — *The Old Royal Plate in the Tower of London*, 1908.

JONES, W. — *Crowns and Coronations*, London 1898.

LYON, A. R. — 'The Imperial Style of the Tenth-Century Anglo-Saxon Kings.' In *History*, New Series, Vol. XL, 1958.

MASKELL, W. — *Monumenta Ritualia Ecclesiae Anglicane*, Vol. II.

PALGRAVE, SIR FRANCIS — *The Antient Kalendars and Inventories of the Treasury of H.M. Exchequer*, 3 Vols., London 1836.

RAYNBERT DE PARIS — *Ogier the Dane.*

RUSSELL, P. E. — The English Intervention in Spain and Portugal in the time of Edward III and Richard II, Oxford 1955.

RYMER, THOMAS — *Foedera* 1830.

SANDFORD, FRANCIS	*The History of the Coronation of King James II.*
SCHRAMM, P. E.	*Herrschaftszeichen und Staatssymbolik.*
	The History of the English Coronation Ceremony, Oxford 1937.
SITWELL, MAJOR-GENERAL H. D. W.	*The Crown Jewels and Other Regalia in the Tower of London*, 1953.
STENTON, SIR F. AND OTHERS	*The Bayeux Tapestry*, London 1957.
STEVENSON, THE REV E. (Editor)	*Chronicon Monasterii de Abingdon*, Rolls Series, 1858.
TAYLOR, A.	*The Glory of Regality*, London 1820.
TENNANT, PROF. J.	*A Description of the Imperial State Crown of Queen Victoria*, 1858.
WALPOLE, HORACE	*Reminiscences*, London 1788.
WICKHAM LEGG, L. G.	*English Coronation Records*, 1901.
YOUNGHUSBAND, SIR GEORGE	*The Crown Jewels of England*, 1919.
	The Jewel House, 1921.

KINGS OF ENGLAND

(Unless otherwise stated, the coronations were held in Westminster Abbey)

BEFORE THE CONQUEST

827 Egbert. Called 'King of England' 828

837 Ethelwulf

856 Ethelwulf's consort, Judith, crowned

860 Ethelbert

866 Ethelred

886 Alfred the Great chosen as king. Crowned at Winchester 891

901 Edward the Elder. Crowned at Kingston-on-Thames or London

924 Athelstan. Crowned at Kingston-on-Thames

940 Edmund I. Crowned at Kingston-on-Thames

946 Edred. Crowned at Kingston-on-Thames

955 Edwy succeeded

959 Edgar the Peaceable. Crowned 973

975 Edward the Martyr. Crowned at Kingston-on-Thames

979 Ethelred the Unready. Crowned at Kingston-on-Thames

1013 Sweyn of Denmark

1014 Canute the Great
     Ethelred again

1016 Edmund Ironside shared the kingdom with Canute. Crowned at Kingston-on-Thames

1035 Harold I

1040 Hardicanute

1042 Edward the Confessor. Crowned at Winchester, Easter Day 1043

1066 Harold II. Crowned in London 5th January

ENGLAND

THE NORMANS

1066   William the Conqueror. Crowned at Westminster Abbey 25th December
        William's consort Matilda. Crowned at Winchester 11th May 1068
1087   William Rufus. Crowned at Westminster Abbey 26th September
1100   Henry I. Crowned 5th August
        Henry's wife, Matilda, crowned 11th November 1100
1135   Stephen. Crowned 26th December
        Stephen's wife, Matilda of Boulogne, crowned 22nd March 1136

THE PLANTAGENETS

1154   Henry II. Crowned 19th December
1170   (Henry, son of Henry II, crowned as co-regent in father's lifetime but died
        1183)
        Marguerite, the wife of the young King Henry, crowned at Winchester 1172
1189   Richard I Cœur de Lion. Crowned 3rd September
1199   John. Crowned 27th May
        John's consort Isabella of Angoulême, crowned 8th October 1200
1216   Henry III. Crowned at Gloucester 28th October. Crowned again at Westminster
        16th June 1220
        Henry III's consort, Eleanor of Provence, crowned 21st January 1236
1272   Edward I. Crowned with consort, Eleanor of Castile, 19th August 1274
1307   Edward II. Crowned with consort, Isabella of France, 25th February 1308
1327   Edward III. Crowned with consort, Philippa of Hainault, 18th February 1327
1377   Richard II. Crowned 16th July
        Richard's consort, Anne of Bohemia, crowned 22nd January 1382

HOUSE OF LANCASTER

1399   Henry IV. Crowned 13th October
        Henry IV's second consort, Joan of Navarre, crowned 1403
1413   Henry V. Crowned 9th April
1420   Henry's wife, Catherine of France, crowned 24th February
1422   Henry VI. Crowned 6th November 1429
        Henry's consort, Margaret of Anjou, crowned 30th May 1445

HOUSE OF YORK

1461   Edward IV. Crowned 29th June
        Edward's consort, Elizabeth Woodville, crowned 26th May 1465
1483   Edward V. Was not crowned
1483   Richard III. Crowned 6th July

HOUSE OF TUDOR

1485   Henry VII. Crowned 30th October
        Henry's consort, Elizabeth of York, crowned 25th November 1487

1509   Henry VIII and consort, Catharine of Aragon. Crowned 24th June
        Henry's second consort, Anne Boleyn, crowned 1st June 1533
1547   Edward VI. Crowned 20th February
1553   Mary I. Crowned 1st October
1558   Elizabeth I. Crowned 13th January 1559

HOUSE OF STUART

1603   James I. Crowned 25th July
1625   Charles I succeeded. Crowned 5th February 1626
1649   Commonwealth
1661   Charles II. Crowned 23rd April
1685   James II. Crowned with consort, Mary of Modena, 23rd April
1689   William III and Mary II. Crowned 11th April
1702   Anne. Crowned 23rd April

HOUSE OF HANOVER

1714   George I. Crowned 20th October
1727   George II. Crowned with consort, Caroline of Anspach, 11th October
1760   George III. Crowned with consort, Charlotte of Mecklenburg, 22nd September
        1761
1820   George IV. Crowned 19th July 1821
1830   William IV. Crowned with consort, Adelaide of Saxe-Meinigen, 8th September
        1831
1837   Victoria. Crowned 28th June 1838
1901   Edward VII. Crowned with consort, Alexandra of Denmark, 9th August 1902

HOUSE OF WINDSOR

1910   George V. Crowned with consort, Mary of Teck, 22nd June 1911
        Edward VIII was not crowned
1936   George VI. Crowned with consort, Elizabeth, 12th May 1937
1952   Elizabeth II. Crowned 2nd June 1953

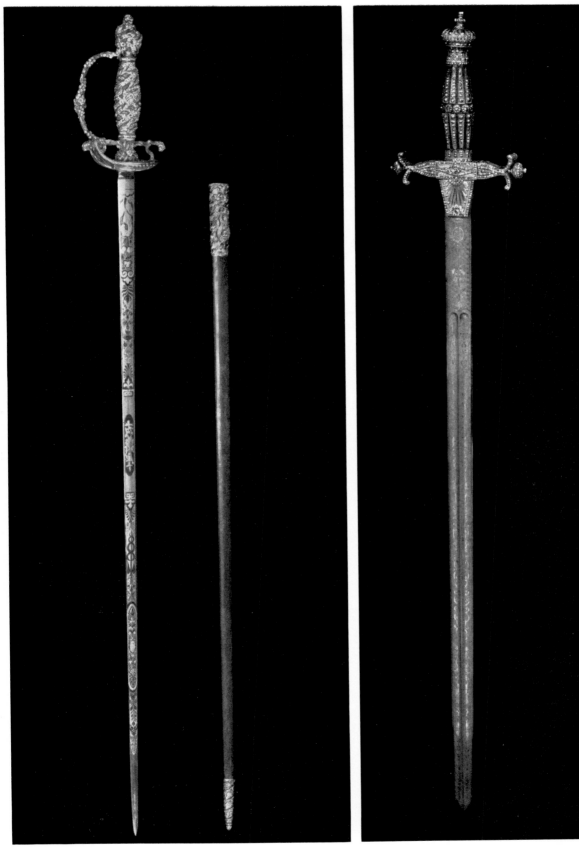

a   *Court dress sword mounted in chased gold in the style of Louis XIV. Made for George II and worn by George IV. Windsor Castle (p. 190)*

b   *Gold sword with richly chased hilt and guard set with hematite. Belonged to Joseph Bonaparte. Windsor Castle (p. 190)*

a   *Crown attributed to King Hunald, Duke of Aquitaine (obiit 774). Bibliothèque Nationale (p. 209)*

b (above, right)   *Reliquary crown of St Louis previously in the possession of the Dominicans at Liège. XIII-Century. The Louvre (p. 222)*

c (above) *XIII-century reliquary crown. Treasury, Amiens Cathedral (p. 222)*

d (left) *Crown attributed to Margaret of Bavaria, who married John the Fearless, Duke of Burgundy, in 1385. Dijon Museum (p. 225)*

CHAPTER EIGHT

FRANCE

The history of the French monarchy is that of seven dynasties or lines of sovereigns—Merovingian, Carolingian, Capet, Valois, Bourbon, Bonaparte and Orleans—covering a period from the v to xix centuries. It was not until the end of the xv century that the general area of land and its boundaries conformed approximately to those which we know as modern France, and they varied considerably from one period to another. But the monarchy became the centre of the development of a distinctive culture which led to the growth of the French nation and which made an outstanding contribution to Western civilisation.

THE MEROVINGIAN DYNASTY

The origin of the Merovingians is obscure, but dates from the time of the Roman withdrawal from Gaul. The first king was said to be Pharamond, but he is a legendary figure whose existence is doubtful. His supposed son, Clodion the Hairy, was King of the Salian Franks in 428–47, and his son-in-law, Merovic, who was the next king, gave his name to the dynasty. In 458 he was succeeded by his son Childeric. At the end of the v century, amid the ruins of the Roman Empire, the Church maintained its position and influence in Gaul, and under Clovis, the son of Childeric, there appeared a substitute for the Emperor in lending military support to the Church. Clovis, having defeated the Merovingian heads of the other Frankish States and after a war with Burgundy, married in 493 Clotilda, the niece of the King of Burgundy who was an orthodox Christian. In 507 he defeated the Alamans, and in 508 the Visigoths, and he decided to be baptised into the orthodox Church,[1] an event of great historical importance. This was the occasion which led to the legend of the *Sainte Ampoule*, which contained the Holy Oil and which was later used for the anointing of the Kings of France, thus giving them a special position among the sovereigns of Europe.

According to the legend, Clovis, as a result of the influence of his wife who implored him to become a Christian, vowed that if he could turn the threatened defeat by the Alamans into a victory, he would be baptised. The legend goes on to say that the tide of battle turned and the Alamans were routed and their king slain. Clovis returned to his capital and preparations were made for the royal baptism. On the appointed day the King stood ready at the font, but the pressure of the crowd prevented the priest with the chrism needed for the sacrament from reaching the baptistry. Waiting in vain, St Remi (Remigius), the saintly Bishop of Rheims in charge of the ceremony, knelt down

1 The word 'orthodox' is used in distinction to the Arian heresy which was very prevalent at the time.

in prayer, and in response to his prayer a dove, whiter than snow, appeared from out of the sky holding in its beak an ampoule with the chrism needed to consummate the sacrament. Thus it came about that Clovis, the first Christian King of the Franks, was anointed with a miraculous chrism divinely presented.[1]

Where and when the baptism occurred has not been accurately determined. There are those who consider that it took place in Rheims in 506 or 507 after the defeat of the Alamans, while others think that it was at Tours in 508 after the defeat of the Visigoths. The case for the latter has been well argued by Oppenheimer.[2] About 507–8 Clovis received from the Emperor Anastasius I the dignity of a Roman consul, and according to some that of a Roman patrician, which legalised his conquest and conferred upon him civil powers. With this honour were sent a golden crown, a purple tunica and a chlamys. These he donned in the church of St Martin at Tours in 508, and mounting his horse he rode to the cathedral distributing largesse to the people. According to Oppenheimer's argument, he was then baptised in the cathedral. Subsequently he is said to have given the crown to the basilica of St Peter.[3] When Clotaire, the last surviving son of Clovis, died in 561, his four sons divided the kingdom between them and completed the conquest of Gaul. The Merovingian kings, who were really little better than warlike chiefs, showed considerable energy down to the death of Dagobert (*obiit* 639), but it was a period of foreign and internecine wars. Thereafter a decline set in and no king reached more than the age of twenty-five. The real power fell into the hands of the Mayors of the Palace who belonged to the Carolingian family. Finally, in 751, Pepin, who was Mayor of the Palace, obtained the consent of Pope Zacharias to send King Childeric III to the Monastery of St Omer, while his son Thierry was confined to another monastery, and the line became extinct.

There is very little information available about the royal ornaments of the Merovingian kings. There is some evidence of the royal state of the early ones in the ornaments found in the grave of Childeric I which was opened at Tournai on 27th May 1753. These included 100 gold coins of the Emperors Marcian, Leo, Zeno and Valentinian; two rings, one of which bears the inscription *CHILDRICI REGIS*; a sword and scabbard; a mantle plate; an armlet; a globe of crystal and a number of ornaments supposed to represent bees 'of the purest gold, their wings being inlaid with a red stone like a cornelian'.

Montfaucon[4] mentions insignia on the statues of Merovingian kings in various churches. These include seven crowns on the statues of Clovis, his Queen and his sons at St Germain-les-Prés; five crowns on statues in the stone portals of the cathedral of Notre-Dame in Paris; two crowns from the cathedral of Chartres; a crown engraved on the tomb of Clotaire in the church of St Médard at Soissons, and others. But as these are not contemporary they are not reliable. They were probably either the fanciful ideas of the artists, or represented insignia in use at a much later time. It is known that Clovis had a passion for imitating conventions at the Byzantine Court and

---

[1] Sir Francis Oppenheimer: *The Legend of the Sainte Ampoule.*
[2] Sir Francis Oppenheimer: *Frankish Themes and Problems.*   [3] *Chronyque de Gauthier*, Tôme 1, p. 2.
[4] B. de Montfaucon: *Les Monumens de la Monarchie Françoise*, 1729, Tôme 1.

therefore it is reasonable to conjecture that he may have adopted the Byzantine insignia. After he had assumed the robes sent to him by the Emperor when he was made a consul, the Merovingian kings continued to use a tunic which was a close-fitting garment with wide-open sleeves, but shorter than that worn by Roman officials in order to reveal the leggings which were a characteristic part of the costume of the Frankish warriors which the King shared with his soldiers.[1] Over these the kings wore a mantle.

We know that in the Treasury of St Denis, a church which was built by Dagobert, there was a golden sceptre ascribed to that king. It was described by Doublet,[2] and he mentions that the antiquaries of his day considered it to be a consular staff. On the summit was a golden eagle on which was sitting a youth, said by some to be Ganymede. The eagle's wings were set with 4 emeralds and a garnet surrounded by 8 pearls. The eagle was based on a globe held by a hand with a little branch garnished with pearls, enamels and coral. Below the hand was a golden rod also enamelled and set with stones. Doublet adds that this sceptre was beautiful and precious. Serious doubts have been cast, however, as to whether any part of the sceptre dates back to the time of Dagobert.

According to Doublet,[3] Queen Nanthilde, the second wife of Dagobert, presented a pair of bracelets which he describes as being 'so rare and exquisite as not to be compared with any other'. Another pair of bracelets of great value was given to St Denis by Pepin. These had belonged to Gayfier, or Wayfer, Duke of Aquitaine who was defeated by Pepin. There is still preserved in the Bibliothèque Nationale in Paris the so-called throne of Dagobert which by tradition was the coronation chair of the Kings of France. Abbé Suger, who had the chair repaired, thought it was one of a pair made for Dagobert by St Eloy, and relates that at an earlier date it was used by the sovereigns to receive the homage of the nobles. But it fell into disrepair and disuse until it was repaired and used by Napoleon at his coronation. It is considered by modern archaeologists to be a Roman curule chair of the late classic period. Originally it was a folding type of chair, but with no back piece.[4]

THE CAROLINGIAN DYNASTY

Pepin, or Peppin, the Short, was the son of Charles Martel, who from 715 until his death in 741 had, as Mayor of the Palace, been king in all but name. Charles divided his power between his two sons—Carloman took the eastern part of the kingdom and Pepin the western. In 747 Carloman abdicated and became a monk, leaving Pepin in sole possession, and in 751 he took the title of King. Expecting resistance if he usurped the Merovingian throne, Pepin took the wise precaution of gaining strong support from the Church and carefully prepared the way for his accession by obtaining the approval of Pope Zacharias for the establishment of the Carolingian dynasty. In November 751 he persuaded Boniface to anoint and crown him in the name of the bishops. This ceremony, which was new to France, gave the sovereign immense prestige and the monarchy a sacred character. After the ceremony at Soissons he was proclaimed King

1 Sir Francis Oppenheimer: *Frankish Themes and Problems.*
2 Jacques Doublet: *Histoire de l'Abbaye de St Denis, 1625.*   3 Jacques Doublet: op. cit.
4 Sir Martin Conway: 'The Abbey of St Denis and its Ancient Treasures', in *Archaeologia*, Vol. 66, 1914–15.

in an assembly of nobles, counts and bishops and took the title *Gratia Dei rex Francorum*. There now followed an event which was second only in importance to the baptism of Clovis. The Papacy could no longer rely on the military protection of the Emperor and the emergence of the strong Lombard kingdom constituted a menace. Pope Gregory III had turned to Charles Martel for aid when in 739 he offered him the Patriciate, but Charles had declined because of his relations with Liutprand, King of the Lombards. By 753 the Pope's position had become perilous. The Lombards had captured Ravenna, the seat of the Byzantine Exarch, threatened to march on Rome, over which the Lombard King claimed jurisdiction, and sought to impose the head tax on Roman citizens. Pope Stephen II travelled to Gaul to seek, by a personal appeal, the support of Pepin, who promised to intervene against the Lombards. In return, the Pope conferred upon the King the Patriciate, and to ensure that the Carolingian dynasty would continue to protect the Papacy, Pepin's two sons, Charles[1] and Carloman, aged eleven and three respectively, were also made Patricians. In the Abbey of St Denis the Pope anointed and confirmed Pepin's Queen and his two sons, and then anointed Pepin and invested him with the insignia and robe of a patrician. That this act should have been performed by the Pope himself, on the first visit of a Pope to France, immensely increased the prestige of the monarchy and confirmed its sacred character. Moreover, it gave the monarchy a special relationship with the Church as its defender and the Papacy as its protector and paved the way for the creation of the Western Empire under Charlemagne. On the death of Pepin 768, Charlemagne became king of the northern parts of the Frankish kingdom known as Neustria, Burgundy and Provence, while his brother was recognised as king of the eastern parts, including Austrasia, Swabia and Thuringia. Charlemagne was crowned at Noyon on 9th October 768 and Carloman at Soissons on the same day. In 771 Carloman died and Charlemagne was recognised at Sorbery as sole King of the Franks. On Christmas Day 800 Charlemagne was crowned by the Pope at Rome as Emperor of the West. On the death of Charlemagne in 814, the disastrous Frankish royal custom of dividing up their inheritance as though it were private property led to a rapid disintegration. By 839 the Empire had been divided into three kingdoms and by 879 these had been split into seven.

Louis the Pious, the sole survivor of Charlemagne's three sons, had been crowned by Charlemagne at Aix-la-Chapelle as Emperor in 813, and in 816 he was crowned with his Empress by the Pope at Rheims. In 817 he divided the Empire between his three sons, associating Lothair, the eldest, with the government of the Empire.

On Louis' death, the Empire was dismembered and Charles the Bald became the first King of the West Franks. He was anointed and crowned at Metz as King of Lorraine by Hincmar, Archbishop of Rheims, in 869. At this ceremony, Hincmar addressed the Court and high ecclesiastics and referred to the chrism of divine origin: 'Charles . . . of the race of Clovis who was baptised and with the heaven-sent chrism, some of which we still possess, anointed and consecrated King.'[2] This is the first reference which we have of the Holy Chrism used at the baptism being associated with the anointing of a king. Hincmar was anxious to establish Rheims as the coronation place of the French

---

[1] Subsequently known as Charlemagne
[2] Sir Francis Oppenheimer: *The Legend of the Sainte Ampoule*. P. E. Schramm: op. cit.

kings, and the fact that the Holy Chrism was still preserved there might have been construed as giving Rheims a special claim.

In 852 Hincmar had been responsible for the second opening of St Remi's tomb, when he transferred the remains to a silver casket. Among the objects found in the tomb were two ampoules. There already existed a legend which related that a dying pagan had begged for St Remi's presence at his bedside because he wished to die a Christian. When St Remi asked the priest in attendance for the chrism for the pagan's baptism, none was available. The legend related that St Remi ordered empty ampoules to be placed on the altar and in answer to his prayer they were miraculously filled. After the pagan had made the necessary renunciation, he was baptised. The salvation of his soul was then followed by the salvation of his body. After the discovery of the two ampoules in St Remi's tomb, Hincmar varied the legend by stating definitely that two ampoules had been placed empty on the altar, one of which was marked for the reception of the Holy Oil and the other for the reception of the chrism, and both were duly filled in answer to St Remi's prayer. During the period of the Carolingian dynasty, the two ampoules were used at the royal anointings, or *sacres*, because of their special connection with St Remi, and with what Oppenheimer calls 'The Legend of the Moribund Pagan'. Although Charles the Bald became King of Lorraine, of Germany and of Italy and received the Imperial Crown in Rome in 875, he was unable to exercise authority over his widespread dominions, and there followed a period of confusion. On the death of Charles in 877 an important constitutional change occurred. Under the Merovingians, succession had been by birth, and under the early Carolingians it had been hereditary. Charles' son, Louis II, the Stammerer, who had, in 866, become King of Aquitaine, succeeded to the Kingdom of the West Franks as a result of his election by nobles and bishops, for which he had to pay heavily by gifts of land and other concessions. He was anointed and crowned by Hincmar in September 877 in the church of St Corneille of Compiègne. In the following year, when Pope John VIII was attending the Council of Troyes, he took the opportunity to be consecrated a second time, on 7th September, but the Pope refused to crown his Queen, Adelaide, sister of Ethelred, King of England, on the grounds that Charles the Bald, his father, had given the Abbey of St Denis to the Holy See and that Louis had refused to recognise this. When Louis II died on 13th April 881, a party of nobles elected the old King's sons, Louis and Carloman, and decided how the kingdom was to be divided among the two provinces, thus depriving the king of the prerogative of choosing his own vassals. The two brothers were anointed and crowned before the altar of St Peter in the Abbey of Ferrières on 14th September 879 by Angesius, Archbishop of Sens. Louis died on 5th August 882 at St Denis and Carloman reigned alone until accidentally killed while hunting on 12th December 884. The nobles then passed over Charles the Simple, the posthumous son of Louis II, and chose Charles II, the Fat, who had been crowned Emperor in February 881. Thus the Empire of Charlemagne was once again re-united under one throne. Charles II was not anointed or crowned King of the West Franks and after a disastrous and feeble reign, he was deposed and died in poverty at Neidingen on the Danube on 18th January 888.

The majority of the French nobility and clergy then elected Odo, Count of Paris, a military hero without any hereditary claim. In 888 he was anointed and crowned by Walter, Archbishop of Sens, in the Château of Compiègne. Fulco, Archbishop of Rheims and Hincmar's successor, jealous of his position *vis-à-vis* the Archbishop of Sens whom he considered had supported an upstart, called together the minority of nobles to elect a rival king, Wido of Spoleto, who was a relation of Fulco. Wido was anointed and crowned King at the Monastery of Tournai on the Saône in 888, but receiving no support, he withdrew. The position was now complicated by another rival, Arnulf, Duke of Carinthia, who had been elected King of the East Franks when Charles the Fat was deposed. But recognising that there were now two distinct kingdoms—German and French—which could not be united, Arnulf reached agreement with Odo whereby the German King, keeping a semblance of paramount sovereignty, offered Odo a quasi-imperial guardianship. Odo did homage to Arnulf and accepted a crown with which Fulco crowned him on 13th November 888.

In 893 Charles the Simple gained the support of a number of nobles and was anointed and crowned King at Rheims on 28th January 893 as Charles III. This ceremony did not take place in the splendid new cathedral, but in the church of St Remi. Oppenheimer[1] argues that Fulco purposely chose the church because the ampoules from St Remi's tomb were preserved there. He claimed that by using one of these, which contained the Holy Chrism associated with St Remi's miracle and, according to Hincmar's statement at the coronation of Charles the Bald, was regarded as that which had been used at the baptism of Clovis, he could strengthen the claim that Rheims should be the place of coronation of the French kings, especially as Charles was the legitimate heir to the Carolingian throne, while his rivals were upstarts.

In 907 Charles married Frederonne, sister of Bovo, Bishop of Châlons. She was anointed and crowned in St Remi's church by Herivée, Archbishop of Rheims and shared her husband's special gratitude by bestowing upon the monastery a part of her dowry which consisted of lands associated with St Remi. Odo allowed Charles III part of Neustria, and on his death Charles obtained possession of the whole kingdom. But the nobles became jealous of Charles whose royal authority was growing, and as a result of discontent, they elected Robert I, brother of Odo, to the throne. He was anointed and crowned at Rheims in 922, but shortly afterwards was killed in battle at Soissons. Robert had insisted that his coronation should take place at the church of St Remi at Rheims so that he could be considered to be as well established on the throne as Charles. Herivée, the Archbishop of Rheims, was dying and so the ceremony was performed by Walter, Archbishop of Sens. The use of one of St Remi's ampoules, which was regarded as a relic, for the consecration of an upstart king and by a rival archbishop was considered outrageous by Richer, the chronicler of Rheims.

After Robert's death, Raoul, or Rudolph, Duke of Burgundy, was elected King and was anointed and crowned at the church of St Médard at Soissons on 13th July 923 by Gothair, Archbishop of Sens. In 924 Raoul became seriously ill. He considered that his condition was due to his having scorned the idea of being anointed with the Holy Chrism from St Remi's relic. As he could not ask for the ampoule to be brought to his sick bed, he travelled to Rheims at great risk and visited St Remi's shrine, and

[1] Sir Francis Oppenheimer: *The Legend of the Sainte Ampoule.*

within four weeks was completely cured. In gratitude he made generous gifts to the monastery.[1] His Queen, Emma, did not make the same mistake as her husband and was anointed at Rheims in 923 by Sully, Archbishop of Rheims. Her decision to go to Rheims was made in case anything might befall her husband who was fighting in Lorraine, so that it would enable her to confirm her rights and to establish her claims.

Charles III was placed in confinement and died at Peronne on 7th October 929. His second wife, Eadgyfu, sister of Athelstan, King of England, fled to England with her son Louis. On the death of Raoul, the nobles chose him as King and although only a boy of fifteen, he returned to France and was anointed and crowned at Laon on 19th June 936. Owing to an outbreak of plague, Rheims was not available for the first king of the restored Carolingian line. Laon was chosen instead, as it was specially connected with St Remi, who had been educated there and had founded the See on which he had bestowed lands which he had received from Clovis. The King was known as Louis IV, the Foreigner, and the ceremony was performed by Artauld, Archbishop of Rheims. During his reign he closely associated himself with the veneration of St Remi. His Queen, Gerverge, was anointed and crowned at the church of St Remi where she was buried.

On Louis' death on 10th September 954 he was succeeded by his son Lothair, who was elected by the Federal Lords in the church of St Remi. The new King, who was only fifteen years old, had been specially dedicated to St Remi to ensure that no adverse consequences should follow his father's coronation at Laon and not at Rheims. He regarded himself as a special ward of St Remi and was anointed and crowned in the saint's church by Artauld, and no doubt one of St Remi's ampoules was used on this occasion. In 979 when Lothair was attempting to regain Lorraine, the succession was threatened by Charles of Lorraine, and the King deemed it necessary to have his son anointed and crowned during his lifetime. The ceremony took place at Compiègne and was performed by Adalbero, Archbishop of Rheims. Compiègne was chosen because the war between Lothair and the Emperor Otto II was still being fought and Rheims was not considered to be safe. He died on 2nd March 986. His wife Emma, daughter of Lothair, King of Lombardy, who had not been anointed and crowned, was accused of poisoning him. On the accession of Louis V there was a ceremony of installation at which oaths of fidelity were made, but this was not a second coronation. Louis died in May 987 and Queen Emma again was accused of having administered poison.

We have very little evidence about the regalia of the Carolingian kings of France, and as several of them were also emperors, it is as such that they were more often depicted. In the Treasury of the church of Conques in the Department of Auvergne is a statue of St Foy (*Plate 97, c*) of wood covered with gold standing about 3 ft high. On the head is a gold crown consisting of a circlet of twelve oblong plates joined together by hinges and decorated with precious stones. The crown is closed with two arches, each formed of four plates with a single plate at the summit and point of juncture. From the circlet between the arches are set fleurs-de-lis ornamented with precious stones. It is considered that the crown dates from the last quarter of the x century or the first quarter of the xi century. There is no evidence as to its origin or of it having been associated

1 P. H. Lauer: *Robert I et Raoul de Bourgogne.*

with any royal personage and it is too small to have been worn. It does, however, provide evidence of a type of royal crown in use at that time.

Oppenheimer[1] has suggested that in accordance with widespread custom, Pepin and his two sons would most probably have given the robes which they had received from the Pope on the occasion of their anointing at St Denis to the abbey for safe keeping. These, says Oppenheimer, would have been the hyacinth-coloured garments enriched with gold which were prescribed in the Court protocol for official robes. Pope Zacharias, who was a Greek, had encouraged the settlement in Rome of Greek craftsmen who had fled from Constantinople at the beginning of the iconoclastic struggle, when the manufacture of works of arts for the Church was forbidden there. Oppenheimer goes on to suggest that the robes bore the pattern *diapré* in imitation of the Byzantine imperial mantle with which these artists would have been familiar, and that the golden pattern was the 'flood of light' symbolising the Holy Ghost, a fitting emblem for the occasion. Oppenheimer argues that this was the origin of the use of the fleur-de-lis in France. The Carolingians preferred their Frankish robes to foreign ones. Charlemagne only wore official Roman dress on two occasions after his anointing at St Denis. One was on the occasion of the visit of Pope Adrian when he put on his patrician's dress, and the other was at his imperial coronation. The annals of Fulda in 876 tell us that after Charles the Bald was crowned Emperor, he laid aside the crowns and dresses of the kings of France, his predecessors, for the diadems and vestments of the Greek emperors, clothing himself in robes that touched his heels over which he wore a broad baldric that descended to his feet, covering his head with a silken hood on which he placed his crown. These he continued to wear on Sundays and feast days, but this was as Emperor and not as King of the West Franks. Louis V wore Roman or Greek robes. This was put down to his youthful vanity, and caused widespread disapproval as he was expected to wear the traditional Frankish royal costume.

The Abbey of St Denis claimed that Charlemagne gave his rich crown to the abbey. This would have been in accordance with custom, but it was not handed down as the so-called Crown of Charlemagne, which appears in the earliest existing inventories which date from the XVI century and was a mere appellation given to later ornaments at the time when the cult of Charlemagne became an important matter. The possession of Charlemagne's sword and other royal ornaments was also claimed. In the same way the name of Charlemagne came to be attached to these at a much later date. According to Doublet[2] Charles the Bald gave to St Denis his crown with four *couplières* adorned with large red uncut stones, large and exquisite emeralds, very beautiful sapphires, very excellent rubies and very excellent oriental pearls. This crown will be further discussed later. There was also kept at St Denis a little crown of an empress which was taken to pieces in the XII century. It may have been that of Richaldes, the second wife of Charles the Bald, who was crowned Empress in 877 and was closely connected with St Denis. In the Bibliothèque Nationale in Paris there is a crown which is attributed to this period. It is a simple round circlet of base metal with a few traces of gilding and with four fleurs-de-lis, between which there were four other ornaments, one of

---

[1] Sir Francis Oppenheimer: *Frankish Themes and Theories.*   [2] Doublet: op: cit.

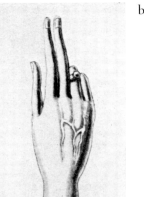

b (left) *Detail of hand showing the ring*

c (right) *The inscription upon the sceptre*

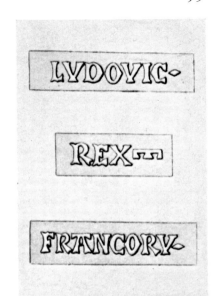

a (left) *Ivory sceptre of Louis XII. From Catalogue of the Earl of Londesborough's Collection (p. 231)*

d (below) *Detail of the knob of the sceptre decorated with fleurs-de-lis and leaves*

e *XV-century painting from an altar-piece depicting the Mass of St Giles. It shows Charles Martel kneeling and wearing crown which agrees with the description of* La Sainte Courone *in the inventory of 1634*

a   *Treasury of St Denis, from Félibien's* Histoire de l'Abbaye de Saint-Denys. *Armoire I,* N *crowns, sceptre and hand of justice of King Henry IV*

b   *Armoire II,* X *coronation crowns of King Louis XIII;* Y *funeral crown of the Empress Anne of Austria*

a   *Armoire III, crown of Maria Theresa;* K *hand of justice of St Louis;* M *sword of St Louis;* P Sainte Couronne
renamed the Crown of St Louis; Q *crowns of Louis XV*

b   *Armoire IV,* H *crown of Charlemagne;* T *crown of Queen Jeanne d'Evreux;* R *sword of Charlemagne;* P *sceptre of
Charles V*

a (left) *The great table diamond of Francis I given to the Crown by letters patent by Francis I. From G. Bapst's* Histoire des Joyaux de la Couronne de France *(p. 234)*

b (below, left) *Jewel with the diamond of the House of Guise. From G. Bapst's* Histoire des Joyaux de la Couronne de France *(p. 252)*

c *Grand Cross of Diamonds from the portrait of Elizabeth of Austria and Charles IX. From G. Bapst's* Histoire des Joyaux de la Couronne de France *(p. 236)*

which is missing and the other three are broken. On the circlet below each fleur-de-lis were precious stones, the settings of some still being intact. It is described as the crown of King Hunald, Duke of Aquitaine (705–74) (*Plate 80, a*). Hunald abdicated in 746 and handed over his duchy to his son as an act of penance for having put out the eyes of his brother. In 769 he emerged from his monastery on the Isle of Ré and led the Aquitainians in revolt against Charlemagne. Hunald fled and fell into Charlemagne's hands. His fate is unknown, but there are many romantic legends regarding it. According to some he went to the Court of Desiderius, King of the Lombards at Pavia, but it is more likely that he was confined to a monastery. This crown has not attracted authoritative attention, but it appears to have been a burial crown of considerably later date than the time of Hunald.

When Louis V died suddenly in 987, the rightful Carolingian heir, Charles of Lorraine, was unacceptable as he was without wealth or influence and absent from the kingdom. At an electoral assembly at Senlis, Adalbero, Archbishop of Rheims, and his able secretary Gerbert, with the support of the reformed Cluniac clergy, elected Hugh Capet, Duke of France, to be King. In his address to the Assembly the Archbishop said: 'The throne is not acquired by hereditary right. We should elevate to this dignity only him who is distinguished not merely by nobility and birth, but by the wisdom of his mind.'

THE CAPET DYNASTY

The real founder of the House of Capet was Robert the Strong who received the Countships of Anjou and Blois from Charles the Bald. He was the father of Odo and Robert I, already mentioned. Robert's son, Hugh the Great, Duke of France and Normandy, who was the most powerful figure in the kingdom, could have gained the throne had he so wished, but preferred to wield the real power and arrange for the election of his own candidates.

The Capets became one of the great families of Europe. For nine centuries one branch or another were Kings of France. They were Dukes of Burgundy from the x century to 1361 and also founded the second ducal house in 1363 through which they formed a union with the Hapsburgs through the marriage of Mary, daughter of Charles the Bald, with Maximilian I who subsequently became Emperor. Another branch became Counts and Dukes of Anjou, members of which became Kings and nobles of Naples and Hungary. In the XIII century Navarre for a time had a Capet on the throne and three members of the house became Emperors of Constantinople.

Hugh Capet's position on becoming King was by no means easy. He had inherited a kingdom of the great feudal lands of Normandy, Champagne, Burgundy, Flanders, Vermandois, Brittany and Aquitaine whose lords had become hereditary and almost independent princes. The political state of the kingdom was disintegrating, and the only bond of unity was the monarchy which, however, was without wealth and the means to enforce its rights. But step by step the kings gradually overcame these difficulties, and by the XIII century the monarchy had become all powerful. This was done by the acquisition of lands, by rallying the great feudal lords against the English, by winning the support of the Church and particularly by the establishment of Rheims as the place of anointings and coronations. Moreover, the dynasty was fortunate in having relatively long reigns— those of the first seven kings averaging thirty-three years—with the result that there were no minorities. To ensure an unbroken succession, their sons were anointed and crowned during their fathers' lifetime, there always being a direct heir available, thus making the monarchy hereditary and weakening the principle of election. The relationship with Germany was made easier by the replacement of the Carolingians by the Saxon House who had no direct connection with France or claim to the French throne.

After his election in May 987, Hugh Capet, the son of Hugh the Great, lost no time in being anointed and crowned, and the ceremony took place at Noyon in July 987, Adalbero officiating. But Charles of Lorraine was still an active rival, and as the legitimate Carolingian heir received some support. Hugh Capet, determined to make the succession of his family secure and having overcome the opposition of Adalbero, who was at first unwilling to have the right of election diminished, Hugh's son Robert II was anointed and crowned as co-King in the Cathedral of Ste Croix at Orleans in December 987. Neither Hugh's wife nor the first two wives of Robert were anointed and crowned, but according to some writers Constance of Provence was anointed and crowned at Orleans. In 1017 Robert, who had succeeded to the throne on his father's death in 996, arranged for his eldest son Hugh to be consecrated as co-King, and the ceremony took place in the church of Corneille at Compiègne. But in 1025 Hugh died and after some argument Henry, the King's next son, was elected co-king and consecrated at Rheims in 1027.

There were various reasons why the first coronations of the Capet dynasty did not take place at Rheims, but the claims of the archbishop now became firmly established. In 999 Pope Sylvester II, who as Gerbert had previous close association with Rheims, first as secretary to Adalbero and then as archbishop, addressed a letter to Arnulf, the then Archbishop of Rheims, appointing him and his successors to be the consecrators of the French kings. The anointing and crowning of Henry at Rheims in 1027 was an important landmark in the history of the French coronations. Oppenheimer has argued[1] that Robert gave his royal authority for the ampoule of St Remi, which had been used at former royal anointings, to be regarded as the *Sainte Ampoule*. There is, in fact, nothing recorded of the use of the *Sainte Ampoule* until the coronation of Louis VIII in 1223, though it is clear that by then its use was accepted as traditional. The case for its identification at the coronation of Henry I must, therefore, be based on circumstantial evidence. Henry I was elected on Whitsunday 1026 and his *sacre* was deferred until Whitsunday 1027. His father, Robert II, personally supervised the preparations for the ceremony. He was well acquainted with coronations because, apart from his own, he had been present at that of his father and had been closely associated with the preparations for that of his eldest son. At this period the cult of relics was very strong and the King, grief-stricken at the death of his eldest son, was anxious to obtain divine protection for his second son Henry. He was a Latin scholar and would have found in Hincmar's writings a description of the consecration of

[1] Sir Francis Oppenheimer: *The Legend of the Sainte Ampoule.*

Charles the Bald on which subsequent coronation forms had been based. Here was recorded the belief that the Holy Chrism used at the anointing of Clovis was preserved at Rheims. He must also have been aware of the importance which the late Carolingian kings attached to Rheims and to their use of one of St Remi's ampoules. For these reasons Rheims was chosen in preference to Orleans as the place of coronation, and the King gained comfort in his distress and anxiety by identifying the ampoule of St Remi, which had been used for the anointing of the former kings, as that which had been sent down from heaven on the occasion of the baptism of Clovis.

We need not probe into the acts, devices and wiles, even to the forging of documents, in which the archbishop and other protagonists indulged with a view to establishing Rheims as the See above all other French Sees, and as the place of the coronation of the French kings.[1] From now on it held that privileged position and only on three occasions—Louis VI at Orleans in 1108; Henry IV at Chartres in 1594 and Napoleon at Paris in 1804—were the *sacres* performed elsewhere and then for special reasons. Moreover, the ceremony was from now onwards performed in the cathedral and not in St Remi's church. At the time of the coronation of Henry the church of St Remi was being rebuilt and, therefore, the cathedral was used, and this precedent was repeated at the next coronation, and it became the permanent place of the consecration of the French kings.

The second ceremony in the cathedral church was performed in 1059 when Henry caused his six-year-old son Philip to be anointed and crowned, thereby confirming the hereditary right of the Capets. On this occasion the election was retained as a mere formality in the coronation service. At the ceremony Gervais, the archbishop, with St Remi's crozier in his hand, addressed the assembly claiming his responsibility for the election of the King and for his consecration as St Remi had baptised and consecrated Clovis, and further asserting that his rights to the primacy and to the consecration of the kings had been conferred by one Pope and confirmed by another.

Although Louis VI, the Fat, was elected to be Associate King in his father's lifetime and was in 1103 styled *Rex Francorum designatus*, he was not anointed and crowned because his father had quarrelled with the Pope over his second marriage and had been excommunicated. When Philip died in 1108 after a reign of forty-eight years which, however, was lacking in achievement, it was a matter of urgency for Louis to be anointed and crowned, and the ceremony was performed at Orleans by the Archbishop of Sens the day after his father's funeral. For this occasion the ampoule of St Martin which was kept at Marmoutier was used.

The reign of Louis VI, which lasted thirty-four years, is of great importance in the history of the French monarchy for by his energy he made his power felt and began the destruction of feudalism. In 1123, when the Emperor Henry V, in alliance with Henry I of England, invaded the kingdom, he rallied the barons and his subjects round the Oriflamme of St Denis and defeated the invaders. The Oriflamme was returned to St Denis and given over to the care of the monks and thereafter was regarded as the Palladium of the kingdom. Louis, like some of his predecessors, had a superstitious fear that his failure to have his *sacre* performed at Rheims would displease St Remi. He

1 This has been dealt with fully by P. E. Schramm in *Der König von Frankreich*.

made it clear that at the time Rheims was under interdict by the Pope and he was at pains to cause his eldest son Philip to be anointed and crowned at Rheims in 1129, and when he died, for his second son, Louis VII, to have his *sacre* at Rheims in 1131. This took place only fourteen days after the funeral of his brother, opportunity being taken of the presence of Pope Innocent II to perform the ceremony. The chronicles of Marigny contain a description of the occasion which gives the first written information about the use of St Remi's ampoule. Having stated that the Pope consecrated the Prince in front of the altar, the passage continues: 'With the oil which St Remi had received from the hands of angels and with which he had anointed Clovis in the Christian faith.'

Louis VII reigned for forty-three years. As a result of his divorce of Eleanor of Aquitaine, his first wife, he later lost Aquitaine to Henry II of England on the latter's marriage to her. It was not until after thirty years of marriage to three wives that an heir —Philip II—was born in 1165. In 1171 the Pope advised the King to have his son anointed and crowned, but the boy fell ill and the ceremony could not take place. Louis vowed to visit the tomb of St Thomas à Becket at Canterbury to pray for the recovery of his son and heir, and when Philip's health was restored, the King summoned the leaders of the realm to Rheims where on All Saints Day 1179 Philip was anointed and crowned. He himself could not attend the ceremony as he was paralysed as a result of a stroke and he died on 18th September 1180.

Philip II Augustus was one of the greatest French kings. By his sagacity and energy he destroyed the Angevin Empire which the Plantagenets had brought to the English Crown and he forged France into a nation. Philip's name had been put forward during the struggle between the Guelphs and Hohenstaufens as a candidate for election as German King, but although this project did not materialise, the French claimed part of the imperial title and the King took the title *Philipus semper Augustus Francorum rex*. His victory at Bouvines over the Emperor Otto IV and the forces brought into coalition by John Lackland in 1214 in which the great feudal lords, the knights and the *bourgeoisie* fought for the King under the Oriflamme, was a national triumph, brought unity to France and gave her the supremacy of the West. So firmly was the hereditary monarchy established that it was no longer necessary for the king's eldest son to be crowned during his father's lifetime. When Philip Augustus died in 1223 his son, Louis VIII, the Lion, succeeded him and he was anointed and crowned at Rheims on 6th August 1223, but his reign was short as he died on 8th November 1226.

Louis VIII's heir, who succeeded as Louis IX, was only nine years old when his father died. His mother, Queen Blanche of Castile, was appointed Regent, an office which she held effectively for ten years. Louis was anointed and crowned at Rheims on 29th November 1226. His reign at home was not very eventful, but he exercised a moral authority which made him be regarded as the ideal king of the Middle Ages, and the prestige and power of the French monarchy was unsurpassed. During the height of a serious illness in 1244 he decided to take the Cross, but did not leave France until 1248, returning in 1256. Before leaving for the Crusade he had purchased from the Latin Emperor in Constantinople, John of Brienne, who was in great poverty, some relics including the Crown of Thorns, parts of the True Cross, the Holy Lance and the

Holy Sponge, and between 1245 and 1248 he built the Sainte Chapelle in Paris as a shrine for them. Louis made a treaty with Henry III, King of England, by which Henry renounced Normandy, Anjou, Touraine, Maine and Poitiers and received certain fiefs and domains of the King of France on condition that he recognised Louis as *liege suzerain*. In 1270 he ventured on his second Crusade, but died of plague in Tunis on 25th August of that year.

St Louis was succeeded by his son Philip III, the Hardy, who was anointed and crowned at Rheims on 30th August 1271. On his death at Perpignan on 5th October 1285 he was succeeded by his son Philip IV, the Fair, who was anointed and crowned at Rheims in May 1286. He died at Fontainebleau on 29th November 1314. Philip IV was succeeded in quick succession by his three sons, Louis X, the Quarreller, who was crowned at Rheims in August 1315 and died at Vincennes on 8th June 1316; Philip V, the Tall, who was crowned at Rheims in December 1317 and who died at Longchamp on 3rd January 1322; and finally by Charles IV, the Fair, who was crowned at Rheims on 1st February 1322 and on whose death at Vincennes on 1st February 1327 the direct line of the House of Capet became extinct.

We have seen how Rheims became the accepted place of coronation of the French kings and how the legend of the *Sainte Ampoule* developed and gave the kings of France a special position among the Christian rulers by virtue of their anointing with holy oil sent down from heaven. We must now deal briefly with the nature of the French coronation service and its special features; with the coronation of French queens, and with crown wearing or feast coronations. We must consider the privileged position attained by the Abbey of St Denis as the place of burial of the French kings and queens and as the repository of the regalia. Then we must take note of the growth of the cult of Charlemagne, of the adoption of the fleur-de-lis as one of the special emblems of the French monarchy, and we must deal with French coronation *ordines* and the regalia used by the French kings up to the end of the first line of the House of Capet.

Under the Capets the coronation ceremony of the kings of France was developed and was subjected to English, German and Roman influences, but several national features were incorporated, the most important being the consecration of the king with the Holy Oil contained in the *Sainte Ampoule*. Because of this, the ceremony became known as the *sacre* rather than the coronation. We are not concerned here with the intricate history of the political and ecclesiastical influences which brought about changes. Those who are interested will find the subject has been well covered by Schramm.[1] The *ordo* of Rheims, which was drawn up between 1260 and 1274 and was the consolidated form of usage under the later Capets, became the basis of the subsequent French coronation ceremonies.

The first part of the ceremony was a constitutional act. As the principle of a hereditary monarchy had come to be accepted, the election of the king, even when it had become a mere formality, disappeared and the principal constitutional feature was the oath. The second part of the ceremony was the consecration or confirmation of the king as a knight. This took the form of four separate acts: the vigil; the investiture with the spurs; the girding on of the sword, and the offering of the sword to the altar of

---

1 P. E. Schramm: *Der König von Frankreich.*

God. The vigil took place on the night preceding the consecration when the king went to the coronation church to pray. On the day of the coronation ceremony, after the king had taken the oath, he put on his coronation vestments over his own shirt and tunic. These consisted of the shoes, the surcoat, which was like a dalmatic, and over this the mantle. The Duke of Burgundy fastened on the spurs to the shoes and then took them off. The archbishop then girded the king with the sword and having un-buckled it from its belt, drew it and handed it to the king, placing the scabbard on the altar. The king then carried the sword to the altar, received it back again from the archbishop and handed it to the seneschal who carried it unsheathed during the rest of the service.

The third part of the ceremony was the anointing. On the morning of the *sacre* the *Sainte Ampoule* was brought in solemn procession from the Abbey of St Remi to the cathedral. Only the Abbot of St Remi and the Grand Prior were allowed to carry the *Sainte Ampoule*. In the procession the Grand Prior carried it in a reliquary fastened round his neck. He rode on a white charger, given by the king, right up to the altar steps. The procession was composed of the monks of the *Sainte Ampoule*, four chevalier barons of the *Sainte Ampoule* who held the poles of a silken canopy over the relic and who were accompanied by four *Seigneurs Hôtages* who originally remained in the abbey as hostages, but were later allowed to join the procession. Escorting the procession was a body of knights numbering from 200 to 300.

On the altar of the cathedral was a paten on which was placed the chrism. The archbishop took a golden style and a drop of the Holy Oil from the *Sainte Ampoule* and with his finger mixed it with the chrism. The king was anointed on the head, on the breast, between the shoulders, on each shoulder and at the jointure of each arm. In the XIV century anointing of the hands was added. This was connected with the miraculous powers which the king was said to possess of healing scrofula. In Hincmar's original description of the baptism of Clovis, the contents of the heaven-sent ampoule were described as 'chrism'. Chrism was a consecrated oil made fragrant and more precious by admixture of balsam and was employed in more solemn rights than those at which consecrated oil was used, including baptism. In the IX century the Church Reform Party at various synods raised objections to the use of chrism for the anointing of sovereigns as this was reserved for bishops and was unacceptable because a king, by using chrism, might feel justified in calling himself *Rex et Sacerdos*. In the second half of the X century the use of a chrism for the anointing of sovereigns in Europe was discontinued, except in France where the claim of the Holy Chrism sent to Clovis established a special position. But in time the contents of the *Sainte Ampoule* came to be described as Holy Oil and this was mixed with chrism at the king's anointing.

After the anointing, the king was invested with the royal ornaments: the ring, sceptre, verge and crown. The ring was used by the West Franks, and we find when Louis VII was consecrated as co-king, his father Louis VI handed him a ring as a token of actual power. In earlier times bracelets were also used and were among the ornaments removed from St Denis by Odo in 888, but by the XIII century they are no longer mentioned. The inclusion of both sceptre and staff in the French regalia corresponded with early English usage, but there the staff was replaced by the orb, an ornament which never featured in the French regalia. The short sceptre is of Roman origin and in France was surmounted by a trefoil which developed into the fleur-de-lis. The staff, which either reached the ground or to the steps of the throne, was in its earlier stages surmounted by a *fleuron* ornament which developed into a fleur-de-lis and which by the time of Louis VII was enclosed in a rhomboid ornament. At some time this was replaced by an ivory hand, and the staff became known as the Hand of Justice denoting the act of swearing an oath symbolising the judicial supremacy of the king.[1]

Although we have no definite evidence, it seems probable that up to the time of Philip Augustus there was no special coronation crown, each king being provided with a new one. This would have been necessary as the king would attend the coronation of his heir as co-king wearing the crown with which he had been crowned, a new one being provided for the junior king. After the crown had been set on the king's head, he was enthroned by the archbishop, a ceremony in which the peers participated by laying their hands on the crown.

When a queen was crowned with her husband, her coronation took place at this point, the king remaining enthroned. The king and queen then received communion in two kinds. The laity had been excluded from the use of the chalice since the XII century, this being a privilege of the clergy. In the *ordo* of Rheims of 1274, the former custom of the king receiving communion in two kinds was retained and although it was an exceptional privilege, it was continued in subsequent *ordines*.

The king, and queen if present, then exchanged their coronation crowns for lighter ones and divested themselves of their coronation robes, and proceeded to the coronation banquet, a part of the ceremony which had no constitutional significance. Subsequently, at least from the time of Louis VIII (1283), the king made a spectacular ceremonial entrance into Paris.

Although the coronation orders made provision for the anointing and coronation of the queen, those of the first Capets were not crowned. The early Capetian kings, crowned in the lifetime of their fathers, were young men and not yet married. Such queens as did undergo a coronation were anointed and crowned at their wedding service, but not at Rheims except when they were already married at the time of the king's *sacre*. There is some suggestion that Constance, the wife of Robert II, was crowned on her wedding day at Orleans, and although the date of the marriage of Louis VI to Adelaide at Savoy is not known, the Pope in a Bull makes reference to her consecration. All three wives of Louis VII were anointed and crowned at their marriage ceremonies, the King also being crowned at the same time. It is considered by some that on the first occasion he was crowned as King of Aquitaine. The second marriage ceremony took place at St Denis. Philip III was crowned with his wife at Vincennes. Louis VIII was married before his coronation and his Queen Blanche of Castile was crowned at the same time as her husband.

---

1 There is no certainty as to when it was introduced. It seems that it first appeared on the seal of Hugh Capet (987–96) but then fell into disuse until Louis X (1314–16) used it on his seals, and it then continued to be used numismatically by his successors. Although the 1505 inventory refers to the Hand of Justice of St Louis it is open to doubt whether such an ornament actually took its place among the royal ornaments of the French kings until the reign of Charles VI (1380–1422).

Originally it was laid down that the queen should be anointed and invested with the ring and crowned. The *ordo* of Rheims in 1274, however, elaborated the ceremony. The queen was anointed with the oil of the catechumen and then invested with the sceptre and staff and crowned. Oppenheimer[1] claims that for the queen's anointing, the second ampoule of St Remi was used. Her enthronement was assisted by the barons and principal ladies. For the banquet she wore a lighter crown.

The coronation of the king at his wedding ceremony, after his own *sacre* at Rheims, can be included in the category of crown wearing, or feast coronations. Certainly since the time of Hugh Capet and probably from the time when the kings of the West Franks were also emperors, it was customary for the king to wear his crown and appear in full regalia on certain feast days. On these occasions the crown was placed on the king's head in church by the archbishop or some other high ecclesiastical dignitary. Similar practices are found in Germany and England. The anointing of Pepin and his sons, Carloman and Charlemagne, and the subsequent close connection of the Carolingians with the Abbey of St Denis led to claims for the coronation of the French kings to be performed there, and at least for the abbey to be closely associated with the coronation. Nothing was spared to substantiate these claims, even to the forging of documents, but the foundation had to be content with being the burial place of the kings, the repository of the regalia and national relics and perhaps, as is suggested by Schramm, of the royal archives.

When Hugh Capet became King, St Denis was the patron saint of his family and his successors paid special reverence to the saint's abbey. It was already a custom for the kings to be buried there, though there were exceptions, one being Louis VII, who was buried at St Maria Barbeux. It was usual for their regalia, which was used at the funeral, to be retained in the possession of the abbey. Thus we find that King Odo in 888 was able to obtain all the royal ornaments and robes besides the ecclesiastical requirements needed for his coronation from St Denis. The ornaments were not always returned though replaced by other gifts. The Abbé Suger, after Louis VI had promised to return his crown to the abbey on his death, interpreted this to mean that all the crowns belonged by right to the saint. There was also a forged document drawn up at the abbey which claimed that the right was established by Charlemagne. It was said that Charlemagne, before leaving for the Holy Land on his fictitious crusade, took the crown from his head and placed it on the altar, thus surrendering his realm into the safe keeping of St Denis.[2] Although this claim was recognised by Philip Augustus, the coronation insignia were not kept there, but in the Royal Treasury in the Louvre until St Louis finally gave over the regalia for safe keeping to the Abbot of St Denis. St Louis showed great interest in the abbey and not only made extensions and improvements to the structure but ordered the monuments for the tombs of his royal ancestors. He also gave a number of his holy relics to the abbey, some of which were incorporated into the regalia. The *ordo* of Rheims confirmed that it was the established custom for the regalia and royal vestments to be kept at the abbey, and this continued until the French Revolution. It was incumbent on the abbot to produce them for the coronations

---

[1] Sir Francis Oppenheimer: *The Legend of the Sainte Ampoule*
[2] L. Buchner: *Die Hut der Krönunginsignien in Frankreich und in Deutschland im Mittelalter.*

at Rheims, and they were ceremoniously taken there and returned after the ceremony under escort. According to Abbé Suger the Empress Mathilda gave one of her crowns to St Denis which was used to embellish a sardonyx vessel *CUM QUIBUSDAM FLORIBUS CORONAE IMPERATRICIS* which is now in the *Cabinet de Medociles* in the Bibliothèque Nationale.

St Denis also became the central point of the cult of Charlemagne in France. The great mediaeval romances, the *Chansons de Gestes*, of which *The Song of Roland* was the most important, date from the XII century. *The Song of Roland* is based on the legendary chronicler known as Pseudo Turpin which purports to be the work of Turpin, Archbishop of Rheims, who died about the year 800, although it is generally considered that the work belongs to the middle of the XII century. This great work relates the fabulous achievements of Charlemagne and the heroic deeds of his Paladins. The great Emperor was supposed to have given over the whole of France to St Denis and the coronation of the French kings was made to depend upon the saint. Other claims were made for St Denis which are rather extravagant, and some authorities consider that they must have been written at St Denis and inserted into the song. The important fact is that *The Song of Roland* gained widespread popularity not only in France but from Scandinavia to Spain and from Italy to the Holy Land. It is not surprising, therefore, that a great national feeling and pride was stimulated and that Charlemagne, who in Germany was revered as a saint, in France became the national hero. The authorities at St Denis were not slow to take advantage of this and they claimed that the Oriflamme was Charlemagne's personal banner presented to him by the Pope in 800 and that the royal sword was *Joyeuse*, the Sword of Charlemagne, and the coronation crown was the Crown of Charlemagne. Philip Augustus, too, made Charlemagne his model. A chronicler relates how the King was found deep in thought and said he had been considering whether God would grant France the power and expansion she had under Charlemagne in his and his successors' time. Before the Battle of Bouvines Philip Augustus blessed his knights in the same way as Charlemagne had done in *The Song of Roland*. Bouvines was fought against the German Emperor under the Oriflamme—the Banner of Charlemagne—and was in the public mind a parallel to Charlemagne's victory over the Saxons. In *The Song of Roland* the name of France was used instead of Gaul, which was interpreted as meaning that the country was free and not subservient to any other. Authors even tried to say that the Capets were descended from Charlemagne. One asserted that Philip Augustus' mother was a descendant of Charlemagne and another that Louis VIII's mother, Isabella of Hainault, sprang from the family of Charlemagne. The strength of the Charlemagne legend was such that it was thereafter accepted without question as establishing the special position and the claims of the French kings. It is a popular belief that the fleur-de-lis was the special emblem of the French monarchy, probably because it was used so profusely. It was, of course, a special royal French emblem, but they did not have a monopoly. It was used by the Carolingians as an imperial as well as a royal emblem, and it was adopted in England and in other Christian kingdoms who developed it according to their own ideas. In France it was developed into a high stylised form, whereas elsewhere it was in the early days a less distinctive type of emblem usually called a *fleuron*. Louis VI in the middle of the XII century introduced the fleur-de-lis on his coins and on his second seal where it surmounts the verge. But even earlier, Robert II, Henry I and Philip I are depicted with their short sceptres surmounted by fleurs-de-lis which also appear on their crowns, though they are less formalised.

In the reign of Louis VI armorial bearings were established and the fleur-de-lis was adopted as the heraldic emblem of the Kings of France. It was later emblazoned on the Oriflamme, and at the victory of Bouvines it was there for all to behold. Schramm[1] says: 'From then on Europe knew that the Kings of France carried the queen of flowers without a thorn on their Arms'. The fleur-de-lis was used either in a group of three at a time, or as a continuous pattern—gold on blue velvet. The love of allegory in the period of chivalry soon led to the belief that it symbolised the teaching of the Sermon on the Mount. By the XIV century a heavenly origin was attributed to it and it was claimed that it was sent from heaven by an angel to Clovis on the occasion of his baptism as a special mark of favour on the part of the Blessed Virgin. In the XVI century at the Council of Trent, the French bishops, when disputing for the precedence of their king, fortified their claim by asserting that the King of France received the fleur-de-lis direct from heaven.[2] We find that for the coronation of Philip Augustus, his father Louis VII prescribed that the Prince wore *ses chausses appelées sandels ou bottines de soye, couleur la azure semée en moult endroits de fleur-de-lis d'or, puis aussi son dalmatique de main coleur et œuvre*. Similarly, in the *ordo* of the *sacre* of Louis VIII among the regalia and robes brought from St Denis was: *Item: Caligis lacintines intextis lilies auries* . . . . Again, the *ordo* for the *sacre* of Louis IX provides for the boots and surcoat to be of velvet embroidered with tissues of fleurs-de-lis. The sceptre, too, bore a fleur-de-lis on top to denote that the Christian symbol surmounted the legal one.

The crowns of the French kings, originally simple circlets, became open circlets ornamented with *fleurons* and later with fleurs-de-lis. Under Philip Augustus these had become developed into a distinctive feature and were great lily crowns, each with four large fleurs-de-lis rising from the circlet. They were much heavier and more distinctive than the earlier circlets and no doubt were intended to give a special character to the French open royal crowns in rivalry to the arched crown of the Emperor.

It has already been noted that the gift of crowns to abbeys and other religious foundations was a practice in Carolingian times. Each king usually had his own personal crowns. There was as yet no national crown in the true sense and the custom of sending the crown used at Rheims to St Denis after the coronation ceremony necessitated the provision of personal crowns to be used on other occasions. Some would have had several. Doublet[3] relates that Charles the Bald gave his crown to the Abbey of St Denis and describes it in some detail stating that it had been used to crown all the subsequent Kings of France down to Henry IV. It is known that Charles the Bald was a generous benefactor to the abbey and his gifts included a thorn from the Crown of Thorns and other relics. We may discount the possibility that the Crown of Charlemagne, which was said to have been given to the abbey, survived. Apart from other reasons, St Denis was subjected to various dangers due to disorders and the abbey was

[1] P. E. Schramm: op. cit.
[2] De La Roque: *Traité Singulier de Blazon*.   [3] Op. cit.

pillaged by the Normans in 865. It was hardly likely that so rich a spoil would have been spared. But we have another piece of information which strengthens the claim that Charles the Bald's crown had a special position and was perhaps used at coronations. The Continuator of Aymon's *Histoire* relates that in the year 877 upon the death of the Emperor Charles the Bald, his widow—Richaldes, his second wife—proceeded to Compiègne to find the new King Louis II, where she handed him the late Emperor's will and with it, in accordance with the terms of the will, the sword known as the Sword of St Peter, the royal vestment, the crown and the golden sceptre set with precious stones, by all of which the late King meant him to stand invested with the kingdom. The same writer relates further that in 879 King Louis II, abandoning all hope of recovery from his illness, sent his son Louis III the crown, sword and other royal ornaments enjoining those who were there with him to cause his son to be duly anointed and crowned. This suggests that there was an idea that the King's rightful successor was to use the royal ornaments of his father, and the regalia may thus come to have been regarded as a dynastic possession. Unfortunately we do not know what regalia was used at the coronations of the co-kings in the early reigns of the Capets. Did the father wear the crown with which he had been crowned and was a new one made for his son, or did the father wear a personal crown and allow his son to wear the traditional coronation crown? If that could be answered, the claim of the Crown of Charles the Bald would be easier to determine. But there are two pieces of evidence which also give some support to the claim. The only representation we have of the French coronation crown, which though somewhat arbitrary, is that in one of the engravings in Félibien's *Histoire de St Denys* (*Plates 80* and *81*). It shows a heavy crown with four great fleurs-de-lis which differs from the crown of St Louis, which though in the same general style is cast in one piece, for it consists of a circlet made of four plates joined together by pins and the four fleurs-de-lis are attached to the circlet as separate pieces. This type of circlet, decorated with precious stones, was in use at the time of Charles the Bald. Moreover, we learn from Du Tillet that Philip Augustus caused the crowns to be renovated. It is reasonable to suppose that with the importance attached to the fleur-de-lis in his reign these ornaments were added at the renovation.

It is clear that despite the custom of depositing the regalia at St Denis, the claim of the abbey had not been permanently established. It may be argued that if Charles the Bald had given his crown to the abbey, how was it his Queen could take it to Compiègne for the use of his heir? The direction contained in his will would no doubt have been sufficiently compelling for the abbot to give it up. The fact that the crown was not continuously kept there and that the abbey reasserted its claim is shown by a passage in Félibien's *Histoire de St Denys* which says:

> After the death of the Kings of France, the marks of their royal dignity, that is to say their crown, mantle and other royal ornaments belonged to the Church of St Denis where it was always the custom to offer them to the patron saint of their person and of their kingdom. King Louis VI, having been told of this custom, came to St Denis accompanied by his wife Adelaide and there in the presence of Bishop Conon, the Legate of the Holy See, he presented the crown of his father, King Philip, who had already been dead twelve years.

The charter is dated 1120 and signed by King Louis, Queen Adelaide, Philip their son and by four chief officers of the Crown. Louis VI had been brought up at St Denis and was no doubt aware of the custom, but it was only in 1120 that he was induced to comply and to make provision for his crown to go to the abbey on his death. It is difficult to distinguish whether it was the coronation crown or the King's personal crown that Philip Augustus handed over after his coronation to the abbey, though whichever it was, it seems to have been taken to the Royal Treasury subsequently, presumably when he decided to have it altered. His son Louis VIII in his will left the gold and precious stones of his crowns to the foundation of the abbey, but this must refer to his personal crowns. At length his successor, St Louis IX, regularised the position in 1260 by formally making the Abbot of St Denis the custodian of the regalia and handed over two large crowns and one small one adorned with precious stones which, according to the document, King Philip Augustus had kept in the Royal Treasury and which he intended should be used at the coronation of the kings and queens. There the matter must rest on the available evidence. Philip Augustus may have had new crowns made, or the old ones adapted, but in any case he laid down a tradition which would at least give permanence to the coronation crowns. Félibien's account of this reads as follows:

> On his return (from the Holy Land) St Louis had previously devoted himself to the affairs of his kingdom and in pious works. On 9th October he was at St Denis in order to celebrate, as was the custom, the feast of the saint. He added to the treasures of this church two big crowns, that which Philip Augustus, his ancestor, had had made for the crownings of the kings and queens, and another smaller crown that the king traditionally wore during the banquet on his coronation day. These three crowns were of gold and were enriched with precious stones. Formerly they were kept in the Treasury, but St Louis preferred that they be looked after at St Denis with the other royal ornaments and clothing used at the anointing and the coronations of the kings and queens. He ordered at the same time that the three crowns which he presented be placed round the altar on special occasions together with those of the former kings which were treasured in the same church. The King obtained from the Abbot Matthew a receipt dated October 1260 and subsequently had sent in his name the charter which we have given in the month of May following. . . .

It is clear enough from the evidence that the two heavy crowns were for the use of the kings and queens. There had been a crown of an empress, probably that of Queen Richaldes, who had close associations with St Denis, but this was dismantled in the XII century. St Louis had a new crown made for his wife, probably because the Queen Mother was still alive and was, therefore, entitled to the crown used at her coronation. At any rate, the crown of Philip Augustus given by St Louis was subsequently used as the coronation crown and at the coronation of King Philip III, the son and successor of St Louis, it was described for the first time as the Crown of Charlemagne.

St Louis, too, gave his own crown to St Denis. It was described as of massive gold enriched with topazes, sapphires, rubies, emeralds and oriental pearls and by a very large uncut stone on which was inscribed: *De capillis Domini, de spines Domini.*

There was a third great crown of the Kings of France which was also kept at St Denis known as the *Sainte Couronne* because it too contained a relic from the Crown of Thorns. What was the origin of this crown we do not know, but it was of the same characteristic pattern as that of the crown of St Louis, the circlet and the four fleurs-de-lis being cast in one piece. It is depicted at a later date, when arches had been added, in the painting known as 'The Mass of St Giles'.

The oldest proper inventory of the Treasury of St Denis known today is that of 1505 and in it we find several items of regalia which were attributed to the first line of Capetian kings. These will be described later in the chapter when the inventories are dealt with, but we may take note now of the list of ornaments belonging to this period.

They include, in addition to the crowns, the clasp and mantle of St Louis; the signet ring of St Louis; the sword of Charlemagne; a sword attributed to Archbishop Turpin; a sword attributed to St Louis; the Hand of Justice of St Louis; the sceptre of St Louis and the sceptre of Charlemagne. Those which bore the name of Charlemagne were given this appellation at the coronation of Philip III in 1271 when the sword of Charlemagne, known as *Joyeuse*, was carried before the King by a cousin . . . *In memoriam tam victioriosimmi principis.* The pommel and guard of *Joyeuse* may be of XI- or XII-century work, but the hilt and blade are of later date. It is still preserved in the Louvre and will be described later with the other royal ornaments kept there.

The sceptre of Charlemagne is not that of Charles V now in the Louvre but an earlier one which had the same appellation. The sceptre and Hand of Justice of St Louis were of silver gilt. Another Hand of Justice with a gold top and a handle made of unicorn horn may have dated from the XIII century. The sword attributed to St Louis is that which the King is said to have brought from the Holy Land. The sword of Archbishop Turpin probably dated from the time when *The Song of Roland* enjoyed popularity. The signet ring of St Louis is still preserved in the Louvre. The clasp of St. Louis was described in the inventory as the clasp of the mantle of Charlemagne.

After St Louis' gifts to St Denis, the next was a bequest of a crown of Jeanne of Burgundy, wife of Philip VI, who died on 21st January 1329 and left to the abbey the crown which she used at Rheims at the banquet on her coronation day. In 1343 Jeanne d'Evreux, wife of Charles IV, gave her crown to St Denis in perpetuity and it was subsequently used, according to Félibien, at the coronation of queens held at St Denis. The Queen directed that on her death it was to be placed on her head by the monks. After her funeral it was to be suspended before the altar with the other crowns at solemn celebrations. It was of gold with eight *fleurons* decorated with rubies, sapphires and pearls. In the inventory of 1739 there is a note to say it had been recently repaired and enriched at the abbey's expense. The crown was unusually heavy for a queen's crown and possibly it was the second heavy crown which Philip Augustus had prepared for the coronation of the queens, and perhaps had been altered to suit the taste of Jeanne d'Evreux.

From ancient times the kings had their own banner which was borne before them in battle. From the X century it was blessed at the coronation. When Louis VI acquired the Countship of Vexin, which was part of the domains of the Abbey of St Denis, he came into possession of the banner of the saint which already had a tradition of having brought victory to the Count of Anjou in 1044. Before going into battle against the Emperor Henry V in 1124, Louis VII went to St Denis and received the banner from the altar. His victory gave the banner and the saint immense prestige and it came to be regarded as the national Palladium. *The Song of Roland* attributed the banner to Charlemagne, who was said to have received it from Louis III at his imperial coronation in 800. It was described as an *orie flambe*, a golden flaming cloth and came to be known as the Oriflamme. As the banner of Charlemagne, its prestige was even greater, especially after it had been present with the King at the victory of Bouvines. The banner was kept at St Denis, and when required for war the King would go to the abbey and the Oriflamme would be measured and a copy made for use in the campaign. Between 1124 and 1186 it was taken by the kings no less than twenty-one times, and it continued to be used until the Battle of Agincourt in 1415. Thereafter it remained at St Denis until the Revolution, when it was destroyed. There is a copy of the Oriflamme preserved in the Treasury of the Abbey of St Denis today, the present one having been made in 1913. Although there is no record of it being taken to Rheims for the coronation ceremony, a copy which was regarded as the royal banner of the king was blessed at each coronation ceremony.

During the period of the Crusades, it became the custom for royal gifts of reliquary crowns to be given to churches. Godfrey de Bouillon[1] is said to have given one to the church of Notre-Dame at Boulogne which disappeared in the Revolution. There is still preserved in the Treasury of the Cathedral at Amiens a crown belonging to the latter half of the XIII century (*Plate 80, c*).

> It is formed of a rigid gold circlet bearing six large and six small fleurs-de-lis. On the circlet are twelve large receptacles for relics. Between these were set two stones, one above the other in cup-like settings, some of which are now missing. Each fleur-de-lis had five stones set in the form of a rose. At times the crown was suspended by chains.

St Louis is known to have given several such crowns. One he gave to the Cathedral of Notre-Dame in Paris. It was of silver gilt and was the setting for various relics including fragments of the clothing of Our Lord, the Holy Sponge, of the Crown of Thorns and the stone from the Holy Sepulchre. It appears in inventories of the cathedral of 1343 and 1416, but was not included in the plate melted down in 1562 and had probably disappeared before then.[2] Another silver gilt reliquary crown in which was a thorn from the Crown of Thorns, probably a gift from St Louis, was preserved at Notre-Dame de Poissy.

The most celebrated of these reliquary crowns is that which St Louis gave to the Dominicans at Liège and which is now in the Louvre and described as the Crown of St Louis (*Plate 80, b*).

> It is of silver gilt and consists of eight plates each surmounted by a *fleuron*, four being larger than the others. They are pinned together with hinges and each pin bears the statue of an angel cast in silver gilt and each holding a scroll describing the relic on the neighbouring plate. The inscriptions which are still visible read: *De ligno v . . . . . —e Corona Du—Ioh. Bapt. Mar. Magd.—Martirib—De Virginib—De Confess—De apostoli—De lances—Du.*

Montfaucon[3] published a drawing of the crown in 1730. In 1794, during the French

[1] F. De Mély: *Les Reliques de Constantinople au XIII Siècle.*
[2] Aubert Marcel: *Documents sur les Fontes du Trésor de la Cathédrale de Paris en 1562.*
[3] Op. cit.

Revolution, the monastery was dispersed and Pierre Mossay took the crown to Germany where he died in the Dominican Rectory of the University of Leipzig. Later and shortly before Napoleon's armies entered the city, the Dominican priests asked for an interview with Princess Max of Saxony, who, as Princess Caroline of Parma, was the granddaughter of Louis XV, and handed her a parcel containing the crown. It remained in the possession of the House of Wettin thereafter, and during the Second World War it was hidden in the Castle of Moritzburg. When the Russian armies threatened that area, Prince Ernest Henry of Saxony decided to take the crown for greater safety to the Castle of Sigmaringen in south-west Germany where his sister Princess Margarethe of Hohenzollern lived. In August 1944, the Nazis imprisoned the Hohenzollerns and the castle was evacuated and used as the residence of the members of the Vichy Government who had fled from liberated France. Prince Ernest Henry took a room in a nearby inn, made contact with some of his sister's servants who were in the castle and persuaded one of them to smuggle the crown out of the castle under his overcoat. The Prince then took it back to Moritzburg. For greater safety he took it to Dresden and locked it in a safe in the estate office of his family at No. 7 Parkstrasse. On the night of 24th February 1945 Dresden was devastated by a bombing attack and No. 7 Parkstrasse was destroyed. When the safe was opened it was found that the papers and some drawings by Dürer were charred to ashes, but the crown was intact, save for a single narrow crack. The Prince then returned it once again to Moritzburg and after various adventures it was again taken to Sigmaringen. The Louvre had for twenty years been negotiating for the acquisition of this relic and finally were able to gain possession of it from Prince Ernest Henry, and it is now on view in the Galerie d'Apollon.[1]

Philip the Fair (1285–1314) gave a bust reliquary of his grandfather, St Louis, to Notre-Dame in Paris. The reliquary was the work of Guillaume Jullien and the head was adorned with a rich fleur-de-lis crown. The reliquary and crown disappeared during the French Revolution but a new bust and crown were made in the XIX century, which are still preserved in the Treasury of Notre-Dame.

THE HOUSE OF VALOIS

On the extinction of the main male line of the House of Capet in 1328, the peers and barons held an assembly and declared that 'no woman nor therefore her son' could, in accordance with custom, succeed to the monarchy in France. Thus, the claim to the French throne of Edward III, King of England, who was grandson of Philip IV, was invalidated. The assembly gave the crown to Philip VI of Valois of the younger branch of the House of Capet.

Philip was crowned at Rheims with his wife Jeanne of Burgundy on 29th May 1328. After prolonged negotiations, Edward reluctantly agreed to do homage to Philip VI for his possessions in Guienne. This ceremony took place in the Cathedral of Amiens in 1329. The French King was surrounded by a brilliant Court and wore the royal robe of velvet powdered with gold fleurs-de-lis with a rich diadem on his head. Holding the golden sceptre in his hand, he sat on a magnificent throne with the King of Navarre on

1 There is an electro-plated copy of it in the Victoria and Albert Museum.

his right and the King of Minorca on his left. King Edward was required to take off his crown, his sword and his spurs before doing homage to the French King as Duke of Guienne. But it was not long before the natural rivalry between the two Kings, personal grievances and economic and political reasons, besides Edward's claim to the French throne, led to what is known as the Hundred Years War. The threat of invasion by the English had been present for some time and this necessitated Philip rearming on land and sea. Despite extra taxation to meet the cost of these preparations, Philip was short of funds and in June 1340 he sought from the Abbey of St Denis the loan of some of the contents of the Treasury. A letter from the King dated 10th June stated that he had received from the abbot seven golden crowns with a rich cross formerly given by King Philip Augustus which was also of gold and, like the crowns, decorated with precious stones. The weight of the gold amounted to 31 marks 6 oz which, together with the pearls and precious stones, were valued at 10,648 livres. The King gave his royal word of honour that he would return the cross and the crowns in the same state in which they had been lent to him before the following Christmas. We know that the cross was returned but have no precise information about the crowns.

Philip VI died in 1350 and was succeeded by his son John II, the Good, who was crowned with his wife Bona of Luxemburg at Rheims in September 1350. The King was taken prisoner by the Black Prince at Poitiers and died in London in 1364. His son and successor Charles V was crowned with his Queen, Jeanne de Bourbon, at Rheims on 19th May 1364. Charles, who was surnamed the Wise, had acquired a remarkable library in the Louvre which contained the manuscripts of two foreign and six French coronation *ordines*. He had acted first as Lieutenant of the Kingdom after Poitiers in 1356 and then as Regent during his father's captivity in England. During this period he caused a new *ordo* to be drawn up for his *sacre* and, although keeping within the framework of previous *ordines*, which in turn were based on the *ordo* of Rheims, the ceremony was considerably lengthened and the ceremonial made more elaborate. The anointing of the hands, which had lapsed, was re-introduced, and to prevent any drop of the Holy Oil being defiled, the King subsequently put on gloves. The gloves, the sword and the ring were all blessed and the prayers, where suitable, were borrowed from the order for the consecration of a bishop. The significance of the ring was that the King was married to his kingdom. The reasons underlying the creation of a new coronation *ordo* are fully discussed by Schramm.[1] It is only necessary here to say that the new *ordo* was intended to emphasise the King's personal views on the subject and the spiritual position of the French kings, and to consolidate the association of Charlemagne with the French monarchy. During his reign the King strengthened the position of and enriched the monarchy. He had an extravagant taste for precious objects, jewels, books and for building which necessitated increasing taxation and the sale of municipal charters and patents. On his death at Vincennes on 16th September 1380 he was succeeded by his son Charles VI, who had been given the title of 'Dauphin' at his birth and was the first heir to the throne to bear the title 'Dauphin' from infancy. He was twelve years of age when he ascended the throne and was crowned at Rheims on 1st November 1380. In 1385 he married Isabel of Bavaria, aged fourteen. She was crowned

1 P. E. Schramm: op. cit.

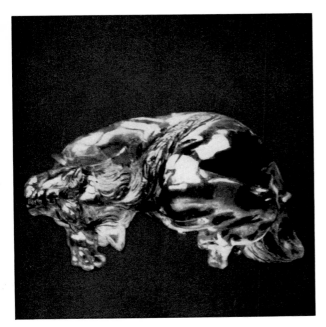

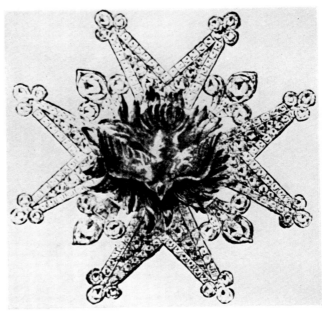

a (above, left) *Ruby known as The Côte de Bretagne. The Louvre* (p. 252)

b (above, right) *Order of St Esprit set with the Œuf de Naples re-cut as a dove and the 'Roman A' recut to represent flames. From G. Bapst's* Histoire des Joyaux de la Couronne de France (p. 252)

c (left) *Toison d'Or with The Côte de Bretagne recut in the form of a dragon, and the Blue Diamond. From G. Bapst's* Histoire des Joyaux de la Couronne de France (p. 252)

d (right) *The Côte de Bretagne in its setting as reconstructed from the description in the inventories by Lucien Hirtz. From G. Bapst's* Histoire des Joyaux de la Couronne de France

a *Frame of crown of Louis XV set with imitation stones. The Louvre* (pp. 250 and 274)

b *Crown of Louis XV from an engraving by Antoine* (p. 249)

at the marriage ceremony at Amiens on 23rd August 1385. Charles VI, who became insane in 1392, lived until 21st August 1422 when he died in Paris. He played little or no part in the government from 1392, and after the defeat of the French by Henry V of England in 1415, when the English King became Master of France, Henry, seeing the state of neglect in which Charles was living, re-organised his household. Charles was succeeded by his son Charles VII but owing to the state of the country it was not immediately possible for him to go to Rheims to be crowned. With the appearance of Joan of Arc, the King was reluctantly persuaded to go to Rheims where he was crowned on 17th July 1429, a ceremony which was considered essential before Charles could be recognised as the rightful King of France. He had married Marie of Anjou, but she was not crowned. Charles VII died on 22nd July 1461 and was succeeded by his son, Louis XI, from whom he had been estranged. The *sacre* of the new King was performed at Rheims on 15th August 1461. At this ceremony Louis XI was dubbed a knight by the Duke of Burgundy. At the two previous coronations the kings had been similarly dubbed, but they had not previously been knighted. Schramm in discussing this concludes that as the King had been a knight from birth, the meaning was clear that it was a hollow honour accorded to the Duke as the King did not require to be made a knight again. The Duke of Burgundy had the privilege of putting the knightly spurs on the King's shoes. In 1429 the Burgundian Order of the Golden Fleece had been founded, and in 1461 there was no French order of chivalry, so that it may have been that this act was connected with making the King a Knight of the Order of the Golden Fleece.[1]

In Louis XI's reign Charles the Bold, who had become Duke of Burgundy in 1467, made the duchy a powerful state and cultivated an ambition to turn it into a separate kingdom. Charles did indeed persuade the Emperor Frederick III to agree to crown him at Treves and he journeyed there equipped with crown and sceptre for the ceremony. But during the night the Emperor decamped and Charles' ambition remained unfulfilled. The Court of Burgundy had become fabulously rich and magnificent, outshining the Royal Courts of Europe. When Charles the Bold was killed at the Battle of Nancy, his treasure was dispersed and some famous Burgundian crown jewels found their way into the Royal Treasuries of France, England and the Hapsburgs. In the Museum at Dijon is a crown which has been attributed to Margaret of Bavaria (*Plate 80, d*), who married John the Fearless, Duke of Burgundy in 1385. Little is known of the origin or purpose of this crown which is of gilded bronze with fleurs-de-lis and other ornaments. It was possibly a funeral crown.

Louis XI died on 30th August 1483 and was buried at Cléry instead of St Denis. He was succeeded by his son, Charles VIII, a boy of thirteen years who was crowned at Rheims on 30th May 1484. On leaving Rheims he went to St Denis in accordance with custom to pray at the tomb of the saint, before making his solemn state entry into Paris. Félibien states that on this occasion he was crowned again, although this ceremony was distinct from the *sacre*. In 1491 Charles married Anne of Brittany who was crowned at St Denis on 13th December of the same year. Charles conceived a project of claiming

---

[1] In 1469 Louis XI introduced the first French Order of St Maurice which got into such disrepute that in 1579 the Order of St Esprit was created.

the rights of the House of Anjou, including the Kingdom of Naples, and to use this as a stepping stone to the capture of Constantinople from the Turks and for his own coronation as Emperor of the East. Having been crowned King of Naples in the Church of St Januaire, he made a state entry into Naples wearing the imperial insignia. On his head was an arched crown and in his left hand an orb, and in his right hand a sceptre. The two former ornaments were alien to French usage. The King has been depicted wearing an arched crown, the first French king to be so represented,[1] and the orb is depicted in the King's hand on a seal of Louis XII. Charles did not survive long and died as a result of an accident at the Château of Amboise on 8th April 1498. As he did not leave any issue, the crown passed to a cousin, Louis of Orleans who became Louis XII.

During the reigns of the first seven kings of the House of Valois, several royal ornaments were added to those already in the Treasury of St Denis. The most important mentioned in the inventory was the golden sceptre 5 ft 10 in. long, surmounted by a gold and enamelled lily on which rests a figure of Charlemagne enthroned. The sceptre, which is still preserved in the Louvre, bears an inscription saying that it was used by the Emperor. This was made for the coronation of Charles V and may have replaced an earlier one dating from the XIII century. There were also the sword and scabbard of Charles VII which was adorned with gold, and the crown of Anne of Brittany consisting of six plates weighing 9 oz, but without precious stones. Anne of Brittany also gave the clasp of a rich mantle to the abbey. On the clasp was an oriental hyacinth surrounded by a form of fillet on which was written in letters of gold *non Mudera*. The clasp also bore the Queen's arms in gold and enamel. It was valued at 12,000 livres. Later, in 1568 and 1677, it was repaired.

Doublet[2] describes the robes of John II and Charles V which were kept in the Treasury of the abbey.

A pair of shoes of velvet *samy*, sewn in lozenges, moons, stars and golden fleurs-de-lis with a border of the old fashion lined with *sandal*. A garment of a sub-dean of velvet blue *samy* sewn lined as above. An *orfray de Cypre* and in front high up a fastening of two plates of gold decorated with 4 oriental pearls each, and a verse inscribed on each of them:

Christe cuum Regem serva regnando Joanen
ut iustam legem servando tollat inanem

Another deacon's garment very similar to that of the sub-deacon which has on the shoulders four large buttons of pearls, each of them decorated in the middle with gold and rubies.

In the same way the rich coat, the shoes and the garments of the above-named people.

The garments of the consecration of King Charles V, his son. A pair of shoes of blue satin lined with red satin sewn with fleurs-de-lis of gold, bordered round the lower part and round the upper opening and in the middle of the back with golden bands sewn with pearls.

A pair of *bouttones* with *avant pied* of blue satin lined with crimson satin sewn with golden fleurs-de-lis, each boot decorated with six buttons of small pearls.

A *surcol* of crimson satin, doubled with sandal wood red, bordered all round with *orfray d'or* sewn with crowns, fleur-de-lis and *K* on the wrist of the sleeves, in front and on the stomach with thirty-eight little golden rings, with three laces (or strings), one of silver gilt and the other of gold.

A garment of a sub-deacon of blue satin, sewn with fleurs-de-lis of gold, doubled with crimson

---

[1] Jean Du Tillet: *Portraits des Rois de France.*   [2] Doublet: op. cit

satin, bordered on the back, the two sides, the neck, on the seam of the sleeves round the shoulders and in front, also on the wrists and the opening of the neck in front, of golden *orfray*, sewn with *las d'amour*, with branches and leaves: on the field in the *las*, and in between with fleurs-de-lis, *K*'s and crowns and all, also the borders of the *orfray* with seed pearls, and on the branches, leaves and fleurs-de-lis, precious pearls, and in the middle a *chiton* of gold decorated with a very large uncut garnet and at the wrists buds of pearls decorated in the middle with a *chalon d'or* and garnets, and in the opening of the neck a golden joint of two pieces which close the neck.

Another garment of a deacon, similar to the ones described above, having on the shoulders four large buttons of large pearls decorated in the middle with a *chalon* of gold and much larger garnets than the ones described above.

A coat of white satin, sewn with golden fleurs-de-lis, doubled with crimson satin, bordered all round with golden *orfray* much larger than the ones mentioned before, sewn with large love-knots of branches and leaves and in these and between the fleurs-de-lis with large *K*'s and larger crowns of seed pearls, larger than the above-mentioned ones, and flowers above these branches and leaves, each flower of 6 large pearls, larger than those below, and in the middle of each flower a *chalon* decorated with gold and a large garnet.

It is not known to what extent the Treasury of St Denis was pillaged during the Hundred Years War, but we know that it was claimed that it had been ravaged by the English. Henry VI of England had been crowned in Notre-Dame in Paris in 1431, but had brought his own crown over from England for the purpose, and as he used an *ordo* based on the English ceremony he probably did not make use of the French regalia at St Denis.

We must now consider that part of the Royal Treasury which can be described as crown jewels, although not part of the regalia. The Merovingians buried their personal ornaments with their owners, a practice which Charlemagne forbade as it led to the loss of too much wealth. But in Carolingian times most of the available gold and precious stones were not used for personal jewellery, except for the royal ornaments, but were used to make ecclesiastical ornaments. During the period of the cult of relics more importance and value was attached to the relics themselves than to the magnificent reliquaries made of gold, precious stones and other rare materials. The presents given to St Denis by Charles the Bold such as *L'écrin de Charlemagne* were particularly notable. These gifts to ecclesiastical foundations were partly due to the religious spirit of the times, but also to the fact that many monasteries had workshops and almost a monopoly of craftsmen. During the reigns of Dagobert I and Clotaire III, no less than three goldsmiths were canonised in France—Eloi, Alban de Fleury and Theau. It was not until the death of St Louis that there was a break away from the traditional austerity in the French Court. By the beginning of the XIII century, secular goldsmiths who employed jewellers became strongly established in Paris. Although jewellery in the form of clasps and buckles, brooches and head-dresses came into fashion, we still find a predilection for jewels of a personal nature such as the rosary of 100 pearls and ten gold ornaments of Queen Jeanne d'Evreux in 1372

The Capetian kings, being less rich, were at first unable to compete with the splendour of the Courts of the feudal lords, but as the domains of the Crown increased and their power was consolidated, the Royal Court became more luxurious. We know that Queen Jeanne d'Evreux had many jewels. In 1349 she gave her best jewels to the Convent of the Grand Carmes of the Blessed Maubert, Paris,[1] to be kept in the Treasury until her death and then to be sold and the money used for buildings. When she died in 1372, the Queen left other jewels including a crown of ten *fleurons* set with emeralds; two smaller crowns; fourteen coronals, of which three were rich—one had emeralds as the principal stone; one with balas rubies and one with sapphires; two jewelled clasps; a pair of lozenge-shaped brooches; three large brooches; one round and one with a cameo in the middle and one square, together with a number of lesser items—brooches, circlets, belts. At her wedding she had worn a large fleur-de-lis clasp to her mantle, an ornament which seems to have been reserved for the royal family.

With the kings of the House of Valois, the luxury and magnificence of the Court increased. It was the age of chivalry with its pageantry and with the growing power of the king it was not only considered right for the splendour of the great ceremonial to be elaborated but kings were in a position to obtain the resources to pay the enormous expense involved. This development was particularly marked in the reigns of John II and Charles V[2] when one prince of the royal blood vied with another in luxurious display. Besides their use for display and magnificence in time of peace, the crown jewels formed a reserve of capital and could be pledged in times of war or financial stringency. The inventories of the Treasuries of these kings show the remarkable collections they accumulated.[3] Charles V at the time of his death had eight splendid crowns for himself; nine for his Queen and twenty-six others, besides coronals, all richly jewelled. These included:

1. The very grand, very beautiful and best crown of the King, four great *fleurons* and four small, decorated with balays, sapphires, diamonds and pearls. The Emperor Charles VI, on a visit in 1378, asked to see this beautiful crown, and it was taken to him at the Château of Beouté sur Marne.

2. Another great crown called the crown of the five emeralds. It consists of four large and four small *fleurons* and in the centre of the circle a large and long emerald. The crown was set with other emeralds, balays, diamonds and pearls.

3. Another great crown called the crown with the stones *à jour*, with six big and six small *fleurons*, balays, sapphires, diamonds and pearls.

4. Another great crown called *La Couronne à Pierrerie Carrée* with six *fleurons* decorated with balays, emeralds, diamonds and pearls.

5. Another great crown of very great style, called the *Couronne de l'Etoile*, consisting of eight plates. It was used by King John at the meetings of the Order of L'Etoile, between 1330 and 1351.

6. The crown of silver the King had made to hold a thorn of the *Sainte Couronne*.

7. Another crown of gold of eight great *fleurons*.

8. Another crown of gold of very ancient fashion with four large and four small *fleurons*.

9. Another, the great crown made for Jeanne de Bourbon with eight large and eight small *fleurons*.

10. A small crown of Jeanne de Bourbon with six large and six small *fleurons*, a circlet formed of twelve plates.

11. The great circlet of Jeanne de Bourbon of seven plates.

[1] Joan Evans: *The History of Jewellery*.   [2] H. Clifford-Smith: *Jewellery*.
[3] Bapst: *Testament de Jean le bon*, 1884. J. Labarte: *Inventaires de Charles V Roi de France*, 1879.

12.–17. Circlets.

18. The great crown of Marie de France (Charles V's daughter) with eight *fleurons*.

19. A small crown of Marie de France of eight *fleurons*.

20–21. Small crowns.

22. A circlet of Madame D'Orléans, daughter of Charles Le Bel.

23–24. Circlets, one with the arms of France, one with the arms of Navarre.

25. A crown.

26. A crown on a basinet with 10 large sapphires, 15 balays, emeralds and Scottish pearls weighing 2 marks. This property belonged to King John, who always wore a crown on his helmet.

27–29. Three crowns.

30. A great crown of seven large and seven small *fleurons*.

31. A crown.

32–36. Circlets.

37. A crown.

38. Another great crown with eight large and eight small *fleurons*.

39. Another great crown of fourteen plates.

40. A great circlet of eight plates.

41–44. Circlets.

45. A princess's crown.

46. A circlet.

47–52. Hair ornaments.

53. Small crown of the King.

54. A small crown of ancient fashion.

55. Nine *fleurons* of a crown.

The first of these crowns is spoken of as the *très belle couronne*. It had four large and four small *fleurons*, all adorned with diamonds, rubies, balas rubies, sapphires and large pearls and had a cap, also adorned with precious stones. Among the stones of the crown was a round *cabochon* balas ruby weighing $262\frac{1}{2}$ carats, a square balas ruby weighing 80 carats and another *cabochon* balas of 93 carats. There were also 2 large sapphires of 63 and $45\frac{1}{3}$ carats. According to remonstrances made to Charles VI by the city and University of Paris on 12th February 1413 the crown had been pledged before that date, probably to gain funds for the struggle between Burgundy and Orleans. As a result of this protest the crown was apparently redeemed, but was shortly afterwards broken up and the *fleurons* pledged separately to various nobles, court officials (in lieu of wages), and merchants, for a total sum of 73,790 fr, probably between 1415 and 1418. Nothing further is heard of the *très belle couronne*. At the same time various other crown jewels were pledged, including the Venetian Balas, which weighed $414\frac{1}{2}$ carats, which was bought by the Duke of Berry in 1408 for 18,000 fr, and the Cavernay *cabochon* balas of 231 carats, the *Rubis de la Mie* and the Berry Pearl, all once the property of the Duke of Berry.[1] In addition, there were six great fleur-de-lis clasps and enormous balas brooches and other ornaments. The brooches were decorated with eagles, griffins and stags.

1 'The Very Beautiful Royal Crown of the Armagnac and Burgundian Era', an essay by J. Deny, Professor of the School of Oriental Studies, *Mélanges offerts à M. Nicolas Iorga par ses amis de France et des Pays de Langue française*, Paris 1933.

Louis XI inherited a lavish display of jewels and we read of his public entry into Paris after his coronation, bringing a display of jewels hitherto unsurpassed. His costume was covered with precious stones and those on the harness of his horse were estimated to be worth one million écus. But he was not interested in the outward display of royalty, except at times to impress Ambassadors when he wore gorgeous robes. He also seems to have had a cynical sense of humour about such matters as is illustrated by the story of the occasion when he witnessed a great feat of gallantry on the part of Raoul de Lannoy in 1477 at the siege of Quesnoy. He placed on his neck a chain of great value, saying: *Mon ami, vous être trop furieux en un combat. Il faut vous enchaîner, car je ne veux point vous perdre désirant me servier encore de vous plusieurs fois.* Louis XI was ungainly in stature with rickety legs and his piercing eyes and long hooked nose gave a certain grotesqueness to his countenance. His ugliness was emphasised by the old felt hat he preferred to wear with a leaden figure of a saint as its only ornament. He liked to travel dressed in grey like a pilgrim and shocked the aristocracy by his bourgeois way of life. While attempting to copy St Louis by giving lavish presents to the shrines of influential saints, he was well practised in the art of bribery and gave generously to the clergy and politicians alike if he saw that there was some gain to be achieved. He was at heart austere and according to his wish was buried without royal apparel. After his death a scarf for his head was found among his belongings sewn with no less than forty-two images of Our Lady of Embrun. His successor, Charles VIII, was not left with the prodigal wealth that his father had inherited, but he attached great importance to outward ceremony.

Charles VIII, having left no male issue, the succession passed to his cousin Louis XII of Orleans, and his *sacre* was performed at Rheims on 27th May 1498 (1499 new calendar). Félibien relates how the King was crowned again at St Denis in the following words:

> The King after his consecration passed through St Marcoul where he made his devotions. Afterwards he rested for some days at St Germain-en-Laye from whence he went to St Denis in order to take the crown. The ceremony of the crowning of those days was distinct from that of the consecration and over a long period of time had been carried out at St Denis. The King was crowned with a gold crown destined for this purpose. Louis XII did not wish to miss any of the saintly practices established by his predecessors. The ceremony of his crowning took place on Sunday, 1st July 1498.

It will be seen that it is now claimed that the second coronation had been established over a long period, although that of Charles VIII was the first which was recorded by Félibien. We have a description of the state entry into Paris.[1] The King wore a tunic of cloth of gold garnished with precious stones with his arms worked delicately on the material. On his head was a toque of black velvet surmounted by a rich plume. He was mounted on a horse richly caparisoned with cloth of gold. The King was preceded by the Grand Ecuyer bearing his helmet ornamented with a crown of gold richly worked and garnished with precious stones. Louis XII had been married at the age of fourteen to Joan the Lame, daughter of Louis XI. But they became estranged and she was

---

[1] Molinet: *Histoire de Choses Mémorables.*

divorced. He then married Anne of Brittany, widow of Charles VIII, who had already been crowned. On her death in 1513 he married Mary Tudor, sister of Henry VIII of England, who was crowned at St Denis on 5th November 1514 and afterwards made a state entry into Paris wearing a robe of cloth of gold ornamented with diamonds, rubies, carbuncles and topazes. But the marriage was of short duration as Louis XII died on 1st January 1515. An ivory sceptre (*Plate 79, a, b, c* and *d*) believed to have belonged to Louis XII was purchased by the Earl of Londesborough from the Debruge collection (Cat. No. 167) in the first half of the XIX century. It is a long ivory rod and on the third finger of the hand is a ring with a small pearl. The knob is decorated with fleurs-de-lis and leaves. The sceptre bears the inscription *LUDOVICUS REX FRANCORUM*. The word *REX* is followed by a label of three pendants similar to one used by Louis XII on his crest when he was Duke of Orleans.

Louis XII left no son and for the second reign running the succession went to a cousin, Francis I of Angoulême. He was crowned at Rheims on 24th January 1515 and proceeded to St Denis where he was crowned again, the notices of the occasion suggesting it was a ceremony carried out with an increased amount of pomp. His queen, Claude, daughter of Louis XII, was crowned on 10th May 1517 at St Denis. Félibien's description is interesting as it represents the fully-developed ceremony of the coronation of queens at St Denis:

Queen Claude of France, daughter of Louis XII and the first wife of Francis I, came to Saint Denis for her crowning. She arrived on Saturday afternoon, 9th May, accompanied by Princes, Princesses and a great number of Lords and Ladies of the Court. The Justices and all the people assembled before Her Majesty, and at the gate of the town four of the principal citizens offered her a canopy. The Queen met on entering the Abbey church several prelates who offered her Holy Water; and at the same time suitable hymns were sung. The King and Louise of Savoy, his mother, who were already there, received her at the door of the chancel from where she was led to the seat which had been prepared for her. She attended prayers, and then retired to her apartment in the Abbey. In the evening she returned to the church to pray by the tomb of the King and Queen, her father and mother, and then attended confession in order to prepare for the Holy Communion which she was to receive the following day.

Everything was prepared for her consecration and her crowning. In the chancel in the middle of the transept was a high canopy with seats covered in cloth of gold surrounding it for the Princesses. On the two sides there were sorts of amphitheatres decorated with rich tapestries. The whole chancel was similarly decorated and the high altar full of reliquaries and covered with the Arms of France and of Brittany on cloth of gold. On the right side on a sideboard, covered by a canopy, were two crowns, with the sceptre, the Hand of Justice, the royal sword and several cups and other vases of gold and silver-gilt. Opposite the sideboard under the arch, which was to the left of the high altar, was the place for the foreign ambassadors. Before the high altar there was a chair for the officiant who was the Cardinal of Luxemburg, Bishop of Le Mans and Apostolic Legate, and two other chairs on each side for the Cardinals of Boisy and of Bourges. On the right side near the Cardinal of Boisy were the Bishops of Laon in Brittany, of Auxerre, of Castres, of Senlis, of Ross in Scotland, of Avranches and several abbots, all in their mitres and wearing their pontifical ornaments.

When warned by the sound of bells that the ceremony was about to start, the Queen left her apartments to go to the church. She wore a skirt of silver and over that she wore a coat of ermine.

A great cloak of blue velvet lined in ermine hung from her shoulders. She was covered in jewels and this added a new glory to the majesty of her person. She was led by the Bishops of Toulouse and Laon, both of the House of France, and was preceded by the Princes of the Blood Royal, Knights of the Order and of other Princes, each according to his station. The Duchesses of Alençon and of Vendôme held each side of the Queen's cloak, and the end was carried by the Lady of Ravestein. The Princesses and the Ladies followed, carrying ducal crowns or circlets of gold on their heads according to their rank of Duchesses or of Countesses. Widows were dressed in black velvet and others were in cloth of gold enriched with precious stones. The Legate and the Cardinals, accompanied by the Bishops, received the Queen at the church door and then the *Te Deum* was sung, whilst the Queen was led before the high altar where she prostrated herself before she knelt down. After the *Te Deum* the Cardinal, who was about to carry out the ceremony of the consecration and of the crowning, started by making an oration and then touched her forehead, chest and shoulders. The Queen was served in this ceremony by Louise of Savoy and by the Duchess of Alençon, her daughter. When all the unctions were completed the Cardinal gave her the sceptre, the Hand of Justice and then the ring. During the ceremony of the crowning, the Duke of Alençon, the High Constable of Bourbon and the Duke of Vendôme supported the crown on the Queen's head. Whilst she was led to her throne the Prince of La Roche-sur-Yons carried the sceptre and the Duke of Guise carried the Hand of Justice. The Duchesses sat on the right of the Queen and the Countesses on her left.

The Cardinal of Luxemburg said the mass which was sung by the choir of the Chapel Royal to the accompaniment of several instruments. The Archbishop of Tours acted as Deacon, and the Bishop of Beauvais as sub-Deacon. At the Gospel the Queen got up, with the crown on her head, the sceptre in one hand and holding in the other the Hand of Justice. The Cardinal of Boisy, accompanied by two prelates and by two Deacons and sub-Deacons, then brought the Book for the Queen to kiss.

During the offering the *Dame de Portion* carried the golden and silvered bread, the Lady of the Chamber the wine in a gold vase and Demoiselle de Lestace thirteen pieces of gold money. The Lady in Waiting, having received these gifts from their hands, got up and presented them to the Duchesses, the bread to the Duchess of Alençon, sister of the King, the wine to the Dowager Duchess of Alençon and the gold to the Dowager Duchess of Vendôme, after which the Queen was led by the Princes to the altar, followed by the Princesses, to make the offering. The mass completed, she returned to the same place as where she had been consecrated and received, kneeling, the Holy Communion with much respect and humility. The officiating Cardinal finished off the ceremony by several orations and by the Blessing, which he gave the Queen, and to all the assembly. The Queen was led back to her apartments in the same order in which she had come to the church, except that on her return she was wearing the crown on her head. The Lord d'Orval carried before Her Majesty the Crown of Charlemagne which had been used in the ceremony and the Princess of La Roche-sur-Yons and of Guise, the sceptre, and the Hand of Justice. There was a magnificent feast afterwards during which music and all sorts of instruments were used to increase the festivities of such an august assembly. The Queen spent another day at Saint Denis and did not leave till Tuesday, 12th May, to make her formal entry into Paris.

Francis was a Prince of the Renaissance and possessed brilliant though superficial qualities. He has been described at the time of his succession as a young, handsome, chivalric and gallant prince, affable, courteous and a brilliant talker with a sprightly wit, a facile poet with some delicacy of feeling and some generous impulses which made him amiable. On the other hand he was at bottom frivolous, profoundly selfish and incapable of consistency or application; his character was at once authoritative and weak.[1] The French monarchy had gradually been tending towards absolutism. Francis made the monarchical authority imperious and more absolute. He was the first king to introduce the rule *du bon plaisir*.

An outstanding occasion in the reign, though it produced few political results, was the celebrated meeting of Francis I and Henry VIII on the Field of the Cloth of Gold. Elaborate arrangements were made on a magnificent and sumptuous scale and each Court competed to outshine the other. But the factor that dominated the period was the rivalry between Francis I and the Emperor Charles V. Francis's defeat at Pavia in 1526 and subsequent captivity in Madrid led to the Treaty of Cambrai in 1529 which, though containing harsh conditions for Francis, did lead to some unexpected pledges of friendship by the Emperor who abandoned his rights to Burgundy, released the French captives in Madrid and bestowed on Francis I the hand of his eldest sister Eleanor of Austria who was the Dowager Queen of Portugal. Francis's first wife, Claude, had died in 1542. Immediately the Treaty had been signed, the Dauphin and the Duke of Orleans escorted Eleanor to Paris. The first town which they entered in France was Bayonne and the Queen wore a collar adorned with three rows of very large pearls with rubies and diamonds which were large and fair and of great value. This no doubt was an ornament from the Portuguese crown jewels. The marriage was celebrated on 17th July 1530 at the Abbey of Clarisses de Beryries near Mont de Marcan. Francis and Eleanor made their state entry into Bordeaux on 20th July, and on this occasion the Queen wore many gems including two as large as nuts which she had brought from Spain.

A month earlier, by Letters Patent dated 15th June 1530, Francis had constituted a treasure of crown jewels which, according to the documents, he did in order to make a gift to his successors. He ordered that at each alteration of these jewels their value, pitch and weight should be verified so as to ensure the obligation to keep them for the successor to the Crown. Francis selected jewels from his personal property for the gift and constituted them 'the property of the State', but on the express condition that they should never be alienated.

It was on the occasion of her state entry into Bordeaux that Francis gave to Eleanor these crown jewels for her use while she was Queen. This collection, which was valued at 272,242 *écus soleils*,[2] contained eight pieces, the most notable being a collar or great necklace of 11 diamonds, either table cut or point cut. These diamonds were set in bezels placed on festoons of friar's knots. They had been so set by Anne of Brittany as a customary emblem of widowhood. Each festoon was separated by knots of gold cord resembling those of the Collar of St Michael and on each of the ends were 14 pearls. The most important stone of this ornament was known as 'The Eye' or *Fusée* of Brittany, valued at 108,240 *écus soleils*. This collar was said to have belonged to Claude of France.[3] The second item in the inventory was a jewel to hang round the

---

1 Julius Isaac in the 11th Edition of the *Encyclopaedia Britannica*.

2 The present-day value of an *écu soleil*, which was of fine gold, would probably be about £2.

3 An engraving depicting the 'restoration of the necklace of France' is reproduced by G. Bapst, in his *Histoire des Joyaux de la Couronne de France* from which work much of the following information about the history of the crown jewels has been taken.

neck by a chain in the form of a 'Roman A'. The principal stone was a pointed diamond called the *Prant Pointe* worth 30,000 écus and a very beautiful ruby worth 25,000 écus. Another piece in the form of a letter 'A' had a great balas ruby in the centre worth 20,000 écus. A brooch had as its centre stone a diamond known to history as the *Pointe de Bretagne*. It had formerly belonged to Anne of Brittany, and she had in 1496 commissioned the diamond merchant Jehan Cayon to 'put it under his little mill so as to re-cut it'. Another brooch had a large table-cut diamond set in the centre of red enamel. From the end of each brooch hung a large drop pearl.

The other ornaments were 2 balas rubies in mountings, one known as the *Côte de Bretagne* was valued at 50,000 écus and the other at the same price. Another balas ruby was valued at 10,000 écus. Finally, there was a great table emerald set in gold and bought by Francis I from Mademoiselle de Beauvoys. Its inclusion in the inventory does not seem to have been intended as the King gave it to Eleanor shortly after her entry into Bordeaux.

Apart from the crown jewels, Eleanor had her own personal collection of jewellery to which at Bordeaux the King added many pieces which he had inherited or bought. These consisted chiefly of ornaments which he had inherited from Claude of France. Francis later frequently gave Eleanor numerous and rich presents of jewellery. He himself had a considerable collection which he could dispose of as he pleased.[1]

The crown jewels could be neither altered nor sold and they were in the custody of the *Chambre de Comptes* which, with the King, was accountable for them. It was not long, however, before the King forebade the councillors to trouble themselves about them and ordered that all papers concerning them should be burnt. Francis was also insistent that his own personal transactions regarding the purchase of jewels should be kept secret, and in 1537 he ordered his 'friends and faithful Councillors of the Chamber of Accounts' to burn all the papers and inventories. It is only by chance that the inventory of 1532 has been preserved.

There have also survived some petty cash accounts which show that between 12th December 1528 and 21st December 1529 no less than 132 different pieces of jewellery were delivered to the King, and between 7th January 1529 and 30th June 1530 a further 41 pieces were delivered.

There is an amusing anecdote of the Countess Chateaubriant who had received a large share of the King's liberality. When she went out of favour, the King demanded back the jewels he had given her, several of which bore intimate mottoes. The Countess delayed obeying the King's demand by feigning illness and sent the jewels to a goldsmith to melt down. She then sent the King the gold ingots, which he returned, saying he only wanted the jewels back for the sake of the mottoes adorning them.

Francis I in 1532 bought a great table diamond (*Plate 82, a*) for 65,000 ecus, an enormous sum at that time, and the stone was one of the largest and finest then known. Later it passed into the crown jewels of the King's personal treasury.

In 1532 Francis again met Henry VIII, this time near Calais at a place called Sandingfield. Henry wore a doublet sewn all over with diamonds and rubies worth 100,000

1 For inventory of this see G. Bapst, op. cit.

écus and wore his celebrated collar of 14 large rubies and 14 diamonds with a carbuncle described as big as a goose's egg. The collar was valued at 400,000 écus. As neither queen was present, the crown jewels did not make an appearance, but Francis was magnificently apparelled and wore 'the finest diamonds that have anywhere been seen'. Anne Boleyn was there and danced with Francis, who gave her a great drop diamond worth some 16,000 écus, and he also gave Henry a jewel described as a sepulchre like a cross mounted as a ring worth 1,500 écus which had been acquired from George Wellgei, a celebrated broker at Antwerp.

Francis arranged with Pope Clement VII for the marriage of his second son Henry to Catherine de Medici, the Pope's niece. The King sent the young Princess a diamond ring valued at 3,000 écus. The marriage was celebrated at Marseilles on 25th October 1533. There was an exchange of presents, the Pope sending the King a narwhal (unicorn) horn which was greatly esteemed, and Francis gave the Princess a great table-cut diamond. The Princess brought with her a large quantity of precious stones and jewels, including the biggest and finest pearls ever seen. These pearls consisted of six ropes and 25 other large pearls. Catherine subsequently, when Queen Mother, gave them to Mary Queen of Scots, who took them to Scotland with her after the death of her husband. Their subsequent history is related elsewhere.[1] The Treasurer of France expressed astonishment at the paucity of gold and silver which composed the dowry, but the Pope's representative replied: 'that besides all these, to make the dowry worthy of such a marriage he had promised him by an authentic document three pearls [sic] of inestimable value of whose possession the greatest kings were desirous and covetous— the towns of Naples, Milan and Genoa'.[2] Naturally the three towns were not given to France, but to merit the saying, three of the most beautiful jewels of the crown were given the names of *Pointe de Milan*; *Table de Gênes*; *Œuf de Naples*. The two former stones were diamonds and the *Œuf* a balas ruby. In order to pay for his niece's dowry, Pope Clement had to pledge one of the finest diamonds of his tiara to the banker Strozzi. On her wedding day the new Duchess of Orleans used a crown of gold specially made for the occasion, and she wore 2 great pearls of 92 and 96 gr given her by Francis I.

Another great ceremonial occasion was on 14th July 1538 when the Emperor Charles V visited Francis I. Francis gave the Emperor a diamond worth 30,000 écus set as an eye in a ring bearing the inscription: *Dilectionis testis et exemplum*. Charles V took with him his own collar of the Golden Fleece and gave it to Francis, who in return gave the Emperor the collar of St Michael. The Emperor also gave to the King's daughter, Princess Margaret, diamonds worth 50,000 ducats and pearls of great price.

Among the notable craftsmen who worked for Francis were Benvenuto Cellini, who was resident in Paris from 1540 to 1545, Etienne Delaune, called 'Stephanus', who had worked under Cellini, and Jean Duvet, known as the Master of the Unicorn and who was goldsmith to Francis I. Pierre Mangot was jeweller to the King from 1531 to 1542, while the King's gem engraver was Matteo del Nasaro.

Francis died on 31st March 1547 and was succeeded by his surviving son Henry II. On 5th April Queen Eleanor returned to the Grand Pantler of France the crown jewels,

---

1 See p. 166   2 Brantôme: *Recueil de Dames*, Vol. VII.

keeping for her own use her personal jewels; except for a diamond known as the *Grande Pointe*, the setting of which she had had altered, the other pieces were as she had received them. The crown jewels were handed over to Catherine de Medici, the new Queen.

Henry II was crowned at Rheims on 26th July 1547. He postponed his state entry into Paris until his queen, Catherine de Medici, had been crowned at St Denis, which ceremony took place on 10th June 1594. Contrary to custom, the King wished to be present and a special stand was built for him. On 18th June the Queen made her state entry into Paris, the King making his two days later. The Queen's crown, which was decorated with her own jewels, was so heavy that it had to be taken off frequently, and her mantle was richly decorated with jewels which were her personal property. Henry II broke away from tradition by using, instead of the great fleur-de-lis clasp on his coronation mantle, one described as a great cross composed of 9 large diamonds with a great pearl hung from the base of the cross. This jewel had belonged to Francis I, who had paid 90,000 écus for it. Catherine possessed necklaces in which the stones were mounted in interlocking X surmounted by a crowned *H*. While the Queen had the use of some of the personal jewels of her husband the King's mistress, Diana of Poitiers, had from the beginning of the reign the keys of the Royal Closet and made use of the King's jewels. In her casket was a great necklace of diamonds and pearls; a close-fitting collar or carcanet made of diamonds with 3 *cabochon* rubies in the centre separated from each other by 4 pearls; another carcanet of emeralds with a pear-shaped pearl hanging from the under-side of the great cross the King had used as a mantle clasp. She also used the great table diamond set with a large drop pearl which Francis I had bought for 65,000 écus, the famous ruby called the *Œuf de Naples* valued at 70,000 écus, another cross of 6 diamonds and 3 drop pearls and another great table diamond with a rose pearl. On the death of the King, all these were returned to the Royal Closet by Diana.

Henry had not the same love of jewels as had Francis I, but he was anxious to increase the collection of crown jewels begun by his father. When he went to war he left behind Letters Patent dated April 1551 stating that the jewels enumerated (those mentioned above as used by Diana of Poitiers) were worthy to figure among those of the House and Crown of France, and he ordered that on his death these jewels should be the inalienable property of the State. The King survived the campaign, but died unexpectedly on 12th July 1559.

He was succeeded by his son, Francis II, who recognising the commands of his father by Letters Patent dated 6th August 1559, gave effect to Henry II's wishes. The document reads:

> After the decease of our late and most honoured lord and father we found in his cabinet and treasure certain jewelled ornaments and precious stones being of great value and price. [There follows a list.] Let it be known that we desire that the said jewels and other precious pearls should remain for ever in the possession of the household and crown of France being worthy of this place and we say and declare that our will and intention is that the said jewels shall remain in the possession of the household and crown of France as precious furnishings of the said house to which we have and do leave give and destine to remain property in the Treasury of precious furnishings of the said house and crown of France, so that they shall never have any cause or occasion to be

extracted sold or otherwise alienated—which selling, alienation or extraction we have and do forbid and perpetuate all these present, given under our hand and seal at Paris on the 4th day of July in the year of grace 1559 in the first year of our reign, signed 'Francis'.

This declaration was drawn up in such terms as to prevent royal mistresses from wearing the crown jewels and later led to some confusion in various attempts to circumvent this provision.

Francis II had married Mary Stuart when he was Dauphin on 24th April 1559. A description of the ceremony informs us that she was dressed in a robe of Persian velvet covered with gems and embellishments of white embroidery in such fashion that it was admirable to look at. Catherine de Medici, contrary to what has been written by some of her detractors, did not lavish extravagant sums on jewellery. It was necessary for her to give expensive presents, but the accounts show that she exercised economy. On the occasion of her son's wedding she gave Mary Stuart a carcanet composed of a great diamond cut in facets shaped like an escutcheon; a great diamond set in a gold ring and a *cabochon* ruby also set in a gold ring. Catherine de Medici also gave Mary Stuart wonderful pearls which she had brought with her from Italy. The carcanet worn by Mary Stuart at her wedding is later described as being composed of 30 pearls, 3 table-cut and 2 point-cut diamonds. One of the points was the stone known as the *Pointe de Milan* and the other was the *Pointe de Bretagne*. Below the carcanet she wore a much larger necklace of friars' knots each separated by 15 diamonds and each adorned with 14 round pearls. It was valued at 49,000 écus. Another necklace consisted of different coloured stones set in different coloured enamels. Another ornament was a *bordure* which could be worn with a bandeau on the hair, or as a carcanet round the neck, or as a bodice trimming. It was composed of 12 emeralds set in bezels, each bezel enamelled in red and white arabesques surrounding crowned 'F's.

Francis was crowned at Rheims on 18th September 1559, but it is not recorded that he went to St Denis or made a state entry to Paris, nor was Mary Stuart crowned at St Denis. She had already been crowned Queen of Scots when an infant, and it is recorded that on the occasion of her wedding when she was only fifteen years of age, she was anointed and crowned at the ceremony which took place at Notre-Dame in Paris. Francis had but a very short reign, as he died on 5th December 1560. While he had added to the crown jewels, he altered some of those which his father had given for posterity, although some of the celebrated pieces, including the *Côte de Bretagne*, the *Fève de Naples*, known henceforth as the 'Roman A', remained in their former state. The resetting was done by François Dujardin, a pupil and successor of Pierre Mangot. He dismantled some of the ornaments given by Francis I and used the stones he took out to make several new ornaments. The first was a touret, or cap, one of the rubies in which, on the marriage of Catherine de Medici, had been given the name of the *Table de Gênes* (Genoa). This ornament was valued at 60,000 écus.

Francis II was succeeded by his brother Charles IX, a boy of ten, who was crowned at Rheims on 15th May 1561. Even when he was declared of age in 1563, he left the government of France very much in the hands of his mother. During the lifetime of her husband Catherine de Medici had little opportunity to wear the crown jewels at state ceremonies as she was thrust into the background by the King's mistress, Diana of Poitiers. Again, during the short reign of Francis II, Mary Stuart held the central position at Court. When Catherine's third son, Charles IX, came to the throne she obtained his signature to a document, which he was probably unable to read, which placed at the Queen Mother's disposal all the crown jewels. But although she was a lover of jewels and had a fine casket of her own, Catherine de Medici made use of the crown jewels for purposes other than personal adornment. She offered the English Ambassadors, Smith and Throckmorton, the most beautiful jewel of the French Crown for Queen Elizabeth in exchange for the English rights to Calais, but the offer was refused.

This was at the time of the religious civil wars which lasted fifty years in France. The Roman Catholic Church in France and the Pope, the King of Spain and the Italian princes all realised that Catholicism would be menaced in their countries if Protestantism won its fight against the French monarchy, and all were thus ready to help to finance the King of France in his struggle. Having drawn upon the riches of the Church, Charles had to turn elsewhere, and the crown jewels were used as pledges against loans from the principal finance houses of Europe. The first loan was from Venice, and as the financiers did not know the value of jewels, four goldsmiths were employed. The value they gave them declared the whole collection to be worth 2,200,000 écus. After some parley, they took the great cross which Francis I had used as a mantle clasp valued at 9,000 écus; the rich pendant with the great table diamond bought by Francis I valued with the setting and pearl pendant at 72,000 écus, and another large diamond in a gold and enamel pendant with a pearl drop valued at 40,000 écus. The transaction was completed on 24th January 1569 and the jewels taken to Venice.[1] About the same time Charles had offered the Duke of Florence the 5 great rubies—the *Œuf de Naples*, the *Côte de Bretagne*, another valued at 28,000 écus and 2 others. The Duke's valuers declared that they were not oriental rubies, but balas rubies and, therefore, worth a good deal less, and they estimated their value at 124,000 écus. After a great deal of wrangling, a contract was signed on 14th April 1569 for a loan of 180,000 écus against the security of the five stones. As the loans were repaid, the jewels were reclaimed, but the repayment called for fresh loans, and in 1571 the King borrowed 60,000 écus from the Canton of Basle on the security of a large gold necklace set with 9 big rubies.

In 1570 the King married Elizabeth of Austria, daughter of the Emperor Maximilian II, who was crowned at St Denis on 25th March 1571. In preparation for the wedding, the crown jewels for the third time were altered, except, of course, those which were pledged abroad. The Queen Mother added to the crown jewels and her gifts were made 'inalienable from the Crown'. These included a series of small pearl ornaments and parures of pearls and coloured stones. The inventory of 5th November 1570 says that there were in the crown jewels complete sets of ornaments consisting of a carcanet, a collar, or great necklace, a *côtière*, or chain, with a pendant and a *bordure* for the head. The total value of the crown jewels at this time was 570,278 *écus soleil*. But owing to the troubles of the times, there was little opportunity for the young Queen to wear

[1] For the full story, see G. Bapst: op. cit.

them. The alteration of the crown jewels was a breach of the Letters Patent and made a precedent for subsequent further breaches which led to the dispersal of most of the collection. But fashions had changed and the strength of the Renaissance was very powerful.

Charles IX died at the age of twenty-four on 30th May 1574 and was succeeded by his brother, Henry III, who, about a year earlier, had been elected King of Poland. The Poles tried to prevent the King's departure, but he arrived in France in 1575. He soon interested himself in the crown jewels and, with his mother, checked them to make quite sure that the widowed Queen Elizabeth had returned them all. Henry was crowned at Rheims on 5th February 1575, but owing to the unsettled state of the country he was unable to go to St Denis for his second crowning in order to make his state entry into Paris. The situation also did not permit his Queen, Louise de Mercœur, to be crowned. Henry was concerned that he might die childless and his only heir was his brother, the Duke of Alençon, who was in poor health. There was, therefore, a strong possibility of the throne of France passing to Henry of Navarre who was a Protestant. The King therefore couched the wording of the Letters Patent, which relieved the Queen Dowager of responsibility for the crown jewels, in such terms that it was clear that he wanted to abolish the Salic Law.

Henry became embroiled in unwise policies and involved the country in financial chaos. John Casimir, Count Palatine, had demanded 8,000,000 livres before he would remove his mercenary troops from the royal lands. When the crown jewels were given to him in pledge he had some waggons of a special design made, with closed cases on platforms, in which he displayed the crown jewels of France to all the people. Moreover, his personal expenditure was on a prodigal scale. The story of his financial operations is a most intricate one, but has been disentangled by Bapst.[1] Having exhausted all means of raising money in France by floating loans at exorbitant rates of interest, by imposing oppressive taxation, by alienating Church property, the King turned to such jewels as he could lay his hands on which he either sold or pledged.

The first transaction took place on 23rd February 1567 when he took the rubies from the reliquaries containing the Crown of Thorns and the Holy Nail in the Sainte Chapelle. They were disposed of without trace. A writer of the time[2] relates that on the night of 10th May 1575 the relic of the True Cross was stolen from the Sainte Chapelle and a riot resulted. People said that this was the result of the schemes and manœuvres of the Queen Mother who was so detested by the people that any misfortune that occurred was laid at her door. It was said that the relic had been sent to Italy as pledge for a large sum of money.

Henry then turned to Charles of Lorraine, a cousin of Queen Louise, and asked for a loan of 100,000 écus. Charles, anxious to gain favour with the King, but being without money, sent the King the jewels of the ducal crown of Lorraine which were 'inalienable from the State Crown' and he was given as surety 4,000 acres of forest at Compiègne. The jewels included a great necklace containing 9 large table-cut diamonds, 8 others and 16 large drop pearls: a necklace adorned with 7 large table-cut diamonds, 4 other diamonds and 16 large pearls: a jewel with a great table diamond

[1] G. Bapst: op. cit.   [2] *Mémoires de Pierre de L'Estoile.*

embellished with 8 others: another great jewel with a big *cabochon* ruby with 8 table diamonds: the Cross of Lorraine containing 9 great diamonds: another stone of which there was particular mention was a great point diamond of 18 carats which the King gave to John Casimir and which Charles was anxious to recover. As the debt was not paid back in time, Charles cut down the forest at Compiègne. Thereafter the King sold or pledged all the crown jewels and but few were redeemed.

Henry III's fear of being childless was fulfilled and having tried by assassination to get rid of the Guises, he was himself assassinated and with his dying breath designated Henry of Navarre as his heir.

THE HOUSE OF BOURBON

Henry of Navarre of the House of Bourbon was a Protestant and his accession found France riven with the struggle between the Popular League and the Protestants, while the nation desired internal unity and religious tolerance. For five years he struggled to conquer his kingdom. On 23rd July 1593 Henry abjured Protestantism and was received into the Roman Catholic Church at St Denis. As Rheims was in the hands of the League, he chose Chartres as the place of coronation and his *sacre* was performed at the church of Notre-Dame on 27th February 1594. The *Sainte Ampoule* not being available, that of St Martin, which was kept in the Abbey of Marmoutier near Tours, was used. The remainder of the ceremony was in accordance with tradition. The regalia had been taken from St Denis to Paris for safety and so new ornaments had to be provided. These included a crown of gold described as *Clause à l'Impériale*[1] and a second one described as a ducal crown of silver gilt which the King wore all the day of his coronation; the sceptre and the Hand of Justice of silver gilt with the sword and two spurs. The King subsequently gave these to the Abbey of St Denis.

Henry IV possessed no personal fortune and he found the royal domains in France almost entirely alienated. Moreover, the Treasury was without funds. The new King had nothing on which to raise credit as the crown jewels were in pawn, the King's *Cabinet* in Paris had been pillaged by the League and only a small portion of the Royal Treasury was saved by Devetz, Councillor of the *Cour des Aides*. With the help of Sillery and Sancy the King succeeded in raising the funds necessary to meet the cost of establishing himself firmly on the throne and in due time to repay his creditors and to put in order the finances of the country.

Nicholas Harlay, Seigneur de Sancy, was a soldier and financier who showed the greatest devotion to the French monarchy, especially to Henry IV. His financial transactions are too complicated to unravel. He was not only a diamond fancier, but understood the value of precious stones for the purpose of raising money. The first notable transaction of this sort of which we know is recorded in a document dated 31st January 1589 which relates to the purchase of some diamonds and other jewels by Henry III from Sancy and their being pledged by Sancy for the purpose of raising troops in Switzerland. A warrant relates to a purchase by the King from Sancy:

[1] Doublet: op. cit.

A great flawless diamond, facet cut, weighing 37 to 38 carats or thereabouts set in a golden frame at the end of which hangs a great round pearl, flawless and perfect, of about 20 carats; also a great heart-shaped ruby set in gold at the base of which hangs a great pear-shaped pearl, for the price of 20,000 écus. The large jewels were pledged and put into the hands of the said Sieur de Sancy that he might pawn them in Switzerland, Germany or elsewhere with the charge that if they were pledged for less than 24,000 écus, His Majesty will only pay to the said Sancy the price for which they were pledged.

Sancy became Colonel General of the Swiss troops of whom there were 12,000, and after the assassination of Henry III he saved the monarchy by bringing them over to Henry IV, the new King. It has sometimes been claimed that the large diamond known as 'The Sancy' or 'Great Sancy' which came into the French Royal Treasury later was identical with the largest diamond pawned by Sancy to raise the Swiss troops. We first hear of the 'Great Sancy' in 1593 when it was already pledged to Roderiques, a money-lender, for one-third of its value. In 1594 it passed to a gentleman of Lucca from whom Sancy redeemed it in 1595. But from a document of 20th February 1595 we learn that the jewels pawned to raise the Swiss troops were then still unredeemed. Moreover, the largest diamond in the warrant of 31st January 1589 weighed 37 to 38 carats, while the weight of the great diamond was $53\frac{1}{2}$ carats. The weight of the smaller stone approximates more closely to a diamond known as the 'Little Sancy' which passed into the Prussian crown jewels and whose weight today is recorded as $34\frac{1}{2}$ carats. The discrepancy in weight can be accounted for by the difference in the carat in various countries until it was standardised, and perhaps by the removal of the gold setting.

If the 'Great Sancy' did not play the vital part that has been attributed to it in saving the monarchy, it certainly was used on various occasions by Sancy for raising money, and although Henry IV at one time thought of buying it, Sancy finally sold it to James I of England in 1604 for 60,000 écus. Since Nicholas de Sancy placed his private fortune at the disposal of the King's cause, it indeed played its part in the history of this period.

Henry IV purchased jewels when he could, the most notable acquisition being a fine diamond bought from the Duke of Epernon on 5th November 1600 for 30,000 écus. The King reconstituted the Crown Treasure, but did not appoint a Crown Jeweller. In 1604, however, by an Order in Council a number of posts of Goldsmith Valets were created to be in charge of the Royal Wardrobe and to have the responsibility for the administration and security of the crown jewels. In 1608 the King gave twenty apartments in the Louvre to twenty artists in the royal employ and among these was a Goldsmith Jeweller of the Crown.

Henry IV married Marie de Medici, niece of the Grand Duke of Tuscany, in 1600, but the Queen was not crowned at the time. In 1610, however, Henry wished to appoint Marie as Regent when he was away at the head of his army and she was, there-fore, crowned at St Denis with great pomp on 13th May of that year. The regalia with the rest of the treasure of the abbey had been returned in May 1598 from Paris, where it had been sent for safe-keeping during the civil war. The ceremonial was materially the same as that used at the coronation of Elizabeth of Austria. This was the last coronation of a Queen of France. After the ceremony the King and Queen proceeded to Paris for the state entry which had been arranged to take place on the following Sunday on a scale of unprecedented magnificence. But on 14th May, the day following the coronation, Henry IV was assassinated by a man named Ravaillac. The heir to the throne being but nine years old, the widowed Queen, Marie de Medici, was appointed Regent. The young King, Louis XIII, was crowned at Rheims on 17th October 1610. The ceremony was performed by the Cardinal de Joyeuse in accordance with established custom. After the ceremony the regalia and the coronation robes were returned to St Denis and the King also gave to the abbey the two crowns which had been made for the occasion—one of gold and the other of silver-gilt. On 30th October he made his state entry into Paris. Owing to the youth of the King and the fact that the Queen Mother observed deep mourning, the crown jewels were not used in the early part of the reign. When, however, Louis XIII obtained his majority on 2nd October 1614 the crown diamonds were taken from their coffers in the cellars of the Louvre.

In 1612 as a matter of policy, Marie de Medici had arranged for Louis XIII to marry Anne of Austria, daughter of Philip III of Spain, and for Princess Elizabeth of France, the King's sister, to marry Philip (later Philip IV), son of Philip III of Spain. The double marriage ceremony took place at the church of St Andrew at Bordeaux on 25th December 1615. For this occasion Marie de Medici ordered from the Crown Jeweller, Corneille Rogier, sets of ornaments for the two future Queens. Anne of Austria's ornaments were set with the crown diamonds and with others added by Rogier. The principal ornament was a crown which was set with a number of stones from the treasury and was enamelled, probably with black arabesques. We have no detailed description of the crown, but various portraits of the Queen show her with a closed crown set with precious stones. The crown cost 800 livres to make and it was taken to the Louvre in a case of green morocco, lined inside, which cost 60 livres. The Queen also received a great chain of gold enamelled in different colours. The chain was set with 29 large diamonds, each in a circle of diamonds, with twenty lesser stones set between. The centre stone was that which Henry IV had purchased from the Duke of Epernon and which was the largest and most beautiful stone in the crown diamonds.

Although it is known that Louis XIII and Anne of Austria and also Marie de Medici made numerous purchases of jewellery, no details are available other than about the Queen's wedding presents, but Bapst[1] recounts three anecdotes relating to them. The first concerns the crown diamonds which were pawned either with Marshal d'Ancre or with his wife. At the end of 1616, on the instigation of a shoemaker called Picard, an infuriated crowd attacked the mansion of the Marshal d'Ancre, broke open the doors and rushed into the house. Having broken up the furniture, the pictures, the statuary and the chests containing the jewels, the crowd gave itself over to pillage, and the Venetian Ambassador relates that the dress the Queen had worn at the King's coronation, which was covered with diamonds of great value, was found in the house torn to fragments. Eight months afterwards an almost identical thing happened at the time of the assassination of Marshal d'Ancre. The Venetian Ambassador wrote: 'There was found with him, besides Bills of Exchange in his name and that of his wife for five million

[1] Op. cit.

écus, jewellery, precious stones and goldsmith's work valued at more than one million gold écus and the larger part of this jewellery and these stones belonged to the Crown.' The King had the jewellery and stones returned to him and sent them to the Queen, his wife, while an Award in Council confirmed the action which the King had taken.

Another Venetian Ambassador reported the third incident: writing on 21st September 1618, he relates that:

> Anne of Austria, finding herself in her room with the ladies attached to her person, placed on a table a necklace of 80 pearls which she had just removed from her neck. Hardly had the Queen turned her back than the necklace disappeared. Surprised and indignant at such an occurrence, she had the doors closed and a search made for the guilty party. A Spaniard named Isabellica, who was second Lady-in-Waiting, was then seen to throw something out of the window. This lady had picked up the necklace from the table and with the most complete unconcern in the world she threw the pearls into the bush under the window. They sent to pick up the pearls, but only found 45. The others were missing.

Each of these pearls was worth 800 écus.

In 1636 Cardinal Richelieu drew up a deed making a donation of part of his property to the Crown. This included his jewelled church plate consisting of an enamelled cross; a chalice with its paten; two cruets; a bust of St Louis; a ciborium and a pyx, all enriched with diamonds, rubies and pearls and valued at 765,000 livres. In addition, there was a notable heart-shaped diamond, rose-cut, with a little table in the upper part of the facets, of very fine water and weighing 19 carats. It was valued at 100,000 livres. From the time it came into the crown jewels this stone was given the name of 'Richelieu'. Richelieu died in 1642 and Louis XIII on 14th May 1643.

Louis XIV was not yet five years old when his father died, and there followed a long Regency under the Queen Mother, who shared the power with her Minister, Cardinal Mazarin. Louis was declared of age in 1651, but his *sacre* at Rheims did not take place until 7th June 1654. After the ceremony the Queen Mother, in accordance with custom, sent the two new crowns made for the occasion—one of gold and one of silver gilt—to St Denis with the other coronation ornaments.

During the long reign of Louis XIV, the longest recorded in the history of Europe, the crown jewels continued to play their traditional role as valuables on which money could be raised to pay for troops and to give splendour to the Court. As was to be expected, the *Grand Monarque* enriched the crown jewels with some most valuable acquisitions. Besides the return to the Treasury of the three great rubies which had been in pawn for many years, the most notable additions were:

> The bequest by Cardinal Mazarin of the famous 18 Mazarin Diamonds, including 'The Sancy' and 'The Mirror of Portugal'.
> The diamonds of the House of Guise, purchased.
> A large number of diamonds and precious stones purchased from the travellers Tavernier and Bazu.
> The jewels purchased from the Estate of Marie Louise de Gonzague, Queen of Poland.
> Various purchases made by the Crown Jewellers.

In 1649 it was found necessary to pledge the crown jewels to the Colonels of the Swiss Regiments. Since the reign of Francis I, the Swiss Cantons had provided troops for service with the French Crown. The agreements between the King's representatives and the Colonels of the Regiment laid down that the troops were to be paid regularly. Since 1570 the Kings of France had also contracted loans with the Swiss Cantons. It will be remembered that in the early years of the reign of Henry IV there was difficulty in repaying the debt contracted by the King's predecessor and the King found it necessary to borrow further sums from this source. By 1602 the principal and accumulated interest due had increased and at the same time the Swiss Regiments had not been fully paid. An arrangement was made for the liquidation of the debt, but by 1649 the pay of the troops, whose loyalty and integrity had never been in doubt, was still in arrears. In order to pacify the soldiers, the crown jewels were given as security for the 300,000 livres which was the pay due to them for the first six months of 1648. It was agreed that if the sum had not been repaid on the specific date, the Colonels could pledge the diamonds to raise money, but they undertook to return them when the back pay was received. During the *Fronde* it was impossible to raise money either to pay the interest, to repay the debt or to pay the soldiers, and so further jewels were given in security for an additional sum of 300,000 livres. This lot of jewels included a pair of ear-rings of incomparable beauty which the King and the Queen Mother wanted for the use of Queen Marie Thérèse. By 1652 three Captains of the Free Companies, who still had not been paid, succeeded in getting hold of the crown jewels and took them to Zurich. Despite persuasions and threats by the French Ambassador and various means adopted by Cardinal Mazarin to obtain them, the Captains remained adamant. It was not until 1665 that the debt was redeemed and the jewels returned to the Crown.

The 3 rubies had been given to a banker named Zamat in pledge for a loan of 120,000 écus in 1581. The sum was to be repaid plus 20,000 écus for interest in 1583. In the event of a default in payment, Zamat was entitled to sell or pawn the stones, though he undertook to repay the King anything in excess of the loan due. It transpired that Zamat was acting on behalf of Pierre Legrand, the King's secretary. In 1602 Legrand's widow handed over the rubies to Sully hoping that this would ensure repayment. On the death of Henry IV Sully gave them to Marie de Medici. In 1616 the widow Legrand died and the stones passed into the possession of her heirs who began a series of legal actions which continued until 1670 when the matter was settled and the stones were returned to the Royal Treasury. The affair was complicated by a claim in 1643 of the Canons of the Sainte Chapelle that these stones were part of the five rubies which had been taken by Catherine de Medici in 1576. Finally, in 1697, this claim was settled when the reliquary of the *Sainte Couronne* was taken from the great shrine and the rubies were tried in the setting. The official report states: 'that the diameters of these settings were considerably greater than the size of the rubies and Montarsy, the King's Jeweller, said that he did not believe that these rubies were those that King Henry III had had removed'. In the face of this declaration the grille of the shrine was closed and the rubies were returned to the King's coffers.

The five great balas rubies of the Sainte Chapelle had been considered to be royal

a   Crown of Marie Leczinska from an engraving by Charles Duclos, 1725 (p. 251)

b   Engraving of crown of Charles X designed by the House of Bapst (p. 270)

c (left)   Funeral crown of Louis XVIII. Treasury of St Denis (p. 269)

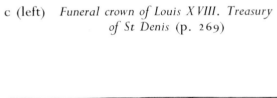

d (right)   Funeral crown of Marie Antoinette. Treasury of St Denis (p. 269)

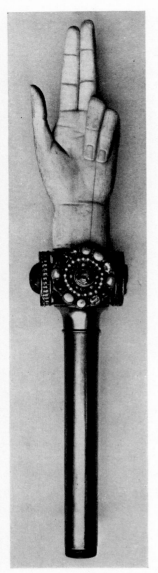

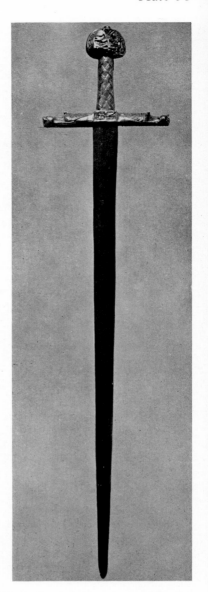

a (extreme left)
Sceptre of Charles V.
The Louvre (p. 275)

b (left)
Hand of Justice.
The Louvre (p. 276)

c (right)   *Coronation*
sword 'Joyeuse'.
The Louvre (p. 275)

d   *Coronation spurs.*
The Louvre
(p. 275)

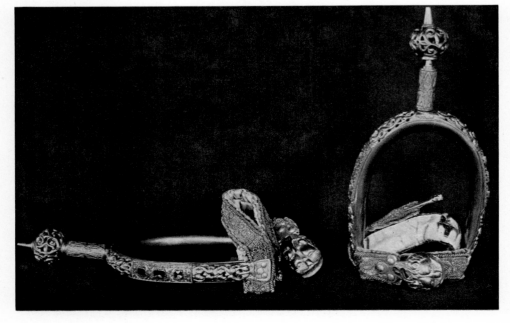

property, having been given by St Louis to the privileged Church of the French kings. Four were set in the vessel containing the Crown of Thorns and the fifth in that containing the Blood of Our Lord. We have a description of them in the official reports of their removal in 1576:

> The first rock-shaped and pierced in three places was estimated at 70,000 écus; the second, approaching a spinel in colour, pierced right through estimated at 30,000 écus; the third a round pierced *cabochon* estimated at 40,000 écus; the fourth an egg-shaped *cabochon* estimated at 40,000 écus; the fifth a *cabochon* estimated at 70,000 écus. As far as can be ascertained these rubies were entrusted to the Ambassadors to take to Italy where they were pawned and nothing more has been heard of them.

In 1644 Queen Henrietta Maria left England for France carrying with her all the English crown jewels on which she could lay her hands. Among these were two notable diamonds, 'The Sancy' and 'The Mirror of Portugal'. She tried to sell these to raise funds to support Charles I's cause and to meet her own needs. She contracted loans to a total of 427,566 livres with the Duke of Epernon, and among the jewels she gave in 1654 as surety were 'The Sancy' and 'The Mirror of Portugal'. As she was unable to repay the loans, the Duke was permitted to retain or sell the two diamonds in return for the extinction of 360,000 livres of the debt. The Duke sold these two diamonds to Cardinal Mazarin, who was a great collector of jewels and who purchased many others which had belonged to Charles I besides some which were the personal jewels of Henrietta Maria and others which had belonged to Queen Christina of Sweden. In his will, the Cardinal left these two great stones to the French Crown and agreed that they should be collected together with sixteen others which he also bequeathed, and be thereafter known as the Mazarin Diamonds.

There is much confusion about the history of 'The Sancy' or 'Great Sancy Diamond'. It has been inaccurately considered to be one of the diamonds that Charles the Bold of Burgundy lost at the Battle of Granson or Morat, but these stories were written in the time of Louis XV, by a writer who was trying to flatter the King as being the possessor of a great historical diamond. The stone takes its name from Nicholas Harlay, Seigneur de Sancy, in whose possession we first hear of it in 1593. Henry IV wished to buy it, but had not the funds, and in 1604 Sancy sold it to James I of England for 60,000 écus. It passed to James's son, Charles I, whose consort was forced to sell it. During the Revolution it was stolen, but was said to have been identified in Spain in 1809 and later was purchased by the Demidoff family in Russia in about 1828. It was purchased by a wealthy Parsee merchant in Bombay in the 1860's for £20,000, but after a short time returned to Paris having been acquired by a firm of jewellers who later sold it to the Maharajah of Patiala. The stone weighs 53¾ carats, is of very fine water, almond-shaped and faceted on both sides in a style peculiar to Indian lapidaries.

The confused history of 'The Mirror of Portugal' is dealt with in Chapter Eighteen.

The other sixteen Mazarin Diamonds were subsequently recut, in some cases more than once, as is shown from the following table taken from the first and last inventories in which they all appear with their weight and size:

No.	Name	Inventory 1691 (Cont'd)		Inventory 1791 (Cont'd)	
		Weight Carats	Value Livres	Weight Carats	Value Livres
1.	Grand Sancy	$53\frac{3}{4}$	600,000	$53\frac{12}{16}$	1,000,000
2.		$33\frac{3}{8}$	260,000	$24\frac{1}{6}$	240,000
3.	Mirror of Portugal . .	$25\frac{3}{8}$	150,000	$21\frac{2}{16}$	250,000
4.		$24\frac{1}{4}$	100,000	$13\frac{10}{16}$	60,000
5.		$21\frac{5}{8}$	120,000	$22\frac{6}{16}$	160,000
6.		$18\frac{1}{4}$	80,000	$19\frac{12}{16}$	140,000
7.	The Grand Mazarin . .	21	75,000	$18\frac{9}{16}$	75,000
8.		$18\frac{1}{4}$	55,000	$14\frac{12}{16}$	30,000
9.		$15\frac{1}{4}$	75,000	$14\frac{14}{16}$	150,000
10.		17	50,000	16	50,000
11.		$17\frac{3}{4}$	40,000	$20\frac{6}{16}$	50,000
12.		17	50,000	17	50,000
13.		13	40,000	$10\frac{4}{16}$	25,000
14.		$11\frac{1}{3}$	35,000	$8\frac{7}{16}$	25,000
15.		$10\frac{3}{4}$	20,000	$8\frac{16}{32}$	12,000
16.		$8\frac{3}{4}$	16,000	6	8,000
17.		$21\frac{1}{2}$	70,000	$21\frac{6}{16}$	25,000
18.		22	70,000	$21\frac{8}{16}$	25,000

The Mazarins were among the crown jewels stolen at the time of the Revolution and only five—Nos. 4, 7, 8, 13 and 16—were recovered, but they are difficult to identify and the one which the authorities decided to preserve and is still in the Louvre and described as 'Mazarin No. 8' does not correspond with the previous descriptions either in weight or colour. Besides this bequest the Cardinal left a spray of 50 diamonds to the Queen, while to Anne of Austria he left a big circular-shaped diamond known as the *Rose d'Angleterre*; a rose diamond weighing 14 carats and a ring with a perfect oriental *cabochon* ruby.

In 1665 Louis XIV purchased from his cousin, Marie of Lorraine, the diamond of the House of Guise which had belonged to Henry, Duke of Guise, who had attempted to gain the throne of Naples. This stone had belonged to the House of Guise since the XVI century. Charles II, Duke of Lorraine, had it in his Treasury and Louis gave it to the Duchess of Elbœuf to enable her to borrow money on its security as ransom for her husband who was a prisoner of war.

In 1669 the celebrated French traveller, Jean Baptiste Tavernier, returned from his travels in the East and was presented to Louis XIV. He had brought back with him a superb collection of precious stones of which Bapst writes: 'their brilliance seemed even more resplendent owing to their distant and somewhat mysterious origin.' The King was fascinated by the purity of the quality of the diamonds which Tavernier showed him and ordered Colbert to buy a number of these stones. Tavernier's bill came to 897,731 livres of which 220,000 livres were accounted for by the Blue Diamond, the remainder being for 44 large diamonds and 1,122 lesser ones. The Blue Diamond, which was officially designated 'The Blue Diamond of the Crown', was a most beautiful stone of brilliant blue weighing $112\frac{3}{16}$ carats. It was cut in the Indian style which was designed to make the best of the stone with the minimum loss of weight. But the style did not achieve the maximum brilliance and the stone was recut in 1673 by Sieur Pitau who cut it heart-shaped which entailed a reduction of the weight to $67\frac{1}{8}$ carats. There is an engraving of the 22 finest diamonds which Tavernier sold to the King.[1] The first is the Blue Diamond and the others are:

A table-cut stone of $51\frac{9}{16}$ carats.
A drop-shaped stone cut in the Indian style of $31\frac{3}{8}$ carats.
A stone of $29\frac{1}{2}$ carats.
Two stones in the rough with a few facets; one of $21\frac{1}{6}$ carats of particularly fine water, and the other of $20\frac{3}{4}$ carats.
A heart-shaped stone of $26\frac{1}{6}$ carats.
A drop-shaped stone of $24\frac{7}{8}$ carats of pale rose colour.
A stone of $13\frac{5}{8}$ carats.
A stone of $10\frac{1}{2}$ carats.
A stone of 9 carats.
A stone of 11 carats.
A rose-coloured stone of $10\frac{5}{6}$ carats.
A stone of 7 carats.
Three uncut stones of 32, $24\frac{7}{8}$ and $10\frac{12}{16}$ carats.
    Most of these stones had been cut by Indian lapidaries and were recut in Paris.

A little while after this transaction, Louis XIV made another purchase, also of great importance, which was arranged by Pitau, the King's Goldsmith. This was in respect of jewels brought to Europe by Sieur Bazu, who also came from India. The total bill was for 504,340 livres and the jewels purchased included 14 big diamonds, of which 1 cost 110,000 livres, and 131 lesser diamonds; a portrait box adorned with diamonds costing 108,000 livres; a balas ruby; 2 fine oriental topazes; 3 fine pearls, of which 1 was round and valued at 40,000 livres, another pear-shaped at 21,500 livres and a third which was rather flat which was valued at 3,300 livres.

At about the same time the King ordered Pitau to buy for him the jewels and plate of Marie Louisa de Gonzague, Queen of Poland, who had died in 1667. The bill for this purchase was 170,000 livres. The jewels included a pair of diamond and a pair of pearl ear-rings, an aigrette of diamonds, 9,795 pearls of different sizes; eight chains, two of which were adorned with diamonds, two with rubies, the third with pearls, rubies and diamonds and one with emeralds and diamonds; fourteen jewels, including rings, set with rubies; a wreath of coral with two diamond crosses and a considerable number of smaller diamonds, rubies, buttons, tags and other jewels.

In 1678 Sieur Alvarez, jewel merchant, who had sold the King a considerable quantity of jewels, was ordered to cut 665 diamonds from the King's latest acquisitions, of which twelve were large stones. Another jeweller and Keeper of the Crown Jewels was Pierre le Taxier de Montarsy, who received considerable orders from the King. When he died in 1710 he should have been in possession of a great quantity of diamonds

1 Published by G. Bapst in *Histoire des Joyaux de la Couronne de France*, and in the English edition of Tavernier's *Travels in India*, the latter being a copy of an engraving in the possession of the Royal Society.

belonging to the King and valued at 300,000 livres, but he had been in debt and had pawned most of the stones. Strong efforts were made to recover them, but it is not known with what result.

During the reign of Louis XIV the French crown jewels were the finest and richest collection of gem stones as yet found in Europe and probably in the world. With the additions made in the next two reigns, the collection attained an even higher state which probably has never been surpassed, certainly in respect of the quality and the number of the large diamonds which were included.

In 1661 the valuation of the crown jewels was as follows:

The old crown jewels	938,800 livres
The Mazarin Diamonds	1,931,000 ,,
Jewels bought by the King	377,400 ,,
Jewels inherited from the Queen Mother	737,000 ,,
Other stones bought by the King	3,260,596 ,,
Other stones taken from the jewels of Queen Marie Thérèsa .	143,500 ,,
Total :	7,388,296 ,,

Another inventory was taken in 1691 and the total value of the crown jewels was then 11,424,181 livres. Of the diamonds whose weights are given, no less than 109 were of 10 carats or more and 273 stones weighed between 4 carats and 10 carats.

Although white diamonds of the purest water continued to be the most highly prized, coloured diamonds began to appear in the crown jewels. Apart from the Blue Diamond, which is described in the inventories of the period as violet blue and because of its size and brilliance was regarded as a unique stone of special distinction, we find other colours being noted. Two are described as rose-coloured; two yellow and one brown. Louis XIV's reign saw great changes in the use to which the crown jewels were put. The early years did not lend themselves to festivities. The King was a minor; the Queen Mother in deep mourning, and the country was in a continual state of war, but by the time Louis was declared of age, the *Fronde* had ended and a period of peace set in. When the King married Marie Thérèse of Spain, only a few of the crown jewels were available for her use, but she was not a pleasure-loving woman, was not fond of luxury, and used the crown jewels but little. Bapst has described her personality as: 'modest rather than plain. A home lover, chaste almost to the point of artlessness; loving the King deeply, she put up with the infidelities of her royal husband without complaint and never rebelled against the success of the mistresses who took her place at festivities.' The King made very few presents to the Queen, the most notable being a very inferior pair of ear-rings as a substitute for the superb diamond pair recorded as one of the most beautiful ornaments of the crown jewels which were in pawn. When the Queen was dying, Louis XIV paid her a visit and said a few affectionate words to her and she replied: 'I die content if it is true you love me still.' When she died the King said: 'This is the only sorrow she has caused me.'

Unlike the Queen, Louis XIV was very fond of jewellery and appropriated the crown jewels to his own use and had them set in buckles, as buttons and in the hilt of his sword, and he introduced the use of jewels in the insignia of Orders of Chivalry which had previously been of gold and silver either plain or enamelled. This was first done in 1663 when he ordered, through Lescot, a cross of the St Esprit in diamonds set *à jour* to the value of 38,500 livres. Later a star and two other crosses were added.

The King had two complete sets of diamond coat and waistcoat ornaments; one consisting of 123 buttons, 300 jewelled buttonholes and nineteen buttonhole decorations for the frock coat and another ninety-six buttonholes for the waistcoat. To this set belonged a 'crocket' of 7 diamonds for the hat, a spray for the frock coat and a cross and wide ribbon. The other set consisted of 168 buttons, 336 buttonholes, nineteen buttonhole decorations for the frock coat; forty-eight buttons and ninety-six buttonholes for the waistcoat and a 'crocket' of diamonds for the hat. In addition there were two pairs of garters to hold up the stockings above the knee; a double pair of shoe buckles and a sword enriched with diamonds which, with its hilt, was valued at 224,000 livres. There was also a set of pearl ornaments somewhat similar to the diamond ones.

The finest ornament in the treasury was a great chain or necklace of 45 diamonds valued at approximately 2,000,000 livres, while other women's ornaments, including a necklace of 25 big pearls, were valued at 250,000 livres. There were three pairs of earrings—one of which was valued at 500,000 livres and set with the 4th, 5th and 6th Mazarins and the Richelieu Diamond. Three pins for the hair were also set with diamonds. The King's sword had a hilt of gold set with 131 diamonds valued at 23,000 livres.

The King was very generous in his presents of jewels not only to friends and courtiers but to important visitors and ambassadors. As there was no Queen to wear the crown jewels, he lent them to princesses, and in his old age he lent to princes some of them which had been set to adorn his own apparel. The princes, the great lords and all who attended Court followed the King's example and spent fabulous sums on jewels with which they bedecked themselves.

Louis died on 1st September 1715; his two sons, his eldest grandson and his great grandson all having died, the third son of Louis, Duke of Burgundy, and Marie Adelaide of Savoy, had unexpectedly become heir to the throne and succeeded his great-grandfather at the age of five. The Duke of Orleans became Regent and died in June 1723, four months after the King had been declared as having attained his majority at the age of thirteen. On 25th October 1722 the King's *sacre* had been performed at Rheims according to the forms in use since Charles IX. In 1691, the titles of the Abbey of St Denis had been suppressed and it lost its independence and came under the authority of the Abbot of St Germain-les-Prés. The coronation regalia continued to be kept there, but a departure was made by the manufacture of a magnificent jewelled crown for the King to wear after his coronation. The frame of this crown was stripped of the diamonds and precious stones after the ceremony and set with imitation stones before it was given to the Abbey of St Denis.

This crown, which was one of the most splendid that has ever existed, was made by Laurent Ronde, the Crown Jeweller, who advertised in the *Mercurye* for the public to come and view it in his workshop in the Louvre. The crown was described in the *Mercurye* and the factual nature of the description suggests that it was the official one given by the Crown Jeweller:

The circlet or diadem of this superb crown is bordered with two strings of pearls and adorned with eight stones of different colours, very large and perfect, between each of which are 3 diamonds linked together by very delicate ornaments.

Eight fleurs-de-lis of diamonds rise above each of the coloured gems on the diadem, and eight *fleurons* or ornaments, composed each of three stones of various colours, are placed between each fleur-de-lis. The heads of the eight fleurs-de-lis are formed of 8 table diamonds known as Mazarins, the arms and centres of the 3 other diamonds and the cross pieces are each a single diamond oblong in shape.

The great and very perfect diamond, weighing 547 grams, known as the Regent, bought for the King by the Duke of Orleans, forms the body and the cross piece of the fleur-de-lis in the front of the crown.

From the eight fleurs-de-lis above spring eight branches or arches which close the crown; they are adorned with diamonds and gems of various colours.

A string of pearls, with two rows of little brilliants, serves to unite the eight arches and as a base for the fleur-de-lis terminating the crown.

Between those eight branches and at the spot where they unite are 8 great drop diamonds shaped like so many springing branches and a kind of sun, if the crown is regarded from a bird's eye point of view.

This fleur-de-lis, which dominates all the others, is isolated. The head is composed of a pear-shaped diamond named the Sancy; the cross arms are composed of 15 diamonds set back to back and joined together by little ornaments to correspond with the size of the Sancy. The bonnet is of violet satin, enriched with 25 diamonds linked together by a very delicate gold embroidery.

This admirable work of art, set *à jour*, weighing about 32 oz was executed under the supervision and from the designs of M. Ronde's son, associated with M. Ronde his father in supplying all the gems of which the King had need, in the same fashion as done heretofore by the Sieurs de Montarsy, father and son, their uncle and cousins, so that for more than seventy years this family was honoured by the King's confidence and entrusted with the gems of the Crown.

Today the frame of the crown (*Plate 84, a*), set with paste facsimiles of the actual stones used, is displayed in the Galerie d'Apollon at the Louvre.

Although the old crown diamonds, including the Mazarins, were used to great effect, they were eclipsed by a new addition to the crown jewels—the Regent Diamond.

As with the stories of most great historical diamonds, the facts relating to the Regent Diamond have been subjected to embellishments. The best account is probably that given by Streeter.[1] The salient facts are that the stone was found by a slave in the Parteal mines on the Kistan in 1701. At that time it weighed 401 carats. The slave succeeded in escaping to the coast with the diamond where he sold it to an English sea captain, who, according to one story, having obtained possession of the stone, flung the slave into the sea. The sea captain sold it for £1,000, probably to Jamchund, who was at that time the largest diamond merchant in the East. The stone was bought from Jamchund in 1701 by Mr Thomas Pitt, Governor of Fort St George, for £20,000.[2] In 1710 Pitt had returned to England and was the subject of scandalous attacks suggesting he had obtained the diamond by foul means, accusations from which he was cleared.

[1] E. W. Streeter: *The Great Diamonds of the World.*
[2] This is confirmed in a letter written by Pitt at Bergen in October 1710 to Colonel H. Yule: *History of the Pitt Diamond*, published by the Hakluyt Society 1888.

Pitt had sent the diamond home to Sir Stephen Evance and it was skilfully cut in London as an almost perfect brilliant of 136¾ carats. The cleavage and dust obtained in cutting was valued at £7,000 to £8,000 while the cost of cutting and polishing was £5,000. According to Streeter the only flaw in the stone was a speck which was invisible in its setting, though Bapst mentions two slight almost invisible clefts.

The possession of the stone brought no happiness to Thomas Pitt. Even after refuting the calumnies on his name, he was constantly haunted by a morbid fear of losing it or being robbed of it, and while it remained in his possession he never slept two nights running under the same roof. In 1717, however, he succeeded in selling it to the Duke of Orleans, who was Regent of France, through Law, a notorious Scottish financier. According to the Duke of St Simon, who also had a hand in the transaction, the Regent was very reluctant to spend so large a sum on the diamond when the Treasury was so empty, but in the end, by flattery, Law and St Simon succeeded in completing the deal and the diamond was sold for a sum of 2,500,000 livres, or £135,000, including £5,000 as Law's reward. It was almost immediately revalued at 6,000,000 livres, and in the 1791 inventory it was valued at 12,000,000 livres, or £480,000. The purchase of the diamond proved popular and its name was changed from Pitt to Regent. The transaction was satisfactory for Pitt, too, as the fortunes of his family were restored, and it is perhaps ironical that the descendants of Thomas Pitt and his son William Pitt should have played so important a part in the struggle against Napoleon, who was helped to power by this diamond.

Before taking its place in the Crown of Louis XV, the Regent Diamond was worn by that young King on two occasions. The first was on 21st March 1721 when the Turkish ambassadors were received in Paris with great magnificence. For the reception of the Ottoman Embassies, the King wore a flame-coloured coat with the diamond buttons and buttonholes of Louis XIV; the Sancy Diamond in a large agraffe in his hat and the Regent Diamond set in a knot of pearls and diamonds on a shoulder ornament. One year later the King attended a solemn *Te Deum* at Notre-Dame to celebrate the alliance concluded between France and Spain. On this occasion he wore a lilac velvet costume and the same diamond ornaments as he had used a year earlier.

On 5th September 1725 Louis XV married Marie Leczinska, daughter of the exiled King of Poland. For this occasion the crown jewels were reset and the old sets of ornaments used by the King were broken up and adapted for the Queen as necklaces, aiguillettes, agraffes, brooches and other pieces of jewellery. The most important ornament was a crown of which an engraving by Duclos (*Plate 85, a*) has been preserved. Bapst describes it as follows:

> Its framework, in silver gilt *repercé à jour* says the legend placed under the print of this crown, was composed as usual of a circlet and of a circle of arches or diadems closing it at the crest.
>
> The circlet was adorned with rose diamonds between alternate rubies, sapphires, topazes and emeralds, each one of which is accompanied by little silver ornaments representing a species of embroidery; two strings of pearls form the borders of the circlet.
>
> The circle was composed of eight fleurs-de-lis of rose diamonds. Between the fleurs-de-lis are little ornaments composed of a coloured stone and 3 diamonds.

The eight diadems, appearing to spring from the fleurs-de-lis and meeting at the summit, were enriched with diamonds and coloured stones set alternately as on the circlet.

The summit was a double fleur-de-lis all of rose diamonds.

There were in the crown 138 diamonds and forty coloured stones. It was 8 in. high and weighed about 16 oz.

It was made under the orders of M. Ronde, jeweller to the King, by Sr Ronde, his nephew.

The Queen wore the crown on her wedding day and also a great mantle of violet velvet sprinkled with golden fleurs-de-lis. The Queen's jewellery conformed to fashion and she wore the necklaces called carcanets set with diamonds which were generally set *en appliqué* on a velvet ribbon around the neck. 'The Sancy' was usually set in the centre of one of these as a pendant, while the Regent served to adorn the hair.

At the marriage of Louise Elizabeth of France to the Infante of Spain, which took place in 1737, the Queen wore a necklace with 'The Sancy' pendant from the centre.

At the first marriage of the Dauphin to Marie Thérèse of Spain, the Dauphin wore 'The Sancy' in his hat, but Marie Leczinska got the diamond back again once the festivities were over and wore it at all the great ceremonies at which she was obliged to appear.

On 29th December 1749 the King ordered Jaquemin, the Crown Jeweller, to mount the *Côte de Bretagne (Plate 83, a)* in the decoration of the Golden Fleece. This insignia was a masterpiece of the jeweller's art besides being an object of great value. To the *Côte de Bretagne* was added one of the most beautiful of the crown jewels, the Blue Diamond *(Plate 83, c)*. The *Côte de Bretagne* was cut in the form of a dragon to obliterate three holes which disfigured it, the weight was thus reduced from 206 carats to 105 carats, but the result was an outstanding success and the stone was considered to be one of the finest examples of the gem-cutter's art. The ruby formed the body and the head of the dragon, whose tail was composed of small diamonds curled around a hexagonal brilliant, one of its curls attached to the ring through which the ribbon of the Order was passed. The wings of the dragon were set with diamonds. The dragon was surrounded by palms in brilliants; flames of gold enriched with topazes issued from its mouth and the fleece hung below it. In the centre of the golden and topaz flames was set the Blue Diamond.[1] The other two Crown rubies, the *Œuf de Naples* and the 'Roman A' had a similar fate. On 4th April 1757 they were sent to Jaquemin to serve as centres for a star of the Order of the St Esprit *(Plate 83, b)*. Jaquemin had the *Œuf de Naples* cut in the shape of a dove and divided the 'Roman A' into several pieces. These pieces, cut and engraved to represent flames, were set around the dove to make the background for the centre of the star. The circumferences of the fleurs-de-lis were in diamonds, several of each colour and mounted on tinsel in accordance with the fashion of the day. As a result of this cutting, the *Œuf de Naples* and the 'Roman A' lost part of their value and in the 1791 inventory both together are only valued at 15,000 livres.

Although during the reign of Louis XV fashions and jewellery underwent considerable changes, the inventory taken in 1774 shows that many sets of ornaments were in the same state as in 1691. Among them the great chain with the diamond of the House of Guise *(Plate 82, b)* and the twelve Mazarins, the set of dress ornaments of the

---

[1] A reproduction of this Golden Fleece is included in *Pierres Précieuses* by Monsieur Pouget.

a (above, left) *Portrait of Napoleon in coronation robes by F. Gerard (1770–1837). The Palace of Versailles* (p. 266)

b (above, right) *Portrait of the Empress Josephine in coronation robes by F. Gerard. Château de Malmaison* (p. 266)

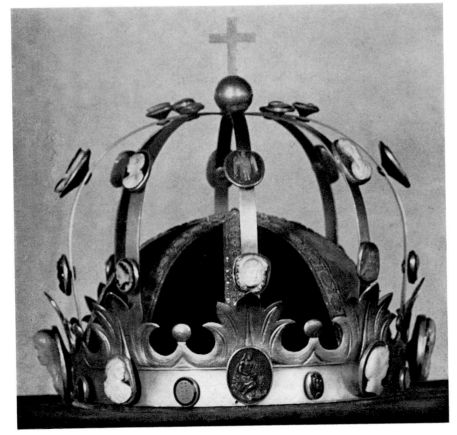

c (left) *Crown of Charlemagne made for Napoleon's coronation. The Louvre* (pp. 266 and 274)

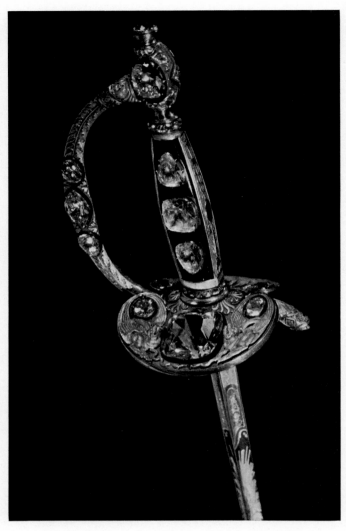

a   *Design of sword for the First Consul, set with the Regent
Diamond. From G. Bapst's* Histoire des Joyaux de la
Couronne de France *(p. 264)*

b   *Napoleon's coronation sword. H.I.H. Prince
Napoleon's Collection (p. 268)*

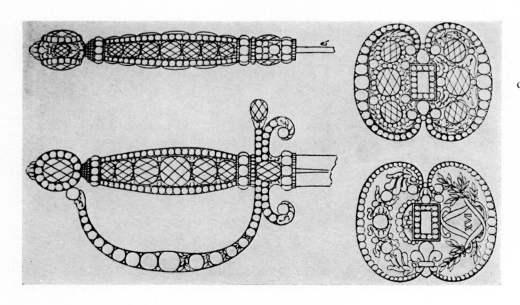

c   *Design of sword of Louis XVI
by Brelet. From G. Bapst's*
Histoire des Joyaux de la
Couronne   de   France
(p. 253)

King with 123 buttons, nineteen *fleurons* for buttonholes and a hat brooch. Louis XV gave his Queen a number of new ornaments including a parure of coloured stones consisting of an epaulette, a belt, a *trousse queue*, a *trousse-robes* and a collar. In addition, a pair of ear-rings of pearls and diamonds, rows of pearls and diamond drops, knots and pendants. The King had made for his own use an Order of the St Esprit in diamonds.

The King died on 10th May 1774 and was succeeded by his grandson, Louis XVI, who was born in 1754, became heir to the throne in 1765 and was married to Marie Antoinette, the daughter of the Empress Maria Theresa, in 1770. The King's *sacre* was performed at Rheims on 11th June 1775 in accordance with the established rites. After the King had been crowned with the Crown of Charlemagne, the jewelled crown of Louis XV, which had been reset, was placed on the King's head. Subsequently the King went to St Denis and offered his gold crown in homage to the Patron Saint of France.

Like his immediate predecessors, Louis XVI did not make use of the crown jewels as security for raising loans, but after the two reigns in which the splendour of the Court had become almost fabulous, that of Louis XVI in contrast returned to simpler forms. The great Court ceremonies in the *Grande Galerie des Glaces* at Versailles gave place to more intimate gatherings at the Trianon.

Marie Antoinette's taste for jewellery was quite different from those of her predecessors and she did not like heavy ornaments, but rather preferred light settings in which, instead of the ornament being designed to show up the qualities of a great stone, the stones were used merely to embellish the design. The great crown diamonds, including the Regent, 'the Sancy' and the Mazarins were set negligently in an aigrette of heron's feathers, or as drops of water on garlands of flowers. As a result most of the stones in the women's ornaments among the crown jewels were taken from their settings and used in an ever-changing number of settings. Marie Antoinette was particularly fond of a set of ornaments comprising a necklace, a pair of ear-rings and pendants and little knots, wreaths for the head and four pom-poms, all in brilliants and oriental rubies. The Queen had added some of her own jewels to the crown jewels used in this setting and it became impossible to distinguish the state jewels from those of the Queen. Marie Antoinette requested the King to give her the jewels in their settings and this he did by decree in 1788.

Another item which Marie Antoinette constantly wore was a pair of girandole earrings which Louis XVI gave her at the beginning of the reign. They consisted of two brilliant drops hung from 4 diamonds.

The King's ornaments among the crown jewels remained intact and Louis XVI added to them. The two chief sets were the white and the coloured. In the white set was a Golden Fleece in gold and brilliants valued at 413,000 livres. An Order of the St Esprit with fleurs-de-lis was worth 324,000 livres. In the coloured set were the Golden Fleece with the *Côte de Bretagne* valued by itself at nearly four million livres; an epaulette worth several hundred thousand livres, and a sword made in 1784. The sword was designed by a celebrated Paris jeweller, Sieur Brelet, and made by G. F. Bapst. The King thought it was an opportunity to introduce the crown rose diamonds which had never been used, and the hilt, which was set with these large rose diamonds and several brilliants, was a masterpiece of the craftsmanship of the jeweller.

The most important change in the crown jewels during the reign of Louis XVI was the recutting of many of the diamonds. In 1784 it was realised that the diamonds which had not been changed for 150 years were very inferior in relation to the modern methods of cutting. It was decided, much to the irritation of the French jewellers, to have them recut in Amsterdam and Antwerp. The cutting took place in 1788 and the stones were returned to the King's Wardrobe. The value of the crown jewels was enhanced, in spite of the loss of the set of ornaments of diamonds and rubies to which, it has already been mentioned, Marie Antoinette was attached. According to one account these appeared later in the Hapsburg Treasury in Vienna, and some jewels were so attributed in the catalogues of the Vienna Treasury in the last century. These jewels were altered in 1858 and reset for the marriage of the Emperor of Austria. Bapst has cast doubt on this because the story that Princess Charlotte, the daughter of Marie Antoinette, took them with her to Vienna after her release in 1796 would have been impossible. As, however, they were the Queen's personal jewellery, she may have caused them to have been sent to Vienna from Amsterdam at the time when they disappeared for some reason that has not been recorded.

In 1789 the Constituent Assembly passed a law establishing a Civil List which gave the King only a usufruct over the Crown property. Thus the crown jewels were, as originally designed by Francis I, only available for the use of the reigning sovereign. The *Garde-Meuble* was placed under the supervision of an officer of the Ministry of the Interior, but the King and Queen kept part of the jewels in 1789, 1790 and 1791. They had, however, all been returned to the *Garde-Meuble* by the time of the Legislative Assembly in 1791.

There is one notorious incident which occurred during the reign of Louis XVI which, though not connected with the crown jewels, is often mistakenly thought to have been so. It is known as the affair of the Queen's Necklace. Boehmer and Bassenge, the Crown Jewellers, had spent a great part of their fortune amounting to 1,160,000 livres in creating a *collier-berthe* made from the most beautiful diamonds at that time on the market,[1] which they offered to the Queen on several occasions, but she always refused, saying on one occasion: 'France has more need of a ship than a diamond ornament.' Marie Antoinette had a particular aversion to Cardinal Rohan, who, whilst Ambassador in Vienna, had revealed the Queen's frivolous conduct, which had drawn a rebuke from her mother, the Empress Maria Theresa. On his return to France the Cardinal wished to regain favour at Court and to become Prime Minister. By chance he met an adventuress and schemer, the so-called Countess de la Motte, a descendant of a bastard of Henry II, who persuaded him that she had influence with the Queen. The jewellers, also believing that the Countess enjoyed the Queen's favour, made use of her to try to sell the necklace. On 21st January 1785 she told them that the Queen would buy the necklace, but left the price to be negotiated by a high person. A little later Rohan arranged the purchase for 1,600,000 livres, payable in instalments. He produced what appeared to be the evidence of the Queen's authority and the necklace was handed over. In accordance with arrangements, the Cardinal handed it over to a

[1] A life-size reproduction of it is given in E. Vanderheym's *Notice Historique sur Les Joyaux de la Couronne*, Paris 1887.

man who was said to be a valet to the Queen. When Boehmer asked the Queen for payment she was astonished and declared that she had neither ordered nor received the necklace. The truth was then revealed and there followed a *coup de théâtre*. On the Feast of Assumption on 15th August 1785 the whole Court, with Cardinal Rohan in his pontifical vestments surrounded by priests, awaited the King and Queen when suddenly the Minister of Marine appeared at the doorway of the *Salle des Glaces* and cried out in a resounding voice: 'Arrest Monsieur the Cardinal Rohan.' The Captain of the Guard stepped forward and carried out the order. A trial followed in which the Cardinal was acquitted and the Countess was sentenced to be branded, whipped and shut up in the Salpêtrière from which she later escaped. Meanwhile, the *soi-disant* Count de la Motte had hurried with the necklace to England where it was broken up and the stones sold. Although now it is generally believed that Rohan was more of a dupe than a swindler and Marie Antoinette was quite innocent in the matter, at that time people believed that the Queen had used the Countess as an instrument to satisfy her hatred of Cardinal Rohan, and as a result the Queen became very unpopular.

Even when the events which led up to the Revolution became menacing, Louis XVI showed himself as being incapable of understanding or being interested in his duties as King. He was very fond of hunting and his exploits in the field took pride of place in his diary. Even on 14th July 1789, the day of the Fall of the Bastille, the sole entry in the diary is: 'Nothing.' Events followed in quick succession: the King's attempted flight in June 1791; the storming of the Tuileries on 20th June 1792; the subsequent imprisonment of the King and Queen in the Temple and their trials and execution in 1793.

During the Revolution the French regalia and crown jewels suffered irreparable loss. There were four distinct incidents: the removal of the coronation ornaments from the Abbey of St Denis and the subsequent melting down, sale and dispersion of most of them; the desecration of the royal tombs at St Denis; the destruction of the *Sainte Ampoule* at Rheims, and the theft of the crown jewels from the *Garde-Meuble*.

We have already traced the history and the special position of the Abbey of St Denis in relation to the coronation ornaments, but we must consider their composition in more detail. Our knowledge of the regalia depends largely on the inventories and the three XVII-century writers—Doublet,[1] Dom Millet[2] and Félibien.[3] There were also a number of small booklets corresponding to modern guide books prepared for the use of pilgrims and visitors.[4]

The oldest inventory of the Treasury of St Denis known today is dated 22nd January 1504 (1505 new style), drawn up by order of Louis XII. A copy of this inventory is still preserved in the Bibliothèque Nationale and was published by Omont.[5] A new inventory was taken between 1st January and 11th October 1634 after the suppression

---

[1] Jacques Doublet: *Histoire de l'Abbaye de St Denis*, 1625.
[2] Dom S. G. Millet: *Le Trésor Sacré*, 1636.   [3] Félibien: op. cit.
[4] A bibliography was published by M. A. Vidier in *Mémoires de la Société de l'Histoire de Paris, et de L'Ile de France*, Vol. XXVI, 1899, pp. 123–4.
[5] H. Omont: *Mémoires de la Société de l'Histoire de Paris*, Vol. 28, 1902.

of the titles of St Denis and when the abbey was taken over by the Reformed Congregation of St Maur. It is very detailed and runs into 433 pages in quarto. There are two copies in the Bibliothèque Nationale and one in the National Archives. It has not so far been published. The next inventory, which was the last, was taken on 3rd July 1739. A copy is in the Bibliothèque Nationale and has been published by Omont.

The more important items of the coronation regalia and the other royal ornaments included the three great crowns; the Crown of Charlemagne[1]; the Crown of St Louis[2]; and the *Sainte Couronne*.[3] The Crown of Charlemagne is described in the 1505 inventory as having four *fleurons* adorned with several spinels, sapphires and pearls valued at 59,923 écus. In the 1634 inventory we are told that it had four plates and four *fleurons* with a large ruby *en cabochon* in the centre of the circlet weighing 200 carats valued at 15,000 livres. The crown had a crimson bonnet and on top of this was once fastened a very fine old ruby weighing 206 carats and round it a description saying that it had belonged to John the Good. The stone was missing in 1634, and a monk who had been there eight years had never seen it.[4]

St Louis' Crown is described in the 1505 inventory as:

Another great crown also of gold with four *fleurons* adorned with several spinels, emeralds and pearls valued at 16,632½ écus. In the 1634 inventory there is a long description given, but at the end the Commissioners who took the inventory say that the crown was taken from the Church of St Croix, Rue de la Bretonnerie where it had been taken for safe-keeping during the Wars of Religion. It was removed by the Duke of Nemours and the big ruby from it by the Duke of Mayenne. The crown was broken up.

It is clear that during the religious wars one of these three crowns was lost but there is great confusion as to which one it was. Doublet writing in 1625 relates that:

Charles the Bald, Emperor and King of France, gave his golden crown with four plates enriched with large red uncut stones with large and exquisite emeralds, very beautiful sapphires, very excellent rubies and very beautiful oriental pearls and to enrich it even more, King John gave a large uncut red stone of great preciousness which he wanted to have attached to the top at the end of the fleur-de-lis. This very rich crown, which had served to crown all the Kings of France since Charles the Bald to Henry the Great, was taken by the Bad League which unfortunately had taken Rheims against His Majesty and caused a detestable sacrilege, the gold of which was melted and the rich precious stones were dispersed to different persons of high standing who ought to give them back to St Denis.

Dom Millet writing in 1636 states that Charlemagne left his crown to St Denis, and adds that Charles the Bald also gave his crown with four plates with red stones, great emeralds, sapphires, rubies and 3 oriental pearls. He repeats what Doublet had said about King John's ruby and that the crown was taken by the League. Félibien has nothing to say about it though he states that the *Sainte Couronne* was a present from the

---

[1] Inventory of 1505, No. 1. Inventory of 1634, folio 2. Inventory of 1739, No. 72.

[2] Inventory of 1505, No. 2. Inventory of 1634, folio 10. Inventory of 1739, No. 55.

[3] Inventory of 1505, No. 205. Inventory of 1634, folio 293.

[4] This is precisely the same weight as the ruby known as the *Côte de Bretagne* and it is possible that the two stones may be identical.

Emperor Charles the Bald. He also relates that Louis VI gave a hyacinth to the abbey to be attached to the Crown of Thorns and he also mentions that a gold crown enriched with gems was still shown in the Treasury of St Denis in which was enclosed a Holy Thorn from the Crown of Our Lord. Conway[1] expressed the opinion that the *Sainte Couronne* was one and the same crown which had been given by Charles the Bald. The confusion is made the greater by the fact that Conway and others have drawn attention to the detailed description of the three great crowns in the 1634 inventory and concluded that they must all have been extant at that date. Actually the entries in the 1634 inventory include items which were no longer at St Denis as they had been taken to Paris for safety.

The *Sainte Couronne* is described in the 1505 inventory as:

A crown named the *Sainte Couronne* with four *fleurons*, two covered at the back with silver gilt for strengthening, adorned in the centre of the circlet in front with a large round *cabochon* spinel, pierced lengthways, weighing 248 carats and under this in its setting a *sendal* and in the *sendal* some thorns and some hairs of Our Lord; the value of the said spinel was 20,000 écus and the other stones and pearls, also the gold and silver of the said crown 2,574½ écus.

In the 1634 inventory the description agrees with that of 1505, except that there is no mention of the actual relics, but on a piece of parchment in the *sendal* on which the inscription, half-effaced, was written. In the centre of the crown was a big round *cabochon* spinel weighing 292 carats and valued at 20,000 écus. There is mention of vacant sockets where pearls once were, and according to the 1505 inventory there was once a reliquary.

If we study the evidence closely it is possible to reconcile the conflicting theories. It is quite clear that the so-called Crown of Charlemagne was that which had been altered by Philip Augustus and had been given to St Denis by St Louis for the coronation of the kings and queens. It may well have been the Crown of Charles the Bald, because the four hinged plates which compose the circlet represent a type of crown in use at the time of that king. The great fleurs-de-lis which were a later form of decoration of French crowns were probably added by Philip Augustus. It can be seen from Félibien's engraving that they were separate ornaments added to the plates. There is no reason why the tradition that this crown had been used for the coronation of the Kings of France since Charles the Bald should not have been based on fact although the crown had been altered. The reference by Doublet and repeated by Dom Millet that this crown had been taken by the League is obviously an error. It is still described as the coronation crown in the 1739 inventory. It must, therefore, have been either the Crown of St Louis or the *Sainte Couronne* which was destroyed by the League.

The monks of Ste Croix made an inventory in 1588 which says in folio 26 that St Louis' Crown had been taken by the Duke of Nemours. Moreover, the 1634 inventory specifically states that the frame of the Crown of St Louis had been carried off during the troubles. The surviving crown was described in the XVII century as being decorated

---

1 Sir Martin Conway (afterwards Lord Conway): 'The Abbey of St Denis and its Ancient Treasures', *Archaeologia*, Vol. 66, 1914–15.

with topazes, among other precious stones, and as containing relics. The only crown of which there is a mention of topazes or relics is the *Sainte Couronne* and it seems reasonably certain that it was this crown which was still preserved at St Denis in 1739 when it is described as 'A gold crown of the same King (St Louis) enriched with several precious stones among which is a ruby of great price in which is enclosed a Thorn of the Crown of Our Lord'.

With regard to the relics there is a description on the tomb of Charles the Bald at St Denis which says that he gave a thorn from the Crown of Thorns and a nail of the Cross to St Denis, but this inscription was made at the time of St Louis. From documents published by Félibien[1] we learn that St Louis was in possession of a number of thorns from the Crown of Thorns and other precious relics. There is also a Charter of 1261 in which St Louis donated three crowns to the Abbey. It is likely that St Louis would have placed some of these relics in one of these crowns, or in the fourth crown, which was his own crown, which he also gave to the Abbey and which bore an inscription *De capillis Domini, de spinis Domini*. The Charter of 1261 states that the three crowns were to be suspended before the High Altar on feast days, together with the other crowns in the Treasury. On Good Friday the *Sainte Couronne* was placed on the head of an ancient wooden crucifix which was said to have miraculously spoken to Dagobert or another. The Holy Nail was attached to one of its feet. This practice continued until the crucifix was burnt by the Huguenots in 1567.

In the 1505 inventory, besides the three great crowns, there are several others, Item 92 being a silver gilt crown valued at 16 écus and Item 93 'another crown also of silver gilt and around it inscribed on the front an *M* and *R*, which was valued at 10 écus'. Item 104 describes a golden crown of eight *fleurons* with precious stones valued at 734½ écus. This was the crown which Jeanne d'Evreux, consort of Charles IV, gave to the abbey and which was used at the coronation of those queens crowned at St Denis, probably as a lighter crown which they wore after the heavy Crown of Charlemagne had been used for the actual act of coronation.

The Crown of Charlemagne and the Crown of St Louis are somewhat summarily depicted in Félibien's plates. The Crown of Charlemagne on Armoire IV R (*Plate 81, b*) and the crown described as the Crown of St Louis, but which is probably the *Sainte Couronne*, on Armoire III P (*Plate 81, a*).

Item 129 was a crown of gold with six hinges without stones, weighing 9¼ ounces, worth 81 ecus. The circlet was inscribed:

> *Anna Britannie Ducissa, Carolo Octavo et Ludovico duodecimo Francorum Regibus connubio iuncta, bis Regina, coronata anno salutis nostrae millicisimo quinquentisimo quarto.*

Item 166 was a crown of silver with narwhal horn around the circlet.

1 Félibien, op. cit., Appendix, p. cxlvi.

Besides the sceptre of Dagobert (Item 87) there were other sceptres, one of silver (Item 88) and another of gold (Item 116) on a rod of wood covered with gold with a golden figure of Charlemagne seated on a chair.

Three Hands of Justice were enumerated. One (Item 89) of German silver set on a silver gilt rod; a Hand of Ivory (Item 81) set on a rod of wood covered with gold leaf; a Hand of Ivory (Item 115) on a wooden rod covered with gold leaf.

There were four swords, one (Item 111) 'said to be that of Charlemagne' in a wooden coffer, was used at the coronation of the King; another (Item 112) said to be that of Archbishop Turpin; another (Item 113) was the sword of St Louis, and another (Item 114) the sword of Charles VII.

A pair of spurs (Item 117) were adorned with gold, silver and gems.

Two clasps are enumerated, one (Item 32) from the mantle of Charlemagne, no doubt the clasp of St Louis, and the other (Item 127) described as a golden lozenge serving to fasten the mantle.

Among four rings was the signet ring of St Louis.

In the 1739 inventory, besides the Crown of Charlemagne and the *Sainte Couronne*, there were many other items of regalia. These included two crowns, a sceptre and Hand of Justice made for the coronation of King Henry IV. Three crowns, the first of gold, the second of silver gilt, which were used at the consecration of Louis XIII, and the third of silver gilt used at the funeral of Queen Anne of Austria. Two crowns, one of gold and one of silver gilt, used at the consecration of Louis XIV. Three silver gilt crowns, one of which was used at the funeral obsequies of Louis XIV, and the other two at those of Louis, Dauphin of France, his son and of Marie Christine of Bavaria, wife of the Dauphin. A crown of silver gilt used at the funeral of Queen Marie Theresa of Spain, wife of Louis XIV. The crown of Jeanne d'Evreux, described as 'of gold enriched with rubies, sapphires and pearls and is used for the coronation of Queens of France, which has lately been repaired and enriched at the Abbey's expense'; three crowns of silver gilt, the first used at the funeral of Henrietta Maria of France, Queen of England; the second at the obsequies of the Dauphin, grandson of Louis XIV, and those of Marie Adelaide of Savoy, his wife; two crowns, one of gold and one of silver gilt adorned with *medoz* stones and imitation red gems to represent the fine crown jewels and of the same shape and size as when the State Crown was used, together with the gold one used at the consecration of Louis XV; two crowns of silver gilt used at the funerals of 'Madame Third of France and of the Duke Anjou', unnamed children of King Louis XV; five crowns of silver gilt, the first used at the funeral obsequies of Philip, Duke of Orleans, brother of Louis XIV; the second at those of Mademoiselle de Montpensier, daughter of Gaston; the third at those of Charles, Duke of Berry, grandson of Louis XIV; the fourth at those of Marie Louise Elizabeth of Orleans, his wife, and the fifth at those of Philip, Duke of Orleans, Regent of France.

Other items of regalia were the Hand of Justice of St Louis of silver gilt. The sword of St Louis brought by him from the Holy Land. A golden ring engraved with fleurs-de-lis adorned by a sapphire on which is a portrait of St Louis with the letters *S* and *L*. A golden sceptre 5 ft 10 in. long, surmounted by an eagle and enamel lily on which is a figure representing the Emperor Charlemagne. An inscription above says it was used by the Emperor. The sword of Charlemagne with his spurs, the guard, hilt and pommel of the sword of gold. Also the guard of the scabbard adorned with precious stones. A Hand of Justice, the top of gold and the handle of narwhal horn.

It will be seen that not all the items in the 1505 inventory had survived to 1739, and of the crowns in the former inventory only those of Charlemagne, the *Sainte Couronne* and the crown of Jeanne d'Evreux still existed. There were plenty of opportunities for ornaments to be lost as in time of danger it was customary to move the treasure to places where it was deemed safe. Félibien records that in 840 it was taken to Ferrières; in 858 the relics were taken to Nogent-sur-Seine; in 864 the monastery was pillaged by the enemies; in 876 the relics were taken to Conserreux. In 887 the monks took refuge from the Normans at Rheims and carried away their relics with them. In 1346 Philip VI was loaned seven golden crowns and a rich cross which had been given by Philip Augustus on which to raise money and which he promised to return before Christmas. The cross was returned, but there is no record of the crowns coming back to the treasury.

In 1432 the treasures which had been taken to Burgundy a few years earlier were returned to St Denis. The treasure was taken to Paris for safety on various occasions: first in 1464, again in 1544 and in 1588. In 1589 it was taken from the Hotel of St Denis to Ste Croix de Bretonnerie for greater safety. In 1567 the abbey was pillaged by the Huguenots.

There is a paucity of pictorial representations of the ornaments and we have to rely on plates in Félibien's work. There is a picture, formerly in the Dudley collection, known as The Mass of St Giles which depicts Charles Martel wearing one of the great crowns. The painter's name is not known, but he was probably a northern French or South Netherlandish master and shows the influence of Hugo van der Goes (*obiit* 1494). Conway has suggested that Charles is depicted wearing the *Sainte Couronne*. There is no reason to dispute this as it has a marked resemblance to the second great crown in Félibien's plates which is erroneously called St Louis' Crown and is almost certainly the *Sainte Couronne*. The only difference is that the crown depicted as being worn by Charles Martel is *clause a l'Imperiale*. The arches are not mentioned in the 1505 inventory and were probably added by Francis I. They would have been detachable. In Félibien's plates the two great crowns and the crown of Jeanne d'Evreux are shown as open crowns as are the ducal crown of Henry IV and the funeral crown of Henrietta Maria. All the others follow the same pattern of circlets surmounted by fleurs-de-lis and closed with four arches. The coronation crowns of Henry IV and Louis XIII and the funeral crowns, except that of the Dauphin, are closed with arches surmounted by a fleur-de-lis. That of the Dauphin is closed with two arches in the form of four dolphins, a heraldic emblem adopted by the eldest son of the kings of France from the time of Philip VI who purchased the domain of Humbert III, Dauphin of Viennois in 1343.

By a decree of the National Assembly of 18th February 1790 the monastic orders were suppressed and on 12th September 1792 the monks of St Denis sang their last office. The Commissioners of the Directory of Paris—Morge, Gamier and Leblond—carried off the royal ornaments. The crowns and some ornaments went into the melting pot.

Others, including the sword *Joyeuse*, were sold on the 25 *Vendémiaire* of the year VI (7th October 1798) while others including the sceptre and Hand of Justice and the spurs remained in the Cabinet des Antiques, probably because they were of little intrinsic value.

At the funerals of the kings of France an effigy of the king, dressed in royal robes, was placed on the coffin. The king's crown, together with the sceptre and Hand of Justice and *Joyeuse* covered with crêpe were also placed on the coffin on a cushion when it arrived at St Denis. When a Mass for the dead king was said, the king's crown, the sceptre and Hand of Justice and the spurs were placed on the altar. For the obsequies of queens, princes and princesses, special funeral crowns of silver gilt were made. It was formerly the custom to bury the kings in their royal robes and with copies of the royal ornaments.

On 31st July 1793 Barrère proposed the destruction of all the 'frightful souvenirs of the former kings' in the Abbey of St Denis. A commission was appointed to preside over the work of destruction and on 6th, 7th and 8th August fifty-one royal tombs were destroyed. Two months later (14th to 25th October) a revolutionary mob entered the crypt and opened the fifty-seven coffins which had been placed there since the time of Henry IV. In a number of coffins items of regalia were found. In that containing the body of Louis VIII were part of a wooden sceptre and a diadem of gold tissue. In the coffin of Philip IV were a gold ring, a diadem of gold tissue and a brass gilt sceptre. In that of Louis X were part of a sceptre and a brass crown, much corroded. A skeleton of Philip V was clothed in royal robes and on his head was a golden crown enriched with precious stones. In the coffin of Charles V there were a crown, a sceptre of gold and a beautiful carved silver Hand of Justice. In the coffin of Jeanne de Bourbon, his wife, were the remains of a crown and a gold ring, a diadem of gold tissue and a brass gilt sceptre. In that of Louis X were part of a sceptre and a brass crown, much rusted. Part of a crown and a silver gilt sceptre were also found in the coffins of Charles VII and his wife Marie d'Anjou.[1]

On 6th October 1793 the National Convention sent a representative named Ruhl to Rheims where he announced that 'for the execution of the laws relative to royalty and to the destruction of all signs and marks pertaining thereto he intended to suppress a reliquary containing what was called the *Sainte Ampoule* which had served for the *sacres* of the would-be kings and which he knew still existed in the city'. He directed that the reliquary containing the *Sainte Ampoule* be brought to him on the following day at 2 o'clock to be destroyed on the Plaçe Nationale in the presence of the people and that 'its dust be cast to the wind'.[2]

The Grand Abbot and two others conceived a plan to substitute for the *Sainte Ampoule* another of similar shape, size and colour, but the chances of success were small and the consequences of discovery grave and so the plan was abandoned. In accordance with the instructions, the *Sainte Ampoule* was carried out to the Plaçe Nationale and placed on the pedestal of the statue of Louis XV where it was smashed with a hammer. The crowd shouted *Vive la République*. A report of the proceedings was sent to the National

---

1 Abel Hugo: *Les Tombeaux de Saint-Denis*.
2 Lacatte-Joltrois: *Recherches Historiques sur la Sainte Ampoule*, Rheims 1823.

Convention, together with the remains of the reliquary wrapped in the shirt of a soldier. But some fragments of the vessel and some of its contents were saved. On the morning of 7th October the reliquary had been taken to the Town Hall where the Curate of St Remi and a municipal officer both extracted particles of the ointment. After the destruction some fragments were collected by the sentries and these were gathered together and in 1819 they were placed in a silver casket designed for the purpose.[1] A new *Ampoule* was made later for the particles of chrism which had been saved.

The crown jewels were lodged in the *Garde-Meuble*, which was not only a furniture repository but also a museum designed to contain the royal treasure. The remains were arranged so as to permit visits to the collections by the public on certain days. The collections included the arms and armour of the French kings; the state beds; precious objects, including Cardinal Richelieu's church plate and the great collection of tapestries. In one of the rooms of the first floor the crown diamonds were kept in glass cases. Thierry, who was in charge of the treasure, fearing burglary, took all the precautions he could to safeguard the jewels. They were placed in eight boxes—the Regent, the Sancy, the pearls and many other precious stones in one, and the remainder, with the unset diamonds which formed the greatest part of the treasure, in the others. The boxes were placed in a marquetry commode, the drawers of which were very strong with a heavy copper secret lock. Another casket of walnut which contained the king's decorations and diamond buttons was too big to go into one of the drawers and therefore was placed on a table in the middle of the room. Later the crown jewels were moved into eleven cabinets.

The *Garde-Meuble* was very poorly guarded and Thierry made repeated representations about the dangers to which the valuable collections were exposed. After the flight to Vincennes it was rumoured that there had been a project to carry off the crown diamonds. As a result a new inventory was made on 25th June 1791. After the arrest of the King, Cambon, the Minister of the Interior, on 16th August 1792 proposed to the National Assembly the sale of the crown jewels and that the money raised should be used as security for the paper currency. On the morning of 17th September 1792 it was discovered that during the night robbers had scaled the colonnade and made their way in through a window overlooking the Place Louis XV. The thieves broke the seals which had been placed on the cabinets and carried off many of the priceless treasures. At the time the crown jewels had been valued at nearly 30 million francs and only stones worth 5,500 francs remained.[2]

The truth about the theft has always remained obscure. The incident was exploited by the various political factions to incriminate their opponents. Madam Roland Danton and Fabre d'Eglantine were said to be the guilty parties, while the last-named asserted that the Girondins were the real thieves. Marat accused the aristocrats, and the Public Prosecutor of the Revolutionary Tribunal laid the blame on Marie Antoinette. The

[1] For a description see *Trésors de Reims*, by P. Tarbe.
[2] There are varying figures of the total value as a result of the different valuations for the Regent. The 1791 inventory gave a valuation of 23,922,197 francs for unmounted stones and 5,186,236 for set stones and other *objets d'art*. Several jewellers considered that there was a gross over-valuation.

keepers naturally came under suspicion, while the story got about that the Government had used the crown jewels to bribe the King of Prussia to evacuate Champagne. The story of the theft is dealt with very fully by Bapst.[1]

Thierry had been the victim of the 2nd September massacre and the supervision of the *Garde-Meuble* now became the responsibility of a man named Sergent, assisted by two Commissioners of the Commune who had taken possession on the pretext that they represented the State. Sergent was arrested on the day of the theft, and according to some accounts he asserted that with a special magnet he could find the stolen treasure. He was taken to a place called the *Allée des Veuves* (Avenue Montaigne) where his eyes were bandaged and he pointed to the foot of a tree. Excavations were made and the hiding place was discovered and a large part of the crown jewels were recovered. The Regent, however, was not among them but was discovered later in an attic, while the Guise and several other less celebrated diamonds were found in the house of one Tavenal. Others were later handed back by their new owners who had carefully kept them against a better day, while Napoleon acquired all those which could be identified as being part of the former crown jewels. But some of the most famous stones were not recovered. Among them the Sancy, the Mirror of Portugal, the Blue Diamond, the *Côte de Bretagne* and all but five of the Mazarins. The Sancy turned up in 1835 and its subsequent history has already been traced. The Mirror of Portugal disappeared altogether. The Blue Diamond was cut up into three pieces, the largest of $44\frac{1}{4}$ carats is believed to be the celebrated Hope Diamond, having been bought by Mr H. T. Hope for £18,000. The second, of $13\frac{3}{4}$ carats, was sold by the Duke of Brunswick at Geneva in April 1874 for 17,000 Swiss francs, or £686. The third stone of $1\frac{1}{4}$ carats was purchased by a firm of Paris jewellers in about 1862 who sold it in 1874 for £300 to Streeter, the Bond Street jeweller. Mr Edwin W. Streeter had an opportunity of examining the two larger stones in juxtaposition and found them identical in colour and quality and the same as the third stone, while the three were different from the other blue diamonds known to exist in Europe at the time.

The *Côte de Bretagne* came into the possession of a man named Cadet who kept it for a long time and in 1796 entrusted it to an *émigré* named Lancry who took it to Hamburg where he possibly wanted to sell it, but more probably with the intention of restoring it to the French, for a reward. The negotiations with the French Government seem to have broken down, but the stone returned to France, though how is not known, and possibly it came into the possession of Louis XVIII. It is now in the Louvre.

During the Directory, France had no less than fourteen armies in the field and the cost of arming and maintaining them was enormous. The National Convention had confiscated the property of *émigrés*, abbeys and churches and these they tried to sell. At Versailles more than 3,000 lots were sold in just over a year while other sales took place all over the country. The articles sold comprised pictures, furniture and *objets d'art* and when they had been dealt with, attention was focused on the diamonds.

The diamonds which had been recovered from the theft were placed in the coffers of the Public Treasury and to these were added jewellery confiscated from

1 Op. cit., Book VIII, chapters 2–7, pp. 447–533.

private owners. It is no wonder that they became hopelessly mixed up and no one was able to identify them or to state their origin.

In 1795 another acquisition was made as a result of the French conquest of Holland. It was discovered that the King of Sardinia had borrowed 760,000 florins from the firm of Renouard and Company, and that as security for this sum he had deposited in the strong-rooms of the firm pearls, diamonds and precious stones worth double the sum borrowed (see page 438). After protracted negotiations as to how the French Government could acquire them as valuables on the security of which loans could be raised, it was decided that in accordance with the laws of war everything belonging to the Governments of the enemies of the Republic was the property of France. The diamonds were handed over to three representatives of the Committee of Public Safety on 30th May 1795, and it was agreed to give Renouard and Company the sums paid to the King of Sardinia on the security of the diamonds. They were taken to Paris and amalgamated with the crown jewels. Whether the King of Sardinia was ever paid or not is not known.

In the same year, when the five Directors took executive power into their hands, the state jewels were revalued, the Regent at six million francs and the rest of the stones at ten million francs. Under the Directory the state diamonds were used in a number of complicated financial transactions, the most important was the double loan agreement made by Parceval, the Adjutant-General in charge of army recruitment. In the one transaction he pawned diamonds, including the Regent, to Treskow, a Berlin banker, for four million francs, and on the other he raised one million francs from the Marquess of Iranda in Madrid. Both these persons supplied horses to the army, and it can be said with truth that in 1797 Lasalle's hussars at Rivoli and in 1800 Kellerman's cavalry at Marengo were mounted on horses procured by the crown jewels. Among the stones given to the Marquess was one of $53\frac{3}{4}$ carats which though unidentified could only have been the Sancy. It was not returned to France, but came into the hands of Godoy, the Prince of Peace, in 1809 and then apparently into the possession of the Spanish Bourbons.

The Regent was taken to Berlin, but was redeemed and then given to a Dutchman named Valenberghem as a guarantee for a series of loans. He lived in sumptuous style and entertained all important people in Amsterdam, displaying the stone prominently in his reception rooms. He confessed later, when he gave it back to the French Government, that it was only a model that had been so displayed and that the real stone was constantly worn by his wife round her neck and under her bodice.

When Bonaparte came to power he and the Finance Minister redeemed all the diamonds, except the Sancy, and put the country's finances in order. At the time of the signature of the Peace of Lunéville and the Peace of Amiens he decided, in accordance with diplomatic usage, that presents of diamonds to the value of 400,000 francs should be given to the plenipotentiaries, and these were taken from the state diamonds. Then to signalise his assumption of power he ordered Nitot to make him a sword on the guard of which was set the Regent diamond.

Another huge treasure of diamonds and precious stones fell into Bonaparte's hands under the terms of the Treaty of Tolentino in 1797 which placed the burden of the cost of Bonaparte's armies in Italy upon the Pope. The Papal Treasury and the treasuries of many churches over which the Pope had jurisdiction were stripped of their riches. It is not clear what happened to this enormous wealth of precious metals and stones, except that the great emerald from the Papal Tiara was placed in the Museum of Natural History, Paris.

In 1803 most of the diamonds which had been given as security for loans were returned with the notable exception of the Sancy, but the bankers Perrin and Cablat had sold some stones in the Levant for three million francs. The Treasury thus again contained a rich store of diamonds, which included some of ancient origin—the Regent, the Guise Diamonds, a five-sided rose-coloured diamond and five Mazarins. Of the diamonds confiscated from the *émigrés* we know but little, except that they included a pair of brilliants each weighing 16½ carats which were set in Bonaparte's sword. There is a detailed inventory of the King of Sardinia's jewels which consisted of men's and women's ornaments, including ear-rings, necklaces, aigrettes, hairpins, knots, waist knots, crosses of the Order of St Maurice; hat brooches, and epaulettes. There were a few large stones, the most notable being a diamond of 17 carats. There was a considerable number of drop pearls, rubies and sapphires, but they do not seem to have been of the first quality.

Josephine wished to be allowed to use the state diamonds and to this the First Consul agreed, and jewels to the value of 254,198 francs were made available, this sum being paid into the Public Treasury by the Private Treasurer to the Consulate.

When Bonaparte was proclaimed Emperor on 18th May 1804 he attached much importance to the ceremony of coronation, and it was arranged that he should be anointed by the Pope and crowned at Notre-Dame, Paris, on 4th December 1804. The reasons for the coronation and the difficulties of the preparations have been covered by several writers,[1] but there is an incident which has been frequently misrepresented and misunderstood. Napoleon is said to have roughly brushed aside the Pope, seized the crown from the altar and crowned himself. The facts are as follows. When Pius VII agreed to come to Paris, he made it conditional that the ceremony of consecration should not be separate from that of coronation. The Pope demanded that there should be no innovation contrary to the dignity of the sovereign pontiff or to the usage which had always been followed when the Emperors of France and Germany were both crowned and consecrated by the Pope. Pius had not demurred, however, at the proposal that the Empress should receive a crown from the Emperor.

When the Pope arrived in France, Napoleon had other ideas and declared 'that he wishes to take the crown so as to avoid all discussion among the grand dignitaries who might claim to give it to him in the name of the people. He thinks that His Holiness may be held to have carried out the essential ceremonial of blessing the crown and uttering a prayer when the Emperor put it upon his head.' The Emperor went on to quote the case of Louis the Debonair and asserted that 'Charlemagne had said, on coming out from St Peter's, that he would never have entered it had he known the Pope had the intention of crowning him, since he was not willing to seem to owe the Holy See a crown which he held only by his sword'. He went on to argue that from thence had arisen the custom of the Carolingian emperors crowning themselves. He was on dangerous ground and quoted no authorities but surprisingly the Pope agreed without a protest.

1 See Frederic Masson: *Napoleon and his Coronation.*

Napoleon was at pains to connect his imperial title not only with Charlemagne but with the earliest French kings. For this reason he chose as an emblem the bees found in the grave of Childeric and not the fleur-de-lis. He also took the eagle as his imperial emblem. Difficulties arose over the regalia. The imperial regalia with the so-called Crown of Charlemagne was no longer at Nuremberg and was not available. The French coronation ornaments were incomplete; the crown had been destroyed and the sword *Joyeuse* sold, and only the sceptre, the Hand of Justice and the spurs were still preserved in the *Cabinet des Antiques*. It was, therefore, necessary to have a new crown made, and an arched crown set with antique gems was provided.[1] A private owner named Léorier produced a sword which antiquaries recognised as being the *Joyeuse*, but embarrassment followed when the blade of another sword which was claimed to be *Joyeuse* also turned up.[2] It was decided to use the first one. The spurs were discarded because they bore the fleurs-de-lis. The sceptre had lost its staff and one used by the Precentor was provided. Napoleon did not consider these ornaments satisfactory and, therefore, determined to have new ones made, although the old ones, which were described as the insignia of Charlemagne, were to be carried in the procession. Although the French kings had never adopted an orb as one of their royal ornaments, Napoleon insisted on having one made, because it was an ornament found among the regalia of the German emperors.

The insignia of Charlemagne thus consisted of the new crown with antique gems called the Crown of Charlemagne (*Plate 87, c*), the Spurs of Charlemagne which had been made for Charles V, the Sword of Charlemagne, *Joyeuse*, and an orb. Napoleon's regalia comprised an open golden crown of laurel leaves (*Plate 87, a*), an imperial sceptre of silver gilt surmounted by an eagle, the Hand of Justice from the French regalia, but with a new decoration of pearls and a staff of silver gilt, a ring and a sword with a golden hilt enriched with diamonds. In addition, there was the Grand Collar of the Legion of Honour and an imperial mantle of purple velvet powdered with golden bees. The Emperor entered Notre-Dame wearing his crown and carrying the sceptre and the Hand of Justice, although he had not yet been crowned. The Empress wore a mantle of purple velvet powdered with golden bees and with the letter *N* in the embroidery. She had a crown of gold set with pearls and coloured stones and also a diadem of gold and precious stones.

With the proclamation of the Empire, all the state jewels became at the disposal of the Emperor. Josephine had already received from the Treasury a pearl necklace valued at 226,500 francs and ruby and emerald parures each worth 15,000 francs. The jewellers Biennais, Foncier, Marguerite and Nitot mounted some of the gems in various ornaments for the coronation and we can get some information from their accounts:

Supplied by Biennais

Golden crown of laurel leaves	8,000 francs
Box to contain same	1,350 francs
Imperial sceptre, silver gilt	3,500 francs
Hand of Justice, the decoration of pearls and orb of silver gilt	2,800 francs
Orb, silver gilt	1,350 francs

---

[1] It is now in the Louvre.　　　　[2] Possibly the sword of Archbishop Turpin.

Supplied by Marguerite, Jeweller

Setting in ring of emerald furnished by Treasurer . . .	48 francs
Golden workmanship of the cordon of the Grand Order . .	13,500 francs
Golden workmanship of the Grand Order	850 francs

Marguerite supplied 2,261 brilliants for 867,368 francs besides different stones for 13,179 francs which were inserted in the crown, diadem and the cordon of the Grand Order.

Supplied by Marguerite, Jeweller for the Empress Josephine

Making of the crown, the diadem and the girdle . . .	15,000 francs
Making of 174 bezels	752 francs
Setting of 42 brilliants in bezels	140 francs
Setting in ring of rubies furnished by the Treasury . . .	48 francs

Supplied by Leroy and Raimbaud

114 dozen emeralds at 12 francs	1,368 francs
Supplying 49 dozen emeralds at 15 francs and 3 emeralds . .	738 francs

In addition the rose-cut diamonds from the crown jewels were set in a girdle.

In 1805 Napoleon ordered some ornaments for his own use, the principal one being a cord and button for his hat, the cost of which was 362,000 francs, including a large diamond of 25⅝ carats. Other ornaments included the collar and Orders of the Legion of Honour, which cost 188,722 francs.

In March 1807 Nitot provided the Empress with a diamond diadem worth 86,259 francs; a comb worth 27,702 francs; a pair of bracelets at 28,131 francs and a rivière of two rows of diamonds at 107,055 francs and a hydrangea garland at 51,777 francs. We also know from a design which has been preserved that Napoleon ordered for Josephine a diadem of rubies and laurel leaves, the stones coming from the crown jewels. Up to the time of Napoleon's marriage with Marie Louise purchases of jewels had been relatively unimportant, but at his marriage 6 million francs were provided for the occasion and many new jewels were purchased, the cost of which came to 6,600,000 francs. As the stones were incorporated into the crown jewels, the Privy Purse was repaid the 6 million available, but the balance remained outstanding.

There were other important purchases, first a necklace of three rows of round pearls at a cost of 317,995 francs and later a necklace of a single row with a parure of pearls which cost 128,408 francs. A further 408 pearls were bought from Nitot for 326,000 francs. A jeweller named Chaine sold the Emperor a large number of diamonds which were to be used for a parure composed of a diadem worth 326,200 francs; a necklace of 24 brilliants worth 409,000 francs, and a pair of ear-rings worth 68,000 francs. Nitot mounted a great diamond parure costing 1,645,466 francs composed of a diadem at 407,404 francs, a necklace at 875,292 francs; a comb at 127,501 francs; a pair of ear-rings at 56,846 francs; a pair of bracelets at 101,150 francs, and finally a belt at 77,252 francs. The diadem had a pendant diamond of 24 carats from the old Crown Treasure in the centre, below this pendant was a 25½-carat stone, oval in shape, thin and of aquamarine water which was bought from Nitot for this purpose for 137,000 francs. Nitot also mounted a series of parures of stones of various colours—rubies, sapphires, emeralds, turquoises in similar sets of ornaments as the great diamond parure. Included among these ornaments were a diadem and a crown. The diadem was composed of drop pearls and cost 221,547 francs. The centre was formed by one of the largest known pearls, egg-shaped weighing 337 gr and valued at 40,000 francs. The crown was closed and composed of pearls valued at 110,279 francs. It was surmounted by a small eagle. Napoleon also had his own ornaments completed or altered. The Consular Sword was broken up in 1811 and a new one made, set with the diamonds including the Regent which had been on the pommel of the old sword. This sword hung from a baldric of white velvet covered with the rose diamonds from the crown jewels.

Louis XV had had among his personal property a collection of eighty-two cameos which he placed in the Bibliothèque Nationale. They had become state property in 1790 by a law of the Constituent Assembly. Napoleon had twenty-four of these cameos set in a great pearl necklace and a parure consisting of a diadem, a comb, bracelets, a pair of earrings, a waist belt and a medallion in which 2,275 pearls were used. The parure at the Bourbon Restoration was regarded as the personal property of Louis XVIII and the remaining fifty-eight cameos were returned to the Bibliothèque Nationale, where they now are.

Napoleon was meticulous in matters of administration and had special arrangements made and regulations drawn up for the care of the crown jewels.

In 1814, when Paris was threatened, Marie Louise and her son, the King of Rome, left the capital on 29th March with a large baggage train for Rambouillet and then Blois. Among the valuables which she took with her were the crown jewels, her own personal jewels and those which had been bought from the Civil List. On 9th April Marie Louise became very anxious about the safety of the jewels and thought that the carriages in her train might be plundered by the enemy soldiers. She therefore wore as many as possible on her own person, believing that no one would dare to be so lacking in respect as to search her. In fact, en route for Orleans some of the carriages were stopped and rifled by the Cossacks, although no jewels were lost. The most awkward and the most valuable ornament was Napoleon's sword (*Plate 88, b*), in which the Regent diamond was set, and which was difficult to hide. A Monsieur Menéval, who accompanied the Empress in her flight, was asked by her to take the sword to pieces. Having no tools at his disposal, he had to snap the blade off the hilt which was then concealed in his coat.

On 11th April Napoleon, who was at Fontainebleau, gave instructions for the crown jewels to be returned to the state coffers, but the stones not belonging to the crown jewels were to be taken from their mountings. Meanwhile, however, an official by the name of Dudon, who had lost favour with Napoleon, arrived at the behest of the Provisional Government to take possession of the state property. He removed the waggons which had accompanied the Empress and which contained 10 million francs worth of gold and silver coinage, silver and silver gilt plate worth 3 million francs, snuff boxes and diamond rings destined as presents to the value of 400,000 francs and the imperial clothing and ornaments. Dudon then presented himself to Marie Louise's lady-in-waiting and demanded from her the pearl necklace the Empress was wearing round her neck. The necklace, a single row of pearls which had cost $\frac{1}{2}$ million francs, had been given to her by Napoleon shortly after her confinement and was her personal property. The Empress was in the crowded drawing-room when the lady-in-waiting brought the message. She unhesitatingly took off the necklace and gave it to the lady-in-waiting, saying, 'Hand it to him and say nothing.'

THE RESTORATION OF THE BOURBON DYNASTY

At the Restoration Louis XVIII took possession of the crown jewels and those of Napoleon. He had the letter N removed from the snuff boxes and he ordered that the great diamond and the emerald parures should be dismantled and the emerald one sold.

On the news of the escape of Napoleon from Elba and his landing in France, Louis XVIII fled by night to Ghent taking with him the crown jewels, those of Napoleon and the cameos from the Bibliothèque Nationale. Napoleon gave Louis a safeguard to leave the country and demanded back the crown jewels, but they were not returned to him.

At the second Restoration, Louis ordered a new inventory to be taken. Apart from the diamond and emerald parures which had been dismantled there were other items missing. These objects had been given as presents to the allied generals and to others. Louis XVIII had intended to present the Duke of Wellington with an estate in France, but he was advised against this gift of land. Instead he presented the Duke with 10 diamonds that were set in the form of the Star and Badge of the Order of St Esprit. These had previously been in the St Esprit of Louis XIV and later had been mounted in the quillons of Napoleon's sword. When the Order of St Esprit was suppressed after 1830 the Duke of Wellington had them mounted as ear-rings for his daughter-in-law, Lady Douro, using the two largest diamonds for this, and the other eight were made into a tiara and necklace. The gift was presented to Lady Douro on the occasion of her marriage on 18th April 1839. The two large drop brilliants weighed $9\frac{3}{4}$ carats and $8\frac{3}{4}$ carats respectively.

Louis had all the parures remounted and for the King there were the sword, a second sword, the royal crown, the hat brooch, an aigrette, an epaulette, a mantle clasp, a pair of shoe buckles, a pair of garters, rosettes for hat and shoes, crosses and plaques of the St Esprit and foreign decorations. As there was no queen, the royal princesses were allowed to wear the crown jewels, there being six parures—one of brilliants, one of rubies, one of pearls, one of sapphires, one of turquoises and one of emeralds (*Plates 90 to 95*). Each parure consisted of a diadem, one or more necklaces, a comb, a pair of bracelets, a waist belt and three dress agraffes. They had been designed by Everard Bapst, the Crown Jeweller, and mounted by Frédéric Bapst. Louis XVIII sold thirteen of the crown diamonds and bought two diamonds, one of $22\frac{1}{4}$ carats and the other of $15\frac{1}{2}$ carats, which were added to the crown jewels in exchange.

In January 1815 the bodies of Louis XVI and Marie Antoinette were removed to St Denis from the Madeleine cemetery where they had been buried after their execution. The funeral crown of Marie Antoinette (*Plate 85, d*), which was made for the occasion in the traditional style, is still in the Treasury of St Denis, as is that of Louis XVIII (*Plate 85, c*), who died on 16th September 1824. Charles X, who succeeded to the throne, decided to revive the coronation ceremony, and it was performed with unrivalled magnificence in May 1825. But despite the gorgeous splendour the occasion was not a success and the obsolete usages were quite out of keeping with the outlook of the times. Indeed it seems strange that the French coronation ceremony had lasted down to the time of Louis XVI, for it had lost much of its constitutional significance by the time that absolutism was fully established. The kings, no doubt, found the oath to the people an unnecessary and irritating anachronism, but the power of tradition prevailed and the ancient privileges claimed by St Remi and St Denis, the heaven-sent oil, the Oriflamme, the fleur-de-lis, the Crown of Charlemagne and *Joyeuse*, all combined to give the kings of France a special, indeed a unique position among the sovereigns of Europe.

Charles X used a splendid diamond crown made by Frédéric Bapst for Louis XVIII. It followed the traditional pattern and the Regent Diamond was set in the great surmounting fleur-de-lis. It was not broken up until 1854, at which date the frame without the stones was still kept in the cellars of the Ministry of Finance. The Crown Jewellers, Messrs Bapst, offered to purchase the crown, set it with facsimile stones and present it to the Louvre. This led to the authorities ordering it to be secretly broken up. The sword used by Charles X at his *sacres* was designed by Everard Bapst and executed by Charles Bapst (*Plate 89, a*). The hilt was entirely set with diamonds of the finest water. It is now in the Louvre. All the parures from the crown jewels were worn at the coronation by the royal princesses. On 28th July 1830, when the political situation looked menacing, the crown jewels were taken in the carriage specially designed for transporting the crown jewels to Rambouillet, where Charles X then was. On 5th August the Paris mob succeeded in overthrowing the Government; a column of fifty to sixty thousand people arrived with pikes, halbards, carbines, and other weapons, and set out for Rambouillet to attack the royal family. On their approach Charles decided to abdicate and leave France, and commissioners were sent to General Pajol, who was the leader of the column, with whom they negotiated the return of the crown jewels. They were handed over and brought back to Paris by the triumphant mob and placed in the Central Treasury of the Finance Ministry, where they were kept in a box locked with five keys held by three officials. The box was then taken to the premises of the Crown Jeweller on the Quai de l'Ecole, where they remained until 1832 when, under a new law regarding the Civil List, they were deposited in the vaults of the Civil List in the Louvre.

THE HOUSE OF ORLEANS

After the departure of Charles X, Louis Philippe of Orleans, Duke of Orleans, was elected King of the French, but he was not crowned. His inauguration ceremony took place in the Palais Bourbon, where a throne surrounded by tricolour flags had been prepared. The Duke of Orleans seated himself on the throne and the Marseillaise was played and a salute of guns fired from the Invalides. The declaration of 7th August was then read which called to the throne 'His Royal Highness of Orleans, Duke of Orleans'. Amidst cries of *Vive le Roi*, Louis Philippe signed the Charter and the Declaration of his Oath, which were to be placed in the archives of the kingdom. Upon this four marshals approached bearing the sceptre, the crown, the sword and the Hand of Justice. Although the Crown of Charles X was used on this occasion, King Louis Philippe in 1831 adopted a new design for the Crown of France, although no such crown was actually made. The fleurs-de-lis were replaced by strawberry leaves and a wreath of oak-leaves was placed round the circlet. The surmounting fleur-de-lis was replaced by an imperial orb with a jewelled band.

In 1846, when Napoleon's remains were brought to Paris from St Helena, General Bertrand handed over to Louis Philippe the Emperor's arms. The King directed that they should become the property of the Crown and they were added to the crown jewels. They consisted of:

The sword Napoleon usually carried and which he wore until his death, on the blade of which he had inscribed 'Sword which the Emperor Napoleon wore at the Battle of Austerlitz'.

The sword worn by the Emperor Napoleon at the *Champ de Mai*, 1815.

A very rich dagger given by Pope Pius IV to de la Valette, Grand Master of the Order of Malta, on the relief of the siege by the Turks in 1563.

A mahogany box inlaid with ebony containing two pairs of large double-barrelled pistols from the Armament Factory at Versailles.

A curved sabre.

During the reign of Louis Philippe neither the King nor Queen Adelaide made use of the crown jewels, which remained locked away in the vaults of the Civil List which were moved from the Louvre to the Tuileries, where the personal valuables of the royal family were also kept.

On 29th February 1848 when a new insurrection broke out and Louis Philippe abdicated a mob entered the Tuileries, but they were interested in finding wine rather than the crown jewels. In the cellars of the Commandant of the National Guard they found 10,000 bottles, upon which they fell, as a result of which orgy twelve bodies were found next morning on the floor of the cellar, which was littered with broken bottles and swimming in wine. Owing to the presence of mind of a labourer named Nô a detachment of the National Guard, under a sergeant, was procured and a scheme was devised to carry the crown jewels to safety on a stretcher, and the valuables of the royal family were so removed. On 26th February, the three keyholders appeared and after a delay it was decided, owing to the deteriorating situation, to remove the crown jewels to the Headquarters of the National Guard. The safe was opened and there being no time to check the inventory they stuffed some of the jewels in their pockets. General Courtais, carrying the crown with the Regent at its summit, ordered the party to follow. They proceeded through a subterranean passage to the Chief-of-Staff's office where the jewels were placed in a corner and covered with a tablecloth. Later in the day the jewel cases were placed in five bags and loaded into a furniture van and, escorted by a detachment of the National Guard, were taken to the Ministry of Finance where the bags were sealed. On 12th March a verification of the inventory was made and it was found that a box containing a hat button in brilliants and two rose diamond pendants valued at 300,000 francs were missing. Despite a widespread search they were not recovered.

On 9th March 1848 the provisional Government had made a decree authorising the

Finance Minister to alienate the crown jewels for a price to be fixed by sworn experts, but apart from a valuation no action was taken.

THE SECOND REPUBLIC

On 4th November 1848 a new constitution was promulgated, setting up a democratic republic, and on 10th December Prince Louis Napoleon, nephew of the former Emperor, was elected President. During the time of the Second Republic the crown jewels remained in the Treasury, unused, but when the Empire was proclaimed in 1852 a *senatus consulate*, dated 12th December of that year, declared that the personal endowments of the Crown included the diamonds, pearls, and precious stones in the Treasury and the jewels were, therefore, placed at the Sovereign's disposal.

THE SECOND EMPIRE

On the marriage of Napoleon III to the Empress Eugenie on 29th January 1853 the crown jewels were taken in hand and the old sets were dismantled and new ones made and so large was the work involved that a number of jewellers were employed; the House of Bapst were reappointed Crown Jewellers, the others being Lemmonier, Kramer, Millerio Beaugrand, Ouzille-Lemoine, Viette and Fester. The firms made the Imperial Crown and decorations for the Emperor, and for the Empress a crown diadem, comb, belt, brooches, spray, head-dress and fan. Alfred Bapst designed the remaining ornaments which were executed by Frédéric Bapst. They consisted of a diadem of palm leaves, two large shoulder knots, a *berthe*, aiguillettes in the Marie Antoinette style, a garland with sixteen aiguillettes, an ivy-leaf ornament for the corsage, a *sévigné* brooch, a so-called reliquary brooch, and another large fantasy brooch, a comb, a chain of thirty-two links, a belt buckle, and two important diadems—one called the 'Russian' and the other the 'Greek' (*Plate 90, a*).

The Greek diadem contained a socket in which the Regent diamond could be inserted when not used in another ornament. The ivy-leaf corsage contained two of the surviving Mazarins, the fourth and the thirteenth, while another, the sixteenth, was in the corsage spray. The comb had in the middle of the band the five-sided diamond and on the left side the eighth Mazarin. The big brooch of pearls and diamonds had in the centre the large egg-shaped pearl of 337 carats which Nitot had provided in 1801, and which had been given the name the 'Regente'. The crown jewels were worn with great effect by the beautiful Empress Eugénie at the brilliant court of the Second Empire and a number of additions were constantly being made. In March 1880 before leaving for Zululand to visit the grave of her son, the Prince Imperial, the Empress Eugénie gave her crown to the Church of Notre-Dame des Victoires at Paris. Some ornaments were displayed at the International Exhibition in Paris in 1855. After the fall of the Empire they were exhibited at the Paris International Exhibition of 1878 and in the *Pavillon de Flora* in 1883.

On 7th August 1870, after the defeat of Marshal MacMahon at Worth, a state of siege was declared in Paris and on 10th August the Minister of the Imperial House, who was

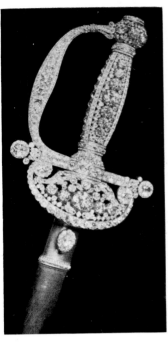

a *Design of sword of Charles X by Everard Bapst. From G. Bapst's* Histoire des Joyaux de la Couronne de France *(p. 270)*

b *Sword of Charles X. The Louvre (p. 275)*

c *The Regent Diamond. The Louvre (p. 274)*

d *The Hortense Diamond. The Louvre (p. 274)*

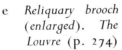

e *Reliquary brooch (enlarged). The Louvre (p. 274)*

a (above)   *Greek diadem* (33); (below) *diadem of emeralds and brilliants* (27) (pp. 272, 284 and 285)

b   *Buckle in brilliants for a girdle in the form of a sun with nine aiguillettes, the centre stone of* $25\frac{5}{8}$ *carats* (29); *seven of the Mazarin diamonds* (65) (pp. 284 and 287)

c   *Two round hairpins set with brilliants* (1); (below) *a sévigné brooch of brilliants* (51); (at sides) *detail of chain of brilliants* (28) (pp. 282, 284 and 286)

d   *Collar of four rows of 222 brilliants weighing 363 carats with two great brilliant shoulder knots* (10) (p. 282)

in charge of the Civil List, considered that the crown jewels should no longer be kept in the Tuileries. Consequently they were packed in a deal box marked with an anchor at each corner. When this had been sealed with the seals of the Treasury of the Privy Purse, the Crown Jeweller and the Minister of the Imperial Household, it was taken to the Ministry of Finance and placed in the central coffers of the Public Treasury. At the end of the month it was decided that the crown jewels should be given in to custody of the Bank of France for safe keeping. M. Rowland, the Governor of the Bank, agreed. But they were never taken to the Bank of France, as M. Rowland asked if they could be sent to the provinces with the bullion held by the bank. The box, which was sealed, was then put into one of the bank's boxes, marked on the outside *Chaînes d'assemblage* and the words 'Special projectiles'. It was then put on to a goods train accompanied by two bank agents and taken to Brest, where, together with the bullion, it was moved to the arsenal. On 20th March the bullion was returned to Paris, but the crown jewels were placed in the hold of a ship named the *Borda*, where they remained until 1872. As a special precaution against attack, the admiral in command at Brest ordered the frigate *Hermione* to be held in a constant state to put to sea and issued instructions that in the event of an alarm the crown jewels were to be put aboard the *Hermoine*, which was immediately to sail for Saigon.

THE THIRD REPUBLIC

On 4th September 1870, when the insurrection broke out in Paris, several people entered the Treasury in search of the crown jewels. All they found were some models of jewellery set with fake stones. This discovery led to a rumour that all the real stones had been taken out of their settings and removed by the Empress. When the Commune began, delegates were sent to the Bank of France to take possession of the crown jewels: they refused to believe the Bank officials who asserted they were not there and it took a lot to persuade the Commune of the truth. The crown jewels were brought back to Paris in 1872 and in the following year they were checked by a commission and then placed in the cellars of the Ministry of Finance. The stones which had been bought from the Civil List and were valued at one hundred thousand francs were handed over to the Empress's representatives.

It was not long before a proposal for the sale of the crown jewels gained favour. The indefatigable protagonist of this proposal was a deputy named Benjamin Raspail. Twenty years previously, in 1848, his father had unsuccessfully brought a similar proposal before the National Assembly. Benjamin Raspail tabled a motion in the Chamber of Deputies on 7th June 1878 but a long time passed before the motion received approval by 342 votes to 85 on 20th June 1882. After that it took four years to pass through the Senate. Although there was a considerable measure of agreement that the crown jewels should be sold there was a great deal of disagreement as to what purpose the proceeds should be put. Finally on 7th December 1886 a modified bill was passed. Under this enactment certain objects of historical, artistic or scientific merit were to be preserved in the Louvre, the Natural History Museum and the School of Mines. The imperial crown and the swords of Louis XVIII and the Dauphin were to be destroyed and the remainder were to be sold by public auction, the proceeds to be converted into Government stocks.

The objects which were destined to be preserved in the Louvre, the Natural History Museum and the School of Mines were handed over without incident. The Imperial Crown consisted of a jewelled circlet on the upper rim of which rested eight Imperial eagles, with elevated wings, between which were leaf ornaments from behind which sprang half-arches of Greek honeysuckle floriations to form an ogee, on which rested an orb and cross.

Benjamin Raspail, who had a personal grudge against Napoleon III, demanded the privilege of destroying the crown. 'I myself will break up this crown and send it to the foundry', he declared. But shortly before the due date he had a fall and was unable to attend and had to content himself with receiving as a present the hammer with which the crown had been demolished.

The crown jewels which were to be sold were taken from the Louvre to the *Salle des Etats* in the *Pavillon de Flora*, where on 20th April 1883 they were put on display until 12th May. The sale, which lasted from 12th to 23rd May, attracted world-wide interest and the crown jewellers of Belgium, Spain, Italy, Russia, Denmark, Sweden and Norway and Persia, besides leading jewellers from England, America, Holland, Portugal, Switzerland, Turkey, Egypt, Havana and Tunis attended. The gross proceeds of the sale were 6,864,050 francs to which may be added the receipts from the value of the gold and stones of the ornaments melted down, part of the furnishings of the sale room and a 5% commission paid by the purchasers, which brought the total to 7,221,360 francs. The expenditure on the sale was 293,851 francs, leaving the net proceeds of the sale at 6,927,509 francs. This money was invested in Government stocks bearing 3% interest. The sale which had been announced a long time ahead had depressed the market and the jewellery trade was greatly relieved when the sale was over.

The articles which it had been decided to preserve because of their historic or artistic interest are still displayed in the Galerie d'Apollon of the Louvre, where the surviving ornaments of the coronation regalia and many other treasures have been assembled.

The most important of these is the Regent Diamond (*Plate 89, c*) which, according to the valuation, represented two-thirds of the value of the crown jewels. Although the stone has been valued on many occasions by expert jewellers using a formula by which diamonds are valued it must be taken as only a theoretical value. Today it is said to be worth £450,000, but it is doubtful if a purchaser could be found for it at that price. Its history has already been traced.

The Hortense (Hydrangea) Diamond (*Plate 89, d*) is a five-sided stone of 20 carats and of a beautiful pink colour. It was wrongly described as the eighth Mazarin at the time of the sale but is probably one of the stones purchased from Tavernier and set in the third *fleuron* for a buttonhole mentioned in the 1691 inventory.

The so-called reliquary brooch (*Plate 89, e*) has nothing about it to justify that name. It is a pendant brooch containing some large diamonds including two of a pink tint weighing about 21 carats, each of which had been among Louis XIV's set of buttons.

Altogether there are 93 brilliants weighing 143$\frac{27}{32}$ carats. The Commission on the Crown Diamonds[1] in their reports of 6th May 1882 and 12th February 1884 described the brooch as 'obviously a work of the period Louis XV'. Vanderheym[2] describes it as containing the first diamonds cut in France in the XV century and states that the setting was made in 1698; no doubt it was for this supposed historical association that it was decided to preserve it. In fact, it was made by Alfred Bapst in 1855 and the design was inspired by an XVIII-century model.

The sword made for the coronation of Charles X (*Plate 89, b*) contains 1,576 brilliants which weigh 330$\frac{3}{4}$ carats chosen from amongst the most beautiful stones in the crown jewels. Vanderheym describes it as so perfectly done that the hilt feels like an ivory one to touch.

The coronation crown of Louis XV has already been described. The frame is set with facsimiles of the original stones which naturally lack the brilliant fire of diamonds and as a result give the crown a rather tawdry appearance which does not do justice to the splendour of the original. But the false stones are of historical interest as they give an idea of some of the celebrated diamonds which were set in the crown in 1722.

The Crown of Charlemagne made for Napoleon has already been noted. It was made by Nitot and the cameos were intended to give an antique appearance.

The reliquary known as the Crown of St Louis, because the saintly King gave it to the Dominicans, was acquired by the Louvre after the Second World War.

The Dey of Algiers' watch is a very fine piece of workmanship. It was given to Louis XIV by Baba Ali, Dey of Algiers, on the occasion of his investiture in 1710.

The Chimera is a jewel in whose centre piece is a fine pearl in an enamel setting of very excellent work. It dates from the XVII century and Louis XIV attached the greatest importance to it as a fetish.

The Elephant of the Danish Order has been preserved as an admirable specimen of enamel work.

Apart from these items which were saved from the crown jewels there are still in the Louvre other coronation ornaments of varying antiquity which were 'restored' for the coronation of Napoleon and Charles X.

The most important item is the Sword of Charlemagne known as *Joyeuse* (*Plate 86, c*). The hilt and the ornamentation of the scabbard and hilt are of gold. The pommel is adorned with the intertwined figures of two fabulous birds resembling phoenixes. The guard terminates with two winged lions, the eyes being of lapis lazuli. The best authorities attribute the handle to the XI and XII centuries although some consider that it has features which could date it back to the Carolingian period. The grip was remade in the XIX century. The blade is of later date and replaced an earlier one. The scabbard dates back to the XII century but was restored for the coronation of Charles X when the blue velvet covering was used. The goldsmith's work on the scabbard is enriched with sapphires, topazes, amethysts, a garnet and a rock crystal. The sword and scabbard in its original state can be seen in Rigaud's portrait of Louis XIV.

The coronation spurs (*Plate 86, d*) are of gold and were restored in the XIX century when some garnets were added and the fastenings of gold and velvet were provided.

---

[1] General Guide to the Louvre Museum, 1952–3.   [2] Vanderheym: op. cit.

The royal sceptre consists of the sceptre proper, a short rod with a lily resting on a ball, on top of which rests an embossed statue of Charlemagne seated on a throne, with a closed crown on his head and a long sceptre in his right hand and an orb in his left. On the step of the throne is the inscription *Sanctus Karolus Magnus, Italia, Roma, Germania*. On the base of the lily are three bas-reliefs of subjects taken from the *Chronicle of Archbishop Turpin*. The first subject is taken from the beginning of the *Chronicle* in which the Apostle St John ordered Charlemagne to deliver Spain and Galicia from the power of the Saracens. The second is taken from Chapter XIX of the *Chronicle*: 'How the lances and axes of the Christian knights were found all flowing and rooted in the earth.' The third subject is from Chapter XXXII of the *Chronicle*, and represents the death of Charlemagne. The sceptre was adapted for Louis XIV into a long sceptre by the addition of a plain gold staff 6 ft high which could be separated into three pieces. The present staff (formerly that belonging to the Precentor of St Denis) bears the following inscription in old French:

> Of silver has this baton been made
> In the year MCC eighty [*sic*]
> Fourteen, neither more nor less
> (Of) those who will hold it in their hands
> Will pray when life is ended
> That his soul shall be transported to heaven
> . . . Let it be kept
> and he looked at great feasts
> For to maintain loyalty
> The Precentor should carry it in his hand.

Today the inscription is covered with purple velvet embroidered with fleurs-de-lis, added for the coronation of Charles X.

The Hand of Justice was made for the coronation of Napoleon (*Plate 86, b*). It is adorned with a gold medallion which is attributed to the Carolingian age.

The clasp of the royal mantle, sometimes called the Clasp of St Louis, is a large lozenge-shaped chased silver plate in the centre of which is a large fleur-de-lis picked out with jewels. Several stones are now missing but 6 amethysts, 6 emeralds and 11 garnets remain while the framework is adorned with 26 garnets and 2 sapphires. Clasps of this sort had been worn by the Kings of France for several centuries and certainly earlier than St Louis, but this one, despite its description in the inventories of St Denis, is attributed to the XIV century and is similar to one described in an inventory of the jewels of Charles V taken in 1379.

The signet of St Louis which was formerly kept at St Denis has on the bezel a pale, table-cut aquamarine in which is engraved the figure of St Louis standing crowned and carrying a sceptre and the letters *S.L.—Sigillum Ludovici*. The setting is of gold and on the hoop of the ring is a fleur-de-lis in *niello*. As the figure of St Louis has a nimbus it must be of a later date than his canonisation in 1297, twenty years after his death.

The coronation ring of Napoleon was given to the Louvre in the early 1950's by M. Lucien Basyangen of Geneva.

Such are all that remain of the former glories of the French coronation regalia and crown jewels. Is it possible that some other ornaments have survived and lie forgotten in some lumber-room? What has happened to the objects connected with the monarchy sold in 1887 and to the ornaments from the royal tombs? Perhaps one day some will be found and added to these relics of the French monarchy.

BIBLIOGRAPHY

AUBERT, M. — *Documents sur les Fontes de Trésor de la Cathédrale de Paris en 1562.*
'Aubert d'Avignon, joallier du roi et garde des diamants de la coronne 1736–85', in *Mémoires de l'Académie de Vaucluse*, 2nd Series, XIX, 1919.

BAPST, G. — *Histoire des Joyaux de la Couronne de France*, Paris 1889.
Testament de Jean le Bon, Paris 1884.

BARBET DE JOUY, H. — *Les Gemmes et Joyaux de la Couronne au Louvre.*

BERTAUD — *Diamants de la Couronne de France*, Paris 1887.

BLOCHE, A. — *La Vente des Diamants de la Couronne*, Paris 1888.

BRUEL, F. L. — 'Deux inventaires de bagues, joyaux, pierreries et dorures de la reine Marie de Médicis', in *Archives de l'Art de France*, new series, 1908, II.

BUCHNER, L. — *Die Hut der Krönunginsignien in Frankreich und in Deutschland im Mittelalter.*

CONWAY, SIR MARTIN — 'The Abbey of St Denis and its Ancient Treasure', *Archaeologia*, Vol. 66, 1914–15.

DARCEL, A. — *Trésor de l'Eglise de Conques*, 1861.

DE MELY, F. — 'Les Reliques de Constantinople au XIII Siècle', in *Revue d'Art Chrétien*, 1899–1900.

DOUBLET, JACQUES — *Histoire de l'Abbaye de St Denis*, 1625.

DURAND, G. — *Monographie de l'Eglise Notre-Dame, Cathédrale d'Amiens*, 1903.

DU TILLET, J. — *Portraits des Rois de France*, Paris.

ENAULT, L. — *Les Diamants de la Couronne*, Paris 1884.

FÉLIBIEN, MICHEL — *Histoire de l'Abbaye Royale de Saint-Denys en France*, Paris 1706.

GODEFROY, TH. — *Le Cérémonial de France*, Paris 1649.

HUGO, ABEL — *Les Tombeaux de Saint Denis*, Paris 1825

LABARTE, J. — *Inventaires de Charles V, Roi de France*, 1879.

LACATTE-JOLTROIS — *Recherches historiques sur la Sainte Ampoule*, Rheims 1825.

LAUER, P.H. — *Robert I et Raoul de Bourgogne.*

MALLAIS, P. DES — *Le Sacre et le Couronnement des Rois de France*, Paris 1927.

MASSON, FREDERIC — *Napoleon and his Coronation.*

MILLET, DOM S. G.	*Le Trésor Sacre*, 1636.
MOLLINGER, E.	'Le Sceptre de Charles V, Roi de France', in *Gazette archaeologique*, Vol. XIV, 1889.
MONTFAUCON, B. DE	*Les Monumens de la Monarchie Françoise*, Paris 1729.
MONTAIGLON, A. DE	'Joyaux et pierreries de la reine Jeanne d'Evreux', in *Archives de l'Art français*, 2nd Series, Vol. I, 1861.
OMONT, H.	'Inventory of the Treasury of St Denis', 1504, in *Mémoires de la Société de l'Histoire de Paris*, Vol. 28, 1902.
OPPENHEIMER, SIR FRANCIS	*The Legend of the Sainte Ampoule*, London 1954. *Frankish Themes and Problems*, London 1952.
SCHRAMM, P. E.	'Der König von Frankreich', in *Zeitschrift der Savigny-Stiftung fur Rechtsgeschichte*, Vols. LVI, 1936, and LVII, 1937.
TARBE, P.	*Trésor de Reims*.
TAVERNIER, J. B.	*Travels*. English translation by V. Ball 1889.
VANDERHEYM, E.	*Notice Historique sur les Joyaux de la Couronne*.
VERLET, P.	'La Couronne de Saint Louis', in *Bulletin des Musées de France*, XIIième année, No. 9, November 1947. *The Apollo Gallery and its Treasures*.

'Inventaire des Joyaux de la Couronne de France en 1560', in *Revue Universelle des Artes*, III, 1856, and IV, 1856.

KINGS OF FRANCE

MEROVINGIANS

	Pharamond (existence doubtful)
428	Clodion the Hairy
447	Merovic
458	Childeric I
481	Clovis the Great
511	Childebert. Paris Clodomir. Orleans Thierry. Metz Clotaire. Soissons
534	Theodebert. Metz
548	Theodebald. Metz
558	Clotaire I, sole ruler
561	Charibert. Paris Gontram. Orleans and Burgundy Sigebert. Metz Chilperic. Soissons

575 Childebert II
584 Clotaire II. Soissons
596 Thierry II. Orleans
      Theodebert. Metz
613 Clotaire II, sole king
628 Dagobert I, the Great
639 Clovis II. Burgundy and Neustria
      Sigebert II. Austrasia
656 Clotaire III
670 Childeric II, sole king
      Thierry III. Burgundy and Neustria
674 Dagobert II. Austrasia
691 Clovis III
695 Childebert III, the Just
711 Dagobert III
715 Chilperic II
717 Clotaire IV
720 Chilperic II again
      Thierry IV
737 Interregnum
742 Childeric III, the Stupid

CAROLINGIANS

752 Pepin the Short. Consort, Berthe, crowned at St Denis
768 Charlemagne. Crowned at Noyon, 9th October
      Crowned at Rome as Emperor of the West, 25th December 800
813 Louis I, the Debonair. Crowned as Emperor at Aix
      Crowned with consort, Hermengarde, at Rheims 816
840 Charles the Bald. First King of West Franks
      Crowned King of Aquitaine at Limoges 854
      Crowned King of Lorraine at Metz, 9th September 869
      Crowned Emperor at Rome 875
876 Louis II, the Stammerer. Crowned King of Aquitaine
      Crowned King of West Franks at Compiègne, September 877
      Crowned at Troyes 878
879 Louis III and Carloman. Crowned at Ferrières, 14th September
884 Charles II, the Fat. Crowned Emperor 881 but never as King of West Franks
887 Odo (Hugh), Count of Paris, elected. Crowned at Compiègne, 13th November
      888
888 Wido of Spoleto. Crowned at Tournai
893 Charles III, the Simple. Crowned at Rheims, 28th January in father's lifetime
      Crowned on marriage with second consort, Fréderonne, at Rheims 907
922 Robert I. Crowned at Rheims; second consort, Constance of Provence, crowned
      at Orleans

923 Rudolph or Raoul of Burgundy. Crowned at Soissons, 13th July. Emma, consort
of Raoul, anointed at Rheims

936 Louis IV, the Foreigner. Crowned at Laon, 16th June

954 Lothair. Elected and crowned at Rheims

979 Louis V, the Indolent. Crowned in father's lifetime at Compiègne, succeeded
986

HOUSE OF CAPET

987 Hugh Capet. Crowned at Noyon and Rheims

988 Robert II, the Strong. Crowned as co-king at Orleans. Succeeded 996

996 (Son Hugh. Crowned as co-king at Compiègne. Died 1025)

?1027 Henry I. Crowned as co-king at Rheims. Succeeded 1031

1059 Philip I, the Fair. Crowned at Rheims as co-king. Succeeded 1060

1108 Louis VI, the Fat. Crowned at Orleans. Consort, Adelaide of Savoy, crowned 1115

1129 (Son Philip. Crowned at Rheims. Died 1131)

1131 Louis VII, the Young. Crowned as co-king, succeeded 1137
First consort, Eleanor of Aquitaine, crowned at Bordeaux
Second consort, Constance of Castile, crowned at Orleans 1154
Third consort, Alix of Champagne, crowned at Paris 1160

1179 Philip II, Augustus. Crowned as co-king, 1st November, succeeded 1180

1180 Philip II succeeds. Crowned at St Denis with consort, Isabella of Hainault,
29th May 1181

1223 Louis VIII, the Lion. Crowned with consort, Blanche of Castile, at Rheims,
6th August

1226 Louis IX, St Louis. Crowned at Rheims, 29th November
Consort, Marguerite of Provence. Crowned at Sens 1233

1271 Philip III, the Hardy. Crowned at Rheims, 30th August
Second consort, Marie of Brabant. Crowned at Vincennes 1274

1285 Philip IV, the Fair. Crowned at Rheims, May 1286

1314 Louis X, the Quarreller, succeeded. Crowned with consort, Clemence of
Hungary, at Rheims 1315

1316 John I

1316 Philip V, the Tall. Crowned with consort, Jeanne of Burgundy, at Rheims,
December 1317

1322 Charles IV, the Fair. Crowned at Rheims, 1st February
Consort, Marie of Luxemburg. Crowned at Paris 1323

? Third consort, Jeanne d'Evreux. Crowned at St Denis

HOUSE OF VALOIS

1328 Philip VI, the Fortunate. Crowned at Rheims, 29th May with consort, Jeanne of
Burgundy

1350 John II, the Good. Crowned with consort, Bona of Luxemburg, September

1364 Charles V, the Wise. Crowned with wife, Jeanne of Bourbon, 19th May

a (left)   *Coronet and diadem of rubies and brilliants from the ruby parure (53 and 54) (p. 287)*

b (above)   *Part of girdle (64); two clasps (59) and one of fourteen buttons (60); a pair of ear-rings (62); and a pendant (63) from the ruby parure (p. 287)*

c (below left)   *Pair of bracelets (55); two neck-laces (56 and 57); and pendant (65) from ruby parure (p. 287)*

d   *Three brilliant ornaments in the form of a rose (4); part of a set of stars (9); comb with 24 brilliants from the Mazarin diamonds (70) (pp. 282 and 287)*

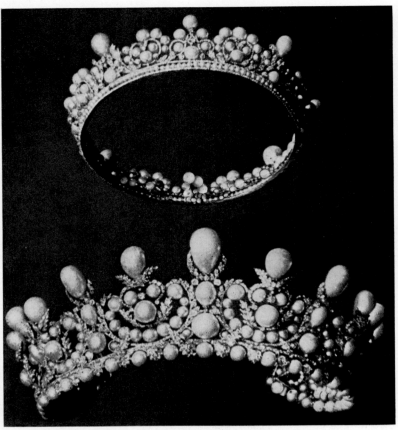

a   *Coronet and diadem of pearls and brilliants* (48) (p. 286)

b   *Collar of four rows of pearls* (40)
(p. 285)

c   *Bracelet of pearls and brilliants* (46); *four plaques of
pearls* (47); *a collar of 38 round and 9 pear-shaped
pearls* (45) (p. 286)

d   *A great brooch of pearls and brilliants with 'La
Regente', a pearl of 337 gr* (50); *four brooches
of pearls and brilliants of the same model* (39)
(pp. 285 and 286)

a (left) *Coronet and diadem from the sapphire parure (38) (p. 285)*

b (below, left) *Bracelet, brooch, pair of ear-rings and necklace from the sapphire parure (38) (p. 285)*

c *The Russian diadem (32) and two diamond fillets (30) (p. 284)*

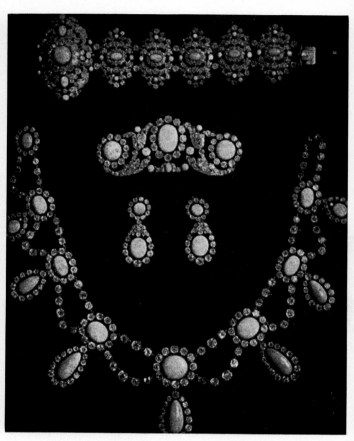

a and c (below)   *Ornaments from a great girdle of brilliants, pearls, rubies, sapphires and emeralds (35) (p. 285)*

b   *Bracelet, brooch, pair of ear-rings and necklace from the turquoise parure (31) (p. 284)*

c

1380   Charles VI, the Beloved. Crowned at Rheims, 1st November
            Consort, Isabel of Bavaria. Crowned at Amiens, 23rd August, on marriage, 1385

1422   Charles VII, the Victorious. Crowned at Rheims, 7th July 1429

1461   Louis XI. Crowned at Rheims, 15th August

1483   Charles VIII, the Affable, succeeded. Crowned at Rheims, 30th May 1484
            Consort, Anne of Brittany. Crowned at St Denis, 13th December 1489

1498   Louis XII. Crowned at Rheims, 27th May and at St Denis, 1st July
            Third consort, Mary Tudor. Crowned at St Denis, 5th November 1514

1515   Francis I. Crowned at Rheims, 24th January, and afterwards at St Denis
            Consort, Claude of Brittany. Crowned at St Denis 1517

1547   Henry II. Crowned at Rheims, 26th July
            Consort, Catherine of Medici. Crowned at St Denis, 10th June 1549

1559   Francis II. Crowned at Rheims, 18th September
            Consort, Mary Queen of Scots. Crowned at Paris

1561   Charles IX. Crowned at Rheims, 15th May
            Consort, Elizabeth of Austria. Crowned at St Denis, 23rd March 1571

1574   Henry III. Crowned at Rheims, 1575

HOUSE OF BOURBON

1589   Henry IV, the Great. Crowned at Chartres, 27th February 1594
            Second consort, Mary of Medici. Crowned at St Denis, 13th May 1610

1610   Louis XIII, the Just. Crowned at Rheims, 17th October

1643   Louis XIV, the Great, succeeded, aged 5. Crowned at Rheims, 7th June 1654

1715   Louis XV, the Well-beloved, succeeded, aged 5, Crowned at Rheims, 25th October 1722

1774   Louis XVI. Crowned at Rheims, 11th June 1775

1793   (Louis XVII)

FIRST REPUBLIC

FIRST EMPIRE

1804   Napoleon I. Crowned at Paris, 4th December

BOURBONS RESTORED

1814   Louis XVIII

1824   Charles X

HOUSE OF ORLEANS

1830   Louis Philippe

SECOND REPUBLIC

SECOND EMPIRE

1852   Napoleon III

APPENDIX

A RECONSTRUCTED CATALOGUE OF THE SALE AND DISPOSAL OF THE
FRENCH CROWN JEWELS, 1887

1. Two round hairpins with 324 brilliants weighing 150 carats. Circular in shape and the surface completely covered with brilliants. Designed by Alfred Bapst in May 1863. Estimated value 35,000 frs. Sold to M. Doutrelon for 40,000 frs.

2. Two great shoulder knots set with 1,341 brilliants weighing $282\frac{5}{16}$ carats. The inspiration of the design was taken from the period of Marie Antoinette. Each consisted of five rows of brilliants with the middle enriched with large stones mounted in claws. Designed by Alfred Bapst in December 1863 for the court mantle of the Empress Eugénie. Estimated value 78,600 frs. Sold to M. Doutrelon for 84,000 frs.

3. Seven aiguillettes set with 222 brilliants weighing $215\frac{25}{32}$ carats hanging from a foundation ornament set with 59 brilliants weighing $18\frac{9}{16}$ carats and 8 rose diamonds. Estimated value 15,000 frs. Sold to M. Bonynge for 25,100 frs. There was keen competition for this item. According to Bloche[1] it was bought on behalf of Queen Victoria.

4. Three ornaments in the form of wild roses set with 522 brilliants weighing $129\frac{11}{16}$ carats and 133 rose-cut diamonds. The first flower had as its centre a brilliant of 6 carats, surrounded by 158 brilliants. The second had a central stone of 5 carats with 166 other brilliants. The third had a central stone of 3 carats set amidst 176 brilliants. Designed by Alfred Bapst in April 1867 and worn by the Empress Eugénie as hair ornaments. Estimated value 50,000 frs. Sold to Mm. Rouvenant and Despres for 44,100 frs.

5. A bow with two tassels set with 2,438 brilliants weighing $136\frac{3}{4}$ carats and 196 rose-cut diamonds. Executed by the House of Kramer in the reign of Napoleon III. The design was inspired by the style of Marie Antoinette. Estimated value 35,000 frs. Sold to M. Emile Schlessinger for 42,200 frs.

6. A setting in which was a brilliant solitaire of 9 carats. It was sometimes used as the centre-piece of the garland of currant leaves (No. 11). Valued at 15,000 frs. Sold to M. Doutrelon for 16,100 frs.

7. A crescent set with 89 brilliants weighing $40\frac{13}{16}$ carats. Designed by Alfred Bapst in March 1860 and made specially for a costume of Diana worn by the Empress Eugénie. Valued at 18,000 carats. Sold to M. Emile Schlessinger for 21,400 frs.

8. A pendant described as a hair ornament but more probably a corsage brooch. It was set with 477 brilliants weighing $65\frac{11}{16}$ carats and 100 rose-cut diamonds. Made by the House of Kramer in the reign of Napoleon III. Estimated value 15,000 frs. Sold to M. Doutrelon for 17,000 frs.

9. Seven stars set with 215 brilliants weighing $49\frac{13}{16}$ carats and 25 rose-cut diamonds. Made by the firm of Bapst and Nephew in the reign of Napoleon III. The first lot of two stars estimated at 6,000 frs sold to M. Bleville for 8,300 frs. The second lot of two stars valued at 6,000 frs sold to M. Aucoc for 8,300 frs. The third lot of one star valued at 3,600 frs sold to Mm. Irmaos and Levy for 5,600 frs. The fourth lot of two stones valued at 6,000 frs sold to Mm. Rouvenot and Despres for 10,600 frs. Total realised 32,800 frs. against a valuation of 21,000 frs.

10. A collar formed of four necklaces with a total of 222 brilliants weighing 363 carats. The first row contained 33 brilliants weighing $55\frac{1}{2}$ carats; was valued at 30,000 frs and sold for 28,300 frs. The second row contained 45 brilliants weighing $64\frac{1}{2}$ carats; was valued at 40,000 frs and sold for 36,500 frs. The third row contained 57 brilliants weighing $96\frac{1}{2}$ carats; was valued at 55,000 frs and sold for 62,500 frs. The fourth row contained 79 brilliants weighing $127\frac{1}{2}$ carats; was estimated at 55,000 frs and sold for 62,500 frs. The clasp contained 8 brilliants weighing 9 carats, which were valued at 4,500 frs and sold for 8,000 frs. The purchaser in each case was M. Tiffany.

[1] Arthur Bloche, *La Vente des Diamants de la Couronne.*

11. A garland of currant leaves in sixteen parts each with a brooch and three pendants or aiguillettes. A total of 2,314 brilliants weighing $517\frac{3}{16}$ carats and 353 roses were used. It was executed in June 1856 by Bapst and Nephew, to the designs of M. Devin, Inspector of the Crown Jewels, and was much favoured by the Empress Eugénie. At the sale the garland was dismantled into eight lots.

Lot 1. One part valued at 28,000 frs sold to M. J. and M. P. Bapst and Sons for 40,000 frs.
Lot 2. One part valued at 28,000 frs sold to M. Pickard for 53,000 frs.
Lot 3. One part valued at 25,000 frs sold to M. Bachruch for 24,600 frs.
Lot 4. One part valued at 25,000 frs sold to M. E. Robert for 23,100 frs.
Lot 5. Two parts valued at 20,000 frs sold to Messrs Garrard for 26,800 frs.
Lot 6. Two parts valued at 14,000 frs sold to M. Tiffany for 23,200 frs.
Lot 7. Two parts valued at 16,400 frs sold to M. Tiffany for 16,400 frs.
Lot 8. Six parts valued at 35,000 frs and sold to M. E. Robert for 34,500 frs.

12. A piece of a jewel in the form of a small flower belonging to the corsage catalogued under No. 8 composed of 58 brilliants valued at 2,500 frs and sold to M. Van Cleef for 2,100 frs.

13. A parcel of brilliants taken from various orders and decorations. One lot containing 14 brilliants weighing $34\frac{1}{8}$ carats valued at 11,600 frs and sold to Madame Chauvet for 18,600 frs. A second lot of 80 brilliants valued at 18,000 frs sold to M. Osiris for 18,200 frs.

14. A parcel of brilliants from various orders and decorations. One lot containing small brilliants and rose-coloured diamonds weighing 40 carats valued at 5,000 frs sold to M. Lepée-Esmelin for 6,200 frs. A second lot of brilliants (*mêlés*) weighing 100 carats valued at 20,000 frs and sold to Mr Welby for 15,000 frs.

15. Six brilliants called *briolettes* in two lots. The first lot of one stone weighing 8 carats valued at 12,000 frs sold to M. Tiffany for 24,500 frs. The second lot of five stones weighing 10 carats valued at 8,000 frs sold to M. Rosenau for 17,700 frs.

16. A parcel of small rose-cut diamonds weighing 40 carats valued at 4,000 frs sold to M. Aucoc for 6,800 frs.

17. A parcel of small brilliants weighing $83\frac{1}{32}$ carats valued at 10,000 frs sold to Mm. Filard and Pelletier for 12,900 frs.

18. A great opal surrounded by brilliants. It could be used on a brooch or on an agraffe and on occasion was suspended to the Order of the Golden Fleece. Valued at 25,000 frs. Sold to the Baron de Horn for 23,000 frs.

19. A sapphire weighing 10 carats and other coloured stones valued at 3,000 frs sold to Madame Asselin for 4,600 frs.

20. Eight round pearls weighing 128 gr valued at 8,500 frs sold to the Countess of Bari, Princess of Bourbon, for 8,300 frs.

21. A lot of brilliants taken from various orders and decorations weighing 154 carats valued at 23,000 frs. Sold to M. J. and P. Bapst and Son for 26,300 frs.

22. A lot of brilliants taken from various orders and decorations weighing $218\frac{1}{2}$ carats and valued at 24,000 frs. Sold to M. Peczenick for 30,700 frs.

23. A lot of brilliants taken from the various decorations weighing $17\frac{1}{2}$ carats valued at 1,200 frs and sold to M. Noury for 2,300 frs.

24. A brilliant with a flat side called 'a portrait' weighing 6 carats valued at 3,200 frs and sold to Baron de Horn for 11,800 frs.

25. Bouquet for the corsage in the form of a diamond brooch. This light and elegant ornament in the form of a bouquet of flowers and leaves with a knot of ribbons composed of 2,637 brilliants weighing $132\frac{5}{16}$ carats and 860 rose-cut diamonds. It was valued at 35,000 frs. It was designed by M. E. Bapst for the Duchess of Berry and sold to M. Bécoulet for 41,100 frs.

26. Six brilliants divided into three lots. The first lot of 1 brilliant of $7\frac{29}{32}$ carats and 1 brilliant of $6\frac{1}{32}$ carats was valued at 10,000 frs and sold to M. Boin-Taburet. The second lot of 1 brilliant of $6\frac{1}{9}$ carats and 1 of $5\frac{1}{2}$ carats valued at 10,000 frs sold to Madame Pilloy for 11,200 frs. The third lot of 1 brilliant of $4\frac{29}{32}$ carats and 1 of $5\frac{1}{16}$ carats valued at 10,000 frs was sold to M. Vever for 17,100 frs.

27. A diadem of emeralds and brilliants. In all 1,031 brilliants weighing 176 carats and 46 emeralds weighing 77 carats were employed. It was made by Frédéric Bapst and Bros. in July 1820 and had been worn successively by the Royal Princess and finally by the Empress Eugénie who particularly esteemed emeralds. It was valued at 50,000 frs and sold to M. Bachruch for 45,900 frs.

28. A chain of thirty-two rectangular pieces linked together by circular links. Altogether 833 brilliants weighing $621\frac{19}{32}$ carats were employed. It was made by Alfred Bapst in December 1867 to support the two anchors in diamonds worn by the Empress Eugénie at a ball given by the Minister of Marine. It was sold in four lots each consisting of eight links. Each lot was valued at 50,000 frs and the first two were sold to M. Doutrelon for 45,500 frs each, the third to M. Peczenick for 45,200 frs and the fourth to M. Friedlander for 45,400 frs.

29. A buckle for a girdle in the form of a sun or a great rose window from which hung nine aiguillettes. In the centre was a brilliant of 25 carats and 295 brilliants weighing 146 carats were employed. It was designed by Alfred Bapst in 1867 and valued at 140,000 carats. It was sold for 132,500 frs to Madame Gal and later was acquired by Mm. Tiffany.

30. Two fillets, one for the brow and one for the hair, set with 27 brilliants weighing 101 carats and 41 brilliants weighing 124 carats respectively. They were made in 1867 by Bapst and Nephew. The first was estimated at 80,000 frs and was bought by M. Vever for 102,500 frs, the second also valued at 80,000 frs was bought by Mm. Alphonse and Louis Ochs for 83,500 frs.

31. A parure of turquoises, brilliants and fancy stones consisting of a diadem, a coronet, a necklace, a pair of bracelets, a comb and a pair of pendant ear-rings. The diadem in a design of arabesques and foliage set with brilliants among which were set larger turquoises set in brilliants. The border was formed by a row of brilliants. The coronet was of a similar design. The necklace was formed of two chains of brilliant settings with large turquoises set between and seven pendant turquoises in brilliant settings. The other ornaments were in similar style. Altogether 3,302 brilliants weighing 434 carats and 265 turquoises and other stones were used. The parure was designed by Everard Bapst and mounted by Bapst Brothers in July, 1820. The coronet which was valued at 18,000 frs was sold to M. Lepée-Esmelin for 22,100 frs. The diadem valued at 30,000 frs was sold to M. Alexandre Lazard for 47,800 frs. The necklace valued at 15,000 frs was sold to M. Hamelin for 19,100 frs. The pair of bracelets valued at 10,000 frs was sold to the Baron de Horn for 11,300 frs. The comb and ear-rings valued at 7,000 frs were sold to Baron de Horn for 18,200 frs.

32. The Russian Diadem composed of a graduation of spiral ornaments set with brilliants. It could be adapted to be worn as on a chain. The number of brilliants used was 1,200 weighing 405 carats, in addition to 442 rose-cut diamonds. This diadem was executed by Bapst and Nephew in 1863 for the Empress Eugénie for a ball given in her honour at the Château of Compiègne. The design was taken from a portrait of a Grand Duchess of Russia. The diadem was valued at 150,000 frs and sold to Messrs Garrard for 180,000 frs.

33. The Greek Diadem. This diadem in a Greek design was made as a setting for the Regent Diamond. It was set entirely with brilliants, 326 in number, weighing $306\frac{19}{32}$ carats and 286 little brilliants weighing 5 carats. It was designed by Alfred Bapst and executed by Bapst and Nephew in June 1867. It was valued at 150,000 frs and sold to Bapst and Sons for 131,500 frs.

34. A *Berthe* or corsage ornament set with 181 brilliants weighing $185\frac{7}{8}$ carats, 27 rubies weighing $18\frac{1}{18}$ carats, 15 sapphires weighing $11\frac{1}{8}$ carats, 35 emeralds weighing 25 carats, 29 hyacinths, 46

garnets, 41 turquoises, 48 amethysts, 2 chrysoprases, 10 topazes and 765 rose-cut diamonds. It was made by Bapst and Nephew in June 1864. The estimated value of this ornament was 30,000 frs and it was sold to Baron de Horn for 36,100 frs.

35. A great girdle set with 34 large rose diamonds weighing 202 carats, 2,414 brilliants weighing $313\frac{3}{4}$ carats, 63 pearls of 1,164 gr and 2 rubies weighing $21\frac{1}{8}$ carats, 4 sapphires weighing $29\frac{1}{8}$ carats, 8 emeralds weighing $49\frac{1}{4}$ carats. It was made in December 1864 from designs of Alfred Bapst for the Empress Eugénie to wear with her costumes at a full dress Fête Parée. It was sold in 9 lots.

> Lot 1. A plaque valued at 25,000 frs sold to M. Lewerson for 34,200 frs.
> Lot 2. A plaque valued at 17,000 frs sold to the Baron de Horn for 16,300 frs.
> Lot 3. A plaque valued at 18,000 frs sold to M. Lehmann for 16,000 frs.
> Lot 4. Two rose-shaped ornaments valued at 18,000 frs sold to M. Michel Ephrussi for 17,000 frs.
> Lot 5. Two rose-shaped ornaments valued at 9,000 frs sold to M. Lindenbaum for 8,100 frs.
> Lot 6. Ten rose-shaped ornaments valued at 20,000 frs sold to M. Tiffany for 20,000 frs.
> Lot 7. Eighteen rose-shaped ornaments valued at 14,000 frs sold to Baron de Horn for 15,200 frs.
> Lot 8. Four pendeloques valued at 5,000 frs sold to the Baron de Horn for 8,100 frs.
> Lot 9. One plaque valued at 40,000 frs sold to M. Tiffany for 31,200 frs.

36. A brooch of yellow diamonds with 65 brilliants weighing $109\frac{29}{32}$ carats, the principal stone weighing 27 carats. It was executed during the reign of Napoleon III by Bapst and Nephew. The brooch was valued at 30,000 frs and sold to Baron de Horn for 20,500 frs.

37. A parure of gold and mosaics consisting of a collar, a brooch and pendant ear-rings. Valued at 4,000 frs and sold to M. Henri Bain for 6,200 frs.

38. A parure of sapphires and brilliants consisting of a diadem, a coronet, a necklace, two bracelets, a comb, a pair of pendant ear-rings, three clasps and an ornamental accessory. In all 3,837 brilliants of $568\frac{3}{16}$ carats and 67 sapphires of $768\frac{1}{4}$ carats were employed. The parure was designed by Everard Bapst and executed in February 1819. It was sold in eight lots. The coronet valued at 35,000 frs was sold to Mm. Boin and Aucoc for 31,600 frs. The pair of bracelets valued at 30,000 frs was sold to Mr Welby for 37,600 frs. The necklace valued at 60,000 frs was sold to J. and P. Bapst and Sons for 86,560 frs. The diadem valued at 100,000 frs was sold to M. Biedermann for 135,000 frs. The comb estimated at 10,000 frs was sold to M. Tiffany for 18,000 frs. The ear-rings valued at 7,000 frs were sold to J. and P. Bapst and Sons for 22,500 frs. The three clasps valued at 10,000 frs were sold to Madame Asselin for 13,700 frs. The ornamental accessory valued at 5,000 frs was sold to M. Friedlander for 5,100 frs.

39. Four brooches in pearls and brilliants of the same model. A total of 266 brilliants weighing $166\frac{11}{32}$ carats, 520 rose-cut diamonds and 28 pearls weighing 1,496 gr was employed. The first valued at 50,000 frs was sold to Sir Ogden Goelet for 43,000 frs. The second valued at 30,000 frs was sold to Bapst et Fils for 31,100 frs. The third valued at 35,000 frs was sold to M. Louis Grub for 21,000 frs. The fourth valued at 30,000 frs was sold to M. Louis Grub for 18,500 frs.

40. A collection of pearl ornaments consisting of: A collar of four rows of 362 pearls of 5,630 gr with a clasp enriched with 4 pearls of 64 gr. Each row was sold separately. The first of 56 pearls weighing 88 gr valued at 70,000 frs was sold to M. Lowenstein Brothers for 48,000 frs. The second of 76 pearls weighing 1,212 gr valued at 85,000 frs was sold to M. Lewerson for 66,300 frs. The third of 100 pearls weighing 1,540 gr valued at 80,000 frs was sold to M. Morel and Ason for 84,500 frs. The fourth of 130 pearls weighing 1,992 gr, valued at 150,000 frs was sold to M. L. Taub for 105,000 frs. The clasp valued at 2,400 frs was sold to M. Ung for 3,600 frs.

41. A collar of pearls composed of eight rows comprising 526 pearls weighing 6,225 gr with a clasp enriched with 16 pearls weighing 160 gr. The first row of 52 pearls weighing 464 gr, estimated at 15,000 frs, was sold to A. Wissian for 16,000 frs. The second row of 51 pearls, weighing 628 gr,

estimated at 25,000 frs, was sold to M. Ecalle for 39,200 frs. The third row of 58 pearls, weighing 676 gr and estimated at 25,000 frs, was sold to M. Tiffany for 30,300 frs. The fourth row of 62 pearls, weighing 740 gr and estimated at 35,000 frs, was sold to M. Friedberg for 45,100 frs. The fifth row of 68 pearls weighing 808 gr and estimated at 50,000 frs was sold to M. Tiffany for 38,600 frs. The sixth row of 71 pearls weighing 873 gr was estimated at 50,000 frs and sold to M. Tiffany for 41,300 frs. The seventh row of 79 pearls, weighing 952 gr, was estimated at 55,000 frs and sold to M. Lowenstein Brothers for 52,000 frs. The eighth row of 85 pearls weighing 1,084 gr estimated at 70,000 frs and sold to M. Tiffany for 70,100 frs. The clasp of 16 pearls weighing 160 gr was estimated at 4,500 frs and sold to M. Grognier-Arnaud for 6,000 frs.

42. A necklace of pearls comprising 47 pearls weighing 684 gr, estimated at 35,500 frs and sold for 34,600 frs to M. A. Bloche.

43. A necklace of pearls, one row of 58 pearls weighing 524 gr estimated at 15,000 frs sold to Mm. Rondel, Barmore Billiens.

44. Collar of pearls, one row of 58 pearls weighing 392 gr and estimated at 10,000 frs sold to Messrs Garrard for 15,000.

45. Collar of pearls consisting of one row composed of 38 round pearls and 9 pear-shaped pearls of a total weight of 1,612 gr. Some of the pear-shaped pearls were among the crown jewels in the time of Louis XV. The row of 38 pearls was purchased in 1810 by Napoleon I as a present for the Empress Marie Louise. Estimated at 120,000 frs, it was sold to M. Louis Grub for 74,300 frs.

46. Two bracelets with pearls and brilliants composed each of five rows of pearls comprising 100 pearls with a large clasp composed of 72 brilliants and one large pendant pearl. The pearls weighed about 2,000 gr, the brilliants about 40 carats. Estimated at 60,000 frs they were sold to Sir Ogden Goelet for 90,200 frs.

47. Five plaques composed of 1 large half-pearl surrounded by pearls, estimated at 4,000 frs and sold to M. Istel for 5,100 frs.

48. A great pearl diadem composed of 998 brilliants weighing $64\frac{7}{32}$ carats. Estimated at 100,000 frs and sold to M. Julius Jacoby for 78,100 frs.

49. 212 pearls weighing 2,452 gr and a coronet of pearls and brilliants weighing 8 carats; also 274 pearls weighing 984 gr and rose-cut diamonds of 2 carats. Made by the House of Bapst and estimated at 30,000 frs they were sold to Sir Ogden Goelet for 38,000 frs.

50. A great brooch of pearls and brilliants containing the great pearl known as 'La Regente' of 337 gr in addition to 4 pear-shaped pearls of 400 gr, 2 pear-shaped pearls, 2 button pearls and 40 large brilliants. Made by the House of Lemonier in the reign of Napoleon III and estimated at 225,000 frs, they were sold to M. J. Rossel for 176,000 frs.

51. A *sévigné* brooch composed of 324 brilliants of $168\frac{3}{16}$ carats and 3 brilliants of 36 carats, the stones included 1 large solitaire of 9 carats made in June 1856 from the design of M. Alfred Bapst by the House of Bapst and Nephew. Estimated at 125,000 frs it was sold to M. Tiffany for 120,000 frs.

52. A suite of breast ornaments containing stones which had been set in the crown of Charles X. The stones are enumerated as:

One pendeloque of 16 carats.	Forty pendeloques of 50 carats.
One pendeloque of 14 carats.	One oval brilliant of 14 carats.
One pendeloque of 14 carats.	One pendeloque of 12 carats.
Two pendeloques of 20 carats.	One pendeloque of 10 carats.
Four pendeloques of 32 carats.	Two pendeloques of 16 carats.
Eight pendeloques of 48 carats.	Two pendeloques of 7 carats.

A number of pendeloques weighing 150 carats and other different brilliants weighing 288 carats.

Although this piece was sold in thirteen lots estimated at 546,000 frs they were all bought by
M. Tiffany for a total sum of 811,000 frs.

Items 53 to 64 inclusive form the ruby parure.

53. A diadem of rubies and brilliants mounted in the style of Louis XII and executed by Messrs
Bapst Brothers in June 1816. Estimated at 175,000 frs and sold to M. Hass for 160,000 frs.

54. A coronet estimated at 100,000 frs and sold to M. Guillemin for 104,000 frs.

55. Two bracelets estimated at 25,000 frs and sold to M. Tiffany for 42,000 frs.

56. A great necklace estimated at 70,000 frs and sold to Bapst and Son for 77,500 frs.

57. A small necklace estimated at 30,000 frs and sold to Bapst and Son for 43,100 frs.

58. A clasp estimated at 2,000 frs and sold to M. Chaland for 4,700 frs.

59. Two clasps estimated at 6,000 frs and sold to M. Beaumont for 8,200 frs.

60. Fourteen buttons estimated at 3,500 frs and sold to the Baron de Horn for 10,000 frs.

61. A rosary estimated at 15,000 frs and sold to M. Pickard for 18,100 frs.

62. A pair of ear-rings estimated at 20,000 frs and sold to M. Boin-Taburet for 25,000 frs.

63. A pendant estimated at 12,000 frs and sold to M. Boin-Taburet for 10,600 frs.

64. A girdle which was sub-divided into ten lots, estimated at 64,000 frs and sold to various bidders
for 80,100 frs.

65. The Mazarin Diamonds—1 pear-shaped rose-coloured diamond of $24\frac{27}{32}$ carats estimated at
70,000 frs sold to M. Tiffany for 128,000 frs; 1 white pear-shaped diamond of $22\frac{1}{4}$ carats estimated at
80,000 frs and sold to M. Tiffany for 81,000 frs.

66. A brilliant *carré* weighing $18\frac{19}{32}$ carats, estimated at 70,000 frs and sold to M. Boucheron for
101,000 frs.

67. A brilliant *coin arrondis* estimated at 125,000 frs and sold to Madame Asselin for 152,000 frs.

68. An oblong pearl of $16\frac{9}{16}$ carats estimated at 60,000 frs and sold to M. Boucheron for 92,000 frs.

69. An oval brilliant of $18\frac{1}{32}$ carats estimated at 75,000 frs and sold to M. Tiffany for 71,000 frs.

70. A comb of 24 brilliants from the Mazarin Diamonds was broken up into seventeen lots:

A brilliant of $10\frac{1}{32}$ carats estimated at 15,000 frs and sold to M. Mortimer for 15,100 frs.

A brilliant of $8\frac{5}{8}$ carats estimated at 16,000 frs and sold to the Baron de Horn for 11,800 frs.

A brilliant of $14\frac{1}{2}$ carats estimated at 30,000 frs and sold to M. Boucheron for 18,000 frs.

A brilliant of $18\frac{5}{8}$ carats estimated at 40,000 frs and sold to M. Boucheron for 56,500 frs.

A brilliant of 17 carats estimated at 34,000 frs and sold to the Baron de Horn for 18,400 frs.

A brilliant of $9\frac{5}{32}$ carats estimated at 15,000 frs and sold to M. Tiffany for 26,400 frs.

A brilliant of $10\frac{21}{32}$ carats estimated at 15,000 frs and sold to M. Pam for 12,800 frs.

A brilliant weighing $8\frac{6}{32}$ carats estimated at 12,000 frs and sold to M. Tiffany for 29,000 frs.

A brilliant of $15\frac{1}{2}$ carats estimated at 30,000 frs and sold to M. Picard for 65,000 frs.

A brilliant of $13\frac{10}{32}$ carats estimated at 20,000 frs and sold to M. Tiffany for 35,200 frs.

A brilliant of $6\frac{28}{32}$ carats estimated at 15,000 frs and sold to M. Boucheron for 25,200 frs.

A brilliant of $8\frac{2}{32}$ carats estimated at 16,000 frs and sold to M. Martial Vernard for 13,000 frs.

A brilliant of 9 carats estimated at 10,000 frs and sold to M. Tiffany for 21,400 frs.

71. Two aiguillettes of 28 brilliants estimated at 80,000 frs and sold to M. Boucheron for 141,000 frs.

72. Two aiguillettes of 28 brilliants estimated at 70,000 frs and sold to M. Tiffany for 60,000 frs.

73. Two aiguillettes of 26 brilliants estimated at 35,000 frs and sold to M. Tiffany for 46,000 frs.

74. Two aiguillettes of 24 brilliants and estimated at 25,000 frs sold to M. Boin-Taburet for
37,000 frs.

75. Two aiguillettes of 35 brilliants estimated at 3,000 frs and sold to the Baron de Horn for
10,000 frs.

76. A lot of sapphires estimated at 500 frs and sold to M. Collot for 400 frs.

77. A cross composed of 10 brilliants estimated at 6,000 frs and sold to M. Boucheron for 11,300 frs.

78. Two ornaments in rubies estimated at 1,500 francs and sold to Messrs Gronier-Arnaud for 3,100 frs.

79. A little eagle in roses from the middle of the Grand Cross of the Legion of Honour worn by Napoleon III and two clasps in brilliants estimated at 3,000 francs and sold to M. Morel for 2,200 frs.

80. An *écrin* containing facsimiles of the crown jewels which had been made to the command of Napoleon III. Estimated at 1,200 frs it was sold to the Baron de Horn for 5,100 frs.

81. A lot of divers stones consisting of 2 pearls, 2 half-pearls, a lot of rose diamonds of $30\frac{1}{2}$ carats, a briolet, 5 little brilliants, a lot of rubies, emeralds, sapphires and amethysts weighing 8 carats, being a debris of the jewels, estimated at 1,200 frs and sold to M. Soaher for 5,350 frs.

82. Debris of gold and silver of 585 gr sold to the Baron de Horn for 1,600 frs.

83. Debris of gold and silver weighing 650 gr sold to the Baron de Horn for 350 frs.

84. Sent to the Museum of the School of Mines. Two brilliants called portraits, 3 briolets, 950 pearls, an opal surrounded by brilliants, 20 opals of which 6 were mounted, 272 turquoises, 187 amethysts, 4 emeralds, 8 tourmalines, 47 emeralds, 3 diamonds, one of $16\frac{24}{32}$, one of $2\frac{18}{32}$ carats; also one of $3\frac{20}{32}$ carats; 2 topazes, the brilliant rose which had ornamented the middle of the comb (see No. 70) and other *objets d'art*, melted down and realised for the Mint.

85. The Imperial Crown, the sword of the Dauphin and the sword of Louis XVIII. These were destroyed.

a and d   *Parts of a garland of currant leaves of brilliants and rose diamonds* (11) (p. 283)

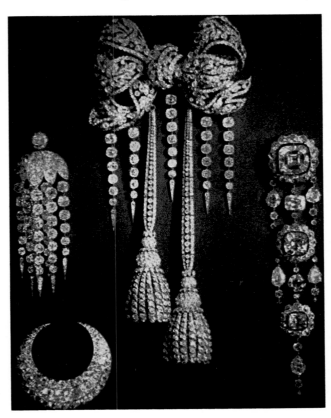

b   *A brilliant bow with two tassels* (5); *one of seven aiguillettes in brilliants* (3) *a crescent set with 89 brilliants* (7); *brooch of yellow brilliants* (36) (pp. 282 and 285)

c   *Bouquet of flowers and leaves set with 2,637 brilliants and 860 rose diamonds* (25) (p. 284)

d and a   *Parts of a garland of currant leaves of brilliants and rose diamonds* (11) (p. 283)

a   *Statue of Charlemagne or Charles the Bald. The Louvre, Paris* (p. 293); b   *X-Century ivory plaque of Christ in Majesty, showing an Emperor, possibly Otto I, with a crown having a single arch. Metropolitan Museum of Art, New York* (p. 297)

c   *Book of the Gospels of Henry II with plaques which are believed to have come from the crown of the Empress Theophano. Bavarian State Library, Munich* (p. 297)

d   *Miniature from the Book of the Gospels of Charles the Bald showing the Emperor wearing a crown with fleurs-de-lis. Residenz Treasury, Munich* (p. 293)

CHAPTER NINE

GERMANY

THE CAROLINGIAN DYNASTY

In early times the leaders of the German tribes were invested with military emblems, the lance, the sword and the helmet and they were elevated on the shield and then placed on a seat. The kings wore their hair long in the regal fashion, and although we know that in the VI century Clovis, King of the West Franks, had a crown, its adoption by other Western kings was slow.

In the middle of the VIII century the position of the Papacy was becoming increasingly precarious. There had for long been a drift from the control of the Emperor in Constantinople and Italy had been disturbed by the iconoclastic controversy. Disorder followed, the Exarch was killed and the Pope resisted and rebuked the Emperor. The Lombards seized this opportunity and descended on the Exarch as champion of the images and on Rome as champion of the Emperor. The Pope was temporarily able to stay the Lombards, but finding himself between a heretic Emperor and a barbaric invader he turned to the West Franks for aid. He first appealed, though in vain, to Charles Martel, who as Mayor of the Palace of the Merovingian kings of the West Franks was the virtual ruler and who had proved his worth as champion of Christianity when he defeated the Spanish Musulmans at Poitiers. Charles died shortly after, at the time when the situation was becoming more urgent and the Pope's need for a powerful ally had become essential. Pope Zacharias was persuaded to agree to the deposition of Childeric III, the old and feeble Merovingian King, and to anoint and crown Pepin, the son of Charles Martel. This gave the first King of the Carolingian line a special sanctity and raised the status of the crown as a royal emblem. The Pope was rewarded by Pepin's assistance, the Lombards were quelled and the northern part of the Italian exarchate was given to the Pope. In return Pepin was given the Roman title of patrician, which ranked next after emperor and consul. Pepin was succeeded in 768 by his son Charlemagne, who had been anointed at St Denis by the Pope on the occasion of his father's coronation (see page 204). The new King united the five or six tribal leagues which composed the German nation and was crowned at Noyon on 9th October 768 being recognised as King of the East Franks. When the Lombards again attacked the Papacy, Charlemagne swept down upon them and finally in 774 he extinguished the Lombard kingdom and himself took the title of the King of the Lombards. In 781 he had his second son, Carloman, crowned King of Italy by Pope Adrian, and his youngest son was crowned King of Aquitaine.

In 796 Leo III succeeded Pope Adrian I and, to show his intention to continue his predecessor's policy, he sent to Charlemagne the banner of the city of Rome and the keys of the Confession of St Peter. Three years later an insurrection broke out and the Pope, whilst in procession through Rome, was attacked by armed men and left for dead. He escaped, however, and made his way to Germany where he conferred with Charlemagne. The latter was occupied in suppressing a revolt in Saxony but sent the Pope back to Rome under the protection of one of his trusted lieutenants and promised to follow himself. In 800 he arrived at Rome and in full synod pronounced the Pope innocent of certain charges of which he had been accused. According to a reliable authority[1] we learn that the Council decided to make Charlemagne Emperor and the Pope agreed. The passage runs:

> and because the name of the Emperor had now ceased among the Greeks and their Empire was possessed by a woman it then seemed to both Leo the Pope himself and to all the Holy Fathers who were present in the assembled Council as well as to the rest of the Christian people that they ought to take to be Emperor Charles King of the Franks who held Rome herself where the Caesars had been wont to sit and all the other regions which he held from Italy and Gaul and Germany; and inasmuch as God had given all these lands into his hand it seemed right that with the help of God and with the prayer of the whole Christian people he should have the name of Emperor also.

On Christmas Day 800, which was two days after the Council had come to their decision, Charlemagne went to the Basilica and there was crowned. Bryce[2] describes this occasion, which was the start of the political union between the Chair of St Peter and the Teutonic Crown, as 'the central event of the Middle Ages'. His description of the coronation is worth quoting in full:

> On the spot where now the gigantic dome of Bramante and Michael Angelo towers over the buildings of the modern city, the spot which tradition had hallowed as that of the Apostle's martyrdom, Constantine the Great had erected the oldest and stateliest temple of Christian Rome. Nothing could be less like than was this basilica of those northern cathedrals, shadowy, fantastic, irregular, crowded with pillars, fringed all round by clustering shrines and chapels, which are to most of us the types of mediaeval architecture. In its plan and decoration, the spacious sunny hall, the roof plain as that of a Greek temple, the long row of Corinthian columns, the vivid mosaics on its walls, in its brightness, its sternness, its simplicity, it had preserved every feature of Roman art, and had remained a perfect expression of Roman character. Out of the transept a flight of steps led up to the High Altar underneath and just beyond the great arch of triumph as it was called: behind in the semi-circular apse sat the clergy, rising tier above tier around its walls; in the midst, high above the rest, and looking down past the altar over the multitude, was the bishop's throne, itself the curule chair of some forgotten magistrate. From that chair the Pope now rose, as the reading of the Gospel ended, advanced to where Charles, who had exchanged his simple Frankish dress for the sandals and chlamys of a Roman patrician, knelt in prayer by the high altar, and as in the sight of all he placed upon the brow of the barbarian chieftain the diadem of the Caesars, then bent in obeisance before him, the church rang to the shouts of the multitude, again free, again the lords and centre of the world. 'To Charles Augustus, crowned by God, the great and peace-giving Emperor, be life and victory.' In that shout, echoed by the Franks without, was pronounced the

---

[1] *Annals of Lauresheim.*   [2] Lord Bryce: *The Holy Roman Empire*, London 1904.

union, so long in preparation, so mighty in its consequences, of the Roman and the Teuton, of the memories and the civilisation of the South with the fresh energy of the North, and from that moment modern history begins.

But the impression which the three contemporary accounts leave is essentially the same. They all show how hard it is to give a technical character to the transaction as an act either of conquest or of election. The Frankish King does not of his own might seize the crown but rather receives it as coming naturally to him, as the legitimate consequence of the authority he already enjoyed. The Pope bestows the crown, not in virtue of any right of his own as head of the Church; he is merely the instrument of God's providence, which has unmistakably pointed out Charles as the proper person to defend and lead the Christian Commonwealth. The Roman people do not formally choose and appoint but by their applause accept the chief who is presented to them. The act is conceived of as directly ordered by the Divine Providence which has brought about a state of things that admits of but one issue, an issue which king, priest and people have only to recognise and obey: their personal ambitions, passions, intrigues, sinking and vanishing in reverential awe at what seems the immediate interposition of Heaven.

Charlemagne died in 814 and was buried at the Basilica of St Mary which he had built and endowed at Aix-la-Chapelle (Aachen), his favourite residence.

Considerable controversy has arisen around the question of Charlemagne's coronation and it is important to our subject to try to determine whether he was crowned with a crown given by the Pope or one in his possession. We can only conjecture, but there are some pointers which suggest that the Pope provided the crown. The most important, perhaps, is that there is no evidence that Charlemagne was consulted beforehand about the coronation, and he declared later[1] that had he known the design of the Pope he would not have gone to church even though it was Christmas Day. According to one of the two contemporary accounts of German origin of the coronation of Charlemagne[2] the Pope placed a golden crown on his head. In another, Roman account[3] written half a century after the event, it is stated that the Pontiff, with his own hands crowned Charlemagne with a very precious crown. The implications are that the crown was a gift bestowed by the Pope. Furthermore, Charlemagne showed his displeasure at the attitude of the Pope by delaying making use of the imperial title for some months. He did not wish it to seem that he held his Empire from the Pope.[4] Ten years later Charlemagne demonstrated his feelings when his youngest and only surviving legitimate son, Louis, was crowned as his successor at Aix on the 11th September 813. Some accounts say that Charlemagne himself placed the crown on Louis' head, others state that, obeying his father's command, Louis took the crown from the altar and placed it on his own head as co-Emperor.

Although Charlemagne had intended his Empire to continue under the supreme authority of one emperor he had divided it into separate kingdoms, each ruled over by a scion of the imperial reigning house. Louis I the Pious (in France *Le Débonnaire*)

---

[1] Einhard: *Vita Caroli.*
[2] *Chronicle of Moissac.*   [3] Anastasius: 'Life of Leo III' in *Vita Pontificum Romanorum.*
[4] Dr F. L. Ganshof: *The Imperial Coronation of Charlemagne. The Theories and Facts,* being the 16th lecture in the David Murray Foundation in the University of Glasgow delivered on 23rd November 1948.

did not possess the qualities to impose his authority. Perhaps to show that papal consecration was necessary Pope Stephen IV journeyed to Rheims and crowned Louis as Emperor in October 816. The Pope brought with him two crowns; one was a golden crown set with jewels which he bestowed upon Louis as a gift *quae Constantini Caesaris antea fuit*[1]; the Pope made a similar gift to the Empress. One authority[2] puts forward the idea that the donation of Constantine was fabricated between the first coronation of Louis in 813 and the second in 816 and the crown bestowed by Pope Stephen IV was, in fact, the very crown which Pope Sylvester I had refused when it was offered to him by Constantine. In July 817 Louis was again crowned at Aix as King of the East Franks. The chaos that marked his reign was continued in that of his eldest son, Lothair I, who was crowned as co-Emperor at Aix in 817 and on 5th April 823 by Pope Pascal I at Rome. His son, Louis II, was crowned King of Italy at Rome by Pope Sergius II on 15th June 844 and as co-Emperor, also at Rome, by Pope Leo IV in 850. According to 'Vita Sergii' in the *Liber Pontificalis* at the coronation in 844 Louis was crowned with a *Spatha b Petri*. On the death of his father in 855 he became sole Emperor and on 18th May 872 he was crowned a second time as Emperor in Rome by Pope Adrian II. On the death of Louis II in 875 Charles the Bald, King of the West Franks and son of Louis I by his second wife, succeeded to the Empire and was crowned King of Italy at Pavia and on 29th December 875 Emperor at Rome by Pope John VIII. In 843 Louis the 'German', the third son of the Emperor Louis I, had received most of the lands east of the Rhine and became King of the East Franks. He is considered by some to be the real founder of the German kingdom. His son, Charles III, the Fat, received from his father the Kingdom of Swabia. He was crowned Emperor in Rome by Pope John VIII in February 881, with a crown from the Treasury of St Peter.[3] While he re-united all the dominions of Charlemagne, his great-grandfather, he was unable to hold the Empire together, was driven out of Italy and deposed at Frankfurt in 887 and he died the following year. Thus ended the legitimate line of Carolingian emperors and the early German kings.

With the assumption of the imperial title the old Teutonic insignia were replaced by those belonging to the imperial dignity. The laurel wreath of the Roman emperor appears on seals and coins though, of course, it was not actually worn. The helmet is replaced by the crown and the lance becomes flagged. We learn from the *Annals of France*, drawn up in the Monastery of Fulda, that after Charles the Bald had been crowned Emperor, he laid aside the crowns and robes of the Kings of the West Franks, his predecessors, for the diadems and vestments of the Greek emperors, clothing himself in robes that touched his heels, over which was a broad baldric that descended to his feet and covered his head with a silken hood on which he placed his crown. The Greek crowns of this period were known as *stemmata*, the main features of which were a rigid gold circlet, the borders of which were often decorated by strings of pearls with precious stones set in a row between, that in front being of outstanding size. The upper rim sometimes carried four or more *fleurons* or other ornaments. A special

---

[1] Eichmann: 'Von der Kaisergewändung im Mittelalter', *Hist. Jahrbuch*, Vol. 58, 1938, p. 276.
[2] Brunner Zeumer: *Die Constantinische Schenkungsurkunde*.
[3] *Brevarium Regum Francorum*, *Monumenta Germanica Historica*.

feature of the *stemmata* of the Eastern emperors was the *pendulae* or *cataseistae*, which it was the exclusive right of the emperor to wear.

Iconographic representations of the early Carolingians are neither very numerous nor reliable guides. They often take conventional forms which the artists had borrowed from earlier Roman examples. Sketches of the celebrated mosaic of the Triclinium of St John Lateran in Rome depict Charlemagne wearing a *stemma* with radii on the upper rim and carrying the sword and banner as royal insignia. The small statuette of an emperor,[1] formerly at Metz and now in the Louvre, shows the emperor wearing a typical *stemma* with four fleurs-de-lis (*Plate 96, a*). In his right hand he carries a sword (which is a XIX-century addition and probably replaced a sceptre) while in his left hand is an orb with a cross. The date of this ornament has not been determined. Contemporary representation of the other Carolingian emperors usually show them wearing *stemmata*.[2] Charles the Bald is sometimes depicted wearing a crown with arches.[3] One seal, of a Bull of Louis II, distinctly shows *cataseistae*. Charles the Bald alone among the Carolingians is sometimes depicted with the orb[4] and was the first to bear the sceptre, which was surmounted by a fleur-de-lis.

In the year 1000 Charlemagne's tomb at Aix was opened by Otto III, and he is said to have found the body of the Emperor sitting on a marble throne robed and crowned with a Book of the Gospels before him on his knee and a golden cross hanging from his neck which Otto unclasped. In 1165 Frederick I transferred Charlemagne's remains to a wooden coffin which fifty years later was placed in a splendid shrine by Frederick II.

A legend, probably of French origin, grew up that the crown, sword and other ornaments were removed from the tomb and subsequently treated as relics. This has been discredited and it is clear that it was never a tradition at Aix, where it was unknown when Petrarch visited Aix in 1333 when the clergy told him of Charlemagne's legends. There are, however, a number of ornaments still preserved which probably belonged to Carolingian times. Among the imperial regalia at Vienna is a weapon known as the Sabre of Charlemagne. By tradition it was said to have been a present from Harun-el-Raschid, whose emissaries, bearing gifts, were received by Charlemagne in 801. Another story was that it was part of the booty obtained from the Avars, but recent research suggests that it came into the regalia at a later date. The French Coronation Sword *Joyeuse* has been claimed to be the Sword of Charlemagne, but, although the hilt may date from that time, the weapon has been restored so many times that it is impossible to identify it in its original form. Among the more curious of Charlemagne's relics still preserved is an ivory horn made from an elephant's tusk given by Harun-el-Raschid. This apparently excited Charlemagne's curiosity and he obtained an elephant from Harun in 802 which died in 810.

---

1 It is usually considered to represent Charlemagne, but it may be Charles the Bald.

2 An early example of this is shown in a miniature in the Book of the Gospels of Charles the Bald in the Treasury at Munich (*Plate 96, d*).

3 *Codex Aureus of St Emmeram. Vivian Bible*. School of Tours, 845–51. *Cod. Paris Bib. Nat. lat 1*, f. 43.

4 *Psalter of Charles the Bald. Cod. Paris Bib. Nat. lat 1152, f. 3 v.*

THE SEPARATION OF THE KINGDOMS OF THE EAST AND WEST FRANKS

AND

THE SAXON DYNASTY

With the extinction of the Carolingian legitimate line in 888, there followed a period of confusion which lasted over sixty years. Charlemagne's Empire was broken up. Arnulf, Duke of Carinthia, an illegitimate descendant of Charlemagne, was chosen King of the East Franks by the Germans: Odo, or Eudes, Count of Paris and son of Robert the Fat, was elected King of the West Franks. Thereafter the East and West Frankish kingdoms were separated. Rudolph proclaimed himself King of Transjurane Burgundy, and Boso, son-in-law of Louis II, became King of Cisjurane Burgundy. Southern Italy still accepted the Emperor of Constantinople, while Berengar of Friuli was chosen King of Lombardy, but was overcome by Wido of Spoleto who became King of Italy and was crowned Emperor at Rome in 891. When he died in 894, his son, Lambert, was crowned Emperor by the Pope. Pope Formosus summoned Arnulf to deliver him from the power of these upstarts. He reached Pavia, where he was crowned King of Italy in 894 but was forced to retreat. In 895 he made another expedition and stormed Rome where he was crowned Emperor by Formosus in the following year. Seized with paralysis, he returned to Bavaria, where he died in 899 and was succeeded by his son, Louis the Child, on whose death in 911 the Carolingian line came to an end.

In Germany, Conrad Duke of Franconia was then chosen King of the East Franks, and on his death Henry the Fowler, Duke of the Saxons, succeeded and laid the foundations of a stable German monarchy. He was the great-grandson of Charlemagne through a female line. Meanwhile Louis III, the Blind, son of Boso, King of Burgundy, procured the imperial title and was crowned Emperor in Rome in February 901 by Pope Benedict IV, but he was captured by Berengar, blinded and returned to his kingdom where he retained his hollow imperial title until his death in 928.

Berengar was crowned Emperor in Rome in 915 with a crown from the Treasury of St Peter.[1] He died in 924, the last of these phantom emperors. Hugh of Burgundy seized the crown of Italy but was forced to flee from Rome without having been crowned. On his death his son, Lothair, became King of Italy, and in 951 Berengar II, who had usurped the crown of Italy, endeavoured to marry Lothair's widow, Adelaide, to his son Adalbert. The Queen refused, was thrown into prison but escaped and appealed to Otto the German king. Otto responded and defeated Berengar, who was compelled to hold his kingdom as a vassal of the East Frankish crown. Otto's first wife, Edith, the grand-daughter of Alfred the Great of England, having died, he married Queen Adelaide himself.

Information about the ceremony of the investiture of the early German kings is very scanty. It seems that Louis the Child underwent a non-ecclesiastical ceremony at Bamberg in the year 900 at which he received a crown. His successor Conrad I, according to three accounts, was anointed in 911 and thus was the first King of the

---

1 *Gesta Berengarii in Monumenta Germanica Historica.*

East Franks to be consecrated. Henry I refused to be anointed after his election but nevertheless wore a crown which had been sent to him by Conrad. The coronation of Otto I at Aix in 936 was probably the first church coronation of a German king. It was carried out according to the practice already established by the West Franks. He was anointed and crowned and invested with sword, ring, sceptre and staff, bracelets and mantle. Henry I had acquired a very precious object known as the Holy Lance. It was once the insignia of the Kingdom of Lombardy, and according to Pope John VIII, writing in 879 to the Archbishop of Milan, the possession of the Italian kingdom was necessary for the attainment of the imperial dignity. Apart from its importance as a royal ornament it was much revered as a relic, as one of the Holy Nails of the Cross was inserted in it. Rudolph of Burgundy acquired the Holy Lance from Samson, Count of Upper Italy. Henry I made strenuous efforts to obtain the Holy Lance and even threatened Rudolph with war, as a result of which Rudolph prudently handed it over, probably in 935. The Holy Lance then superseded another lance which had been handed over to Henry with a crown as a token of his right to the succession by the dying King Conrad I. Henry died before he could be crowned emperor, to be succeeded by his son Otto. During Otto's reign the Holy Lance gained great prestige as an invincible weapon in battle. It was placed on the cross-beam of the imperial cross, except when carried in procession before the king when it was mounted on a shaft. It was given the credit for the victory of Birten in 939, while at the Battle of Lechfeld in 955 Otto grasped it in his hand and defeated the Hungarians, who had become the Terror of Europe, and his army greeted him with a shout of *Imperator, patra, patriae.*

There is an even greater paucity of information or pictorial representation of the regalia of the pre-Ottonian period than in the Carolingian era. On their seals the emperors are usually shown in conventional or stylised forms with the dress and insignia of Roman emperors. In the case of Arnulf the Emperor bears an orb which is now surmounted by a cross on a long stem. There is no reason to suppose, however, that an orb was actually included in the regalia. German kings are depicted wearing *stemmata* and with a spear and shield.

Otto I had already in 951 assumed the title of the King of the Lombards, and in 960 Pope John XII, who was hard-pressed by Berengar II, invited him to go to Italy, promising to crown him Emperor. Otto began to make preparations for the journey, but it was not until 961 that he reached Pavia and on 2nd February 962 he was crowned by the Pope, John XII, with his Queen Adelaide in the church of St John Lateran. After the coronation Otto confirmed the rights and privileges which had been conferred on the Papacy while the Romans promised obedience. Pope John took an oath of fidelity to the new Emperor, but he did not keep his word and Otto ordered his deposition and appointed Leo VIII in his stead. The Romans were compelled to swear that they would elect no further Pope in future without the imperial consent, and in 966 this was confirmed by Leo VIII.

In 972, after some difficult negotiations, Otto succeeded in obtaining the consent of the Eastern Emperor, John Tzimiskes, to the marriage of his son, Otto II, to Theophano, daughter of the Emperor Romanus II. Otto I died in 973 and was buried at Magdeburg. He was succeeded by his son who had been chosen German King at Worms and crowned at Aix on 26th May 961 at the age of six. On 25th December 967 he was crowned co-Emperor at Rome by Pope John XIII. He died at Rome in 983, a few days before his son Otto III, aged three, was crowned German King at Aix on 25th December, the news not having reached the Germans until after the ceremony. During the new King's minority, the government of Germany was in the hands of his mother, the Byzantine Princess Theophano, who exercised a strong influence on her son. When he was fifteen he came of age, crossed the Alps and was recognised and probably crowned as King of the Lombards at Pavia. He proceeded to Rome, where he was crowned Emperor by Pope Gregory V on 25th May 996.

Otto III, who had an erratic and contradictory character, dreamed of making Rome once more the capital of an Empire which included both the Roman and Byzantine realms. He nominated a succession of popes of whom Gregory V was a German and a cousin, and Sylvester II was French and his tutor. He introduced the feudal system into Rome and the Pope himself treated it with favour. The simple German Court was transformed by the elaborate ceremonial of the Byzantine Court,[1] which he adopted although it gave offence to his German courtiers. In the year 1000, the millennium of the birth of Christ, Otto III went to Aix and opened the tomb of Charlemagne. Two years later Otto died unexpectedly in Italy at the age of twenty-two, in the year 1002, leaving no direct heir. His kinsman, Henry II, surnamed the Saint, a grandson of Henry the Fowler, now sought the German throne. Archbishop Heribert of Cologne brought the Emperor's body, together with the imperial insignia, to Aix. Henry II demanded from the archbishop, by right of inheritance, the *insignie regnis*. When the archbishop hesitated he was arrested and Henry took possession of the imperial regalia, except for the Holy Lance which the archbishop had sent on ahead. Henry II was elected King at Mainz and crowned there on 7th June 1002. In 1001 he had married Kunigunde, daughter of Siegfried, Count of Luxemburg. As Henry was prevented from taking possession of the kingdom by being enthroned in the Chair of Charlemagne at Aix he received the Holy Lance instead, and investiture with the Lance was repeated later at Merseberg. At this time the Crown and Lance were still considered to be essential emblems of leadership in Germany. Although in May 1004 he went to Italy and was crowned King of the Lombards at Pavia he returned to Germany, and it was not until 14th February 1014 that he was crowned Emperor in Rome by Benedict IV, whom he had recognised as the rightful Pope against a rival. He died in 1024 and was buried at Bamberg, where he had founded and richly endowed a bishopric. Henry was the first to take the title of the King of the Romans after his

---

1 J. B. Bury in his article on the later Roman Empire in the XI edition of the *Encyclopaedia Britannica* states: 'the court ceremonial of Constantinople, which forms such a marked contrast to the ostentatiously simple establishments of Augustus and the Antonines, had in its origin a certain constitutional significance. It was introduced by Aurelian and Diocletian not, we must suppose, from any personal love of display, but rather to dissociate the Emperor from the army at a time when the State had been shaken to its foundations by the predominance of the military elements and the dependence of the Emperor on the soldiers. It was the object of Diocletian to make him independent of all with no more particular relation to the army than to any other elements in the State; the royal court and the inaccessibility of the ruler were calculated to promote this object. The etiquette and ceremonies were greatly elaborated by Justinian and were diligently maintained and developed.'

a   *Drawing of reliquary bust with crown of Otto II.
From Hallesche Heiltumsbuch. Bavarian
National Museum (p. 297)*

b   *Crown attributed to Otto III on crucifix. St Eusebius's
Cathedral, Vercelli (p. 298)*

d   *Crown attributed to Otto III on statue of the Virgin Mary.
The Minster, Essen (p. 298)*

c (left)   *Crown on the bust of St Foy. Abbey of Conques
(pp. 207, 298 and 308)*

a   *Burial crown of Emperor Conrad II (obiit 1039). Speyer Cathedral (p. 302)*

b   *Burial crown of Empress Gisela (obiit 1043). Speyer Cathedral (p. 302)*

c   *Burial crown of Emperor Henry III (obiit 1056). Speyer Cathedral (p. 302)*

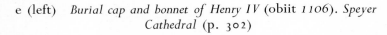

d   *Burial crown of Emperor Henry IV. Speyer Cathedral (p. 302)*

e (left)   *Burial cap and bonnet of Henry IV (obiit 1106). Speyer Cathedral (p. 302)*

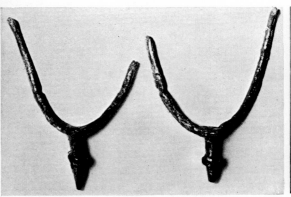

f   *Pair of spurs found in grave of Henry V. Speyer Cathedral (p. 302)*

g   *Burial orb of Emperor Henry III. Speyer Cathedral (p. 302)*

coronation in Germany, which was used subsequently between the time of the German coronation and the coronation at Rome when the title of Emperor was taken.

We have more information about the regalia of the Saxon line of kings and emperors than of any of their predecessors, although there still remain a good many gaps and the evidence is sometimes too slender to make anything certain, but sufficient to justify reasoned argument. In the Metropolitan Museum at New York there is an ivory plaque which is one of a series which probably decorated the antependium of an altar in Magdeburg Cathedral which had been founded by the Emperor Otto I. The plaque shows a figure which is taken to be Otto wearing an imperial crown with an arch (*Plate 96, b*). The Museum authorities consider that it belongs to the second half of the x century and was made in Milan or Reichenau. Some writers have claimed that the crown on Otto's head is unmistakably the Imperial German Crown now in Vienna, but apart from the single arch there is no particular likeness to the peculiar characteristics of the Vienna Crown. Deckerhauf[1] has argued convincingly enough for Schramm and other authorities that the Vienna Crown was made for Otto I. Luitprand of Cremona relates that in 962 Otto arrived for his coronation in Rome *miro ornatu novo apparatus* and that the Emperor's robes were specially made for him. It is considered that the new ornaments were borrowed from those worn by the High Priests in the Old Testament and include the celestial mantle with *tintinnabulae* described in the Wisdom of Solomon, xviii,24: 'For in the long garment was the Holy Word and in the four rows of the stones was the glory of the Fathers graven and Thy Majesty upon the diadem of His Head.' Among the ornaments so borrowed from the High Priests was the mitre on which was set the crown. It was because of this that the single arch was given to Otto's crown. Otto I and his successors uninterruptedly are represented wearing a crown closed with two arches on their seals. The double-arched crown is also shown but not exclusively in other representations. This matter and questions relating to the Vienna Crown will be discussed later. Otto II and his Greek wife, Theophano, are shown on an ivory relief of Byzantine work[2] wearing Byzantine imperial crowns with *cataseistae*, but as the object is by a Greek artist it may not be representative of the actual ornaments they used but those which he remembered being in use at the Court of Constantinople. Nevertheless it is possible that Theophano had possessed a Byzantine crown and fragments of it may have been used to decorate a cover of a Book of the Gospels of Henry II (*Plate 96, c*) formerly in the cathedral at Bamberg. This has an elaborate decoration including twelve enamelled plaques bearing portraits in the Byzantine style which may have once formed part of a crown. A useful piece of evidence of one type of crown in use at that period is a very careful drawing in the *Hallesche Heiltumsbuch* of a crown that adorned a reliquary bust of Otto II (*Plate 97, a*) in the Monastery of Berge. This monastery was founded by Otto I, but according to the *Hallesche Heiltumsbuch* of 1520 the crown had belonged to Otto II. This was probably recorded as a tradition which existed in the monastery to the effect that the crown was a bequest from Otto II. Technical opinion considers the filigree work to belong to

---

1 Hansmartin Deckerhauf: *Herrschaftszeichen und Staatssymbolik*, Ch. 25.
2 In the Cluny Museum, Paris, No. 1035.

the x or xi centuries, though other details suggest an earlier date. Rademacher[1] suggests that it came from the same workshop as the earliest of the Essen crosses which were a gift of the Abbess Mathilda who was the grand-daughter of Otto I. The crown is a rigid open gold circlet bordered by rows of small pearls and precious stones with larger stones set between. From the circlet rise large ornaments at the front and sides with small ornaments set between. The ornament in front is of special interest as it consists of a lily mounted on round ornaments. The earliest examples of lilies on crowns date from the ix century[2] but the round ornaments are of a later date, probably from the middle of the x to the middle of the xi centuries. The arrangement of four precious stones on the round ornament, together with the large stone in the centre of the brow band, could be taken to represent a cross. Rademacher suggests that the crown must have been made between 961, when Otto II was made King of Germany, and 967, when he was crowned Emperor. This need not necessarily have been the case, especially when it is remembered that Otto was only six when he was crowned at Aix and thirteen when he was crowned Emperor. It was probably made as the Emperor's personal crown by the Byzantine artists who had been brought to the imperial court as a result of his marriage in the year 972 to Princess Theophano. The reliquary bust is of much later date, probably the first third of the xiv century. As the crown is shown to fit the bust closely, the bust was probably made for the purpose. Another crown of the Ottonian period is on the head of a crucifix in the Cathedral of St Eusebius at Vercelli (*Plate 97, b*). It is a gold circlet covered with filigree work on which are set a number of precious stones. In the front is a large cross affixed to the inside of the circlet. The crown is said to date from about the year 1000 and it is thought that it may have been presented by Otto III, who made his Logothete, Leo, Bishop of Vercelli and bestowed many favours upon the Church there. There is in the Minster at Essen a statue of the Madonna on which is a small crown 12.5 cm in diameter (*Plate 97, d*). It is considered by art historians to be work of the end of the x century. The crown is a gold circlet richly set with precious stones between two rows of pearls and with four fleurs-de-lis on the rim. It is, in fact, the earliest fleur-de-lis crown still extant. One authority[3] suggests that it was the crown with which Otto III was crowned when three years old on Christmas Day 983. Otto III's sister was the abbess of the convent at Essen.

When Henry II went to Rome for his imperial coronation in 1014 he took with him a crown which he gave to the altar of St Peter and was crowned with a new crown presented by the Pope. It was on this occasion that we first come across an actual orb. Pope Benedict VIII ordered an orb and sceptre to be made for the coronation. The golden globe was girdled by a jewelled band and surmounted by a cross. The Pope presented Henry II with this orb with the admonition that it represented the earth ruled by the Cross which the Emperor would rule over in a manner deserving the Cross's protection. Henry accepted the ornament and thanked the Pope. Subsequently Henry

---

[1] F. Rademacher: 'Eine Krone Kaiser Ottos II' in *Deutches Verein für Kunstwissenschaft*, Journal, I, 79, 1934.

[2] The Crown on St Foy at Conques (*Plate 97, c*). Crown on the Statue of the Virgin at Essen is an early extant example.

[3] Professor Hermann Schnitzler: Director of the Schnütgen Museum in Cologne.

gave his imperial coronation crown, the sceptre, the orb, his golden vestment and a crucifix to the Monastery of Cluny.[1] In 1030, during a great famine, the monks broke up these ornaments and distributed the proceeds to the poor. In the Treasury at Munich is the crown attributed to the Empress Kunigunde, consort of Henry II, and this is dealt with elsewhere.[2] At the coronation of Henry II the celestial mantle and the bracelets, which were an old German royal ornament, were used for the last time. We have already mentioned that Otto I probably introduced the imperial mitre among his coronation ornaments. Eichmann states that the oldest document of a mitration of an emperor by the Pope occurs in the *ordo* of the crowning of emperors named after Censius which he considers to date from Ottonian times.

On the death of Henry II in 1024 the Saxon line of German kings and emperors came to an end. A great assembly of the German princes was held early in September 1024 on the banks of the Rhine below Worms and Conrad, Duke of Franconia, was chosen as German King. After his election Kunigunde, widow of Henry II, sent the new King her late husband's insignia. He was known as Conrad II and because he was a descendant, through a female line, of Otto the Great and Charlemagne he was surnamed the Salic or Salian. At his election he gained the decisive support of the German bishops, especially Aribo, Archbishop of Mainz, who crowned him in his cathedral on 8th September but refused to crown his wife Gisela, widow of Ernest I, Duke of Swabia, because she was within the prohibited degrees of affinity. Gisela was crowned at Aix by Pilgrim, Archbishop of Cologne, some days later. In 1026 Conrad was crowned King of Lombardy at Pavia and on 26th March 1027, in the presence of the Kings of Burgundy and Denmark, was crowned Emperor at Rome by Pope John XIX.

An important event of Conrad's reign was the accession of Burgundy to the Empire. The last king, Rudolph III, had promised the succession to the Emperor Henry II, but did not extend this promise to Conrad on Henry's death. Tumult followed but in 1028 at Basle Rudolph met Conrad and promised him the succession. In September 1030 Rudolph died and Conrad marched into Burgundy and took the Burgundian crown at Peterlingen (Payerne) in 1033, driving out his rival Odo, Count of Champagne. He was recognised in 1034 at Geneva by a great assembly of nobles of Germany, Burgundy and Italy, a ceremony sometimes referred to as a second coronation. Conrad died in 1039 and was buried in the cathedral at Speyer, the building of which he had begun. According to *Vita Hugonis Abbatis*[3] Conrad gave his *insignia quae romane gestabet* to the Monastery at Cluny, where in 1030 it shared the fate of the ornaments given by

---

1 Cluny was a great Benedictine monastery founded in 910 which became the centre of a revival and reform of monasteries and by the middle of the XII century the head of 314 monasteries in all parts of Europe and the Holy Land and the abbot had entire control of all the monks, sometimes estimated at 10,000, in these houses. Its influence was even more widespread. Although supporting the religious and ecclesiastical reforms of Hildebrand in the struggle between the Empire and the Papacy, the abbots of Cluny managed to steer a middle course. From the middle of the X century to the middle of the XII century the Abbot of Cluny was the most important and powerful ecclesiastic after the Pope in the Roman Church. It is not surprising, therefore, that the emperors, especially of the Saxon and Franconian line, treated the abbot with great respect, and there are several instances of royal ornaments being presented to the abbey: e.g. the orb and crown of Henry II and the crown of Conrad II.

2 See Chapter Two—Bavaria.   3 *Acta Sanctorum III.*

Henry II. It was during Conrad's reign that the present arch and cross on the Vienna Crown was added. Deckerhauf suggests it was because the old arch was damaged but it may have been for dynastic reasons.

Henry III, surnamed the Black, was the only son of Conrad II and had been designated his father's successor in 1026 and crowned at Aix on 14th April 1028. In 1038 his father formally handed over to him the Kingdom of Burgundy, although he was only given the title of *Dux et rector Burgundiae*. He was crowned at Arles in 1042, but it was not until 1046 that he was crowned at Milan, and after deposing two rival popes and forcing another to resign, was crowned Emperor on the 25th December by his nominee, Pope Clement II. He had been given by Pope Gregory VI a *preciosissum diadema*.[1] He was recognised by the Romans as hereditary patrician and wore the emblems of the office—the green mantle and golden circlet. Henry was granted by a Roman Synod the right of nominating the popes and used his power to appoint a succession of Germans to the Holy See. Thereafter the title of a German king to receive the imperial crown was never seriously disputed. Henry died in 1056 and was succeeded by his son, Henry IV, who at the age of three had been chosen German King at Tribur and crowned at Aix on 17th July 1054.

Henry's long minority, the manner in which he was brought up and his personal failings ill-fitted him for a contest with such a formidable opponent as Hildebrand, who had become Pope as Gregory VII. The Pope issued his famous decree that was to enforce the celibacy of the clergy, the extinction of simony and the prohibition of lay investiture of the clergy. Henry countered this attempt to undermine the imperial authority by calling a synod of German bishops who declared the Pope deposed. Gregory replied by excommunicating Henry. The Imperial Diet decided that Henry should be tried by an assembly under the Presidency of the Pope. This combination of both temporal and spiritual forces was too much for the King. He decided to submit and humiliated himself before the Pope, who absolved him. Gregory proclaimed that to the Pope, as God's Vicar, all mankind was subject, all rulers were responsible and that he who gave the crown had the right to excommunicate and depose. Henry's respect and power was thus weakened in Germany and on his return there from Italy he found that Rudolph, Duke of Swabia, had been chosen German King and on 27th March 1077 had been crowned at Mainz. In the succeeding wars, Rudolph, who was supported by the German bishops and princes, while Henry commanded the loyalty of the cities and the people, gained victories. Gregory again excommunicated Henry, who on three occasions declared the Pope deposed and succeeded in having Clement III elected as anti-Pope. Rudolph was finally beaten and slain in 1080 and Henry descended on Italy to obtain the imperial coronation. He was crowned King of Lombardy at Pavia in 1081, but it was not until 1084 that he entered Rome and, having received the patrician authority and having been presented with a crown by the Romans, was crowned Emperor by Pope Clement III. We learn[2] that the Pope had in his possession a crown designed for the imperial coronation. In the following year Gregory died in exile.

Meanwhile Henry's opponents had chosen Hermann, Count of Luxemburg, in

---

[1] *Ottonis frisingensis Chronicle VI.*
[2] *Bernoldis 1083. Monumenta Germanica Historica,* ss. 5.

Henry's stead, but he found Henry too strong for him and failed to get himself crowned. A third anti-king, Egbert Margrave of Meissen, was chosen but was murdered in 1090 and peace then ensued in Germany.

In Italy, where the Papacy remained his implacable enemy, there was further trouble and Henry's son, Conrad, who had been crowned King of the Germans at Aix in 1087, was persuaded to oppose his father and was crowned King of Lombardy in Monza in 1093. But in 1098 the Pope declared Conrad deposed and chose the Emperor's son Henry V as German King, and he was crowned at Aix on 6th January 1099. Although he promised to take no part in the affairs of the Empire during his father's lifetime, the younger Henry led a revolt against his father, who was taken prisoner in 1105 and forced to abdicate. He escaped but died in 1106 at Liège, where he was buried. The body was removed, however, to Speyer, where it was placed in an unconsecrated grave until 1111 when the sentence of excommunication was cancelled and the remains were interred in the cathedral which he had reconstructed on a magnificent scale.

Under Henry V the struggle over the investitures continued. Despite the expostulations of Pope Pascal II, the German King continued to invest bishops with ring and crozier. Henry went to Italy with a large army and entered Rome, where he took the usual oaths, and on 12th February 1111 presented himself at St Peter's to receive the Imperial Crown. The text of the Treaty which Henry had made with the Pope in which he renounced the rights of investiture in return for coronation and the restoration to the Empire of all lands given by German kings and emperors to the German Church since the time of Charlemagne was read out, and amidst a tumult the Pope refused to crown the King. Henry thereupon seized Pascal and the cardinals and carried them away from the city, whereupon the Pope relented and having confirmed the rights of investiture, promised to crown the King, which he did on 13th April 1111. Henry was crowned with a heavy imperial crown consisting of seven lilies and a cross which later his widow Mathilda brought to England. By 1116, however, Pascal had withdrawn his consent to lay investiture and excommunicated Henry, who, however, drove him from Rome and was crowned Emperor a second time by Burdinas, Archbishop of Braga. In 1122 by the Concordat of Worms a compromise was made and Henry renounced the right of investiture with ring and crozier but was allowed the right of investing with the sceptre in respect of the estates of the Church held under the Crown. Henry died at Utrecht in 1125 and was buried at Speyer. He was married to Mathilda of England, but there were no children and the line of Franconian or Salian emperors became extinct.

The portraiture of the Franconian emperors shows the development of the regalia. On most coins and seals the crown continues to be depicted as a closed *stemma*, although in some cases it is an open circlet. But the single arch worn from ear to ear which first appeared in the reign of Henry II persists in respect of Conrad II and Henry III.[1] The sceptre surmounted by a bird appears for the first time on the seals of Conrad II and is

---

1 Conrad II. Fresco in the choir apse, Cathedral of Aquilega, Northern Italian work of 1031. *Book of the Gospels of Henry III*, Echternach School, c. 1046 Upsala University Library, f. 3, V. MS. in the *Book of the Gospels* Reichenauer School mid-xi century (*Berlin Kupferstichkab.* 78, A 2, f. 1a).

repeated in the portraiture of all four emperors and on a seal of the anti-king Rudolph. At first the bird had open wings but later they have become closed.

In the *Hildesheim Annals* of 1031 and in the *Acta Ezonis*, it is related that Conrad II was sent two crowns by Queen Richenza of Poland (who was a German princess), one of which belonged to her and the other to her husband, King Michael II. In the year 1000 Otto III had anticipated the Pope making Boleslav Chrobry, Duke of Poland, a king by himself placing a crown on the Duke's head. In 1025 Boleslav was again crowned in the cathedral at Gnesen by the archbishop, and on his death in 1027 Michael II crowned himself and his wife Richenza. The ecclesiastical coronation of 1025 was considered in Germany to have been an injury to his overlord the Emperor, and Michael had to return his father's crown to the Emperor. There is no record of what happened to these crowns.

In August 1900 the imperial graves in Speyer Cathedral were opened and the remains were removed to a new mausoleum. In the coffins were found a number of royal ornaments of great importance and interest as being among the oldest still preserved. They are now kept in the crypt of the cathedral. The burial ornaments of the Franconian emperors and empresses included:

Conrad II (obiit 1039)

A crown (*Plate 98, a*) consisting of a circlet of copper gilt, to the upper rim of which are riveted a cross and three trefoil ornaments. On the circlet is inscribed: *PACIS ET URBIS AMATOR.* A mantle and hose of patterned silk.

The Empress Gisela (obiit 1043)

A circlet (*Plate 98, b*) of copper with a cross and three fleurs-de-lis riveted to the upper edge. On the circlet is the inscription: *GISELA IMPERATRIX.*

Henry III (obiit 1056)

A crown (*Plate 98, c*) in the form of a circlet of copper gilt surmounted by four fleurs-de-lis. On the lower edges are two protruding pieces of copper. An orb of wood (*Plate 98, g*) covered with leather surmounted by a cross.

Henry IV (obiit 1106)

A crown of copper gilt (*Plate 98, d*) surmounted by four fleurs-de-lis and with a single arch from back to front. Inside the crown was a bonnet of silk with a broad brow-band and two bands of gold embroidery resembling arches on a crown (*Plate 98, e*); a gold ring with a sapphire and pearls inscribed: *ADALBERO EPS.*

Henry V (obiit 1125)

A lead cross which was probably on the funeral crown. A pair of iron spurs sprinkled with gold (*Plate 98, f*).

The spurs in Henry V's grave are the first example of such ornaments to be found as part of the regalia. The crowns of Conrad and Gisela are the earliest extant known to bear a cross on the circlet. The crown of Henry II is the oldest extant with a single arch while the orb of Henry III is the oldest that is still preserved. It is to be noted that in none of the graves was there a sceptre.

On the death of Henry V, his young widow Mathilda inherited the Emperor's crowns and other treasure. The Archbishop of Cologne succeeded in obtaining the German crown and other ornaments which were regarded as the imperial insignia, in order to strengthen his support of Lothair of Supplinburg against the candidature of Frederick of Swabia as German King. Mathilda shortly afterwards left Germany for England. She took with her a considerable treasure including a number of royal ornaments and vestments, which were considered to have been the late Emperor's personal possessions. These she intended to go to the Benedictine monastery of Bec Hellouin at Rouen. Included in these possessions was not only a substantial part of the crown treasure but valuables from the imperial chapel.[1] The imperial mantles were afterwards converted to liturgical use at Bec Hellouin. The inventory mentions two golden crowns one of which is described as:

> a crown of massive gold and precious stones with which the imperial son, Henry, was later crowned King, so heavy was it that when the King or Emperor is crowned with it, it is borne to and fro supported by two silver rods. It requires the full strength of a man's two arms when it is taken up to the treasury strong room. However, when once it is placed on the brow of the wearer a stone of great price and size is worn along with a cross of solid gold. In like manner is there another small golden crown which the Emperor uses on important feast days.

We know from the description of the coronation of Henry V that the crown was composed of a cross and seven lilies. Mathilda gave her husband's crown to her son Henry II of England who was crowned with it in 1135 and thereafter it was used as the coronation crown of the early Plantagenet Kings of England.

The choice of the successor to Henry V led to a protracted election. The House of Hohenstaufen had supported Henry IV, while Lothair, Count of Supplinburg, had supported Henry V against his father, and as a reward was made Duke of Saxony. The efforts of Adalbert, Archbishop of Mainz, and the supporters of the Papacy succeeded in obtaining the election of Lothair at Mainz on 30th August 1125. Lothair was crowned King at Aix on 13th September 1125. The King claimed some of the Hohenstaufen estates of the late Emperor as Crown property but Frederick the One-Eyed, Duke of Swabia and Lothair's unsuccessful rival to the kingship, and his brother Conrad (later the Emperor Conrad III) resisted and civil war followed.

At the behest of Pope Innocent II, who visited the King at Liège, Lothair went to Rome accompanied by Innocent. As St Peter's was in the hands of the anti-Pope Anacletus II, Lothair was crowned Emperor by Innocent in the Lateran Church on 4th June 1133. Subsequently he received as Papal fiefs the extensive estates of Mathilda, Marchioness of Tuscany. Lothair was submissive to the Pope and was the first emperor to perform the menial service of holding his stirrup at his coronation. It seems that the Pope claimed the Emperor as his vassal, as is shown by the inscription: *Post homo fit papae sumit quo dante coronam* in the audience hall of the Lateran Palace in Rome. Although Lothair was acknowledged vassal of Eric II, King of Denmark, and Boleslav III, Prince of Poland over tribute, while the Byzantine Emperor John Comnenus implored his aid against the King of Sicily, the power of the German monarchy was in

---

1 An inventory will be found in Etienne of Rouen's *Draco Normannicus*, edited by R. Howlett.

decay. Most noteworthy was the enhanced position and independence of the German princes and dukes. The part they played in choosing Lothair as King was an important development in the election of emperors.

THE SWABIAN AND HOHENSTAUFEN DYNASTY

Conrad III, Duke of Swabia, had, on the death of Henry V, become titular King of Burgundy. During the civil wars Lothair had gained the support of Henry the Proud, Duke of Bavaria, by giving his daughter Gertrude in marriage and granting him the administration of the Kingdom of Burgundy. Conrad thereupon obtained his election as German King in opposition to Lothair on 18th December 1127 and was acknowledged in Northern Italy and crowned at Monza in June 1128. He came to terms with Lothair in 1135 and on the Emperor's death he was again chosen King at Coblenz on 7th March 1138 in the presence of the Papal Legate and crowned at Aix six days later. The imperial insignia were in the possession of Henry the Proud, and when the new King demanded them to be handed over the Duke in return asked for his investiture with the Saxon Duchy, which Conrad was unwilling to give. There were further internal struggles in Germany and Henry IV and his son, Henry the Lion, disputed Conrad's title. In 1146, despite the confusion within the Empire, Conrad, having secured the election and coronation of his younger son Henry, took the cross and went to the East, not returning until 1149. Although he had repeated invitations from the Romans to take the Imperial Crown, it was not until the end of his reign that he agreed to go, but he died in 1152 at Bamberg before the preparations for the journey had been completed.

Conrad's son, Henry, who had been crowned King in 1146, had died and the Emperor passed over his second son owing to his youth and nominated Frederick II, Duke of Swabia, as his successor. The princes accepted Conrad's advice and chose Frederick early in March 1152 at Frankfurt, and the new King was crowned at Aix on 9th March. Frederick I, surnamed Barbarossa, was one of the greatest German kings and emperors; his reputation has been passed down in history as a great national hero. He was anxious to restore the Empire to the position at which it had stood under Charlemagne and Otto the Great.[1] His first task was to restore order in Germany; his second to come to terms with the Pope. A treaty between Frederick and Pope Eugenius III was made at Constance in 1553. The Pope undertook to crown Frederick as Emperor provided that the King promised not to make peace with Roger II, King of Sicily, nor with the rebellious Romans and to defend the Papacy. When Frederick

---

[1] Frederick I added to the customary title 'Roman Empire' the epithet of 'Holy'. It is sometimes suggested that there was an earlier origin of the use of the title 'Holy Roman Empire' but there is no documentary trace. The first occasion on which it occurs is believed to be in the Privilege of Austria granted by Frederick in the fourth year of his reign and the second of his Empire, which says: *Terram Austriae quae clypeus et cor sacri imperii esse dinoscitur.* (Pertz: *Monumenta Germanica Historica 4.*) The title of 'Holy Roman Empire' was used occasionally by Henry VI and Frederick II and more frequently by their successors until after Charles IV's time when it became habitual and the familiar description in current speech of the Germanic State.

arrived in Italy in 1159 he met the new Pope, Adrian IV,[1] near Nepi. The Pope demanded that the King should hold his stirrup, which he at first refused to do but when Adrian threatened to refuse to crown him, Frederick submitted. The coronation took place at St Peter's on 18th June 1155. On 9th June 1156 the Emperor was married at Würzburg to Beatrix, daughter and heiress of Renaud III, Count of Upper Burgundy. In October 1157 he received the homage of the Burgundian nobles at Besançon. At the ceremony the Legate read out the Papal letter which referred to the Imperial Crown as a benefice confirmed by the Pope, and when in answer to shouts of indignation the Legate (afterwards Pope Alexander III) said: 'From whom then if not from our Lord the Pope can best your King help his Empire', great disorder followed. The situation was restored by Frederick in a manifesto in which he declared that he held the Empire from God alone. In 1158 Alexander III excommunicated Frederick who supported the anti-Pope Victor IV and on his death Pascal III. In 1164 Frederick had his son, Henry, aged four, chosen King at Bamberg in June and crowned at Aix on 15th August. In 1166 Frederick obtained from the anti-Pope the canonisation of Charlemagne, which was celebrated with great magnificence at Aix. Later in the year he procured the enthronement of Pascal, who then crowned his wife Beatrix. In July 1177 Pope Alexander III rescinded the ban of excommunication and made a treaty with Frederick at Venice. Frederick recognised Alexander as the rightful Pope, knelt before him and kissed his feet.[2] The ownership of Mathilda's estates was to be fixed by arbitration. On 30th July 1178 Frederick was crowned King of Burgundy at Arles during an interval of leisure. In 1184 Frederick's son Henry was betrothed to Constance, daughter of Roger I, King of Sicily and aunt and heiress of the reigning William II. This important event, which meant the eventual incorporation of Sicily within the Empire, led to further estrangement with the Papacy and Pope Lucius III refused to crown Henry as co-Emperor. Frederick then staged a great ceremony at Milan where his son Henry was crowned King of Italy and married Constance who was crowned Queen of Germany. In 1188 Frederick took the cross and marched into Asia Minor where he was drowned.

Henry VI was Regent at the time of his father's death which had been shortly preceded by the death of his wife's nephew William II, King of Sicily. In 1190 he obtained a promise from Pope Clement IV to crown him Emperor but by the time he arrived in Rome, Clement had died and had been succeeded by Celestine III, who refused to crown him. With the aid of the Romans and his army Henry persuaded the Pope to change his mind and was crowned as Emperor on 14th April 1191. Meanwhile in Sicily Tancred had been chosen King and was supported by the Pope. Richard I of England, having fallen into captivity in Henry's hands on his return from the crusades, bought his release by paying a huge ransom which Henry used to equip a large army with which he descended on Italy and was crowned King of Sicily at Palermo on 25th December 1194. He then endeavoured to carry out his ambitions of universal Empire. Richard I had acknowledged Henry's supremacy; Henry had presented him with a crown

---

[1] The only Englishman to become Pope.
[2] This scene is represented in a picture in the Great Hall of the Ducal Palace, Venice.

but as he was, at the time, invested with the Kingdom of Burgundy his homage was probably as a fief. Henry claimed Tunis and Tripoli and demanded from the Eastern Emperor the cession of the Balkan Peninsula in return for a promise of aid, while the Kings of Cyprus and Armenia asked for investiture by his hands. Having obtained a reconciliation with the Pope the Emperor sought for the recommendation of his son Frederick as his successor. The German princes did not like this proposal which suggested that the Imperial Crown might become hereditary and feared to become entangled in Italian politics. The Emperor succeeded, however, in obtaining the election of his son Frederick II, aged two years, as German King at Frankfurt in 1196 but was unable to persuade Pope Celestine to crown him King of the Romans. Henry died in 1197 and was buried at Palermo.

Frederick II's election as King was set aside because he was still a child. Philip, Duke of Swabia, Bishop of Würzburg and a brother of Henry VI, was elected German King at Mühausen on 8th March 1198 and crowned at Mainz on 8th September but a number of princes who were hostile to Philip chose as anti-King, Otto, son of Henry the Lion, Duke of Saxony and Mathilda, daughter of Henry II, King of England, who had been brought up at the English Court. He was crowned at Aix on 12th July 1198. Civil war followed but Philip prevailed and was crowned a second time with great pomp at Aix on 6th January 1205. In 1197, having given up his ecclesiastical calling, he had married Irene, daughter of the Eastern Emperor, Isaac Angelus, and widow of Roger II, King of Sicily. On 21st June 1208 Philip was murdered at Bamberg at the instance of Otto of Wittelsbach to whom he had refused to give one of his daughters in marriage.

Otto was now chosen King a second time and betrothed to Philip's second daughter Beatrix. He was crowned Emperor at Rome on 4th October 1209, but a breach with Pope Innocent III followed and in 1210 he was excommunicated and declared deposed by an assembly of German princes. He continued the struggle without success and died in 1218 and was buried at Brunswick.

Frederick II, son of Henry VI, a member of the Hohenstaufen family, with Norman blood running through his veins through his mother Constance, daughter of Roger I, King of Sicily, had been brought up in Sicily which was riven with anarchy. His election as German King in 1196 was ineffective but in 1198 at the age of four he had been crowned King of Sicily. In 1208 he married Constance, daughter of Alphonso II, King of Aragon and widow of Emeric, King of Hungary. On Otto's deposition as German King in 1211, a number of princes met at Nuremberg and invited Frederick to be King. Overcoming the opposition of his wife and the Sicilian nobles and having acknowledged the supremacy of the Pope he caused his son to be crowned King of Sicily and himself proceeded to Germany. On 5th December 1212 he was formally elected German King at Frankfurt and crowned four days later at Mainz. On 25th July 1214, following the liberation of Rhineland, he was again crowned King at Aix and subsequently undertook to go on a crusade. In 1220 he entered Rome and was crowned Emperor on 22nd November. Frederick then returned to Sicily to restore order, and it was not until 1227 that he set out for the Holy Land.

His first wife had died in 1222 and in 1225 he married Yolande, daughter of John,

Count of Brienne, titular King of Jerusalem and Frederick himself took the title of King of Jerusalem. Forced back to Italy by a pestilence which struck his army, the Emperor was excommunicated by Pope Gregory IX. After the death of his second wife Isabella in 1228 he set out again to the Holy Land securing Jerusalem where he crowned himself King on 18th March 1229 and the following year returned to Italy.

Meanwhile in Germany Frederick's elder son, Henry, had been Regent; however, disapproving of the Privilege of Worms of 1231 by which Frederick had made the German princes virtually independent sovereigns, he rebelled but was captured by Frederick. In 1237 Frederick's second son Conrad, afterwards Conrad IV, was elected German King, which act was subsequently confirmed by a Diet at Speyer, and he ruled Germany in his father's absence. A great Diet was held at Mainz in August 1238 at which Frederick married Isabella, daughter of John, King of England. There followed a prolonged quarrel with the Papacy and Frederick was twice more excommunicated. In June 1245 he was deposed at the Pope's instigation and the princes in 1246 chose Henry Raspe, Margrave of Thuringia, as anti-King, but when he died in 1247, William, Count of Holland, was chosen as his successor. But the Hohenstaufen rule in Germany continued. At this time, when Frederick seemed to be at the zenith of his power, two disasters overtook him in Italy. Despite some success with his efforts to restore his fortunes the great Emperor retired to Southern Italy and died on 13th December 1250. He was buried at Palermo Cathedral.

Frederick had by his will nominated his son Conrad to succeed him in Sicily and Germany and his son Henry, by Isabella of England, to the kingdoms of Jerusalem and Burgundy, neither of which, however, he was able to obtain. Conrad was acknowledged in Germany but in 1251 he went to Italy and was engaged in fighting until his death in 1254. His youthful son Conradin made a bid for the Kingdom of Sicily but was defeated, captured and beheaded. Thus the great house of Hohenstaufen was extinguished and Italy was inextricably lost to the Empire. In Germany the prodigal disposal of the property of the Crown, particularly by Philip and Otto IV in order to gain adherence to their causes, led to the weakening of the central authority and a gain in power to the princes, while the Privilege of Worms had virtually led to a breakdown in the German kingdom.

Lord Bryce in his *Holy Roman Empire* writes:

> With Frederick fell the Empire. From the ruin that overwhelmed the greatest of its houses it emerged living indeed and destined to a long life but so shattered, crippled and degraded it never more could be to Europe and to Germany what it once had been.

It was during the period of the Hohenstaufens that many questions connected with the regalia became regularised. The lily crown which was originally introduced by Constantine the Great had been adopted in Western Europe and developed. It was used by the French and German kings and introduced into England at the time of Edgar. Other kingdoms followed suit and the fleur-de-lis was recognised as a royal and imperial badge. But the heyday of lily crowns was in the period subsequent to the battle of Bouvines in 1214 when the French King, Philip Augustus, defeated the Emperor Otto IV and the prestige of the French crown became pre-eminent. The oldest existing lily crown is that on the Madonna at Essen, which has already been described. But the arched crown had also been introduced into Western Europe in the IX century. Schramm[1] has drawn attention to drawings by Peiresc of an arched crown which King Boso of Burgundy (*obiit* 887) gave to a bust reliquary of St Maurice in the Cathedral Church of Vienne. From the same source we learn of another drawing also by Peiresc of a second crown which belonged to the bust reliquary of St Maurice at Vienne. This had been the crown of King Hugo of Italy, who died at Arles in 948 and was also an arched crown. We also have the crown of St Foy at Conques (*Plate 97, c*) which although it may not be of royal origin is evidence of a type of crown in use in the middle of the X century. It is not only closed with two arches but also is adorned with the fleur-de-lis.[2] A feature of these double arches was that they were flat and formed a cross on top of the head. This is clearly to be seen when these crowns are looked upon from above and may have been used symbolically to place the cross of Christ on the head of the Lord's Anointed. When Otto I introduced the imperial mitre it was necessary from a practical point of view to have only a single arch which also, instead of being flat, had to rise steeply to go over the mitre. But the single arch does not appear on seals nor was it used frequently iconographically. An imperial double arched crown was developed which had steeply rising arches and was surmounted by a cross and from the time of Conrad III by a globe and cross and this form of crown can be seen on the seals of subsequent reigns. Deér[3] points out that lesser sovereigns and provincial kings had taken unto themselves the lily crown and the arched crown and that it was Lothair III who first stiffened the attitude towards the imperial symbolism of the arch and suggests that the initiative for the Western imperial ceremonial starts with Lothair II, although it was completed by the Hohenstaufens.

Henry VI inherited, through his marriage, the rich treasure of the Norman Kings of Sicily which consisted not only of bars of gold, jewels and rich silk cloth from the celebrated Saracen-Sicilian workshops but many royal ornaments and relics. He had been crowned at Palermo with the Sicilian coronation crown on Christmas Day 1194, and after settling the affairs of the kingdom returned to Germany in 1195. A contemporary writer tells of how the treasure was carried across the Alps by 150 mules. Unfortunately no inventory nor accurate description has come down to us of the treasure Henry VI brought to Germany from Sicily. Some items were dispersed to Bamberg, Halberstadt and other cathedrals by Henry and his successors, while some of the ornaments and vestments may have been used for royal burials. Some of the surviving objects are now in the Vienna Treasury and include the State Sword, which became the Imperial Sword of Ceremony; a girdle of blue silk; a belt for the Sword of St Maurice; the dalmatic; the alb; the gloves; the hose; the shoes decorated with precious stones and the coronation mantle. These were added to the imperial ornaments and relics, the oldest of which had been handed down since the Ottonian period. These include the imperial crown and the imperial cross, the orb, the Sword of St

[1] P. E. Schramm: *Herrschaftszeichen und Staatssymbolik*, Vol. II, p. 398.

[2] Although there is no evidence as to this crown being a royal ornament, the fact that it is adorned with fleurs-de-lis suggests that it had some royal association. (See footnote, p. 98.)

[3] Josef Deér, *Die Abendländische Kaiserkrone des Hochmittelalters*.

Maurice and the Holy Lance. The Emperor frequently took his treasure on his travels and the crown and the cross were placed on a table in the imperial tent, as though on an altar from which Mass was said. At one time the treasure was kept in the Monastery of Limburg in the Hardt. In 1061 it was transferred to the cathedral at Speyer which had just been completed. Later it was brought to the Castle of Trifels where the oldest inventory which exists includes the golden cross with precious stones containing a piece of wood from the True Cross, the golden crown with golden cross, two swords with scabbards decorated with precious stones, the golden orb and cross, the Emperor's mantle decorated with precious stones, three golden spurs, a white mitre, two gloves with precious stones, a velvet coat, two gilded shoes decorated with stones, the lance of St Maurice, Our Lord's Nail and various other relics and small items. Great importance was attached to the possession of the imperial insignia which was considered to strengthen the claim of a candidate to the Empire. Possession of the insignia undoubtedly had a great political significance and influenced the elections. Pretenders struggled to acquire them, legitimate inheritors found their real strength if they possessed them. Importance was also attached to the coronation at Aix which set the seal on the legal and constitutional title of the German King. During the civil wars Aix was sometimes in the hands of the anti-king's party but when liberated the rightful king was at pains to undergo coronation there, even though he might have been crowned before and the imperial insignia may not have been in his possession.

Frederick II, who besides being King of the Romans was King of Sicily and Jerusalem, King of Lombardy and King of Burgundy, had a number of crowns. Mathew Paris relates that:

> when Frederick was deprived of the Imperial Crown he said, full of scorn, 'Where is my pack saddle which contains my portable treasury?', and when it was brought and upon his order opened before his eyes, he said: 'See whether my crowns are already lost.' When one was found he placed it upon his head and crowned stood up and said publicly: 'I have not yet lost my crown.'

Schramm[1] and Deér[2] have dealt very fully with the types of crowns used by Frederick II which may be divided into various categories. The first was the Imperial Crown at Trifels with the single arch which he inherited from the Saxons and Franconians. Secondly there were the crowns with double arches which were based on the German imperial tradition derived from the Carolingians. Thirdly there was the *kalemaukion* derived from Sicily where the Normans had borrowed from Byzantine custom. Fourthly there was a circlet crown with or without lilies and sometimes decorated with eagles, a symbol which he had borrowed from imperial Rome, and fifthly the crown Frederick wore on his helmet. He was also shown on coins with the laurel wreath of the Augusti. The actual crowns we know of are the *Kalemaukion* found in the tomb of his widow, the Empress Constance; possibly two crowns on a reliquary at Stockholm, one with arches which may have been made to be worn by Frederick and the other made for an empress but never actually used; three crowns in Poland, one a king's crown and one

---

[1] Schramm: *Herrschaftszeichen und Staatssymbolik*, Ch. 39, *Kaiser Friedrichs II Herrschaftszeichen*.
[2] Josef Deér: *Der Kaiserornat Friedrichs II*.

a queen's crown at Cracow, which have been made into a cross, the third a king's crown at Plock; and the crown of Queen Beatrix of Castile, formerly in the Cathedral of Seville. In addition we hear of the crown which he placed on the head of St Elizabeth of Hungary when he attended her burial in 1121 at Marburg. We also know of another imperial crown which belonged to Frederick II and which was described as *Corona Oloferni*. The story runs that Parma, a great stronghold of the imperial authority in the north of Italy, was surprised and captured by the Guelphs. Frederick took strong steps to regain it and built a wooden town outside its walls to house his court and army. It was named Vittoria because the astrologers had predicted the success of Frederick's armies. One day in February 1248 while the Emperor was away hunting, the imperial camp was stormed, the Emperor's forces routed and the Treasury and imperial regalia, Frederick's harem and many of his trusted servants fell into the hands of the victorious Parmesans. Several authors who describe the defeat draw special attention to the imperial crown having fallen into the hands of the Parmesans. Tristan Calchus says that a Parmesan known as Curtpassus took the *Corona Aurea* home with him as booty. Another author mentions that a certain Curtepassis, during the plundering of the town, took possession of the *Corona Oloferni*, which, however, in 1281 came into the possession of the town of Parma and was placed in the vestry of the Episcopal Palace. Another account,[1] is in the Chronicle of the Franciscan Salimbene, which states:

> and they took all his ornaments and his imperial crown which was of great weight and value for it was all of gold inlaid with precious stones with many images of goldsmith's work standing out and much grave work. It was as great as a cauldron for it was rather for dignity and for great price than for his head; for it would have slid off his head even had it not been raised to stand higher by means of a cunningly disposed piece of cloth. This crown I have already in my hands for it was kept in the sanctity of the cathedral of the Blessed Virgin in the City of Parma. It was found by a little man of mean stature who was called ironically Cortopasso (short step) and who bore it openly on his fist as a man bears a falcon, showing it to all who could see it, in honour of the victory they had gained and the eternal disgrace of Frederick so the aforesaid crown was bought by the men of Parma from their fellow citizen and they gave him for it 200 imperial pounds and a house near the Church of St Christina where in old days had been a pool to wash horses and they made a statute that whosoever had aught the treasure of Vittoria should have the half himself and should give half to the community; wherefor poor men were marvellously enriched with the spoils of so rich a prince.

Although there is no evidence the possibility cannot be ignored of this crown being the same as that in the Treasury of Munich and known as the Crown of St Henry.[2] This splendid crown consists of six plates of gold surmounted with fleurs-de-lis held together by pins on which are figures of angels. On the inside are slots on one of the plates in the front and on one at the back for fixing the imperial arch and cross and a spare slot is provided on a plate next to the one at the back to enable the crown to be made smaller by the removal of one plate and yet able to carry the arch. Technical opinion has so far attributed the crown to the first part of the XIV century. This may be true of the decoration, although some alterations must have been made at a later date

---

1 Coulton: *From St Francis to Dante.*   2 See Chapter Two—Bavaria, p. 27.

as is shown by the presence of a XVI-century cameo at the back, but the frame of the crown may be of an earlier date. It is of a distinctive form in use in the middle of the XIII century. The arch and cross are missing. It can be imagined that a great crown falling into the hands of people bent on plunder would almost certainly be the subject of pilferage. No doubt the cross and arch, which were detachable, were wrenched off and this is suggested by the damage, which is still visible, to the slot for the arch at the back of the crown. The precious stones could have been prised out of their settings and the jewels on the strong pins in the hinges of the six plates knocked off. Only the metal frame would have remained. Once in the hands of the Bishop of Parma, means would have been available to repair the damage and when the crown was returned to the Emperor Henry VII as liberator of Italy it would have been an occasion worthy of decorating it with a profusion of precious stones including a cameo of the late Roman Empire to add to the significance of its association with the imperial title. The surmounting cross having been lost, the stones on the front plate were set in the form of a cross. The large size of St Henry's crown and the angels fit in with the description given by the Franciscan, Salimbene. Henry died on August 1313 in Italy but it would have been appropriate for his successor, Louis the Bavarian, who was the benefactor of the cities, to do honour to Bamberg and at the same time expunge the name of *Olofernes* which had been given to the crown because of the hostility to the Church of its original owner Frederick II.

There had been some innovations into the imperial coronation ceremony during this period. At the coronation of Frederick I in 1155 at Rome, the Pope gave the Emperor a sword which he girded, brandished and returned to its sheath. The sceptre was then delivered, after which the Pope crowned him. At the coronation of Henry VI and the Empress Constance in 1191, the ring was added to the regalia. It is noteworthy that before the coronation of Frederick I there had been no mention of a sceptre being delivered[1] although in portraiture the king has carried a sceptre since at least the time of Otto I. No such ornament has come down either as being recorded among the treasure of the times or as a grave ornament, until the reign of Lothair II in whose grave at Königslutter, near Brunswick, a sceptre was found.

Mention has already been made of the presentation of an orb to Henry II at the time of his coronation in Rome. There is no further reference to the emperors receiving the orb at their coronations until Henry VI although an orb was found in the grave of Lothair III (*Plate 99, c*). This was lost during the Second World War. It is likely, however, that an orb was regarded as part of the imperial ornaments and was placed on the altar at the coronation though not delivered. Pope Celestine III delivered the orb to Henry VI at his coronation in 1191 and Henry received it with some suspicion as it was an innovation and this incident has subsequently been magnified into a conflict. Thereafter the orb was regularly delivered and was included in the coronation *ordo* of Otto IV as King of the Romans at Aix in 1191.

Two empresses' or queens' crowns were given to Bamberg cathedral by Philip of

---

1 Although a sceptre and staff were delivered at the German coronation at Aix, a practice borrowed from the West Franks.

Swabia and his consort, either on the occasion of their coronation in 1199, or at the time of the reburial of the remains of St Kunigunde in 1201. They disappeared in the XIII century but there still exist engravings of these by Ludewig[1] (*Plate 99, a*) and they were described by C. G. von Murr.[2] They were very tall open crowns of a type used at the Byzantine Court in the Comnenus period. One crown was richly decorated with pearls in a style characteristic of the Sicilian workshops.[3] On this crown is a Gothic crucifix which was probably added to replace a large precious stone removed because of its value.

When Otto IV received the imperial insignia as a legacy from Philip of Swabia he caused the pommel of the Sword of St Maurice to be engraved with the Arms of his family and with the imperial eagle.[4]

When Frederick's grave was opened at Palermo he was found to be wearing a silver fleur-de-lis crown with a sword by his side, a ring on his finger and a globe by his head. No crown was found in the grave of Philip of Swabia at Speyer although he was garbed in a mantle and girdle, shoes and iron spurs.

THE INTERREGNUM 1197–1273

With the extinction of the House of Hohenstaufen there followed a period known as the Interregnum which ended with the election of Rudolph of Hapsburg as German King in 1273. William, Count of Holland, had been elected anti-king in 1247 after the death of Henry Raspe, who had been elected anti-king following Frederick II's deposition. After a long siege William succeeded in taking Aix, where he was crowned on All Saints Day, 1248. According to the Chronicler Belgicus the imperial insignia was not available and William was crowned with a silver crown. Four contemporary writers relate that the regalia used at his coronation and many other crown jewels were subsequently destroyed by fire on the night of William's marriage to a daughter of the Guelphs in Brunswick. So fierce was the conflagration that William and his consort narrowly escaped with their lives. William died on 28th January 1256.

There followed a series of intrigues as to who was to be chosen German King. In Germany the princes had extended their authority and that of the king had been weakened, his election being in the hands of the seven magnates of the realm who were, in fact, sole electors. Two candidates were supported: Alphonso X, King of Castile, and Richard of Cornwall, brother of Henry III, King of England and brother-in-law of the Emperor Frederick II. Neither had landed property in Germany but were considered wealthy enough to support the dignity of the Crown and to reward those who voted for them. Richard was elected by a bare majority. In December 1256 the Archbishop of Cologne came to London and on 26th December solemnly offered him the crown averring that the electors had been unanimous. Actually Richard had only three votes, although Ottokar of Bohemia, having voted for Alphonso, changed sides,

---

[1] *Scriptores rerum episcopatus Bambergensis*, Bamberg 1718.
[2] *Merkwürdigkeiten der fürstbischöflischen Residenzstadt*, Bamberg 1799.
[3] Josef Deér: op. cit.
[4] The sword did not receive the appellation 'St Maurice' until the middle of the XIV century.

a   *Empresses crowns formerly at Bamberg* (p. 312)

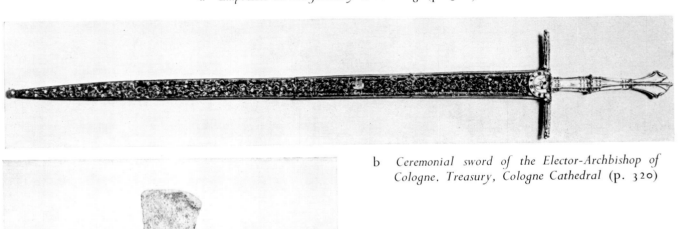

b   *Ceremonial sword of the Elector-Archbishop of Cologne. Treasury, Cologne Cathedral* (p. 320)

c (left)   *Orb found in the grave at Königslutter of the Emperor Lothair II (obiit 1137). Formerly in the Herzog Anton Ulrich Museum, Brunswick* (p. 311)

a   Plates of a crown of Ferdinand II. Treasury, Vienna (p. 327)

b   Frame of imperial crown of Charles VII.
Residenz Treasury, Munich (pp. 321 and 327)

c   Sceptre of Emperor
Charles VII. Resi-
denz   Treasury,
Munich (p. 327)

e   Orb of Emperor Charles VII. Residenz
Treasury, Munich (p. 327)

d (left)   Frame of crown of Empress Maria Amelia

thus giving Richard a majority. Alphonso never left his Spanish kingdom. Richard was crowned at Aix with his consort, Sancha of Provence, on 17th May 1257.

Early in 1259 Richard returned to England and only paid three further visits to his German kingdom. The second was in June 1260 when he intended to journey to Rome for his imperial coronation, but having reached Worms in September he decided not to proceed but to return home. Despite a subsequent summons from the Pope he made no further attempt to obtain the Imperial Crown. The third visit was in 1262 when he presented to the Dean and Chapter of Aix a memorandum in which he bequeathed to their keeping a crown, a sceptre and orb and a set of royal vestments to be used at the coronation of all future kings. The fourth visit was in 1264 when he married his third wife, Beatrice von Falkenburg, at Kaiserleuten.

In his description of his coronation[1] Richard declares with pride that he received the old imperial insignia. This has been interpreted by English writers that he was crowned with the proper regalia. There is a letter from Urban IV to Richard of Cornwall in 1263 which states that Richard received at his coronation at Aix 'that with which the King of the Romans was adorned when he entered Rome'. The regalia were kept in the Castle of Trifels in the custody of Philip of Falkenstein. One report states that he brought the regalia to Aix for the coronation, but doubts are cast on this by Schiffers,[2] who admits, however, that Philip was not in opposition to Richard and may even have attended his coronation. Five days after the coronation Richard invested Philip with the office of Chamberlain and the Trusteeship of the regalia. It was quite customary at the time, however, for more than one crown to figure in the coronation. In England and France two crowns were used and the coronation crown was not worn at the subsequent great banquet. It is possible, therefore, that both the Imperial Crown and Richard's personal crown were used, or at least that the Imperial Crown was carried in the procession in order to show that it was in his possession. Another writer in the *Kilnar Chronicle* relates that at the time of his coronation procession into Aix, Rudolph was in possession of the imperial insignia which were in the Upper Rhine, thanks to the generous expenditure of gold by his family to gain possession of them.

When on his third journey to Germany Richard presented his insignia to the cathedral at Aix these must have been either those ornaments which he had provided for his coronation or a set he had specially made for the purpose.

THE HOUSES OF HAPSBURG, LUXEMBURG, BAVARIA AND OTHERS

On the death of Richard of Cornwall in 1272, the German princes, enjoying their power and relative independence, were reluctant to elect a new king. Pope Gregory X, however, found his revenues declining owing to the disorganisation in Germany and threatened to appoint a king himself if the Electors did not choose one. Largely due to the efforts of his brother-in-law, Frederick III of Hohenstaufen, Rudolph of Hapsburg

---

1 *Annales Monasterii de Burton in Ann. Mon.*, Vol. I; *Neues Archiv*, XIII, 219. *De Antiquis Legibus Liber; Chronica Maiorum et vice comitum.*　　　　　2 Schiffers: op. cit.

was elected German King at Frankfurt on 29th September 1273 and was crowned at Aix on 24th October. The *Ordo* used at his coronation at Aix[1] continued as the standard *ordo* at all subsequent coronations at Aix with very minor changes. The consecrator was the Archbishop of Cologne assisted by the new Archbishop of Mainz and Treves who received the Emperor elect at the entrance to the church. After mass and the Sequence Litany, the Archbishop of Cologne put six questions to the King, one of which asked whether he would maintain the laws of the Empire, another that he would maintain justice, and the sixth whether he would show due submission to the Pope. After the King had taken the oath, he was anointed on the breast and shoulders with the oil of the catechumens and then on the hands. The King was then invested with sword, ring, sceptre and orb and crown.

Rudolph did not go to Rome to be crowned Emperor but to win the Pope's approbation he renounced all imperial rights in Rome and the papal territory of Sicily and then admitted in a letter that the Germans owed the Imperial Crown to the Papacy. Rudolph's reign was more important to his House, of whose greatness he was the founder, than to Germany, but he failed to persuade the princes to elect his son Albert as his successor and thus make the monarchy hereditary.

On his death in July 1291 the Electors chose Adolf, Count of Nassau, on 5th May 1292 and he was crowned at Aix on 1st July, of that year, although the imperial regalia were not in his possession. He was deposed at Mainz on 23rd May 1298 and Albert the son of Rudolph I, was chosen in his stead. Adolf was killed in battle on 2nd July 1298 and was buried at Rosenthal but in 1309 his remains were reburied at Speyer.

On 27th July 1298 Albert I, son of Rudolph of Hapsburg, was chosen King at Frankfurt and on 24th August of the same year was crowned at Aix. He was in possession of the imperial regalia but there is no evidence that he was crowned with them. Albert was murdered in 1308. Although he had been summoned to Rome by the Pope he never went there to be crowned.

On 27th November 1308 the Electors chose Henry VII, Count of Luxemburg, as German King and he was crowned at Aix on 6th January 1309. Henry's ambition was to restore the imperial authority. He descended into Italy in 1310 and he was crowned at Milan on 6th January 1311.

He reached Rome in May 1312 but, being unable to gain St Peter's from his foes, he was crowned in St John Lateran on 29th June, by some cardinals who at first refused but agreed under the threats of the people.

It was on his journey from Lombardy that Ghibertius ruler of Parma came to Henry's camp at Brixen in solemn delegation and presented to him the Imperial Crown of Frederick II which had been looted at the sack of Vittoria in 1248. In 1281 it had come into the possession of the town of Parma and was kept in the vestry of the Episcopal Palace.

Henry died in August 1313, and on 19th October Frederick the Fair, Duke of Austria,[2] was elected by a minority and crowned six days later at Bonn by the Arch-

---

[1] G. H. Pertz: *Monumenta Germanica Historica*.

[2] A golden crown of five pieces which had belonged to Albert I or Frederick the Fair was pawned together with other objects of value at Basle in 1354.

bishop of Cologne with, it is asserted, the imperial regalia which were in his possession. Louis the Bavarian was elected by a minority at Frankfurt on 20th October 1314 and was crowned at Aix on 25th November. After they had come to terms an attempt to rule as joint kings failed and Louis prevailed.

The reign of Louis IV, known as the Bavarian, was noteworthy for the death blow given to the Papal claim to political supremacy. The Pope, fearing the increasing powers of the German King, claimed that the German crown could only be worn by the candidate who had received the approval of the Pope and demanded that Louis should abdicate. Louis indignantly refused and was declared excommunicated and deposed by Pope John XXII. Louis marched on Italy, was crowned at Milan in May 1327 and proceeded to Rome, summoning John to return there from Avignon. The Pope refused and, having gained the support of the Roman people, Louis was chosen senator. Sciarra Colonna, prefect of the city and three other syndics, were authorised to perform the coronation. On 17th January, 1328, Louis was accordingly crowned in St Peter's by lay hands assisted in the religious part of the ceremony by bishops who had been excommunicated by John. Louis, with the approval of the Romans, then deposed John and proclaimed a Franciscan friar as Pope under the name of Nicholas and the Emperor himself placed the tiara on the Pope's head. This reversal of precedent led to the German Estates, at two Diets held at Frankfurt in 1338 and 1339, declaring in a pragmatic sanction that the Empire was held from God alone and that the sovereign was duly chosen by the Electors without the necessity of any confirmation or approval by the Pope. This was confirmed by the Electors at a conference held at Rhens where they made a similar declaration.

After the death of Louis IV in 1347 Edward II, King of England, was elected German King but Parliament forbade him to accept. In January 1349 Gunther of Schwarzburg was elected King but was opposed by Charles, King of Bohemia, and after a few months' struggle Gunther gave up and shortly after died without having been crowned. John of Luxemburg had married Elizabeth, sister of Wenceslas III, who was the last King of Bohemia of the Premyslide dynasty and thus became King of Bohemia. After his death at the Battle of Crécy his son Charles succeeded him as King of Bohemia. Charles had been brought up at the French Court and had married Blanche, sister of the future King Philip IV of France. He was chosen German King at Rhens in 1346 and crowned at Bonn on 26th September, and on the deaths of Louis IV and Gunther, Charles was crowned a second time at Aix on 25th July 1349. On neither occasion did he have the imperial regalia, which did not come into his possession until 1350. Charles's true interests were centred in Bohemia, where he enjoyed the reality of power and used his conspicuous political and administrative qualities for the benefit of that kingdom. He made concessions to Pope Clement VI and confirmed the Papacy in wide territorial possessions. He agreed to take no part in Italian affairs while he promised to defend and protect the Church. In 1354 he crossed the Alps without an army and was crowned at Milan on 6th January 1355. He then proceeded to Rome and was crowned Emperor by a cardinal on 5th April 1355, immediately afterwards leaving the city in accordance with a promise made to Pope Clement VI, though against the wishes of the Romans. Returning to Germany he promulgated the famous Golden Bull in 1356 with the intention of regulating once and for all the election of German kings. On 4th June 1365 he was crowned King of Burgundy at Arles. He visited Italy once more in 1368, where he secured the succession of the Empire to his son Wenceslas. He died at Prague in 1378.

The reign of Charles IV is of great importance in the history of the German regalia. It saw the removal of the imperial insignia to Bohemia; the association of the royal ornaments with the name of Charlemagne; the beginning of a tradition of treating the regalia as relics; the promulgation of the Golden Bull which established the position of the Electors and the formal use of the imperial insignia; and it saw the development of the romantic idea of three crowns being made of three different metals.

It was not until 26th May 1349 that Louis of Brandenburg, son of Louis IV, promised to hand over 'the imperial relics and insignia' to Charles IV. The actual transfer did not take place until after Charles's Aix coronation, when he received them at Munich on 12th March 1350. Charles at once sent them to Prague where on arrival they were taken to St Vitus's Cathedral in solemn procession and received by the Emperor, priests and people. On Charles's orders they were shown to the people at Neustadt. They were kept in Prague for a time and later taken to the Castle of Karlstein, which Charles had built a few miles from the city. On one day every year they were brought in solemn procession to Prague. Only on one occasion during Charles's reign did they leave Bohemia, when in 1361 they were taken to Nuremberg for the baptism of Charles's son Wenceslas, after which they were again returned to Prague with great ceremony and exhibited to the people.

During his sojourn at the French Court Charles had learned of the legend which was current in France but unknown in Germany at that time, that the German insignia had been taken from Charlemagne's tomb. Charles was an admirer of the great Emperor and fostered the Charlemagne cult. He was particularly fond of Aix, which he visited on several occasions, the first being for his coronation in 1349 with his second wife Anna, daughter of Rudolph II, Count of Palatine of the Rhine. He had his third wife Anna, daughter of Henry II, Duke of Schweidnitz, crowned there in 1354.

Charles gave the Cathedral of Aix some notable relics of Charlemagne—the great Emperor's teeth in 1349 and in 1372 a portion of his arm bone. In a letter addressed to the Chapter of the Cathedral, probably written in 1377, the year before his death, Charles exhorted them to lay more stress on the Charlemagne cult, to pay more reverence to the Emperor than in the past and to celebrate his feast day annually.

The association of the name of Charlemagne with the imperial insignia is first mentioned in accounts of the marriage of Frederick the Fair to Elizabeth of Aragon in 1315 at Basle. The relics and regalia were exhibited to the people on a raised stand by a Cistercian monk. One observer, who was an attendant of the Princess, mentioned that the imperial regalia were displayed, among them 'the Crown and Sword of Charlemagne', while in the *Chronicle of Matthias of Nuremberg* we find a reference to the regalia being displayed including 'the lance, the nail, a portion of Our Lord's Cross, the Crown, the Sword of Charlemagne' and others. Basle would, of course, have been within the sphere of the French cultural influence and it is probable that the appellation was only given loosely except to the sword. There already existed a legend that God Himself had sent down from heaven a sword to Charlemagne, and this first appears associated with a sword borne before Philip III of France at his coronation in 1271, although later both the sword at Aix and that in the imperial insignia were sometimes claimed as the sword in the legend.

An inventory of the regalia was taken on the occasion of their being handed over to Charles IV on 12th March 1350, the list includes:

A golden cross decorated with precious stones and 10 pearls complete and not displaced, and on the same cross is the Lance with the Nail of Our Lord and therein a piece of the Holy Cross.

The tooth of St John in a crystal.

St Anne's arm.

Also there are two swords, the one of St Maurice and the other of St Charles with gilded scabbards.

Also is there unmoved and whole the so-called Holy Crown of the Emperor Charles with the cross and arch that belonged to it covered all over with precious stones among them the special one called *Der Waise* (the Orphan).

Also is there a white coat of St Charles, the arms decorated with precious stones and pearls. The red coat of St Charles decorated with two rows of good stones and pearls and gold also is there the golden orb with the golden cross of St Charles.

Two silk gloves with stones, pearls and gold.

The silver sceptre.

A large ring with 1 large ruby, 4 large sapphires and 4 pearls, originally belonging to the Duke of Brunswick.

Another ring with 1 ruby.

Three golden spurs.

A gilded orb with cross and sceptre.

A golden incense vase.

Two large pieces of wax.

An orb.

A blue tunic with gold and pearls.

A brown tunic with black eagles.

A belt.

Two gloves and two shoes of the same material.

A chair with gold and precious stones.

Another chair.

A monstrance and a whole crystal with a golden cross.

It will be seen that the name of Charlemagne is now officially given to many of the ornaments, although it was not until later, probably in 1414, that they became commonly known in Germany as the insignia of Charlemagne. With the exception of the sword, however, this appellation was not necessarily taken to mean that the ornaments had actually belonged to Charlemagne.

In the XIV century the cult of relics was almost at its height and the imperial insignia came to be regarded as relics. We have already seen that some of the ornaments were referred to as relics when they were displayed at the marriage of Frederick the Fair in 1315. In 1322, when Frederick had been defeated by Louis IV at the Battle of Mühldorf and taken prisoner, the imperial insignia fell into Louis's hands and were brought to Nuremberg, where people flocked to see it. The priestly chroniclers regarded them as relics and when they were taken to Munich they were placed in a church where every day four monks celebrated mass.

Charles was an assiduous collector of relics and not only gave some to Aix but detached part of the Nail of the True Cross in the Sacred Lance and gave it to the Cathedral of St Vitus in Prague, where it is still preserved. Charles also gave the name of St Maurice to the Sicilian sword, to which Otto IV had added the imperial eagle and his family arms.

The Golden Bull of 1356 settled and regulated in a formal manner the duties, rights and privileges of the Electors, who were given sovereign rights within their own districts. The Archbishop of Mainz was the senior Elector with the right of invoking the other princes and presiding over the elections. The second Elector was the Archbishop of Treves, who was the Arch Chancellor of the Holy Empire for Italy and to whom belonged the dignity and also the duty of first imposing the royal diadem on the King of the Romans. The third Elector was the Archbishop of Cologne. The fourth Elector was the King of Bohemia, the Arch Cup Bearer of the Holy Empire. The fifth was the Count Palatine of the Rhine who was Arch Steward of the Holy Empire. The sixth was the Duke of Saxony, the Arch Marshal of the Holy Empire and the seventh the Margrave of Brandenburg. The Golden Bull laid down that in accordance with the tradition, which it was asserted had from time immemorial been continuously observed, the election of the King of the Romans and future emperor should be held in the city of Frankfurt, the first coronation in Aix and that his first imperial Court should be celebrated in the town of Nuremberg. In Chapter 22 it stated:

> In order to fix the order of proceedings which we mentioned above, of the Prince Electors in the presence of the emperor or king of the Romans when he is walking, we decree that, so often as, while holding an imperial court, the prince electors shall in the performance of any functions or solemnities, chance to walk in procession with the emperor or king of the Romans and the imperial or royal insignia are to be carried: the duke of Saxony carrying the imperial or royal sword shall directly precede the emperor or king and shall place himself in the middle, between him and the archbishop of Treves. But the count palatine, carrying the imperial orb, shall march in the same line on the right side and the margrave of Brandenburg, bearing the sceptre, on the left side of the same duke of Saxony. But the king of Bohemia shall directly follow the emperor or king himself, no one intervening.

Chapter 26 stated:

> On the day upon which a solemn imperial or royal court is to be held, the ecclesiastical and secular prince electors shall, about the first hour, come to the imperial or royal place of abode, and there the emperor or king shall be clothed in all the imperial insignia; and, mounting their horses, all shall go with the emperor or king to the place fitted up for the session, and each one of them shall go in the order and manner fully defined above in the law concerning the order of marching of those same prince electors. The arch-chancellor, moreover, in whose Arch-Chancellorship this takes place, shall carry, besides the silver staff, all the imperial or royal seals and signets. But the secular prince electors, according to what above has been explained, shall carry the sceptre, orb and sword. And immediately before the archbishop of Treves, marching in his proper place, shall be carried first the crown of Aix and second that of Milan: and this directly in front of the emperor already resplendent with the imperial adornments; and these crowns shall be carried by some lesser

princes to be chosen for this by the emperor according to his will. The empress, moreover, or queen of the Romans, clad in her imperial insignia, joined by her nobles and escorted by her maids of honour shall proceed to the place of session after the king or emperor of the Romans, and also at a sufficient interval of space, after the king of Bohemia, who immediately follows the emperor.

During the XIV century the fact that the emperor had to undergo three coronations led to allegoric meanings being attached to the three crowns, each of which was said to be of a different metal corresponding to the dignity of the realm. Thus the Italian crown was iron, the German silver and the imperial golden. Actually the German crown was made of silver-gilt, while the Italian and the imperial crowns were made of gold. Each had the same feature of an iron ring inside holding the plates together. The first reference to the three metals appears to be mentioned by Matthew Paris, who must have obtained his information from northern Italy. In 1260 he refers in his *Historia Anglorum* to the three crowns of the emperors which he shows on a coat of arms of Otto IV as *argentea, aurea, ferrea*. Another of the early references to the metallic differences of the three crowns is a treatise of Italian origin of about 1350, which states:

> The Roman emperors must after their election be crowned with three crowns, first he must be crowned with the silver crown by the Archbishop of Cologne at Aix. Secondly he must be crowned with the Iron Crown by the Archbishop of Milan and in the third place he must be crowned with the Golden Crown in the city of Rome by the Pope or by the special Legate of the Apostolic throne in the Church of St Peter before the altar of St Maurice.

The matter was confused by Italian writers, evidently chagrined by their being allotted the junior metal, who argued with elaborate reasons that the German crown was of iron and the Italian of silver. It was no doubt in order to solve this difficulty that the growth of the belief in the legend of the iron ring in the Lombard crown was fostered. Various explanations of the allegory have been made. Peterus à Beck, a chronicler of Aix, wrote in 1620 of the rightful meaning of the metals. Iron represented strength and valour; silver—justice; and gold—nobleness and supremacy. Attention was also drawn to the fact that it was with these three metals that the Roman tribute was paid. It was said that the three crowns bestowed on the emperor the lordship of the 'whole world which is divided into three parts, namely Europe, Asia and Africa'. The Golden Bull had made it clear that there were three actual crowns, and German writers have been at pains to prove that the crown at Aix on the bust of Charlemagne was the silver crown with which the German kings were crowned,[1] though the actual ceremonies at which there is evidence that it was used are few.

It is doubtful whether the crowns ever appeared together. The Golden Bull makes it clear that the authors had in mind ceremonial occasions, both in Germany and Italy but it would have been difficult for the Aix and Monza crowns, which had national as well as reliquary status, to have been removed from their kingdoms and there is nothing to show that they ever were. If a ceremony did take place in which the three crowns were carried, no doubt substitutes from the emperor's private treasury would have sufficed.

[1] For the theories regarding the origin of this crown, see pages 348 and 350.

On certain ceremonial occasions it was likely that the emperor, in accordance with the literal directions of the Golden Bull, would not only have worn the imperial vestments but would have been adorned with the crown, sceptre and orb and that the Count Palatine of the Rhine and the Margrave of Brandenburg would in addition have carried an orb and sceptre respectively.

There is in the Munich Treasury an orb which was used by the Elector in virtue of his office and in the Prussian Treasury there is similarly a sceptre which was used by the Elector of Brandenburg. In the Saxon Treasury there is an electoral sword which may have been used in place of the imperial sword of ceremony on certain occasions. The Archbishop of Cologne also had a state sword (*Plate 99, b*) which is still preserved in the Treasury of Cologne. The Elector's dress consisted of a crimson robe trimmed with ermine and a hat turned up with ermine with an ermine tuft on top. Examples have been handed down in the Saxon and Prussian collections.

Wenceslas, son of Charles IV, was born in 1361 and crowned King of Bohemia in 1363. In 1376, during his father's lifetime, he was chosen German King at Frankfurt on 10th June and crowned at Aix on 6th July. As the imperial insignia were not brought from Prague for the ceremony it is likely that the crown on the bust of Charlemagne was used. On his father's death in 1378 he was recognised as King but he confined his interest chiefly to Bohemian affairs. In 1400 the four Rhenish Electors met at Rhens on 21st August and declared Wenceslas deposed. They elected Rupert, Count Palatine of the Rhine, in his stead and he was crowned at Cologne on 6th January 1401, Aix holding out for Wenceslas. Although he hoped to receive the Imperial Crown at Rome, Rupert was unable to reach the city and died in 1410.

On 20th September 1410 three of the Electors chose Sigismund, King of Hungary and step-brother of Wenceslas, as German King, but the other Electors voted for his rival Jobst of Moravia, who, however, died a few months later.

Sigismund was not crowned at Aix until 8th November 1414. We have more than one account of this coronation,[1] and possess more details of the ceremony than of any previous one. Eigil von Sassen relates:

> Duke Louis of Bavaria bore an orb with a cross above as the Elector's emblem. Then came the Duke of Saxony bearing the naked sword. Then Burgrave Frederick of Nuremberg with the golden sceptre and the Bishop of Cologne anointed the King and Queen in the presence of the other bishops and priests and then crowned them both. Then the King was seated on the Coronation Chair. Then the King read the Gospel in the alb and mantle and with the crown of the Emperor Charlemagne on his head and then the Queen was crowned. The crown was valued at 40 doz. guilden and was that of the old Emperors.

Another account by the Ambassador of Savoy is contained in a letter to Count Amadeus VII of Savoy. He writes that from the entry of the King into the city and to the door of the precincts 'the statue of Charlemagne was carried which had a golden crown upon its head'. After describing the coronation ceremony it concludes with: 'The Archbishop of Cologne and other archbishops and bishops took the crown from the head of Charlemagne and set it on the King's head'. This evidence is interesting as

---

[1] Schiffers: op. cit.

it is the first definite information that the crown on the bust of Charlemagne was used for crowning a German king.

As Sigismund was not in possession of the imperial regalia it must have been the crown of the bust of Charlemagne that was used. The imperial insignia were still in Bohemia in the possession of Wenceslas, who, despite persistent demands which had been made by Rupert, refused to give them up, no doubt because he still had a thought of regaining his throne.

Sigismund's attempts to obtain the regalia were also abortive. In fact, at the reconciliation between the step-brothers on 19th July 1411 Sigismund promised to arrange for Wenceslas to be crowned Emperor in Rome and it was agreed that the relics of the Holy Empire should remain with Wenceslas as long as he lived. On 19th June 1416 a new pact was made whereby Sigismund expressly acknowledged that Wenceslas during his lifetime should be styled King of the Romans and promised not to claim the relics and the other regalia of the Holy Roman Empire. On the death of Wenceslas in 1419 Sigismund became King of Bohemia and the imperial insignia came into his possession in October 1420 after having to fight for the possession of the Castle of Karlstein where they were kept. During the Hussite Wars, Karlstein was in danger of attack and Sigismund, in 1421, removed them to his Kingdom of Hungary, first to Blindenburg Castle near Ofen and then ceremoniously to Ofen itself. They were brought out on great feast days and a witness relates how they were carried in the King's procession at Mass on Christmas Day.

On 7th June 1421 the Diet of the Bohemian Estates deposed Sigismund from the Bohemian throne, giving as one of their reasons the fact that he had removed the imperial regalia without their knowledge. On 22nd March 1424 Sigismund had the regalia removed to Nuremberg for perpetual safe keeping. The relics of the Empire, as they now came to be called, were received with a great ceremonial procession, men and women going barefoot. The relics were placed in a shrine suspended on a chain high above the choir and the jewels were placed in a cupboard in the upper vestry of the Church of the Holy Ghost. At the same time a number of ornaments connected with the coronation of the German kings, which were kept at Aix but were not vested in the cathedral there, were also brought to Nuremberg and added to those which Sigismund had brought from Hungary.

An inventory was taken and the reliquary character of the regalia was underlined, the authorities of Nuremberg being enjoined to ensure that the relics were exposed to the people by the clergy each year fourteen days after Good Friday and that on these occasions the relics must be associated with a celebration of Mass. Sigismund wrote to the Pope asking for permission for these exhibitions and in reply the Papal authority was given for the insignia to be kept at Nuremberg and the reliquary character of the imperial regalia was thereby confirmed.

There are records of several occasions on which Sigismund appeared in full regalia. After his coronation at Aix he made an entry into Constance where a general council was held, and he carried his own royal ornaments with him. On Christmas Day at the Pope's matins he chanted the Gospel adorned with the sword, sceptre and crown which he again used at the fifteenth General Session of the Council on 6th July 1415. In April

1417 at Constance he attended a ceremony wearing a high golden crown with the other insignia borne before him. On 29th January 1418 Pope Martin V had the King crowned at a solemn service 'as was usual at such coronation feasts'. On 8th May of the same year at an enfeofment in the market place at Constance Sigismund wore his Imperial Crown on his head. Just before his death at Znaym in 1437 he had himself clothed as a Roman emperor with his alb, mantle and Imperial Crown and his personal ornaments. On all these occasions the imperial insignia were not available and, therefore, personal regalia from the Emperor's private treasury must have been used. We know, too, that in 1403 he had managed to purchase from the Royal Treasury at Prague some costly treasures including a richly decorated and costly crown. This is thought to have been the crown which had been used by one of the consorts of Charles IV and with which Barbara, the wife of Sigismund, was crowned at Aix in 1414. On his seals and in other contemporary portraiture Sigismund is shown wearing a crown with two high crossing arches. For the previous century the German kings had been depicted on their seals wearing open fleur-de-lis crowns, and this innovation was perpetuated down to the reign of Frederick III.

Sigismund received the Lombard crown at Milan on 25th November 1431, and after negotiating for his coronation as Emperor from Siena he was crowned at Rome by Pope Eugenius IV on 31st May 1433. It is not known whether the regalia was taken from Nuremberg but it may be assumed that it was. We know that a delegation consisting of Councillor Erhart and Paulus Haller, Franz Rummel and Martin Haiden attended the coronation and they were knighted by the Emperor at the Tiber Bridge,[1] and there is another description of the ceremony.[2] These printed sources are supported by entries in the Nuremberg archives detailing the expenses paid to the delegation although the insignia are not mentioned.

With the death of Sigismund in 1437 the House of Luxemburg became extinct. Sigismund had designated his son-in-law, Albert II, as his successor, and although he was crowned King of Hungary on 1st January 1438 and King of Bohemia in June that year, he was not crowned at Aix after his election at Frankfurt on 18th March 1438 owing to his preoccupation in defending Hungary from the Turks, and he died in 1439. Although his reign was short, it was notable for the fact that thereafter with one exception, there was an unbroken line of Hapsburg emperors.

On 2nd February 1440 Frederick III, the senior member of the Hapsburg family, was chosen German King at Frankfurt, but owing to his absence from Germany he was not crowned at Aix until 17th June 1442. For this occasion Frederick III applied to the authorities at Nuremberg for the relics and regalia so that he could use them for his coronation. His requests were violently opposed by the Council, who used the argument that by the law the insignia were relics and subject to Papal authority and thus were not at the disposal of the German King. Fearing that the King might later vent his wrath on the city, they eventually gave way after the King had bound himself in writing to hand the insignia back to the Nuremberg Ambassadors immediately after

---

[1] E. Hermann: *Records of the Deutsche Reichstag*, Vol. 10, Gotha 1906, pp. 728–39.

[2] 'Nuremberg Chronicle of the Time of the Emperor Sigismund to 1434 with a Continuation to 1441', published in *Chronicles of German Cities, Nuremberg*, Vol. 1, Leipzig 1862, p. 387.

the coronation, the Council insisting that they should not remain in his possession over-night. Among the arguments used by the King for wanting the Nuremberg regalia was that the royal ornaments which he had ordered to be made for him, by a Nuremberg goldsmith, would not be ready in time. There is a record in the Nuremberg City Council[1] concerning the despatch of the insignia to Aix, and they were used during the coronation of Frederick III on 17th June 1442. The relative passage reads:

> At the earnest request and command of our Gracious Lord and King to Master Johannes our secretary we sent the Emperor Charles' clothing, crown and sceptre with which His Gracious Majesty was in fact crowned on the above mentioned Sunday 17th June.

In 1451 Frederick travelled to Rome and was crowned Emperor on 10th March 1452 by Pope Nicholas V. On this occasion he again used the regalia from Nuremberg, and Aeneas Silvius Piccolomini, afterwards Pope Pius II, was unable to understand why Frederick had sent for the insignia of Charlemagne instead of availing himself of his own newly made insignia. In his account of the coronation the imperial Minister, Kasper Enenkel, states that the Emperor attended the coronation Mass 'clothed with the Holy Robes of the Emperor Charles which had happened to no Emperor for many hundreds of years and which were all treasured for the great honour and the especial mercy of God'. Both these pieces of evidence indicate that it was at least considered unnecessary and unusual for the imperial insignia to be used at the Roman coronation. The despatch of the insignia is recorded in the *Nuremberg Archives*.[2] The relevant passage reads:

> In reply to a question from N. Muffel, the Council informed him that: 'he should keep the Regalia in his charge, until they were needed and, as soon as they had been used, take charge of them again'. This concerns the items of the regalia which Muffel, as Nuremberg's representative, was to take to Italy for the coronation and of which he had already taken charge. This is more clearly expressed in the following letter of 14th December, in which the Council writes: 'Should the ceremony be unduly extended, postponed or perhaps cancelled' Muffel should return with the regalia. If the Emperor wished to retain the regalia, Muffel should draw his attention to the instructions for the safe keeping of the insignia, 'if it were not available for others and could not be produced that would bring an open scandal'.
>
> Another letter dated 15th February, being a reply to a letter of 24th January from Muffel, written from Ferrara, in which he enquires as to whether, in the event of his being detained at the court after the coronation, he should send the insignia in advance in the care of his servants, the Council replied that he must decide for himself, for in Nuremberg they had no information over the progress of the war in Italy. In any case they would be pleased when the regalia were back in their safe keeping.
>
> On 22nd May the Council wrote to Muffel again concerning the regalia: 'It is clear that in the circumstances it would be best that the regalia should be given into the care of trustworthy merchants, who, at a suitable time, could hide them in their wool-sacks and so transport them back.'

Frederick's son, Maximilian, was elected German King on 16th February 1486 at

---

1 The original is in 'Nuremberg Archives', printed in Vol. 16 of *Deutsche Reichstagsakten*, by H. Herre and L. Quidde, Stuttgart, 1928.

2 G. Hirschmann: *Muffel Family in the Middle Ages*. Historical Society of Nuremberg, Vol. 41, 1950, p. 319.

the age of twenty-seven, and during his father's lifetime he was crowned at Aix on 9th April the same year. In the Nuremberg archives is a list of the items of the regalia sent to Aix for this occasion. It is headed *List of Regalia and Crown Jewels* that were sent to Aix and used at the coronation of the Emperor Maximilian I, 1486.[1]

1. A white silk ceremonial robe decorated with pearls, jewels and gold.
2. A large golden stole with pearls and black eagles.
3. A brown silk cape with black eagles.
4. A silk maniple.
5. A red silk dalmatic completely decorated with a great eagle, and gold pieces set with pearls and jewels.
6–9. Also used at the same time—St Charles' crown, orb, sceptre and sword.

The regalia were in the charge of Messrs Gabriel Nuetzel and Ulma Stromeyr.

Maximilian had greatly strengthened the Hapsburg inheritance by his marriage in 1477 to the daughter of Charles the Bold, Duke of Burgundy, and thus succeeded to Burgundy and the Netherlands. Later, by the marriage of his son Philip, who predeceased him, to Joanna the daughter and heiress of Ferdinand and Isabel, he gained the Kingdom of Spain.

In 1493 at the death of Frederick III Maximilian became the sole ruler of Germany. He set out for Italy to be crowned Emperor at Rome, but Venice refused his passage and at Trant on 4th January 1508, with the consent of the Pope, he assumed the title of Roman Emperor without having undergone the Roman coronation. This was an unprecedented step. He died in 1519 and was buried at Innsbruck. Maximilian enriched the imperial relics and regalia by giving a splendid silver-gilt cover to the Book of the Gospels of Charlemagne, while he ordered to be made at Nuremberg the rich receptacles for the Holy Tablecloth, and the piece of the Holy Apron. He also added the Sword of Investiture to the regalia.

On his assumption of the imperial title, although he had not received the mitre from the Pope, he added a mitre to his Imperial Crown. Since Charles IV the mitre appears within the Imperial Crown on the imperial portraiture. In St Catherine's Chapel in the Castle of Karlstein, Charles IV is shown with a low mitre worn with the horns above the forehead and back of the head and below the single arch of the Imperial Crown. It should be noted that the arch has the characteristic decoration of the Aix crown and not that of Conrad II's arch. Sigismund, on the imperial seal, wears a tall mitre in the same way but under a crown with two high arches. Frederick III is depicted on his seal wearing the Imperial Crown with the mitre with horns over the temples, the crown having a single arch and a cross in front. There is a portrait in the Treasury, Vienna, by an unknown artist, of Frederick III wearing a mitre crown (*Plate 107, a*), probably that made for him by a Nuremberg goldsmith (see p. 323). Maximilian is shown on his imperial seal with a small mitred crown. Maximilian's mitred crown is also worn by the figure of the Lord on the cover of the Book of the Holy Gospels. Maximilian's crown is fully described in the documents relating to the sale of certain jewels in Madrid in 1555.[2] Apart from the crown itself, there were two side parts to form

[1] Nuremberg Archives, Coronation File, No. 4, folio 7.   [2] Rudolph Beer: 'Kunstbestubungen Karls V und Philipps II', *Jahrbuch der Kunsthistorischen Sammlungen des Allerhöchsten Kaiserhaus*, Vienna.

the mitre, made of silver thread embroidered with pearls and decorated with precious stones. This is the earliest example of which there is a record of an actual mitre. Since the crown and mitre on Maximilian's seal is very similar in shape as that on Frederick III's seal, this may well have been Frederick's crown and mitre which Maximilian inherited in 1493, but perhaps did not use until 1508, although it is depicted on the cover of the Book of the Gospels which was made about the year 1500.

On Maximilian's death in January 1519 his grandson Charles, already King of Spain, was after some difficulty elected German King and was crowned at Aix on 23rd October 1520. The report on the coronation of Charles V states that the 'two representatives of the Nuremberg Council brought the royal ornaments to Aix'.[1] This is supported by extracts from the Nuremberg archives[2] which record that Messrs Leonhard Groland and Hans Ebner were sent to represent the Honourable Council. They took with them the same items as in 1486, and in addition:

A brown ceremonial robe.
A black ceremonial robe.
A golden stole.
A pair of gloves set with pearls and precious stones.
A pair of shoes set with pearls and precious stones.
A leather belt set with chalcedony.
A golden belt.

In 1521 part of the regalia was taken by two representatives of the Council to the first Reichstag which Charles V held at Worms. The list enumerates the order in which the ornaments were put on.[3]

A pair of red knee stockings.
A pair of stitched shoes with pearls and precious stones.
A brown silk cap with black eagles.
A white alb or dalmatic set with precious stones and pearls.
A large golden stole decorated with pearls and black eagles.
A golden money belt with which His Royal Majesty girdled the stole to him.
A blue maniple on his arm.
A red pallium stitched with pearls and precious stones.
Following this the Crown of Charlemagne was set on his head.

The following were carried before him:
A golden orb set with pearls and jewels.
A silver gilt sceptre.
The Emperor Charles's sword.

As a result of the Reformation the imperial insignia underwent a further change in status because the Church of the Holy Ghost in Nuremberg went over to the Protestants. The differentiation that had been made between the regalia and the relics and their

---

1 *Deutsche Reichstagsakten juengere Reihe*, Vol. II, pp. 65ff., Gotha 1896.
2 *Nuremberg State Archives* Coronation File, No. 4, Folio 19.
3 *Nuremberg State Archives*, Folios 19 and 11.

public display was discontinued. The Catholics were indignant that the old regalia, and especially the relics, should remain under Protestant supervision and throughout the XVII century made intermittent attempts to have them removed.

Charles V had, like Maximilian I, taken the title of Roman Emperor Elect without waiting for his coronation in Rome. In 1530 he was to undergo the imperial coronation, but the Pope was unwilling to receive him in Rome because he had not forgotten the events of 1527 when Charles's army had sacked the Holy City with great ferocity and had held Clement VII himself as captive. The Pope agreed, however, to meet Charles at Bologna, where he received the Lombard crown, and subsequently in the Church of St Petronius the Pope crowned Charles as Emperor. Although two representatives of the city of Nuremberg attended the ceremony there is no record in the archives of the regalia having been taken there, nor is there any mention in the descriptions of the coronation of the Nuremberg regalia having been used. The fact that the two representatives only took four horses to Italy with them would make it seem unlikely that they could have taken the regalia.

In 1555 Charles expressed his determination to abdicate his several crowns giving the sovereignty of Spain and the Indies, the Netherlands and Naples to his son Philip and his German possessions to his brother Ferdinand, who had been elected German King in 1531.

We have some interesting information about Charles's personal regalia in the inventories taken in Spain in 1555 and 1563.[1] They include objects taken from the King of Tunis, including a golden crown, and one imperial crown and mitre of Maximilian I; two crowns and mitres of Charles V; a sceptre and orb of Charles V; one sword of Maximilian and two of Charles V; a baton and also gloves, shoes, cords, tassels, pectorals, stoles, maniples, embroideries, tunicles, a tunic, cloth, fringes, capes, hoods and a gold belt. They were all sold on 14th July 1564.[2]

Ferdinand, after his election as German King at Cologne, was crowned at Aix in January 1531 while Charles V was still on the throne. Two representatives of the Nuremberg City Council attended and took with them the regalia in the same way as for the coronation in 1520.[3] On the abdication of Charles, which in the case of his German possessions was postponed and did not become effective until 1558, Ferdinand was crowned Emperor at Frankfurt on 24th March of that year. This was an entirely new departure and Pope Paul IV would not recognise the new Emperor, but in 1559 his successor, Pius IV, did so through the mediation of Philip II of Spain. Thereafter the coronations at Aix, Milan and Rome were abandoned and there was but one German coronation at Frankfurt. There is no record in the Nuremberg archives of either the regalia or representatives being sent to Frankfurt for the coronation, but this is probably due to the fact that the main source, the Cash Book for 1558, had been lost. There is other evidence to show that the Nuremberg regalia were used at this and at subsequent coronations at Frankfurt.

[1] Rudolph Beer: op. cit.
[2] Rudolph Beer: op. cit. and Pedro de Madrazo: 'Über Krönungsinsignien und Staatsgewänder Maximilians I und Karls V und ihr Schicksal in Spanien', *Jahrbuch der kunsthist Samml.* Vol. 9, Vienna 1899.
[3] *Nuremberg Archives*, Coronation File No. 4, Folio 19 (1531).

Maximilian II was elected German King in November 1562 and crowned at Frankfurt on 24th November 1562. This was an important innovation. According to Ranke,[1] the fact of the reformation led to the enfranchisement of the Empire itself from the dependance in which it had hitherto been upon the Pope. At the election of Maximilian even the Catholic princes expressly insisted upon the omission of any mention of the Pope and expressed the hope that in the future the Pope would rather seek his confirmation from the Emperor than the Emperor from the Pope. When the Imperial Vice-Chancellor drew up an elaborate report to prove the Pope had no more right to claim an influence over the election of an Emperor than over the accession to the throne of any other sovereign, the imperial dignity, in fact, lost its European and Christian significance and became essentially German in character. At his death on 12th October 1576 Maximilian was succeeded by his son Rudolph II, who had already been crowned King of Hungary in 1572 and King of Bohemia in 1575, had been chosen King of the Romans at Ratisbon in October 1575 and had been crowned at Frankfurt on 1st November 1575. In 1602 Rudolph added to the regalia a splendid crown known as the *Hauskrone*, which was used as the personal crown of the Emperor and later became the imperial crown of Austria[2] and is still preserved in Vienna. It incorporated in permanent form the mitre into the crown. His successor Matthias, who was crowned at Frankfurt on 24th June 1612 added the sceptre and orb and probably the sword which later formed part of the Austrian imperial regalia. He was succeeded by his cousin Ferdinand II, who was crowned at Frankfurt on 9th September 1619. In the Vienna treasury there are some fragments of a crown which was broken up in 1872, which had belonged to Ferdinand II, but as the workmanship is of the time of Rudolph II it may only have been inherited by Ferdinand II. They include four plates (*Plate 100, a*) bearing in relief representations of the evangelists and suggest that the crown was octagonal like the so-called Crown of Charlemagne.

Ferdinand II was succeeded by his son Ferdinand III, who was crowned at Frankfurt in 1636 and whose son Ferdinand was chosen German King in 1653 but died the following year. The imperial title then passed successively to Ferdinand III's second son Leopold I, who was crowned at Frankfurt on 1st August 1658, his son Joseph I, who was crowned in 1705, and the latter's brother Charles VI, who was crowned on 22nd December 1711. Charles had no male heir, and while his daughter Maria Theresa claimed the inheritance to the Hapsburg lands her husband Francis was a candidate for the imperial title. But Charles the Elector of Bavaria also set claim to the Hapsburg lands and title and was elected German King on 24th January 1742 and crowned Emperor at Frankfurt on 17th February, with his consort.

Charles VII was unable to get possession of the imperial regalia and had two crowns, a sceptre and an orb (*Plate 100, b, c, and e*), specially made for the occasion. These are still preserved in the Munich Treasury.[3] On his death Francis I was elected German King on 13th September 1745 and was crowned at Frankfurt in 1745 with Maria Theresa who became co-Regent over the hereditary dominions.

Joseph II, son of Francis I and Maria Theresa, was crowned as German King at

1 Prof. Leopold Ranke: *Frederick I and Maximilian II*, 1853. 2 See Chapter One—Austria.
3 See Chapter Two—Bavaria.

Frankfurt in his parents' lifetime on 3rd April 1764. For this occasion copies were made of the crown, orb and sceptre and many of the vestments. According to the account left by Goethe, who was present at the ceremony, the Emperor wore the new regalia, which were copies of the old. On the other hand Prince Khevenhuller, a Court official of Maria Theresa, relates:

> This *corona fictitia* was only carried before the Emperor by the treasurer instead of the Nuremberg crown on the return from the church. For the procession to the church the original and veritable Nuremberg Crown was carried before him as a symbol of the highest imperial dignity. The Emperor wore his personal crown all the time. The King of the Romans wore, on the outward journey, his own newly made archducal hat, richly beset with brilliants and pearls and on the way back the Nuremberg Crown.

This would seem to be the correct version. It was necessary for the King to be crowned with the Nuremberg crown, and therefore the Emperor had to have a second crown made so that he too, should have the imperial emblem. The crown he wore was that made for Rudolph II. The duplicate ornaments were melted down in 1872 but the vestments are still kept in the Vienna Treasury.

At the coronation of Leopold II on 9th October 1790 at Frankfurt the Emperor wore the Rudolph crown on the way to the church with the Nuremberg crown and other insignia borne before him.

The last imperial coronation was that of Francis II at Frankfurt on 14th July 1792. In 1796 Nuremberg was captured by the French. It was decided to remove the treasure elsewhere to a place of safety, and it related that they were hastily placed in a dung cart and driven from the town. During this adventure some of the objects were lost, including the spurs, the bracelets, a humeral and the cap belonging to the dalmatic embroidered with eagles. There are, however, contemporary pictorial records of the contents of the treasury by Delsenbach. The imperial treasures were taken to Prague, whence Baron Alois von Hugel conveyed them to Ratisbon disguised as his personal baggage and there deposited them in the resting place of the city archives; they were taken thence to Passau and to Linz and finally to Vienna. The three objects which had been at Aix were taken to Paderborn in 1798 and from there to Vienna, all the ornaments which had not been lost being reassembled there in the years 1800 and 1801. During the Napoleonic wars they again had to be moved—in 1805 to Ofen; in 1809 to Temesvar; and it was not until 1813 that they were returned to Vienna where they remained until the *Anschluss* in 1938 when, by the orders of Adolf Hitler, they were removed to Nuremberg. During the Second World War they were hidden in a salt mine but in 1946, at the end of the war they fell into the possession of the Americans, were brought back to Vienna and are today again on public exhibition in the secular Treasury.

By a declaration dated 6th August 1806 the Holy Roman Empire came to an end. Francis II in his Instrument announced that, finding it impossible in the altered state of things to fill the obligations imposed by the engagements taken at his election, he considered as dissolved the bonds which attached him to the Germanic body, released from their allegiance the Estates of which it consisted and retired to the government of

German Imperial Crown. Treasury, Vienna (p. 329)

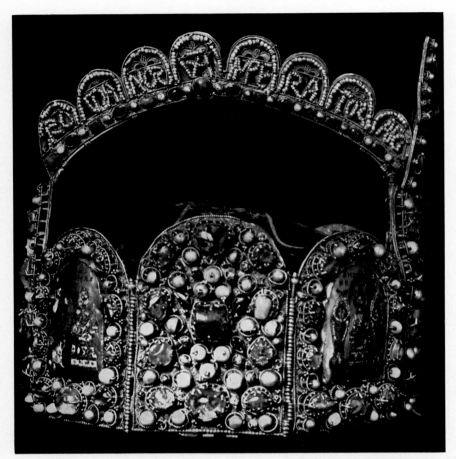

a *German Imperial Crown,*
right side (p. 329)

b *German Imperial Crown,*
left side (p. 329)

his hereditary dominions under the title of Emperor of Austria. Napoleon, who considered himself to be the successor of Charlemagne, had been crowned Emperor in 1804, and the following year Francis began to use the title of Hereditary Emperor of Austria. With Napoleon's subsequent victories, the title of Emperor, as related to the old Empire, became meaningless. In 1700 Prussia had been raised to the position of a kingdom, and in 1805, and 1806, Bavaria, Württemberg, and Saxony also became kingdoms while Hanover was recognised as a kingdom in 1814.[1]

In 1849 an attempt was made to revive the Empire, and the imperial dignity was offered to the King of Prussia, but, although twenty-nine of the German princes had expressed their approval of the scheme, it appeared that there might be jealousy among some of the other sovereigns and he, therefore, refused the offer. On 18th January 1871, King William of Prussia was proclaimed German Emperor making Germany a single state. There was, however, no coronation though for heraldic purposes crowns were adopted for the Emperor, the Empress and the Crown Prince. Models of these were made and were kept in the Hohenzollern collection.

In describing the insignia and relics connected with the German Kingdom and Empire it will be convenient to divide them into groups:

1. The insignia and relics of the Holy Roman Empire in the Secular Treasury of the Hofburg, Vienna.
2. The ornaments which no longer exist but which were described by von Murr[2] and illustrated by Delsenbach.[3]
3. The ornaments which are still preserved in the Treasury of the Minster at Aix-la-Chapelle.
4. Other royal and imperial ornaments which are still preserved in Germany.

1. *The Insignia and Relics of the Holy Roman Empire in the Secular Treasury of the Hofburg, Vienna*

The German Imperial Crown (Plates 101, 102)

This crown, which is one of the most venerable and most historic royal ornaments still preserved in Europe, has been called by various names. It is sometimes referred to as the Crown of Charlemagne or the Nuremberg Crown or the Vienna Crown but the most fitting description, perhaps, is the *Reichskrone*, and the nearest English translation to this is the German Imperial Crown.

The crown consists of eight gold plates rounded at the summit, fastened together by gold pins which fit into beaded slots and each is topped by a pearl. This arrangement made it possible for the circlet to be taken to pieces or to be laid flat when not in use and this facilitated the transportation of the crown on its frequent travels. The plates at the front and the back and those at the sides are profusely decorated with precious stones and are set alternately with four smaller plates which bear enamelled figures on a gold background within a frame of precious stones. Decker-Hauf[4] in collaboration

---

[1] The regalia and crown jewels of these kingdoms are dealt with under separate chapters.
[2] Von Murr: op. cit.　　　[3] Delsenbach: op. cit.
[4] Hansmartin Decker-Hauf: *Herrschaftszeichen und Staatssymbolik*, Ch. 25.

with Schramm, has made an exhaustive analysis of the arrangement of the precious stones and their mystical meanings. The front and back plates are each decorated with four rows of three large precious stones. The two side plates are each decorated with seventy-two precious stones and pearls with a particularly beautiful emerald forming the centre of the design. Decker-Hauf's closely reasoned conclusions are that the front and side plates symbolise the Revelation of St John the Divine and the back plate the High Priest's Robe. He draws special attention to two stones which he calls 'guiding stones' which were set in the crown one on top of the front plate and one on top of the plate at the back. The stone in front was usually described as a white milky opal, although it has sometimes been called a jasper. By tradition the stone was brought back by Archduke Ernest from his adventurous journeys in the East. Albertus Magnus names it *Orphanus* and describes it as follows:

> *Orphanus* is a stone which is in the crown of the Roman Emperor and none like it has ever been seen. For this very reason it is called *Orphanus*. It is of a subtle vinous tinge and its hue is that of pure white snow, flashing and sparkling of bright red wine and all are overcome by its radiance. It is a translucent stone and there is a tradition that formerly it shone in the night time but now in our age it does not sparkle in the dark. It is said to guard the regal honour.

It became famous in romantic legends, was frequently referred to in XII- and XIII-century poetry and was last mentioned in the XIV century. It was very highly prized, and Decker-Hauf suggests it symbolised 'the chosen of God'. It was officially described as *Der Waise*, and the last record of it is in the inventory taken in 1350 when Louis of Brandenburg handed over the imperial regalia to Charles IV. One writer,[1] asserts that Charles IV removed the opal from the crown in Prague in 1350 and had it placed in the Bohemian Crown. While it is true that Charles had removed part of the Holy Lance and given it to St Vitus Cathedral there is no opal in the Crown of St Wenceslas nor is one mentioned in the inventories of the Bohemian regalia. The stone has been replaced by a purplish grey Indian sapphire which does not fit into its setting. The original stone at the back was thought to have been a red stone which was replaced by a very large sapphire which appears to have been lost at the coronation of 1764. It was replaced by a hyacinth. The other precious stones with which the crown is studded are mostly uncut but polished gems of the finest water surmounted by pierced pearls. Sapphires are the stones most frequently employed, some of a large size, and many are encircled with garnets. Emeralds, rubies, amethysts and other stones are also used. Most of the stones are perforated which is a sign of previous use. They are set *à jour* with the gold work at the back cut away so that the light may play through. The other four plates bear scenes from the Old Testament in delicate cloisonné enamel. The first of these is the Lord Enthroned in Majesty between a cherub and seraph surmounted by the inscription *PER ME REGES REGNANT*. The second enamel plate bears a representation of King Solomon with the inscription: *REX SALOMON* and the King holds a scroll with the words: *TIME DOMINUM ET RECEDE MALO*. On the third enamel plate is a representation of King David inscribed *REX DAVID*. The King also bears a scroll with the words: *HONOR REGIS IUDUCUM DELIGIT*. The fourth plate shows King Hezekiah with the

---

1 Johann David Kohler: *Teutscher Reichs-Historie*, 1751.

Prophet Isaiah and is inscribed: *ISAIAS PROPHETA EZECHUAS REX*. The Prophet is holding a scroll with the words: *ECCE ADACIAM SUPER DIES TUOS XV ANNOS*. All these inscriptions are taken from the formula used in X- and XII-century coronations and perhaps earlier. The plaque showing the Prophet Isaiah and King Hezekiah bears a quotation from the Book of Isaiah, Chapter 38, in which the Prophet tells the sick King that he will not die but live for fifteen years longer. The eight plates form an octagon, a feature which is unique in European crowns. The octagonal shape is of special symbolical significance and was connected with the imperial dignity. It was used architecturally in two buildings with close imperial connections, the Palatine Chapel built by Charlemagne at Aix and the Basilica of San Vitale in Ravenna. The number 'eight' was regarded as the symbol of perfection and of achievement and it was said that it transcends the earthly sphere, and thus is a symbol of eternal life in the world to come and illustrates the heavenly Jerusalem.

There are various other features of the crown which command attention. On the inside there are three sockets on the two side plates and on the back plate, and the front plate has only one, although there may have been two others which have been removed. The middle socket is vertical and the other two point outwards. One suggestion has been that these sockets were for fixing the mitre or the pileus and another is that they were to hold crossed arches but both these have been rejected and it is considered that they were used to fix fleurs-de-lis ornaments. The only representation of this crown decorated with fleurs-de-lis is on a piece of canvas in the Art Historical Collection of the city of Vienna on which is a copy of the crown with fleurs-de-lis on the upper rim of the circlet. At the bottom of the two side plates there are also three small horizontal hollow sockets which were for the purpose of fixing the pendants or *cataseistae*, consisting of three chains, bearing pendant precious stones. At the bottom of the inside of the plates is an iron ring which holds the plates together. The second ring above it was added at a later date. The single arch and cross were added by Conrad II. The arch extends over the top of the crown from front to back and on it there is an inscription in small pearls mounted on gold wire which reads: *CHUONRADUS DEI GRATIA ROMANORU[M] IMPERATOR AUG[USTUS]*. The arch consists of eight small arcades which rise from a connecting band composed of two filigree strips, the space between being set on both sides with small pearls. In each of the apertures under the arches and above the inscription are golden fleurs-de-lis of a late XI-century pattern. The arch is attached to the front and the back plates of the crown by golden pins which are movable. At the front of the arch is fixed a Latin cross of gold. At the back of the cross is a figure of Christ crucified engraved on the gold plate. Over the head is the inscription: *JCH NAZARENUS REX JUDEORUM*. The cross is fixed by narrow wedge-shaped gold tongues to a socket in the shield beneath it. The crown itself and the cross are of 21 carat gold but the arch is of 22 carat gold. The diameter between the front and the back plate is 20·9 cm and between the two side plates it is 22·2 cm. The total weight is twelve Viennese marks, three and a half ounces.

The origin of the crown has been the subject of various theories. Bock and Weixlgärtner favour the idea that it was made in a workshop in Treves or Mainz in 993 for Rudolph III, King of Burgundy, and that on his death it passed to the Emperor, Conrad

II, who had married Rudolph's niece. Another theory is that it was a gift from Pope Benedict VIII to the Emperor Henry III. It is now generally accepted that the crown was made in the workshops of the Monastery of Reichenau on Lake Constance, which was also the seat of the Imperial Chancellery, and that it was probably made for Otto I about 961. The cross is thought to have come from the same workshop and dates from the same time as the crown but was probably first used as a pectoral cross. The arch which was a later addition probably replaced an earlier arch.

There is also in the Vienna Treasury a leather case made for the crown for Charles IV after he had taken the crown to Bohemia in 1350. The leather work is beautifully decorated and painted and bears the imperial eagle and the Bohemian lion. It is of the same workmanship as the case made for the crown of St Wenceslas at Prague in 1347.

The most puzzling thing about the crown is its status. There have been many theories about this which have not always been backed by solid evidence and in some cases national sentiments have been allowed to influence the conclusions. One fact which is very clear is that at least from the time of Henry II possession of the crown was considered to be a matter of great importance and materially strengthened the chances of a candidate to be chosen as German king. We have already seen that Henry II even arrested Archbishop Heribert so that he could seize the imperial insignia. There are various other examples such as when Mathilda, on the death of Henry V, had to hand over the imperial insignia to the archbishop although she was allowed to keep the personal regalia of the late Emperor. In the XIII century we find in a poem of Walther von der Vogelweide the idea that he who wears the crown with the *Orphanus* was the real emperor for only the emperor could wear the *Orphanus* and therefore a rival not being in possession of the crown with the *Orphanus* had no valid claim to the throne. Apart from the possession of the insignia it was also considered necessary for the German king to be crowned at Aix, but we find examples of a king in possession of the proper crown being unable to be crowned at Aix and being crowned elsewhere while a rival king in possession of only a personal crown is crowned at Aix. It was usual, however, for the rightful king to undergo a second coronation at Aix at the first opportunity.

Some writers seem to have taken it for granted that the German Imperial Crown was that with which the emperors were crowned by the Pope in Rome. It must first be said that for centuries no importance seems to have been attached to a particular crown being used at a coronation. It is fairly certain that in Carolingian times the Pope provided the crown for the imperial coronation and that in the case of Louis I an attempt was made to connect this with the Donation of Constantine. This led the popes to claim that they were the source of the imperial dignity, which is exemplified by the declaration of John VIII that Charles the Bald owed his crown to the Pope alone. We have definite information, at least in the cases of Louis II in 844, Charles III in 881 and Berengar in 915, that the doubtful crowns used were the gifts of the popes. It is dubious whether Otto I was crowned Emperor with the crown he had had made, although he may have included it in the new set of ornaments which he took to Rome. If we are to accept the deep religious symbolism of the crown and the emphasis on Otto's position as *Rex et Sacerdos* it seems likely that the Pope would have been reluctant to place such an ornament on Otto's head. Conversely Otto was the first German king to be crowned at Aix with all its associations of Charlemagne and to sit on the throne of his great predecessor. As Charlemagne's heir he might have been reluctant for the Pope to crown him with an ornament in which he had been at pains to symbolise the special position which he claimed. It seems more likely that Otto wore his crown on his entry into Rome and was crowned by the Pope with another crown. There is no record as to what crowns were used at the coronations of Otto II or Otto III but Henry II was crowned with a new crown which was a gift of the Pope. With the Franconian or Salian emperors we know definitely that the Pope provided crowns for Conrad II, Henry III, Henry IV and Henry V. There is no record of the crowns which were used in the subsequent coronations down to that of Frederick II, who seems to have taken the imperial insignia to Rome in 1212, as we know he returned them to Germany, but he may not have been crowned with them. After this there is no evidence until Frederick III in 1452. Frederick III was a devotee of Charlemagne and the account of the coronation by the imperial Minister, Kasper Enenkel, states that the Emperor attended the coronation mass 'clothed with the Holy Robes of the Emperor Charlemagne which had happened to no Emperor for many hundreds of years and which were all treasured for the great honour and the especial mercy of God'. We know, too, that Aeneas Silvius Piccolomini, afterwards Pope Pius II, exclaimed that he was unable to understand why Frederick had sent for the insignia of Charlemagne instead of availing himself of his own newly-made insignia (*Plate 107, a*). For the last coronation of an emperor in Italy, that of Charles V in Bologna, in 1530, the German Imperial Crown was not used. After this all coronations were held in Frankfurt and the crown was definitely used to crown the emperor on each occasion. It is probably because of this that the notion gained widespread belief that the crown was the ancient coronation crown with which all the emperors had been crowned. An indication as to the use of the German Imperial Crown at Rome is contained in a letter from Pope Urban IV to Richard of Cornwall in which he states that Richard had used at his coronation at Aix the insignia worn by the German kings on their entry into Rome for their imperial coronation.

There are some writers who, while not claiming that the crown was used at imperial coronations, assert that it was the coronation crown of the German kings. There is no evidence of the crown being used at the coronations of the kings of the Saxon and Franconian dynasties. We know that Conrad III was unable to gain possession of the regalia for his coronation, as they were in the possession of Henry the Proud, Duke of Saxony and Bavaria, his rival, and as his successor Frederick I did not come to terms until 1159 with Henry the Lion, into whose possession the crown had passed, it would not have been available for his coronation in Aix in 1152. William, Count of Holland, was not in possession of the regalia at the time of his coronation at Aix, and according to the Chronicler *Belgicus* the regalia used at William's coronation, and many other crown jewels, were subsequently destroyed by fire on the night of William's marriage to a daughter of the Guelphs in Brunswick. We are uncertain as to what crown was used by Richard of Cornwall but the indications are that he may have used the German Imperial Crown. According to the Saxon *Weltschronik* Richard's successor, Rudolph of Hapsburg, was crowned with the 'Holy Roman Crown which had not happened to any king so they say since Charlemagne'. At the next coronation, that of

Adolf of Nassau, the imperial regalia were not in his possession. The next king, Albert, had possession of the regalia but there is no evidence that he used them, while we have also no information as to the crown used at Henry VII's coronation at Aix in 1309. Frederick, the Fair had possession of the regalia at the time of his coronation at Bonn in 1313, but not so his rival, Louis IV, who was crowned at Aix in the same year. Charles IV only came into possession of the regalia in 1350 after he had been twice crowned as German King. Charles's son, Wenceslas, was crowned at Aix in 1376 during his father's lifetime, but the imperial regalia were at Prague and were not brought to Aix for the occasion. When he was deposed in 1400 he refused to hand over the regalia which were, therefore, not available either for the coronations of Rupert in 1401 or Sigismund in 1414. For the coronation of Frederick III in 1442 the regalia were sent to Aix from Nuremberg and were used. Again in 1486 they were sent to Aix for the coronation of Maximilian I. In 1520 they were sent to Aix for the coronation of Charles V but may have arrived too late to be used, which possibly accounts for the fact that Charles wore them the following year at his first Reichstag. It is clear, therefore, that till the time when the crown was kept at Nuremberg it was not in regular use at the Aix coronations.

The next aspect of the status of the crown is its use iconographically. The earliest representation in which the crown can be actually identified is on the gravestone of Rudolph of Hapsburg at Speyer, which, although restored in the XIX century, is believed to follow the original. It might be thought that the status of the Imperial Crown would have been placed so high that it would have been used iconographically on coins and seals, but it was never so used as a symbol of the imperial office. Instead the heraldic crown with two arches was used from the time of Conrad III, and this was to some extent replaced from the time of Frederick III and Maximilian I by the mitre crown. But in the reign of Frederick III a special group of commemorative coins was made for the Aix coronation and the German Imperial Crown was used as the appropriate symbol of the King of the Romans. It was used, too, very occasionally on coins minted in Nuremberg during the period that the regalia were kept in that city, but in relation to the position of the King of the Romans.[1] But generally speaking numismatic use of the German Imperial Crown was very rare, and the few occasions on which it was depicted were exceptional. It does not appear in portraiture either until the time of Dürer,[2] who painted a picture of Charlemagne invested in the imperial insignia of later times with the German Imperial Crown on his head.

It is clear, therefore, that the crown which from the start was a rich and magnificent work of art, and steeped in mystical religious symbolism so beloved in the Middle Ages, underwent various changes of status. Its possession meant that the holder would be elected German king and thus become emperor, and it was perhaps this meaning that made it the practice for the King of the Romans to make his state entry into Rome wearing the German Imperial Crown for all to behold. The actual crown which the Pope placed on the emperor's head was not considered to be of any particular significance and was frequently given by emperors to some church or monastery. As time passed the

---

[1] Eduard Holzmair: *Nuremberger und Rudolfinische Kaiserkrone im Spiegel der Numismatik*, Vienna 1947.

[2] There is also an engraving by Delsenbach of Charlemagne attired in coronation robes and with the imperial insignia (*Plate 103*).

original symbolism became forgotten, and in the xiv century the crown became associated with the name of Charlemagne. This association is first mentioned in 1315 and was officially accorded in the 1350 inventory by Charles IV, who did much to foster the cult of Charlemagne. At about the same time the imperial insignia began to be regarded as relics, although it was not until Sigismund removed the regalia to Nuremberg in 1424 that the reliquary character of the imperial ornaments was confirmed by Papal authority, and so these ancient objects came to be revered. The Imperial Crown became the supreme emblem of the sovereign who had been chosen as German king, who had been crowned at Aix taking the title of *Rex Romanorum Semper Augustus* and who thus by right was entitled by his coronation in Rome to take the imperial title.

The Sceptre (Plate 104, a).

Although the sceptre came to take its place as a second ornament in the regalia it was not delivered at early coronations. It was, however, used in the portraiture of the German kings and emperors, particularly on their seals. It was probably first delivered at an imperial coronation in Rome when Frederick I was crowned in 1155. The first mention of a sceptre in the imperial regalia is in the inventory of the regalia in the offer to Charles IV by Louis of Brandenburg which included two such ornaments, one of which has disappeared. The other of gilded silver is in all probability the one which is still in existence today. It is of early xiv-century workmanship of simple design and apart from some small pearls is unadorned with precious stones. It consists of a hollow six-sided shaft terminating at the top in a fleur-de-lis and at the bottom in a pomellum. This pomellum is encircled by a ring and a smaller ring is placed a little way up the shaft so as to mark off the place for holding the sceptre. These rings are adorned with little circlets of pearls set in a groove. A third plain ring is set midway between the top of the sceptre, while a fourth similar in design to the lower two is placed on the top of the shaft immediately under the terminating ornament. From this last ring spring six large oak leaves, three of which curve upwards and their ends, which are turned in, support an acorn. The other three leaves curve downwards, their pointed tips covering the terminating ring of the shaft.

A second ornament, which has erroneously been described as a sceptre, is also preserved at Vienna. It was not used as such at coronations and there is little doubt that it was originally the *Aspergillum* or Holy Water sprinkler (*Plate 104, a*). In the Middle Ages it was customary for the Holy Water to be taken by means of a Holy Water sprinkler held in the right hand. A sponge saturated with the Holy Water was placed in the cone-shaped top of the sprinkler which was furnished with a screw which could be undone for the purpose of inserting the sponge. The exterior of the cone was perforated with little holes through which the Holy Water could be sprinkled. The *Aspergillum* consists of a shaft composed of a slender rod covered with silver plate fastened to the rod by riveting nails. There is a pomellum at the foot and another gilded knob half-way up the rod. A stiff foliage ornamentation of a formal design surmounts the staff on which rests the perforated hollow cone in which the sponge was formerly placed. The lower part of the screw for unfastening the cone is still visible, but the latter is now firmly welded to the staff. A piece of metal in the lower pomellum, perhaps there by accident, gives out a ringing sound when the sceptre is moved. This ornament is of early xiii-century workmanship.

The Orb (Plate 104, a).

The imperial orb belongs to the second half of the xii century and is of West German workmanship, possibly from Cologne. It is a hollow sphere 61·5 cm high and composed of six golden plates soldered together. The gold is of 24 carats. A narrow filigree band runs round the orb horizontally dividing it into two halves. Two further bands intersected at the poles encircle the orb vertically, the points of intersection being covered with plaques ornamented with filigree foliage work. The vertical bands on the upper half of the orb are ornamented with gems and bisected with pearls set in smooth capsules serrated at the top. The orb contains a filling of resin to prevent it from becoming dented. The cross surmounting the orb is, in shape and decoration, somewhat similar to the pectoral cross worn by some Byzantine emperors and later by the Western bishops. It is of 21 carat gold, each of the cross arms terminating in a fleur-de-lis. The cross is decorated on both sides with precious stones and bisected pearls. The spaces between the gems are filled with a very fine design of leaves and blossoms in filigree. The stones are sapphires, most of which have evidently been previously used for another purpose as they have been bored through the centre, amethysts, garnets and emeralds. In the centre of the back of the cross at the junction of the arms is a sapphire of the first water. It probably formerly adorned an older signet ring, for on the inner surface is a deeply engraved monogram. Owing to its position it is difficult to decipher but is evidently of Byzantine workmanship. On the sides of the cross is a curious decoration consisting of a narrow groove inside which is set, at regular intervals, little gold rings strung on a strong silk thread.

The Sabre of Charlemagne (Plate 104, c (i)).

The German king was girt with this weapon at the coronation at Aix with the words 'receive this sword by the hands of the bishops'. It was suggested by von Murr that it was a gift to Charlemagne from Harun-el-Raschid, and a later theory was that it was part of the booty Charlemagne took from the Avars. Later investigation[1] identifies it as a sceptre which the widowed Queen Anastasia of Hungary, Mother of King Salomon, presented to Otto of Northeim, Duke of Bavaria, and it passed into the possession of Luitpold Merseburg and then to Henry IV. According to a legend at that time it was the sword of Attila, King of the Huns. Another legend claimed that it was the sword which had been brought to Charlemagne by an angel from heaven. Some confusion arose as to whether the legend applied to this weapon or to the ceremonial sword, both of which have at times borne the name of Charlemagne. It is considered that it probably dates from the end of the IX century and is of Eastern European origin.

The Imperial Sword of St Maurice (Plate 104, b).

This sword is of German work of the XI century although it has been altered subsequently at various times. Since the time of Charles III it has been known as the Sword of St Maurice after the Christian leader of the Thebaean Legion who perished before the gates of Cologne in A.D. 297. It was made as a cermonial sword to be carried with the point upwards in which position an inscription can be read. It was always carried before the emperor in the coronation procession and is the only piece of the regalia that has been consistently used until the end of the Hapsburg monarchy in 1918. It was carried before the emperor when he in person opened the Austrian and Hungarian parliaments, and it was last used at the coronation of Charles, as King of Hungary in 1916. The pommel and cross-piece are slightly gilded and the hilt is bound with silver wire added in the XVI century. On the pommel is an inscription and the imperial eagle added by Otto IV. On the cross-bar are the inscriptions *CRISTVS: VINCIT: CRISTVS REINAT*, and *CRISTVS REIGNAT: CRISTVS INPERAT*, which is the last verse of the Laudes. The scabbard is of olive wood and covered with gold foil and fourteen enamel plates bordered with garnets and pearls. The plaques bear the figures of the German rulers probably beginning with Charlemagne. As the fourteenth of the German kings was Conrad II it was thought that the sword was made for his successor Henry III.

[1] P. E. Schramm: *Herrschaftszeichen und Staatssymbolik.*

Engraving by Delsenbach of Charlemagne wearing German imperial coronation robes (p. 334, footnote 2)

a   *Imperial sceptre, aspergillum and orb. Treasury, Vienna (p. 335)*

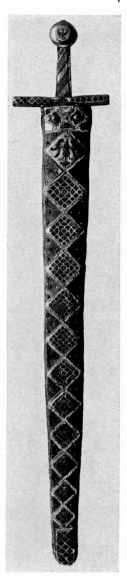

b   *Sword of St Maurice. Treasury, Vienna (p. 336)*

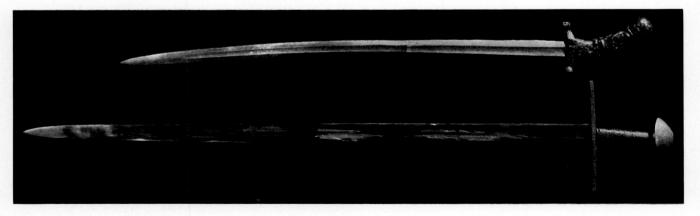

c   (i) *Sabre of Charlemagne;* (ii) *imperial sword of ceremony. Treasury, Vienna* (pp. 336 and 337)

The Imperial Sword of Ceremony (Plate 104, c (ii)).

The Imperial Sword of Ceremony was made in the workshops of Palermo for Frederick II. The hilt and cross-bar are of wood and covered with gold plaques richly decorated with enamel and filigree. The pommel is ornamented with the imperial eagle and Bohemian lion which were added by Charles IV. It was placed on the grave of the Empress Constance together with the *kamelaukion* in the Cathedral Treasury at Palermo. Later it was used for dubbing as knights the emissaries who brought the regalia from Nuremberg for the coronations.

The Dalmatic

The first ceremonial garment to be put on at coronations was the *tunica talaris*. This garment reached to the feet and was adjusted to the stature of the wearer by a girdle. Only the lower hem and the extremity of the sleeves were visible under the alb. It was also called the dalmatic. It was made in the royal workshops in Palermo between 1130 and 1154. It is of heavy material rather like serge in texture and of very dark purple called by the Byzantines *purpura imperialis*. The tunic is bordered at the hem and at the ends of the sleeves with a crimson facing embroidered in gold thread. The lower hem has a recurring pattern containing a heart-shaped ornament in the centre of which is a formal design, probably intended for an Arabian palm tree but not unlike a fleur-de-lis. The hem is bordered on either side with a triple row of pearls. The sleeve opening is also edged on either side with three rows of pearls and is very skilfully and richly embroidered. A formal plant ornament rises in the centre between two root leaves. The outlines of this ornament, instead of being embroidered in gold thread are composed of little tubes of gold, like glass beads, sewn on to the material beneath. This central plant is surrounded by other foliage decoration of an obviously Saracenic character. The lower border is decorated by little circles of gold plate, attached to the material beneath through small eyelet holes, and covered with designs in enamel. These are very similar in design to the gold plates on the imperial mantle and this, together with the oriental character of the embroidery, leaves no doubt that the tunic was made in the royal factory at Palermo for the Norman kings by Saracen-Sicilian embroiderers. The tunic is unlined; it is open at the neck so that it can easily be slipped over the head, is rather close fitting at the waist and is broadened out towards the feet by the insertion of additional pieces of material at the side seams.

The Alb

After the emperor had donned the *tunica talaris* he was handed the Imperial Alb by two canons, with whose help he put it on. It was then shortened by means of a girdle so as to expose to view the richly decorated border of the tunic. The Imperial Alb is an exact copy, both as regards cut and decoration, of the ecclesiastical alb of the XII century. The original material was a heavy white silk, but in the XVIII century this was covered by a white silk taffeta, probably owing to damage from wear and tear. Round the hem of the Alb runs a broad border of violet silk, richly embroidered in gold. This border is divided into five, a wide central stripe adorned with plant and animal decoration and two narrow strips on either side. The outermost and narrowest strips are patterned with a Latin inscription in Roman lettering, repeated eight times the English translation of which reads that the Alb was made in the Royal Workshops in Palermo for King William II in 1181. On the slightly broader divisions inside these strips is an Arabic inscription, also repeated eight times, a rough translation of which would run:

(This Alb) belongs to those vestments which were made by the command of the most honourable King William II whom may God strengthen, His omnipotence succour and His power give victory, Lord of Italy, Lombardy, Calabria and Sicily, the support of the Pope of Rome, the defender of the Christian religion—in the well furnished royal workshops, dated by the little chronology, the year 1181, of the era of Our Lord Jesus the Messiah. In the fourteenth year of the Indication.

The embroidery of lions and griffins on the central broad strip is executed in a thin and flexible gold wire and has preserved its original freshness undamaged to this day. At the neck of the Alb there is a square insertion of purple material, patterned with embroideries of gold and pearls. On the sleeves, where in older times the metal bracelets were worn, and also at the openings, are two further strips of gold and pearl embroidery.

The Coronation Mantle

The Coronation Mantle was brought to Germany by the Emperor Henry VI and was probably selected by the Emperor Frederick II for his coronation in Rome in 1220. It is the richest and most sumptuous vestment of the imperial robes and can be regarded as the high watermark of the art of the Saracen-Sicilian embroiderers and goldsmiths. The shape is that of the ecclesiastical pluviale or cappa, i.e. semi-circular with an opening down the front. The Mantle measures a little over 10½ ft round the hem and is nearly 5 ft in length. The material is a scarlet red silk, with a faint pattern on the outer side. As the manufacture of silk was unknown in Sicily before the middle of the XI century, it is probable that this scarlet material was imported from Byzantium. Down the centre of the back of the Mantle is a date palm tree embroidered in oriental gold thread. The branches are outlined by a double row of pearls. On either side of this central date palm is embroidered a lion fighting with a camel; the lion is pinning down the camel with his claws. The aurefrisia or bordering strip which runs round the neck and down the front edges of the Mantle is adorned with alternating four-petalled roses and diamonds outlined with a double row of pearls and surrounded with foliage work, also of pearls. The centre of the roses is a lily-like ornament in gold embroidery; the diamonds are filled with small gold plates decorated with transparent enamels. The hem of the Mantle is edged with a triple row of pearls and contains an inscription in Arabic characters. It was the custom in the East for caliphs and emirs to have such inscriptions embroidered on their ceremonial robes. The inscription states that the Mantle was made in Palermo at the royal factory in the Year of the Hegira 528. This corresponds to the year A.D. 1133 and shows that the Mantle was made for the Norman King of Sicily, Roger II. These court factories for the production of silk stuffs and gold and pearl embroideries were established near the palaces of all the important Musulman dynasties, and there is no doubt that the Norman rulers took under their protection the Palermo factory established by their Saracen predecessors in Sicily.

In the front of the Mantle, just below the neck and immediately above the heads of the embroidered lions, are two gold medallions, one on either side, covered in enamels in a geometric design. These gold medallions are set in the centre of a four-petalled rose of filigree work, studded with precious stones. They seem to serve no purpose except of adornment, for the fastening of the Mantle was effected by means of two wrought gold fibulas or staples, placed at the opening of the neck, which could be fastened by a gold pin.

Not the least interesting part of the Mantle is the lining, which is of about the same date as the rest of the Mantle but is composed of three separate materials. On both sides of the opening is a very curious cloth of gold tissue with a woven design illustrating the Fall of Man. Bock considers that this cloth of gold tissue may once have formed part of the state robe of one of the Saracen Emirs of Sicily and afterwards, because of its beauty, have been used to form the lining of the Mantle of their Norman successors. This would account for the bird and dragon tissues, obviously a different part of the Emir's robe. The design, with certain variations, is repeated at intervals enclosed in a polygonal frame. In the centre is the Tree of Knowledge, with little apples on the branches; the head of the serpent appears here and there among the branches. On either side of the tree stand Adam and Eve. In some of the designs Eve is offering the apple to Adam; in others Adam has taken it from her. The greater part of the back of the Mantle is lined with a very beautiful design of sea-green leaves on a brownish ground with occasional flowers of a pale yellow colour. Two other designs in cloth of gold tissue are visible in places, one known as the bird-tissue, the other as the dragon-tissue. The reason for the good state of preservation of the lining is that at some time during the late Middle Ages it was covered by an outer lining of green silk. This has only recently been removed.

On either side of the front opening the original lining has been covered with a facing of figured damask, of North Italian manufacture of the xv century. This damask has a design of flowers and foliage in gold and colours on a red ground. This was probably added, owing to wear and consequent damage to the gold tissue beneath, when the coronation vestments were repaired by the Clarissine nuns in 1520.

The Stole

The Imperial Stole differs from the usual ecclesiastical stole of the Middle Ages by its much greater length and breadth. It is over 8 in. wide and, excluding the fringes, has the abnormal length of nearly 19 ft. It was worn crossed over the breast and looped up by a girdle. Even so, it is difficult to see how its inordinate length could have been bestowed, but Bock considers that a loop was made at the back and the inner edges sewn together at the neck, the joined portion being worn as a hood or cape down the centre of the back either inside or outside the Mantle.

The Stole is made of a yellow silk material, interwoven with threads of gold and is probably of North Italian manufacture. It is ornamented by black imperial eagles in medallions alternating with gold plates decorated with enamel work. Both eagles and gold plates are bordered with a double row of pearls. Of the sixty-eight gold plates, eighteen are large and the remaining fifty somewhat smaller. The smaller plates are set alternately with eagles along both sides of the stole, and are mostly in the shape of twelve-pointed stars. The larger plates are placed down the centre and are mostly shaped like four-petalled roses. The eagles are embroidered in black silk on a gold ground; the silk threads, which perhaps suffered damage in dyeing, have almost completely disappeared. The ends of the Stole are decorated with a fringe of a rather unusual type. It is nearly 7 in. long and is composed of tassels alternately of green and violet silk, wrapped round with gold thread and enclosed in a fine net of seed pearls. These tassels divide into two, the two parts being subdivided again into three. The edges of the Stole are bordered with a double row of pearls. It is lined with a plain red taffeta of no particular interest which projects beyond the pearl border on either side. The exact date of the stole is unknown but it is considered to belong to the early part of the xiv century and before 1348.

The Dalmatic embroidered with Eagles

This Dalmatic is one of the most beautiful ornaments of the imperial regalia and as such is described here, but it cannot be proved that it was ever worn during the coronation ceremony. In shape it resembles the usual dalmatics or deacons' vestments of the xiii and xiv centuries. The richness of the decoration suggests that it is unlikely that it was worn as an undergarment, but the narrowness of the sleeves and the neck opening makes it improbable that it could have been worn over the voluminous Alb. It is certain that it was not worn at the later coronations, but it is possible that it was assumed during part of the earlier ceremonies; it may, for instance, have been donned as an upper garment by some of the emperors when they in their role as deacon sang the Gospel at the coronation mass; or possibly at Aix when they were formally appointed as canons of the coronation church.

This Dalmatic is of German workmanship of the early XIV century and is first mentioned in the 1350 inventory. The figured purple material of which it is composed is of Chinese origin. Over the surface of this material are scattered circular embroidered medallions containing imperial eagles. The embroidery is not sewn on to the material itself but on to strong linen, which is first covered with gold thread, over which the eagles are embroidered in black silk, the eyes being formed of small rubies, emeralds and garnets. The hem, neck and armholes, and the ends of the sleeves are edged with a very fine border of embroidery containing royal portraits in irregular circular frames, interspersed with foliage work, whose naturalistic design is typical of the late Gothic period. In the centre of the hem is the portrait of an old, bearded emperor, probably intended to represent Charlemagne, the other circles contain male and female figures in full royal and imperial attire. There was formerly a hood to match this dalmatic which was unfortunately among the lost Nuremberg regalia.

The Girdles

Two girdles are still preserved in the Vienna Treasury; one is a military girdle and was used to gird on the Sword of St Maurice; the other is ecclesiastical in pattern, and was originally used to fasten the Alb but latterly for the purpose of securing the stole.

The military girdle is of Sicilian workmanship of the late XII or early XIII century. It is of silk, interwoven with gold, and has a silver gilt buckle and clasp. The eyelet holes for the insertion of the tongue of the buckle are composed of small metal rings, but the belt must originally have been made for a wearer of no small proportions, for the distance between the buckle and the first eyelet hole is 46 in. Consequently the fabric of the belt shows traces of wear at various places where the tongue of the buckle has been inserted to suit the proportions of less ample figures. The fabric of the belt has been woven on a special ribbon-loom and is of a fashion no longer practised. Three strips, divided by woven lines, once deep red but now faded, compose the belt. The central strip is adorned with woven plant and animal figures, while the outer strips have a woven inscription in versal letters which reads:

CRISTVS RIEHGNAT CRISTVS INQ PARAT DDEVS (vincit).

A similar inscription adorns the guard of the Sword of St Maurice:

The ecclesiastical girdle is of a heavy blue silk; it is fastened by means of two silk cords attached to the lining. The ends of the girdle were used to adjust the Stole across the breast in the form of a cross. The lining is of the same material the joining seams being covered with gold thread. The girdle is only ornamented at the ends; here are sewn on at intervals three gold plates on each side. These gold plates, which are ornamented with a geometric design in pierced filigree work, fill the whole width of the girdle; the central plate on each side is broad, the two others narrow. The cords for fastening the girdle are of red and blue silk and are just over 2 ft long. The geometric design of the filigree plates show that the girdle is of Saracen-Sicilian workmanship of the late XII century.

The Gloves

The Gloves are of Saracen-Sicilian workmanship, probably of the early XIII but possibly of the late XII century. The characteristic patterns of the enamel work on the Gloves, which bears a close resemblance to the enamel plaques on the Mantle and tunic, are evidence of the origin in the royal workshops of Palermo but the imperial eagle embroidered on the palms shows that they were made for the Hohenstaufen successors to the Norman kings, probably for the Emperor Frederick II.

The Gloves are made of that heavy silk material called by French archaeologists *Lance-Croise*, sewn together by strong stitches. They are a deep reddish purple in colour. A curving foliage and tendril pattern in gold embroidery adorns the backs of the Gloves; the spaces between the tendrils are adorned by uncut rubies and sapphires, surrounded with seed pearls. The remainder of the surface is studded with seed pearls, attached singly with white silk threads. The first and third fingers of the left glove and the first finger of the right are ornamented at the base by thin gold plates, on which are figures of sirens in cloisonné enamel on a dark blue ground. Just below the knuckle joint of the middle finger of the left hand is a further irregularly shaped gold plate, upon which is the figure of an angel in niello, set in a frame of pearls. There is a similar frame of pearls on the right glove but the gold plate is much smaller and bears a geometrical design, the remaining space being filled with pearls. Below these plates, on both gloves, is a further gold plaque bearing an enamelled design of a fleur-de-lis, while on either side are two further plaques with birds heads in enamel. The fleurs-de-lis are similar in shape to those in the royal arms of France from the XIII century onwards and to those on the *kamelaukion* found in the time of Constance II in Palermo Cathedral. The arrangement of the gold plates and precious stones is most skilfully designed so that the gloves are quite flexible and do not impede the movement of the hands. The border of the gloves has a double row of pearls above and below; the space between on the back of the gloves is decorated in enamels. The central plate is surrounded on either side by two uncut rubies also set with pearls. All the gold plates show traces of damage and some have become half detached from the material beneath. The palms of the gloves are decorated with various foliage and tendril designs in gold embroidery. The embroidery on the fingers forms zigzag and geometrical designs. The centre of the palms of the gloves is filled by a gold embroidered imperial eagle with wings outspread. The borders are set with enamelled plates and precious stones corresponding to the borders of the back of the Gloves.

The Hose

The Imperial Hose, or Stockings, are also cut according to an ecclesiastical pattern and the inscription round the top shows that they also were made in the royal workshops at Palermo; this inscription is closely akin to that running round the hem of the Alb, which makes it probable that the stockings are of about 1181.

The Stockings are composed of three pieces of material; one piece, which has been left un-adorned, covers the instep; the second covers the legs and heels, while an embroidered border runs round the top. The stockings are 23 in. long from heel to top. The material of which they are composed is a heavy crimson silk, without pattern, of similar texture and colour to that of which the Gloves are made. The plain instep piece is attached to the leg pieces on the ankle and in the centre of the sole of the foot. The leg pieces are also joined under the heel in a manner which would hardly seem to be comfortable to the wearer. It was customary in the Middle Ages, however, for the feet and legs to be swathed in strips of linen. This accounts for the fact that the Stockings are unlined and show few traces of wear or soiling on the inside. The exteriors, too, are in a comparatively good state of preservation, only in places showing traces of wear and tear.

The leg pieces of the Stockings are embroidered in gold with four-petalled roses whose centres are filled with cruciform ornaments. The upper border is woven of a bright green material with an inwoven pattern in gold. Round the top and bottom runs a strip of material bearing an Arabic inscription to the effect that the stockings were destined for the Norman King William II of Sicily. The inscription is incomplete, but the wording is similar to that on the Alb. It is probable that these ribbons containing inscriptions were woven on long continuous strips on a special loom and were then used for decoration purposes without regard to the available space; this would account for the incompleteness of the inscription.

The Shoes

There were formerly three pairs of shoes or sandals among the regalia but two of these disappeared with other articles of insignia during the flight from Nuremberg in 1796. The remaining pair, however, is mentioned in an inventory of 1424; being of medium size these shoes were probably those used at coronations until the end of the XVIII century. The Sicilian origin of the shoes is established by the character of the embroidery and enamel work, the fact that the material of which they consist is the same as that of which the Imperial Mantle is made, and their strong resemblance in decoration to the funeral crown of Henry VI in Palermo Cathedral. The shape of the shoes is strongly reminiscent of the old Roman sandal. It is known that in the time of Constantine the Great, both the Emperor and the Pope wore such sandals, which later became the pattern for ceremonial ecclesiastical foot coverings. It can be established by documentary evidence that Pope Innocent II expressly granted permission for Roger II of Sicily to wear such sandals, a permission which was later confirmed by Pope Lucius II. There can, therefore, be little doubt that these shoes formed part of the treasure brought to Germany by Henry VI.

The upper part of the shoes consists of a strong red silk material which is joined to the thick leather soles by firm stitches. A broad strip of cloth of gold runs down the centre of the foot. This strip has a woven pattern of circles containing fantastic animals. Alternating with these circles are other circles of pearl embroidery surrounding an inset uncut gem, either an amethyst or a pearl, in a strongly projecting setting. Similar strips of cloth of gold with inwoven animal figures decorate the back of the heel and the sides of the shoes, but the central figure of the side strips is a siren or mermaid. The spaces between the cloth of gold strips are filled with pearl embroideries. The inside of the shoe is lined with a red silk material, much damaged by age and wear. On the instep, near the ankle opening, are slits in the material through which the embroidered stockings could be seen; the slits are edged with pearls. The narrow bands of material between these slits are furnished with eyelet holes through which the strong silk laces for fastening the shoes were passed.

Copies of the Imperial Vestments made in the XVIII Century

During the reign of Francis I copies of the regalia and of many of the vestments were made for the coronation of his son Joseph II in 1764 at Frankfurt. It was not possible for Joseph to use the proper regalia and vestments and for his father to wear the substitute set. A copy of the crown, sceptre, and the orb were melted down in 1872, but the vestments are still kept in the Vienna Treasury and consist of:

1. The *Tunicella* of dark blue silk, edged with gold embroidery. On the borders of the sleeves are set small pates of gold covered with enamel.
2. The Stole of gold brocade ornamented with alternating black imperial eagles and gold and enamel plates.
3. The Alb of white silk with broad insertions of gold embroidery at the front and back of the neck. Further gold embroidery adorns the hem and the edge of the sleeves, the latter in addition being set with rubies and sapphires.
4. The Gloves of red silk, with touches of lilac, richly adorned with gold embroidery, rubies and plates of gold and enamel.

5. The *Cingulum Pontificum* of blue silk decorated with gold plates and rubies.
6. The Sword Belt of gold tissue with a gold clasp.
7. The Stockings of rose-coloured silk, with touches of lilac and embroidered in gold.
8. The Shoes of rose-coloured silk with touches of lilac, ornamented with gold embroidery, sapphires, rubies and emeralds.
9. The Sword, mounted in gold and formerly adorned with precious stones of which only the rubies and one transparent stone on a red ground remain.
10. The Coronation Mantle of rose-coloured silk with touches of lilac. Instead of the pearls which adorn the old Imperial Mantle this Mantle is decorated with silver plates. On the shoulders the plates are of gold and enamel set with precious stones. The gold clasps are likewise set with gems and are in addition decorated with a fine engraved design of foliage work in the baroque style. The lining is of apple green silk.

Of the other ornaments and reliquaries there are but a few and only the most important need be dealt with here.

The Imperial Cross (Plate 105, a)

The imperial cross was from the first designed as a reliquary and is of German origin, probably of about the year 1032. It seems to have been ordered by Henry II but was not finished until the reign of his successor Conrad II.

It is of wood overlaid with silver gilt plates. The front of the Cross is adorned with precious stones, pearls and filigree work, the side with ornamental inscriptions in niello, while on the back are other representations in niello—in the centre the Lamb and on the arms of the Cross the Twelve Apostles, with the signs of the four evangelists at the extremities. Cavities have been hollowed out of the wood of the Cross to form receptacles for relics. In one cavity in the horizontal arms of the Cross there is a fragment of the Sacred Lance, and in the perpendicular arms a piece of the True Cross. The cavities are sealed by gold plates which can be either opened or taken away altogether. The niello inscription on the sides of the Cross reads: *ECCE CRUCEM DOMINI FUGIAT PARS HOSTIS INIQUI HINC CHUONRADE TIBI CEDANT OMNES INIMICI.* The style of the lettering makes it certain that the Conrad referred to is Conrad II, and the marked resemblance between filigree work and the settings of the gems on the front of the Cross and the similar work on the Crown are of great help in determining the date of the latter. The silver gilt pedestal on which the Cross stands is an addition of a later date. As the inscription round the base bears witness, it was made for Charles IV in 1352. The inscription runs: *ANNO MILLENO TERCIO QUINQUAGENO SECUNDO CAROLUS AUGUSTUS ROMANUS REX QUE BOHEMUS HOC LIGNUM DOMINI TALI PEDE SIC DECORAVIT.* The pedestal is adorned with two shields, one bearing the Bohemian Lion and the other the one-headed eagle.

The Holy Lance (Plate 105, b)

The origin of this lance has already been traced. In the reign of Henry III it became known as the Lance of St Maurice, and in the reign of Charles IV, by whom so many of the articles of the regalia were renamed, the name of St Maurice was transferred to one of the imperial swords and the lance became known as the Lance of the Passion and was considered to be the weapon with which the Roman soldier Longinus pierced the side of Christ at the Crucifixion. It is thus described in the Nuremberg *Heilthumsbüchlein*, and as such was exhibited in the annual procession of relics and regalia in that city.

There is no doubt that the lance is of very ancient origin and experts have declared its shape to be typical of similar weapons of the Carolingian period; it may well date back to Charlemagne himself.

The blade is made from the steel of Siegen, which in the early Middle Ages was rather rare and valuable and therefore much prized. In the early Middle Ages a piece was removed from the centre of the blade and a nail, supposed to be from the True Cross, was fastened in the oblong opening this formed by means of a lashing of silver wire. The hole thus made weakened the blade which is cracked beneath the opening. Over this crack has been placed a broad iron band covered with a thick plating of silver. An inscription in Latin characters running along a gilded strip shows that this repair was carried out during the reign of the Emperor Henry III. The inscription reads: *CLAVUS DOMINICUS HEINRICUS DEI GRATIA TERCIUS ROMANORUM IMPERATOR AUGUSTUS HOC AGENTUM IVSSIT FABRICARI AD CONFIRMATIONEM CLAVI DOMINI ET LANCEE SANCTI MAURICII. SANCTUS MAURICIUS.* In the reign of Charles IV this earlier repair was entirely covered by another broad band, this time of gold, on the front and back of which are the words: *LANCEA ET CLAVUS DOMINI.* It is considered probable that this gold band was added to conceal the fact that the lower third of the sacred nail is missing. It is thought that Charles removed this and presented it to his beloved Church of St Vitus in Prague; at any rate the treasury of St Vitus contains a relic, said to be a fragment of a Nail of the Cross and about 8 cm in length, which may well be the missing piece. The nail in the lance is of an unusual and ornamental shape. There is no shaft to the lance and the head fits the cavity in the horizontal arms of the Imperial Cross hollowed out for its reception. There is no documentary evidence to prove the exact date at which the Holy Lance ceased to be an article of regalia. It is first mentioned as being enclosed in the reliquary Cross in the inventory of 1350, on the occasion of the handing over of the regalia to Charles IV by Louis of Bavaria.

The Book of the Holy Gospels (Plate 105, c)

This Book of the Gospels played an important part in the coronation ceremony, for upon it the emperor took the coronation oath by laying two fingers on the first page of the Gospel of St John. Tradition states that the Book was found on the knees of Charlemagne in his tomb. There is no doubt that the manuscript is of great antiquity and may possibly date back to the days either of Charlemagne himself or at any rate of his immediate successors. In spite of much research the actual date has never been ascertained, but both the style of the lettering and the curious sharply detailed pictures of the evangelists with their flowing draperies which precede each Gospel are evidence of a Carolingian origin and show an influence of Byzantine ix-century art. On the first page of the Gospel of St Luke is the name of the writer—*DEMETRIUS PRESBYTER.* The writing is in gold uncial characters on parchment stained a deep violet colour.

The binding is of very much later date and is the work of Hans von Reutlingen (c. 1500); the maker's mark together with the hallmark of Aix-la-Chapelle can be seen on the inside of the clasps. It is of silver gilt having the embossed figure of the Saviour in the centre wearing the Imperial Crown of Maximilian I with smaller figures of the Archangel Gabriel on the right and the Virgin on the left. In the four corners are the symbols of the four evangelists. The central figure has been erroneously supposed by some writers, notably von Murr, to represent Charlemagne.

2. *The Ornaments which no longer exist but which were described by von Murr[1] and illustrated by Delsenbach*

When the imperial regalia were removed to Nuremberg a number of ornaments which were connected with the coronation of the German kings but which were not vested in the Minster at Aix-la-Chapelle were also removed there and were deposited in the Church of the Holy Ghost. The XIV- and XV-century inventories give a complete list of these ornaments, but many of the less important items were lost when Nuremberg was captured by the French under Jourdain in 1796. How these came to be lost is obscure, but it is possible that when it was decided to remove the contents of the treasury elsewhere for safety there was only room for a limited number of articles, and it was natural that the less important and less valuable were left behind. We have, however, a pictorial record of these articles in the copper plate engravings of Delsenbach, of which the following being the more important are worthy of notice.

Delsenbach depicts two orbs which were formerly kept at Nuremberg besides that in the imperial regalia. They were both of very simple form and were made of silver gilt unadorned by precious stones. It is supposed that these were regarded as the state orbs and were used and carried at the various ceremonies in place of the Imperial Orb which was actually presented at the coronation and would only be allowed to leave the precincts of the church on special occasions. One of these orbs is divided into two halves by a horizontal embossed circle with borders of filigree work. The cross stands on a pomellum and the arms terminate in circular enlargements. The other orb has no dividing band. The cross also stands on a pomellum and the three arms terminate in fleurs-de-lis. It is difficult to determine the exact date and origin, but Bock considers that the similarity of the fleurs-de-lis on the two orbs with those on the crown on the bust of Charlemagne at Aix makes it possible that the plainer orb was among the regalia presented by Richard of Cornwall to the Minster at Aix.

The Spurs

Delsenbach also depicts a pair of spurs which it may be presumed were used at the coronation ceremony. They were probably of Sicilian workmanship of the XIII century. The outer rim of the heel piece is ornamented with a zigzag pattern and the point of the rowel projects from a lion's jaws. The spurs were attached by means of narrow ribbons of woven golden thread.

The Gloves

These were also used at the earlier coronations but not at the later ones. The pair represented by Delsenbach were probably of dogskin, cut in one piece, the seams being stitched with red silk. They had borders of purple silk stitched with seed pearls in a foliage pattern. They probably dated from the XIII or XIV centuries and were deposited in the Nuremberg Treasury by King Sigismund.

1 Von Murr: op. cit.

The Shoes

In an inventory of the time of Sigismund these are mentioned as 'St Charles's Under Shoes'. There is some doubt as to how these were worn, but possibly they were only used when the youth of the king to be crowned made the usual imperial shoes too large. The uppers of these shoes were of strong crimson silk twill. Narrow stripes, decorated with a pattern of gold and pearls, divided the instep part into two halves. On either side of these was an eagle surrounded by a leaf-patterned design in gold. The soles were of sheepskin.

Delsenbach also mentions another pair of shoes or sandals. The uppers and the heel were thickly covered with embroidery of a Sicilian-Saracen design, which makes it probable that they were made for one of the Hohenstaufen emperors, who were also Kings of Sicily at the end of the xii or beginning of the xiii centuries. These sandals were much smaller than the imperial pair now in the Vienna Treasury and this, together with the fact that they were of a more secular design, makes it probable that they were worn by the queens and empresses.

The Girdles

It is known that there were in the Nuremberg treasury several girdles or belts which were used in the coronation ceremony either for girding up the alb and tunic, for fastening the stole, or as sword belts. Delsenbach gives pictures of two, which have since disappeared. The first was a girdle of strongly woven scarlet silk, with patterns of interwoven gold thread and an inscription in woven thread *Ottoni regum virtus cui crescat acris ea precelso vincimina sic*. The girdle had an unusual decoration in the form of five gold *bullae* attached by means of twisted cords of dark purple silk. The clasps of the belt were made of plates of beaten gold, in the form of lion's jaws, which each held a pearl. It is doubtful whether the girdle dated from the first, second or third Otto. The second girdle shown by Delsenbach was of silver gilt wire work with a plain silver gilt buckle. It was probably used as a sword belt. The plates fastening the buckle to the belt are ornamented with filigree work very similar to that in the sides of the scabbard of the sword described by the old chroniclers as 'Charlemagne's Sword' and both are probably the work of the same Sicilian artist and date from the xiii century.

The Stole

There was also in the Nuremberg treasury a stole woven of gold threads in a plaited pattern and decorated at regular intervals by arabesques of Saracenic design of plants and animals, surrounded by an irregular circular border. It was probably of the xiii century like the plain girdle mentioned above and was of Palermo weaving.

The Ring

The ring played a definite part in the coronation ceremony and two are mentioned in an inventory of the reign of Charles IV (1350). One was a large ring with a big ruby in the centre, having 4 small sapphires round it in the form of a cross; between the sapphires were 4 small pearls. This ring is mentioned in the inventory as belonging to the Duke of Brunswick. Possibly it was either given by the Duke of Brunswick to the

Emperor or it may have been the property of Otto, the son of Henry the Lion of Brunswick, who, on the death of his rival Philip, became the Emperor Otto IV. The other ring was of simpler form and earlier date. It was decorated with a single uncut ruby only. By their shape, both rings must date from the Roman, or from the early Gothic period. They resemble the rings found in the tombs of the Hohenstaufens in Palermo Cathedral, among which is the *annulus regalis* found on the finger of the Empress Constance II, wife of Frederick II. A similar ring was found in the grave of Bela of Hungary. Many signet rings of the XII, XIII and XIV centuries which are still preserved have a like shape. Both these rings appear to have disappeared from the regalia in very early days, for they are not mentioned in the Nuremberg register of insignia of 1424. They may have been kept by Charles IV as memorials of his coronation and they may have been lost by Sigismund when, during the Hussite wars, the insignia were removed from the Castle of Karlstein in Bohemia to Hungary. We know from various ceremonials of coronation and from liturgical prayers that rings continued to be used in coronations after this time, so it can only be supposed that in succeeding coronations the ring used was the personal property of the king and did not belong to the royal treasury.

Ceremonial rings of the XIII and XIV centuries were usually of beaten gold, the portion round the finger rather narrow and that containing the stone measuring longer vertically than horizontally and set with uncut stone, generally a ruby or a sapphire, which was sometimes cut as an intaglio with a monogram.

A Pair of Bracelets

These bracelets are included by Delsenbach but do not appear in the old inventories, the reason probably being that they were not worn at the coronation; the rich embroidery of the sleeves of the alb shows that no such bracelets could have been worn; but, like the sword and spurs, they formed part of the secular regalia. The bracelets are engraved in the Byzantine style. On one is represented the Birth of Our Lord, on the other the Presentation in the Temple. In the centre of the first the Virgin is lying on a couch; behind her is the Child in a richly decorated cradle, with the ox and the ass at the back. On the left of the Virgin are the shepherds and the angels announcing the good tidings, on the right Joseph, to whom angels are confiding the secret of the salvation of mankind. Above the figures runs the inscription: *Quem lex tota sonat, datur orbi gratia donat.* On the second bracelet is engraved the aged Simeon receiving the Child from the Virgin Mary. On one side is a group of Jews and scribes, on the other Joseph with the turtle doves to be presented according to the law. The inscription over this group runs: *Tradita Jura thoris servat regina pundoris.* These two engravings on the bracelet appear to stand in close relation to the embroideries on the king's tunic, and may have been worn with it. The groups of figures are outlined in gold on a background of blue *émail champlevé.* On the lower border, which runs parallel to the upper one with the inscription, can still be seen in places some traces of four-petalled roses in white enamel. The bracelets were slightly curved inwards and at the four corners were small holes by means of which they could be fastened to the upper arm. On the lower outer border, which was decorated with a row of pearls, was a small eyelet hole, through which ribbons of gilded leather could be threaded for fastening purposes.

The life-like figures with their flowing draperies, the lettering of the inscriptions and the technique and colouring of the enamelling make it almost certain that these bracelets dated from the last half of the XII century. They were evidently of German origin, and from their similarity to the enamel altar paintings at Klosterneuburg, and to the enamel work still to be found in many Rhenish churches, were almost certainly the work of Cologne enamel workers and goldsmiths, who were at this time famed for their craftsmanship.

3. *The Ornaments which are still preserved in the Treasury of the Minster at Aix-la-Chapelle*

In the Minster at Aix is a marble chair on which the body of Charlemagne was said to have been seated in his tomb. The German kings were enthroned in this chair after their coronations and received the homage of the princes and nobles of the empire, and it was from here that the new knights received the accolade. In the Treasury is a silver gilt reliquary bust of Charlemagne on the head of which is a XIV-century crown (*Plate 106, a, c* and *d*). This bust has generally been attributed to Charles IV, who was well known for his devotion to Charlemagne and for his development of the Charlemagne cult. Moreover he had given a bust of St Wenceslas to the Cathedral of St Vitus in Prague and placed on it the Bohemian coronation crown. The bust of Charlemagne at Aix has no inscription nor has it the Bohemian Lion, a symbolic representation which Charles IV was wont to inscribe on his gifts.[1] Schramm suggests that he may have donated the gold for the reliquary or in some way provided the funds for the cost. The crown consists of a circlet on the forehead band of which is an embossed border of great simplicity. From the circlet rise fleurs-de-lis alternating with four petal-shaped ornaments. The crown is covered with a thick gilding which is very little damaged, and Bock considers that from the highly polished style and technique of the work it must be of the XIII century. The crown is ornamented with 3 large pearls, fifteen cut stones and fifty-five more or less uncut stones including amethysts, rubies, sapphires and emeralds but also including one of coloured paste. The setting of the stones is peculiar to this period. Each is held on a lectula to which it is secured on four sides by little claw-like hooks. The lectulae are held by funnel-shaped projecting tubes which are more or less round and not faceted like those of the Bohemian crown. The arch rises abruptly from the front and then descends gradually in the form of an ellipse so that the top of the arch is not in the middle of the crown but towards the front. It is evidently of a later date than the crown itself. The arch is ornamented with a very beautiful chased design of clover leaves, with the stems and veins of the leaf in high relief. In the front is a simple cross. Bock considers the arch and cross to date from the middle of the XIV century. The crown fits the head of the reliquary bust.[2]

[1] P. E. Schramm: *Herrschaftszeichen und Staatssymbolik.*

[2] The late B. Witte, who until his death in 1937 was goldsmith to the Minster at Aix and had many opportunities of examining the crown and on occasion repairing it, privately conveyed to the author the view that beyond doubt the bust had been made for the crown which fits it perfectly. He added that it could be assumed with assurance that the crown had been used at coronations. It is certain that the crown on the head of the bust of Charlemagne was used at least at one coronation, that of Sigismund and it may have been used at others.

a   *The Imperial cross c. 1032. Treasury, Vienna* (p. 343)

b   *The Holy Lance. Treasury, Vienna*
(p. 343)

c   *The cover of the Book of the Gospels,
depicting the Saviour wearing the
mitre crown of Maximilian I.
Treasury, Vienna* (p. 344)

b   *Head of sceptre attributed to Richard of Cornwall. The Minster, Aix-la-Chapelle* (p. 350)

a   *Crown on bust of Charlemagne. The Minster, Aix-la-Chapelle*
(p. 348)

c   *Detail of crown on the bust of Charlemagne*

d (right)   *Detail of crown on the bust of Charles*

Bock and others consider the crown on the head of the bust of Charlemagne should be regarded as the *Corona argentea* of Germany.

There has been a great deal written about this crown and there have been fierce controversies as to its origin. The protagonists of Aix have tried to prove that it must have been the crown of Richard of Cornwall, and they draw attention to the fact that Richard in 1262 presented to the coronation church of the Holy Virgin at Aix in perpetuity and in formal Deed of Gift a set of regalia which was his personal property and which was said to have been used at his coronation. This authentic Deed of Gift, which is still preserved in the original archives at Aix, and is quoted by several writers, states that:

> This is the manner and form which the illustrious King Richard of Germany, son of the King of England and of English birth, being in good health and at Aix, did bequeath of his own free will to the Chapel of the Holy Mary at Aix a gold crown most beautifully adorned with rubies, emeralds, sapphires, pearls and other costly stones, and a pair of royal vestments from his own insignia with a sceptre and an orb both of silver gilt.

It is clear that King Richard, who appears to have held the coronation town of Aix in great affection, evidently attached great importance to this gift, for in the same document it is emphatically stated that the regalia which formed the present should be kept in perpetuity in the Treasury of the Coronation Church not only under the seals of the provost, deacons and chapter but also under those of the civil authorities of the town. The document states that when the insignia were used at a coronation they were to be returned to the Treasury immediately after the conclusion of the ceremony. The document ends by saying with great emphasis that this gift to the coronation church should 'neither under stress or circumstances, not on account of war, not for the King, nor for anyone else in the world, be taken away or sold'. In conclusion the donor threatens those who disobey the commands set forth in this deed with the inescapable punishment of God. It seems to me most improbable that in the face of such a stern order the Chapter, who were very jealous of their rites concerning the coronations, should not have exerted every effort to carry out their trust. There is, moreover, no evidence to show that they did not. Huyskens,[1] however, has stated that the deed is in the form of a will and that as Richard died ten years after the document was signed it is likely that the bequest was not carried out, and there is equally no evidence to show that it was. Kirn,[2] on the other hand, claims that, although in the form that was common to wills in those days, the document could be and probably was concerned with a *donatio inter vivos*, an immediate gift. Schramm comes down heavily in favour of the crown having been given to Aix by Charles IV. It must be pointed out that Richard's successor Rudolph did not recognise his predecessors Conrad, William and Richard as fully legalised kings. He avoided the mention of their names and dated his reign and his acts of Government back to the Emperor Frederick II, as his last legal predecessor. He even repealed all the acts of Richard's reign and in view of this attitude it is most

---

[1] A. Huyskens: 'Noch einmal der Krönungsschatz des Königs Richard von Cornwalls'. A counter to P. Kirn in *Annalen d. hist. Vereins f. d. Niederrhein*, 118, 1136–43.

[2] P. Kirn: 'Zur Geschichte der Deutschen Kroninsignien'. An answer to Huyskens in *Annalen d. hist. Vereins f. d. Niederrhein*, 119, 169–73.

unlikely that he would have given his endorsement to Richard's deed regarding the regalia or to have recognised the regalia in any way. It is related that he was crowned with the German Imperial Crown, which seems to have been considered as a very unusual step, and this may have been to have emphasised the disfavour with which he looked upon the crown given by Richard. It is possible that he may have destroyed it, but there is no evidence of this. While Schramm's arguments, especially about the setting of the stones in the crown, must be given full weight the possibility of the frame in the crown being that given by Richard of Cornwall cannot be entirely dismissed. It could have been embellished and redecorated by Charles IV, but one notable point to which attention should be drawn is that the fleurs-de-lis on the Aix crown are of the same characteristic shape and style as those on the funeral crowns of Richard's brother, Henry III of England, and his Consort Eleanor of Provence at Westminster, which no doubt were intended to represent the English crown of the time.

There is another crown in the Treasury of the Minster at Aix. It is of gilded silver studded with pearls and diamonds with a cross in front. The stones are set on enamelled ornaments which take the form of the Rose of York. There is an inscription which relates the crown to the Princess Margaret of York (*Plate 107, c*), sister of Edward IV. This was the bridal crown of the Princess who married Charles the Bold of Burgundy in 1475 and it is said he gave it as a votive offering to the Minster at Aix. It was restored in the middle of the XIX century.

In the Treasury at Aix is a thick simple rod of wood covered with silver gilt at the upper end of which, on a round flat pomellum, is an heraldic bird. Originally the sceptre (*Plate 106, b*) was only 21 in. long, it has been lengthened by a further 12 in., and a central pomellum was added to conceal the join. In spite of its simplicity the carvings of the heraldic bird show great craftsmanship, especially in those of the broad and much curved breast and in those of the neck and back which are emphasised by means of raised dots. Bock and others consider that it dates from early XIV century. Although some writers have tried to show that the bird was an eagle there can be little doubt but that it is meant to represent a dove. In the XII and XIII centuries most of the Continental sceptres were surmounted by floral or foliage ornaments and in England alone was the sceptre surmounted by a dove. It is, therefore, the supposition that this sceptre was that included in Richard's Deed of Gift at Aix.

In the inventory of the Treasury of the Minster at Aix taken in the last quarter of the XVII century there is mention of a globe set with pearls which may well be the orb donated by Richard of Cornwall. In 1794 the contents of the Treasury were taken to Paderborn, where they remained for ten years. On their return to Aix an inventory was taken and in the first box were found five little silver gilt globes, in the ninth six little silver gilt globes and in the eleventh 'the globe and sceptre of the Holy Virgin all gilded'. It seems that these were not royal ornaments and that the earlier globe had disappeared.

4. *Other royal and imperial ornaments which are still preserved in Germany*

There are two crowns which are worthy of some mention. The first is that on the reliquary bust of St Oswald, King of Northumbria (*Plate 107, b*), in the Cathedral of

Hildesheim, and the second is a burial crown of Anne of Austria (*Plate 108, a*) now at Wiesbaden.

The reliquary bust at Hildesheim consists of an octagonal pedestal with a dome-shaped top on which is a head modelled in silver on which, in turn, rests a valuable crown. The eight plates of the pedestal bear portraits of eight kings enthroned and each with a crown, sceptre and orb: St Oswald in the centre and round him Kings Athelwulf, Alfred, Edward, Edmund, Edgar, Ethelred II and Canute. There is also a text. King Oswald gave 'himself and all he had to the Lord the Head of the Executioner which is here hidden in gold'. The silver gilt head has silver eyes with dark blue stones as pupils. The crown consists of eight trapezoidal plates which Schramm[1] has shown must have been made originally from the parts of a pair of bracelets. The crown has been repaired and added to from time to time and parts of the original material date from about 1000 and from the first half of the XII century. Various theories have been put forward about the origin of the reliquary. According to tradition the relics of St Oswald were transferred from England to Flanders in 1038, but since the head was kept in a different place to the body it is by no means certain that it was sent to the Continent at the same time. According to some it was made in England and it is significant that the portraits are of English kings, although some have thought that one depicts King Sigismund of Burgundy who was killed in 524. Stephen Beissel considers that the crown and reliquary were a product of a Hildesheim goldsmith. He considers that it may date from a little time before 21st March 1286, on which date Pope Honorius III in a Papal Bull gave a remission to visitors of the cathedral on the Festival of St Oswald, and this was at the time when the veneration of St Oswald was taking on a new lease of life in Hildesheim. The fact that this ornament is made from materials of an older origin makes it impossible to state exactly when it was made. St Oswald had been revered in many places on the Continent and there is an interesting picture of the King in the Convent of Nonnberg at Salzburg. He is depicted with a crown with *fleurons*, a sceptre and an orb surmounted by a bird. The painting dates from 1440.

The burial crown of Queen Anne, consort of Rudolph I, is of silver gilt with a broad, simple circlet to which are riveted four large fleurs-de-lis, each decorated with four precious stones, including a large sapphire which in 1510 was valued at 40 gulden. The Queen, whose original name was Gertrude, was the daughter of the Count of Hohenberg and Haigerloch and in 1245 she married Count Rudolph of Hapsburg, bringing as her dowry a castle and land in Alsace. On 29th October 1273 she was anointed and crowned with her husband at Aix, after he had been elected German King, and she took the name of Anne. She died in Vienna on 16th February 1281 and, in accordance with her wishes, her body was taken to Basle and interred behind the high altar of the minster there. In 1356 an earthquake occurred, which necessitated the transfer of her remains to a new tomb, which still exists and on which is her effigy. In 1510 the canons of the minster were, according to the chronicle, 'so bitten with curiosity that they opened the royal grave'. The crown was removed and cleaned and placed in the Treasury of the minster. In 1836 the canton of Basle was divided into city and county, and the treasures of the

---

1 P. E. Schramm: *Herrschaftszeichen und Staatssymbolik*, Vol. II, Ch. 23, page 544.

cathedral were apportioned and some, including the crown, were sold. The crown was purchased at an auction for 351 francs by an antiquary named Oppenheim, who resold it in Berlin, where it found its way into the Schloss Museum. In 1945 it was found in Thuringia and taken into the collection of those Prussian works of art which had been recovered and assembled at Wiesbaden, where it now is.

After the proclamation of the German Empire at Versailles on 18th January 1871, consideration was given to the question of a new imperial crown. Designs were drawn, but although models were manufactured, actual crowns were never made. These designs were, however, used for heraldic purposes and the models (*Plate 108*, *b* and *c*) were kept in the Hohenzollern Museum in the Schloss Monbijou, Berlin. During the Second World War they disappeared and have never been recovered.

The new Imperial Crown[1] followed the octagonal shape of the old German Imperial Crown, now in Vienna. The eight plates were of gold. That in the front was decorated with a large diamond cross with four smaller crosses, and this design was followed on the plate at the back and on those at the sides. The intermediate plates were decorated with an eagle set with diamonds. The crown was closed, with two arches carrying a design of arcades reminiscent of the decoration of the single arch of the old German Imperial Crown. The arches formed an ogee at the point of junction, on which rested an orb surmounted by a cross.

The crown designed for the Empress consisted of a head circlet with eight flower ornaments set with diamonds and rubies. It was closed with two arches, which were decorated with a row of pearls and diamonds on the edges. The ogee design and the orb and cross were similar to those in the design for the new imperial crown. The cap was of gold brocade.

There was also a design for a crown for the Crown Prince, somewhat similar to that of the Empress's crown, but carrying the design of crosses and eagles from the new Imperial Crown.

BIBLIOGRAPHY

ALFÖLDI, A.	'Die Ausgestaltung des monarchischen Zeremoniells am römischen Kaiserhofe' in *Mitteil. des deutschen Archiol. Inst. Rom, Abt. XLIX*, 1934.
	'Insignien und Tracht der römischen Kaiser', ibid., Vol. L, 1935.
ARENS, F.	*Die Essener Münsterkirche und ihre Schatzkammer*, Essen 1906.
BASSERMANN-JORDAN, E. VON AND SCHMID, W. M.	*Der Bamberger Domschatz (Bayerischer Kirchenschatz I)*, Munich 1914.
BAUMANN, J.	*Die Öffnung der Kaisergräber im Dom zu Speyer im Sommer 1900*, Speyer 1949.

---

[1] E. Doepler: 'Reichsadler und Kaiserkrone' in *Deutscher Herold*, XX, Berlin 1889.

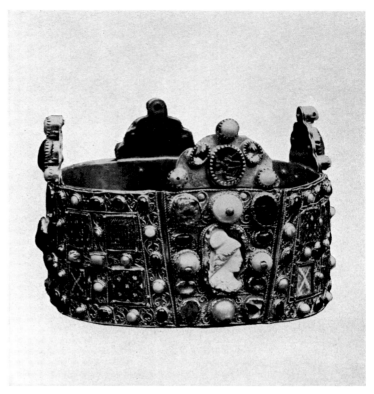

b   *Crown from reliquary bust of St Oswald. Cathedral Treasury, Hildesheim* (p. 351)

a (left)   *Portrait by an unknown artist of the Emperor Frederick III wearing a mitre crown. Treasury, Vienna* (p. 324)

c   *Crown of Margaret of York. Minster Treasury, Aix-la-Chapelle* (p. 350)

a *Burial crown of Anne of Austria, from her tomb in Basle Cathedral. Schloss Museum, Wiesbaden* (p. 351)

b *Model of imperial crown, 1872*

c *Model of crown of Empress, 1872*

Formerly in the Schloss Monbijou, Berlin (p. 352)

BEER, R.
'Kunstbestubungen Karls V und Philipps II', *Jahrbuch der Kunsthistorischen Sammlungen des Allerhöchsten Kaiserhauses.*

BEISSEL, S.
Die Aachenfahrt. Verehrung der Aachener Heiligtümer seit den Tagen Karls des Grossen bis in unsere Zeit, Freiburg 1902.

BOCK, F.
Die Kleinodien des Heiligen Römischen Reiches deutscher Nation, Vienna 1864.

BÖCKLER, A.
Das Perikopenbuch Heinrichs II, Berlin 1946 (*Kunstbrief*).

BRIZIO, A. M.
Vercelli, Cataloge delle cose d'arte e di antichita d'Italia, 1935.

BRYCE, LORD
The Holy Roman Empire, London 1910.

BÜHLER, A.
Die Alttestament. Deutung der deutschen Kaiserkrone, Münster 1952.

BURCKHARDT, R. F.
Der Basler Münsterschatz in den Kunstdenkmälern der Stadt Basel, Basle 1933.

DECKER-HAUF, HANSMARTIN
Herrschaftszeichen und Staatssymbolik, Chapter 25.

DEER, JOSEF
Die Abendländische Kaiserkrone des Hochmittelalters.
Der Kaiserornat Friedrichs II, Berne 1952.
Herrschaftszeichen und Staatssymbolik, Chapter 18.

DELSENBACH, J. A. AND
MURR, C. GIVON
Délinéation exacte des Ornements Impériaux, 1790.

DIEMAND, DR A.
Das Ceremoniell der Kaiserkrönungen von Otto I bis Friedrich II, Munich 1894.

DOEPLER, E.
'Reichsadler und Kaiserkrone', *Deutscher Herold,* XX, Berlin 1889.

EICHMANN, E.
'Von der Kaisergewändung im Mittelalter', *Hist. Jahrbuch,* Vol. 58, 1938.
'Die Mitra des Abendländischen Kaisers', in *Festschrift Sebastian Merkle,* Düsseldorf 1922.

FAYMONVILLE, K.
Die Kunstdenkmäler der Stadt Aachen, I, Düsseldorf 1916.
'Das Münster zu Aachen', in *Kunst der Denkmälerei der Rheinprovinz,* Düsseldorf 1922.

FILLITZ, H.
Die Insignien und Kleinodien des Heiligen Römischen Reiches, Vienna 1954.
Katalog der weltlichen und der geistlichen Schatzkammer des Kunsthistorischen Museums, Vienna 1954.

GANSHOF, DR F. L.
'The Imperial Coronation of Charlemagne, The Theories and Facts', being the 16th Lecture in the David Murray Foundation in the University of Glasgow delivered on 23rd November 1948.

GROSSE, W.
Die Geschichte einer der deutschen Kaiserkrone in Sachsen und Anhalt, VI.

HAGENBURG, N. AND
MAXWELL, SIR W. S.
The Procession of Pope Clement VII and the Emperor Charles V after the Coronation of Bologna, Edinburgh 1875.

HAUPT, G.	'Zur Entstehung der deutschen Kaiserkrone' in *Die Oberrheinische Kunst*, 1927.
HERMANN, E.	*Records of the Deutsche Reichstag*, Vol. 10, Gotha.
HERRE, H. AND QUIDDE, L.	*Deutsche Reichstagsakten*, Vol. 16, Stuttgart 1928.
HIRSCHMANN, G.	*Muffel Family in the Middle Ages*, Historical Society of Nuremberg, Vol. 41, 1950.
HOLZMAIR, E.	*Nürnberger und Rudolfinische Kaiserkrone im Spiegel der Numismatik*, Vienna 1947.
HUYSKENS, A.	'Der Plan des Königs Richard von Cornwallis zur Niederlegung eines deutschen Krönungsschatzes in Aachen', in *Annalen d. hist. Vereins f. d. Niederrhein*, 115, 1929.
	'Noch einmal der Krönungsschatz des Königs Richard von Cornwalls', ibid., 118, 1932.
KALLSTRÖM, O.	*Ein neuentdecktes Majestätsdiadem ottonischer Zeit.*
KÄSTNER, K. W.	*Das Münster in Essen*, Essen 1929.
KEMMERICH, DR M.	*Die deutschen Kaiser und Könige im Bilde*, Leipzig 1910.
KIRN, P.	'Mit welcher Krone wurde König Siegmund in Aachen gekrönt?' in *Annalen d. hist. Vereins f. d. Niederrhein*, 118, 1931.
	'Zur Geschichte der Deutschen Kroninsignien', ibid., 119.
KÖHLER, J. D.	*Teutsche Reichshistorie*, 1751.
KOHN, DR H.	*Der Essener Münsterschatz*, Essen 1950.
LEIDINGER, P.	'Evangeliarium a. dem Domschatz von Bamberg', in *Miniaturen der Bayer. Staatsbibl.*, V, Munich 1914.
MADRAZO, P. DE	*Über Krönungsinsignien und Staatsgewänder Maximilians I und Karls V und ihr Schicksal in Spanien, Jahrbuch der Kunsthist. Samml.* Vol 9, Vienna 1889.
RADEMACHER, F.	'Eine Krone Kaiser Ottos II', in *Zeitschrift des Deutschen Vereins für Kunstwissenschaft*, 1934.
ROMER-BUCHNER, DR B. J.	*Die Wahl- und Krönungskirche der deutsche Kaiser zu St. Bartholemai in FrankfurtamMain*, Frankfurt 1857.
RÖTTGER, B. H.	'Funde von der Öffnung der Kaisergräber im Jahre 1900', in *Kunstdenkmäler der Pfalz, Stadt und Bezirksamt Speyer*, Munich 1954.
SCHIFFERS, H.	*Die Deutsche Königskrönung und die Insignien Richards von Cornwallis*, Aix 1936.
	Der Reliquienschatz Karls des Grossen, Aix 1951.
SCHLOSSER, J. VON	*Die deutschen Reichskleinodien*, Vienna 1920.
SCHULTE, A.	*Die Kaiser- und Königskrönungen zu Aachen 813–1591*, Bonn and Leipzig 1934.

SCHRAMM, P. E.   *Die deutschen Kaiser und Könige in Bildern ihrer Zeit.* Published by the Research Institute of the University of Leipzig 1928.
Herrschaftszeichen und Staatssymbolik, Stuttgart 1955–6.
Kaiser Friedrichs II Herrschaftszeichen, Göttingen 1953.
Sphaira, Globus, Reichsapfel.

WEIXLGÄRTNER, A.   'Die weltliche Schatzkammer,' in *Jahrbuch der Kunsthist. Samml. N.F., 1.2. 1926–28*, Vienna.
Guide to the Weltliche Schatzkammer, Vienna 1929.
Geschichte im Widerschein der Reichskleinodien, Baden bei Wien, Leipzig 1938.

ZEUMER, BRUNNER   *Die Constantinische Schenkungsurkunde.*

Chronicles of German Cities   *Nuremberg*, Vol. I. 'Nuremberg Chronicle of the Time of the Emperor Sigismund to 1434, with a Continuation of 1441', Leipzig 1862.

Description de la Cathédrale de Basle, 1842.

Franconia Sacra, Munich 1952.

Masterpieces of Mediaeval and Modern Christian Art kept in the Cathedral at Aachen, Aix 1939.

LIST OF CORONATIONS OF GERMAN KINGS, EMPERORS AND HOLY ROMAN EMPERORS

(For Italian Coronations see Chapter Fourteen, Italy)

768   Charlemagne. Crowned King of East Franks, Noyon, 9th October
              Crowned Emperor at Rome, 25th December 800
813   Louis the Pious, the Debonair. Crowned at Aix, 11th September
              Crowned Emperor at Rheims 816
              Crowned King of East Franks at Aix, July 817
817   Lothair. Crowned co-Emperor at Aix
              Crowned Emperor at Rome, 5th April 823
844   Louis II. Crowned King (? of Italy) at Rome, 15th June
              Crowned co-Emperor at Rome 850. Crowned Emperor at Rome, 18th May 872
875   Charles the Bald. Crowned Emperor at Rome, 29th December
881   Charles III, the Fat. Crowned Emperor at Rome, February
891   Wido of Spoleto. Crowned Emperor at Rome
894   Lambert. Crowned Emperor at Rome
895   Arnulf. Crowned Emperor at Rome
895   Louis III. Received crown at secular ceremony
              Crowned Emperor at Rome 896
900   Louis IV, the Child. Invested at secular ceremony and received crown as King of the East Franks at Bamberg

SAXON DYNASTY

911   Conrad I. Consecrated King of East Franks
915   Berengar
918   Henry I, the Fowler. Invested with crown and lance
936   Otto I, the Great. Crowned King of East Franks at Aix
         Crowned Emperor at Rome with his consort Adelaide, 2nd February 962 in St John Lateran
961   Otto II, the Bloody. Crowned King of East Franks at Aix, 26th May
         Crowned co-Emperor at Rome, 25th December 967
983   Otto III, the Red. Crowned King of East Franks at Aix, 25th December
         Crowned Emperor at Rome, 25th May 996
1002   Henry II. Crowned and took the title of King of the Romans at Mainz, 7th June
         Crowned Emperor at Rome, 14th February 1014

SALIAN DYNASTY

1024   Conrad II, the Salic. Elected at Worms in September
         Crowned at Mainz, 8th September
         Wife Gisela crowned at Aix, 10th September
         Crowned Emperor at Rome, 26th March 1027
         Crowned King of Burgundy at Peterlingen 1033
1026   Henry III, the Black. Designated successor
         Crowned in father's lifetime at Aix, 14th April 1028
         Crowned King of Burgundy at Arles 1042
         Crowned Emperor at Rome, 25th December 1046
1054   Henry IV. Chosen at Tribur
         Crowned at Aix in father's lifetime, 17th July
         Crowned Emperor at Rome 1084
1077   Rudolph of Swabia. Chosen German King. Crowned at Mainz, 27th March
?   Hermann of Luxemburg. Chosen as anti-king
?   Egbert, Margrave of Meissen. Chosen as anti-king
1087   Conrad, son of Henry IV. Crowned King of the Germans at Aix. Deposed 1098
1099   Henry V. Crowned at Aix, 6th January
         Crowned Emperor at Rome, 13th April 1111. Crowned a second time 1116
1125   Lothair II, of Supplinburg. Elected German King at Mainz, 30th August
         Crowned German King at Aix, 13th September.
         Crowned Emperor at St John Lateran, Rome, 4th June 1133

HOHENSTAUFEN DYNASTY

1127   Conrad III, Duke of Swabia. First chosen, 18th December
         Chosen at Coblenz, 7th March 1138
         Crowned at Aix, 13th March 1138
1146   Henry. Elected and crowned at Aix. Predeceased his father

1152   Frederick I, Barbarossa. Elected at Frankfurt, March
                     Crowned at Aix, 9th March 1152
                     Crowned at Rome, 18th June 1155
                     Consort, Beatrix, Crowned 1166
                     Crowned King of Burgundy at Arles, 20th July 1178
1146   Henry VI. Elected in his father's lifetime at Bamberg
                     Crowned in his father's lifetime at Aix, 5th August
                     Crowned Emperor at Rome, 14th April 1191
1196   Frederick II. Elected at Frankfurt in father's lifetime
1198   Philip of Swabia. Elected German King at Mühlhausen, 8th March
                     Crowned German King at Mainz, 8th September
       Otto IV, the Superb. Crowned at Aix, 12th July
1205   Philip of Swabia. Crowned again at Aix, 6th January
1209   Otto IV. Re-elected King and crowned at Rome as Emperor, 4th October
1212   Frederick II. Re-elected at Frankfurt, 5th December
                     Crowned at Mainz, 9th December
                     Crowned at Aix, 25th July 1214
                     Crowned Emperor at Rome, 22nd December 1220
                     Crowned King of Jerusalem, 18th March 1229
1237   Conrad IV. Elected
1246   Henry Raspe, Margrave of Thuringia. Elected

INTERREGNUM

1247   William of Holland. Elected anti-king, crowned at Aix, 1st November 1248
1256   Alphonso of Castile
1257   Richard of Cornwall. Crowned at Aix with consort, Sancha of Provence, 17th May

HAPSBURGS, LUXEMBURGS AND BAVARIANS

1273   Rudolf of Hapsburg. Elected at Frankfurt, 29th September
                     Crowned at Aix, 24th October
1292   Adolf, Count of Nassau. Elected at Frankfurt, 5th May
                     Crowned at Aix, 1st July
1298   Albert I. Elected at Frankfurt, 27th July
                     Crowned at Aix, 24th August
1308   Henry VII of Luxemburg. Elected German King, 27th November
                     Crowned at Aix, 6th January 1309
                     Crowned Emperor at St John Lateran, Rome, 29th June 1312
1313   Frederick the Fair of Austria. Elected at Frankfurt, 19th October
                     Crowned at Bonn, 25th October
1314   Louis IV, the Bavarian. Elected at Frankfurt, 20th October
                     Crowned at Aix, 25th November
                     Crowned at Rome, 17th January 1328
1349   Gunther of Schwarzburg. Elected in January
1346   Charles IV. Elected German King at Rhens and crowned at Bonn, 26th September

1349   Charles IV. Re-crowned at Aix, 13th July with second consort, Anna of the Palatine
               Third consort, Anna of Schweidnitz 1354
               Crowned Emperor at Rome, 5th April 1355
               Crowned King of Burgundy at Arles, 4th June 1365

1376   Wenceslas. Elected Frankfurt in father's lifetime, 10th June
               Crowned at Aix in father's lifetime, 6th July

1401   Rupert, Count Palatine. Elected and crowned at Cologne, 6th January

1410   Jobst of Moravia. Elected King, September

1410   Sigismund. Elected, 20th September
               Crowned at Aix with consort, Barbara, 8th November
               Crowned at Rome, 31st May 1433

HOUSE OF AUSTRIA

1438   Albert II. Elected Frankfurt, 18th March, not crowned as German King

1440   Frederick III. Elected Frankfurt, 2nd February
               Crowned at Aix, 17th June 1442

1452   Frederick III. Crowned Emperor at Rome, 10th March

1486   Maximilian I. Elected, 16th February
               Crowned at Aix, 9th April, in father's lifetime

1500   Maximilian I. Took title without being crowned, 4th January

1519   Charles V. Elected. Crowned at Aix, 23rd August 1520
               Crowned Emperor at Bologna 1530

1531   Ferdinand I. Elected Cologne, crowned January at Aix
               Crowned Emperor, 24th March 1558 at Frankfurt

1562   Maximilian II. Crowned at Frankfurt, 24th February

1575   Rudolph II. Elected German King at Regensburg, October, crowned at Frankfurt, 1st November

1612   Matthias. Crowned at Frankfurt, 24th June

1619   Ferdinand II. Crowned at Frankfurt, 9th September

1636   Ferdinand III. Crowned at Frankfurt

1658   Leopold I. Crowned at Frankfurt, 1st August

1705   Joseph I. Crowned at Frankfurt

1711   Charles VI. Crowned at Frankfurt, 22nd December

1740   Maria Theresa

1742   Charles VII, Elector of Bavaria. Crowned at Frankfurt, 17th February

1745   Francis I. Crowned at Frankfurt with Maria Theresa his wife as co-regent

1764   Joseph II. Crowned at Frankfurt in parents' lifetime. Succeeded 1765

1790   Leopold II. Crowned at Frankfurt, 9th October

1792   Francis II. Crowned at Frankfurt, 14th July. Last imperial coronation

HOUSE OF HOHENZOLLERN

1871   William I. No coronation

1888   Frederick

1888   William II

a   Crown of King Otto of Greece, formerly in Hohenschwangau Castle (p. 360)

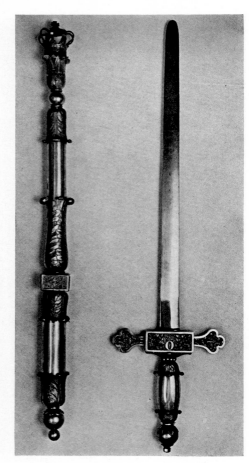

b (left)   Sceptre of King Otto of Greece, formerly in Hohenschwangau Castle (p. 360)

c (centre, left)   Sword of King Otto of Greece, formerly in Hohenschwangau Castle (p. 360)

d   Sceptre and sword of King Otto of Greece in the Bavarian National Museum, Munich (p. 361)

CHAPTER TEN

GREECE

The modern Kingdom of Greece dates from the Convention of London of 1832, at which Greece was declared an independent kingdom under the protection of Great Britain, France and Russia. Prince Otto, the eighteen-year-old second son of King Louis I of Bavaria, was selected as the first King and landed in Greece in February 1833 accompanied, since he was not yet of age, by a Council of Regency composed of Bavarians. His Bavarian Chancellor, together with his regiments of Bavarian troops, were retained perhaps somewhat unwisely by the young King when he came of age two years later, and although he was honest, well intentioned and possessed of a great affection for the country of his adoption, it was not long before he became very unpopular, largely owing to his reliance on foreign advisers and to his autocratic tendencies, both of which were abhorrent to the ardent patriotism and fierce democracy of the Greek people. In 1843 he was compelled to grant a constitution, but being unable to gain either the love or the trust of the nation he was finally deposed in 1862 and forced to leave the country, whence he retired to Bavaria and there died five years later. Although no coronation ceremony had been introduced into the new kingdom, King Otto ordered a set of regalia which he took with him on his departure from Greece. The regalia were for a time on display in the Castle of Hohenschwangau, but today they are kept in Munich and are not shown to the public.[1] Before describing the regalia, however, it will be as well to relate briefly the further vicissitudes of the Greek monarchy down to the present day.

In 1863, by the election of the National Assembly and with the sanction of the three protecting powers, Prince George of Schleswig-Holstein-Sonderburg-Glücksburg, son of King Christian IX of Denmark, came to the throne. The reign started most auspiciously, the national spirit having been flattered by the cession of the Ionian Isles to Greece by Great Britain, and by the wisdom of the young King in adopting, at his father's suggestion, the motto: 'My strength is the love of my people'. On his death fifty years later, Greece had attained a new prestige and the dynasty had become correspondingly popular, but unfortunately the trend of political events both during and immediately after the First World War caused the country to become a pawn in the hands of the Great Powers. The national policy of King Constantine was in general misunderstood and his Queen's close relationship to the Kaiser was unjustifiably exploited to such an extent that he was at last forced to abdicate.

There followed an unhappy interlude in Greek affairs. The young King Alexander's death, as the result of a monkey bite, led to the recall of King Constantine by his

[1] Information supplied by the General Director of the Wittelsbach Ausgleichfonds. Since going to press it has been learned that the regalia of King Otto was presented to King Paul of the Hellenes by the head of the Wittelsbach family and was handed over on the 20th December 1959.

people, but although popular in his own country he was not recognised by the Great Powers and his position after the debacle in Asia Minor became impossible. He was, therefore, once more compelled to abdicate and died shortly afterwards.

His son, King George II, after a brief reign of two years, was expelled from the country in 1923, but he was recalled in 1935 by the will of his people. In 1941, when Greece was over-run by the Germans, the King transferred the seat of Government first to Crete and then to Cairo. In 1944, with the Germans defeated, civil war broke out and King George was advised not to return until order was restored. He returned in 1946 by popular request, but died in the following year when he was succeeded by his brother Paul.

The crown of King Otto (*Plate 109, a*) was made by Fossin and Son of Paris and is of chased silver gilded a dull gold, unadorned with precious stones. The circlet, which carried the design of a laurel wreath, is surmounted by a decorated band from which rise eight strawberry leaves with a gracefully depressed curve between each. From behind the leaves there spring eight half-arches in the pattern of acanthus leaves, which are depressed at the centre where they meet in the form of an ogee. Inside, there is a cap of crimson velvet. Resting on the ogee is an orb of burnished gold with dull gold bands, and this is surmounted by a byzantine cross, the limbs of which, terminated with trefoils, have a burnished outline in contrast to the dull gold of the centre pieces.

The sceptre of King Otto (*Plate 109, b*), by the same makers, is a long golden shaft surmounted by the royal crown in gold with rich chasing. Its base takes the form of a knob, the bottom of which is chased. Both base and grip are smooth and highly polished. Above the grip are the two main sections of the shaft, each rod rising from a flower-shaped ornament, the lower being richly chased with acanthus and the upper smooth and burnished. Separating these is a dull gold cube, the edges of which are ground off and the facets polished; two of its sides bear a white cross on a blue ground in enamel, and the other two sides heraldic lions facing away from each other in gold. A second cube, identical except that the lions are replaced by the letter O in relief, surmounts the upper rod, and on this rests a golden bell-shaped ornament which in turn supports the crown.

Although unadorned with jewels this sceptre possesses a distinctive appearance and its design is most effective, the contrasts between the dull and the polished metal producing an impression of simple grandeur.

The Royal Sword (*Plate 109, c*), which is sometimes miscalled the Coronation Sword, was made by Manceaux of Paris, who was arms maker to King Otto. Its sheath, which is slightly convex, is of gilded metal and down each side runs a seam of burnished strips. Immediately below the guard there is a strip decorated above with the letter O in relief, in the centre with the white cross of Greece on a blue ground, in enamel, surmounted by a crown; and below with a gargoyle, while at each side is a curled snake forming the eyelets from which the sword sling is fastened. Both crown and gargoyle are in dull gold, as are the two chased bands which interrupt the polished expanse of the major part of the sheath, and the rich chasing with which it is terminated. The latter is divided into three panels and decorated in the first with the letter O in relief, in the second with a heraldic crest and the Goddess of Victory, and in the third with Dolphins and Neptune's trident burnished. A polished tip rounds off the scabbard, which is identical on both sides except for the addition of the maker's name on the reverse. The hilt of the sword is of lapis lazuli and has on each side a narrow chased mounting in dull gold with burnished edges, while the pommel and cross-bar are of solid metal covered with dead gold, the former bearing on each side the head of the Madonna and the latter a man's head on its centre-piece and that of a lion on either end. The blade is of dull damascened steel.

In the National Museum of Munich there are another sceptre and sword which had belonged to King Otto (*Plate 109, d*). They were given to the National Museum in 1878 by King Ludwig II of Bavaria. It is not known when they were made or for what purpose they were used but it is thought that they may be of earlier date than the other set of regalia. They are of somewhat heavier design and do not call for any special comment.

The Danish dynasty did not introduce a coronation ceremony or regalia into Greece. When a sovereign ascends the throne he swears an oath to the Constitution before Parliament after which ceremony he attends a *Te Deum*. At royal funerals plain crowns are placed on the coffin.

SOVEREIGNS OF THE MODERN KINGDOM OF GREECE

1832	Otto I, King of Greece
1863	George I, King of the Hellenes
1913	Constantine
1917	Alexander
1920	Constantine (again)
1922	George II
1924	Republic
1935	George II (again)
1947	Paul I

a   *King's crown and sceptre and the princess's crown* (p. 365)

b   *King's crown* (p. 365)

c (centre, right)   *Princess's crown* (p. 365)

d (right)   *Nuptial crown, given to Queen Charlotte of England by George III on their marriage* (pp. 370 and 371)

CHAPTER ELEVEN

HANOVER

The early history of Hanover is merged in that of the Duchy of Brunswick and its off-shoots. In 1610 the seven sons of Duke William (1535–92) made an agreement that the duchy should not be divided and that only one of the brothers should marry and continue the family. They cast lots to determine the question and the lot fell upon the sixth brother George. In 1692 Ernest Augustus, the youngest son of George, who had become the Protestant Bishop of Osnabrück, succeeded to the duchy. He was ambitious for his house and determined to secure for himself the position of Elector. In return for a promise of assistance to the Empire and the Hapsburgs, the Emperor Leopold I granted him as Duke of Brunswick-Lüneburg the title of Elector and the office of Arch-Treasurer and Standard Bearer of the Holy Roman Empire. Owing to opposition, especially from France and Sweden, it was not until 1708 that Ernest Augustus's son and successor, George Louis, was recognised as Elector by the Imperial Diet. In 1658 Ernest Augustus had married Sophia, daughter of the Elector Palatine, Frederick V, and Elizabeth, daughter of James I of England. By the English Act of Settlement of 1701 the eldest son of this marriage, George Louis, became heir apparent of Great Britain and Ireland. George Louis had married his cousin Sophia Dorothea, the only child of George William of Lüneburg-Celle. On the death of his uncle and father-in-law in 1705 he united the duchy with Lüneburg-Celle and his paternal inheritance of Kalenberg or Hanover. He sometimes used the title of Elector of Brunswick and at others that of Elector of Hanover. On the death of Queen Anne in 1714, George Louis succeeded as King of Great Britain and Ireland with the title of George I.

The Electorate of Hanover thereafter suffered many vicissitudes and for a time part of it was incorporated into the Kingdom of Westphalia by Napoleon. In 1814 the Congress of Vienna raised Hanover to the status of a kingdom.

In 1833, to regulate the succession of the Kingdom of Hanover, some alterations were made to the House Law of the House of Brunswick, which had been adopted in 1831. Provision was made to exclude women from the succession as long as agnates or male members of the family survived. On the death of William IV in 1837, the Crown of Hanover thus did not pass to Victoria but to Ernest Augustus, Duke of Cumberland, the fifth and only surviving son of George III. Ernest Augustus died in 1851 and was succeeded by his son, the blind King George V. In 1866 the Prussians occupied Hanover and the King was driven out and the kingdom was annexed to Prussia. On the death of George V in 1878 his son Ernest Augustus, Duke of Cumberland, continued to maintain his claim to the crown of Hanover and refused to be reconciled to Prussia. Because of this attitude the German Government would not allow him to take possession of the

Duchy of Brunswick, which he had inherited on the extinction of the elder branch of the family in 1884. The present head of the family has taken the title of Prince of Hanover and Duke of Brunswick-Lüneburg.

By virtue of their office of Arch-Treasurer of the Holy Roman Empire, the Electors charged their armorial bearings with the Crown of Charlemagne. We learn from documents in the archives of Hanover something about the Electoral Bonnet and the ducal coronet. In 1800 Sir Isaac Heard of the College of Heralds in London wrote to Hanover asking a series of questions about the use of the Electoral Bonnet. These were answered in a memorandum drawn up by the Hanoverian Court Chamberlain's office dated 5th January 1801. This correspondence originated in respect of the modification of the Royal Arms and titles following the union of Great Britain with Ireland. Heard's questions were:

(1) Does the Elector of Brunswick upon any occasion wear the Electoral Bonnet?
(2) Is there preserved among His Majesty's regalia the Electoral Bonnet?
(3) Do any of the princes, sons of the Elector, wear a bonnet of the same form upon any public solemnity?
(4) If not, did they wear any bonnet of inferior degree?
(5) Is the Electoral Bonnet ever carried on cushions or otherwise before the sons of the Elector in public procession?
(6) Is the Electoral Bonnet or any bonnet of inferior degree assigned to be borne by the princes, sons of the Elector, over their armorial achievements?

The memorandum which was sent in reply stated that there were various occasions on which the Elector wore the Electoral Bonnet, the most important being the imperial coronation. It was, however, no longer customary for the Temporal Electors to attend coronations in person but to be represented by Ambassadors. The Ecclesiastical Electors of Cologne, Treves and Mainz, however, attended the imperial coronations and wore their Electoral Bonnets. The Electoral Bonnet of Hanover was preserved in the Court offices of Hanover, and a painting of it by Ramberg was forwarded with the memorandum. It was a flat, shallow, round cap of carmoisine red velvet surmounted by an ermine tail upon a rectangular piece of the same velvet. Round the base of the cap was an ermine fringe with eight points with a double row of ermine tails. The inside lining was of blue silk. The Electoral Bonnet was only worn or used on armorial achievements by the Elector and not by his sons during their father's lifetime. On solemn occasions the sons wore ducal coronets.

On 20th January 1801 Heard again wrote asking for details of the ducal coronet. No specific information could be given, but five sketches were sent. All but one were taken from representations of heraldic coronets. The first was a ducal coronet of four arches surmounted by an orb and cross with a cap inside turned up with ermine which hid the circlet. This was of Brunswick-Wolfenbüttel origin. The second was the ducal coronet of Ernest Augustus (c. 1688) before he was made an Elector. It was an open circlet surmounted by eight strawberry leaves. The third was a combination of the open ducal coronet and the Electoral Bonnet, but it was closed with two plain broad arches and surmounted by an orb and cross. The fourth depicted the actual coronet of Duke

Ferdinand of Brunswick (*obiit* 1792). It was similar to the Electoral Coronet of Ernest Augustus, except that the bonnet had a fringe of ermine which was worn inside the crown showing above the circlet. The fifth, which was taken from the frame of a portrait of Duke Frederick William of Brunswick (*obiit* 1815), was similar to the previous two, but with a row of pearls on the centre of the arches and the ermine fringe was worn outside the circlet.

With his first letter Heard had sent a sketch of an Electoral Bonnet depicted on a medal struck to commemorate the Act of Settlement and also displayed on the Garter plates of George I (13th March 1702) and George II (1710). The Hanoverian Court Chamberlain pointed out that the bonnet was too high and was surmounted by an orb and cross instead of an ermine tail.

After the elevation of Hanover to the status of a kingdom, the Royal Crown was frequently depicted emblematically in England as of the general shape of the stylised royal crowns of the period, although unusually high and with a red cap inside with a tall fringe of ermine outside and hiding the circlet. This probably represented the Hanoverian Electoral Bonnet and not the English Cap of Maintenance.

In the official account of the funeral of George III at Windsor in 1820 it is stated that the crown and sceptre of Hanover were carried at the ceremony, but there is no record of these ornaments being made or of what happened to them subsequently.

At the funeral of Queen Caroline in Hanover and Brunswick, a crown of Great Britain was brought across and borne at the obsequies at Hanover and Brunswick by a representative of the Lord Chamberlain from the English Court.

On the occasion of the marriage of Crown Prince George to Princess Marie of Saxe-Altenburg in 1843, the King ordered a crown and sceptre and a princess's crown to be made (*Plate 110, a*). The contract for the three ornaments was signed in December 1842 by the Finance Minister, von Schulte, on behalf of the King and the Court Jewellers, Knauer and Lameyer. It provided for the delivery of these ornaments within four weeks. The contract laid down that the crown (*Plate 110, b*) was to be of gold with 4 sapphires and 10 oriental garnets, but on delivery it contained an additional 2 sapphires and 6 oriental garnets. It was of the modern heraldic shape of royal crowns, though somewhat taller than those in use in other kingdoms. A cap of red velvet and ermine was made to be worn inside the crown. Settings were provided for additional stones which were to be taken from the king's reserve of jewels for each particular occasion, a practice which was in use under the Hanoverian kings in England. At the present time there are 4 emeralds, 6 sapphires and 10 oriental garnets adorning the crown.

The golden sceptre is ornamented with 16 rubies, 14 emeralds, 16 diamonds and 16 oriental garnets. At a recent date some damage was done to the shaft of the sceptre which can, however, be repaired.

The princess's crown (*Plate 110, c*) was worn by the royal bride at the wedding ceremony in 1843. It is a small golden crown unadorned with precious stones. No queen's crown was made, as the King's Consort, Queen Frederica, had died in 1841.

In 1866 the Prussians required Hanover to side with Prussia against Austria but the King and his Ministers declared that they wished to remain true to the Constitution of the German Federation and to preserve neutrality. Only two hours were granted for a reply, and, as this was unacceptable, 80,000 Prussian troops crossed the border and occupied the kingdom. There was little time to save much, as the invasion was unexpected. The subsequent events and the successful steps taken to remove the crown jewels to a place of safety are graphically described in a Memorandum written by Baron de Mahertie.[1] He states that:

> The crown jewels as well as the Queen's private jewels and the rich treasures of plate, the so-called 'Silber Kammer' were still in the Castle when the Prussian soldiers occupied it, placing sentries at every gate and door and it became a matter of anxious thought how to remove these valuable treasures from the Prussian grasp. It was particularly difficult to save the gold and silver plate on account of its great bulk.
>
> There was enough to dine 2,000 people from gold and silver plates, whilst the huge centre pieces, monumental candelabra, old-fashioned wine coolers and salvers, some pieces measuring 3 and 4 ft in height, took up a great deal of room, indeed these immense and bulky quantities had required three large railway vans, when brought back from England after her Majesty's succession, when the heirlooms of the Georges were equally divided amongst the two branches of the family, Hanover receiving in addition all objects formerly belonging to the Electoral treasure.

The Baron goes on to describe how, with the assistance of 100 devoted labourers, the royal officials and servants managed to pack the treasure into large wine barrels, which were removed under the very eyes of the Prussian soldiery to the royal cellars, and thence by a disused and almost forgotten subterranean passage to the vaults beneath the old market church, tenanted by a patriotic wine merchant, who little by little sent them, among barrels containing wine, some to England by ship from Hamburg, Bremen and Antwerp, and the remainder by rail to Vienna. Although a sum of 20,000 thalers (almost £3,000) had been offered by the Prussians as a reward for the finding of the treasure, no one betrayed the secret.

The Queen's private jewels proved relatively easy to move. The Baron's father was Lord Chamberlain and his mother the Mistress of the Robes, and they took the jewels in a royal coach, which made three journeys from Herrenhausen to their house, where they were buried in a corner of the garden.

The crown jewels presented a more difficult problem. According to the Baron's account they consisted of the crowns of the King and Queen, a sceptre, orb, wand of justice, jewelled collars and stars of the Order of the Garter, of the Order of St George and other Guelphic and foreign orders of knighthood, a jewelled sword of state and other swords.[2]

---

[1] This interesting document entitled *Twixt You and Me, Hanoverian Crown Jewels*, is in the Royal Archives at Windsor. The author has been given permission to make use of it by Mr R. Mackworth Young, the Librarian of Windsor Castle. It is written in romantically dramatic language and, as there has been no attempt to economise in the use of words, it is too long to quote in full, but the salient facts have been extracted.

[2] The crown described as the Queen's was probably the Princess's crown which had been taken into use for the Queen. There is no subsequent reference to the orb, wand of justice (presumably a Hand of Justice) or the jewelled sword of state, and these ornaments do not seem to have been preserved.

They were smuggled out of the Castle by the Lord Chamberlain after a formal authority had been signed by the Queen and the Minister of the King's House.[1]

The Prussians were naturally chagrined by the removal of so valuable a treasure, particularly as this had occurred during and not previous to their occupation. Fearing that the hiding place might be discovered, the Chamberlain decided to remove the treasure to the ducal vaults beneath the Royal Chapel. Taking one of the late King Ernest Augustus's English valets into his confidence, the Baron and his own confidential servant, Henry, a hunchback, chose a dark night and dug up as much of the treasure as could be stowed in ample pouches stitched inside their long winter mantles. They stealthily approached the inner courtyard and were admitted to the chapel by the English valet through a side door used by the bellringers and descended into the vaults. The jewels were deposited on the altar while a suitable hiding place was sought for. Only three of the dusty and becobwebbed sarcophagi proved to be easily accessible, those of the Electress Sophia (mother of George I of England), of the Princess Ahlen, and of a stillborn child, supposed to have been the premature daughter of the first Queen of Prussia.

The Chamberlain decided that the tomb of the child, a large one, would be the least likely to rouse suspicion. Producing two sets of housebreaking implements, the English valet and Henry slowly and cautiously opened the tomb, the tools having to be muffled to avoid the slightest noise. At last the lid was removed; the inner coffin proved to be so small that there was plenty of room. Two crowns and other insignia were placed in the tomb, the lid was replaced and the party returned as silently as they had come.

Further journeys were necessary, the greatest difficulty being the transport of the Sword of State and other swords 'which could not be left behind and could only be carried by having double scabbards placed inside their trousers'. However, this was accomplished in two or three more journeys. So as to avoid suspicion, these had to be made on dark nights, but not consecutively. The tomb of Princess Ahlen was opened, but the Chamberlain shrank from disturbing the ashes of the great Electress, and eventually the tomb of a young electoral prince received the Queen's personal jewels.

Here the jewels remained for several years until the threat of war following on Prince Leopold of Hohenzollern's claim to the Spanish throne, when the King decided the jewels must be removed to England. The Countess Julie Kielmansegge, an old lady of eighty, and other ladies, offered to escort them to Vienna. The Chamberlain and his helpers removed the jewels by the same stealthy means as before. Going first to the house of the pastor of the chief town church, the Chamberlain and Henry changed into hunting dress, while the valet removed picnic baskets and large hampers from the Chamberlain's coach and substituted the jewels for the provisions contained in them, the swords replacing the guns in the gun cases. They then drove to the house of a royal forester and stowed the hampers in the forester's bedroom, the crown being placed in a small toilet bag. The forester met Countess Kielmansegge at the nearest station. The account goes on: 'It appears that it was no easy matter to hide the crown in the Countess's lace bonnet, however it was done and the courageous, wonderful old

1 The King and Crown Prince had joined the army at Göttingen.

lady travelled all the way to Vienna with this heavy ponderous piece of jewellery on her head'. The jewels were sewn into the clothes of five ladies, the swords following them to Vienna in specially made gun cases.

Together with the barrels of plate, the whole treasure was eventually transported to England.[1]

In the Windsor Archives, attached to the Memorandum, is a note, dated December 1948, by the late Queen Mary, which reads:

> After reading the enclosed story about the saving of the Hanoverian Crown Jewels in 1866, I remembered that my Aunt the Grand Duchess of Mecklenburg-Strelitz had told me that when she was coming to England on a visit in 1870, when she arrived at Calais to embark in her special steamer (in those days every member of the royal family was given a special steamer for crossing the Channel), a Hanoverian lady she knew met her and asked whether the Grand Duchess would give her a passage to England because she had the Hanoverian crown jewels sewn into her dress and that the crown was inside her hat, she was to deposit them in the Bank of England in London for safe keeping. Of course the Grand Duchess consented readily. This lady must have been the Countess Kielmansegge mentioned in this story.

With the dissolution of the personal union of the two crowns in 1837, an attempt was made to decide which of the possessions and heirlooms in England had belonged to the family as such, and should now return to Hanover, and which of them belonged to the Sovereign of England and were, therefore, heirlooms of the British Crown.[2] It was inevitable that difficulties would arise in determining to whom all the possessions belonged. The first two Hanoverian kings spent a great deal of time in Hanover and under George I some of his English possessions were removed there. On Queen Anne's death, before the arrival of the new family, there had been a great clearance of the Queen's jewels and many of those which remained were distributed by the new King amongst his German favourites. The only piece of jewellery which the Hanoverians seem to have inherited from Queen Anne was a pearl necklace which had been given her by her Consort, Prince George of Denmark. George II was particularly scrupulous in separating and keeping in each country whatever belonged to England or Hanover.[3] Among the valuables inherited from Queen Anne by George I had been a set of golden knives, forks and spoons. George I took these to Hanover, where they were found by George II, who brought them back to England.

George II left in his will the jewels in his personal possession, half to George III and half to his fourth son, the Duke of Cumberland. George III bought the latter for £50,000 to give to his bride Princess Charlotte of Mecklenburg-Strelitz as a wedding present. The evening before the ceremony he led her into a room where they were all laid out. They included a diamond crown. The Queen kept them in a chest separate from her other jewels and in 1804 ordered the Court Jewellers, Rundell and Bridge,

---

[1] It is interesting to note that, as a result of these adventures the sceptre has been broken. Was this by accident or by intent, to symbolise the extinction of the kingdom? There are several representations of broken sceptres, such as in the tapestries in the National Museum at Copenhagen (*Plate 38*) and Robert Elstrack's engraving of Richard III, which symbolise the forced termination of a reign.

[2] G. M. Willis: *Ernest Augustus, Duke of Cumberland, King of Hanover*, London 1954.

[3] *Horace Walpole's Reminiscences*, edited by Paget Toynbee, Oxford 1924.

to fit the cases with small brass plates engraved with an inscription relating their origin. She bequeathed them to her descendants according to the House Law of Hanover. William IV was not so meticulous as George II had been about keeping his Hanoverian and his English jewels apart.

After William IV's death in 1837 King Ernest Augustus expected to receive the Hanoverian jewels from the executors, but the Whig Law Officers of the Crown advised the Queen that it was by no means clear that the jewels belonged to the Hanoverians. The King, therefore, made a legal claim and on the recommendations of his friend, Lord Strangford, employed Mr Leigh Pemberton as his solicitor. Pemberton asked to see the inventory, which was in the hands of the executors, but this request was refused. He feared that his lack of success might lead his client to consider him to be incompetent. As he was suspicious that the other side was dragging out the proceedings until all the witnesses, who were already of great age, were no longer living, he took depositions from a number of persons including the servants of Queen Charlotte, who had charge of her jewels, as well as those of George IV. The Law Officers of the Crown asserted[1] that the status of the Crown of Hanover was that of a 'corporation sole' and, therefore, could not hold property. Such property they said would only be held in the personal capacity of that one person at any given time. As entailed, the property became automatically his to dispose of as he pleased without reference to the stipulations of the original testator. It must follow that upon the death of William IV the property was escheated to the British Crown. Pemberton pointed out that the crown of a sovereign state did not fall into this category, and that even if it did and the jewels became the unrestricted personal property of William IV they would not, upon his death, be escheated to the Crown, but would follow his testament like the remainder of his personal possessions. As no agreement could be reached, the British Government at last appointed a commission of three High Court Judges—Lord Lyndhurst, Lord Langdale and Chief Justice Tindal—to investigate the matter.[2] There were considerable delays in dealing with the case and on the very day on which the commission was to have met to make the award Chief Justice Tindal died. As the other two members did not agree no award could be given. The Lord Chancellor, Lord Cottenham, refused to renew the commission and the dispute remained in abeyance.

The dispute had led to some coolness between the two Courts, although it was the Whigs who had exploited it as a manifestation of their antagonism towards the King of Hanover, who had been a formidable political opponent when he sat in the House of Lords. The King, when visiting England in 1843, pressed upon Queen Victoria the necessity for bringing the affair to a settlement, but the interminable delays which continued wearied the King and he said he would allow the Queen to retain the jewels with the exception of a few which were important to the Hanoverian Crown.[3]

In 1857 the British Government decided that the dispute ought to be settled and a

[1] They had to make a case because Queen Victoria, in the absence of advice to the contrary, had worn them in public. See *Letters of the King of Hanover to Viscount Strangford*, London 1925.

[2] Greville's *Journal of the Reign of Queen Victoria, 1852–60*, Vol. II, 29th December and 31st December 1857.

[3] Willis: op. cit.

new commission was appointed consisting of Lord Wensleydale, Vice-Chancellor Page Wood and Sir Lawrence Peel (an ex-Indian judge). One of the reasons why the surviving members of the first commission failed to reach agreement was that they did not have before them the will of George III which was available to the new commission. In arriving at their award, the commission divided the jewels into two categories: those which were undoubtedly Hanoverian and those left to Queen Charlotte by George III in his will and disposed of by Queen Charlotte in hers. The commission was unanimous in its award[1] which contained four main points.

First, the jewels which were to be awarded to the King of Hanover.

Secondly, the King of Hanover was entitled to a certain pearl necklace formerly belonging to the Electress Sophia containing 37 pearls, but on the evidence produced these pearls could not be identified.

Thirdly, the King of Hanover's title to any other jewels in the possession of the Queen was negatived.

Fourthly, that on receipt of the jewels the King of Hanover was to give the Queen a full release and discharge of all claims and demands on all jewels which are or were in the Queen's possession.

Lord Lyndhurst, a member of the first commission, told Greville that he was satisfied that the award was correct and that had George III's will been before the first commission they would have given a similar award. The value of the jewels claimed had been greatly exaggerated and Lyndhurst put their real worth at £150,000. Prince Albert had told him that the pearls were the finest in Europe. This remark relates to the famous pearls frequently but misleadingly described as the 'Hanoverian pearls' which Mary Queen of Scots was given by her husband the Dauphin and by his mother Catherine de Medici. They were purchased by Queen Elizabeth I for £3,000 and inherited later by James I, who gave them to his daughter Elizabeth, Queen of Bohemia. Thus, although they had been handed down by inheritance from the Electress Sophia, they were in fact Stuart heirlooms. The jewels were handed over to Count Kielmansegge, the Hanoverian Ambassador at the Court of St James on 28th January 1858 and taken to Hanover and given to King George V. King Ernest Augustus had died some six years earlier and therefore never saw the jewels; but the Hanoverian Court was satisfied that his claim to them had been vindicated.

The beautiful diamond crown (*Plate 110, d*) which Queen Charlotte received from George III passed to the King of Hanover in accordance with the terms of settlement in 1858, and since has been used as the Hanoverian royal wedding crown in place of the princess's crown made in 1842. It follows the established style of English royal crowns, the circlet carrying alternate crosses *patées* and fleurs-de-lis. It is closed with two arches surmounted by an orb and cross. The crown is profusely set with brilliants, many of them being of notable size. It has a unique feature. From the junction of the arches spring four golden rods, which are slightly curved and from the end of each of which is a pendant formed of a large solitaire pendaloque diamond, which greatly adds to the

---

[1] The official version of the award is published in full as an Appendix to this chapter. Public Record Office London, F.O. 34–96.

effect when the crown is worn. A plate is fixed to the outside of the case which bears the inscription: 'CR This box contains the crown which I found at my arrival in the year 1761.'

Another important jewel which may have been returned to Hanover is a diamond known as 'The Cumberland'. This was presented to Prince William, Duke of Cumberland, in 1746 by the City of London after his return from his victory at the Battle of Culloden. The diamond must have been an unusually fine one because the purchase cost the City of London Corporation £10,000. According to Streeter[1] it is not exactly known what happened to this stone, though he states that it is understood to have been restored to Hanover by Queen Victoria in 1866. If this was so, it would not have been restored as a Hanoverian crown jewel as such, but as an heirloom of the Dukes of Cumberland. It is possible that this stone is identical with one which was sold at Christie's on 16th December 1953.[2] It is described as 'an important diamond brooch composed of a large triangular-shaped diamond in a diamond border of hexagonal form supported by a single diamond in a lozenge-shaped collet, a pear-shaped diamond drop'. The description in the catalogue adds that the above triangular-shaped diamond is reputed to have belonged to the crown jewels of Hanover. The sale was on behalf of Lord Grantley and the brooch was purchased by P. Lindsay for £1,700. The reduction in value would be explained by the fact that it was not brilliant cut and the value of stones not so cut has depreciated considerably in modern times.

Another interesting jewel which was in the possession of the Dukes of Brunswick in the last century was a blue drop diamond weighing 13¾ carats. This stone was examined in juxtaposition to the famous Hope Blue Diamond and was found to be identical in colour and quality. This led experts to believe that it was part of the celebrated French Blue Diamond stolen with the crown jewels from the Garde Meuble in Paris in 1792.[3] In April 1874 the Duke of Brunswick sold some jewels at Geneva and this stone was bought by Messrs Oakes Brothers of Paris for 17,000 francs, or £680.[4]

BIBLIOGRAPHY

DULSEN, T. VAN — *Memoirs.*
GREVILLE, C. C. — *Journal of the Reign of Queen Victoria 1852–60*, Vol. II.
MAHERTIE, BARON DE — 'Twixt you and me', MS. in the *Royal Archives*, Windsor.
STREETER, E. W. — *The Great Diamonds of the World*, London 1882.
Christie's Catalogue, December 11th 1953.

[1] E. W. Streeter: *The Great Diamonds of the World.*
[2] Christie's Catalogue, 16th December 1953, Item 127.
[3] Streeter, op. cit.
[4] See catalogue of the sale published at the time by Messrs Rossel and Son, Geneva. At the same sale a number of other outstanding stones were sold including a large rose-tinted diamond which fetched £2,842, 7 diamonds weighing from 27 to 81 carats, and a Chinese idol cut out of a single ruby.

WALPOLE, H.   *Reminiscences*, Ed. Paget Toynbee, Oxford 1924.

WILLIS, G. M.   *Ernest Augustus, Duke of Cumberland, King of Hanover*, London 1954.

ELECTORS AND KINGS OF HANOVER

ELECTORS

1692   Ernest Augustus, created Elector of Hanover

1698   George Louis (George I of England)

1727   George Augustus (George II of England)

1760   George William Frederick (George III of England)

KINGS

1814   George William Frederick (George III of England and first King of Hanover)

1820   George Augustus Frederick (George IV of England)

1830   William Henry (William IV of England)

1837   Ernest Augustus, Duke of Cumberland

1851   George V, son of Ernest Augustus

APPENDIX

AWARD OF THE ARBITRATION TRIBUNAL
AND
COUNT KIELMANSEGGE'S RECEIPT FOR THE HANOVER CROWN JEWELS
JANUARY 23, 1858

(Public Record Office Copy No. 2387 without certificate F.O. 34–96)

Whereas a question has long been pending as to certain Jewels in the possession of Her Majesty claimed by His Majesty The King of Hanover; and in order to put an end to that question Her Majesty some time since, with the consent of His Majesty The King of Hanover, caused a Commission to be issued under the Great Seal directed to the Right Honourable James Lord Wensleydale, the Right Honourable Sir Lawrence Peel, Knight, and Sir William Page Wood, Knight, one of the Vice-Chancellors of the Court of Chancery, directing them to enquire into the said claim, and to report thereon to Her Majesty:—And Whereas the said Commissioners enquired into the said claim accordingly, and made their Report in the month of December last, and they thereby reported that in their opinion His Majesty The King of Hanover was entitled to the Jewels in the possession of Her Majesty enumerated in the Schedule hereto annexed, being Jewels which had been bequeathed by the Will of Her late Majesty Queen Charlotte, Consort of His late Majesty King George the Third, but they negatived the title of His said Majesty to any other Jewels in the possession of Her Majesty, except only that they considered that His said Majesty was entitled to a certain Pearl necklace formerly belonging to the Electress Sophia, containing thirty seven Pearls, but the evidence before them did not show whether those Pearls, or any of them, were in the possession of Her Majesty, on which point therefore they desired further evidence. And Whereas both Her Majesty and the King of Hanover are satisfied that no further evidence can be offered on this subject, there being no means of ascertaining whether these Pearls ever came to the possession of Her Majesty, or if they did, then whether they do not form part of the Pearls included in the said Schedule:—And Whereas Her Majesty, being desirous fully to satisfy all just claims on the part of His Majesty The King of Hanover, has placed in the Hands of the Right Honourable George Earl of Clarendon, one of Her Principal Secretaries of State, all the Jewels comprised in the said Schedule, with directions to deliver the same up to His said Majesty The King of Hanover, or to any person having authority in that behalf, on receiving such a discharge as is herein contained:—And Whereas Adolphus Count Kielmansegge, the Envoy Extraordinary and Minister Plenipotentiary of His Majesty The King of Hanover at the Court of Her Majesty, has received from His Majesty The King of Hanover full power, on receipt of the Jewels comprised in the said Schedule, to give to Her Majesty a full release and discharge of all claims and demands whatever in manner hereinafter contained:—And Whereas the said George Earl of Clarendon, in obedience to the commands of Her Majesty, has this day delivered up to the said Adolphus Count Kielmansegge on behalf of His said Majesty, The King of Hanover, the whole of the Jewels comprised in the said Schedule, as the said Count hereby admits:—Now therefore He the said Count doth hereby, by the authority and in the name of His Majesty The King of Hanover, release and discharge Her Majesty, Her Heirs and Successors, from all claims and demands whatever which His Majesty The King of Hanover or His late Royal Father has or had in respect of any Jewels whatever which now are or ever were in the possession of Her Majesty, whether derived from the said Will of Her late Majesty Queen Charlotte, or from His late Majesty King George the Second, or from any of Her Majesty's Royal Progenitors, or otherwise howsoever; it being clearly understood that the Jewels so delivered up are to be accepted and taken by His Majesty The King of Hanover in full satisfaction of all claims and demands whatever:—As witness my Hand, this Twenty third day of January, One Thousand Eight Hundred and Fifty Eight.

A. KIELMANSEGGE

SCHEDULE OF JEWELS

1. Two brilliant Sleeve Bows.
   A pair of three dropped brilliant earrings.
   A pair of single dropped brilliant earrings, set with several brilliants at the back.
   A large stoned brilliant necklace; and a brilliant cross.
2. A large brilliant Stomacher.
3. A beautifully set brilliant Crown, small, to put on the head-dress.
4. A large pearl necklace; and large pearl dropped earrings.
5. A large brilliant nosegay.

A. KIELMANSEGGE

CHAPTER TWELVE

THE HOLY SEE

The earliest occasion on which we know that a Pope received secular honours was when John I in 526 was sent by Theodoric on an embassy to the Emperor Justin in Constantinople, when he was received with the same ceremonial as was accorded to a basileus on his entry into a city. Pope Constantine I was similarly received when he visited Constantinople at the end of 710. In the *Liber Pontificalis* we find further information about the Emperor's instructions to his governors in Italy as to how to receive the Pope on his return journey. Constantine was to be acclaimed, banners were to be unfurled and members of the highest aristocracy were to render the service of bridle and stirrup to the Pope—*de officium stratores*. The *Liber Pontificalis* also mentions that Constantine I had been accustomed to wear in Rome a head-dress in the shape of a pointed hood which was described as *camelaucum*, and that he wore this head-dress on his visit to the Emperor in Constantinople.

Until the XI century it was customary for the clergy to remain bare-headed during divine service, thus complying with the injunction of St Paul: 'every man praying or prophesying having his head covered dishonoureth his head', and: 'for a man ought not to cover his head for as much as he is the image and glory of God'.[1] The *camelaucum* was worn by the Pope because temporal officials of equivalent status wore it, and it was either conferred upon him as an imperial grant or assumed by him with the agreement of the imperial Court.[2] It is probable, however, that its introduction ante-dated Pope Constantine I, perhaps in the time of the Syrian and Greek Popes in the VII century, or possibly even in the VI century.

In the VIII century the Popes began to claim that they had been invested with the Empire. They based this claim on the *Constitum Constantini* or the Donation of Constantine which purported to be the gift made to Pope Sylvester by the Emperor Constantine the Great. This document is first quoted in the IX century, and although its genuineness was doubted at an early date—the Emperor Otto III and Arnold of Brescia both called it a lie—it was not until the XV century that it came to be seriously attacked.

Today it is generally accepted as a forgery, probably fabricated between 750 and 760. It was no doubt based on an existing tradition, as it is clear that Constantine had made important gifts to the Church—three lists of these gifts are to be found in the *Liber Pontificalis*. But the important point is that it was widely accepted and several

1 I Corinthians, xi, 4, 7
2 P. E. Schramm: *Herrschaftszeichen und Staatssymbolik*, Vol. I, Chapter 2.

Popes based claims on it.[1] According to the document Constantine the Great, in thankfulness for being cured of leprosy, granted to the Pope imperial honours, making him Chief Judge over the clergy, bestowing upon him the primacy over Antioch, Constantinople, Alexandria and Jerusalem and offering him the imperial crown. The clergy were given the rank of senators with the privilege of riding upon white saddle cloths. Lastly, but most important of all, the Pope was to have dominion over all Italy including Rome. The wording is: *Italiae seu occidentalium Regionum*, but later Popes translated *seu* as *et* and thus claimed all Western Europe.[2] The English translation of the passage about the regalia reads:

> We concede and by this present do confer our Imperial Lateran Palace which is preferred to and ranks above all the palaces in the whole world; then a diadem, that is, the crown of our head, and at the same time the phrygium; and also the shoulder band—that is, the collar that surrounds our imperial neck; and also the purple mantle and crimson tunic, and all the imperial raiment; and the same rank as those presiding over the imperial cavalry, conceding also the imperial sceptres, and, at the same time the spears and standards[3]; also the banners and different imperial ornaments and all the advantage of our high imperial position, and the glory of our power.

But according to a later passage, Sylvester did not take the diadem, as he refused to place the imperial crown on the Crown of St Peter—the tonsure. The passage reads:

> We also decreed this, that this same venerable one our Father Sylvester the supreme Pontiff and of Pontiffs his successors, might use and bear upon their heads—to the praise of God and for the honour of St Peter—the diadem; that is, the crown which we have granted him from our own hand, of purest gold and precious gems. But he the most Holy Pope did not at all allow that crown of gold to be used over the clerical crown which he wears to the glory of St Peter; but we placed upon his most Holy Head, with our own hands a phrygium, of gleaming white splendour representing the glorious resurrection of Our Lord and holding the bridle of his horse out of reverence for St Peter we performed for him the duty of groom; decreeing that all the Pontiffs his successors and they alone may use the phrygium in processions.

The papal phrygium seems to have been the *camelaucum* under another name and like the latter, it symbolised the temporal authority of the Pope. It was a high cylindrical hood with a point on top, but it is not known if it had the characteristic of the original phrygium, the point of which tipped forward. It took its name from *Phrygia*, now Karamania, where it was worn by priests and kings. It is possible that the papal phrygium is related to the old Testament high priests' head-dress. We find in Exodus xxviii, 39: 'and thou shall make the mitre of fine linen'. There is much confusion surrounding the biblical head-dress which is variously called mitre, pileus, tiara, corona, *regnum*, among other terms. It has been claimed that the biblical head-dress of the high priest was borrowed by the Phrygians, Lydians, Trojans and others.[4] It was not long before

---

[1] Urban II claimed Corsica by virtue of it; and Anselm, Gratian and Ivo of Chartres all received it into their collections of canon law, while Adrian IV relied on it in claiming the right to dispose of Ireland. See E. Henderson: *Select Historical Documents of the Middle Ages.*

[2] E. Henderson: op. cit.

[3] *Signa*, which may be taken to include the eagle and the orb.

[4] Those who are interested should refer to Schramm, op. cit.

a (left) *Innocent III (1198–1215). Lateran Library* (p. 377)

b (right) *Benedict XII (1334–42) by Paolo de Siena, 1342, in the Vatican Grotto* (p. 378)

c *Boniface VIII (1294–1303) from his tomb in the Vatican Grotto* (p. 377)

d *Tiara with three circlets from the tomb of Urban VI (1378–89) in the Vatican Grotto* (p. 378)

a   *Fresco by Fra Angelico showing Nicholas V (1446–55) wearing the tiara of St Sylvester. Vatican (p. 379)*

b   *Martin V (1417–31) from his tomb in St John Lateran by A. del Polloiolo (p. 379)*

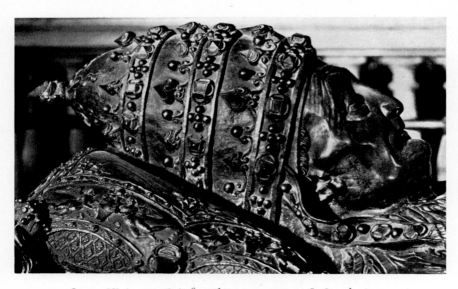

c   *Sixtus IV (1471–84) from his monument in St Peter's (p. 379)*

d   *Tiara of Paul II in portrait of Alexander VI (1492–1503) in the Sala dei Misteri of the Borgian Apartment in the Vatican (p. 379)*

the papal phrygium was referred to as *regnum*, a name used as early as the v century in the *Liber Pontificalis* as referring to terrestrial crowns. This term is first used in the *Ordo Romanus IX* which dates from the first half of the ix century. According to this *ordo*, a layman of low degree placed the *regnum* on the Pope's head after his consecration. The Pope was then conducted to his *cathedra* and, although not strictly a coronation, these two acts not only elevated the Pope above his clergy, but resembled the crowning and enthronisation of the Emperor.

In the xi and xii centuries the papal phrygium, or *regnum*, grew taller and more imposing and the tubular form became onion-shaped with a point on top which was sometimes surmounted by a ball. The colour remained white or cream, although artists' licence sometimes depicted it otherwise.

If we ignore Benzo of Alba's reference to the coronation of Pope Nicholas II (1059), for he was a notoriously unreliable and prejudiced writer, we do not find evidence of the metal circlets until a much later date. The original form was a band round the lower edge of the phrygium similar to that of a mitre which acted as a stiffening, sewn together at the back with the two ends falling behind as pendant bands, as with the mitre. At some time the band, or fillet, instead of being made of stuff, was made of metal, a step which was no doubt necessary for the phrygium to hold its shape when it became tall. It was perhaps natural that the metal circlet came to be regarded as a crown. Benzo certainly suggested that when he accused Hildebrand of crowning Nicholas II with a regal crown. Schramm[1] mentions passages from various writers, including one from Abbé Suger of St Denis, in his reference to Pope Innocent II when he appeared at the Council of Rheims in 1131, which show that the band had become decorated with gold and precious stones and looked like a crown. There are several representations of the xii century which show the papal head-dress with a circlet band. One is of the coronation of Lothair II by Innocent II in 1125. Another—a miniature of about 1174—depicts a phrygium on which two circular bands are shown. A contemporary mosaic (*Plate 111, a*) in the Lateran Library depicts Innocent III (1198–1216) wearing a tall head-dress of a chequered pattern with a broad band at the base and the two pendant fillets hanging down on to the Pope's shoulders.

Innocent III was the first Pope to make a canonical ruling as to when the Pope was to wear the episcopal mitre and when the phrygium, which was appropriate for him alone. The mitre was to be worn *pro sacerdotis* at all pontifical proceedings; the phrygium, which was now usually called the *regnum*, was to be worn *pro regna*, but only outside the church in festival processions at which he showed himself as a terrestrial sovereign.

Under Boniface VIII (1294–1303) the hood of the *regnum* was lengthened and the circlet was greatly enriched with precious stones, while towards the end of his papacy a second circlet was added (*Plate 111, c*). The increased length had the symbolical meaning of dominion of the *una sancta ecclesia* over the earth, and demonstrated the meaning of the papal *unam sanctum*. In the inventory of 1295[2] the second year of Boniface's papacy the head-dress, which is now usually referred to as a tiara, is described

1 Op. cit.

2 E. Müntz: 'La Tiare Pontificale du VIII au XVI Siècle', in *Mémoires de l'Académie des Inscriptions et Belles Lettres Paris XXXVI, Paris 1898.*

as enriched with 48 rubies balas, 72 sapphires, 45 *praxini* or emeralds, numerous little balas rubies and emeralds and 66 large pearls. At the summit was a very large ruby.

Boniface VIII was succeeded in 1303 by Benedict XI, who took the tiara to Perugia. After his death in 1304 there was a period of eleven months before a new Pope succeeded. The Archbishop of Bordeaux was chosen and took the title of Clement V. He removed the papal seat from Rome to Avignon and the tiara was brought to Lyons from Perugia for his coronation on 14th November 1305. In the inventory which was taken in 1315–16 Boniface VIII's tiara is again described and can be identified by the mention of the large ruby, which is recorded as missing. It is described as having three circlets *corona quae vocatur, regnum cum tribus circuitis auries*. It therefore must have been between the taking of the two inventories in 1295 and 1315 that the second and third circlets were added to the tiara. It was during this period that the fleur-de-lis was used to decorate the circlets. The tiara was kept in the Papal Treasury at Avignon until Gregory XI took it back to Rome, which he entered on 17th January 1377. In 1378 Robert of Geneva was elected anti-Pope taking the style Clement VII, and he removed the tiara to Avignon. When the Spaniard, Pedro de Luna, was elected anti-Pope in 1394 styling himself Benedict XIII, he took the tiara from Avignon to Spain, where it remained until Alphonso V of Aragon failed in his attempt to renew the schism, and on his withdrawal of his support from the anti-Pope Clement VII in 1429, the tiara was returned to Rome.

Although by this time the actual tiara possessed three crowns, it continued to be depicted sometimes as having only one or two. The memorial of Benedict XI at Perugia shows only one crown; a statue of Benedict XII (*Plate 111, b*) in the Vatican Grotto depicts the tiara with two crowns, though on that Pope's tomb at Avignon three crowns are shown. On the tomb of Urban VI in the Vatican Grotto the tiara is depicted with three circlets (*Plate 111, d*).

The allegorical meanings attributed to the three crowns have been many and various. One theory is that they symbolise the three churches—militant, suffering, triumphant. Others are that they are an allusion to the Holy Trinity, to the three theological virtues, or to the three powers—sacerdotal, royal and imperial. Another theory is that the Pope has three missions—Father of Kings, Rector of the World and Vicar of Christ. Yet another suggests that they expressed the papal rule over the three parts of the world at the time they were introduced. But it seems more likely that the symbolism was suggested by the idea that took shape in the XIII and XIV centuries that the Emperor was crowned with three crowns—the silver crown of Germany at Aix-la-Chapelle, the iron crown of Lombardy at Milan or Monza and the golden imperial crown at Rome, and therefore the Pope, too, should wear three crowns.

In the XIV century the tiara of Boniface VIII began to be called the Tiara of St Sylvester, and it became venerated and considered as a relic. This was no doubt suggested by the Donation of Constantine, but it now came to be used only at the coronation of Popes, starting with Gregory XI in 1370 and his successor Urban VI in 1378. It was used at no other ceremonies and was kept in the Lateran Treasury. It was last used at the coronation of Nicholas V (1446–55), and in 1485 it was stolen and no more was heard of it. It is depicted on the head of Nicholas V in the fresco of Fra Angelico in the Vatican (*Plate 112, a*).

As the tiara of St Sylvester was not available except at coronations, the Popes had to provide others for their own use. Martin V (1417–31) had one made by a celebrated sculptor-jeweller, Lorenzo Ghiberti (*Plate 112, b*). His successor, Eugene IV, commissioned the same artist to make one for the sum of 38,000 florins, and in 1431 ordered another from a Roman jeweller, Nardo de Pietro. It was described as being made of silver, the metal weighing 5 lb, while additional gold and handiwork cost 31 florins. A few months later Eugene purchased an emerald for 20 florins, which he added to it. In 1439 the Pope pledged this tiara to the Florentines for 40,000 florins. Calixtus III (1455–8) in 1456 made heroic efforts to arm Christendom for the common defence against Islam and sold all his precious stones and plate to equip a fleet against the Turks. Paul II (1464–71), a Venetian, and Sixtus IV (1471–84) had their own tiaras. That of Paul II can be seen in several pictures in the Vatican Gallery, notably in portraits of Sixtus IV and Alexander VI (*Plate 112, d*). A characteristic feature was that the spaces not taken up by the three crowns were entirely covered with pearls. At the time it was made it was valued at 110,000 florins, but Julius II pawned it to the Chigi for only 40,000 florins. It was redeemed by Clement VII (1523–34).[1] Finally it was dismantled at the time of the Sack of Rome, as was one which was made for Paul II's successor, Sixtus IV who, just before his death in 1483, had ordered a new tiara (*Plate 112, c*) from the Venetian, Bartelemmeo Tommaso, which was specially magnificent and cost 10,817 ducats.

Under the pontificate of Julius II (1503–13) the tiaras became exceptionally rich. He had one made for his coronation which he adorned with a large balas ruby of 120 carats, for which he paid 7,300 florins. Another most notable tiara was made by Caradosso, a celebrated sculptor, medallist and goldsmith from Milan, at a cost of 200,000 ducats. It is depicted in a water-colour by Bertoni, now in the British Museum (*Plate 113, a*).

There is a description of the tiara written by John Talman, who had owned the drawing, which reads as follows:

> The rich Tiara or Triple Crown made by Pope Julius ye 2nd kept in the Castle of Saint Angelo att Rome.

The wholle Crown is covered with large Pearles; the lower circle is of beaten Gold wherein are these words *IULIUS LIGUR II PONT. OPT. MAX. ANNO SEPTIMO* in letters composed of small diamonds, the other three circles are likewise of beaten Gold enameled, and sett with Jewels viz; very fine Jacinths, Balasses, and Saphirs. In the space over the lower circle (exclusive of ye small one at ye bottom) are 3 Carbuncles or Ruby-spinels of extraordinary value, and a very beautiful and large Saphir, all hanging loose; and behind on ye back part is another saphir of equal size; there are also some very large Pear-Pearls hanging loose and severall fine Diamonds; On ye top is a very beautiful and large Emeraud, placed there by Gregory ye 13th whose name is ingraved in ye fascia in ye middle of ye said stone, viz GREGORIUS XIII PONT. OPT. MAX. supported by Two golden Dragons enamelled (ye arms of ye Boncompagni, a Noble Family of Bologna, of which Pope Gregory was). When ye foundations were preparing for ye new Edifice of St. Peters in ye Vatican, a Laborer digging struck his Pickaxe on a stone coffin and broke it; upon

---

1 Not to be confused with Clement VII (1375–94), the anti-Pope.

examination it was found to be ye burial place of ye Empress. . . . Upon notice of this accident ye Pope ordered ye Tomb to be opened, when ye Body was found to be dust, but ye Jewels which in great quantity adorned ye body all over were taken out; and ye ashes, being gathered into a small urn, were honourably interred in ye Crypts of ye New Church. With part of ye Jewels ye Pope caused this magnificent Tiara to be adorned, to ye value of 200,000 Roman Scudi (he made also ye rich miter sett with part of these Jewels which he sent to ye Bishop of Loretto). This Triple Crown with 3 others and 2 miters which were made by ye Popes Pius 5 and Paul 5th are kept in ye Castle St. Angelo, and may not be taken thence but when ye Pope celebrates Mass Pontifically in St. Peters or St. Maria Maggiore at their being taken out, there must be present The Treasurer, and Commissary of ye Chamber, the Publick Notary, The Chivaro that is ye keeper of ye keyes & ye Castellano or Governour of St. Angelo, where they are kept in a small round Room at ye top of ye Castle. In this Room is an oblong chest, into which the crowns with their Labels are putt; (after they have been all strictly examined, and an account taken by ye notary what Stones or Pearls are wanting, and an Instrument drawn, whereby they promise to deliver all in ye same manner as they received them). Then They proceed to St. Peters through ye covered Gallery, preceeded by a Guard of 12 men armed cap-a-pie. The 6 Chaplains extramuros robed carry these Crowns and Miters before ye Pope when he goes to St. Peters.

The Labell belonging to the Tiara of P. Julius ye 2nd sett all over with Pearles. The Jewels were adorned with foliage of Gold in relievo. The borders are of beaten Gold enameled, the Pendants are of Gold, and ye lining on ye inside is of a rich gold Ganza or Brocades.[1]

At the time of the Sack of Rome this tiara was in pawn and thus escaped destruction. Benvenuto Cellini in his memoirs described how at that time in 1527 Pope Clement VII,

desiring to save the tiaras and all the mass of jewels belonging to the Apostolic Camera, ordered me to come before him. Then he shut himself in a room with only Cavalierino and me . . . now when the Pope, Cavalierino and I were shut up in this room, the tiaras and all the jewels of the Apostolic Camera were placed before me and His Holiness ordered me to take them out of their gold settings. This I did and then rolled each in a little piece of paper and sewed them into the lining of the clothes which the Pope and Cavalierino wore.

New tiaras were made for Paul III (1534–49) (*Plate 113, c*), Pius V (1566–72) (*Plate 113, d*), Clement VIII (1592–1605) and Urban VIII (1623–44). In 1789, although the tiara of Julius II seems still to have been in use, Pope Pius VI wanted a more elegant one and ordered a new tiara to be made. This contained 3 diamonds of rare size; 36 other medium or small diamonds; 24 large balas rubies; 22 large sapphires; 24 emeralds; 12 medium and 2 small rubies; a mass of oriental pearls with six cordons of very large oriental pearls and 1 extraordinarily large pearl; the large emerald from Julius II's tiara was placed at the summit. Clement XI (1700–21) also had a new tiara made. It is depicted in a drawing of 1700 by Pietro Santi Bartoli, which is now in the British Museum (*Plate 113, b*). It was surmounted by a large balas ruby with a cross.[2]

[1] Notwithstanding what is written below, which was 'copyed from the description quoted by John Talman Esq. (whose drawing this once was) the account is otherwise given by Flaminicus Vacca a Roman Antiquary, who wrote that these Jewels were found and made up by Pope Paul 3rd and were found in a large coffine or urne of Red Egyptian Granite. See *Monfauconi Diarium Italicum*, p. 276, but how to reconcile his acct with the Inscription in the circle of the Crown?'

[2] The drawing came into the possession of an eminent jeweller, Peter Dubens of Leicester Fields, who made a valuation from a close inspection of the drawing. His estimate, described as sagaciously imagined, came to £102,450.

a   Tiara of Julius II (1503–13) from a water-colour by Bertoni. British Museum (p. 379)

b (right)   Drawing of tiara of Clement XI by Bartoli in 1700. British Museum (p. 380)

c   Paul III (1534–49). Statue on the Church of Aracoeli (p. 380)

d   Pius V (1566–72). Funeral monument in St Maria Maggiore (p. 380)

a (left) *Tiara given to Pius VI by Napoleon in 1804. Papal Treasury (pp. 381 and 384)*

b (right) *Tiara given to Leo XIII in 1888 by the City of Paris. Papal Treasury (pp. 383 and 384)*

c (left) *Tiara given to Pius IX by the Catholics of Belgium. Papal Treasury (pp. 383 and 384)*

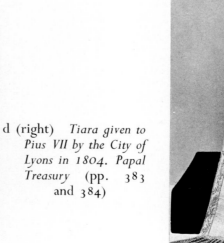

d (right) *Tiara given to Pius VII by the City of Lyons in 1804. Papal Treasury (pp. 383 and 384)*

In 1797 Bonaparte, by the Treaty of Tolentino, imposed upon the Pope a payment of ten million lira in money and five million lira in diamonds and precious effects. In order to meet this, the Papal Treasury was denuded of all its riches and all the tiaras were broken up, except that of Gregory XIII (1572–88) which was very simple and light.

In 1804, when Pius VI agreed to go to Paris to anoint Napoleon, the treasury was so depleted that there was no tiara available of appropriate magnificence for such an occasion. Napoleon made good the omission by ordering a new one which he gave to the Pope as a present (*Plate 114, a*). We have a full description of this in the *Imperial Decree of Messidor 29 of the year XII*.

The tiara given to the Pope by the Emperor Napoleon is of the shape, consecrated by custom, of an elongated pearl bulging slightly in the middle. The central part is of white velvet. The three golden crowns are each composed of a large hoop surmounted by flowers with leaves wrought in gold.

The middle of the hoop of each crown is occupied by a bas-relief worked in gold in the form of an elongated hexagon.

1st bas-relief.—The Re-establishment of Worship. Inscription on the front:

> *Auspice Primo Cos. Bonaparte*
> *Sacer cultus solenniter restit.*
> *Parisiis in Basil. Beatae Virginis.*
> *Die Paschali 1802.*

8 emerald flower-ornaments, 54 rubies, 819 brilliants, 111 rose-diamonds, 412 pearls.

2nd bas-relief.—The Concordat. Inscription:

> *Pii VII summi Pontif*
> *Cum Bonaparte Reip. Gallic. Cos.*
> *De Rebus Ecclesiae componendis Partic.*
> *Parisiis 14 Julli 1801.*

8 flower-ornaments of rubies, 54 emeralds, 815 brilliants, 104 rose-diamonds, 430 pearls.

3rd bas-relief.—The Consecration of the Emperor. Inscription:

> *Napoleo Gallorum Imperator*
> *Sacro inunctus oleo*
> *A Pio VII Summo Pontif.*
> *Die 2 decembr. 1804.*

8 flower-ornaments of sapphires, 54 rubies, 828 brilliants, 119 rose-diamonds, 385 pearls.

Above, the emerald from the tiara of Pius VI weighing 2^O, 5^V $\frac{1}{2}$ 30 gr. It bears the engraved inscription:

> *Gregorius XIII. Pont. Op. Max.*

Around it, 8 rubies, 24 pearls, above a cross of 12 brilliants and 18 rose-diamonds.

The tassel: 12 rubies, 2 emeralds, 36 brilliants, 233 pearls.

The slip buckle: 1 large ruby, 45 pearls.

The bands: 70 rubies, 280 pearls, 56 smaller rubies, 2 sapphires, 4 rubies, 4 emeralds, 116 brilliants, 816 pearls, and 364 pearls.

In all, there were employed 3,345 precious stones and 2,990 pearls.

There is also an account detailing the cost.

Account of a tiara studded with rubies, emeralds, oriental sapphires, diamonds, and pearls; ornamented with three bas-reliefs in gold representing The Concordat, the Re-establishment of Worship by the Emperor, and The Consecration of his Majesty by Pius VII, with the bands, as well as the tassel, enriched with precious stones like those mentioned above, the whole mounted in gold on a ground of white velvet.

By H. Auguste, Goldsmith and Jeweller

1,522 brilliants re-cut, from a carat to $\frac{1}{8}$, weighing together . . . . 306 c. $\frac{1}{4}$ $\frac{1}{8}$

Plus 1,114 brilliants not re-cut . . . . 51 c. $\frac{1}{8}$ $\frac{1}{16}$

Total: 2,646 brilliants, weighing . . . . 357 c. $\frac{2}{4}$

At 160 fr the carat, average price . . . . Fr 57,207

For the cross: 12 brilliants re-cut, of the first quality, at 440 fr the carat, weighing 18$\frac{7}{16}$ 8,107.10

For the cross: 352 rose-diamonds of Holland at 1·50 fr 528

For the cross: 267 Orient rubies of different sizes weighing together 229 c. $\frac{3}{4}$. $\frac{1}{8}$. 30,000

For the cross: 68 emeralds of different sizes weighing together 143 c. $\frac{3}{4}$ $\frac{1}{16}$ . . 25,000

For the cross: 10 Orient sapphires, the largest weighing 77 gr. $\frac{1}{2}$. The whole 91 c. $\frac{1}{4}$. $\frac{1}{8}$ 9,000

34 string of pearls for the fringe of the bands, weighing 2 gr 5 gr, in all 816 pearls 9,000

12 strings of pearls for the fringe of the tassel, 189 pearls weighing 4 gr 24 gr at 9·50 fr 1,800

394 pearls for the ornaments of the two bands, the tassels, the buckles, etc. . 1,379

1,591 pearls for the hoops of the crowns and the borders of the bands, at 10 fr . 15,910

For the cutting of the precious stones, the setting and fitting of the diamonds, the threading of the pearls, the gold jewel weighing 7^m, 5^0 at 20 carats, the embroidery, the decorated cases, the arrangement of all the necessary expenses of the transmission from Paris to Milan wholly at the charge of H. Auguste . . 24,000

181,931.10

The estimated cost had been for 179,800 fr and the agreement for 180,000 fr. This did not include an emerald of a very large size which had adorned the tiara of Pius VI and after the Treaty of Tolentino had been deposited in the Museum of Natural History in Paris.

The tiara is still preserved in the Papal Treasury today, but all the precious stones, except the emerald and 8 small oriental rubies which decorate the pedestal on which the emerald rests, have been replaced by imitation stones. Similarly, the gold plates in the hexagonal frames which bore inscriptions relating to Napoleon have been removed and replaced by others. This was probably done at the behest of Consalvi, the very able secretary of Pius VII, who was incensed at the tactlessness of Napoleon, particularly in the manner in which the emerald had been restored to the Pope.

Another tiara was given to Pius VII on his return from Fontainebleau by the city of Lyons (*Plate 114, d*)—though in the inventory it states that it was given by a shopkeeper of Lyons.

In 1835 Pope Gregory XVI had a new tiara made (*Plate 115, b*) which was modified by Pius IX (1846–78). This has been the tiara most used in modern times, especially since Leo XIII (1878–1903). It was used in the coronation of Leo XII and his successors Pius X, Benedict XV, Pius XI and Pius XII, and at the last coronation, that of John XXIII on 4th November 1958. It is of silver network and the crowns are of gold leaf and are decorated with 540 pearls, 146 coloured precious stones and 11 diamonds. It was valued at 9,500 gold fr at the end of the XIX century. Pius IX was given another tiara by the Palatine Guard in 1877 (*Plate 115, c*) which is of very similar form to that of 1835. It is still sometimes used, especially when a tiara is placed upon the altar during a ceremony, but not worn. Another tiara given to Pius IX was a magnificent one presented by Queen Isabel II of Spain (*Plate 115, a*). It weighs 3 lb and is adorned all over with 18,000 diamonds and 1,000 coloured stones. It is said to have cost £20,000. It was first worn at the proclamation of the Dogma of the Immaculate Conception in 1854. Pius IX received yet another tiara from the Catholics of Belgium (*Plate 114, c*).

Leo XIII received two tiaras: one given by the Diocese of Paris in 1888 and the other, which was made at Bologna, was given by the Catholics of the World on the occasion of his Jubilee in 1903 (*Plate 115, d*). A tiara was presented to Pius XI in 1922 by the people of Milan (*Plate 116, a*). It weighed nearly a kilogram, was adorned with some 2,000 precious stones, including an emerald of great value; 242 other emeralds; 397 rubies and 79 diamonds. The diocese subscribed more than 250,000 lira besides a quantity of jewellery and precious stones. It is kept in the Pope's private apartments. In April 1959 Pope John XXIII received a gift of a new tiara from the people of Bergamo (*Plate 116, b*), of which district he was a native. At the Pope's request the original design was simplified and the money saved given to the poor. It follows the traditional design but the three crowns are decorated with figures of saints and martyrs, adorned with 68 rubies. At the summit is a golden globe encircled by a band of 16 emeralds and at the top is a cross of white gold with 30 diamonds. This tiara also is kept in the Pope's private apartments and is used by Pope John XXIII, who wore the Milan tiara of 1922 on his first visit to St John Lateran.

There are at present eight tiaras preserved in the Papal Treasury in the Sacristy of the Sistine Chapel. An inventory was made in the early years of the XIX century and a new one is due to be made. The inventory describes the tiaras as follows:

(1) Tiara of silver gauze with three golden crowns set with diamonds completely embedded. Each circle has fairly large diamonds and also four bosses formed by small emeralds and also four ovals formed by small rubies. The crowns themselves are made of leaves entirely of diamonds with 8 big imitation pearls in each crown. It is surmounted by a ball made of sapphires with a cross and circle of diamonds. The fillets are of silver cloth covered with gold and set with pearls. The fringe is formed of a string of pearls and two strips of silver and gold threads.

   Gift of Queen Isabel of Spain to Pius IX (some of the diamonds in the crown are missing).
(2) Another of silver cloth of very special quality with three gold crowns set with 40 good

diamonds both big and small; rubies, emeralds, garnets, amethysts, topazes, etc., and each crown has two rows of oriental pearls. It is surmounted by a small cross made up of diamonds which stands on a ball of lapis lazuli. The fillets are covered in gold and are set with 10 good diamonds with Pius IX's arms in enamel. Gregory XVI had this tiara made and it was used for the first time on 19th April 1835.

(3) Another of silver gauze with three golden crowns set with imitation stones of various colours. It is surmounted by a cross set with diamonds which stands on a ball of lapis lazuli with a circle of diamonds. The fillets are worked in gold with Pius IX's arms.

   Given by the Palatine Guard in 1877.

(4) Another of silver foil with olive leaves and circles and various figures chiselled into the silver, with three golden crowns with inscriptions, but no diamonds. The fillets are extremely simple with the arms of Leo XIII. Given by the Catholics of the World for the Holy Father's Golden Jubilee; worn only on this occasion.

(5) Another of white velvet with three golden crowns weighing 1,500 kilograms, set with imitation pearls and big imitation gems of various colours and a cross of imitation diamonds. The base of the cross is made up of a big rare emerald and this inscription chiselled on it: 'Greg. XIII Pont. Max.' This emerald rests on a gold circle with pearls and 8 small rubies.

   Gift of Napoleon to Pius VI. Was used for the first time on 29th June 1804. Cannot be used as it is of wood.

(6) Another of a special kind of silver tissue (a kind of silver thread) with three gold crowns weighing roughly 1 kilogram set with various imitation gems and pearls as likewise on the cross. The fillets are very simple with little crosses at the extremities.

   Gift of the city of Paris to Leo XIII in 1888 when Cardinal Richard was its archbishop. Cannot be used.

(7) Another of special silver material with thin red thread and three gold crowns set with coloured imitation gems. On the upper edge of the crowns there are leaves set with oriental pearls, small diamonds, emeralds, rubies and amethysts. The cross is set with real gems and pearls. The fillets are very simple. Both the tiara and the crowns are of novel shape.

   Belgian gift to Pius IX. Not useable.

(8) Another of silver material with embroidery and three crowns worked in gold and set with coloured talc imitation gems of various shapes and hues. It is surmounted by a small gold cross. The fillets are very simple.

   Given to Pius VII by a shopkeeper of Lyons and used for the first time on 15th August 1821. Not useable.

In the Treasury of St Peter's there is a large tiara of silver gilt set with imitation stones which is used to crown the head of the statue of St Peter on 29th June each year (*Plate 116, c*). This practice is believed to have begun in 1736, and the tiara dates from the XVIII century.

The occasions on which it is laid down that the Pope shall wear the tiara are:

(1) At Mass for the coronation of the Pope.

(2) At Mass for the feasts of the Epiphany, the Annunciation, Easter, the Ascension, St Peter and St Paul, All Saints and the third Mass for Christmas Day.

(3) When the Pope celebrates Mass pontifically.

In addition it is worn on special occasions such as canonisations. The late Pope, Pius XII, rarely wore the tiara and only put it on for the shortest possible time during the essential moments of the ceremonies at which, according to protocol, he must do so.

a (left)   *Tiara given to Pius IX by Queen Isabel of Spain, c. 1854. Papal Treasury*
(p. 383)

b (right)   *Tiara made for Gregory XVI in 1835. Papal Treasury*
(p. 383)

c (left)   *Tiara given to Pius IX in 1877 by the Palatine Guard and used at present time. Papal Treasury*
(p. 383)

d (right)   *Tiara given to Leo XIII by the Catholics of the World in 1903. Vatican Treasury* (pp. 383 and 384)

a (left) *Tiara given to Pius XI in 1922 by the people of Milan. Papal Private Apartments* (p. 383)

b (right) *Tiara given to John XXIII in 1959 by the people of Bergamo. Papal Private Apartments* (p. 383)

c *Statue of St Peter wearing tiara from St Peter's Treasury. XVIII Century* (p. 384)

Folz[1] suggests that in imitation of the Emperor and the Kings of England and France, who wore their crowns at great religious feasts, the Popes from the XI century always wore the *regnum* on the most solemn occasions—thus Gregory VII at Christmas 1075. In support of this he quotes the restoration of the Liturgy of the Stations which was the work of Leo IX. Eighteen Stations were said to be 'crowned'. The first Pope to be crowned on the day of his succession was Pascal II in 1099 and this custom became usual during the XII century.

The Papal coronation rite is very simple.[2] The Pope, who before election is already a bishop, proceeds to St Peter's and begins the Mass. After the *Confiteor* he takes his seat before a faldstool between his throne and the altar. Prayers are then said by the Cardinal-Bishops of Albano, Porto and Ostra. The Pope then returns the reverence of the cardinals and prelates who kiss his feet and face. He then goes to the altar and is invested with the *Pallium* by the Deacon of St Laurence. After more prayers and the singing of the *Laudes*, the Mass proceeds. At the end of the Mass the Pope moves in procession to the stage erected on the steps at the west end of the Basilica. There the *Prior diaconorum cardinalium* removes the Pope's mitre and sets the tiara on his head, the people crying *Kyrie eleison*. The Pope then goes to the gallery overlooking the Piazza and blesses the people. At the coronation of John XXIII on 4th November 1958 the actual crowning took place in the gallery overlooking the Piazza.

In a work compiled by Anonymous in Rome written between 1030 and 1155 entitled *Libellus Graphia Aureae Urbis Romanea*, which was, in fact, a book which purported to set out the ceremonial used at Court, there are listed ten crowns which were said to belong to the emperors. The ninth crown is described as formed of peacock's feathers and which it was said the Pope used to carry by imperial authority.[3] In a description of the coronation of Boniface VIII at the end of the XIII century it is mentioned that the Pope wore peacock's feathers in his crown and a symbolical meaning was attached to them, but Schramm records this as an error which crept in and was perpetuated by copyists. Richard of Hovenden, however, writing in 1186 relates that the Pope sent Henry II of England a golden crown decorated with peacock's feathers in 1185. With this Henry was to crown John King of Ireland. But nothing came of it and no more is heard of the crown.[4] Today the two great fans or *flabeli*, which are carried behind the Pope when he is borne aloft in the *sedia* on his way in solemn processions, are made of peacock's feathers.

While the tiara is the supreme ensign of the temporal and sovereign power of the Pope, there are two other emblems: the Keys and the Pavilion which are considered to represent the temporal power of the Church.

The Keys represent the authority given by Christ to St Peter by the words: 'I will give unto thee the keys of the kingdom of Heaven.'[5] The earliest representation of St Peter holding the keys is in the v century, but it was not until the XIII century that they came into general use as the emblems and objects of the papacy.

1 Robert Folz: *L'Idée D'Empire en Occident du V au XIV Siècle.*
2 See the Rev. R. M. Woolley: *Coronation Rites.*   3 P. E. Schramm: *Kaiser, Rom und Renovatio.*
4 P. E. Schramm: *Kaiser, Rom und Renovatio* and *History of the English Coronation.*
5 St Matthew xvi, 19.

The Pavilion, or *Ombrelliono*, was originally a large sunshade striped yellow and blue[1] which went through many variations in shape. Down to the time of Innocent VIII it was carried before the Pope by an armed man on horseback, though in modern times the size of the Pavilion has been reduced so that it can be carried by a man on foot. Since the time of Martin V the Pavilion has been used heraldically. Since the middle of the XVI century it has sometimes been surmounted by a cross and in the XVIII and XIX centuries occasionally by the dove representing the Holy Ghost.

BIBLIOGRAPHY

BECK, EGERTON	'The Mitre and Tiara in Heraldic Ornament', *Burlington Magazine*, September 1913.
BRAUN, J.	*Die liturgische Gewändung*, Freiburg 1907.
FOLZ, ROBERT	*L'Idée D'Empire en Occident du V au XIV Siècle.*
GALBRAITH, D. L.	*Papal Heraldry*, Cambridge 1930.
HENDERSON, E.	*Select Historical Documents of the Middle Ages*, London 1925.
MASSON, F.	*Napoleon and his Coronations.*
MÜNTZ	*La Tiare Pontificale du VIII–XVI Siècle in Mémoires de l'Académie des Inscriptions et Belles Lettres Paris XXXVI, 1898.*
SCHRAMM, P. E.	*Herrschaftszeichen und Staatssymbolik.*
	History of the English Coronation.
	Kaiser Friedrichs II Herrschaftszeichen, Göttingen 1955.
	Kaiser, Rom und Renovatio.
WOOLLEY, THE REV. R. M.	*Coronation Rites.*

1 D. L. Galbraith: *Papal Heraldry.*

CHAPTER THIRTEEN

HUNGARY

The invasion of Eastern Europe by the Magyars under Arpad, the semi-mythical founder of their monarchy, in 895 drove the Slavs from the land which is now Hungary, which they occupied. This led to the Slavs being divided: the northern from the southern, and the eastern from the western by a non-Aryan race, and to those in the West coming under the Christianising and civilising influences from Germany. The Magyars became the terror of Europe and not only defeated the Germans at Lechfeld in the x century but ravaged the German provinces of Thuringia, Swabia, Bavaria and Lotharingia. When they were eventually checked by the Germans they turned their attention to the Eastern Empire and even reached Constantinople, where they were bought off. Italy and Burgundy also claimed their attention, and in 955 the Emperor Otto I proclaimed them the enemies of God and humanity and finally decisively defeated them at the second Battle of Lechfeld, when only seven Magyars escaped.

This catastrophe convinced the ruling classes that they must adapt themselves so that they could live alongside the Empire and that they should become Christians. Christian influence had already been introduced, principally through the captives taken on their raids. The Eastern Church was the first to establish itself, and Hierothus, a Greek monk, who had been brought as a captive from Constantinople, was consecrated in about 972 as the first Bishop of Turkia. Under the Macedonian dynasty the Eastern Empire revived and its power extended to the Danube. Duke Geza, who became ruler in 972, decided that it was expedient to court the more distant Western Empire rather than the Eastern. In 973 he sent an embassy to Otto II at Quedlinburg and two years later he and his family were baptised. Geza had to act with great statesmanship to preserve the independence of Hungary and was assisted by the fact that the people resolutely remained pagan.

On the death of Geza in 997 his son Waic, who had been given the name Stephen at his baptism in 975, succeeded to the ducal throne. In the year 1000 Stephen was anointed and crowned. According to a strong tradition, which will be examined later, he received a crown from the Pope and the title of Apostolic Majesty to demonstrate the fact that he had surrendered the kingdom to the Apostolic See. With papal approval Stephen established an archbishopric at Esztergom (Gran) and nine bishoprics, and he laid the foundation stone of a great basilica at Székesfehérvar (also called Alba and Stuhlweissenberg) which was to become for several centuries the place of coronation of Hungarian kings. We have a description of the building[1]:

> In that city of the royal residence which is called Alba, under the eternal title and the praise of the same Virgin, he began to construct a large and celebrated basilica of marvellous workmanship, with the walls in the choir adorned with carvings and the floor covered with marble slabs . . . he caused innumerable kinds of *pallia*, accoutrements and other ecclesiastical trappings to be in that place; on the altars were several *tabulae* made of pure gold containing on them rows of most precious stones; a ciborium was erected with wonderful skill over the sacrificial table of Christ and the treasury completely filled with all kinds of crystal, onyx, gold and silver vessels.

Stephen encouraged religious orders to found monasteries and in particular the Benedictines, who established four centres, notably the foundation of Pannonhalma, whose charter, given by Stephen in 1001, is still preserved. These monasteries were not only religious centres but focal points from which civilisation spread. The King was dependent on foreigners as his advisers, and with their aid he built up a sound administration and vested the greater part of the land in the Crown, which ensured his predominant position. The State became based on two elements, the king and the Magyar people, although he prudently did not interfere with the right of the nobles occasionally to meet in general assembly or to elect their ruler.

Esztergom became the capital and the King's favourite place of residence, although the Court was peripatetic. In 996 Stephen married Gisela, daughter of Duke Henry the Quarreller of Bavaria and sister of the future Emperor Henry II. In the same year Otto III, who had been elected to the German throne at the age of three in 983, was crowned Emperor at Rome, and in April 999 Gerbert, Archbishop of Ravenna (and previously Archbishop of Rheims) was elected Pope and took the name Sylvester II. This remarkable and learned man had received great benefits from the Emperors Otto I and Otto II and his policy was influenced by his gratitude towards them. His power in the West Frankish kingdom had been very great, and it was said of Gerbert and Adalbero, Archbishop of Rheims, that their influence alone sufficed to make and unmake kings. He was for a time tutor in arithmetic to Otto III, and the great dream of a restored Empire with its capital in Rome has been attributed to him. Schramm[2] and other recent writers have, however, reassessed the position and have shown that the young Otto III was a strong and independent character who on his own account planned for a universal empire.

Otto III died in 1002 and Pope Sylvester II in the following year and with them the idea of the universal empire also died. The next emperor was Stephen's brother-in-law, Henry II, and this was particularly fortunate for Hungary, which enjoyed a long period of close and friendly relations with Germany, this speeded up the process of civilisation. It is noteworthy that many of Stephen's reforms were not just Western but were German in character. When Henry II died in 1024 his successor Conrad attacked Hungary but was repulsed, which strengthened the position of the young kingdom.

---

[1] *Legenda Maior S. Stephani Regis*. Translation quoted from Patrick J. Kelleher: *The Holy Crown of Hungary*, American Academy in Rome, 1951.

[2] P. E. Schramm: *Kaiser, Rom und Renovatio*, Leipzig 1929.

Stephen, like his father Geza, showed considerable statesmanship in maintaining Hungary's independence between the two empires. He took the side of the Eastern Emperor Basil II against the Bulgarians in 1019, and there are several records of the exchange of gifts and other manifestations of friendship. When Stephen died in 1038 he had no surviving sons and in order to avoid the succession passing to his pagan relations he had chosen Peter Orsioli, son of the Doge of Venice, who had married his daughter, to be the next king. There followed a troubled period when the resentment towards the pro-German policy of Stephen and the lingering strength of paganism led to revolts and to the persecution of Gisela, the German Queen Mother, and the Church. The pagan, Aba Samuel, who had married Stephen's sister, deposed Peter, who as a foreigner was unpopular, and was himself elected king. Peter sought the aid of the Emperor Henry III and Aba Samuel was defeated at the Battle of Ménfö in 1044, the usurper's lance and according to some a crown falling into the hands of the victors.

The following year, during a visit to Hungary, Henry III received from the hands of Peter the golden lance, and possibly the crown which had been taken from Aba Samuel, as a sign of submission of the kingdom to the Empire. But chaos continued for many years, and of the six kings who succeeded Stephen, three met violent deaths and three were continually fighting internal and external foes. Andrew (1047–60) did succeed in restoring the independence of the kingdom, but the Arpad kings incurred the hostility of the Pope and were faced with the danger of becoming vassals of the Emperor. It is not surprising, therefore, that good relations with the Eastern Empire should have been established. It is believed that the Emperor Constantine Monomachus sent Andrew a crown, the plates of which are in the National Museum at Budapest, in recognition of his suppression of the revolts of the pagans and re-establishing Christianity.[1]

When Henry IV effectively became German King in 1069 he soon became embroiled with Pope Gregory VII over the Contest over the Investitures. The Hungarian King, Salomon, had married Henry's sister Judith and the close relations between the two Courts were equally unpopular among Salomon's subjects and the Holy See.

Gregory VII was elected Pope in 1073 and being a vigorous reformer it was not long before he claimed with much vehemence that the Kingdom of Hungary belonged to the Holy See. Writing to Salomon in October 1074 he asserted that Stephen had surrendered his kingdom with all its rights and powers to St Peter, and that the Emperor Henry III had sent the lance and crown given to him by King Peter to the shrine of St Peter and had thus recognised that the authority belonged to him. The Pope severely reproved Salomon for having accepted the kingdom as a fief from the German King and threatened that he would lose it unless he recognised that his kingdom was a fief of the Apostolic See and not of the German King.[2]

In two letters in 1075[3] Gregory supported Duke Geza the elder son of Bela I in

1 Magda Bárány-Oberschall: *The Crown of the Emperor Constantine Monomachus.* The author emphasises that there is no proof of this theory but it is a supposition in keeping with the practice of the time. Another possibility is that it was loot brought to Hungary by returning Crusaders.

2 *Gregory VII Registrum,* edited Joffé. *Bibliotheca Rerum Germanicum,* Vol. II. Quoted by R. W. and A. J. C. Carlysle: *History of Mediæval Political Thought in the West,* London 1915–17.

3 *Gregory VII,* ibid., Vol. II, ii, 63, and ii, 70.

his claim to the Hungarian throne on the grounds that Salomon had forfeited his right by receiving it as a fief from the German King.

Duke Geza and his brother Ladislas led a rebellion and defeated Salomon. Geza shrewdly applied to the Pope for assistance and submitted to accept his kingdom from him as a fief of the Holy See. Geza also established good relations with the Eastern Empire. He rendered signal services to the Emperor Michael Dukas in 1070–1 and again later. After his assumption of the Hungarian royal title in 1074 Michael Dukas sent a crown to the Hungarian Court.

Hungary was fortunate in having two outstandingly able successors to Geza, his brother Ladislas (1077–95), who was subsequently canonised, and Salomon (1096–1116), who was the son of Geza. Although the boundaries of the kingdom were extended to the Adriatic coast and thus became a danger to the vigorous Comnenus dynasty who ruled the Eastern Empire, peaceful relations were maintained by Ladislas and Salomon. In 1104 an alliance was sought with Salomon as a result of which the Hungarian Princess Pyriska, who took the Greek name of Irene in 1104, married the son of the Emperor Alexius Comnenus, who was to become the Emperor John II Comnenus (1118–43). After the death of Salomon in 1116 a quarrel broke out over the succession. The succession in Hungary normally passed to a younger brother and not from father to son. Salomon wished his son, to whom he had given the name Stephen, to succeed him and to ensure this he blinded his brother, Almos. Almos fled to Constantinople, where he gained the support of the co-Emperor John II and his wife Irene; Stephen invaded the Empire and hostilities continued intermittently for forty years.

This is a convenient point in Hungarian history to discuss the origin of the Holy Crown. This ornament has a peculiar, indeed unique position among European regalia, because for centuries it has been regarded as essential for rightful kings of Hungary not merely to be in possession of it but to be crowned with it. In fact Hungary became a crowndom rather than a kingdom and the three elements of the nation were the Holy Crown, the people and the land. It was the source of power from which all constitutional acts were derived.

The earliest works on the regalia appeared early in the XVI century.[1] Since then there have been numerous treatises and essays,[2] but it was not until 1790 that scholars were given the opportunity of examining the crown, and there have been only nine occasions on which such an examination could take place.[3] It was only after the first

1 The first was by Peter Revay. *De Sacrae Coronae Regni Hungariae Ortu, Virtute, Victoria, Fortuna, Annos Ultra DC Clarissimae Brevis Commentarius* (Augustae Vindelicorum, 1613).

2 The bibliography in Patrick J. Kelleher's work, which is by no means exhaustive, runs into some 130 items.

3 (1) In 1790 on the occasion of the coronation of Leopold II. (2) In 1792 on the occasion of the coronation of Francis I. (3) In 1853 after the discovery of the regalia in the swamps of Orsova where they had been buried by Hungarian Nationalists. (4) In 1880 when permission was given to the Hungarian Academy of Sciences to examine the crown. (5) In 1896 during the celebration of the Hungarian millennium. (6) In 1916 after the coronation of Charles IV. (7) In 1928 at the exhibition of the crown to the Congress of the International Association of Museums. (8) In 1938 on the occasion of the 900th anniversary of the death of St Stephen. (9) In 1945 when the regalia come into the possession, at the end of the Second World War, of the U.S. Army Monuments, Fine Arts and Archives staff.

examinations that the Greek inscriptions were translated, and not until 1801 that Kollar[1] drew attention to the fact that the crown was not one piece but made up of two quite different upper and lower parts.

Although photographs of the crown were first taken in 1896 and at some of the subsequent examinations, those taken in 1945 are the only ones which can be regarded as adequate for scientific study. When the Holy Crown was in the hands of the United States military authorities a unique opportunity arose for a more thorough investigation of the crown than had ever been undertaken before. This has resulted in a work by Kelleher,[2] which is the most exhaustive and authoritative study which has yet been published. It has the advantage of being in the English language, which will make it more readily available to students, few of whom could understand the Hungarian in which previous literature on the subject had been written. Moreover, until recently the value of the opinions of most writers was vitiated by their nationalistic or religious inhibitions. Even now it seems unlikely that Kelleher's conclusions will be acceptable to all, and lively controversies are likely to continue over some of the most important questions relating to the origin of the crown and its place in history and art history.

Although unsupported by contemporary documentary evidence it is generally accepted by historians that Stephen, the first King of Hungary, was anointed and crowned in the year 1000 with a crown sent by Pope Sylvester II. The question as to whether the King was crowned at the will of the Emperor or the Pope is one which in modern times has been the subject of sharp controversy between historians especially Zoltan Tóth and Josef Deér.[3]

The evidence available is very scanty. The first mention of Stephen's coronation appears in the XI-century *Chronicles of Thietmar*, Bishop of Merseburg, which relates: 'Through the kindness and encouragement of the before mentioned Emperor, Waic son-in-law of Henry, Duke of Bavaria, founded Episcopal Sees in his kingdom and received a crown and benediction.'

This statement is too ambiguous to permit any proper meaning to be attached to it. It has, in fact, been the subject of various interpretations, on the one hand[4] to show that the relationship of Hungary with the Empire necessitated the Emperor's approval for the dukedom to be raised to the status of a kingdom, while on the other hand it has been argued that the coronation was enacted with the authority of the Pope who sent a crown and a benediction.

In 1083, the year in which Stephen was canonised, there appeared an anonymous work entitled the *Major Life of St Stephen* in which it is stated that Stephen was anointed and crowned with the diadem of royal dignity in the fifth year of his reign. A later work known as the *Minor Life of St Stephen* makes no mention of the coronation. A third *Life of St Stephen* written by Bishop Hartwig between 1112 and 1116 for Salomon I is

---

1 Joszsef Kollar: *De Sacra Regni Ungariae Corona Commentarius*.

2 Patrick J. Kelleher: *The Holy Crown of Hungary*, American Academy in Rome, 1951.

3 Zoltan Tóth: *Critical Review of the Hartwig Legend. The Question of the Origin of the Holy Crown* 1942. *Concerning the Actual State of our Historical Research*, 1943. Josef Deér: *The Foundation of the Hungarian Kingdom*, 1942. *Emperor Otto III and Hungary in the Light of Recent Historical Writing*, 1944.

4 Tóth: op. cit. Deér: op. cit.

largely based on the previous lives but has certain additions, one of which gives the first account of the donation of the crown by Sylvester II. Since this account has been the main supporting evidence about the gift of the Holy Crown which has been accepted for centuries and has been responsible for the subsequent position which it has been given in the history of the Hungarian nation, it is worth quoting in full.

In the fourth year after the death of his father, at the instigation of the divine clemency (Stephen), sent that Bishop Astric (who was called by the other name of Anastasius) to the threshold of the Holy Apostles that he might ask from the successor of St Peter, Prince of the Apostles, that he (the Pope) might extend an ample benediction over the newly arisen Christian community in the Pannonian regions, sanction of the church at Gran as a metropolitan see by the authority of his signature and strengthen the remaining bishoprics through his benediction. Further (he asked) that he might deign to fortify him with a kingly diadem in order that supported by such an honour he might through the Grace of God stabilise what had been undertaken.

At the same time by chance Miesko, Duke of the Poles, having embraced the Christian faith with his own people, sent messengers to the Head of the Roman See and asked to be confirmed with the apostolic blessing and to be crowned with a kingly diadem. Assenting to his petition, the Pope had already caused a crown of marvellous workmanship to be made which he had resolved to send him for the glory of the realm.

But because the Lord knows those who are His (He) Who after two apostles had been selected by lot for the apostolic office by the other apostles, preferred Matthias and caused him to fill the apostle number . . . had decided to distinguish auspiciously His own chosen Stephen with this temporal crown . . . he Stephen who would be adorned later and even more auspiciously with an eternal crown.

And during the night which preceded the appointed day on which he was to have sent the prepared crown to the Duke of the Poles as he had determined, a messenger of the Lord appeared to the Pope in a vision and said to him, 'Tomorrow in the first hour of the day, you will see messengers coming to you from an unknown people who will demand a royal crown from you for their Duke together with the gift of the apostolic blessing. You will therefore take care that the crown which you have caused to be prepared will be handed over to their Duke, without delay, as they will ask. For you must know that it, together with the glory of the kingdom is owed to him on account of the merits of his life.'

Therefore, after the manner of this vision, Bishop Astric came to the Pope at the appointed hour of the following day, executing his enjoined duty prudently and reporting on the deeds of the Holy Duke in due order. . . . After that he asked from the Apostolic See that insignia we mentioned before, indicating that such honour and dignity to be deserved by him who had subjugated many peoples through the Grace of God and had converted many infidels to God through his power.

The Roman pontiff, hearing all these things was greatly pleased and granted all which they asked benevolently. In addition he sent a cross to be borne before the king as a sign of apostledom saying, 'I am apostolic, he, in truth (is) by merit, an apostle of Christ through whom Christ converted so many people to himself'.[1]

We have already seen that before this *Life* was produced the Holy See claimed that the King of Hungary was a vassal on the Pope and that this was based on the idea that Stephen had received his crown from Pope Sylvester II, together with the apostolic

[1] This translation from the original is taken from Kelleher, op. cit.

title, which Deér[1] points out first appeared in a charter in 1001. Tóth considers it improbable that Stephen would have been given the apostolic title as the King had only been a Christian for four years and Christianity had not been firmly established at the time of his coronation. Against this may be set the importance the Pope attached to the influence of the Holy See in Central Europe and the vigorous way in which Stephen had set about Christianising the country, his military defeats of the pagan rebels, his zealous energy in establishing bishoprics and encouraging the religious orders and his apparent willingness to surrender the kingdom to the Pope. These might surely be taken to have been of sufficient importance to have outweighed the short period since Stephen's baptism.

Over the question of whether the crown was sent by the Pope with the approval of the Emperor it is impossible to give a clear answer. It seems likely, however, that the Hungarian duke would have approached his brother-in-law with whom he was on good terms and sought his support. The Emperor Henry III at any rate seems to have been aware that Stephen had surrendered the Hungarian nation to St Peter, for he sent to Rome to be placed over the tomb of St Peter the golden lance and crown taken from Aba Samuel at the Battle of Ménfö and presented to him by King Peter. Both Tóth and Deér agree that the golden lance was not a part of the coronation regalia. That there was also a crown is first mentioned by Pope Gregory VII, but a xvii-century writer[2] records that the crown and lance and the insignia of the King of Hungary were sent to the tomb of the Blessed St Peter by the Emperor Henry who had defeated the King and the Kingdom of Hungary. Tóth has suggested that the crown was that of St Stephen and that it was returned to Hungary later, but Ciampini's evidence refutes that. Deér on the other hand considers it to have been a helmet crown and this would seem to be the most probable explanation.

We are therefore left to consider the reliability of Bishop Hartwig's account. Tóth has argued in the clearest terms that the passage already quoted was written at the instigation of King Salomon. The King had sided with the Pope in the contest over the Investitures, and in 1106 on the death of Henry IV Salomon, believing that the papacy would prevail, agreed to give up his rights of investiture. But in 1111 Pope Pascal II became the prisoner of the Emperor and Salomon took the opportunity to regain the privileges he had given up. According to Tóth the King persuaded Hartwig to write in his history a version of the grant of the apostolic title and the Holy Crown so as to justify and give authority for his actions.

In view of the manner in which Hartwig's account was accepted as proof of the special position of the Hungarian King it seems strange that it was later found necessary to produce another fabrication to reinforce it. The reason seems to have been a dispute between Frederick III and the Pope on the question of the right of the Hungarian King to regulate Church affairs. The importance of the document lies in the fact that Bishop Ipolyi, in his work on the Holy Crown,[3] accepted it as being genuine and based his reasoning as to the origin of the crown on this false evidence. This forgery is sometimes

---

[1] Deér: op. cit.   [2] G. C. Ciampini: *De Sacris Aedificiis*.

[3] Arnold Ipolyi: *History and Description of the Hungarian Holy Crown and Coronation Insignia*, Budapest 1886.

called the Sylvester Bull and sometimes described as a letter. It first appeared in 1644 in Inchofer's *Annales*[1]; he had obtained it from a Franciscan friar named Raphael Levakovics, who asserted that the copy had been made by Antonius Verancsis, who subsequently became Archbishop of Esztergom, from the original which had been preserved in the Chapter House at Trau in Dalmatia, the archives of that foundation being moved to Vienna about that time. That it was a forgery was established from a letter written by the friar which reads:

> The Hungarians have a strong conviction that the Pope had no right in their kingdom, being converted to God by their own king. In order to generate a better opinion in them, I have given certain letters of Pope Sylvester and I shall arrange that they come to light in some manner; I had thought of having them promulgated as being found in Rome but I did not dare without the permission and knowledge of Your Eminence.[2]

Kelleher rightly concluded that in the absence of adequate historical documentary evidence it must be left to art historians to attempt to identify the origin and date of the crown. There is no need here to go into the long and detailed arguments which he and other authors have put forward in support of their views.[3] It must be noted that Kelleher had a unique opportunity of making the most thorough examination of the Holy Crown, and his findings must be treated with respect although they are not necessarily acceptable to all.

The Holy Crown (*Plate 117*) may be divided into five distinct parts: the lower part or diadem; the triangular and small semi-circular ornaments surmounting the diadem; the arches; the cross; the *cataseistae*.

The diadem consists of a circlet of green gold, the upper and lower edges of which are bordered by a row of pearls between which are set eight precious stones and eight enamelled plaques. Attached to the upper rim and part of the diadem are two oblong semi-circular shields, that in front being higher than that at the rear.

On the front shield there is an enamelled figure representing the *Pantocrator* seated on a cushioned backless throne with a cross-nimbus and the right hand giving the blessing and in the left hand the Book of Life. On either side of the throne is a tree above which are Greek inscriptions by which the figure can be identified. Immediately below the *Pantocrator* in the middle of the diadem above the brow is a large polished sapphire. On either side of the sapphire are enamelled plates bearing figures of the Archangels Gabriel and Michael. Going round towards the centre of the diadem a large *cabochon* stone is set in the diadem next to each of the archangels and then there are two more enamelled plates bearing the figures of the two soldier saints, George and Demetrius, beardless and carrying lances and shields. In the figures of St Cosmas and St Damian, both of whom were physicians, one holds medical instruments and an open box and

1 Melchiore Inchofer: *Annales Ecclesiastici Regni Hungariae*, Rome 1644.
2 Kelleher, op. cit. See also *Gerbert Epistles*, ed. J. Havet, 1889.
3 The most important are: Magda Bárány-Oberschall. 1. 'Problems around the Holy Crown.' *Antiquitas Hungarica*, I (1947). 2. 'Localisation of the Enamels of the Upper Hemisphere of the Holy Crown of Hungary,' *The Art Bulletin*, XXXI, 1949 (in Hungarian). Josef Deér: 'The Circlet of St. Stephen's Crown in the Framework of the Byzantine Tradition', in *Herrschaftszeichen und Staatssymbolik*, Vol. II, in *Schriften der Monumenta Germaniae historica*, 13/11.1955 (in German).

the other a closed box tied with string. In the next two compartments are single large oblong sapphires. This brings us to the back of the crown where the central figure is on the shield set on top of the diadem. This bears a representation of the Emperor Michael Dukas. He is bearded and stares out to the front. He wears the *tunica talaris et manicata* with the *loros* crossed over the chest. Around his neck is the jewelled golden collar called *maniakion*. In his right hand he holds the labarum and his left hand is on the scabbard of his sword. On his head is an open stemma and behind a nimbus. On the background of the shield is an inscription in Greek meaning *Michael Dukas, Faithful in Christ, Emperor of the Romans*.

Immediately below the central shield is a large octagonal sapphire. To the right of this is a shield bearing the figure of the co-Emperor. Like his father he stares to the front, carries the labarum and wears an open stemma. He also wears the *tunica talaris* but there are certain differences in his dress appropriate to his rank. On the shield is a Greek inscription which reads: *Constantine Porphyrogenitos, Emperor of the Romans*.

To the left of the octagonal sapphire is a plaque bearing the enamelled figure of Geza, the Hungarian King. His eyes are turned towards the co-Emperor, he wears a simple open diadem with a semi-circular shield in front and carries a Patrician's staff surmounted by an anchor cross. His left hand holds the scabbard of his sword. The plaque bears a Greek inscription which reads: *Geobitz (Geza), Faithful King of Turkey*.

It is evident that the ensemble and the carefully executed details of the figures are designed to convey a special meaning. In the front the *Pantocrator* holds the central position and the two archangels and four saints that flank him on a lower plane have their eyes turned upon him in adoration. The *Pantocrator* and the archangels represent the Supremacy of Christ and the Church while the four saints represent the arts of war and peace. At the back of the crown the Emperor holds the centre but on a slightly lower plane to that of the *Pantocrator*. The co-Emperor in position and in his dress is shown as the junior partner and the Hungarian King is in a lower position still.

The figures of the Emperor and Geza and the inscriptions provide the clearest of evidence that it was a gift from the Byzantine to the Hungarian Royal Court. But there is some doubt as to the reason for the present and as to whether it was given to the King or his Queen. Geza became King of Hungary in 1074 and Michael Dukas lost the imperial throne in 1078, so the gift must have been between those two dates. Gifts of this sort from Byzantium to foreign rulers and princes and nobles at the imperial Court were not uncommon, and there was usually some political motive. Either in war or in peace it was advantageous for both that Hungary should resist all attempts by the German emperors to incorporate the kingdom in the Western Empire and her position was strengthened if she was an ally of the Eastern Emperor. The four saints may thus symbolise the dual alliance. There is nothing either on the crown or in the circumstances of the time to suggest that the gift meant that Geza became the vassal of Michael Dukas—rather it may be taken as a sign of Geza ascending the throne as King and receiving recognition from the Eastern Emperor.

Bárány-Oberschall has pointed out that it would have been unusual for a crown to be presented to a king with a picture of himself on it, and that in any case the diadem bears the characteristics of a woman's crown. Deér strongly supports this view that it was a female crown but concludes that it was made for a person of a lower rank than that of Empress. He further points out that the portrait of Geza himself on the crown makes it impossible that it could have been a crown for the King to wear. Both writers consider that the crown was intended for Bela's queen, Synadene, who came from a Byzantine noble family. Kelleher on the other hand refutes these arguments and emphasises that the representation of the *Pantocrator*, the two Emperors and the King would not be borne on a woman's crown but rather by the independent ruler of a state. Moreover it was a personal crown and he contends that the figures represent a recognition of the sovereignty of Geza by the donor. Kelleher also deals with the significance of the two shields which are part of the diadem. He shows that the son of the Emperor wore four such shields on his crown or *stephanos*, while a son-in-law of the Emperor bore only one. The fact that there are two such shields on this diadem indicates that Geza held a rank of importance and an exalted position among the Byzantine hierarchy of nobles of the first rank.

We must now return to the crown and it will be noted that on the upper edge of the circlet certain additions have been made. These consist of eight plates decorated in translucent enamels with fish-scale designs in green and indigo with a beaded frame. Each enamel is surmounted by precious stones, four of the plates are triangular in shape and the other four have a small circle shape at the top. These plates cover the front half of the crown but on the back are 18 pearls set on gold pins. The circlet is closed with two intersecting arches each consisting of four plaques of red gold decorated with enamel figures in filigree frames, and mountings set with diamonds and pearls. At the point of intersection at the summit is a ninth plate which bears a figure of Christ. Each of these plates is adorned with two enamel plaques which represent eight of the twelve Apostles. On the front plate are enamels of St John and St Bartholomew and on the back plate St John and St Thomas. On one side plate St Paul and St Andrew and on the other St Paul and St Philip. The name of each saint is inscribed on his picture in Roman characters.

From the central plate rises a simple cross with bulbous terminations. This cross leans at an angle of 12 degrees and has become a special and popular feature of the Holy Crown. It seems that the damage must have been done some time between 1613 and 1793, for in Revay's work of 1613 the cross is depicted in an upright position, while in the works of Deczey of 1793 and of Kollar in 1801 the cross is depicted as slanting. From the lower rim on either side hang *cataseistae* each consisting of nine golden chains terminating with precious stones, and pearls set in trefoil mountings. It is generally assumed that the cross slants because it has been damaged, but a correspondent in the London *Times*,[1] who had an opportunity of examining the crown in 1896 when it was taken from the Castle of Buda to the National Museum to be prepared for the King's arrival to open the new Houses of Parliament, states:

from this examination it appeared that the screw which fastened the cross into the small gold ball at the top of the dome has never been bent and shows no signs of violence. The shaft by which the

[1] R. P. Mahaffy: *The Times*, 28th January 1938.

Crown of St Stephen, front view (pp. 391 and 394)

a   *Metal chest containing Hungarian regalia. Formerly in the Royal Palace, Budapest* (p. 406)

b   *Metal chest containing Hungarian regalia*

ball is secured to the dome leaves the ball at a point not directly opposite to the joint at which the cross is screwed into the same ball.

He goes on to say that whoever made up the crown therefore intended that the cross should be crooked.

It has long been the belief that the crown of St Stephen was composed of two original crowns, the lower part being that sent to King Geza by Michael Dukas, the other part that which Pope Sylvester sent to St Stephen. The detailed examination to which the crown has been subjected in recent times has led to a reassessment of this view. Kelleher considers that the workmanship of the upper part of the crown dates from the year 1000 and was a product of the Ratisbon school. He suggests that the plates were taken from the original ornament which was not a crown but probably a book cover. It might have been ordered by Stephen and Gisela as a gift to the Basilica of Székesfehérvar or it might have been a gift to St Stephen from Henry I, or Otto III or Henry II. As to the date of the assembly of the crown there have been various theories, and the reader who is interested should study them, but Kelleher's conclusions demand respect and are worthy of quoting:

Irene[1] was sent to Constantinople in 1104. The Council of Guastalla at which Salomon gave up his rights of investiture took place in 1106. The *Minor Life* which appeared about 1108 makes no reference to the crown of St Stephen. Three years later Pope Pascal II became prisoner of the German Emperor and the Hungarian King seized the opportunity to reclaim his privileges. The *Hartwig Life* dating between the years 1112 to 1116 gives a detailed account of the Stephen Crown and its origin as a papal donation. Isabella became Empress in 1118 and her portrait in Hagia Sophia dating probably from the same year pictures a crown which possesses motives identical with those on the Holy Crown. It seems probable, therefore, that the date of assembly took place in the years between the writing of the *Minor Life* and the *Hartwig Life* since no mention of the crown is made in the former yet full documentation appears in the latter. Isabella's quarrel with Stephen II occurred only after his accession to the throne on the death of his father in 1116. From this chronological sequence it seems logical to postulate that Isabella had gone to Byzantium as the daughter-in-law of the Emperor, saw the new stemmata of Alexius I and his son John pictured in the coronation mantle of the Barberini Psalter, and when the existing Holy Crown was being assembled by Salomon I sent the arch and gabled motives, the pendant chains and the surmounting gold cross as a gift to complete the decorations necessary to duplicate the new Imperial Crown of Byzantium.

That the Holy Crown is an imitation of the new stemmata of the Eastern Empire is borne out by a comparison between the Hungarian head-dress and the crown worn by the two Emperors in the miniature of the Vatican Psalter, for one finds the same features in both, the closed crown shape, the gabled acroteria, the surmounting cross and the pendant chains. . . .

There can be no doubt that the arch and gabled enamels are of Byzantine origin. If Isabella sent them from Constantinople as a gift it must have taken place before 1116, since after that year her relationship to her homeland was ruptured by her quarrel with Stephen II. . . . In the light of the background the appearance of the arch and gabled decorations of the crown of the Empress herself can be explained as revealing her desire to illustrate to all in graphic terms her Hungarian origin, her relationship to the royal crown of the kingdom and her prerogative to sponsor Almos as the

1 Princess Pyriska, daughter of St Ladislas, who was married to the co-Emperor in 1104.

legitimate king against a usurper, to summarise the existing Holy Crown of Hungary as a facsimile of the imperial stemmata of Byzantium which appeared first in the Eastern world at the time of the accession of John II Comnenus with his father Alexius I in the year 1092. The assembly of the crown and the provision of supporting documentary evidence can be attributed to Salomon (1095–1116): from literary and historical sources the date of assembly can be placed between the years 1108–16. The elements chosen for the unification were for the most part materials selected for their historical sentimental value as well as for their suitability for adaptation to the *corona clausa* prototype. The principal purpose of the creation was to provide a dynastic crown for the kingdom. To give tradition and to surround the object with significance documentary evidence was provided through the commission of the Bishop Hartwig biography of St Stephen. That the assembled crown was accepted in subsequent years as the original crown of St Stephen sent to Hungary by the papacy through Heavenly intervention is confirmed by the fact that the existing Holy Crown in its entirety was identified for centuries with the putative Sylvester donation and was believed to assume the last position of importance in the conception of the Hungarian state.

After the death of Stephen the Arpad dynasty continued through the reigns of eleven more kings until 1308. In all, twenty kings of the dynasty were said to have been crowned, but the records are very scanty and it is not possible to say with any certainty how many of them actually were crowned. During the last period of the dynasty the country relapsed into a state of complete anarchy and the kings had to fight for their very lives. The last Arpad king of talent, Bela IV (1235–70), settled much of the unoccupied part of the country with pagan Kumanian immigrants, and to ensure their loyalty to the Crown of St Stephen he married his son, afterwards Stephen V (1270–2), to a Kumanian girl. Stephen V, in an attempt to resist the aggressions of Ottakar II of Bohemia, formed an alliance with the powerful Angevin dynasty then ruling in Naples, who were on good terms with the Pope. His successor Ladislas III (1272–90) was so completely in the power of the pagan Kumanians that the Pope, who claimed suzerainty of Hungary by virtue of Geza's agreement, felt compelled to intervene and after a terrible and bloody struggle in which Ladislas and after him the last of the Arpads, Andrew III (1290–1301), valiantly endeavoured to retain the supremacy of the native dynasty, the Holy See was successful and Charles Robert of Naples became the first Angevin King of Hungary.[1]

The Crown of St Stephen, which according to documents dating from the reign of Bela IV (1235–70) had been designated the Holy Crown, was first committed to the care of the Prior of Székesfehérvar.[2] It was sought after by Pretenders to the throne and Ladislas, the son of Geza II, obtained the possession of it for six months, while Stephen IV (1162–3) also took it by force and had himself crowned with it. The widow of Bela III, after the death of her children, took the crown with her to the Court of the Emperor Frederick I, but it was brought back again by Andrew II after a successful war, and it remained in the kingdom until the end of the Arpad dynasty. In the confusion that followed one party proclaimed Wenceslas King and he took the crown to his father in Bohemia. On his abdication it fell into the hands of Otto of Bavaria, another Pretender

1 Charles Robert's father, Charles Martel, had been crowned titular King of Hungary at Naples on 8th September 1292.
2 It was kept in the Basilica of St Stephen.

to the throne, and it was nearly lost. He had enclosed the crown in a wooden box and tied it to his saddle bow. It fell to the ground unnoticed and when the loss was discovered it was only retrieved after prolonged search. Otto was crowned with it but lost it to Apor, Voivode of Transylvania. Meanwhile Charles Robert, having become King, was crowned at Székesfehérvar with a proxy crown, and although it was consecrated by a Papal Legate sent specially for the purpose from Rome and the Holy Crown itself was placed under interdict until returned to its legitimate owner, this coronation was not considered to be valid. Charles Robert is said to have been crowned again at Esztergom in 1301 and at Buda on 15th June 1309, on neither of which occasions was the Holy Crown available but these may only have been enthronements. In 1310, however, the crown was returned and Charles Robert was again crowned at Székesfehérvar with the Holy Crown. This historical event is depicted in a painting made by the direction of Henry, Provost of Székesfehérvar.

By the end of the xv century it became a popular belief that the king and possessor of the Holy Crown was the first person of rank in the kingdom and the head of the nation, but unless crowned with the Holy Crown with the approval of the States his position was not legalised. Each landowner became known as 'a member of the Holy Crown' and the rest of the people were considered to be 'subjects of the Holy Crown'.

The House of Anjou produced only two Kings of Hungary, Charles I (1310–42) and Louis I (1342–82), who was crowned at Székesfehérvar on 21st July 1342. They brought with them from Italy a knowledge based on experience of good government as understood at that time, and they had the ability to put it to good effect. During their reigns the old Magyar nobility which had been decimated in the civil wars was replaced by a new aristocracy on a feudal basis. With the aid of an imported educated class they restored law and order and put the frontiers of the country into a state of defence. The return of internal organisation and strength, coupled with an enlightened policy in foreign affairs, led to a considerable expansion of the boundaries of Hungary.

Charles I married Elizabeth, sister of Casimir the Great of Poland, and his son Louis, in consequence of a compact made by his father, added the Polish crown to that of Hungary. Louis I, the Great, left two infant daughters, one of whom, Maria, was to share the throne of Poland with her betrothed, Sigismund of Pomerania. The other, Hedwig, sometimes known by her Polish name Jadwiga, was to rule over Hungary with her husband William of Austria. This plan was upset by Louis's wife.

Elizabeth, the mother of the two princesses, wished to rule both kingdoms during their minority. Immediately after her father's death Maria, her favourite, was crowned Queen of Hungary on 17th September 1382. In 1384 Hedwig, although she preferred Hungary to Poland, was crowned Queen of Poland at Cracow and was forced to marry Jagiello, Grand Duke of Lithuania. In Hungary, however, the rule of women was not regarded with favour and the great house of Horvathy offered the Crown of St Stephen to Charles III of Naples. In spite of a promise to the contrary he accepted the offer and was crowned King of Hungary, as Charles II, on 31st December 1385. On 7th February 1386, after a reign of only thirty-eight days, he was treacherously attacked in Elizabeth's apartments at her own instigation and a few days later died of his wounds. The Horvathys, however, soon had their revenge. In July that year, whilst Elizabeth was on a pleasure trip, they kidnapped her and in the presence of her daughter Maria tortured her to death. Maria was saved by the influence of Sigismund, her betrothed. Within six months the latter was elected King and married to her and was crowned on 31st March 1387. Together they ruled over Hungary as joint sovereigns until in 1395 she was accidentally killed. Sigismund continued to rule Hungary for forty-three years after his wife's death. He was elected Emperor and also became King of Bohemia. Although his record as Emperor was undistinguished, he ruled Hungary with great ability and built up the country's defences, especially against the Turks. These invaders, whose forebears first crossed the Hellespont into Europe in 1353, destroyed the Eastern Empire and became in the succeeding centuries the chief menace to the peace of Hungary.

Charles Robert had instituted greater precautions for safeguarding the Holy Crown and he had carried it around the country with him. Under Sigismund it was first kept at Buda and later at Esztergom; finally it was taken to Visegrad which was so strongly fortified that it could only be taken by fraud and not by force. Sigismund's only child was a daughter, but fifteen years before his death he made provision for her and for the future protection of Hungary by marrying her to Albert, Duke of Austria. When Sigismund died Albert became King of Hungary and was crowned at Székesfehérvar on 1st January 1438 being in the same year elected King of the Romans and crowned King of Bohemia. He ruled for less than two years, for in 1439 he fell sick and died during a campaign against the Turks. His only living children were two daughters, but his widow Elizabeth was known to be with child. The succession was, therefore, uncertain and since the Turks were pressing upon the eastern frontier of the country the prospects were dismal and embarrassing. To avoid a long regency or rule by a woman a section of the nobles offered the crown to Ladislas III, King of Poland. Elizabeth, however, was determined to keep open the succession for her unborn child, should he be a son, and she obtained possession of the Holy Crown. One of her ladies, Helen Kattaner, hid it in a cushion and carried it off in the Queen's train to Komarom, where the Queen gave birth to a boy who was named Ladislas Posthumous. On 15th May 1440 when only four months old, he was invested by the Primate with the crown as he lay in his mother's arms at Székesfehérvar. Elizabeth hoped that as the Magyar nobility attached so much importance to the Holy Crown of St Stephen they would in consequence recognise him as their sovereign. But they had already determined on Ladislas, King of Poland, who they made King at Buda, where he was crowned on 17th July 1440. As the Holy Crown was not available the crown from St Stephen's reliquary was used. After his coronation civil war broke out and although her forces occupied a portion of Hungary, Elizabeth fled first to Pozsony[1] and then to Vienna. She took the Holy Crown with her camouflaged as the baby's porringer and carried it in his cradle amongst the bedclothes, upside down with a spoon inside. In Vienna the Queen was forced to pledge the crown to the Emperor Frederick III for 2,500 Hungarian florins. Three years later she died and the civil war came to an end.

During the civil war the Turks had been attacking the eastern borders of Hungary but had been held back by the efforts and leadership of John Hunyady, Ban of Szoreny.

---

[1] The German name for this town is 'Pressburg', and the Czech 'Bratislava'.

a (above, left)   *Sceptre and orb. Formerly in
the Royal Palace, Budapest* (p. 406)

b (above, right)   *Head of sceptre* (p. 406)

c   *Top view of sceptre* (p. 406)

a   Coronation sword. XVI Century. Treasury,
St Vitus's Cathedral (p. 407)

b   Apostolic cross. Treasury of the Metropolitan Church,
Gran (p. 408)

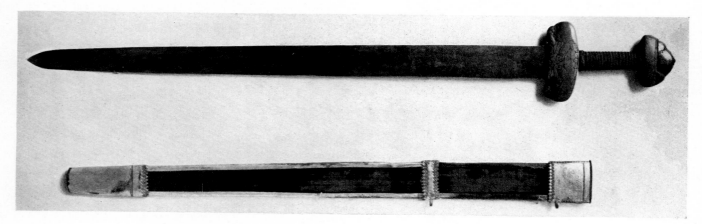

c   Sword and scabbard of St Stephen. Treasury of St Vitus's Cathedral, Prague

The civil war being over the Pope favoured a Holy War against the Turks and Ladislas, by now established as undisputed King, promised to lead it. The Turks, however, offered favourable terms and on the advice of John Hunyady, Ladislas signed a peace treaty with them. The Papal Envoy did not acquiesce. He absolved Ladislas from keeping the treaty and persuaded him to resume hostilities. Within a few months Ladislas and the flower of Magyar chivalry were slaughtered at Varna. In this hour of peril the Magyar gentry elected Hunyady as Governor of Hungary, and when he died decided to elect one of his sons as King.

Ladislas Posthumous, who still claimed the throne, plotted the death of Hunyady's elder son, but died himself shortly afterwards. Matthias Corvinus, son of Hunyady, was then elected King of Hungary. Matthias inherited his father's genius and restored order throughout his kingdom. He built up a famous army which kept the Turks out of the country and the over-powerful magnates under control within it. He redeemed the Holy Crown from the Emperor Frederick III for 60,000 gold florins (or according to some for 80,000 gold florins). Archbishop George Paloczy of Esztergom, the former guardian, was called upon to identify it, and having certified the crown as intact it was brought first to Sopron where it was exposed for three days and then to Buda. Matthias, who had ruled for six years without coronation, was crowned on 25th March 1464 and was recognised as legal King. Shortly after his coronation he caused the Diet to pass a law prescribing that the crown was to be given protection in the future. The declaration ran:

> Therefore we desire as we ought by a common consent and wish of the Lord Prelates, of the barons and of the nobles of our kingdom to provide in this place for the worthy protection and consecration of this Holy Crown an accustomed place and suitable presence for it lest another time (may God avert it) this crown be alienated from this kingdom.

As he had no legitimate heir, his natural son Janos Corvinus was accepted during Matthias's lifetime as his successor. But when Matthias died the nobles asserted their power again, refused Janos Corvinus and on 15th July 1490 chose instead Ladislas, King of Bohemia, who was known to be a singularly weak monarch.[1] His reputation was entirely deserved, for when he died in 1516 the Kingdom of Hungary had fallen almost into anarchy. Territory was lost to Austria, the Royal Treasury was reduced to bankruptcy and there was a peasants' rising against the extortions of the magnates who did what they pleased without fear of royal reproof or punishment. In 1500 the Holy Diet prescribed the appointment of two permanent keepers of the Holy Crown which was to be kept in the fortress at Visegrad.

Ladislas VI had two children, Louis and Anne, who were betrothed as infants, Anne to an Austrian archduke and Louis to an Austrian archduchess. Louis had been crowned King of Hungary on 4th June 1508, and on 11th May 1509, when about three years old, his father had him crowned King of Bohemia at St Vitus Cathedral at Prague. At this ceremony Anne, then six years old, burst into tears because she was not crowned too, so Ladislas crowned her as well. This incident being considered propitious, a sudden exclamation burst forth from the nobles and deputies who were present. They instantly declared her the successor to her brother should he die without issue and the

---

1 His nickname was King All Right.

King on his part promised not to give her in marriage without the approbation of the estates. Seven years later Ladislas died and his son Louis, then a child of ten, was pronounced of age in order to prevent the possibility of the appointment of foreign guardians. Such was the disorganisation and poverty that it is related that the boy King frequently had to go without clothes and with but little food. In 1522 he married his betrothed, Maria of Austria. Four years later, when Hungary was in the depths of her decline, there came the news that Sultan Suliman had left Constantinople at the head of a vast army to conquer Hungary. The Diet proclaimed Louis Dictator. But it was too late. Louis had only time to assemble some 25,000 ill-equipped feudal levies and with these he marched towards the Turkish host, which he met on the plain of Mohacs. There, on 29th August 1526 the Hungarians were annihilated. The King, two archbishops, five bishops and over 24,000 men perished on the field after a battle lasting about two hours. The Turks, surprised at the lack of resistance, entered Buda, ravaged the country and returned to Constantinople with more than 100,000 captives.

No sooner had the Turks quitted Hungarian territory than John Zapolya, Voivode of Transylvania, made a bid for the throne. John had made previous efforts to obtain it. He had courted Princess Anne, daughter of Ladislas VI, but to remove him from Court and to prevent such a possibility he had been appointed Voivode of Transylvania. On the death of Ladislas VI he had been made Governor of Louis II and after the latter's death, as the Electors greatly feared the alternative prospect of a Hapsburg sovereign, he was elected King at Tokay on 14th October 1526 and crowned with the Holy Crown at Székesfehérvar in the following month.

The Emperor Ferdinand in 1521 had married Anne, daughter of Ladislas II. He now claimed the Crown of Hungary in her name and was elected by a packed assembly at Pozsony. The incident of his wife having been crowned at the same time as her brother, Louis II, greatly contributed towards securing his election, after which he drove John Zapolya out of Buda and in November 1527 was in turn crowned King of Hungary at Székesfehérvar. John Zapolya after his coronation had placed the Holy Crown in the custody of one Peter Pereney, but the latter had delivered it to Ferdinand in time for his coronation. Three years later, in 1530, the Holy Crown fell into the hands of Sultan Suliman, who sent it to John Zapolya, whose widow Isabella finally restored it to its legal owner, Ferdinand I.

There were now two persons alive who had been crowned King of Hungary with the Holy Crown, and civil war broke out. With Turkish support John made himself master of two-thirds of the kingdom while Ferdinand had the rest. By the Treaty of Grosswardein it was provided that on John Zapolya's death the whole of Hungary should be reunited under the Hapsburg dynasty. When he died, however, his son Sigismund claimed his father's dominions. Sigismund was attacked and defeated by the Emperor, who was in turn defeated by the Turks. The Turks re-established Sigismund as ruler of half his former lands, keeping the rest for themselves. Hungary was thus divided into three parts—Royal Hungary, the part ruled by the Hapsburgs from Vienna or Prague; Turkish Hungary; and Transylvania, ruled by Sigismund. The Holy Crown and other regalia were taken by the Emperor Frederick to Prague where the insignia remained for more than half a century.

Ferdinand was succeeded by Maximilian, who was crowned at Pozsony on 8th September 1563. On his death in 1572 he was succeeded by Rudolph II, who paid little attention to Hungary, but his brother Matthias, who deposed him, went to Hungary in 1608 and was crowned at Pressburg. The following account of his coronation is given in *History of the Empire*, written by Heiss:

> The King, in a rich Hungarian habit, on horseback, was conducted by the whole body of nobility to the portal of the great church accompanied by the Cardinal Archbishop of Strigonia and the clergy. At his side was the Archduke Maximilian, his brother and before him went several lords carrying the crown, the sceptre, the sword, the glove and ten banners with the arms of the ten provinces of the kingdom. On arriving at the church, Matthias dismounted and placed himself in the choir, near the high altar, where the Cardinal Forgatz, who was to perform the ceremony, was seated. The King was presented to him by the principal nobles and officers of the crown, who addressed the Cardinal thus: 'We have brought here a hero, whom we desire for our king, and to wear the crown of Hungary.' The Cardinal enquired if he was a person qualified for such a station. They answered, 'Yes', and gave a detail of his great qualities and merit. Some prayers were then said and the Mass of the Holy Ghost chanted. The Palatine, lifting up the crown, asked thrice of all present if they chose the Archduke Matthias for their king; to which the assent was unanimous. The crown was then placed on the head of the monarch and the sword of St Stephen given to him with a benediction. With this sword the King then created twenty-eight knights, and being seated on his throne, the Palatine exclaimed, 'Long live Matthias II, our King!' This was followed by the acclamations of the spectators, the ringing of bells, trumpets sounding, organs and the thanksgiving canticle. This ceremony over, the King left the church, mounted on horseback and with the crown on his head rode out of the city to a theatre which had been raised and on which was a magnificent throne, and here he took and received the usual oaths, the hands being held up at the same time, and thus ended the coronation.

At the time of this coronation the nation had insisted upon the crown being kept at home. Its return to Pressburg from Prague was a regular triumph. The Diet passed an Act whereby it was henceforward to be kept in one of the towers of the Fortress of Pressburg. The guards were to be Peter Revay and Count Stephen Palffy, Governors of Turecz and Pressburg. Revay was the first person to publish a book on the Holy Crown, which he did in 1613.

Although the Holy Crown, symbol of Hungarian national pride, was once more on Hungarian soil, the country remained divided into three parts, each of which suffered continually from rebellion and civil war. It was not re-united until after the final advance of the Turks into Central Europe, which culminated in the siege of Vienna, 1683. Then, mainly by the efforts of John Sobieski, King of Poland, the Turks were defeated and within twenty years were so far driven back that they no longer remained a menace to Central Europe. During these struggles the Holy Crown, carefully guarded at all times by the crown-keepers, was taken for safety first to Vienna and later to Linz and Passau before it could be returned again to Pressburg, but it still seems to have been subjected to unexpected dangers. Shortly before the coronation of Ferdinand II the tower in which it was kept at the Fortress of Pressburg was struck by a thunder-bolt, but the crown escaped damage.

Although Hungary was once more re-united, it was not under a national dynasty, it was so divided and exhausted that Leopold I, who had been chosen King of Hungary in 1655, succeeded in having the crown made hereditary in the House of Hapsburg at a packed Diet held at Pressburg in 1687, and his elder son, Joseph, was crowned Hereditary King of Hungary. The Magyar people, nobles and commoners alike, were distrustful and resentful of Hapsburg rule. The Hapsburgs themselves ruled from Vienna and made little contact with their Hungarian subjects who were subjected to constant attempts to Austrianise them. There were more rebellions, which only ceased after Maria Theresa came to the throne. She was crowned at Pressburg on 28th June 1741. Maria Theresa took great interest in the Hungarians, especially in view of their loyalty to her in the war of the Austrian Succession and introduced a series of welcome reforms that benefited all classes including the peasantry.

Joseph II, the next sovereign, did not inherit his mother's good sense in handling his subjects. He abolished the old county assemblies, declined to be crowned in Hungary and had the Holy Crown taken away to Vienna. These blows to Magyar national pride made Hapsburg rule thoroughly unpopular and when Joseph died the country was ripe for another revolt. Leopold II, who succeeded Joseph, however, appreciated the position correctly and as well as making a new compact with the Hungarian state, which was declared to be a 'free independent and unsubjected kingdom, governed by its own laws and customs', he arranged to restore the Holy Crown to Hungarian territory and to be crowned with it at Pressburg. The return of the Holy Crown occasioned remarkable public rejoicings. Triumphal arches were erected along the route of its passage through Hungary. Every town was a scene of festivity, numbers flocked from all quarters to swell the cavalcade and at Buda exulting multitudes, crowding to the cathedral, welcomed the precious symbol of their national splendour and freedom. At night the crown was removed into the chapel of the palace and guarded by two magistrates with drawn sabres. The whole city was illuminated and was *en fête*. The streets resounded with cries of joy and on every side was heard the exclamation of, 'Long Live the Liberties of the Hungarian People'. When the coronation on 15th November 1790 was over the crown was taken to the Royal Palace at Buda, known also as the Castle of Ofen, its new resting place. Leopold's successor, Francis, had his son Ferdinand V crowned as King of Hungary in 1830 during his own lifetime. Ferdinand's consort, Caroline Augusta, was subsequently crowned on 25th September 1835.

Although the Hapsburg dynasty continued to rule Hungary until 1918 the adventures which befell the Holy Crown were not at an end. During the revolution of 1848 the Council for National Defence ordered it to be handed over to Louis Kossuth, leader of the Nationalist Party. The Holy Crown was at that time still held in great esteem as the symbol of Hungarian national pride and patriotism. The country was still a crowndom rather than a kingdom and whoever ruled it could only do so by the name of the Holy Crown. Kossuth was overwhelmed by the Emperor's forces but before he and his party fled across the Turkish frontier he had the crown and other regalia hidden in an iron chest and buried in a marshy field in the valley of Orsova. In 1853 its whereabouts was made known to the Austro-Hungarian Government. The outer cover was found to have been badly eaten away by rust. The mantle was spoiled with mould and

a (above, left) *Plaque of crown of Constantine Monomachus in the Hungarian National Museum* (p. 408)

b (above, right) *Plaque believed to have belonged to Constantine Monomachus (front view) in the Victoria and Albert Museum* (p. 408)

c *Reconstruction of crown of Constantine Monomachus from Bock's* Kleinodien (p. 408)

a   Crown found in grave of Bela III (obiit 1196), now in the Hungarian National Museum (p. 409)

b   Crown found in grave of Anne of Chatillon, Consort of Bela II, now in the Hungarian National Museum (p. 409)

c   Regalia found in grave of Bela III, now in the Hungarian National Museum (p. 409) the sword blackened but fortunately the crown, sceptre and the orb, being of gold, suffered no serious damage; they were brought back to Buda amid scenes of rejoicing. The crown was formally shown to the people by the archbishop and then taken to the Royal Palace in a golden coach.

In 1867, as a symbolic act to demonstrate a reconciliation between the House of Hapsburg and the Hungarian nation, the Emperor Francis Joseph was crowned with the Holy Crown. An account of the ceremony states that:

> The ceremony of the coronation, which did not last less than six hours, comprehended four principal parts. First the procession went to the sacristy of the church, where the King put on the coronation costume, and the traditional mantle, embroidered by the Queen of Hungary in the XII century; then it returned to the interior of the church, to the grand altar. The chanting of litanies then commenced during which the King and Queen remained kneeling, and the royal crown was placed on the altar. The Emperor assisted by the great dignitaries of the kingdom then rose and advanced to the foot of the altar, where he prostrated himself while he was anointed with holy oil on the forehead and breast. Count Andrassy, acting as palatine, took the crown from the altar and gave it to the archbishop and they together placed it on the head of His Majesty; they then removed it and held it upon his right shoulder for a short time, then replaced it. The archbishop placed the royal sceptre in the right hand of the King, and the glove in his left, and when the King, ornamented with these insignia, took his place again on the throne, a *Te Deum* was sung and a salvo of artillery announced the solemn moment to the people who shouted *Eljen Kiraly!*

> The crowning of the Queen was attended with somewhat similar ceremonies. During the rest of the day Her Majesty wore a silver crown[1] studded with diamonds and pearls. This had been made for Maria Theresa, who never used it, being entitled to wear the ancient one as queen-regnant.

> The coronation of the King and Queen having been performed, Mass commenced, and was concluded by the apostolic benediction. A procession was then formed to the square in front of the church, where, ascending the steps of a platform in the open air, the King pronounced in Hungarian with a loud voice, his oath to maintain the liberties and constitution of the kingdom. This finished, His Majesty with the crown on his head, the old mantle on his shoulders, and a large sword in his hand, mounted a noble cream-coloured charger and rode alone up the *Krönungshügel*— an artificial mound, composed of soil brought from every province in the kingdom. A stroke with the sword was dealt by the King towards each of the four points of the compass and managing his steed with dexterity that elicited bursts of applause from his Hungarian subjects, who are noted for horsemanship, he rode down the hill.

> The banquet followed this part of the coronation ceremonies and the King must have experienced considerable relief when the holy, sacred, apostolic but heavy crown of St Stephen was, at length, lifted from his head, having worn it the greatest part of the day.

After the coronation of Francis Joseph the crown and the regalia were taken to the Royal Palace at Buda. The crown was last used for the coronation of King Charles in 1916. The ceremony followed the same lines as that of Francis Joseph described above. Charles was forced to abdicate in 1918 and the following year the crown fell into the hands of the Communist leader Bela Kun who offered it to a British trading company for £4,000. This offer was refused, but before the crown could be broken up for its gold and jewels Bela Kun had to leave the country. After this the crown was kept closely guarded in the Royal Palace at Budapest. During the regency of Admiral

---

[1] For description see Chapter One—Austria.

Horthy the crown was treated as the symbol of royal power and the elections of new custodians for the crown were carried out with all the traditional ceremony.

At the end of the Second World War a heavy metal chest (*Plate 118*), held with triple locks and bearing on its front surface the arms of the Kings of Hungary, was intercepted by the American forces on its route to Switzerland, where it was being sent for safe keeping by the Regent of Hungary, Admiral Horthy. Although the Communist Government has on several occasions demanded its return to Hungarian soil it remains in American custody. Besides the Holy Crown the other ornaments belonging to the Hungarian coronation regalia include the sceptre, the orb, the sword and the coronation mantle.

The sceptre (*Plate 119, a, b* and *c*) consists of a staff which is a hollow cylinder of gold plate, surmounted by a crystal ball, of about 7 cm in diameter. The rock crystal is engraved with figure of lions on the three sides. Alföldi considers that King Stephen inherited this ball sceptre from his father, and that the crystal is the work of the x century from Egypt. From the crystal hang ten chains ending in little balls which hang loose and which when moved give out an attractive ringing sound possibly intended to give warning of the approach of the King.

The orb first appears to have been used by the Hungarian kings by Andrew III, the last of the Arpad dynasty. The ornament (*Plate 119, a*) at present in the Hungarian regalia is a hollow ball of silver gilt surmounted by a double cross. Both the orb and the cross on its summit are quite plain and without carving or filigree work. The only adornments are two small escutcheons in the shape of a shield, soldered on to the side of the globe beneath. The escutcheons bear in coloured enamels the arms of the dynasty reigning at the time of their manufacture. On a quartered field are the red bars of Hungary on a white ground; in the opposite corners the golden lilies on a blue ground of the Neapolitan House of Anjou. The orb must therefore have been made either for Charles I or Louis the Great. The great prosperity enjoyed by Hungary during the long reign of Louis, together with the shape of the escutcheons and the style of the enamel work, make it probable that the orb dates from the reign of the second Angevin king—from 1342 until 1382. This is borne out by the great resemblance between the escutcheons on the orb and the coats of arms on the two reliquary tablets still preserved in the Cathedral Treasury of Aix-la-Chapelle which are known to have been a gift from him. Louis had a great affection for Aix and we know he built a chapel there in honour of the patron saint of Hungary, close to the Palatinate Chapel. This was pulled down in 1767 and replaced by an Italian dome in rococco style, but the place is still known as the Hungarian Chapel. The chapel was furnished by the royal donor with many costly church vessels and richly embroidered vestments adorned with his own coat of arms; amongst those surviving are a pectoral brooch and two silver gilt candlesticks, all of which bear a coat of arms almost identical with that on the escutcheons belonging to the orb.

The coronation mantle was originally a chasuble made under the direction of Queen Gisela, wife of St Stephen and sister of the Emperor Henry II, for the Church of the Holy Virgin at Székesfehérvar. This vestment was used by celebrants on feast days as well as for coronations during the mediaeval period but later it became wholly identified with the office of the coronation and took the place of a pall. Originally a closed vestment, it was opened down the front for the coronation of Maria Theresa. At that time also a cape was added. The mantle is made of silk material which is almost certainly Byzantine. Its original colour was purple with some figuring in blue or dark green. The pattern is now indistinguishable and the colours have run together. The mantle is embroidered in heavy gold thread. A strip of gold embroidery runs up the centre of the back, dividing two-thirds of the way up to form a Y shape. Two other gold bands run round the mantle, one half-way up, the other a few inches above the hem. At the centre of the back, within the branches of the golden Y, is a gold-embroidered figure of the Saviour surrounded by the other persons of the Trinity and the Virgin Mary. Below the branches of the Y but above the medial band of gold, stand fifteen prophets. Their numbers are uneven because one was lost when the robe was opened. Below the prophets are the twelve Apostles each portrayed with the symbols appertaining to him. Between the hem and the gold band which runs round the robe below the apostles stand twelve royal figures separated each from each by a pair of peacocks. The royal figures to left and right of the central gold bands represent Queen Gisela and St Stephen. Queen Gisela is crowned and clad in royal garments; in her right hand she carries, as donatrix, the model of a church. St Stephen wears a *tunica talaris* and over that a royal pall or *chlamys*. His crown is a low circlet decorated with four crosses. In his left hand he carries an orb with a cross, in his right a lance-like sceptre. The other royal figures are similarly equipped. Although the cape was added much later the material from which it is made is considered to be XI-century work. The mantle was amongst the regalia buried by Kossuth's party at Orsova and it was much damaged by the bog waters. After its recovery it was kept with the crown jewels at the Royal Palace at Buda.

The coronation sword (*Plate 120, a*) is thought to date from the first half of the XVI century. It seems probable that a previous coronation sword was lost in the Turkish invasions of that period or was lost in the civil wars that followed and had to be replaced. It may be that the present sword took the place of St Stephen's Sword which is preserved in the Cathedral Treasury at Prague (*Plate 120, c*); but it cannot be its immediate successor because that sword had found its way to Prague a century and a half before the coronation sword was made. The sword was a blade of 28 in. in length, double edged with a regular taper, the blade is stiffened by a single central rib which runs down the blade almost to the point. There is some engraving near the hilt and there are also traces of former gilding but these embellishments have been much damaged by rust. The sword has a plain hilt with a grip covered with red velvet. The scabbard, which is also plain, is made of the same material.

There are two crosses associated with the Hungarian regalia. The first is a processional cross which is still preserved in the Treasury of the Metropolitan Church of Gran. The Hungarian kings held it aloft in their right hands at their coronations when swearing that they would diligently maintain the rights and privileges of their country according to the old institutions. It has been converted into a reliquary by the addition of a capsule in the centre. At the junction of the four arms is placed a large four-petalled rose, outlined in filigree, the middle of which is filled by a filigree cross with arms of equal length. Within the cross is a crystal case which contains the relics. The whole four-petalled ornament is evidently a later addition for the purpose of containing the relics, for traces of the original filigree decoration have been discovered underneath it.

The *pacificale* itself is of thin gold plate. The ends of the arms terminate in the trefoil ornamentation characteristic of the late Romanesque period. The topmost leaf of the trefoil is again divided into three, while further semi-circular additions adorn the angles between the curves of the lower leaves of the trefoil and the cross arms. The base of the cross is probably XVI century, much inferior both in design and workmanship. The whole front surface of the cross is decorated with a rich design in filigree and is studded with precious stones. The back of the cross is also adorned with filigree work but of a much simpler design and without inset gems. The central receptacle is closed with a gold plate ornamented in XVI-century style with the standing figure of the Virgin, with an inscription in blue enamel *Regina coeli, Patrona Ungariae*.

The other cross is known as the Apostolic Cross (*Plate 120, b*) and is also preserved at Gran. It is claimed that from the days of St Stephen the Kings of Hungary have enjoyed the title of *Rex Apostolicus*, which gave them the privilege of having an Apostolic Cross, and it is possible that originally such a cross was presented by the Pope. The present cross cannot have been made earlier than the end of the XV century and its design is of north-Italian art. The cross consists of two parts, a crucifix and a staff. The figure of Christ is of silver. His crown, hair and loincloth are gilded. At the ends of the arms of the cross are figures of St John and the Virgin Mary in relief. At the top of the cross is a pelican and at the foot a bust of the Magdalene. The cross itself is of silver, the strongly defined border is gilded and the surface chased. Several of the background surfaces of the front of the cross are filled in with dark blue enamel, under which, in a strong light, the patterns on the silver plate beneath are clearly distinguishable. This device is very characteristic of Italian Renaissance work. The back of the cross also merits attention. On the ends of the cross arms are busts of the four evangelists in niello while in the centre also in niello is a bust of the Virgin Mary. The cross arms are decorated with a beautiful ornamental design typical of Italian work at the close of the Middle Ages.

In 1860 and 1861 the National Museum bought from a certain Janos Huszar eight gold plaques which he said he had found while ploughing at Nytra-Ivanka. In 1870 the Museum purchased another plaque, a small setting for a precious stone and some gold fragments from another man who said they had been found with the first eight plaques. Two of the plaques are small round medallions slightly over an inch in diameter. The remaining seven range from 3 to $4\frac{1}{2}$ in. in height and from slightly under to slightly over 2 in. in width. Each of these plaques has one end square and the other rounded and bears a full-length enamel figure. These plaques, which are believed to have formed a Byzantine crown (*Plate 121, a*) have been fully dealt with by Bárány-Oberschall in a monograph entitled *Konstantinus Monomachos Czászár Koronaja*. This author does not agree with Bock's reconstruction but suggests a reconstruction as a simple diadem (*Plate 121, c*). There is a gold plaque now in the Victoria and Albert Museum which was at one time thought to have been part of this crown (*Plate 121, b*). The plaque was acquired from a collector and although it appears to have emanated from Hungary it is not known where it was first found. Some doubts have been cast upon

a   *Crown found in a grave on Margaret Island, c. XIII Century. Hungarian National Museum* (p. 410)

b   *XVII-century crown on head of reliquary bust of St Ladislas, King of Hungary (1077–95).   Cathedral Treasury, Györ* (p. 410)

d   *Crown from the reliquary bust of St Dorothea.   Silesian Museum, Wroclaw* (p. 411)

e and f   *Bracelets attributed to Queen Maria I (obiit 1395). Hungarian National Museum* (p. 409)

c   *Crown and orb found in the grave of Sigismund (obiit 1437). Hungarian National Museum, Budapest* (p. 410)

a *Coronation of Ferdinand V at Pozsony (Pressburg) on 28th September 1830. The King, who is wearing the Holy Crown, swears to defend the four corners of the kingdom* (p. 404)

b *Coronation of Francis Joseph and Queen Elisabeth at Budapest on 8th June 1867* (p. 405)

the genuineness of these plaques, but the authoritative opinion today is that they were plaques belonging to the crown but possibly later additions.

In the xvi century the Turks destroyed the coronation church at Székesfehérvar and despoiled the royal tombs. During the xix century some of the remaining royal graves were excavated, including those of King Bela III (*obiit* 1196) and his wife Anne of Chatillon (*Plate 122, a* and *b*). In the graves were found several items of royal insignia wrought of precious metal but of very simple design. The regalia made for King Bela's funeral appear to have been specially and hastily made. The crown (*Plate 122, a*) buried with the King was a plain circlet of silver-gilt adorned only with four silver-gilt crosses in shape similar to a cross *pattée* roughly and irregularly cut and fastened to it with plain rivets. The crown buried with his queen was of similar design but slightly smaller. In the King's grave was also found a silver-gilt staff or sceptre, very plain but decorated at the top with what appears to have been a miniature crown. Beside the crowns and the sceptre, a sword (*Plate 122, c*) and a pair of spurs were found. These are considered likely to have been personal possessions of King Bela. The sword was typical of those in use in the late Romanesque period, and although the grip has lost its covering, the blade and terminal pommel of the hilt are sufficiently well preserved for it to be evident that this was not just a symbolic sword made only for burial furniture. The spurs are of special interest as few spurs from the Romanesque period have been preserved. They are of plain and simple shape without ornamentation. The old German imperial spurs which were lost at the end of the xviii century were of a much more ornamental design.

There were also found in the grave the upper part of a *virga* or *baculus regalis*, a pectoral cross and two rings.

These ornaments which were found in 1848 were kept in the National Museum until 1862 when they were reburied in the coronation church at Budapest; but models of the two crowns, the sword, the sceptre and the spurs were made and are still in the National Museum.

During the xix century the remains of a simple yet richly decorated and delicately shaped crown were found in a grave on Margaret Island. No inscriptions were found in or on the grave and it has not been possible to identify the personage buried there. By some it is thought to be the grave of Stephen V (*obiit* 1272). The diadem consists of eight hinged gold plates fastened together to form a narrow circlet. Each of the eight gold pins which hold the hinges projects upward and branches into three beautifully worked vine leaves. Every gold plate is decorated at both ends with a single precious stone in a projecting setting. From the centre of each plate rises a lily cut from gold plate. These lilies are very similar in design to the fleur-de-lis on the Bohemian crown. They are decorated with 3 pearls and one precious stone alternating with three precious stones and 1 pearl. On the circlet, at the base of each lily, is set a six-petalled rose worked in gold. Each rose is set with a precious stone projecting from its centre and a pierced pearl at the point of each petal. The crown was found in a damaged state with many of the stones and pearls missing. It is now in the National Museum at Budapest.

Also in the National Museum are two richly decorated gold bracelets which, according to tradition, once belonged to Queen Maria I, who died in 1395 (*Plate 123, e and f*).

These bracelets are supposed to have been found during the excavation of the ruins of the old Episcopal Church of Grosswardein where they had been dropped into a well when that stronghold was stormed. The bracelets are both of similar design but one is larger than the other, both in circumference and width, and is more highly ornamented. They are smaller than the imperial *Armillae* formerly kept at Nuremberg, and this indicates that they were probably made for a woman. Each consists of two curved gold plates joined by a hinge. Round the edges of each bracelet run three rows of raised cordon work in gold, more elaborately executed on the larger bracelet than on the smaller one. The main surface of each is decorated with polygonal gold ornaments with filigree knobs which alternate with small precious stones mounted in raised settings incorporating more cordon work. The design of these bracelets is considered by some experts to be of Eastern origin. Some authorities, however, are of the opinion that the bracelets now in the Museum are not the original ones found at Grosswardein but only imitations. There are known to be copies in existence elsewhere.

In the National Museum there are a crown and orb (*Plate 123, c*) which were found at Nagyvarad in the grave of the Emperor Sigismund, who died in 1437. The crown consists of a narrow circlet to which are riveted eight slightly projecting plates surmounted by fleurs-de-lis. Each plate is decorated with ten precious stones set in strongly projecting settings somewhat similar to those on the Margaret Island crown (*Plate 123, a*). Five stones are set on each fleur-de-lis and five on the plates below them. Many of these stones are now missing. The crown is attributed to the XIV century and the wealth of the stones suggests that it was used as a personal crown by Sigismund during his long reign as King of Hungary. The orb is a plain globe surmounted by a cross equal in height to the globe itself. Neither the ball nor the cross have any traces of decoration. In this way it resembles the Coronation Orb, which is of slightly earlier date. It must be remembered that Sigismund and Maria were co-sovereigns and, therefore, a second orb would probably have been made for their coronation. This may be it. It only remains to note that while the Hungarian Orb bears a double cross, Sigismund's has a plain single one.

There are three crowns on reliquary busts of Hungarian origin which are still extant. The first is that of St Ladislas (*Plate 123, b*) in the Cathedral Treasury at Győr (Raab). A bust was originally made for the King's tomb in the Cathedral of Nagyvarad, but this was destroyed by fire in 1406. The existing bust was then made to replace it. In the XV century it was removed from Nagyvarad and was discovered in a neglected condition by Demeter Napragi, Bishop of Győr, who purchased it and placed it in his cathedral, where it still is. The bust and crown were in need of repair and, according to an inscription on the inside of the crown, Bishop Napragi had both repaired in Prague in 1600. It seems that the crown was entirely remade and it is thought by some, although it has now been established with certainty, that part of the old crown is incorporated with the new one. The circlet of the crown is adorned with rosettes decorated in enamel and set with precious stones. From the circlet rise twelve large, leaf-like ornaments, each set with a precious stone in the centre. Between these are twelve small fleurs-de-lis, which may have formed part of the original crown.

The second is a crown on a head reliquary of St Coloman. This Irish prince, who was a descendant of the Arpad Dynasty on his mother's side, was killed in 1072 while returning from the Holy Land. He was buried at Melk, but his body was later reinterred in Hungary. It was again brought back to Melk and buried in the Benedictine Abbey there. His head reliquary was preserved in the Royal Basilica at Székesfehérvar and was brought to Melk in 1517 by the Emperor Maximilian.[1] The crown is of Hungarian work of the middle of the XII century. It is an open crown decorated with fleurs-de-lis.

The third crown is on the reliquary bust of St Dorothea (*Plate 123, d*) in the Silesian Museum at Wroclaw (Breslau). The reliquary bust is of silver gilt and was made in Hungary about 1435. The crown is possibly also from the XV century but seems to have been added later as it is too large for the head of the bust. The crown consists of a circlet decorated with enamel and precious stones from which rise eight small and eight large leaf-like ornaments.

BIBLIOGRAPHY

BARANY-OBERSCHALL, M.	'Localisation of the Enamels of the Upper Hemisphere of the Holy Crown of Hungary', *The Art Bulletin*, XXXI (1949).
	'Problems around the Hungarian Holy Crown' (in Hungarian), *Antiquitas Hungarica*, I (1947).
	The Crown of the Emperor Constantine Monomachus. Arch. Hung. XXII, Budapest 1937
BOCK, F.	*Die Kleinodien des heiligen römischen Reiches deutscher Nation*, Vienna 1864.
	'Die ungarische Reichsinsignien', *Mittheilungen der k.k. Central-Commission*, II, 1857.
CIAMPINI, G. C.	*De Sacris Aedificiis.*
CZOBOR, B.	*The Hungarian Holy Crown and the Coronation Mantle* (in Hungarian), Budapest 1900.
CZOBOR, B., AND RADISICS E. DE	*Les Insignes Royaux de Hongrie*, Budapest 1896.
DEER, JOSEF	*The Foundation of the Hungarian Kingdom* (in Hungarian), Budapest 1942.
	'Emperor Otto III and Hungary in the Light of Recent Historical Writing' (in Hungarian), *Szazadok*, 1944 (1–3), Budapest.
ECKHART, F.	'The Holy Crown of Hungary', *The Hungarian Quarterly*, IV (1940–41).
GARADY	'History of the Hungarian Holy Crown' (in Hungarian), *Hazank*, I, 1858.
GRABAR, A.	*L'empereur dans l'art Byzantin*, Paris 1936.
IPOLYI, A.	*History and Description of the Hungarian Holy Crown and the Coronation Insignia* (in Hungarian), Budapest 1886.

[1] The author visited the Abbey of Melk in 1959 but was unable to locate it. The priest-in-charge stated it had been removed to Sigmaringen.

KELLEHER, P. J.	*The Holy Crown of Hungary*, American Academy in Rome 1951.
KOLLAR, J.	*De Sacra Regni Ungariae Corona Commentarius.*
MIHALIK, A.	'Eleventh-Century Crowns', *The Hungarian Quarterly*, IV (1938–39).
MORAVCSIK, G.	'The Holy Crown of Hungary', *The Hungarian Quarterly*, IV (1938–39).
REVAY, P.	'De Sacrae Coronae Regni Hungariae ortu, virtute, victoria, fortuna', *Augustae Vindelicorum*, 1613.
	'De Sacrae Coronae Regni Hungariae ortu, virtute, victoria, fortuna Commentarius cum iconae', *Viennae excudebat Matthaeus Cosmerovius*, 1652.
SCHRAMM, P. E.	*Kaiser, Rom und Renovatio*, I–II, Leipzig 1929.
TÓTH, Z.	*Critical View of the Hartwig Legend* (in Hungarian), Budapest 1942.
	Concerning the Actual State of our Historical Research. The Question of the Origin of the Holy Crown (in Hungarian), Budapest 1943.

KINGS OF HUNGARY

(The records of early Hungarian Coronations are very incomplete)

997 Waic or St Stephen. Crowned 1000 and received from the Pope the title of Apostolic Majesty
1038 Peter the German, son of Orsioli, Doge of Venice
1041 Aba Samuel
1044 Peter again
1047 Andrew I
1061 Bela I
1064 Salomon
1076 Geza I
1077 Ladislas the Pious
1095 Salomon
1114 Stephen II
1131 Bela II
1141 Geza II
1162 Stephen III (and Stephen IV). Crowned at Székesfehérvar 1161
1173 Bela III
1196 Emeric
1204 Ladislas II
1205 Andrew II
1235 Bela IV
1270 Stephen V. Crowned as Junior King in father's lifetime, 1254
1272 Ladislas III

1290 Andrew III

1292 Charles Martel of Anjou. Crowned titular King of Hungary at Naples on 8th September

1301 Wenceslas of Bohemia and Otto of Bavaria

1309 Charles I, Robert of Anjou. Crowned at Székesfehérvar, 27th August 1310

1342 Louis the Great. Crowned at Székesfehérvar, 21st July 1342

1382 Maria. Crowned at Székesfehérvar, 17th September 1382

1385 Charles II of Durazzo. Crowned at Buda, 31st December 1385

1387 Mary and Sigismund, King of Bohemia. Sigismund crowned King of Hungary at Székesfehérvar, 31st March 1387

1392 Sigismund alone

1437 Albert, Duke of Austria. Crowned at Székesfehérvar, 1st January 1438, with consort, Elizabeth

1439 Elizabeth alone

1440 Ladislas V, Posthumous. Crowned at Székesfehérvar, 15th May 1440

1440 Ladislas IV (III of Poland). Crowned at Buda, 17th July 1440

1445 John Hunyady. Regent

1458 Ladislas V again

1458 Matthias Corvinus. Crowned at Székesfehérvar, 25th March 1464

1490 Ladislas VI, King of Bohemia

1516 Louis II. Declared king but previously crowned King of Hungary on 4th June 1508 and King of Bohemia in 1509

1526 John Zapolya, Voivode of Transylvania. Crowned at Székesfehérvar, 11th November 1526

1526 Ferdinand I, King of Bohemia. Crowned King of Hungary at Székesfehérvar, November 1527, as rival king

1540 Ferdinand I alone

1563 Maximilian I. Crowned at Pozsony (Pressburg), 8th September 1563

1572 Rudolf. Crowned at Pozsony 1572

1608 Matthias II. Crowned at Pozsony, 1608

1618 Ferdinand II

1625 Ferdinand III. Crowned at Pozsony, 16th December 1625

1647 Ferdinand IV. Crowned at Pozsony, 16th June 1647

1655 Leopold I

1687 Joseph I. Crowned at Pozsony, 1687 in father's lifetime

1712 Charles (VI of Germany). Crowned at Pozsony, 22nd May 1712

1741 Maria Theresa. Crowned at Pozsony, 28th June 1741

1780 Joseph II

1790 Leopold II. Crowned at Pozsony, 28th June 1790

1792 Francis I

1835 Ferdinand V. Crowned as co-King at Pozsony, 28th September 1830. His Consort, Caroline Augusta, crowned at Pozsony, 25th September 1835

1848 Francis Joseph. Crowned at Buda with his consort, Elizabeth, 8th June 1867

1916 Charles IV. Crowned at Buda with his consort, 1916

lifetime he was not crowned as King of Italy, probably because the union of Germany and Italy made the Italian kingdom inseparable from the imperial dignity. This was emphasised when Otto II had his son Otto III, aged three, elected King of Italy at Verona in 983 and then sent him to Aix-la-Chapelle to be crowned King of Germany and Italy. At this ceremony the Archbishop of Ravenna attanded as the representative of the *Regnum Italium*.[1] Kroener claims, with some later Italian writers, that the fact that Otto III was crowned at Monza cannot be substantiated, though we must take note that Bombelli, in supporting the belief that the coronation of Otto III took place at Monza and not at Pavia because of party strife, and goes on to relate that because no suitable crown was available the so-called 'Iron Crown' which hung over the altar in the church of St John as *donatio Longobardo* was taken down and used for the coronation, although it was too small. When Otto III unexpectedly died in 1002 the national anti-German party in Italy caused the Margrave Ardouin of Ivrea to be elected King, and on 15th February 1002 he was crowned in St Michael's church at Pavia. In 1004 Henry II, who had been elected German King, crossed the Alps and was elected and crowned in St Michael's church, Pavia, on 14th May, although on Henry's departure Ardouin took the throne again.

Although there was a national movement to break away from the German union on Henry II's death, internal agreement could not be reached and the Archbishop of Milan was, therefore, sent to Conrad, who had succeeded to the German throne, at Constantine in 1024, where he did homage and promised to crown him as King of Italy. Conrad was crowned in Milan Cathedral on 23rd March 1026 by the Archbishop of Milan. Eleven years later Conrad was again in Italy and wished to wear his crown according to custom but, as the archbishop had turned against him, all the churches except a small one were closed to him. Neither Henry III nor Henry IV were crowned, the latter because of his excommunication by the Pope, and it came to be generally accepted that the German kings were automatically Kings of Italy. Conrad, elder son of Henry IV, was crowned at Monza in 1103, but after his deposition Henry V, his younger brother, was not crowned, although he went to Italy in 1110. Neither he nor his successor, Lothair III, considered it to be necessary to be crowned in Italy. Lothair, however, wore his crown at a Court Day at Mincio in 1136. On 29th June 1128 Conrad III, the anti-King, was crowned at Monza, Pavia being in the hands of Lothair, his rival. The coronation took place in St Michael's church, where it was stated the 'Iron Crown' was kept, but afterwards the King went in procession to St John's church for the coronation Mass. Conrad's successor, Frederick Barbarossa, was crowned at St Michael's church, Pavia, on 24th April 1155. In 1158 Frederick wore his crown at Monza, but this was a 'crown-wearing' ceremony and not a coronation. Frederick had his son, Henry VI, crowned at Milan with his consort on the occasion of their wedding, and it was stated that Frederick was crowned at the same time. It seems to be reasonably well established that Henry's coronation was as King of Italy, although his wife, who had not been crowned at Aix-la-Chapelle, may have received the German crown. Frederick was unlikely to have been crowned again, and as far as

---

[1] P. E. Schramm: 'Die Krönung in Deutschland bis 1028', in *Zeitschr. f. Rechtsgesch.* 55 Kan. Abt. 24, 1935.

he was concerned it is more likely to have been a 'crown-wearing' ceremony. After Henry VI's reign, there was civil war in Germany and of the two rival kings Philip did not go to Italy, and although Otto IV was received by the Lombard nobles at a ceremony there is no mention of a coronation until some time later, so it is unlikely that he was crowned. There were no further coronations until that of Henry VII on 6th January 1311 at Milan, which was chosen by all the Italian authorities except those of Monza. His successor Louis of Bavaria was crowned at Milan with his Queen on 31st May 1327, and Charles IV was crowned at Milan on 6th January 1355. Charles IV's two immediate successors were not crowned as Kings of Italy, Wenceslas never went to Italy and Rupert, although he crossed the Alps in 1401, was defeated and therefore could not be crowned. Sigismund, who succeeded Rupert, entered into negotiations with the Duke of Milan and others and as a result was crowned in Milan on 21st November 1431. Frederick III was also crowned King of Italy by Pope Nicholas V in Rome on 16th March 1452, though not without opposition from the Italian notables who felt that Milan had been slighted. Frederick's successor, Maximilian I, was not crowned but his successor, Charles V, was crowned at Bologna on 22nd February 1530 by Pope Clement VII two days before he received the imperial crown. Charles V was the last German emperor to cross the Alps and to receive the Italian crown. In 1805 Napoleon decided to be crowned King of Italy and the ceremony took place on 26th May of that year in the Cathedral of Milan, Napoleon placing the crown on his head and pronouncing the traditional words: 'God gave it to me, let all who touch it beware.' In 1816 Francis I, Emperor of Austria, became King of the new Lombardo-Venetian kingdom, and on 6th September 1838 his successor Ferdinand I was crowned at Milan. This was the last coronation.

It has been necessary to trace in some detail the story of Italian coronations in order to follow more clearly the place in history of the celebrated 'Iron Crown' of Lombardy. This ornament is still kept in the Basilica of St John in Monza in a glass case in a square recess placed in an elevated position over an altar and shut by a hinged door, and as it is adored as a relic a ceremony has to be performed when it is shown to visitors. A copy hangs before the altar.

The 'Iron Crown' (*Plate 126, a*) consists of six detachable parts, each part is a riveted gold shield. The crown has a circumference of about 48 cm, a diameter of about 15 cm and it is 5·3 cm high. Each shield is made in one piece but on the outside each is divided into two panels, one oblong and the other square, with the exception of the one at the back of the crown which is ornamented only with one stone and enamel roses. The other panels are ornamented with 3 uncut stones, a sapphire, a garnet and an amethyst which are set one by the other in oval settings. The spaces between the stones are covered with a deeply incised leaf ornamentation of a simple design which has been carried out in a technically imperfect manner. On the centre of the square panel are set single uncut gems fronting which are four chased rosettes and the four corners are filled with a leaf design in enamel work. The cloisonné enamels are of excellent workmanship and very well preserved. The six shields are held together by gold wire pins which are undecorated at the top and just bent over so that they cannot be easily drawn out. The slots into which they are fixed are barred on the outer side and ornamented with gold filigree work which besides serving as an ornament adds strength to the slots. The uncut gems in the crown are 7 garnets, 4 amethysts

a   Crown plate of a helmet of King Agilulf, VI Century. National Museum, Florence (p. 416)

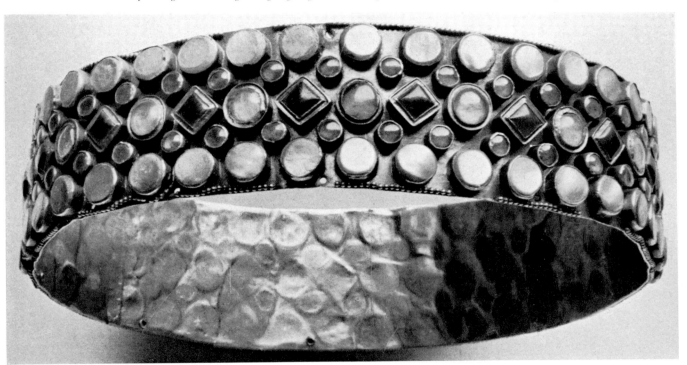

b   Crown of Theodolinda, VI Century. Monza Cathedral (p. 417)

c   Crown of King Agilulf on coronation
medal of Napoleon as King of Italy,
1805. British Museum (p. 418)

a   *The Iron Crown of Lombardy, IX Century. Monza Cathedral* (p. 420)

b   *Iron crown of Lombardy and Kazan Armilla from Bayer's* Opuscula (p. 421)

c   *The tympanum. Monza Cathedral* (p. 424)

d   *Marble plaque depicting the coronation of a King of Italy. Monza Cathedral* (p. 424)

2 true sapphires, 7 lynx sapphires and 2 paste stones, one of which has an intensive blue colour like a true sapphire and a silvered back surface, while the other is dark yellow like a hyacinth. The gold plates are held together by a narrow strip of iron which runs around the inside of the crown and it is secured to the inner surface of the golden circlet in rather a rough manner by three rivets. There are also eight large holes in the iron strip which are not utilised.

Many theories have been put forward by art historians as to the origin and date of the crown, but today it is generally accepted as being a work of the middle IX century. Elze[1] has put forward an hypothesis which is perhaps the most acceptable, although it cannot be proved with certainty. His conclusion is that it was originally a coronet worn at the German Court in the mid-IX century and that it had belonged to Gisela, the daughter of the Emperor Louis the Pious, who had married Count Eberhard of Fruili. In his will Eberhard left his possessions to be divided between his four sons and three daughters and there was included in his treasure *coronam auream cum ligno Domini* which went to his eldest son Unroch. Elze concludes that Gisela's possessions were similarly divided on her death in 874 and that her son Berengar I inherited her coronet and gave it to the church at Monza. He was the only notable of the period who is known to have been a benefactor of Monza and he gave the church a cross in the same style as the Iron Crown, which is still kept in the Treasury there. Frisi and Barbier de Montault quote two lists of treasures of the Chapel of King Berengar I the first of which includes two crowns and the second only one. Several writers, including Bock, Kondakov and Haase, have considered the crown to be a bracelet because of its small size. Bock drew attention to the remarkable similarity of the Monza crown to a pair of ornaments in the Imperial Museum at St Petersburg, which were found at Kazan in 1730. Originally they were thought to be diadems but later it was suggested that they were *armillae*. An illustrated article on the subject appeared in the publication of the Imperial Academy of Science at St Petersburg. A treatise was also written by T. S. Bayer,[2] who produced an engraving of one of the Kazan ornaments with an engraving of the Monza crown for comparison (*Plate 126, b*). The Kazan ornaments each consisted of eight plates against the six of the Monza crown but the ornamentation and the setting of the precious stones were the same. We know nothing of the history of the Kazan ornaments, which were lost in the XIX century, but it is reasonable to conclude that they originated from the same place and were used for the same original purpose as the Monza crown. In other words, they were both coronets and their small size is accounted for by the fact that they did not have to fit the head but sat on top of the head affixed to a veil, which accounts for the small holes on the rim.

We must now consider the legends which have grown up around the Monza crown. It is usually said that it originates from the time of Constantine the Great, whose mother, St Helena, gave her son two of the nails of the True Cross. One of these was made into a bridle for the Emperor's horse, and from the other a diadem was fashioned. These precious relics remained in Constantinople on the death of the Emperor Constantine until they were brought to Rome as a present to Pope Gregory the Great, who

---

[1] Reinhard N. Elze: op. cit. [2] T. S. Bayer ed. *Opuscula*, 1770.

gave the diadem made from the Holy Nail to Queen Theodolinda, who in turn gave it to the Church of St John which she had built at Monza. According to the story it was subsequently used for the coronations of all the Lombard kings and all the German emperors and kings who became Kings of Italy.

There appears to be sufficient evidence to substantiate the claim that St Helena did have a diadem incorporating one of the Holy Nails she acquired, but there is silence about the Nail or diadem being among the gifts given to Pope Gregory the Great by Constantine, Tiberius Augustus, or by Pope Gregory to Theodolinda, or by Theodolinda to the church at Monza, and it seems unlikely that so important a relic should not have been mentioned. We have already seen that there is no evidence to show that the kings or queens of Lombardy were crowned or, in fact, that any coronation took place at Monza until possibly that of Conrad II in 1093, the usual place of coronation being Pavia or Milan. It seems hardly likely that the contemporary Lombard historians would have failed to have referred to Monza as the place of coronation or to have mentioned that a special crown was kept for the coronations and that it contained a relic as precious as a Holy Nail. Other stories which are similarly unsupported by evidence claim that the crown was given by Maximilian, by Theodoric or by Charlemagne.

It was not until the XI or XII centuries that Monza endeavoured to establish the fact that it was the coronation town and that the coronation crown was kept there. The first mention of the 'Iron Crown' is in 1230 in the *Chronicle of John Codagnellus of Piacenza*, which contains many legends and stories of the old times and claims that the 'Iron Crown' had been presented to the church at Monza by Theodoric the Great and that the sovereign of Italy used it to receive the *Regnum Italie*. This story, sometimes with embellishments, was subsequently repeated by other writers. In 1260 Matthew Paris, who must have obtained his information from Northern Italy, refers in his *Historia Anglorum* to the three crowns of the emperors which he shows on a coat of arms of Otto IV as *argentea, aurea, ferrea*. Writing in 1288, or 160 years later, Bonviceinus de Ripper states that the king was crowned with the 'Iron Crown,' but this does not mean that the crown was so described before the XIII century.

There were three inventories taken in Monza, in 1275, 1345 and 1353, the entries being: In 1275:

> Item. in primis sunt quatuor corone, quarum una est magna cum cruce aurea cum ornamentis et lapidibus.
> Item. corona parva cum cruce et omnibus ornamentis suis.
> Item. corona una auri cum cruce et lapidibus suis et ornamentis.
> Item. alia corona aurea cum crucibus geminus lapidibus et ornamentis suis.

There are also mentioned briefly in 1345:

> Corone quatuor auri cum una patena. March(arum) XVII Unz(iarum) V.

and there are described in 1353:

> Item. corona una magna auri larga et ampla ornata zafiliis et aliia lapidibus pretiosis; cum cadenellis auri pendentibus et cum lapidibus XIII intus qui videntur esse zafilii, et uno loco carente za filio et alio lapide, et ornata perlis LV gorssis ad astrorum et uno cristallo grosso et multis aliis perlis et lapidus parvis.

Item. una alia corona auri ornata lapidibus preciosis minutis.
Item. una alia corona auri cum uno circulo ferri et cum quindecim lapidibus pretiosis intus.
Item. corona una auri ornato fatharis et quam pluribus lapidibus.

In the last inventory the third crown is described as *cum uno circulo ferri*, and although only fifteen stones are mentioned against the twenty-two now in the crown it is reasonable to suppose that this is the ornament today known as the 'Iron Crown'. The iron ring, which was later claimed to be the Holy Nail, was a feature in other crowns made of several plates which needed to be held together when in use. The German Imperial Crown in Vienna, for instance, has such a narrow strip of iron for this purpose.

There were no Italian coronations between that of Henry VI, 1186, and Henry VII, 1311. When preparations were being made for the coronation of Henry VII the King enquired about the 'Iron Crown' and sent a letter to Monza in which he commanded, under pain of excommunication and interdict, that the King's envoy should be told where the 'Iron Crown' and the documents necessary for the coronation were located. But since 1273 the 'Iron Crown' had been missing. During the struggle between the Guelphs and the Ghibellines the pro-Guelph, Della Torre, had pledged many of the objects in the Monza Treasury, including the 'Iron Crown', to a Jew and no one knew where they were to be found. The 'Iron Crown' did not reappear until 1319 when it was redeemed by Matteo Visconti of Milan and returned to Monza. Meanwhile Henry VI had to provide a crown for his coronation on 6th January 1311 and one was made in the shape of a laurel wreath of polished steel set with valuable pearls. It was subsequently designated *Laurea* and given to the Monastery of St Ambrose in Milan for safe keeping, with instructions that it should be used for the coronation of Henry's successors. Louis of Bavaria used it for his coronation in 1327 because the Monza crown was again not available. In 1323 the monks of St John at Monza, fearing that the 'Iron Crown' might again be stolen during the disorders, buried it. In 1324 it went with the whole of the Monza Treasury to Avignon and it was not returned to Monza until 20th March 1345. The coronation of Charles IV at Milan in 1355 was planned to follow that of Henry VII in every particular. Since there was now confusion between *Laurea* that was sometimes referred to as the 'Iron Crown' and the 'Iron Crown' at Monza, it is not clear which one Charles used. There was no subsequent coronation until that of Sigismund, 1431, and it seems that the Monza crown was used, as at that time the *Laurea* was described as an 'iron crown full of rust', and it was subsequently lost. The Monza crown was used at the coronation of Frederick III in Rome, and on 2nd February 1530 it was brought to Bologna from Monza by messenger for the coronation of Charles V. According to Muratori the first mention of the significance of the iron ring being a Holy Nail was made by Bazatus in 1587. He was followed by Zucchius, whose violation of the truth Muratori holds it charitable to attribute to gross carelessness. In 1585, two years before the publication of Bazatus's book, a letter sent from the Archbishop of Monza to Pope Sixtus V, quoted by Muratori, speaks of the 'Iron Crown' as the most precious possession of his church and as having been used during early times for the coronations of emperors. But he distinguishes it from the relics and makes no allowance for it having been wrought from a Nail of the True Cross. From the XVI century onwards the belief gained strength, but having been discredited by the searching enquiry of Muratori, worship of the crown as a sacred relic was alternately suspended and reinforced by decrees and counter-decrees of the ecclesiastical authorities until in 1688 the matter was laid before the Congregation of Relics at Rome. A process was instituted which lingered on until 1715 when a diplomatic sentence was pronounced leaving the chief point—the identity of the iron ring with the Holy Nail—undecided but sanctioning it being exposed to the adoration of the faithful and being carried in processions. Despite the judgment of the Congregation of Relics, Visconti, the Archbishop of Milan, gave his decision that 'the iron ring in the Monza crown should be considered as one of the Nails of the Holy Cross and as an original relic'. To this day there are many who have faith in this decision, and the ecclesiastical guardians of the crown at Monza assert that there is not a single speck of rust on the 'Iron Crown' although it has been exposed for fifteen centuries.

At Monza there are two objects which might be considered to give some evidence about the 'Iron Crown', but a close analysis of them makes it clear that while they contain much which is of interest, as far as our subject is concerned their purpose seems to be propaganda in favour of Monza being the repository of the 'Iron Crown' and the place of coronations. First is the *tympanum* (*Plate 126, c*) or sculptured panel over the main entrance of the cathedral, and the second is the panel of marble in an *ambo* in the cathedral which depicts in bas relief the coronation of a king of Italy. Oppenheimer[1] has made a detailed analysis of the *tympanum*. He concludes that the apse of Theodolinda's first church was, during her lifetime, embellished by a pair of superposed mural paintings in keeping with the habits of the day. In the first rebuilding in the XII century the original compositions were repainted and, some contend, modified and enriched. In the rebuilding in the XIV century drastic changes were introduced and the scenes designed for the glorification of Theodolinda were moved from the lower to the upper register and thus given greater prominence. These scenes include Theodolinda offering the 'Iron Crown' of Lombardy to St John the Baptist and also depicts three other crowns hanging upside down as votive crowns. The 'Iron Crown' is depicted with a sloping cross as a sign of humility[2]. The figure of Matteo Visconti, who was responsible for the return of the Treasure to Monza in 1319, was added in the XIV century.

The second plaque (*Plate 126, d*), in the cathedral, has been dealt with fully by Kroener, who concludes that it dates from not earlier than the second half of the XIV century and that the details of the relief may have been taken from Morigias's description of the supposed coronation of Otto IV at Monza in 1209, which he wrote about in 1345, but in any case the plaque does not give us a factual representation of a coronation. We may note four votive crowns are shown above the altar, but the crown which the archbishop is placing on the King's head bears no resemblance to the 'Iron Crown'.

The first coronation *ordo* of the Italian rite belongs to the IX century and consists of only four prayers. There is no mention of anointing or investing or of the coronation of the queen. By the XI century a much longer rite was in use containing the whole of the English 'Egbert *Ordo*' and Roman forms borrowed from the Frankish rite. The

1 Sir Francis Oppenheimer: *Frankish Themes and Problems*, London 1952.
2 See page 105 footnote 2.

a   *Regalia of Napoleon as King of Italy, 1805. Risorgimento Museum, Milan* (p. 425)

b   *Ferdinand I with coronation regalia as King of Lombardo-Venetia. Water-colour by A. Weissenböck. Treasury, Vienna* (p. 425)

c   *Coronation sword of Ferdinand I, King of Lombardo-Venetia. Treasury, Vienna* (p. 425)

b   *Crown attributed to King Roger II. Basilica of St Nicholas, Bari (p. 429)*

a (left)   *Mosaic depicting the coronation of King Roger II. Church of Martorana, Palermo (p. 427)*

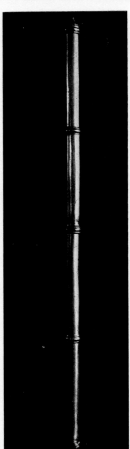

d   *Crown on reliquary bust of St Agatha. Treasury, Catania Cathedral (p. 431)*

c   *Sceptre attributed to Charles II, King of Naples, c. 1289. Basilica of St Nicholas, Bari (p. 432)*

king was anointed and invested with the crown, the sceptre, the verge, the sword and the ring. The Queen was also crowned. The *ordo* used at the coronation of Henry VII and Queen Catherine at Milan in 1311 was more elaborate. After the anointing the King was invested with the ring, the sword, the crown, the sceptre and the verge. Following the Benediction the King was solemnly led to the throne and seated upon it by the archbishop, who then delivered the orb.

It is impossible to say definitely for which coronations the 'Iron Crown' was employed but it was probably brought into use not later than the XI century and thereafter was used regularly when available. There is no indication as to whether the rest of the regalia were Italian or the personal ornaments of the emperors. The Monza inventory of 1275 mentions *virga una argentea circumdata*, but Oppenheimer[1] considers this to be the ceremonial fan depicted on the Monza *tympanum*. In 1805 Napoleon used the 'Iron Crown' at his coronation at Milan. He brought it back from Paris where it had been taken in 1797. He also had a special set of regalia (*Plate 127, a*) made for the occasion which is now preserved in the Museo del Risorgimento in Milan. It consists of the following ornaments:

A royal crown of gold with two arches surmounted by an orb and cross which is set with imitation stones of paste and mother-of-pearl.

A sceptre of silver gilt surmounted by a crown of rays, on which rests the Lion of St Mark. The sceptre bears the monogram *N*.

A Hand of Justice with an outstretched ivory hand surmounting a long silver gilt staff.

For the coronation of Ferdinand in 1838 a special set of coronation ornaments was made and are depicted in a water-colour by A. Weissenböck (*Plate 127, b*). A special royal crown was made for the occasion, on the bonnet of which the 'Iron Crown', being too small to be worn, was fixed. It was closed on top with royal arches surmounted by a cross. The other ornaments were a sceptre, an orb and a sword. The crown, the sceptre and the orb were broken up and sold in 1871–2. But the sword (*Plate 127, c*) is still preserved in the Vienna Treasury, it was made by Mayerhofer and Klinkosch and designed by Peter Fendi.

The handle of the sword is of gilded silver with the scabbard covered with blue velvet, the blade, which was made by the Viennese steel craftsman Hans Schleifer, has etchings with gold inlay. The blade bears the following inscription:

RECTA TERI beneath the Austrian imperial crown. On the other side *FERDINANDUS AUSTRIAE IMPERATOR: FRANCISCI: IMP(ERATORIS) LOMB(ARDIAE) VENET(IAE) PRIMI REGIS FILIUS INSIGNI CORONAE MEDIOL (ANEA) MDCCCXXXVIII SYMPTAE PRIMUS,*

and above the inscription the Arms of Lombardy and Venetia.[2] There are also preserved in Vienna the coronation mantle of blue velvet and ermine, richly embroidered in gold with the 'Iron Crown' repeated on the border, and also the undergarment and sword belt.

To commemorate his coronation Napoleon instituted the Order of the Iron Crown.

1 Sr. Francis Oppenheimer: op. cit.
2 H. Fillitz: *Catalogue of the Crown Jewels*, etc., Vienna 1956.

425

Francis I revived Napoleon's Order of the Iron Crown in 1816, and in 1838 Ferdinand held a great ceremony of the Order in the Doges Palace at Venice. The Austrian Order fell into disuse in 1868 when the first King of Italy founded the Italian Order of the Crown of Italy. A mantle and collar of the Austrian Order are preserved in the Vienna Treasury. In 1859, when the Austrians evacuated Lombardy, they took the 'Iron Crown' to Vienna, where it remained until 1866. When the unification of Italy had been completed and Victor Emmanuel II of Sardinia was proclaimed King of Italy the people of Monza petitioned for the return of their crown. The Emperor of Austria agreed to its return and the 'Iron Crown' was brought from Vienna to Turin and presented to the King. It was taken to Monza on 6th December 1866. In 1878 it was placed on the coffin of King Victor Emmanuel, and in 1900 it was again taken from Monza with traditional ceremony and laid on the coffin of King Humbert and at the funeral the Master of the Ceremonies bore the crown immediately behind the coffin. Once each year it is taken out and carried in public in a solemn procession.

THE NORMAN KINGDOM OF SICILY

In 1046 Robert Guiscard, the sixth son of Tancred of Hautville, a petty noble of Coutances in Normandy, set foot in southern Italy where three of his elder brothers had already established themselves over Apulia and Calabria. In 1057 Robert succeeded his brother Humphrey as Count of Apulia and having been joined by his youngest brother, Roger, he conquered southern Italy. The Papacy recognised the Normans and, anxious to secure them as allies, Pope Nicholas II invested Robert Guiscard with the title 'By the Grace of God and St Peter, Duke of Apulia and Calabria, future Lord of Sicily'. With his brother Roger he invaded Sicily and in January 1072, having taken Palermo, he invested Roger as Count of Sicily. Robert died in 1085 and on the mainland was succeeded by one of his sons. In Sicily Roger established a firm rule and, while tolerant to the Greeks and Moslems, he created new Latin bishoprics and turned the Archbishopric of Palermo into a Catholic See. As a reward in 1098 the Pope granted him and his heirs the Apostolic Legateship in the island.

In 1101 Roger I died at the age of seventy and was succeeded by his younger son Roger II, who was then eight years old and began to rule personally in 1112. Roger now claimed all the Hautville possessions on the mainland as well as in Sicily, and though resisted by Pope Honorius II he was in 1129 recognised as Duke of Naples, Capua and the other Hautville possessions. Honorius II died in February 1130 and two rival Popes, Anacletus II and Innocent II, were elected. Roger gave his support to Anacletus and Innocent fled to France. Roger considered that in order to hold his possessions together it was essential for him to obtain the royal title. On 27th September 1130 Pope Anacletus in a Bull granted Roger the title of King of Sicily, Apulia and Calabria, Roger was crowned in Palermo on Christmas Day 1130, and took the more pretentious title of King of Sicily and Italy. In 1138 Anacletus died and Roger sought the confirmation of his title from Innocent II, who, having been defeated by Roger at Galuccio, invested him with the title of *Rex Scilliae Ducatus Apuliae et Principato Capuae*. Roger now became one of the greatest kings of Europe and established Sicily as the leading maritime power of the Mediterranean. He died at Palermo on 26th February 1154 and was succeeded by his fourth son, William I, the Bad, who had been crowned in his father's lifetime in 1151. William was not recognised by Pope Adrian II until 18th June 1156, but after Alexander III had succeeded to the Papacy in 1159 William became the champion of the Pope against the Emperor. In fact, in November 1165, Alexander III was installed in the Lateran by a guard of Normans. William I died on 7th May 1166 and was succeeded by his son William II, the Good, who came of age in 1171. In February 1177 he married Joan, the daughter of Henry II of England, and she was crowned at Palermo. William II died in November 1189 leaving no children and the crown passed to Tancred, the illegitimate grandson of King Roger. He was crowned at Palermo in January 1190. Constance, the daughter of King Roger and wife of the Emperor Henry VI, established a rival claim to the Sicilian throne, and although Tancred was recognised by the Pope in 1192, after he had surrendered the royal legateship in Sicily, he only survived until 1194, when he died a few days after his son Roger, whom he had made joint king. His Queen, Sibilla, was appointed Regent for her second son William III, but the Emperor Henry VI descended upon Sicily and claimed the crown, which he received at Palermo on Christmas Day 1194. Tancred's family fell into his hands and William III appears to have died in Germany in 1198. Henry only remained in Sicily a few months and left his wife Constance as Regent. He returned in 1197 and died at Messina on 28th September of that year and was buried at Palermo.

The Norman Kings of Italy, while following the Roman liturgical practice, borrowed from the Eastern Empire forms of court ceremonial, particularly with regard to their insignia. During the periods such as in 1143 and 1158, when there was a rapprochement between the Sicilian and Byzantine Courts, Greek artists were encouraged to emigrate into Sicily, and during the intervening period, which was one of bitter emnity, King Roger's Admiral George of Antioch raided Thebes and the Peloponnesus and carried off silk workers and others to Sicily as prisoners. These were established in a workshop attached to the palace, where they engaged in silk weaving and embroidery and also in the manufacture of gold and jewelled ornaments, while other artists and their Sicilian pupils produced the wonderful mosaics of the Cathedrals of Cefalu and Monreale and the royal castle and Palatine Chapel at Martorana.[1] These workshops turned out numerous vestments and crowns and other royal ornaments, the style of which was copied from Byzantium, as can be seen in numerous iconographic representations of the kings. In the Church of Martorana in Palermo there is a mosaic depicting the coronation of Roger (*Plate 128, a*), and at Monreale is one of the coronation of William II. Both these show the Kings being crowned by Christ, which is characteristic of Byzantine iconography following the end of the iconoclastic controversy in the IX century, when the Patriarch's part in the coronation ritual had been established. It may, however, be that the Kings wished to demonstrate that they received their crowns from God and not from the Pope. In each case the King is wearing a crown in the Byzantine style. On their coins and seals the Norman kings invariably wore the arched

[1] These have been exhaustively analysed by Dr Otto Demus in the *Mosaics of Norman Sicily*. See also Prof. di Pietro's *I Musaici Siciliani dell' eta Normanna*, Palermo 1946.

Byzantine crown or *kamelaukion*, but in accordance with the usage in Constantinople which they copied they had crowns of various shapes which they wore on numerous ceremonial occasions. We know, however, that the Norman kings had a special coronation crown given to Roger II in 1130 by Pope Anacletus II. This was the *Corona Regni Siciliæ et Calabriæ et Apuliæ* and it was regarded as indispensable for each legitimate king to receive it at his coronation.[1] This was still in use at the coronation of Henry VI, and it was probably used at the coronations of Frederick II in 1198 and his son Henry in 1212.

In the Basilica of St Nicholas at Bari there is a metal plaque representing the coronation of King Roger. It is oblong in shape and is said to have been placed on the architrave of the Tabernacle by the King himself. It portrays in enamel a scene of St Nicholas in the act of crowning the King. The King is dressed in a flowered tunic with a stole and holds in his left hand an orb, and in his right hand a Byzantine *labarum*, on the panel of which is the inscription *Rogerius Rex*. St Nicholas is clothed in pontifical dress and with his left hand is grasping a crozier, while with his right hand he places on Roger's head a crown in the form of a rigid circlet. Underneath is the legend *Sanctus Nicholaus*. According to local tradition this scene gives expression to what is believed to be a historical fact that it was by the intercession of St Nicholas that Roger returned to the fold of the church and obtained the legitimate title of the King of Sicily, Duke of Apulia and Prince of Calabria.[2] Contrary to Byzantine practice, the orb had in fact been delivered at the first Sicilian coronation and the words in the German coronation *ordo*, which was used on this occasion, were altered from *sceptrum et baculum* to *sceptrum ac regnum*,[3] *regnum* being used to describe the orb in the Sicilian kingdom. In 1170, when William II held a coronation festival, the instructions laid down that the king should appear with diadem, sceptre and orb, and on the occasion of his wedding in 1177 the King wore his diadem and bore the sceptre and orb, while the sword, shield and lance were carried before him. According to a letter from the Senate and people of Rome to King Conrad III, Pope Eugenius III granted King Roger the verge and ring and the dalmatic, mitre and sandals, but Schramm[4] argues against this and concludes that, although it may have been contemplated, the right to use the mitre was not, in fact, conferred upon the Kings of Sicily. Among the other royal vestments depicted by Norman kings was the Byzantine *lorum*, which was brought into use by Roger II.

Although Roger de Hovenden asserts that the graves of Tancred and his son Roger were despoiled of their regalia this was not the case, as it was not the custom for the Norman kings to be buried with regalia. No royal ornaments were found in the graves of Roger II or William I, and the protocol describing the opening of the grave of Henry VI in 1491 states explicitly that no jewels were found. In this the kings seem to have followed Byzantine practice, and in the case of William I and Henry VI it was found that the Kings' heads were wrapped round with silken bands from each side of

---

[1] Josef Deér: *Der Kaiserornat Friedrichs II*, Berne 1952.
[2] This information was given to the author by the Prefect of Bari in June 1938.
[3] P. Schramm: *Sphaire, Globus, Reichsapfel*.
[4] P. Schramm: *Herrschaftszeichen und Staatssymbolik*, Vol. I page 78 ff.

which hung strips of the same material.[1] In the Treasury of the Basilica of St Nicholas of Bari a royal crown (*Plate 128, b*)[2] is preserved which is attributed to King Roger II, who was the first benefactor of the Basilica. According to local tradition, after his reconciliation with the Church, Roger was obliged to cause the crown with which, in 1131, the anti-Pope Anacletus II had crowned him [*sic*] to be hung beside the tomb of St Nicholas, who was buried there in 1087.[3] Schramm[4] suggests that it is a votive crown. Certainly the poor workmanship and the crude manufacture makes it improbable that it was a crown for personal use, and it seems more likely to have been made as a votive crown to be hung above the tomb of St Nicholas.

The crown is a narrow circlet of bronze with a plaque bearing a figure of an angel set in front and similar plaques at each side. There was a fourth plaque on the back of the crown but this is now missing. These plaques are roughly riveted to the rim and are more than twice the height of the circlet, the top part conforming in general outline to a crude form of fleur-de-lis. Between each plaque are set one large and two small precious stones and below these stones are a series of holes. On the upper rim is another series of holes similar but more numerous. The bronze between the stones is chased with a design of leaves which are enamelled. The circlet is 26 cm in diameter.

On the death of Henry VI the Kingdom of Sicily was inherited by his son Frederick, a member of the Hohenstaufen family and heir of the Norman kings through his mother. Although not yet four years of age he was crowned at Palermo on 17th May 1198. His mother, who had assumed the Government, died a few months later leaving Pope Innocent III as Regent of the kingdom and guardian of the young King. When he was fourteen Frederick was declared of age and in the following year married Constance, daughter of Alphonso II of Aragon and widow of King Emeric of Hungary. Despite the reluctance of his wife and the Sicilian nobles he accepted an invitation to go to Germany to succeed the Emperor Otto IV, who had been declared deposed. He recognised the papal supremacy in Sicily, and Pope Innocent III agreed to the coronation of his son Henry as King of Sicily, which took place in 1212. Henry's reign was of no importance as he, too, soon went to Germany, where he was crowned King of the Romans, and having rebelled against his father died in obscurity in Italy as a prisoner. His father, who became the Emperor Frederick II, had a greater affection for Sicily than for any other of his realms; he died on 13th December 1250 and was buried at Palermo. He left the Kingdom of Sicily to his son Conrad IV, who had been chosen King of the Romans in 1237. Although he assumed the Sicilian royal title he died four years after his father and was nominally succeeded by his son Conradin. Manfred, a natural son of Frederick II, who had been administering the kingdom with success in the absence of his half-brother Conrad IV and his nephew Conradin, was, however, crowned King of Sicily at Palermo on 10th August 1258, as a result of a report which later proved to be false that Conradin had died. The Pope excommunicated Manfred and

---

1 Deér: op. cit.

2 F. Nitto di Vito: 'S. Nicola Tesore', in *Noblessima*, Vol. 12, Naples 1093. Hubert Graf Waldburg-Wolfegg: *Vom Südreich der Hohenstaufen*, Munich 1954.

3 Information provided by the Prefect of Bari in 1938.

4 P. Schramm: *Herrschaftszeichen und Staatssymbolik*, Vol. III, p. 908.

declared his coronation void, but the King was undeterred and gained much support in Italy. He retained the Sicilian crown, promising to leave the kingdom to Conradin on his death. Pope Innocent IV determined to crush the Hohenstaufens and offered the Kingdom of Sicily in turn to Richard of Cornwall and in 1255 to Henry III of England for his son Edmund Crouchback. In 1262 Pope Urban IV, a Frenchman, offered Charles, Count of Anjou, brother of Louis IX of France, the Kingdom of Sicily and Naples. After prolonged negotiations Urban's successor, Clement IV, confirmed the arrangements and Charles accepted the Kingdom of the Two Sicilies as a fief of the Church. He went to Rome, where he was crowned by the Pope in 1265. He then collected an army and marched against Manfred, who was defeated and perished at the Battle of Benevento, in 1266. Conradin then took up the contest but he, too, was defeated, taken prisoner and beheaded, and with his death the House of Hohenstaufen became extinct.

The Emperor Henry VI, by his marriage in 1186 to Constance, daughter of King Roger II, aunt and heiress of William II, had inherited the treasure of the Norman kings at Palermo. He was not able to take possession of it until he entered Palermo and was crowned King of Sicily on 25th December 1194. Early in the following year he moved the treasure to Germany, and contemporary writers relate that it needed 150 pack animals to transport it across the Alps. Unfortunately there is no detailed list of the treasure which was taken to the Hohenstaufen Castle of Trifels, where the imperial treasure was kept, but many of the items were disposed of as gifts, especially to churches. Deér[1] deals with this fully. It seems improbable that the Sicilian coronation crown was taken, but Schramm[2] suggests that two women's crowns of Sicilian origin which were for a time in the Treasury of Bamberg Cathedral may have come from this treasure. By the time that Henry's son, Frederick II, became Emperor there were included in the imperial treasure kept at Trifels a coronation mantle of King Roger II, the alb and dalmatic made in 1185 for King William II, the red stockings probably also made for William II and a belt or *cingulum* dating from the XII century. It seems that Frederick II used these at his imperial coronation and that they thus became part of the imperial ornaments, though one writer[3] has argued that the Sicilian vestments did not come into general use until the Hapsburgs. But they did, in any case, come into regular use and are today in the Vienna Treasury.

In 1781 the tombs of Frederick II and his wife, the Empress Constance of Aragon, at Palermo were opened.[4] In the tomb of Frederick II the Emperor was found to be clothed in coronation robes, on his head was a silver crown decorated with very small pearls and stones, at his left side was a short sword, on his finger was a ring with a large emerald, and a plain metal globe without decoration or a cross, lay by his head.

In the grave of Constance of Aragon, who had been crowned Empress with Frederick II in 1220 and had died in 1222, was found a very distinctive crown (*Plate 129, a*). This was placed in the Cathedral Treasury, where it still is, but it did not attract much serious attention until recently. The crown has been dealt with thoroughly by Deér,[5]

---

[1] Deér: op. cit.   [2] P. E. Schramm: *Herrschaftszeichen und Staatssymbolik*, Vol. III p. 830 ff.
[3] G. Haupt: *Die Reichsinsignien.*
[4] Dom F. Danielli: *Regali Sepolleri del Duomo et Palermo*, Napoli 1859.   [5] Deér: op. cit.

whose conclusions are of great interest. The crown is a *kamelaukion*, hemispherical in shape, with a cap which fits the head closely on which is a circlet of pearls; it is set with precious stones in tubular settings on gold ornaments. From the circlet rise two arches of similar design with a large pear-shaped ruby at the point of intersection. Round the lower edge of the cap is a row of small fleurs-de-lis and on each side hangs a pendant ornament. As Deér has conclusively shown that arched crowns were not worn by women, the crown must have been one belonging to Frederick II, who is known to have continued to have made use of the Palermo workshops for the manufacture of rich ornaments. Frederick had several crowns, and this must have been one which he used as King of Sicily. Schramm[1] gives as the explanation as to how one of Frederick's crowns would have been found in his wife's tomb that the twenty-seven-year-old King, feeling strong emotion at the death of his wife, put his own crown into her grave, a piece of himself, and thereby a guarantee of insoluble unity in their destiny until the day of the Last Judgment.

In the Treasury of the Cathedral at Catania there is a reliquary bust of St Agatha on whose head there is a crown (*Plate 128, d*). On the reliquary bust there is an inscription saying it was made by Giovanni de Bartoli and his father. At that time Marzial, Bishop of Catania, was Chancellor to the Emperor Frederick III who in 1373 sent him on a mission to the Papal Court at Avignon. Marzial died at Avignon and his successor, Bishop Elias, brought the reliquary back with him to Catania where it was received on 3rd December 1377.

According to tradition the crown on the bust was the gift of Richard Cœur de Lion while on a visit to his brother-in-law on his way to the Crusades. There is little authentic information about the crown but it is improbable that it was the gift of Richard. Churchill[2] draws attention to the similarity of this crown with one described in an inventory taken in the first half of the XIV century of the jewels belonging to Duke Amadeus of Savoy.

The crown weighs 818 grams of gold. Mr C. C. Oman of the Victoria and Albert Museum has provided the author with the following comment:

> The crown is formed of thirteen oblongs embossed with oak-leaves. Each is set with an oval stone and is surmounted by a fleur-de-lis which is decorated with garnets, sapphires, etc., and with transfixed pearls on the edges. The general appearance of the crown suggests a period considerably later than the Hohenstaufens, at earliest the late XIII century.

THE KINGDOM OF THE TWO SICILIES

The coronation of Charles I of Anjou as King of Naples and Sicily opened up a new chapter in the history of the monarchy in southern Italy. Having become master of the two kingdoms he instituted an oppressive, ruthless and cruel despotism in Sicily which eventually led to a popular rising on Easter Day, 1282, which is known as the Sicilian Vespers. It resulted in the murdering of almost all the French in the island, which was

1 P. Schramm: *Herrschaftszeichen und Staatssymbolik.*
2 S. J. A. Churchill: *Burlington Magazine,* Vol. X, 1906.

left to its own people. The following September Peter of Aragon, who through his marriage to Constance, the daughter of Manfred, claimed the rights of the House of Hohenstaufen, landed in Palermo and was chosen King. Affairs in Aragon demanded his attention and he was unable to spend much time in Sicily. In 1285 both rival Kings died. The death of Peter led to Sicily and Aragon being separated. His elder son, Alphonso, became King of Aragon and his second son, James, King of Sicily. Despite a papal interdict James was crowned King at Palermo, but in 1291 Alphonso died and he left Sicily to take up the throne of Aragon, leaving his brother Frederick as lieutenant of the island kingdom. Meanwhile Charles II, son of Charles I, was a prisoner in the hands of the King of Sicily. He was liberated on the understanding that he would retain Naples but leave Sicily to the King of Aragon. On his return to the mainland in 1289 he went to Rieti to meet the new Pope, Nicholas IV, who absolved him of all his inconvenient promises and crowned him King of the Two Sicilies. There is in the Basilica of St Nicholas of Bari a sceptre (*Plate 128, c*) which, according to tradition, Charles II, in order to show his humility, placed on the tomb of St Nicholas to indicate that he was a vassal of the great Saint of Myra and Protector of Bari. It is a steel rod covered with gilded copper, 38 cm long. It is broken at the top and was originally much longer than at present.[1]

When James succeeded to Aragon he made peace with Charles II in 1295 and renounced Sicily, receiving in exchange Sardinia and Corsica and the hand of Charles's daughter, but the people of Sicily would not accept this arrangement and in 1296 Frederick III was crowned King at Palermo on 25th March.[2] He then had to defend Sicily against attacks from the mainland, and he suffered reverses which led to a treaty in 1305 by which Pope Boniface VIII acknowledged him as King of Trinacria for life, Frederick agreeing not to use the name of Sicily. Charles II died in 1309 and was succeeded by his second son, Robert, who was crowned King of the Two Sicilies at Naples on 3rd August 1309. The terms of the treaty which Frederick had made with the Pope were never properly carried out, and Frederick again took the title of King of Sicily, which was also used, on his death in 1337, by his son Peter, who succeeded him. There were now two Kingdoms of Sicily and two Kings, although as a matter of convenience the King of the mainland was usually spoken of as King of Naples.[3] Both Peter and Robert died in 1342. Peter left an infant son, Louis, and the island kingdom kept its independence until 1416 when it was united with Aragon under King Alphonso, who in 1435 became King of Naples and Sicily. Sicily and Naples were again separated from 1458 to 1553 when the crowns were united with that of Spain. Subsequently there were two further separations, the first from 1713 to 1720 and the second from 1806 to 1815, but at other times the island formed part of the Kingdom of the Two Sicilies. In Naples Robert's son having died, his grand-daughter Joanna, wife of Andrew of

[1] Information supplied by the Prefect of Bari in 1938.

[2] Although he was the second Frederick of Sicily he took the title of Frederick III because his predecessor of that name was well known as the Emperor Frederick II, and he, himself, was the third son of King Peter.

[3] The title King of Naples was only used formally by Philip of Spain, Joseph Bonaparte and Joachim Murat.

a   *Crown found in grave of the Empress Constance. Treasury, Palermo Cathedral* (p. 430)

b   *Coronation of Victor Amadeus as King of Sicily in Palermo, 1713. Formerly in the Royal Palace, Turin* (p. 433)

a (above, left)   *Portrait of Charles, King of Naples and Sicily. National Museum, San Martino, Naples* (p. 436)

b (above, right)   *Portrait of King Ferdinand IV. National Museum, San Martino, Naples* (p. 436)

c   *Portrait of Queen Maria Isabella. National Museum, San Martino, Naples* (p. 436)

Hungary, succeeded to the throne. Andrew was murdered and his brother, Louis, King of Hungary, came to Italy and drove out Joanna. The anti-Pope Clement VII refused to recognise his claims and he returned to Hungary. Joanna was now recalled and with her husband, Louis of Taranto, she was crowned at Naples by the Pope's legate in 1352. Pope Urban IV now declared Charles of Durazzo, great-great-grandson of Charles II, to be King of Sicily and Naples. In 1381 he conquered the kingdom and murdered Joanna, and he himself died in 1386. There were now two rival claimants to the throne, Louis II of Anjou, who had been nominated heir by Joanna and was crowned by the anti-Pope Clement VII, and Ladislas, the seven-year-old son of Charles III, who was crowned by Pope Boniface IX in 1389. Ladislas died in 1414 and was succeeded by his sister, Joanna II. During a rather sordid reign she nominated one of her lovers, Alphonso of Aragon, to succeed to the throne on her death, which occurred in 1435. Alphonso had already inherited Sicily in 1416 and thus reunited the kingdoms. On his death in 1458 he left Naples to his illegitimate son, Ferdinand I, and Sicily, Sardinia and Aragon to his brother John. Ferdinand was not crowned as Pope Calixtus III declared the line of Aragon to be extinct and the kingdom a fief of the Church. Ferdinand died in 1394 and was succeeded by his son Alphonso II, who was crowned on 8th May 1494, but Charles VIII of France invaded Italy with a view to claiming the rights of the House of Anjou. He entered Naples and was crowned in the Church of St Januaire, and Alphonso abdicated in favour of his son Ferdinand II, who, however, died two years later, in 1496, and he was succeeded by his brother Frederick. In 1502 the whole kingdom passed to the Spanish crown and was ruled by Spanish viceroys for the next 203 years. The Archduke Charles of Austria became King of Naples in 1707, and in 1713 Duke Victor Amadeus of Savoy was crowned King of Sicily at Palermo (*Plate 129, b*), although he exchanged his kingdom for that of Sardinia in 1718. In 1734 Charles of Bourbon, son of Philip V of Spain, conquered Naples and Sicily and was crowned at Palermo on 3rd July of that year.[1] This was the last coronation in Sicily. In 1759 Charles III succeeded to the Spanish throne and abdicated the Two Sicilies in favour of his eight-year-old son Ferdinand. When in 1799 the French took Naples the King established his court at Palermo. He returned to Naples in 1802 but was again forced to flee to Sicily in 1805. Napoleon appointed his brother Joseph Bonaparte as King of Naples, and he entered his capital in 1806. In 1808 Napoleon conferred the crown of Spain on Joseph and appointed his brother-in-law Joachim Murat as King of Naples. In 1816 Ferdinand having returned to Naples proclaimed himself King of the Two Sicilies and in 1825 he died. His son Francis I succeeded to the throne but died in 1830, and was succeeded by his son Ferdinand II until his death in 1859, when his son Francis II, the last King of the Two Sicilies, came to the throne. On 18th February 1861 Victor Emmanuel became King of Italy, and Naples and Sicily ceased to be a separate kingdom.

There is no single work dealing with the coronation ceremonies and regalia of the Kingdom of the Two Sicilies. In the catalogues of the National Library at Naples there are many references to documents relating to the claims of the Holy See to rights over

[1] According to Harold Acton in *The Bourbons of Naples* this was the nineteenth coronation at Palermo.

the Kingdom of Naples and the disputes concerning them. It is necessary, therefore, to collect such scanty particulars as there are on our subject from various sources.

When Robert the Wise was to be crowned on 3rd August 1309 no record could be found of the ceremony of the coronation of his father Charles II at Rieti by the Pope on 28th May 1289. Pope Clement V instructed Cardinal Giacomo Stefaneschi Gaetani, Cardinal-Deacon of S. Giorgio al Velabro, to compose an *ordo ad coronandum et inundendum regem Cicilie.*[1] This *ordo* with subsequent amendments and with the elimination of all mention of King Robert was inserted in the 'Cerimonial' of Cardinal Stefaneschi.[2] The following are the most important features. The coronation of kings was performed by the proper Metropolitan with the assistance of the bishops of the kingdom.[3] Before the Mass the king was presented and took the oath. The king was anointed with the oil of the catechumens in the form of a cross on the right arm and between the shoulders. The king then donned a garment like a dalmatic and the royal mantle. In the second part of the ceremony the king was invested with the royal sword which he handed to his swordbearer who sheathed it. The crown was placed on the king's head by the archbishop jointly with the other bishops after which he received the sceptre and the orb. The king was then enthroned and received the acclamation of the people. The oath of the King of the Two Sicilies required him to pay 'liege homage' to the Holy See *pro regno Siciliae ac tota terra quae est citra Pharum usque ad confina terrarum ejusdem Romanae Ecclesiae . . . excepta civitate Beneventana cum toto territorio . . . et pertinentis suis,* but the extent of the pontifical claims was sometimes disputed.

Some details are available about the coronation of Alphonso II in 1494. One account[4] runs:

on the 8th day of May on Thursday, the Ascension Day of Our Lord Jesus Christ, in the year 1494, it having been appointed that the aforesaid Lord King be crowned and anointed in the principal church of Naples by Cardinal Giovanno Borgia, Archbishop of Monreal, Cardinal of the title of Santa Suzanna, Envoy of the Pope Alexander VI, the wings of the main altar were well adorned with the church draperies and seats provided for the Christian Embassies and also for the Grand Turkish Embassy and the Mass was celebrated and the aforesaid Majesty was anointed and crowned and supplied with everything as the aforesaid Majesty desired to ride on horseback in the City with crown, sceptre and globe preceded by the standard and also the sword. The steed was adorned with reins, crownpiece and saddle and the King's attire was of brocade and pearls, the horse being covered by the brocade mantle. The steed's bridle was held by the honoured sire duke *de trajecto* and the illustrious Alphonso *de piccolominibus* the Duke of Amalfi and other seigneurs and barons and gentlemen on foot and running persons went scattering silver coins.

---

[1] The original text of this *ordo* appears to be that shown in one of the codices relating to the Papal Liturgy preserved in the Municipal Library at Avignon. MS. 1706 Fol. 18–20.

[2] *Andrieu, Mich. Le Pontifical Romain at Moyen-age* T. III. Vatican City 1940, pp. 41–320, 667, 669.

[3] The first two kings of the Two Sicilies were crowned by the Pope himself, and subsequently the Pope, on several occasions, sent a special legate to perform the ceremony.

[4] Notar Giacomo: *The Chronicle of Naples.* MS. of the Brancaccian Library published by P. Garzilli, Naples 1845.

Another account[1] follows the general lines of the description already quoted but adds some details of the regalia. It says that the 'King rode in the City on a white horse and adorned with silver brocade', adding that this adornment was embellished with many precious stones and the King had on his head the crown 'estimated by many craftsmen to be worth more than one million thirty thousand ducats'. He also wore a solid gold buckle with two clasps estimated to be worth ninety thousand ducats and carried in his hand a rod with a dark red carbuncle on the top thereof estimated to be worth fifty thousand ducats. He was followed by the Grand Chamberlain Ettore Carafa bearing in his hand the royal sword 'that never was so beautiful nor so rich that was estimated at ten thousand ducats'; also by the Grand Master of the Stables bearing the King's shield of gilt, silver and precious stones and by a seigneur who bore the royal helmet, the vizor thereof had a 'buckle worth two hundred and twenty thousand ducats'. The chronicler expresses wonder at such a display of precious objects and luxury surrounding the entire ceremony.

The writer Mazella[2] devotes a chapter to 'the coronations of the Kings of Naples' in which he maintains that only a few enjoyed the prerogative of the coronation and anointment by order of the Pope. The ceremony was attended by the seven great officers of the kingdom clad in purple garments lined with white ermine with rich head-pieces, and by the mayor of the city of Naples. The king was dressed with sandals embroidered with jewels and pearls, with the dalmatic and with the cope or mantle. He states that the anointing on the shoulder and on the right arm denoted that the king would bear the weight of the affairs of the kingdom and that he would employ the sword to preserve it. Afterwards the king was dressed with a regal robe of purple falling down to his feet and lined with sable richly adorned with gold and jewels to signify charity. There then followed the delivery of the gold sceptre, the top of which was wrought with pearls and jewels with which the king was enjoined religiously to command the people. He was invested with the naked sword in the right hand with which to pursue the enemies of the Christian name. The ring was then placed on his finger and the bracelet on his arm in order that he be faithful and pure in good deeds. The king was invested with the golden globe 'to figure in the kingdom in order that he uphold the same with singular piety, virtue and constance'. Finally the apostolic legate placed the imperial crown on the head of the King of Naples. It was 'divided in two parts adorned with many jewels to denote glory'. The king was enthroned on a 'chair covered with gold brocade' and received the homage. The king then rode through the city, under a canopy embroidered in gold. Another writer, Troyli[3] expresses doubts at the assertion of Mazella and others that since the time of Charles I of Anjou the Kings of Naples had used the closed crown similar to the imperial crown.

Troyli also gives a description of the crown used by Charles III at his coronation at Palermo in 1735:

> This majestic extremely rich and well-devised crown was of pyramidal shape composed of a covered circle from which there protruded five carved rods sustaining an entirely spherical globe

1 Giuliano Passero: *Journals*, edited by V. M. Altobelli in 1785.
2 Scipione Mazella: *Description of the Kingdom of Naples*.
3 P. Troyli: *General History of the Kingdom of Naples*, Vol. IV, Part III, 1751.

representing the world, surmounted by a golden cross. The entire weight of the crown was 19 oz, i.e. 5 oz diamonds, 13 oz gold and 1 oz silver, which served as a setting for the 361 diamonds adorning the crown, and though the diamonds were all large and perfect, one there was on the central arch that surpassed all the others in size weighing 168 gr, but it was not also entirely perfect.

The value of this marvellous crown amounted to one million two hundred thousand ducats. The clever designer and craftsman who made the crown was Claudio Imbert of Avignon, who was at that time held in the King's service.

There are two descriptions of the coronation of Charles III; one is entitled 'the account of the Solemn Entrance, Acclamation and Coronation of Charles, King of the Two Sicilies, of Jerusalem etc. . . . which took place in Palermo on 30th June 1735'. The other is to be found in MS. XV.G. 32 in the National Library at Naples.

Although subsequent Bourbon Kings of Naples were not crowned a formal royal crown was adopted for heraldic purposes, and after the proclamation of the union of the crowns of Naples and Sicily in 1816 a distinctive crown appears to have been made, and can be seen in portraits of Ferdinand IV[1] and his consort (*Plate 130, b and c*). The king's crown had four arches each with a row of pearls with a jewelled circlet surmounted with fleurs-de-lis and crosses, also set with jewels. The queen's crown was in a similar style but smaller. The king's sceptre was a jewelled rod like a military baton. Joseph Bonaparte is depicted in an engraving with a crown and sceptre, but these were probably personal ornaments which he may have taken to Spain with him as they do not appear in the reign of Murat.

THE KINGDOM OF SARDINIA

The House of Savoy ruled over the territory of Savoy and Piedmont for nine centuries. Although at first they were only counts we learn from an inventory taken in 1344 of the treasure of Duke Amadeus VI, popularly known as the Conti Verde, that they possessed crowns. Three fleur-de-lis crowns are mentioned of which one is described as:

a golden crown which has twelve fleurs-de-lis and twelve clusters, and in each fleur-de-lis there is a ruby in the middle and 4 emeralds set around a large ruby surmounted by a pearl. In six of the clusters there are rubies and the other six emeralds. Each of the clusters has 9 pearls; the weight is given as two marks six oz.

In 1416 the Emperor Sigismund conferred upon Count Amadeus VIII the rank and title of Duke. In 1439 Amadeus VIII was chosen as Pope, although a layman. He abdicated the ducal title, assuming that of Pope Felix V, but in 1449 he renounced the tiara and died in retirement two years later. After the abdication of Amadeus VIII a succession of dukes ruled Savoy. The fourteenth duke, Charles Emmanuel II, who died in 1675, was succeeded by his only son, Victor Amadeus II, who was still a boy and whose imperious mother, Jeanne of Savoy-Nemours, was known as Madame Reale and acted as Regent. Victor Amadeus I married Anne of Orleans, granddaughter of

---

[1] Ferdinand I as King of the Two Sicilies and IV of Naples and Sicily.

Henrietta Maria and Charles I of England. In 1713, by the Treaty of Utrecht, he was made King of Sicily and was crowned with his consort at Palermo. But in 1720 the Powers obliged him to give up his kingdom and take Sardinia in exchange for Sicily. This arrangement allowed the House of Savoy to continue to rule over Savoy and Piedmont and to enjoy the royal title. As the King had already been anointed and crowned it was considered unnecessary to him to be crowned again as King of Sardinia. In 1730 he abdicated in favour of his son, Charles Emmanuel I, who, on his death in 1793, was succeeded by his son Victor Amadeus II, who in turn was succeeded by his son Charles Emmanuel II in 1796. The Court had been established at Turin, and although there was no coronation ceremony the kings and queens possessed crowns and sceptres, which are depicted in a series of portraits which are still preserved in the former royal palace there. The ducal regalia, which had consisted of an open coronet, a sceptre and a sword, can be seen in a painting of the wedding of Emmanuel Philibert to Margaret of Valois (*Plate 131, d*) (1553–80).

Some confusion arises by the sovereigns sometimes being numbered as Dukes of Savoy and at others as Kings of Sardinia. Thus King Victor Amadeus I was III as Duke of Savoy and King Charles Emmanuel I was III of Savoy.

There are several portraits of Victor Amadeus I (1720–30) showing different crowns, although the sceptre takes the form of a military baton bearing the cross of Savoy. One crown has four flat arches and is embellished with diamonds; a second has four tall arches and is set with flat diamonds and coloured stones *en cabochon*; a third (*Plate 131, a*) also has four high arches and is much more richly decorated with brilliants. In each the King wears a jewelled collar of the Savoy Order of the Annunziata. Charles Emmanuel I (*Plate 131, e*) (1730–73) is shown in his portraits with a simple royal crown with depressed arches and a plain short sceptre. The crowns continued to change their form in each reign, which suggests that they were personal crowns.

Victor Amadeus II (1773–96) is depicted with a crown with eight *ogee* half-arches and a short sceptre (*Plate 131, b*). Victor Emmanuel I (1802–21)[1] is shown with a crown with four arches set with pearls and the old military baton (*Plate 131, c*). A portrait of Charles Felix (1821–31) in the Palazzo Chiablese shows a crown in the Empire style (*Plate 132, a*), the circlet surmounted by triangular ornaments with crosses set between and there are eight tall *ogee* half-arches. The King has a military baton in his hand and over the royal mantle he wears the Collar of the Annunziata.

The queens also had crowns. A portrait of Maria Antonia Ferdinanda of Spain (*Plate 132, b*), consort of Victor Amadeus II, shows an elegant crown with a narrow circlet adorned with 16 pearls set in pairs between eight ornaments set with brilliants. On the circlet are eight strawberry leaves, each set with a large pearl from behind which rise eight half-arches decorated with brilliants and held by a ring of pearls. On the summit is a gold globe and a brilliant cross. Maria Giovanna Battista, the second wife of Charles Emmanuel II, has a different crown (*Plate 132, c*), the strawberry leaves being set with large diamonds and the arches each with a row of pearls. A portrait of Elisabeth Teresa di Lorena shows a crown with diamonds and pearls and also a sceptre.

1 In 1805 Sardinia was merged into Napoleon's Kingdom of Italy, but in 1814 Victor Emmanuel I was restored.

When Victor Emmanuel II, the last King of Sardinia, became King of Italy in 1861 the Iron Crown of Lombardy became the official crown of the Kingdom of Italy and, although a formal modern royal crown was used heraldically, the crowns, sceptres and batons used by the Kings of Sardinia were not preserved.

We have some information about the jewels of the House of Savoy. In the inventory of the crown jewels of the Ducal House dated 19th October 1679 the principal stone described was:

'a large table diamond set in a gold, black and white enamelled rim in the antique style weighing 54 carats with 3 appended pearls, pear-shaped, amongst which pearls is the "Pilgrim" weighing 45 carats and the other two 38 and 36 carats respectively. The gem was bequeathed to the Crown by Christine of France by her will dated 5 April 1562.'

This jewel was not mentioned in the inventory of 1772 in a manner in which it can be identified but the diamond may have been recut.

At the end of the XVIII century Victor, King of Sardinia, had sent some of his jewels to the Bank of Amsterdam, where they were deposited as security for a sum of 760,000 florins borrowed from the House of Renouard and Company. In 1795, when the French army occupied Amsterdam, these jewels fell into the hands of the French Republican Government. Some were handed over to Renouard in satisfaction of the debt, while the remainder were taken into the French Treasury and subsequently under the Empire were incorporated into the French crown jewels. The inventory of these jewels is still preserved and gives the following information:

Chapter I
A box containing hair ornaments, bows, strings of pearls, ear-rings, aigrettes and two epaulettes all in brilliants and pearls . . .

162,352 florins

Chapter II
A box containing three collars, two pairs of ear-rings, one aigrette, four bouquets of rubies, a great chain and two epaulettes all in diamonds . . .

196,486 florins

Chapter III
A box containing collars, ear-rings, bracelets and two crosses in brilliants and pearls . . .

229,759 florins

Chapter IV
A box containing necklaces, ear-rings, bows, hat ornaments, aigrettes, bracelets, crosses of the Orders of St Maurice and St Lazarus and others all in brilliants, sapphires and pearls . . .

190,239 florins

Chapter V
A box containing rings set with pearls, hat ornaments, aigrettes, crosses, etc., in brilliants . . .

172,883 florins

Chapter VI
A box containing ear-rings, brooches, bows, aigrettes, bracelets of pearls, emeralds, diamonds, etc. . . .

630,570 florins
_____
1,014,776 florins

a   *Detail of crown from portrait of King Victor Amadeus I* (p. 437)

b   *Detail of crown and sceptre from portrait of Victor Amadeus II* (p. 437)

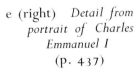

d   *Ducal coronet, sceptre and sword from a painting of the wedding of Emmanuel Philibert to Margaret of Valois. XVI Century* (p. 437)

c   (left)   *Crown and sceptre from portrait of Victor Emmanuel I* (p. 437)

e   (right)   *Detail from portrait of Charles Emmanuel I* (p. 437)

All in the Royal Palace, Turin

a   *Portrait of Charles Felix. Chiablese Palace, Turin*
(p. 437)

b   *Portrait of Queen Maria, consort of Victor Amadeus II*
Royal Palace, Turin (p. 437)

c   *Crown from portrait of Queen Maria, second wife of*
Charles Emmanuel II. Royal Palace, Turin (p. 437)

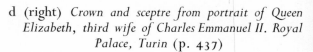

d   (right) *Crown and sceptre from portrait of Queen*
Elizabeth, third wife of Charles Emmanuel II. Royal
Palace, Turin (p. 437)

The only notable stone seems to have been a diamond of 17 carats which at the sale of the French crown jewels in 1887 fetched 18,400 francs.

More recently the House of Savoy possessed a famous furlong of pearls which is to be seen in a portrait of Queen Margherita by Gardigiani. This consisted of an historic pearl necklace bequeathed by her mother-in-law, Queen Maria Adelaide, to which a string of pearls was added on each anniversary of Queen Margherita's wedding. In all there were thirty-two strings of pearls which became family heirlooms.

BIBLIOGRAPHY

ACTON, HAROLD — *The Bourbons of Naples*, London 1956.

ANTOLINI, F. — *Li Re d'Italia inauguratio no con la Corona Ferrea du Odocare firo Ferdinando I*, Milan 1838.

BAPST, G. — *Les Joyaux de la Couronne de France*, Paris 1889.

BARAGGIA, G. LES — *La Regina Theodolinda.*

BARBIER, DE MONTAULT — 'Inventaires de la Basilique royale de Monza', in *Bulletin Monumental*, 46, 1880.

'L'Église royale et collégiate de Saint Nicholas à Bari', in *Revue de l'art Chrétien* 1883. *Le Sceptre de Charles II d'Anjou.*

BAYER, T. S. — 'De duobus diadematibus in museo imperatorio', in *Commentarii acad. scient. imperialis Petropolitane*, Vol. VIII, St Petersburg 1741.

BELLANI, A. — *La Corona Ferrea del Regno d'Italia*, Milan 1819.

BOCK, FRANZ — *Die Kleinodien des heiligen römischen Reiches deutscher Nation*, Leipzig 1864.

BOMBELLI, R. — *Storia Della Corona Ferrea dei re d'Italia*, 1870 Florence.

BOSEA, P. P. — *Disputatio de Corona Ferrea . . . cum responsione ad Muratorum*, MS. in Libraria del Capitolo di Monza.

BUNT, C. — *The Goldsmiths of Italy*, London 1926.

BURGESS, W. — 'Memoir on the relics of Theodolinda at Monza', in *Archaeological Journal*, Vol. XIV.

CHURCHILL, S. J. A. — 'Giovanni Bartelo of Siena', in *Burlington Magazine*, Vol. 10, 1906.

DANIELLI, DOM F. — *Regali Sepolleri del Duomo di Palermo*, 1784.

DEÉR, JOSEF — *Der Kaiserornat Friedrichs II*, Berne 1952.

DEMUS, DR OTTO — *Mosaics in Norman Sicily*, London 1948.

ELZE, REINHARD N. — *Herrschaftszeichen und Staatssymbolik*, Chapter 19.

FONTANINI, G. — *Dissertatio de corona ferrea Longobardorum*, Rome 1717.

FRISI, A. — *Memorie della chiesa Monzese*, 1770.

Memorie storiche di Monza e sua corte, Monza 1794.

FUMIGALLI, C., AND BELTRAMI, L. — *La Cappella della Regina Theodolinda in Monza*, Milan 1891.

GIACOMO, NOTAR	*The Chronicle of Naples, 1845.*
HAASE, K.	*Die Königskrönungen in Oberitalien und die 'eiserne' Krone,* Strassburg 1901.
KROENER, A.	*Wahl und Krönung der Deutschen Kaiser und Könige in Italien,* Freiburg 1901.
MAURICE, E.	*'L'Arte in Onore de Sancta Agata', in L'Arte Roma, IX.*
MAZELLA, SCIPIONE	*Description of the Kingdom of Naples.*
MELY, F. DE	*'La Couronne de Fer', in Gazette des Beaux Arts, 3, S, XVII, 1897.*
MURATORI, L. A.	*Antiquitates Italiae.*
	'De corona ferrea . . . commentarius', in Anecdota Latina, Rerum Ital. Script. XIV, Vol. II, 1698.
NITTO DI VITO, F.	*'S. Nicola Tesore', in Noblissimi, Vol. 12, Naples 1903.*
OPPENHEIMER, SIR FRANCIS	*Frankish Themes and Problems,* London 1952.
PASSERO, GIULIANO	*Journals, 1785.*
PIETRI, PROFESSOR	*I Musaici Siciliani dell' eta Normanna,* Palermo 1946.
	De Culta Coronae Ferrarae.
SCHRAMM, P. E.	*Herrschaftszeichen und Staatssymbolik.*
	Sphaire, Globus und Reichsapfel, Stuttgart 1958.
TROYLI, P.	*General History of Naples.*
WALDBURG-WOLFEGG, GRAF HUBERT	*Vom Südreich der Hohenstaufen,* Munich 1954. 1954.
WEIXLGÄRTNER, A.	*Führer durch die weltliche Schatzkammer,* Vienna 1937.
ZUCCHI, B.	*Historica della Corona Ferrea,* Milan 1607.

KINGS OF ITALY

LOMBARDY

575	Authéri elected. Married Theodolinda	701	Ragimbert
		701	Arimbert II
592	Agilulf. Also married Theodolinda	712	Ansprand elected
615	Adaloald	712	Luitprand
625	Arioald	744	Rachis
636	Rothari	749	Aistolf
652	Rodoald	756	Desiderius. End of Lombard Kingdom. Charlemagne assumes title of King of Lombardy
653	Aribert I		
661	Bertharit and Godebert		
662	Grimoald		
671	Bertharit again	780	Pepin. Crowned king in father's lifetime in Rome
686	Cunibert		
700	Luitbert	812	Bernard
		820	Lothair

GERMAN EMPERORS AND OTHERS

The German Emperors considered themselves to be kings of Italy by virtue of their election as German kings. Some did not consider a separate Italian coronation necessary.

875	Charles the Bald. Not crowned as King of Italy
877	Carloman. Not crowned
879	Charles III, the Fat. Crowned at Ravenna 880
888	Berengar I. ? Crowned in Pavia
920	Hugh of Provence
945	Lothair II
950	Berengar II
968	Berengar II and son, Adalbert, received crown from Byzantine Emperor
1002	Ardouin of Ivrea. Elected and crowned at Pavia on 15th February
1004	Emperor Henry II. Elected and crowned at Pavia on 14th May
	Ardouin again
1026	Emperor Conrad II. Crowned at Milan 23rd March
1026	Emperor Henry III. Not crowned as King of Italy
1054	Emperor Henry IV. Not crowned as King of Italy
1093	Conrad. Crowned at Monza. Deposed
1128	Conrad III. Crowned at Monza 29th June
1155	Emperor Frederick I Barbarossa. Crowned at Pavia 24th April
	From 1209 to 1308 the German Emperors were also Kings of Italy but were not crowned as such
1311	Emperor Henry VII. Crowned at Milan with his consort 6th January
1327	Emperor Louis IV, the Bavarian. Crowned at Milan with his consort 31st May
1355	Emperor Charles IV. Crowned at Milan 6th January
1376	Wenceslas. Not crowned
1401	Rupert. Not crowned
1431	Sigismund. Crowned Milan 21st November
1452	Frederick III. Crowned as King of Italy by Pope 16th March
1493	Maximilian I. Not crowned as King of Italy
1530	Charles V. Crowned at Bologna 22nd February
	From 1556–1792 German Emperors were not crowned as Kings of Italy
1805	Napoleon I. Crowned at Milan 26th May
1816	Emperor Francis I of Austria became King of new Lombardo-Venetian Kingdom
1838	Emperor Ferdinand I of Austria. Crowned at Milan, the last Italian coronation
1848	Emperor Francis Joseph

KINGS OF ITALY

1861	Victor Emmanuel II declared King of Italy
1878	Humbert I
1900	Victor Emmanuel III
1946	Humbert II. Abdicated June 1946

KINGS OF SARDINIA

1720 Victor Amadeus I of Savoy
1730 Charles Emmanuel I
1773 Victor Amadeus II
1796 Charles Emmanuel II
1802 Victor Emmanuel I
1805 Sardinia merged with Italy under Napoleon I
1814 Victor Emmanuel I restored
1821 Charles Felix
1831 Charles Albert
1849 Victor Emmanuel II

KINGDOMS OF NAPLES AND SICILY
(Norman Dynasty of the Kingdom of Sicily)

1046 Robert Guiscard invaded Southern Italy
1058 Roger I
1101 Roger II. Crowned King of Sicily, Apulia and Calabria at Palermo 25th December 1130
1151 William I, the Bad. Crowned in lifetime of his father
1166 William II, the Good. Consort, Joan of England, crowned at Palermo 1177
1189 Tancred. Crowned with consort, Sibilla, 1st January 1190. Created son, Roger, co-king 1194
1194 William III. Crowned
1194 Constance and her husband, the Emperor Henry VI. Crowned 25th December
1197 Emperor Frederick II. Crowned at Palermo 17th May
1212 Henry, son of Frederick, crowned in father's lifetime died 1250
1250 Conrad IV
1254 Conradin
1258 Manfred. Crowned at Palermo 10th August
1266 Charles of Anjou. Crowned at Rome

SEPARATION OF KINGDOMS 1282
Naples

1282 Charles I of Anjou
1285 Charles II. Crowned at Rieti 28th May 1289
1309 Robert the Wise. Crowned at Naples 3rd August
1343 Joanna I. Crowned with second husband, Louis of Taranto, Naples 1352
1381 Charles III of Durazzo
1382 Louis I of Anjou
1385 Louis II. Crowned at Naples in 1386
1386 Ladislas of Hungary. Crowned at Naples 1389
1414 Joanna II and Alphonso

Sicily

1282	Peter I of Aragon. Elected at Palermo	1342	Louis
		1355	Frederick III
1285	James I. Crowned at Palermo 1291	1376	Maria and Martin
		1402	Martin I
1295	Frederick III. Crowned at Palermo 25th March 1296	1409	Martin II
		1410	Ferdinand I
1337	Peter II	1416	Alphonso I

KINGS OF NAPLES AND SICILY

1435 Alphonso I
1458 Ferdinand I. Not crowned
1458 John of Aragon
1479 Ferdinand the Catholic of Spain
1494 Alphonso II. Crowned at Naples 8th May
1494 Charles VIII of France. Crowned at Naples
1495 Ferdinand II
1496 Frederick II

THE CROWN UNITED WITH SPAIN

1503 Ferdinand III of Spain
1516 Charles 1 (V of Spain)
1556 Philip I (II of Spain)
1598 Philip II (III of Spain)
1621 Philip III (IV of Spain)
1665 Charles II (of Spain)
1700 Philip IV (V of Bourbon)

KINGDOM OF NAPLES

1707 Charles III of Austria
1713 Victor Amadeus of Savoy. Crowned at Palermo with consort, Anne of Orleans

THE TWO SICILIES

1734 Charles IV (III of Spain). Crowned at Palermo 3rd July (last coronation)
1759 Ferdinand IV

KINGDOM OF NAPLES

1806 Joseph Napoleon Bonaparte
1808 Joachim Murat

ITALY

THE TWO SICILIES

1815   Ferdinand I, formerly Ferdinand IV of Naples and Sicily
1825   Francis I
1830   Ferdinand II
1859   Francis II
1861   Victor Emmanuel II of Sardinia as King of Italy

CHAPTER FIFTEEN

NETHERLANDS

In 1806 Napoleon created Holland into a kingdom and his brother Louis Bonaparte was proclaimed King. He was not crowned, however, and no regalia were made. His reign had lasted only four years when he abdicated. Holland was then united to France until its independence was restored and Belgium annexed to its dominions, and the Prince of Orange was proclaimed sovereign prince of the United Netherlands. On 16th March 1815, after Napoleon's return from Elba, the Prince of Orange assumed the title of King of the Netherlands, under the style of William I, and was solemnly proclaimed in The Hague. After the defeat of Napoleon, William made a state entry into Brussels for his accession proclamation. For this occasion a set of regalia was hurriedly made and is still preserved in the royal palace at The Hague (*Plate 133, a*). The ornaments, which are very simple in design, consist of a crown, a sceptre, an orb and a standard.

The crown of silver gilt is of the modern heraldic shape consisting of a broad fillet set with large single precious stones. Resting on the circlet are eight strawberry leaves with an imitation pearl in metal between each. From behind these spring the arches decorated with imitation pearls in metal and depressed at the point of junction. The crown is surmounted by a plain orb and cross.

The sceptre is of silver gilt unadorned with precious stones. It is somewhat short and on either side of the centre grip it is decorated with a leaf design. The top is surmounted by a royal crown.

The orb is of plain silver gilt and is of very simple design. The equator and horizontal band is represented by a thin rib. It is surmounted by a cross *pattée*. The standard is of silk and bears the arms of the kingdom on an orange background.

In 1831 Belgium was separated from Holland and the 1815 regalia were no longer appropriate for the reduced kingdom. When William I abdicated on 7th October 1840 it was found necessary to obtain a new set of regalia for the so-called coronation ceremony (*Plate 133, b*). Among the royal archives of the Netherlands is a document relating to the new regalia which reads as follows:

On 27th November 1840 supplied by my father Heer V. A. Bonebakker, of the firm of A. Bonebakker & Son, to H.M. King William II at The Hague to be used at his coronation:

One fine silver gilt royal crown, according to the known peculiar model, with stones and pearls mounted in gold as per attached sketch, with velvet cap for the inside, in a white *worte-houten* case dressed with fringes of velvet cloth.

For the silver and gold used for gilding, florins 1470.

As is known by the order and the prices agreed to the stones and pearls could not be genuine. Payment of the above-mentioned royal crown will be made on 3rd July 1841.

The crown, although generally following the design of that of 1815, is much more elegant and of much superior workmanship. The arches are not so depressed and the cross surmounting the orb is smaller.

The sceptre is of a different design and is longer. It is of silver gilt decorated with imitation pearls. At the top of the sceptre is a leaf design in which rests an orb and cross.

The orb is of silver gilt adorned with imitation precious stones. It has a broad band as equator and two upward bands as meridians. It is surmounted by a large cross. Both orb and sceptre were made by the Court Jewellers at The Hague.

The State Sword has a gilded handle set with imitation stones and pearls and with a scabbard of crimson velvet.

The Standard is similar to that of 1815, except that the background is of white silk and the arms of the kingdom are painted on. The artist was Van Hone.

These ornaments are kept in the royal palace at The Hague.

There is no true coronation ceremony. The sovereign proceeds to the Nieuwe Kerk at Amsterdam, where a religious service takes place during which the oath to the constitution is taken. The regalia are placed with a copy of the constitution of the realm on a table before the throne, and the sword and standard are carried by high officials. The existing regalia were used at the ceremony for William II in 1840, for that of William III in 1849, at that of Queen Wilhelmina in 1898, and at that of Queen Juliana in 1948. The regalia are not used at the State Opening of Parliament. At the funeral of the sovereign they are placed on the coffin.

Apart from the regalia there are no crown jewels in the proper sense, all State jewellery being the private property of the royal family. Streeter,[1] however, mentions two large diamonds as being in the possession of the royal family, one weighing 36 carats and known as the Bantam, and the other the Holland, also of 36 carats.

SOVEREIGNS OF THE NETHERLANDS

1815	William I
1840	William II
1849	William III
1890	Wilhelmina
1948	Juliana

[1] E. W. Streeter: *The Great Diamonds of the World.*

a *Regalia of King William I.*
Royal Palace. The Hague.
(p. 445)

b *Regalia of King William II.*
Royal Palace, The Hague
(p. 445)

a   *King's crown, 1818. Norges Bank,
Trondheim* (p. 454)

b   *Queen's crown, 1830, Norges Bank,
Trondheim* (p. 454)

c   *Crown prince's crown, 1846.
Norges Bank, Trondheim*
(p. 455)

CHAPTER SIXTEEN

NORWAY

From earliest times the kings in Norway were elected in a manner similar to that found in other European countries with a Teutonic population. There were twenty-nine districts or *fylker* and in each there was a king. He was elected by an Assembly of the people. A man of high standing proposed the most suitable man of the royal family as a candidate and named him king. The Assembly gave its consent for the transfer of the kingdom to the elected king by beating their weapons against their shields. Trondheim, which was then known as Nidaros, later became the heart of the kingdom and there was a common Thing or Assembly.

According to tradition the royal family was a branch of the great Yngling dynasty of Upsala which claimed descent from the god Frey, and the family increased its power through conquest, inheritance and marriage until, in the reign of Halfdan the Black, the kingdom covered a wide area. Halfdan's son, Harold Haarfager, created the United Kingdom of Norway. The people in Trondelag, which was a canton of Trondheim, and the surrounding country claimed the right to choose and pay homage to the King of United Norway at their Assembly of the Øre (The Øreting). The first time that a king was so elected was in 935 when Haakon Adelsteinfatre returned home from the Court of the English King, Athelstan, where he had been brought up. He was presented to the peasants at the Øreting by the Earl Sigurd Haakonsson, who proposed him as King. Haakon then stepped forward and asked the peasants to call him King and to give him their support. He, in his turn, promised to give them back the allodial possession of which Harold Haarfager had deprived them. The story ran round the Assembly that the candidate for the throne was really Harold Haarfager, who had returned rejuvenated, and with great shouting they gave their consent and made him King.

When Olaf Tryggvesson, the great-grandson of Harold Haarfager who had been converted to Christianity when in exile, returned to Norway from England in 995 there was a similar ceremony to that at which Haakon I had been elected King. Olaf was unanimously accepted as King and received homage at all the Assizes. When he was killed at the Battle of Svolder in the year 1000 there was an interregnum until 1015 when Olaf, another descendant of Harold Haarfager, returned to Norway and declared himself King. In 1029 he was expelled by his people whose loyalty he had strained by crushing the aristocracy and enforcing rigorously the acceptance of Christianity. He returned to Norway in 1030 and fell at the Battle of Stiklestad fighting against his own subjects, who were supporting a Danish invader, Canute the Great. But the misrule and disunion under the Danes made Olaf's memory sweet and his own errors were forgotten and his service to Norway, especially his support of the Church, were remembered. In 1164

Olaf was made a saint and declared Patron Saint of Norway, though he was not canonised. The axe became the royal symbol in Norway in his memory, as he was said to have been killed by an axe in the battle. Miracles were worked at his tomb and his fame spread throughout Scandinavia and beyond, even to England where churches were dedicated to him.

The rights of the Trönders to elect the Kings of Norway had from the start been disputed, and with the stronger royal power and the progress of Christianity there was growing opposition, and for the next hundred years, especially when the line of Harold Haarfager came to an end, there were disputed successions. In order to ensure the succession of his family, Sigurd I Jorsalfar (1103–30), had his son Magnus IV, the Blind, accepted as his successor during his lifetime, and he received homage throughout the country. On his father's death Magnus only received the homage of the King's men at Oslo. But a rival claimant appeared on the scene who was accepted as King and received homage in some parts of the country. A period of anarchy followed. The necessity for establishing the order of succession became a matter of great importance and about 1160 a powerful baron, Erling, claimed the throne for his son Magnus on the grounds that the boy's maternal grandfather was King Sigurd Jorsalfar. As descent through females was not valid, Erling sought the support of the Church and succeeded in interesting the powerful Archbishop Egstein of Nidaros to his claim.

After tedious negotiations the clergy agreed to introduce coronation into Norway and to crown Magnus as King. On his part the King was required to pledge himself in his coronation oath to surrender and offer up his crown to St Olaf, at whose shrine in the Cathedral of Nidaros it should be kept. In a secret document the King declared that the symbolic surrender of the crown indicated that he received the kingdom in everlasting feud from the patron saint of the country. The Church interpreted this as meaning that the King held his crown as a fief of the Norwegian Church, and thus their power was immensely strengthened. At the same time an assembly of the people was summoned and new legislation was passed, particularly in regard to the succession. The new law provided that the kingdom should be indivisible and that the succession should devolve on the eldest legitimate son of the King. In the case of the eldest son being unworthy or unqualified, a new king should then be elected at Nidaros within a month of the king's death. In the event of an election being necessary, the conclusive influence of the clergy was assured. The coronation of Magnus V took place at Bergen on 10th August 1163 in the presence of a papal legate, Stephen of Orvieto, the act of crowning being performed by the archbishop.

But the promises which Erling had made on behalf of King Magnus to the hierarchy of the Church were not acceptable to many people and a new Pretender, Sverre, became the leader of a party known as Birkebeiner. Although Magnus had the support of the Church and the majority of the aristocracy, Sverre's military genius led to his defeat in several engagements and he was finally killed in the Battle of Nordnes in 1184. Sverre gained the support of the small landowners and was able to build a powerful monarchy; he appreciated the importance of coronation and negotiated with Archbishop Eric and later with the Pope. But the Church put up most strenuous resistance to his efforts to cut down their prerogatives and refused to crown him. The archbishop left the country and from Denmark placed his whole See under interdict. Sverre nevertheless forced the remaining four bishops to anoint and crown him at Bergen on St Olaf's Day, 27th July 1194. Sverre died in 1202 and was succeeded by his son Haakon III who, however, died, perhaps through poison, in 1204. His son Haakon IV ascended the throne and opened negotiations with the papal Court to obtain approval for his coronation. Public opinion had undergone a change and the importance of the legitimacy of the candidate for the throne was recognised as a pre-requisite for the anointing and coronation. After protracted negotiations, which were several times broken off and resumed and which lasted for years, Haakon was at last given papal dispensation and William, Cardinal Archbishop of Sabina, went to Norway as the Pope's legate to anoint and crown the King. We learn from the saga that this event was regarded as Norway taking her place among the civilised kingdoms of Christendom.

The coronation took place on St Olaf's Day 1247. Besides the cardinal there were also present Archbishop Sigurd, the Bishops of Bergen, Stavanger, Oslo, Hamar and Hole (Iceland), ten abbots, the archdeacons and the deans from all the bishoprics; the King's three sons; the son of Haakon the Mad; nine feudatories, five judges of the Assizes; the royal bodyguard; the Court functionaries and the most eminent men from each shire.

As it had been raining hard, the road from the King's Court to the church was not only paved, but covered with green and red cloth. The procession was led by eight bodyguards in full uniform and equipment. The sceptres were carried by Sigurd the King's son, and Munan the son of the Bishop of Bergen. The crown was carried by Haakon the Young, and the coronation sword by Knut Earl. The King himself was escorted by the archbishop and two bishops and was received at the door of the church by the cardinal and two other bishops who accompanied him to the altar. After the service the archbishop and the bishops went with the King to the King's Court, a big boat-house 60 yards long and 40 yards wide which had been fitted up as a Guildhall for the occasion. Outside and inside the walls were covered with coloured cloth. Silk cushions lay on the seats and besides the head table, twelve other tables were laid. As there was insufficient room for all, tents had been pitched outside for the King's guests.

King Haakon sat on the throne of the hall. To the right were the cardinal, archbishop and bishops and other prelates and clergy. To the left were the Queen, her mother, the King's daughter, a sister of the Queen and the other ladies. Opposite to the King sat Haakon the Young and at his side Knut Earl and the King's sons, and at both sides sat the feudatories. The first dish was carried in by the four most distinguished feudatories and the first cup was filled for the King by the young Haakon, for the cardinal by Knut Earl and for the Queen by Sigurd the King's son, and for the archbishop by Munan son of the Bishop of Bergen. After the banquet the cardinal spoke. First he thanked God because the task the Pope had charged him with had been so well carried out. He then addressed some cordial words to the Norwegian people, telling them that everything he had seen in the country had been a pleasant surprise to him. Nothing had been in keeping with the inconsolable and discouraging ideas which he had on his journey up to Norway. He concluded with a benediction over the King, the Queen, the bishops, the clergy and the entire Norwegian people. The cardinal then departed, but he remained until the Virgin Mary's hymn had been sung. The King then thanked everybody who was present and returned to the King's Court. The general festivities continued for another two days.

The next coronation was that of Magnus VI Haakonson in 1261 at the time of his marriage to the Danish Princess Ingebord which had taken place three days before.

The ceremonial was the same as at the coronation of his father. The sceptres were carried by two feudatories while Knut Earl, supported by two men, carried the crown and another feudatory carried the sword. In the procession the old King walked by the side of his son. The Queen Ingebord was crowned after the King, but did not take part in the procession. The Guildhall, which had now been reconstructed, was used for the first time on this occasion for the coronation banquet, which was of great splendour. Magnus VI made preparations for the coronation of his son Eric II, Magnus, towards the end of his own reign, but he died before the coronation actually took place on 2nd July 1280. The clergy were strongly represented on this occasion, and after negotiations that caused a delay, they succeeded in getting the coronation oath drawn up to their advantage. A year later the young King was married to Margaret, the daughter of the King of Scotland. According to a clause in the marriage contract she was crowned on her wedding day, the only occasion in Norway when a queen was crowned separately.

All these coronations took place in Bergen, but when Haakon V, who had formerly been Duke of East Norway and Oslo, was crowned with his wife Eufemia the ceremony took place in St Helvard Church in Oslo in November 1299. When in 1319 Haakon V died, the male line of Harold Haarfager's family became extinct. Haakon's daughter Ingebord had married Duke Eric of Sweden and in 1319 their three-year-old son Magnus succeeded to the Norwegian and Swedish thrones. He was crowned in Stockholm in 1336 and having received the homage at Hange, was crowned at Oslo in the autumn of 1337. In 1343 Magnus handed over Norway to his youngest son Haakon VI, who married Margaret, daughter of King Valdemar IV of Denmark. There is no record of his coronation which may have taken place at Oslo. Haakon VI died in 1380 and his son Olaf V succeeded and received homage at Trondheim on 29th July 1381, but he died in 1387 and the royal line became extinct.

According to the statutes, a new sovereign should have been elected, but Margaret was acknowledged as Queen. Two years later Eric of Pomerania, the great nephew of Margaret, received homage as King at Nidaros, and in 1397 Eric was crowned at Kalmar as King of Norway, Sweden and Denmark. Eric's successor, Christopher of Bavaria, was crowned in all three kingdoms, the first the Norwegian coronation being performed at Oslo on 2nd July 1442. When in 1449 it was necessary to elect a new king, Aslak Bolt, Archbishop of Nidaros, pressed the claims of Trondheim as possessing the ancient privilege of being the place of homage and coronation.

In 1449 Christian of Oldenburg was elected in Oslo and received homage in Manstrand, and it was agreed that within a certain time he should appear at Trondheim to be crowned, but Charles VIII of Sweden disputed the throne and went to Trondheim, where he received homage and was crowned by the archbishop after he had promised the Norwegian Church certain privileges. Charles was not able to maintain his position as King of Norway, and after the death of Aslak Bolt, Christian came to Trondheim with a fleet and was crowned on St Olaf's Day 1450. This became a precedent and in 1483 Christian's son, Hans, arrived at Trondheim, where he was crowned on 20th July 1483. The Union with Sweden had been dissolved in 1450, but that with Denmark became stronger. From 1506 to 1511 Christian II was Vice-Regent of

Norway and tried several times to persuade the archbishop to crown him. But his requests were refused. When he ascended the throne in 1513 he was crowned in Oslo, and this was the last coronation which took place in Norway for nearly three hundred years. At this time Norway became little more than a province of Denmark and was ruled by Danish officials. The Lutheran Church was introduced in 1539 and the churches and monasteries were sacked by the Danes, and pastors of the Danish Lutheran Church were installed.

Christian II was deposed and his uncle Frederick I succeeded to the throne, but, although he promised by charter to be crowned at Trondheim or in any other suitable place, he never visited Norway. His son Christian III visited Oslo with his young Queen in 1529, where he stayed for two months. He wished to receive the homage as successor to the throne, but the Archbishop Olaf Engelbrektsson refused and he never returned to Norway. In 1548, however, he sent his son to receive homage as successor to the throne, but after his accession he only paid a short visit to Norway. Christian IV (1588–1648) paid more attention to Norway than his predecessors and had intended to receive homage at Trondheim. In 1591 he wrote a letter to the Feudal Lord, Ludvig Munk, to repair the coronation seat in the cathedral, but he did not go there, though in the same year he went to Oslo and received homage with great pomp and stayed in the Akerhus. In 1610 he sent his son Christian to receive homage as successor to the throne in the same place, but he did not become king. In 1647 Frederick III, accompanied by Queen Sophie Amalie, received homage at Oslo, and in 1656 he accompanied his son Christian when he went to Oslo to receive homage as heir to the throne. The last homage in Norway was held in 1661 when the Danish monarchy became hereditary and absolute. It was subsequently discontinued as being constitutionally unnecessary.

On 14th January 1814, by the Treaty of Kiel, Frederick VI of Denmark and Norway ceded Norway to Sweden. It was an act of political expediency as the Danes had backed Napoleon. Bernadotte, who had been elected heir to the Swedish throne in 1810, joined the allies and after the Battle of Leipzig he marched on Denmark. The people of Norway had not been consulted about the change in sovereignty, and in May 1814 at a meeting of national delegates held at Eidsvold a new constitution was adopted and the Danish Governor, Prince Christian Frederick, was elected King. Bernadotte thereupon invaded Norway and at a convention held at Moss agreement was reached, and in November of that year the Storthing agreed to Norway being declared a 'free, independent and indivisible kingdom united with Sweden under one king'. It was laid down in the constitution that the King of Sweden and Norway must undergo a separate coronation as King of Norway at Trondheim. Bernadotte succeeded to the throne as Charles XIV in 1813, and in 1818 he was crowned King of Norway at Trondheim as Charles Johan XIV. His successor Oscar I refused to undergo the ceremony, but the next King, Charles XV, and his consort, Queen Louise, were crowned at Trondheim on 5th August 1860. The next King, Oscar II, and Queen Sophie were crowned on 18th July 1873. As a result of a national movement and after prolonged negotiations King Oscar relinquished the crown of Norway on 27th October 1905 and the Union with Sweden came to an end. Prince Charles of Denmark was elected King on 18th November and took the title of King Haakon VII. The new King and his consort were crowned at Trondheim on 22nd June 1906 as the first king of the once more independent Kingdom of Norway. In 1908 the Constitution was amended to make the coronation ceremony permissive but not mandatory. King Olaf VI, who succeeded his father in 1957, was not crowned but on 22nd June 1958 he underwent a ceremony in the cathedral at Trondheim which was described as the King's Hallowing. The King knelt before the altar and the bishop placed his hands upon his head and gave a blessing.

Little evidence is available regarding the early Norwegian regalia. In the Museum at Bergen there is an effigy of King Eystin Osten Magnusson (*obiit* 1123) which shows the King to be wearing a crown with his name engraved on the circlet from which rise four crosses. This was originally in the monastery at Munkelir. We know from the description of the coronation of Haakon IV that the king's regalia consisted of a crown, two sceptres and a sword. Haakon IV had received a present from Henry III of England of a crown made by Edward of Westminster. This was probably used as a personal crown. In the cathedral at Stavanger there is an effigy of King Magnus VI (1263–80) wearing a circlet with four leaf-like ornaments. The representations of kings on seals cannot be taken as reliable as they are formalised pictures of the king sitting in majesty. They all show a king with an open crown, sometimes with a sceptre and sword and sometimes with a sword alone. The orb first appears on the seal of Magnus Ericksson, though this was probably copied from elsewhere and does not necessarily mean that it was part of the coronation regalia, though it persists on later seals. The Oldenburg dynasty introduced it into Denmark and probably brought it to Norway. Queen Blanca is shown with a crown and a sceptre. We learn something from a document still preserved in Stockholm[1] which is a receipt dating from the early 1340's for valuables kept in the Royal Treasury at Bohus which included:

> three gold rings which belonged to King Sverre (*obiit* 1202); a royal sceptre together with a pentagonal state wand . . . a set of coronation robes, namely a mantle, a toga, a tunic and a pair of boots. Further a silken banner Norwegian. Further a cloth banner Norwegian. Further the King has placed in the Treasury for his daily use the Swedish banner of silk and all Norwegian banners of *saeian*.[2]

It may be that the three gold rings were simple circlets or crowns. The fate of St Olaf's crown and the coronaion regalia is not precisely known, but at the time of the Reformation in 1530 the last Archbishop of Trondheim loaded the relics and contents of the Treasury of Trondheim Cathedral on to two ships. One ship sank in Trondheim fjord and the other went to Holland where the treasure was sold. The regalia, or at least the coronation crown, may have been included among these treasures for the crown was always kept with the relics of St Olaf, although the other regalia ornaments were the personal property of the king.

The modern Norwegian regalia dates from 1818 when, on the death of King Charles III (during whose reign Norway had obtained recognition as a separate kingdom), his successor Charles Johan XIV provided on his own initiative a crown and royal banner of

---

[1] Baron Rudolph Caederstrom: *De Svenska Riks Regalierna.*
[2] *Saeian* = a cloth of middling quality.

Norway. These were carried at his funeral by the Prime Minister, Peder Anker, and Major Marstack. The new royal crown was made of gold set with precious stones. For his coronation at Trondheim, in accordance with the new constitution, the King also ordered to be made a royal sword, a sceptre and orb, and a horn for the anointing oil. There was indignation in Norway that the coronation insignia should be made outside the kingdom and a motion was brought into the Storthing by Councillor Floor, proposing that the Government should immediately be asked to have the regalia made in Norway. The motion was defeated on 30th March 1818 and it was agreed by a narrow majority that:

> The Storthing throws out the proposal since it has learnt that insignia for Norway have already been made in Stockholm. The Storthing accepts with appreciation His Majesty's kindness, in the expectation, however, that these insignia, being the property of Norway, will always be kept in the kingdom.

The regalia were brought under military escort from Stockholm to Trondheim, and on the coronation day they were taken to the Government House under the escort of an officer and 100 *chasseurs* and there were placed under a guard of officers until the procession started. Before the conclusion of the coronation ceremonies no decision had been taken regarding the regalia, which were considered to be the King's private property. By the Royal Resolution of 11th September 1818 the King deferred to the Storthing's decision that the royal insignia should be kept in Norway and decided to defray from his private purse all the expenses incurred in making the regalia, laying down that in future they should be kept in Trondheim Cathedral in charge of the senior magistrate of the town.

In connection with the coronation of Queen Desideria in 1830 a crown, sceptre and orb were provided out of the funds granted for this purpose. At the same time it was decided that the regalia and royal banner should be taken from Trondheim to Christiania (now Oslo) and kept in the Regalia Tower of the Akerhus Fortress, where they remained for some years until removed to the safes of the Ministry of Finance. Whenever the regalia were used for coronations at Trondheim, or for royal funerals at Stockholm, they received a military escort for the journey.

For the preparation of the coronation of King Oscar I and Queen Josephine (which did not take place), it was decided by a resolution of January 1846 to provide out of the sum voted for the coronation: two coronation mantles, a canopy over the throne with the royal coat of arms embroidered in gold, a gilt coronation chair bearing the royal emblem, a new coat of arms for the royal banner, gilt chairs for the royal princes, red velvet cushions for the Queen's regalia and other coronation accessories, together with a crown costing about 300 ducats for the Crown Prince. The regalia and coronation accesories have not been added to or undergone any special change since that time. At the coronation of 1873, 2,200 specie dollars were spent on putting the regalia in order and partly renewing the coronation robes.

Since Norway has been an independent kingdom the regalia have been kept in the Norges Bank at Trondheim and their care is the responsibilty of the Regalia Commission set up by Royal Resolution of 2nd March 1837 and 4th July 1893. During the

German Occupation the regalia remained in the Norges Bank, and although they were cause for anxiety they were not interfered with by the Germans.

The king's crown (*Plate 134, a*), which is of striking appearance, is made of gold and was the work of the Stockholm jeweller, Eric Linderoth. The broad circlet is decorated with gold laurel leaves and is adorned with eight large precious stones in heavy gold settings, with 3 pearls set between each stone. In the front of the crown is a fine great chrysoberyl which King Charles Johan XIV obtained through the Brazilian Consul in Stockholm in 1818. On the circlet are eight gold strawberry leaves, of which seven bear a precious stone in the centre. Between the strawberry leaves are pairs of oak leaves, each with an acorn represented by a large pearl. From the oak leaves on the front, back and sides spring broad golden arches decorated with laurel leaves and pearl acorns with fine precious stones on each arch. From the remaining strawberry leaves spring delicate intermediate arches formed of branches of gold laurel leaves. The arches are depressed in the centre and at their junction rests a large globe enamelled blue and powdered with stars. The equator and vertical band are formed of pearls. From the orb rises a beautiful cross composed of 5 diamonds. Inside the crown is a crimson cap powdered with gold crowns and with pearls. The stones used to adorn the crown include 5 amethysts; 4 alexandrites; 4 chrysoprases; 1 emerald; 1 opal; 1 ruby; 1 sapphire; 1 topaz; 5 tourmaline and 96 pearls besides 28 half-pearls.

The king's sceptre (*Plate 135, a*) is a long rod of silver gilt unadorned with precious stones. It is surmounted by an elaborate design of oak leaves on which rests a small orb and cross.

The king's orb (*Plate 135, b*) is of silver gilt, with an equator and horizontal band unadorned with precious stones. It has two peculiar features, the one being that its base is a flat stand, the other that it is surmounted by an orb and cross which are decorated with pearls.

The sword (*Plate 135, a*) has a handle of silver gilt and the blade is that of a sword which King Charles Johan XIV had carried at the head of the allied troops at the Battle of Leipzig before becoming King. The blade has the Swedish and Norwegian royal emblems stamped on it but is very worn. The handle is decorated with mother of pearl.

The queen's crown (*Plate 134, b*) of gold is much smaller than the king's. It was designed by the artist Joachim C. Frick and made by Herman C. Oiset. The design is based on the crown of Queen Ulrica Leanora of Sweden and amethysts are used as the principal precious stones. The broad circlet is chased in gold and is adorned with eight large and eight small precious stones between which is set a rose formed by 7 pearls. The lower rim is decorated by a row of imitation pearls and the upper rim by a string of oriental pearls. On the rim rest semi-circular bands supported by 16 small pearls set in pairs. At the junction of these bands are eight leaf designs in gold each with a precious stone set in the centre. Each leaf is separated from the next by a large round pearl. From behind the leaves spring eight arches, each set with seven precious stones. At the point of intersection of the arches, which are depressed, is a circle of pearls on which rests the orb with an equator and two horizontal bands of pearls. From the orb rises a cross formed of pearls. Inside is a cap of crimson velvet embroidered with a leaf design in seed pearls.

The queen's sceptre (*Plate 135, a*) is a silver gilt rod, the lower portion of which is richly traced. On the top is a large ornament of leaves, above and below which hang long pendants of precious stones. It is surmounted by a small orb and cross.

The queen's orb (*Plate 135, b*) has an equator decorated with twelve precious stones, the meridian with six.

The horn for the anointing (*Plate 135, c*) is of plain silver gilt and rests on a chased stand. The point of the horn is surmounted by a royal crown and the broad end is closed by a lid secured by a chain.

The crown of the Crown Prince (*Plate 134, a*) was considered necessary because in 1818 Crown Prince Oscar had to borrow a Swedish prince's crown. Its provision was the subject of a competition. The design and work was carried out at Christiania, and it is the only ornament in the regalia made in Norway. The crown has never, however, been used by any member of the royal family. It is of gold and costs 300 ducats. It is an open crown of very handsome design. The broad circlet, lavishly decorated with oak leaves and scroll work in gold, is set with eight precious stones and 8 pearls representing acorns. From the circlet rise eight pointed rays each surmounted by a delicate mass with a pearl set in the centre. Each ray is decorated with gold scroll work on which are set two precious stones and 1 pearl. Between the rays are branches of oak leaves with a pearl acorn set in the centre. Inside is a cap of crimson velvet heavily embroidered in gold.

The regalia are not used at the State Opening of the Storthing but the crown was placed on King Haakon's coffin at the lying-in-state in 1957. The king's crown, sceptre, sword, orb and banner were displayed at the Hallowing of King Olaf at Trondheim in 1958 and were on show to the public for a few days afterwards.

BIBLIOGRAPHY

CAEDERSTROM, BARON RUDOLF	*De Svenska Riks Regalierna*, Stockholm 1942.
DAAE, A.	*De Norske Hylding og Kroning*, Christiana 1906.
KROHN-HANSEN, T.	'De Norske Kronregalier', *Norges Handverk*, 1958, No. 4.
OVERLAND, O. A.	*Illustreret Norges historie* 1906.
	Hyldinger og kroninger i Norge.
SCHRAMM, P. E.	*Herrschaftszeichen und Staatssymbolik.*
VINSNES, J. F.	*Kongerkroningen* 1906.

Memorandum prepared from official sources by Norwegian Foreign Office.

SOVEREIGNS AND CORONATIONS

872	Harold I Haarfager
930	Eric Bloody Axe
935	Haakon I, the Good
961	Harold II, Greycloak
970	(Earl Haakon of Lade)
995	Olaf I, Tryggvesson
1000	(Earls Eric and Haakon)
1016	Olaf II, the Saint
1030	Svein, son of Canute the Great
1035	Magnus I, the Good
1046	Harold III, Hardrada
1066	Olaf III, the Quiet
1066	Magnus II

1093	Magnus III, Barefoot
1103	Egstein I
1103	Sigurd I Jorsalfar
1103	Olaf IV
1130	Magnus IV
1130	Harold Gille
1136	Sigurd II, Mund
1136	Egstein II
1136	Inge
1161	Haakon II
1162	Magnus V. Crowned at Trondheim, 10th May 1163
1184	Sverre. Crowned at Bergen, St Olaf's Day, 29th July 1194
1202	Haakon III
1217	Haakon IV, the Law Mender. Anointed and crowned at Bergen on St Olaf's Day 1247
1263	Magnus VI and Queen Ingeborg. Crowned at Bergen 1261
1280	Eric. Crowned at Bergen, 2nd July 1280. His consort, Margaret of Scotland, crowned at Bergen 1281
1299	Haakon V and Queen Eufemia. Crowned at Oslo, 10th August 1299
1319	Magnus VII. Also King of Sweden. Crowned at Oslo 1337
1343	Haakon VI. Probably crowned at Oslo
1381	Olaf V. Received homage. Crowned at Trondheim, 29th July 1381
1387	Margaret
1389	Eric of Pomerania. Received homage at Trondheim. Union of crowns of Norway, Sweden and Denmark. Crowned King of the three kingdoms at Kalmar, 17th June 1397
1450	Union of crowns of Norway and Denmark
1442	Christopher. Crowned at Oslo, 2nd July
1483	Hans. Crowned at Trondheim, 20th July
1513	Christian II, King of Denmark and Norway. Crowned at Oslo
1814	Charles XIII. Not crowned as King of Norway
1818	Charles Johan XIV. Crowned King of Norway 1818
1844	Oscar I. Not crowned King of Norway
1859	Charles XV and Queen Louise. Crowned at Trondheim, 5th August 1860
1872	Oscar II and Queen Sophie. Crowned at Trondheim, 18th July 1873
1905	Norway becomes independent kingdom. Haakon VII and Queen Maud. Crowned at Trondheim, 22nd June 1906
1957	Olaf VI. Ceremony of King's Hallowing, 22nd June 1958

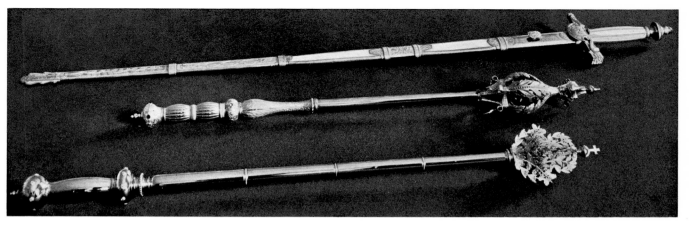

a   *Coronation sword and sceptres of the king and queen. Norges Bank, Trondheim* (p. 454)

b   *Orbs of the king and queen. Norges Bank, Trondheim* (p. 454)

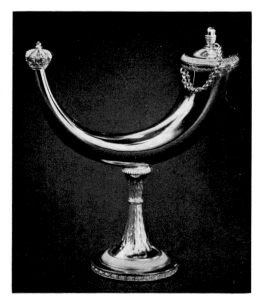

c   *Horn for the anointing oil. Norges Bank,*
Trondheim (p. 454)

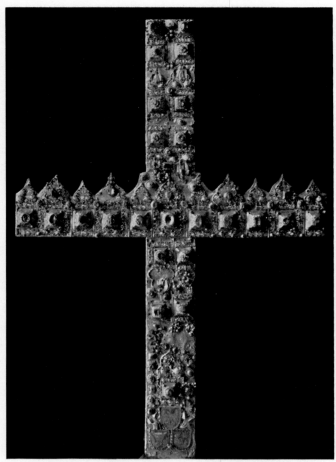

a   Cross made from two royal crowns. XV Century.
Cracow Cathedral (p. 459)

b   Reliquary bust of St Sigismund with crown made in
1601. Plock Cathedral (p. 460)

c   Detail from cross made from two royal crowns (p. 459)

d (right)   Reliquary bust of St Sigismund. Back view

CHAPTER SEVENTEEN

POLAND

Prior to the end of the x century our knowledge of the history of Poland is very scanty. Duke Miesko (Michael) I (962–92) was the founder of the Piast dynasty. Although Christianity had been first introduced into the country by Greek Orthodox monks Miesko was baptised by Jordan, the Catholic chaplain of his consort the Bohemian Princess Dobrawa. Miesko's son Boleslas I, Chrobry The Great (992–1025), understood the political necessity of establishing a national church as a means of perpetuating the independence of the Polish nation. He founded at Gniezno (Gnesen) in Great Poland a church which was to be the national shrine, and there he deposited the relics of the martyred missionary, St Adalbert of Prague. He also obtained from Pope Sylvester the elevation of Gniezno to be the Metropolitan See. Boleslas amassed an immense treasure which greatly impressed the Emperor Otto III, who in the year 1000 came to Gniezno to visit the tomb of St Adalbert. The Emperor acknowledged Boleslas as King, placing a crown upon his head and presenting him with a spear or lance. These ornaments were said to be exact copies of those used by the Emperor, and in the case of the spear, which still exists, this is true, as it is an exact copy of the Lance of St Maurice, which was one of the ornaments of the imperial regalia. It is half a metre in length and the head contains a Holy Nail.

Another gift which was later sent to Boleslas by the Emperor was a golden throne which was said to have been found in Charlemagne's tomb. It is true that after leaving Gniezno Otto journeyed to Aix-la-Chapelle, where he was present when the tomb of Charlemagne was opened. But the story that he took out a number of ornaments as relics has been discredited. We can get an idea of the shape of the thrones in use at the time from the contemporary royal seals and miniatures. They were made in the form of folding chairs to facilitate their being carried on the king's travels when they were required for ceremonial purposes.

Although Boleslas used the royal title, which the Emperor had bestowed upon him, he had doubts about the validity of his coronation, as it was without religious significance. He therefore sought the approval of the Pope for his coronation by the archbishop. As no reply was received, he gave orders to the clergy to crown him without the Pope's permission. The ceremony took place at Gniezno in 1025. According to some authorities Boleslas crowned himself, while according to others he was crowned by the archbishop assisted by the Polish bishops. Boleslas died in the same year and was succeeded by his son Miesko II, who in 1027 crowned himself at Gniezno with his father's crown and also crowned his consort the German Princess Richenza. When in 1031 Miesko II was overthrown his Queen returned to Germany with the crowns with which she and her husband had been crowned, and these she presented to the Emperor Conrad II.[1] The significance of the gift of these crowns lies in the fact that in Germany the ecclesiastical coronation of 1025 was regarded as an affront to the Emperor who was the King's overlord. We have no knowledge of the shape of these crowns, although there existed until 1857 a miniature of a scene representing Mathilde, daughter of Hermann, Prince of Swabia, offering Miesko II, King of Poland, in the year 1027 a liturgical manuscript entitled *Ordo Romanorum*. A letter from the Princess to Miesko is written at the beginning of the manuscript; the picture of the King and the Princess follows.[2]

For the next half-century the country was in chaos and stripped of its treasures. Poland at this time has been described as a smoking wilderness and wild beasts made their lairs in the ruined and desecrated churches. In 1076 Boleslas Smialy gained sufficient power to crown himself at Gniezno on 26th December of that year. There is no reliable information as to what regalia was used at this ceremony, but new royal ornaments were probably made for the occasion as the lance was the only item available. Boleslas II died in 1079, and from that date until 1295 the monarchy lapsed and the country was ruled by numerous princes. During this time the regalia of Boleslas II was kept in the cathedral in the Wawel at Cracow. From the middle of the XI century to the end of the XIII century the dukes and princes of Poland were depicted on the coins and seals with helmet, lance and sword.

In 1295 Premyslas, Prince of Greater Poland, having obtained papal approval, was anointed by the archbishop assisted by four bishops: he then crowned himself at Gniezno. For this occasion the regalia, consisting of the crown, the lance and for the first time the sceptre, were brought from the Wawel at Cracow to Gniezno. To commemorate the day the King ordered his effigy to be engraved on his seal wearing his full coronation robes, with his crown on his head and holding the sceptre. Premyslas only survived a year and was murdered in 1296. Then Wenceslas, King of Bohemia, gradually conquered Poland and was crowned at Gniezno in 1300. His death and that of his son left the country disunited and riddled with internal struggles. Ladislas I, Lokietek, The Short, a Polish prince, who had been in exile, returned to Poland in 1306 and was recognised as King, but was not crowned until 1320. In the intervening period the royal ornaments were lost, except for the lance which was in the safe-keeping of the cathedral at Cracow, but was not used any more at coronations. Ladislas I, Lokietek, Duke of Great Poland, reunited Great and Little Poland when he received the royal title and dignity. While waiting to receive the approval of the Pope for his coronation he ordered a new set of regalia and coronation vestments to be made. The ceremony, which he determined should be one of great splendour, took place at Cracow on 20th January 1320.

The new crown was formed of nine or ten gold plates one of which could be removed so as to fit the King's head. Each plate had the shape of a fleur-de-lis and

---

[1] *Hildesheim Annals of 1031*: Acta Ezonis.

[2] This document, which had eighty-three parchment pages, was in the library of the Cistercian abbey at Neuenzell on the Oder. Later it went to the library of the Church of St Hedwig in Berlin, from where it disappeared in 1857.

together they formed a circle and were joined by hinges. At a later date two arches and an orb and a cross were added. At the base of each fleur-de-lis were set three precious stones, with a large one above, flanked by 2 pearls with two small stones above. The fleurs-de-lis themselves were decorated with a large stone set among a number of smaller ones in the centre, with others on either side and a rosette of pearls at the top. Altogether 117 large stones and 180 smaller stones, mostly rubies, sapphires and emeralds, and 90 pearls were used in the decoration of the crown. After the crown the most noteworthy ornament was the coronation sword which Lokietek received from his uncle, Boleslas, son of Conrad. The sword is romanesque in style rather short and similar to those used by the crusaders at that time. The hilt, which takes the shape of a cross covered with gold leaf, was surmounted by figures representing symbolically the four evangelists. St John is represented by an eagle, with his name inscribed in Latin below. The second figure is of an angel holding a ribbon draped round him inscribed St Matthew. On the other side of the hilt is St Mark in the form of a winged lion, while an ox symbolises St Luke. Below these figures on both sides is an *Agnus Dei* holding a triumphal flag, with blood streaming from its chest. The guard also has the same four symbols with the inscription engraved below: *QUINCUNQUE HAEC NOMINA DEI I SECUM TULERIT NULLUM PERICULUM ET OMNINO NOCEBIT.*

On the reverse side of the guard appears another darker, cabalistic inscription, originally of Arabic words, but these have been somewhat changed and are difficult to translate: *CON. CIT. OMON CEVE SEDALAI EBREHEL.* In the XIX century when the sword was being renovated in Paris two new plates were added and the original inscription was altered. It now reads: *ISTE EST GLADIUS PRINCIPIS ET HAEREDIS BOLESLAI DUCIS POLONIAE ET MASOVIAE LANCIEAE.* On the knob are the letters *ALPHA* and *OMEGA.*

The original coronation sword of Boleslas Chrobry was known as *Szczerbiec (Plate 140, b and c)* which means 'Notch'. According to tradition Boleslas struck a blow with his sword when entering the golden gate of the city of Kiev. In order to perpetuate the tradition Lokietek's sword was given the old name of *Szczerbiec*, and in the same way his crown came to be called the Crown of Boleslas Chrobry.

On the death of Ladislas I, Lokietek, in 1333, his son Casimir III, The Great, succeeded him and was crowned at Cracow. On his death in 1370 the male line of the Piast dynasty came to an end.

There are three crowns in Poland which can be identified as having belonged to the Hohenstaufens and were probably among the treasures of the Emperor Frederick II, which his sons Conrad IV and Manfred sold and pledged in order to raise money. They were probably acquired by either Ladislas Lokietek (1320–33) or by his son Casimir the Great (1333–70). Two of these—one a king's crown and the other a queen consort's crown—were adapted to decorate a cross which was given to the cathedral at Cracow by a bishop who had officiated there from 1471–88 (*Plate 136, a and c*). Eleven pieces of one crown covered the cross beam and the twelfth is on the lower part of the upright beam. The second crown, also of twelve plates, was cut up and apart from one pair the plates were used singly. In each crown the plates are alternately large and small, the larger being surmounted by an eagle, which was the Hohenstaufen emblem. The scroll decoration of the king's crown depicts hunters and ladies of royal rank, and men jousting on foot and on horseback. These two crowns have been treated somewhat roughly in their application to the cross. It is considered that they date from between 1225 and 1235. The king's crown was probably that of the German King Henry VII[1] and the other that of his consort, Margaret of Babenberg, whom he married in 1225. The third crown was placed on a head reliquary of St Sigismund which Casimir the Great gave to the Cathedral of Plock in 1370 (*Plate 136, b* and *d*). This crown must have suffered damage as according to an inscription it was replaced in 1601 by a new crown which was made by a goldsmith of Plock who apparently was instructed to copy the pattern of the old crown as closely as possible. The crown is somewhat similar to the king's crown on the cross at Cracow except that the scroll work carries a design of birds and small figures. It is evident that parts from the original crown were used for making the new one. It is believed that the original three crowns were made in the workshop of the goldsmith Dietrich of Cologne.[2]

In 1910 a jewelled crown was found buried with a helm beneath an oak tree near Sandomierz (*Plate 138, a*). Considerable controversy arose as to the origin of this crown and, among others, the late Sir Guy Laking interested himself in it but disagreed with the general opinion that it was the crown of Ladislas I, Lokietek, his opinion being that it was the crown of that King's successor Casimir III. Subsequent research has failed to identify definitely the origin of this crown, and it has even been suggested that it is the crown of Witold, Grand Duke of Lithuania, who, although he obtained the consent of Ladislas Jagiello to the right to wear the kingly crown, died before he was crowned. The crown was placed in the Treasury of the Cathedral of St Stanislas at Cracow. It consists of four plates, each with a brow band set with precious stones in the form of a cross and surmounted by fleurs-de-lis, each set with five precious stones also in the form of a cross. The plates are fastened together with pins topped by small fleurs-de-lis. The stones are uncut but polished; they include some opals. The crown was worn over a helmet in battle and at state entries into cities. It belongs to the period of Ladislas I, Lokietek, and Casimir III, but it is of an earlier date than the burial crown of Casimir III. In the cathedral treasury at Cracow there was also preserved copies of a crown and a sceptre found in the grave of Casimir III. The original crown was made of copper thickly gilded and adorned with sapphires, amethysts, topazes, rubies and crystals. In form it was a rigid circlet with five large fleurs-de-lis. The circlet was adorned with a row of precious stones, the larger ones arranged in the form of a cross. The copy was made of copper gilt set with paste (*Plate 138, b*). The sceptre (*Plate 137, b*) was a short staff surmounted by a knob surrounded by fleurs-de-lis, below which were four branches decorated with fleurs-de-lis.

In default of male issue of the Piast dynasty the Polish throne passed to Louis of Anjou, known as the Great, King of Hungary, the nephew of Casimir III. He was crowned at Cracow on 17th November 1370. The Archbishop of Gniezno tried hard to get the regalia back to Gniezno and Louis promised that they should be kept there, but after his coronation he returned to Hungary and took the Polish regalia with him, where they were strictly guarded. The regal ornaments taken were described[3] as

---

[1] Son of the Emperor Frederick II, not to be confused with the Emperor Henry VII.
[2] P. E. Schramm: *Herrschaftszeichen und Staatssymbolik*, Vol. III, Ch. 39.   [3] Dlugosy: *Historya*, Vol. III.

coronam regni Poloniae, sceptrum, pomum, gladium et cetera Regni Insignia. This is the first mention of an orb among the Polish regalia. Such an ornament was included among the Hungarian coronation insignia at that time and it seems probable that Louis introduced it into Poland. Poland formed but a small part of his dominions and he therefore appointed his mother Queen Elizabeth, who was the daughter of Ladislas I, Lokietek, as Regent and he ruled the country through her. On Louis' death there followed an interregnum of two years during which fierce civil wars were waged by the various claimants to the throne. In 1383 the Poles finally made an agreement with the Queen Mother of Hungary to accept as their Queen the infant Princess Jadwiga, daughter of Louis and grand-daughter of Ladislas I, Lokietek.

Owing to the fear of the powerful Teutonic Order it was found expedient to unite Poland and Lithuania, and Jagiello, Grand Duke of Lithuania, was chosen to be King of Poland and to be married to Queen Jadwiga, who was, however, most reluctant as she was already engaged to Duke William of Austria. On 15th February 1386 Jagiello was crowned at Cracow by the Archbishop of Gniezno, assisted by two bishops, in the presence of Queen Jadwiga. He took the title of Ladislas II. Jadwiga was married to Jagiello three days later. She had not been allowed to bring back to Poland the coronation regalia of Ladislas I, Lokietek, and two new sets of ornaments were made specially for the occasion. There is no detailed information about these ornaments except that the king's crown was of gold set with precious stones. In 1412 King Sigismund of Hungary met King Ladislas II, Jagiello, at Lubwola and from there they journeyed to Koszyce and Buda where political negotiations took place. Shortly after Ladislas had left Buda, Sigismund decided to return the golden crown, sword, sceptre, orb and many other jewels belonging to the Polish realm. The return of the national regalia was solemnised by a great religious ceremony on the Feast of the Assumption, at which Ladislas placed the royal ornaments on the altar in the Church of St Mary at Cracow so that the people might behold them. Afterwards they were taken to the Wawel. Andrew Rozena, the knight who brought the regalia to Cracow, was rewarded by the gift of four villages and he also took back gifts for King Sigismund. After the death of Queen Jadwiga her regalia and a number of relics which commemorated her virtuous life were deposited in the Treasury. At that time there were in the Treasury four crowns, besides sceptres, orbs, coronation vestments and other valuables. The burial sceptre and orb (*Plate 139, a*) are still preserved.

Ladislas Jagiello died in 1434 at the age of eighty-three. During his reign of forty-five years the former pagan Lithuanian chieftain had, as Catholic King of Poland, raised his country to a great power. He was succeeded by his son Ladislas III, who later became King of Hungary, and was crowned at Cracow on 25th July 1434. He fell in the field at Varna at the head of a Magyar army against the Turks in 1444. Casimir IV, the second son of Ladislas II, Jagiello, succeeded his brother and was crowned at Cracow in June 1447. The first full inventory of the treasury was made during the reign of Casimir IV in 1475. Two crowns are listed, 'The crown for the coronation of the Polish kings' and 'The second crown for the homage' which had become a separate ceremony from the coronation. This crown was most probably that which had been made for Ladislas II, Jagiello's, coronation which took place after the return of regalia. Included in the

461

inventory are two sceptres, two orbs, the sword Szczerbiec, a number of ecclesiastical ornaments, many relics, an ampulla 'Vascula crystallina ad unguendas reges' and other valuables.

On the death of Casimir IV in 1492 he was succeeded by his brother John Albert, who died after a short reign of five years and was succeeded by his brother Alexander, whose coronation is depicted in an illuminated manuscript of the beginning of the xvi century known as *Pontyfikal Erazma Ciolka* (*Plate 137, a*) in the Museum of the Princes Czartoryski at Cracow.

Alexander died in 1506 after a reign of only five years and was succeeded by his brother Sigismund I, the fifth son of Casimir IV. In 1538 Pope Paul III sent to Sigismund I a sword (*Plate 140, d*). This was in accordance with papal practice of sending a sword, known as a *stocco*, and a *biretto*, or Cap of Maintenance, which were solemnly blessed on the night of the Nativity and sent to a son of the Church as a reward for signal service done in the cause of Christianity and in defence of Christendom.[1] This sword was very highly prized by the Polish people, who regarded it almost as a national palladium and it was kept in the cathedral at Cracow. On the death of Sigismund II in 1572 the House of Jagiellon came to an end and the blade of the papal sword was deliberately broken as a sign that Poland's glory had departed. In 1848, after the annexation of Poland by the Russians in the previous year, Sigismund's sword was broken for the second time. On Sigismund's death in 1548 his son, Sigismund II, Augustus, ascended the throne and was crowned with his Calvinist consort Barbara Radziwill on 7th December 1550 at Cracow. Sigismund II, Augustus, was only a boy of ten when he was crowned, and this necessitated certain new coronation vestments being made for the occasion to fit him. These included sandals, tibialia, a dalmatic of red velvet embroidered with gold thread, gloves and a small sword. The sword is sometimes taken to be that which later found its way into the Hohenzollern collection, but this was more probably another sword from the private collection of Sigismund I, who had it made for dubbing knights and who left it to Sigismund II, Augustus. During the reigns of Sigismund I and Sigismund II, Augustus, the royal treasure was divided into state property and the private property of the Kings. Both these Kings were patrons of the arts and acquired for their private treasury special crowns and many beautiful jewels which were kept in the royal castle at the Wawel in Cracow. With the death of Sigismund II, Augustus, on 6th July 1572 the great Jagiello dynasty came to an end.

After an interregnum during which five candidates sought election to the throne, Henry of Valois was elected King on 11th May 1573. He was crowned at Cracow shortly afterwards, but after a reign of thirteen months he left his uncomfortable throne in Poland to succeed his brother as King of France. After another interregnum of eighteen months Stephen Bathory, Prince of Transylvania was elected King. The reform of the constitution, which was introduced just before the election of Henry of Valois, turned Poland from a limited monarchy into a republic with a king as chief magistrate. The king was deprived of most of his former power, the hereditary principle was abandoned and the king had no say in the choice of his successor; in religious matters he

---

[1] Charles E. Beard: 'The Polish Art Treasures', in the *Connoisseur*, August 1955.

was compelled to remain neutral; his traditional leadership of the militia was severely restricted and he had to marry a wife selected by the senate. Four senators were in constant attendance on the king in order to supervise his actions.

One of the conditions which Stephen Bathory had to accept on his election was his marriage to Anne Jagiello, the somewhat elderly sister of Sigismund II, Augustus. They were crowned together on 1st May 1576 at Cracow at a ceremony of unprecedented magnificence. A feature of the ceremony was the investiture of the Queen with the orb which, being an emblem of sovereignty, cannot properly be used as a royal ornament by a queen consort. In the Cathedral Treasury at Cracow there is a copy still preserved of Queen Anne's burial crown (*Plate 139, c*), which is a silver gilt circlet with large and small fleurs-de-lis: there is an inscription on the circlet giving her name and style. There is also preserved the original simple gold orb engraved with the Polish Eagle and surmounted by a cross which is said to be the original ornament used by Anne (*Plate 139, d*). The probable explanation is that, as a token of the continuity of the national dynasty, Queen Anne was invested with all the emblems of royal power at her coronation. It also seems probable that Jadwiga, the wife of the first Jagiello king, used an orb, there being two in the treasury at the time of her coronation. In this case she had been chosen as a Queen Regnant two years before Jagiello ascended the throne. It was probably on this occasion that the Polish crown was first actually closed with arches, although an arched crown is shown on the sword sent to Sigismund I by Pope Paul III in 1538. The first actual example of a Polish arched crown is the Burial Crown of Stephen Bathory, a copy of which is still preserved (*Plate 140, a*).

Anne had inherited from her brother Sigismund II, Augustus, his treasure including regalia, royal robes and jewellery as he did not wish them to leave the country. She was pressed several times to return the state insignia and for a long time she refused but in the end had to give way. Things were made so unpleasant for her in the Seym that eventually, on 1st May 1576, at the first council meeting held after the coronation she agreed to hand back Sigismund II, Augustus', regalia to the treasury as state property. The original sceptre and the Chain of the Polish Order of the White Eagle of Sigismund II, Augustus, are still preserved in the National Museum at Warsaw (*Plate 139, b*).

We learn from an inventory of the Treasury taken after Stephen Bathory's death the richness of the Polish royal treasure at this time. The list includes:

I   Crowns
1. Gold crown of Boleslas Chrobry.
2. Gold crown of the Queen.
3. Gold crown for the Homage.
4. Silver gilt burial crown for the occasion of the funeral of Sigismund I.
5. So-called Hungarian crown of gold consisting of eight large plates four of them adorned with sapphires and four with rubies. This was left by John Zapolya in his will to Sigismund II, Augustus, to whom he was related.[1]
6. A gold crown which, in the will of Sigismund II, Augustus, was described as having been bought.

[1] Sigismund I had married Barbara the sister of John Zapolya, King of Hungary; after her death he married Bona Sforza, and Isabella, daughter of this union, married John Zapolya.

II	Tray	A silver gilt tray with a picture of the Blessed Virgin Mary engraved in the centre and Greek letters round the edges. This was the tray on which the crown was carried. It had been included in the 1475 inventory.
III	Sceptres	1. Silver gilt sceptre of the Kings of Poland. (In the same set as crown No. 1.)
		2. Sceptre of wood with a crystal. (In the same set as crown No. 2.)
		3. Small gilt sceptre. (In the same set as crown No. 4.)
		4. Gold sceptre with cross. (In the same set as crown No. 5.)
IV	Orbs	1. and 2. Two gilt orbs surmounted by small crosses. (In the same sets as crowns Nos. 1, 2 and 3.)
		3. Silver orb with small cross. (In the same set as crown No. 4.)
		4. Gold orb with cross. (In the same set as crown No. 5.)
V	Coronation Sword	Small sword of Boleslas Smialy (also known as Chrobry). Sheath made of silver gilt with four evangelists on handle. (Appeared in 1475 inventory as Szczerbiec.)

VI Crosses

1. *Crux altaris.*	3. *Crux pectoralis.*
2. *Crux stationalis.*	4. *Crux pacificalis.*

VII Coronation Bible. (Included in 1475 inventory.)

VIII Coronation robes, including sandals, alb, tunic, dalmatic, mantle and humeral, all richly embroidered with gold and silver.

IX Two thrones.

Also liturgical relics; effigies; vessels of precious materials; and a number of jewels including chains, medals, necklaces, bracelets, pendants, rings, etc., etc., profusely adorned with rubies, sapphires, emeralds and other precious stones and pearls. For the first time diamonds are enumerated in the inventory and the weights of the larger stones are given, the largest being a table cut stone of 22 carats. In all about 250 items of jewellery are listed. In addition there were in the treasury many items of richly decorated armour, swords, saddles, helmets, weapons and a fine collection of Gobelin tapestries.

Sigismund II, Augustus, had a great passion for jewellery and much of this treasure was collected by him.

There appear to have been three sets of funeral ornaments for Sigismund II, Augustus, and Stephen Bathory. The first was probably carried in the funeral procession and was made of silver gilt. These ornaments were removed from Poland in 1668 but copies were made of copper. Ornaments made of less valuable materials were buried with the kings. When the tomb of Stephen Bathory was opened the commissioners were unable to state definitely what materials they were made of. In the treasury of the cathedral at Cracow there are preserved the copies of the burial crown of Sigismund II, Augustus (*Plate 139, e*), which is a plain open crown, and the funeral crown of Stephen Bathory (*Plate 140, a*), which is decorated with strawberry leaves and closed with two arches surmounted by an orb and cross. There are also copies of a burial sceptre and orb (*Plate 140, a*).

After the death of Stephen Bathory, Sigismund Vasa son of John III, King of Sweden, was elected to the Polish throne. He was crowned at Cracow on 27th December 1587 as Sigismund III. While his predecessors had been at pains to keep the royal treasure intact

a   *Coronation of King Alexander Jagiello from a miniature in the Pontifical of Erasmus Ciolek. Czartoryski Museum. Cracow,* (p. 462)

b (right)   *Ivory sceptre of Sigismund III* (p. 465)

d   *Painting by Bacciarelli of the Polish coronation crown known as the Crown of Boleslas Chrobry* (p. 468)

c (left)   *Sword presented to John Sobieski by Pope Innocent XI* (p. 466)

a   *Helmet, crown and spearhead found at Sandomierz, attributed to King Casimir III, the Great. Polish National Collection*
(p. 460)

b   *Copies of the burial crown, sceptre, orb and spurs of Casimir III, the Great. Polish National Collection (p. 460)*

Sigismund III took out a number of pieces of jewellery for his own use, others he gave to Queen Anne and others he disposed of to pay for the wars in which he involved Poland.

The items he took for himself included:

A girdle with 15 diamonds.
Three rings with cut diamonds.
A globe on a gold cord containing musk.
Two pear-shaped containers, enamelled and set with precious stones.
A casket with the royal coat-of-arms.
A black crest.
A large clock, a gift from Prince Anspach.
A pendant with a large diamond.
Twelve dozen pearls of different sizes.

Among the jewels which the King gave to Queen Anne were:

A necklace with 2 diamonds, 3 rubies and 8 pearls.
A necklace with 7 diamonds, 6 rubies and 13 pearls.
Two necklaces made in the form of enamelled chains.
A necklace described as particularly beautiful. It consisted of two rows, one of diamonds with enamelled links and the second of rubies also with enamelled links. Below this hung a pendant with the letters *ZYGMUNT AUGUST* set in diamonds. Sigismund III kept the pendant but sent the necklace to Anne.
One diamond ring and two rings with rubies.

There is no evidence that Sigismund III sold any of the jewels, but there are records of several items being pawned and although some were redeemed a great many never appeared again. Among the items which he pawned were:

A rose diamond.
A necklace with a big ruby and three plates set with diamonds.
Gold harness including a complete saddle.
A gold goblet set with precious stones and pearls.
Reins of drawn gold.

There were many other jewels placed in pawn but which were not listed. In Sigismund III's wills there is mention of a crown bequeathed to him by Sigismund II, Augustus, which was pawned to one Jan Tudesco and redeemed for 20,000 zlotys. Sigismund appears to have considered it as his own property and took it with him to Sweden for ceremonial use there. It is probable that this is the ornament which is described in later inventories as the 'Swedish Crown'.[1]

On the death of Sigismund III in 1632 his son Ladislas IV ascended the throne. During his reign another crown known as the 'Russian' was added to the regalia. This

1 In 1937 the author saw an ivory sceptre in Belgrade which has a Polish origin (*Plate 137, b*). It is of very fine work. The top ball represents the battle of Nikopol. On a square compartment below are displayed the Arms of Poland and a portrait of King Sigismund III of Poland wearing an arched crown. On the shaft and the round compartment below it are scenes from the coronation of Sigismund III. The sceptre dates from the early part of the XVI century. It is believed that the sceptre was removed from a Russian museum by a soldier during the Revolution in 1917 who sold it to a Russian General who escaped to Yugoslavia. The subsequent fate of the sceptre is not known.

addition was probably made after the Treaty of Polyankone (28th May 1634) by which the Russians re-ceded Smolensk and the Eastern Provinces which had been lost during the reign of Sigismund II. This crown was left by Ladislas IV to the state in his will. Ladislas IV died in 1648 and was succeeded by his brother John Casimir, the third and last Vasa king of Poland. During his reign Poland suffered from the Cossack rebellion and from Russian and Swedish invasions and the King was compelled to flee. He had already sold part of the royal treasure to pay for the army before he went into exile. He journeyed to France in 1668 taking with him a large part of what was left in the treasury. Only a few items are listed and these include:

> The silver gilt burial crown of Sigismund I.
> The silver gilt burial crown of Stephen Bathory.
> Two gilt orbs.
> A Bible with a silver gilt cover.
> A gold cross with many precious stones and pearls.
> A picture with a gold frame.

John Casimir left these ornaments to Anna Gonzaga and she in turn left them to the Benedictine Abbey at Saint Germain-des-Prés near Paris. During the French Revolution they completely disappeared. It was suspected that the King had melted down the 'Russian' crown, but this was untrue as the crown appears again later on.

In 1669 a Polish nobleman Michael Wisniowieck was elected to the throne by the unanimous free vote of his countrymen. But the Polish Commander-in-Chief, John Sobieski, plotted against his King and himself ascended the throne in 1674. The reign of John III, Sobieski, was marked on the one hand by brilliant military achievements, the King's victory over the Turks giving him great renown, while on the other hand the position in the kingdom deteriorated. Sobieski received Poland's second *stocco* or sword (*Plate 137, c*) from Pope Clement X for his victory over the Turks at Choczym on 11th November 1673 but actually it was not sent to the King until 1686 by which time Innocent XI had become Pope. It is decorated in the rococco style and is in the Hermitage in Leningrad. Sobieski received another *stocco* and *biretto* from Pope Innocent XI for his victory over the Turks who were besieging Vienna in 1683. This is a sword of great beauty of design. It is 6 ft 6 in. in length, there is an elaborately chased two-hand hilt of silver gilt and it carries the Polish eagle amongst the decorations. The blade is etched and gilded with the name of the Pope. Both the sword and the *biretto* have survived. For some reason the Polish authorities have wrongly identified the *biretto* as the Bonnet belonging to the mantle of the French Order of the Holy Ghost. The *biretto* is of a different shape and richly embroidered with pearls, while in front is a representation of the Dove of the Holy Ghost which probably was the cause of the wrong identification. In 1696 Sobieski died a broken-hearted man, prophesying that disaster lay ahead. During his reign a great many crown jewels vanished, although the King did not take them for himself. The only ornament recorded as sold was a necklace with a table-cut diamond weighing $22\frac{1}{4}$ carats valued at 12,000 ducats, and a pear-shaped pearl. When the Swedes invaded the country the contents of the treasury were removed and hidden, so as to prevent them from falling into the hands of the invaders. The regalia, however, were returned to the treasury of the cathedral at Cracow. On the death of John Sobieski no less than eighteen candidates presented themselves for election to the Polish throne. Austria supported James the son of the late King; France's candidate was Louis, Prince of Conti, but the successful claimant was Frederick Augustus, Elector of Saxony. The adherents of the Prince of Conti tried to prevent the coronation by making a hole in the wall of the treasury and taking out the regalia, which they hid at Lubwola.

As a result of this action the King found it necessary to provide himself with a new set of regalia for his coronation at Cracow in 1697. The work was entrusted to Johann Frederick Klemm, a Freiburg goldsmith who had set up at Dresden. The crown (*Plate 141, a* and *c*) did not resemble any of the crowns in the Polish treasury and it was not made of gold but of gilt, and semi-precious stones and paste were used in its decoration. A sceptre (*Plate 141, b*), orb (*Plate 141, d*) and sword were also provided. After his coronation Frederick Augustus caused an effigy of himself to be made and clothed with his coronation robes and regalia. This was displayed in Dresden to impress his Saxon subjects. The regalia then disappeared until they were discovered by accident in the theatrical property store of the Dresden Museum in 1929 when the effigy wearing royal robes and bearing the regalia was again placed on display. For the funeral of Frederick Augustus I in 1733 another crown was made. It was of gilt unadorned with precious stones with two arches depressed at the centre and surmounted by an orb and cross. This crown may subsequently have been used at the funerals of the Kings of Saxony. It was probably that sold by the Property Department of the House of Wettin after the First World War.

In 1700 the 'Russian' crown was placed in pawn with the Elector of Brandenburg for the sum of 400,000 thalers and was never redeemed. In 1704 Charles XII of Sweden declared Stanislas Leszczynski to be King of Poland, and he was crowned at Warsaw but he only retained the title until 1709. On the death of Frederick Augustus I, Stanislas Leszczynski, who had become the father-in-law of Louis XV of France, attempted to regain the throne with French aid. But in June 1734 the son of Frederick Augustus I gained the throne and was crowned as Augustus III. As the national regalia were not available new ornaments were made for the King and his wife, Maria Josef. Each set consisted of a crown, sceptre and orb and there were also two swords (*Plate 142, a, b* and *d*). These ornaments were probably made in Dresden. The King's crown (*Plate 142, a*) was formed of a circlet richly adorned with large precious stones and diamonds set between two rows of diamonds. On top of the arches, instead of the usual orb and cross, was a large precious stone *en cabochon*. The Queen's crown (*Plate 142, c*) was similar but of smaller design, with the precious stones in less profusion. In 1934 the National Museum at Warsaw bought these royal ornaments from the Dresden collection.

In September 1764 Stanislas Poniatowski was elected King and was crowned at Warsaw on 25th November that year. The old regalia had been returned to the royal treasury during the previous reign and were sent to Warsaw for this, the last, national Polish coronation. After the ceremony they were returned to Cracow. The crown was renovated for the occasion, the arches being renewed and a new plate added. A drawing of the crown was made by Bacciarelli (*Plate 137, d*) and it was also depicted in a painting by K. J. Werner.

The disastrous reign of Stanislas Poniatowski saw the three partitions of Poland, the end of the monarchy and the loss of the regalia in 1794. A new inventory of the crown jewels had been taken in 1792 and this gives more detailed information than was contained in the previous ones:

Crowns	1.	Gold crown called *originalis sive privilegiata*, given by the Emperor Otto III to Boleslas Chrobry. Composed of ten parts. Used at coronation of King Stanislas who added a golden arch and inserted an additional plate. Adorned with rubies, sapphires, emeralds and pearls, altogether 474 stones.
	2.	Gold crown used to crown Polish queens, composed of eight parts in which there were 142 precious stones and pearls.
	3.	Gold crown called *homagialis*, of nine parts in which there were 178 precious stones and pearls.
	4.	Hungarian crown of gold filigree work formed of eight parts.
	5.	So-called Swedish crown of nine plates with 21 diamonds and 255 other stones and pearls.
Sceptres	1.	Gold sceptre adorned with nine precious stones.
	2.	Small sceptre of gold belonging to the Hungarian crown terminating with three gold leaves.
	3.	Sceptre of silver gilt with a hole at the top.
	4.	Sceptre of silver gilt with a form of nosegay on the top.
Orbs	1.	Gold orb on which a map of the world was traced, surmounted by a cross decorated with pearls and rubies.
	2.	Gold orb with cross which was used with the Queen's crown.
	3, 4 and 5.	Three other orbs with crosses; silver gilt.
Swords	1.	*Szczerbiec.*
	2.	Sword of Sigismund.
	3.	Sword with Polish royal coat-of-arms with an eagle on top.
	4.	Sword with coat-of arms of Lithuania.

The crown described as that of Boleslas Chrobry was in fact that of Ladislas I, Lokietek, and had been used as the national coronation crown. As it had originally ten plates the one added by Stanislas must have been made to replace one that was lost. The crown for the Homage was probably that made for Ladislas II, Jagiello.

When Sigismund III succeeded his father King John III of Sweden to the Swedish throne, he was crowned at Upsala on 19th February 1594. He took with him the crown which had been described in an earlier inventory as 'bought'. The crown was of gold composed of five large parts and five smaller parts and had been decorated with balas rubies and pearls. On top was an orb with a small cross. When the inventory was taken in 1792, most of the stones had been taken out, only seven remaining, and alongside the crown were two cases containing the rubies and a second one with the pearls. An emerald and a sapphire were also wrapped up and kept with the crown. The sceptre which went with this crown was, in 1792, dismantled and in twenty-one pieces.

The orb was of silver-gilt and could also take to pieces. It had engraved on it a *sphaera mundi* or map of the world, a feature which had hitherto been unique on the orb made for the coronation of Eric XIV of Sweden in 1561.

Eric's son, John III, had married Catherine Jagiellonica, sister of Sigismund II, the last king of the Jagiello dynasty of Poland. At the coronation of John III at Upsala in 1569, contrary to established Swedish custom, Queen Catherine was invested with an orb as well as her husband. There is no record of this second orb being made for her, but when she died King John's second wife Gunilla was crowned and a new orb was made. It is possible, therefore, that Catherine's orb was made similar to that of her husband's and was considered as her personal property and passed to her son Sigismund and was brought by him to Poland.

The second sword was provided by Sigismund I for dubbing knights, while the third and fourth swords were carried at the coronation to represent the king's sovereignty over Poland and Lithuania. They were said to have been sent to Ladislas II, Jagiello, by the Teutonic knights before the battle of Grünewald in 1410. The second sword bore the inscription *SIGISMUNDUS REX JUSTUS*. It was a small weapon in the renaissance style. Until 1939 it was preserved in the Hohenzollern Museum in the Schloss Monbijou at Berlin.

Compared with the previous inventories the total number of items is small but there were still included a number of reliquaries, necklaces, saddles, helmets, swords and chains. Two important items which were used at the coronation ceremony were missing the silver gilt tray on which the crown was carried and the ampulla. The tray no doubt was sacrificed when depredations were made on the treasury to pay for the wars. The ampulla most probably became absorbed in the ecclesiastical treasury.

In 1794 the Poles abandoned Cracow, but no steps were taken to remove the regalia. On 15th June the town was entered by Prussian troops. Generals Elser and Ruets who were in command had received orders not to pillage the town but they decided to despoil the castle and they did so ruthlessly. A retired artillery captain named Zabrzycki betrayed the place where the regalia was kept and having obtained the keys from the governor of the castle a systematic search was made. For the time being the room containing the iron chest in which the regalia was kept was left intact but everything found in other parts of the castle which was of any value was looted. Furniture, mirrors, hangings and coverings were all taken and even the door handles and the parquet floor were removed. The Director of the Cathedral Choir, Francis Xavier Kratzer, who died in 1818, wrote his memoirs and described how in the early days of October 1794 he went to the treasury with three officers and a locksmith from Breslau. They had great difficulty in breaking down the six iron-covered doors and even the use of cannon was suggested. According to Kratzer, a Cracow craftsman suggested that the floor underneath the door be knocked out and access made through the breach. When in January 1796 the Austrians took over the occupation of Cracow, their commander General Baron Foullon was unwilling to take the responsibility for the state of affairs he found in the castle and asked the municipal authorities to appoint a delegation to make an inspection and draw up a report. This they did and their report was placed in the city archives. It stated that all the locks on the doors of the treasury had

469

been forced and all the chests broken. The hasps of the chest containing the regalia had been sawn off. Nothing of value was left and the only trace of the regalia was six records of inspections of the treasury which had been made in the XVIII century.

Nothing, however, was said by any Polish authorities. Not even the last custodian of the treasury, Father Sierakowski, nor the Bishop Felix Turski nor Professor Jacek Przybylski who had taken the last inventory, revealed the truth. When conditions became more settled in the next century the plunder of the treasure by the Prussians began to be mentioned in memoirs and other works, but no public or official statement was made except that the Prussians declared that they had found nothing in the treasury. Its fate, however, must have been known to several people. Among reports that were circulated was one that when Felix Lubienski in 1798 was received in audience in Berlin by King Frederick William III he was overcome by emotion when he recognised the diadem and necklace the Queen was wearing as jewels formerly in the Polish royal treasury. When asked what was the matter he confessed the truth. Augustus Frederick, Duke of Sussex and uncle of Queen Victoria, related that when on a visit to Berlin he was shown the Hohenzollern treasury and the crown of Poland was placed upon his head. But despite these stories it became widely believed in Poland that the coronation regalia had been saved. In 1829 when Nicholas I was crowned at Warsaw the Paris newspaper *Constitutionel* published an article about the Polish regalia. This article related that the insignia had been rescued by two monks who, assisted by six locksmiths, broke into the treasury at the Wawel, removed the regalia and took them to a monastery in Lithuania where they were hidden. This legend gained currency and various persons were mentioned as being the rescuers. Speculation was centred in the Capuchin monastery at Vladomierz in Eastern Poland as being the repository of the lost regalia. So firmly was this believed that in 1920 the Polish Government ordered special inquiries to be made but the search was fruitless. Nevertheless the story persisted that the regalia was hidden in some secret recess and would reappear when Poland again had a king.

In 1931, however, seven secret documents from the Prussian treasury came to light and although they were incomplete they solve the mystery of the missing Polish crowns.[1]

The first three documents relate to King Frederick William's instructions for the regalia to be taken from Cracow in great secrecy via Cosel to Breslau and the report by General von Ruets of their despatch. They are dated between 28th June 1794 and 8th October 1795.

In 1815 the Congress of Vienna settled that the Tsar of Russia should assume the title of King of Poland in respect of that part of Poland that was apportioned to Russia. Alexander I claimed the Polish regalia but they were not forthcoming. In 1817 the coronation sword *Szczerbiec* was identified in the Hermitage in St Petersburg. The museum authorities stated that they had purchased it with some other objects from a collector

1 They were published in 1935 by Dr Charles Estreicher in a pamphlet entitled *Zniszczenie Polskick Insigniow Koronyeh* (*The Destruction of the Polish Insignia*). The same author published another work in English entitled *The Mystery of the Polish Crown Jewels*. English translations of the original documents are given in an appendix to this chapter. The German authorities are believed to have destroyed the originals.

a Burial sceptre and orb of Queen Jadwiga. Polish National Collection (p. 461)

c Copy of crown of Queen Anne Jagiellonica. Polish National Collection (p. 463)

b (left) Sceptre, sword and chain of the Order of the White Eagle of Sigismund II, Augustus. Polish National Collection (p. 463)

d Orb of Queen Anne Jagiellonica. Polish National Collection (p. 463)

e Copies of burial crown, sceptre and orb of Sigismund II, Augustus. Polish National Collection (p. 464)

a   *Copies of burial crown, sceptre and orb of King Stephen Bathory. Treasury, Cracow Cathedral*
(p. 463)

b (left) *obverse and* c (right) *reverse of* 'Szczerbiec', *the Polish Coronation Sword. Polish National Collection* (p. 459)

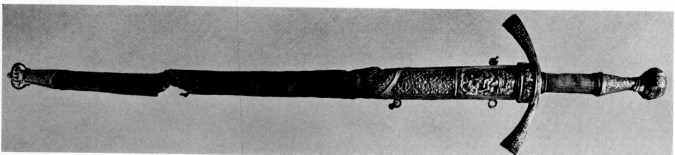

d   *Sword sent by Pope Paul III to Sigismund I in 1538 and which was broken at the funeral of Sigismund II Augustus. Polish National Collection* (p. 462)

who claimed that he had bought the sword in an antique shop. It was returned to Poland in accordance with the terms of the Treaty of Brest-Litovsk, after the First World War.

In 1829 Nicholas I was crowned at Warsaw, and as the Polish regalia were not available, he had to provide a set for the occasion.

The second set of four documents are all dated 1836. They are letters exchanged between the Prussian Minister of War, Karl von Witzleben, and the Court Minister, Prince Wittgenstein, and a letter addressed to the latter by an official of the archives in Berlin. In the final document Wittgenstein definitely states that the six crowns[1] from Cracow were dismantled on an order from the King on 17th March 1809, and on a further order of 18th June 1811 they were taken to Königsberg and destroyed. On 27th July 1811 there were delivered to the Chancellor of State 25 lb 27 oz (Loths) of gold and 9 lb 77.8 oz of silver which had been obtained from the Polish crowns. The precious stones and pearls were to be handed over to the Maritime Trading Company (Hauptseehandlungskasse), with instructions to dispose of them.

But the evidence provided by these documents can be corroborated and the story taken a step further by a passage which includes quotations from other official documents in Paul Seidel's work on the Prussian Crown Treasury.[2] In the year 1806 as the result of the invasion of Prussia the Court had been compelled to take flight to East Prussia and the regalia and crown jewels were also taken there. In 1809 Frederick William III decided that such part of the crown treasure as could be easily convertible into cash should be placed at the disposal of the state. The gold plate of Frederick the Great and silver plate frames and fittings were melted down and the metal sold. The Prussian crown jewels were sent from Königsberg to the Maritime Trading Company in Berlin, but as, owing to the disturbed conditions, the current market values had fallen to one-quarter of what they had been, the idea of their sale was given up. Besides the Prussian crown jewels there were also sent to Berlin a number of articles previously kept at Königsberg. Among these were six crowns 'some with cut sones, some with uncut stones and some of fine gold only not set with gems'. There were also a silver-gilt sceptre, the top of which was missing, decorated with coloured cut stones; two swords, one dagger sheath set with gems; two reliquaries; one golden orb; two heavy gold chains; two sceptres; and three metal orbs.

An order signed by Altenstein, Minister of State, declares:

> At the command of the All Highest the King himself certain articles kept in the Treasury shall no longer be preserved but used for the benefit of the State; Privy Councillor for War, Zenker, as Treasurer is hereby instructed by His Majesty that he shall in secret dismantle and do his utmost to take to pieces certain known effects in his care in the Treasury either himself or through experts. He shall then make a confidential statement thereon and then be prepared to melt down the metals to be found in them and to execute any other instructions as to the remainder. His Royal Majesty gives Privy Councillor Zenker by this command renewed proof of the confidence of his All Highest and is the more assured of the prompt fulfilment of his orders.

Dated 17th March 1809, signed 'Altenstein'.

1 The sixth was the 'Russian' already pawned to the Hohenzollern Treasury in 1700.
2 Paul Seidel: *Die Insignien und Juwelen der Preuszischen Krone*, Leipzig 1913.

This written order was only a confirmation of Zenker's instructions which had actually been carried out already. In the Minister's presence one of the six crowns was broken up and destroyed, the others handed over to Zenker for destruction and sorting out of the component parts. At the same time it was advised that the destruction of certain pieces, such as the Polish sword and its bejewelled sheath, should not be made public. The Königsberg jeweller, J. C. Groat, valued the jewels and the pearls from the dismembered articles at a total of Reichsthalers 25,762. Among the items enumerated were:

A single table-cut diamond of $108\frac{1}{2}$ gr valued at Rs. 16,000.
Two smaller table-cut diamonds of $28\frac{1}{4}$–$20\frac{1}{4}$ gr valued at Rs. 1,500.
Two rose diamonds of $25\frac{3}{4}$ and 29 gr, valued at Rs. 800 and Rs. 1,000.

The main part of the gems consisted of a large number of sapphires, rubies and emeralds which were valued at an exceptionally low figure. For example, a cut sapphire of $140\frac{1}{7}$ carats was valued at only Rs. 400. A smaller stone of bad colour weighing 84 carats was valued at Rs. 200, and an uncut emerald of 45 carats at Rs. 45. A cut sapphire of 31 carats was valued at Rs. 71. The numerous pearls, including fourteen necklaces, were also priced below their real value. Only 'an elliptical pearl, as a pendant, which with the gold setting weighs $40\frac{1}{2}$ carats and perhaps about 34 without gold' was worth 1,200 thalers by itself without the gold.

The next document referring to this action is dated 18th June 1811 and is signed by the King himself. It was a Royal Order in Cabinet addressed to Henderbenberg and read as follows:

Inasmuch as the destruction of the six crowns until now preserved in the Treasury took place at Königsberg on my orders and by word of mouth to Freiherr von Altenstein, Minister of State, I find therein nothing to draw attention to and approve that the gold and silver shall be minted. The gold content shall be assigned to the savings stock and the endowment fund. You should endeavour to dispose of the gems and pearls gradually as opportunity offers and the proceeds should be assigned towards the liquidation of the national debt. Signed: 'Frederick William', Potsdam, 18th June, 1811.

In pursuance of the order Henderbenberg directed Privy Councillor Zenker to hand over to be minted 27 lb 27 loths of gold and 9 lb $7\frac{7}{8}$ loths of thick silver-gilt which he had obtained from the ornaments and the jewels and pearls were to be handed over to the Maritime Trading Company.

The last coronation of a King of Poland was that of Alexander II, Tsar of Russia, in April 1856. The regalia provided for the coronation of Nicholas I were used on this occasion. These ornaments belong properly, however, to the Russian crown jewels, among which they have been preserved.

The regalia were so closely connected with the coronation ceremony that it is of interest to trace the development of Polish coronations. The first three were held without papal sanction, although that of 1025 was a religious ceremony. The manuscript of 1027 depicting Princess Mathilde holding a manuscript bearing the words *Ordo Romanorum* suggests that the service was based on the Roman *ordo*. The coronation of Premyslas was the first with papal sanction and which included the anointing. The

Roman *ordo* was probably used on this occasion but the King crowned himself as his predecessor, Miesko II, had done. The Roman coronation *ordo* was used without modification from the coronation of Wenceslas in 1300 to that of Ladislas II, Jagiello, in 1386. The right to crown the king was vested in the Metropolitan Archbishop of Gniezno and the first five coronations were held in his cathedral. Ladislas Lokietek transferred the ceremony to his capital at Cracow, where all subsequent coronations, except two held at Warsaw, took place. The right of the Metropolitan Archbishop was, however, confirmed by the Privilege of 1451, the decree of Sigismund II, Augustus, of 1550, the Bull of Pope Sixtus V of 1589, and the Constitution of 1736.

The special Polish national features were introduced for the coronation of Ladislas III, Jagiello, on 25th July 1434. They were borrowed mainly from the Bohemian national formula which had been established in the XIV century. The Archbishop of Gniezno was substituted for the Archbishop of Prague, the altar of St Stanislas for the altar of St Guy, the chapel of St Catherine for the chapel of St Wenceslas, the Marshal of the Crown for the Usher of the Bohemian Kingdom, and on the eve of the coronation the Polish King was required to make a pilgrimage to the Skalka near Cracow where the remains of St Stanislas were kept, in the same way that the Bohemian King made a pilgrimage to Vyschrad. But in the details of the service the authors held to the Roman *ordo*. This *ordo* was used at subsequent coronations, although in the XVI century a special ceremonial was established, which was used not only for the ceremonies in the church but those outside such as the homage and the banquet.

In the final form the King was conducted in procession to the church where he was met by the Metropolitan Archbishop, the bishops, mitred abbots and other clergy who conducted him to the High Altar where the senators carrying the regalia placed the royal ornaments on the Holy Table. The senators carrying the standards stood around the throne. After some prayers the King knelt down and took the oath, laying his hands on the Book of the Gospels. The King then lay on the floor with his arms outstretched in the form of the cross. All the clergy said prayers over the prostrate King, who then rose and knelt before the archbishop, who anointed him on the right arm as far as the elbow, the forehead and breast, though later the shoulders were substituted for the breast. While the Mass was being celebrated the King was conducted to the chapel where he was dressed in sandals, a stole, a dalmatic, a humeral and a maniple. So vested he returned to the High Altar, where the archbishop girded him with the sword. The King unsheathed the sword and with it made the sign of the cross to the four parts of the world. Then the King knelt down and the archbishop placed the crown on his head. After this the archbishop placed the sceptre in his right hand and the orb in his left. The King then received Holy Communion. After the Mass was over, the Primate and the Bishop of Cracow led the King to the throne and the service ended with the singing of the *Te Deum*.

The next day the King accompanied by a big suite rode on horseback to the Great Square. In the procession the sceptre, the orb and the unsheathed sword were borne before him by three high dignitaries. In the town hall the King was dressed in his coronation robes and placed on his head the crown called *Homagialis*. He took his place on the throne set high up under a canopy in the Square near the town hall where he could be seen by all the people. The King then dubbed those to be created knights. Then the magistrates in the name of the city and the citizens swore the oath of homage and faithfulness and handed to the King the keys of the city gates. The procession then solemnly returned to the royal castle and the celebrations ended with a splendid banquet.

It is not certain when the homage was first introduced as a separate lay ceremony, but it was already performed at the time of Casimir IV (1445). It may be thought that this ceremony was instituted out of consideration for the king so that he should not become fatigued by the long proceedings, or in order to give the people a chance of participating, since the cathedral was situated in the Wawel and only privileged spectators could attend. It is more probable that it became necessary after the Union with Lithuania, where two-thirds of the people professed the Greek Orthodox religion. After the Union with Lithuania all the chief officers of state were duplicated, there were standards and swords of state for each country, and the oath specially provided for the preservation of the rights of Lithuania.

The coronation of the queen was somewhat similar to that of the king. The anointing was different, and neither political nor judicial power was officially given to her. The king conducted his consort to the altar and asked the archbishop to crown her. She was then anointed and the archbishop placed the crown on her head and invested her with the sceptre and in some cases with the orb, although in the coronation *ordo* there is no mention of this ornament. The special circumstances in which Jadwiga and Anne Jagiello received the orb have already been mentioned. We know definitely that it was delivered to Elizabeth of Austria. It so often happens at coronations that once an innovation is introduced it persists.

In all twenty-seven kings and twenty-four queens were crowned. Queens were crowned with their husbands if married at the time or otherwise on the occasion of their wedding. But several queens were not crowned at all, either because they were not Roman Catholics or because they were not of royal rank. When, on 1st September 1939 the Germans attacked Poland and started an aerial bombardment of Cracow, the Polish national treasures were housed in the castle at Wawel, and it was decided to prevent them from falling into the hands of the invaders. On 4th September they were loaded upon a barge and floated down the Vistula for six days. On 10th September they were transferred to farm carts and made a long and dangerous journey southwards into Roumania. On reaching Bucharest the Polish Legation informed the guardians of the treasure that arrangements had been made for their safe custody in the Roumanian royal palace, but the guardians thought it would be safer to lodge them in the British Embassy. Later, with the approval of the Polish Government in exile in London, they were removed by sea to France, shortly before the German invasion. It was necessary to remove them hurriedly from this new danger and fortunately the Polish ship *Batory* was available in a French port at that time and she took them to Canada in June 1940. They were at first stored at the National Experimental Farm at Ottawa. After the war, when a Communist Government was set up in Poland, claims were put forward for the return of the treasures, which by that time had been deposited, by their custodians, in the Bank of Montreal in Ottawa. Fearing that a court order might be made for the

a   Crown, sceptre and orb of Augustus II, the Strong. Historical Museum, Dresden (p. 467)

b   (right)   Sceptre of Augustus II, the Strong. Historical Museum, Dresden (p. 467)

c   Crown of August II, the Strong. Historical Museum, Dresden (p. 467)

d (right)   Orb of Augustus II, the Strong. Historical Museum, Dresden (p. 467)

a   Crown and orb used at the coronation of Augustus III. Polish National Collection
(p. 467)

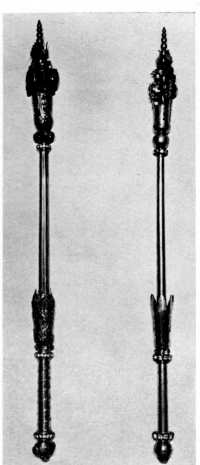

b   (right)   Sceptres of Augustus III and Queen Maria
Joseph. Polish National Collection (p. 467)

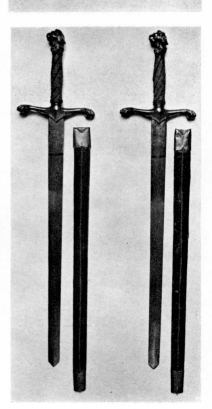

c   Crown and orb used at the coronation of Queen Maria Joseph. Polish
National Collection (p. 467)

d (right)   Coronation swords of Augustus III. Polish National Collection (p. 467)

bank to hand over the treasures to the Communist Government of Poland the guardians removed them and placed them in two convents in the province of Quebec and Mr Du Plessys, who at the time was Premier of Quebec, managed to have them placed under police protection rather than under a Federal guard, and asserted that the treasures were the property of a Roman Catholic Poland and were not available for return to a Communist Government, who might not respect or preserve them. Meanwhile the Canadian Government had answered the Polish Government by informing them that the proper course for them to adopt was to appeal either to the Canadian courts or to the International Court at The Hague. This the Polish Government appeared to be reluctant to do. The treasures were later under an armed guard in the Quebec Provincial Museum, and a complication arose through the death of one of the guardians. Anxiety existed that some of the objects of the treasure, particularly the tapestries, were in need of attention for their possible preservation, but there are no funds available for the purpose.[1]

[1] As this book was going to press information has been received that agreement has been reached for part of the Polish Treasure in Canada to be returned to Poland but it is not known whether the regalia are included in this arrangement.

APPENDIX

DOCUMENT I

To Major-General von Ruets

My dear Major-General von Ruets,

I have received your note of the 22nd instant and, concerning the Polish Royal Insignia, my instructions are that you should take steps for their safe keeping and ensure that none of them are disposed of.

I remain your affectionate King,

FREDERICK WILLIAM

H.Q. Konsky.
28th June, 1794.

DOCUMENT II

To Major-General von Ruets

My dear Major-General von Ruets,

I gave orders to the Privy Councillor and Chamberlain von Hoym to take steps to have the Polish Royal Insignia, which are in Cracow, transported from there with safe-conduct to Cosel and thence to Breslau. It is necessary that this should be done with greatest possible secrecy and you must co-operate with Privy Councillor von Hoym, with whom you should make exact arrangements, especially that the former depository of the Insignia shall be carefully guarded and that no one who could reveal the removal of the Regalia should be allowed to approach it. You should act with the greatest caution and arrange all in agreement with Privy Councillor von Hoym in the best possible way that circumstances permit.

I am your very affectionate King,

FREDERICK WILLIAM

Potsdam.
24th September, 1795.

DOCUMENT III

To His Majesty the King

I report most humbly the manner in which the Polish State Insignia was sent from here to Breslau to the State Minister, Count von Hoym, on the 4th October. According to the orders of Your Majesty the utmost caution was exercised and I gave Privy Councillor von Hoym the assistance of Captain von Holtzmann, Captain von Losthin and Lieutenant von Freuend. The greatest difficulty was experienced in destroying six doors mounted with iron work and provided with complicated locks and in opening the iron case in which the regalia was preserved. The edge-tool maker of Breslau, who was employed for this purpose, was bound by an oath beforehand and is being sent back immediately.

I remain for life with the most inviolable faithfulness and homage,

VON RUETS

Cracow.
8th October, 1795.

DOCUMENT IV

To the Lord High Chamberlain and Privy State Minister von Wittgenstein

106 KM
  A

At yesterday's audience I submitted to His Majesty the King several cabinet orders, which have recently been discovered, regarding the Polish State Insignia. His Majesty the King recollected that these state Insignia were formerly in the treasury and were only delivered when His Majesty the Emperor Alexander of Russia, in consequence of the Vienna Congress, became King of Poland.

I now beg Your Highness most obediently to reveal all that Your Highness knows about the State Insignia.

VON WITZLEBEN

Berlin.
1st January, 1836.

DOCUMENT V

Berlin.

7th January, 1836.

To His Excellency von Witzleben

Your Excellency informed me in his honoured letter of the 1st of this month that Your Excellency submitted to His Majesty the King several cabinet orders which have recently been discovered concerning the Polish State Regalia which were formerly in the treasury. Your Excellency asked me at the same time to communicate to him all that may be known to me regarding these Insignia.

I have caused the necessary researches to be made in the archives, and I have the honour to transmit to Your Excellency herewith the results of these researches. Since it is uncertain to which Insignia of the Kingdom of Poland the above orders refer, I beg Your Excellency to be kind enough to let me know what further researches may be of special value for furnishing the evidence required.

WITTGENSTEIN

DOCUMENT VI

Berlin.

26th January, 1836.

The negotiations requested on the 15th of this month from the Royal Privy Office and Archives concerning the Polish Coronation and State Insignia found in the year 1795 in Cracow, will be with the documents which, by command, were presented in 1824 to the Department for Foreign Affairs, relative to the occupation and revenue of the district of Cracow, and its incorporation with Silesia, Vols. I and II. I have not been permitted to obtain possession of these documents.

I remember, however, that His Excellency, the late Privy State Minister, Count von Hoym, presented His Majesty the King with a report about the discovery of these Insignia and that these, in consequence, if I am not mistaken, were sent to the treasury at Berlin.

PAULI

DOCUMENT VII

Berlin.

27th January, 1836.

To His Excellency von Witzleben

As Your Excellency on the 11th instant was kind enough to give me more detailed particulars about the Polish State Insignia, which Your Excellency first mentioned in his letter of the 1st of this month, I have the honour to inform Your Excellency that since then every effort has been made to find some trace of the documents concerning this matter. In the Privy State and Cabinet Record Office nothing could be found about this subject, nor in the Silesian Archives of the former Minister, Count von

Hoym, was there anything which suggested negotiations of the year 1795 as communicated by Your Excellency. This matter was treated, as it is proved by these negotiations, with the utmost secrecy and an employee of the old Silesian Archives remembered, however, that the Polish State Insignia brought from Cracow were later delivered from Breslau to the Treasury in Berlin. This is also confirmed by the documents of the Treasury. According to them there were six crowns in the Treasury. One of them was, without doubt, the crown of the Czars,[1] which I mentioned in the annexe to my letter of the 7th instant; the other five crowns—besides them there is also mention of a Polish sword—are probably the Polish State Insignia brought from Cracow at a time which, up till now, has not been ascertained and were delivered to the Treasury.

All six crowns were dismantled and a royal order notified by the Privy State Minister, von Altenstein, to the treasurer, the Privy Councillor for War, Zenker, on the 17th March, 1809. As His Majesty the King, by royal order of the 18th June, 1811, deigned to approve the destruction of these ornaments which had been carried out as a result of the oral command at Konigsberg, the treasurer Zenker was charged by the Chancellor of State on the 27th July 1811 to use up in coining the gold and silver obtained from the crown which formerly had been preserved in the treasury and which amounted to 25 pounds and 27 ounces of gold and 9 pounds and 77·8 (*sic*) ounces of silver. The precious stones and pearls were ordered to be sent to the Directors of the Sea Trading Company, who had received instructions to sell them.

Nothing could be found out regarding the delivery of the Polish Crown to His Majesty the Emperor Alexander of Russia.

WITTGENSTEIN

BIBLIOGRAPHY

BALZAR, O.	*Skarbiec I Archivum Koronne*, Lwowie 1917.
BEARD, CHARLES E.	'The Polish Art Treasures', in the *Connoisseur*, London, August 1955.
BOVET, M. A.	*Cracovie*, 1910.
ESTREICHER, DR CHARLES	*The Destruction of the Polish Crown Insignia*.
GLOGER, Z.	*Encklopedja Staro-Polska*, Warsaw 1902.
KOPERA, C. F.	*Dzieje Skarbca Koronnego*, Cracow 1904.
LAKING, SIR GUY	*Record of European Arms and Armour*, 1920.
MORELOWSKI, M.	'Korona i helm zvalzione w Sandomierza a sprawa korony Witolda i grabowiow dynastcznych w Wilnie', in *Ateneum Wilenskie* R. VIII, 1930.
ORGELBRAND	*Encyclopaedia Powszechna*, Warsaw 1864.
PRZEZDZIECKI	*The Lance of St Maurice*.
RADZIKOWSKI	*Szczerbiec, miecz Boleslawowski*, 1898.
SADOWSKI	*Szczerbcem*, Cracow 1892.
SCHRAMM, P. E.	*Herrschaftszeichen und Staatssymbolik*.
SEIDEL, PAUL	*Die Insignien und Juwelen der Preuszischen Krone*, Leipzig 1913.

[1] In fact it had already been pawned to the Elector of Brandenburg.

TOMOWICZ   *Szczerbiec*, Cracow 1928.
WLOCZNI, O.   *Zwanej S. Maurycego*, Warsaw 1861.
WOLANSKI, A.   *Losy Regaljow, Polskieh*, Cracow 1921.

KINGS AND CORONATIONS

962   Miesko
992   Boleslas I. Crowned in the Year 1000 at Gniezno by Emperor Otto III
      Crowned in 1025
1025 Miesko II. Crowned himself in 1027 at Gniezno, and also his consort Richenza
1041 Casimir I
1058 Boleslas II, the Intrepid. Crowned at Gniezno, 26th December 1076
1081 Ladislas I, the Careless
1102 Boleslas III, Wry Mouth
1138 Ladislas II
1146 Boleslas IV, the Curled
1173 Miesko III, the Oldest
1177 Casimir II, the Just
1194 Lesko V, the White
1200 Miesko III. Restored
1202 Ladislas III
1227 Boleslas V, the Chaste
1279 Lesko VI, the Black
1295 Premyslas. Crowned himself in 1295 at Gniezno.
1300 Wenceslas, King of Bohemia. Crowned at Gniezno in 1300
1306 Ladislas the Short, Lokietek. Crowned on 20th January 1320 at Cracow
1333 Casimir III, the Great. Crowned at Cracow
1370 Louis, King of Hungary. Crowned on 17th November 1370 at Cracow
1383 Jadwiga and Jagiello (who became Ladislas II). Her future husband, Jagiello,
      was crowned on 15th February 1386 at Cracow, and married Jadwiga three days
      later
1434 Ladislas III, King of Hungary. Crowned on 25th July 1434 at Cracow
1444 Casimir IV. Crowned in June 1447 at Cracow
1492 John Albert
1501 Alexander
1506 Sigismund I
1548 Sigismund II, Augustus. Crowned on 7th December 1550 at Cracow with his
      consort Barbara Radziwill
1573 Henry of Valois. Crowned in 1573 at Cracow
1575 Stephen Bathory. Crowned on 1st April 1575 with his consort, Anne Jagiello, at
      Cracow
1587 Sigismund III. Crowned on 27th December 1587 at Cracow
1632 Ladislas IV

1648 John Casimir
1669 Michael Wisniowieck
1674 John Sobieski. Crowned on 14th February 1676
1697 Frederick Augustus. Crowned on 15th September 1697 at Cracow
1704 Stanislas Leszczynski. Crowned on 24th September 1705 at Warsaw
1709 Frederick Augustus (again)
1734 Augustus III
1764 Stanislas Poniatowski. Crowned in 1764 at Warsaw
1829 Nicholas I. Crowned in 1829 at Warsaw
1856 Alexander II of Russia

CHAPTER EIGHTEEN

PORTUGAL

Towards the end of the xi century Spain attracted crusading knights from all over Europe to play a part in driving out the Moors. Among them was Henry, Count of Burgundy, a grandson of Robert, the first Duke of Burgundy. This ambitious warrior won the favour of Alphonso VI, King of Leon, and was given the hand of his natural daughter, Theresa, and as part of her dowry he received the County of Portugal.[1] It was not long before he was able to annex the County of Coimbra to the south. When he died in 1112 he left the Regency in the hands of his widow, Theresa, for his son Alphonso Henriques, who was aged three. In 1128 Alphonso Henriques overthrew his mother and became undisputed Count of Portugal. He became one of the warrior heroes of mediaeval romance[2] and has been revered by the Portuguese as a saint on account of his personal character and because not only was he born in the country he ruled but devoted his whole life to its interests and was the founder of their kingdom. The annals of his reign, written two centuries later, contain a mass of picturesque legends which do not bear the authority of contemporary chroniclers. They were, however, widely believed and were not without their effect on the position and prestige of the Portuguese monarchy.

Alphonso Henriques's most famous exploit was his victory over the Moors at the Battle of Ourique on 25th July 1139. The legend relates that, on the evening before the battle, Christ crucified appeared to Alphonso in his tent and promised him victory. This tradition was perpetuated by the five wounds of Christ being borne upon the Coat of Arms of the Kings of Portugal. The story goes on to assert that five kings were defeated on this occasion and that two hundred thousand Mohammedans were slain. After the battle the Portuguese soldiers are said to have raised Alphonso on their shields and hailed him as King. Another story, which is probably also legendary, tells how after the Battle of Ourique Alphonso fought another battle in Galicia against the French Counts Raymond and Henry in which he was wounded. The question of the independence of Portugal was then settled by a chivalrous contest known as the Tourney of Valdevez. The Portuguese knights vanquished the Champions of Leon and Castile, and in consequence of this victory Alphonso Henriques assumed the title of King of Portugal. The later chroniclers then relate that in 1143 Alphonso assembled a Cortes at Lamego, where he received the crown from the hands of the Archbishop of

1 The old *Terra Portucalense*, the name of which was derived from the town of *Portucale*, now known as Oporto situated at the mouth of the Douro.

2 Among his contemporaries were Henry II of England, Philip Augustus of France and the Emperor Frederick Barbarossa.

Braganza, Portugal was declared free from the Crown of Leon and constitutional laws were passed. Modern research has questioned these fables, but it can be established that Alphonso began to use the royal title in 1140, though the King of Castile did not recognise it until 1143. In order to safeguard his new kingdom, Alphonso appealed to Pope Lucius II for protection and placed Portugal under the Holy See as a feudal fief. The Papacy accepted his allegiance and tribute, but it was not until 1176 that Pope Alexander III first addressed Alphonso as King. In the circumstances of the establishment of the Portuguese monarchy the ceremony of coronation was not introduced, though on various occasions, particularly when there was a change in the direct line of descent, a ceremony did take place at which the king received the crown, usually from the archbishop, who had first delivered the oath; but there was no anointing.[1] The Kings of Portugal did, however, adopt a royal crown as a symbol of their status. That used from 1140 to 1279 was a simple circlet from which rose a number of rays.

In 1185 Alphonso Henriques died and his next four successors kept the kingdom in being, though at times rather precariously. They were able to contain the Moors and to establish permanent boundaries of the kingdom. An important act by Alphonso III, who took the throne after the deposition of Sancho II by the Pope in 1246, was to abandon the semi-ecclesiastical titles of Visitor and Defender of the Realm and to proclaim himself King, which act reduced the large measure of control which the Church and nobles had exercised over the monarch. During the long reign of King Diniz (1279–1325) the kingdom was consolidated, the supremacy of the crown was recognised and great progress was made. Diniz changed the design of the crown, which became an open circlet decorated with fleurs-de-lis and strawberry leaves. Diniz was succeeded by his son Alphonso IV (1325–57). During his reign his son Peter, who was heir to the throne, took as his mistress Inez de Castro, a lady-in-waiting to his late wife, and they had several children. A group of nobles persuaded the King that the succession was being compromised and reluctantly he consented to Inez's murder. It is related that when Peter succeeded to the throne he ordered her body to be exhumed; dressed in a royal robe, with a crown on her head, the corpse was enthroned beside the King and the assembled nobles paid homage to the Queen, swearing fealty on her withered hand. This story is today considered to be fictitious and it is certainly not mentioned by Fernão Lopes, the most notable chronicler of the day. Peter (1357–67) was succeeded by Ferdinand (1367–85), and on his death a rebellion broke out owing to the danger of the succession resulting in a union of the crowns of Portugal and Castile. On 16th April 1385 a Cortes held at Coimbra declared the Crown of Portugal elective and Dom John, Master of the Order of Aviz and natural son of Peter I, who already had the title of Defender of the Realm, was chosen King. In August 1385 with the help of a body of English archers, the King of Castile was defeated at the Battle of Aljubarrota, the independence of Portugal was secured and the title of the House of Aviz to the throne was made sure. On 9th May 1386 the Treaty of Windsor was signed, which declared that the kingdoms of England and Portugal were to be united

---

[1] Pope Eugenius IV (1431–47) granted the King of Portugal the right of anointment and coronation which was never used.

a   *Portrait of Queen Maria Joanna, XV Century.*
     National Museum of Antique Art, Lisbon

b   *Portrait of Maria I and King*
     Peter III with crown, 1777,
     National Museum of Antique
     Art, Lisbon (p. 485)

a   *Royal crown, XIX Century, 1817. Ajuda
        Palace, Lisbon* (p. 488)

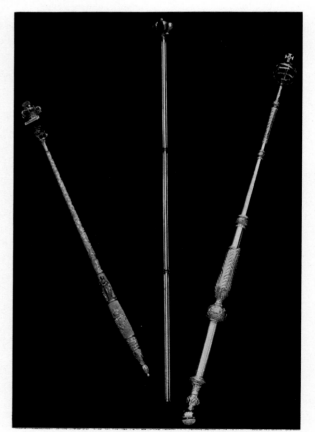

b   *Three sceptres, XVIII and XIX Centuries*
            (p. 489)

henceforth in the closest bonds of friendship and alliance. The Treaty has remained in force down to the present time. Shortly after, King John married Philippa, daughter of John of Gaunt.

Seven kings of the House of Aviz reigned from 1385 to 1578. In 1415 began the series of discoveries which led through an heroic and golden age to the establishment of the Portuguese Empire. The pages of Portuguese history of this time are illuminated with such great names as Henry the Navigator, Vasco da Gama, Albuquerque and John de Castro. Their expeditions led them round Africa to India and the China seas, and in the first half of the XVI century to Brazil. In many places settlements were established while Brazil was colonised. As a result of these enterprises the kings of Portugal became fabulously wealthy and the richest sovereigns in Europe. Perhaps to demonstrate his enhanced status, King John II in 1481 introduced the arched crown with strawberry leaves, a style which remained in force until the end of the monarchy. But after the reign of Manuel (1495–1521) decadence set in. The king had become absolute, the patriotism of the nobility had been transferred to a personal worship of the king and corruption spread to every department of government. The population became seriously depleted through emigration, wars, plague, famine and pestilence leading to the importation of hordes of slaves, which had the effect of discrediting manual labour. The position was further worsened by the persecution of the Jews and the establishment of the Inquisition.

Into this situation Sebastian, a boy of three, came to the throne. His upbringing was dominated by Jesuits and he came of age in 1568, a weak-minded but obstinate ascetic. Although the dynasty was threatened with extinction he refused to marry and absorbed his whole energies in planning a crusade against the Moors in Africa. Sebastian appealed to the Pope for help, but Gregory XIII only sent him an arrow of St Sebastian. His appeal for aid from his uncle Philip II of Spain was also fruitless. Although most of his seasoned troops were overseas and his treasury was depleted, the King was undaunted and on 24th June 1578 he set sail with his fleet and his polyglot army. Ten days before, the archbishop had solemnly blessed a banner which had been worked with the Arms of Portugal and an imperial crown. Sebastian also borrowed the sword of Alphonso Henriques, which was kept in the Convent of Santa Cruz at Coimbra, and he had a rich crown made as an emblem of sovereignty over the African Empire he sought to establish. But a few weeks later, on 9th August, at El-Kesr-el-Kebir, the dream of the African Empire was destroyed when the Portuguese were overwhelmed, the King and 9,000 of his army were killed and all but fifty of the survivors were taken prisoner. When the news reached Lisbon the whole country was stunned—the King, the army and the country's reputation had all been lost in the disaster, while much of what remained of the national wealth had to be used to ransom the hundreds of nobles and knights who were prisoners of the Moors. The only surviving prince of the Aviz dynasty was the Cardinal Prince Henry, who was old and feeble minded and incapable of dealing with the situation. Nevertheless Cardinal Henry was solemnly crowned King but died after a reign of little over a year. Portugal was now faced with the problem of the succession to the throne. There were seven candidates but only two could be considered seriously. Dom Antonio, Prior of Crato, an illegitimate nephew of King

Manuel, proclaimed himself King at Santarem and entered Lisbon without opposition. But Philip II of Spain, who had a better claim, brushed aside Antonio's makeshift army and the Prior fled to France and England taking with him a valuable collection of jewels which he used, without success, to enlist the support of Queen Elizabeth.

Philip II made a solemn entry into Lisbon and received the Portuguese Crown in the presence of a Great Cortes held at Thomar on 15th April 1581 at which he swore an oath promising that Portugal should remain a separate kingdom and be joined to Spain only by a personal union. These promises were, however, broken and Portugal endured a period known as 'the sixty years captivity'.

In 1640 the discontent with Spanish rule had reached a high pitch and advantage was taken of Spain's resources being taxed by her war with France, and a revolution in Catalonia, to stage a rebellion. John VIII, Duke of Braganza, who was a descendant of King Manuel, was chosen as leader. The revolt broke out on 1st December 1640 and was completely successful. On 3rd January 1641 John entered Lisbon amidst great popular rejoicing and on 15th January he was solemnly crowned as John IV in the Cathedral of Lisbon. On 19th January 1641 a Cortes was assembled at Lisbon which accepted John IV as King and his son as heir to the throne. On this occasion the King was again crowned by the archbishop, who also gave him the sceptre. The Sword of the Kingdom was carried by the High Constable. In 1656, when John IV died, he was succeeded by his second son, Alphonso VI, a vicious and feeble boy of thirteen, who in 1662 seized the royal authority which had been exercised by his mother as Regent. His marriage with Princess Marie, daughter of Henry IV of France, was dissolved after four months and Marie married Alphonso's brother, Dom Pedro, who became Regent. On Alphonso's death in 1683 he received the crown as Peter II. When he died in 1706 he was succeeded by his eldest son, John V (1706–50), who in turn was succeeded by his son Joseph (1750–77). During the period of these two reigns Portugal, despite the loss of much of the wealth she had drawn from the Orient, enjoyed unparalleled riches. Important discoveries of gold, diamonds and other precious stones were made in Brazil and King Peter prudently avoided making the goldfields a royal monopoly but took one fifth of the annual export which brought in some £300,000 per annum. The Portuguese sovereign, with his splendid and luxurious Court, again became celebrated all over Europe. Much of the wealth was spent on the Church. Enormous sums were given and lent to the Popes, who in return accorded the King of Portugal the title of 'Most Faithful Majesty'.[1] In Portugal, too, there was lavish expenditure on ecclesiastical buildings. The decoration of a single chapel in the Church of San Roque in Lisbon cost £225,000 while £4,000,000 was spent on the convent palace of Mafra. On 1st November 1755 a terrible catastrophe overtook Lisbon, half of which was laid in ruins by a severe earthquake and tidal wave, and further destruction was caused by fire and by depredations and looting by the mob. Thousands of people perished and many artistic and historical objects were lost.

On the death of King Joseph in 1777 his daughter Maria I succeeded to the throne and married her own uncle Dom Pedro, a younger brother of King Joseph, and re-

---

[1] John IV had replaced the mediaeval title of 'Highness' by that of 'Majesty'.

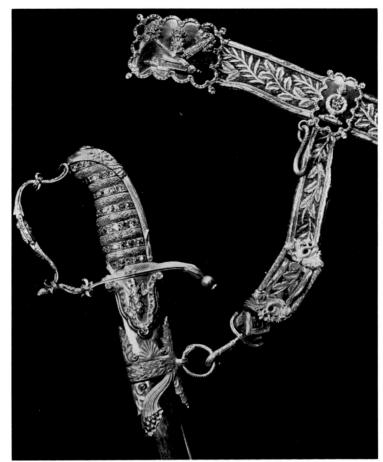

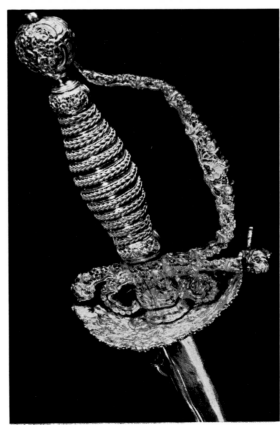

a (above)   *Court sword set with diamonds. Ajuda Palace, Lisbon* (p. 489)

b (above, right)   *Sabre of Dom Miguel set with diamonds. Ajuda Palace, Lisbon* (p. 489)

c (right)   *Court sword with chased gold handle. Ajuda Palace, Lisbon* (p. 489)

a *Grand Cross of three Portuguese military orders set with brilliants, rubies and emeralds, 1789* (p. 489)

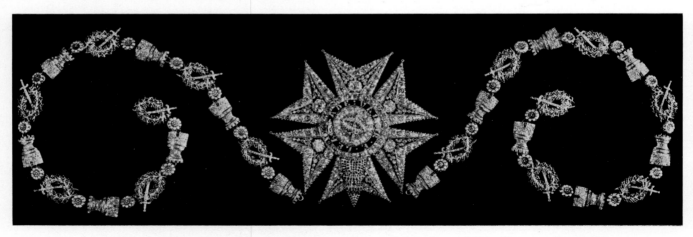

b *Collar and Grand Cross of the Order of the Tower and Sword in gold, brilliants and emeralds.*
Ajuda Palace, Lisbon (p. 489)

a   *Grand Cross of three Portuguese military orders set with brilliants, rubies and emeralds. First half of XVII Century* (p. 489)

All in the Ajuda Palace, Lisbon

b (above)   *Golden Fleece of gold, brilliants, rubies and a large sapphire. First half of XVIII Century* (p. 489)

c (left)   *Grand Cross of the Order of Our Lady of the Conception set with diamonds, 1832* (p. 489)

d (right)   *Small Golden Fleece made for Queen Amelia set with rubies and brilliants, XIX Century* (p. 489)

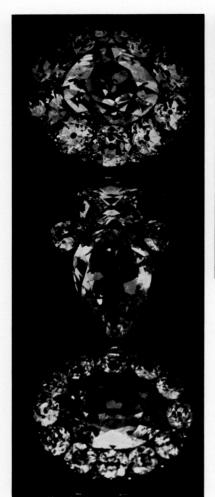

b   *Diadem with stars set with brilliants, 1878. Ajuda Palace, Lisbon* (p. 490)

a (left)   *Epaulette with three large brilliants, 1784. Ajuda Palace, Lisbon* (p. 490)

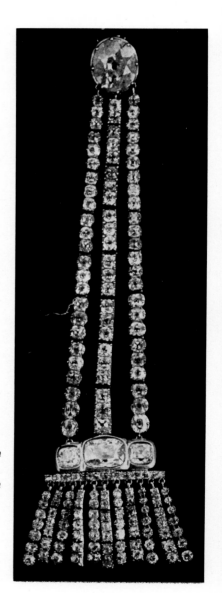

c (left)   *Collar with stars set with brilliants, 1876. Ajuda Palace, Lisbon* (p. 490)

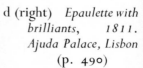

d (right)   *Epaulette with brilliants, 1811. Ajuda Palace, Lisbon* (p. 490)

ceived the crown jointly.[1] A few years after the death of Peter III in 1786, which was followed by the death of his eldest son, Dom John took charge of affairs and in 1799 was declared Regent. When Portugal was overrun by the French armies in 1807 Dom John proclaimed a Council of Regency and sailed with the royal family to Brazil. Although the British subsequently evicted the French from Portugal, Dom John continued to reside in Brazil for fourteen years. In 1816, on the death of Queen Maria, the Prince Regent was proclaimed King as John VI. In 1821, John VI returned to Portugal and solemnly swore to recognise the new constitution and to rule as a constitutional monarch. His consort, Queen Carlotta, and her son Miguel, refused to take the oath and were consequently banished. Meanwhile, after his departure from Brazil, the country declared its independence and John's eldest son Peter was elected Emperor. In 1824 John recognised Peter as Emperor of Brazil and returned to Rio de Janeiro to spend the rest of his days in peace. In Portugal the Regency passed to John's daughter, Isabel Maria, after John's death in 1826, although Peter was King. Peter's position was now difficult as he was devoted to Brazil, where his liberal ideas made him popular. He drew up a new constitution for Portugal and abdicated the throne on the condition that Maria married her uncle, Dom Miguel, who was required to swear fidelity to the new constitution which was known as the Charter. Miguel, who was an extreme absolutist, landed in Lisbon in February 1828. He had previously been solemnly betrothed to Maria and had sworn to abide by the Charter, whereupon Peter appointed him Regent. Regardless of his promises he dissolved Parliament and convened a Cortes of the old type which offered him the crown, and on 7th July 1828 he took the oath as King. In this he was supported by his mother Queen Carlotta, whose enormous wealth was at his disposal. Peter then intervened and having abdicated the Brazilian throne in favour of his son Peter II in 1831, he led an expedition to Portugal and ousted Dom Miguel in 1834, declaring that his daughter Maria was of age, although she was only fifteen. Having established her on the throne he died in the following September. Dom Miguel was permitted to keep all his personal possessions so long as he left Portugal and never returned. Maria was twice married, her first husband dying only four months after their marriage. She then married Ferdinand of Saxe-Coburg, who received the title of King Consort. On her death in 1853, Ferdinand acted as Regent until his son, Peter V, came of age in 1855. Peter V died of cholera in 1861 and was succeeded by his brother Luis, who like Peter left the government of the kingdom in the hands of his Ministers. He died in 1889 and was succeeded by his son Dom Carlos I and shortly afterwards in Brazil the Emperor Peter II abdicated and a republic was declared. In Portugal itself republicanism grew rapidly, and finally Dom Carlos I and the Crown Prince were assassinated in 1908. King Manuel II reigned for two years when a revolution established a republic in 1910 and he left the country and went into exile in England. During the last century no more crowning ceremonies

---

1 A painting of Queen Maria I and King Peter III (*Plate 143, b*) depicts their joint sovereignty. The crown is placed on a pedestal between them and Maria places her left hand on it and carries the sceptre in her right hand to show that she is the hereditary sovereign. The King makes a gesture with his right hand above to symbolise his share in the royal title.

took place but the king swore an oath to the constitution before the Cortes, the crown and sceptre being displayed on a table.

Although during the period of the Aviz dynasty the Kings of Portugal amassed great wealth, we have little precise information about the crown jewels. When Antonio, Prior of Crato, was displaced by Philip II of Spain in 1581 he took with him a large collection of diamonds and precious stones which, according to Froude,[1] were part of the crown jewels of Portugal. On these he borrowed 200,000 écus from a Portuguese Jewish financier named Alvaro Mendes, and among the stones was one 'of great worth' on which Mendes had personally loaned 20,000 écus. Antonio tried to interest Queen Elizabeth in his cause, and in exchange for a promise of help he handed over all his jewels. Although Queen Elizabeth did not extend any assistance to him she did not give the jewels back. These, according to Froude, were diamonds of the Crown of Portugal, but some doubt has been thrown on this by M. de Vilhena Barbosa, who carried out researches which questioned the possibility of Antonio having made off with the crown jewels. He was able to show that the treasury of the royal household and the Governors of the kingdom had had time, before the arrival of Antonio at Lisbon, to put the crown jewels in a place of safety, as these officials were loyal to the cause of Philip II. The King bestowed honours and dignitaries on these officials, and it is unlikely that he would have done so had they not looked after his interests. On the other hand, when in 1583 Antonio was condemned to death *in absentia*, the judgement specifically stated that he had removed the diamonds of the Crown of Portugal. It seems likely, therefore, that some of the crown diamonds had fallen into his hands, although he is known to have acquired a number of precious stones and valuables which were given to him by his supporters and also looted convents and churches. Among the stones given to Queen Elizabeth was a table-cut diamond of 30 carats mounted in a chain of gold, enamelled and surrounded by flowers, which was known as 'The Mirror of Portugal'.[2] This later passed into the crown jewels of France. During the period of the personal union of the Crown of Portugal with that of Spain, Philip II and his two successors would have had the use of the Portuguese crown jewels. We hear of a diamond also known as 'The Mirror of Portugal', which was worn by Philip IV of Spain on the occasion of the marriage of Louis XIII with Anne of Austria. No doubt as Portugal regained her independence by a rebellion the crown jewels were not returned from Madrid. During the period from 1725 to 1755 the Portuguese kings obtained great wealth from Brazil. Apart from the goldfields, diamonds were discovered in 1725 in Minas Geraes and by 1727 there was danger of a slump in diamond prices. The Dutch merchants who controlled the Indian output asserted that any diamonds from Brazil were of inferior quality, but the Portuguese began to ship diamonds from Brazil to Goa and export them to Europe as Indian stones. For the next twenty years the output from Minas Geraes was about 144,000 carats annually, but it was not until 1772 that the Government of Brazil started to work diamond mines on its own account and, in fact, it became a royal monopoly, but the King had already established a royal right to every stone above 20 carats in weight that was won, which continued until the

---

[1] Froude: *History of England*, 1886, Vol. II.   [2] See page 146 (*Plate 50, c*).

a (above, left) *Diamond rivière of 55 brilliants, 1787. Ajuda Palace, Lisbon* (p. 490)

b (above, right) *Small decoration of three military orders set with brilliants, rubies and emeralds. Ajuda Palace, Lisbon* (p. 490)

c (right) *Diamond rivière of 32 brilliants, 1787. Ajuda Palace, Lisbon* (p. 490)

a   *Corsage ornament with emeralds and brilliants, 1 emerald of 47·91 carats and 1 brilliant of 23·89 carats.
First half of XVIII Century (p. 490)*

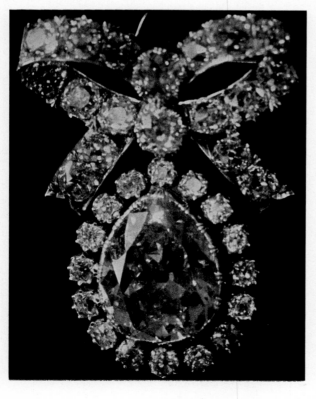

b   *Pendant brooch with drop brilliant of 31·93 carats (p. 490)*

c   *Pendant brooch with sapphire of 100 carats and 2 other large sapphires. Ajuda Palace, Lisbon (p. 490)*

severance of Brazil in 1834.[1] It was estimated that he obtained an income of £100,000 a year by a contract entered into with a syndicate of English diamond merchants. Other precious stones were also found in Brazil, including topaz, ruby, aquamarine, tourmaline, chrysoberyl, garnet and amethyst. In the Lisbon earthquake of 1765 many of the royal treasures including, it is believed, the regalia, were lost, but this loss was replenished from the mines in Brazil. The most famous stone which came to the Portuguese Royal Treasury was the so-called Braganza diamond. Not only do the stories of this stone differ but there is also confusion between it and another stone. The most acceptable account of its discovery is that given by Mawe.[2] He writes:

a few leagues to the north of the Rio Plata is the rivulet named Abaïté, celebrated for having produced the largest diamond in the Prince's possession, which was found about twelve years ago. Though this circumstance has been already briefly stated it may be allowed me in this place to relate the particulars as they were detailed to me during my stay at Tejuco. Three men (elsewhere named Antonio de Sousa, Jose Feliz Gomez and Thomas de Sousa) having been found guilty of high crimes were banished into the interior and ordered not to approach any of the capital towns or to remain in civilised society on pain of perpetual imprisonment. Driven by this hard sentence into the most unfrequented part of the country they endeavoured to explore new mines or new productions in the hope that, sooner or later, they might have the good fortune to make some important discovery, which would obtain a reversal of their sentence, and enable them to regain their station in society. They wandered about in this neighbourhood, making frequent searches in its various mines, for more than six years, during which time they were exposed to a double risk by becoming the prey of the anthropophagi, and in no less danger of being seized by the soldiers of Government. At length they, by hazard, made some trials in the River Abaïté at a time when its waters were so low in consequence of a long season of drought that a part of its bed was left exposed. Here, while searching and washing for gold, they had the good fortune to find a diamond nearly an ounce in weight [sic]. Elated by this providential discovery, which at first they could scarcely believe to be real, yet hesitating between a dread of the rigorous laws relating to the diamond, and a hope of regaining their liberty, they consulted a clergyman, who advised them to trust to the mercy of the State, and accompanied them to the Villa Rica, where he procured them access to the Governor. They threw themselves at his feet, and delivered to him the invaluable gem on which their hopes rested, relating all the circumstances connected with it. The Governor, astonished at its magnitude, could not trust the evidence of his senses, but called the officers of the establishment to decide whether it was a diamond, who set the matter beyond all doubt. Being thus, by the most strange and unforeseen accident, put in possession of the largest diamond ever found in America, he thought proper to suspend the sentence of the men as a reward for their having delivered it to him. The gem was sent to Rio de Janeiro from whence a frigate was dispatched with it to Lisbon, whither the clergyman was also sent to make the proper representations respecting it. The sovereign confirmed the pardon of the delinquents and bestowed some preferment on the holy father.

On arrival in Lisbon it went to the Royal Treasure, and John VI did not have it cut but wore it suspended from his neck on gala days. The weight of the stone has been variously given but the authentic weight is believed to be 1,680 carats or a little over

[1] It is estimated that the production from 1740–71 was 1,700,000 carats and from 1772–1818, when it was a royal monopoly, 1,304,770 carats.
[2] J. Mawe: *Travels in Brazil*, 1812.

11 oz. Romé Delysle estimated its value at three hundred million sterling but this, of course, was quite unrealistic, and even the Jeffrey's method of calculation, which would make it worth £5,644,800, could hardly be accepted. It is generally believed that the stone is not a diamond at all, and Mawe, who examined it, considered it to be a white topaz of little value, but it was kept jealously guarded in the Portuguese Treasury against all inquisitive sightseers and the authorities were anxious that it should be regarded as a genuine diamond.[1]

It is sometimes claimed that the great diamond known as the Sancy was at one time among the crown jewels of Portugal, but Bapst in his *Histoire des Joyaux de la Couronne de France* has clearly shown that this would not have been possible. It seems that confusion may have arisen through Dom Antonio of Crato disposing of a large diamond to Nicholas Harlay, Seigneur de Sancy, who gave his name to another famous diamond. Another large diamond, found in the River Abatio, came into the possession of John VI when he was Regent and became known as 'The Regent of Portugal'. It is a round-shaped stone and its weight in its uncut state was 215 carats. John VI's collection of diamonds and precious stones was said to be worth three million pounds sterling. Some of this wealth was pledged to raise money to continue war with France. When in 1801 France and Spain declared war on Portugal the Prince Regent contracted a loan of twelve million florins from the Houses of Hope of Holland and Baring of London on the security of the diamonds coming from Brazil. When the royal family went to Brazil they took some crown jewels with them, but they left behind in Lisbon two thousand carats of brilliants and these were subsequently seized by General Junot.

The Portuguese crown jewels which have survived the vicissitudes of the nation's history are today kept in the National Palace of Ajuda at Lisbon. The collection contains the crown and sceptres, jewelled insignia of the Portuguese Orders, the crown jewels set in personal ornaments, weapons, plate and other items. Dom Miguel, before leaving Portugal after the Convention of Evera Mont, sent by his *valet de chambre* boxes containing the jewels in his possession, with a letter to his brother asking him to return to the Crown those which were crown property. These boxes were deposited in the State Bank, where they remained until 1954 when a settlement was reached regarding the jewels between members of the former Royal House and the Portuguese Government. A selection of 115 of these ornaments was arranged in the Ajuda Palace in 1954 but are not on show to the public. They are enumerated in a beautifully produced catalogue.[2]

The royal crown (*Plate 144, a*) was made in the workshop of Antonio Gomes da Silva in Rio de Janeiro in 1817 and the inscription on the crown reads *Inacio Luiz da Costa O Fez*, which gives the name of the artist who carried out the work. It is of chased gold and no precious stones are used in its decoration. The circlet is decorated with a chased wreath of laurel leaves and on it rests

[1] E. W. Streeter: *The Great Diamonds of the World*. Recent inquiries have failed to obtain any information as to what has happened to the stone. There is among the crown jewels a large, rough, uncut aquamarine, the weight of which is given as 1,750 carats, approximately sufficiently close to the weight of the so-called Braganza Diamond to make it possible for the two stones to be identical. It could have been worn by being held by clasps. The catalogue states that this aquamarine was formerly the property of Dom Miguel.　　　[2] José Rosas Júnior: *Catálogo das Jóias e Platas da Coroa*.

eight strawberry leaves set alternately with eight fleurs-de-lis. From behind the strawberry leaves spring eight half-arches having a pronounced bulge which form an ogee at their junction, on which rests a polished globe surmounted by an elegant cross. On each arch is a graduated row of gilded pearls. Inside the crown is a cap of red velvet.

There are three sceptres (*Plate 144, b*); the first is a slender rod of gold and enamel surmounted by an elegant lily. It is of English work of the second half of the XVIII century and bears an inscription which reads *Honest Vivere—Alterum Non Ladere—Tribuerius Suum Cuique—*. The second was made in Rio de Janeiro in 1817 by the same jeweller as the crown. It is a golden rod with an elaborately chased ornamentation, and on the handle is the Portuguese Coat of Arms. At the summit is a dragon bearing a pedestal on which rests a miniature copy of the royal crown. The third sceptre was made in London in 1828. It is a golden rod of chased work surmounted by an astrolabe and a cross. It bears the monogram of D. Maria II and the inscription *Os Portugueses leais à Senhora D. Maria II—Londres 1828*.

Among the weapons are two swords and a cavalry sabre (*Plate 145, b*) which had belonged to Dom Miguel. One of the swords (*Plate 145, a*) and the sabre have handles of gold set with brilliants, and the second sword has a richly decorated gold chased handle (*Plate 145, c*).

The Portuguese Order of Christ was founded by King Diniz in conjunction with Pope John XXII in 1318 on the abolition of the Order of Templars. It was secularised in 1789 and its religious aspect was abandoned in Portugal though the papal branch survives as a distinct Order. The insignia of the Order are of gold and enamel. There are three Portuguese Military Orders—the Tower and the Sword founded in Brazil in 1808 as a revival of an older Order of the Sword dating from 1459; the Order of St Benedict of Aviz founded in 1162; and the Order of St James (of Compostella) and the Sword, a branch of an Order traditionally founded in Spain in the X century but historically dating from 1175. In 1789 these three Orders were united and granted a common badge. The collection contains notable examples of the insignia.

The first is a plaque of Grand Cross of the three Military Orders (*Plate 146, a*) in gold set with brilliants, rubies and emeralds, which was made in Lisbon in 1789 by Ambrósio Pollet. Another Grand Cross (*Plate 147, a*) is also of gold set with brilliants, rubies and emeralds and contains some large brilliants of outstanding quality. It is Portuguese work of the first half of the XVII century. There is also the Collar of the Grand Cross of the Tower and the Sword (*Plate 146, b*) in gold, brilliants and emeralds which is the work of Antonio Gomes da Silva and made in Rio de Janeiro in 1813. A similar decoration of the three Orders in gold with brilliants, rubies and emeralds was made by Ambrosio Pollet in Lisbon in 1790.

A plaque of the Order of Our Lady of the Conception (*Plate 147, c*) set with brilliants and rose-cut diamonds was made by Antonio Gomes da Silva in Lisbon in 1832.

Apart from the Portuguese Orders there is a splendid Golden Fleece (*Plate 147, b*) of gold, brilliants, rubies and a large sapphire. It was made in the first half of the XVIII century and was worn by John VI and Dom Miguel.

A small decoration of the three Military Orders set with brilliants, rubies and emeralds (*Plate 149, b*).

A small decoration of the Order of Charles III of Spain. XVIII century (*Plate 151, d*).

Another Golden Fleece (*Plate 147, d*) made in Lisbon in the second half of the XIX century for Queen Amelia is of gold set with rubies and brilliants.

An Order of the Elephant of Denmark is of gold and enamel set with brilliants.

489

There are also twenty-six other foreign Orders unadorned with precious stones including the Insignia of the Order of the Garter dating from the second half of the XIX century.

Apart from the Insignia of the Portuguese Orders there are three jewelled epaulettes which were worn with the Grand Cross of the three Military Orders. The first was the work of Adam Gottlieb Pollet and made in Lisbon in 1784 (*Plate 148, a*). It contains three large brilliants, one of which is drop-shaped, set among other brilliants of fine quality. The second epaulette was made in Lisbon in the second half of the XVIII century and it contains 3 large and 19 lesser brilliants and 2 large rubies. The third was made by A. G. da Silva in Rio de Janeiro in 1811 (*Plate 148, d*) and is set with brilliants.

The remaining jewellery contain ornaments for personal adornment; the most important are:

A collar or necklace of eighteen stars, nine large and nine small, with large brilliants in the centre of each, surrounded with smaller stones, made for Queen Maria Pia by Estevao de Sousa in Lisbon in 1876 (*Plate 148, c*).

A diadem of twenty-five stars in brilliants made by Estevao de Sousa in Lisbon in 1878 for Queen Maria Pia (*Plate 148, b*). Each star is set with a large brilliant in the centre, that in the front being a stone of unusual size.

Two rivières of 55 and 32 brilliants respectively mounted in gold (*Plate 149, a and c*), both the work of Ambrosio Pollet of Lisbon in 1787.

A magnificent corsage ornament in the form of a bow (*Plate 150, a*) set with 28 emeralds of 301·44 carats including one stone of 47·91 carats, in the centre; and brilliants weighing 195·72 carats, the largest being 23·89 carats. It was the property of Queen Maria Anna of Austria, consort of John V, and was the work of the first half of the XVIII century.

Twenty-three large and twenty small buttons (*Plate 151, a*) set with brilliants, of Portuguese work of the second half of the XVIII century.

Two trefoil brooches in brilliants and rose-cut diamonds set in platinum (*Plate 151, c*), made in Portugal in the second half of the XIX century.

A brooch in the form of a pendant with a large drop brilliant of 31·93 carats, surrounded by 16 other brilliants pendant from a brilliant bow (*Plate 150, b*). This is Portuguese work of the first half of the XVIII century.

A pendant with a large sapphire of 100 carats and 2 large drop sapphires set with small brilliants (*Plate 150, c*). It was the property of the Infanta Isobel Maria, daughter of John VI, at the time of the regency of the Queen, and was acquired by the State in 1874. It is Portuguese work of the first half of the XIX century.

A gold ring with large brilliant (*Plate 151, e (i)*)—Portuguese work of the first half of the XIX century.

A gold ring with a large brilliant similar to the above which had been the property of Dom Miguel (*Plate 151, e (ii)*).

A ring with a miniature on ivory of the Infanta D. Francesca de Paula, daughter of Charles IV of Spain (*Plate 152, b*), made in the second half of the XVIII century.

A pendant with a miniature set with brilliants on ivory of D. Manuel de Godoy, Duke of Alcudia (*Plate 152, a*), made in the second half of the XVIII century.

A pendant with a miniature on ivory, set with brilliants of Charles III of Spain (*Plate 152, a*); work of the second half of the XVIII century.

A pendant with miniature on ivory, set with brilliants, of D. Carlotta de Borbón (*Plate 152, a*); work of the second half of the XVIII century.

A ring with a miniature set with brilliants of an Infante of Spain (*Plate 152, b*); made in the second half of the XVIII century.

a   *Two sets of buttons set with brilliants, XVIII Century. Ajuda Palace, Lisbon* (p. 490)

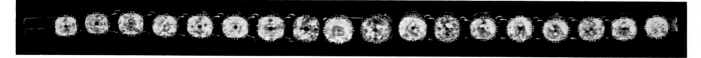

b   *Bracelet with 18 brilliants. Ajuda Palace, Lisbon* (p. 490)

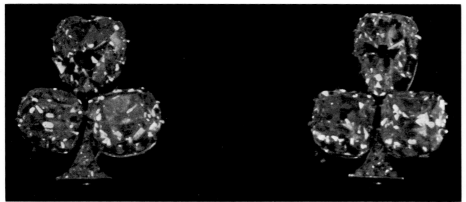

c   *Two trefoil brooches with large brilliants, XIX Century. Ajuda Palace, Lisbon*
(p. 490)

d   *Small decoration of the Order of Charles of Spain, set with brilliants, rubies
and emeralds. Ajuda Palace, Lisbon* (p. 489)

e (i) (left)   *Gold ring with
large brilliant, XIX Cen-
tury;* (ii) (right)   *Gold
ring with large brilliant,
formerly the property of
Dom Miguel. Ajuda
Palace, Lisbon* (p. 490)

a   *Pendants with miniatures of* (left) *D. Carlotta of Bourbon;* (centre) *Charles III of Spain and* (right) *Godoy, Duke of Alcudia. Ajuda Palace, Lisbon* (p. 490)

b and c (left)
*Gold ring with miniature,
XVIII Century.
Ajuda Palace,
Lisbon
(p. 490)*

d   *Handle of a cane with brilliants the largest of 24·32 carats, XVIII Century. Ajuda Palace, Lisbon* (p. 491)

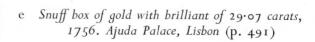

e   *Snuff box of gold with brilliant of 29·07 carats, 1756. Ajuda Palace, Lisbon* (p. 491)

A bracelet set with 18 brilliants (*Plate 151, b*); Portuguese work of the second half of the XVIII century.

An uncut aquamarine of 1,650 carats, formerly the property of Dom Miguel.

Two unset brilliants from Brazil of 7·07 and 7·01 carats.

The handle of a cane of gold set with brilliants, with a brilliant of 24·32 carats (*Plate 152, d*); work of the second half of the XVIII century.

A snuff box of gold set with brilliants and emeralds with a brilliant of 29·07 carats (*Plate 152, e*). It is inscribed *Jacqmin Joiallier de Roi—Paris* and on the inside *L. Roucel à Paris le 29 Juillet 1756*. It was the property of King Joseph.

There are four crowns in the treasury dating from the second half of the XVIII century which were used to adorn the heads of religious images. Two are ornamented with brilliants, rubies and emeralds.

Although not truly belonging to our subject it may be mentioned that the regalia made for the Emperors Peter I and Peter II of Brazil have been preserved. The crowns of the two Emperors, and the great and lesser sceptre, the coronation mantle and a tippet of toucan's feathers are in the Museum of Petropolis, near Rio de Janeiro. The present head of the imperial family, H.I.H. Dom Pedro of Orleans and Braganza, has in his possession the imperial orb, the coronation sword, habit and a splendid Golden Fleece in diamonds which was made for Peter I, and the Collar of the Order of the Rose.

BIBLIOGRAPHY

ALMEIDA, FORTUNATO DE	*Historia de Portugal*, 6 vols., Coimbra 1927–9.
FROUDE, J. A.	*History of England*, Vol. I.
JOSÉ ROSAS JÚNIOR	*Catálogo das Jóias e Platas da Coroa.*
MAWE, J.	*Travels in Brazil*, 1812.
NOWELL, C. E.	*A History of Portugal*, Princeton, New Jersey 1952.
STEPHENS, H. M.	*Portugal*, London 1891.
STREETER, E. W.	*The Great Diamonds of the World.*
WILLIAMS, H. S. (Editor)	*The Historian's Histories of the World*, 'Portugal'.

KINGS AND QUEENS OF PORTUGAL

1139	Alphonso I, Henriques. Declared King
1185	Sancho I
1212	Alphonso II
1223	Sancho II
1248	Alphonso III
1279	Diniz
1325	Alphonso IV
1357	Peter (Pedro) I
1367	Ferdinand I
1385	John I. Master of the Order of Aviz

1433	Edward
1438	Alphonso V
1481	John II
1495	Emmanuel (Manuel)
1521	John III
1557	Sebastian
1578	Henry
1580	Antonio, Prior of Crato
1580	Philip II, King of Spain
1598	Philip III, King of Spain
1621	Philip IV, King of Spain
1640	John IV, Duke of Braganza
1656	Alphonso VI
1683	Peter II
1706	John V
1750	Joseph Emmanuel
1777	Maria I and Peter III
1786	Maria I alone
1792	John, Regent
1816	John VI
1826	Peter IV
1826	Maria II
1828	Dom Miguel
1833	Maria III. (Her husband, Ferdinand, had the title of King Consort)
1853	Peter V
1861	Luis I
1889	Carlos I
1908	Manuel II
1910	Republic declared

CHAPTER NINETEEN

PRUSSIA

The history of the rise of modern Prussia is inseparable from that of the House of Hohenzollern. During the course of five centuries the Hohenzollerns added to their Electorate of Brandenburg various other scattered territories, and particularly the districts known as East and West Prussia, from which the modern state took its name, until the kingdom of their own creation became the most powerful and the leading state in a great empire. It is natural, therefore, that the Prussian regalia and crown jewels should be connected with the Hohenzollern family and that they should be regarded as the property of that dynasty and not of the state.

The origin of the House can be traced back to Tassilon, who is said to have built a castle at Zollern in the IX century, but the first historical mention of the name is in the Chronicon of a certain Berthold (*obiit* 1088), who refers to 'Burchardus of Zolorin'. This man appears to have been a Count of Zollern and to have met his death in 1061. The great-grandson of Burchardus married Sophia, daughter and heiress of Conrad, Burgrave of Nuremberg; in 1192 he succeeded his father-in-law as Burgrave, obtaining also some lands in Austria and Franconia. His successors played an unimportant part in German history until in 1415 Frederick, the sixth Count of Hohenzollern and Margrave of Nuremberg, purchased from the Emperor Sigismund, for the sum of 400,000 florins, the Margravate of Brandenburg with the rank and title of Elector and Prince of the Holy Roman Empire. He was solemnly invested by the Emperor, to whom he made homage, at Constance on 14th April 1417. Prussia at that time was under the suzerainty of Poland, and was not a part of the Holy Roman Empire. The population was not German at all but Lithuanian. These Lithuanians had remained pagans and barbarians until they were half conquered and half exterminated by the Teutonic Knights in the XIII and XIV centuries, after which their country became Germanised by a constant immigration from the west. The Teutonic Order governed the territory and in 1525 Albert, the Grand Master of the Order, having become a follower of Luther, converted it into a duchy for himself and his descendants, under the suzerainty of Poland. In 1618 his family died out and in accordance with an arrangement made in 1569 the duchy and part of Brandenburg became hereditary in the Hohenzollern family. In 1656 Duke Frederick William, the Great Elector, proclaimed himself Duke, Sovereign, and King of Prussia. Although in the following year Poland, by the Treaty of Wehlau, recognised the duchy as an independent sovereign state, the Emperor would not recognise it.

The insignia of the Elector consisted of the Electoral Hat or Bonnet, the robe of scarlet velvet trimmed with ermine, the sword, the sceptre and, in the second half of the XVI century, the crown. When each of these ornaments was introduced is not certain; we know that a ceremonial sword was used from an early date, but it does not seem to have been called the electoral sword until the time of the Great Elector (*Plate 153, a*). The weapon which became the electoral sword was consecrated and given by Pope Pius II in 1460 to Albert Achilles, then Margrave and who in 1470 became Elector of Brandenburg.[1] The Pope himself relates how, wishing to enlist the aid of the Margrave against the Turk, he sent a cardinal with a present of 10,000 gold pieces and two horses to meet Albert as he approached Mantua. At the Feast of the Epiphany he made him a ceremonial present of this sword, so that 'the most worthy prince in the world should be decorated with it for the birth of Our Lord'. Later in the year the Pope also bestowed on the Margrave a gold cross set with 10 diamonds and 4 pearls.

The sword (*Plate 153, a*) has on several occasions been altered and restored, but the original blade remains. Von Lessing, who minutely examined it and compared it with a very similar sword in the Armoury at Madrid, suggests that the now undecipherable inscription on the blade ran as follows: *ACCIPE SCM GLADIUM MVNVS A DEO QVO DECIICIES AD VERSARIOS PPLI MEI XPOANI*, a slightly altered rendering of the text from 2 Maccabees xv,16: 'Take this holy sword, a gift from God, with the which thou shalt wound thy adversaries.' At the upper end of the blade, concealed under the hilt, are the arms of the Piccolomini on five half-moons. (Pope Pius II was the famous humanist *Aeneas Sylvius Piccolomini*.) Above are the crossed keys and the papal tiara. In the centre of the inscription can be seen the traces of a small round engraving of the Apostle Peter. Of the original hilt only the silver grip decorated with flat acanthus leaves and the silver mussel-shell in the centre of the guard remain. The original pommel, which was cut from a chalcedon, has been replaced by a metal knob decorated with tendril work and the guard by late Gothic foliage work in the form of a bow. On the old guard must have been inscribed, as in other similar swords, the Pope's dedication.

The scabbard has been restored in cast silver-gilt. From a vase-shaped ornament at the mouth-piece spring traceries of acanthus foliage patterns, containing three lozenge-shaped shields at regular intervals on each side. Originally the arms and symbols of Pope Pius II must have decorated the shields, but they have been replaced by the various parts of the electoral coat-of-arms. On the flat now undecorated aperture and point of the scabbard were originally the papal arms in coloured enamels. The sword was restored at the time of the Reformation and the Brandenburg coats-of-arms substituted in enamel on silver plates. The shape of the ornaments on the pommel and guard of the hilt date from about 1530 to 1540 and make it probable that the sword was altered at that date. The six coats-of-arms are those of Brandenburg, Kassubien and Pommerania on the front and Rügen, Nuremberg and Zollern on the back.

There are several representations of former electors in which the sword is depicted, in particular the portrait of the Elector Albert Achilles on the altar of the Order of the Swan in the Chapel of St George of the Church of St Gumperts in Anspach. This shows the Elector in a kneeling position; behind him, also kneeling, are the Graf zu Linden und Ruppin, carrying in his hands an ermine hat, and the Ganz Edler Herr zu Pulitz, bearing a sword on his shoulder. This sword does not greatly resemble the electoral sword, but it must be remembered that in paintings of those days exact reproduction

---

[1] For the origin and history of this sword see Lessing: 'Die Schwerter des Preuszischen Krontresors' in *Jahrbuch der Königlich Preuszischen Kunstsammlungen*, 1895.

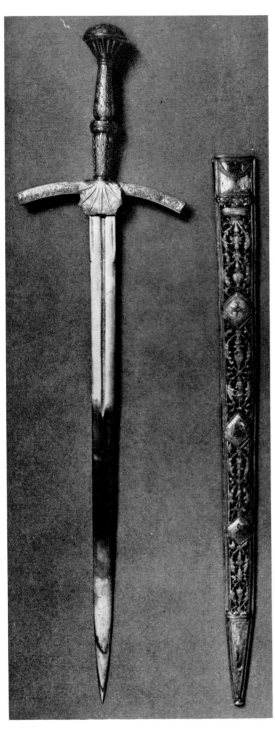

a   *Electoral sword, 1466 (p. 494)*

b   *Sword of Prussian sovereignty, XVI Century*
(p. 495)

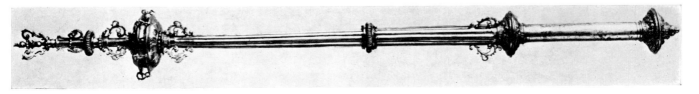

c   *Electoral sceptre, XVI Century. Hohenzollern Museum (p. 496)*

a   *Portrait of the Elector John Sigismund, 1608* (p. 495)

b   *Portrait of Crown Prince Karl Emil (1655–77)
with electoral crown and hat* (p. 496)

c   *Electoral hat, c. 1786*
(p. 496)

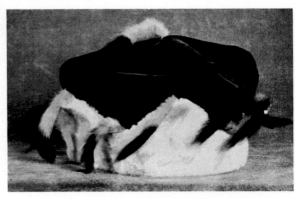

cannot be expected. It is worth noting that even then a Herr zu Pulitz was a sword-bearer. In a painting of the Elector Johann Sigismund (*Plate 154, a*) there are eight coats-of-arms instead of six. The probable explanation is that Joachim I, owing to his piety, would have been unlikely to have destroyed the papal emblem; his successor, Joachim II, was at pains to keep the coats-of-arms which were in use at the time of the Reformation, and the additional ones shown in the picture are also the imaginings of the artist, who represented the eight coats-of-arms which were in use at that date. According to Laking,[1] another sword of the same period preserved in the Vatican shows that it was made by the Florentine goldsmith Simone di Giovanni. For two centuries prior to 1810 it was preserved in the *Zeughaus* in Berlin, passing thence to the *Kunstkammer*. In 1857 it was placed among the crown regalia of Prussia.

A second sword is that known as the Sword of Prussian Sovereignty (*Plate 153, b*), which first appears as such at the funeral of the Great Elector. This sword, as its form and decoration show, was originally intended to be a weapon and not a ceremonial sword.

The scabbard and hilt are silver-gilt; only the pommel and the blade are steel. On the front of the pommel is an inset medallion of Duke Albert of Prussia and his wife, Dorothea of Denmark, with an inscription stating that the sword was made for the Duke in 1540–1 in Königsberg by Jobst Freudner of Ulm. On the left and right of this medallion are copies of old Roman coins which from the inscriptions are known to be those of Nero and Hadrian. The front of the hilt and scabbard are decorated with a number of plates on which are engraved in relief scenes from the Old Testament; the plates are surrounded and joined together by strips of tendril and foliage work. On the hilt is represented God the Father as Creator, with the inscription *In principio creaunt deus celum et terram*. On the scabbard the plates show the Fall of Man, the Murder of Abel, the Sacrifice of Isaac, Jacob's Dream, Samson with the gates of Gaza, and Samson and Delilah. It is difficult to see any connection between these decorations and the purpose and design of the sword. The designs are taken from various sources but are especially after the manner of the 'Little Masters', such as Virgil Solis, Aldegraver, Hans Sebald, Beham, Altdorfer, and others. The goldsmiths and silversmiths, as was common among the artists at the close of the Gothic period, seem to have paid more attention to the possibilities of exploiting their material than to the purpose for which the article was designed. The back of the hilt and scabbard are decorated in a much simpler style. On the pommel is inset a copy of an Italian plaque of the *Rape of Ipheginia* by Valerio Balli, or Vicentino, the original of which was preserved in the Kaiser Friedrich Museum. On the left and right of this inset are, as in the front, copies of heads of Roman emperors. The back of the grip is ornamented with tendril and foliage work, behind which a bear can be seen. The back of the scabbard is undecorated on the upper part where it would touch the body of the wearer and is provided with holes for fastening. The lower half is adorned with beautiful foliage and tendril work after the manner of Aldegraver. The blade dates, according to the opinion of Von Heydens, from about 1500; it is undecorated but beautifully shaped and fitted to its purpose. The maker's mark resembles that of Wiersburg von Solingen, who first became famous in the beginning of the XVII century. The splice which runs down the centre of the blade to the extreme point is very skilfully joined to the hilt in such a manner that the sword retains its elegance of form while losing none of its strength.

The sword was formerly thought to be the work of an Augsburg or Nuremberg craftsman, but there is authoritative evidence that at least the hilt and scabbard were

1 Sir Guy Laking: *A Record of European Arms and Armour.*

made in Königsberg itself by the goldsmith Jobst Freudner of Ulm. He was working in Königsberg at that date and, according to old documents, was employed in 1527 in the making of two swords. One of these swords was almost certainly the *Reichsschwert*, which in style and design belongs to that period. Moreover, the silver work on the scabbard and hilt is stamped with an *I*, which must stand for the Christian name of the goldsmith—Jobst Freudner. A similar initial is stamped on the silver sceptre of the University of Königsberg, which documentary evidence shows was made in 1544 by Freudner.

Another sword still preserved is known as the Pomeranian Sword, which was given to Duke Bogislaw of Pomerania by Pope Alexander VI (Borgia) on Christmas Day 1497. According to the papal accounts in the Vatican[1] it was originally made entirely by the goldsmith Angelino di Domenico de Sutri, but of his work only the scabbard remains. The hilt and blade were remade in Germany in the second half of the XVI century. Duke Bogislaw deposited it in the Church of St Otto in his Pomeranian home but at a later date removed it to his treasury. In 1638 on the extinction of his line of the family the contents of the treasury were inherited by the Duchess Anna, widow of the Duke Ernest von Croy-Havre, and were taken to Stolp. The sword was inherited by her son Ernest Bogislaw von Croy, and on his death in 1684 he left it by will to the Great Elector of Prussia, who placed it in the *Zeughaus* of Berlin, where it remained until 1810, when it was removed to the Hohenzollern Museum.

By the Golden Bull of Charles IV of 1356, it was laid down that the Margrave of Brandenburg as Arch-Chamberlain of the Empire had the right to carry the imperial sceptre. By virtue of this right the sceptre was borne on the coat-of-arms of Brandenburg, and with the Red Eagle is frequently found as the emblem of the electorate. The Electors of Brandenburg thus also included a sceptre among their insignia and one dating from the end of the XVI century has been preserved.

This sceptre (*Plate 153, c*) has a fluted rod with a plain handle. It is ornamented at the top by a large and a smaller *pomellum* and some scroll work. It is recognisable as that shown in the portrait of Elector Johann Sigismund, 1608, in the former royal collection, although in the picture the sceptre appears to have been set with jewels, as are others shown in XVII-century portraits.

The electoral hat (*Plate 154, c*) was round in shape and made of scarlet velvet turned up with a broad fringe of ermine with tails and an ermine tuft on top. One which has been preserved is probably not older than the funeral of Frederick the Great (*obiit* 1786). In 1656 when the Great Elector proclaimed himself Duke, Sovereign and King of Prussia, a crown was made which was worn over the electoral hat. In a portrait of Crown Prince Karl Emil, 1655–77 (*Plate 154, b*), son of the Great Elector, in the former royal collection, the Prince is depicted carrying a jewelled royal crown with two arches surmounted by orb and cross, with the electoral hat inside the crown. In the funeral procession of the Great Elector in 1688 the electoral hat with the royal crown with four arches was borne in the procession. The frame of the crown was kept in the Royal Treasury and only set with jewels, usually diamonds and pearls, on special ceremonial occasions.

[1] Laking: op. cit.

a *Frame of crown of King Frederick I, 1701*
(p. 502)

b *Frame of crown of Queen Sophia Charlotte, 1701*
(p. 502)

c *Frame of crown of King William I, 1861*
(p. 508)

d *Frame of crown of Queen Augusta, 1861*
(p. 508)

All in the Neues Museum, Wiesbaden

a   Crown of King William II,
    1889. Schloss Hohenzollern
              (p. 509)

b (left)   Head of royal sceptre,
    1701. Neues Museum, Wies-
    baden (p. 502)

c (right)   Royal orb, 1701. Neues
    Museum, Wiesbaden (p. 502)

The funeral of the Great Elector provided an occasion on which the electoral insignia were developed to its fullness, additional items having been added perhaps because of the Elector's claim to the title of Sovereign Duke. The ornaments carried in the procession were:

> the Sword of Prussian Sovereignty;
> the Electoral Sword;
> the English Order of the Garter;
> the Helmet;
> the Military Baton;
> the Electoral and Royal Seal;
> the Crown and Electoral Hat;
> the Electoral Sceptre.

The military baton or *Regimentsstab* had not been mentioned before and is described as 'a staff of government covered with blue velvet and richly embroidered with gold and silver'. It has been preserved, and in general form resembles the baton of a modern field marshal. The state helmet or *Reichshelm* was made for the occasion of this funeral and was subsequently regularly used at funerals of male members of the Hohenzollern family until 1918, and is still preserved. It is of silver gilt decorated with wrought copper ornamented at the throat with a medallion of the Great Elector and surmounted by a plume of ostrich feathers. Although not mentioned in the description of the funeral, it was the custom for a pair of spurs to be carried at electoral funerals. These were usually borrowed from the armoury for the occasion, but later, although the date is uncertain, a silver gilt pair which has been preserved came to be kept in the Treasury.

The Crown Prince Karl Emil having died, the Great Elector was succeeded by his son Frederick III, who became the twelfth Elector of Brandenburg. Frederick continued the policy of the Great Elector and had a large and efficient army with which he gave assistance to the Emperor Leopold. He was very fond of pomp and ceremony, and tried to model his Court on that of Louis XIV. He was anxious to obtain for himself and his successors the title of King and this engaged much of his energies for some years. Despite the military assistance he rendered to the Emperor, it was not until November 1700 that Leopold gave his imperial sanction to Frederick's request, having first obtained various conditions of which further military aid was the most important. Pope Clement XI made a furious protest.[1] The King did not waste any time, and crowned himself as Frederick I, King of Prussia, at Königsberg at a ceremony of characteristic magnificence on 18th January 1701. A full description of the coronation has been left by Besser, who was the Master of the Ceremonies. The King wore a robe of scarlet with rich gold embroideries and large diamond buttons and over it a mantle of purple velvet embroidered with crowns and eagles and lined with ermine. Contrary

---

[1] Bryce: *The Holy Roman Empire*: states, 'His prophetic spirit dreaded and denounced in Hildebrandine fashion the admission of a heretic to the most sacred and secular offices'.

to established custom in other kingdoms, he went to the church wearing his crown and carrying his sceptre. The Queen was dressed in flowered gold brocade with a large diamond corsage. Her mantle and crown were like the King's except that the crown was worn over her own thick curling coal-black hair instead of over a wig. On her right breast she wore an aigrette of pearls. At the coronation ceremony the King having been anointed, crowned himself and then crowned his Queen in token of his independence, to show that he was no vassal of the Emperor and no subject of the Pope. The action was symbolical and the sign was more fully understood by posterity than by those who witnessed it, or even by the King himself, although he perceived the wisdom of 'sowing for the future', one of his favourite expressions.

The regalia consisted of three crowns for the King, the Queen and the Crown Prince, and the royal sceptre and orb, and in addition the other ornaments carried in the procession were:

> the Electoral Sword;
> the Electoral Hat;
> the English and Danish Orders;
> the State Seal;
> the Sword of Prussian Sovereignty;
> the Banner.

To enable the public to make an inspection, for three days after the coronation all the royal ornaments were displayed and made accessible in the castle under the protection of the Swiss guard.

When Frederick died in 1713 the funeral was carried out with great pomp. The corpse was arrayed for the lying-in-state in full coronation dress, crown on head, and the other insignia at the side. The body, clothed in a long dress of cloth of gold, was laid in an open coffin covered with a brocade pall embroidered at the head with the crown and at the foot with the chain and the Order of the Black Eagle. In the funeral procession the regalia were carried in front of the coffin with the exception of the banner, which followed behind it.

Frederick's successor, Frederick William I, was a man of opposite tastes to his father. He was frugal in habit, simple in tastes, and had a complete contempt for the trappings of royalty. The coronation ceremony was dispensed with and the regalia put away. One of his first acts on his accession to the throne was to dismiss from the palace every unnecessary official. He regulated the royal household on principles of the strictest parsimony. Even the greater part of the beautiful furniture was sold. At his funeral he was buried in military dress instead of in royal robes. At his death in 1740 he was succeeded by his son, Frederick the Great, who accepted as a precedent his father's act of dispensing with the coronation. During his reign many of the gold ornaments in the Treasury were melted down and the gold thus obtained used for the making of Frederick's famous gold dinner service, afterwards melted down in the time of the Napoleonic Wars to meet the needs of the empty Treasury. Frederick the Great was succeeded on his death in 1786 by his nephew Frederick William II, but even this break in the direct descent did not occasion a revival of the coronation.

In fact the only occasions on which the regalia appeared during these and the successive three reigns were at the funerals of the kings.

On his death Frederick William III succeeded to the throne in 1797. During his reign Prussia was defeated and humiliated by Napoleon and many of the King's valuable possessions were sacrificed to replenish the national Treasury. His successor Frederick William IV (1840–59) had a romantic temperament, and would have liked to have revived some of the kingly ceremony. He was a great believer in the divine right of kings, and in spite of being a Protestant hoped for the restoration of the Holy Roman Empire, although he refused the offer of the imperial crown. However, he showed no practical interest in the ceremonial side of his office. On the accession of his brother William I, however, the coronation was revived for political reasons. The ceremony took place as before at Königsberg on 10th October 1861.

About half-past ten in the morning, the King in one procession, and the Queen in another following, left the royal apartments for the church adjoining the castle, preceded by the heralds in blue costumes and numerous state dignitaries, including the Grand Master of the Wardrobe bearing the royal mantle on a velvet cushion, the bearers of the Great Seal, the Orb, the Sword of State (naked and borne upright) and the Sceptre on a cushion. Immediately after followed Prince Radziwill carrying the Crown, and next came the King in a General's uniform, covered with the mantle of the Order of the Black Eagle, his plumed helm in his hand. He was followed by other dignitaries, and General Wrangel bearing the state Banner. The Queen, attired in white silk with ermine, came next, accompanied by her entourage.

The King and Queen took their places at the foot of the two pillars in front of their thrones, facing the altar. After the usual liturgy of the Lutheran Church and sermon, the coronation service commenced. Whilst the *Salvum fac Regem* was sung the bearers of the Crown, Sceptre and Orb approached the altar, laid the regalia on it and retired. The high officials also who bore the Sword of State and the Great Seal stood near the altar, to which the King ascended, knelt and prayed. On his rising, the Crown Prince approached the King and took off the Black Eagle mantle and collar, while the court officials placed on His Majesty the coronation robes.

The King then went forward and, taking the Crown from the altar with both hands, placed it on his head. He then took the Sceptre and Orb and, turning towards the spectators, waved the latter twice or thrice, and then laid it down on the altar, and passing the Sceptre from the left hand to the right, he grasped the Sword of Justice. The Queen, after being arrayed in her coronation robes, approached the altar, and the King placed the Crown on her head. Their Majesties both knelt and prayed, after which the procession left the church, and on entering the palace the Queen retired.

The King, in coronation robes, with Crown and Sceptre, appeared on the platform in the great hall, and received the three addresses from the Upper House, from the Chamber of Deputies, and from the witnesses to the coronation. His Majesty replied, and waved his Sceptre thrice. The list of decorations to be given away was read by the Minister of the Interior. The chief Herald and four others advanced and exclaimed in a loud voice, 'Long live King William the First' and whilst the grand chorale, *Nun danket alle Gott*, was being sung by thousands of voices, the King re-entered the palace, and the ceremony, which lasted about four hours, terminated.

As a result of the successful outcome of Bismarck's policy, King William I of Prussia was proclaimed German Emperor after the capture of Paris. To spare the feelings of the minor sovereigns of Germany the new title was 'German Emperor', not

'Emperor of Germany', as the latter title would have implied that the territories of other sovereigns were situated in a land belonging to the holders of the title, while the former means simply 'the head of the German *Reich*'. There was no coronation ceremony, but the proclamation took place in the Palace of Versailles before all the German sovereign princes.

On the death of King William I in 1888, his son Frederick III reigned for but a few months and was succeeded in his turn by William II as King of Prussia and German Emperor. William ascended the throne on 15th June 1888 and a few days later he attended his accession ceremony at which he took the oath, and at which the crown was carried on a cushion. During his reign the crown was used at various national ceremonies but was carried on a cushion and never worn.

We do not know much about the Prussian Crown Treasury before the time of Frederick William, the Great Elector. In 1646 he had married Louisa Henrietta of Orange, who became the mother of the future King Frederick. A statement with a valuation of the jewels and silver effects in her possession was drawn up by the jewellers Charles Codde and Laurens Ravens of The Hague and witnessed by Frederick William and his consort on 4th June 1647 as was also a valuation of the jewellery and silver effects of their marriage settlement.[1] Another inventory sets out the presents given to Frederick William by his wife. The Orange inheritance included four pearl necklaces, the first consisting of 35 round pearls of unusually large size which were valued at 24,000 guldens. The numerous diamonds mostly described as table-cut or rose-cut were apparently only small and not highly priced. Some gold vessels were valued at 66,854 guldens. The jewels presented by Frederick to his consort included a number of table- and rose-cut diamonds of striking size and beauty, and were valued at 78,350 guldens. Frederick and his brother Louis inherited from their grandmother Amelia of Solms, the widow of the Stadtholder Frederick Henry, a fourth part of her jewels, among which were several valuable ornaments. They were listed in an inventory dated 1677. That Frederick attached great importance to these jewels is testified by several other inventories which indicate the constant changes of ownership, but a great part of his inheritance was given to his wife Henrietta of Hesse-Cassel. The last of these inventories is dated 11th February 1688, some three months after the death of the Great Elector.

From the year 1681 Frederick, then an electoral prince, started to purchase jewels from the Court Jeweller, Jost Liebmann. He started on a modest scale, the amount of that order being 3,772 Reichstalers. His annual expenditure with Liebmann only exceeded this sum in 1684 and 1687. In 1684 Frederick married his second wife Sophia Charlotte of Hanover, the sister of King George I of England. This occasion offered an opportunity for costly presents, which included a ring with big-faceted diamonds costing 300 rtlrs[2] which the Electoral Prince, on giving to his wife, remarked: 'Just for a beginning'. A little later the Princess received from her husband a portrait with a big-faceted diamond costing 1,500 rtlrs. A month later he gave her two bracelets with big-faceted

[1] This and a number of other inventories and documents relating to the Prussian crown jewels were printed in full in Seidel's work.

[2] The expression 'faceted diamonds' used at this time almost certainly referred to rose-cut diamonds.

a   *The Orange Pearls as set in 1703* (p. 504)

b   *The Diamond Suite with the Little Sancy of* $34\frac{1}{8}$
carats, XIX Century (pp. 503 *and* 509)

a   *Tiara of brilliants and pearls with large sapphire* (p. 509)

b   *Bracelet of brilliants and pearls with large sapphire* (p. 509)

c   *Suite of sapphires, brilliants and pearls* (p. 509)

diamonds for 3,000 rtlrs, an ornament with large and fine emeralds and diamonds for 2,500 rtlrs, and other pieces were given, while her Hanoverian courtiers also were presented with numerous gifts. In 1687 when the Great Elector was seriously ill and Frederick's succession was almost a certainty his expenditure on jewellery increased. In the following year on his succession he presented nine ambassadors with his portrait wearing an electoral hat which cost some 519 rtlrs each. He bought for his personal use two big-faceted diamonds at a price of 20,000 rtlrs, a chain of twenty-two faceted stones at 4,400 rtlrs, and as a present for the Electress of Hanover a ring with a big-faceted diamond at 6,000 rtlrs. He continued to make considerable purchases from Liebmann, including golden daggers, rings, crosses of Orders, buttons, sprays of brilliants, etc., and some idea of the scale of this expenditure is shown by Liebmann's account for the year 1697 amounting to nearly 261,000 rtlrs. Until the time of Frederick the jewels in possession of the electoral family were regarded solely as personal ornaments, and there is little or no documentary evidence concerning them. It was not until 1710 that he formally included his jewels in his house entails. In a document entitled *The Specification of the Commission of Entail* we find a paragraph in which Frederick I, King of Prussia, orders that the following shall belong to his house entail:

> All and everything inherited by us, as given to us, or as bought, or jewellery which came to us included in a special specification, or which we may in future inherit, buy or in any other way acquire, it is laid down that these shall be held as crown jewels of our Royal House as in the case of other Royal Houses and shall never or under any pretext be alienated, given away or put to any other use.

The special specification has not been preserved, but what can be regarded as a valid substitute is an inventory of the 'jewels, gold and pearls in store on the death of the late King Frederick I of blessed memory'. This document in the archives of the Royal House is dated 29th September 1713.

Since only two months elapsed between the grant by the Emperor of the title of King to Frederick and the coronation at Königsberg, there was too little time available for the elaborate preparations which were necessary for what was evidently a carefully planned ceremony. It would seem, therefore, that Frederick must have begun his arrangements in anticipation of the Emperor's approval of his request to be recognised as King. Not only did Frederick have to make a long journey to Königsberg, but it was necessary for the three crowns, the sceptre, the orb and the other ornaments, and the royal robes to be designed and made.

> The King's crown consisted of a circlet around the lower rim of which was a row of fine pearls with a large drop pearl set between each of the arches. The circlet was covered with rose-cut diamonds. From behind the circlet rose four arches set with rose diamonds, at the junction of which rested a gold orb covered with blue enamel and surrounded by a girdle and equator of diamonds with a diamond cross on top. Altogether 135 rose-cut diamonds, 2 table-cut diamonds and 8 drop pearls were used. The crown was of a large size because, as was the fashion at the time, the King wore a wig. The Queen's crown was of similar design, though smaller, and was adorned with 147 rose-cut diamonds, 25 brilliants, 8 drop pearls and 48 round pearls. The Crown Prince's

crown was adorned with 110 rose-cut diamonds, 8 brilliants, 8 drop pearls and 83 round pearls. The stones were fastened to the gold frames with wire so that they could be removed and used for other requirements when needed.

The frames of the King's crown and the Queen's crown (*Plate 155, a* and *b*) with their jewelled orbs have been preserved, but that of the Crown Prince was broken up in 1737. There are, however, still preserved the leather boxes in which the crowns were kept.

The sceptre (*Plate 156, b*) is of a very striking design. It is of gold, and the handle is separated by two *pomella* in the usual style; the staff is decorated in enamel work, and at the top is a large oriental garnet which, according to Besser, was presented to the Elector by Peter the Great to commemorate his visit to Königsberg in 1697. This garnet is held by a gold clasp and is used as a pedestal for the ornament which forms the head of the sceptre. This takes the form of a Prussian eagle invested with the Prussian regalia. The head of the eagle is surmounted by the crown of Prussia, the wings are spread, and in the right claw is held the sceptre and in the left the sword. These miniatures of the sceptre and sword are of gold, and the sceptre is an exact replica of the original and in turn holds a miniature itself. The body of the bird is formed by a large oriental garnet, while the wings and feathers are represented by diamonds.

In an inventory of the crown jewels made in 1765 the following valuation was placed upon the component stones and gold of the sceptre, in rtlrs:

690 diamonds weighing 130 carats	3,380
In the eagle a great oriental garnet	25
Two ditto on top of the sceptre	50
332 small oriental garnets	27:16
At the bottom of the sceptre an oriental ruby . . .	300
3½ marks of 18 carat gold	498:18

making a total value of 4,281 rtlrs and 10 gr. This sceptre has been associated with the name of Peter the Great in various ways. Apart from the oriental garnet, which is sometimes erroneously described as a big ruby and which forms the body of the eagle, it has been stated in several places in connection with the coronation of 1861 that Peter presented the whole sceptre to the Elector, but Seidel was unable to find any proof of this, and imagined that the statements are founded on misinterpretation. It is also related that during his visit to Königsberg Peter praised the sceptre. This does not seem to have been very probable if it were the electoral sceptre which he was shown, because it was a plain ornament of no artistic merit, nor of a striking design. It is possible that Frederick had already had the sceptre made, but what is more likely is that Peter the Great, who had a fine sceptre surmounted by three eagles made for his coronation, praised his own sceptre, which may have suggested to the Prussians to have the head of their sceptre also adorned by their eagle. It is noteworthy that the imperial Russian sceptre made for the coronation of Catherine II nearly a century later is also surmounted by an eagle and bears some resemblance to the Prussian sceptre. A leather box to contain the sceptre has still been preserved.

The orb (*Reichsapfel*) (*Plate 156, c*) was also made for the coronation of 1701. It is of 18-carat gold enamelled all over in blue. The globe is encircled by a girdle which is joined from the top by four similar bands. The girdle and the bands are set with diamonds and rubies. The orb is surmounted by a cross.

The 1765 inventory valued the orb as follows:

50 diamonds weighing 25 carats	700
36 rubies and garnets	72
1 mark of 18 carat gold	142:12

a total value of 914 rtlrs and 12 gr. The value of the enamel work was not taken into account.

A new seal of the kingdom was made for Frederick I which depicted the King sitting on the throne robed in the coronation mantle. The seal was carried in the coronation procession and a new one was made subsequently in each reign. A state banner was made for the coronation in 1701 and, following Swedish practice, was carried behind the king. It was also used at the royal funeral. In the Inventory of the Armoury of 1718 it is described as:

A banner of white damask embroidered with a black eagle on the breast of which is the letter F, the staff covered with blue velvet and with a gold and silver gilt ornament on the top; round the banner is a double gold fringe.

At a later date the letter F on the eagle's breast was replaced by the initials F. W. R. and the old white damask was changed for cloth of silver, presumably on account of wear. Both these alterations were probably made by Frederick William II for the funeral of Frederick the Great.

The Great Elector had much admiration for the Order of the Garter, of which he was a knight. He was particularly anxious that his son should also become a Knight of the Garter. To commemorate the ceremony of his coronation, Frederick I instituted the Order of the Black Eagle, and in certain respects he copied the foundation of the Order of the Garter. The chain of the Order was used at coronations and funeral ceremonies as part of the regalia. It is of silver gilt and enamel; the cross of the Order is of gold. It is not certain whether this is the original chain of the foundation of the Order in 1701.

Unfortunately the documents of transactions between the King and his jeweller at the time of the coronation are incomplete. It seems that some of the stones needed for the regalia were only loaned, for in the records is an entry dated 16th May 1701 which states that 'Jewels in the Queen's crown valued at 6,000 rtlrs were to be handed back'.

In the early days of Frederick I's reign there were disputes over the terms of the Orange necklaces. On 28th July 1702 Frederick I entered into a contract with the Princess of Nassau as the trustee of Princes John, William and Friso about the jewels and furniture belonging to the legacy of Frederick Henry of Orange. It was agreed that the King could take immediate possession of the Little Sancy diamond and should give up all right to the other jewels except the legacy rights of the late Princess Amelia of Orange. The Little Sancy was a diamond of 34½ carats valued at 300,000 rtlrs (*Plate 157, b*) and became the premier stone in the Prussian crown jewels. It has sometimes been confused with the Sancy, a celebrated stone of 53½ carats. The stone was formerly in the collection of Nicholas Harlay, Seigneur de Sancy, who died in 1627, and was a collector of diamonds. Following his death the collection was disposed of by the family and the two largest stones were named the Great and the Little Sancy. The latter was bought by Frederick Henry of Orange.

The principal item in the legacy of Frederick's grandmother Amelia of Solms was a necklace of 36 pearls and this, according to the bequest, was to go first to Princess Henrietta Catherine of Anhalt-Dessau, the sister of Frederick's mother, for her lifetime and then to pass to Frederick. This was confirmed by an agreement between Frederick and his aunt dated 5th February 1703. Nevertheless the necklace came into the possession of the King in the same year. It was then broken up and the pearls used with others to form some beautiful chains, which were known as the Orange pearls (*Plate 157, a*).

There is no information as to what happened to the jewels of Queen Sophie Charlotte when she died in 1705. There is an inventory which records the jewels given by Frederick I to his third wife Sophia Louise of Mecklenburg-Schwerin which 'shows the high regard the King held his royal dignity and the decorations which should support it'. The list is notable for the number of emeralds that feature in it. On Frederick I's death all the jewels except a few pieces which his widow kept as mementos were handed back and taken to the apartment of the new Queen Sophia Dorothea.

The will of Frederick I enumerated a relatively small number of female ornaments —some rings, a pair of ear-rings, two bracelets and numerous pearls. The majority of items included Orders set with diamonds, jewelled buttons, shoe buckles, daggers, swords, canes and other articles of personal adornment or ceremonial insignia for the use of the King. The seven jewelled Orders included in the will were three sets of insignia of the Order of the Garter, of which one was decorated with 13 big pearls valued at 4,000 rtlrs; two Danish Orders and two unspecified Stars, which were probably the Order of the Black Eagle, of which one was set with 15 large and 385 small brilliants. There were 120 diamond-studded buttons. When on 27th December 1741 these stones were removed 26 of the largest diamonds were certified as weighing from $5\frac{1}{8}$ to $16\frac{3}{8}$ carats. An oblong ornament set with brilliants which the King used to wear on his shoulder to fasten the Ribbon of an Order was of special costliness. Of the seventy-two rings listed one was of exceptional value and contained a large oval brilliant which the King had acquired in 1710 for 42,000 rtlrs. There were ten daggers and swords set with jewels and ten canes similarly decorated. The origin of the pearls is not given, but there were 128 in all, of which 29 were large round ones and one a drop-shaped pearl which the King had bought from Liebmann in 1712 for 12,000 rtlrs.

Liebmann's accounts appear to have been very haphazard and the numerous deliveries were badly catalogued. As early as 1697 a total account which was called for stated that Liebmann had delivered jewels to the value of 52,000 rtlrs 19 gr when Frederick was Electoral Prince, and 208,936 rtlrs and 23 gr when Frederick was Elector. Frederick was 19,744 rtlrs and 16 gr in arrears, but this sum included an advance by Liebmann on the Grumkowschen inheritance taken over by the Elector. After Frederick I's death a claim was made by the jeweller for 106,418 rtlrs. Liebmann's widow and son were arrested and money, gold and jewels found in the house

a (left)   *Pair of ear-rings of rubies and brilliants*
(p. 509)

b   *Two brooches of rubies and brilliants* (p. 509)

c (below)   *Necklace of rubies and brilliants* (p. 509)

d   *Suite of rubies and brilliants* (p. 509)

a   *Two pearl necklaces of Queen Elizabeth and the Empress Frederik with large drop pearl and a round pearl* (pp. 508 and 509)

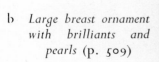

b   *Large breast ornament with brilliants and pearls* (p. 509)

were kept in the custody of the Court Treasury. A commission was appointed by the Privy Council to inquire into the claims. Liebmann's son appealed to the King for protection, and without prejudice declared that neither his mother nor his family had played any part in the matters contained in the suit. He renounced all claims either to the amount involved in the suit or the property worth 100,000 rtlrs which had been seized. He prayed, however, that the King should return a sufficient portion of the goods in custody to satisfy the creditors of the family.

The Liebmann case can be taken as characteristic of the tightening up of the state administration in the new reign. Frederick I had undoubtedly achieved a lot in advancing Prussia towards its future greatness, but his extravagances had exhausted the accumulated treasure left by the Great Elector, had necessitated high taxation, and had reduced the kingdom to financial chaos. Frederick William I brought the same strict economy to the court and to the administration of the kingdom as he practised in his private life. As a result, by the time of his death he had raised the annual revenue of the state to 7 million rtlrs, had paid off his father's debts, and left his successor a well-filled treasury. Frederick William I made no additions to the crown jewels, and, in fact, sold a number of jewelled ornaments. He disconcerted von Luck, who was responsible for the inventory, by removing a number of jewels from the treasury from time to time surreptitiously and without informing the officials, so that the removals could not be catalogued. Among the articles removed were ten jewelled canes, while on 20th August 1714 2 brilliants valued at 1,200 and 1,000 rtlrs respectively were taken and presented by the King to the Queen. On the 1st March 1732 a big ring and two crystal buttons were similarly taken. In the same year other articles, including golden chains of Orders and a silver ink-stand and a ring with large brilliants in it were also taken. On 13th December 1732 the King made all those present stand aside, and broke something off with his scissors. No one could see what, but the King's attendant carried it out in a covered silver dish. In March 1733 a little casket of jewels in which von Luck recognised one diamond button, many buckles and rings, and some loose gems and hairpins, etc., was taken, while in June 1734 a handsome casket of jewels was also taken.

The jewellery of Queen Sophia Louise was given by the King to his wife on 15th December 1715. The Queen herself wrote a specification of the stones in her own hand in December 1719. In January 1720 the jewels in this list were sent to Amsterdam to be sold. Among them were 58 large, 38 medium and 8 little brilliants; 41 large and 63 little rose diamonds; 6 large and 1 medium emerald; and 8 large and 16 medium rubies. As the stones were only valued at 200,000 rtlrs, the King signed an instruction to try for a higher price. The King's attitude was that it was not in accordance with his policy to have such a large capital sum locked up lying idle in jewellery in the treasury, although later he spent large sums on silver vessels which he intended, however, should be melted down and minted in case of need, and, indeed, they served Frederick the Great as his war chest. Unfortunately the time of the sale of the jewels at Amsterdam was not well chosen. In their daily letters to the King and Minister von Greuz, his two representatives von Dershau and Sobbe constantly complained that bad news from Paris about the financial operations of the well-known John Law and the Indies Company had destroyed the market.[1] On 13th February Dershau writes: 'All posts from France bring bad tidings of the well-known Law and these hinder all our designs. There are many people who come to view the jewels, but few buyers.' A few days later he wrote that people had lost both the desire and the courage to use jewels 'which at the moment is forbidden in France. As a result the buyers are scared away and the price of jewels has fallen by at least 50%.' Finally von Dershau advised the King that he was sure the jewels could not be sold at the price desired, and that the cost of the stay of the Commission in Amsterdam was unwarranted. Frederick William then decreed on 14th March that the Commission should return. They had, however, sold a number of articles bringing in a total of 142,590 rtlrs. One ornament of four rosettes which had at one time cost 120,000 guldens was sold for only 28,000.

On the death of Frederick William I on 31st May 1740 the crown, sceptre and orb were removed from the Treasury for the funeral and were replaced immediately afterwards. On 14th November 1741 the King had the insignia and jewels removed from Fredersdorf, and on his instruction the jewellers Quentin and Funster removed the stones from some of the settings in the presence of Queen Elizabeth Christine. Among these were the pearls and gems from both crowns. It is recorded that the Little Sancy was removed from the crown and given to the Queen for her use, together with some other diamonds. This is the first mention we have of the Little Sancy being in the crown, and no doubt it was put there by Frederick I because of its pre-eminence. The Queen used the stone in an arrangement of 4 large and 5 little brilliants as a bouquet to which the Little Sancy was attached.

Frederick the Great's mother Sophia Dorothea died in 1757 and in her will she left everything to her son the King except certain specified jewels to her daughters. The crown jewels already having been in the valuation there is no mention of them in the will. An earlier will leaves 'the necklace of 37 large pearls belonging to our House' to her son, and 2,000 rtlrs worth of jewellery to each of her six daughters. It was not until the end of the Seven Years War that Frederick the Great could make use of his mother's bequest. In April 1763 he had the coffers sent to Potsdam and incorporated the contents with the crown jewels. It was from the time of the third wife of Frederick I that it became customary for the queens to incorporate in the crown jewels the jewels given to them by their husbands. In 1765 when Frederick William, heir to the throne, married his first wife Elizabeth Christine of Brunswick, the jewels of Queen Sophia Dorothea were made over to the bride. This was also done at the Prince's second marriage to Princess Frederick of Hesse-Darmstadt in 1769, by whose will the jewels were returned to the crown treasury in 1805. Only the pearls were left by the King's order to Queen Louise.

During the reign of Frederick the Great the crowns were not used, but on his death in 1786 it was necessary to prepare the King's crown for the funeral. The frame with the arches attached was brought out of the Treasury together with the jewels, and the

---

[1] Law was a Scotsman who became Controller General of Finances in France. He set up a fabric of false credit subsequently called 'Law's Bubble', and although the shares went up in 1718 to twentyfold the original value and were worth more than eighty times the amount of all the current specie in France in 1720 the Bubble burst and spread ruin throughout the country.

crown re-assembled under the supervision of the Queen Dowager, by the jeweller Soheren Baudessen, a process that took six hours. When the crown was ready the Queen displayed it, on a green velvet cushion, to those who were staying with her. It was then packed and taken to Berlin, where it was inspected by Frederick William II and members of the royal family. After the funeral it was taken to pieces and all the jewels together with 6 big brilliants were returned to the Queen Dowager. When she died in 1797 she left her private jewellery to Frederick William II, his second wife Louise and to the Crown Princess.

In his will Frederick the Great had made provision for an income of 20,000 rtlrs a year for his widow. The Queen was to hand over all her personal jewellery to her nephew the eldest son of the Prince of Prussia (afterwards Frederick William II), and some to his brother Prince Henry. After Prince Henry's death Prince Frederick William agreed in 1780 that some of the jewels could be used by the Queen to pay certain debts incurred during the Seven Years War. The Queen withdrew this agreement from the treasury on 25th May 1784. How far she used her personal jewels for this purpose is not known, but she left the King, her nephew, a jewel collection of great value.

A practice grew up for the crown jewels to be worn at the weddings of members of the royal house. In 1793 the Crown Prince married Louise of Mecklenburg-Strelitz, and it is recorded that her bridal crown (Plate 161, a) was set with 47 large and 5 small brilliants, 6 drop pearls set with little brilliants and 30 round pearls which were taken from the treasury. In addition she also had from the crown jewels for the occasion a pair of ear-rings set with 8 large, 10 medium and 35 small brilliants, a necklace of 65 rose-cut diamonds, a breast ornament of 107 large and small rose-cut diamonds, a pair of bracelets and an ornament for her arm in which there were 62 and 48 medium rose-cut diamonds respectively. The same jewels were worn two days later by her sister at her wedding with Prince Louis, and on 13th February 1797 by Princess Augusta of Prussia at her wedding with the Heir Presumptive, later the Elector William II of Hesse-Cassel. At the wedding of the daughter of Frederick William III the use of the bridal jewellery became even greater, because after the death of Queen Louise there was no reigning queen and so it fell to the bride of the day to display the riches of the house in jewellery. Queen Louise often had worn the Little Sancy in the setting used by Queen Elizabeth Christine, but its use at a wedding is first mentioned at that of Princess Alexandrine in 1822, when it was set as a pendant of a necklace of 22 or more rose diamonds and was subsequently repeatedly used as a bridal decoration. It was later set in a similar necklace of brilliants and handed down in this form (Plate 157, b). The princesses were allowed to use the jewellery for balls and festival occasions, if they had the King's written permission. When Queen Louise went to Prussia for the Oath of Allegiance ceremony in 1798 she took a number of brilliants and pearls with her which she kept for future ceremonial and court occasions. There were strict regulations as to how these jewels were to be kept at the various royal residences and on journeys. When the country was over-run by Napoleon the crown jewels and insignia accompanied the flight of the court to East Prussia in 1806. Frederick William III was prepared to make any sacrifices for the country's dire needs, and placed at the disposal of the state a large part of the crown treasury which contained valuable material and was therefore easily convertible into cash. Silver decorative objects such as mirror frames, tables, folding screens, etc., were melted down. Only the silver plate for the tables was excepted. The total weight of the silver was 9,259¾ lb, and the estimated value was 150,980 rtlrs 13 gr. The gold plate of Frederick the Great was melted down at Hamburg and was valued at 229,619 rtlrs. The King even wished to sell the crown jewels themselves, and was only prevented from doing so by the fact that the chaotic conditions of the time had caused their value to fall to one quarter of what they were formerly worth. In preparation for a possible sale the crown jewels were sent from Königsberg to Berlin and a valuation was made which came to a total of 525,259 rtlrs and 4 gr. The valuation in 1741 was 1,427,320 rtlrs more than this. The brilliants had in any case been excepted from the intended sale, but in fact none of the jewels were sold. According to von Bailleu, not long before her death Queen Louise said about her pearls, 'I loved them very much and kept them back when I had to give up my diamonds (in 1809). They were better suited to me for they signified tears, and I have shed so many.' When she died on 19th July 1810 an inventory was taken and her jewels and pearls were handed over to the Treasury.

In 1815 an interesting item came into the crown jewels. It was a suite of brilliants (*Plate 162, a*) taken from the travelling coach of Napoleon after the Battle of Belle Alliance by the Fusilier Battalion of the 15th Infantry Regiment, and sent to the King by Major von Hellier, whom the King thanked. It contained 22 solitaires and 121 little brilliants, and was valued in March 1819 between 16,000 and 20,000 rtlrs.

For the coronation of William I in 1861 the old regalia was used except for the crowns, it being necessary to make a new crown for the King owing to the fact that the wearing of wigs had gone out of fashion, and a new crown was also made for the Queen. They were both of similar design to the old crowns, and were set with the great rose diamonds. The frames of these crowns have been preserved (*Plate 155, c* and *d*).

By her will Queen Elizabeth, consort of Frederick William IV, left her very rich collection of jewels valued at 162,300 rtlrs to the Crown Treasury, but she made provision that they were to be available for the use of Princess Victoria (afterwards the Empress Frederick), provided they were not bequeathed or alienated to anyone else. Among the ornaments were a tiara of brilliants with a large sapphire in the centre, a suite of sapphires and brilliants consisting of necklace, ear-rings, two pendant brooches and a fan; a necklace of large pearls; a suite of rubies and brilliants consisting of a necklace, bracelets, a pair of ear-rings and brooches; a large aquamarine set in brilliants which according to tradition had adorned the clasp of the coronation mantle of Napoleon; an emerald with a bas-relief head of Tippoo Sahib; a large drop pearl; and a yellow diamond from Anspach. She left a set of opal ornaments to her nephew Prince Frederick Charles of Prussia for his wife, which was to become the property of his line, but should this become extinct they were to return to the royal treasury. She also left to the Hohenzollern Treasury by word of mouth a clasp of rubies and brilliants, a pearl pendant and a decoration of the Order of the Swan. Frederick William II directed that the Order of the Swan was never to be worn by anyone as an ornament, as he proposed to revive the Order which, however, for various reasons was never done.

After the death of the Empress Frederick the jewels were worn by the Empress

a   *Hohenzollern nuptial crown, XVIII Century* (p. 507)

c   *Brooch with great sapphire, brilliants and drop pearl* (p. 507)

b   *Diadem of brilliants and drop pearls belonging to the Empress Augusta* (p. 509)

a   *Diamond ornaments taken from Napoleon's coach after the Battle of Belle Alliance, 1815 (pp. 508 and 509)*

b   *Brooch of brilliants (p. 509)*

d   *Aquamarine said to have been in the clasp of Napoleon's coronation mantle, 1804 (pp. 508 and 509)*

c (left)   *Brooch and cross of emeralds and brilliants (p. 509)*

Augusta, though part were given to the Crown Princess on the occasion of her wedding. The will of the Empress followed tradition and left part of her jewellery to the crown treasury for the use of the wife of the existing king. The jewellery had come to the Queen on her marriage, and one brooch was valued for probate at 150,000 marks.

In 1889, a year after having ascended the throne, William II ordered a new crown to be made. The Emperor addressed the following letter to the Court Minister:

> I have decided to have the Royal Crown reconstructed. It is to be made of beaten gold in accordance with the drawings you have laid before me. The circlet is to be set with twenty-four large roses. Over each pair of stones on the circlet the eight clover-leaves stand, each set with three greater roses and a smaller one. From the clover-leaves eight half-arches, each adorned with ten to twelve roses, rise to the apex on which rests the Orb, consisting of a large sapphire and the Cross set with brilliants. Between the clover-leaves there are eight upright ornaments, each of which is set with a rose and a large drop pearl. The Crown is to be furnished with a full purple lining reaching up to the arches. You are to take further action accordingly.
>
> (Sgd) WILHELM R.
>
> Berlin.
> 27th February 1889.

The crown was made by the court jewellers Jumbert and Son.

> The rose diamonds have been used to great effect and are admirably set off by the large drop pearls placed between each arch. The old blue enamel orb has been replaced by a beautiful sapphire, cut *en cabochon*. The 142 rose diamonds employed have a total weight of $723\frac{3}{32}$ carats, the 8 pearls $155\frac{3}{4}$ carats. Apart from the large sapphire there are also 18 brilliants of $6\frac{1}{16}$ carats used in the decoration of the cross.

At the time of William II's Jubilee in 1913, the principal items of personal jewellery among the crown jewels included:

The Orange Pearls (*Plate 157, a*), consisting of three ropes and three pearl pendants.

A brilliant suite (*Plate 157, b*), consisting of a necklace of 22 brilliants with the Little Sancy as a pendant, a large breast ornament and two solitaire ear-rings.

A suite of sapphires, brilliants and pearls (*Plate 158*), consisting of a tiara, a bracelet, a necklace, two pendants, a pair of ear-rings and a fan.

A suite of rubies and brilliants (*Plate 159*), consisting of a great and a small necklace, a bracelet, a pair of ear-rings and two brooches.

Two pearl necklaces (*Plate 160, a*) of Queen Elizabeth and the Empress Frederick, a round pearl and a drop pearl ornament.

A large breast ornament (*Plate 160, b*) of brilliants and pearls.

A diadem of brilliants and pearls (*Plate 161, b*).

A brooch (*Plate 161, c*) with a great sapphire, brilliants and a drop pearl.

A suite of brilliants (*Plate 162, a*) found in Napoleon's coach after the Battle of Belle Alliance, consisting of a necklace, a hat brooch, another brooch and a pair of ear-rings.

A brooch of brilliants (*Plate 162, b*).

A brooch and cross of emeralds and brilliants (*Plate 162, c*).

An aquamarine (*Plate 162, d*) said to have been in the clasp of Napoleon's coronation mantle, 1804.

A tiara of brilliants (*Plate 163, a*).

A tiara of brilliants and emeralds (*Plate 163, b*).

A suite of brilliants and rubies (*Plate 163, c*), consisting of a collar, pendant brooches, ear-rings and a ring.

A suite of emeralds and brilliants (*Plate 164, a*), consisting of a necklace, a brooch with pendant, another brooch and a pair of ear-rings.

A cameo suite, including a bracelet (*Plate 164, c*) and a comb (*Plate 164, b*).

A hat of Frederick I with a diamond and pearl agraffe.

A chain of the Order of the Swan.

An emerald with a bas-relief head of Tippoo Sahib.

A yellow diamond from Anspach.

In 1918 when the Emperor William II abdicated he was allowed to keep the family property, including the crown which had been made for him in 1889. At the end of the Second World War it was taken from Berlin to Bückeburg where it was hidden by being bricked up in the crypt of the Kleine Kirche, but it was found by British troops and returned to the Hohenzollern family. The contents of the castle at Potsdam and other Hohenzollern treasures were seized by the Russians and their whereabouts are not known, but most of the royal ornaments from the Hohenzollern Museum in the Schloss Monbijou in Berlin were saved and are in safe custody at Wiesbaden. Some ornaments which remain in the possession of the Hohenzollern family are preserved in Schloss Hohenzollern where they are on public display. These include the crown of William II; the Pomeranian sword which was discovered in 1951 and purchased by the family, although the scabbard was missing, and the field marshal's baton. In 1954 the castle was burgled by a man named Fallk who, having doped the watch-dog, cut his way through the iron bars covering the windows and stole a number of articles including some valuable golden snuff boxes set with diamonds. He threw the stones into the river Neckar and kept the gold. He also took the baton which he buried in the grounds just below the castle. When he was arrested he said that he looked at the crown, but valuable though it must have been, he was unable to bring himself to steal this symbol of Prussia's greatness.

The only other ornament that need be mentioned was the ampulla, which was used at the two coronations for the anointing of the kings. It was made in lapis lazuli and kept in the Treasury of the Royal Chapel in the castle at Königsberg.

BIBLIOGRAPHY

BRYCE, LORD	*The Holy Roman Empire*, London 1904.
LAKING, SIR GUY	*A Record of European Arms and Armour.*
SEIDEL, P.	*Die Insignien und Juwelen der preuszischen Krone*, Leipzig 1913.
STILLFRIED, GRAF R.	*Die Attribute des neuen Deutschen Reiches*, Berlin 1879.

MARGRAVES OR ELECTORS OF BRANDENBURG

1134 Albert I, the Bear, first elector of Brandenburg
1170 Otho I
1184 Otho II

a   *Tiara of brilliants*
(p. 509)

b   *Tiara of brilliants and emeralds*
(p. 509)

c   *Collar, pendant brooches, ear-rings and a
ring of brilliants and rubies* (p. 510)

a   *Suite of emeralds and brilliants* (p. 509)

b   *Comb of brilliants with intaglio* (p. 509)

c   *Bracelet of brilliants with intaglio* (p. 509)

1206	Albert II
1221	John I and Otho III
1266	John II
1282	Otho IV
1309	Waldemar
1319	Henry I, the Young
1320	(Interregnum)
1323	Louis I of Bavaria
1352	Louis II, the Roman
1365	Otho V, the Sluggard
1373	Wenceslas, of Luxemburg
1378	Sigismund, of Luxemburg
1388	Jossus, the Bearded
1411	Sigismund, again Emperor
1415	Frederick I of Nuremberg (of the House of Hohenzollern)
1440	Frederick II, surnamed Ironside
1470	Albert III, surnamed the German Achilles
1476	John III, his son; as margrave, the Cicero of Germany

Elector 1486

1499	Joachim I
1535	Joachim II
1571	John-George
1598	Joachim-Frederick
1608	John Sigismund

DUKES OF PRUSSIA

1618	John Sigismund
1619	George William
1640	Frederick William, the 'Great Elector'
1688	Frederick III

KINGS OF PRUSSIA

1701	Frederick I (Frederick III, Duke of Prussia). Crowned at Königsberg, 18th January 1701 with Queen Sophie Charlotte
1713	Frederick William I
1740	Frederick II, The Great
1786	Frederick William II
1797	Frederick William III
1840	Frederick William IV
1859	William I, brother. Crowned at Königsberg, 10th October 1861, Emperor of Germany, 1871
1888	Frederick III
1888	William II

CHAPTER TWENTY

ROUMANIA

Roumania was one of the modern kingdoms of Europe, and although there is evidence from frescoes and other pictorial representations that the rulers of the principalities, which later formed the kingdom, used various royal ornaments, none of these survived the period of Turkish vassalage from 1504 to 1714. After a period of upheaval the first step towards unifying the Roumanian nation was accomplished in 1857. The Powers decided that the principality should be governed by its own prince, and in 1859 the election of Prince Cuza was ratified by the Powers and by the Porte. During his seven years' reign this Prince effected a great number of reforms, but when he attempted to force others through too autocratically he was forced to abdicate in February 1866. The Council of Regency invited the brother of the King of the Belgians to be the new ruler, but he declined, whereupon the Powers and the Porte, who still controlled the destinies of the country, decided that the new prince or *Hospidar* should be a native of Roumania. After a referendum, however, which was almost unanimous, Prince Charles (Carol) of Hohenzollern-Sigmaringen was elected and in 1881 was proclaimed King. On 23rd May 1881 he and his consort, Princess Elizabeth of Wied, 'Carmen Sylva', were crowned in the cathedral at Bucharest (*Plate 165, a*).

The new royal couple soon consolidated the position of their country. The King died in 1914 two months after the outbreak of the First World War, and his son, Ferdinand, took the side of the Entente. Roumania emerged from the war with additional territory and on 15th October 1922 King Ferdinand and Queen Marie were crowned at Alba Julia, the ancient capital of Transylvania. His successor, King Charles (Carol), was never crowned; nor was the last King of Roumania, Michael, whom the Communist Government forced to abdicate in 1948.

The Roumanian coronation ceremony introduced in 1881 was simple and brief. The king wore a royal mantle of purple velvet trimmed with a double row of ermine which bore the name of *Cabanta* and the queen a rich mantle. On arrival at the church a procession was formed with the clergy at its head followed by the standards of all the regiments. To the sound of pealing bells and chanting choirs it moved into the church. One of the Metropolitans read the Gospel, the Metropolitan Primate recited the exhortation of the Almighty to shower benefits on the Throne, and another Metropolitan recited the ritual prayers, while the deacons and archpriests recited in a high voice the passages of the *Ectenies*. The choir sang the hymn *Dignum Est*. The Metropolitan Primate then delivered the king's crown to the President of the Senate and the queen's crown to the President of the Chamber. The religious service being finished, the sovereigns mounted the *parvis* of the church whence the coronation procession moved

513

forward to the grand *arroi*. The canopy under which the coronation was performed was supported by the four generals commanding army corps. The President of the Senate then presented the crown to the king who placed it on his own head, after which the President of the Chamber delivered the queen's crown to the king who crowned his consort. After this the sovereigns received the ovations of the crowd to the sound of peals of bells and salvoes of artillery and the Act of Coronation, signed by the high authorities, was given by the king to the Minister of Public Instruction to be deposited in the State archives.

The Roumanian coronation ceremony was very degenerate, with no religious significance whatsoever. There was no unction nor oath and no delivery of the sceptre or any other ornament. It has been said that the practice of the king crowning himself and his queen derived from the precedent of Napoleon, but this was not so. It was borrowed from the Eastern Orthodox rite which at that time was in use in Russia where the Tsar always crowned himself and his Empress. It was necessary for the crown to be handed to the king by two statesmen because there was no ecclesiastic present at that part of the ceremony, and this may have been borrowed from the similar Scandinavian practice. It also emphasised that the actual crowning was a civil rite, as was the signing of the Coronation Act at the end of the ceremony.

The very simplicity of the Crown of Roumania commands respect. It was made from the steel of a cannon captured from the Turks in the last war which the Roumanians fought against them to gain their independence, and bears the proud name of the *Couronne d'Acier* (*Plate 165, b*). As Charles I said: 'It will show to future generations the heroism of the Roumanians of today and the intimate union of the country and its sovereign.' The crown is in a modern form and is somewhat plain. The circlet has a number of emblematic gems embossed upon it, and arranged at intervals around it are eight emblems in the shape of shields, but not unlike certain forms of the fleur-de-lis. Between them are eight emblems in the form of strawberry leaves. From the shields rise the four arches with lines of imitation pearls. The arches are depressed at the centre and have at their junction a simple orb with an equator and two meridional bands. Surmounting the orb is a cross, the extremities of which are decorated to form octagons on which there are engraved crosses. The cross bears the inscription *Le passage du Danube* which refers to the victory at Plevna. Inside the crown is a cap of crimson velvet.

The sceptre is simple in form, being made of Transylvanian gold unadorned by precious stones. It is short and is surmounted by a fleur-de-lis, the traditional symbol of the *voivodes*, which was the title previously used by the Princes of Moldavia and Wallachia.

The crown with which Queen Elizabeth was crowned has not been preserved. The design of Queen Marie's crown (*Plate 165, c*) followed that of Despina Doanna, the consort of a Prince of Wallachia who is depicted in the frescoes of the ancient church at Curtea D'Argesh. It is made of gold from Transylvania and is in beaten arabesques after the classic style, and set with moonstones, amethysts, turquoises, emeralds and rubies, polished but uncut in the ancient manner, and with *pendulae* which were a feature of many mediaeval crowns.

a   *Coronation of King Charles I and Queen Elizabeth at Bucharest, 23rd May 1881. Sketch by M. Száthmári, Court artist*

b   *King Ferdinand wearing the* Couronne d'acier, *1922*

c   (right)   *Queen Marie's crown made in France of Transylvanian gold, 1922*

a   *Cap of Constantine Monomachus* (pp. 517 and 525)

b   *Crown of Kazan* (pp. 517 and 525)

c   *Crown of Tsar Michael Theodorovitch, also called the
Crown of Astrakhan* (p. 525)

d   *Cap of Monomachus of the Second Order or the
Crown of Kiev, Vladimir and Novgorod, also called
the crown of Ivan V* (pp. 521 and 525)

These four crowns are in the Kremlin Museum, Moscow

CHAPTER TWENTY-ONE

RUSSIA

According to Nestor of Kiev, the oldest Russian chronicler, in 862 three brothers, Ruric, Sineus and Truvor, Princes of Rus—a land generally supposed to be a part of Sweden—accepted an invitation from the tribes occupying part of what is now known as Russia to found a dynasty. It was not long before they set about conquering neighbouring territories and in 882 Oleg, the Regent during the minority of Ruric's son, Igor, gained the Duchy of Kiev. In 945 Igor made a treaty with the Byzantine Emperor and Christianity was permitted to be practised at Kiev. Olga, the widow of Igor, embraced the Christian faith in 957, but it was not until the reign of Vladimir I, Great Prince of Kiev and grandson of Olga, that the Greek Church was established as a state religion. Vladimir had sent envoys to report on the religions practised by neighbouring states. They did not form a good opinion of what they found either in Germany or in the Muslim states, but in Constantinople the magnificence of the ceremonial made an overwhelming impression and they reported to Vladimir strongly in favour of establishing the Orthodox Church in his domains. The Emperor Basil II, in return for Vladimir's conversion, offered his sister Anne in marriage. Vladimir was baptised and married at Kherson in 988. This was only the second occasion on which a Byzantine princess had married abroad, her sister Theophano being married to the Emperor Otto II in 972. Like her sister, she introduced into her new country artists, writers and courtiers, who had an important effect on the development of art and the introduction of Byzantine court ceremonial to Kiev. Vladimir's subjects quickly followed their ruler's example. The ancient wooden idol, Penour, was thrown down, dragged at horses' tails, scourged in derision and cast into the river, in whose waters the people were then baptised. Vladimir and his son, Yaroslav (1019–54) strengthened their position by matrimonial alliances with the reigning families of Poland, Sweden, Norway, France and Hungary.

These events led to the aggrandisement of the grand dukes and the introduction of great splendour to their Court. As early as 1075 Burhard, the Ambassador of the Emperor Henry IV, was astonished at the incalculable treasures which he saw at the Court of Sviatoslav.

But the numerous family of the Ruric dynasty regarded the country as their estate and there were serious family quarrels. After the death of Yaroslav in 1054, disintegration set in and during the next 170 years no less than sixty-four principalities had a passing existence, 293 princes claimed the succession and there were eighty-three civil wars. The most notable ruler during this time was Vladimir II, Monomachus (1113–25) who defeated the Polovtsi and married Gyda, or Gytha, the daughter of Harold II of England.

In 1224 Russia was invaded by the Tartars under Ghengis Khan, who, however, withdrew, but in 1235 there was a second invasion and the invaders stayed, setting up their capital at Sarai on the Volga. This western section of the Mongol Empire was known as the Golden Horde. Alexander Nevski, Grand Prince of Vladimir (1252–63), who is considered to be the Russian national hero and saint, displayed a mixture of military prowess, which enabled him to defeat the Swedes and the Teutonic knights, and diplomatic skill, which kept the Tartars from attacking Russia. His son, Daniel, founded the line of Moscow princes of the Ruric dynasty who in 1380 formed a coalition of Russian princes and gained a great victory over Kulivkovo, the Khan of the Golden Horde. Thereafter they extended their domains and set up various principalities.

Ivan III (1462–1505) may be said to be the real founder of the Russian Empire, and by his rout of the Golden Horde and his absorption of Perm, Novograd and other independent principalities he started what was to become an uncontrolled central monarchical authority.

After the fall of Constantinople to the Turks in 1453, the idea was fostered that the Grand Dukes of Muscovy, as the most powerful potentates in the Eastern Orthodox sphere, were the political heirs and successors to the Byzantine emperors as the protectors of the Orthodox faith. After the death of Ivan III's first wife, Maria of Tver, in 1467, Pope Paul II, hoping to strengthen the bonds between Russia and the Holy See, suggested that Ivan should marry Sophia Palaeologus; she was the daughter of Thomas, the despot of Morea, the claimant to the throne of Constantinople, and the niece of the last Eastern emperor. The marriage took place in 1472 and she took the name of Anna.

From this time on, a great change took place in the position of the sovereign, who became sacrosanct, held aloof from the Boyars, and the patriarchal system of government disappeared. Under the influence of the Princess, Byzantine customs and Court ceremonies were introduced and Ivan assumed, as the Arms of Russia, the double-headed eagle as token of his succession to the inheritance of Rome and Byzantium. Ateliers were set up and Greek craftsmen were brought from Constantinople, while a search was instituted throughout the country for deposits of precious stones and metals.

In 1498, Ivan decided to crown Demetrius, his heir by his first wife, as co-Regent. On this occasion the ceremony, which took place on 4th February of that year, was conducted according to the ancient Byzantine rules. Five bishops led by the Metropolitan Simon attended. The Metropolitan handed Ivan a cap or crown which had been used by the Princes of Vladimir at their installation ceremonies. Ivan placed the cap on the head of Demetrius and invested him with another family heirloom, the *barmi* or collar. The Metropolitan then blessed the young Prince. Demetrius, however, did not reign, as through the influence of Anna Palaeologus, it was arranged that her son, Vassili, or Basil, should succeed Ivan. According to some authorities Basil was crowned on 14th April 1502, but the historian Kostromaroff disclaims this, remarking: 'maybe he was not anxious to pass through a church service which brought fetters to the first Prince who was distinguished by it'. Basil continued the work of unification and, when he died in 1533, he was succeeded by his son, Ivan IV, known to history as Ivan the Terrible. Ivan revived the coronation and a record of the ceremony has been preserved.

Ivan's father and grandfather had coveted the title of Tsar, but had not dared to assume it publicly in Russia, although they had occasionally used it in addressing other sovereigns. Ivan IV at his coronation on 16th April 1547 took the title of 'Tsar of all Russia' instead of that of 'Grand Prince of Muscovy'. He was also the first to be anointed with the consecrated oil on the forehead, mouth and chin and to take the Holy Sacrament at the ceremony. Great importance was attached to these innovations which strengthened the conceptions of national unity by making the sovereign a person apart, the Lord's anointed, as well as successor to the inheritance of the Russian Empire and the bearer of a title embracing all the Russian principalities.

Claims were also put forward to show that the coronation crown itself had been a gift from the Byzantine Empire. In an epistle of Joassaph, Patriarch of Constantinople, addressed to Ivan IV and written on parchment in 1561 with the seal and the signature of the Patriarch and thirty-four metropolitans and archbishops, not only is a blessing bestowed on the coronation of the Tsar but mention is made of the royal heirlooms consisting of a pectoral cross suspended on a golden chain; a crown, or cap, of gold; a collar or *barmi*; an orb and a vessel of cornelian which by tradition had come down from the Emperor Augustus. These it was said had been sent by the Emperors Basil and Constantine and brought by their envoys, the Metropolitans of Ephesus and Antioch, for the coronation of his ancestor, Vladimir, Grand Prince of Kiev in 988. While there is no reason to suppose that gifts of this nature, including a crown, were not sent by the Emperors on this occasion, Ivan IV preferred to associate the regalia with Vladimir II, Monomachus (1113–25), who was a grandson of the Emperor Constantine Monomachus and thus a direct heir of Byzantium. As most authorities ascribe the workmanship of the original part of the crown to the XII or XIII centuries, rather than to the X century, Ivan's preference is the more likely theory. From the time of Ivan IV the crown has always borne the official title of the 'Cap of Monomachus'. Ivan IV was succeeded by his son, Theodore I, in 1584 and the new Tsar was crowned and anointed according to the established rights on 31st May of that year. Being of weak intellect, the actual government fell into the hands of a Boyar, Boris Goudonov, who had married the Tsar's sister, Irene. One of Boris Goudonov's achievements was to gain the formal assent of the Eastern Orthodox Church for Russia to have its own Patriarch. This was popular with all classes, and when Theodore, the last survivor of the House of Ruric, died in 1598, Boris was elected Tsar and solemnly crowned on 1st September. The ceremony was performed by Job, the first Patriarch of Russia, and in view of Boris's somewhat slender claims to the throne, he used the words: 'God praises not the birth of a man, but his virtues.' Boris's son, Theodore, who had been carefully prepared for the throne, was proclaimed Tsar on his father's sudden death on 13th April 1605 but on the appearance of the False Demetrius I he was foully murdered in his apartments in the Kremlin on 10th July of that year.

Ivan IV had had a younger son who was murdered in 1591 while still a child, and according to popular belief, Boris Goudonov had instigated his death. In 1603 a man calling himself Demetrius claimed to be the rightful heir to the throne and gained the support of those Boyars who regarded Boris as a usurper. Even the Patriarch Job was impressed by his claims. Demetrius was forced to flee to Lithuania and then to Poland, where he gained support, was converted to the Roman Catholic Church and baptised. At the head of a force of supporters he entered Russia, and the sudden death of Boris enabled him to be accepted by the people as the true Pretender to the throne. On 30th July 1605 he was crowned by the Patriarch Isidore, a Greek whom he had chosen. On 8th May 1606 he married Marina Miniszek, the daughter of a Polish magnate who had supported him. No Tsarina had been crowned before, but on this occasion he crowned Marina. It was the Russian custom to stand during services in church, but in accordance with the Roman Catholic practice two thrones were installed in the Uspenski Cathedral, one of which had been a present to Ivan IV from the Shah of Persia. This led to much discontent and Demetrius was seen to be a Tsar alien to the deeply rooted usages, religious rules and superstitions of the time, while the Tsarina was a Roman Catholic and a Pole. Moreover, the arrogant behaviour of the Polish troops during the subsequent festivities aroused the hostility of the Muscovites, who, under the leadership of a cunning and influential Boyar, Basil Shouisky, made a sudden *coup d'état*, entered the Kremlin and slew Demetrius. Marina was allowed to depart and later was married to the second False Demetrius. Basil Shouisky was now proclaimed Tsar (19th May 1606) and crowned on 1st June, but he was not generally recognised and on 19th July 1610 he was deposed. Then followed a period of great danger to Russia. Sigismund III, King of Poland, revealed his plan to obtain the throne for himself, which aroused anti-Catholic feeling throughout the land, while the Swedes, who had become rivals of the Poles, set up a Pretender of their own in Novograd who became known as the False Demetrius III. But the invaders were repelled and the Grand National Assembly elected as Tsar Michael Romanov, the young son of the Patriarch Philaret, who was related by marriage to the last dynasty.

We have some information of the crowns and other regalia in the Moscow Treasury at this time from the writings of several authors. Jacques Maigret,[1] a Burgundian captain who served under Boris Goudonov and the first False Demetrius, describes the Treasury (*raskhodnia Kasna*) before the Polish occupation of 1611 to 1612 as being filled with all sorts of jewels and plate. He mentions four crowns, three of the Emperor and one with which the grand dukes were crowned, besides an unfinished one which the first False Demetrius had made for his wife. There were two sceptres and two orbs, but during the Polish occupation much of the plate was melted down, and we learn from Samuel Maskeivitch's Journal (1594–1621) that some of the regalia was sacrificed. This included the crown of Boris Goudonov and the unfinished crown of Marina Miniszek. The Polish troops demanded money from the Council of Boyars who replied that they had no money and were not willing to use the riches of the Treasury which were needed for the coronation of Ladislas, the son of Sigismund III, King of Poland. Since, however, the memories of Boris Goudonov and the False Demetrius were detested, there was no feeling about pledging their crowns, together with some other ornaments including two or three narwhal horns, a cross made of narwhal decorated with diamonds and a hussar saddle embellished with stones and fine pearls which had belonged to Demetrius. The stones and pearls in Boris Goudonov's crown were valued

---

[1] J. Maigret: *Estat de l'Empire de Russe.*

at 20,044 roubles and those in Marina's crown at 7,872 roubles, the saddle was valued at 6,570 roubles and the narwhal cross with its gold chain at 7,625 roubles.

Of the other crowns mentioned by Maigret, one can be identified as the Cap of Monomachus and one of the others would have been the crown which Ivan gave to the Khan Ediguer of Kazan when he embraced Christianity in 1553 and took the name of Simeon. It seems that besides the coronation crown, the Tsars had their own personal crowns, and the third crown mentioned by Maskeivitch was probably such a one. The sceptre and orb which form part of the regalia may have survived what became known as 'The Time of Troubles'. But apart from three thrones there are very few other ornaments in the Treasury today which date back to the period before the Romanovs.

When the young Michael Romanov was elected Tsar on 21st February 1613 he was in the care of his mother at the Ipatievsky Monastery near Kostroma, and it was not until 24th March that he was discovered by the delegates of the National Assembly. His mother tried to dissuade him from accepting the throne, but in the end he consented. According to Abraham Palitzine[1] he was offered by the town of Kostroma the 'Cross of the Tsars' which was placed in his hand. He then took his seat on the throne and was proclaimed 'The elect of God, the true great Sovereign Tsar and Grand Prince Michael Theodorovitch, Autocrat of all Russia'. So much damage had been done to the capital that Michael had to wait several weeks at the Troitska Monastery before he could enter Moscow. The young Tsar was crowned on 11th July 1613 according to the ancient rites, the Cap of Monomachus being used. There was acute dissension among the Boyars as to who was entitled to carry the royal ornaments.

The Tsar's Treasury, or *Kasna* had been organised in the Kremlin in the reign of Ivan III and is first mentioned in 1494. The Crown Treasury contained the regalia. There was also an Armoury and Store Room. Attached to the Treasury were workshops where not only armour but also gold and silver and jewelled ornaments, were made. During 'The Time of Troubles' these ceased to function and the craftsmen were dispersed. On the accession of Michael, the Treasury and workshops were re-established and foreign artists and craftsmen were recruited. Thence onward there was an enormous output of artistic treasures. Although the records of the contents of the Treasury go back as far as the XVI century, the inventories of the XVII century are fuller and give a precise description of each ornament with its weight and number of jewels employed. However, historical information is scanty.

Michael had several royal ornaments made. One was a personal crown which, while following the general shape of the Cap of Monomachus, was surmounted by an arched crown similar to those in use in Western Europe. It is sometimes described as the *Bonnet Franc*. The globe of the Russian Empire and the ancient *Sceptre de Grande Parade* were both probably made, or at least re-made, in Michael's reign and are included in the inventory of 1642 which describes them as Frankish work. This no doubt refers to the foreign craftsmen who were employed and to the Western influences which were coming into Russia.

The *barmi* or collar in the regalia is usually attributed to the reign of Alexis, and

---

[1] A. Palitzine: *Mémoires du cellérier.*

Weltman[1] states that it was ordered by Tsar Alexis from Constantinople and that there is a receipt dated 1665 for 18,325 roubles paid to Ivan Jouriev for the work. He also states that the bow-and-arrow case made for Alexis was ordered from Constantinople in 1662 when it was made by the same artist who was a Greek. Maskell[2] and other writers prefer to attribute them to Russian workmanship, although agreeing that the enamelled plaques with religious subjects and Greek inscriptions belonging to the *barmi* are of Byzantine origin. Maskell suggests that Ivan Jouriev was a Russian workman, or at least employed in Moscow. The inventory of 1642, which was made while Michael was still on the throne, describes an embroidered *barmi*. In any case, it seems very unlikely that any such royal ornaments would have been ordered from Constantinople which was at that time under Turkish dominion. There is also preserved in the Kremlin a throne of Tsar Michael, although Weltman does not include this in his list.

These new ornaments have a dynastic flavour about them. On the one hand the crown, sceptre and the orb all bear the name of Monomachus, thus emphasising the heritage of the Russian monarchy, while the new ornaments, with their mixture of Eastern style and Western influence, give a new and distinctive appearance to the regalia of the first of the Romanov tsars.

On the death of Michael in 1645, his son, Alexis, succeeded to the throne and was crowned on 28th September of that year. During the reign of Alexis, the artistic activities of the workshops in the Oruzhania Palata reached a very high standard under the enlightened administration of Khitrovo, who did not hesitate to encourage new ideas and Western influences. The output of arms and ornaments of various kinds was enormous. As has already been indicated, we must discount Weltman's assertion that Alexis ordered the *barmi*, sceptre and orb from Constantinople, although a new orb was made by Ivan Jouriev in 1662 and a new sceptre in 1665. It seems as though the *barmi* was also altered in 1665. Weltman also considered that the splendid throne of Alexis was ordered at the same time as the regalia and was made at Ispahan in Persia. In a register known as the Book of Embassies, it is recorded that a throne was sent to Alexis in 1660 by Ichto Modevlet who was a member of the Court of the Shah of Persia. Maskell, however, casts doubt on this origin and considers that it was made by the Moscow goldsmiths and quotes Viollet le Duc and other writers in support. One theory which seems to be the most probable is that a throne was received from Persia, but was embellished and made more magnificent in the Moscow workshops.

On Alexis' death in 1676, his son Theodore III, a youth of fifteen succeeded him and was crowned on 18th July of that year. Although he had a fine intellect and noble disposition, he was afflicted from childhood with a mysterious disease which horribly disfigured him and made him half paralysed. He died after reigning six years. A personal crown was made for Theodore but was broken up in the next reign. Alexis had been twice married. Ivan V, the second son of his first wife was next in order of succession, but he was almost an imbecile and so Peter, a son of the second marriage, was proclaimed Tsar. But Ivan's ambitious sister, Sophia, managed to persuade the standing

[1] A. Weltman: *Le Trésor de Moscou*.   [2] A. Maskell: *Russian Art*, London 1889.

army to upset this arrangement and after a tumult and some assassinations, Ivan and Peter were proclaimed joint Tsars with Sophia as Regent. This necessitated a double coronation which took place on 25th May 1682. Ivan V was crowned with the Cap of Monomachus and for Peter a new crown similar to the original was made and was described in the inventories as the Cap of Monomachus of the Second Order. Another crown of gold lace brocade known as the Cap of the Third Order was made for Ivan in 1684, while in 1687 caps, or crowns, of the traditional shape, but richly adorned with diamonds, were made for each Tsar. Two orbs were available for the coronation, but a new sceptre was made for Peter. It was also necessary for there to be a double throne and for this purpose an old throne was altered and provided with two seats. Ivan died in 1689 which left Peter as sole Tsar, although until his mother's death in 1694, he was not absolutely free to follow his own inclinations.

The reign of Peter the Great brought about great changes in Russia. Foreign, and particularly Western, influences had already been at work and Peter with ruthless vigour continued the process. He was no respecter of tradition and despite the unwillingness of the majority of his subjects, much of what they treasured as established customs was swept away, including many of the ceremonial rituals which his predecessors had scrupulously observed. He abolished the Patriarchate, thus subordinating the Church to the monarchy. He built St Petersburg as the new capital of Russia and on 22nd October 1721 he was proclaimed 'Father of the Fatherland, Peter the Great, Emperor of all Russia'.

Peter the Great brooked no opposition, and his only son, Alexis, who was suspected of supporting the opponents to reform, was brutally killed. Peter decided to pass over Alexis' son, the Grand Duke Peter, as his successor and to appoint his wife Catherine, a woman of obscure and humble origin, to succeed him. The throwing aside of the principles of primogeniture shocked the people, but when he announced that he was going to crown Catherine as Empress they were appalled. Apart from Marina, no woman had ever been crowned in Russia and this proposal was considered to be a scandalous innovation. Nevertheless, Peter crowned Catherine in Moscow on 7th May 1724 and made it an occasion of great pomp and splendour.

Another innovation was the crown used at the ceremony. Instead of the old style cap, a new crown was made following in general the shape of the Western Imperial Crown made for the Emperor Rudolph in 1602, which was used extensively for heraldic purposes at the time and with which no doubt Peter was familiar since his visit to Vienna. From the circlet rose mitre-shaped sides with a single arch from the front to the back and the crown was surmounted by a large balas ruby on which rested a cross, the whole being richly decorated with diamonds—2,536 in number—besides pearls. A contemporary description of the crown records:

> The Imperial Crown was rich in diamonds and brilliants, a great number of them being of remarkable size. The diadem was set off with oriental pearls all of equal water and extraordinary dimensions. In the whole crown there was but one coloured stone, a ruby or spinel of peerless beauty and of greater size than a pigeon's egg. It certainly was the most remarkable ruby known at the time. The stone was placed on top of the diadem in the middle of the crown and was surmounted by a cross with brilliants.

This spinel was probably one which was presented to Catherine I by Menchikov who had obtained it from Prince Galzarine who, when Governor-General of Siberia, was executed for bribery. The frame of the crown, without the jewels, is still preserved. Thereafter the Cap of Monomachus was no longer used as the coronation crown. It was not considered necessary to provide a new sceptre or orb and those in the existing regalia were used. The *barmi* was not included in the Empress's regalia and was, in fact, never used again. Peter the Great died in 1725 and Catherine was accepted as Empress, but she only lived until 1727. The succeeding years saw great uncertainty in the succession and, in fact, in the thirty-seven years between the death of Peter until the accession of Catherine II in 1741, no less than seven sovereigns reigned. On the death of Catherine I, the Grand Duke Peter, grandson of Peter the Great, was recognised as Tsar and was crowned as Peter II on 24th February 1728. He died in 1730 and Anne, the daughter of Ivan V, was offered the throne and was crowned on 28th April of that year. A new crown was made for Anne which was somewhat larger, but of the same style as that of Catherine I from which the diamonds were taken to decorate it. This crown was used later at the coronation of Alexander II in Warsaw as King of Poland. Anne, having no male issue, selected Ivan, the infant son of her niece Anna, Duchess of Brunswick, as her successor. On the death of the Empress in 1740, though still a child Ivan was proclaimed Emperor as Ivan VI, but in a little over a year he was dethroned and Princess Elizabeth, daughter of Peter the Great and Catherine I, became Empress and was crowned on 25th April 1742, for which occasion a new crown was made. This crown has not been preserved.

Elizabeth disliked the Germans, but she was unable to find among the surviving descendants of Michael Romanov anyone who could be called a genuine Russian. She therefore chose as her heir-apparent a son of her deceased elder sister, Peter, Duke of Holstein-Gottorp, who, despite her attempts to Russianise him, remained a thorough German. On Elizabeth's death in 1761 he succeeded her, but was so detested that within a few months of his succession and before he had had time to be crowned, he was de-throned and assassinated. His wife, a German princess, was then proclaimed Empress as Catherine II. She was crowned on 22nd September 1762 and introduced several new features into the ceremony. She placed the crown on her own head and took Communion, entering the gates of the Iconostasis, the screen adorned with icons separating the chancel from the nave in Russian churches, and in which, according to custom, women were not entitled to enter.

For her coronation Catherine ordered a new crown from Lubie, the Court Jeweller, and it was designed by Jeremie Posier, an artist from Geneva. It was not ready in time for the coronation, but it was used as the coronation crown at each subsequent coronation. In his memoirs Posier referred to the permission which had already been granted him to break up some old jewellery, and continues:

> The extracted materials were to be used for a new crown which H.M. wishes to have for her coronation. H.M. bade me consult M. Betsky about everything. I was very pleased with this order because it relieved me of any responsibility or trouble I might have had with the persons administering the Treasury. I made up my mind at once to agree in all with M. Betsky (who longed to satisfy his ambition) and I contented myself with helping him with all that concerned my task.

I recommended to him a very skilful Frenchman named Aurole who did his work splendidly. I chose among the objects everything that was suitable, and as the Empress wished the crown to remain unchanged after the coronation, I picked out the biggest stones, diamonds as well as coloured gems, most suitable for mounting, and I thus obtained the richest object that ever existed in Europe. In spite of my greatest care to make the crown as light as possible by using only the strictly necessary materials to fasten the stones, it yet proved to weigh 5 lb.

Actually the crown was changed during Catherine's reign and the coloured stones were removed and replaced by diamonds, while a great spinel was set on top of the crown. This stone is the one which is said to have been purchased in Peking in 1672 for the Tsar Alexis by Nicholas Spahany, the Russian Ambassador at the Court of the Emperor Kam-hi. The price was said to have been 2,672 roubles, but according to another story it was paid for with a 'load of gold ingots'.

The Imperial Sceptre was also made during the reign of Catherine II. It was designed by Troitinski and at the top was set the famous Orloff diamond.

Catherine gave orders for the orb of the Empress Elizabeth to be used at her coronation, but at the eleventh hour it was found that it had been broken up and its gold used for making other objects. A new orb was made in a great hurry, possibly by Posier, who arrived in Moscow with six assistants a week before the ceremony. Together with the sceptre, it became part of the permanent coronation regalia.

Other state ornaments made for Catherine were the great diamond clasp for her mantle attributed to Posier, and the jewelled insignia of the Order of St Andrew which can be seen in portraits of the Empress. Peter the Great and the Empress Elizabeth had laid the foundation of what was to become the most magnificent collection of personal jewellery in the world, and Catherine II added very considerably to this. The more important objects will be described later.

Catherine died in November 1796 and was succeeded by her son, Paul, who during his mother's lifetime had been kept in a state of semi-captivity. He was crowned on 5th April 1797 and for the first time—with the exception of Marina—his consort, Marie Feodorovna, was crowned too. But in making this concession to his consort he also made this occasion an opportunity to issue a proclamation banning women from the right of accession to the throne. A crown in the same style as that of the Emperor but smaller was made for the Empress and was used at subsequent coronations. Paul, whose sanity was in doubt, having made himself very unpopular, was assassinated in March 1801 and was succeeded by his son Alexander I.

The coronation of Alexander I on 15th September 1801 and the subsequent ceremonies of Nicholas I on 22nd March 1826, of Alexander II in August 1856, of Alexander III on 15th May 1883 and of Nicholas II on 26th May 1896 all followed the same procedure.

Some time before the event a proclamation was made informing the population of the date of the ceremony. A day or two before the ceremony the tsar made a state entry into Moscow riding on horseback surrounded by the grand dukes and high military officers, with the empress and grand duchesses following in gilded state coaches. On the actual day the tsar and tsarina proceeded to the Uspenski Cathedral under a canopy in solemn procession, the regalia being carried before them. In 1856, besides the crowns, the sceptre and the orb, there were added the great diamond chain of the Order of St Andrew, the Imperial Banner, the sword and shield of the Empire and the State Seal. In 1895 a third crown had to be made for the dowager empress who attended the ceremony. It was similar in size and design to that of the empress. The emperors wore military uniform and the only coronation vestment—the mantle—was also carried in the procession. On arrival in the church, some prayers were said by the Metropolitan, who blessed the mantle and the crowns, which were then handed to the tsar who placed the Imperial Crown on his own head. The Metropolitan then delivered the Sceptre and the Orb. The tsar, having seated himself on the throne, summoned the tsarina. The tsar took off his crown and with it touched the brow of the tsarina and replaced it on his head. He then set a smaller crown on the tsarina's head and she assumed the purple robe of the Order of St Andrew. After some prayers, invoking God's help in the tsar's acts and judgment, and an anthem, the Metropolitan anointed the tsar on the forehead, eyes, nostrils, ears, breast and on both sides of the hands and the tsarina on the forehead only, with chrism. They were then asked by the Metropolitan to pronounce the long version of the Creed. The tsar was conducted through the royal gates and received the Holy Sacrament in both kinds separately as if he were a priest. The tsarina communicated in the usual way at the royal gates. The archdeacon then proclaimed the titles of the sovereigns and the clergy and assembled company did homage by making their obeisances. The Metropolitan presented the cross for the tsar and tsarina to kiss, after which the imperial procession left the church. After the service the sovereigns, with the crowns on their heads and wearing their coronation mantles, appeared before the people and were acclaimed, bowing three times on each side.

Reference has already been made to the ancient *Kasna*, or Treasury, of the Kremlin instituted by Ivan III. It suffered severe loss from frequent fires and from the melting down of a large quantity of the plate during the war with Poland and the Time of the Troubles. In 1737 a great fire destroyed a large part of the armoury. In 1812, during the French invasion, the whole treasure, including the regalia, was moved to Novograd and though there were some losses, it was returned to Moscow in 1814. In 1850 the entire collection was transferred to the newly completed Oruzhania Palata. In the 1920's the collection was re-examined and the remains of the Grand Treasury and other items of real artistic merit were retained, while the rest was dispersed to other museums.

The collection was originally divided into three parts: the Grand Treasury in which were kept the regalia; the Armoury and the Store House for costumes, robes, uniforms and arms for the Tsar, his court and bodyguards. Attached were extensive workshops where not only arms and armour were made, but icons were painted and gold and silver and jewelled ornaments manufactured. In 1835 a full catalogue was prepared containing more than 10,000 items.

The regalia kept in the Treasury included eleven crowns; two collars or *barmis*; four sceptres; two orbs, besides crosses, chains, coronation robes and thrones. In the Armoury there were preserved some personal and ceremonial weapons of the tsars besides the banner, sword and shield of the Empire. The oldest crown is known as the Cap of Monomachus (*Plate 166, a*). It is described in the inventory of 1696 as:

> The cap of gold filigree called 'Monomachus', is surmounted by a plain cross having at the extremities 4 pearls; above the dome (or apple) between 3 pearls are three large stones, a topaz, a sapphire and a ruby, all in gold settings. On the crown are 4 emeralds and 4 rubies set in gold and 25 pearls of Ormuz. The cap is bordered with sable fur and lined with red satin.

By tradition this crown was a gift from the Byzantine Emperor to St Vladimir in 988, but the modern view is that it probably dates from the XII or XIII centuries. We only know for certain that it was used as a coronation crown by Ivan IV in 1547 and that it was subsequently used at the next eight coronations. The epithet 'Monomachus' was added by Ivan IV. The crown consists of eight plates which completely cover the head which make it a sort of *camelaucum*, the type of closed crown introduced to Constantinople at the end of the XI century by the Comnenus dynasty. The original filigree decoration, which includes a pattern of flowers, is in exquisite taste. The other part of the crown and jewels were added later, probably for the coronation of Ivan IV. The dome, which is a peculiar feature and repeated in subsequent crowns is sometimes described as 'apple' which suggested that it was intended to represent the orb or globe. After Peter the Great had proclaimed the Empire, several of the crowns in the Treasury were associated with parts of the country and the Cap of Monomachus was sometimes designated 'The Crown of the Crimea'.

The next oldest crown in the Treasury is the Crown of Kazan (*Plate 166, b*). It is described in the inventories as:

> 'The Cap of the Tsar Simeon of Kazan. It is in filigree with niello. On the summit is a yellow ruby (topaz) and on either side 2 great pearls. The cap is adorned with 33 rubies, 18 large and 12 small turquoises and 12 cut in two. The border is of black sable fur. The value of the cap is 684 roubles 20 altimes.'
>
> The cut-out plates which form the crown are oriental in character and the arabesques are in Persian style, but it is regarded as having been the production of a Russian workshop. The topaz was added in 1625 and replaced the great ruby which was taken for the crown of Tsar Michael.

Other caps or crowns still preserved in the Kremlin Museum are:

> The crown of Tsar Michael Theodorovitch (*Plate 166, c*) is formed of plates *à jour* in enamel surmounted by an arched crown on top of which is a large emerald. The crown is decorated with 45 diamonds, 36 rubies, 21 sapphires, 22 emeralds, 15 'sparkling' emeralds and 51 pearls of Ormuz. The border is of sable fur. Originally the crown was surmounted by a cross with 23 diamonds, 3 pearls of Ormuz and a great ruby, but this was removed and placed on a new cap made for the Tsar Ivan V in 1687. At a later date this cap was designated 'The Crown of Astrakhan'.
>
> A group of four crowns was made for the joint reign of Ivan V and Peter I. The first is a simple one resembling the Cap of Monomachus and was known as the Cap of Monomachus of the Second Order, though later it became designated 'The Crown of Kiev, Vladimir and Novgorod' (*Plate 166, d*).
>
> In 1684 a cap of golden lace brocade was made for Ivan V. The diamonds with which it was adorned were taken from a crown of Tsar Theodore Alexievitch. It was known as *Altabasnaya* because it is made of gold lace and was also designated 'The Crown of Siberia' (*Plate 167, a*). In the inventory of 1702 it is valued at 909 roubles.

In 1687 a diamond crown was made for Ivan V and another for Peter I. The crown of Ivan (*Plate 167, b*) still followed the traditional form of a pyramidal cap surmounted by a dome and a cross, and is surrounded by a circlet of plates hinged together and decorated with double-headed eagles set between *fleurons* and rosettes, all richly decorated with diamonds. Below the cross is a great ruby in three circles of gold set with diamonds. In the 1702 inventory this crown was valued at 15,211 roubles.

The diamond crown of Peter I (*Plate 167, c*), while in the same general design as that of Ivan, had some distinctive features. The circlet is surrounded by 4 large rubies and 8 emeralds set *à jour* on top and with pliant and nodding stems. The front plaque is specially richly adorned with diamonds and there are 847 diamonds employed in the decoration of the cap, apart from those in the circlet. On top, under the cross, is an immense uncut balas ruby. In the inventory of 1702 the cap was valued at 16,930 roubles.

The next crown in order of antiquity is that made for the coronation of Catherine I. Only the frame (*Plate 168, a*) stripped of its jewels remains, but it is of interest as being the first example of the Western style mitre-shaped crown used in Russia.

The mitre-shaped crown of the Empress Anne Ivanova is still preserved (*Plate 168, b*). It is decorated with 2,500 diamonds and several rubies. Under the cross is a great ruby which some identify as that purchased in Peking in 1676 which, however, is generally thought to be the one now in the Imperial Crown. In the inventory of 1725 this ruby was valued at 60,000 roubles. The crown was used by Tsar Alexander II for his Polish coronation in Warsaw in 1852 and was subsequently designated 'The Crown of Poland'.

The Crown of Malta of the Order of St John of Jerusalem was offered to Tsar Paul in 1798 when Bonaparte occupied the island. The Order possessed two crowns, one adorned with fine pearls which was taken by the French, and the other of gold and enamel which was sent to Paul and was first kept at St Petersburg, but transferred to Moscow in 1827.

In 1798 George XIII, the last King of Georgia, approached the Russians for help against the Persians and renounced his crown in favour of the Tsar. There is in the Treasury a Crown of Georgia in the conventional style of a circlet with four arches surmounted by an orb and cross. It is described as the Crown of Georgia, but it is not known if it was transferred from Georgia, or made especially when it became a Russian province in 1801.

The Royal Crown of Imeretia was kept in the Treasury of the Cathedral of the Virgin in the Convent at Gelati, but it is not known whether it has survived.

In some works on regalia a crown of Finland is depicted. In 1809 such a crown was designed and was used heraldically but no actual crown was made. The design is of a royal crown with a single arch going from side to side with an orb and cross on top. In the centre of the circlet rises a double-headed eagle surmounted by an imperial crown.

The Eastern emperors used as part of their regalia a collar or kind of tippet of brocade adorned with gold and enamelled plates and decorated with precious stones. It is referred to in the donation of Constantine, see p. 376. These are sometimes described as diadems, probably because they were fitted with a kind of decorated hood which could be drawn over the head. It is claimed that such a collar was sent by the Emperors Basil and Constantine to St Vladimir in 988 together with other regalia. The Russians gave the name *barmi* to the collar, although in the inventories they are described as diadems. Mention of them is found in the wills of the grand princes where they are always inseparable from the gold cap. Such an ornament formed part of the coronation regalia from Ivan IV to Peter the Great.

There are two such collars preserved in the Treasury. The oldest was found with other ornaments in 1882 in a cache in the ruins of the town of Ryazan. These ornaments had probably been

a   *The Altabasnaya Cap of Tsar Ivan V*

b   *Diamond crown of Ivan V*   c   *Diamond crown of Peter I*

These three crowns are in the Kremlin Museum, Moscow

a   *Frame of crown made for Catherine I (p. 526)*   b   *Crown of the Empress Anna Ivanova (pp. 522 and 526)*

c   *The Alabastron (p. 530)*   d, e and f   *Heads of sceptres of Tsar Alexis, Georgia and Peter I*
(p. 527)

All these objects are in the Kremlin Museum, Moscow

hidden during one of the Tartar invasions. The *barmi* (*Plate 169, a*) consists of eleven jewelled plaques with enamelled figures. Four plaques represent the crucifixion; the Virgin Mary; St Barbe and St Irene. Two large double plaques ornamented with precious stones and fine pearls bear a representation of a grand prince holding a cross in his right hand. On his head is a nimbus and on the two sides are lilies. It is unquestionably of Byzantine workmanship.

The second *barmi* (*Plate 169, b*) is of much later date. A *barmi* embroidered in spun gold on dark violet satin with pearls is described in the 1642 inventory and may have been the basis of the present collar. The plaques, however, are attributed to the reign of Tsar Alexis and there is a receipt dated 1685 for the sum of 18,325 roubles paid to Ivan Jouriev for the work of a collar. This *barmi* is very rich and consists of seven plaques fixed on brocade and adorned with enamel, diamonds, sapphires, rubies and emeralds. The large plaque in the centre bears a representation of the Virgin Mary bearing in her arms the Infant Jesus. It is decorated with 60 diamonds. The plaque on the right represents the True Cross being found by the Emperor Constantine and St Helena, his mother, and bears a Greek inscription. It is decorated with a sapphire, 7 large emeralds, 48 diamonds and 28 rubies. The plaque on the left bears the same ornamentation with a representation of the Miracle of St Mercury performed by Julian the Apostate. The four small plaques placed between the three large ones represent the Creation; King David surrounded by a choir singing the Psalms; the Kings, the Apostles and the Prophets; and the Church with the Holy Ghost descending on the officiating priest.

Although it was sometimes claimed that the Russian sceptre was part of the original gift of regalia made by the Eastern emperors, the oldest one still preserved probably dates from the reign of Tsar Michael (*Plate 168, e*). In the inventory of 1642 it is described as 'a sceptre of chased gold with various enamels and precious stones, diamonds, rubies and emeralds, surmounted by three eagles in enamel. Below the eagles is a crown with a sapphire at the summit'. The sapphire of the sceptre was lost and has been replaced by an emerald.

A second sceptre was made for Tsar Alexis in 1665 (*Plate 168, d*) and is described as after the form of the royal ensigns of the Emperor Constantine the Great. It was valued at 2,600 roubles. It is of gold *taillé à jour* and adorned with precious stones and enamel. At the top is a globe on which rests a crown on either side of which is a double-headed eagle. The sceptre bears twelve medallions with representations in niello of the twelve great fêtes of the year.

A sceptre was made for the coronation of Peter the Great (*Plate 168, f*). At the summit are three double-headed eagles with spread wings. A fourth sceptre described as the Sceptre of Georgia (*Plate 168, e*) is covered with emerald green enamel enriched with diamonds and rubies and surmounted by a double-headed eagle. It bears the cypher of Paul I.

While an orb was included in the list of the regalia said to have been sent from Constantinople to St Vladimir, the oldest one in the Treasury is of a much later date and was probably made or re-made for Tsar Michael (*Plate 170, a*). It has usually been described as Byzantine work, but the 1642 inventory says it is of Frankish work by which is probably meant that it was made by Western craftsmen in the Moscow workshops. The golden globe is 7½ in. in diameter and with the tall cross 12 in. high. It is very richly decorated with translucent enamels and precious stones. There are in all 58 diamonds, 89 rubies, 23 sapphires, 56 emeralds mounted in gold and enamel and 37 fine pearls. In addition there are enamel pictures representing the anointing of David, his victory over Goliath, his return after the victory, and the persecution of Saul. Between these are four symbolic figures—the eagle, the lion, the griffin and the unicorn.

The second orb (*Plate 170, b*) was made in 1662 by Ivan Jouriev who was paid 7,917 roubles for his work. The globe rests on an elegant stand and has a richly jewelled equator. On top is an open crown with a small enamelled globe from which rises a cross. The orb is decorated with 159 large and small diamonds, 8 large and 196 small sapphires and 136 other stones described as 'sparkling'. They are all set on a background of green enamel.

There are a number of crosses among the regalia, the most important being the cross of the tsars given to Tsar Michael at Kostroma. The cross has two bars decorated with ciselé enamel and at the summit is a two-headed eagle crowned and adorned with precious stones. A copy was made for Peter the Great on the occasion of his double coronation with Ivan V.

In the inventories of 1629 and 1632 the crosses of the Tsarina Eudoxia Lukianovna are described. One is of German work and made of ebony encrusted with silver. Another is called the Greek Great Cross. In the registers it is recorded that in the year 1658 on 11th June in the Golden Chamber of the Grand Seigneur, the Tsar and Grand Prince Alexis Michailovitch was presented by John Anastahow, a Greek of Constantinople, with a gold cross enriched with diamonds, emeralds and rubies valued at 219 roubles. There are in the Treasury three Indian crosses given by the Tsar Michael to his son Alexis. They are of Indian wood chased and enriched with enamel and precious stones.

There is also an ivory cross formed of seven pieces of ivory surmounted by a globe and a double-headed eagle. The ivory is carved with representations of six Kings of Israel and the Twelve Apostles.

In the Treasury are a number of great chains. One of Arabian gold has seventy-six links in a filigree in the form of oblong hexagons. It is claimed to be the actual chain of the cross sent from Byzantium to St Vladimir. Another chain is formed of 160 links encrusted with niello. The chain of Tsar Michael has eighty-eight gold links on some of which are engraved the titles of the Tsar and a prayer to the Holy Trinity. Another chain has 103 gold links, the sides of which are chased with various coloured enamels. A chain of Tsar Theodore Alexievitch consists of twenty-four gold plaques enamelled with alternating crosses and serpents. The latter are adorned with fine pearls weighing 700 gr. Another chain of Tsar Theodore is formed of two rosettes in enamel fixed on red satin enriched with rubies and pearls.

In the Uspenski Cathedral is a carved wooden throne called 'The Throne of Vladimir Monomachus', but according to modern opinion it is considered to have been made for Ivan IV in 1551 and because it was damaged during the Polish occupation, to have been restored by Tsar Michael. It is the traditional coronation chair of the tsars. The chair is made of walnut and lime and decorated with relief and pierced carving painted dark brown. Traces of gold suggest that it was originally gilded. On the cornice fringe and on the door panels are a series of inscriptions in Slavonic characters. The throne stands on four sculptured mythical beasts. On the side panels and on the door are twelve carved bas-reliefs depicting scenes from the life and campaigns of an unidentified Russian prince. Above the throne is a tent-like octagonal canopy on top of which is a double-headed eagle.

In the Treasury there are no less than twenty thrones but only seven need be noted. The oldest was brought by Sophia Palaeologus from Constantinople in 1472 when she married Ivan III. It is made of ivory plaques. The original panels represent the Legend of Thrace. A number of the original panels have disappeared and been replaced, probably in the XVII or XVIII centuries, by new ones depicting battle scenes with the warriors in German costume. The throne was restored in 1856 for the coronation of Tsar Alexander II. The next oldest throne is known as 'The Persian' and is said to have been sent to Tsar Ivan IV by the Shah of Persia. The throne is embellished with 1,325 rubies and hyacinths, 539 turquoises, 164 pearls, 25 sapphires, 15 amethysts, 21 chrysolites and some false emeralds.

The throne of Boris Goudonov was a present from Abbas, Shah of Persia, in 1604. It is adorned with 825 turquoises, including one of remarkable size, 552 rubies, 177 fine pearls and 700 pearls cut in two. In addition there are numerous small turquoises forming the border.

a (i)–(iv)　*Barmi found at Old Ryazan.　Kremlin Museum, Moscow* (p. 527)

(i)

(iv)

(ii)

(iii)

b　*Barmi of Tsar Alexis Michael. Kremlin Museum, Moscow* (p. 527)

a   The orb of Tsar Michael. Kremlin Museum,
Moscow (p. 527)

b   The orb of Tsar Alexis Michael, 1662. Kremlin
Museum, Moscow (p. 527)

The *Book of Embassies* mentions another throne sent to the Tsar Alexis in 1660 by Ichto Modevlet, who was attached to the Court of the Shah. It was made by an Armenian, Zachary Saradarow, who was paid 22,591 roubles 20 altimes for it. According to Weltman it probably came from a workshop of Ispahan. Other writers have cast doubt on this because of the unmistakably Russian workmanship of parts of the throne. The probable explanation is that a throne was received from Persia and was sent to the Moscow workshops to be enriched. According to the 1676 inventory it is adorned with 876 diamonds of various sizes; 1,223 amethysts in addition to rubies and turquoises and three strands of pearls surrounding an inscription which reads: *Potentissimo et invictissimo Muscovitarum Imperatori Alexio, in terris feliciter regnanti, hic thronus, summa arte et industria fabrefactus, sit futuri in coelis et perennis faustum felix que omen, Anno Domini 1659.*

For the joint coronation of Ivan V and Peter I, a double throne had to be provided. A throne which had belonged to Tsar Michael and stood in the Golden Room was chosen for the purpose. It was decorated with four sculptured symbolic figures—the eagle, the lion, the griffin and the unicorn—which date from the time of Ivan III. The throne has two seats under an elaborate canopy supported by chased silver pillars.

The Throne of Poland was, in 1833, in the Throne Room of the royal palace at Warsaw and was used for the coronation of Nicholas I and the Empress Alexandra. It consists of two seats of gilded wood under a baldaquin embroidered in gold and bearing the cipher of the Emperor.

The coronation robes of the tsar originally consisted of a kaftan or tunic and a mantle lined with ermine. From the time of Peter II military uniform was worn instead of the coronation tunic. There are eight coronation kaftans preserved in the Treasury. They are made of Damascus silk, richly embroidered with gold brocade. There is also the kabab, or dalmatic, of Tsar Alexis. The coronation robes of four empresses regnant and four empresses consort are also preserved: some are particularly rich in decoration and embroidery. There are also various coronation mantles.

The sword never played an important part in the Russian coronation regalia as it did in the West, but in 1856 a banner, a sword and a shield of the Empire were made. The tsars had always possessed banners and several are still preserved in the Armoury, including that of Ivan IV and one of 1664. The latest one followed the old design and was made to replace an old banner which had become worn out.

From the reign of Ivan IV onward the tsars were anointed at their coronations, and according to tradition the ampulla was a vessel of cornelian said to have originally belonged to the Emperor Augustus. It was included among the gifts said to have been sent to St Vladimir by the Emperors Basil and Constantine in 988. This tradition was strengthened by the fact that in the wills of the grand princes the vessel of cornelian mounted in gold was passed down from father to son as an heirloom and a sacred object inseparable from the Crown. If such a vessel was sent to St Vladimir, it could hardly have been intended for the coronation chrism, as anointing was not introduced into the Byzantine coronation ceremony until the coronation of the first Latin Emperor Baldwin I in the first part of the XIII century. It is in any case difficult to identify such a vessel today, unless it is one known as the *Alabastron* to which a similar tradition is attached.

The preparation of the Holy Oil for distribution to various churches throughout the Empire was a great ceremony which took place in Holy Week. The preliminary mixing of oil, wine, herbs and a variety of different ingredients began in the fourth week of Lent. In Holy Week these ingredients were ceremonially prepared, two large boilers, several bowls and sixteen vases being used. All are of great size and of massive silver, being a gift from Catherine II in 1762. In addition there was the highly venerated Alabastron which was always kept on the altar of the sacristy of the Synodal Treasury. Each year a small quantity of the chrism it contained was taken to mix with the newly prepared Holy Oil from which an equal quantity was restored.

> The Alabastron (*Plate 168, c*) is a long-necked flagon with a bulbous body. The vessel is made of copper inlaid with mother-of-pearl cloisonné in gold. The neck has a collar set with turquoises and surmounted by a cross set with rubies. It is supposed to be of Persian workmanship, but it is more likely that it was made in Moscow some time in the XVII century, no doubt to replace the cornelian vessel which had been lost. It was not actually present at the coronation ceremony as the chrism was contained in a vessel from the Ecclesiastical Treasury of the Uspenski Cathedral. Its traditions and the fact that it was the original source of the coronation chrism give it a special position.

We must now turn to what is known variously as the Russian Treasury of Diamonds and Precious Stones, the Diamond Fund or the Russian Crown Jewels.

The last occasion on which the Imperial Crown was used was the opening of the Duma by the Tsar in 1906, but the personal jewellery was still used on various occasions at Court. The Court Jewellers were the well-known house of Fabergé. In 1913 Agathon Fabergé, who was a great connoisseur of precious stones, recommended that the whole collection of crown jewels should be overhauled and re-catalogued.[1] The permission of the Tsar was obtained and at the beginning of 1914 he had begun this formidable task in St Petersburg. The setting of every stone was examined, and starting with the less important objects, by the summer he had come to the regalia. Having completed the work on the insignia of the Order of St Andrew, the orb and the sceptre, he was about to begin on the crowns when he received a telephone message from the Chief of the Cameral Department of the Cabinet of the Tsar who directed him immediately to stop the examination and to despatch the crown jewels under guard to Moscow because of the danger of war. War, in fact, broke out a few weeks later. The jewels, in eight or nine boxes, were sent to the Kremlin, where they were stored and remained untouched until after the war. During the Revolution Agathon Fabergé was twice arrested and imprisoned. When he was released, Trotsky sent him a message asking him to go to Moscow to sit on a commission to value the regalia and crown jewels. He excused himself on the ground of his health, but a month later the invitation was repeated and again refused. A third invitation was brought at 3 o'clock in the morning by two Red soldiers bearing a personal letter from Trotsky couched in very friendly terms. This time he accepted, provided he was properly treated, especially in respect of comfortable accommodation. The work lasted from the autumn of 1921 until the spring of 1923 and each item was photographed and whenever possible the weight of each stone was recorded. In 1926 the jewels were publicly displayed and later a catalogue was published in four languages—Russian, English, French and German. It seems it was the intention of the Soviet Government to sell the collection, but this decision was retracted and after a short while the catalogue was withdrawn. Actually a number of items were sold to a syndicate who brought them to England and most of

[1] H. C. Bainbridge: *Peter Carl Fabergé*.

these were offered for sale at Christie's on 16th March 1927. The collection that was sold included some important ornaments, but the intention seems to have been to retain as part of the national heritage those ornaments which were of historical importance or artistic merit.

The collection of diamonds exceeds 25,300 metric carats in weight, including 70 large ones totalling 1,500 m.c. Other first-class stones from 5 to 12 carats weighed about 1,800 m.c. The best stones are of Indian origin, but there are some good Brazilian stones and there are a few from South Africa.

With regard to other precious stones, there are 1,700 m.c. of large sapphires and 2,600 m.c. of smaller ones. The rubies are not numerous, but of high quality, the large stones totalling 60 m.c., the small 200 m.c. The pearls are of great beauty.

Although Peter the Great practised austerity, he did acquire many jewels for his consort, Catherine I, and about 20% of the collection dates from his reign and that of his daughter Elizabeth. Catherine II, whose extravagance in dress and luxury reached standards experienced neither before nor since, added about 40% of the collection. The Empress paid particular attention to Russian sources of precious stones and the collection contained aquamarines, alexandrites, chrysolites and other stones from the Urals and Siberia. About 25% was added by Alexander I and Nicholas I and the remainder by later tsars. Not all ornaments made for the tsars were included in the crown jewels: they were not considered to belong to the State Treasury until they were definitely added to it either by gift or bequest. Some of the ornaments were made for the use of the grand duchesses and only passed into the State Treasury when they died.

The Office of the Treasury had the duty of providing presents on certain anniversaries and the value of these presents was very large. The value of gifts by the Tsar between the end of 1796 and the beginning of 1801 was $3\frac{1}{2}$ million roubles. These mostly went to the imperial family, especially as wedding gifts.

Catherine II reigned at a time of very high standards of artistic work and she was able to obtain the services of highly skilled jewellers such as Posier and Duval. Unfortunately much of the beautiful XVIII-century work was broken up to produce new ornaments in the poorer taste of the XIX century. Some, indeed, were made for transitory use or for some special occasion such as a fancy dress ball and not much importance was attached to artistic taste or careful and skilled workmanship. There was a continual passage of ornaments through the Treasury for remodelling and in the case of rose diamonds for recutting as brilliants. In the reign of Alexander III the House of Fabergé was appointed Goldsmiths and Jewellers to the Court and this led to a return of the higher craftsmanship and artistic merit being applied to the imperial gifts of jewellery, especially the famous Easter Eggs, down to the end of the tsarist regime. In 1906 a number of ancient jewels were sold for a fraction of their present value.

Some of the items that have disappeared in the course of time included some notable pieces. One of these was a diamond of 120 carats known as 'The Moon of the Mountains'. It has sometimes been confused with 'The Orloff', but has quite a different history.[1] Originally it belonged to the Mogul emperors, but passed with the rest of their possessions to Nadir Shah. It is said to have been

1 E. W. Streeter: *The Great Diamonds of the World*, London 1882.

531

one of the two large diamonds which decorated Nadir's throne, the other being 'The Sun of the Sea'. In 1747, shortly after retiring to Persia with his fabulous loot, Nadir was murdered and his treasure plundered by his troops. A short time afterwards an Afghan soldier, so runs the story, who had been in his service, appeared at Basra with 'The Moon of the Mountains', an emerald rare in size and beauty, a splendid ruby, a magnificent sapphire and some lesser gems. These he took to an Armenian jeweller who made a very handsome offer for them. However, as he had to borrow money to effect the payment he told the Afghan to return in a few days. This made the latter suspicious and he disappeared as mysteriously as he had arrived. He then appears to have made his way to Baghdad where he disposed of the treasure to a Jew for a sum equivalent to £500 and two thoroughbred Arab horses. The Armenian also paid a visit to Baghdad and by chance came upon the Afghan. He saw that he was living in a riotous manner, followed him and learned of the way in which he had disposed of the jewels. After fruitless bargaining with the Jew who declined to sell any of them, he resolved to murder him together with the Afghan who alone knew the motive. With his two brothers as confederates, the Armenian invited both the Afghan and the Jew to a party at which the wine flowed to excess, and he found an opportunity of poisoning both their cups. In the night both bodies were placed in sacks and thrown into the Tigris. The three brothers now quarrelled over the distribution of the spoils, so the Armenian disposed of his brothers in the same way and their bodies, too, went to the Tigris. He then prudently departed with his spoil and journeyed to Constantinople and thence through Hungary and Silesia to Holland where he set up as a dealer in jewels.

After a time his repute reached the Courts of Europe. Catherine the Great was much taken by descriptions of the famous diamond and the Armenian was invited to St Petersburg. There he was offered 10,000 roubles and a title in exchange for the stone, but he refused and would agree to no less than 60,000 roubles. The Tsarina then set her astute Councillor, Count Pania, on to the Armenian whom he led into such extravagant ways that he became heavily in debt. One day he was ordered to pay his debts immediately and was informed that he would not be allowed to leave the country until they were paid. Nothing daunted he somehow raised the money, paid his debts and suddenly departed. Ten years later he was discovered at Astrakhan. After protracted negotiations he was persuaded to sell the diamond to the Tsarina for the original offer of 10,000 roubles and it thus passed into the Russian Treasury. Its present whereabouts is unknown.

Until 1783 a famous necklace, known as 'The Azra' was among the Russian crown jewels. It consisted of 110 perfectly matched pearls with a large round black pearl at the junction of the two ends from which, suspended from a diamond cross, was a great black pear-shaped pearl of beautiful form and fine lustre known as 'The Azra' (*Plate 175, b*). Catherine II gave it to her favourite Potemkin in 1783 and he bequeathed it to his niece, Princess Tatania Youssoupoff. Since then it has been handed down in the Youssoupoff family who also had acquired 'La Pelegrina', the 'Incomparable Pearl' (*Plate 175, b*), which was formerly a part of the Spanish crown jewels. The two pearls were displayed together in the Exhibition of Russian Art held in London in 1935.

Other famous items were the wonderful purple amethyst 'gleaming by night like red fire' which Catherine II had obtained from the Urals: a quantity of celebrated Alexandrites and some notable iridescent enamels.

The collection of Russian crown jewels is so important and interesting that it deserves a fairly full description based on the authority of the catalogue made in 1922. It is not possible to differentiate between the actual weight and estimated weights in every case, but the estimates were made by outstanding experts and, thereafter, may be taken to approximate to the actual weight. In the inventory some weights are given

Imperial crown of Russia, front view (p. 533)

a   *Imperial crown of Russia, side view* (p. 533)

b   *Imperial crown of Russia, back view*   c   *Imperial crown of Russia, view from above*

in old carats and some in metric carats. These are differentiated in the descriptions by 'cts' being used for old carats and 'm.c.' being used for metric carats. Unless specific mention is made of the weight of a single stone, the weights given refer to the total where more than one stone is mentioned. For purposes of reference, the numbers given in brackets after the short description of the pieces refer to the numbers in the 1922 inventory.

This magnificent collection of regalia and personal jewellery in the Imperial Russian Treasure can conveniently be divided into groups of similar types of ornaments. These groups include regalia; jewelled head-dresses, necklaces, brooches, other body ornaments, bracelets, ear-rings, head ornaments, dress ornaments and miscellaneous items.

Regalia

The Imperial Russian Crown (No. 1) (*Plates 171* and *172*) ordered for the coronation of Catherine II in 1762, but not completed in time, is one of the most exquisite and richest ever made. It was designed and made under the supervision of Posier. It contains 4,936 diamonds weighing 2,858 carats. The circlet of the crown is composed of a row of large and medium-sized diamonds set between claw-like ornaments with a diamond band above and below. The largest stone is an oblong Indian pear of $12\frac{5}{8}$ cts. There are two with a total weight of $10\frac{15}{16}$ cts; another sixteen stones with an average weight of over 5 carats each. The remainder—595 in number—weigh $423\frac{1}{8}$ cts. They are all beautiful stones of various tints, some pinkish.

From the circlet rises the mitre composed of six palm-like ornaments, four parts of square ornaments and two side bands with oak leaves and acorns. In all, 2,075 diamonds weighing 1,386 cts, the largest stone being $7\frac{1}{4}$ cts, decorate this part of the crown.

The inner borders of the mitre are set with two rows, each of 37 perfectly matched pearls weighing 763 carats. While the circlet would be regarded as a piece of jewellery of high merit by any standards, the mitre-shaped sides give a superb effect because the diamonds, despite their profusion, have been subordinated to the beauty of the design. But the single arch, or diadem as it is described in the inventories, has a magnificence which must make it one of the most splendid pieces of jewellery ever created. It carries a design of oak leaves and acorns, but its glory is a row of large solitaire brilliants. At the bottom in front are 2 large brilliants, one of $55\frac{22}{32}$ cts, eight-sided and stepped, with a slight tint, and the other of $41\frac{5}{16}$ cts. Then there is a four-sided brilliant of $18\frac{3}{8}$ cts; a pink pendant of $21\frac{7}{8}$ cts, and a bevelled four-sided and oblong stone of $17\frac{3}{8}$ cts. There follow other stones up to the centre: a triangular Indian-cut brilliant of pinkish-brown tint of $17\frac{3}{16}$ cts, an oval boat-shaped bluish-white stone of $17\frac{1}{8}$ cts, a long pendant with a light golden tint of $12\frac{3}{4}$ cts, a perfectly white rhomboid of $16\frac{1}{2}$ cts, and a four-sided thick stone of pink water of $12\frac{1}{4}$ cts. There are eight other stones of from $9\frac{1}{2}$ to $12\frac{1}{2}$ cts and 115 others of $240\frac{24}{32}$ cts with 1,600 smaller stones weighing about 163 carats. On the top of the arch is a rosette with 16 brilliants of $38\frac{7}{8}$ cts and 201 others of $20\frac{11}{32}$ cts. From the rosette rises a magnificent spinel (*Plate 178, f*) of 414·30 m.c. (389 old carats) and surmounting this is a brilliant cross.

The crown of the tsarina (No. 82) (*Plate 173, a*) follows the same general style as the Imperial Crown, but is smaller and squatter. The circlet is formed of a row of large solitaire brilliants set between the borders of smaller diamonds. There are 25 solitaires weighing $130\frac{1}{2}$ cts or an average of a little over 5 cts each. Above the centre of the circlet are 3 brilliants of over 6 cts each, from behind which rises an arch; on the summit of this is a circular ornament containing a brilliant of $8\frac{1}{2}$ cts; above this is a diamond cross. In addition 140 brilliants weighing $162\frac{27}{32}$ carats and 2,200 roses are used to adorn the crown. The stones are described as of very good quality, some from India and others from Brazil. The crown was made in 1801 by Duval for the Tsarina Elizabeth, Consort of Paul I. The cost was 37,854 roubles and 12½ copeks.

A similar crown was made in 1896 for the Dowager Tsarina Marie to wear when attending the coronation of her son, Nicholas II. Although it is to be seen near the orb in the display of the Russian Imperial Treasure (*Plate 170, a*) in Plate I of the catalogue of the Imperial Russian Treasure, it is not listed in the catalogue and it is not known what happened to it.

The Imperial Sceptre (No. 3) (*Plate 174, a, b* and *c*) is a beautiful burnished rod divided into three compartments and with eight rings of brilliants, including 15 weighing 14 cts, and various others weighing 30 cts. At the top is the celebrated Orloff Diamond (*Plate 174, d*) surmounting which is a double-headed eagle, crowned, bearing the sceptre and orb and with the Arms of Russia in enamel on its breast. It was designed by C. N. Troitinski for Catherine II *c.* 1784. In the old inventories the weight of the Orloff was given as 185 cts, but when Agathon Fabergé was cataloguing the crown jewels in 1914, the stone fell out and he weighed it and although he did not make a note of the weight at the time and he could not remember it exactly, he thought it to be rather heavier than previously recorded and its official weight today is 194¾ m.c. In appearance the stone is like a large rose, Indian cut, and pure white with a tendency to a slightly bluish-green water. It is a fragment of a large octahedron and has two small visible cracks and a slight network of cracks which gives it a yellow-brown spot.

There have been various versions of the history of the Orloff. The story generally accepted[1] is that it originally formed one of the eyes of a statue of Brahma in the temple in the island of Sheringham in Mysore. A French deserter pretended to be converted to the Hindu religion and by a show of devotion was given access to the statue whose eye he removed at the first favourable opportunity. He sold it for £2,000 to an English sea captain who in turn sold it in London to a Jew for six times that amount. The Jew disposed of it to a Persian merchant called Khojeh who sold it to Prince Orloff in Amsterdam for a sum equivalent to £90,000, an annuity of £4,000 and a patent of nobility. At the time Orloff had fallen into disfavour with his mistress, the Empress Catherine II, and he thought that he might regain her favour by presenting her with the gem, especially as she had previously refused to purchase it on the grounds that the price demanded was too great. Orloff did not, however, benefit by the gift to the extent which he desired which was to become the husband of the Empress, but she gave him a marble palace at St Petersburg.

As has already been mentioned the Imperial Orb (*Plate 174, e*) was made hurriedly in 1762 for the coronation of Catherine II, probably by Posier. It is a great ball of burnished gold resting on a stand. It carries an equator and meridian of good quality Brazilian diamonds set on silver brocade in massive silver. This does not fit the globe properly and was evidently a piece of jewellery already in existence and adapted to the purpose. In all there are 49 diamonds weighing 102 carats, including 5 of about 5 cts each. In the centre where the two bands join is a large diamond of 46.92 m.c. (*Plate 178, e*). This is described in the inventory as a wonderful stone of old India, perhaps from Golconda. The cleavage surface is almost flat while the front is covered with fine Indian cuttings. It is pure white with a barely noticeable bluish water. On the top of the orb is a large Ceylon sapphire of 200 carats set *à jour* in a collar of brilliants. Resting on this is a cross with large and good-quality brilliants, most of which are Brazilian, but some are Indian stones with a yellowish tint and one is bright pink.

According to the catalogue, the clasp of the coronation mantle was made for Tsarina Elizabeth about 1750 (*Plate 176, a*). The brilliants are described as old stones of varied quality and value and

[1] E. W. Streeter: *The Great Diamonds of the World*, p. 103.

a   *Crown of the empress, 1801* (p. 533)

b   *Nuptial crown (sold at Christie's, 1927).*
XIX Century (p. 550)

c   *Head of imperial sceptre*

a   *Imperial sceptre,*
c. *1784* (p. 534)

b   *Handle of imperial sceptre, side view*

d   *Orloff Diamond, side view*

e (right)   *Imperial orb,*
1762 (p. 530)

compared with first-class stones, many are of low value, yellow or with blemishes. The quality of the stones does not, however, detract from the effectiveness of the very beautiful design. The largest stone weighs 6 carats and in addition there are 116 brilliants weighing 281 carats besides various other diamonds with a total weight of 95 carats.

The principal Russian Order of Knighthood is the Order of St Andrew the First Called. It was founded by Peter the Great on St Andrew's Day 1698. Later, admission to the Order carried with it membership of the Order of St Anne founded in 1735 by Charles Frederick, Duke of Holstein-Gottorp in honour of his wife, Anne, daughter of Peter the Great, and of the Order of Alexander Nevski, founded in 1725 by Catherine I, and the Order of the White Eagle, a Polish Order adopted by Russia in 1831.

The insignia of St Andrew was worn with the coronation dress and consisted of a collar composed of three members alternately—the Imperial Eagle bearing on a red medallion a figure of St George slaying the dragon; the badge of the Grand Duchy of Moscow, and the cypher of the Emperor Paul I in gold on a blue ground surmounted by an imperial crown surrounded by a trophy of weapons and green and white flags and a gold star with a blue St Andrew's cross.

Among the crown jewels there are various sets of insignia, the most important being the great diamond chain or collar (No. 4) and cross and star (No. 5) made for Paul I.

The chain (*Plate 177, a*) has twenty links covered with 3,229 brilliants of $1,039\frac{27}{32}$ carats. The cross is decorated with 1 brilliant of 9 carats; 24 of $46\frac{1}{2}$ carats and various small brilliants of 32 carats. The star has 18 brilliants of 50 carats; 325 of 106 carats and 350 roses. In addition there is a spare part of the chain with the monogram of Peter the Great.

The small chain of the Order (No. 6) (*Plate 177, b*) consists of twenty-three links with brilliants of 180 m.c. and 5,000 small roses. A cross (No. 7) (*Plate 177, c (i)*) that goes with it has 7 brilliants of $6\frac{1}{2}$ carats and small stones of 32 carats. Another cross (No. 7, item 8) has brilliants of 13 carats, and another (No. 7, item 10) has brilliants of 65 m.c., including a stone of $5\frac{1}{2}$ m.c. with a pale violet tint.

A star of the Order (No. 7, item 11) (*Plate 177, c (ii)*) has 55 brilliants of 43 m.c. and various other stones of 17 carats. Another star (No. 8) has 269 brilliants of 20 carats. There is one (No. 40) with high old Indian roses and a small brilliant in each of the eagle's eyes and one (No. 41) with the eagle in smoky topaz. Another (No. 171) has 18 brilliants of 50 carats and 325 of 106 carats, besides 350 roses, while a particularly fine cross (No. 172) has one very good and perfectly pure stone of 5·03 m.c.; two pendants of $3\frac{1}{2}$ m.c. besides 127 brilliants of 7 carats and roses of 3 m.c.

A cross for the hat of the Order (No. 174) (*Plate 177, c (iii)*) has thirteen good old stones in a light blue silver setting of which one weighs 6 carats; six of 18 carats; six of 14 carats and 28 small brilliants of 1 carat.

A cross (No. 209) has a perfectly pure and very good bevel stone of 5·03 m.c.; two pendants of about $3\frac{1}{2}$ m.c.; 127 brilliants of 7 carats and roses of 3 carats.

A chain of twenty-three links and a cross (No. 211) covered with brilliants of 90 m.c. on the chain with 122 single facet stones and 6,000 roses, while on the cross is a very good pendant of 432 carats, besides other stones of $48\frac{1}{2}$ carats.

There are four stars and two crosses of the Order of Alexander Nevski:

A star (No. 7, item 7) (*Plate 177, c (iv)*) with blue enamel and brilliants and roses with a total weight of 54 m.c.

A star (No. 7, item 9) with blue enamel and brilliants weighing 33 carats.

A star and cross (No. 39) with 163 brilliants weighing $94\frac{1}{4}$ carats, including a yellow stone of 6 carats, and also a single-facet stone weighing 11 carats.

A star and cross (No. 173) with old brilliants and roses mounted in massive silver.

There is one star of the Order of Anne (No. 7, item 25) set with diamonds weighing $9\frac{1}{2}$ carats and one star of the White Eagle (No. 177) but without diamonds.

The Order of Catherine is represented by an Order (No. 38) in the form of half a wheel surmounted by a cross covered with brilliants weighing $55\frac{1}{2}$ carats, besides 129 single-facet stones and 30 roses, and a star (No. 206) also set with diamonds.

The only foreign Order in the Treasure is a Golden Fleece (No. 189) (*Plate 193, a (i)*) ornamented with brilliants weighing 16 carats.

Jewelled Head-dresses

A (1) A large diadem with pearls (No. 9) (*Plate 180, a*). This beautiful XIX-century tiara is set with 340 brilliants weighing $287\frac{1}{2}$ carats and others weighing 84 carats besides 500 roses. The largest stone is $10\frac{7}{8}$ carats, but has spots. The large pearls weigh $35\frac{3}{4}$, 42, 29, 26, 25, 24, 23, $22\frac{3}{4}$, 22, 19, 17 and 14 carats, respectively, and the remainder numbering 101 weigh $339\frac{1}{2}$ carats.

A (2) A diadem with brilliants (No. 51) (*Plate 180, b*). This magnificent ornament dates from between 1820–30. A row of diamonds are set as pendants so that they swing with the movement of the body of the wearer. The centre pendant is a heart-shaped stone weighing $10\frac{1}{2}$ m.c. Below it is a large rounded stone of 11 m.c. Above, the three centre large white stones weigh 20 m.c. There are 202 other brilliants weighing 171 m.c. and 406 smaller stones weighing 60 carats. They are all very good Brazilian stones.

A (3) A 'Kokoshnik' (No. 72), or Russian national head-dress (*Plate 181, a*), with large brilliants and pearls. The band of gold cloth is bordered by two rows of pearls and is set with 6 large brilliants weighing $7\frac{9}{32}$, $6\frac{5}{32}$, $9\frac{11}{32}$, $6\frac{10}{32}$, $5\frac{25}{32}$ and $14\frac{20}{32}$ carats. They are beautiful pure stones with the exception of the second which has black spots. Between these are set 9 large drop-pearls weighing 150 m.c. There are twenty-nine other medium stones of 18 m.c. besides a number of smaller ones.

A (4) A brilliant diadem (No. 124) in the form of a bandeau like a garland (*Plate 181, b*). This ornament belonged to Elizabeth Petrovna in 1761.

There are 27 brilliants some of which are yellow weighing $34\frac{1}{2}$ carats, and various small stones weighing 62 carats.

A (5) A diadem of brilliants (No. 137) (*Plate 180, c*) with 18 pear-shaped pearls. 529 brilliants weigh 118 m.c. and some small roses 2 m.c. The pearls weigh 250 m.c.

A (6) A diadem of brilliants and emeralds (No. 139) (*Plate 181, b*) belonging to a parure. The brilliants are good South African stones and weigh 225 m.c. The large emerald weighs 23 m.c.; the other 10 emeralds 64 m.c.

A (7) A diadem of brilliants and sapphires (No. 140B) (*Plate 182, a*) belonging to a parure. There are 163 brilliants weighing 197 m.c. and 550 smaller stones weighing 200 m.c. They are good South African stones. The total weight of the 16 large sapphires is 222 m.c.:

1 weighs 33 m.c.;
2 weigh 55 m.c.;
2 weigh 30 m.c.;
2 weigh 45 m.c.;
2 weigh 30 m.c.;
2 weigh 10 m.c.;
5 weigh 16 m.c.

A (8) A diamond diadem with oriental turquoises (No. 154) (*Plate 182, b*) dated from 1895. 176

a *Display of Russian crown jewels* (p. 533)

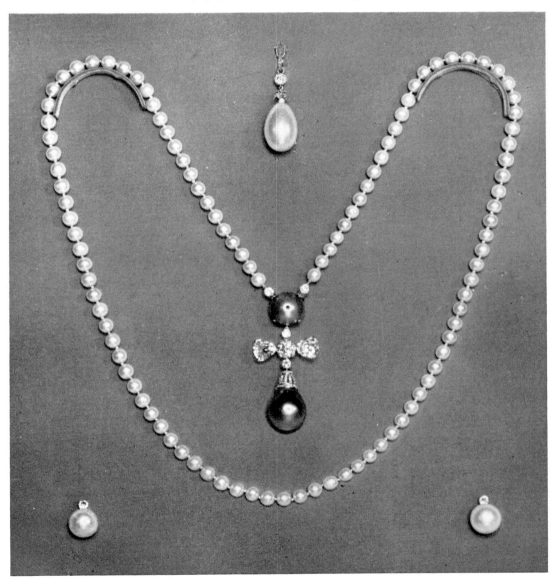

b *'La Pelegrina', the Incomparable Pearl and the Azra Black Pearl* (p. 532)

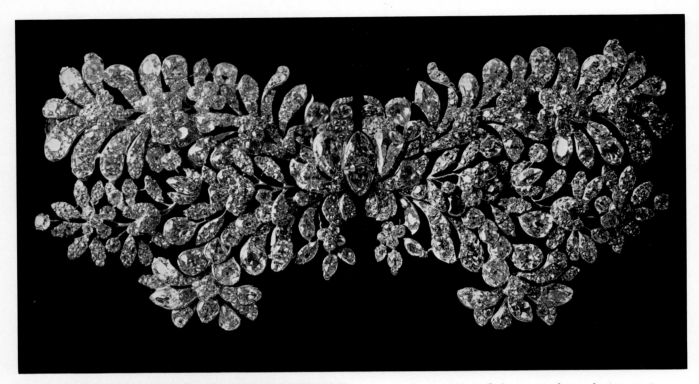

a   *Clasp of the imperial mantle* (p. 534)

b   *Diamond court sword* (S 119) (p. 550)

brilliants weigh $79\frac{28}{32}$ carets; 649 double-facet stones weigh $86\frac{13}{32}$; 348 single-facet stones $26\frac{23}{32}$ carats besides 334 roses. There are 54 turquoises, but their weight has not been recorded in the inventory.

A (9) A diamond diadem with Indian brilliants (No. 159) (*Plate 182, c*). In the centre is a large stone which is described in the inventory as: 'The flat blood-red 10 carat.' It is probably the historically celebrated pink diamond which was among the treasures of Paul I. It is mounted on silver-foil and its actual weight is 13.35 m.c. It is a very pure and beautiful stone with a very delicate pink colour. There are in the diadem 39 beautiful briolettes of old Indian cut, some being slightly yellowish. The largest stone is 9 carats, the remaining 38 weigh 115 carats. In addition there are a number of Brazilian brilliants of which 2 weigh $13\frac{1}{4}$ and 2 weigh $10\frac{11}{16}$ carats; 132 others weigh $226\frac{3}{8}$ carats, besides which there are single-facet stones weighing 8 carats and 1,200 roses.

A (10) A diadem with large sapphires (No. 178) (*Plate 183, a*). The diamonds are Brazilian stones. One is a large flat pendant of 9 carats; 560 others weigh $177\frac{1}{4}$ carats, besides which there are 750 roses. The large sapphire in the centre weighs 70 carats; and there is 1 of 26 carats, 1 of 20 carats and 2 of 9 carats.

A (11) A pearl diadem (No. 194) (*Plate 183, b*). This is a beautiful piece of jewellery of the XIX century. The 12 large drop pearls are set in diamond cups with spiky diamond ornaments in between. At the bottom of each is a medium-sized brilliant. The weights are not recorded in the inventory.

A (12) A diamond diadem with sapphires (No. 204). There are 8 brilliants of 12 m.c.; 28 of 28 m.c.; 320 of 8 m.c.; and 92 roses. There are 9 sapphires weighing 145 m.c., including one of 34·20 m.c.

Necklaces

B (1) A necklace of 26 large pearls weighing 506·5 carats with a brilliant clasp (No. 11) (*Plate 184, a (i)*).

B (2) A pearl necklace of three rows with two diamond clasps (No. 34) (*Plate 185, b*). The first row contains 54 pearls of 199 carats. The second row has 60 pearls of 270 carats, and the third row 68 pearls of $354\frac{3}{4}$ carats. In one clasp there is 1 brilliant of 6 carats and 1 of $5\frac{1}{2}$ carats, as well as 18 other brilliants of $13\frac{1}{32}$ carats, three single-facet stones and 36 roses. The inventory records that in 1898 it was in the possession of Marie Feodorovna.

B (3) A string of large pearls (No. 142) consisting of 38 pearls of 565 m.c.

B (4) A necklace of brilliants, strings of pearls and clasps with emerald and ruby (No. 43) (*Plate 192, b (i)*). Two rows of 76 pearls weigh 210 m.c. and three rows of brilliants containing 210 stones weigh 135 m.c. One clasp is set with a ruby of 18.05 carats surrounded by 8 brilliants of about 15 m.c. and roses of about $1\frac{1}{2}$ m.c. In the other clasp is an emerald of 18.10 m.c. set with 12 brilliants weighing 19 m.c. and roses of about $1\frac{1}{2}$ m.c.

B (5) A necklace with brilliants and pearl pendants (No. 70) (*Plate 184, b*). It consists of 15 pear-shaped brilliant pendants of 11 m.c. and various Brazilian brilliants and roses of 120 carats. There are 15 drop-shaped pearls of 250 m.c. and 29 round pearls of 270 m.c.

B (6) A necklace with pearls and brilliants (No. 71). The brilliants are Brazilian of medium quality and include nineteen large stones of 20 m.c. Nine in the upper setting of about 15 m.c.; sixty on the upper rim of 65 m.c., besides 560 small brilliants of 75 m.c.

B (7) A magnificent diamond rivière of forty-five stones (No. 28) (*Plate 184, c (i)*). The total weight is nearly 294 carats. They are Indian stones in silver bezels with a gold outer rim. It is not mentioned in the inventories before 1922:

No. 1 stone is described as being of a somewhat bluish water and unique. It weighs $19\frac{20}{32}$ carats.

No. 2 stone weighs $18\frac{30}{32}$ carats.
No. 3 stone weighs $17\frac{6}{32}$ carats.
No. 4 stone weighs $10\frac{25}{32}$ carats.
No. 5 stone weighs $12\frac{8}{32}$ carats.
No. 6 stone weighs $12\frac{8}{32}$ carats.

There are two stones of over 9 carats, three of over 8 carats, four of over 7 carats, six of over 6 carats, three of over 5 carats, eleven of 4 carats or more; the remainder all being between 2 and 4 carats.

B (8) A necklace of brilliant solitaires (No. 29); a rivière of 23 large Indian solitaires of a total weight of $165\frac{1}{2}$ m.c. (*Plate 184, c (ii)*). The stones vary in quality, but there are some excellent blue stones from Golconda. Some others include yellow or bluish stones and some are rather flat. In general, however, the stones are beautiful and elegant.

B (9) Diamond fringe necklace (No. 33) (*Plate 185, a*). This striking piece consists of forty-three pear-shaped pendants and includes some excellent Indian pendants and some very good Brazilian stones. The largest pendant is $5\frac{1}{2}$ carats, the remaining forty-two weigh 25 m.c. There are also large stones weighing 65 carats and small stones weighing 80 carats.

B (10) A diamond rivière (No. 44) or necklace (*Plate 186*). Esclavage of 36 large brilliants having a total weight of $475\frac{30}{32}$ m.c.—i.e. an average of over 13 m.c. per stone. The stones are of excellent quality; 21 solitaires form the base of the rivière and the other 15 are set as pendants which swing freely. The inventory states: 'the beauty of the stones and their general impression, perhaps unique in the world, is altogether staggering'. Although there are a few defective stones with black spots, there are others which are unchipped solitaires of bluish or delicate pink water. 'All these shades of colour mingle with a general sparkling gamut, enchanting in appearance and deeply artistic in its general effect.' On the necklace are the following stones:

1 brilliant solitaire, four-sided, good water, $32\frac{15}{32}$ carats;
1 brilliant solitaire, oblong, best water, $23\frac{29}{32}$ carats;
1 brilliant solitaire, oblong, but decomposed and white, $17\frac{8}{32}$ carats;
1 brilliant solitaire, with a large defect in the centre, $19\frac{19}{32}$ carats;
1 brilliant solitaire, a large oblong, but very decomposed, $16\frac{5}{8}$ carats.

The other stones weigh $16\frac{4}{32}$, $13\frac{27}{32}$, $12\frac{14}{32}$, $11\frac{11}{32}$, $10\frac{4}{32}$, $8\frac{24}{32}$, $8\frac{15}{32}$, $7\frac{20}{32}$, $6\frac{9}{32}$ and $16\frac{6}{32}$ carats respectively.

The fifteen pendants described:

1 brilliant very much decomposed, darkish water, $26\frac{19}{32}$ carats;
1 brilliant thoroughly good, regular shape, yellowish, 25 carats;
1 brilliant similar to the last, $20\frac{9}{32}$ carats;
1 brilliant of good water, regular in shape, $17\frac{20}{32}$ carats;
1 brilliant similar to above, $16\frac{6}{32}$ carats;
1 oval, very decomposed, white, $12\frac{15}{32}$ carats;
1 brilliant, $14\frac{24}{32}$;
1 brilliant, pinkish, $14\frac{22}{32}$ carats;
1 brilliant, four-sided, oblong, flat, $4\frac{14}{32}$ carats.

The other six stones weigh $14\frac{13}{32}$, $7\frac{28}{32}$, $7\frac{12}{32}$, $7\frac{5}{32}$, $6\frac{12}{32}$, $6\frac{11}{32}$. There are 15 small brilliants of a total weight of $12\frac{1}{16}$ carats set between the necklace and the pendants.

B (11) Small chain necklace (No. 149). Consists of forty-seven parts with base decorated with 27 brilliants of 13 carats and 322 single-facet stones of 24 carats.

B (12) Diamond rivière (No. 195) of 25 large brilliants weighing about 60 m.c.; 598 small brilliants of 20 m.c. and 24 roses (*Plate 193, c (i)*). Described as a beautiful collection of old stones.

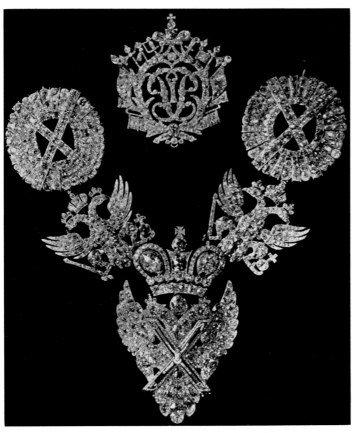

a   *Diamond Cross and Collar of the Order of St Andrew.*
Late XIX Century (p. 535)

b   *Diamond Collar of the Order of St Andrew*
(p. 535)

c   (i) *Cross of the Order of St Andrew;* (ii) *Star of the Order of St Andrew;* (iii) *Hat ornament of
the Order of St Andrew;* (iv) *Star of the Order of Alexander Nevski* (p. 535)

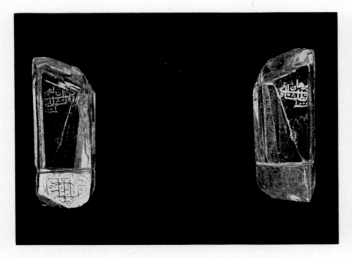

a   *The Shah Diamond of 87·70 carats (p. 549)*

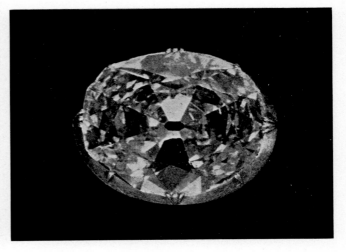

b   *Indian solitaire of $53\frac{12}{32}$ carats (C5) (p. 540)*

c   *Indian solitaire of $40\frac{12}{32}$ carats (S100) (p. 551)*

d   *Brooch with solitaire of $22\frac{16}{32}$ carats (C6) (p. 540)*

e   *Indian diamond of 46·92 carats from the imperial orb (p. 534)*

f   *Cross and spinel of 413·30 carats from the imperial crown (p. 533)*

a   (right) *Brooch of sapphires and brilliants* (C50) ; (left) *brooch clasp with brilliants and various coloured stones* (C46)
(p. 542)   (p. 542)

b   *Necklace of brilliants and sapphires* (B15) (p. 539)

a   *Large diadem with pearls* (A1)
(p. 536)

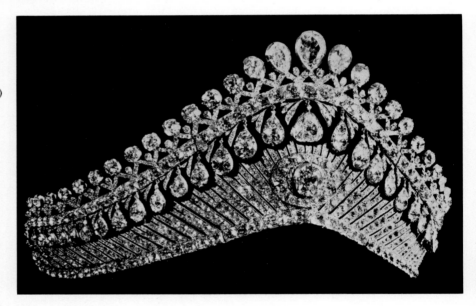

b   *Diadem with brilliants* (A2)
(p. 536)

c   *Diadem with brilliants and 18
pear-shaped pearls* (A5) (p. 536)

B (13) A diamond rivière (No. 205, item 1) composed of 28 good bezels, some with black spots. The brilliants are from India and Brazil and the total weight is $88\frac{2}{33}$ carats, single stones varying from $2\frac{13}{32}$ to $5\frac{26}{32}$ carats.

B (14) A diamond and sapphire necklace (No. 35) (*Plate 187, a*). There are 16 sapphires including a very fine one of 159.25 m.c. and 1 of 15.5 m.c. The remaining 14 weigh 150 m.c. The brilliants number 414 with a total weight of 204 m.c., the largest being 4 m.c. There are also 1,050 roses of 7 m.c.

B (15) A necklace of brilliants and sapphires (No. 138). There are 10 sapphires of 200 m.c. and brilliants weighing 210 m.c. The brilliants are Brazilian stones of medium quality with some South African stones mixed in.

B (16) A necklace of brilliants and sapphires (No. 140A). There are 58 sapphires weighing 260 m.c. and twelve large, good-quality South African stones as pendants weighing 400 m.c. with other brilliants weighing 120 m.c.

B (17) An esclavage necklace (No. 73) of brilliants, pearls and emeralds. The brilliants are Brazilian of medium quality and weigh 225 m.c. There are 39 emeralds with a total weight of $344\frac{1}{2}$ m.c. The largest weighs 32 m.c. 1 weighs 30 m.c. and another 25 m.c.

B (18) A necklace of emeralds and brilliants (No. 139B). There are 15 round emeralds weighing 125 m.c. and 3 square weighing $22\frac{1}{4}$ m.c. The brilliants, which are good South African stones, include fifteen large stones weighing 45 m.c. and 610 small stones of 150 m.c. The necklace forms part of a parure, there being a companion diadem and a plastron.

B (19) A large diamond necklace of rubies and spinels (No. 89) (*Plate 187, b (ii)*). There are 13 rubies varying in weight from just under 1 ct to $7\frac{24}{4}$ cts, and 5 spinels from $12\frac{31}{32}$ to $2\frac{20}{32}$ cts. One stone described as a shorl is $13\frac{15}{32}$ cts, while two small stones are undetermined; 209 brilliants of about 50 cts and 22 roses are in the surrounding setting.

B (20) An esclavage bow with brilliants and a red spinel (No. 90) (*Plate 187, b (i)*). This is described as a wonderful piece of jewellery of 1760, towards the end of the sumptuous Elizabethan period. The spinels number 21 and weigh about 150 m.c. The weight of the brilliants is not given.

B (21) A necklace and aigrette with amethysts (No. 231).

Brooches and Similar Ornaments

C (1) A diamond spray brooch (No. 21) with brilliants and a large pink solitaire of 38.75 m.c. from Old Golconda. It is described as rather old, but a thick, sparkling stone. The petals and leaves are set with old Brazilian stones of a total of 120 m.c. which have been selected with great care.

C (2) A solitaire of pure bluish-grey of Indian origin of 20.5 m.c. set as a brooch (No. 31) (*Plate 184, c (iv)*). The stone is not of the highest quality.

C (3) A brooch (No. 49) in the form of a rose with leaves. On the roses and leaves are 500 brilliants and roses of 80 m.c. Those on the roses are yellow and those on the leaves white. The stalk is set with beautiful delicate yellow rose-diamonds, and on the bud are other yellow stones of a lovely tone.

C (4) A diamond brooch clasp with a pink brilliant in the centre (No. 77) (*Plate 187, c(i)*). The centre stone is of delicate pink water, oval in shape and weighs $17\frac{8}{32}$ carats. It is set on a scroll with small roses surrounded by 12 oval, flat brilliants with a total weight of 24 carats. From the lower side hang 3 large diamonds. In the centre is a flat, pear-shaped stone of Indian cutting and origin weighing $28\frac{8}{32}$ carats. On either side are two flat, pear-shaped stones of similar type weighing $8\frac{1}{32}$ and $8\frac{14}{32}$ carats respectively. It is thought that the largest stone was bought in 1834 from a Hungarian merchant named Bitterman.

C (5) A brooch (No. 85B) (*Plate 178, b*) with an Indian solitaire of $53\frac{12}{32}$ carats. It is described as a white stone of pure water, but with some black spots, but nevertheless a beautiful stone. In the 1898 inventory it was valued at 200,000 roubles.

C (6) A brooch (No. 87) (*Plate 178, d*) with a large ancient Indian solitaire weighing $22\frac{16}{32}$ carats. It is described as an intersting delicate greenish water stone with black speckles, engraved '16 April 1841'.

C (7) A bow brooch of brilliants (No. 128). The stones are old Brazilian of good quality with slightly yellowish tint, some old fashioned in cut.

C (8) A diamond brooch with large emerald brilliants (No. 162) (*Plate 188, a (vi)*). There are eight large and good Brazilian stones weighing $8\frac{1}{2}$ m.c., twenty-four medium stones weighing 6 m.c. and 136 small single-facet stones of a total of $4\frac{1}{2}$ m.c.

C (9) A diamond brooch in the form of a spray (No. 185), of Brazilian stones of medium quality, consisting of two pears weighing 10 m.c., 7 brilliants of 9 m.c., 158 small briolettes of 10 m.c.

C (10) A rose brooch (No. 12) with a large pearl and leaves of brilliants (*Plate 184, a (ii)*). A beautiful piece with the leaves set with 215 small white brilliants of 22 m.c. In the centre is a large pearl of 52·1 m.c.

C (11) A diamond brooch-coulomb (*Plate 188, b (i)*), with 2 large pearls and pink brilliants (No. 96). This is a piece of jewellery of great value and artistic beauty. The upper piece consists of a beautiful round pearl of 38 cts on a scroll setting surrounded by 10 large pure white Brazilian brilliants of $24\frac{15}{16}$ carats. Below this, forming the centre of the ornament, is a round pink Brazilian brilliant of $9\frac{11}{16}$ carats, described as a good and rare stone. From this hangs the lower part of the ornament in the centre of which is a beautiful drop-shaped pearl of 77 carats surrounded by 14 brilliants of good quality and pure water, but with a slightly yellowish tint, weighing 15 carats. There are also 90 roses.

C (12) A diamond brooch with 1 round and 3 pear-shaped pearls (No. 97) (*Plate 188, b (iii)*). In the centre of the frame set with brilliants is a fine, round pearl of 25 m.c. From this frame hang 3 pear-shaped pearls of 64.10 carats. There are 5 large brilliants of $7\frac{1}{2}$ m.c., 32 medium of about 14 m.c., 53 small brilliants of $2\frac{1}{2}$ m.c. and 192 roses of about 1 carat.

C (13) A large brooch set with brilliants and pearl pendants (No. 133) (*Plate 189, a (i)*). There is 1 excellent first-class brilliant from old India, described as of a pleasing triangular shape and remarkable thickness. It weighs 11.35 m.c. The other stones are good, old stones from Brazil and include two pendants of about 4 m.c. and one good, round stone of $3\frac{1}{2}$ m.c. There are 6 brilliants of 7 m.c., and 6 of 3 m.c., and a number of smaller stones weighing 30 m.c., and 6 pearls weighing 85 carats.

C (14) Brooch-aigrette with branches of brilliants and pearl pendants (No. 146) (*Plate 189, b (iv)*). The brilliants, which are good, old Brazilian stones on brocade, weigh about 43 carats. One pearl weighs 8 m.c., and of the others, 2 weigh 15 m.c.

C (15–21) Seven brooches (*Plate 190, b (i)*) with large red stones and brilliants (Nos 14–20):

(15) A brooch with a spinel of 50 carats set with 400 solitaires of 9 carats and 8 brilliants of 9 carats.

(16) A brooch with a spinel of 42 carats set with 12 brilliants of about 20 m.c.

(17) A brooch with a spinel of 32 carats set with 12 brilliants of about 12 m.c.

(18) A brooch with a spinel of 23 carats set with 11 brilliants of 12 carats.

(19) A brooch with a ruby of 13 carats with 11 brilliants of 11 m.c.

(20) A brooch with a spinel of 22 carats set with 11 brilliants of 10 m.c.

(21) A brooch with a spinel of 13 m.c. set with 10 brilliants of 13 m.c.

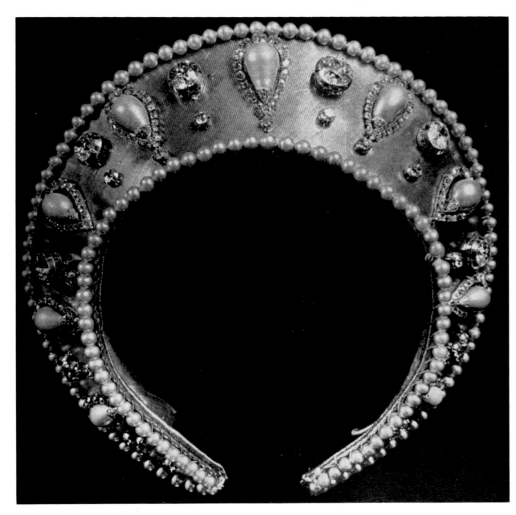

a *Kokoshnik with large
   brilliants and pearls*
   (A3) (p. 536)

b *Diadem with brilliants*
   (A4) (p. 536)

a   *Diadem of brilliants and large sapphires* (A7)
(p. 536)

b   *Diadem of brilliants and Eastern turquoises*
(A8) (p. 536)

c   *Diadem of Indian brilliants* (A9)
(p. 537)

C (22) A diamond brooch with a large balas ruby and portrait (No. 100) (*Plate 192, a (i)*). The balas ruby of 11.56 m.c. is surrounded by 9 good Brazilian brilliants of 17 carats, below which are 4 pearls of 7 m.c. suspended and attached to a diamond ribbon from which hangs a portrait of Alexander II set in diamonds of about 8 carats. Below is another ribbon with a brilliant of 2 m.c. and a pear-shaped pearl of 5 m.c.

C (22a) Order with portrait of Peter I (No. 101) (*Plate 192, a (ii)*). The portrait itself is surrounded by 12 brilliants of good water of a total weight of 31 cts. On the upper side, on a lug to take a ribbon, there is a large square yellow brilliant of about 12 cts surrounded by roses.

C (23 and 24) Two brooch clasps of brilliants and spinels (No. 129). There are 14 spinels, 7 in each, of a total weight of 20 m.c. These are set with 228 Brazilian brilliants weighing $29\frac{10}{32}$ carats.

C (25) A diamond brooch with a large ruby (No. 164) (*Plate 188, a (iv)*). This is a magnificent brooch with a ruby of $39\frac{19}{32}$ carats surrounded by some Indian solitaires of the following weights:

(1) $6\frac{16}{32}$ cts.   (2) $7\frac{16}{32}$ cts.   (3) 8 cts.   (4) $6\frac{21}{32}$ cts.   (5) $5\frac{18}{32}$ cts.   (6) 6 cts.   (7) $10\frac{16}{32}$ cts.

C (26) A diamond brooch with brilliants and a large square sapphire (No. 58) (*Plate 190, a (v)*). The sapphire weighs 197 m.c. and is set with 25 large Brazilian brilliants of 50 m.c. and small stones of 4 m.c.

C (27) A brooch clasp with brilliants and a Ceylon sapphire (No. 59) (*Plate 190, a (iv)*). The sapphire weighs 65.18 carats and is set with 20 large brilliants of 20 m.c. and 6 small brilliants and roses of $1\frac{1}{2}$ carats.

C (28) Brooch with brilliants and a large *cabochon* sapphire (No. 61) (*Plate 190, a (vi)*). The sapphire weighs 161 carats and there are 20 good, old Brazilian brilliants of 35 m.c., besides a number of small brilliants and roses of 3 m.c.

C (29) Brooch clasp with brilliants and a large sapphire (No. 134) (*Plate 189, a (iii)*). The sapphire weighs 260 m.c., and there are 18 good Brazilian brilliants of 60 m.c., besides a number of small brilliants and roses.

C (30) Diamond brooch with Ceylon sapphire (No. 161A) (*Plate 188, a (i)*). The sapphire weighs 249.35 m.c. and is set with 26 brilliants of 20 m.c. around it.

C (31) Diamond brooch with Ceylon sapphire (No. 161B) (*Plate 188, a (ii)*). The sapphire is 142 m.c. and is set around with 24 brilliants of 16 m.c.

C (32) Brooch clasp with large sapphire (No. 236). The weight of the sapphire is not recorded: the clasp is set with 20 yellow brilliants of 15 m.c., probably South African stones.

C (33) Diamond brooch clasp with large Indian sapphire (No. 237). The sapphire weighs 33 m.c. and is set with 12 brilliants which are old, white Brazilian stones of medium value of total weight of 12 m.c. There are also many roses.

C (34 and 35). Two large brooches with sapphire and yellow brilliants (No. 238). The weight of the sapphire is not recorded. There are yellow brilliants of 10 m.c. besides roses of $3\frac{1}{2}$ carats.

C (36) Brooch bow with large sapphire (No. 240). The sapphire weighs 75 m.c. and in the bow there are 19 large brilliants of 60 m.c. and 264 small brilliants of 50 m.c. In the medallion are 12 large brilliants of 22 m.c. and a number of small stones of 5 m.c.

C (37) Diamond brooch with brilliants and large, square emerald (No. 56) (*Plate 190, a (i)*). The emerald weighs 136·25 m.c. There are 6 large white Brazilian solitaires of about 25 m.c., 150 small brilliants of 10 carats and 150 small roses.

C (38) A square brooch with brilliants and a square emerald (No. 57) (*Plate 190, a (iii)*). The emerald weighs 41·5 m.c. and is set with 4 large, good Brazilian brilliants weighing respectively 3·95, 4·25, 4·50 and 4·68 m.c. There are also 12 large brilliants of medium quality of 10 m.c.

C (39) Brooch clasp with brilliants and a large *cabochon* emerald (No. 60) (*Plate 190, a (ii)*).

The emerald weighs 42·35 m.c. and is set with 16 large, good Brazilian brilliants of 32 m.c. besides roses of a total weight of 1 m.c.

C (40) Brooch with large *cabochon* emerald (No. 135) (*Plate 189, a (ii)*). The emerald weighs 153·75 m.c. and is set with 20 very good, old Brazilian brilliants of 35 m.c.

C (41) Brooch coulomb with large emerald (No. 136) (*Plate 189, a (iii)*). The large emerald is drop-shaped and weighs 110 m.c. A second emerald is square and weighs 6 m.c. There are 18 good, large Brazilian brilliants of 10 m.c. and 26 small brilliants and 18 roses of 1½ carats.

C (42) Brooch *sévigné* with emeralds (No. 165) (*Plate 191, a (i)*). There are 3 emeralds weighing 140, 174·10 and 21.90 m.c. respectively. The brilliants are Brazilian of yellow tint and varying quality and were taken from other pieces of jewellery; 15 weigh about 32 m.c.; 3 solitaires of about 5½ m.c.; 48 brilliants 38 m.c. and 24 brilliants 4 m.c.

C (43) Brooch with large emerald (No. 163) (*Plate 188, a (v)*), having an Arabic inscription, with 24 Brazilian brilliants of about 24 carats. On the gold setting is engraved ' $\frac{540}{\text{CXXXIV}}$ '.

C (44) Brooch with hexagonal emerald (No. 168) (*Plate 191, a (iv)*). The emerald weighs 40 carats and is surrounded by 26 Brazilian brilliants of 50 carats.

C (45) Gold brooch with square emerald (No. 235). The emerald weighs 4½ m.c. and is set with 2 pear-shaped Brazilian brilliants, each weighing 6·35 m.c.

C (46) Brooch clasp with brilliants, emeralds, sapphires and other stones (No. 141). A balas ruby weighs 65 m.c., an emerald 40 m.c., a sapphire 17 m.c., 2 topazes 50 m.c., and they are set with 1 brilliant of bluish water of 5 m.c., 1 of medium quality and 4½ m.c., 4 of 9 m.c. and 202 of 62 m.c.

C (47) Brooch clasp with topaz and brilliants (No. 13) (*Plate 190, b (ii)*). The topaz weighs 45 m.c. and is in a setting of 16 large brilliants weighing 27 m.c., 4 of ¾ m.c. and 333 good, old roses.

C (48) Brooch with yellow-green beryl (No. 64) (*Plate 191, b (i)*). The weight of the beryl is not given, but there are 8 large brilliants, 4 pear-shaped and 4 square-shaped, of a total weight of 10 m.c., besides 200 roses and small brilliants.

C (49) Diamond brooch with Eastern turquoises (No. 153) (*Plate 185, c*). There are 7 turquoises, the weight is not recorded, but they are set with 180 brilliants having a total weight of about 83 carats.

C (50) Gold brooch (No. 239) in the shape of a crown with a miniature. It is set with a regular rhomboid of good water of 3½ m.c., one portrait stone of 4 m.c., 3 brilliants of 3½ m.c. and 116 small brilliants of 5 m.c.

C (51) Brooch belonging to a parure of brilliants and sapphires (No. 140C). There are 7 sapphires weighing 150 m.c. The brilliants are good South African stones, 5 pear-shaped weigh 28 m.c., and the remaining 77 weigh 78 m.c.

C (52) Large bouquet with emerald leaves and flowers of brilliants (No. 27) (*Plate 194, b*). The emeralds forming the leaves weigh 50 m.c. The brilliants are excellent stones, mostly very thick, mounted upon coloured foil or on brocade. A special characteristic is that they are pinkish shade and are pear-shaped, blunt angled and very flat stones. The outstanding stone is a large flat brilliant pendant of 15⅛ carats of a delicate violet shade, the only stone of the bouquet set *à jour*, which has a large 'feather' flaw in the middle and a small crack, but is nevertheless considered to be a very valuable stone of Old Golconda. There is a second large and beautiful stone of 10 carats of a somewhat steely tint. Another good stone is of irregular shape with a slight tint weighing 4½ carats; 6 yellow brilliants weigh about 15 carats and a single yellow stone is 1¾ carats; 34 other brilliants weigh 26 carats and there are a number of double-faceted stones of 17 carats and single-facet stones weighing 50 carats. The bouquet is mentioned in the 1760 inventory.

a   *Diadem with large sapphires* (A10) (p. 537)

b   *Diadem of brilliants and pearls* (A11) (p. 537)

a (above, left)   (i) *Necklace of 26 large pearls* (B1) (p. 537)
                 (ii) *Rose brooch with a large pearl of 52·1
                      carats* (C10) (p. 540)

b (above, right)   *Necklace with brilliants and pearl
                   pendants* (B5) (p. 537)

c (left)   (i) *Diamond rivière of 45 stones* (B7) (p. 537)
          (ii) *Necklace of brilliant solitaires* (B8) (p. 538)
         (iii) *2 solitaires of 20½ and 19·55 carats as ear-
               rings* (E4) (p. 546)
          (iv) *Solitaire of 20·5 carats set as a brooch* (C2)
               (p. 539)

C (53) Aigrette bouquet holder of sapphire and brilliants (No. 62) (*Plate 195, a*). One sapphire weighs 65 carats, 1 weighs 30 carats, 4 weigh 18 carats and 75 weigh 5 m.c.; 37 brilliants weigh 24 carats and double- and single-facet stones weigh 47 carats. The work is probably of the time of Paul I (1800).

C (54) Medallion with brilliants and aquamarine (No. 63) (*Plate 191, b (vi)*). A large aquamarine weighs 231·65 m.c.; 7 large good-quality Brazilian brilliants weigh 10 carats and other diamonds 16 carats. Probably of the time of Alexander I.

C (55) Rose-coloured tourmaline as fruit (No. 65) (*Plate 191, b (iii)*). The tourmaline is cut to represent fruit and weighs 266 m.c.

C (56) Two large spinels in bezels (No. 66) (*Plate 191, b (ii)*). The settings are plain without diamonds; the spinels weigh 100 m.c. and 56 m.c. respectively.

C (57) Medallion with large chrysolite (No. 67) (*Plate 191, b (iv)*). The chrysolite weighs 192·75 m.c. and is set with 30 brilliants of 24 carats.

C (58) Medallion with large alamandine (No. 68) (*Plate 191, b (v)*). The alamandine is set with 35 Brazilian brilliants, but no weight is recorded of any of the stones.

C (59) Spray of flowers with bright sapphires (No. 53). There are 180 sapphires of 110 carats set with a large number of small brilliants of 130 carats.

C (60) Aigrette like a fountain with brilliants and large sapphires (No. 54). There are 11 sapphires of which one weighs 50 m.c., one 30 m.c., one 15·45 m.c. and one 8 m.c. There are 4 brilliants weighing $1\frac{1}{2}$ carats and single-facet stones weighing 17 carats.

C (61) Pin with a pink brilliant (No. 74) (*Plate 187, c (i)*). The pink brilliant weighs $3\frac{5}{16}$ carats.

C (62) Pin with blue brilliant (No. 75) (*Plate 187, c (ii)*). The blue brilliant weighs 7 carats.

C (63) Pin with diamond briolette (No. 76) (*Plate 187, c (iv)*). This is an excellent Indian stone of pale brownish golden water weighing $11\frac{15}{16}$ carats. On one side it is cut as an Indian briolette. On the other as a brilliant. The other stone is set as a small coronet with 11 brilliants.

C (64) Diamond medallion with portrait of Nicholas I (No. 99) (*Plate 192, a (iii)*). The brilliants are good white Brazilian stones, except 1 large, flat oval brilliant of yellow water with a weight of about 7 m.c., and the other 12 weigh 50 carats, and 30 small stones $1\frac{1}{3}$ m.c. There is also a good portrait stone of about 6 m.c.

C (65) Amethyst ornament (No. 104) (*Plate 193, b (ii)*). The amethyst weighs $4\frac{3}{4}$ carats and is set with 1,245 brilliants with a total weight of 72 carats.

C (66) Diamond aigrette with pearl pendants (No. 145) (*Plate 189, b (i)*). 1 pearl weighs $9\frac{7}{8}$ carats and 3 weigh 21 carats. The brilliants are good Brazilian stones and are on brocade. Two pendants weigh 7 carats and 68 other brilliants weigh 24 carats.

C (67) Pin in Louis XV style with pearls and brilliants (No. 147). A small pin which in the inventory is described as being like a dagger; 1 pearl weighs 11 carats and 1 weighs 3 carats. There are 16 Brazilian brilliants of poor quality weighing $3\frac{1}{2}$ carats.

C (68) Diamond bow ornament (No. 115). The brilliants are described as good Brazilian stones, mostly single-facet on brocade. Twenty-four stones weigh 21 carats and a number of smaller ones weigh 28 carats.

C (69) Bow of brilliants with rays (No. 119) (*Plate 193, b (iii)*). There are 12 brilliants of 8 carats, a large table-cut diamond of Indian cut on top and a number of single-facet stones of 18 carats.

C (70) Bouquet of brilliants (No. 122). One yellow pendant weighs $3\frac{1}{2}$ carats. One pinkish brilliant 2 carats. One four-sided yellow stone $2\frac{1}{2}$ carats and 37 others weigh 90 carats and double- and single-facet stones 28 carats.

C (71) Bow of brilliants with pearls (No. 127). The 156 brilliants weigh 16 carats.

C (72) Ornament like a bow of gold with rubies and small brilliants (No. 130). 2 rubies weigh $3\frac{1}{2}$ m.c., 8 weigh 7 m.c. and 16 weigh $1\frac{1}{2}$ m.c.; 26 brilliants weigh 7 carats and other small stones 21 carats.

C (73) Diamond clasp in the style of Louis XV (No. 150). There are 8 brilliants of 4 carats; a number of single stones of $5\frac{1}{2}$ carats, and 44 pearls of 7 carats.

C (74) Bouquet of narcissi (No. 156). This ornament contains 3 yellow brilliants of $4\frac{1}{2}$ carats and other brilliants of a total weight of 50 carats.

C (75) Bouquet of enamel leaves and sapphires and rubies (No. 157). There are 309 brilliants of good quality weighing 14 carats and 249 rubies weighing 21 carats.

C (76) Gold cross with 4 large brilliants and spinel (No. 160) (*Plate 188, a (iii)*). The 4 brilliants, which are very good old Indian stones, weigh $9\frac{1}{32}$ carats; $10\frac{9}{32}$ carats; $13\frac{12}{32}$ carats and $11\frac{23}{32}$ carats respectively. There is a spinel of 7 m.c. surrounded by 8 brilliants of $9\frac{1}{2}$ carats.

C (77) Pendant with large emerald (No. 169) (*Plate 191, a (v)*). The weight of the emerald is estimated to be between 240 and 250 m.c. It is set in gold with a border of 54 brilliants.

C (78) An ornamental set with chrysolite (No. 176). This consists of a bow with a large chrysolite in the centre; a pair of ear-rings each with three chrysolite pendants; three brooches, one large with 5 pendant chrysolites, the other two similar, but smaller with 2 and 3 chrysolites respectively. They are set with Brazilian brilliants with silver on brocade, but the weights of the stones are not given in the inventory.

C (79) Four antique pins with emeralds and diamonds of the time of Peter I (No. 179). The weight of the emeralds is not given. There are 64 diamonds of 7 carats.

C (80) Small bouquet of brilliants on coloured foil (No. 184). 9 yellow brilliants weigh $9\frac{1}{2}$ carats and other small stones weigh $16\frac{1}{2}$ carats.

C (81) Aigrette spray with three flowers (No. 186). 25 good-quality Brazilian brilliants on brocade weigh $21\frac{3}{4}$ carats; a number of small stones of 6 carats of poor quality and yellowish.

C (82) Diamond ornament (No. 191) (*Plate 193, a (v)*). This is an elegant ornament composed of brilliants and a large solitaire in the centre.

C (83) Small aigrette with pearl (No. 232). The pearl weighs $14\frac{1}{2}$ carats and there are 7 brilliants of white water on foil weighing 4 carats and four single-facet stones of 3 carats.

C (84) Large aigrette with pearl pendants (No. 233). 7 brilliants weigh $4\frac{3}{8}$ carats.

C (85) Aigrette with 2 large emeralds (No. 234). The emeralds weigh 20 and 12 carats respectively. The brilliants, which are of high quality, weigh 21 m.c.

C (86) Medallion with a flat rose diamond (No. 246). The rose is very flat and weighs $3\frac{1}{2}$ carats. It is a very beautiful and pure stone set with large triangular brilliants of 2 carats and 200 roses.

C (87) Medallion with flat Brazilian aquamarine (No. 247). There are 18 brilliants of 10 m.c. and 12 small ones. The weight of the aquamarine is not recorded.

C (88) Oval medallion with emerald cameo (No. 248) (*Plate 191, a (vi)*). There are 20 good brilliants of $6\frac{1}{2}$ m.c. and roses of about 1 m.c.

C (89) Pendant with large solitaire (No. 250). A beautiful and simple pendant with a medium-sized brilliant on top and a large solitaire trapezoidal in shape which is described as a wonderful Indian stone of clear water weighing $12\frac{3}{32}$ carats.

C (90) Diamond pendant with sapphires (No. 253). There are five pendants. The first two are *en pair* and contain a large sapphire of 40 carats, brilliants of 4 m.c. and roses of $1\frac{1}{2}$ m.c.

No. 4 contains a sapphire of 45 m.c., yellow brilliants of 8 m.c. and roses of 2 m.c.

No. 5 contains a sapphire of 50 m.c., brilliants of 10 m.c. and roses of about 2 m.c.

C (91) Six pendants of black flint agate (No. 256).

C (92) Pin with a double rose (No. 259). A peculiar pin with a slender, somewhat cracked rose of $1\frac{1}{4}$ carats in a silver setting. On the flat side is a doubled rock crystal cut like a rose.

C (93) Pin with 2 Scottish pearls (No. 260). The pearls weigh 9 and 8 carats respectively.

C (94) A pin as a water nymph and large baroque pearl (No. 261).

C (95) Five pins with pierced sapphires of a total weight of 80 carats (No. 262).

C (96) Two pins with Russian diamonds (No. 264). 1 diamond is $\frac{3}{16}$ m.c. and the other one $\frac{1}{4}$ m.c. These were the first diamonds to be found in Russia in the Groblagodatski region of the Urals.

C (97) A pin like a star with roses (No. 265). The star has 8 triangular antique cut roses of $1\frac{1}{4}$ carats.

C (98) Three pins with enamelled leaves (No. 266). The brilliants weigh $\frac{10}{32}$, $\frac{3}{16}$ and $\frac{1}{16}$ carats and are of yellow-blue and white tints respectively.

C (99) Three pins with sapphires weighing 4 carats and brilliants of 10 m.c. (No. 269).

C (100) Seven bezels with spinels (No. 273) weighing 6, 14, 10, $12\frac{3}{4}$, 4, $9\frac{1}{4}$ carats respectively.

C (101) Old emeralds with total weight of about 300 m.c. in gold bezels (No. 274).

C (102) Two pins with emeralds (No. 277). There are 4 brilliants of 3 carats and five single-facet stones of $1\frac{1}{2}$ carats.

C (103) Pins with 6 emeralds of 100 carats (No. 278).

C (104) Three pins with a pearl like a star (No. 279). 1 pearl weighs 20 carats and is set with a brilliant of $\frac{3}{4}$ carat, and 12 small brilliants of 1 carat. In the second pin the pearl weighs 16 carats and 5 brilliants 2 carats, and in the third pin the pearl weighs 10 to 12 carats and there are 4 brilliants of $\frac{1}{2}$ carat.

C (105) Three pins with emeralds (No. 282). In two pins there are no diamonds and the emeralds weigh 25 and 22 carats respectively. The third pin has an emerald of $5\frac{1}{2}$ carats and 15 brilliants of $1\frac{1}{2}$ carats.

C (106) Two silver pins with rubies and spinels (No. 284).

Bracelets

D (1) A gold bracelet with an immense flat diamond (No. 42) (*Plate 192, b (iii)*). A gold bracelet with coloured enamel and clasp in Gothic style with a large flat surface like a mirror. The latter is covered by an irregular triangular rather thick table stone—a portrait diamond of rare purity and exceptional beauty and size. The stone weighs about 25 m.c. A scientific specification of this stone has been made in Dr Fersman's *Historic Stones of the Diamond Fund* in the Bulletin of the Russian Academy of Science, 1925.

D (2) A bracelet with four rows of bezels with brilliants (No. 52) (*Plate 195, c*). In the clasp are three somewhat muddy stones having a total weight of $15\frac{1}{4}$ m.c. and 26 brilliants of 10 m.c. On the bracelet are 54 brilliants of 87 carats and 14 of 28 carats.

D (3) A bracelet of large pearls with clasp, ornamented with brilliants and a sapphire (No. 98) (*Plate 188, b (ii)*). The sapphire weighs 23.9 m.c. and set round it are 10 large brilliants of a total weight of about 18 carats. Each are pure white Brazilian stones. At either end of the pearls are 3 small brilliants. There are 54 pearls of 175 m.c.

D (4) A bracelet of large brilliants with a portrait of Nicholas I Alexandrovitch (No. 102) (*Plate 192, a (iv)*). In the clasp is a portrait of Nicholas, brother of Alexander III, on a good portrait brilliant surrounded by 12 large brilliants of 80 m.c. All are first-class Brazilian stones. This fine piece of jewellery was made in the second half of the XIX century.

D (5) A bracelet belonging to the parure of brilliants and sapphires (No. 140). There are 11 sapphires weighing 43 m.c., 10 brilliants of 23 m.c., 1 of $\frac{3}{4}$ m.c. and 152 of 12 m.c. They are all good South African stones.

D (6) A pair of bracelets with pearls and lamels of stags' hoof (No. 228).

D (7) A pair of bracelets with various coloured stones (No. 229). In the first there are 6 brilliants of 9 carats, 23 of 2 carats and 350 roses. In the second, 8 brilliants of 6 carats and 375 roses.

D (8) A pair of gold bracelets (No. 230). One is inscribed 'd. 18 April 1818' and on the other 'D.U. 3 Sept. 1840 Jusqu'au 16 April 1841'.

Ear-rings

E (1) A pair of ear-rings of brilliants (No. 23). 2 brilliants weigh 22 carats, 2 of 12, 2 of 7 carats, and 4 of 14 carats, besides which there are small brilliants and roses.

E (2) A pair of diamond ear-rings with pearls (No. 24). There are 3 drop-shaped pearls on each ear-ring and the 6 weigh 40 m.c. They are set with small brilliants of a total weight of 3 m.c.

E (3) A pair of diamond ear-rings with pearl pendants (No. 25). There are 2 drop-shaped pearls on each ear-ring, the 4 weighing 13 m.c. They are set with 2 brilliants of 2 m.c., and 6 of 2 m.c., besides small stones weighing 4 m.c.

E (4) Two solitaires as ear-rings (Nos. 30 and 32) (*Plate 184, c (iv)*). The first is a solitaire of old Indian origin of pink water and ideal purity—an excellent rare stone of $20\frac{1}{2}$ m.c. The second is an old Indian stone not of high quality weighing 19·55 m.c.

E (5) A pair of ear-rings in the form of a cascade with brilliants and sapphires (No. 55). There are 8 sapphires of 60 m.c. and 14 of 17 m.c. in a solid silver setting encased in gold. The work is of Elizabethan period about 1740.

E (6) A pair of ear-rings—pendants—with spinels (No. 91) (*Plate 187, b (iii)*). There are 18 spinels weighing 29 carats set with 10 brilliants of 8 carats, 28 of 17 carats, 40 of 16 carats and 146 of 10 carats.

E (7) A pair of gold ear-rings with aquamarines (No. 112). There are 126 single-facet Brazilian brilliants of 11 carats. The weight of the 4 aquamarines is not given. Made about 1780.

E (8) A pair of gold ear-rings with aquamarines (No. 173). 118 brilliants weigh $21\frac{1}{4}$ carats with 130 single-facet stones of 14 carats and 60 roses. The weight of the 4 aquamarines is not recorded. Made about 1770 to 1780.

E (9) A pair of silver ear-rings with aquamarines (No. 114). The brilliants number 144 and weigh about 13 carats. The weight of the 4 aquamarines is not recorded. Made about 1775 to 1785.

E (10) A pair of ear-ring pendants with brilliants (No. 116). There are 6 pendant brilliants of original antique cut and beautiful water weighing about 18 carats. Also 2 oblong and good brilliants of 9 carats, 2 brilliants of 3, and 4 of 3 carats. Small stones weigh 32 carats.

E (11) A pair of ear-rings with brilliants on coloured foil (No. 123). These were made about 1750–70 and are in the form of 2 roses with sapphires and a bee. There are 2 large oval brilliants and 4 pear shaped on coloured foil weighing 20 carats. 8 other brilliants weighing $7\frac{1}{4}$ carats and other stones of 18 carats.

E (12) A pair of diamond ear-rings with pendants and rubies (No. 131). There are 8 rubies weighing 30 carats. The brilliants are Brazilian with a slight tint. 8 weigh $6\frac{1}{2}$ carats and 124 weigh 12 carats.

E (13) A pair of ear-rings with large pendant pearls (No. 143) (*Plate 189, b (ii)*). The pearls weigh 24·81 and 23·4 m.c. respectively. Above them are 2 large Brazilian brilliants of white water of 9·35 m.c. and small Brazilian stones of about 1 carat, together with a number of small roses.

E (14) An ear-ring with very rare Indian briolette (No. 144) (*Plate 189, b (iii)*). The pendant is made as an ear-ring of a superb large white briolette of $40\frac{1}{2}$ carats of Indian cutting in a delicate gallery which holds it. The stone is old Indian with small feather flaws and a large deep cut at the back which suggests that the briolette was formerly set in some other manner and that this cut was made separately for that purpose. The other two briolettes are 2 small brilliants and above each are flat and blind brilliants of 5 carats.

a   *Diamond fringe necklace* (B9) (p. 538)

b   *Pearl necklace of three rows* (B2) (p. 537)

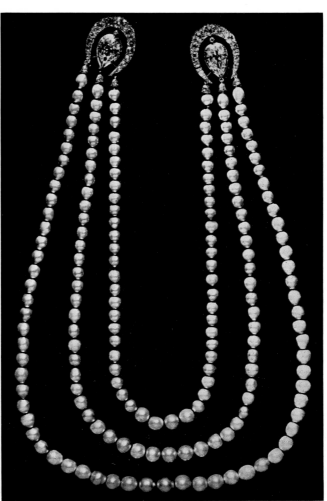

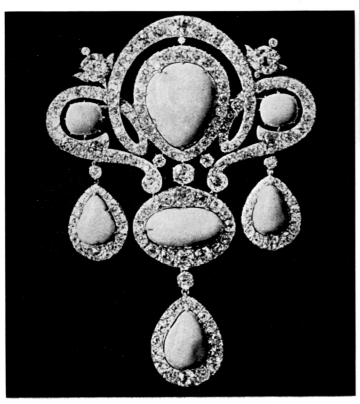

c   *Diamond brooch with oriental turquoises* (C49)
(p. 542)

Diamond rivière of 36 large brilliants, the largest weighing $32\frac{15}{32}$ *carats* (B10) (p. 538)

E (15) A pair of ear-rings with emerald pendants (No. 166). These ear-rings were made in 1840 and contain 1 emerald of 15 carats, 1 of 20 carats and 2 of 6 carats. They are set with 60 brilliants of $9\frac{1}{2}$ carats.

E (16) A pair of ear-rings with turquoises (No. 249).

E (17) A pair of ear-rings with brilliants and roses (No. 251). There are 2 large old Brazilian brilliants of 15·5 m.c.; 2 of $2\frac{1}{4}$ carats, 8 of $1\frac{1}{2}$ carats and roses of about 3 m.c.

E (18) A pair of ear-rings with brilliants and blue glass (No. 254). Each ear-ring has 1 brilliant of about 2 carats in the centre.

E (19) A pair of ear-rings with splendid high roses (No. 255). They are described as good-shaped, pointed facets of pure water weighing $6\frac{1}{2}$ carats.

E (20 to 24) Five pairs of ear-rings with rose-coloured garnets (No. 257). There are 88 garnets of 16 carats and 143 single-facet brilliants of 10 carats.

Head Ornaments

F (1) A pair of diamond hatpins (No. 22). On the top are single stones weighing $2\frac{1}{4}$ and $2\frac{3}{4}$ m.c. In the uppermost row of each are 6 small brilliants and 24 roses. In the lower row of each are 3 large brilliants totalling $3\frac{1}{2}$ carats in each pin. On each of the lower wheels are 20 roses and on each of the spirals are 54 stones weighing 26 and 29 m.c. respectively.

F (2) A hairpin of brilliants in the form of a Horn of Plenty (No. 46). The stones are Brazilian of good quality and include two in the first class in the shape of inserted pendants of the most beautiful bluish water. The 2 brilliants weigh 7 carats. Another stone weighs $1\frac{1}{2}$ carats and twelve others 10 carats. There are also a number of double- and single-facet stones weighing 23 carats.

F (3) Two hairpins as baskets of flowers (No. 47). Each has 4 brilliants of 4 m.c. and various stones of 16 m.c. between them.

F (4) A haft for Sultan's plume with emeralds (No. 50). This ornament in modern times is described as a hatpin or garland and is decorated with 30 emeralds set *à jour* weighing 10 carats and 22 brilliants besides a number of small stones. One brilliant pendant weighs $2\frac{3}{4}$ carats and the remaining twenty-one weigh 16 carats. Two small stones weigh $2\frac{1}{4}$ carats.

F (5) Three diamond hatpins as bows (No. 108). These are excellent pieces of the Catherine period. The stones are from Brazil and are of good quality mounted on brocade. The two bows have 2 brilliants of $5\frac{1}{2}$ carats and 20 of 7 carats, besides a number of small stones of 24 carats. The fasteners are of silver. The bows screw into the pins, but may be used as buckles. On the pins is one blunt-headed old stone, white, of $3\frac{3}{4}$ carats and forty-six stars of 21 carats, with some small stones of 20 carats.

F (6) A Sultan's plume with feathers and pearls (No. 121).

F (7) Hairpin in the form of a laurel branch with emeralds (No. 175). The weight of the emeralds is 10 carats and small brilliants 1 carat.

F (8) Hairpin as a flower with brilliants and pearl pendant (No. 183). The pearl weighs 12·60 m.c. One brilliant pendant $2\frac{1}{2}$ m.c. and thirteen small pendants weigh 7 m.c.

F (9) Three silver hairpins with brilliants (No. 187). There is 1 brilliant of $\frac{7}{8}$ carats and 29 of 3 carats.

F (10) Two pearl headpins (No. 193).

F (11) Hatpin with large emerald (No. 258). The emerald weighs 23·80 m.c. There are 12 white Brazilian brilliants and 24 small roses.

F (12) Hairpin in the form of a dragonfly with rubies and brilliants (No. 270). The gold wings are covered with 100 old white brilliants on foil of $1\frac{1}{4}$ carats. 1 ruby weighs $1\frac{1}{4}$ carats and 1 of $\frac{3}{8}$ carat and $1\frac{1}{4}$ carats.

F (13) Three silver hairpins with brilliants (No. 271). There are 32 brilliants weighing $4\frac{1}{8}$ carats.

F (14) A hairpin with pearl (No. 272).

F (15) A hairpin with sapphires (No. 279).

F (16) A hairpin with sapphire (No. 276).

F (17) Three diamond hairpins for the hair in silver (No. 280). In the first there are 78 brilliants weighing 9 m.c. On the under side is engraved: '1763 19 (P.aude) 80, 27/32, 163 br. C.F.E'. These figures have not been deciphered. The date corresponds to the first year of the Catherine period giving these ornaments an historical and museum interest. The other two hairpins have 34 brilliants of $4\frac{1}{4}$ carats.

F (18) Diamond hairpins (No. 283). There is 1 brilliant of $1\frac{1}{2}$ carats and 29 of $3\frac{1}{2}$ carats.

Dress Ornaments

G (1) Diamond cord with tassels (No. 103) (*Plate 193, b (i)*). There are 28 brilliants of 23 carats; 84 of 8 carats and 1,580 single-facet stones of 66 carats, besides 24 pearls of 45 carats.

G (2) Twelve diamond buttons (No. 105). These belong to the early Catherine period and are good old Brazilian stones (*Plate 195, b (ii)*). The weights are engraved on the under side in the case of six stones and are as follows:

11 of 15 m.c.; 4 of 13 m.c.; 2 of 14 m.c.; 5 of 13 m.c.; 3 of 14 m.c.; 6 of 12 m.c.

The remaining six were sold at Christie's with other crown jewels.

G (3) Diamond sash with two tassels (Nos. 79 and 120) (*Plate 196, c*), One-half of the sash is 32·4 cm by 6·1 cm, the other 31·7 cm by 4·2 cm, and the tassels are 6·2 by 3·6 cm. The sash and tassels are entirely composed of good brilliants of uneven tone. Two have large black spots. The numbers and weights are not recorded.

G (4) Six silver buckles with brilliants (No. 118). On each buckle is 1 large brilliant, 11 medium and 76 small brilliants. Of the large ones, 2 are bevelled flat stones; 2 pear-shaped very good quality and also 2 pear-shaped with a tint. The 6 large ones weigh 11 carats, 3 others weigh 3 carats and 58 of $21\frac{1}{2}$ carats. The number of small stones weigh 36 carats.

G (5) Epaulet with brilliants with tassels (No. 125) (*Plate 196, b (i)*). The stones are very large Brazilian, but generally not of much value. Mostly irregular in shape and in various shapes, cuts and purity. There are two diamond pendants of 2 carats, twenty-four of 24 carats and 172 of 52 carats.

G (6) Epaulet of brilliants in gold (No. 126) (*Plate 196, b (ii)*). 1 large brilliant in a large bow is a flat, oval stone with slight tint of 9 carats; 1 large brilliant, flat, in a small bow of 6 carats. There are 6 of 9 carats, 10 of 10 carats, and 124 of 84 carats, besides facet stones of 22 m.c. and roses.

G (7) Diamond buckles with spinels and brilliants (No. 132). There are four curbed buckles for shoes containing 12 spinels, 4 of 40 carats, 5 of 5 carats and 1 of $5\frac{1}{2}$ carats; 1 of $5\frac{1}{8}$ carats and 107 of $3\frac{7}{8}$ carats. They are set with 8 brilliants weighing 8 carats and 223 brilliants of 36 carats.

G (8) A plastron (No. 139C) of diamonds and emeralds being part of a parure. There are 5 emeralds of 50 m.c. and 228 good South African brilliants and roses of 85 m.c.

G (9) Diamond dress ornament 'kaftan' (No. 151). There are 365 pieces for sewing on and are good Brazilian stones on brocade. They are for the general decoration of a dress and there are 13 brilliants of $15\frac{1}{8}$ carats, 68 of 62 carats, 195 of 148 carats, 1,708 of 495 carats and single-facet stones of 600 carats. In addition there are pieces for the decoration of the pockets which include 1 brilliant of $3\frac{1}{2}$ carats, 4 brilliants of 11 carats, 6 of $13\frac{1}{2}$ carats and 359 of $148\frac{1}{4}$ carats and single-facet stones of 44 carats.

G (10) Dress ornaments of brilliants (No. 152). These consist of 123 pieces for sewing on and on each piece are 20 small brilliants of a total weight of $1\frac{1}{2}$ to 2 m.c. The stones are old and good and mostly single facet mounted on silver or brocade.

a *Diamond and sapphire necklace including one sapphire of 159·25 carats (B14) (p. 539)*

b (i) *Esclavage bow with brilliants and red spinels (B20) (p. 539)*
   (ii) *Large necklace of brilliants, rubies and spinels (B19) (p. 539)*
   (iii) *Ear-ring pendants with spinels (E6) (p. 546)*

c (i) *Diamond brooch (C4) (p. 539)*
   (ii) *Pin with pink brilliant (C61) (p. 543)*
   (iii) *Pin with blue brilliant (C62) (p. 543)*
   (iv) *Pin with diamond briolette (C63) (p. 543)*
   (v) *Diamond brooch with various stones and pearl pendants (S108) (p. 551)*

a   (i) *Diamond brooch with Ceylon sapphire (C30) (p. 541)*
  (ii) *Diamond brooch with Ceylon sapphire (C31) (p. 541)*
  (iii) *Gold cross with 4 large brilliants and spinel (C76) (p. 544)*
  (iv) *Diamond brooch with large ruby (C25) (p. 541)*
  (v) *Brooch with large emerald and Arabic inscription (C43) (p. 542)*
  (vi) *Diamond brooch with large emerald and brilliants (C8) (p. 540)*

b   (i) *Diamond coulomb brooch with 3 large pearls and pink brilliants (C11) (p. 540)*
  (ii) *Bracelet with large pearls, brilliants and sapphires (D3) (p. 545)*
  (iii) *Diamond brooch with 1 round and 3 pear-shaped pearls (C12) (p. 540)*

G (11) Ten diamond buttons of early XIX century (No. 212). The buttons are covered with brilliants with beautiful engravings on the back. Evidently date from the early time of Alexander I, i.e. about 1810 to 1820. There are five large buttons with excellent quality and very high Brazilian brilliants each of 9 m.c. In addition there are roses of $\frac{3}{4}$ m.c. There are also five smaller buttons of poor material, each of 7 m.c. and roses of $\frac{3}{4}$ m.c.

G (12) Buttons with spinels (No. 213). Two pairs of buttons with a total of 4 spinels of 7 carats and around them 40 Brazilian brilliants of 8 carats.

G (13) Twelve diamond buttons with emeralds (No. 204). Six of these were sold at Christie's in 1927 and six remain. The weights are not recorded.

G (14) A pair of gold cuff buttons with brilliants (No. 215). Each contains an oval blunt formed brilliant on brocade with a combined weight of $3\frac{1}{4}$ carats.

G (15) Brilliant ornaments for sewing on (No. 216). Forty-five small pieces each containing brilliants of $\frac{1}{4}$ to $\frac{1}{2}$ carat, and all very varying in quality and value.

Miscellaneous

There are a number of miscellaneous objects in the Treasure which do not fall into any of the above categories, but which are deserving of mention. Among these are parts of the celebrated Pitt or Regent Diamond. When this stone was cut in London, the debris left after the cleavage was valued at £7,000 and rose diamonds were cut out of it and sold to Peter the Great, but it is improbable that they could be identified today.

The Shah Diamond (No. 86) (*Plate 178, a*). This important single stone formerly weighed 95 carats, but after re-cutting weighs 88·7 carats. It has a yellowish tint and is of very unusual shape being a narrow oblong with cleavaged faces, only the fourth side being faceted. The three cleavage faces are beautifully engraved with the names of three Persian rulers. Apart from the 'Jehan Ghir Shah' it is the only diamond known to have had engravings carved upon it in the East, but the difficulty of engraving diamonds has led it to be thought that it may be a phenacite. It is said to have been found in the second half of the XVI century and was among the Persian crown jewels until it was presented to Nicholas I by Prince Chrostoes, the younger son of Abbas Mirza in 1843 when he visited St Petersburg. It does not appear ever to have been worn by the Russian imperial family, although round the edges is another cleavage to allow a spring to be fixed so that it can be worn as a pendant.[1]

Rings being articles of a very personal nature do not feature prominently in the catalogue. There are some wedding rings (No. 241) and a ring with an emerald of $5\frac{1}{4}$ m.c. surrounded by 18 brilliants (No. 242).

There is a sabre decorated with brilliants (No. 202). On the knob of the hilt there is a large brilliant of $5\frac{1}{2}$ m.c. of the first water, surrounded by two rows of brilliants of medium size. Altogether on the sabre there are 440 stones of 65 carats, besides 345 small roses.

Among the miscellaneous ornaments are a gold rattle and whistle ornamented with brilliants (No. 186). A gold Georgian chain (No. 207). An antique Russian silver cross (No. 208) and a snuff box (No. 80). The snuff box is of French workmanship and is decorated with various brilliants and 2,071 roses of about 75 m.c.

The above list is not exhaustive and excludes those ornaments which can be identified as sold at Christie's on 16th March 1927. This sale included some important items which had been purchased by a syndicate in the United Kingdom and appears to include some items not in the inventory of the Imperial Russian Treasure and which may have been the private property of the Russian royal family. Some details are given in an Appendix to this chapter.

[1] For a detailed description of the diamond see article by A. E. Fersman: 'Diamond Shah', *News of the Russian Academy of Science*, 1922.

APPENDIX

Summary of Russian State Jewels, mostly dating from the XVIII century, sold by auction on behalf of a syndicate by Messrs Christie, Manson, Woods, on Wednesday, 16th March 1927.

In the following list the first number refers to that in Christie's catalogue, and the second number prefixed with 'No.' refers to the numbers in the inventory of the Imperial Russian Treasure. The names of the purchasers and prices paid are given where known.

S62 (No. 37). *Nuptial Crown (Plate 173, b).*

The historical origin of this crown is not known. It was placed in a special case, the work of the jewellers Nicholls Planke about 1840 which dates it from not earlier than the second half of the Nicholas period. It was used at weddings for members of the Russian royal family. The crown was apparently hastily made up from old embroideries of Catherine evidently taken from half a belt of brilliants. These embroideries with brilliants were sewn on and some solitaires, also sewn on, to the purple velvet to which they were fastened by unusually inaccurate silver threads, rather uneven, unsymmetrical and crooked. The embroideries themselves were on black riband: eighty pieces held with 4 large brilliants, 320 brilliants of 182 carats and about 1,200 single-facet stones of 80 carats. On the top under the cross are 3 moderate-sized solitaires in silver settings weighing about 6 carats. On the cross itself there are six stones of about 15 carats. (£6,100—Fourres)

S60 (No. 93)

Star of the Order of St Catherine with red enamel centre with diamond motto and crown, surrounded by a circle of diamonds in border of diamond rays. (£300—Wartski)

S61 (No. 94)

The badge of a Maid of Honour in diamonds with monogram of Catherine II surmounted by a crown. (£210—Harrison, Sir A. Black)

S119 (No. 203)

A Court sword, the hilt and guard composed entirely of brilliants. The blade is triangular in shape of partly blued steel and the fittings of those of the scabbard have diamond mounts. There are 3 white brilliants of $3\frac{1}{2}$ carats; 882 various brilliants weigh 150 carats and roses 12 carats. (£1,700—Curiel)

S117 (No. 10)

A pearl and brilliant tiara: a XIX-century ornament (*Plate 196, a*). There are 25 large drop pearls weighing a total of $311\frac{7}{8}$ carats, the largest being $19\frac{1}{4}$ carats. There are 5 brilliants of $7\frac{14}{32}$ carats, two of $\frac{13}{32}$ carat, 22 of $17\frac{1}{2}$ carats, 115 of 45 carats and single-facet stones of 40 carats and 900 roses.

S116 (No. 45)

A diamond tiara designed as wheat-ears and foliage ornamented with brilliants and sapphires (*Plate 194, a*). There are 37 Indian briolettes of especial beauty, of wonderful water and rarity of workmanship, pointed at either end. There are 6 brilliants of 9 carats, 5 of $6\frac{1}{2}$ carats, 8 of 8 carats, 35 of $24\frac{1}{2}$ carats. Various others of 115 carats, besides 800 roses. The large stone in the centre is a white sapphire of 37 carats. This piece was added to the Russian Treasury on the death of Marie Feodorovna, wife of Paul I, in 1829.

S41 (*Not identified*)

Diamond necklace composed of fifteen oval links. (£240—S. J. Phillips)

S71 (No. 205)

A diamond necklace of 25 graduated collets, set in foliage-patterned borders of smaller diamonds. The stones are old Indian and Brazilian and in general are of pure and rare selection and beauty. The total weight of the brilliants is $133\frac{30}{32}$ carats and individual stones vary from $13\frac{21}{32}$ carats to $2\frac{18}{32}$ carats, eleven weighing 5 carats or over. (£2,700—S. J. Phillips)

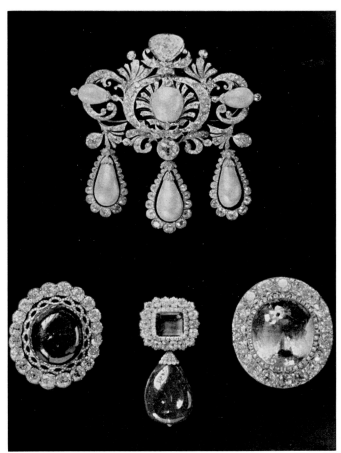

a (i) *Large brooch set with brilliants and pearl pendants* (C13) (p. 540)
(ii) *Brooch with large cabochon emerald of* 153·75 *carats* (C40) (p. 542)
(iii) *Brooch coulomb with large emerald of* 110 *carats* (C41) (p. 542)
(iv) *Brooch clasp with brilliants and large sapphire of* 260 *carats* (C29) (p. 541)

b (i) *Diamond aigrette with pearl pendants* (C66) (p. 543)
(ii) *Ear-rings with large pearl pendants* (E13) (p. 546)
(iii) *Ear-ring with very rare Indian briolette* (E14) (p. 546)
(iv) *Brooch-aigrette with branches of brilliants and pearl pendants* (C14) (p. 540)

a (i) *Diamond brooch with brilliants and large square emerald* (C37) (p. 541)
(ii) *Brooch-clasp with brilliants and a large cabochon emerald* (C39) (p. 541)
(iii) *Square brooch with brilliants and a square emerald* (C38) (p. 541)
(iv) *Brooch-clasp with brilliants and a Ceylon sapphire* (C27) (p. 541)
(v) *Brooch with brilliants and large sapphire* (C26) (p. 541)
(vi) *Brooch with brilliants and a large cabochon sapphire* (C28) (p. 541)

b (i) *Seven brooches with large red stones and brilliants* (C15–21) (p. 540)
(ii) (centre) *Brooch-clasp with topazes and brilliants* (C47) (p. 542)

a   (i) *Brooch sévigné with 3 emeralds weighing 140, 174·10 and 21·90 carats respectively* (C42) (p. 542)
(ii) *Ear-rings of emeralds with emerald pendants* (E15) (p. 547)
(iii) *Two pendants with globe emeralds*
(iv) *Brooch with hexagonal emerald* (C44) (p. 542)
(v) *Pendant with large emerald estimated at 240–250 carats* (C77) (p. 544)
(vi) *Medallion with emerald cameo* (C88) (p. 544)

b   (i) *Brooch with yellow-green beryl* (C48) (p. 542)
(ii) *Two large spinels in bezels* (C56) (p. 543)
(iii) *Rose-coloured tourmaline as fruit* (C55) (p. 543)
(iv) *Medallion with large chrysolite* (C57) (p. 543)
(v) *Medallion with large alamandine* (C58) (p. 543)
(vi) *Medallion with brilliants and aquamarine* (C54) (p. 543)

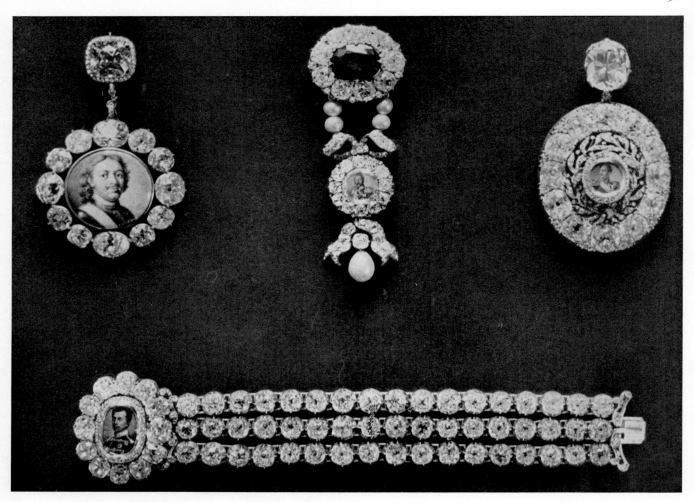

a (i) *Diamond brooch with large balas ruby and pendant of brilliants with portrait of Alexander II* (C22) (p. 540)
   (ii) *Russian Order with pendant of brilliants and portrait of Peter I* (C22a) (p. 540)
   (iii) *Diamond medallion with portrait of Nicholas I* (C64) (p. 543)
   (iv) *Bracelet of brilliants with portrait of Nicholas I* (D4) (p. 545)

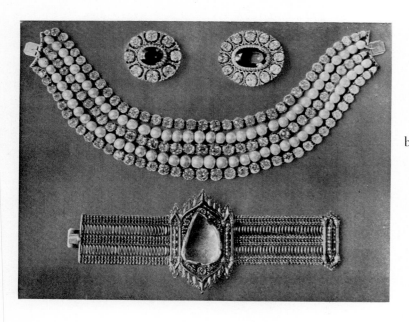

b (i) *Clasps of emerald and ruby* (p. 537)
   (ii) *Necklace of brilliants with strings of pearls* (B4) (p. 537)
   (iii) *Bracelet of gold with large flat diamond of 25 carats* (D1) (p. 545)

S81 (*Not identified*)

A diamond necklet composed of oval- and riband-patterned links. (£310—S. J. Phillips)

S110 (*Not identified*)

A diamond necklace of velvet and riband design. (£230—S. J. Phillips)

S1 (No. 222)

A garnet suite consisting of a long necklace with pendant cross; a pair of four-row bracelets and two chains, gold mounted. (£58—Walker)

S2 (No. 218)

A smoky crystal (topaz) suite consisting of a pair of two-row bracelets with drop and a pair of ear-rings, gold mounted. (£58—Fourres)

S3 (No. 222)

Five smoky crystal shuttle-shaped hair ornaments. Twelve shuttle-shaped pins and six circular pins. (£27—Fourres)

S4 (No. 223)

A garnet suite consisting of a four-row necklace; a cluster-patterned necklace; a pair of bracelets; three buckles and six clasps. (£37—Frumkin)

S5 (No. 220)

A chrysophase suite with diamond bands consisting of a necklace; a pair of ear-rings and six pins. (£265—Fourres)

S80 (No. 104)

An amethyst and diamond necklace with foliage-patterned centre and a spray pin *en suite*. The amethyst weighs $4\frac{3}{4}$ carats and there are 1,305 brilliants of 72 carats. (£470—S. J. Phillips)

S100 (No. 85a)

A magnificent, oval brilliant with a fine, rosy-white or pinkish tint mounted as a brooch (*Plate 178, c*). The stone is described as sparkling and of ideal purity, first class in its quality, though somewhat too long in the oval. It is of Indian origin and weighs $40\frac{12}{32}$ carats.[1] (£11,800—Fourres)

S108 (No. 78)

A magnificent brooch with diamond foliage-patterned groundwork (*Plate 187, c (v)*). At the top is set a superb emerald of 6 m.c., an oblong spinel of 22 m.c. and 2 sapphires in the centre of 16 m.c. with three large pearl drops of 50 m.c. The diamonds are described as of superlative beauty and the pearls weigh $13\frac{1}{2}$ m.c.

S10 (No. 188)

A pair of sapphire and diamond spray brooches. (£175—S. J. Phillips)

S56 (No. 190)

An ornament formed as a bird and foliage, set with sapphires, rubies, emeralds and diamonds (*Plate 193, a (iii)*). (£180—S. J. Phillips)

S59 (No. 108)

Two diamond Knot-of-Riband brooches with cluster centres (*Plate 195, b (iv)*). (£300—S. J. Phillips)

S94 (No. 234)

An emerald and brilliant ornament with 2 large square emeralds in brilliant scroll borders. Of these 1 emerald weighs 20 carats and the other 12 carats. (£4,300—Fourres)

S93 (No. 185)

A diamond brooch with two large pear-shaped drops. The two pairs weigh 10 m.c., 7 brilliants 9 m.c., 158 small brilliants 10 m.c. (£520—S. J. Phillips)

---

[1] This may be the stone described as the Polar Star by Streeter: op. cit.

S95 (No. 146)

A pearl and diamond ornament designed as a spray of foliage with pear-shaped diamond drops. There are 3 drop pearls and 1 *bouton* pearl; 2 pearls weigh 15 m.c., 1 weighs 8 m.c. and 1 weighs 50 m.c.; 2 brilliants weigh 7 carats, 2 weigh 4 carats, 9 weigh 8 carats, one round stone on the stem 2 carats, fifty-six various weigh 10 carats.   (£680—Landsberg)

S96 (*Not identified*)

A diamond sapphire spray ornament.   (£580—Nyburg)

S99 (? No. 97)

A pearl and diamond foliage spray ornament with 1 large baroque pearl in the centre and 3 drop pearls. The baroque pearl weighs 25 m.c., and 3 drop pearls 64·10 m.c.   (£350—S. J. Phillips)

S107 (*Not identified*)

A diamond pendant with large oblong centre stone and riband-patterned borders of small diamonds.   (£170—Nyburg)

S118 (*Not in inventory*)

A cameo pendant with onyx cameos of Queen Victoria and the Prince Consort in a border of brilliants with brilliant crown and loop.   (£310—Schavarian)

S7 (No. 281)

Two olivine and diamond fly pins and a rose diamond pin with a star-shaped top.   (£18—Fink)

S11 (*Not identified*)

A pair of ruby and brilliant cluster pins.   (£65—Black)

S13 (*Not identified*)

A set of three diamond pins of scroll design, the largest being an oval centre.   (£220—S. J. Phillips)

S15 (*Not identified*)

A sapphire and marquise pin.   (£58—Black)

S16 (*Not identified*)

A set of three single brilliant pins.   (£25—Punt)

S19 (*Not identified*)

A ruby and diamond cluster pin.   (£28—S. J. Phillips)

S20 (*Not identified*)

A large ruby and diamond cluster pin.   (£48—S. J. Phillips)

S21 (*Not identified*)

A pin with oblong spinel with diamond borders.   (£92—S. J. Phillips)

S22 (No. 180)

A set of sapphire and diamond pins of flower design.   (£180—S. J. Phillips)

S26 (No. 188)

A set of three diamond sprays mounted as pins.   (£310—S. J. Phillips)

S24 (No. 193)

A pair of pearl and diamond pins of small design.   (£185—Curiel)

S30 (No. 183)

A pearl and diamond flower spray pin with a drop pearl and a pear-shaped brilliant.   (£300—Fourres)

S39 (*Not identified*)

An emerald and diamond pin of scroll design.   (£78—S. J. Phillips)

S40 (*Not identified*)

A similar emerald and diamond pin of scroll design.   (£50—Mrs Caulfield)

a   (i) *Golden Fleece* (p. 536)
    (ii) *Pair of pearl and diamond pins* (S24) (p. 552)
    (iii) *Ornament formed as a bird and foliage* (S56)
                    (p. 551)
    (iv) *Pair of single diamond ear-rings* (S74) (p. 555)
    (v) *Diamond ornament with large solitaire* (C82)
                    (p. 544)

b   (i) *Diamond cord with tassels* (G1) (p. 548)
    (ii) *Amethyst ornament* (C65) (p. 543)
    (iii) *Brilliant bow with rays* (C69) (p. 543)

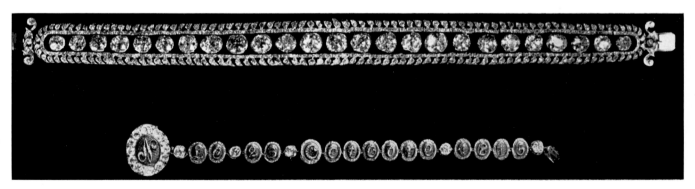

c   (i) *Diamond rivière* (B12) (p. 538); (ii) *bracelet of enamel and brilliants* (S14) (p. 554)

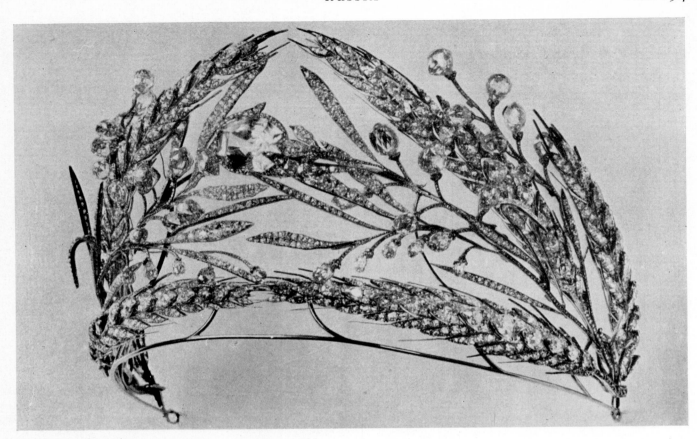

a (above)   *Diamond tiara designed as wheat ears and foliage. XIX Century (S116) (p. 550)*

b (left)   *Large bouquet with emerald leaves and flowers. XVIII Century (C52) (p. 542)*

S43 (*Not identified*)
A pearl and diamond ornament of riband design. (£125—S. J. Phillips)

S45 (*Not identified*)
A pair of pendants of foliage and cluster design with large centre stones and pear-shaped drops.

S51 (*Not identified*)
A pear-shaped emerald and diamond drop. (£50—Landsberg)

S53 (*Not identified*)
A pearl and diamond pin with 3 drop pearls. (£120—S. J. Phillips)

S54 (*Not identified*)
A diamond pin formed as a spray of foliage. (£90—S. J. Phillips)

S57 (*Not identified*)
An emerald and diamond pin with pear-shaped emerald drop. (£135—Esmerian)

S58 (*Not identified*)
A pear-shaped emerald pin and a *cabochon* emerald pin with pearl drop. (£55—S. J. Phillips)

S97 (*Not identified*)
Five sapphire drops mounted as pins and pendants. (£380—Fourres)

S109 (*Not identified*)
Three emerald and diamond pins with emerald centre and diamond border. (£120—Walker)

S111 (*Not identified*)
A pearl and diamond pin set with 4 pearls and a diamond cross. (£105—S. J. Phillips)

S 24 (*Not identified*)
A pair of diamond clasps of foliage design with pear-shaped centre stones. (£300—Franklin)

S25 (*Not identified*)
A set of gold shuttle-shaped diamond slides with large centre stones. (£195—Fourres)

S29 (*Not identified*)
A set of four diamond slides of scroll design with cluster centres. (£280—Curiel)

S47 (*Not identified*)
An emerald and diamond square clasp. (£90—Withers)

S48 (*Not identified*)
A similar emerald and diamond square clasp. (£100—Curiel)

S49 (*Not identified*)
An oval emerald and diamond square clasp. (£70—Chester Street Gallery)

S75 (No. 182)
An emerald-and-diamond clasp with a large oblong emerald in borders of small diamonds.
(£820—S. H. Harris)

S76 (No. 182)
Another with square emerald in diamond borders.

S77 (No. 182)
Two emerald and diamond oblong clasps with oblong emeralds in borders of 8 diamonds and a small ditto nearly similar.

S78 (*Not identified*)
A diamond flower spray ornament composed of white and coloured stones and mounted as a pin.
(£250—S. J. Phillips)

S83 *(Not identified)*
    A ruby and diamond flower spray ornament.   (£370—Franklin)

S84 *(Not identified)*
    An emerald foliage spray ornament mounted as a pin.   (£240—Fourres)

S34 *(Not identified)*
    A pair of sprays formed as fruit and ribands.   (£255—Fourres)

S35 *(Not identified)*
    A pair of sprays formed as fruit and ribands.   (£240—S. J. Phillips)

S36, 37 (No. 188)
    A pair and a set of three diamond flower sprays.   (£360 and £370—Fourres)

S66 *(Not identified)*
    A set of three diamond sprays formed as fruit and ribands.

S67 *(Not identified)*
    A set of three diamond sprays formed as fruit and ribands.   (£300—S. J. Phillips)

S68, 29 (No. 188)
    Two pairs of diamond flower sprays.   (£230 and £230—S. J. Phillips)

S70 (No. 188)
    One pair of diamond flower sprays.

S88–90 *(Not identified)*
    Three pins as diamond fruit-shaped sprays.

S92 *(Not identified)*
    46 shuttle-shaped diamond slides with flower-spray centres. The back dated 1764.
                                        (£1,150—S. J. Phillips)

S104, 106 (No. 188)
    Two pins of diamond foliage-patterned sprays.

S105 (No. 188)
    One pin of diamond foilage-patterned sprays.   (£200—S. J. Phillips)

S8 (No. 245)
    A turquoise and diamond forget-me-not bracelet.   (£70—S. J. Phillips)

S14 (No. 196)
    A bracelet *(Plate 193, c (ii))* with oval links with blue enamel centres and diamond borders set in diamonds and the initial 'N' and the inscription: *Le 23 Octobre 1815.*

S18 (No. 226)
    A pair of bracelets with diamond flowers and amethysts and other stones. (£310—S. J. Phillips)

S38 *(Not identified)*
    A rose diamond bracelet of foliage and riband design.   (£33—Mrs Shalit)

S44, 48 *(Not identified)*
    A pair of diamond bracelets with bands of foliage design of knot-of-riband centres with large oval centre stones. These are 2 brilliants weighing 8 m.c., 8 are 8 m.c., 38 are 25 m.c., and various other stones 60 m.c., described as beautiful craftsmanship of 1870.   (£3,400—S. J. Phillips)

S6 *(Not identified)*
    A ruby and rose diamond chatelaine hook and gold buckle set with 4 diamonds.
                                        (£26—S. J. Phillips)

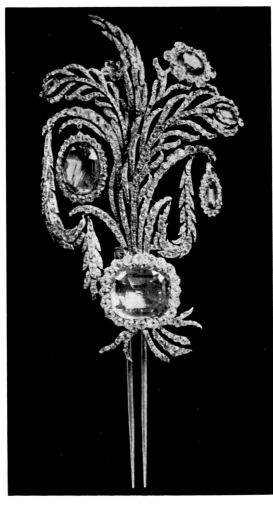

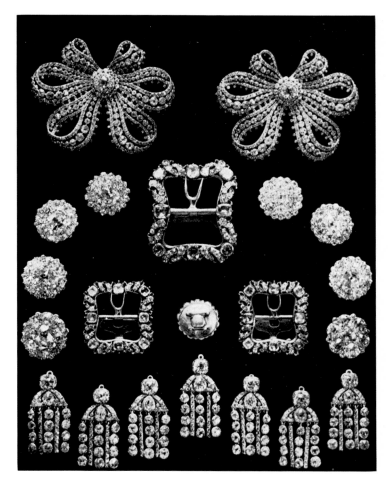

a *Aigrette bouquet holder of sapphires and brilliants (C53) (p. 543)*

b   (i) *Two diamond knot riband brooches (S59) (p. 551)*
  (ii) *Nine of twelve diamond buttons (G2) (p. 548)*
  (iii) *Diamond and sapphire buckle (p. 555)*
  (iv) *Pair of diamond and sapphire shoe buckles (S9) (p. 555)*
  (v) *Seven diamond tassels with single stone top (S33) (p. 555)*

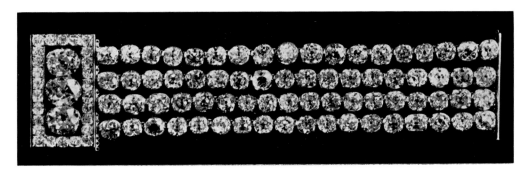

c   *Bracelet with brilliants (D2) (p. 545)*

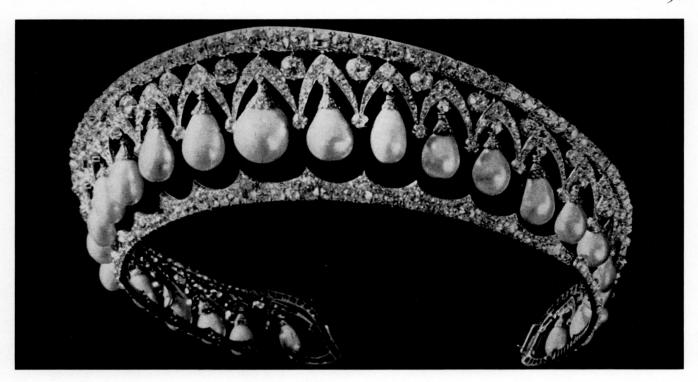

a   *Pearl and brilliant tiara* (S117) (p. 550)

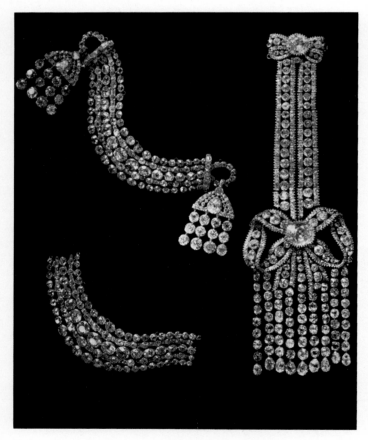

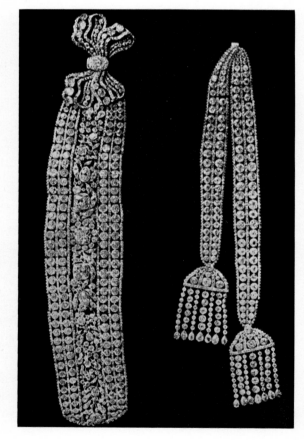

b (i)   *Epaulette with brilliants and tassels* (G5); (ii) *Epaulette of brilliants in gold* (G6) (p. 548)

c   *Diamond sash and tassels* (G3) (p. 548)

S17 *(Not identified)*
Three chains of smoke crystal buttons, each set with a diamond in the centre.   (£110—Frumkin)

S46 (No. 105)
A set of six diamond *pavé* buttons, the backs dated 1764.   (£2,250—Fourres)

S52 (No. 214)
Six emerald and diamond cluster buttons and clasps.   (£170—Wartski)

S98 *(Not identified)*
Four emerald clasps with diamond brooches.   (£330—Mrs Bennett)

S32 (No. 106)
A pair of diamond tassels with single stone tops.   (£480—Mrs Morgan)

S31–33 (No. 106)
Seven diamond tassels with single stone tops *(Plate 195, b (v))*.

S63, 64, 65, 85, 86, 87, 101, 102, 103, 112, 113, 114 (No. 106)
Pairs of diamond tassels with single stone tops.

S9 (No. 107)
A pair of sapphire and diamond square shoe buckles *(Plate 195, b (iv))*; 16 sapphires weigh 20 m.c. and 16 others 9 m.c.   (£48—Phillips)

S23 (No. 110)
A pair of amethyst and diamond ear-rings with amethyst centre and diamond foliage-patterned borders.   (£295—S. J. Phillips)

S27 (No. 111)
A pair of amethyst and diamond ear-rings with cluster tops and pear-shaped drops.
(£135—S. J. Phillips)

S55 *(Not identified)*
A pair of pearl and diamond ear-rings of riband design, each set with pear-shaped and 2 drop pearls.
(£240—S. J. Phillips)

S72 (No. 112)
A pair of aquamarine and diamond link ear-rings with cluster tops and drops and riband-patterned clusters.   (£230—S. J. Phillips)

S73 (No. 113)
A pair of aquamarine and diamond link ear-rings with cluster tops and drops and riband-patterned clusters, nearly similar.   (£160—S. J. Phillips)

S74 (No. 192)
A pair of single diamond ear-rings.   (£270—S. H. Harris)

S79 *(Not identified)*
Four agate and diamond ear-rings with riband-patterned centres.   (£320—S. J. Phillips)

S82 (No. 242)
A ring with a large brilliant in border of small diamonds chased gold hoop set with small diamonds and partly enamelled blue. The brilliants weigh about 10 m.c. and are of a somewhat violet colour in tone, slightly misty and with small black spots. There are 89 roses of about 1 carat.
(£260—Mrs Shalit)

S91 (No. 197)
A green jasper snuff-box mounted with gold borders finely chased with flowers and foliage in

vari-colour gold in the style of the period of Louis XV. Two panels and borders are highly over-laid with baskets and sprays of flowers, trophies and foliage in white and fancy coloured diamonds.

(£2,600—Levy)

S120 (No. 36)

A fan with tortoiseshell sticks, the outer sticks set with the Russian arms in fine brilliants with brilliant borders, the mount painted with views of Paris by E. de Liphart. (£800—Wall)

S121 (No. 200)

Another fan with mother-of-pearl sticks overlaid with gold and the outside sticks richly studded with rubies, sapphires and diamonds and with jewelled tassels attached. The mount painted with the coronation of a tsar and shipping on the Neva on the reverse by G. Lasellaz. (£800—Walker)

S122 (No. 80)

A Louis XVI gold *étui* chased with trophies and emblems and with diamond thumb-piece.

S123 (No. 198)

A Louis XVI tablet case with Vernis-Martin panels painted with garden scenes and arabesque in gold ground and with gold borders chased with foliage.

S124 (No. 201)

A gold cup cover and stand, finely chased with foliage and engraved with a Russian inscription stating that the cup was presented by the Government and people of St Petersburg to General Ivan Petrovitch Soltykov in 1790: weight 72 oz 14 dwt. (£260—S. H. Harris)

The total sum realised from those items recorded as sold was £52,609, but out of the 124 items in the catalogue, thirty do not appear to have been sold, perhaps because they did not reach the reserve price. It is probable that most of these were sold privately. They included some important items such as two tiaras (No. 116 and No. 112) and a magnificent brooch (No. 108) and these might well have increased the total to £75,000.

BIBLIOGRAPHY

BAINBRIDGE, H. C.	*Peter Carl Fabergé.*
BELOYERSKOI, N.	*The Coronations of the Czars in Russia* (in Russian), St Petersburg 1827.
CHRISTIE, MANSON AND WOODS	Catalogue, 16th March 1927.
CONWAY, SIR MARTIN	*Art Treasures in Soviet Russia*, London 1925.
FERSMAN, DR A. E.	*Russian Treasury of Diamonds and Precious Stones*, Moscow 1924.
MAIGRET, JACQUES	*Estat de l'Empire Russe.*
MASKELL, A.	*Russian Art*, London 1889.
METALLINOS, E.	*Imperial and Royal Coronations*, London 1902
PALITZINE, ABRAHAM	*Mémoires du cellérier.*
STREETER, E. W.	*The Great Diamonds of the World*, London 1882.
STROGANOV, S.	*Antiquities of the Russian Empire*, 1852.
VOYCE, A.	*The Moscow Kremlin*, London 1955.
WELTMAN, A.	*Le Trésor de Moscou.*

Mémoires du Règne de Catherine, Amsterdam 1729.

DUKES OF KIEV

850	Ruric
879	Oleg
913	Igor I
945	Olga, widow, Regent
955	Sviatoslav I
973	Jaropalk I
980	Vladimir the Great
1015	Swiatopalk
1019	Yaroslav I
1054	Isiaslav I
1073	Sviatoslav II
1078	Wsewolod I
1093	Swiatopalk II
1113	Vladimir II, Monomachus
1125	Mitislav
1132	Jaropalk II
1138	Wiatschelav and Wsewolod II
1146	Isiaslav II and Igor II
1153	Rostislav
1149	George I

GRAND DUKES OF VLADIMIR

1157	⌠ Andrew I
1175	⌡ Michael I
1177	Wsewolod III
1213	George II and Constantine (1217–18)
1238	Yaroslav II
1252	Alexander Nevski the Saint
1263	Yaroslav III
1270	Basil I
1275	Demetrius I
1281	Andrew II
1294	Daniel Alexandrovitch
1303	George III
1305	Michael III
1320	Basil II
1325	George IV
1327	Alexander II

GRAND DUKES OF MOSCOW

1328	Ivan I
1340	Simeon the Proud

1353 Ivan II
1359 Demetrius II
1362 Demetrius III
1389 Basil III, Temnoi
1425 Basil IV

TSARS OF MUSCOVY

1462 Ivan III
1498 (Demetrius. Son of Ivan. Crowned as co-Regent 4th February)
1505 Basil V. Crowned 14th April 1502
1533 Ivan IV, the Terrible. Crowned 16th April 1547
1584 Theodore I. Crowned 31st May
1598 Boris Goudonov. Crowned 1st September
1605 Theodore II
1605 Demetrius II. Crowned 30th July 1605. Consort, Marina, crowned on marriage 8th May 1606
1606 Basil Shouisky. Crowned 1st June
1610 Ladislas of Poland
1613 Michael Romanov. Crowned 11th July
1645 Alexis. Crowned 28th September
1676 Theodore III. Crowned 18th July
1682 Ivan V and Peter I, brothers. Crowned 25th May together

EMPERORS AND EMPRESSES

1698 Peter the Great alone
1724 Catherine I, his wife. Crowned in husband's lifetime in Moscow, 7th May
1725 Catherine I succeeded
1727 Peter II. Crowned 24th February 1728
1730 Anne of Courland. Crowned 28th April
1740 Ivan VI
1741 Elizabeth. Crowned 25th April 1742
1761 Peter III, not crowned, and Catherine II
1762 Catherine II alone. Crowned 22nd September
1796 Paul. Crowned with consort, Marie Feodorovna, 5th April 1797
1801 Alexander I. Crowned 15th September
1825 Nicholas I. Crowned with consort, Alexandra, 22nd March 1826
1855 Alexander II. Crowned August 1856
1883 Alexander III. Crowned with consort, Marie, 15th May
1896 Nicholas II. Crowned 26th May

CHAPTER TWENTY-TWO

SAXONY

The origin of the Royal House of Wettin can be traced back to the year 1095. In 1423 the Emperor Sigismund bestowed upon Frederick, a Prince of the House, the vacant electoral Duchy of Saxe-Wittenberg and the title Elector was substituted for the title of Duke of Saxony. In the Golden Bull of the Emperor Charles IV of 1356 it was laid down that the Duke of Saxony, as Arch-Marshal of the Empire, should on occasions when a solemn imperial or royal Court be held bear the Sword of State directly in front of the Emperor. The sword thus became the special emblem of the Electors of Saxony and they bore two swords on their coat of arms.

There are preserved in the Historical Museum at Dresden, among the magnificent collection of arms and armour, three electoral swords. The first was that of Frederick the Magnificent which dated from 1425 (*Plate 197, a*). The second was that given to Duke Maurice by the Emperor Charles V on 24th February 1548 at Augsburg and which was used subsequently by the electors as part of their insignia (*Plate 197, c*). The third was an electoral sword made for the Elector Augustus in 1566 (*Plate 197, b*).

The sword given by Charles V was according to Laking[1] the culminating point of all that is elaborate in the nature of design and richness of material as applied to sword mounting. He states:

> that the whole of the hilt and the scabbard are of silver gilt embossed and the surface chased with emblematic figures, trophies of weapons and swages of paint and flowers in the finest German renaissance taste. From the maker's mark the sword can be identified as the production of a famous goldsmith, Lorenz Trunck of Luxemburg (1500–74). The blade is probably of Solingen make and is deeply etched with scroll work. An inscription records the date and occasion of its gift.

Apart from the sword, the elector wore as part of his insignia an electoral hat. An example of this is kept in the Historical Museum at Dresden and is made of scarlet cloth trimmed with ermine (*Plate 197, d*).

In 1694 Frederick Augustus, known as Augustus the Strong, became Elector and in 1697 he was elected to the throne of Poland, but he only used the royal title in his capacity as King of Poland. Augustus was a man of luxurious and extravagant tastes and he endeavoured to model his Court on that of Versailles. He caused the erection of some outstanding buildings at Dresden which he filled with remarkable collections

---

1 Sir Guy Laking: *A Record of European Arms and Armour*, Vol. II, London.

of rare and costly treasures of sculpture and painting, of porcelain and *objets d'art*. He had a set of regalia made for his coronation in Poland, and these are displayed in the Historical Museum at Dresden.[1]

Augustus the Strong was succeeded by his son Frederick Augustus II, who was also elected King of Poland as Augustus III. He, in turn, was succeeded as Elector by Frederick Augustus III, who became the first King when Saxony was raised to a kingdom in 1806. The royal line continued until 1918 when the last King abdicated.

Towards the end of the Second World War Dresden was very seriously damaged by an aerial bombardment. The centre of the city was obliterated and the notable buildings including the royal palace and the Historical Museum were completely destroyed. The collections were taken to a place of safety and fell into the hands of the Russians who have returned them to Dresden, where they are again on display in the rebuilt museums.

The Kings of Saxony did not introduce a coronation ceremony, but it is believed that a set of regalia consisting of a crown, a sceptre, an orb and a sword were made by an unknown Dresden jeweller and removed by the royal family on the abdication of the last King in 1918.[2]

In the accounts of the funerals of the kings it is recorded that the royal crown rested on the coffin and that other royal ornaments were displayed. For heraldic purposes a formal royal crown with four arches was used.

Although the Saxon regalia were unimportant there was a remarkable collection of crown jewels originally established by Augustus the Strong, and added to by his successors. Augustus had prepared a series of eight rooms on the ground floor of the royal palace to house his collection of precious stones and *objets d'art* of bronze, ivory, silver, enamel and gold. These rooms were given the name of the Green Vault and the decoration of their interior was designed by Raymond le Plat of Paris and his two assistants, Longuelune and Knoffel, in the ornamental style invented by the celebrated French decorator and designer Jean Berain. The floors and door frames were of marble and the walls were panelled in fine woods and set with gilded framed mirrors from which rose ornamental brackets towards the vaulted ceilings. The whole was an example of the best taste of the Baroque period. There were altogether more than 3,000 objects in the collection. Most of these were curiosities illustrating human skill and ingenuity, but many of them possessed remarkable artistic merit. Several pieces were the work of the famous Dresden goldsmith, Johann Melchior Dinglinger, and many more showed his influence. The eighth room (*Plate 198*) contains the collection of crown jewels, which were arranged in suites of ornaments comprising swords, hair combs, buttons, bows, rings and jewelled orders. There were separate suites in diamonds, emeralds, sapphires, rubies, tortoiseshell and cornelians. The Order of the Golden Fleece is carried out in no less than eleven different settings.

Following the example of Louis XIV, Augustus the Strong used the stones for personal adornment. Some idea of the richness of the collection may be obtained from the fact that apart from the pearls and semi-precious stones the total weight of diamonds,

[1] These are described in the Chapter Seventeen—Poland.
[2] This information was given to the author in 1938 by the Director of the Historical Museum.

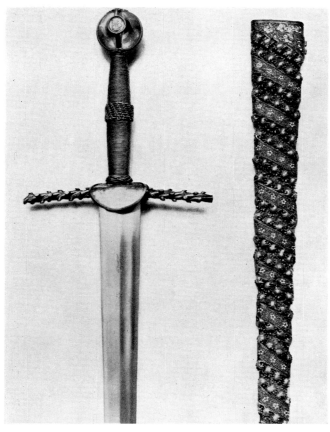

a (above, left)   *Electoral sword of Duke Frederick I, 1425.*
Historical Museum, Dresden (p. 559)

b (above, right)   *Electoral sword of Duke Augustus, 1566.*
Historical Museum, Dresden (p. 559)

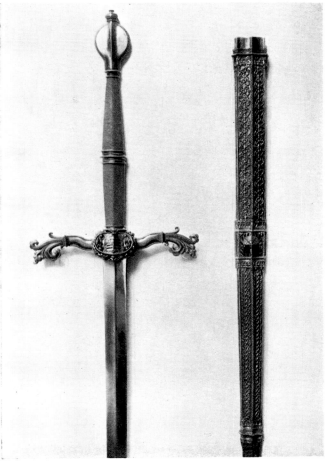

d   *Electoral hat. Historical Museum, Dresden* (p. 559)

c (left)   *Electoral sword of Duke Maurice, 1548.*
Historical Museum, Dresden (p. 559)

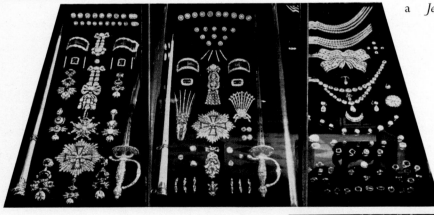

a　*Jewel Chamber in the Green Vault,*
Dresden, 1932 (p. 560)

b　and　c　*Cabinet of crown jewels*
in the Green Vault (p. 561)

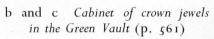

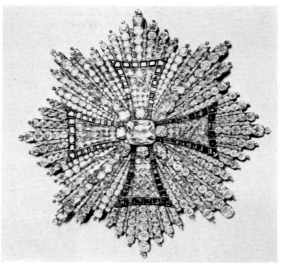

a (above, left) *Large shoulder knot in the form of a bow with 51 large and 611 small brilliants, the largest being* $21\frac{6}{8}$ *carats. Green Vault, Dresden (p. 562)*

b (above, right) *Star of the Polish Order of the White Eagle, set with rubies and 225 diamonds, the largest of* $11\frac{4}{8}$ *carats. Green Vault, Dresden (p. 561)*

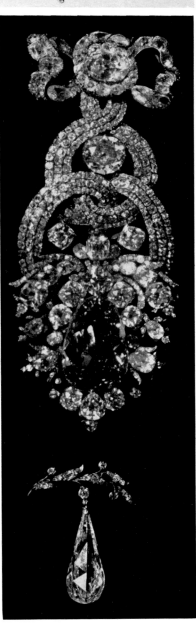

d *Pair of ear-rings. Green Vault, Dresden (p. 562)*

c *Hat agraffe with brilliant of 40 carats and 2 other large brilliants. Green Vault, Dresden (p. 562)*

e *Shoulder knot with green brilliants of* $48\frac{4}{8}$ *carats, and pendant with pendeloque brilliant of* $17 \cdot 55$ *carats. Green Vault, Dresden (p. 561)*

a   *Diamond necklace of 38 large brilliants of a total weight of* 489·44 *carats. The pendant weighs* 30 *carats and the next largest stone* 24$\frac{4}{8}$ *carats. Green Vault, Dresden* (p. 562)

b   *Shoulder knot with 20 large brilliants. The centre stone weighing* 40$\frac{6}{8}$ *carats. Green Vault* (p. 561)

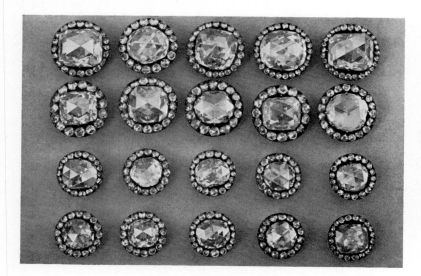

c (left)   *Large coat and waistcoat buttons set with diamonds. The largest stone weighing* 12$\frac{1}{2}$ *carats. Green Vault, Dresden*

d   *Two large sapphires weighing* 194·5 *and* 548 *carats respectively. The one on the right is known as Peter the Great's Nose. Green Vault* (p. 563)

b   *The cornelian suite* (p. 563)

a   *Ornaments from the*
    emerald suite.
    (p. 562)

c   *Ornaments from the*
    cornelian suite
    (p. 563)

All in the Green
Vault, Dresden

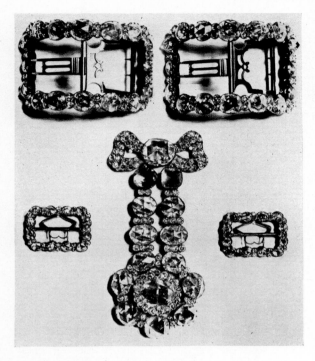

b *Buckle from the sapphire suite of Augustus the Strong* (p. 563)

a *Pair of belt buckles, pair of shoe buckles and hat agraffe from Augustus the Strong's suite of faceted stones* (p. 561)

c *Clasp from the emerald suite of Augustus the Strong* (p. 562)

d (i) *Small Golden Fleece with 3 cats-eyes and 57 brilliants;* (ii) *Golden Fleece with 3 emeralds, 2 large brilliants and 70 medium and smaller brilliants* (p. 561)

e *Golden Fleece with 3 cornelians surrounded by 132 brilliants*

f *Golden Fleece with 3 irregular-shaped rubies and 70 brilliants* (p. 562)

(All in the Green Vault, Dresden)

a   Golden Fleece with brilliants
and Brazilian topazes

b   Golden Fleece with oriental
topazes

c   Golden Fleece with brilliants
and onyxes

d   Golden Fleece with brilliants
and 3 Indian opals

e   Golden Fleece with 318 brilliants and 3 garnets

f   Golden Fleece with 255 brilliants and hyacinths

(All in the Green Vault, Dresden) (p. 561)

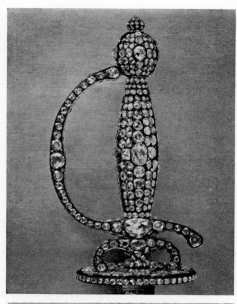

a (left) *Hilt of sword set with 780 rose diamonds. Green Vault, Dresden (p. 561)*

b (right) *Hilt of dress sword set with 1,898 brilliants. Green Vault, Dresden (p. 562)*

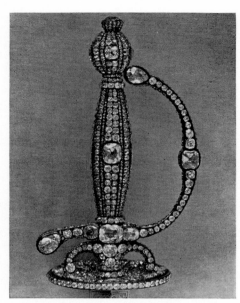

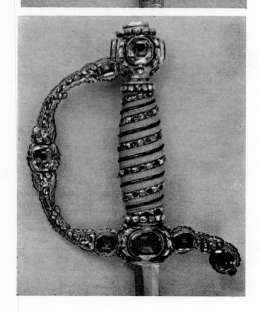

c (left) *Hilt of sword set with brilliants and emeralds. Green Vault, Dresden (p. 562)*

d (right) *Hilt of sword set with brilliants and rubies. Green Vault, Dresden (p. 563)*

e (left) *Hilt of sword set with brilliants and sapphires. Green Vault, Dresden (p. 563)*

f (right) *Hilt of sword set with brilliants and cornelians. Green Vault, Dresden (p. 563)*

emeralds, sapphires and rubies was over 7,000 carats, and in 1938 the total value was estimated at ten million Reichsmarks or a little under one million pounds sterling.

The collection is displayed in cabinets, the most important pieces being in a cabinet with six divisions (*Plate 198, b* and *c*). Between the two world wars some rearrangement was made because, as the result of a settlement with the House of Wettin, some of the jewelled ornaments were returned to the former Royal Houses.

The first division contains ornaments in which rose-cut diamonds are the principal stones. These include:

A set originally of thirty large coat buttons and thirty waistcoat buttons (*Plate 200, c*) set with diamonds, the largest weighing $12\frac{1}{2}$ carats.[1]

A large hat agraffe (*Plate 202, a*) of 15 diamonds weighing $62\frac{1}{2}$ carats and 103 small stones. The middle stone in the pin weighed $24\frac{3}{8}$ cts and one on the rosette $15\frac{5}{8}$ cts.

A pair of shoe buckles (*Plate 202, a*) with 32 large and 72 small rose diamonds.

Two belt buckles and four hatpins set with diamonds.

A shirt stud with a large rose diamond of $12\frac{1}{2}$ cts.

A shoulder knot (*Plate 200, b*) with 20 large and 216 small rose diamonds, the centre stone weighing $40\frac{6}{8}$ cts.

Two Orders of the Golden Fleece with topazes and diamonds (*Plate 203 a* and *c*).

A large Golden Fleece with 83 brilliants.

A small Golden Fleece (*Plate 202, d (i)*) with cats-eyes and 57 brilliants.

A Golden Fleece (*Plate 203, d*) with 3 Indian opals and 101 rose diamonds.

A Golden Fleece (*Plate 203, e*) with 318 brilliants and 3 garnets, one of which weighs $46\frac{6}{8}$ cts.

A Golden Fleece (*Plate 203, f*) with hyacinths and 255 brilliants.

The Polish Order of the White Eagle (*Plate 199, b*) with rubies and 225 rose diamonds including one of $11\frac{4}{8}$ cts.

A sword with the hilt (*Plate 204, a*) set with 780 rose diamonds, the largest weighing $8\frac{1}{8}$ cts.

A cane set with rose diamonds.

The second division contains ornaments in which brilliants are the principal stones:

Thirty coat buttons set with brilliants weighing from 5 to 30 cts.

Thirty waistcoat buttons with brilliants.

Two large and two small shoe buckles set with brilliants.

Four hatpins set with brilliants.

A shoulder knot (*Plate 199, e*) with a green brilliant of $48\frac{4}{8}$ cts, 2 white brilliants of $38\frac{4}{8}$ cts and $20\frac{4}{8}$ cts, and a large number of other brilliants. The Green Brilliant, or Dresden Green, is the most famous in the collection. It was purchased at the Leipzig Fair in 1743 from a Dutch merchant. According to Kluge the price paid was 200,000 thalers or about £30,000. It is usually stated that it was purchased by Augustus the Strong, but as he had died ten years earlier it must have been Frederick Augustus II. Nothing is known of its previous history, but it is probably of Indian origin. It is of a beautiful apple-green colour, faultless and of the purest water.

A hat aigrette in gold with brilliants.

[1] Where the weights are given in fractions old carats are referred to; where they are shown in decimals the metric carat is indicated.

A hat aigrette with a slide set with brilliants.

A small agraffe in the form of a palmette set with brilliants.

A hat agraffe set with brilliants including a very pure stone of 40 cts and 2 brilliants of $38\frac{4}{8}$ and $20\frac{4}{8}$ cts (*Plate 199, c*).

Two cuff links, one with a cloudy brilliant of $13\frac{2}{8}$ cts and the other a yellowish stone of $15\frac{2}{8}$ cts.

A set of 4 yellow brilliants, the largest weighing $29\frac{2}{8}$, 23·19 and 13·48 cts respectively.

A dress sword (*Plate 204, b*) with 1,898 brilliants, the largest of $9\frac{4}{8}$ cts.

A cane set with brilliants.

The Star of the Polish Order of the White Eagle set with rubies and brilliants, the largest weighing $19\frac{6}{8}$ cts.

The third division contains pearls and diamond ornaments which had belonged to Queen Eberhardine of Hohenzollern, the consort of Augustus the Strong.

A four-row necklace of 228 oriental pearls.

A four-row necklace of 177 Saxon pearls from the River Elster but lacking in lustre.

A beautiful diamond pendant with a single pendeloque stone of 17·55 cts (*Plate 199, e*).

A large shoulder knot in the form of a bow of 51 large and 611 small brilliants. The largest stone of $21\frac{6}{8}$ cts (*Plate 199, a*).

A diamond necklace (*Plate 200, a*) of 38 large brilliants of a total weight of 489·44 cts, the pendant stone weighing 30 cts and of the purest water, the next largest stone weighing $24\frac{4}{8}$ cts. One stone is of brownish colour and several are Indian stones of bluish white hue.

A pair of brilliant ear-rings (*Plate 199, d*), the stones weighing $12\frac{4}{8}$ and $16\frac{4}{8}$ cts respectively.

A suite of hair ornaments including one set as a sun with 127 brilliants set *à jour*, one set as a half moon with 65 brilliants and two stars with 91 brilliants.

Forty-eight rings set with diamonds, 1 of which is a brown stone, 2 rose coloured, 1 yellow and 2 bluish.

The fourth division contains the emerald suite (*Plates 201, a and 202, c*).

Thirty-six coat buttons and thirty-six waistcoat buttons besides three large buttons set with emeralds.

Five buckles set with emeralds.

A belt buckle set with emeralds (*Plate 201, a*).

A Golden Fleece (*Plate 202, d (ii)*) set with emeralds.

A hat ornament with large emeralds.

A hat ornament with 4 large emeralds.

A neck ornament of the Polish Order of the White Eagle set with emeralds and brilliants.

Two swords set with emeralds and brilliants, one (*Plate 204, c*) with 90 emeralds and 220 brilliants.

The fifth division contains the ruby suite.

Thirty-eight coat buttons and thirty-six waistcoat buttons set with rubies and brilliants.

Two shirt links set with rubies.

Nine buckles set with rubies and brilliants.

Two large pendant spinels weighing 48 and $59\frac{4}{8}$ cts.

The Star of the Polish Order of the White Eagle with 381 brilliants and 268 oriental rubies.

A neck ornament of the Polish White Eagle with emeralds and 16 rubies and 480 brilliants.

A Golden Fleece (*Plate 202, f*) with 70 brilliants and 3 rubies.

A hat ornament with 12 large rubies and 96 brilliants.

A gold snuff-box set with rubies.
A sword (*Plate 204, d*), the hilt of which is set with rubies and diamonds.
A cane set with rubies.

The sixth division contains the sapphire suite.

Thirty-six waistcoat and forty-eight coat buttons set with sapphires.
Five small and three large buckles set with sapphires and brilliants.
A breast ornament with brilliants and large sapphires.
A shoulder knot set with brilliants and large sapphires.
2 large sapphires (*Plate 200, d*) weighing 194·5 cts and 548 cts respectively, given by Peter the
    Great. The larger is known as Peter the Great's nose.
The Cross of the Polish Order of the White Eagle set with sapphires.
A sword (*Plate 204, e*) set with 19 large and 46 small sapphires and 389 rose diamonds.
A cane set with sapphires.

In another cabinet is a tortoiseshell suite which consisted of buttons, buckles, snuff boxes, swords, a Golden Fleece and an Order of the White Eagle, the ornaments being made of tortoiseshell with gold and brilliant settings. In yet another cabinet was the Cornelian suite (*Plate 201, b*) made for Augustus the Strong in 1719. This included thirty-six coat and thirty-six waistcoat buttons each set with a large cornelian, one large and five small buckles set with brilliants and cornelians, a Golden Fleece (*Plate 202, e*) set with 3 large cornelians and brilliants, a sword (*Plate 204, f*), a hunting dagger, a walking stick, a riding whip and various other ornaments set with cornelians and brilliants. In addition there are two sets of coat and waistcoat buttons set with Saxon topazes and a number of necklaces, girdle chains, pendants and rings of the XVI and XVII centuries. A large collection of Foreign Orders and decorations include the Insignia of the Order of the Garter given to the Elector George IV at the end of the XVII century.

BIBLIOGRAPHY

ERBSTEIN, DR JULUS   *Das Königliche Grüne Gewölbe zu Dresden*, 1906.
LAKING, SIR GUY   *A Record of European Arms and Armour*, Vol. II.
SPONSEL, DR   *Fuhrer durch das Grüne Gewölbe zu Dresden*, 1921.

LIST OF KINGS AND ELECTORS

ELECTORS

1423	Frederick I		
1428	Frederick II. His sons Ernest and Albert divided the state		
1464	Ernest	1464	Albert
1486	Frederick III	1500	George
1525	John	1539	Henry
1532	John Frederick	1541	Maurice
1548	Maurice		

SAXONY

1553	Augustus
1586	Christian I
1591	Christian II
1611	John George I
1656	John George II
1680	John George III
1691	John George IV
1694	Frederick Augustus I. King of Poland 1697
1733	Frederick Augustus II. King of Poland as Augustus III
1763	Frederick Augustus III. King of Saxony 1806

KINGS

1806	Frederick Augustus I
1827	Anthony Clement
1836	Frederick Augustus II (nephew)
1854	John
1873	Albert
1902	George
1904	Frederick Augustus III. Abdicated 1918

CHAPTER TWENTY-THREE

SCOTLAND

The first evidence of a coronation of a Scottish king is that of Malcolm IV, who succeeded at the age of ten in 1153. It is recorded that he was crowned at Scone, and the matter-of-fact account of the event suggests that it was in accordance with long-established practice. At the accession of his brother and successor, William the Lion, the practice of proclaiming the royal descent by a public recitation of the king's genealogy is first mentioned. At William's death in 1214 he was succeeded by Alexander II, and it is recorded that his coronation at Scone was attended by the seven Earls of Scotland, one of whom, the Earl of Fife, enjoyed the special privilege of placing the crown on the King's head. It is probable, at any rate from the time of the next King, Alexander III (1249–86), that the Honours of Scotland, as the Scottish regalia have with affectionate pride been called by historians, consisted of a crown, sceptre and sword. On his death there was a period of confusion, the nobles forming themselves into two hostile parties supporting two of the rival claimants to the throne, John Baliol and Bruce the Old, both descendants in the female line of David the Younger, brother of William the Lion. Edward I, King of England, supported the claims of John Baliol, who was crowned at Scone on 26th December 1292. But Baliol rebelled, and in 1296 his followers were defeated at Dunbar. Edward now seized and removed to England John Baliol's regalia consisting of the royal robe, sceptre, sword, crown and ring,[1] and the Black Rood, the Coronation Stone of Scone, St Margaret's Fragment of the True Cross and many documents. When Robert the Bruce raised the standards of independence he was recognised as King and crowned at Scone on 27th March 1306. Two days later the ceremony was repeated in order to accede to the claim of Isabella, Countess of Buchan, that to her family the MacDuffs, Earls of Fife, belonged the right to place the Scottish king on the throne. In the following June Bruce was defeated at Methuen, and the golden circlet which had been hurriedly made for the coronation fell into the hands of the English.[2] Whether Bruce had new regalia made after Bannockburn we do not know. Reid[3] supposes he did, but this can only be conjectured as there is no evidence. For the coronation of David, the infant son of Bruce, on 24th November 1331 a special sceptre of small size had to be made, and a record for the payment of this still exists.[4] This was the first coronation at which the king was anointed, which rite appears to have

---

[1] Wyntoun: *Cronykil*, Book viii, Chapter xii.   [2] Rymer: *Foedera*, 1012.
[3] John J. Reid: 'The Scottish Regalia', *Proceedings of the Society of Antiquities of Scotland*, Vol. XII, 1889–90.
[4] *Exchequer Rolls*, Vol. 1, 382.

been conferred by the Pope, John XXII, in a Bull[1] which authorised the Bishop of St Andrews or the Bishop of Glasgow to perform the anointing and coronation.

We have no record of the regalia during the next five reigns, but as the kings were crowned—Robert II in Scone in March 1371, Robert III at Scone in August 1390, James I at Scone on 21st May 1424, James II at Holyrood in March 1437 and James III at Kelso in 1560 at the age of nine—the regalia must have been available on these occasions. On the coins and medals from the time of Robert the Bruce the crown is depicted as an open circlet with fleurs-de-lis. Arches first appear on the groat and half-groat variously ascribed to James III and James IV. On one of the panels of the altar-piece, formerly in the Collegiate Church of the Trinity and now preserved in Holyrood Palace, the crown is depicted, which Brooke[2] states is thought to represent with reasonable accuracy the crown worn by James III and James IV. It is a ridged circlet with ten fleurs-de-lis cast in one piece and with crosses fleury which appear for the first time soldered on between each fleur-de-lis. It is decorated with sapphires, rubies and pearls. In the reign of James IV, who was crowned at Scone in June 1488, the arched crown is definitely established, not only on coins but can also be seen on the heads of the King and his Queen Consort, Margaret, daughter of Henry VII of England, in miniature in a prayer book printed about 1500[3] (Plate 205, c and d).

The crown had two arches rising steeply upwards in the 'imperial' shape and surmounted by an orb and cross. This was no doubt borrowed from English practice. There was never an orb among the Scottish regalia nor were the kings depicted with one, which follows the French practice. In the reign of James IV there were other additions to the regalia. In 1494 the Pope Alexander VI sent the King a golden rose and a sceptre by the hands of a prothonotary named Forman. It was greatly altered by James V but is still among the regalia. In 1502 the Lord Treasurer's accounts showed the payment to Robert Selkirk Cutlar for a great sword of honour with a sheath. In October 1502 another gilt sword was delivered to the King at Falkland. In 1507 Pope Julius II sent a *stocco* or sword and a *biretto* or consecrated Cap of Maintenance as a gift to James IV which was delivered with great solemnity in the Church of Holyrood by the papal legate and the Abbot of Dumfermline. This was in accordance with the custom instituted by the Popes in the IX century, to consecrate such ornaments on the night of the Nativity and to send them as a gift to the son of the Church who best deserved them. The sword is still among the regalia.

James V became King when seventeen months old, on the death of his father on the field of Flodden. During his reign many important changes were made to the Honours of Scotland. In 1539 an inventory was taken of the Royal Wardrobe and Jewel House which enumerates:

a crown of gold set with 68 oriental pearls, 20 diamonds and other precious stones, [and it is stated that one fleur-de-lis was missing] a sceptre with a great beryl and a pearl set on top; two

---

[1] Printed in Theiner's *Vetera Monumenta*, p. 244.
[2] Alexander J. S. Brooke: 'Technical Description of the Regalia of Scotland', *Proceedings of the Society of Antiquities of Scotland*.
[3] Vienna Cod. lat. 1897.

a   *Portrait of James IV;* b (right)   *Portrait of Queen Margaret of Denmark, consort of James IV*

Both portraits formerly part of an altarpiece in the Collegiate Church of the Trinity, now in Holyrood Palace (p. 566)

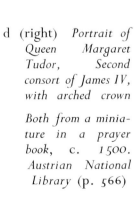

c   (left)   Portrait of
James   IV   with
arched crown

d   (right)   Portrait of
Queen   Margaret
Tudor,   Second
consort of James IV,
with   arched   crown

Both from a minia-
ture   in   a   prayer
book,   c.   1500.
Austrian   National
Library (p. 566)

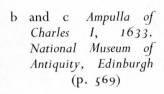

a *Royal crown, 1539–40; royal sceptre, 1494, remade 1536; state sword, 1507, in Edinburgh Castle (pp. 566, 574 and 575)*

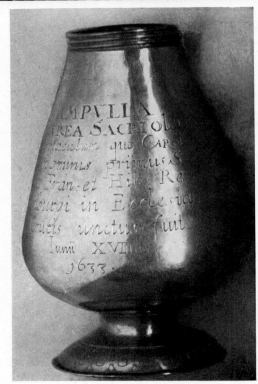

b and c *Ampulla of Charles I, 1633. National Museum of Antiquity, Edinburgh (p. 569)*

swords of honour and two sword belts; the cap sent by the Pope; the insignia of the Orders of the Golden Fleece, the Garter and St Michael of France.

The King soon after ordered the crown to be remade, and in the account of the Lord High Treasurer of Scotland there is a record of a payment on 15th January 1540 to John Mossman, a goldsmith of Edinburgh, for making and fashioning the crown, with a further £19 6s. for the supplying of stones. John Paterson was paid 34s. for making a case for the crown, and Thomas Arthur 72s. 6d. for supplying velvet and satin and for making a bonnet for the crown. The crown was delivered to the King at Holyrood on 13th February. According to a MS. diary of Lord Fountainhal, preserved in the Advocate's Library at Edinburgh, it is stated 'that the crown of Scotland is not the ancient one but was casten of new for James V'. If we take into account the price charged, it seems probable that the materials of the old crown were used and others added to make the crown larger, heavier and more magnificent. The claim that materials from a crown made for Robert the Bruce after Bannockburn were used cannot be substantiated by evidence, though if such a crown did exist it is probable that the materials were incorporated into the successor crowns. The arches, however, do not seem to have been remade, for the quality of their gold is different from that used in the crown. It seems probable that they were taken from the old crown and added. The orb and cross surmounting the arches and the leaf ornaments are of French workmanship, and it has been conjectured that James had them made when he visited Paris in 1536. This crown was made for James V and is that which is still preserved today as the Crown of Scotland (*Plate 206, a*).

James V also had the sceptre remade (*Plate 206, a*), and according to the accounts of the Lord High Treasurer an Edinburgh goldsmith, Adam Leys, was paid £26 4s. for providing 11½ oz silver and for remaking and gilding the sceptre. In January 1537 Pope Paul III sent James V a sword with the exhortation to draw it against his kinsman Henry VIII of England. In the inventory of 1579 only one sword, described as the Sword of State (*Plate 206, a*), is mentioned, the other three having disappeared. We first learn of a queen's crown in the portrait of Margaret of Denmark, Queen of Scotland, on one of the panels of the altar-piece formerly in the Collegiate Church of the Trinity (*Plate 205, b*). She is represented with an open crown enriched with pearls and precious stones. In another portrait of Margaret of Denmark by Van Der Goes[1] the Queen wears side pieces consisting of a network of gold and pearls and on top a richly decorated circlet or coronet. Margaret of Denmark died in 1485, and seven years later James IV married Margaret, daughter of Henry VII of England. There is a record of a crown being made for the Queen directly after her marriage. Mungo Bradie, a goldsmith, was commissioned to undertake the work. The cost of the materials was £77 0s. 5d. and £20 was charged for the workmanship. Although there is no mention of the arches this may be the crown in the miniature portrait of the Queen in a prayer book in Vienna already referred to. There is a record[2] of another queen's crown being made in 1539. This

---

[1] In the collection of Her Majesty the Queen in Holyrood House and now on loan to the National Gallery of Scotland.

[2] Accounts of the Lord High Treasurer, 5th October 1539.

would have been for James V's second wife, Mary, daughter of the Duke of Guise, whom the King had married in 1538. It was made by John Mossman and cost £65. The fate of this crown is not known. Four months later a sceptre was made for the Queen. Its weight was 31½ oz of silver and the total cost £54 1s. 9d. It is described by John Tennand on 28th November 1542 as 'ane sceptour with ane qukyte hande'. This suggests beyond reasonable doubt that it was a Hand of Justice and took this form in view of the Queen's French origin.

On the death of James V on 14th December 1542 he was succeeded by his infant daughter Mary, who was crowned on 9th September 1543 at Stirling, when nine months old. On 24th April 1558, at the age of fifteen years, she was married to Francis, King of France. Francis died in August 1561 and Mary returned to Scotland and she brought with her many of the rich jewels which she had received in France. When in 1568 Mary crossed the border her adherents retained possession of Edinburgh Castle and other strongholds of the kingdom. Edinburgh Castle was held by Kirkaldy of Grange, and there the Honours of Scotland were kept, and were, therefore, not available for the King's party who wished to hold a Parliament at Stirling in 1571. For this occasion a new set of regalia was made by the goldsmith Mungo Bradie, consisting of a crown, a sceptre of silver gilt, a sword and a royal robe. These ornaments were used on 17th January 1572, and until 1573. On 25th April 1573 the Governor of Edinburgh Castle refused to deliver the regalia to Sir William Ivary, commanding the English besieging force, but a month later the King was forced to surrender, and the King's adherents, having gained possession of the regalia, the Civil War came to an end. James VI was crowned on 29th July 1569 at Stirling, on the abdication of his mother, Mary Queen of Scots. When he married Anne of Denmark in 1590 the Queen was crowned on 17th May at Holyrood. The ceremony seems to have been somewhat of an ordeal as it lasted from 10 a.m. until 5 p.m. There was no singing of any kind, and the unfortunate Queen had to listen to six discourses, three addresses and three sermons, the last being in English, French and Latin. After this Mr Andrew Melville recited 200 lines of a poem of his own composition.[1] The Queen received a sceptre from Mr Melville and the King handed the crown to the Duke of Lennox, who placed it on his head. At this time the Honours of Scotland were lodged in Edinburgh Castle, and by an Act of Parliament in April 1585 the custody of the Honours was vested in the Captain of the Castle. When James succeeded to the English throne in 1603 they remained in Scotland, although he took with him many of the jewels in his possession. On James's death in 1625 his son Charles succeeded to the throne and on 18th June 1633 was crowned at Holyrood. We have very little information about Scottish coronations before this time. In eight cases the ceremony had to take place so soon after the death of the preceding king that there was no time for elaborate preparations. Furthermore, ten of the sovereigns were but children at the time of their coronations and in some cases mere infants. Except in four cases the coronations had all taken place at Scone, but as the church there was in ruins Charles chose Holyrood. The service was drawn up by Laud, who was at the time Bishop of London. We

[1] The Rev. R. M. Woolley: *Coronation Rites.*

have two fairly full accounts of the ceremony.[1] A long time was taken in the preparations of the ceremonial, and although Sir James Balfour was consulted the coronation was performed in accordance with the rites of the English Church[2] which caused some ill feeling and acrimonious criticism. There are only a few points which need be noted. The regalia consisted of the crown, sceptre and the sword, and the spurs were added for the first time. The anointing was a matter of some confusion. The draft of the ceremony directed that a silver ampulla should be carried by Lyon.[3] Lyon in his report mentions two jugs of oil carried by Lyon, one of which was given to the Marischal and the other to the Constable, who gave this to the bishops. Bute, who takes this description from the two official documents regarding the coronation, says that the Bishop of Dunblane handed Lyon a golden vessel containing the oil which Lyon describes habitually as the *sacred* oil. This golden vessel has come to light in recent years. Cooper[4] states that 'the golden ampulla or vial with the sacred oil' referred to in the official records still exists in the custody of Sir George Grant Suttie. In 1907 it was shown to the Scottish Ecclesiastical Society during a visit to Seaton Chapel. The minister, Mr Anderson, said at the time that the ampulla was known to have been kept very private from George IV when he had visited Preston Grange. It is not known how the ampulla came to Balgone. It has been suggested that it might have been furnished for the coronation by George Guthrie, who was then Treasurer at Edinburgh and may have retained it after use.[5] The ampulla next appears in March 1948 when it was offered for sale in London, but the trustees of the Suttie Estate agreed to it being withdrawn from the auction to be purchased by the National Museum of Antiquities of Scotland. The ampulla (*Plate 206, b* and *c*) is made of gold and is 5 feet high and weighs 3½ oz troy. It consists of a pear-shaped vessel on a low pedestal which is closed on top with a lid which is provided with two horns through which the oil can be poured. It bears the inscription:

> AMPULLA
> *Avrea Sacri olei*
> *Receptaculum quo Carolvs eius nominis primus Scotiae*
> *Anglie Fran; et itib; Rex*
> *Edinburg; in Ecclesic*
> *S:Crucis unctus fuit*
> *Iunii xviii*
> *1633.*

We must now return to the narrative of the regalia. In 1637, at the outbreak of the Civil War, the Honours were removed from Edinburgh Castle to Dalkeith. In 1639, however, they fell into the hands of the Covenanters and were used at the Assembly of Parliament in August of that year and on the occasion of its reassembly on 11th June 1640.

1 *The form of King Charles I, His Coronation in Scotland, June 11th 1633.* Written with Mr Dell's own hand; Secretary to the late Archbishop of Canterbury, Dr Laud. Sir James Balfour: *Annals of Scotland*, Vol. IV, p. 383.

2 See John, Marquis of Bute: *Scottish Coronations*.

3 Sir James Balfour.   4 J. Cooper: *Four Scottish Coronations*.

5 Robert B. K. Staples: 'Charles I's Coronation Ampulla', in *Proceedings of the Society of Antiquities of Scotland*, Vol. XXXII, 1947–8.

Later, however, they fell into the hands of the Presbyterian party and were held in the custody of the Lord Treasurer at Edinburgh Castle, except during the Sittings of Parliament when the Earl Marischal took on the responsibility. It is recorded that they were so used in Edinburgh on 15th May and 5th July 1650. After the Battle of Dunbar on 3rd September 1650 the English took Edinburgh Castle, but the Honours had been removed, and although it has not been recorded where they were kept it may possibly have been at Dunnottar Castle. They were brought out for the sittings of Parliament at Perth on 26th November and 30th December of that year and for the coronations of Charles II at Scone on 1st January 1651. This coronation, the last to be held at Scone and in Scotland, followed very much the lines of that of Charles I, but it was performed as a Presbyterian rite and the unction was omitted. The crown was placed on the King's head by the Marquis of Argyle and the King received a sceptre from the Earl of Crawford. He was girt with the sword by the Great Constable and the Earl Marischal put on the spurs.

After the coronation the Honours were again used at the sittings of Parliament on 13th and 31st March 1651 at Perth, and on 23rd May at Stirling. At the last sitting of Parliament on 6th January 1651 it was ordained that the Earl Marischal should take the Honours to Dunnottar Castle for safe keeping. The Earl Marischal, however, had been taken prisoner by the English, but he managed to convey a message to his wife together with the key of the strong-room in which the regalia were lodged, bidding her to deliver it to George Ogilvy of Barras, to whom he gave the governorship of the castle, which he was to hold in the name of the King. With a garrison of only forty men, two sergeants and a lieutenant, Ogilvy busied himself with stocking the castle with provisions during the weeks that lapsed before the arrival of the English, a task he found difficult even for so small a garrison. In November the English forces arrived at Dunnottar. Twice they summoned Ogilvy to surrender but each time he emphatically refused, declaring that he held the castle in the name of the King. Dunnottar was perched high on a precipitous rock projecting into the North Sea and was a strong natural position, almost impregnable if properly garrisoned. With his small number of men and the shortage of provisions the position became precarious, and Ogilvy explored the possibilities of removing the regalia by sea, but this proved to be impossible. The months went by and the English commander did not seem to realise how lightly the Castle was held and took no steps to harry the garrison. He even permitted non-combatants to pass freely through the lines. This latter fact enabled a bold but simple plan to be devised by Mrs Ogilvy, who was in the castle with her husband. Mrs Granger, the wife of the minister of a neighbouring parish, obtained permission to visit Mrs Ogilvy and the two of them hatched a plot to remove the regalia to a place of greater safety. There are several stories as to how the Honours were actually removed, but the one which is given popular credence is that which stated that Mrs Granger concealed the crown in her lap and the sword and the sceptre in a bundle of flax carried by her serving woman. The two women had to pass through the English lines, and it is said that the gallant but unsuspicious English general assisted the ladies to mount their horses. Whatever may be the truth of how the Honours were actually removed, there can be no doubt that it was a bold plan which was carried through successfully only by the bravery of those concerned. It was said that Ogilvy was kept in ignorance of the plan until after it had been successfully executed, but this would seem to be improbable. The Honours were safely conveyed to the Grangers' bedroom and were hidden in the bottom of a bed until Mrs Granger had the opportunity of burying them. This was done with the assistance of her husband in Kinneff Church.

Although the safe removal of the Honours must have been a great relief to Ogilvy he doggedly continued to keep the English at bay until, on 4th June 1652, after a siege of six months, he surrendered, honourable terms being granted by the English commander. One of the articles of the capitulation read: 'That the Croun and Scepter of Scotland, together with all other ensigns of Regallitie, be delivered to mee, or a good account thereof, for the use of Parliament, etc. But when they took possession of the castle and its contents the English found no trace of the regalia, and great was their wrath and indignation. Ogilvy explained that the regalia had been removed to France by John Keith, the younger son of the Countess Marischal, and in spite of there being evidence to strengthen the possibility of this story Ogilvy and his wife were heavily fined and imprisoned.[1]

Although Mrs Ogilvy died from the effects of her treatment and the Grangers also suffered from persecution, no word of the secret was betrayed. For some nine years the regalia lay hidden in Kinneff Church. Ogilvy occasionally visited the Grangers and brought fresh linen. The Honours would then be disinterred and taken into the Manse, where, according to Mrs Granger, they were 'ayred in night tyme before ane fyre'. Wrapped in the fresh linen they were reburied. At the Restoration the Countess Marischal was the first to inform Charles II that the regalia was in safe keeping, and she received a written order from him to produce them at the forthcoming meeting of Parliament. Unfortunately there followed a quarrel between the Keith and Ogilvy families in regard to the part each had played in the saving of the Honours. These two families and the Grangers had all done their parts well and deserved to be rewarded for the service which they had rendered to their country. The King was not ungrateful for what they had done and bestowed upon them what he considered to be suitable rewards. The unseemly quarrel that ensued as to the proper reward that each should have merely detracted from the heroic service that they had undoubtedly rendered. Finally the Countess's son was created Earl of Kintore with the office of Knight Marischal and was given a salary of £400 a year, while Ogilvy, in spite of his bravery and after sacrificing a large part of his fortune in the defence of the regalia, received the somewhat empty reward of a baronetcy and an augmented blazon of arms. The Scottish Parliament awarded Mrs Granger two thousand merks as a testimony 'of their

[1] John Keith, having remained in France for some two years, followed Middleton to Holland with the intention of joining his expedition. He arrived too late, however, and proceeded to Scotland. Landing in Fife he was arrested by the English but escaped in disguise, and after several adventures he joined Middleton until the skirmish at Lochgarry on 26th July 1654 which finally scattered the Royalist troops, who took refuge in the hills. During this time Keith obtained from Middleton a receipt for the Honours purporting to have been given in 1652 in Paris, 'tho it was trewly subscribed at Capoch in Lochwaber'. When he finally surrendered to the English he produced this receipt and was questioned as to the part he took in carrying the Honours to France, with the result that all search for them in Scotland was given up.

sense of her service' in preserving the Honours of the Kingdom.[1] The Honours were restored to Edinburgh Castle with due ceremony.

When the Scottish Parliament met on 8th May 1662 the regalia took their long-established place and were honoured with salutes of guns. At the adjournment on 15th September 1662 they were conveyed from Edinburgh Castle in the Commissioner's coach with six horses, trumpets sounding and guns firing salutes. Similar ceremonies were held whenever the Honours were brought from the castle or returned there during each succeeding Scottish Parliament. In 1689 occurred an incident which does not seem to have attracted much attention. It was believed that Charles I had wanted the Scottish regalia to be taken to England in order that he might be crowned with them there.[2] Sir Walter Scott[3] writes:

there is a constant tradition for which we are not able to produce a written or distinct authority that Charles I desired to have the crown of Scotland sent up to London to be used for his coronation there but this having been declined by the Scottish Privy Council as contrary to the law of the Kingdom he was induced to undertake a journey to Scotland in order to be there crowned king.

The idea of the Honours crossing the border was, of course, an anathema to all true Scots, but on 24th April 1689, after the accession of William III and Mary to the throne of England, we find in the Proceedings of the Estates in Scotland a record which reads:

The person moved that the State should proffer the names of three members, one of each Estate, who were to wait on their Majesties with the offer of the crown and it was carried by a Vote that the three members should be the Earl of Argyle, Sir James Montgomery and Sir John Dalyrimple. Lord Cardross obtained the permission of the Estates to go to London.

There is then the official account described as:

an account of what passed in the Banqueting House at Whitehall on 11th day of May 1684 at the Delivery of the Crown of Scotland.[4] The Earl of Argyle, Sir James Montgomery of Skelmarly and Sir John Dalyrimple, the Commissioners sent by the Meeting of the Estates of Scotland to offer their Majesties the Crown of the Kingdom; about three of the clock met at the Council Chamber and from thence were conducted by Sir Charles Cottrel, Master of the Ceremonies, attended by men of Nobility and Gentry of that Kingdom who reside in and about this place to the Banqueting House where the King and Queen came attended by many persons of quality the Sword being carried before them by Lord Cardross (and their Majesties being placed on the throne under a rich canopy) they concluded themselves of their commission as follows; in the last place the coronation oath was tendered to their Majesties which my Lord Argyle pronounced distinctly word by word and their Majesties repeated it after him holding up their right hands according to the custom of taking

---

[1] The part played by the Keith family appears in *Papers Relative to the Preservation of the Honours of Scotland in Dunnottar Castle, 1651–2*; edited with an introduction and notes by Charles Howden in Vol. XXVI of the Publications of the Scottish History Society in December 1896. The part played by the Ogilvy family is contained in a book by D. C. Barron entitled *In Defence of the Regalia* published in 1910.

[2] James Grant: *Memorials of Edinburgh Castle*.

[3] Sir Walter Scott: *Memorandum on the Scottish Regalia on Miscellaneous Prose Works*.

[4] This event is also briefly referred to by John Evelyn in his *Diaries*.

the oath in Scotland. Then their Majesties signed the oath in the presence of the Commissioners. God save King William and Queen Mary. *Finis*.[1]

There are several records of the year 1689 of the Honours continuing to be required at the meetings of Parliament and also when the royal assent was given to Acts of Parliament by touching the documents with the sceptre. On these occasions the procession known as 'The Ryding of the Parliament' was recognised by orders of the Privy Council, showing that the regalia took its place in due order. When the Act of Union was passed in 1707 the discussions became somewhat acrimonious when it was reported that the Honours were to be taken to England, and in order to prevent such a possibility an article was introduced into the Treaty which reads:

> That the croun, sceptre and Sword of State, Records of Parliament, etc., continue to be kept as they are within that part of the United Kingdom called Scotland; and that they shall so remain in all time coming notwithstanding the Union; on 16th January 1707, the Treaty of the Union was solemnly ratified and touched with the Sceptre by the Earl of Seafield, Lord Chancellor.

On 26th March 1707 the Honours of Scotland were locked up in the oak chest in the Crown Room of Scotland under bolt and bar, and a deposition was made to the fact that this was done.

After many years, suspicions were aroused that the Honours had been removed, contrary to the Treaty, to England, but no steps were taken to prove this. In fact, the Crown Room was left undisturbed until, in 1794, a royal warrant was issued for the room to be opened to ascertain whether some missing documents were stored there. The documents were not found, but the commissioners saw the great oak chest in which the regalia were supposed to be contained, but, having no legal power to open it, they departed, having first locked the room and secured it.

The regalia might have been lying hidden in the chest to this day had it not been that Sir Walter Scott and others interested themselves in the fate of the Honours. At length, George IV in 1817 agreed to issue a royal warrant to the Scottish officers of state and certain public persons, including Sir Walter, to open the Crown Room and see whether the regalia were intact. Sir Walter has himself described the scene thus:

> The chest seemed to return a hollow and empty sound to the strokes of the hammer, and even those whose expectations had been most sanguine felt at the moment the probability of disappointment and could not but be sensible that, should the search confirm their forebodings, it would only serve to show that a national affront and injury had been sustained, for which it might be difficult, or rather impossible, to obtain any redress. They joy was therefore extreme when the ponderous lid of the chest being forced open, at the expense of some trouble and labour, the Regalia were discovered lying at the bottom covered with linen cloths exactly as they had been left in the year 1707. . . . The rejoicing was so general and sincere, and so plainly to show that,

1 While it is clear that the Sword of State was carried at the ceremony it is not so evident that the crown was brought to London for the occasion. The words in the record 'to wait on their Majesties with the offer of the crown' could be metaphorical. But the description of 'The Delivery of the Crown of Scotland' seems to be more explicit, though it would have been contrary to popular feeling for the crown to have been brought across the border.

however altered in other respects, the people of Scotland had lost nothing of their national enthusiasm which formerly had displayed itself in grief for the loss of these emblematic Honours, and now was expressed in joy for their recovery.

The following year royal instructions were issued for the safe keeping of the regalia, and arrangements were made for the public to be admitted to view them. A few years later William IV added the lesser ornaments which could claim a Scottish origin.

Since then the regalia have been on display in the Crown Room of the castle, and in 1953 were taken to St Giles Cathedral in Edinburgh, where they were presented to Queen Elizabeth II during her State visit following her Coronation in London.

The Crown of Scotland is very elegant in design. It consists of a circlet or band of gold which is surmounted by ten gold crosses fleury and ten gold fleurs-de-lis set alternately. From the circlet spring two full arches, the sign of independent and hereditary monarchy, which are depressed at the centre, thus making it a 'Royal' as opposed to an 'Imperial' crown. At the point of intersection of the arches there rests an orb, symbol of sovereign authority and majesty. From the orb rises a cross *pattée*. All the gold used in the crown is probably of Scottish origin. The decorations include enamel, diamonds, pearls and precious stones. Inside is a bonnet of crimson silk velvet trimmed with ermine and the total weight is 56 oz 5 dwt troy. It rests on a crimson silk velvet cushion of recent manufacture, trimmed with gold lace and with gold tassels at the corners.

A closer inspection of the Crown will reveal a number of points of interest. The circlet is adorned with 22 semi-precious stones set equidistant and with a pearl between each pair. These stones, which are set in projecting gold collets, have been cut in various styles. There are 9 carbuncles, 4 jacinths, 4 amethysts, 2 white topazes, 2 rock crystals foiled to resemble emeralds and 1 white topaz with yellow foil behind. According to tradition, all these stones are of Scottish origin, but this has been proved to be impossible except perhaps in the case of the rock crystals, and even the origin of these is doubtful. They all belong to species which were of considerably greater value in former days and to which special magical properties were attributed. Carbuncles were said to keep away poison, plague, sadness, evil thoughts and wicked spirits; jacinths were believed to procure sleep, riches, honour and wisdom; amethysts, it is said, dispelled sleep, sharpened the intellect and were an antidote against poison; whilst to the topaz was attributed the power to discover poison and to quench the heat of boiling water, and its powers increased and decreased with the rising and the waning of the moon. Of the 20 pearls on the circlet 13 are oriental and 7 are Scottish.

The fleurs-de-lis are of plain gold unadorned but each cross fleury was originally adorned with 4 pearls with a table-cut white topaz in the centre. One of the white topazes has been lost and replaced by a pearl, while in five other crosses one or more pearls are missing. Below each cross fleury and fleur-de-lis there was formerly a setting containing alternately a diamond and blue enamel. There are now only 8 diamonds, and one of the blue enamel fillings is also missing. The diamonds were cut in an ancient Indian style and this has assisted the experts in ascertaining the date of the crown.

The arches are of gold decorated with enamelled oak-leaves. The workmanship is considered to be French and it is obvious that they were added to the crown at a later date. Resting on the arches is the orb or celestial globe. It is of gold, enamelled blue and is powdered with stars, a peculiarity found elsewhere only in Norway and Sweden. Above rises a large cross *pattée* which is decorated with 8 pearls and 1 amethyst. The bonnet has at each quarter a large Oriental pearl mounted on a gold ornament. Formerly the bonnet was of purple; English crowns are the only others in which ermine is used.

The Scottish Sceptre was presented to James IV in 1494 by Pope Alexander VI. It is no longer in its original state, for James V, who apparently thought that he could improve on the existing regalia ordered it to be altered; and so, in 1536, it was almost entirely remade. On its arrival in Scotland it weighed but 15 oz and was a fine example of delicate Italian workmanship. By James's orders more gold was added thus bringing the weight up to 26½ oz which, no doubt, he thought to be more in keeping with the dignity of a King of Scotland. In spite of its enhanced weight, much of the beauty of the workmanship was lost, for the Scottish goldsmiths had never reached a very high standard of craftsmanship. The sceptre may be divided into three parts: first the rod and handle; second, the head; and third, the rock crystal globe and finial.

The rod is hexagonal in shape and is divided by three knobs into a handle and two shafts each decorated on three of the six sides. The lower shaft is decorated with engraved fleurs-de-lis and thistles, while the upper shaft is decorated with grotesques, cups and foliage. On the plain sides of the lower shaft are engraved the letters *I* and *R* and the figure 5 for Jacobus Rex V. Resting on the upper shaft is a capital from which rises the head of the sceptre. The head of the sceptre is divided into three by three dolphins, between which are three figures on corbels. In the first is the Virgin Mary, wearing an open crown, holding in her right hand the Infant Christ, and in her left hand a mound with a cross. On her right is St Andrew in an apostolic robe and with a halo on his head. In the saint's left hand is an open book and in his right hand St Andrew's cross, the upper part of which has been broken off. On the left of the Virgin Mary is St James wearing a loose, flowing robe. His right hand holds an open book, and in the left hand he carries a pilgrim's staff. Each figure is surmounted by a Gothic canopy. On the capital rests a pedestal from which rises a cuplike clasp of three bands of twisted wire which hold in place a globe of rock crystal. This globe is cut and polished smooth all over and weighs 7 oz 1 dwt. A natural fissure runs through it diagonally. The three bands are held in position at the top by a leaf ornament from which rises an open ornament formed of six bands of wire. This ornament is, in turn, surmounted by a leaf ornament holding an egg-shaped finial of silver gilt on the top of which rises a Scottish pearl.

The whole sceptre is of silver and has been gilded all over. It is not surprising that, during the adventures the regalia experienced, the top of the sceptre suffered damage and at one time the rock crystal globe sloped at an angle. There are signs of this having been repaired, but the damage can only be detected by a close examination.

The Sword of State and belt are a fine piece of Italian workmanship presented to King James IV in 1507 together with a consecrated hat, and both gifts delivered at the

Church of Holyrood with great solemnity by the papal legate. Bishop Lesley, in his *History of Scotland*, states:

> Julis the Second, Paip for the tyme, send ane ambassadour to the King, declaring him to be Protectour and Defendour of Christian faythe, and, in sign thereof, send unto him ane purpour diademe wrocht with flouris of gold, with anew sword, having the hiltis and skabert of gold, sett with precious stains.

He appears to have confused two embassies sent by the Pope, for the title of Protector and Defender of the Faith was bestowed in 1537.

The total length of the sword is more than 4 ft 6 in. The pommel and grip of it are of silver gilded over and decorated with delicate *repoussé* work. The handle is of a graceful form ending in oak-leaves and acorns. The blade is very thin and in the course of time it has become very much damaged. At the top end of the blade are etched the figures of St Peter and St Paul, while in the centre is an etched inscription filled in with gold: *JULIVS II PONT MAX N*. On one side this inscription is very faint, probably accounted for by the fact that the blade was once broken and had to be welded and reground. The scabbard is made of wood and covered with crimson silk velvet on which is mounted silver gilt *repoussé* work. On the front of the scabbard are the Arms of Pope Julius II in enamel. Other enamel plates have been lost but the *repoussé* decoration is intact and depicts acorns, oak-leaves, dolphins and grotesque mask. The decoration on the back of the scabbard has suffered much damage from the ravages of time but there remains much of the *repoussé* decoration which elaborates a design of acorns, oak-leaves and grotesque masks. Some of the damage appears to have been repaired by Scottish goldsmiths. The sword belt formed part of the original papal gift and bore the Arms of Pope Julius II and an elaborate decoration. When the regalia were removed from Dunnottar Castle this belt was retained by Governor Ogilvy as a piece of evidence that the regalia had been in his custody. Long afterwards it was discovered carefully concealed in a wall of the house of Barras. In 1889 it was found to be in the possession of a descendant of Ogilvy of Barras, and it is now with the original sword. It has, however, suffered very much during the course of its adventures and its former beauties are no longer discernible.

There is a second sceptre or rod among the regalia today which since 1817 has been described as the High Lord Treasurer's mace. It is a rod of silver gilt a little more than 3 ft long. The top is surmounted by an oval globe of rectangular crystal cut with square facets and held in position by four bands. On top of the crystal rests a cross *pattée* decorated at each extremity and in the centre with coloured balls. Sir Walter Scott in his *Papers* relative to the regalia states that as there is no mention of this ornament in the Act of Delivery of the Regalia and Deposition which was made when the regalia were placed in the chest in 1707 this proves it to be the Mace of Office peculiar to the Treasurer of Scotland. Although it had probably been deposited in the chest by the Earl of Glasgow it is thought from the marks on the mace that it was made before 1519, and it has been surmised by some authorities that this was the queen's sceptre. This suggestion, however, is hardly acceptable, as from the description it is clear that the queen's sceptre was surmounted by a Hand of Justice. It seems likely that it was made as a royal ornament because the crystal globe and cross are emblems only suitable for a king or queen and it would have been most unusual for the mace of a great officer of state to have been decorated with a crystal. It seems likely, therefore, that it was an old royal sceptre, possibly that in use before the papal gift. Apart from the Honours of Scotland there are also a number of ornaments which were deposited in the Crown Room on 18th December 1830 by William IV. They include a collar and a George of the Order of the Garter, the latter being decorated with 118 rose- and table-cut diamonds, and a St Andrew of the Order of the Thistle. The origin of the Scottish Order of the Thistle is obscure, but it was revived or possibly instituted in 1540 by James V, and today it exists as one of the great Orders of Europe. This jewel of St Andrew is oval in form, and the centre is a chalcedony cut with a cameo of St Andrew with his cross and with a Scottish thistle below. Around the cameo set in a gold band are 12 large rose diamonds. On the reverse is a garter, inlaid with blue enamel, bearing the motto in gold *NEMO ME IMPUNE LACESSIT*. Within this garter is a small compartment, oval in shape, covered by a lid. Beneath the lid is a miniature, painted in watercolours on ivory, of Princess Clementina Maria Sobieski, who in 1719 married Prince James Francis Edward Stewart, son of James VII. On the lid itself is enamelled a Scottish thistle and leaves. This beautiful ornament is the work of different artists and their names are unknown. The exquisitely cut cameo is probably the work of a London jeweller. This ornament is the only one of those shown in the Crown Room at Edinburgh Castle which has recently been used. When the sovereign is in residence at Holyrood the insignia of the Order of the Thistle are sometimes worn, including this jewel.

A ruby ring which was among the ornaments bequeathed by Cardinal York to George II is of gold and has a peculiar arrangement inasmuch as it may fit fingers of any size. It is jointed like a bracelet and there are a number of notches by which its size may be regulated. It is surmounted by a large ruby which, however, is very thin, and the colour of which is rather pale. On the upper surface or table is engraved a cross. Around the ruby is a girdle of 26 small diamonds. According to tradition this is the Coronation Ring of Charles I, but there is no record of such a coronation ring, and thus proof is not possible.

The oak chest is a fine specimen of such chests as were in common use in Scotland in the XVI and XVII centuries. The oak is from Danzig, but the workmanship is Scottish. It is so large that it cannot be taken through the door of the Crown Room and, therefore, it must have been assembled inside. When the search was made for the regalia in 1817 the keys could not be found and the chest had to be forced open.

BIBLIOGRAPHY

BUTE, JOHN MARQUIS OF	*Scottish Coronations.*
BROOKE, ALEXANDER J. S.	*Technical Description of the Regalia of Scotland.*
COOPER, J.	*Four Scottish Coronations.*
GRANT, JAMES	*Memorials of Edinburgh Castle.*

SCOTT, SIR WALTER — 'Memorandum on the Scottish Regalia', in *Miscellaneous Prose Works*.

STAPLES, ROBERT B. K. — *Charles I's Coronation Ampulla*.

WOOLLEY, THE REV. R. M. — *Coronation Rites*.

KINGS AND CORONATIONS

1153 Malcolm IV. Crowned at Scone
1165 William the Lion
1214 Alexander II. Crowned at Scone
1249 Alexander III
1292 John Baliol. Crowned at Scone on 26th December 1292
1306 Robert the Bruce. Crowned at Scone on 27th March 1306
1331 David. Crowned on 24th November 1331
1371 Robert II. Crowned in March 1371
1390 Robert III. Crowned in August 1390
1424 James I. Crowned on 21st May 1424
1437 James II. Crowned in March 1437 at Holyrood
1460 James III. Crowned in 1560 at Kelso
1488 James IV. Crowned in June 1488 at Scone
        James V
1542 Mary. Crowned on 9th September 1543. (Her husband was King of France and their marriage took place in 1558)
1569 James VI. Crowned on 29th July 1569. His wife, Anne of Denmark, was crowned on 17th May 1590 at Holyrood
1625 Charles I. Crowned on 18th June 1633 at Holyrood
1650 Charles II. Crowned on 1st January 1651

CHAPTER TWENTY-FOUR

SPAIN

Strictly speaking there are no Spanish crown jewels. Apart from some formal items made in the XIX century a number of important ornaments have survived, but these in no way form a collection of regalia, as their incidence and origins are diverse and their survival has been in the main accidental. Probably the most important reason for this is that proper coronations in the three main Spanish kingdoms were abandoned early. The coronation ceremony in Castile, which could trace its origins to the Visigothic ceremony, the first in Western Europe, came to reflect the certainties and uncertainties of the royal succession and was abandoned at the end of the XIV century when the Trastamaran dynasty felt itself secure. The Aragonese ceremony lasted a little longer, retaining its full glory and traditional importance until the beginning of the XV century when it suddenly ceased, for reasons which can only be conjectured. The ceremony in Navarre, with elevation on the shield, lasted until the Spanish part of the kingdom was conquered by Ferdinand the Catholic in 1512. Thus by the time Spain was finally welded together there was no coronation ceremony and no need for permanent attributes of royalty. And though the newly found wealth of America with its great riches in precious stones and pearls would have enabled the Spanish Hapsburgs to have created one of the greatest collections of crown jewels in Europe, it probably never occurred to this austere dynasty to do so. Personal ostentation was controlled by sumptuary laws, and the craftsmen under royal patronage tended to concentrate on ecclesiastical ornaments.

With the exception of the swords in the Royal Armoury in Madrid no royal ornaments were handed down through successive generations of monarchs for any length of time, and this is particularly true of the Middle Ages. None of those pieces which have survived have done so in circumstances in which they could have been used by future rulers. In fact they only survived because they were in the custody of a great church, or buried in an undefiled grave or, in the case of the Visigothic crowns, in the ground. Not surprisingly these survivors are mostly unconnected with each other and are uncharacteristic of the ornaments of their day. The more normal ones have disappeared for a variety of causes. In the Middle Ages many pieces were pawned or sold, others were broken up and remade, and this practice was most common when new styles of goldsmith's work became fashionable in the XVI century.[1] The XIX century saw the destruction of two of the great mediaeval pantheons. The graves of the Aragonese kings at the Monastery of Poblet were destroyed in the disturbances of the 1830's, while Napoleon's troops broke open the royal tombs at St Isidore's in Leon and afterwards watered their horses in the empty stone coffins. Among other instances of looting

[1] For several examples see Baron Ch. Davillier: *Recherches sur l'Orfévrerie en Espagne*, Paris 1879, pp. 132–4.

in the Peninsular War it is said that the French removed ten campaign wagons of silver and gold from the Escorial. More recently burglaries have removed some of the surviving items, as when the Guarrazar crowns were stolen from the Royal Armoury in 1921.

The fact that most of the surviving ornaments are unconnected and uncharacteristic may explain why this subject as a whole has not attracted Spanish writers. Although a number of extremely valuable monographs have been published on most of the surviving ornaments, the nearest there is to a complete account of Spanish royal ornaments are the relevant chapters of Schramm's *Herrschaftszeichen und Staatssymbolik*.[1] There is, however, plenty of material to work on. In Castile there is a wealth of miniatures from the XI century, and the accumulative evidence of these supported by such other sources as seals and coins gives us a clear idea of how the crowns developed. From the middle of the XIV century these pictorial sources are augmented by royal wills and from the XV century by inventories. In Aragon, where there are fewer contemporary miniatures, there are a number of very detailed inventories from 1303 onwards. The material has been published in a number of different places, but has not been previously collated and assessed. Undoubtedly there are other inventories and accounts in the rich archives of Castile and Aragon which have not yet been published. There are also many fields for further research. One of the most interesting would be the question of the extent to which the crown jewels were regarded at various times as being part of the 'state treasure' or as the personal possessions of the monarchs.

THE VISIGOTHIC KINGDOM

The Visigoths first entered the Iberian Peninsula under their second king, Ataulf, in A.D. 414. His successors established themselves at Toulouse, at times acting as allies of the Romans, at others expanding their kingdom at the expense of Rome. From these early days there is evidence that the royal treasure of the Visigoths played an important part in their conception of sovereignty. When King Theodored was killed at the Battle of Chalons 451, at which the Roman–Visigothic alliance defeated Attila, his eldest son Turismund was elected King on the field. He would have pursued Attila had not the Roman commander, Aetius, advised him to return to Toulouse lest his brothers should sieze the royal treasure and usurp the throne.

Between 453 and 507, under Theodoric, Euric and Alaric, the Visigothic kingdom expanded over a large part of the peninsula. Towards the end of this period, however, their lands in the south of France were being attacked by the Franks and Burgundians, and after the death of Alaric they lost the greater part of their Gallic possessions. From 511 to 526 the Ostrogoth Theodoric ruled the Visigoths as regent for his nephew, Alaric's son Almaric. In 511, when Carcassonne was threatened by the Franks, Theodoric removed the Visigothic royal treasure to Ravenna. According to Procopius this treasure included trophies from the sack of Rome by Alaric I in 410, among them being loot from the Temple of Jerusalem destroyed by the Emperor Titus, above all a 'table of Solomon'[2] which it is tempting to identify with that looted by the Arabs in Toledo

---

[1] P. E. Schramm: *Herrschaftszeichen und Staatssymbolik*, Stuttgart 1954–6.

[2] Davillier (op. cit.: pp. 7–8) points out that the term *Solomonis* might merely mean that the article was extremely precious and not necessarily that it was attributed to King Solomon.

200 years later. Part at least of this treasure was returned to the Visigothic court, now established at Toledo, after the death of Theodoric in 526.

In the middle of the VI century, when Justinian was attempting to revive the Roman Empire, an opportunity for him to intervene in Spain occurred. A rebellion broke out against King Agila (549–54), who lost most of the royal treasure to the rebels at Cordoba. With the outward sign of monarchy in their hands the latter elected a rival king, Atangild, who asked for Byzantine assistance. Justinian sent troops who secured the throne for Atangild and then settled the south-east coastlands. Atangild's successor, Leovigild (568–86), brought most of the peninsula under Visigothic control, conquering the Suevian kingdom of Galicia in 585. Leovigild campaigned successfully against the Byzantine colonists, capturing Cordoba from them in 572, but it was left to Svinthila (621–31) finally to drive them out. They left a permanent Byzantine influence on the art of Visigothic Spain. According to St Isidore, Leovigild was the first Visigothic king who appeared with full regalia; he probably copied them from his Byzantine enemies.

The Visigoths had long been Christian but had early adopted Arianism. The Catholics, however, were growing in influence despite persecution, and in 587 Recared (586–601), a few months after his accession, was converted to the Catholic faith. The Church soon became a powerful force in the state, and in 631 joined in a successful alliance with the nobility to depose Svinthila in favour of Sisenand. The rebels bought the aid of Dagobert, King of the Franks, with the promise of a gold *missorium* which Aetius had given Turismund as a reward for his assistance against Attila. But when Dagobert's emissaries were carrying it to France they were waylaid by the Visigoths who removed the *missorium* and returned it to the royal treasure at Toledo; instead Sisenand paid Dagobert a large sum as compensation.

Thenceforth, however, the approval of the Church replaced the possession of the royal treasure as the manifestation of sovereignty. The Fourth Council of Toledo, held under the chairmanship of St Isidore in 633, proclaimed the Church's right to take a major share in the government, including the confirmation of the king's election to the throne; this seems to have been conceded by Sisenand in recognition of the vital part played by the Church in his successful usurpation.

At some stage between the Fourth Council of Toledo and the accession of Wamba in 672 the coronation ceremony was introduced.[1] By the time of Wamba it consisted of two parts, the oath to the people and their oath to the king, followed by the anointing and investiture. The notices in the chronicles of the intervening kings give no indication, but the writings of St Julian suggest that the coronation of Wamba was not the first, as he refers to it as if it were a customary ceremony. Equally significant is his account of

1 Although St Isidore refers to Recared's accession in the following terms, *Leovigildo defuncto, filius ejus Recaredus regno est coronatus . . .*, it is doubtful whether Recared was actually crowned. The ceremony would have occurred before his conversion, and it is unlikely that St Isidore would have recognised an Arian coronation. The early chroniclers naturally varied their style in recording each accession, and *coronatus* is no more evidence that Recared was crowned than *sceptra paterna est adeptus* in Sampiro's chronicle is evidence that Ordoño II ever possessed a sceptre. It should also be remembered that St Isidore eulogised Recared for his conversion to Catholicism, and this may explain the use of the somewhat extravagant term *coronatus*.

how Count Paul, sent by Wamba to put down a Basque rebellion, crossed into Septimania and had himself elected King and crowned at Narbonne with a votive crown which had been given to the shrine of St Felix by Recared. It seems unlikely that he would have committed so great a sacrilege if the act of crowning had not already become the necessary confirmation of a king's election. Indeed it seems likely that both parts of the coronation ceremony were a result of the Fourth Council of Toledo itself. The final canon speaks of the king as the Lord's anointed, and refers to the oath sworn by him. The theoretical works of St Isidore had already equated the kingship with priesthood. Further evidence is provided by the canons of the Sixth Council of Toledo (638) which refer to the accession oath as if it had been in existence for some years; it is again mentioned in the canons of the Eighth Council (653). This was the first coronation ceremony in Western Europe and, although the Visigoths may have known of the anointing of Clovis in 496 when he was baptised into the Christian religion, it seems to have derived purely from St Isidore's study of the Bible.

The first textual evidence of anointing is St Julian's eye-witness account of the coronation of Wamba on 19th September 672. The king, who had previously sworn the customary oath to the people, knelt before the altar of the Church of St Peter and St Paul in Toledo, while Bishop Quiricius poured the holy oil on his head with *benedictionis copia*. Unfortunately no forms of the coronation rite exist, although fragments survive.[1] Diego de Valdes writing at the beginning of the XVII century repeats a legend that soon after the holy oil had been administered to the crest of Wamba's head it evaporated and a pillar of smoke rose in the air and vanished from sight.[2] This legend was probably invented many years after the coronation in order to rival that of the *Sainte Ampoule* and make the King of Spain seem more favoured by God than the other kings of Christendom.

Ervigic in 680, Egica in 687 and Witiza in 700 are said by the chroniclers to have been anointed king at Toledo, the last sharing the throne with his father until the latter's death in 702. On the death of Witiza in 708 civil war broke out, and when at last Roderick was elected king in 710 he had to deal with the Moorish invasion. At the Battle of Guadalete in 711 Roderick and his army were destroyed and the Mohammedan rule of Spain began. It was nearly 800 years before all Spain was Christian again.

Many accounts show that the Moors were astonished at the riches of the Visigoths. Ben Kartabus in his *Kitab-al-Iktifa*, writing of the conquest of Tarik relates:

> In the main church of the said city he found the Table of Solomon. . . . And he found besides twenty-five crowns or diadems adorned with precious stones, belonging to the monarchs who had ruled that land, for each time a king died he left a crown there, and they wrote on it his name and his titles and condition and how long he had lived and how long he had reigned.[3]

1 M. Ferotin (ed.): *Liber Ordinum*, Paris 1904, pp. 499–504. In particular there is an anthem *De inordinatio sive natalicio regis* in the Mozarabic *Antiphonarium* at Leon Cathedral, a facsimile edition of which was published in Madrid in 1953.

2 Diego de Valdes: *De dignitate regum regnorumque Hispaniae*, Granada 1602, p. 125.

3 P. de Gayangos: *The History of the Mohammedan Dynasties in Spain*, London 1840. Other Arab writers give different accounts of the finding of the 'Table of Solomon'.

The sole survivors of this treasure are the crowns of Guarrazar. There are several stories about the finding of these, the most common one being that they were found by accident on 25th August 1858 by a peasant and his wife in a cache of masonry by a well, which had been exposed when the topsoil was washed away by heavy rain. A little later pieces of ancient jewellery appeared in the Toledo shops and came to the notice of José Navarre, goldsmith to Queen Isabel. He purchased as many pieces as he could find, and although some must have been melted down, and at least one is thought to have been thrown in the Tagus to avoid discovery, he was able to reconstruct nine votive crowns. Navarre had no confidence that he would be adequately rewarded in Spain so he smuggled his treasure into France, and in January 1859 sold it to the French Government. From then until 1940 these crowns (*Plate 207, a*) were kept at the Cluny Museum at Paris. Then six of them were moved to Madrid, where they still are at the National Archaeological Museum, under an 'exchange', the terms of which have never been settled. In 1861 two other crowns were found in the cemetery of Guarrazar; these were acquired by the Spanish Government and kept at the Royal Armoury in Madrid until they were stolen in 1921.

The most important of the Guarrazar crowns were those of Svinthila, which was in the Royal Armoury, and Recevinthus, which was at the Cluny Museum and is now in Madrid.

The crown of Svinthila (621–31) (*Plate 207, b*) consisted of a circlet, formed by two plates, hinged at one end and secured by a bolt at the other. The crown, which was constructed of a double layer of thin gold, was set with three rows of stones, the middle row being composed of large rosettes the centres of which were large coloured stones *en cabochon* and standing out from the garnets set in the open work of the rosettes. From the lower rim of the circlet a number of letters (cut from gold plate and set with small garnets) hung on small chains, and though some were missing *SVINTALANUS REX OFFERET* could be read with certainty; below each letter hung other stones. The crown was suspended by four chains, with links shaped as pear leaves, from a large piece of rock crystal. From this hung another chain, passing through the centre of the circlet and terminating in an ornate and curiously shaped cross.

The crown of Recevinthus (653–72) consists of plates constructed of two layers of gold, hinged and bolted as in Svinthila's crown. The edges of the hoop so formed consist of two bands of cloisonné work with incrustations of cornelian. Between these outer bands are three rows of stones *en cabochon*, the intervening spaces being pierced in open work and engraved to represent foliage or flowers. From the lower rim hang letters, set with garnets or coloured glass, reading *RECCESVINTHUS REX OFFERET*. The crown is suspended from a globe of rock crystal in the same way as that of Svinthila. As with that crown a cross, though of more normal design, is suspended through the centre of the circlet.

Only one of the other crowns has a definitely royal association, the remainder being representations of crowns especially made for votive purposes. The exception is the crown of Sonnica, who may have been a Visigothic queen, which is still in the Cluny Museum.

Sonnica's crown is formed of a smooth band of gold, divided like the others into two semi-circles. The decoration consists of three lines of large, various coloured stones *en cabochon*. From the lower rim of the circlet hang several irregular-shaped stones. The cross which hangs from the crown is decorated with great oval and rectangular stones and on the reverse is inscribed *IN Dn/NOM/INE/OFFERET SONNICA/SCE/MA/RIE/IN S/ORBA/CES*. Various interpretations have been put on this inscription, the two most usual being that it refers to a votive offering made either to the church of St Mary in Sorbas in Southern Spain or to Santa Maria de Abaxes in Toledo.

When the crowns were first discovered they caused a furore among archaeologists and historians which was heightened by the way in which the crowns were smuggled to France. A considerable controversy arose as to whether the two most important crowns had been worn or had been made as votive ornaments. Despite the eminence of those engaged in the controversy, the major protagonists being Amador de los Ríos and Ferdinand de Lasteyrie,[1] their motives do not appear to have been entirely scientific. If the crowns had been royal ones, as Amador de los Ríos claimed, they might have ranked as national regalia, heirlooms of the state, and their transfer to France might have been deemed contrary to international practice. On the other hand if they were purely votive offerings no such question would arise. A dispassionate view of the evidence available does not lead to any firm conclusion. The crowns of Svinthila and Recevinthus were of a size suitable for wearing and their plates were hinged; on the other hand the other crowns found at the same time, the size of which suggests that they were not intended to be worn, also consist of two hinged plates. The crown of Svinthila, however, had small rings on the inside which might have been to attach it to a cloth lining. Lasteyrie, in arguing against the possibility that they were worn, considered that the pendeloques were very long, and although they could have been added later the chains attached to the crown of Recevinthus appeared to have been made at the same time as the crown.[2] This argument is hardly conclusive. The history of the Visigothic treasure does not throw much additional light on the problem. The crowns do not match the description given by Ben Kartabus—that itself, of course, may have been apocryphal. If they had, they could have been considered as royal crowns donated to churches on the death of their owners. On the other hand the story of Count Paul shows that crowns of this nature could have been worn. This argument can probably never be resolved and it does not seem of very great importance. The crowns themselves, whether worn or purely votive, are a fine example of Visigothic art.

THE KINGDOM OF CASTILE
(Including Asturias, Galicia and Leon)

The Arab conquest completely destroyed the Visigothic state, and Arab rule soon extended over the whole peninsula. In 718, however, a group of fugitive Visigoths defeated an Arab detachment at Covadonga and were able to establish a small Christian state in the Asturian mountains, their leader, the semi-legendary Pelayo, being pro-

---

[1] José Amador de los Ríos: *El arte latino-bizanto en España y las coronas visigodas de Guarrazar, Memórias de la Académia de San Fernando*, Madrid 1861; F. de Lasteyrie: *Description du trésor de Guarrazar*, Paris 1860.

[2] The *pendilla* or *cataseistae* were a feature of Byzantine imperial crowns and could be worn only by the emperors, but there are several examples of this feature being borrowed by the West, no doubt to demonstrate that their rulers were not inferior to the Eastern emperors.

claimed king in about 721. His son Favila (737–9) and his son-in-law Alphonso I (739–57), who took advantage of a civil war among the Moors to reconquer Galicia, were in turn elected King and the monarchy, although still elective, remained in Alphonso's family.

The Visigothic coronation ceremony probably represented the Church's confirmation of the election of a new king. The ceremony seems to have been reintroduced in Asturias by Alphonso II (791–838), perhaps as part of a deliberate policy of imitating the Visigoths to support his claims that the Asturian kings were the direct heirs of the Visigothic monarchy and the rightful owners of all Spain,[1] or perhaps for the more practical reason that the solemn and public anointing by the Church was the best method of confirming an election at a time when the elective principle was no longer generally accepted.

A further impulse to the growing kingdom was given by the policy of Ordoño I (850–66) of re-populating empty conquered territory with Christian colonists, his major success being the re-population of Leon which was begun in 856. This policy was continued by Ordoño's son Alphonso III (866–910) and his successors, and one of the results was that the juridical system of Asturias, Leon and Castile became based on the concept of empty or reconquered land being in the power of the crown and occupied on its authority with the consequent superiority of the state, rather than on the feudalism which obtained elsewhere. Naturally allied to this was the Visigothic concept of the indivisibility of the realm, that the kingdom was passed down undivided to the next ruler. Towards the end of Alphonso's reign, perhaps due to the influence of his Frankish wife, he put his sons Garcia, Ordoño and Fruela respectively in charge of Leon, Galicia and Asturias, each with the title of 'King'. This seems to have been purely for the purpose of administration and was not intended to be a partition of the kingdom. Somewhat naturally the sons wanted to ensure that they retained their own kingdoms, and they successfully rebelled against their father in the last years of his reign, forcing him to abdicate in their favour. The concept of indivisibility prevailed, for on the death of Garcia in 912, Ordoño ruled both Leon and Galicia and on his death in 923 Fruela reunited the whole kingdom, which was not divided again under the Asturian dynasty. Indivisibility had an even wider meaning in the time of Alphonso III at least, that Spain itself was indivisible and was the lawful patrimony of the Asturian kingdom.

About 906 Alphonso III began to take the title of Emperor of Spain.[2] It seems more likely that this was to square the political and administrative position with the political

---

[1] This is the implication of the passage in the *Albedan Chronicle* which has been taken as evidence that Alphonso II reintroduced the coronation ceremony: *Omnemque gotorum ordinem sicuti Toledo fuerat, tam in eclesia quam palatio in Obete cuncta statuit.* It is tempting to read too much into this and the chronicler may be rationalising after the event. In fact the *Visigothic Chronicle* says of Alphonso I: *unctus est in regno,* but this may be an error as there are no other notices of coronations until Alphonso II. On the whole question of succession to the throne see Claudio Sánchez-Albornoz; 'La succesion al trono en Leon y Castilla', in *Boletín de la Académia Argentina de Letras,* xiv, No. 50, p. 45.

[2] There has been much literature on the imperial title of the Kings of Leon. See, e.g., Ramon Menendez Pidal: *El Imperio Hispanico y los cinco reinos,* Madrid 1950; R. Folz: *L'idée d'Empire en l'Occident,* Paris 1953.

concepts outlined above than that it was intended to proclaim that Asturias was independent of and equal to the Empire of Charlemagne. In his own realm Alphonso was a king over three other kings, which would have been a good reason for assuming the title of Emperor. Moreover, it would demonstrate his claim to be the legitimate heir to all Spain, as it would place him above Sancho Garcia of Navarre, who had assumed the title of King in 905, and above the Moorish emirs.

In 906 the clergy of Tours Cathedral, as a part of their efforts to raise funds for the rebuilding of the cathedral which had been destroyed by the Huns, wrote to Alphonso offering to sell him an imperial crown of gold and precious stones, Alphonso replied asking that they should convey the crown to him; if he liked it he would buy it, if not he would repay the expenses of the messengers. Doubts as to the genuineness of Alphonso's letter now seem to have been resolved, but there is no evidence that this crown was ever brought to Spain. Indeed the work of the jewellers of Oviedo at that period, as exemplified by the celebrated 'Cross of the Angels' and 'Cross of Victory', was of such high standard that the importation of a crown would have been unnecessary unless there was a very special reason for doing so. It is therefore likely that Alphonso was interested in acquiring this crown as tangible evidence of his claim to the title of Emperor.

During the x century, clerical theory seems to have moved from the principle of electing kings to the idea that the monarchy might be hereditary. This idea gained ground slowly, but the accession of Ramiro III as a minor in 966 may be taken as evidence that the hereditary principle was generally accepted by then. Throughout the century, however, there were disputes and wars of succession after the death of most kings. This background of changing political theory makes it easier to understand the importance accorded to the Leonese coronation rite by the early chroniclers, and indeed the form of the rite itself with its concentration on the unction and the mutual oaths between king and people instead of investiture with specific royal ornaments. Whatever principle, elective or hereditary, might be in vogue the oaths gave the seal of lay approval on the succession and the unction the approval of the Church. And the unction itself set the King of Leon apart from other unanointed kings (such of those of Navarre) and supported the assumption of the title of Emperor which frequently appears in the charters of the later kings of the Asturian dynasty. Finally the rite provided continuity with the Visigothic state and thus supported the claims to sovereignty over the whole peninsula.

Despite the imperial pretensions of the Leonese the most powerful Spanish monarch in the first half of the xi century was Sancho the Great of Navarre, who built up a considerable kingdom on the southern slopes of the Pyrenees at the expense of both his Moorish and Christian neighbours, including in it the County of Castile which had become independent of Leon during the reign of Ramiro II (931–50). On his death in 1037 Sancho divided his kingdom among four sons, one of them, Ferdinand, who was married to the sister of Bermudo III of Leon, taking a truncated Castile with the title of King. Two years later he defeated and killed Bermudo and became King of Leon in the name of his wife.

Although Ferdinand on becoming King of Leon followed local custom and was crowned and anointed in Leon Cathedral, he introduced from Navarre the Germanic doctrine which looked on the land of the king, as that of the nobles, as a personal estate, divisible among heirs, and which held that the relations between the nobles and the king were not based on the superior universal order of the state but on a personal bond freely entered into between the sovereign and his vassals, the most important element being the provision of mutual protection and allied services. On his death in 1065 Ferdinand divided his kingdom between his sons, Sancho taking Castile, Alphonso Leon and Garcia Galicia. Sancho, the eldest, naturally adopted the theory of the indivisibility of the realm and set out to reunite his father's kingdom by force. He had practically succeeded in this when he was assassinated while besieging Zamora. Alphonso, returning from exile, was recognised by the nobles as King of Castile (after swearing an oath that he was not implicated in his brother's assassination) and Leon, and defeated Garcia, reincorporating Galicia into the kingdom. Alphonso became the premier Christian king of Spain and greatly extended Castile at the expense of the Moors, taking Toledo in 1085. After successfully defending his conquests against the Almoravides he began to style himself *Toletanus imperator* or *Toletanis imperii magnificus triumphator*. Previously he had occasionally used the title *Totius Hispaniae imperator*, or in correspondence with the Arab princes of Andalusia, 'Emperor of the two religions'. The association of Toledo, the Visigothic capital, with the imperial title underlines the claim to be the heir to the Visigoths.

Alphonso VI was succeeded in 1109 by his daughter Urraca, the wife of Alphonso I of Aragon who now styled himself *Rex et Imperator*. Urraca so mismanaged the kingdom that a party in Galicia set up her son (by a previous marriage to Raymond of Burgundy) as the legitimate heir to the throne. On his mother's death in 1126 he as Alphonso VII inherited the whole Kingdom of Castile and Leon, despite the claims of Alphonso of Aragon, and the following year an agreement was made whereby the latter abandoned Castile to his rival and foreswore the title of Emperor. Alphonso VII went from strength to strength, and his step-father's successor in Aragon even recognised him as his over-lord and paid him homage. From 1126 onwards Alphonso increasingly used the imperial title, and finally in 1135 he was crowned at Leon as Emperor of Spain, the Pope after-wards confirming him in this title. Present at this coronation and thus acquiescing in the use of the imperial title were the Count of Barcelona and the King of Navarre, Garci-Ramirez, who had succeeded in separating his kingdom from Aragon to which it had been united since 1076 and who had become a vassal of Alphonso in return for his support.

It was probably more to prevent a fratricidal war on his death than to the acceptance of the doctrines of his forefathers that Alphonso VII divided his kingdom between his sons Sancho (Castile) and Ferdinand (Leon), one of the effects of this division being the final extinction of the claim to the title of Emperor. During the XII and XIII centuries primogeniture became the generally accepted method of succession, and Ferdinand III, having succeeded as King of Castile where his mother Berenguela abdicated in his favour, was accepted as King of Leon as the eldest son of his father Alphonso IX, despite the latter's attempts to disinherit him. Ferdinand's son Alphonso X attempted to give legal force to royal succession by primogeniture, but before this could be ratified by the Cortes his eldest surviving son, Sancho, who would have been disinherited by this law in favour of the sons of his deceased elder brother, Ferdinand de la Cerda, rebelled, and on his father's death was in a sufficiently strong position to be crowned King.[1] Thereafter primogeniture prevailed.

The Navarrese and Burgundian dynasties seem to have regarded the coronation ceremony more as a political measure than as a traditional act of continuity with the Visigoths, and continuity would have been even further lost by the replacement of the Mozarabic rite by the Roman one during Alphonso VI's reign. It may be significant that there is no textual evidence of anointing after Alphonso VII, except for Alphonso XI. As far as is known Sancho II was not crowned in Castile nor was Alphonso VI in Leon on the death of their father, but when Sancho had driven his brother out of Leon he had himself crowned there in 1072 and, in his turn, Alphonso VI was crowned at Burgos on becoming King of Castile. Alphonso VII underwent two coronations prior to his imperial one in 1135. When he was set up as King of Galicia in 1111 he was crowned and anointed at Santiago at an improvised ceremony, and on his mother's death he was crowned at Leon. The coronation ceremony during this period seems to have been used in every case to reinforce a doubtful claim, and this becomes even more apparent after Alphonso VII. There is no mention in the chronicles of the coronation of those kings whose succession was entirely free from doubt, except for Alphonso X and XI, and they were probably crowned through piety or love of pomp and ceremony. Otherwise there seem only to have been coronations when a king or usurper wished to affirm that his claim to the throne was legitimate. Thus the coronation or accession ceremony of Henry I can be attributed to the fact that he was an infant. Ferdinand III was crowned King of Castile at Valladolid in 1217 because he succeeded on the abdication of Berenguela, and as King of Leon at Toro in 1230 because of his father's attempts to deprive him of his inheritance. Sancho was crowned at Toledo in 1284 to set the seal of respectability on his usurpation, and his ten-year-old son Ferdinand IV was crowned at Toledo in 1295 as a political move in the war of succession following Sancho's death. Similarly Ferdinand IV's uncle, John, the pretender to the throne, also underwent a form of coronation in Leon in 1296. Another usurper, Henry of Trastamara, was crowned at Burgos when he invaded Castile in 1366, but he did not repeat the ceremony when he eventually won the throne from Peter I in 1396. Henry's son John I would have wished to assert his lawful right to the throne against the claims of Peter's daughter Constance and her husband John of Gaunt. His piety may have been another reason for his coronation. The marriage of John's son Henry to Catherine of Lancaster removed this threat to the dynasty and, there being no need for them, no other coronations are recorded in Castile. They were replaced by a simple accession ceremony at which the royal standard was flown and the new monarch acclaimed by the assembled people.[2] It is

---

[1] Louis, the grandson of Ferdinand de la Cerda, was crowned King of the Fortunate or Canary Islands by Pope Clement VI in 1342 and invested with a gold crown and a sceptre, but he was never able to occupy his throne.

[2] Schramm has drawn attention to the significance in this context of the act of uncrowning a dummy of Henry IV at Avila in 1465 by a confederacy of rebel nobles. An effigy of the king, robed and wearing royal ornaments, was placed on a throne on a scaffold. After a manifesto had been read the leaders of the confederacy removed first the crown, then the sceptre, then the sword and finally the rest of

noteworthy that Alphonso XI at his coronation in 1330 crowned himself,[1] presumably in imitation of his brother-in-law Alphonso IV of Aragon, and that this practice was also followed by John.

From the time of Ferdinand I no city remained the royal capital for more than two or three generations, one consequence being that no city or church had the monopoly of coronations and from the XI century they took place at seven different centres. Thus no great church or abbey became the custodian of the regalia. This seems to have been one of the reasons why regalia in the western kingdoms of Spain never assumed the importance they did elsewhere. Another seems to have been that the turbulent history of the kingdoms and the changing political background to the coronation ceremony were such as to preclude the development, as there was in other countries, of special significance being accorded to any particular royal ornament. Even the famous swords, the Lobera of St Ferdinand and Tizona and Colada of the Cid, which were part of the Castilian royal treasure, although bearing romantic names were not associated with the coronation ceremony as, for example, was *Joyeuse* in France. At the time when the coronation ceremony was of major importance there seems to have been no concept of a state treasure, but from the XIV century onwards, when this idea was developing, the coronation ceremony was losing its importance. Nor were the monarchs prior to Peter I able to build up great personal treasures, as they frequently had to sell or pledge their jewellery in times of crisis, the earliest record of this being when Sancha, wife of Ferdinand I, sold all her jewels to raise an army to fight the Moors.

There is some evidence from early miniatures that the kings of the Asturian dynasty wore helmet crowns, but it can hardly be considered conclusive. It seems fairly certain, however, that the new dynasty of Ferdinand I introduced a crown decorated with fleurs-de-lis. Prior to his accession in 1037 there do not seem to be any representations of kings wearing fleur-de-lis crowns, but from the second half of the XI century until at least the death of Alphonso VII there is ample evidence that the Leonese and Castilian monarchs possessed a crown, the upper decoration of which consisted of a few simple and rather small trefoil ornaments.[2] The most detailed representation of this type of

the royal insignia before pulling the dummy off the throne. Investiture with regalia evidently remained significant in the minds of the people even though the coronation ceremony itself had been abandoned.

[1] A coronation ceremonial had previously been prepared for Alphonso by Ramón, Bishop of Coimbra, in which the King was to be crowned and invested with a mitre by the archbishop. Claudio Sánchez Albornoz: 'Un ceremonial inedito de coronacion de los reyes de Castilla', in *Logos* (Revista de la Facultad de Filosofía y Letras, University of Buenos Aires), III, p. 75. The bishop was evidently not familiar with the traditional Leonese ceremonial, for apart from the introduction of the mitre there are several minor points which do not tally with what is known of previous coronations. In the event it seems certain that his ceremonial was not used at Alphonso's coronation, for in the contemporary account of it there is no reference to the mitre, while the King crowned first himself and then the Queen.

[2] The first representation in Castile of the trefoil or fleur-de-lis crown on the head of a king is in a miniature of a Book of Hours at Santiago University (*Plate 208, a*) which is contemporary with Ferdinand I. Crowns of this type also appear in the portraits of Ferdinand I, Alphonso VI and Alphonso VII in the collection of donations at Santiago Cathedral known as the *Tumbo A*. The last two portraits were contemporary, or nearly so, with their subjects, and the individuality of the earlier portraits raises the possibility that they may have been copied from earlier miniatures which were contemporary with the monarchs portrayed.

crown is the XII-century engraving on the tomb of Prince Garcia in the royal pantheon of St Isidore at Leon:

> The crown is formalised to some extent but the details shown are consistent with the requirements of a royal crown. It appears to be made in two pieces, the lower being a circlet set with oval stones alternately horizontal and vertical with a diamond-shaped one in the middle. Above this is another band which acts as a base for four *fleurons* on curving stems.

The major figure in Spanish history during this period was Rodrigo Diaz de Vivar, the Cid, who had been Sancho II's standard bearer and chief-of-staff and who occupied high positions under Alphonso VI, whose cousin Jimena he married. But the king never forgave him for playing a leading part in administering the oath that he was not concerned in Sancho's assassination and on two occasions exiled him. The second time he carved out a territory for himself at Valencia and married his daughters to the Count of Barcelona and the Infante of Navarre, his grandsons becoming the Kings of Aragon and Navarre. On the Cid's early death in 1099 Jimena ruled Valencia for three years until Moorish attacks forced her to call for assistance from Alphonso VI, who decided to abandon the town. The great treasure that the Cid had accumulated was brought back to Castile, part of it being passed down as royal heirlooms. During the reign of John II (1406–54) a part of this treasure was found buried under a pillar in the Madrid palace of Alvaro de Luna. It then included the Cid's swords Tizona, Colada and Guiosa[1] and the girdle of Jimena. The latter was said to have been a girdle of diamonds, pearls, sapphires, rubies and emeralds which had belonged to the Sultana Zobeida, wife of Haroun el Raschid, and which had come into the possession of the Moorish ruler of Valencia, Al Cadir. He was murdered by rebels under Ibn Jahhaj, and when the Cid occupied Valencia the latter was made to swear that he had not murdered Al Cadir and had not taken the girdle. He was then allowed to retain his post of Cadi on condition that if the girdle was found in his possession the Cid would withdraw his protection and possibly put him to death as a regicide. Later the Cid suspected him of treachery and tortured him until he admitted possession of Al Cadir's jewels, including the girdle. The Cid accordingly had Ibn Jahhaj burnt alive and gave the girdle to Jimena.

A royal inventory of 1503[2] mentions Tizona and Colada, and today in the Royal Armoury at Madrid there is the blade of a Christian sword of the XI to XIII centuries which corresponds to the description of Tizona in the 1503 inventory:

> It is a narrow two-edged blade with a rounded point, with a channel running down the centre for nearly all its length. The channel for the first third of its length on both sides has various letters and devices cut into the steel and filled with gold.

After the division of Castile and Leon on the death of Alphonso VII coins and contemporary miniatures[3] representing monarchs of both kingdoms show them wearing

---

1 The Spanish version of *Joyeuse*. The practice of giving special names to swords may have been adopted in Spain under the influence of the romances of Charlemagne.

2 J. Ferrandis: *Inventarios reales (Juan II a Juana la Loca)*, *Datos documentales para la Historia del Arte en España, III*, Madrid 1943, p. 69. For the appearance of a sword named Tiçon in Aragon, see p. 604, note 1.

3 E.g., the *Tumbo A* portrait of Alphonso IX and the miniature of the donation of the Castle of Ucles in the National Historical Archives, Madrid, showing Alphonso VIII and Eleanor of England.

a   *Visigothic crowns. The crown of Recevinthus is in the centre, and the crown of Sonnica on the extreme left. Formerly in the Cluny Museum, Paris* (p. 583)

b   *Crown of Svinthila. Formerly at the Royal Armoury, Madrid* (p. 583)

a   *Detail from miniature of Ferdinand I showing crown and staff with animal's head.* Book of Hours, *Santiago University* (p. 589)

b   *Miniature of Alphonso of Castile (1252–84), on horseback. From a collection of donations and miniatures known as the* Tumbo A. *Santiago Cathedral* (p. 592)

c   *Crown with the castles, early XIII Century. Toledo Cathedral* (p. 591)

crowns in which balls replace the fleur-de-lis as the decoration above the circlet. Although this might be an over-formalised representation of a fleur-de-lis a fragment of a carving on the XII-century tomb of Ordoño in the royal pantheon at St Isidore provides evidence that there was an actual 'crown with balls'. The crown in the carving on Ordoño's tomb resembles that on Garcia's tomb in that it is divided into two horizontal bands set with stones, but in place of the *fleurons* on the upper rim of the circlet there are large balls, apparently set with small stones. Significantly during this period the earlier fleurs-de-lis crown largely disappears from the miniatures of kings.

One crown of a different, and indeed unique, style has survived from the first half of the thirteenth century. In 1948 the tomb of Sancho IV (1284–95) at Toledo Cathedral was opened, and a crown was found on the head of the embalmed body of the King. It is now in the cathedral treasury.

The crown (*Plate 208, c*) consists of eight plates, probably of silver with an overlay of gold, fastened by hinges. Each plate is 7 cm long (the crown is 55 cm when extended) and 4·5 cm high, and each is surmounted by a heraldic castle 4 cm high and 4·5 wide, apparently worked from the same piece of metal as the plate. These castles have three towers, the centre one being slightly higher than those at the flanks, and contain rose windows and Gothic arches identical in style to those of the heraldic castles on the sarcophagus of Alphonso VIII and Eleanor at Las Huelgas de Burgos. The plates are set alternately with large sapphires and cameos, one to each plate, the settings being Romanesque in style, with conventional *fleurons,* and riveted to the plates. The sapphires are cut to show a somewhat curved surface and are polished almost smooth. The cameos are very old. Two of them are male profile busts, ivory coloured on a blue ground. The other two, perhaps female busts, are in agate so worked as to draw out the different colour effects of each stone: the background dark, the faces clear and the hair coloured. One of the figures has over the shoulders and hair a lion's skin and head worked in the same stone. The other has a gold net finely engraved into the hair.

The fact that only the castle, the heraldic device of Castile, features in the crown has led both Hüffer[1] and Schramm to the view that it dates from the separation of Leon and Castile. Immediately after the reunion the lion of Leon appears to have been joined with the castle in royal wear on every possible occasion. Schramm goes further and refers to it as the 'Crown of Alphonso VIII', and this title has been repeated by Biehn.[2] It seems more likely, however, that this crown was made for Ferdinand III between 1217 and 1230 while he was still King of Castile only (the size of the crown precludes it from having been made for Henry I who was only twelve at his death). The style of the castles on the crown is so similar to that of Alphonso's tomb, and so different from any other representation of the heraldic castles of Castile, that it is most likely that if they are not the work of the same hand they were at least executed within a short time of each other. Alphonso VIII died in 1214 and Queen Eleanor died, broken-hearted, twenty-six days later. The romantic circumstances of their deaths suggest that the idea of the double tomb was considered appropriate after the death of Eleanor, and indeed

---

1 H. Hüffer: 'Los hallazgos en la Catedral de Toledo y la corona real castellana', in *Clavileno*, II, no. 7 (1951).

2 H. Biehn: *Die Kronen Europas und ihre Schicksale*, Wiesbaden 1957.

Gomez Moreno[1] states that the tomb was not completed until late in the reign of Ferdinand III. Unfortunately the only external evidence as to the existence of this crown is a reference in the second will of Alphonso X dated at Seville 21st January 1284 and that is of little help in dating it. Until further material comes to light it would be safer to refer to this crown as the 'crown with the castles' rather than to attribute it to any individual monarch.

Hüffer considers that the crown might have been placed in Sancho's tomb to safeguard it during the dynastic struggle following his death, but as it was no longer used by then and was of little intrinsic value this seems unlikely. It is more probable that this is a case of an obsolete crown being used as a burial crown instead of a special funeral crown being made (as for example in XIV-century Aragon). It appears that at the time of Sancho's death it was customary to embalm and robe royal corpses. A number of tombs have been opened at Las Huelgas de Burgos, among them that of Ferdinand de la Cerda, Sancho's elder brother, who was dressed in rich robes and on whose head was a cap embroidered with the arms of Castile and Leon. On the other hand although the tombs of several other kings have been opened no other crowns have been found.

Following the reunion of Castile and Leon the representations of monarchs in contemporary miniatures[2] and on coins and seals show them wearing crowns decorated with a few fleurs-de-lis, larger and more gothic in style than those of the XI and XII centuries. These representations appear during the latter part of the reign of Ferdinand III and throughout Alphonso X's reign, but disappear almost completely under Sancho IV, although they reappear on the early seals of Alphonso XI. One explanation of this would be that a crown of this design existed but that it was then pawned by Alphonso X in the last years of his reign and never redeemed. The Arab Ibn Khaldun,[3] writing in the time of Peter I, stated that Alphonso X had pawned 'the crown of his ancestors' to Yacub Ibn Abd el Haec, in return for money and troops to resist Sancho's rebellion, and that this crown was still kept in the palace of the Beni Abd el Haec at the time when he wrote.

Five royal swords from the XIII century have survived. In the Royal Armoury in Madrid there are the supposed *Lobera* of Ferdinand III and another sword which has been attributed both to Ferdinand III and Alphonso X, and at Seville there is yet another sword attributed to Ferdinand III. In Sancho's tomb at Toledo a sword was found as well as a crown, and one was also found in the tomb of Ferdinand de la Cerda at Burgos, but these are of minor importance.

Lobera (Plate 209, b). This has a plain double-edged blade with a broad groove down the centre; on both sides of the blade the letters 'SI SI NO NO' are engraved in gold in the groove. This is presumably a reference to the advice given in a book *Noblezay lealtad* written by twelve wise men of Ferdinand's council: 'Señor, your yea should be yea, and your nay nay which is a very great virtue

[1] M. Gomez Moreno: *El panteón real de las Huelgas de Burgos, Madrid* 1946, p. 14.

[2] E.g., many miniatures in the works of Alphonso X, and the *Tumbo A* portraits of Ferdinand III and Alphonso X (*Plate 208, b*).

[3] M. Dozy: *Recherches sur l'histoire d'Espagne*, 2nd edition, Leyden 1860, Vol. I, p. 118.

in a prince, or in any other true man, and a great security for his vassals and his possessions'. This sword is very likely the Lobera given by Ferdinand on his deathbed to his younger son Manuel, who later bore it at the Battle of Salado. The hilt was added later, being the work of the famous Toledo swordsmith Salvador de Avila, who died in 1539.

Sword of Ferdinand III or Alphonso X. The blade is double-edged with a wide channel along the centre. In this are engraved concentric circles between double parallel grooves which end in a cross. The guard is of solid silver overlaid with gold; in its centre the arms of Castile are engraved on the one side and those of Leon on the other. The two arms of the guard curve inwards towards the blade with a trefoil inside each curve. The handle is of wood with thin silver plates and the pommel, also covered in silver plates, is of iron wrought in the form of a very formal fleurs-de-lis. The richness of the sword and the royal emblems on it are sufficient evidence of its origin.

Sword of Ferdinand III at Seville. The blade has a deep channel in the middle in which there are vestiges of engraved letters, probably rubbed away by repeated cleaning. The guard is silver plated and has various designs on it in Arab style, and is also enriched with pieces of jasper or red marble. The pommel is a flattened circle of rock crystal bound at the edge with silver. The hilt is also of crystal and it is likely that these pieces were later additions. Gestoso[1] thinks that this is the sword which was held in the right hand of the richly dressed statue of King Ferdinand which was in the Royal Chapel of Seville Cathedral until the second half of the xvii century.

The evidence of the miniatures, coins and seals as to other royal ornaments is confusing and probably unreliable. The *Book of Hours* at Santiago University shows Ferdinand I carrying a staff topped with the head of an animal (*Plate 208, a*); it resembles a wolf, but might have been intended to represent the lion of Leon. The xii-century miniatures show the kings carrying short sceptres of varying styles, some with animals heads, some with fleurs-de-lis and some of peculiar design, resembling a club with stalks protruding from it, possibly an attempt at representing the rod of Aaron. The most common representation is of a fleur-de-lis sceptre, at least until the time of Alphonso X. The orb first appears on a seal of Alphonso VII, but is represented in such a peculiar fashion, being held between thumb and forefinger, that it seems most likely that no orb was in use and that the idea of incorporating one in the seal was borrowed from a foreign source to support Alphonso's claim to the title of Emperor. Similarly the appearance of the orb on the coins of Ferdinand II and Alphonso VIII and its occasional use in miniatures[2] is likely to be a copy from elsewhere. Alphonso X, who was a candidate for election as Holy Roman Emperor, in rivalry with Richard of Cornwall, is often depicted with a plain orb and with a sceptre surmounted by an eagle, which may be a Hohenstaufen eagle inherited from his mother, Beatrice of Swabia, or an imperial one assumed as part of his claim to the Empire. One instance is known of Alphonso X's Queen, Yolande, sister of Peter III of Aragon, being depicted holding an orb, which is unusual as she was not a queen regnant. Flores,[3] writing in the xviii century, mentions a seal affixed to a donation to a church in Astorga showing Yolande enthroned with a sceptre in her right hand with an eagle on it with an orb surmounted by a cross in her left. Yolande's sister-in-law, Queen Constance of Aragon, is also

---

1 José Gestoso y Perez: *Recuerdos de San Fernando* in *Museum IV*, Barcelona 1914, p. 191.
2 E.g., miniatures of the *Tumbo de Toxos Outos* in the National Library at Madrid.
3 H. Flores: *Memorias de las Reynas Catholicas*, 2nd ed., Madrid 1770, Vol. II, p. 530.

depicted on one seal with an orb.[1] In the absence of evidence as to the dates of the respective seals it would seem more likely that Yolande copied the orb from Constance, who as the heir to the Hohenstaufen throne of Sicily might be considered a queen regnant and so entitled to have an orb.

The seal of Sancho shows him with an orb with a large cross on it in his left hand and a sceptre surmounted by an eagle in his right hand, and this is repeated in the early seals of Alphonso XI. In his later seals, however, the sceptre is replaced by a sword. There is no other evidence to show whether any such sceptres or orbs really existed or were merely depicted on the seals, etc., in imitation of other countries; there is an ebony sceptre said to be from this period on the tomb of Ferdinand III in Seville Cathedral, but it does not seem to have been properly examined and may well prove to have been made later by the cathedral authorities. One of the interesting questions yet to be answered is the extent in which the eagle was used in actual royal devices in mediaeval Castile; it may be significant that it is embroidered on the pillow which was beneath the head of Ferdinand de la Cerda (the grandson of Beatrice of Swabia and the son of the claimant of the Holy Roman Empire) in his tomb at Burgos.

A miniature in the National Library at Madrid shows Alphonso X with a closed crown, presumably as Emperor. Alphonso's son Sancho had prepared for his infant son a description of the attributes and symbolism of royalty, and this includes a description of the king wearing a closed crown, carrying a sword in his right hand and in his left an orb with a cross on top. A sceptre is also mentioned among the regalia of the king. These are the only occurrences of the closed crown in Castile apart from the dubious identification of two miniatures in the Pontifical of the Columbus Library in Seville as John I.[2]

The coins of Alphonso XI show a new crown with a number of large *fleurons* interspersed with smaller ones. We do not know definitely whether Alphonso actually had a crown of this style, but his son Peter I almost certainly did. Peter's will,[3] dated 18th November 1362, is a most important document for the study of mediaeval Spanish jewellery. After stating that in the absence of male heirs his kingdom should devolve on his eldest daughter Beatrice, who with her sisters had been legitimised by act of the Cortes in the previous year, he makes a large number of specific bequests of regalia and jewellery, among them three crowns. To his second daughter Constance he intended to leave 'the crown with the cameos which was of the King my father, whom God pardon, and the crown with the eagles which belonged to the Queen of Aragon, my aunt'. For obvious reasons the cameo crown cannot be identified as the one found in Sancho's tomb; the crown with the eagles, however, was in Seville Cathedral until the XIX century and was known as the crown of St Ferdinand. It is clearly Aragonese in

---

[1] See p. 602.

[2] The National Library miniature has been published by A. Ballesteros y Biretta: *Historia de España y su influencia en la historia universal*, Barcelona 1922, Vol. III, p. 13. For Sancho's symbolism see *Los castigos* of Sancho IV, Chapter 11, published in *Biblioteca de autores españoles*, No. 51, Madrid 1860, p. 111. For the Columbus Library miniatures, see p. 599.

[3] Published in P. Lopez de Ayala: *Crónica del Rey Don Pedro, Crónicas de los Reyes de Castilla*, Madrid 1779, Vol. I, p. 558; and J. B. Sitges: *Las mujeres de Don Pedro I de Castilla*, Madrid 1910, p. 250.

a   Crown with the eagles. Formerly in Seville Cathedral from where it was stolen in 1871 (p. 605)

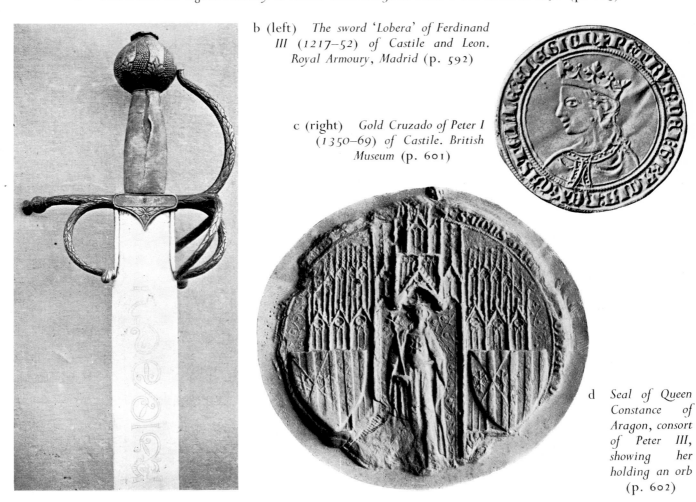

b (left)   The sword 'Lobera' of Ferdinand III (1217–52) of Castile and Leon. Royal Armoury, Madrid (p. 592)

c (right)   Gold Cruzado of Peter I (1350–69) of Castile. British Museum (p. 601)

d   Seal of Queen Constance of Aragon, consort of Peter III, showing her holding an orb (p. 602)

b   Seal of Peter IV of Aragon (1336–87), obverse. Date of seal 1344. Shows the probable form of regalia of that period (p. 607)

a   Double crown of Martin of Aragon (1396–1410). A votive crown, unique of its kind, composed of two coronets and with an obscure motto on its base. Barcelona Cathedral (p. 608)

c   Reverse of (b). Showing shield of Barcelona with a coronet closely resembling those in double crown of Martin of Aragon (p. 608)

d   Crown with the pelicans. Currand Collection, National Museum, Florence (p. 613)

origin and is described at page 605. To his third daughter, Isabel, Peter intended to leave 'the French crown which belonged to Blanche, daughter of the Duke of Bourbon'.[1] Among his other bequests were two *alhaytes* (a Moorish word meaning collar or breast ornament) made in Seville and each containing one of the great balas rubies Peter had obtained from King Bermejo of Granada; these were to go to Beatrice and Constance. To his natural son John he intended to leave his Castilian sword ornamented with stones and pearls and a very rich saddle. He also partitioned between the sisters the jewels of their mother, Maria de Padilla, his minor jewels and his silver. Finally he stated that the heir to his kingdom should take the residue of his treasure.

It is noteworthy that although Beatrice was to inherit the kingdom she was not left a crown, but only some specific personal ornaments. The inference from this is that the items listed in the will were Peter's major personal ornaments and that there were other ornaments of state, including a crown, which would pass automatically to his successor. It is also noteworthy that although there is a strong tradition that Peter took 3 balas rubies from Bermejo only 2 are mentioned in the will. As he seems to have considered these gems to be particularly important it is quite likely that he would have set the third in a place of honour in his state crown, which would probably be the one depicted on the coins with a number of large *fleurons* interspersed with smaller ones. It is possible to go further and deduce that the *Courone d'Espaigne* in the English inventories was Peter's state crown. We have already seen[2] that there is strong circumstantial evidence that this crown came into the English treasury as part payment for the troops which the Black Prince led into Spain to recover Peter's throne. It consisted of seven large and seven small *fleurons* and was set with a great balas ruby, which was not only given an individual value but an individual weight, a great rarity in those days, which might imply that it was a stone of great importance. It contained no cameos nor eagles and thus cannot be identified with the crowns Peter intended to leave to Constance, and although it is possible that it may have been Blanche's crown; the description of the latter in the will implies that, unlike the other two, it did not have any major decorative feature. If it had contained a great balas, it seems strange that this was not mentioned. On the other hand the crown in the English inventories tallies with the shape of crowns on Peter's coins (*Plate 209, c*). Although the evidence is far from being conclusive it seems reasonable to infer that the crown in the English inventories is the state crown of Peter and that the main ruby set in it is the third balas of Bermejo. From the inventory the following description of the crown can be deduced:

The band had the great balas set in the middle in the front and also had 6 other very large balas rubies, alternating with 7 smaller sapphires. Above each balas in the band rose a very large *fleuron*, each being set with a lesser balas (valued at £13 6s. 8d. each as against £603 6s. 8d. for the central balas in the circle and £100 each for the others, but still large enough to warrant the inventory description 'gross'), 1 ruby, 3 sapphires and 22 pearls. The arrangement of the stones in each *fleuron* might well have been the ruby in the stem, the balas in the centre and a sapphire in each leaf. Above each sapphire in the band was a smaller *fleuron* set with a small balas (valued at £5), a

---

1 Peter's legal wife whom he had repudiated. She died in prison in July 1361.
2 See Chapter Seven—England, p. 175.

small sapphire and some 6 small pearls. The number of stones that the inventory shows were in the large *fleurons* indicates that the depictions on coins, etc., of the crowns of Peter and his successors with their very high fleurs-de-lis in proportion to rather narrow circlets were not fanciful.

Peter's will was never executed. In 1366, after his natural half-brother, Henry of Trastamara, had invaded Castile, he fled from Seville to Bayonne with as much of his treasure as he could take with him. He had to dispose of all this to pay the troops in Gascony. The same English inventory gives full descriptions of a sword and a saddle which seem likely to have been those mentioned in the will, and also a gold *pallet* or helmet.[1] The rest of Peter's treasure fell into the hands of the Trastamarans.

Peter's eldest surviving daughter, Constance, married John of Gaunt, who after the death of Peter in 1369 claimed the Castilian throne in the name of his wife and now entitled himself 'King of Castile and Leon, Duke of Lancaster'. He was not, however, accorded precedence in England as a king until 8th March 1386, shortly before his departure for the invasion of Castile. On that occasion Richard II presented him and Constance with gold crowns to be used at the coronation ceremony in Burgos if the expedition was successful. In the event the invasion ended in stalemate, and in 1387 John of Gaunt came to terms with John I of Castile, who had succeeded his father in 1379. John of Gaunt abandoned his claims in return for a substantial pension and the marriage of his daughter Catherine to John's heir Henry. A clause of the settlement provided that the title 'Prince of Asturias' should be bestowed on Henry, in imitation of the English 'Prince of Wales', and this title of the heir to the Spanish throne was retained until the end of the Spanish monarchy in the xx century. At the conclusion of the main negotiations John of Gaunt sent to John, by the hand of Constance, the crown which Richard had given him for his Castilian coronation. John was so moved with this gift that he presented Constance with the town of Huete in addition to his other cessions under the settlement.

We have considerable superficial knowledge of the Trastamaran royal ornaments from chronicles and royal wills as well as from pictures, coins and seals, but no certain knowledge of the style or design. John left some crowns to his queen, and the royal crowns and the swords *de virtud*[2] to his successor, Henry III. On the latter's death his son John II was an infant. Queen Catherine and Henry's brother Prince Ferdinand, who later became King of Aragon, secured the throne for John, but in the troubled times of the regency the royal treasure was dispersed. John more than made up for this when he came of age, as he was a great collector of jewels. In particular he despoiled the rebellious nobles who had grown over-powerful during the regency.

After the death of one of these, Alvaro de Luna, the treasure of the Kings of Castile was found buried beneath a pillar at his palace in Madrid. It included the swords of the Cid and the girdle of Zobeida, mentioned above, and a gold crown of Peter. There

---

[1] The sword was valued at £1,218 13s. 4d.; the saddle at £1,141 13s. 4d. and the helmet at £1,708.

[2] The exact significance of this phrase is elusive. It may refer to state swords used for ceremonial entries into cities and for dubbing knights, but there is no evidence that the kings had more than one of these. On the other hand the phrase may have been intended to refer to, or include, the swords with a historical and romantic significance, such as the swords of the Cid.

are not, however, sufficient details to identify this with any of those mentioned in Peter's will. On John's death these were inherited by Henry IV, who kept great treasures in the *Alcazar* of Segovia, where, according to the *Reminiscences of Leon de Rosmital* of a journey in Spain and Portugal in 1465–7,[1] were kept thirty-four golden effigies of Spanish kings, sitting on royal thrones, holding sceptres and orbs. Isabel the Catholic inherited all this treasure when she succeeded Henry IV in 1474.

From pictures, notably an altar-piece by Peter Serra, coins and seals it appears that the Trastamaran crowns consisted of very narrow diadems set with gems and pearls, from which rose some four very tall *fleurons* with smaller ones between them. On the coins these *fleurons* sometimes took the shape of the Cross of St James of Compostella, as indeed they had done on some of the coins of Peter. Some of the seals show the kings with orbs, but they all hold swords instead of sceptres. Once again the only ornaments which have survived are swords, two of which are now in the Royal Armoury:

> *The Pontifical*[2] *sword of John II*, given to him by Pope Eugenius IV in 1446, has a straight blade with bevelled edges and a channel in the centre. There is an engraved inscription near the guard, which is of gilded silver, forming a cross whose ends are formal *fleurons*. The hilt resembles a balustrade, and the pommel is pear shaped. An inventory of 1503 shows that there was originally considerable enamelwork on the sword, but this has now vanished.
>
> *The blade of the Pontifical sword of Henry IV*, given to him by Pope Calixtus III in 1458, to encourage him to fight against the Moors. The 1503 inventory shows that this sword was originally very rich; all that remains is an engraving on the blade showing a shield with a bull, surmounted by the tiara and the keys and with this inscription: *ACCIPE. S.C.M. GLADIUM. MUNUS. A. DEO. I. QUO. DEI. CIES ADVERSARIOS. P.P.LI. MEI..XPIANI.*

THE KINGDOM OF NAVARRE

When the Moors reached the Pyrenees they met with similar resistance to that encountered in the Asturian mountains. The mountain tribes maintained an uneasy independence for some two centuries and in 905 their leader Sancho Garcia took the title of King. In the next century, under Sancho the Great (*obiit* 1035), Navarre was briefly the greatest Christian kingdom in Spain, but when Sancho divided his kingdom on his death it never regained this position, and remained a buffer state controlling the western passes of the Pyrenees. Its neighbours made many attempts to absorb it, both by force of arms and by dynastic marriages, and at various stages of its history Navarre formed part of Aragon and France. But between these periods of uneasy annexation the little country maintained its independence, and it was not until 1512 that Spanish Navarre was finally incorporated into the united Kingdom of Spain by the troops of Ferdinand the Catholic.

Patriotic local historians have claimed that from the first there was an inauguration

---

[1] Cited by Ferrandis, op. cit., p. xv.

[2] These pontifical swords were known as 'Stocco'. Each year on Christmas Eve the Pope consecrated a sword which he sent as a gift to a son of the Church, normally to the one who best deserved it, but on occasions to one who was dilatory with an exhortation to encourage him to attack the Church's enemies. See Chapter Twenty-three—*Scotland*, p. 566.

ceremony for the kings of Navarre in the simple Teutonic form of elevation on a shield and the swearing of mutual oaths. This ceremony is mentioned in the early *fueros* of Navarre and is indeed very old, but it is impossible to date it. In 1234 when Theobald I, Count of Champagne, became King of Navarre he added anointing to the ceremony, supposedly in imitation of the Kings of France, but equally in imitation of his fellow Spanish monarchs in Castile and Aragon. Louis Hutin, son of Philip IV of France and heir to the French throne, was crowned King of Navarre in 1307 with all the formalities prescribed by the *fuero*, despite the fact that his father had told him that it was unnecessary for him to be crowned in his Spanish kingdom.

From the detailed description of the coronation of Charles III[1] on 13th February 1390 we know that the regalia included a crown, sword, sceptre and shield. After the King had been anointed he changed back into his robes and went to the high altar on which were the sword, crown and sceptre. After the Bishop of Pamplona had said the appointed prayers the King took the sword and girded it on with his own hands. He then unsheathed it, waved it on high as a sign of justice and re-sheathed it. Then, after more prayers had been said, he took the crown and crowned himself. Finally he took the sceptre in his hand and mounted on the royal shield which had the arms of the kingdom painted on it. The shield was carried by the barons, and the procurators of the three districts of Pamplona, and the great crowd, shouted, '*Real! Real! Real!*' while the King showered largesse. When he dismounted he was led to the throne and enthroned by the papal legate and the two senior bishops. Then followed a *Te Deum* and a general acclamation, after which the Bishop of Pamplona celebrated a sung mass and the King offered the customary gifts.

On the death of Charles III in 1425 he was succeeded by his daughter Blanche. She seems to have been proclaimed at Olite separately from her husband, Prince John of Aragon. The latter entered Navarre at the head of an army to be proclaimed King, and his wife sent him from Olite the royal standard with the arms of Navarre. John was then proclaimed King in front of his army. This use of the royal standard is similar to that in Castile at the accession ceremonies following the abandonment of coronations. In Navarre, however, coronations in the traditional style continued until the kingdom was conquered by Ferdinand the Catholic.

None of the ornaments of the Navarrese regalia have survived. It appears that the Navarrese dynasty introduced the fleur-de-lis crown to Castile, and the inference is that it already featured on the crowns in Navarre. The lily emblem was certainly venerated there from an early date, for in 1048 Garcia IV created the Order of the Lily of Navarre in honour of the Virgin.[2] From miniatures and coins it appears that in the XIV century the Navarrese crowns were similar to those in the neighbouring kingdoms with tall fleurs-de-lis interspersed with small ornaments, and in the XIV century these intermediate ornaments became almost as large as the fleurs-de-lis themselves. We also know a little about the crowns from the few inventories which have been published:

1 Quoted in J. Yanguas y Miranda: *Diccionario de Antigüedades del Reino de Navarra*, Pamplona 1840, Vol. I, p. 263.

2 G. J. Osma: *Las divisas del Rey en los pavimentos de 'obra de Manises' del Castillo de Napoles. Textos y Documentos Valencianos*, No. III, Madrid 1909, p. 54.

for example an inventory taken in 1362 of jewels sent from Bruges for Queen Joan, wife of Charles II, mentions several gold crowns, including one with eight *fleurons*.[1] The documents of the mediaeval Navarrese royal treasury have been catalogued[2] and further research will probably provide more information. One manuscript which would repay detailed study is the *Ceremonial de los reyes de Navarra* at Pamplona Cathedral, an illustrated contemporary record from the time of Charles III, which includes a miniature showing two bishops putting a crown with tall fleurs-de-lis on the head of a king seated on a throne. Another is the *Pontifical Hispalense* at the Columbus Library in Seville, which is said to have been written by the Bishop of Calahorra about 1390 for the Queen of Navarre. It contains a miniature showing a king wearing a crown with an arch and holding a sceptre with an orb on top. This king has been stated to be John of Castile,[3] but practically the only place in which the arched crown and the combined sceptre and orb appear simultaneously is England. It would be more likely for English influence to be found in Castile than Navarre at that time, but there is only one other representation known to the writer of a Castilian king with an arched crown, and the connection of this miniature with Navarre cannot be entirely dismissed.

THE KINGDOMS OF ARAGON AND MALLORCA

Aragon was a tiny county in the central Pyrenees which was incorporated into the Kingdom of Navarre in the x century. On the death of Sancho the Great of Navarre in 1035 his natural son Ramiro inherited Aragon as King. There is a dubious tradition that Pope Benedict IX anointed him and blessed his crown and sceptre. By the beginning of the XII century the little kingdom had expanded southwards towards the Ebro by encroaching on the Moors and eastwards along the southern slopes of the Pyrenees at the expense of the short-lived kingdom of Sobrarbe and a number of counties of the Spanish Mark, and had temporarily added Navarre to its domains. The reign of Alphonso I, the Quarrelsome (1102–34), who is said to have been crowned at Huesca, marked the ascendency of Aragon among the Christian states of the Peninsula. His marriage with Urraca of Castile united for a time the three Christian kingdoms, and Alphonso styled himself Emperor of Spain. The time was not ripe for such a union, and Alphonso had to relinquish first the Castilian kingdom and then the imperial title to his step-son Alphonso VII of Castile. Alphonso I, however, expanded Aragon across the Ebro and gave the reconquest a strong religious character. On his death, childless, he bequeathed his kingdom to the Templars and the Knights of St John of Jerusalem. The people of Aragon were not content with this solution and proclaimed Alphonso's brother, Ramiro, who was a monk, as King. Ramiro reigned long enough to marry, become the

---

1 Davillier, op. cit., p. 41, note. An inventory of goods of Iñes, Countess of Foix, sister of Charles II of Navarre, includes a gold crown which her mother gave her. P. Fernando de Mendoza: *Los Plateros de Carlos el Noble*, Pamplona 1925, p. 85.

2 José Ramon Castro: Archivo General de Navarra, *Catálogo de la Seccion de Comptos*, Pamplona 1952, etc.

3 E.g., F. J. Sánchez Cantón: *Los retratos de los reyes de España*, Barcelona 1948, p. 60.

father of a daughter, Petronilla, and betroth her to Count Ramon Berenguer IV of Barcelona. He then retired to his monastery, Ramon Berenguer becoming ruler of Aragon and Navarre regaining its independence under Garci-Ramirez.

At the time of the union the County of Barcelona was much more important than the Kingdom of Aragon in terms of wealth and population, and had already absorbed a number of smaller counties of the Spanish Mark. Catalonia, as these counties came to be called, had cultural and linguistic ties with the south of France, and the city of Barcelona itself had a flourishing Mediterranean trade, particularly with Italy. Henceforth Aragon was not only a Spanish state, expanding down the east coast to well south of Valencia, and at times united with Navarre, but also the centre of a Mediterranean empire which at various times included the Balearic Islands, parts of Southern France, Corsica, Sardinia, Sicily and Naples. It was never possible, however, for the Aragonese kings to wield the scattered and heterogeneous peoples of this empire into one realm. Instead James I (1213–76) and Peter III (1276–85) successively regarded Mallorca and Sicily as separate kingdoms for their younger sons to inherit.

The son of Ramon Berenguer and Petronilla, Alphonso II (1162–96) extended his power to the north of the Pyrenees, acquiring the counties of Provence and Roussillon, which he left to his second son on his death, and accepting the homage of Béarn and Bigorre. His will contains the first mention of a crown in the Kingdom of Aragon, for he left in perpetuity to the Monastery of Poblet *regiam coronam meam*. A contemporary miniature[1] suggests that this crown was of plain design consisting of several plates. His son Peter II (1196–1213) continued his French policy, and partly to win papal support for this went to Rome in 1204, and acknowledged the Pope as his feudal overlord, promising to pay an annual tribute to the papacy. In return he was to be protected by papal authority and was accorded a papal coronation. He was anointed by the Bishop of Portuense, crowned by Innocent III and invested with the mitre, sceptre, orb and mantle. This unusual investiture of a king with a mitre has not been satisfactorily explained; it was not perpetuated in the Aragonese coronation ceremony, presumably because of the argument as to the Church's part in it. Blancas[2] relates a story that Peter believing that the Pope's custom was to place his feet on the crown as a part of the ceremony had the crown made of unleavened bread set with gems, so that the Pope had to put it on with his hands. This crown was offered at the altar at St Peter's, together with the sceptre; Schramm infers from the fact that the descriptions of the ceremony do not refer to this as a gift that it was merely symbolical and that Peter returned home with his crown, but to have made such a gift would have been in accordance with occasional practice.

One interesting effect of this coronation appears on Peter's seals. Prior to 1204 they showed him holding a sword and a sceptre decorated with a fleur-de-lis; after 1204 the sword is replaced by an orb with a cross. The seals both before and after 1204

---

1 A diploma of 1195 at Jaca Cathedral. In general the miniatures in Aragon are a less valuable source than they are in Castile, largely because the latter country tended to be isolated from the main streams of European art, forcing the local artists to draw on their own experience rather than to copy contemporary fashion, while the Aragonese artists were much more open to foreign influence.

2 Geronimo de Blancas: *Las coronaciones de los Reyes de Aragon*, Saragossa 1641.

depict Peter's crown decorated with crosses; his coins, however, show crowns with balls, which may have been in imitation of the Kings of Castile of that period.

Peter's acknowledgment of the feudal supremacy of the Pope was deeply resented in Aragon, and the feudal dues were not paid. His son James, who inherited the throne at the age of three, was not crowned, although in 1221 he attended Mass with his bride at Tarragona and girded himself with his sword at the altar. His early seals reflected this, for he was depicted without an orb or a sceptre and with a sword across his lap. At some time between 1231 and 1238 an orb was added to the seals, and it is likely that this shows the influence of his second marriage to Yolande of Hungary in 1234. At the end of his reign James made a journey to see the Pope at the Council of Lyons in 1274 and requested a papal coronation. The Pope refused to crown him unless he renewed the vassalage acknowledged by his father and paid the arrears of the feudal dues. This James refused to do, and he returned home uncrowned. He had taken with him to Lyons a particularly rich crown worth over 100,000 sueldos. James's own account[1] describes it as being better than any other in Lyons, and we can suppose that it was newly made for the occasion in Gothic style with large fleurs-de-lis similar to contemporary crowns in other countries, and that it replaced the earlier style of crowns with crosses or balls which continued to be reproduced on James's seals and coins. Certainly when James's son Peter III came to the throne in 1276 his coins showed a crown with large fleurs-de-lis.

Peter was crowned with his Queen, Constance, daughter of Manfred of Sicily, at Saragossa on 16th November 1276. It seems likely that this coronation was inspired partly by his father's disappointment and partly by his desire to underline the claim of Constance to the throne of Sicily, from which her family had been displaced by Charles of Anjou. In order to overcome the difficulties of acknowledging papal supremacy he gave the ceremony a peculiarly Aragonese twist. Although he and Constance were crowned by the Archbishop of Tarragona, to whom the Pope in 1204 had given the right to crown the Kings of Aragon, Peter had previously made a solemn protest before the notables of the realm that did not receive the crown in the name of the Roman Church. He was also careful not to use the royal ornaments or the title of King before his coronation, presumably to underline that it was an act of confirmation in the title by the people of Aragon. His successor, Alphonso III, was in Mallorca at the time of his accession in 1285 and used the title of King in despatches before being crowned, at which the nobles protested greatly, even though Alphonso had been acknowledged as heir by the estates of the realm at the time of his father's coronation. Alphonso also made a protest that he received his crown *nec pro ipsa ecclesia nec contra ecclesiam* and stated that he would not prejudice his successors from being crowned elsewhere than at Saragossa. It seems likely that at his coronation Peter was invested with a stole in recognition of his wife's claim to the throne of Sicily, where this vestment had previously been in use; certainly the stole featured in the Aragonese coronation ceremony after his reign and the Sicilian connection makes it probable that it started with Peter. With his coronation also the sceptre reappears on the royal seals, so that the kings were

[1] M. Flotals and A. de Bofarull: *Historia del Rey de Aragon Don Jaime I*, Madrid 1848, p. 413.

shown with an orb in their right hand, a sceptre in the left and a sword across the lap. In one seal[1] (*Plate 209, d*) Constance is shown holding an orb surmounted by a double cross—this is sometimes known as the Patriarchal cross. Little is known of the significance of this symbol, which appears from time to time throughout Europe. It occurs on the reverse of coins minted in Aragon (but not Catalonia) from the time of James I to that of Peter IV and also on some Mallorcan coins and in miniatures in the Mallorcan Book of Privileges; there is also a notable double processional cross in the Episcopal Museum at Vich. Its use on the orb of Constance may thus have derived from a local tradition. On the other hand the double cross on the orb is associated in Hungary with the Angevin dynasty, and it is possible that they had introduced it also into Sicily when they displaced Manfred, and that it was borrowed, at least heraldically by their Aragonese Hohenstaufen rivals. Constance was presumably depicted holding an orb as Queen of Sicily, as orbs were not usually given to queens consort, although her sister-in-law Queen Yolande of Castile is depicted with one.[2]

James I had conquered the Moorish kingdoms of Valencia and the Balearic Islands. The former was incorporated into the Kingdom of Aragon but the latter, together with Roussillon and Montpellier, were left to his second son James with the title of King of Mallorca. After the Sicilian Vespers in 1282 Peter III drove the French out of Sicily and accepted the kingdom on behalf of his wife, being crowned at Palermo on 2nd September 1282. His French wars brought him into conflict with his brother, who acknowledged French overlordship for his lands in Provence, and at the end of his reign he sent a fleet to the Balearic Islands under his son Alphonso. On Peter's death Alphonso succeeded to the Aragonese throne and soon completed the conquest of the Balearics. Peter's second son James became King of Sicily. On Alphonso's death, childless, in 1291 James succeeded to the throne of Aragon; he was careful only to use the title of King of Sicily until his coronation, at which he made a protest in the same form as his brother had, adding that he took the throne as the eldest surviving son of Peter III and not as his brother's heir. For a short time Sicily and Aragon were united, but in 1294 by the Peace of Agnani James agreed to return Sicily to the Angevins in exchange for Sardinia and Corsica, which he had incorporated into his kingdom by the end of his reign. The Sicilians, however, did not accept this treaty and elected James's younger brother Frederick, who had been left in Sicily as governor, as their King, and successfully maintained their independence; the Catalan mercenaries who helped them to do so subsequently entered the Byzantine Empire and founded the Sicilian Duchy of Athens. James also restored the Kingdom of Mallorca to his uncle and namesake, but remained as its feudal overlord.

From the reign of James II we learn more about the Aragonese royal ornaments from letters, receipts and inventories. At least five separate crowns can be identified from these, and there were probably more in existence. Two of them were queens'

---

1 F. de Sagarra: *Sigillografia Catalana*, Barcelona 1915, Vol. I, p. 234.
2 See p. 594.

crowns which may for convenience be described as the 'Crown of the Queen of Aragon' and the 'Emerald crown of Blanche of Anjou'.

The Crown of the Queen of Aragon. This crown of nine pieces was given by James to his Queen, Blanche of Anjou, in August 1304.[1] After her death in 1310 the crown reverted to the Treasury and is mentioned in a document dated at Valencia on 20th April 1311. The same crown, identifiable by the number of pieces and jewels, was given in 1315 as a wedding present to James's second Queen, Mary of Cyprus. In her will dated 2nd April 1319 she left it to the Infanta Violante. In the letter authorising the gift to Queen Mary the crown is described in sufficient detail for its shape to be deduced. Each of the nine pieces was surmounted by a 'pinnacle', eight of these being set with a large pearl each and one, presumably the central one, with a large balas. The plates themselves were each set with one large stone and four smaller ones. Where the large stone was a balas the smaller ones were sapphires or emeralds; where it was a sapphire the smaller ones were balases. Thus the central plate was set with a large balas and 4 emeralds, and the two on each side of it each with a large emerald and 4 balases. Next to these were two each set with a large balas and 4 sapphires, and the two next to these were each set with a large sapphire and 4 balases. The two plates at the back were each set with a large balas, one of them having 4 emeralds and the other 4 sapphires. The crown also contained numerous smaller stones and pearls. With its alternating and contrasting stones it displayed a symmetry unusual in jewellery of this period, and it would be most interesting to know more of its origin.

The Emerald Crown of Blanche of Anjou. In a document dated 23rd October 1313 James ordered his treasurer Arnald Messeguer to transfer to his[2] daughter Isabel a number of jewels and other items which had belonged to Queen Blanche. These included two garlands, one of nine pieces with 5 great sapphires and other jewels, and the other decorated with twenty roses, two gold *fleurons* from a crown, a dress decorated with eagles and a crown. The crown was of sixteen pieces with sixteen pinnacles made in the form of *fleurons*, and was set with 8 large emeralds, 8 rather smaller ones, 64 small emeralds and 87 garnets. The fact that the only important stones in this crown were emeralds shows an unusual sense of style, and as in the case of the previous crown it would be interesting to know more of its origin.

We also know of three other crowns, one with thirteen pieces and two that each had eleven pieces. The major stones of the thirteen-piece crown were 16 balases, 6 emeralds and 53 large pearls; on the rim were gold ornaments, presumably *fleurons*, set with pearls and turquoises. This crown was evidently not the most important that the King possessed because it was twice deposited as a guarantee for a loan: in 1312, together with two others, with the Master of Calatrava, and in 1318 with the Archbishop of Tarragona; on both occasions it had two stones missing, and we can infer that it was not used sufficiently for it to be worth repairing. Also deposited with the Master of Calatrava in 1312 was a crown of eleven pieces set with balases, emeralds, sapphires and pearls; this crown is listed after the others in the inventory and less details of it are given, the implication being that it was comparatively unimportant. The third crown deposited with the Master of Calatrava was also of eleven pieces. Although the number of jewels are not listed a peculiarity in the description makes it identifiable with another crown of eleven plates to be found in an inventory of goods in

1 All references to letters and other documents of the reign of James II, unless otherwise stated, may be found in J. E. Martinez Ferrando: *Jaime II de Aragon*, Barcelona 1948.

2 H. Finke: *Acta Aragonesa*, Berlin 1922, Vol. III, p. 239.

the Royal Chamber in 1323.[1] This in turn can be identified by the number and type of stones with a crown of eleven pieces redeemed from the Templars in 1303. This crown, which is fully considered below, is of particular importance for art historians, but does not seem to have been James's main crown. In the 1312 receipt it appears after the crown with thirteen pieces as *item aliam coronam auri* . . ., neither its place nor its description being consistent with its being the King's main crown. We may therefore deduce that James had yet another crown which was his most important one.

Three letters between 1321 and 1323 tell us of the fate of three of these crowns. On 1st November 1321 James wrote from Tortosa to the Bishop of Barcelona telling him to return to safe custody the crowns and other ornaments which he had taken out as it was extremely dangerous to do so; he was not to take them out again without the King's permission. On 9th July 1322 James wrote from Barcelona to Charles IV of France; he had been seriously ill and had wanted to sell his crown and other jewels to pay his debts. Charles had heard of this and wanted to buy the crown, and James now had to write and say that he could not sell them to him as they were in the custody of the Bishop of Barcelona; he therefore advised Charles to send emissaries to the Bishop to inspect these ornaments. The implication of this letter is that the King's main state crown was to be sold. Finally on 29th November 1323 James wrote to the Bishop of Barcelona and told him to sell 'those three gold royal crowns of ours'. The wording of this final letter implies that the three crowns are the same ones whose sale had already been considered and which had been in the Bishop's care for some time; they would therefore not have included the eleven-plated crown which had been in the Royal Chamber a few months previously.

The importance of this other crown is that its description tallies with the photograph of the crown which was stolen on 30th April 1873 from Seville Cathedral, where from time to time it adorned the statue of the *Virgen de los Reyes*. From this photograph, which was the only evidence available, and the local tradition which called it the 'Crown of Saint Ferdinand' Schramm made a series of deductions. The photograph showed that the crown had remarkable similarities in style to those nailed to the cross at Cracow, which Schramm has attributed to the workmen of Henry (1225–35), son of the Emperor Frederick of Hohenstaufen. Schramm considered that the Seville crown was probably made in the Rhineland in the early XIII century, and that it came to Spain when Beatrice of Swabia (who was first cousin of the Emperor Frederick) married

---

[1] F. Martorell y Traball: *Inventari del bens de la cambra reyal en temps de Jaime II. Anuari de l'Institut d'Estudis Catalans*, Any IV, 1911–12, p. 561. The 1312 inventory reads as follows: *item aliam coronam auri undecim peciarum in qua sunt baleys grossi et minuti et saffiri grossi et minuti, et maracdi et safiri et perle.* The 1323 inventory is in Catalan and in much greater detail, but is in the same order of 'large and small balases, large and small sapphires, emeralds and sapphires and pearls'. The unnecessary double occurrence of sapphires in both inventories suggests that they were both taken from an earlier inventory, possibly the 1303 one amended when the extra sapphires were added to the crown. The two different spellings 'saffiri' and 'safiri' also occur in the 1323 inventory as 'safirs' and 'saffirs' but probably are without significance. The first item in the 1323 inventory reads: i. *espaha appeilada Ticon.* On his deathbed James I had sent his eldest son, later Peter III, a sword of this name, and this is presumably the same one. In his autobiography James said that the sword gave such virtue to those who carried it that he preferred it to a lance: M. Flotals and A. de Bofarull, op. cit., p. 188.

Ferdinand III in 1219. Although he considered the passage in the will of Peter I of Castile where he wished to leave to his daughter Constance 'the crown with the eagles which belonged to the Queen of Aragon, my aunt' and recognised that the crown might have had an Aragonese origin, he preferred to call it 'The Crown of Beatrice of Swabia', a name which has been repeated by Biehn.

The crown (*Plate 209, a*) depicted in the photograph consisted of a number of plates; Davillier, who evidently visited Seville a few years after the theft, said ten, and Schramm, relying on the photograph, twelve. The photograph certainly gives the impression that there were eleven or twelve. The centre plate was surmounted by a crowned double-headed eagle of the type used by the Hapsburgs, clearly a xvi-century addition. The other plates of the crown are in an entirely different style. The two either side of the centre plate are each set in the middle with one very large oval stone surrounded by a number of very small stones, and have one smallish oval stone in each corner of the plate. The background is of foliage worked in relief. Surmounting these two plates are 'pinnacles' topped with what is probably a large pearl surrounded by 6 very small garnets, and with two smallish stones set in each side. Standing out from each pinnacle is an eagle with a wrought surface with wings outstretched. Each eagle has a largish stone set in the middle of its breast and three small stones in each wing. The next two plates, flanking those just described, are less clear in the photograph. They appear to be wider and to be divided into two parts: one-half being a repetition of the first two plates with a large stone set in the centre of a square with four smaller ones in each of the corners, the other consisting of a rosette of 7 pearls above which a very small wrought eagle is joined to the plate itself. Above the square of stones in these plates are 'pinnacles' set with stones and larger eagles in the same way as the two plates already described. The setting of the stones has been thoroughly considered by Schramm and there seems no reason to doubt his conclusion that the peculiar type of setting with the stones protruding from the plates on metal 'stems' is similar to that of the Cracow crowns and originated in Sicily. On the other hand if the crown in the photograph is to be identified with that in the inventory of James II's Royal Chamber, Schramm's theory that it was the crown of Beatrice of Swabia must be abandoned.

Three points aid this identification. First the number of plates: the crown in the inventory had eleven plates; the one in the photograph eleven or twelve. But the centre plate of the latter was clearly added or altered later, and so even if we consider, as Schramm does, that the photograph shows twelve plates the number can be equated with that of the inventory crown. Secondly the inventory describes the crown as having eagles which were apparently set with stones in the same way as the ones shown in the photograph; it does not seem likely that two crowns decorated with this type of eagle existed, one in Castile and one in Aragon.[1] Finally there is the historical evidence of Peter's will. 'The Queen of Aragon, my aunt' was Eleanor, sister of Alphonso XI of Castile, who married James II's son and successor Alphonso IV. Alphonso would probably have given his new Queen a crown in the same way as his father had given crowns to his two Queens. Peter presumably obtained it when he had his aunt murdered in 1359. He held the city of Seville in special regard and began the construction of the royal chapel in the old cathedral; it is not unlikely that he would have presented this crown to the cathedral at some time between the making of his will in 1362 and his flight to Bayonne in 1365.

The only positive evidence to support the claims of Beatrice, i.e. the traditional attribution of the crown to St Ferdinand, is explicable by the fact that it 'belonged' to the statue of the *Virgen de los Reyes*, which is said to have been given by St Louis of France to Ferdinand and by him to the

[1] For a quite different eagle crown of Isabel I, see p. 611. Although the eagle was not a common emblem in Spain up to the xiv or xv centuries thereafter it became quite common.

cathedral. It is easy to see that a later donation of the crown might have been confused with the original donation of the statue. Indeed the confusion might have been deliberate on the part of the Trastamaran propagandists who attempted to conceal any good deeds of Peter. A further consideration is that if Alphonso X had had access to the crown, as he would have done even if it had been donated to Seville Cathedral by Ferdinand, he would almost certainly have used it, with the eagles as evidence of his Hohenstaufen connection, in his campaign to become Emperor. There is, however, no evidence that he did so.

We cannot be certain of the origin of this crown, but some light is shed by its earlier history. A comparison of the jewels in the 1323 inventory with those of the eleven-plated crown, which together with two sceptres, a 'flor' and an orb was redeemed from the Templars in 1303,[1] shows them to be so nearly identical as to make it almost certain that it is the same crown. Unfortunately it is not possible to work out an arrangement of the stones which fits exactly with those shown in the photograph, although the numbers are approximately right, if pearls are included. This is only to be expected in view of the XVI-century alteration. The set of regalia pawned to the Templars might well have been James's Sicilian regalia put to this use after Sicily had regained its independence. Alternatively they may have belonged to James's mother, Queen Constance, who died in 1300. Both these possibilities fit with Schramm's theory of the Sicilian origin of the settings of the stones and his view that the eagles have a Hohenstaufen significance.

Neither of the previous ideas as to the origin of this interesting crown, the traditional attribution to St Ferdinand and Schramm's attribution to Beatrice of Swabia, correspond to the existing evidence. Further research may well throw more light on its history, and until we can be more certain it would be safer for it to be called the 'Eagle Crown' than for it to be attributed specifically to any person.

From 1299 James's seals depict him holding an orb with the double or patriarchal cross, but we have no means of knowing whether this was merely heraldic. The orb redeemed in 1303 was of hollow gold and surmounted by a cross, whether ordinary or partiarchal the inventory does not relate. It was set with 5 sapphires and 5 balases, and the cross with 12 pearls. The *flor* had a great ruby at its head with a pearl set above the ruby. One of the sceptres was a rod of gilded silver and the other was of gold surmounted by a large piece of crystal above which was a cross made from 4 pearls, a balas and a sapphire.

Alphonso IV, who succeeded his father in 1327, made a change in the coronation ceremony. Instead of making the protest as his predecessors had done he reduced the part played by the Church by more direct means. He girded the sword on himself, and after being anointed crowned himself and invested himself with sceptre and orb. Muntaner[2] has given a full eyewitness account of this coronation, including details of the regalia. The crown was of gold with sixteen very high 'pinnacles' set with very large pearls, almost the size of pigeons' eggs. The crown was also set with rubies, balases, sapphires, turquoises and emeralds, and had in front a great carbuncle. It was so heavy that Alphonso changed it for a lighter one on returning to the palace. The description of the crown makes it seem likely that it was a new one made for the occasion, and that it followed the contemporary style, having large *fleurons* with smaller

---

1 J. Delaville Le Roulx: *Les joyaux de la couronne d'Aragon en* 1303, Paris 1889.
2 R. Muntaner: *Cronica*, ed. *Arxiu Historich*, Barcelona 1886, p. 585.

ones between them. On the other hand this type of crown does not appear on the seals until the 1340's, well into the reign of Peter IV (*Plate 210, b*). The coronation sceptre was three handbreadths long and had a great ruby on top. Alphonso's earliest seals show a fleur-de-lis on the sceptre, but from 1333 they show sceptres topped by eagles, and this is generally followed in all the seals until the reign of Martin. The orb was surmounted by a golden 'flower' in turn surmounted by a cross, but there is no evidence as to whether or not this cross was double, as depicted on Alphonso's seals.

Alphonso's son Peter IV, the Ceremonious, also placed the crown on his own head at his coronation in 1336, but only after long arguments with the clergy. Later in his reign he drew up a new coronation order for the Kings of Aragon and invented an order for queens, in which the king crowned the queen and invested her with other royal ornaments including the orb.[1] No queen had been crowned since Constance in 1276 as no king since Peter III had been married at the time of his accession, although in the festival at the time of the marriage of James II with Blanche the King placed the beautiful Queens' Crown on her head.[2] Now Peter had his fourth wife, Sibilia, crowned, presumably with the new order. It was most unusual for queens consort to be invested with an orb, and there is no ready explanation as to why Peter incorporated this in his ceremony. Possibly he was familiar with the seals showing Constance with an orb and copied the practice from them.

Peter seems to have considered the crown with which he was crowned to be of exceptional importance, as there are constant references to it throughout his reign. In a letter of 20th April 1342[3] he ordered to be pawned the gold crown with precious stones and pearls *quam portavimus die coronationis nostre*; at the same time the sceptre and orb were to be pawned, the latter having 12 pearls and 10 stones, the same number as in the orb redeemed in 1303. In 1343 Peter finally conquered Mallorca from the vassal dynasty and reunited it to the Kingdom of Aragon. In a letter dated 1st June 1343[4] he instructed his treasurer to send him for his coronation in Mallorca his coronation crown, the orb with the rubies and the *sella* (which might have been a saddle or a portable throne), and there is a note on the letter to say that the treasurer had done this. The coronation crown was still in existence in 1372, as there is a letter from the heir to the throne, John, dated 9th April in that year in which he says that there is no crown available for his bride, Martha of Armagnac, as the King had only his coronation crown left, while the Queen had had all her crowns taken to pieces. Four days later the King ordered a crown to be constructed for Martha.[5] Despite these constant references we have no information as to the style of Peter's crown; it may have been

---

1 Two slightly different versions of this order have been published: Blancas, op. cit., p. 117, and in *Coleccion de documentos ineditos del Archivo General de la Corona de Aragon*, Vol. V, Barcelona 1850, p. 267.

2 Muntaner, op. cit., p. 355.

3 Josep Rius: 'Mes documents sobre la cultura catalana', in *Estudis Universitaris Catalans*, XIII, Barcelona, p. 164.

4 *Coleccion de documentos ineditos del Archivo General de la Corona de Aragon*, Vol. XXXI, Barcelona 1866, p. 20.

5 Josep Madurell i Marimon: 'Les noces de l'Infant Joan amb Martha D'Armanyac', in *Estudis Universitaris Catalans*, XIX, Barcelona, p. 54.

the same crown previously used by Alphonso or even the quite different one later used by Martin. One inventory of this reign which gives a full description of crowns was the list made in 1356[1] of the goods left by Queen Maria to the Infantas Constance—who at that time was heir to the throne—and Joanna. These goods included four crowns, none of them particularly remarkable, having between eleven and fifteen *fleurons* or pinnacles above the circlet.

One further document from this reign is worth citing. In a letter dated at Tarragona 28th February 1360[2] Peter refers to the steps he was having taken over the construction of a sword to be used at the coronations of his successors. The scabbard was to have nineteen enamels, each one depicting one of the Kings of Aragon or Counts of Barcelona, an idea possibly borrowed from the sword of St Maurice in the German imperial regalia. The implication of this letter, taken with Peter's constant reference to his coronation crown, is that he wanted to build up a permanent, inalienable set of regalia for use at the ceremonies which he had rewritten. Even if he succeeded in this design the results did not survive the end of the dynasty in 1410.

Peter's son John I was married at his accession in 1387, but although he crowned himself according to his father's rite his wife was not crowned. On John's death in 1395 he was succeeded by his younger brother Martin, who delayed his coronation until 1399 so that he could be crowned on the same day as his son, Martin the Younger, was crowned King of Sicily. At the ceremony Martin crowned his consort Maria de Luna, who was invested with the orb, apparently according to Peter's rite. Immediately before the coronation the crown was in pawn, and we therefore have a full description of it.[3]

> The crown consisted of a circle of gold decorated with five large and four small rosettes of precious stones. Corresponding to these were five large and four small pinnacles, presumably *fleurons*. The most remarkable feature of the crown was that it contained 30 diamonds and must be one of the earliest crowns anywhere in Europe set with these stones. Each of the large rosettes had a large emerald, 4 balases and 4 diamonds, while each of the large pinnacles was set with 4 balases, 2 diamonds and a number of emeralds and pearls. The small rosettes and pinnacles were also set with balases, emeralds and pearls.

In Barcelona Cathedral is preserved a curious crown known as the garland of Martin, mainly of xv-century work but with xix-century additions.

> This crown (*Plate 210, a*) is of gilded silver and consists of two open diadems mounted one above the other, each diadem having thirty-two small *fleurons*. These narrow diadems resemble the heraldic coronet surmounting the arms of Barcelona on the reverse of royal seals (*Plate 210, c*). The lower diadem, which is the larger, is mounted on a circle of tubular metal turned like the thread of a screw and inscribed repeatedly with the word *SYRA* separated by small ornaments resembling seals. The smaller diadem is joined to the lower one by four hoops which curve upwards and inwards. From it hang sixteen decorations, half being strings of pearls and half being in the form of fruit. The hoops curve upwards from this diadem to close the crown at the top where they are

---

1 A. Rubió y Lluch: *Documents per l'Historia de la Cultura Catalana Mig-eval*, Barcelona 1908, Vol. I, p. 172.   2 A. Rubió y Lluch, op. cit., Vol. I, p. 191.   3 D. G. Llagostera: 'Itinerari del Rey En Martí', in *Anuari D'Institut D'Estudis Catalans*, Any IV, 1911–12, p. 140.

surmounted by a cross on a small globe, undoubtedly a modern addition. There seems little doubt that this crown, probably votive in origin, was intended to depict the double crown of Aragon, the device of an order founded by John I.[1] There also seems no reason to doubt Schramm's interpretation of the ornaments on the tubular base as being a punning representation of *cudere*, to stamp or seal, so that when taken with the inscription the word 'Syracuse' can be descried. The inscription presumably has some reference to Sicily but its exact significance is uncertain.

Also at Barcelona Cathedral is a beautiful silver throne, collapsible and portable, which is believed to have belonged to Martin, and a rich embroidered belt of his, which has been much restored.

On Martin's death in 1410 the dynasty of the Counts of Barcelona came to an end and there was an interregnum. Eventually in 1412 Prince Ferdinand, uncle of John II of Castile, was chosen as King. Both he and his Queen were crowned with Peter's order. Martin's crown had disappeared, but Ferdinand's fellow monarchs sent him others. His nephew sent him the crown he had worn at his accession ceremony, and the Queen of Navarre also sent a crown. Nevertheless Ferdinand had a new crown made in Barcelona and crowned his consort, Leonora, with the Castilian one. The Barcelona crown had fourteen plates, from each of which rose a 'pinnacle', and its main stones were rubies and balases. The sceptre had a great balas like a dove's egg on top, and may have been the same one used by Alphonso IV.

This was the last coronation in Aragon. Ferdinand's son Alphonso V was not crowned in Spain and this has never been satisfactorily explained. Possibly he followed the example of his cousins in Castile and considering that his title to the throne was secure saw no reason to continue this tradition. He was, however, crowned King of Naples after he had captured it in 1443. On his death he left his Italian possessions to his illegitimate son, Ferdinand, while the Aragonese territories went to his brother, John II, who was already King Consort of Navarre. On John's death Aragon was united with Castile when his son Ferdinand the Catholic, husband of Isabel of Castile, came to the throne.

We know little of the ornaments of the later kings. While Alphonso was still heir to the throne he had a crown with a large number of *fleurons*, but in August 1424 this was dismantled.[2] It is also recorded that he pawned a crown to raise funds during his siege of Naples. The coins and seals indicate that his crowns and those of John II were adorned with very tall *fleurons* shaped rather like crosses interspersed with smaller ornaments. The sceptres from the time of Martin no longer are topped with eagles, perhaps because Martin had no need to emphasise Aragon's connection with Sicily when his son was King of that island. From about 1441 Alphonso's seals reverted to an orb with a single cross, or occasionally one without a cross at all, in place of the orb with the patriarchal cross. This probably had some connection with his conquest of Naples, as when John II succeeded to Aragon but not to Naples the orb with the patriarchal cross again appeared on the seals. An interesting feature of the seals from the middle of the reign of Peter IV is the *Chimera* or dragon helmet of the Kings of

1 A. van de Put: *The Aragonese Double Crown*, London 1910.
2 E. G. Hurtebise: 'Inventario de los bienes muebles de Alfonso V de Aragon como Infante y como Rey', in *Anuari de l'Institut d'Etudis Catalans*, 1907, p. 165.

Aragon, an example of which is preserved in the Royal Armoury at Madrid; it is fairly certain that this is one used by Martin at a festival in Mallorca in 1407.

The most celebrated of the ornaments of John II was the balas collar which was given as a betrothal present to Isabel of Castile. It had been pawned to the University of Valencia as security for money to prosecute John's war against France. The university was unwilling to give it up, but after eight months of negotiations and argument that it was necessary to impress the Castilians they gave way.

One of the tragedies of the XIX century was the sacking of the royal monastery of Poblet, which contained the pantheon of the Kings of Aragon, first by the French and then by revolutionaries during the disturbances of the 1830's and 1840's. We do not know exactly what treasure Poblet had at the end of the XVIII century, whether it then still possessed the royal crown left to it by Alphonso II or the gold belt bequeathed by James I. The royal graves, however, certainly contained some burial ornaments when they were destroyed in 1835. Peter IV had left instructions that he should be buried in his coronation robes with a silver gilt crown set with stones of crystal on his head and the sceptre and orb in his hands, and John I left similar instructions.[1] Ferdinand in his will also gave instructions that he should be buried in full regalia, but ordered that the real ornaments and not replicas should be used. The fate of these burial ornaments is not known, but by 1870 a belief had grown of the existence of a great buried treasure from Poblet and many people searched for it. Among the most determined of these treasure hunters was a certain Pere Palan who consulted a Barcelona medium. This lady described the treasure which included:

> The crown of the Kings of Aragon of solid gold . . . so heavy that the kings with great effort could only support it for a certain time on their heads . . . in the centre of each *fleuron* is a fat emerald, on the top a cross or an eagle.[2]

This description appears to be a mixture of the surviving information concerning several of the Aragonese crowns. Unfortunately when Pere Palan dug according to the medium's instructions he failed to find this interesting crown, or indeed anything else.

It is convenient to relate here what little is known of the regalia of the independent Kingdom of Mallorca. The coronation ceremony was introduced there by the first independent King, James the son of James I of Aragon, presumably so that he should not seem to be less than his elder brother Peter III, who revived the ceremony in Aragon. James's coins show him wearing a fleurs-de-lis crown with large *fleurons* interspersed with small ornaments, and with an orb and a sceptre topped by an open hand; this was presumably in imitation of the Kings of France whose overlordship James recognised in respect of Roussillon and Montpellier. His successors had similar coins. A Book of Privileges in the Historical Archives of Mallorca[3] contains several miniatures showing the coronations of James I of Aragon as King of Mallorca and of

---

[1] F. Marés Deuloval: *Las tumbas reales de Poblet*, Barcelona 1952. In 1522 the Cathedral of Barcelona had a silver orb and sceptre given on the occasion of the burial of King John; Josep Mas: *Inventari de la sagrista de Barcelona pres en 1522*, Barcelona 1923. The reference may well be to John II.

[2] E. Toda y Guell: *La destruccio de Poblet*, Poblet 1935, p. 367.

[3] J. Pons y Marqués: 'El Códice de Privilegios de Mallorca,' in *Panorama Balea* No. 12, Palma 1952.

James II and Sancho of Mallorca. The book was begun in 1334 and the value of the miniatures as regards past events is questionable. The crowns shown have four wide and elaborate *fleurons*, quite different from those shown on the coins. Sancho is shown enthroned with a sword in his right hand and in his left a staff surmounted by a cross, the four arms of which are terminated in small double crosses. This symbol recurs in another miniature in the book in which a bishop standing near a king is holding a double processional cross.

THE KINGDOM OF SPAIN

The marriage of Isabel of Castile and Ferdinand of Aragon, the Catholic monarchs, led to the effective unification of the two kingdoms on the death of the latter's father John in 1479. The rest of the Peninsular then comprised the Moorish Kingdom of Granada and the Christian Kingdoms of Portugal and Navarre. Granada was conquered by Ferdinand and Isabel in 1492, Portugal was brought into their orbit by the turn of the century by means of dynastic marriages, and Ferdinand's troops overran the Spanish part of Navarre in 1512. Although Portugal remained independent, except for a short period from 1580–1621, the other kingdoms which had made up the Iberian peninsular remained united and instead of warring amongst themselves and against the Moors were able to concentrate on imperial enterprises in both Europe and America.

There is some reliable information concerning Isabel's main crown in a series of inventories and receipts, although no pictorial representation which exactly accords with the inventory description has survived.[1] At some time before 1477 she had ordered it to be made by the Valencian silversmith Garcia Gomez, a great part of the materials coming from other pieces of jewellery in her treasury. However, the circumstances of her reign seldom enabled Isabel to wear this crown. It was remade on several occasions and at other times gems were taken out of it as gifts or for sale. The crown itself was constantly in pawn. Indeed the only occasion at which we are certain that Isabel wore it was at the wedding of her son John with Margaret of Austria in 1496, and even then it had to be borrowed from the city of Valencia to which it was pledged. It was again pawned to Valencia in 1500, and on this occasion the crown was fully described in the inventory or receipt[2]:

> The crown was of gold and consisted of eight members, worked in the form of foliage and roses enamelled in colour. From each piece rose two *fleurons*, one large and one small. At the joins of the eight pieces were eight eagles of solid gold, of which four were enamelled and four plain. The crown was set with 9 diamonds cut in various fashions and 7 rubies 1 large and 6 small; presumably a diamond and a ruby were set in each of seven pieces with the large ruby in the centre piece in front, and 2 diamonds in one of the pieces at the back. The crown was also profusely set with pearls.

We do not know for certain what became of this crown after the pledging in 1500.

[1] The various references have been conveniently brought together by D. Angulo Iñiguez: *Isabel la Catolica, sus retratos, sus vestidos y sus joyas*, Santander 1951. One representation which may resemble Isabel's crown is that in the Hispano-Flemish retable from St Thomas at Avila, now in the Prado, which shows Isabel wearing a crown similar to that described in the inventories, except that it does not feature eagles. The crown of Ferdinand shown on the same retable is extremely formalised.

[2] Ferrandis, op. cit., p. 170.

It may have been the one referred to in a letter of 1542 as having been deposited in 1508—that is after the death of Isabel—at the Monastery of St John at Burgos in connection with the payment of the dowry of Catherine of Aragon. There is in Toledo Cathedral a crown for the Virgin of the Sacristy which consists of a narrow jewelled circlet with imperial arches and mitre-like side pieces added. It is said that the circlet belonged to Isabel, and if this is correct it may well be the one just described. Several accounts in the cathedral archives, which have been published, imply that the whole crown was made in the XVI century, but this may be due to loose wording and the reference may only have been intended to apply to the arches which were certainly made then.[1] This crown does not seem to have been the subject of serious study and presents scope for further research.

At the Royal Chapel of Granada Cathedral, where the Catholic monarchs are buried, there are a crown and sceptre of Isabel and a sword of Ferdinand. Because of the poor workmanship and the nature of the materials, and in the case of the sceptre its size, it seems unlikely that the crown and sceptre were used by the queen and they may be funeral ornaments. On the other hand a document from the time of Charles V, detailing the order of a procession to be held at Granada on the first Sunday of the year in memory of the Catholic monarchs, mentions that a crown is to be carried at the head of the procession as well as the sword of Ferdinand. It is, therefore, possible that the crown and sceptre were made especially for this purpose.

The crown (*Plate 211, c*) is of gilded silver and consists of a smooth band, probably originally covered by an outer band set with gems which has disappeared, surmounted by open relief-work, mainly in the form of pomegranates, the heraldic emblem of Granada.

The sceptre (*Plate 211, d*) is also of gilded silver. It is very large with a globe towards the top surmounted by fruit.

The sword (*Plate 211, b*) is the one used at the conquest of Granada and left to the Royal Chapel by Ferdinand. The pommel, the handle and the guard, which last is in the form of a cross whose arms curve towards the blade, are covered with arabesque engraving. Otherwise this weapon is unremarkable.

The ceremonial sword of the Catholic monarchs is kept, together with its sheath, in the Royal Armoury at Madrid, where there are also two non-ceremonial swords of Ferdinand.

The former is a two-edged sword with no chasing on the blade other than the mark of an unknown swordsmith. The two-handed guard is made of iron, gilded and engraved, in the form of a cross with short, straight arms ending in half-moons, on one of which there is the motto *TANTO MONTA* and on the other the invocation *MEMENTO MEI O MATER DEI MEI*. The pommel is formed of a cross in the ogival style, on one side of which can just be seen the image of St John the Evangelist and the yoke, the emblem of Ferdinand, and on the other the bundle of arrows, the emblem of Isabel. The hilt is covered with red velvet and wire. This sword is probably the one which in the time of the Hapsburgs was carried unsheathed at the accession of kings and at their ceremonial entrances into cities. According to the 1503 inventory it was used in the time of the Catholic monarchs for dubbing knights.

[1] J. F. Rivera: *Le Cathèdrale de Tolède*, Barcelona 1957. Davillier, op. cit., pp. 206 and 237; F. J. Sánchez Cantón (ed.): *Documentos de la Catedral de Toledo*, Madrid 1916, II, p. 47. One of the difficulties is that several crowns seem to have been made for this Virgin.

Isabel's great wealth of jewels included some noteworthy ornaments, four of which may be described here:

The collar of the balases was, as we have seen, given by Ferdinand to Isabel on their betrothal. Like the crown this was frequently in pawn, in 1487 to Cordoba and in 1489 to Valencia,[1] where it remained until 1505. This may also be the collar which with the crown was deposited at the Monastery of St John at Burgos in 1508 in connection with the dowry of Catherine of Aragon. In 1489 this collar consisted of 7 balas rubies each set in a piece made in the form of a flower alternating with 8 pearls each set over a rose. Between each of these jewels were three pieces made in the form of yokes in red and white enamel. These yokes had been added since the collar first came into Isabel's possession, but it had lost a great unset pierced balas ruby from which hung a large pearl in the shape of a pear.

The collar of the cordones, also pledged in 1487, consisted of twenty-four pieces of gold with 20 balas rubies, 10 very large and 16 not so large, 60 large pearls, 30 smaller ones and 50 very small ones, all strung on three ribbons of silk. It was more than three times as heavy as the collar of the balases.

The collar of the arrows, also pledged in 1487 and again to Valencia in 1500, consisted of sixteen bundles of gold arrows, enamelled in green on the shafts and in black and white on the feathers, and was also set with 20 large table balases and 20 pearls in the shape of pears from which hung gold and enamel roses. A collar of this nature, but not exactly corresponding to the description is carved on the funeral statue of Queen Joan the Mad at Granada.

The Salamandria jewel, also pledged in 1487, was formed of two salamander heads, the eyes of one being rubies and the eyes of the other being diamonds. It was set with 9 other rubies, 9 other diamonds and 7 large pearls, one hanging between the two heads.

There has been considerable research into the story that Isabel sold her jewels to help pay the cost of fitting out Columbus's fleet.[2] There is no evidence at all to support this tradition nor is there evidence that any of the many transactions of this period when jewels were pledged were directly connected with Columbus, but of course the additional expenses entailed in subsidising his voyage may have been an indirect cause of the pledging of jewels on other occasions.

Two interesting reliquary crowns of which little is known have survived from this period:

A reliquary bust of Ferdinand the Catholic (Plate 211, a), formerly in the Spitzer collection, was in 1959 sold by Frank Partridge and Sons Ltd of New Bond Street to Mr R. J. Grog of Paris. The head is crowned with a narrow diadem rising into a number of *fleurons* with curled leaves. In the band beneath each *fleuron* are set three gems and there is one larger stone between each group of three. The identification of the bust with Ferdinand is not definite, but as the style of the work is of the late XV century, and as there is a Saragossa silversmith's mark on the neck it is fairly certain. The style of the crown is simpler than those depicted in pictures and other representations of the late XV century, but early in the next century there seems to have been a reversion to more simple styles and the crown may not in fact be entirely apocryphal.

A crown *(Plate 210, d)* believed to be a XV-century Spanish reliquary crown is in the Carrand collection at the National Museum in Florence. It consists of seven plates of gilded silver, six of which are surmounted by large curled leaves, the seventh leaf being broken off. Five of the hingepins

---

1 For the pledging of these jewels, see Angulo Iñiguez, op. cit., pp. 31–33.
2 E.g., C. Fernandez Duro: *Tradiciones Infundadas*, Madrid 1888, p. 359.

are topped by smaller curly leaves, the other two are missing. Six of the plates have in their centre a round enamel with a formal foliage design, and the remains of such an enamel can be seen on the other plate, and in the centre of each of the hinge-pin tops is another such enamel. Six of the plates have two small metal flowers, one each side of the enamel, but on the seventh these are replaced by cherubs' heads. In the middle of the leaf of this last plate is a medallion with a formal foliage design. The other leaves each have similar medallions but these show pelicans 'in their piety', that is, pecking their breasts. The origins of this unusual crown are unknown.

Charles V (as he is always called even in Spain where he should be Charles I) ascended the throne of Spain in 1516 and in 1519 he was elected as Holy Roman Emperor. Until his abdication in 1556 Spain was merely an instrument in the creation of a Hapsburg Empire. Philip II, who succeeded Charles, continued this policy allied to one of regaining the Protestant parts of Europe for the Roman Catholic Church. The tastes of Philip and his successors were austere and, although they still possessed a crown and sceptre, now that there were no coronations the occasions on which the regalia were used were rare. In 1564 Philip sold some personal ornaments of the imperial regalia which he had inherited from Maximilian I and Charles V, but these had no connection with Spain.[1] There was, however, another crown sold at the same time which had belonged to the Moorish King of Tunis which had been described in a receipt of 1555 as:

> A crown of gold in the form of a diadem with a large carbuncle-type stone in the middle, which appears to be false, and with a large eight-sided sapphire and 2 medium sapphires, 2 small spinels which appear to be garnets and 2 large pearls of irregular shape, and with 54 large and small pearls, the total weight with the stones and pearls being $56\frac{1}{2}$ oz.[2]

In some coins of Charles V minted at Valencia and in Sicily he is depicted with an imperial arched crown. In 1554 Philip II married Mary Tudor, who had ascended the throne of England in 1553. This led to the temporary adoption by Spain of the closed crown with four arches. Philip and Mary are depicted on their seals with crowns of this type surmounting the arms of the two kingdoms, and there is a particularly good example in the stained glass at Lambeth Palace.[3] Philip is also shown with a crown of this type on the coins minted in some parts of his dominions. This temporary adoption of the closed crown was clearly due to the wish that the Spanish crown should not be inferior to the English Tudor crown with closed arches. After Mary's death in 1558 the Spanish coins reverted to depicting crowns without arches until 1589 when a crown with a single arch appears on Philip II's Castilian coins. In the reign of Philip IV this is replaced by a crown with four raised arches. Crowns with depressed arches do not appear generally on the coins until the reign of Charles II (1665–1700), although there are earlier instances. On the other hand an engraving of Philip II in the *Chronicle of Cremona* (1582) depicts a very stylised single-arched crown, while another engraving of the period shows his fourth wife, Anne of Austria, daughter of the Emperor Maxi-

[1] See Chapter Nine, Germany, p. 326.
[2] Rudolf Beer: 'Acten, regesten und inventare aus dem Archivo General zu Simancas', in *Jahrbuch der Kunsthistorischen Sammlungen des Allerhöchsten Kaiserhauses*, Vienna 1891, Vol. XII, p. CLIII.
[3] F. Sydney Eden: *Ancient Stained and Painted Glass*, 2nd edition Cambridge 1933, p. 191.

a   *Reliquary bust of Ferdinand the Catholic (1479–1516). Formerly in the Spitzer Collection now owned by M. Grog of Paris (p. 613)*

b (above, right)   *Sword of Ferdinand the Catholic. Granada Cathedral (p. 612)*

c   *Crown of Isabel the Catholic, probably a funeral ornament. Granada Cathedral (p. 612)*

d   *Sceptre of Isabel the Catholic. Granada Cathedral (p. 612)*

a   *Crown from a painting of 'The Family of Philip V', by Michael van Loo* (p. 615)

b (left) *La Peregrina*
(p. 616)

c (right)   *Portrait of Charles II, aged four. Spanish School. Royal Collection*
(p. 615)

milian, wearing a crown with two arches surmounted by a cross. A late seal of Philip II (1597), however, depicts an open crown. In Her Majesty's collection in London there is a portrait of Charles II at the age of four (about 1665) which shows a crown with two raised arches surmounted by a cross (*Plate 212, c*).

At the end of the XVI century the new wealth from the Americas made Spain one of the richest countries in the world. Precious metals and stones were available in profusion and Spain entered a period of luxuriance, which neither the austere example of the monarchy nor the numerous sumptuary laws could curb. The great emerald mines of Peru provided an immense source of this beautiful stone, and other precious stones were also available. In 1581 Philip II annexed Portugal, and although he made various promises to the Portuguese he took to Madrid the Portuguese crown jewels which came into his possession. But once again the only royal ornaments which have survived are the swords in the Royal Armoury where the following are kept:

> The imperial sword of Charles V, the hilt being added in the reign of Philip III (1598–1621).
> The blade of a pontifical sword of Charles V, given by Clement VII in 1529.
> The blade of a pontifical sword of Philip II when a prince, given by Paul III in 1547.
> A pontifical sword and the blade of another pontifical sword of Philip II as King, the latter given by Pius IV in 1560 and the former by Clement VIII in 1593.
> The blade of a pontifical sword of Philip III when a prince, given by Gregory XIV in 1590.
> A pontifical sword of Philip IV when a prince, given by Paul V in 1618, and several other ceremonial swords of princes and military swords of kings.

Charles II was the last of the Spanish Hapsburgs. He was succeeded in 1700 by the Duke of Anjou, grandson of Louis XIV of France, who took the title of Philip V. The Bourbon dynasty continued until Napoleon proclaimed his brother Joseph as King. During this dynasty the regalia were of no importance, although they appear formally in a number of royal portraits[1] which show crowns consisting of a circlet set with stones and pearls above which are formal trefoils. From the trefoils rise four flattened arches set with pearls, surmounted by an orb with a cross. One set of regalia is said to have been destroyed when fire damaged a large portion of the old palace in Madrid in 1734, but from later portraits it seems probable that these were replaced, and there is a story that on his abdication in 1808 Charles IV handed the Spanish crown to Napoleon.

Joseph Bonaparte reigned for only five years, and after the Battle of Vittoria he retired altogether from his kingdom. At Vittoria he lost his baggage train including his crown and sceptre. These have completely disappeared and were doubtless looted. It seems probable that his regalia were personal ornaments which he had used previously as King of Naples. On the restoration of the Bourbons in 1814 a new crown and sceptre were made of a formal heraldic design, and a small crown of this type is shown in the portrait of Queen Isabel II by Winterhalter (*Plate 213, b*). This crown and sceptre were plain and of a formal heraldic design and were used only occasionally, such as for the opening of the Cortes by the sovereign in person.

---

[1] E.g., Charles IV, by J. A. Ribera (Royal Palace, Madrid); Philip V, by Hiacinthe Rigaud (Prado); the Family of Philip V, by Michael van Loo (Prado) (*Plate 212, a*).

The so-called Spanish crown jewels were in fact family heirlooms and not the property of the state. Charles IV, while in exile from 1808 to 1814, and his son Ferdinand VII disposed of many of these jewels. In 1868, when Queen Isabel II was expelled from Spain, the family jewels were divided between the Queen and her sister, the Duchess of Montpensier. Ten years later, in July 1878, some of the Queen's jewels were sold at the Hotel Druot at Paris and realised more than a million and a half francs. Among the ornaments sold were a butterfly brooch which fetched £4,777, a diamond necklace (£8,000), a brooch in the form of a flower (£3,260), thirty-one emerald balls with as many brilliants (£3,064), and a celebrated pendant (£12,000). The Cortes had discussed the ownership of the jewels at considerable length but the Queen established her right to them as personal porperty.

When the monarchy was restored in 1870 there was no mention of any crown jewels under King Amadeo of Savoy, although a crown and a sceptre appear in his portrait by C. L. Rivera. These ornaments were probably made earlier in the century and certainly existed but were only used occasionally, for instance at the opening of the Cortes by the sovereign in person. Before the Civil War the author was informed by the authorities that these ornaments were preserved in the vaults of the Cortes, and they may still be there.

In 1878 King Alphonso XII married Princess Mercedes, who died a few months later. He gave his bride a crown set with 5,000 brilliants, several weighing 16 carats, besides other precious stones of great value. Queen Eugenie, the Consort of King Alphonso XIII, had some notable jewels, including a coronet given on the occasion of her wedding by the ladies of Catalonia. Its design embodied the Arms of England, the fleurs-de-lis of the House of Bourbon and the four bars of Catalonia inset with rubies and diamonds.

Among the Spanish crown jewels until the time of Joseph Bonaparte was the most celebrated of the American pearls, *La Peregrina*, or Philip II Pearl (*Plate 212, b*).

> Various stories have been told of its discovery, but some are plainly apocryphal. It seems that it was found at the Pearl Islands off Panama by a negro slave who was rewarded with his freedom. The stories differ as to the date of the discovery, but it must have been before 1554, as Philip gave it to Mary Tudor on their marriage and she is shown wearing it in portraits, at the Prado, Hampton Court and Winchester Cathedral. On Mary's death it was returned to Spain, and according to Garcilasso de la Vega at one time decorated the crown of the celebrated Virgin of Guadalupe. Jacques de Treco, Court Jeweller to Philip II, is credited with saying that it might be worth 30,000, 50,000 or 100,000 ducats as one might choose to estimate, as its value was so remarkable as to go beyond any standard valuation. *La Peregrina* was worn by the Queens of Spain while posing for their state portraits[1] and on important state occasions. For example Queen Margarita, wife of Philip III, wore it at the celebrations in Madrid of the signing of the treaty of peace between Spain and England in 1605, and Queen Isabel, wife of Philip IV, wore it at the ceremony at which Prince Balthasar Charles took the oath as Prince of Asturias in 1632.[2]

[1] Portrait of Queen Eleanora, by Mabuse (Hampton Court); Margarita of Austria, by Pantoza de la Cruz (Prado); anonymous portrait of Isabel of Bourbon, first wife of Philip IV (Prado); anonymous portrait of Maria Luisa of Orleans, first wife of Charles II (Prado).

[2] Anon: *Noticia de Ceremonial Antiguo para el juramento del Principe de Asturias*, Madrid 1850, p. 30.

Saint Simon, Grand Seigneur at the Court of King Louis XIV, twice mentions *La Peregrina* in his Memoires[1] in relation to Philip V of Spain. In the first in 1706 he relates how the Queen of Spain sent her husband, who was at Versailles, all their jewels by the hands of a French valet named Vaut. Among them was *La Peregrina*. The second reference is dated 1722, 'I saw and handled at my ease the famous *Peregrina* that the King of Spain had that evening on the fold of his hat, hanging from a beautiful clasp of diamonds . . . [it] is perfectly shaped and bell-mouthed like those little pearls which are musk scented.'

The pearl remained among the crown jewels of Spain until Joseph Bonaparte abdicated in 1813 and took the pearl away with him. After his death it passed to Hortense, his step-niece by marriage and from her to Prince Louis Napoleon. Lord Frederic Hamilton has related how it came into the possession of his father, the then Marquis of Abercorn.[2] 'The Prince came to see my father one day and confided to him that he was in great pecuniary difficulties. He asked my father to recommend him an honest jeweller who would pay him the price he wanted for "*La Pelegrina*" [sic]. He named the price, and drew the great pearl out of his pocket. My father, after examining the jewel and noticing its flawless shape and lustre, silently opened a drawer, drew a cheque, and handed it to Prince Louis without a word. That afternoon my father presented my mother with "*La Pelegrina*". To my mother it was an unceasing source of anxiety. The pearl had never been bored, and was so heavy that it was constantly falling from its setting. Three times she lost it; three times she found it again. Once at a ball at Buckingham Palace, on putting her hand to her neck, she found that the great pearl had gone. She was much distressed, knowing how upset my father would be. On going into supper, she saw "*La Pelegrina*" gleaming at her from the folds of the velvet train of the lady immediately in front of her. Again she lost it at Windsor Castle, and it was found in the upholstery of a sofa. . . . When it came into my brother's possession after my father's death, he had "*La Pelegrina*" bored, though it impaired its value, so my sister-in-law was able to wear the great jewel as often as she wished without running the constant danger of losing it.'

The pearl is in the possession of the present Duke of Abercorn. In 1913 it was polished and was certified to weigh 203·84 gr.

La Peregrina should not be confused with another fine pearl *La Pelegrina* which belongs to the Youssoupoff family and which according to their family records also formed part of the crown jewels of Spain until it was given by Philip IV to his daughter Maria Theresa on her marriage to Louis XIV of France. It was not heard of again until it was bought by Princess Youssoupoff in Moscow. It was then described as being the most perfect pearl in existence, a practically globular Indian pearl of singular beauty weighing 28 carats. Actually it was ovoid in shape.[3]

Another famous pearl found in 1691 was presented to Charles II and named after him. The Charles II pearl was similar in size to *La Peregrina*, and for many years these two pearls were worn as ear-rings by successive Queens of Spain, until the Charles II pearl was destroyed in the fire at the old Palace at Madrid in 1734.

1 Marquis de Saint-Simon (ed.): *Mémoires du Duc de Saint-Simon*, Paris 1829–30, Vol. V, p. 100 and Vol. XX, p. 100.

2 Lord Frederic Hamilton, *Here, There and Everywhere*, London 1921.

3 G. F. Kunz and C. H. Stevenson: *The Book of the Pearl*, London 1908. See *Plate 175, c* (Russia).

BIBLIOGRAPHY

AMADOR DE LOS RÍOS, JOSÉ — *El arte latino-bizantino en Espana y las coronas visigodas de Guarrazar, Memorias de la Acadamia de San Fernando*, Madrid 1861.

ANGULO IÑIGUEZ, D. — *Isabel la Catolica, sus retratos, sus vestidos y sus joyas*, Santander 1951.

BLANCAS, GERONIMO DE — *Las coronaciones de los reyes de Aragon*, Saragossa 1641.

COUNT DE VALENCIA DE DON JUAN — *Catalogo Historico-decriptivo de la Real Armeria de Madrid*, Madrid 1898.

DAVILLIER, BARON CH. — *Recherches sur l'Orfévrerie en Espagne*, Paris 1879.

FERRANDIS, JOSÉ — 'Artes decorativas visigodas', in *España Visigoda*, Vol. II, of Historia de España, directed by R. Menendez Pidal.
Inventarios reales (Juan II a Juana la Loca), Datos documentales para la Historia del Arte en España III, Madrid 1943.

HEISS, ALOÏS — *Descripcion General de las Monedas Hispano-cristianas*, Madrid 1865–9.

LASTEYRIE, F. DE — *Déscription du trésor de Guarrazar*, Paris 1860.

MADRAZO, P. DE — *Coronas y cruces del tesoro de Guarrazar, Monumentos Arquitectonicos de España*, Madrid 1879.

MENENDEZ PIDAL, RAMON — *Historia de España*, Madrid 1935 onwards.

SAGARRA, F. DE — *Sigillografia Catalana*, Barcelona 1915.

SÁNCHEZ-ALBORNOZ, CLAUDIO — 'La succesion al trono en Leon y Castilla', in *Boletín de la Acadamia Argentina de Letras*, XIV, No. 50.

SÁNCHEZ CANTÓN, F. J. — *Los retratos de los reyes de España*, Barcelona 1948.

SCHRAMM, P. E. — 'Die Krönung in Katalanisch-Aragonesischen Königreich', in *Homenatge a Antoni Rubió i Lluch*, Barcelona 1936.

SCHRAMM, P. E. — *Herrschaftszeichen und Staatssymbolik*, Stuttgart 1954–6.

WAY, ALBERT — 'The Votive Gold Crowns recently found near Toledo', in *The Archaeological Journal*, Vol. XVI, September 1859.

YANGUAS Y MIRANDA, J. — *Diccionario de Antigüedades del Reino de Navarra*, Pamplona 1840.

MONARCHS AND CORONATIONS

THE VISIGOTHIC KINGDOM

410 Ataulf. Invaded Spain 414
415 Sigeric
415 Valia
418 Theodered
451 Turismund
453 Theodoric
466 Euric
484 Alaric II
507 Gesaleric
511 Almaric (Theodoric the Ostrogoth, Regent 511–26)
531 Theudis
548 Theudisclo
549 Agila
554 Atangild (elected King by rebels in 551)
568 Liuva I
568 Leovigild
586 Recared I (possibly crowned)
601 Liuva II
603 Viterius
610 Gundemar
612 Sisebert
621 Recared II
621 Svinthila
631 Sisenand
636 Khintila
639 Tulga
642 Khindasvintus
653 Recevinthus
672 Wamba. Crowned at Toledo, 19th September 672
680 Ergivic. Crowned at Toledo, 680
687 Egica. Crowned at Toledo, 687
702 Witiza. Crowned at Toledo, 700, as Governor of Galicia and acknowledged heir Egica
710 Roderick. Killed at Guadalete, 711

THE KINGDOMS OF ASTURIAS, LEON AND GALICIA

721 Pelayo
737 Favila
739 Alphonso I, the Catholic (possibly crowned)

757 Fruela I
768 Aurelio
774 Silo
783 Mauregato
788 Bermudo I, the Deacon
791 Alphonso II, the Chaste. Crowned
842 Ramiro I
850 Ordoño I
866 Alphonso III, the Great. Crowned. Took title of Emperor
910 Garcia. (King of Leon)
913 Ordoño II. (King of Galicia, 910–13.) Crowned at Leon, 913
924 Fruela II. (King of Asturias, 910–24)
925 Alphonso IV, the Monk
931 Ramiro II. Crowned
950 Ordoño III
956 Sancho I, the Fat
966 Ramiro III. Crowned
985 Bermudo II. Crowned as pretender to the throne, 982
999 Alphonso V. Crowned
1027 Bermudo III. Killed, 1037

THE KINGDOM OF CASTILE

1035 Ferdinand I, the Great. Crowned King of Leon, 1037
1065 Garcia. King of Galicia. Disenthroned by Sancho II and Alphonso VI
1065 Sancho II. Crowned at Leon, 1072
1072 Alphonso VI. (King of Leon, 1065–72.) Crowned at Burgos, 1072
1109 Urraca, married Alphonso I of Aragon
1126 Alphonso VII. Crowned King of Galicia, 1111, at Santiago, of Leon, 1126 and Emperor of Spain, 1135 at Leon

CASTILE		LEON	
1157–1158	Sancho III, the Desired	1157–1188	Ferdinand II
1158–1214	Alphonso VIII, the Noble	1188–1230	Alphonso IX
1214	Henry I. Possibly crowned		
1217	Berengaria		
1217	Ferdinand III, the Saint. Crowned King of Castile at Valladolid, 1217, and King of Leon at Toro, 1230		
1252	Alphonso X, the Wise. Crowned at Seville		
1284	Sancho IV, the Brave. Crowned at Toledo		
1295	Ferdinand IV, the Implacable. Crowned at Toledo		
1312	Alphonso XI. Crowned with his consort, Maria, at Burgos, 1330		
1350	Peter I, the Cruel		

1369   Henry II of Trastamara. Crowned as Pretender at Burgos, 1366
1379   John I. Crowned at Burgos
1390   Henry III, the Lazy
1406   John II
1454   Henry IV, the Impotent
1474   Isabel I, the Catholic
1504   Philip I, the Handsome

THE KINGDOM OF NAVARRE

Early kings are doubtful
 905   Sancho Garcia I
 925   Garcia II
 970   Sancho II, Abarca
 994   Garcia III, the Trembler
1004   Sancho III, the Great
1035   Garcia IV
1054   Sancho IV
1076–1134   Kings of Aragon
1134   Garci-Ramirez or Garcia V
1150   Sancho V, the Wise
1194   Sancho VI, the Strong
1234   Theobald I, Count of Champagne. Crowned at Pamplona, 1234
1253   Theobald II
1270   Henry I
1274   Joan, married to Philip IV of France
1304   Louis Hutin of France. Crowned at Pamplona, 1307
1316   John
1316   Philip, the V of France. Crowned, 9th January 1317
1322   Charles I, the IV of France
1328   Joan and Philip of Evreux. (Joan alone from 1343.) Crowned at Pamplona, 5th March 1329
1349   Charles II, the Bad
1387   Charles III, the Noble. Crowned at Pamplona, 13th February 1390
1425   Blanche, married John II of Aragon
1441   John II of Aragon
1479   Eleanor
1479   Francis Febo. Crowned Pamplona, 6th November 1482
1483   Catherine, married John of Albret. Both crowned at Pamplona, 1494

THE KINGDOM OF ARAGON

1035   Ramiro I. (Succeeded his brother Gonzalo in the Kingdom of Sobrarbe in 1038)
1067   Sancho I. (King of Navarre from 1076)

1094   Peter I
1102   Alphonso I, the Quarrelsome (possibly crowned)
1134   Ramiro II, the Monk
1137   Petronilla. Married Ramon Berenguer, Count of Barcelona
1162   Alphonso II
1196   Peter II, the Catholic. Crowned at Rome, 1204
1213   James I, the Conqueror
1276   Peter III, the Great. King of Sicily from 1282. Crowned with his consort, Constance of Sicily, at Saragossa, 16th November 1276, and at Palermo, 2nd September 1282
1285   Alphonso III, the Frank. Crowned at Saragossa, 14th April 1285
1291   James II. (King of Sicily, 1285–95). Crowned at Saragossa, 24th September 1291
1327   Alphonso IV, the Benign. Crowned at Saragossa, 3rd April 1328
1336   Peter IV, the Ceremonious. Crowned at Saragossa, 1336. Fourth consort crowned 1380
1387   John I. Crowned at Saragossa, 1387
1396   Martin, the Humane. Crowned with his consort, Maria, at Saragossa, 1399
1410–1412   Interregnum
1412   Ferdinand I, the Honest. Crowned with his consort, Leonora, at Saragossa, 11th February 1414
1416   Alphonso V, the Magnanimous. King of Naples from 1443
1458   John II. Also King of Navarre
1479   Ferdinand the Catholic

THE KINGDOM OF MALLORCA

1276   James II. Crowned 1276
1311   Sancho. Crowned 1311
1324   James III. Driven from Mallorca by Peter IV of Aragon

THE KINGDOM OF SPAIN

1516	Charles I (or V)	1759	Charles III
1556	Philip II	1788	Charles IV
1598	Philip III	1808	Joseph Bonaparte
1621	Philip IV	1814	Ferdinand VII
1665	Charles II	1833	Isabel II. 1868. Republic
1700	Philip V, Duke of Anjou	1870	Amadeo, Duke of Savoy. 1873. Republic
1724	Louis I	1875	Alphonso XII
1724	Ferdinand VI	1886	Alphonso XIII. Abdicated 1931

a   *Portrait of Joseph Bonaparte by Pradier, 1813, showing his crown. National Museum, San Martino, Naples* (p. 615)

b   *Portrait of Isabel II by F. X. Winterhalter. Royal Palace, Madrid* (p. 615)

a   (i) *Sword of the Realm made for Gustavus Vasa in 1540; (ii) the second sword of state. State Bank, Stockholm*
(pp. 633 and 651)

b   *King's sword made for the coronation of Gustavus III,*
1771 (pp. 646 and 653)

c   *Sword belonging to the insignia of a royal duke at*
the coronation of Gustavus III, 1771 (p. 646)

CHAPTER TWENTY-FIVE

SWEDEN

The history of the early rulers of Sweden is largely legendary and the sources of information about their installation ceremonies and their regalia are slender. Even the chronological order and enumeration of the kings is based on a computation of Archbishop Johannes Magnus in the XVI century, which is without any historical foundation.

We learn from the *Ynglinga Saga*, which is based on the earlier poem known as the *Ynglintal*, that the kings and earls were installed at the ceremony of the 'Ale'. The king sat on a stool below the throne and a goblet known as the *Brage-full* was brought to him. The king stood up to receive it, swore an oath and drank from the goblet. He was then led to the hereditary throne and was enthroned on the seat of his father.

Another ceremony of installation took place at the Mora stone which was situated north of Upsala. Here the king was raised on the stone and received the homage. This ceremony, which was the formal confirmation of the election of the king and probably preceded any religious service connected with the king's accession, was no doubt of Germanic origin and somewhat similar to other such ceremonies performed in North-West Europe at this time. Some authorities consider that this ceremony was not discontinued until the accession of Christian I of Sweden, Denmark and Norway (1457–63). In order to secure the succession, he arranged for his son to be elected during his lifetime as his successor and King of the Union of the three kingdoms at Stockholm, and the Mora ceremony was not considered necessary. The stone itself had certainly disappeared before Gustavus Vasa ascended the throne in 1523. That the Mora stone was used subsequent to the introduction of the Christian coronation is shown by the survival of two of the stones set up to mark the homage received there, which can be identified by their inscriptions. They bear the names of Eric XIII of Pomerania, who received the homage in 1397, and Charles VIII, who received it in 1448.

Upsala was the ancient capital of Sweden and the residence of the kings. There was a great temple there which is described in *Adam of Bremen's History* as one of great splendour and covered with gilding. In it stood the statues of the three deities, Thor, Odin and Fricco. A great festival was held there every nine years attended by representatives from all over Sweden. Large numbers of animals and even men were sacrificed and their bodies were subsequently hung up on trees in a neighbouring sacred grove.

The first Swedish king to be baptised was Olaf Skøtkonung in the year 1000, and his three successors were likewise Christians, but there followed a period of reversion to paganism and a struggle for power. Towards the end of the XI century the old pagan religion was overthrown, and while the Christian Church consolidated its position, on the political side the Swedes and Goths became a single monarchy. This was achieved by Eric IX (c. 1150–60), a zealous churchman who organised the Church on the same lines as it had already been established in other kingdoms. The first Swedish cathedral had been built at Upsala in about the year 1140, and an Archiepiscopal See was established there in 1163, thus converting the heathen temple into a Christian place of worship. According to the legend Eric was attacked during Mass and murdered while leaving the church, and for this reason he was given the surname of 'the Holy' and became the national saint of Sweden, although the cult of St Eric did not gain strength until a century later. The rivalry that existed between the houses of Eric and Sverker continued, and the two successors of St Eric also met violent deaths. Both sides sought aid internally from the Church and externally from Denmark. Although coronation had been introduced into Norway in 1164 and into Denmark in 1170 there is no evidence of such a ceremony in Sweden before 1210, when Eric X, the grandson of St Eric, was anointed at Upsala. He had succeeded in gaining the support of the Church, and the ceremony was performed by the Archbishop of Upsala, assisted by all the subordinate bishops and with the approval of the nobility. The act of anointing was confirmed by Pope Innocent II in 1216.

Eric X's successor, John I, was anointed and crowned at Linköping in 1219 and the next King, Eric XI, was crowned at Upsala in July 1224. This period saw the rise of the Folkungar family, which contracted marriages with the royal families of Sweden, Norway and Denmark. A leading member of this family, Birger Jarl, married Ingeborg, the King's sister, and Eric XI in 1243 married Katherine, a member of the Folkungar family. On Eric XI's death in 1250 the line of St Eric became extinct and Birger Jarl became the Regent on the proclamation as King of his young, weak and incompetent son Waldemar I. Waldemar was crowned at Linköping in 1251, but in 1275 he was dethroned by his brother Magnus, who was crowned with his consort, Helwig, at Upsala in 1276. On the death of Magnus I in 1290 his son Birger II was crowned with his consort, Margaret, at Söderköping, in December 1302. There followed a period of confusion which lasted until 1319, when Magnus II, the infant son of Duke Eric, was elected King at the Mora Stone. He had already succeeded to the throne of Norway, and for a time the two crowns were united, though not very happily. When he came of age he was crowned with his consort, Blanche of Namur, at Stockholm on 21st July 1336. It will be noted that these two coronations did not take place at Upsala despite the fact that in 1296 the Upland's law had laid down in the 'king's code' that the king should 'be consecrated to the crown in Upsala Church by the archbishop and the suffragan bishops'.

Although Magnus lived until 1374 the latter part of his reign was marked by serious troubles, and in 1358 having failed to pay his debts to the Pope he was excommunicated. Meanwhile his son Eric XII had taken advantage of the difficulties of his father and had assumed the title of King in 1356, but he died in 1359 without having been crowned. In 1363 Albert of Mecklenburg, whose mother was a daughter of Duke Eric of Sweden, was invited to accept the Swedish throne, and having defeated Magnus he became King but was not crowned. He was forced to leave the country in 1395 after being defeated by Margaret, who was Regent of Norway and Denmark and had been proclaimed Regent of Sweden in 1388. Eric of Pomerania, a nephew of Margaret, who had already been elected King of Norway and Denmark, was chosen as King of Sweden in 1396 and was crowned King of the three kingdoms at Kalmar on 17th June 1397. He married Philippa, the thirteen-year-old daughter of Henry IV of England, who was crowned Queen in October 1406.

While Margaret lived she ruled over the three countries with wisdom and moderation, but on her death in 1412 Eric XIII, who was weak and incompetent, assumed the reins of Government. In 1439 as a result of rebellions Denmark and Sweden withdrew their allegiance to Eric, and Christopher of Bavaria was elected in his stead and was also proclaimed King of Norway in 1442. Christopher III was crowned at Upsala on 14th September 1441, and his consort, Dorothea of Brandenburg, was crowned at Copenhagen on 14th September 1445. He was also crowned separately in the other two kingdoms, which demonstrated that the Union had ceased to exist. On his death in 1448 Karl Knutsson was elected King of Sweden and was crowned as Charles VIII at Upsala on 29th June 1448, and his consort, Katherine, was crowned three days later. Meanwhile the Danes had elected Christian of Oldenburg as their King and he also succeeded in procuring his election as King of Norway, but the peasants did not accept this and proclaimed and crowned Charles as their King. However, Charles renounced the Norwegian crown and Christian was crowned at Trondheim. In Sweden Charles VIII quarrelled with the clergy and with some of his subjects, and in 1457 Christian I supplanted him as King of Sweden and was crowned at Upsala on 2nd July of that year. On his death in 1470 he was succeeded in Denmark by his son Hans, but in Sweden and in Norway (until 1483) there was an interregnum. Hans succeeded in establishing his authority in Sweden in 1497 and was crowned in Stockholm in that year, his consort, Christina, being crowned at Upsala in 1499. Hans died in 1513 and was succeeded in Denmark and Norway by his son Christian II, whom the Swedes declined to recognise. In 1519, however, he gained possession of Stockholm, where he was crowned on 4th November 1520. The Swedes became exasperated by his rule and found an able native leader in Gustavus Vasa, who in 1521, following a rising, was appointed administrator at Vadstena and in June 1523 was proclaimed King at Strengnäs, and Sweden withdrew from the Union.

Since the modern Swedish regalia date from the period subsequent to the dissolution of the Kalmar Union it will be convenient here to take note of such information as is available about the royal ornaments before this date. The earliest representations are on coins and seals. In the XI century a king is shown with the Teutonic golden helmet. Later Knut Ericsson (1167–96) is shown with an arched crown, a sceptre and an orb, but it is improbable that such ornaments were actually in use and it is more likely that they were borrowed from depictions of kings 'Enthroned in Majesty' which were in use in other kingdoms.

When St Eric was murdered in 1160 he was buried at Gamle Upsala, the seat of the early pagan kings. In 1273 the King's body was transferred to a shrine in Upsala Cathedral. Between 1574 and 1579 during the reign of John III the contents of the shrine were examined and a crown was found in the tomb. It is a circlet of eight segments decorated with incised ornaments and adorned with glass jewels. It was taken out of the tomb and kept in the cathedral until a few years ago when the tomb was re-opened and the contents again examined. The original crown was returned to the tomb, but a copy was made and is now in the Historical Museum at Stockholm. This crown has been fully dealt with by Dr Thordeman.[1]

Schramm[2] has suggested that while the presence of a crown in the tomb indicates that the kings used crowns at that time the crown itself was not made to be worn. He concludes that it was originally on a statue of Christ and was placed in the tomb to show the relationship between the earthly and heavenly king. At this time in Scandinavia open circlets resembling crowns were in common use by the nobility and by other persons on such occasions as weddings. It was therefore necessary to associate the royal crown with Christ the King, and there are several examples of crowned figures of Christ still in existence in Sweden and Denmark.[3]

We have evidence of a queen's crown on the effigy of Queen Katherine (*obiit* 1250), consort of Eric XI, on her tomb at the Monastery of Gudhem. The crown is open with four large and four small leaf-like ornaments resting on the circlet. There is also in the Kestner Museum at Hanover a crown-case which is considered to have been for the circlet of Mechthild of Holstein, widow of King Abel of Denmark, who subsequently married (*c.* 1261) Birger Jarl, Duke of Sweden. It was found on a farm near Walkenried in the Harz Mountains about 1850 and was acquired by the museum in 1887.[4]

Such documentary evidence that is still preserved respecting the regalia is of great interest. In 1311 when King Birger II had to leave the country he wrote to the Chapter at Upsala '. . . we are sending into your safe keeping . . . the royal crown, sceptre and orb; the royal ceremonial robes namely subtile, dalmatic, mantle, breast-piece, linen, shoes, an eagle of gold, a belt of silver, a book about the coronation of kings'. These evidently were the coronation regalia and vestments which the King had used in 1302, and it is interesting to note that an orb already featured among the royal ornaments. The eagle was probably the clasp of the royal mantle.

Another document is a receipt dating from the early 1340's for valuables, textiles, weapons, etc., which were kept in the royal treasury in the Castle of Bohus. The list included:

> three gold rings which belonged to King Svere [*obiit* 1202]; a royal sceptre together with a pentagonal state wand . . . a set of coronation robes, namely a mantle, a toga, a tunic and a pair of boots. Further two silken banners which are called 'banner', Swedish; further two banners of cloth, Swedish; further a silken banner, Norwegian; further the King has placed in his treasury for his daily use a Swedish banner of silk and two Norwegian banners of *saeian*.[5]

King Svere had been King of Norway, and it seems probable that some of these ornaments, including the three gold rings and the pentagonal state wand, had formed part

---

1 *Erik den Helige*, edited by Bengt Thordeman, Stockholm 1954.
2 P. E. Schramm: *Herrschaftszeichen und Staatssymbolik*, Vol. III, p. 922 ff.
3 See Chapter Six p. 63 and Plate 37.
4 Dr Monica Rydbeck: *Birger Jarl's Kronfodral*. Hans Wentzel: *Der Kronkasten der Eolkunger*.
5 A cloth of middling quality.

SWEDEN

of the Norwegian regalia. The three gold rings may have been simple circlets or crowns
or they could have been bracelets which were in common use in Scandinavia. The
Castle of Bohus, situated near the Norwegian border, had been recently completed
and was a convenient place for King Magnus II, who was King of Norway and Sweden,
to keep his regalia and treasure.

We find a suggestion that an attempt had been made to establish a national regalia
for use at the coronation of Swedish kings in an entry in the Diary of the Monastery of
Vadstena dated 3rd January 1454. It reads:

> To him (Karl Knutsson) were brought two golden crowns which his predecessor King Eric
> (XIII) had deposited in the monastery on the agreed condition that . . . if a new king were
> crowned in the kingdom he should be permitted to use them for his coronation against indemnity
> or if the monastery fell upon hard times they could be sold to afford relief to the monastery. When
> he saw the crowns and all the other costly treasure which Queen Philippa had bequeathed to the
> monastery the King said to the Confessor and the Brethren: 'These costly treasures you are holding
> in the monastery against the rule of the Saviour and to the peril of your souls'.
>
> And he declared that with the approval of the Convention, he would exchange them for some-
> thing which would be of value and profit to the monastery in the manner of a fee. And Queen
> Philippa's crown was valued at 1075 Stockholm Marks, but King Eric's at 700 marks, two less in
> Swedish currency. . . . These monies of gold did King Karl send to the monastery, just as he had
> said and there are letters to prove what has been told here. . . . And when all these had been
> taken and assessed, they were carried to the Sacristy and laid once more in the depositary of the
> monastery.

When we come to look for evidence as to whether these crowns were used at
coronations subsequent to Queen Philippa's bequest made at the time of her death in
1430 we can only find one item which may have some bearing on the matter. This is a
letter dated 6th August 1445 from King Christopher addressed to the abbess, the general
confessor, the sisters and the brethren of Vadstena saying that he was sending with this
letter his chaplain, the Canon of Upsala, Dr Claues Ryting, to fetch 'the very best and
most costly crown which you have' as 'we are agreed with our beloved council that
our betrothed [Dorothea of Brandenburg] shall be crowned on the second or the third
day of our nuptials'.

In the Diary of the Monastery of Vadstena as well as in the *Sture Chronicles* there is a
description of a visit by Charles in 1455:

> a great throng
> that time King Karl the evangilum sang.
> A crown of gold on his head he wore,
> a golden orb in his right hand he bore,
> and in his left hand a golden sceptre.
> And a knight went before him with a naked gilded sword.

The Diary adds that the King was clothed in a mantle and a fine white robe.

When Charles had obtained possession of the crowns he removed them from
Vadstena. In 1457 when he had to flee the country and left Stockholm for Danzig he
deposited the crowns with the Dominicans at Stockholm. Christian I obtained an order
from the Swedish Council of State for Charles's property to be confiscated and he

627

accused the late King of having taken the crowns with him in his flight. The crowns are described as those 'which had been presented to the state in memory of Queen Margaret and Philippa'. This suggests that the crown of Eric XIII which had been given to Vadstena had originally been that of his aunt Queen Margaret. Christian's accusation proved to be untrue as in 1461 the Dominican monks revealed that they were in possession of the treasure.

Christian in his turn was accused of removing the crowns and other treasures which he had received from the Dominican monks. One of the accusations reads:

> Item think also how he [Christian I] took away from the monastery of the black brothers in Stockholm, the costly treasures, the gold, silver and other coins and particularly the two golden crowns with precious stones which King Karl had redeemed from the monastery of Vadstena to the honour and profit of the kingdom . . . and removed them all against his oath.

At any rate from this time they disappeared and, although they may have been used at several coronations, they had become too closely identified as symbols of the unpopular union to be regarded as a national loss.

Two more royal ornaments are mentioned in Charles's will of 1470. These were 'Our great gilded sword and our golden sceptre' which he left to his son Karl. It is uncertain whether the young Karl ever came into possession of these ornaments as his legitimacy was not recognised. But we find a reference to 'the sword of the kingdom' which was pledged by Charles's nephew and political heir, Sten Sture the Elder, to a powerful Stockholm alderman, Jacob Kuste, some time before the administration of the estate was executed on 11th June 1477.

There is no evidence of a special ampulla being provided for the oil for the anointing at the coronation rite. It is unlikely, as in most kingdoms use was made of ordinary ecclesiastical vessels generally to be found in church treasuries. It is possible, however, that for the coronations at Upsala an ampulla (*Plate 225, c*), still preserved in the silver room of the cathedral, was used. It is of jasper ornamented with silver and enamel and is considered to be of French workmanship of the XIII century.

Since the time of Albert of Mecklenburg (1364–89) the Swedish coat of arms has borne three open crowns. The three crowns actually first appear before that date, probably about 1275, and the origin and meaning of this badge has not been fully determined. It is sometimes asserted that the three crowns indicate the sovereignty over the Swedes, the Goths and the Wends. A mistaken idea too is that they represent the Union of the three kingdoms of Sweden, Norway and Denmark. There are those who associate the badge with the three Magi whose relics were brought to Cologne in 1164. We find other examples of the use of three crowns which have not been properly explained such as in the cult of Arthur; on the seal of Oxford; in the arms of the See of Ely, which are said to be the mythical coat of arms of St Ethelreda. They are found too on the badge of the English Order of the Bath, and on the continent on the coat of arms of the City of Cracow; on the coat of arms of the Koninck family in the Netherlands and on those of Du Faure in France. It seems likely that the origin of the three Swedish crowns will continue to be wrapped in mystery.

The reign of Gustavus I Vasa opens up a new chapter in the history of Sweden and the development of the coronation ceremony and of the royal ornaments. During his reign many important changes and reforms were effected, among them being the declarations of the Diet of Vesterås in 1544 which abolished the Roman Catholic Church in Sweden and made the succession to the throne hereditary in the House of Vasa. We have not much information about Gustavus I Vasa's coronation. Although he had been proclaimed King in 1523 and there was a wish that he should be crowned as soon as possible, some five years passed before the ceremony took place. A superstition had grown up against the coronation taking place at Stockholm as three kings who had been crowned there had met with a tragic fate. Bishop Hans Brask issued a warning against holding the coronation at Stockholm 'as an untimely death had always followed after . . .'. Upsala was therefore restored to its position as the place of coronation and Gustavus was crowned there on 12th January 1528. Peter Swart's *Chronicle* records that it took place 'with all the pomp and solemnity proper to such an occasion and there were present all the persons of rank in the kingdom'. The golden orb was borne by Thure Jensen, the sword by Larntz Siggeson, who was appointed High Constable, and the sceptre by Holinger Carson. There is no mention of the crown, which had probably been placed upon the altar.

There is a record in the Treasury book of 1527 of the making of the crown which appears under the heading 'Gifts'. It reads: 'Item iiij goldsmiths swains who made my lord and master's crown in Stockholm VIII mrk'. This is possibly the same crown as is mentioned in 1562 in the Treasury book, which has a marginal note stating that this inventory was made on the death of the late King. It is recorded as being in the keeping of the Chamberlain Carl, and is described as a golden crown with 6 large rubies, 2 large diamonds, 7 small rubies, 7 small diamonds, 6 sapphires and 84 pearls.

Gustavus I Vasa was married three times. His first consort was Katherine of Saxe-Lauenburg to whom he was married on 24th September 1531, on which occasion she was crowned Queen of Sweden. The Queen bore him a son, the future Eric XIV, and after an unhappy union she died on 23rd September 1535. A year later Gustavus became betrothed to Margaret Leijonhufvud, a member of one of the great Swedish families. The marriage took place at Upsala on 1st October 1536 and Margaret was crowned Queen a few days later. Margaret died on 26th August 1551 having borne the King five sons and five daughters; among those surviving was one who later became John III. On 22nd August 1552 Gustavus married his third wife, Katherine Stenbock, a girl of sixteen years, who survived him by sixty years. She was crowned Queen the day after her wedding.

In August 1560 Gustavus was taken seriously ill and died on 27th September at the age of sixty-four. There are letters still preserved which show that the King took a close interest in the arrangements for his burial. The body was embalmed and was dressed in a long black velvet coat adorned with rows of the initial *G* beneath an open crown. A crown was placed on his head, a sceptre of silver gilt in his hand and under his crossed hands was placed a richly ornamented sword. The body lay in state for eight weeks. It had been decided that the two Queens who had predeceased him—Katherine of Saxe-Lauenburg and Margaret Leijonhufvud—should be reinterred with the King at

Upsala. On 17th December an impressive funeral procession left Stockholm for Upsala, the journey taking three days. The funeral took place on 21st December 1560. In the procession life-like waxen images of the King and his two Queens were placed on the coffins. These effigies wore crowns decorated with precious stones on their heads and carried sceptres in their hands. There is an account dated 3rd March 1561 showing that a sum was paid to the goldsmith Hans Rosenfelt for five crowns and five sceptres together with other articles for the funeral. A dramatic feature of the funeral ceremony occurred when the coffin was carried down into the vault. Svanti Sture, who carried the Great Sword of State unsheathed, stepped forward to the entrance of the vault to face the heir to the throne, Duke Eric. Three times he turned the sword downwards and set its point on the floor of the church, proclaiming in a loud voice that the Most Sovereign King Gustavus was dead. Then he delivered the sword to 'His Royal Majesty, by God's Grace Eric the fourteenth, King of the Swedes, Goths and Wends' exhorting him to wield it and to reign as his royal father had done before him. The handing over of the sword of state signified the transfer of power to the new King. Two years previously, a funeral ceremony had been held in Brussels for the Emperor Charles V at which Prince William of Orange, who was carrying the sword, in a like manner proclaimed the death of the Emperor and the accession of Philip II. This ceremony was copied in many courts and no doubt it was borrowed for this occasion in Sweden.

Gustavus I Vasa's third wife Katherine Stenbock lived until 13th December 1621, when Gustavus II, Adolphus, was on the throne. She had lived through six reigns. She was buried in the crypt where the remains of her husband and her two predecessors rested.

In 1886 when the cathedral was undergoing restoration the Vasa tombs were opened and the regalia found in them were placed in the silver room of the cathedral, where they are still preserved. In 1945 the tombs were again opened and subjected to a thorough examination. The coffins were restored and replaced in their former position in the crypt. The results of the investigation have been fully recorded with illustrations in a fine work edited by Martin Olsson.[1]

At the first opening in 1886 a crown (*Plate 221, a*), sceptre (*Plate 223, a*), and sword (*Plate 224, a*) were found in the tomb of the King. The sword was one which Gustavus had used during his lifetime, but the crown and sceptre had been specially made for the funeral before the King's death. This explains why Rosenfelt made only five crowns and five sceptres instead of six. All the representations of the crowns in use during the King's lifetime show that only the open crown was still in use. It seems therefore that the arches and surmounting orb and cross were added by Eric XIV, who had determined to adopt the arched crown, between the time of the King's death and the funeral. A black bonnet was found in the tomb which would have been the crown cap.

There is nothing which has been found to show whether Queen Katherine of Saxe-Lauenburg was buried with regalia after her death, though it is possible that a crown and sceptre of gilded wax were placed in the coffin. On the occasion of her re-burial

[1] M. Olsson: *Vasagraven i Uppsala Domkyrka* (with a summary in English), Stockholm 1956.

an arched crown (*Plate 221, b*) was placed on her head and a sceptre (*Plate 223, b*) in her hand. Queen Margaret Leijonhufvud was originally buried with an open crown of gilded wax and a sceptre with an iron shaft covered with gilded wax (*Plate 224, c and d*). These ornaments were found in her coffin when it was opened in 1945 and were removed and placed in the silver room of the cathedral. According to an account paid to the painter Urban another crown and sceptre were placed on the coffin at her funeral in 1551. On the occasion of her re-burial in 1560 a crown (*Plate 221, c*) and sceptre (*Plate 223, c*) were placed in her coffin.

The two Queen's crowns of 1560 are of the same design and are closed with arches though they are of a different pattern to that of the King. The three sceptres buried with the King and the two Queens in 1560 were of the same design with slight differences. The King's sceptre is longer than the others but it carries at the top a gilded pearl on a short rod. That of Queen Katherine is similar but in the case of Queen Margaret there is a difference because she was not of princely birth and there is no short rod under the pearl.

In 1886 a small crown of pearls (*Plate 221, d*) was found in the coffin of Queen Katherine Stenbock which had been made specially for the burial. This is now in the silver room of the cathedral.

After the death of Gustavus I Vasa, his son, Eric XIV, turned his attention to his forthcoming coronation. The former Swedish coronation rite had not contained many features which could be identified as distinctly national and had probably been based on the Roman *Ordo*. Eric was determined to celebrate his coronation in a manner befitting the new regime and the changed and enhanced status of a Protestant, hereditary and national monarchy. It was decided that the ceremony should take place at Upsala on 29th June 1561, and preparations were put in hand in the previous year. The King addressed a letter to his *legatus perpetuus* in London, one Dionysius Beurreus, who was to return to Sweden for the coronation, in which he was instructed to 'bring back notes to divers ceremonies, and how such matters are duly conducted at other royal courts when such occasions are being solemnised'. Unfortunately the legate's report has not survived. We may conjecture, however, that the King was anxious that the Swedish royal ornaments should not be in any way inferior to those of other kingdoms. The only coronations that had been conducted with a Protestant rite were those in England, in 1547, 1553 and 1559, and in Denmark, in 1559.

Eric also took active steps regarding the manufacture of the royal ornaments which would be worthy of becoming permanent regalia now that the monarchy was hereditary. In February 1561 he sent delegates to Antwerp to arrange for a crown, a sceptre and an orb to be made there. In a 'Register of that which shall be commanded for the Coronation of Our Most Gracious Majesty' we find the following opening item.

> In the first place His Majesty the King desires that His Majesty's Crown shall be made in Antwerp, together with the sceptre and the orb, and that the crown shall be set with diamonds and rubies with a few large pearls and a great round sapphire on top, and there shall also be precious stones on the sceptre and on the orb likewise. And His Majesty the King also desires that a sword shall be ordered to match these things.

A few months later one of the delegates, Nils Gyllenstierna, wrote from Antwerp requesting a remittance of some thousand thalers for appurtenances for the coronation:

> principally for the Crown, Sceptre, Orb and Sword which shall then be borne before Your Majesty and for which most of the designs have already been made and all sorts of precious stones, rubies, emeralds, diamonds, sapphires and some large pearls, which are required for them, have been ordered here from a jeweller named Hans Glaser, who formerly served Your Majesty's father the late King of august memory and who previously worked on Your Majesty's Sword and poignard.

According to another delegate on 20th May 'payment was made to Hans Glaser on account of His Majesty the King's Crown, Sceptre, Orb and Sword—3000 thaler'. For some reason or other, perhaps because of the heavy cost, these ornaments were not sent to Sweden. Even in 1568 there is a record that 'the crown and sceptre which His Majesty our Most Gracious Lord and King had caused to be commanded from Antwerp have not arrived in the kingdom although His Majesty had often had letters written on the subject'.

In March 1561 an order was placed with a Flemish goldsmith in Stockholm named Cornelius ver Weiden (or Wijin) for a crown and a sceptre, and some gold and precious stones were handed over for the purpose. The crown that was delivered to the King was a fine example of the jeweller's art. Attached to the gold circlet were a number of plaques beautifully enamelled and set with precious stones. The King's initials E.R. in pale blue enamel and flanked by two female figures symbolising the seven cardinal virtues and *Caritas Humana* were repeated four times. Eight large and arched enamelled ornaments each with a precious stone set in the centre rested on the rim, and between these were set eight small ornaments. From behind the large ornaments the two arches sprang. They were richly enamelled and set with precious stones and were not depressed at the centre but took the imperial shape, which no doubt was copied from the Tudor Crowns in England. A gold and enamelled orb rested on the point of intersection of the arches, but it is not known what form the surmounting cross took.

Incorporated into the enamel decorations are lions bearing halberds borrowed from the Norwegian coat of arms and the leopards and hearts taken from the Danish coat of arms. The use of the latter was in reply to the refusal of Denmark to remove the three Swedish crowns from their coat of arms. The crown weighed 6 sterling marks and 1 oz. The precious stones used were: 2 large emeralds, 2 small emeralds, 2 large sapphires, 2 large rubies, 6 small rubies, 8 large diamonds, 8 small diamonds, 12 large pearls, 4 medium pearls and 24 small pearls. Although it has been much altered this crown has been passed down to the present time as the Crown of the Realm of Sweden.

Ver Weiden deputed the manufacture of the sceptre to a goldsmith of Stockholm named Hans Heidernrich, and provided for the purpose 3 sterling marks of gold, which proved to be insufficient and had to be supplemented in June. He also provided 1 large emerald, 1 large sapphire, 1 large topaz, 3 small diamonds and 3 small rubies. In the course of time various alterations have been made to the sceptre, but it is still the King's sceptre among the regalia.

The Orb of the Realm (*Plate 216, c and e*) was also made for the coronation of Eric

a   *Crown of Eric XIV. State Bank, Stockholm* (p. 649)

b   *Reconstruction of crown of
Eric XIV. State Bank,
Stockholm*

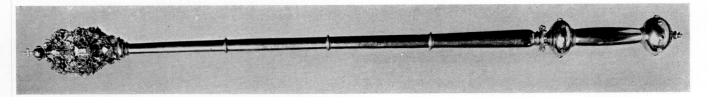

a   *King's sceptre, 1561. State Bank, Stockholm (pp. 632 and 649)*

b   *The ampulla. State Bank, Stockholm (pp. 640 and 651)*

c   *Orb of the Realm, 1561, front view. State Bank, Stockholm (pp. 633 and 649)*

d   (left) *Keys of the Realm of Eric XIV and Ulrica Leonora, 1720. State Bank, Stockholm (pp. 633, 644, 650 and 652)*

e   (right) *Orb of the Realm, 1561, back view*

XIV either by Cornelius ver Weiden or his brother Petter ver Weiden. There is a record of the latter being given some gold for the cross on the orb, but when in the autumn of 1561 he went to England, he was believed to have taken the gold with him. The orb has a feature which today is unique in the form of a map of the world engraved on its surface. This orb is still preserved among the Swedish regalia.

Eric XIV introduced a new ornament into the Swedish regalia in the form of the Key of the Realm (*Plate 216, d*). It was delivered by the goldsmith nine days before the coronation. It is still among the regalia.

At this time the sword still enjoyed precedence over all the other royal ornaments including the crown. There were two swords which had belonged to Gustavus Vasa which were available and they were included among the regalia and are still in existence today. The oldest or Great Sword of Gustavus I Vasa was known as the Sword of the Realm (*Plate 214, a*). It not only represented a personal link with the founder of the dynasty but the Old Testament scenes on the blade depicting Joseph, after many vicissitudes, attaining power and glory, and Moses leading his people out of the thraldom of Egypt, were regarded as symbolic of Gustavus Vasa's own story and achievements. The sword was purchased in Augsburg in 1540 by Claus Heier, a merchant of Augsburg, who had been appointed to a position at the Swedish Court. He paid 30 gulders and 15 crowns for the weapon. For the coronation of Eric XIV the hilt was gilded.

There is more than one description of the coronation of Eric XIV, the best and most detailed record being that of Laurentius Petri Gothus, Court Chaplain. The ceremonial used on this occasion was based on ancient tradition with the addition of new features to mark the changed conditions and status of the monarchy. It is of special interest not only because it was the first Protestant rite used in Sweden but because it formed the model on which all subsequent coronations down to 1873—a period of over 300 years—were based.

The first matter to be noticed is the order of precedence given to the regalia in the procession:

> The Key borne by Gustav Johansson.
> The Orb borne by Birger Nilsson Grip.
> The Sceptre borne by Court Steward Per Brahe.
> The Crown borne by Sten Ericksson Leijonhufvud.
> The Sword borne by the Lord High Constable, Svante Sture.
> The King.
> The Royal Robes borne by five young noblemen.

The sword, which was still regarded as the most important royal ornament, took precedence over the crown and was carried immediately in front of the King. The robes included a white tunic, gloves, a ring, a sword and the royal mantle.

The King was met at the door of the cathedral by the archbishop, the bishops and the 'ordinaries', who greeted him with the words, 'blessed be he who cometh in the name of the Lord', followed by a prayer. The King having placed himself in the royal chair and the dukes and others having taken their places the archbishop preached a sermon on the 'duties and office of the sovereign' in which he exhorted the congregation not to look upon the ceremonies merely as a spectacle and a pageant 'but should rather have a special significance, more important and memorable, particularly as the ceremonies performed at royal coronations and the like are no new or recently instituted custom, but have always, from time immemorial, been practised not only in one country or kingdom but over the whole world'.

After the sermon the King went into the chancel and entered 'the prepared chamber or tent of silken cloth outspread to the right of the altar' where he donned other robes. He re-entered the chancel bearing a large gilt offertory filled with dalers which he set upon the altar as an offering. After he had prayed the King gave affirmative answers to questions put by the archbishop, who asked if he would 'honour, strengthen, defend and by force maintain the true religion, the pure word of God, the true faith etc.'. The King then took the oath. After further prayers the archbishop anointed the King, who was stripped to the waist, first on forehead and breast, then on shoulders and back and finally on arms and hands. The King was then clothed in a white tunic and the archbishop put on the coronation gloves and the ring saying, 'God Who has called thee to the knowledge of the Gospels, keep thy faith pure and clear to the end.' Then the King was girded with the little sword with the prayer: 'God, for whom all things are possible, strengthen and comfort thee so that thou mayest perform thy task manfully, in the imitation of the King of Whom it has been written: "Bind thy sword to thy side thou Hero, decked with praise and glory, and be thou prosperous in all thy splendour." Amen.'

While the great royal mantle was then laid on the King's shoulders, there was a reading from the Gospels, during which the King held the great Sword of State in his right hand. The King then ascended his royal throne, which stood on a dais in the centre of the chancel. Over the throne hung a canopy with the royal coat of arms. The archbishop took the crown from Sten Eriksson's hands and 'set it upon His Majesty's bare head' with the words:

> Almighty God and Merciful Father, who has given thee the Crown of the Kingdom (the symbol of Royal Honour and Glory), let his blessing fall richly upon thee and so strengthen thee with all kingly virtues that country and kingdom may prosper through thy good rule, and that thou, after this temporal and transient kingdom mayest inherit the everlasting and receive the crown which God shall ever give to His chosen saints.

Then 'all those who stood around hailed him for their King, with the acclamation of the common people' and the archbishop gave the King the sceptre saying:

> Almighty God, Who has given thee power and royal might, and commanded that thou shalt rule and judge thy people with righteousness (of which this sceptre is the symbol), so endow thee with gentleness and mercy therefore that thou in thy rule mayest follow the Everlasting and Heavenly King, Jesus Christ, of whom it is written The Sceptre of Thy Kingdom is the Sceptre of Righteousness. Thou lovest righteousness and hatest iniquity or ungodliness. Through the Same, Lord Jesus Christ. Amen.

The orb was then delivered to the King by the archbishop with the words:

God Who has set thee up as an all-powerful and reigning king over a whole, mighty and Christian Kingdom (of which the orb and cross are symbols), grant thee His Divine Grace that thou mayest defend it for his honour and glory and for the happiness and benefit of the people of Sweden. Through Jesus Christ Our Lord. Amen.

Finally the King received the great Sword of State from the archbishop who recited the following prayer:

God, who has commended into thy hands this sword that thou therewith mayest defend the good and punish the evil, grant thee His Holy Grace that thou mayest be comforted and undaunted manfully to fulfil that which has been commanded of thee, to the honour and glory of His Holy Name, and to the peace, freedom and great comfort of thy people, through Jesus Christ Our Lord. Amen.

The King having received all the royal ornaments 'sat in Majesty' on the throne, with the crown on his head, the sword in his right hand and the orb and sceptre in his left. Then the herald who stood behind the throne cried loudly: 'Now is the Most Sovereign and Illustrious Prince and Lord Eric XIV, anointed and proclaimed King of Sweden.' Having repeated these words twice more the nobles and common people replied: 'God grant our King happiness and salvation and a long and prosperous reign.' In the church the trumpets sounded while outside the soldiers and the cannons gave a salute.

The royal dukes, the counts, barons and knights then did their homage and the procession moved back to the castle. The Treasurer cast money to the people, wine and ale flowed from barrel and vat, the coronation oxen, roasted whole and stuffed with calves, ducks and chickens were cut up and distributed among the people to feast upon. At the castle the coronation banquet was held and during the next five days there were tournaments, bear-baiting and firework displays.

Although the Order of the Seraphim was said to have been founded in the second half of the XIII century, the insignia were not worn at coronation ceremonies until the middle of the XVIII century. Eric XIV was anxious to receive the French Order of St Michael, which had been conferred upon his father, Gustavus I Vasa. But his two attempts to obtain it were unsuccessful, as was one to obtain the Order of the Garter. In the absence of anything better he had made a jewel with a badge in the form of a salvator and a chain decorated with the Swedish coat of arms. This he wore at his coronation. Although this insignia looked like that of the foreign orders he coveted he did not turn it into an Order of Chivalry and there is no record of it having been conferred on anyone else.

In 1560 shortly before his death, Gustavus Vasa had conferred dukedoms upon his younger sons, a step which laid the foundation for further troubles, as they enjoyed a measure of independence. When the crown of Sweden was elective there was, of course, no heir to the throne, but in 1544 when the crown became hereditary the heir to the throne became entitled to assume the insignia of his rank. Eric XIV went to his coronation in procession wearing the princely mantle and crown and at the ceremony his step-brothers appeared in their ducal raiment, namely in their tunics sewn with pearls and stones and with their crowns. We have some information about these early princely crowns. A German chronicler states that at the coronation of Eric XIV, Dukes John,

Charles and Magnus wore violet-brown mantles trimmed with ermine and with collars and trains which reminded him of the dress of the German electors. On their heads they wore a hat with a crown which bore four clover leaves.

Apparently Eric was not altogether satisfied with his regalia for on 12th February 1563 the crown and sceptre were handed over to a Swiss goldsmith in Stockholm named Hans Beijer, who was instructed to make considerable alterations. Beijer did not hand back the crown until 25th May 1563. He had remade the crown and demanded 4,000 marks for the work he had done, as well as payment for 16 small pearls. This sum was considered to be too much, but it is not known how much he was paid. He died the same year. While the stones in the sceptre were removed there is no account of any work done to it. In December 1565 it was placed in a sealed cupboard in the King's wardrobe together with a sealed box containing the stones belonging to it. In 1563 the orb was also handed over to Beijer, and on the orders of the King it was sent to his brother Frans Beijer in Antwerp, and it was not returned until 1568 when Frans came to Sweden and was paid 2,230 marks for the work he had done.

Eric XIV had been unsuccessful in his matrimonial schemes. In 1561 the news of his father's death reached him on the eve of his contemplated departure for England to press in person his suit for the hand of Elizabeth I. Among others whose hand he sought was Princess Renata of Lorraine. But in the end he decided to marry his mistress, Karin Mansdatter, the daughter of a common soldier. The marriage took place on 4th July 1568 at Stockholm and the following day Karin was crowned Queen of Sweden. In the preparations for the wedding the King ordered a crown, a sceptre and an orb to be made for his Queen. It was the generally accepted custom in Europe, though there were one or two exceptions, that the orb, being a symbol of sovereignty, could not be used by a queen consort. In Sweden there is no evidence of a queen consort being invested with an orb at her coronation before Karin Mansdatter, but this custom was subsequently always followed. The reasons for this unusual custom have not been satisfactorily explained, and we must therefore search for the reasons that inspired the idea. There is a portrait of Margaret Leijonhufvud (*Plate 217, b*) at Gripsholm Castle which shows the Queen with an open crown and carrying a sceptre and orb. The portrait is considered to be a copy of an earlier one painted in 1544, seven years before the Queen's death. It is possible that the regalia were added when the copy was made to conform to what was established practice. But if it can be proved that the orb had been painted in the original then the custom must have been introduced in the reign of Gustavus Vasa. Gustavus had received an orb at his coronation, but one was not included among the regalia with which he was buried or among the ornaments which adorned his effigy at his funeral. There is no evidence that any of his consorts were invested with the orb at their coronations, nor was an orb included among their funerary regalia. On the existing evidence it seems that the custom started at the coronation of Karin Mansdatter.

If we look for reasons to explain this custom, the first that suggests itself is that in the reign of Gustavus Vasa the queens consort were crowned as Queens of Sweden. This gave them a special status, as in other kingdoms queens consort were usually known by their personal names and not as queen of the kingdom over which their husbands ruled. In the case of Karin there were other special circumstances. The King had been estranged from his brother John and the marriage was the occasion of a reconciliation, a condition being that John recognised the legality of the wedding and Karin's children as the successors to the throne. On the day of the Queen's coronation her infant son, Gustavus, was proclaimed Prince Royal. It may be that the delivery of the orb to the queen was to emphasise her position as the mother of the future king. But we cannot overlook the possibility of Polish influence. In 1552 John had married Katherine Jagiellonica, the sister of Sigismund II, King of Poland. In 1386 when Ladislas II, Jagiello, Grand Duke of Lithuania, became King of Poland his wife Jadwiga was already Queen of Poland and at her coronation had been invested with the orb. It seems that the custom was perpetuated in Poland both in respect of queens regnant and queens consort. Katherine Jagiellonica was already in Sweden at the time of the preparations for Eric's wedding, and it is possible that she inspired the idea.

The only incident we know of which occurred at the wedding is that at the feast the Chancellor, Nils Gyllenstierna, dropped the King's crown on the floor. A year after the wedding Eric XIV, whose sanity had for some time been in doubt, was formally deposed. On 30th September 1568 John III was proclaimed King by the army and the nobility. This was confirmed by a *Riksdag* on 25th January 1569. Eric was kept in captivity and was a great anxiety to the Government, as there were several rebellions in his favour. On 10th March 1575 an assembly of notables at John's request pronounced a formal sentence of death upon Eric, and on 24th February 1577 he died suddenly in his new prison at Orbyhus. It was said that he was poisoned by John's orders. Eric XIV was buried in the cathedral at Vesterås and a tombstone inscribed with a verse from the Bible was erected over his grave. In 1787 Gustavus III erected a sarcophagus in place of the tombstone. There is a letter written by the Consistory at Upsala to the County Lieutenant's Office at Vesterås on 15th March 1797 which contains the following passage: 'Regarding the transfer of the crown and sceptre now kept in the Sacristy at Upsala Cathedral to Vesterås to be placed there on the Sarcophagus of King Eric XIV's tomb according to the order given by H.M. King Gustavus III on 16th July 1787.' This led to a belief that Gustavus III had thought that the time was due for John III to repay his debts to his brother. One version of the story asserted that Gustavus had broken off the bronze sceptre from the marble statue of John III at Upsala and had placed it on Eric's tomb. Another that the crown and sceptre referred to were those which had been used at John's funeral and had then been preserved in the silver room of the cathedral. This story was given credence by Sohlberg, a chaplain to the army and head of the archives at Vesterås Cathedral in 1834.[1] This view was supported by Lindegren,[2] architect to the Drottingholms Palace, writing in 1898. But Hahr[3] has pointed out that John's funeral regalia had been destroyed by fire at Upsala Cathedral in 1702. He tells us that John's marble statue had been made in Danzig in 1594 by a Netherlands artist where it remained until it was brought to Sweden by Gustavus III. The monument had been kept in a store-room at Danzig and the crown and sceptre which had been made for it had been kept on a table in front of the monument. These were the ornaments

1 Lars Gustaf Sohlberg: *Historical Description of the Cathedral at Vesterås*, 1934.
2 Agi Lindegren: *Maria Church at Vesterås*, 1898.
3 August Hahr, Professor at Upsala University 1923: *Vesterås Cathedral*.

637

which Gustavus III ordered to be brought to Vesterås. The crown is of gilded bronze and closed with arches. The circlet is decorated with heads and figures of nude women. The crown is profusely adorned with imitation precious stones made of glass and mother-of-pearl. It is of fine workmanship dating from the end of the XVI century. The sceptre is also of gilded bronze and the orb of gilded wood. Thus they do not come into the category of funeral regalia but of monumental ornaments of the same sort that are used to adorn the tombs of Swedish kings, especially those in the Riddarholm Church at Stockholm.

John III and his consort, Katherine Jagiellonica, were crowned at Upsala on 10th July 1569. The ceremony followed the general pattern of the coronation of Eric XIV, and the existing regalia were used with the addition of a new item—the State Seal or Secret—which was borne in the procession between the orb and the key. The chain of an order is also mentioned as having been carried in the procession. It was apparently John's intention to found a Swedish Order, but this was not carried out. It is not certain whether John used Eric XIV's salvator or had a new chain and order made. It is known, however, that he added an *Agnus Dei*. But it remained the King's personal order and was not conferred on anyone else. As a queen was being crowned at the same coronation ceremony an innovation was made whereby having entered the church the regalia was laid upon the altar, the King's on the right and the Queen's on the left. A new prayer to explain the meaning of the coronation ring was also added.

Queen Katherine Jagiellonica died in 1583 and was buried in a crypt below a special chapel in Upsala Cathedral. Her burial regalia consisted of a golden crown (*Plate 222, b*) set with pearls and precious stones and a sceptre which may have been used by the Queen during her lifetime. It is made of rings of ebony and mother-of-pearl wired together. The handle is of gold with enamel work and jewels and the ornament at the top is of gold and precious stones. These ornaments are still preserved in the silver room of Upsala Cathedral.

John III gave a silver votive crown to be hung over the shrine of St Eric and another one to be hung from the arch of the chapel below which Katherine Jagiellonica is buried.

On 21st February 1585 John III married his second consort, Gunilla Bielke, at Vesterås. For this ceremony a new set of ornaments was made for the Queen consisting of a crown, a sceptre (*Plate 217, e*) and an orb (*Plate 217, d*). They were given the un-usual term of *reginalia*. The work was given to Gillis Coyet, an artist from the Nether-lands who had become goldsmith to the King in 1574 and had made the furnerary orb of Katherine Jagiellonica. But time was short and several other goldsmiths had to be em-ployed. The Queen's crown which was described as 'coarse and gross work', was decorated with enamel and closed with arches surmounted by an orb. It was set with pearls, emeralds and 'kareleska' rubies. These last stones were unusually clear garnets which were mined in 1582 in the newly found deposits in Karelia. The crown did not survive, for in an inventory taken two days after John's death we find an entry that Queen Gunilla's crown had been dismembered. The Queen's sceptre was made by Anthony Grott or Grooth, who was also from the Netherlands. It followed the general design of the sceptre of Eric XIV, though smaller and with a more slender shaft. It was decorated with 10 emeralds, 2 'kareleska' rubies and 8 pearls and the total cost was 160 daler. The orb is a simple golden globe on a small stand with an equator and meridian set with pearls and a cross with pearls. In its very simplicity it is effective. In all 27 pearls were used. The gold is described as Hungarian and Rhenish, and some of it seems to have been supplied by the Treasury, as the bill only came to 3 dalers.

The sceptre and orb were kept together as the queen's regalia for a hundred years, and thereafter the orb was on occasion used by the king.

John III, in 1584, the year before his second marriage, had Eric XIV's crown 'improved' by his goldsmith Gillis Coyet. It was probably on this occasion that the 16 baroque pearls were added in pairs in order to obliterate the initials E.R., which would have been hateful to John.

John III died in 1592 and his body was embalmed and arrayed in royal robes and invested with burial regalia. His son Sigismund, who was heir to the Swedish throne, had been elected King of Poland in 1587 and the funeral was postponed until the new King could be present. Meanwhile the coffin was taken to the royal chapel where it rested until February 1594, when in the presence of Sigismund it was taken to Upsala and buried in the Vasa vault. Gunilla Bielke died in 1597 and was also buried in the Vasa vault at Upsala.

The regalia found in the royal tombs are now in the silver room of Upsala Cathedral. The crown of John III (*Plate 222, a*) is of gold and set with precious stones. It is described as 'a perfect example of a renaissance crown in manneristic style'. The sceptre (*Plate 223, d*) is in a different style and there is also a simple orb (*Plate 222, d*). The regalia of Gunilla Bielke are of silver gilt and are described as 'inferior and provincial'. The ornaments are a crown (*Plate 222, c*), a sceptre (*Plate 223, e*) and an orb (*Plate 222, e*). The King's sword was a rapier (*Plate 224, b*).

Although Sigismund was a Roman Catholic he was crowned in accordance with the established Swedish rite, but not until he had consented to the 'maintenance of the pure evangelical religion in Sweden'. The ceremony took place at Upsala on 19th February 1594, and his consort, Anne of Austria, was crowned at the same time. On 14th July 1594 he returned to Poland leaving his uncle, Duke Charles, and the senate to rule Sweden. As it was claimed that the King had failed to keep his promises Duke Charles was appointed Regent for life. Sigismund in 1598 landed at Kalmar with an army and was well received in the country but he suffered a defeat from Duke Charles at the Battle of Stångebro, and left the country never to return. He was formally deposed in 1599 and in 1604 Charles assumed the title of King as Charles IX.

Sigismund had wanted to take the Swedish king's regalia back to Poland with him, but this was not allowed. We find, however, in the inventories of the Polish regalia a set of royal ornaments which is called the 'Swedish'. The ornaments consisted of a crown, sceptre and orb. It is of particular interest to note that in the inventory of 1609 the orb is described as having engraved on it a *Sphaera mundi*. Of the origin of these ornaments there is no record, but they continued to feature among the Polish regalia until it was destroyed by the Prussians.[1]

Charles IX and his consort, Christina of Holstein, were crowned at Upsala on

1 See Chapter Seventeen, Poland, pp. 264–5.

15th March 1607. There were several innovations, the most important of which was the provision of an ampulla in the form of a horn as one of the coronation ornaments. This beautiful piece was made by the Stockholm goldsmith Peter Kempe. It was borne in the coronation procession by the archbishop. The ring was carried as one of the royal ornaments for the last time and Charles IX's coronation ring is still preserved in the Royal Armoury. It is of gold set with a large crystal. An innovation was a prayer which was recited when the Key of the Realm was delivered, in which the King was exhorted to 'close all the doors of the kingdom against all heretical foes and infidels' and 'to open the doors for the poor and those in sore distress'. At Sigismund's coronation the King had not worn any insignia of a Swedish Order but wore that of the Golden Fleece. Charles IX re-introduced a personal order which took the form of a chain with the Jehovah badge. This was made by Anthony Grott and is still preserved in the Royal Armoury. Charles died in 1611 and was buried in the Cathedral of Strengnäs, where his Queen, Christina, was also buried. The regalia found in their tombs and now in the silver room of the cathedral are particularly noteworthy. The King's crown (*Plate 226, a*) is of rich workmanship of gold and enamel decorated with pearls and chrysolites and is closed with two arches surmounted by an orb and cross. The King's sceptre and orb (*Plate 226, b and d*) are both of gold and enamel and were the work of Peter Kempe. They are also set with precious stones. Queen Christina's crown (*Plate 226, c*) is that of a widowed queen, *dule* and unjewelled. It is of gold and black enamel with a design of roses, pansies and small star-shaped flowers and is closed with arches. Her sceptre and orb (*Plate 226, b and e*) are simpler than those of her husband.

Charles IX was succeeded by his seventeen-year-old son Gustavus II, Adolphus, who proved to be one of the most able and most famous of the Swedish kings. He was crowned at Upsala on 12th October 1617. The number of bearers of the regalia in the procession was reduced from ten at the previous coronation to six. The state seal no longer appeared among the royal ornaments, the mantle and key were carried by one bearer and the King wore his coronation vestments on the way to the church (a custom which had started in the reign of Charles IX). The sword for the first time gave precedence to the crown.

The regalia had appeared at a ceremony in 1616 before the coronation when the King received the Dutch ambassadors. On this occasion the sword, crown, sceptre and orb were placed on a marble table on the right of the King.

In November 1620 Gustavus Adolphus married Maria Eleanora of Brandenburg, and she was crowned Queen of Sweden on 28th November 1620 at Stockholm. As Queen Christina the elder, widow of Charles IX, was still alive the existing queen's regalia was at her disposal and orders were given for a set of royal ornaments to be made for the new Queen Consort. The crown (*Plate 217, a*), which was closed with two arches, was decorated with 422 diamonds and 12 rubies. It was subsequently altered and put to other uses but is still preserved among the Swedish regalia. Although sufficient time had been allowed for the making of the crown, the sceptre and orb had to be made in great haste. From a letter written by the King on 15th September 1620 it appears that the Treasurer, despite the King's order, had forgotten to place an order for these ornaments. Two designs were submitted for the King's approval

a   Crown of Maria Eleanora. State Bank, Stockholm (p. 651)

b   Portrait of Margaret Leijonhufvud. Gripsholm Castle (p. 636)

c (left) Reconstruction of crown of Maria Eleanora, 1620 (p. 640)

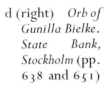

d (right) Orb of Gunilla Bielke. State Bank, Stockholm (pp. 638 and 651)

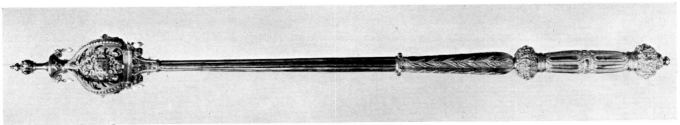

e   Sceptre of Gunilla Bielke. State Bank, Stockholm (pp. 638 and 651)

a   *Crown of Queen Louisa Ulrica. State Bank, Stockholm* (p. 652)

b (left) *Engraving of crown of Louisa Ulrica by J. E. Rehn* (p. 645)

c   *Orb of Maria Eleanora, 1620. State Bank, Stockholm* (p. 645)

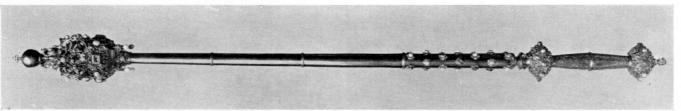

d   *Sceptre of Maria Eleanora, 1620, State Bank, Stockholm* (p. 651)

with the comment that the one based on the old sceptre would take six months to execute and the new one could be completed in six weeks. On 3rd October the King ordered that it should be ready in three weeks. Actually an extension of time was found to be possible and the sceptre, which was of simpler work than the crown, was made ready in time. The orb was also made in haste, which necessitated a simple design. These three ornaments were made by or under the supervision of Rupert Miller, an outstanding goldsmith who was established in Stockholm from 1606 to 1623. He was not only a distinguished artist but an outstanding enameller. Miller's bill came to 2,000 thalers. Besides the stones in the crown the sceptre was set with 70 diamonds and 14 rubies and the orb with 8 diamonds and 14 rubies. It seems that these stones were provided from the Treasury and the bill represented wages. The colour scheme of these ornaments—gold, black enamel, white diamonds and red rubies—was inspired by the heraldic colours of the two royal houses: that of Gustavus Adolphus black and red; and of Brandenburg red and white.

As though he had a premonition that he would not live to see Sweden again, Gustavus Adolphus in 1629 chose his burial place in the Riddarholm Church at Stockholm, and on 19th May 1630 he solemnly took leave of the estates of the realm holding in his arms the little Princess Christina, his only child and heiress, and tenderly committed her to the care of his loyal and devoted people. He then left for Germany to support the Protestant cause. He was killed in somewhat obscure circumstances on 6th November 1632 at Lützen. He was buried in the Riddarholm Church on 22nd July 1634. On the lid of the coffin is a cushion with crown, sceptre and sword. Queen Maria Eleanora died in 1655 and was buried in the Gustavian chapel near to her husband. Her tomb was opened a few years ago and it was found that the Queen had been buried with an elaborately decorated crown (*Plate 227, b*) on her head and a sceptre and an orb in her hands. These ornaments were photographed undisturbed in the tomb.

Gustavus II was succeeded by his only child Christina, who was six years old at the time of her father's death. When she was eighteen she assumed the reins of power on 8th December 1644, but was not crowned until 20th October 1650. Her advisers were against her decision to be crowned at Stockholm, but she was insistent, and she made the following declaration: 'There is but one thing which could conflict with this resolution, namely the opinion held by the common people concerning Upsala and they make a great stir about it. But it would not be much to respect the wishes of Her Majesty, since the happiness of Her Majesty does not depend on any place, but on God.' The Queen's later misfortunes were blamed on the fact that she had been crowned at Stockholm and not at Upsala.

Christina adamantly refused to marry despite the pressure which was brought to bear upon her to wed a suitable husband. A candidate who was particularly favoured was Charles Gustavus, son of John Casimir, Count Palatine of Zweibrücken, and Katherine, sister of Gustavus Adolphus. But Christina was fixed in her determination to remain unmarried. She decided, however, that Charles Gustavus should be declared to be her heir. There was much opposition both from her advisers and the senate, but she overcame this and in 1650 the *Riksdag* declared the Swedish crown to be hereditary in Charles and his male heirs.

Christina's coronation took place on 20th October 1650, and the major innovation was that the ampulla was no longer carried in the procession among the royal ornaments, but was borne by the archbishop, who met the Queen at the door of the church. The Queen chose the crown of her mother, Maria Eleanora, which was altered by the goldsmith Jurgen Dargeman. The old crown had two arches, and it was thought that it would be more fitting for the crown of a queen regnant to have four arches. The new arches were each set with 9 diamonds instead of 6 used in the original. The queen was invested with all the royal ornaments used by a sovereign regnant, including the Sword of State and the key. For the first time the coronation order was printed.

Charles Gustavus only arrived in Stockholm on 1st October, and at a Council held on 3rd October Christina reminded her councillors that the Hereditary Prince had always used a special dress at coronations consisting of a crown, a hat and a mantle. There was little time for these to be prepared, and it was not until 12th October, but a week before the coronation, that Dargeman received an order to make a crown and received an advance of 200 ducats for the purpose. Dargeman dismantled the crown of Queen Christina the Elder, mother of Gustavus Adolphus, to provide the material, and only the frame and surmounting orb and cross of the old crown remained. The crown had originally been made by Rupert Miller in 1606. The new crown consisted of a circlet from which rose eight triangular plates topped by pearls. The whole was very richly ornamented with enamel work and set with 143 large and small diamonds, 3 large sapphires, 47 large pearls, 14 rubies and 32 small pearls. Charles wore this crown over a hat of purplish brown velvet with silver and gold flames embroidered on it (*Plate 219, a*). After the coronation the crown was taken to the house of the Court-Intendant, where it was kept until 1661, when it was placed in the royal wardrobe.

Shortly after her coronation Christina set her mind on abdicating the throne, but her final decision was deferred until 1654. On 6th July of that year a solemn ceremony of formal abdication took place at the Castle of Upsala in the presence of the estates and the great dignitaries of the realm. The Queen wearing her royal mantle, with the crown on her head and the sceptre and orb in her hands, entered the great hall of the castle. On either side was a minister of state, one bearing the great Sword of State and the other the key of the realm. The Queen took her seat on a silver throne and the act of renunciation of the throne was signed by the senate and then read aloud, and the Hereditary Prince, whose chair was a little to the rear of the throne, placed the deeds in her hands. The Queen then stood up and took the crown off her head and handed it to Count Brahe, who received it kneeling. The Queen then divested herself of the other attributes of royalty which were placed on a table near the throne, and then she addressed the assembled company on the past struggles and glories of Sweden and its prospects.

On leaving Sweden Christina was openly accepted into the Roman Catholic Church at Innsbruck, and although she twice returned to Sweden in the vain hope of recovering her throne she finally settled at Rome, where she died on 19th April 1689. When in Rome she deposited in the Church of Our Lady at Loreto (near Ancona) a crown and sceptre. She was previously heard to say: 'So people will have it that I shall go to Loreto and deposit my crown and sceptre at the feet of the Virgin Mary. I gave up

a   *Crowned hat of Prince Charles Gustavus (p. 642)*

b   *Crown of the Crown Prince (p. 652)*

c   *Prince's crown made for Prince Charles, 1772*
(pp. 646 and 652)

d   *Prince's crown made for Prince Frederick Adolphus*
(pp. 646 and 652)

e   *Princess's crown made for Princess*
Sophia Albertina (pp. 646 and 653)

(All these crowns are in the State Bank,
Stockholm)

a (left)   *Princess's crown made for Princess Hedwig.*
State Bank, Stockholm (pp. 647 and 653)

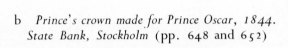

b   *Prince's crown made for Prince Oscar, 1844.*
State Bank, Stockholm (pp. 648 and 652)

c (left)   *Princess's crown made for Princess Eugenie,*
1860. State Bank, Stockholm (pp. 648 and 653)

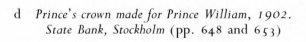

d   *Prince's crown made for Prince William, 1902.*
State Bank, Stockholm (pp. 648 and 653)

these symbols of royalty in Sweden, and if I had any other to dispose of, I would present them to the poor King of England.' These ornaments were kept in the church treasury until 1797 when, in order to comply with the terms of the Treaty of Tolentino imposed by Bonaparte, the contents of the Treasury, including the crown and sceptre, were melted down as a contribution towards the payment of the huge sum demanded from the Pope.[1]

Charles X was crowned at Upsala on 6th June 1654, and on 24th October he married at Stockholm Hedwig Eleonora, the daughter of Frederick III, Duke of Holstein-Gottorp. She was crowned Queen of Sweden the following day. Charles died at the early age of thirty-seven and was buried in what is known as the Caroline Chapel in the Riddarholm Church in Stockholm. On the metal coffin rests a tall, gilded crown with four arches. The funeral regalia of Charles X is still preserved in the Royal Armoury and consists of a crown (*Plate 227, c*), sceptre, orb, key and parts of a sword (*Plate 227, d and e*).

Charles X was succeeded by his only son, who reigned as Charles XI. He was only in his fourth year when his father died. He came of age when he was seventeen (1672), and was crowned at Upsala on 28th September 1675. On this occasion the orb suffered some damage. It was carried by the Chancellor of the Realm, Magnus Gabriel de la Gardie, whose horse stumbled, throwing its rider, and the orb received a large dent, damaging the black enamel which filled the engraving of the map. In 1680 Charles married Ulrica Leonora (the Elder) of Denmark, who was crowned Queen of Sweden at Stockholm on 25th November 1680. She died in July 1693 and Charles died in April 1697. They were both buried in the Caroline Chapel of the Riddarholm Church and tall, gilded crowns closed with four arches rest on the lids of their coffins. They had commanded before their deaths that no burial regalia should be made for them and thereafter no king or queen of Sweden was buried with regalia.

The only surviving son of Charles XI and Ulrica Leonora the Elder now succeeded to the throne as Charles XII at the age of fifteen, and he was crowned at Stockholm on 14th December 1697. As he was mounting his horse after the ceremony the crown fell off the King's head. It was during this reign that the initials *C.R.S.* in diamonds were probably added to the crown. The regalia had been used on one occasion before the coronation when in 1662 the young King received the Russian Embassy and the royal ornaments were displayed on a table near the throne. Charles fell at the siege of Fredriksten on 11th December 1718 at the early age of thirty-six. Immediately after the King's death his sister Ulrica Leonora was elected Queen of Sweden and was crowned at Upsala on 17th March 1719. For the occasion a change was made in the decoration of the sceptre, 14 small sapphires being set in the part above the handle in place of 14 small pearls. The ampulla was also repaired, some rubies which had fallen out were replaced and the safety chain for the lid was added. In 1720, with the agreement of the Estates, Ulrica resigned her sovereign powers in favour of her husband Frederick, Prince of Hesse. He was crowned as Frederick I at Stockholm on 3rd May 1720. Ulrica Leonora attached great importance to her right to the emblems of sovereignty even after her husband's coronation. It was necessary for the coronation of Frederick

1 Information given to the author by the ecclesiastical authorities at Loreto in 1957.

to have a second Key of the Realm made so that the Queen too should have one in her own right. The new key, which was slightly heavier than the older one, was probably made by the German goldsmith, Nicholas von Bleichert. On the ring of the handle is the inscription: *V.E.D. G.R.S.* [*Ulrica Eleonora Dei Gratia Regina Suevicae*] *d.3. maij.A 1720.* Queen Ulrica Leonora died in 1741 and was buried in the Caroline Chapel of the Riddarholm Church, where her father was also buried, and where her husband Frederick I was buried on his death in 1751. On the sarcophagus of Charles XII is a crown, sceptre and sword, and that of Frederick I a crown, sceptre and orb.

During Frederick's reign two political parties grew up known as the Caps and the Hats. The latter led the country into war with Russia as a result of which Finland was lost. When Queen Ulrica Leonora died childless the question of the succession became a matter of importance. The Hats saw a chance of retrieving the position in Finland and a bargain was made with the new Russian Empress Elizabeth for the restoration of the greater part of Finland so long as her cousin, Adolphus Frederick of Holstein-Gottorp, was elected successor to the Swedish crown. The terms of the Empress were accepted, and on the death of Frederick in 1751 Adolphus Frederick became King. He was crowned with his consort, Louisa Ulrica, the imperious sister of Frederick the Great, at Stockholm on 26th November 1751. Although Queen Leonora the Younger had been a Swedish princess, her husband Frederick I was German, and now Sweden was to be ruled by a King who was German and married to a Prussian. That the monarchy at this time was no longer national in outlook is well brought out in the next reign, that of Gustavus III, when in 1771 for the first time for over a hundred years a King of Sweden addressed the Diet in its native tongue. It is therefore not surprising that less importance was attached to national traditions. It is true that the coronation rite survived with little alteration, though henceforth it was always performed at Stockholm and not at Upsala, but the regalia of Eric XIV for a time no longer appeared to be regarded as especially associated with the coronation ceremony. Frederick I had been crowned with the crown of Maria Eleanora, but he found it heavy and uncomfortable, so in 1731 he reverted to the use of the crown of Eric XIV. Adolphus Frederick also used Maria Eleanora's crown, though he was invested with Eric XIV's sceptre and, perhaps because it was lighter, he used the orb of Gunilla Bielke.

Adolphus Frederick opened Parliament in person in 1751 before he had been crowned, and the question arose as to whether he should wear the crown. It had been laid down in 1723 that the King should open Parliament wearing his royal mantle with his crown on his head and the sceptre in his hand. The question of what Adolphus Frederick should wear was brought up for discussion in the Chancellor's office. Tessin, while emphasising the King's right to wear the crown, advised against it 'in order to avoid any comment by the public on what they might consider an untimely and perhaps illegal infringement of the royal prerogative, if His Majesty the King should on that occasion show himself with crown on head before the coronation and anointing ceremony had taken place, it would be wiser and best for the King to be clad in royal mantle and for the regalia to be placed on a table beside the throne'. Charles XII in 1697 had worn the crown before his anointing and this had been considered to be a bad omen.

a   *Burial crown of Gustavus
Vasa. Upsala Cathedral*
(p. 630)

b (above, left)   *Burial crown of Katherine of Saxe-Lauenburg. Upsala Cathedral*
(p. 631)

c (above, right)   *Burial crown of Margaret Leijonhufvud. Upsala Cathedral*
(p. 631)

d   *Burial crown of Katherine Stenbock. Upsala Cathedral (p. 631)*

a   *Burial crown of John III. Upsala Cathedral*
(p. 639)

b   *Burial crown of Katherine Jagiellonica. Upsala
Cathedral* (p. 638)

d   *Burial orb of John III.*   e   *Burial orb of Gunilla*
Upsala Cathedral   *Bielke. Upsala Cathe-*
(p. 639)   *dral* (p. 639)

c   *Burial crown of Gunilla Bielke. Upsala Cathedral*
(p. 639)

For the coronation the regalia was overhauled. The scabbard of the State Sword was given a new covering of pale purple and the sword itself was cleaned. Although the King preferred to have the crown of Maria Eleanora the crown of Eric XIV was repaired and provided with a new circlet. The initials *C.R.S.* which Charles XII had added had already been removed in 1731. A new cap of satin heavily embroidered with gold encrusted with pearls was also provided. Eric XIV's orb, although apparently not used, also underwent repair. The black enamel of the engraving of the map was removed and replaced with blue enamel, and the small celestial orb and cross was replaced by that on Maria Eleanora's orb. Louisa Ulrica showed great interest in the arrangements for the coronation, and especially in the new crown which was made for her use. This was designed by John Eric Rehn, who had just returned from Paris. His design (*Plate 218, b*) showed the pronounced influence of French contemporary art, and it is clear that he was familiar with the crown made for Marie Leczinska.[1] This crown had been carefully depicted in an engraving by Duflos, and Rehn followed this example and made an engraving of Louisa Ulrica's crown. The Crown consists of a circlet on which rest a number of ornaments from behind which spring eight half-arches with a blue enamelled orb surmounted by a short cross. The crown is set with 695 diamonds of which the 44 largest had been placed at her disposal on the occasion of her wedding. After the coronation these stones were removed from the crown and replaced by Swedish rock crystals, although when the crown was later brought into use again the real diamonds were reset in it. The orb surmounting the crown instead of being powdered with stars bore the three Swedish open crowns.

The principal change in the coronation ceremony was the precedence given to the Sword of State. At the funeral of Frederick I it had lost its place immediately after the crown and was borne after the sceptre. At the coronation it was again given only third place among the royal ornaments. In 1748 Frederick I had reconstructed the Order of the Seraphim, and although the insignia did not form part of the regalia and was not carried in the coronation procession it was worn by the King in his coronation attire.[2]

Adolphus Frederick died in 1772 and was buried in the Gustavian Chapel of the Riddarholm Church. His consort, Queen Louisa Ulrica, who died in 1791, was also buried there. He was succeeded by his son, Gustavus III, who with his consort, Sophie Magdalena of Denmark, was crowned at Stockholm on 28th May 1772. The King took a great interest in the detailed arrangements for his coronation and the order of ceremonial contains marginal notes in his own hand. From his portrait by Lorenze Pasch the Younger it can be seen that he used the same regalia as his father, although additionally the State Sword of Eric XIV is also depicted. At the coronation the Sword of State returned to its former position immediately after the crown, and the mantle was given junior position by being carried in front of the other royal ornaments. The King wore a princely mantle and the crown made for Charles X Gustavus as Hereditary Prince. When he was divested of these they were placed upon the altar. Eric XIV's crown was provided with a new cap of purple velvet, though the rich embroidery was retained.

[1] See Chapter Eight, France, p. 251.

[2] The jewelled insignia worn by the King as Sovereign of the Order are to this day the property of the Order and are not included among the crown jewels.

The large sapphire at the top of the crown was replaced by a blue enamelled orb. The orb of Maria Eleanora was provided with a silver base. The right arm with the sword on the figure of Justice adorning the ampulla broke off and was replaced. Up to this time the sword used for girding the King had been a personal weapon, though no doubt richly ornamented, but there was no special coronation sword. Gustavus III made good this deficiency and provided a special king's sword. It was made in a classic antique form with the hilt in the form of a cross, and was adorned with brilliant and coloured precious stones. The blade dates from the time of Gustavus Adolphus. This sword, which is still preserved, was used at the next three coronations, but when it became the custom for the king to wear military uniform this sword fell into disuse, as a military weapon was considered to be more appropriate. Two similar swords (*Plate 214, c*) were made for the royal dukes attending the coronation.

It was also found necessary to provide crowns for the King's brothers, Prince Charles and Prince Frederick Adolphus, and for his sister, Princess Sophia Albertina. The Court Jeweller was commissioned to make three gold crowns but without cost to the state purse. The King ordered that instead of the usual *fleurons* the Vasa sheaves were to be used to decorate the crowns. The Princes maintained that they should use the Holstein arms, and a dispute ensued. The Princes declared that they would not wear the crowns of the King's pattern, and if necessary would not attend the coronation ceremony. But the King's will prevailed and the new crowns were made bearing the Vasa sheaves. The jewels for these crowns were taken from three silver crowns and from other ornaments which were in the treasury. In Prince Charles's crown were set 232 brilliants, rose-cut and table diamonds, 40 emeralds and 132 pearls, while a similar number of jewels were used to adorn that of Prince Frederick Adolphus. The former crown is hall-marked but the latter crown was altered in 1866 and the hall-mark was probably destroyed. Princess Sophia Albertina's crown was decorated only with diamonds and pearls, there being 85 on the circlet and 8 on the points of the rays. These three crowns followed the same pattern. On the circlet was a theme of the three crowns interspersed by large precious stones. The upper rim carried a border of a string of pearls above which rose eight rays bearing a leaf design and set with precious stones with the Vasa sheaf set between each ray. Inside was a cap on which the three-crown motif was embroidered. Gustavus III had added two black enamelled wheatsheaves to the front and the back of the crown of the Hereditary Prince. Since the XVI century the sheaf had been used heraldically and the origin was probably a play on the name of the Vasa dynasty, the word *vasar* meaning sheaf. Gustavus III did much to restore the identity of the monarchy with national aspirations and showed particular pride in the Vasa sheaves as a dynastic emblem. The origin of the triangular ray-like ornaments has not been determined. They give the Swedish crowns an appearance not dissimilar to Byzantine radiated crowns, and while they may have been adopted by chance or for some native reason, it has been suggested that they may have been used to bring in an eastern motive symbolising Sweden's geographical position twixt East and West.

During Gustavus III's reign the crown of Louisa Ulrica was used by Queen Sophie Magdalena. For the coronation the rock crystals were replaced by real diamonds, although these were removed again four days after the ceremony. On other occasions when the crown was used it was reset with diamonds. At the time of the coronation a large rose diamond of $8\frac{7}{8}$ carats and specially fine water was placed in the centre ornament. This stone had been in a ring belonging to Ulrica Leonora the Elder, and on 6th September 1693 Charles XI had ordained that in remembrance of the late Queen it should always be kept with the King's crown, 'whereas it . . . was a betrothal ring first between His Majesty's father . . . and her well-remembered and Respected Majesty as well as also between His Majesty himself and her late most Blessed Majesty the Queen'.

On 21st August 1772 following a *coup d'état* that restored some of the prerogatives of the crown, Gustavus III appeared before the assembled Estates in full regalia and delivered a famous philippic. Another occasion on which the royal family appeared in full state was at the christening of the heir to the throne, Gustavus (IV) Adolphus, on 10th November 1778. The hereditary prince's crown, which since the time of Adolphus Frederick had been used as the crown prince's crown, was placed on a table beside the cradle—a custom which continued. The King and Queen and the princes wore their crowns and a new one had to be made for Princess Hedwig Elizabeth Charlotte. This followed the pattern of the 1771 crowns, although it took a somewhat simpler form.

Gustav III died on 29th March 1792 after he had been shot while attending a masquerade in the opera-house at Stockholm. He was buried in the Gustavian chapel of the Riddarholm Church, where his consort, Queen Sophie Magdalena, was also buried on her death in 1813. He was succeeded by his son Gustavus IV, who married Frederica Dorothea of Baden on 31st October 1797. The King's reactionary views caused him to avoid calling together a Diet, and in consequence his coronation had to be postponed. In March 1800 events compelled him to summon the Estates and he and his consort were crowned at Stockholm on 3rd April. On 29th March 1809 Gustavus IV voluntarily abdicated, but on 10th May the Estates declared that not only the King but his family had forfeited the throne. On 5th June the regent, Duke Charles, the son of Adolphus Frederick, was proclaimed King with the title Charles XIII. Gustavus IV went to Germany and in 1812 having divorced his consort settled in Switzerland where he died in 1837. Later Oscar II caused his body to be brought back to Sweden and buried in the Riddarholm Church. Charles was crowned with his consort on 29th June 1809. On this occasion the King used the crown and sceptre of Maria Eleanora. Charles XIII was childless and infirm and the question of the succession was becoming urgent. Prince Charles Augustus of Augustenburg, Stadtholder of Norway, was elected Crown Prince, but he died suddenly and mysteriously in 1810 and the Estates elected Bernadotte, one of Napoleon's marshals, as Crown Prince. He was adopted by Charles XIII and received the homage of the Estates on 5th November 1810, assuming the name Charles John. In 1814 Charles XIII became the first King of Sweden and Norway. On 5th February 1818 the King died and was buried in the Riddarholm Church. His consort, Queen Hedwig, died in the same year and was also buried there.

The Crown Prince now came to the throne as Charles XIV and was crowned at Stockholm on 11th May 1818. For this coronation the crown of Eric XIV was again brought into use and was subjected to a thorough overhaul, which included some important alterations. The work was done by the German jeweller Michael Benedicks, who had set up business in Stockholm in 1796 and had been appointed Court Jeweller.

On the circlet the eight enamelled ornaments each set with a pair of pearls were removed and replaced by eight large rosettes of diamonds. The pearls surmounting points of the ornaments rising from the circlet were replaced by diamonds. The original orb and cross surmounting the crown was also removed and replaced by a large blue enamelled celestial orb, powdered with stars and with a large brilliant cross on top. Charles's consort, Eugénie Désirée Clary, was crowned as Queen Desideria on 21st August 1829. Charles XIV died on 8th March 1844 and was buried in the Bernadotte Chapel in the Riddarholm Church, where his wife was also buried on her death in 1860. He was succeeded by his son Oscar I, who was crowned with his Consort, Josephine de Beauharnais, on 28th September 1844, at Stockholm. At this ceremony the King's two eldest sons, Prince Charles (XV), aged eighteen, and Prince Gustavus, aged seventeen, wore the princes' crowns which had been made in 1771. The third son, Prince Oscar (II), was aged fifteen and attended the ceremony. This necessitated a new crown having to be made. It was ordered from the firm of Giron and Co. and followed the pattern of the 1771 crown of Prince Frederick Adolphus. The supply of loose stones in the treasury was somewhat depleted and economies were made by halving some of the pearls, of which 2 were from Eric XIV's crown. A large emerald of $21\frac{1}{4}$ carats was placed in the centre of the circlet, which was taken with other settings from an epaulette of Gustavus III. The third stones to the right and left of the central emerald are described as 'spurious round emeralds'. The brilliants had originally been the property of Gustavus III but came to the State Treasury when Gustavus IV left Sweden. Some of the pearls are described as Swedish and others as Scottish. Although it was the heraldic rule that only the Crown Prince's crown should have a sheaf in the centre, the rule was broken in the case of this crown.

On the death of Oscar I on 8th July 1859 his eldest son came to the throne as Charles XV. He had married Princess Louisa of the Netherlands and they were crowned at Stockholm on 3rd May 1860. At the ceremony the Queen wore one of the existing princesses' crowns before she was crowned, and the other was worn by Princess Sophie. There was now another princess—Eugenia—of age to attend the coronation, and it was necessary for a new crown to be made for her. The order which was placed with Edward Emmanuel Petterson stipulated that the crown should be ready by 20th April, only about eight weeks later. The design of Princess Hedwig's crown was followed, and some pearls and the cross from Eric XIV's crown were placed at the jeweller's disposal. Charles died on 18th September 1872 leaving only one child, a daughter. He was succeeded by his brother Oscar II, whose consort was Princess Sophia Wilhelmina of Nassau, and they were crowned on 12th May 1873. This was the last coronation in Sweden as the next King, Gustav V, who succeeded to the throne in 1907, considered that the coronation ceremony was no longer in keeping with the times and conditions in Sweden. Another prince's crown was made, however, in Oscar II's reign. After his coming of age Prince William was to attend the Opening of Parliament on 17th January 1903, and there was no crown available for him. The firm of C. G. Hallberg was entrusted with the making of this crown, the order being placed on 22nd August 1902. The design was made by Agi Lindegren, the palace architect, and followed that of the crown made in 1844, except that the front ornament was a ray instead of a sheaf.

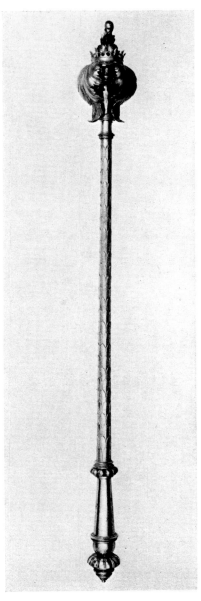

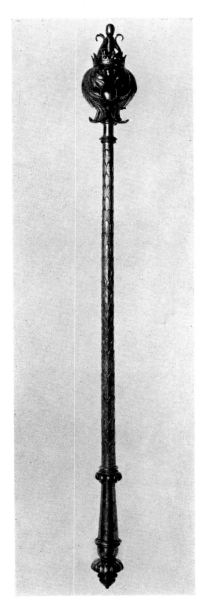

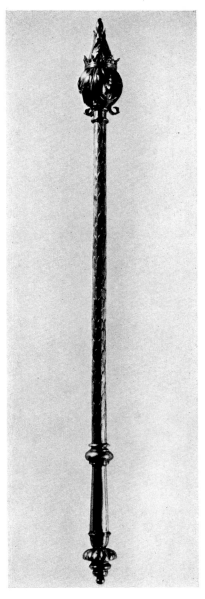

a   *Burial sceptre of Gustavus   b   *Burial sceptre of Katherine   c   *Burial sceptre of Margaret
        Vasa (p 630)*   of Saxe-Lauenburg (p. 631)*   Leijonhufvud (p. 631)*

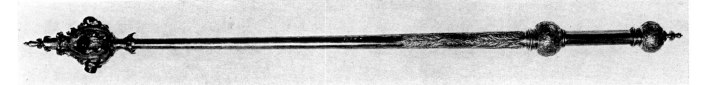

d   *Burial sceptre of John III (p. 639)*

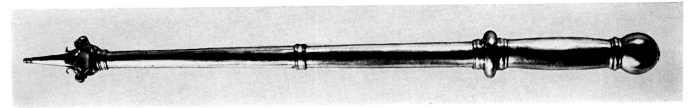

e   *Burial sceptre of Gunilla Bielke (p. 639)*   All in Upsala Cathedral

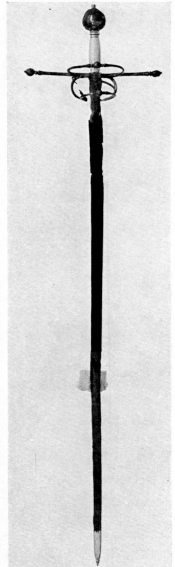

a (above)   *Burial sword of Gustavus Vasa* (p. 630)

b (above, centre)   *Burial sword of John III* (p. 639)

c (above, right)   *Gilded wax sceptre of Margaret*
Leijonhufvud (p. 631)

d (right)   *Gilded wax burial crown of Margaret*
Leijonhufvud (p. 631)

All in Upsala Cathedral

Although there is no longer a coronation ceremony the regalia is still used when the king opens Parliament in person and the crown and sceptre are placed on a table by the throne. In 1909 before this ceremony King Gustav V ordered the crown to be restored. The diamond rosettes set in the circlet in 1818 were accordingly replaced by the original ornaments of enamel and pearl. At the funeral of Gustav V the crown was carried near the coffin. The crown which had been made for the funeral of Louisa Ulrica, widow of Adolphus Frederick and mother of Gustavus III, had been kept with the other royal ornaments and had been used at royal funerals, and at the funeral of Gustav V it was placed on the lid of the coffin.

The Swedish state regalia is today in the care of the Keeper of the Royal Armoury and are kept in the vaults of the State Bank of Sweden in Stockholm. The keys are held in the possession of seven officials of the Treasury and the State Bank. It will be convenient to recapitulate with a brief description of how these ornaments are today.[1]

The King's Crown (No. 4) (Plate 215, a and b)

This crown was originally made for Eric XIV in 1561 and has been altered on several occasions since. It is richly decorated with enamel, diamonds, pearls and precious stones. On the front and back of the circlet are large rubies. The large ornaments which rise from the circlet have a coloured stone in the centre and are topped by a large diamond. There are two arches at the intersection of which rests an orb with a large cross of brilliants. The orb is enamelled blue and powdered with stars. Inside is a richly embroidered cap of purple velvet covered with gold embroidery set with pearls. Authoritative opinion considers that the cap detracts from the artistic merit of the crown which is of a very high order. The crown is 23·7 cm high and the diameter is 18 × 20·4 cm. It weighs 1·715 grams.

The King's Sceptre (No. 5) (Plate 216, a)

The sceptre is a golden rod 80·9 cm in length and it weighs 1·417 grams. It was made for the coronation of Eric XIV in 1561 and has been subjected to alterations at various times. There is a beautifully and elaborately worked ornament at the top, set with pearls and precious stones. It was originally surmounted by a large sapphire representing an orb but this has been replaced with a blue enamelled orb and cross. The lower part above and below the handle is elaborately decorated with pearls and precious stones and the handle itself is chased.

The Orb of the Realm (No. 9) (Plate 216, c and e)

The Orb of the Realm was made for the coronation of Eric XIV in 1561. On the golden globe is engraved a map of the world which is a feature not found on any other orb among European regalia extant. Details of the map are well described by Baron Rudolf Caederström in *Svenska Riks Regalierna*, who writes:

No doubt this is an expression of the King's broad humanistic education and originality. Geography is well represented in his personal library, of which we have fortunately a catalogue dated 1568 and it includes two editions of Ptolemy, one of them *Tolemai Geographia*, clearly the vernacular edition of the 1561 *La Geographia di Claudio Tolemeo*, while the other *Ptolemy Cosmographia* must be one of the editions of *Claudi Ptolemei veri Alexandrieni Cosmographia*. The catalogue also mentions *De Usi Globi Astronomiae et Cosmographia*. Moreover it is known that the King owned a copy of Strabo's *De Situ Orbis*, probably in the edition which was published in Venice

1 The numbers given in brackets after each ornament's title are those of the present inventory.

in 1516. As neither of these works contain illustrations from which the engraving of this map is copied, it was probably just in order to obtain a good modern map that the orb was sent to the goldsmith Francis Beijer of Antwerp, since Antwerp at that time was one of the main centres of the cartographers. At first sight the map engraved on the orb seemed rather confused. It does however, look as if by mistake the engraver used the die back to front for the northern hemisphere, so that the geographical outlines appear as in a mirror. The geographical names have been placed in what would approximately be the correct position on the globe if the map had been the right way round. For instance India is on the eastern side between the inverted contours of the inner Mediterranean, etc. If the map outlines of the northern hemisphere are turned the right way round they are seen to represent the full extent of the geographical knowledge of the period. It would seem, however, that the engraver borrowed certain limits from maps other than a global map, as details such as the compass points of a pair of dividers could consequently have been taken from the latter. The great age of this global map does, however, merit geographical analysis.

The globe is divided by a beautifully chased and enamelled equator and a single meridional band, and these are decorated with pearls and lion masks. It also has two other unusual features. It is surmounted by another small orb powered with stars and it is on a flat stand. This small orb was originally made for the orb of Maria Eleanora in 1620, but in 1779 it was exchanged for the original. The only other examples of royal orbs being surmounted by small celestial orbs are to be found in the Norwegian regalia and the idea was, of course, borrowed from Sweden.

The Key of the Realm (No. 12) (Plate 216, d)

The Key of the Realm is an ornament peculiar to the Swedish regalia and was introduced by Eric XIV at his coronation in 1561. It is an emblem of sovereignty and can only be used by a king or queen regnant. Perhaps it was introduced because of the custom of investing queens consort with the orb, which should properly be regarded as an emblem of sovereignty, making it desirable for the sovereign to have an additional emblem. The key is 43 cm long and being a ceremonial key it has an old-fashioned type of bit. It appears originally to have been kept in the king's silver room but in 1583 it was transferred to the wardrobe where the rest of the regalia were kept.

The Sword of the Realm (No. 13) (Plate 214, a (i))

At the time of the coronation of Eric XIV in 1561 the Sword of the Realm took precedence over all the other royal ornaments, even the crown. It is generally thought that the choice of the motif of the decoration of the blade was intended to depict in an allegorical manner the vicissitudes of Gustavus Vasa's own life and rise to power. The blade, which is 107 cm long and 4·7 cm broad, is gilded all over and has been etched by a very skilful German artist. The etchings on one side represent a number of episodes from the story of Joseph. First Joseph tells of his dream. He is lured into the well. He is sold, flees from Potiphar's wife and is imprisoned. Then Pharaoh dreams, the fat and the lean kine; the brothers coming to buy corn; the cup is found in Benjamin's sack; Jacob comes to Joseph; Jacob's coffin is carried from the land; and at the tip of the sword is Jacob's grave. On the other side there is the story of Moses, beginning with the burning bush; the staff turned into a snake; Moses and the Egyptian priests; the plague of toads, of pestilence, of boils and of hail; the slaughter of the first born; the Paschal Lamb; and Pharaoh and his army perish and the Israelites cross the Red Sea.

The hilt may have been of a later date than the blade and it was in any case gilded in 1561 for the coronation of Eric XIV.

a (above, left)   *Tomb of Eric XIV with crown, sceptre and orb.*
Vesterås Cathedral (p. 638)

b (above, right)   *Helmet crown of Gustavus Vasa. Royal Armoury,*
Stockholm (p. 653)

c (left)   *Ampulla in Silver Chamber of Upsala Cathedral*
(p. 628)

a   *Burial crown of Charles IX. Strengnäs Cathedral* (p. 640)

b   *Burial   sceptres   of Charles IX and Queen Christina* (p. 640)

c   *Burial crown of Queen Christina of Holstein. Strengnäs Cathedral* (p. 640)

d and e (right)   *Burial orbs of Charles IX and Queen Christina. Strengnäs Cathedral* (p. 640)

The Second State Sword (No. 14) (*Plate 214, a (ii)*)

The second state sword is somewhat smaller, the blade being 102·7 cm in length and 4·3 cm broad at the hilt tapering to a point. The blade at least is thought to be older than that of the Sword of the Realm. In form it is characteristic of a double-handed knight's sword of the late Middle Ages, but it has been made into a ceremonial sword by the rich gilt etchings which cover the blade. The motifs are stories from Roman history. One scene depicts Caius Musieus Scaevola before King Porsenna and the other the generosity of the Emperor Trajan. These same stories are to be found on other contemporary German swords[1] and it is probable that the blade was manufactured towards the end of the 1520's, while the marks are those of the episcopal workshops at Passau. The grip, the pommel and the cross guard probably date from the XVI century and the very skilful ornamentation of gold and silver hammered into the steel was most likely done in the workshops of Arboga. This sword first appears in the wardrobe in 1557.

The Ampulla or the Horn for the Oil (No. 15) (*Plate 216, b*)

This beautiful and much admired ampulla was made in 1606 for the coronation of Charles IX. It is of gold and ornamented with enamel of fine workmanship and set with 10 diamonds and a number of red stones, probably garnets. It is 15·5 cm in height and 12 cm in breadth.

Gunilla Bielke's Sceptre (No. 7) (*Plate 217, e*)

This sceptre was made in 1585 for Queen Gunilla's coronation. It is a golden rod and only pearls are used in its decoration. It is 68 cm long and weighs 847·5 grams.

Gunilla Bielke's Orb (No. 10) (*Plate 217, d*)

This orb was made at the same time as the sceptre. It is a simple golden globe with an equator and meridional band set with 27 pearls. It is surmounted by a simple gold cross with 3 pearls. It has a stand which screws into the globe to allow it to be placed easily on a table. It is 17·9 cm high and the greatest width is 12·1 cm. It weighs 494·5 grams.

Maria Eleanora's Crown (No. 2) (*Plate 217, a*)

This crown is today described in the inventory as 'King's Crown', because, although it was originally made for Maria Eleanora, it was taken into use by Frederick I and was used by some of his successors. It is 18·4 cm high and the circlet is 17·8 × 21·4 cm in diameter. It consists of a circlet of gold set with diamonds and coloured stones with a large ruby in front. Originally it had two arches, but today it has four, the change being made for the coronation of Queen Christina. On the circlet are eight large ornaments of gold set with diamonds, and between these are small flower-like ornaments with a ruby set in the centre. The gold arches are set with diamonds and they are surmounted by a celestial orb and cross. The orb is of blue translucent enamel with sun, moon and stars in diamonds.

Maria Eleanora's Sceptre (No. 6) (*Plate 218, d*)

This sceptre is also described in the inventory as 'King's Sceptre', although it was made for the coronation of Maria Eleanora. It is a golden rod 74·1 cm in length and weighs 756 grams.

---

1 The Scaevolo story appears on three other blades, two formerly in the Arsenal in Berlin (P.C. 8190 and P.C. 8274) and one in the Museum at Dresden (M. 54), while the Trajan story is also found on one of the two swords (P.C. 8274) in the former Berlin Arsenal.

The ornate top ornament is surmounted by a small orb and cross; the orb is covered with blue enamel.

Maria Eleanora's Orb (No. 8) (Plate 218, c)

This is a simple golden globe with an equator and a meridional band set with rubies and diamonds. The small orb, which surmounts it with a cross set with 3 pearls on top, was originally on the Orb of the Realm. The change was probably made for the coronation of Adolphus Frederick and Ulrica Leonora in 1751. The orb is 13·3 cm high and the diameter of the globe is 11·2 cm. It weighs 410 grams.

The Key of Ulrica Leonora (No. 11) (Plate 216, d)

This key was made for Queen Ulrica the Younger when she ceded the Government to her husband Frederick I but wished to keep for her own use the emblems of sovereignty. It is a copy of the old Key of State, though it weighs slightly more than the other.

The Crown Prince's Crown (No. 16) (Plate 219, b)

This was originally made for Charles X as Hereditary Prince and later came into use as the Crown Prince's crown. It was made largely from an older crown of Queen Christina the Elder. It is an open circlet of gold richly decorated with precious stones and pearls and enamel. From the circlet rise eight triangular rays also richly decorated and between these pearls. Gustavus III added two black-enamelled Vasa sheaves, one in the front and one at the back. In the front of the circlet is a fine sapphire. The crown is 14·5 cm high and the diameter of the circlet is 20·3 × 17·8 cm. The crown weighs 1,334 grams. Inside the crown is a cap of light blue satin with gold embroidery.

Crown of Louisa Ulrica (No. 3) (Plate 218, a)

This crown, which was made for the coronation of Queen Louisa Ulrica in 1751, is composed entirely of diamonds in a silver frame. The circlet, the ornaments which rise from it and the arches are openwork set with diamonds. The globe is covered with translucent polished enamel and is covered with groups of three open crowns. The diamonds in the surmounting cross are set à jour. Inside is a cap of red velvet embroidered with silver spangles. The crown is 12·6 cm high and the inside diameter is 13·1 cm. It weighs 527·5 grams.

Crown of Prince Charles (XIII) (No. 17) (Plate 219, c)

This crown, which was made for Prince Charles on the occasion of the coronation of his brother Gustavus III in 1772, is an open circlet of gold with eight rays with Vasa sheaves set between. On the circlet are the three Swedish crowns set with diamonds between which are crosses formed by an emerald as the centre stone surrounded by 4 diamonds. On top of the circlet is a single row of pearls. The rays are decorated with palm leaves in bas relief, each ray with 4 emeralds. The Vasa sheaves are in black enamel with a white outline. Inside the crown is a cap of dark blue satin dotted with gold crowns. The height is 13·7 cm, the diameter 17·3 × 20·8 cm and the weight 1·145 grams.

Crown of Prince Frederick Adolphus (No. 18) (Plate 219, d)

This crown followed the same design and general decoration of that of Prince Charles. The height is the same but the diameter varies slightly being 17·8 × 20·1 cm and the weight is 1,158 grams.

Crown of Princess Sophia Albertina (No. 20) *(Plate 219, e)*

This crown follows the same design as those of the two princes but is only set with diamonds. The height is 11·3 cm, the diameter 13·2 cm and the weight 651 grams.

Crown of Princess Hedwig Elizabeth Charlotte (No. 21) *(Plate 220, a)*

This crown, which was made seven years after the others, follows the same pattern, though the majority of the stones are coloured, some being semi-precious stones. The height is 10·6 cm, the diameter 12·5 cm and the weight 501 grams.

Crown of Prince Oscar (No. 19) *(Plate 220, b)*

This crown, which was made in 1844, differs from the previous ones. The front ornament on the circlet is a Vasa Sheaf which is heraldically incorrect. Beneath this is a large emerald of 21¼ carats, and then alternately round the crown circlet are groups of three crowns set with brilliants alternating with emeralds set with diamonds. Two of the emeralds are described as spurious. The rays are set with half-pearls and the tips are surmounted with single round pearls. The height is 14·05 cm, the diameter 17·3 × 20·6 cm and the weight 1,248 grams.

Crown of Princess Eugenie (No. 22) *(Plate 220, c)*

This crown follows the general design of the previous princesses' crowns. There are 80 pearls on silver thread forming a border to the top of the circlet. On the circlet itself there are eight coloured stones, and the rays have both diamonds and coloured stones. The height is 11·3 cm, the diameter 12·9 × 13 cm and the weight 733 grams.

Crown of Prince William (No. 19½) *(Plate 220, d)*

This crown follows the traditional pattern with a ray and not a sheaf in front. The row of pearls, 146 in number, is threaded on silver thread. The circlet is engraved with palm and laurel leaves set with diamonds and emeralds. The pearls came from a bracelet of Princess Hedwig Elizabeth Charlotte which had been supplied in 1774 by the Court Jeweller of the Duke of Orleans. The twelve stones round the 3 emeralds under the back ray were originally in the cross of the orb of Eric XIV. The crown is 13·8 cm in height, the diameter is 17·1 × 20 cm and the weight 1,248 grams.

The King's Sword (No. 23) *(Plate 214, b)*

This sword was made for the coronation of Gustavus III to be used for the girding. It was subsequently used at the next three coronations. The hilt is decorated with diamonds and precious stones. The blade may have been from a sword of the time of Gustavus II, Adolphus. The sword belt which Gustavus used was not the one made for the purpose but an older one which had a clasp set with brilliants made by the Court Jeweller Franz Berg, which is still preserved, though partly altered, in the Treasury.

Apart from the ornaments included among the regalia there are certain other items which are deserving of attention. In the Royal Armoury there is a crowned helmet of iron inlaid with gold *(Plate 225, b)*. The crown is fastened to the helmet with rivets. The helmet is of a Polish type and was made in Nuremberg by Kunz Lochner about 1540. It was bought by a merchant who was the King's agent. It appears in a still extant inventory of 1540 and it was used at the King's funeral. It then passed into the possession of John III.

In the National Historical Museum at Stockholm there is an open circlet, the plates of which are joined together by pins and on the rim of which are fleur-de-lis ornaments. It is sometimes called the crown of Badeboda (*Plate 228, b*) having been found in a hoard of treasure with other silver objects at that place. Although fleur-de-lis ornaments on a crown usually suggest that it had some royal association it seems that this emblem was not esteemed as a royal badge in the north to the same extent as elsewhere in Europe. It was the custom during the XIV century for the nobility, especially women, to wear crowns, and this circlet of silver gilt may have been worn by a noblewoman.[1]

In the same museum is a very valuable reliquary which consists of a gold-mounted agate bowl with a richly jewelled foot and lid. On the bowl is a large and particularly splendid crown, the circlet of which is decorated with crosses and fleur-de-lis (*Plate 228, d*). The crown is closed on top with two arches (*Plate 228, c*). Inside the bowl was probably the skull of some saint. The bowl is considered to be of Roman origin, the mounting dating from the X and XI centuries while the foot and lid as well as the crown probably date from the first half of the XIII century. Schramm[2] and Deér[3] have expressed the opinion that the crown is really two crowns of German origin, made to be worn and which probably belonged to the Hohenstaufens. The Swedish authorities do not agree with this view and consider that it is one crown which was made for the reliquary. It came to Stockholm from some unknown German cathedral, probably as loot. Because the workmanship of the foot of the reliquary resembles that of some works at Goslar it is still sometimes called the Goslar Reliquary[4] (*Plate 228, a*).

[1] Baron Carl R. af Ugglas: 'Personhistoria och medeltida silversmide', in *Svenska Kulturbilder*, new series, 6, XI–XII, pp. 152 ff.

[2] P. E. Schramm: *Kaiser Friedrichs II Herrschaftszeichen*, Göttingen 1955.

[3] Josef Deér: *Der Kaiserornat Friedrichs II*, Berne 1952.

[4] B. Thordeman: 'Det stora Stokholms-relikvairet i ny belysning', in *Fornvannen* 1955.

BIBLIOGRAPHY

ÅMARK, MATS	*A guide to Upsala Cathedral*, Upsala 1937.
BERGQUIST, E. H.	*Strängnäs domkyrka, is Sörmkandsbygden*, 1957.
	Södermanlands hembygdsförbunds årsbok, Eskilstuna 1957.
BREHMER, CHRISTOPHER J.	*De Regalibus Regni Sveo-Gotticci*, Stockholm 1733.
CAEDERSTRÖM, BARON RUDOLF	*De båda rikssvärden, Gustav Vasa Minnen*, Stockholm 1938.
	Regalie Utställningen, Stockholm 1938.
	De Svenska Riks Regalierna, Stockholm 1942.
DEÉR, JOSEF	*Der Kaiserornat Friedrichs II*, Berne 1952.
HAHR, AUGUST	*Vasterås Cathedral*, 1923.
LENK, TORSTEN	*Rikssymbolerna*, Stockholm 1948.
	'Johan III's Salvator och Agnus Dei', in *Journal of Royal Armoury*, Vol. VII, 2.

LINDEGREN, AGI	*Maria Church at Vasteras,* 1898.
OLSSON, MARTIN	*Riddarholm Church,* Stockholm 1937.
	Vasagraven i Uppsala Domkyrka, Stockholm 1956.
RYDBACK, DR MONICA	*Birger Jarl,* Kronfodral.
SCHRAMM, P. E.	*Herrschaftszeichen und Staatssymbolik,* Bd. III.
	Kaiser Friedrichs II Herrschaftszeichen, Göttingen 1955.
SOHLBERG, LARS GUSTAF	*Historical Description of the Cathedral at Vasterås,* 1834.
STENEBERG, KARL ERIK	*Kronprinskronen och Arvfurstehatten,* Stockholm 1938.
THORDEMAN, BENGT	*Erik den Helige,* Stockholm 1954.
	'Det stora Stokholms-relikvairet', in *Fornvannen,* 1955.
UGGLAS, BARON CARL R.	'Personhistoria och medeltida silversmide', in *Svenska Kulturbilder,* new series, 6, XI–XII, pp. 152 ff.
UPMARK, GUSTAF	*Upsala Domkyrkas Silfrekammer,* Upsala 1927.

SWEDISH SOVEREIGNS AND CORONATIONS
(The dates of the early kings are problematical)

RAGNAR-LODBROK'S LINE

1001 Olaf Schtøkonung. Styled King *c.* 1015
1026 Edmund or Emund Colbrenner
1051 Edmund or Emund Slemme
1056 Stenkil
1066 Halstan
1090 Ingo I, the Good, Stenkilsson
1112 Philip Hallstensson
1118 Ingo II, Hallstensson

SVERKER'S LINE

1132 Sverker Kolsson
1150 Eric IX, Jedvardsson, the Saint
1160 Charles VII
1167 Knut Ericksson
1195 Sverker Karksson
1210 Eric X, Knutsson. Crowned at Upsala, 1210
1216 John Sverkersson. Crowned at Linköping, 1219
1222 Eric XI, Ericksson, the Stammerer. Crowned at Upsala, 1224

FOLKUNGAR LINE

1250 Waldemar I, Birgersson. Crowned at Lingköping, 1251
1276 Magnus I, Ladulaes. Crowned with his consort, Helwig, at Upsala, May 1276

655

1290   Birger II, Magnusson. Crowned with his consort, Margaret, at Söderköping, December 1302

1319   Magnus II, Ericksson, the Luxurious. Crowned with his consort, Blanche of Namur, at Stockholm, 21st July 1336

1350   Eric XII

MECKLENBURG LINE

1363   Albert

UNION OF CROWNS

1389   Margaret

1412   Eric XIII of Pomerania. Crowned at Kalmar as King of the three kingdoms, 17th June 1397
      His consort, Philippa of England, crowned at Lund, October 1406

1440   Christopher of Bavaria. Crowned at Upsala, 14th September 1441
      His consort, Dorothea of Brandenburg, crowned at Copenhagen, 14th September 1445

1448   Charles VIII, Knutsson (King of Sweden only). Crowned at Upsala, 29th June 1448
      His consort, Katherine, crowned at Upsala, 2nd July 1448

1457   Christian I. Crowned at Upsala, 2nd July 1457

1483   Hans. Crowned at Stockholm, 26th November 1497
      His consort, Christina, crowned at Upsala, 1499

1502   Christian II. Crowned at Stockholm, 4th November 1520

1523   Sweden separated from Denmark and Norway

VASA DYNASTY

1523   Gustavus I Vasa. Crowned at Upsala, 12th January 1528
      His first consort, Katherine of Saxe-Lauenburg, crowned at Upsala, 24th September 1531
      His second consort, Margaret Leijonhufvud, crowned at Upsala, 6th October 1536
      His third consort, Katherine Stenbock, crowned at Upsala, 23rd August 1552

1560   Eric XIV. Crowned at Upsala, 29th June 1561
      His consort, Karin Mansdatter, crowned at Stockholm, 5th July 1568

1569   John III. Crowned with his first consort, Katherine Jagiellonica, at Upsala, 10th July 1569
      His second consort, Gunilla Bielke, crowned at Vesterås, 21st February 1585

1592   Sigismund of Poland. Crowned with his consort, Anne of Austria, at Upsala, 19th February 1594

1604   Charles IX. Crowned with his consort, Christina of Holstein, at Upsala, 15th March 1607

a   *Burial crown of St Eric IX. Upsala Cathedral* (p. 626)

b   *Burial crown of Maria Eleanora. Riddarholm Church* (p. 641)

c   *Funeral crown of Charles X. Royal Armoury, Stockholm* (p. 643)

d   *Funeral orb of Charles X. Royal Armoury, Stockholm* (p. 643)

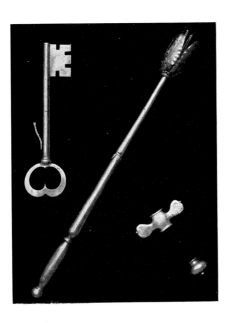

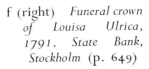

e (left)   *Funeral key and sceptre from the funeral regalia of Charles X. Royal Armoury, Stockholm* (p. 643)

f (right)   *Funeral crown of Louisa Ulrica, 1791. State Bank, Stockholm* (p. 649)

b   Crown of Badeboda. Historical Museum,
Stockholm (p. 654)

c   Arches of crown on Goslar Reliquary

a   The so-called 'Goslar Reliquary'. Historical Museum, Stockholm
(p. 654)

d   (below)   Circlet of crown on Goslar Reliquary

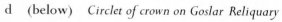

SWEDEN

1611   Gustavus II, Adolphus. Crowned at Upsala, 12th October 1650
       His consort, Maria Eleanora, crowned at Stockholm, 28th November 1620

1633   Christina. Crowned at Stockholm, 20th October 1650

1654   Charles X, Gustavus. Crowned at Upsala, 6th June 1654
       His consort, Hedwig Eleonora, crowned at Stockholm, 25th October 1654

1660   Charles XI. Crowned at Upsala, 28th September 1675
       His consort, Ulrica Leonora the Elder, crowned at Stockholm, 25th November 1680

1697   Charles XII. Crowned at Stockholm, 14th December 1697

1718   Ulrica Leonora. Crowned at Upsala, 17th March 1719

1720   Frederick I of Hesse. Crowned at Stockholm, 3rd May 1720

HOLSTEIN-GOTTORP DYNASTY

1751   Adolphus Frederick. Crowned with his consort, Louisa Ulrica, at Stockholm, 26th November 1751

1771   Gustavus III, Adolphus. Crowned with his consort, Sophie Magdalena, at Stockholm, 28th May 1772

1792   Gustavus IV, Adolphus. Crowned with his consort, Frederica, at Norrköping, 3rd April 1800

1809   Charles XIII. Crowned at Stockholm, 29th June 1809, with his consort, Hedwig Elizabeth Charlotte

BERNADOTTE DYNASTY

1818   Charles XIV, John. Crowned at Stockholm, 11th May 1818
       His consort, Desideria, crowned at Stockholm, 21st August 1829

1844   Oscar I. Crowned with his consort, Josephine, at Stockholm, 28th September 1844

1859   Charles XV. Crowned with his consort, Louisa, 3rd May 1860

1872   Oscar II. Crowned with his consort, Sophia, at Stockholm, 12th May 1873

1907   Gustav V. Not crowned

1950   Gustav VI, Adolph. Not crowned

CHAPTER TWENTY-SIX

WURTEMBERG

The name of Wurtemberg was adopted by a certain Conrad von Beutelsbach, who took the title of Count of Wurtemberg in the year 1080, and it was subsequently given to a hill in the vicinity of Stuttgart, on which the ancestral castle was built. The family gained possession of extensive lands which were augmented on the death of Conradin of the House of Hohenstaufen in 1268 by part of the Duchy of Swabia. Count Eberhard I (*obiit* 1325) doubled the size of his county and transferred his residence to Stuttgart. The family lands were several times divided, but in 1482 they were declared indivisible and were united under Count Eberhard V. In 1495 this arrangement was confirmed by the Emperor Maximilian I and the Imperial Diet, and the county was raised to the rank of duchy. On the occasion of the creation of the duchy, the Emperor presented the new Duke with a sword with the advice: 'Use it for justice, for the protection of the widows and orphans, for the punishment of the wrong.' The sword is still preserved in the castle at Stuttgart. The hilt and scabbard are plated with silver gilt, decorated with a German Gothic tracery design with a shield with the arms of Teck, which were introduced when the country was raised to a duchy. The Teck arms also appear on the wheel pommel. According to Laking[1] the proportions of the hilt are those of the bastard sword. The blade, which is the original though much worn, bears the running wolf mark.

In 1532 the ruling family adopted the Lutheran faith. On 1st January 1806 the duchy was advanced to the rank of kingdom, and the Duke took the simple title of King of Wurtemberg. In 1918 the reigning King, who was the fourth to bear that title, abdicated and resumed the title of Duke of Wurtemberg. On his death in 1921 the headship of the family passed to Duke Albert of Wurtemberg of the senior and Roman Catholic branch of the family, the Protestant branch having become extinct.

Although no coronation ceremony was introduced into the Kingdom of Wurtemberg, a sceptre was made in 1806 and a royal crown in 1822.

The royal crown of Wurtemberg (*Plate 229, a*), being closed with arches slightly depressed at their junction, follows the pattern of the crown of an independent and hereditary king and bears a close resemblance to the modern royal crown in heraldic use on the Continent of Europe. It is made of gold and decorated with diamonds, emeralds and pearls in the late rococo style, and inside there is a red velvet Cap of Estate. The circlet is bordered by rows of well-matched pearls, those in the upper row being larger than those in the lower. Between these are sixteen round ornaments of

---

[1] Laking: *A Record of European Arms and Armour.*

floral design in three different patterns, each ornament being separated from its neighbour by two small studs set one above the other, these being alternately small diamond rosettes and emeralds in brilliant *collets*. Resting on the circlet are eight graceful arcs picked out in small brilliant cut diamonds, and at the junction of each arch is a golden strawberry leaf, having in its centre a flower composed of brilliants with a small diamond rosette on either side and below, similar to those on the circlet. The four arches spring from behind the strawberry leaves, and are composed of narrow gold convex bands encrusted with a row of jewelled ornaments. At the junction of the arches is placed the golden orb surrounded by an equator from which rise the meridional bands, dividing the upper part into four quarters. These bands are of gold set with small brilliants. Into the top of the orb there is screwed a cross. The screw, which is made of gold, passes through the middle of the orb and is secured under the junction of the arches by a nut. On the head of the screw is a knob around which are set small diamonds, and to this the cross is fixed. The setting of the cross is gold, but nothing of the metal is seen for the surface is entirely covered with brilliants, a large stone being placed in the centre and two lesser stones radiating from it to each arm, set amidst a profusion of small brilliants. The limbs have been gracefully curved and at the extremities there has been placed a small lozenge-shaped brilliant. In all, 55 emeralds, some 220 pearls and innumerable diamonds have been used in its composition. The crown was made by the Court Jeweller August Heinrich Kuhn.

The royal sceptre (*Plate 229, c*) is a slender rod of polished gold, divided into five sections by bands of small diamonds. The base is a short knob, ovoid in shape, and above the lowest diamond band is a convex grip. Between the next two bands the rod is pronouncedly concave, tapering thence to its summit, the edges of which are patterned like petal ends, with a round stud upon which a large emerald, set in a gold band, rests on one of its corners so as to give it the appearance of a square lozenge. The fine emerald is surmounted by a cross, similar in shape, though smaller, to that on the crown. At the foot of the cross is fixed a large oblong diamond in a gold setting, above which are 4 round brilliants in invisible settings, the brilliant in the centre and at the top of the cross being the largest. On each of the arms are 3 round brilliants. The sceptre was designed by the jeweller Thouret.

These ornaments are still preserved at Stuttgart together with a fine diamond diadem of the last Queen, Charlotte (*Plate 229, b*), which was made by the jeweller Edward Foehr. Another crown jewel is the Harlequin Diamond of 22 carats which was originally set in a Golden Fleece for Duke Karl Alexander (1733–7), from whose collection stones now in the regalia were taken. The Harlequin is now set as a pendant in a splendid three-row diamond necklace, which has a total of 97 stones (*Plate 229, d*).

KINGS

1805   Frederick I
1816   William I
1864   Charles I
1891   William II. Abdicated 1918

a   *Royal crown of Wurtemberg. Wurtemberg Landesmuseum, Stuttgart* (p. 659)

b   *Diamond diadem of Queen Charlotte. Wurtemberg Landesmuseum, Stuttgart* (p. 660)

c (left)   *King's sceptre. Wurtemberg Landesmuseum, Stuttgart* (p. 660)

d (right)   *The Harlequin diamond set as a pendant in a splendid three-row diamond necklace which has 97 stones. Wurtemberg Landesmuseum, Stuttgart* (p. 660)

a   *The regalia of the Karageorgevitch dynasty made for the coronation of King Peter in 1909. Formerly in the Royal Palace, Belgrade (p. 662)*

b   *Bas-relief of a coronation of an XI-Century King of Croatia. Split Cathedral (p. 661)*

CHAPTER TWENTY-SEVEN

YUGOSLAVIA

Modern Yugoslavia comprises a number of small states with a very chequered history. They rose and fell as principalities, kingdoms and even empires, and were submerged by the Bulgarians, the Byzantine Empire, the Hungarians, the Turks, the Austrians, Napoleon and more recently by the Germans. Their early history was complicated by the struggle between the Greek Church and the Eastern emperors on the one side and the Roman Catholic Church and the Powers on the other.

Serbia, the most important of these states, was raised to the status of a kingdom when Michael Voislavich became King in 1077 and received a crown from Pope Gregory VII. After his death the country was over-run by civil wars until Stephen Nemanya brought all the Serb countries under his rule, although he did not take the title of king. He was succeeded by his eldest son, Stephen, who was crowned King of Serbia by a legate sent by Pope Honorius III in 1217. But in 1222 he was again crowned according to the Greek rites by his brother, Sava, the first Orthodox Archbishop of Serbia and the patron saint of the country, with a crown sent by the Greek Emperor from Nicaea. The coronation took place at Ushitze, and a fresco depicting the ceremony is to be found in the monastery there. In 1345 Stephen Dushan proclaimed himself Emperor of the Serbs and Greeks and was solemnly crowned with an imperial crown at Skolpje (Uskub) on Easter Day 1346. At the same time his wife, Helena, was crowned Empress and his son, Urosh, was crowned King of Serbia. The last Serbian emperor was killed in the disastrous Battle of Kossovo in 1389.

The crown jewels disappeared at Kossovo and there are only iconographic representations of the regalia of the period. A former Serbian diplomat told the author that when stationed at Constantinople he had identified some jewellery in the Sultan's treasury as having belonged to the former Serbian crown jewels.

The early history of Croatia is vague and the records are scanty. Early in the VIII century Duke Tomislav became the first independent national ruler, although the authorities disagree as to whether he called himself king or not, some maintaining that the first 'proper' king was Drzislav (c. 978–1000). The Kingdom of Croatia reached its zenith under Zvonimir, who was crowned as a papal vassal in 1076 (Plate 230, b). After his death in 1089 Helena, the Queen-widow, and rebellious nobles, called in Ladislas I of Hungary. The latter was accepted as King in return for promises to respect the laws and institutions of the land. Thereafter Croatia remained one of the lands of the Holy Crown of Hungary until 1918, when it finally broke away from Hungarian rule and became in the same year part of modern Yugoslavia.

Bosnia, until 1353, was ruled by governors or 'bans' the last of whom, Stephen

Kostromanic, was succeeded by his nephew Tvrtko, who in 1376 was crowned as 'Stephen I, King of Bosnia, Serbia and the Sea-coast', the Serbian Tsar Lazar retaining his own title though with diminished authority. In 1463 the major part of Bosnia succumbed to the Turks, under whose rule it continued with a turbulent history until 1878 when it was occupied by the Austro-Hungarians, who finally annexed it and Herzogovina in early 1914. In 1918 Bosnia and Herzogovina became part of Yugoslavia.

The small principality of Montenegro was proclaimed a kingdom in 1910, but was absorbed into the Kingdom of the Serbs, Croats and Slovenes in 1918. A formal modern royal crown was adopted for heraldic usage.

Serbia was declared an independent kingdom in 1882, but the first King, Milan, was not crowned. Upon his abdication his son, Alexander, was anointed and crowned at the ancient monastery at Zica. In 1903 King Alexander and his Queen were murdered in Belgrade and the Obrenovitch dynasty came to an end. Peter Karageorgevitch was elected King and was crowned in Belgrade on 21st September 1904. For the occasion a new set of regalia was made (*Plate 230, a*). The crown was made from the bronze of a cannon captured from the Turks by Karageorge, the Serbian leader in the War of Independence. It is in the style of a modern royal crown though rather taller. It is decorated with white enamel and semi-precious stones. On the circlet are four fleurs-de-lis and four enamelled double-headed white eagles. Inside is a cap of crimson velvet. When Serbia became part of the Kingdom of Yugoslavia this crown became the crown of the new Triune Kingdom, but it is really a dynastic crown. The other ornaments of the Serb regalia, the sceptre, orb and a clasp for the royal mantle, were made in the same style.

Until the German invasion of Serbia in the Second World War the regalia were kept in the chapel in the royal palace of Belgrade, but was subsequently moved to the Monastery of Zica.

SERBIAN RULERS

c. 1052	Michael
1077	Michael proclaimed King
c. 1081	Constantine Bodin

RASCIA

1083	Vukan
	Dates uncertain—Grand Zupans—Urosh I and II
	Desa
	Tichomir
c. 1167	Stephen Nemanja
1196	Stephen the First. Crowned
1217	Stephen the First. Crowned, proclaimed King
1228	Stephen Radoslav
1233	Stephen Vladislav

1242 Stephen Urosh I
1276 Stephen Dragutin
1282 Stephen Urosh II Milutin
1321 Stephen Urosh III Decanski
1331 Stephen Dushan proclaimed Tsar 1345. Crowned 1346 with consort, Helena
1355 Tsar Stephen Urosh. Crowned with father in 1346
(1366 King Vukashin)
1371 Prince Lazar
1389 Stephen Lazarevitch. Despot from 1402
1427 George Brankovitch
1456 Lazar Brankovitch

HEREDITARY PRINCES

1829 Milosch (Obrenovitch I). Abdicated 1839
1839 Michael II
1840 Michael III
1842 Alexander Karageorgevitch
1858 Milosch Obrenovitch again
1860 Michael III
1868 Milan Obrenovitch IV. King 1882
1889 Alexander. Crowned at Zica.
1903 Peter I (Karageorgevitch). Crowned at Belgrade, 21st September 1904
1921 Alexander Karageorgevitch. King of Serbs, Croats and Slovenes. King of Yugoslavia 1929
1934 Peter III
1945 Republic proclaimed

GENERAL BIBLIOGRAPHY

A select bibliography has been given at the end of each chapter, but there are a certain number of general works which belong to the whole. A selection of these is given below.

ABBOT, M.   *Jewels of Romance and Renown*, London 1933.

ABDUL AZIZ   *The Imperial Treasury of the Indian Mughuls*, Lahore 1942.

BOAK, A. E. R.   'The Imperial Coronation Ceremonies in the Fifth and Sixth Centuries', *Harvard Studies in Classical Philology*, Vol. XXX, 1919.

BRADFORD, E.   *Four Centuries of European Jewellery*, London 1953.

BRIGHTMAN, F. E.   'Byzantine Imperial Coronations', in *Journal of Theological* Studies, II.

CARLYLE, SIR R. W., CARLYLE, A. J.   *A History of Mediaeval Political Theory in the West*, 6 vols., London 1950.

CLIFFORD-SMITH, H.   *Jewellery*, London 1908.

DIEULAFAIT, L.   *Diamonds and Precious Stones*, London 1874.

EMMANUEL, H.   *Diamonds and Precious Stones*, London 1867.

Encyclopaedia Britannica, 11th edition, Cambridge University 1910.

Encyclopaedia Italiana.

EVANS, J.   *English Jewellery*, London 1921.
     A History of Jewellery 1100–1870, London 1951.

FILO, B.   *L'ancien Art bulgaire*, Berne 1919.

FISCHER, W.   'Eine Kaiserkrönung in Byzantium', in *Zeitschr: fur Allg. Gesch.*, Vol. IV, 1887.

FOLZ, R.   *L'idée d'Empire en Occident du Ve–XIVe Siècles*, Paris 1953.

FOX-DAVIES, A. C.   *A Complete Guide to Heraldry*, London 1909.

GERLACH, M.   *Atlas des Couronnes*, Vienna 1877.

GRABAR, A.   *L'empereur dans l'Art byzantin*, Paris 1936.

Haydn's Dictionary of Dates, 1910 edition.

HENDERSON, E. F.   *Select Historical Documents of the Middle Ages*, London 1925.

HERMANN, C. F.   *Disputatio de sceptrie regie antiquate et origine*, Göttingen 1851.

HERBERT-SMITH, G. F.   *Gem-stones*, 6th edition, London 1930.

HOFFMANN, C. C.   *De Origine et Jura Sceptrum*, Frankfurt 1736.

JONES, W.   *Crowns and Coronations*, London 1898.

KRÜNITZ, DR J. G.   *Oeconomische Encyclopaedie oder allgemeines System der Staats-, Stadt-, Haus- und Landwirtschaft*, Brunn 1793.

KUNZ, G. F., STEVENSON, C. H.   *The Book of the Pearl*, London 1908.

LABARTH, M. J.   *Handbook of the Arts of the Middle Ages and Renaissance*, London 1855.

MAWE, J.   *A Treatise on Diamonds and Precious Stones*, London 1815.

PORPHYROGÉNÉTE, C.	*Le Livre des Cérémonies*, 2 vols., ed. A. Vogt, Paris 1935.
ROSSI, F.	*Italian Jewelled Arts*, London 1957.
SCHLUMBERGER	*L'Épopée byzant.*
	Un Empereur byzant.
SCHRAMM, P. E.	*Herrschaftszeichen und Staatssymbolik*, Stuttgart 1955–6.
	Sphaire, Globus, Reichsapfel.
SELDEN, J.	*Titles of Honour*, London 1631.
STEINGRÄBER, E.	*Antique Jewellery*, London 1957.
STOPFORD, F.	*The Romance of the Jewel*, London 1920.
STREETER, E. W.	*The Great Diamonds of the World*, London 1882.
	Precious Stones and Gems, London 1898.
TWINING, L.	*Symbols and Emblems of Early and Mediaeval Christian Art*, London 1855.
WEINSTEIN, M.	*Precious and Semi-precious Stones*, London 1930.
WESTROPP, H. M.	*A Manual of Precious Stones*, London 1874.
WOODWARD, J.	*A Treatise on Heraldry, British and Foreign*, London 1896.
WOOLLEY, THE REV. R. M.	*Coronation Rites*, Cambridge 1915.

INDEX

Compiled by

G. Norman Knight, M.A., M.S.ind. and Terence Miller, M.S.ind.

INDEX

Page numbers in bold type indicate the more important references.
Italicized numbers denote the *Plate numbers* of illustrations or their captions.
The names of Popes, Libraries, Museums and Treasuries are grouped under those headings.
(*bis*) denotes two, and (*ter*) three, references on same page.

G

M

Y

Z